W9-CUU-468

Florida Statistical Abstract 2007

Forty-first Edition

Bureau of Economic and Business Research
Warrington College of Business Administration

Order books from Bureau of Economic and Business Research
Warrington College of Business Administration
221 Matherly Hall, Post Office Box 117145
Gainesville, Florida 32611-7145
phone (352) 392-0171, ext. 212
fax (352) 392-4739
e-mail: info@bebr.ufl.edu
http://www.bebr.ufl.edu

ISBN 978-1-932901-12-2
ISSN 0071-6022

Printed in the United States of America on acid-free paper

Cover photograph of the Jacksonville sklyline at night by Warren Flagler, photographer, South Miami, Florida

Contents

Preface

This year marks the 41st edition of the *Florida Statistical Abstract*. Since 1967 the *Abstract* has been widely considered the state's data book and has provided a comprehensive collection of the latest statistics available on the social, economic and political organization of Florida. This 41st edition continues the tradition but with some subtle, yet significant, changes.

Data are primarily presented at the county level, although the *Abstract* also includes information about Florida Metropolitan Statistical Areas, cities, planning districts, other sub-state units, and comparisons of Florida to other Sunbelt and populous states, the U.S., and other countries. This volume contains a selection of data collected by public and private entities. State of Florida and federal government agencies contribute the majority of the data. A listing of source agencies appears in the section introductions at the beginning of each chapter.

Every effort is made to publish the most up-to-date figures possible; however, these data cover a wide range of activities reported for different time periods so uniformity is impossible. Statistics in this edition are generally for the most recent year or period available by the fall of 2007. Each table title indicates the time period for the data and exceptions are footnoted. Sources are cited at the bottom of each table and online root source addresses and access dates are provided. More statistical detail and comprehensive discussion of methods and definitions than can be included in the *Abstract* are usually available from the source. Data not released in either a printed or online publication by our print deadline are identified in the source citation as either "unpublished data," or as a "prepublication release."

Each year all tables are reviewed: new tables of current interest are added, continuing series are updated or revised to reflect changes in source definitions or methods, and less timely data are eliminated. Some tables of "benchmark" data, although not timely, are repeated. The reader is encouraged to use tables in earlier editions of the *Abstract*.

Organization of the volume. Six divisions, each of which is subdivided into sections, make up the organizational structure. The first division (Sections 1.00 through 7.00) generally includes tables presenting data on characteristics of the population; demographics, housing, education, income, employment, and welfare. Except for Section 8.00, which presents data on physical geography and the environment, the next three divisions (Sections 9.00 through 23.00) refer primarily to establishments engaged in economic, social, and political activities. Establishments are classified in most sources according to the North American Industry Classification System (NAICS), which is defined with a listing of major industry groups in the Glossary.

The fifth division of the *Abstract* contains tables of a comparative nature: economic and social trends. Time series showing the fluctuations of major economic indicators such as prices and employment are included in Section 24.00. Selected statistics of the economic, social, and physical environments of Florida, other Sunbelt and other populous states, and the U.S. comprise Section 25.00. The final division, Section 26.00, globally compares Florida characteristics to the United States and other specified countries.

Changes in this edition. New tables appearing in this edition include expanded population projections data by race and sex; tables showing mortgage status and monthly housing costs; student discipline data; harvested fish and fishing anglers; value of construction work; airport instrument operations; state parks and areas acreage and attendance; and employment in sports-related businesses in the state.

Bureau of Economic and Business Research (BEBR). BEBR's mission is twofold: (1) to produce, collect, analyze, and disseminate economic and demographic data on Florida; and (2) conduct applied research and publish findings on topics relating to the state's ongoing economic growth and development. BEBR's activities are organized around three research programs: population, economic analysis, and survey research. To learn more about BEBR's research and for information about other publications, visit www.bebr.ufl.edu.

Acknowledgments. As Editor, Eve Irwin researched current and new data sources; reviewed current tables, prepared layout instructions, and planned new entries; directed production and monitored changes; prepared all of the section contents and paginated the current volume. Eve also developed and implemented quality control standards for the numerous online data sources used in table preparation.

Assistant Editor, Phoebe Wilson, prepared all of the table layouts, maps, and charts, the cover, and all promotional materials. Phoebe managed production and production staff and worked with a myriad of data downloads from various online and electronic sources. She also produced the *Abstract* CD-ROM for distribution and prepared the volume for printing.

Xochlit Buitrago provided significant publication proofing for this volume, assisted by Krishna Kotapati and Paula Ivey. Xochilt and Krishna also entered data and performed quality control tasks.

As always, we rely on other BEBR staff for assistance and to provide data. Martin Smith offered invaluable computer support to meet our data needs and Matt Collins provided technical support to the program. Stefan Rayer provided unpublished data from the BEBR Population Program; Jim Dewey furnished retail price data from the Economic Analysis program; and the BEBR UF Survey Research program provided household income data. Pamela Middleton provided valuable marketing consultation to the Senior Editor and coordinated the distribution of all incoming order requests; assisted by Janet Fletcher, Paula Ivey, and Xochilt Buitrago.

Suggestions for improvements to the *Abstract* are encouraged and welcomed.

Susan S. Floyd
Senior Editor
Gainesville, Florida
October 2007

Counties and Metropolitan Statistical Areas Effective December 18, 2006 to present

Cape Coral-Ft. Myers MSA
Lee County

Deltona-Daytona Beach-Ormond Beach MSA
Volusia County

Ft. Walton Beach-Crestview-Destin MSA
Okaloosa County

Gainesville MSA
Alachua County
Gilchrist County

Jacksonville MSA
Baker County
Clay County
Duval County
Nassau County
St. Johns County

Lakeland MSA
Polk County

Miami-Ft. Lauderdale-Pompano Beach MSA
Broward County
Miami-Dade County
Palm Beach County

Naples-Marco Island MSA
Collier County

Ocala MSA
Marion County

Orlando-Kissimmee MSA
Lake County
Orange County
Osceola County
Seminole County

Palm Bay-Melbourne-Titusville MSA
Brevard County

Palm Coast MSA
Flagler County

Panama City-Lynn Haven MSA
Bay County

Pensacola-Ferry Pass-Brent MSA
Escambia County
Santa Rosa County

Port St. Lucie MSA
Martin County
St. Lucie County

Punta Gorda MSA
Charlotte County

Sarasota-Bradenton-Venice MSA
Manatee County
Sarasota County

Sebastian-Vero Beach MSA
Indian River County

Tallahassee MSA
Gadsden County
Jefferson County
Leon County
Wakulla County

Tampa-St. Petersburg-Clearwater MSA
Hernando County
Hillsborough County
Pasco County
Pinellas County

POPULATION

Non-Hispanic Black Population, 2006 (%)

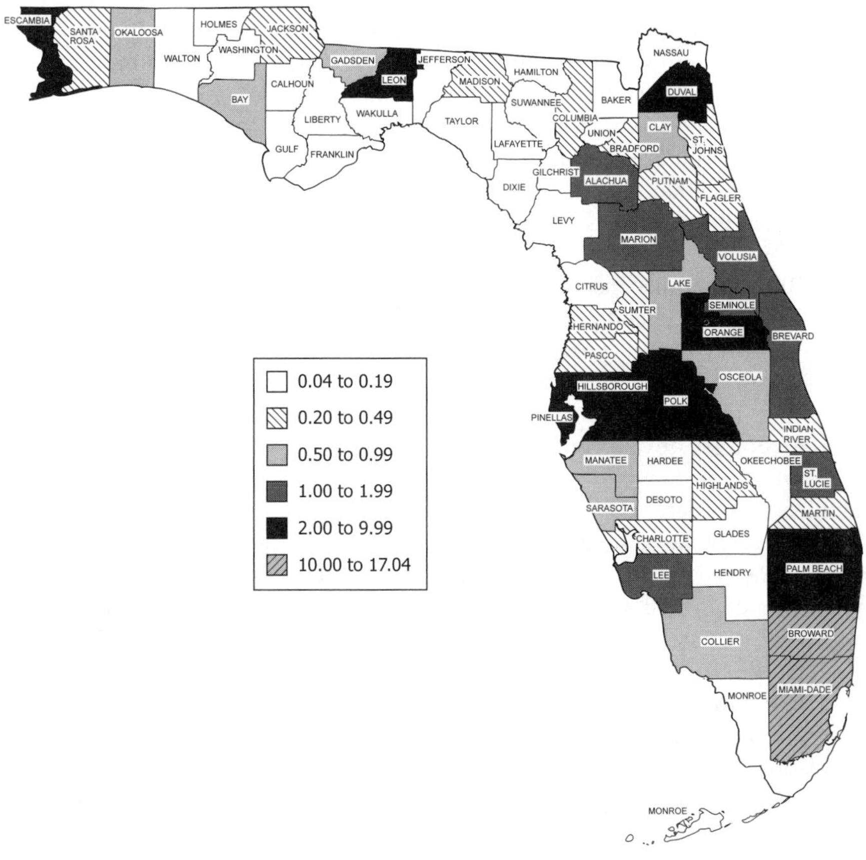

- 0.04 to 0.19
- 0.20 to 0.49
- 0.50 to 0.99
- 1.00 to 1.99
- 2.00 to 9.99
- 10.00 to 17.04

Source: Table 1.36

Section 1.00
Population

This section presents population estimates and projections for the state and counties of Florida. The primary source of the data is the Bureau of Economic and Business Research (BEBR). BEBR is contracted by the state to produce the official annual intercensal statewide population figures.

Census data. The Census of Population, taken once every ten years by the U.S. Census Bureau, provides basic statistics about population and serves as benchmark data for this section. Decennial census counts from the 2000 census appear in various tables throughout Section 1.00.

In 1994, BEBR published the *1990 Census Handbook – Florida*, a collection of 1990 Florida county-level census data complete with 1980 comparative data. This volume is an excellent source of historical county-level census data.

In addition to the decennial censuses, the Census Bureau issues a series of *Curent Population Reports*. These reports contain national, regional, and sometimes state population statistics resulting from periodic surveys, special censuses, and cooperative estimation and projection efforts between the individual states and the Census Bureau. Many of these reports can be found on the Census Bureau's Internet Web site at www.census.gov.

Tables 1.03 and 1.10 provide historical census population series beginning as early as the 1830 census for the state and 1940 for counties. Various tables throughout this section include 2000 census counts for comparison with the current intercensal population estimates. Census population estimates for states and the United States for July 1, 2006, appear on Table 1.11.

Population estimates and projections. BEBR produces intercensal population estimates and projections in five-year increments for the state of Florida. These estimates are published annually in *Florida Estimates of Population* and in the *Florida Population Studies* series, the sources used for numerous tables in this section. Discussion of the methodology used in the estimation and projection process can be found within each source.

A series of county-level intercensal population estimates for 2002 through 2006 appear in Table 1.20. Extreme caution must be exercised when deriving annual changes from successive estimates. Calculating such changes can lead to inaccurate conclusions regarding population growth, especially for small places. The best base of any estimate of population change is generally the most recent census enumeration. City-level population estimates appear in Table 1.25. Estimates by age, race, sex, and Hispanic origin can be found on various tables starting with Table 1.30 through 1.39. Projections for specified years through 2030 are found in tables 1.40 through 1.64.

Area designations. Counties and municipalities are legal and political entities, but from a sociological point of view the community of which a person considers himself or herself to be a part may not correspond to such an entity. Terms like "Greater Jacksonville" or "the Miami area" are used to indicate the real community. People do not hesitate to cross city or county limits or even state lines to work, to buy or sell, or to seek cultural, medical, recreational, or social services. For this reason, the U.S. Office of Management and Budget (OMB) has designated areas known as Metropolitan Statistical Areas (MSAs) and, beginning in 2003, Micropolitan Statistical Areas.

Current MSA standards were defined on December 18, 2006, and include designations for Micropolitan Statistical Areas and Core Based Statistical Areas, which refer collectively to metropolitan and micropolitan statistical areas. (See the Glossary for an explanation of criteria for each type of area.) Where possible, MSA data are presented using the current definitions, although some data may be presented using an earlier designation due to data availability limitations. Area differences are minimal and comparisons can be made using the information located on the Census Bureau's Web site at www.census.gov. A note will appear at the bottom of tables using earlier designations. An MSA area map as defined as of 2006 is presented at the front of this volume.

In Florida, MSAs are defined in terms of entire counties. Population living in MSAs may be referred to as the metropolitan population. Table 1.12 contains population figures for Florida's MSAs as defined in December 2005.

Various state government agencies have grouped counties into designated districts. There are eleven planning districts, each with common interests and needs for planning community development. The map accompanying Table 1.66 presents Florida's counties by planning district.

Sources. Most of the outside data sources used in the *Abstract* may be found on the Internet. Several state agencies provide data throughout the volume. A state agency Web site directory can be found on the state's official Web site at www.myflorida.com. Because Web addresses change frequently, only root addresses are provided on tables throughout this volume when an online source is used.

BEBR provides unpublished median age, projections, and elderly population statistics. Voting-age population estimates and projections are presented in Section 21.00.

Homeless population estimates and some immigrant data are provided by the Florida Department of Children and Families. Other data on immigrants are from the Office of Immigration Statistics in the U.S. Department of Homeland Security. Data about veterans are from the U.S. Department of Veterans Affairs. Financial information about veterans at the county level can be found in Section 23.00.

Section 1.00
Population

Tables listed by major heading

Tables listed by major heading

Tables listed by major heading

Table 1.01. CENSUS COUNTS AND ESTIMATES: GENERAL POPULATION CHARACTERISTICS IN THE STATE OF FLORIDA, APRIL 1, 2000 AND 2006

Characteristic	2000 Number	2000 Percentage	2006 Number	2006 Percentage
Total population	15,982,378	100.0	18,089,889	100.0
Male	7,797,715	48.8	8,878,166	49.1
Female	8,184,663	51.2	9,211,723	50.9
Age (years)				
Under 5	945,823	5.9	1,117,630	6.2
5 to 9	1,031,718	6.5	1,055,789	5.8
10 to 14	1,057,024	6.6	1,127,349	6.2
15 to 19	1,014,067	6.3	1,174,594	6.5
20 to 24	928,310	5.8	1,154,089	6.4
25 to 34	2,084,100	13.0	2,247,135	12.4
35 to 44	2,485,247	15.5	2,602,876	14.4
45 to 54	2,069,479	12.9	2,534,472	14.0
55 to 59	821,517	5.1	1,107,702	6.1
60 to 64	737,496	4.6	934,136	5.2
65 to 74	1,452,176	9.1	1,452,008	8.0
75 to 84	1,024,134	6.4	1,171,721	6.5
85 and over	331,287	2.1	410,388	2.3
Median	38.7	(X)	39.8	(X)
18 and over	12,336,038	77.2	14,071,245	77.8
Male	5,926,729	37.1	6,819,812	37.7
Female	6,409,309	40.1	7,251,433	40.1
21 and over	11,736,378	73.4	13,379,437	74.0
62 and over	3,245,806	20.3	3,591,104	19.9
65 and over	2,807,597	17.6	3,034,117	16.8
Male	1,216,647	7.6	1,316,672	7.3
Female	1,590,950	10.0	1,717,445	9.5
Race				
One race	15,606,063	97.6	17,773,002	98.2
White	12,465,029	78.0	13,767,248	76.1
Black or African American	2,335,505	14.6	2,778,549	15.4
American Indian and Alaska native	53,541	0.3	54,150	0.3
Asian	266,256	1.7	393,427	2.2
Native Hawaiian and Other Pacific Islander	8,625	0.1	9,125	0.1
Some other race	477,107	3.0	770,503	4.3
Two or more races	376,315	2.4	316,887	1.8
Hispanic or Latino (of any race)	2,682,715	16.8	3,642,989	20.1
Mexican	363,925	2.3	563,110	3.1
Puerto Rican	482,027	3.0	682,432	3.8
Cuban	833,120	5.2	1,054,371	5.8
Other	1,003,643	6.3	1,343,076	7.4
Not Hispanic or Latino	13,299,663	83.2	14,446,900	79.9
White	10,458,509	65.4	11,040,168	61.0
Persons in households, total	15,593,433	97.6	17,677,671	97.7
Householder	6,337,929	39.7	7,106,042	39.3
Spouse	3,192,266	20.0	3,443,569	19.0
Child	4,171,924	26.1	4,799,474	26.5
Other relatives	954,061	6.0	1,276,586	7.1
Nonrelatives	937,253	5.9	1,052,000	5.8
Unmarried partner	369,622	2.3	432,372	2.4

(X) Not applicable.

Source: U.S., Department of Commerce, Census Bureau, American FactFinder, General Demographic Characteristics, Internet site <http://factfinder/census.gov/> (accessed 21, September 2007).

Table 1.02. CENSUS COUNTS: TOTAL POPULATION, APRIL 1, 1990 AND 2000, IN THE STATE AND COUNTIES OF FLORIDA

County	1990	2000	Percentage change	County	1990	2000	Percentage change
Florida	12,938,071	15,982,824	23.5	Lake	152,104	210,527	38.4
				Lee	335,113	440,888	31.6
Alachua	181,596	217,955	20.0	Leon	192,493	239,452	24.4
Baker	18,486	22,259	20.4	Levy	25,912	34,450	32.9
Bay	126,994	148,217	16.7	Liberty	5,569	7,021	26.1
Bradford	22,515	26,088	15.9	Madison	16,569	18,733	13.1
Brevard	398,978	476,230	19.4	Manatee	211,707	264,002	24.7
Broward	1,255,531	1,623,018	29.3	Marion	194,835	258,916	32.9
Calhoun	11,011	13,017	18.2	Martin	100,900	126,731	25.6
Charlotte	110,975	141,627	27.6	Miami-Dade	1,937,194	2,253,779	16.3
Citrus	93,513	118,085	26.3	Monroe	78,024	79,589	2.0
Clay	105,986	140,814	32.9	Nassau	43,941	57,663	31.2
Collier	152,099	251,377	65.3	Okaloosa	143,777	170,498	18.6
Columbia	42,613	56,513	32.6	Okeechobee	29,627	35,910	21.2
DeSoto	23,865	32,209	35.0	Orange	677,491	896,344	32.3
Dixie	10,585	13,827	30.6	Osceola	107,728	172,493	60.1
Duval	672,971	778,879	15.7	Palm Beach	863,503	1,131,191	31.0
Escambia	262,798	294,410	12.0	Pasco	281,131	344,768	22.6
Flagler	28,701	49,832	73.6	Pinellas	851,659	921,495	8.2
Franklin	8,967	9,829	9.6	Polk	405,382	483,924	19.4
Gadsden	41,116	45,087	9.7	Putnam	65,070	70,423	8.2
Gilchrist	9,667	14,437	49.3	St. Johns	83,829	123,135	46.9
Glades	7,591	10,576	39.3	St. Lucie	150,171	192,695	28.3
Gulf	11,504	14,560	26.6	Santa Rosa	81,608	117,743	44.3
Hamilton	10,930	13,327	21.9	Sarasota	277,776	325,961	17.3
Hardee	19,499	26,938	38.2	Seminole	287,521	365,199	27.0
Hendry	25,773	36,210	40.5	Sumter	31,577	53,345	68.9
Hernando	101,115	130,802	29.4	Suwannee	26,780	34,844	30.1
Highlands	68,432	87,366	27.7	Taylor	17,111	19,256	12.5
Hillsborough	834,054	998,948	19.8	Union	10,252	13,442	31.1
Holmes	15,778	18,564	17.7	Volusia	370,737	443,343	19.6
Indian River	90,208	112,947	25.2	Wakulla	14,202	22,863	61.0
Jackson	41,375	46,755	13.0	Walton	27,759	40,601	46.3
Jefferson	11,296	12,902	14.2	Washington	16,919	20,973	24.0
Lafayette	5,578	7,022	25.9				

Note: Includes all revisions to 2000 census figures as of May 14, 2004.

Source: University of Florida, Bureau of Economic and Business Research, Population Program, *Florida Estimates of Population, April 1, 2006.* Census data from U.S. Census Bureau.

Table 1.03. CENSUS COUNTS: HISTORICAL CENSUS COUNTS IN THE STATE AND COUNTIES OF FLORIDA, 1940 THROUGH 1980

County	1940	1950	1960	1970	1980	Percentage change 1940-1950	1950-1960	1960-1970	1970-1980
Florida	1,897,414	2,771,305	4,951,560	6,791,418	9,746,961	46.1	78.7	37.2	43.5
Alachua	38,607	57,026	74,074	104,764	151,369	47.7	29.9	41.4	44.5
Baker	6,510	6,313	7,363	9,242	15,289	-3.0	16.6	25.5	65.4
Bay	20,686	42,689	67,131	75,283	97,740	106.4	57.3	12.1	29.8
Bradford	8,717	11,457	12,446	14,625	20,023	31.4	8.6	17.5	36.9
Brevard	16,142	23,653	111,435	230,006	272,959	46.5	371.1	106.4	18.7
Broward	39,794	83,933	333,946	620,100	1,018,257	110.9	297.9	85.7	64.2
Calhoun	8,218	7,922	7,422	7,624	9,294	-3.6	-6.3	2.7	21.9
Charlotte	3,663	4,286	12,594	27,559	58,460	17.0	193.8	118.8	112.1
Citrus	5,846	6,111	9,268	19,196	54,703	4.5	51.7	107.1	185.0
Clay	6,468	14,323	19,535	32,059	67,052	121.4	36.4	64.1	109.2
Collier	5,102	6,488	15,753	38,040	85,971	27.2	142.8	141.5	126.0
Columbia	16,859	18,216	20,077	25,250	35,399	8.0	10.2	25.8	40.2
DeSoto	7,792	9,242	11,683	13,060	19,039	18.6	26.4	11.8	45.8
Dixie	7,018	3,928	4,479	5,480	7,751	-44.0	14.0	22.3	41.4
Duval	210,143	304,029	455,411	528,865	571,003	44.7	49.8	16.1	8.0
Escambia	74,667	112,706	173,829	205,334	233,794	50.9	54.2	18.1	13.9
Flagler	3,008	3,367	4,566	4,454	10,913	11.9	35.6	-2.5	145.0
Franklin	5,991	5,814	6,576	7,065	7,661	-3.0	13.1	7.4	8.4
Gadsden	31,450	36,457	41,989	39,184	41,674	15.9	15.2	-6.7	6.4
Gilchrist	4,250	3,499	2,868	3,551	5,767	-17.7	-18.0	23.8	62.4
Glades	2,745	2,199	2,950	3,669	5,992	-19.9	34.2	24.4	63.3
Gulf	6,951	7,460	9,937	10,096	10,658	7.3	33.2	1.6	5.6
Hamilton	9,778	8,981	7,705	7,787	8,761	-8.2	-14.2	1.1	12.5
Hardee	10,158	10,073	12,370	14,889	20,357	-0.8	22.8	20.4	36.7
Hendry	5,237	6,051	8,119	11,859	18,599	15.5	34.2	46.1	56.8
Hernando	5,641	6,693	11,205	17,004	44,469	18.6	67.4	51.8	161.5
Highlands	9,246	13,636	21,338	29,507	47,526	47.5	56.5	38.3	61.1
Hillsborough	180,148	249,894	397,788	490,265	646,939	38.7	59.2	23.2	32.0
Holmes	15,447	13,988	10,844	10,720	14,723	-9.4	-22.5	-1.1	37.3
Indian River	8,957	11,872	25,309	35,992	59,896	32.5	113.2	42.2	66.4
Jackson	34,428	34,645	36,208	34,434	39,154	0.6	4.5	-4.9	13.7
Jefferson	12,032	10,413	9,543	8,778	10,703	-13.5	-8.4	-8.0	21.9
Lafayette	4,405	3,440	2,889	2,892	4,035	-21.9	-16.0	0.1	39.5
Lake	27,255	36,340	57,383	69,305	104,870	33.3	57.9	20.8	51.3

Continued . . .

Table 1.03. CENSUS COUNTS: HISTORICAL CENSUS COUNTS IN THE STATE AND COUNTIES OF FLORIDA, 1940 THROUGH 1980 (Continued)

County	1940	1950	1960	1970	1980	Percentage change 1940-1950	1950-1960	1960-1970	1970-1980
Lee	17,488	23,404	54,539	105,216	205,266	33.8	133.0	92.9	95.1
Leon	31,646	51,590	74,225	103,047	148,655	63.0	43.9	38.8	44.3
Levy	12,550	10,637	10,364	12,756	19,870	-15.2	-2.6	23.1	55.8
Liberty	3,752	3,182	3,138	3,379	4,260	-15.2	-1.4	7.7	26.1
Madison	16,190	14,197	14,154	13,481	14,894	-12.3	-0.3	-4.8	10.5
Manatee	26,098	34,704	69,168	97,115	148,445	33.0	99.3	40.4	52.9
Marion	31,243	38,187	51,616	69,030	122,488	22.2	35.2	33.7	77.4
Martin	6,295	7,807	16,932	28,035	64,014	24.0	116.9	65.6	128.3
Miami-Dade	267,739	495,084	935,047	1,267,792	1,625,509	84.9	88.9	35.6	28.2
Monroe	14,078	29,957	47,921	52,586	63,188	112.8	60.0	9.7	20.2
Nassau	10,826	12,811	17,189	20,626	32,894	18.3	34.2	20.0	59.5
Okaloosa	12,900	27,533	61,175	88,187	109,920	113.4	122.2	44.2	24.6
Okeechobee	3,000	3,454	6,424	11,233	20,264	15.1	86.0	74.9	80.4
Orange	70,074	114,950	263,540	344,311	470,865	64.0	129.3	30.6	36.8
Osceola	10,119	11,406	19,029	25,267	49,287	12.7	66.8	32.8	95.1
Palm Beach	79,989	114,688	228,106	348,993	576,758	43.4	98.9	53.0	65.3
Pasco	13,981	20,529	36,785	75,955	193,661	46.8	79.2	106.5	155.0
Pinellas	91,852	159,249	374,665	522,329	728,531	73.4	135.3	39.4	39.5
Polk	86,665	123,997	195,139	228,515	321,652	43.1	57.4	17.1	40.8
Putnam	18,698	23,615	32,212	36,424	50,549	26.3	36.4	13.1	38.8
St. Johns	20,012	24,998	30,034	31,035	51,303	24.9	20.1	3.3	65.3
St. Lucie	11,871	20,180	39,294	50,836	87,182	70.0	94.7	29.4	71.5
Santa Rosa	16,085	18,554	29,547	37,741	55,988	15.3	59.2	27.7	48.3
Sarasota	16,106	28,827	76,895	120,413	202,251	79.0	166.7	56.6	68.0
Seminole	22,304	26,883	54,947	83,692	179,752	20.5	104.4	52.3	114.8
Sumter	11,041	11,330	11,869	14,839	24,272	2.6	4.8	25.0	63.6
Suwannee	17,073	16,986	14,961	15,559	22,287	-0.5	-11.9	4.0	43.2
Taylor	11,565	10,416	13,168	13,641	16,532	-9.9	26.4	3.6	21.2
Union	7,094	8,906	6,043	8,112	10,166	25.5	-32.1	34.2	25.3
Volusia	53,710	74,229	125,319	169,487	258,762	38.2	68.8	35.2	52.7
Wakulla	5,463	5,258	5,257	6,308	10,887	-3.8	0.0	20.0	72.6
Walton	14,246	14,725	15,576	16,087	21,300	3.4	5.8	3.3	32.4
Washington	12,302	11,888	11,249	11,453	14,509	-3.4	-5.4	1.8	26.7

Source: University of Florida, Bureau of Economic and Business Research, *The Urbanization of Florida's Population: An Historical Perspective of County Growth, 1830-1970,* and *Florida Population: Census Summary, 2000*. Data from U.S. Census Bureau.

Table 1.10. CENSUS COUNTS: TOTAL, URBAN, AND RURAL POPULATION IN FLORIDA, CENSUS YEARS 1830 TO 2000

Census year and date	Total Number	Total Change from previous census Number	Total Change from previous census Percentage	Urban Number	Urban Percentage of total	Rural Number	Rural Percentage of total
Previous urban definition 1/							
1830 (June 1)	34,730	(X)	(X)	0	0.0	34,730	100.0
1840 (June 1)	54,477	19,747	56.9	0	0.0	54,477	100.0
1850 (June 1)	87,445	32,968	60.5	0	0.0	87,445	100.0
1860 (June 1)	140,424	52,979	60.6	5,708	4.1	134,716	95.9
1870 (June 1)	187,748	47,324	33.7	15,275	8.1	172,473	91.9
1880 (June 1)	269,493	81,745	43.5	26,947	10.0	242,546	90.0
1890 (June 1)	391,422	121,929	45.2	77,358	19.8	314,064	80.2
1900 (June 1)	528,542	137,120	35.0	107,031	20.3	421,511	79.7
1910 (April 15)	752,619	224,077	42.4	219,080	29.1	533,539	70.9
1920 (January 1)	968,470	215,851	28.7	353,515	36.5	614,955	63.5
1930 (April 1)	1,468,211	499,741	51.6	759,778	51.7	708,433	48.3
1940 (April 1)	1,897,414	429,203	29.2	1,045,791	55.1	851,623	44.9
1950 (April 1)	2,771,305	873,891	46.1	1,566,788	56.5	1,204,517	43.5
1960 (April 1)	4,951,560	2,180,255	78.7	3,077,989	62.2	1,873,571	37.8
Current urban definition 2/							
1950 (April 1)	2,771,305	873,891	46.1	1,813,890	65.5	957,415	34.5
1960 (April 1)	4,951,560	2,180,255	78.7	3,661,383	73.9	1,290,177	26.1
1970 (April 1)	6,791,418	1,839,858	37.2	5,544,551	81.6	1,244,892	18.3
1980 (April 1)	9,746,324	2,954,906	43.5	8,212,385	84.3	1,533,939	15.7
1990 (April 1)	12,937,926	3,191,602	32.8	10,970,445	84.8	1,967,481	15.2
2000 (April 1)	A/ 15,982,824	3,044,898	23.5	14,270,020	89.3	1,712,358	10.7

(X) Not applicable.

A/ Includes revisions made to total population census counts by the U.S. Census Bureau; urban and rural population counts were not revised.

1/ Figures have been adjusted to constitute a substantially consistent series based on incorporated places of 2,500 or more persons with additional areas defined as urban under special rules.

2/ The current urban definition defines the urban population as all persons living in urbanized areas and in places of 2,500 or more persons outside urbanized areas. An urbanized area comprises an incorporated place and adjacent densely settled surrounding area that together have a minimum population of 50,000. Population not classified as urban constitutes the rural population. Rural classification need not imply farm residence or a sparsely settled area because a small city is rural as long as it is outside an urbanized area and has fewer than 2,500 persons.

Source: U.S., Department of Commerce, Census Bureau, Census 2000 Summary File 1 (SF1) 100-Percent Data, Internet site <http://factfinder.census.gov/> (accessed 22, February 2007), and previous census reports.

Table 1.11. STATES: CENSUS COUNTS, APRIL 1, 2000, AND ESTIMATES, JULY 1, 2006
IN FLORIDA, OTHER STATES, AND THE UNITED STATES

State	Census April 1 2000 (1,000)	Estimates July 1 2006 (1,000)	Per-centage change 2000 to 2006	State	Census April 1 2000 (1,000)	Estimates July 1 2006 (1,000)	Per-centage change 2000 to 2006
Florida	15,982	18,090	13.2	Missouri	5,595	5,843	4.4
				Montana	902	945	4.7
Alabama	4,447	4,599	3.4	Nebraska	1,711	1,768	3.3
Alaska	627	670	6.9	Nevada	1,998	2,496	24.9
Arizona	5,131	6,166	20.2	New Hampshire	1,236	1,315	6.4
Arkansas	2,673	2,811	5.1	New Jersey	8,414	8,725	3.7
California	33,872	36,458	7.6	New Mexico	1,819	1,955	7.5
Colorado	4,301	4,753	10.5	New York	18,976	19,306	1.7
Connecticut	3,406	3,505	2.9	North Carolina	8,049	8,857	10.0
Delaware	784	853	8.9	North Dakota	642	636	-1.0
District of				Ohio	11,353	11,478	1.1
Columbia	572	582	1.7	Oklahoma	3,451	3,579	3.7
Georgia	8,186	9,364	14.4	Oregon	3,421	3,701	8.2
Hawaii	1,212	1,285	6.1	Pennsylvania	12,281	12,441	1.3
Idaho	1,294	1,466	13.3	Rhode Island	1,048	1,068	1.8
Illinois	12,419	12,832	3.3	South Carolina	4,012	4,321	7.7
Indiana	6,080	6,314	3.8	South Dakota	755	782	3.6
Iowa	2,926	2,982	1.9	Tennessee	5,689	6,039	6.1
Kansas	2,688	2,764	2.8	Texas	20,852	23,508	12.7
Kentucky	4,042	4,206	4.1	Utah	2,233	2,550	14.2
Louisiana	4,469	4,288	-4.1	Vermont	609	624	2.5
Maine	1,275	1,322	3.7	Virginia	7,079	7,643	8.0
Maryland	5,296	5,616	6.0	Washington	5,894	6,396	8.5
Massachusetts	6,349	6,437	1.4	West Virginia	1,808	1,818	0.6
Michigan	9,938	10,096	1.6	Wisconsin	5,364	5,557	3.6
Minnesota	4,919	5,167	5.0	Wyoming	494	515	4.3
Mississippi	2,845	2,911	2.3	United States	281,422	299,398	6.4

Note: Includes person in the Armed Forces residing in each state.

Source: U.S., Department of Commerce, Census Bureau, Population Division, "Annual Estimates of the Population for the United States and States, April 1, 2000 to July 1, 2006," Internet site <http://www.census.gov/> (accessed 6, June 2007).

Table 1.12. METROPOLITAN AREAS: CENSUS COUNTS, APRIL 1, 1990 AND 2000, AND ESTIMATES APRIL 1, 2006, IN THE STATE AND METROPOLITAN AREAS OF FLORIDA

Metropolitan Statistical Area (MSA)	Census 1990	Census 2000	Estimates 2006	Percentage change 1990–2000	Percentage change 2000–06
Florida	12,938,071	15,982,824	18,349,132	23.5	14.8
MSA, total	12,138,672	14,973,519	17,177,268	23.4	14.7
Cape Coral-Ft. Myers	335,113	440,888	585,608	31.6	32.8
Deltona-Daytona Beach-Ormond Beach	370,737	443,343	503,844	19.6	13.6
Ft. Walton Beach-Crestview-Destin	143,777	170,498	192,672	18.6	13.0
Gainesville	191,263	232,392	260,482	21.5	12.1
Alachua County	181,596	217,955	243,779	20.0	11.8
Gilchrist County	9,667	14,437	16,703	49.3	15.7
Jacksonville	925,213	1,122,750	1,314,619	21.4	17.1
Baker County	18,486	22,259	25,004	20.4	12.3
Clay County	105,986	140,814	176,901	32.9	25.6
Duval County	672,971	778,879	879,235	15.7	12.9
Nassau County	43,941	57,663	68,188	31.2	18.3
St. Johns County	83,829	123,135	165,291	46.9	34.2
Lakeland	405,382	483,924	565,049	19.4	16.8
Miami-Ft. Lauderdale-Miami Beach	4,056,228	5,007,988	5,478,171	23.5	9.4
Broward County	1,255,531	1,623,018	1,753,162	29.3	8.0
Miami-Dade County	1,937,194	2,253,779	2,437,022	16.3	8.1
Palm Beach County	863,503	1,131,191	1,287,987	31.0	13.9
Naples-Marco Island	152,099	251,377	326,658	65.3	29.9
Ocala	194,835	258,916	315,074	32.9	21.7
Orlando-Kissimmee	1,224,844	1,644,563	2,032,877	34.3	23.6
Lake County	152,104	210,527	276,783	38.4	31.5
Orange County	677,491	896,344	1,079,524	32.3	20.4
Osceola County	107,728	172,493	255,903	60.1	48.4
Seminole County	287,521	365,199	420,667	27.0	15.2
Palm Bay-Melbourne-Titusville	398,978	476,230	543,050	19.4	14.0
Panama City-Lynn Haven	126,994	148,217	165,515	16.7	11.7
Pensacola-Ferry Pass-Brent	344,406	412,153	451,075	19.7	9.4
Escambia County	262,798	294,410	309,647	12.0	5.2
Santa Rosa County	81,608	117,743	141,428	44.3	20.1
Port St. Lucie-Ft. Pierce	251,071	319,426	401,960	27.2	25.8
Martin County	100,900	126,731	142,645	25.6	12.6
St. Lucie County	150,171	192,695	259,315	28.3	34.6
Punta Gorda	110,975	141,627	160,315	27.6	13.2
Sarasota-Bradenton-Venice	489,483	589,963	687,711	20.5	16.6
Manatee County	211,707	264,002	308,325	24.7	16.8
Sarasota County	277,776	325,961	379,386	17.3	16.4
Sebastian-Vero Beach	90,208	112,947	135,262	25.2	19.8
Tallahassee	259,107	320,304	363,438	23.6	13.5
Gadsden County	41,116	45,087	48,195	9.7	6.9
Jefferson County	11,296	12,902	14,353	14.2	11.2
Leon County	192,493	239,452	272,497	24.4	13.8
Wakulla County	14,202	22,863	28,393	61.0	24.2
Tampa-St. Petersburg-Clearwater	2,067,959	2,396,013	2,693,888	15.9	12.4
Hernando County	101,115	130,802	157,006	29.4	20.0
Hillsborough County	834,054	998,948	1,164,425	19.8	16.6
Pasco County	281,131	344,768	424,355	22.6	23.1
Pinellas County	851,659	921,495	948,102	8.2	2.9

Note: Data are for MSAs based on December 2005 designations. See Glossary and map at the front of the book.

Source: University of Florida, Bureau of Economic and Business Research, Population Program, *Florida Estimates of Population, April 1, 2006.* Census data from U.S. Census Bureau.

Table 1.14. COUNTY RANKINGS AND DENSITY: POPULATION ESTIMATES, RANK PERCENTAGE DISTRIBUTION, LAND AREA, AND DENSITY IN THE STATE AND COUNTIES OF FLORIDA, APRIL 1, 2006

County	Estimates			Land area 1/ (square miles)	Density	
	Number	Rank in state	Percentage of state		Persons per square mile	Rank in state
Florida	18,349,132	(X)	100.00	53,937.2	340	(X)
Alachua	243,779	23	1.33	874.3	279	22
Baker	25,004	52	0.14	585.3	43	51
Bay	165,515	25	0.90	763.7	217	28
Bradford	28,551	49	0.16	293.2	97	38
Brevard	543,050	10	2.96	1,018.5	533	12
Broward	1,753,162	2	9.55	1,208.9	1,450	2
Calhoun	14,113	63	0.08	567.4	25	60
Charlotte	160,315	28	0.87	693.7	231	27
Citrus	136,749	32	0.75	583.6	234	26
Clay	176,901	26	0.96	601.1	294	20
Collier	326,658	15	1.78	2,025.5	161	33
Columbia	63,538	39	0.35	797.2	80	42
DeSoto	33,164	48	0.18	637.3	52	47
Dixie	15,677	59	0.09	704.1	22	63
Duval	879,235	7	4.79	773.9	1,136	6
Escambia	309,647	17	1.69	663.6	467	13
Flagler	89,075	35	0.49	485.0	184	32
Franklin	11,916	64	0.06	534.0	22	62
Gadsden	48,195	42	0.26	516.2	93	40
Gilchrist	16,703	57	0.09	348.9	48	49
Glades	10,796	65	0.06	773.5	14	66
Gulf	16,509	58	0.09	565.1	29	57
Hamilton	14,517	61	0.08	514.9	28	59
Hardee	27,186	51	0.15	637.4	43	52
Hendry	38,678	46	0.21	1,152.7	34	56
Hernando	157,006	29	0.86	478.3	328	18
Highlands	96,672	34	0.53	1,028.5	94	39
Hillsborough	1,164,425	4	6.35	1,051.0	1,108	7
Holmes	19,502	56	0.11	482.6	40	53
Indian River	135,262	33	0.74	503.3	269	24
Jackson	50,246	43	0.27	915.8	55	45
Jefferson	14,353	62	0.08	597.8	24	61
Lafayette	8,060	66	0.04	542.8	15	65
Lake	276,783	19	1.51	953.1	290	21
Lee	585,608	8	3.19	803.6	729	8
Leon	272,497	20	1.49	666.8	409	17

See footnotes at end of table. Continued . . .

Table 1.14. COUNTY RANKINGS AND DENSITY: POPULATION ESTIMATES, RANK PERCENTAGE DISTRIBUTION, LAND AREA, AND DENSITY IN THE STATE AND COUNTIES OF FLORIDA, APRIL 1, 2006 (Continued)

County	Estimates			Land area 1/ (square miles)	Density	
	Number	Rank in state	Percentage of state		Persons per square mile	Rank in state
Levy	38,981	44	0.21	1,118.4	35	55
Liberty	7,772	67	0.04	835.9	9	67
Madison	19,814	55	0.11	692.0	29	58
Manatee	308,325	18	1.68	741.2	416	16
Marion	315,074	16	1.72	1,579.0	200	30
Martin	142,645	30	0.78	555.7	257	25
Miami-Dade	2,437,022	1	13.28	1,944.5	1,253	4
Monroe	80,510	38	0.44	997.3	81	41
Nassau	68,188	40	0.37	651.6	105	36
Okaloosa	192,672	24	1.05	935.8	206	29
Okeechobee	38,666	45	0.21	774.3	50	48
Orange	1,079,524	5	5.88	907.6	1,189	5
Osceola	255,903	22	1.39	1,322.0	194	31
Palm Beach	1,287,987	3	7.02	1,974.2	652	10
Pasco	424,355	12	2.31	745.0	570	11
Pinellas	948,102	6	5.17	280.2	3,384	1
Polk	565,049	9	3.08	1,874.9	301	19
Putnam	74,416	37	0.41	722.2	103	37
St. Johns	165,291	27	0.90	609.0	271	23
St. Lucie	259,315	21	1.41	572.5	453	15
Santa Rosa	141,428	31	0.77	1,015.8	139	35
Sarasota	379,386	14	2.07	571.8	664	9
Seminole	420,667	13	2.29	308.2	1,365	3
Sumter	82,599	36	0.45	545.7	151	34
Suwannee	38,799	47	0.21	687.7	56	44
Taylor	21,471	54	0.12	1,042.0	21	64
Union	15,028	60	0.08	240.3	63	43
Volusia	503,844	11	2.75	1,105.9	456	14
Wakulla	28,393	50	0.15	606.7	47	50
Walton	55,786	41	0.30	1,057.7	53	46
Washington	23,073	53	0.13	579.9	40	54

(X) Not applicable.
1/ Land area figures represent the total area in the counties in 2000 and are not adjusted for lands which cannot be developed (government-owned parks or reserves) or are uninhabitable (swamps or marshes).

Source: University of Florida, Bureau of Economic and Business Research, Population Program, *Florida Estimates of Population, April 1, 2006.* Census data from U.S. Census Bureau.

Table 1.20. COUNTIES: CENSUS COUNTS, APRIL 1, 2000, AND POPULATION ESTIMATES APRIL 1, 2002 THROUGH 2006, IN THE STATE AND COUNTIES OF FLORIDA

County	Census 2000	Estimates 2002	2003	2004	2005	2006	Percentage change 2000 to 2006
Florida	15,982,824	16,674,608	17,071,508	17,516,732	17,918,227	18,349,132	14.8
Alachua	217,955	228,607	231,296	236,174	240,764	243,779	11.8
Baker	22,259	22,992	23,383	23,963	23,953	25,004	12.3
Bay	148,217	152,186	154,827	158,437	161,721	165,515	11.7
Bradford	26,088	26,517	26,972	27,740	28,118	28,551	9.4
Brevard	476,230	494,102	507,810	521,422	531,970	543,050	14.0
Broward	1,623,018	1,669,153	1,698,425	1,723,131	1,740,987	1,753,162	8.0
Calhoun	13,017	13,231	13,439	13,610	13,945	14,113	8.4
Charlotte	141,627	148,521	151,994	156,985	154,030	160,315	13.2
Citrus	118,085	123,008	125,804	129,110	132,635	136,749	15.8
Clay	140,814	149,901	156,011	163,461	169,623	176,901	25.6
Collier	251,377	277,457	292,466	306,186	317,788	326,658	29.9
Columbia	56,513	58,372	58,890	60,453	61,466	63,538	12.4
DeSoto	32,209	32,798	33,713	34,105	32,606	33,164	3.0
Dixie	13,827	14,459	14,688	14,928	15,377	15,677	13.4
Duval	778,879	809,394	826,279	840,474	861,150	879,235	12.9
Escambia	294,410	299,485	303,310	307,226	303,623	309,647	5.2
Flagler	49,832	56,785	61,541	69,683	78,617	89,075	78.8
Franklin	9,829	10,161	10,480	10,649	10,845	11,916	21.2
Gadsden	45,087	45,911	46,491	46,857	47,713	48,195	6.9
Gilchrist	14,437	15,023	15,517	15,900	16,221	16,703	15.7
Glades	10,576	10,664	10,729	10,733	10,729	10,796	2.1
Gulf	14,560	15,202	15,615	16,171	16,479	16,509	13.4
Hamilton	13,327	13,925	14,025	14,303	14,315	14,517	8.9
Hardee	26,938	27,437	27,400	27,787	27,333	27,186	0.9
Hendry	36,210	36,154	36,511	37,394	38,376	38,678	6.8
Hernando	130,802	136,484	140,670	145,207	150,784	157,006	20.0
Highlands	87,366	89,038	90,393	92,057	93,456	96,672	10.7
Hillsborough	998,948	1,055,617	1,079,587	1,108,435	1,131,546	1,164,425	16.6
Holmes	18,564	18,708	18,940	19,012	19,157	19,502	5.1
Indian River	112,947	118,149	121,174	126,829	130,043	135,262	19.8
Jackson	46,755	47,707	48,991	48,870	49,691	50,246	7.5
Jefferson	12,902	13,261	13,552	14,064	14,233	14,353	11.2
Lafayette	7,022	7,205	7,353	7,535	7,971	8,060	14.8
Lake	210,527	231,072	240,716	251,878	263,017	276,783	31.5

See footnote at end of table.

Continued . . .

Table 1.20. COUNTIES: CENSUS COUNTS, APRIL 1, 2000, AND POPULATION ESTIMATES APRIL 1, 2002 THROUGH 2006, IN THE STATE AND COUNTIES OF FLORIDA (Continued)

County	Census 2000	Estimates 2002	2003	2004	2005	2006	Percentage change 2000 to 2006
Lee	440,888	475,073	495,088	521,253	549,442	585,608	32.8
Leon	239,452	248,039	255,500	263,896	271,111	272,497	13.8
Levy	34,450	36,013	36,664	37,486	37,985	38,981	13.2
Liberty	7,021	7,157	7,227	7,354	7,581	7,772	10.7
Madison	18,733	18,932	19,139	19,498	19,696	19,814	5.8
Manatee	264,002	277,362	286,884	295,242	304,364	308,325	16.8
Marion	258,916	271,096	281,966	293,317	304,926	315,074	21.7
Martin	126,731	131,051	134,491	137,637	141,059	142,645	12.6
Miami-Dade	2,253,779	2,312,478	2,345,932	2,379,818	2,422,075	2,437,022	8.1
Monroe	79,589	81,140	80,537	81,236	82,413	80,510	1.2
Nassau	57,663	61,094	63,062	65,016	65,759	68,188	18.3
Okaloosa	170,498	176,971	181,102	185,778	188,939	192,672	13.0
Okeechobee	35,910	36,551	37,236	38,004	37,765	38,666	7.7
Orange	896,344	955,865	983,165	1,013,937	1,043,437	1,079,524	20.4
Osceola	172,493	193,355	210,438	225,816	235,156	255,903	48.4
Palm Beach	1,131,191	1,183,197	1,211,448	1,242,270	1,265,900	1,287,987	13.9
Pasco	344,768	361,468	375,318	389,776	406,898	424,355	23.1
Pinellas	921,495	933,994	939,864	943,640	947,744	948,102	2.9
Polk	483,924	502,385	511,929	528,389	541,840	565,049	16.8
Putnam	70,423	71,329	71,971	73,226	73,764	74,416	5.7
St. Johns	123,135	133,953	139,849	149,336	157,278	165,291	34.2
St. Lucie	192,695	203,360	211,898	226,216	240,039	259,315	34.6
Santa Rosa	117,743	124,956	128,889	133,721	136,443	141,428	20.1
Sarasota	325,961	339,684	348,761	358,307	367,867	379,386	16.4
Seminole	365,199	387,626	394,900	403,361	411,744	420,667	15.2
Sumter	53,345	61,348	63,001	66,416	74,052	82,599	54.8
Suwannee	34,844	35,727	37,198	37,713	38,174	38,799	11.4
Taylor	19,256	19,800	20,646	20,941	21,310	21,471	11.5
Union	13,442	13,794	13,726	14,620	15,046	15,028	11.8
Volusia	443,343	459,737	470,770	484,261	494,649	503,844	13.6
Wakulla	22,863	24,217	24,938	25,505	26,867	28,393	24.2
Walton	40,601	45,521	47,066	50,543	53,525	55,786	37.4
Washington	20,973	21,649	21,913	22,434	23,097	23,073	10.0

Note: Estimates are unrevised and are subject to future revisions.

Source: University of Florida, Bureau of Economic and Business Research, Population Program, *Florida Estimates of Population, April 1, 2006,* and previous editions. Census data from U.S. Census Bureau.

Table 1.25. COUNTIES AND CITIES: CENSUS COUNTS, APRIL 1, 2000, AND POPULATION ESTIMATES APRIL 1, 2006, IN THE STATE, COUNTIES, AND MUNICIPALITIES OF FLORIDA

Area	Census 2000	Estimates 2006	Percentage change
Florida	15,982,824	18,349,132	14.81
Incorporated	7,905,318	9,331,989	18.05
Unincorporated	8,077,506	9,017,143	11.63
Alachua	217,955	243,779	11.85
Alachua	6,098	7,657	25.57
Archer	1,289	1,225	-4.97
Gainesville	95,447	120,919	26.69
Hawthorne	1,415	1,401	-0.99
High Springs	3,863	4,576	18.46
LaCrosse	143	190	32.87
Micanopy	653	626	-4.13
Newberry	3,316	4,414	33.11
Waldo	821	821	0.00
Unincorporated	104,910	101,950	-2.82
Baker	22,259	25,004	12.33
Glen St. Mary	473	466	-1.48
Macclenny	4,459	5,433	21.84
Unincorporated	17,327	19,105	10.26
Bay	148,217	165,515	11.67
Callaway	14,233	14,789	3.91
Cedar Grove	5,367	6,325	17.85
Lynn Haven	12,451	16,436	32.01
Mexico Beach	1,017	1,164	14.45
Panama City	36,417	37,540	3.08
Panama City Beach	7,671	10,005	30.43
Parker	4,623	4,688	1.41
Springfield	8,810	9,017	2.35
Unincorporated	57,628	65,551	13.75
Bradford	26,088	28,551	9.44
Brooker	352	355	0.85
Hampton	431	425	-1.39
Lawtey	656	667	1.68
Starke	5,593	6,053	8.22
Unincorporated	19,056	21,051	10.47
Brevard	476,230	543,050	14.03
Cape Canaveral	8,829	10,317	16.85
Cocoa	16,412	17,395	5.99
Cocoa Beach	12,482	12,785	2.43
Indialantic	2,944	2,961	0.58
Indian Harbour Beach	8,152	8,696	6.67
Malabar	2,622	2,872	9.53
Melbourne	71,382	76,742	7.51
Melbourne Beach	3,335	3,308	-0.81
Melbourne Village	706	715	1.27
Palm Bay	79,413	96,683	21.75
Palm Shores	794	949	19.52
Rockledge	20,170	25,225	25.06
Satellite Beach	9,577	10,938	14.21
Brevard (Continued)			
Titusville	40,670	44,020	8.24
West Melbourne	9,824	15,777	60.60
Unincorporated	188,918	213,667	13.10
Broward	1,623,018	1,753,162	8.02
Coconut Creek	43,566	48,283	10.83
Cooper City 1/	27,914	29,859	6.97
Coral Springs	117,549	129,615	10.26
Dania Beach	20,061	28,555	42.34
Davie	75,720	84,057	11.01
Deerfield Beach 1/	64,585	75,603	17.06
Ft. Lauderdale	152,397	175,836	15.38
Hallandale	34,282	35,844	4.56
Hillsboro Beach	2,163	2,234	3.28
Hollywood 1/	139,368	143,287	2.81
Lauderdale-by-the-Sea 1/	3,221	5,831	81.03
Lauderdale Lakes	31,705	32,161	1.44
Lauderhill	57,585	63,134	9.64
Lazy Lake Village	38	41	7.89
Lighthouse Point	10,767	10,899	1.23
Margate	53,909	55,332	2.64
Miramar	72,739	110,322	51.67
North Lauderdale	32,264	41,584	28.89
Oakland Park	30,966	42,427	37.01
Parkland	13,835	21,913	58.39
Pembroke Park 1/	5,384	5,740	6.61
Pembroke Pines	137,427	151,786	10.45
Plantation	82,934	84,891	2.36
Pompano Beach	78,191	101,103	29.30
Sea Ranch Lakes 1/	734	730	-0.54
Southwest Ranches 2/	0	7,415	(X)
Sunrise 1/	85,787	89,669	4.53
Tamarac	55,588	59,259	6.60
Weston	49,286	61,629	25.04
West Park 2/	0	13,804	(X)
Wilton Manors	12,697	12,546	-1.19
Unincorporated 1/	130,356	27,773	-78.69
Calhoun	13,017	14,113	8.42
Altha	506	562	11.07
Blountstown	2,444	2,476	1.31
Unincorporated	10,067	11,075	10.01
Charlotte	141,627	160,315	13.20
Punta Gorda	14,344	16,952	18.18
Unincorporated	127,283	143,363	12.63
Citrus	118,085	136,749	15.81
Crystal River	3,485	3,737	7.23
Inverness	6,789	7,240	6.64

See footnotes at end of table.

Continued . . .

Table 1.25. COUNTIES AND CITIES: CENSUS COUNTS, APRIL 1, 2000, AND POPULATION ESTIMATES APRIL 1, 2006, IN THE STATE, COUNTIES, AND MUNICIPALITIES OF FLORIDA (Continued)

Area	Census 2000	Estimates 2006	Percentage change
Citrus (Continued)			
Unincorporated	107,811	125,772	16.66
Clay	140,814	176,901	25.63
Green Cove Springs	5,378	6,381	18.65
Keystone Heights 1/	1,345	1,411	4.91
Orange Park	9,081	9,034	-0.52
Penney Farms	580	633	9.14
Unincorporated 1/	124,430	159,442	28.14
Collier	251,377	326,658	29.95
Everglades	479	527	10.02
Marco Island	14,879	15,719	5.65
Naples	20,976	22,970	9.51
Unincorporated	215,043	287,442	33.67
Columbia	56,513	63,538	12.43
Ft. White	409	463	13.20
Lake City	9,980	10,919	9.41
Unincorporated	46,124	52,156	13.08
DeSoto	32,209	33,164	2.97
Arcadia	6,604	6,755	2.29
Unincorporated	25,605	26,409	3.14
Dixie	13,827	15,677	13.38
Cross City	1,775	1,768	-0.39
Horseshoe Beach	206	274	33.01
Unincorporated	11,846	13,635	15.10
Duval	778,879	879,235	12.88
Atlantic Beach	1,634	1,604	-1.84
Baldwin	13,368	14,015	4.84
Jacksonville	735,617	834,789	13.48
Jacksonville Beach	20,990	21,544	2.64
Neptune Beach	7,270	7,283	0.18
Escambia	294,410	309,647	5.18
Century	1,714	1,755	2.39
Pensacola	56,255	55,033	-2.17
Unincorporated	236,441	252,859	6.94
Flagler	49,832	89,075	78.75
Beverly Beach	547	513	-6.22
Bunnell	2,122	2,513	18.43
Flagler Beach (part)	4,878	5,457	11.87
Marineland (part)	6	9	50.00
Palm Coast	32,732	67,832	107.23
Unincorporated	9,547	12,751	33.56
Franklin 1/	9,829	11,916	21.23
Apalachicola	2,334	2,507	7.41
Carrabelle	1,303	1,282	-1.61
Unincorporated 1/	6,192	8,127	31.25
Gadsden	45,087	48,195	6.89
Chattahoochee	3,287	3,833	16.61
Greensboro	619	652	5.33
Gretna	1,709	1,741	1.87
Havana	1,713	1,764	2.98
Midway	1,446	1,683	16.39
Quincy	6,982	7,300	4.55
Unincorporated	29,331	31,222	6.45
Gilchrist	14,437	16,703	15.70
Bell	349	452	29.51
Fanning Springs (part)	273	345	26.37
Trenton	1,617	1,686	4.27
Unincorporated	12,198	14,220	16.58
Glades	10,576	10,796	2.08
Moore Haven	1,635	1,626	-0.55
Unincorporated	8,941	9,170	2.56
Gulf 1/	14,560	16,509	13.39
Port St. Joe	3,644	3,791	4.03
Wewahitchka	1,722	1,949	13.18
Unincorporated 1/	9,194	10,769	17.13
Hamilton	13,327	14,517	8.93
Jasper	1,780	1,705	-4.21
Jennings	833	805	-3.36
White Springs	819	774	-5.49
Unincorporated	9,895	11,233	13.52
Hardee	26,938	27,186	0.92
Bowling Green	2,892	3,084	6.64
Wauchula	4,368	4,454	1.97
Zolfo Springs	1,641	1,551	-5.48
Unincorporated	18,037	18,097	0.33
Hendry	36,210	38,678	6.82
Clewiston	6,460	6,573	1.75
La Belle	4,210	4,571	8.57
Unincorporated	25,540	27,534	7.81
Hernando	130,802	157,006	20.03
Brooksville	7,264	7,322	0.80
Weeki Wachee	12	8	-33.33
Unincorporated	123,526	149,676	21.17
Highlands	87,366	96,672	10.65
Avon Park	8,542	8,792	2.93
Lake Placid	1,668	1,762	5.64
Sebring	9,667	10,218	5.70
Unincorporated	67,489	75,900	12.46

See footnotes at end of table.

Continued . . .

Table 1.25. COUNTIES AND CITIES: CENSUS COUNTS, APRIL 1, 2000, AND POPULATION ESTIMATES APRIL 1, 2006, IN THE STATE, COUNTIES, AND MUNICIPALITIES OF FLORIDA (Continued)

Area	Census 2000	Estimates 2006	Per-centage change
Hillsborough	998,948	1,164,425	16.57
Plant City 1/	29,760	32,834	10.33
Tampa	303,447	330,886	9.04
Temple Terrace	20,918	23,035	10.12
Unincorporated 1/	644,823	777,670	20.60
Holmes	18,564	19,502	5.05
Bonifay 1/	2,665	2,732	2.51
Esto	356	379	6.46
Noma	213	213	0.00
Ponce de Leon	457	477	4.38
Westville	221	226	2.26
Unincorporated 1/	14,652	15,475	5.62
Indian River	112,947	135,262	19.76
Fellsmere	3,813	4,628	21.37
Indian River Shores	3,448	3,722	7.95
Orchid	140	307	119.29
Sebastian	16,181	21,666	33.90
Vero Beach	17,705	18,160	2.57
Unincorporated	71,660	86,779	21.10
Jackson	46,755	50,246	7.47
Alford	466	492	5.58
Bascom	106	111	4.72
Campbellton	212	208	-1.89
Cottondale	869	918	5.64
Graceville	2,402	2,500	4.08
Grand Ridge	792	899	13.51
Greenwood	735	776	5.58
Jacob City	281	293	4.27
Malone	2,007	2,300	14.60
Marianna	6,230	6,562	5.33
Sneads	1,919	1,996	4.01
Unincorporated	30,736	33,191	7.99
Jefferson	12,902	14,353	11.25
Monticello	2,533	2,520	-0.51
Unincorporated	10,369	11,833	14.12
Lafayette	7,022	8,060	14.78
Mayo	988	1,025	3.74
Unincorporated	6,034	7,035	16.59
Lake 1/	210,527	276,783	31.47
Astatula	1,298	1,591	22.57
Clermont 1/	9,338	22,097	136.64
Eustis	15,106	17,766	17.61
Fruitland Park	3,186	3,628	13.87
Groveland 1/	2,394	5,923	147.41
Howey-in-the-Hills	956	1,156	20.92
Lady Lake	11,828	12,805	8.26
Leesburg	15,956	18,841	18.08
Lake (Continued)			
Mascotte	2,687	4,270	58.91
Minneola	5,435	9,440	73.69
Montverde	882	1,183	34.13
Mount Dora	9,418	11,125	18.12
Tavares	9,700	12,552	29.40
Umatilla	2,214	2,672	20.69
Unincorporated 1/	120,129	151,734	26.31
Lee	440,888	585,608	32.82
Bonita Springs	32,797	43,518	32.69
Cape Coral	102,286	154,499	51.05
Ft. Myers	48,208	65,729	36.34
Ft. Myers Beach	6,561	6,874	4.77
Sanibel	6,064	6,321	4.24
Unincorporated	244,972	308,667	26.00
Leon	239,452	272,497	13.80
Tallahassee	150,624	176,336	17.07
Unincorporated	88,828	96,161	8.26
Levy	34,450	38,981	13.15
Bronson	964	1,130	17.22
Cedar Key	790	924	16.96
Chiefland	1,993	2,140	7.38
Fanning Springs (part)	464	587	26.51
Inglis	1,491	1,731	16.10
Otter Creek	121	143	18.18
Williston	2,297	2,425	5.57
Yankeetown	629	759	20.67
Unincorporated	25,701	29,142	13.39
Liberty	7,021	7,772	10.70
Bristol	845	957	13.25
Unincorporated	6,176	6,815	10.35
Madison	18,733	19,814	5.77
Greenville	837	852	1.79
Lee	352	380	7.95
Madison	3,061	3,106	1.47
Unincorporated	14,483	15,476	6.86
Manatee	264,002	308,325	16.79
Anna Maria	1,814	1,847	1.82
Bradenton	49,504	54,911	10.92
Bradenton Beach	1,482	1,553	4.79
Holmes Beach	4,966	5,038	1.45
Longboat Key (part)	2,591	2,598	0.27
Palmetto	12,571	13,756	9.43
Unincorporated	191,074	228,622	19.65
Marion	258,916	315,074	21.69
Belleview	3,478	3,859	10.95

See footnotes at end of table.

Continued . . .

Table 1.25. COUNTIES AND CITIES: CENSUS COUNTS, APRIL 1, 2000, AND POPULATION ESTIMATES APRIL 1, 2006, IN THE STATE, COUNTIES, AND MUNICIPALITIES OF FLORIDA (Continued)

Area	Census 2000	Estimates 2006	Percentage change	Area	Census 2000	Estimates 2006	Percentage change
Marion (Continued)				Monroe	79,589	80,510	1.16
Dunnellon	1,898	2,014	6.11	Islamorada	6,846	7,057	3.08
McIntosh	453	446	-1.55	Key Colony Beach	788	857	8.76
Ocala	45,943	51,853	12.86	Key West	25,478	25,319	-0.62
Reddick	571	516	-9.63	Layton	186	206	10.75
Unincorporated	206,573	256,386	24.11	Marathon	10,255	10,605	3.41
				Unincorporated	36,036	36,466	1.19
Martin	126,731	142,645	12.56				
Jupiter Island	620	628	1.29	Nassau	57,663	68,188	18.25
Ocean Breeze Park	463	421	-9.07	Callahan	962	1,345	39.81
Sewalls Point	1,946	1,995	2.52	Fernandina Beach	10,549	11,815	12.00
Stuart	14,633	16,661	13.86	Hilliard	2,702	2,964	9.70
Unincorporated	109,069	122,940	12.72	Unincorporated	43,450	52,064	19.83
Miami-Dade 1/	2,253,779	2,437,022	8.13	Okaloosa	170,498	192,672	13.01
Aventura	25,267	29,451	16.56	Cinco Bayou	377	382	1.33
Bal Harbour	3,305	2,973	-10.05	Crestview	14,766	19,494	32.02
Bay Harbor Islands	5,146	5,208	1.20	Destin	11,119	12,098	8.80
Biscayne Park	3,269	3,320	1.56	Ft. Walton Beach	19,973	20,882	4.55
Coral Gables	42,249	44,404	5.10	Laurel Hill	549	581	5.83
Cutler Bay 2/	0	37,103	(X)	Mary Esther	4,055	4,264	5.15
Doral 2/	0	32,541	(X)	Niceville	11,684	13,221	13.15
El Portal	2,505	2,552	1.88	Shalimar	718	730	1.67
Florida City	7,843	9,195	17.24	Valparaiso	6,408	6,537	2.01
Golden Beach	919	942	2.50	Unincorporated	100,849	114,483	13.52
Hialeah	226,419	228,344	0.85				
Hialeah Gardens	19,297	20,476	6.11	Okeechobee	35,910	38,666	7.67
Homestead	31,909	43,167	35.28	Okeechobee	5,376	5,673	5.52
Indian Creek Village	33	59	78.79	Unincorporated	30,534	32,993	8.05
Islandia	6	6	0.00				
Key Biscayne	10,507	11,464	9.11	Orange	896,344	1,079,524	20.44
Medley	1,098	1,288	17.30	Apopka	26,642	37,253	39.83
Miami	362,470	391,355	7.97	Bay Lake	23	28	21.74
Miami Beach	87,933	92,145	4.79	Belle Isle	5,531	5,891	6.51
Miami Gardens 2/	0	107,579	(X)	Eatonville	2,432	2,547	4.73
Miami Lakes 2/	0	27,292	(X)	Edgewood	1,901	2,160	13.62
Miami Shores	10,380	10,456	0.73	Lake Buena Vista	16	19	18.75
Miami Springs	13,712	13,723	0.08	Maitland	12,019	16,055	33.58
North Bay	6,733	5,794	-13.95	Oakland	936	1,933	106.52
North Miami	59,880	59,734	-0.24	Ocoee	24,391	32,175	31.91
North Miami Beach	40,786	40,688	-0.24	Orlando	185,951	224,055	20.49
Opa-locka	14,951	15,487	3.59	Windermere	1,897	2,682	41.38
Palmetto Bay 2/	0	25,142	(X)	Winter Garden	14,351	28,440	98.17
Pinecrest	19,055	19,530	2.49	Winter Park	24,090	28,620	18.80
South Miami	10,741	10,528	-1.98	Unincorporated	596,164	697,666	17.03
Sunny Isles Beach	15,315	18,121	18.32				
Surfside	4,909	5,635	14.79	Osceola	172,493	255,903	48.36
Sweetwater	14,226	14,281	0.39	Kissimmee	47,814	60,241	25.99
Virginia Gardens	2,348	2,371	0.98	St. Cloud	20,074	30,035	49.62
West Miami	5,863	5,744	-2.03	Unincorporated	104,605	165,627	58.34
Unincorporated 1/	1,204,705	1,098,924	-8.78				

See footnotes at end of table.

Continued . . .

Table 1.25. COUNTIES AND CITIES: CENSUS COUNTS, APRIL 1, 2000, AND POPULATION ESTIMATES APRIL 1, 2006, IN THE STATE, COUNTIES, AND MUNICIPALITIES OF FLORIDA (Continued)

Area	Census 2000	Estimates 2006	Percentage change
Palm Beach 1/	1,131,191	1,287,987	13.86
Atlantis	2,005	2,138	6.63
Belle Glade	14,906	16,894	13.34
Boca Raton	74,764	85,488	14.34
Boynton Beach	60,389	67,071	11.06
Briny Breezes	411	418	1.70
Cloud Lake	167	164	-1.80
Delray Beach	60,020	64,095	6.79
Glen Ridge	276	265	-3.99
Golf Village	230	232	0.87
Greenacres City	27,569	31,734	15.11
Gulf Stream	716	736	2.79
Haverhill	1,454	1,554	6.88
Highland Beach	3,775	4,157	10.12
Hypoluxo	2,015	2,463	22.23
Juno Beach	3,262	3,637	11.50
Jupiter	39,328	50,028	27.21
Jupiter Inlet Colony	368	371	0.82
Lake Clarke Shores	3,451	3,469	0.52
Lake Park	8,721	9,113	4.49
Lake Worth	35,133	36,412	3.64
Lantana 1/	9,404	10,121	7.62
Manalapan	321	360	12.15
Mangonia Park	1,283	2,539	97.90
North Palm Beach	12,064	12,562	4.13
Ocean Ridge	1,636	1,640	0.24
Pahokee	5,985	6,419	7.25
Palm Beach 1/	9,676	9,706	0.31
Palm Beach Gardens	35,058	48,176	37.42
Palm Beach Shores	1,269	1,366	7.64
Palm Springs	11,699	14,512	24.04
Riviera Beach	29,884	33,408	11.79
Royal Palm Beach	21,523	30,334	40.94
South Bay	3,859	4,666	20.91
South Palm Beach 1/	1,531	1,526	-0.33
Tequesta Village	5,273	5,702	8.14
Wellington	38,216	55,564	45.39
West Palm Beach	82,103	107,617	31.08
Unincorporated[1]	521,447	561,330	7.65
Pasco 1/	344,768	424,355	23.08
Dade City	6,188	6,856	10.80
New Port Richey	16,117	16,645	3.28
Port Richey	3,021	3,205	6.09
St. Leo 1/	590	1,250	111.86
San Antonio 1/	684	948	38.60
Zephyrhills	10,833	12,579	16.12
Unincorporated 1/	307,335	382,872	24.58
Pinellas 1/	921,495	948,102	2.89
Belleair	4,067	4,144	1.89
Belleair Beach 1/	1,632	1,619	-0.80
Belleair Bluffs	2,243	2,232	-0.49
Pinellas (Continued)			
Belleair Shore 1/	75	71	-5.33
Clearwater 1/	108,789	110,602	1.67
Dunedin	35,691	37,574	5.28
Gulfport	12,527	12,935	3.26
Indian Rocks Beach	5,127	5,345	4.25
Indian Shores	1,705	1,803	5.75
Kenneth City	4,400	4,551	3.43
Largo	69,371	75,850	9.34
Madeira Beach	4,511	4,514	0.07
North Redington Beach	1,474	1,509	2.37
Oldsmar	11,910	13,829	16.11
Pinellas Park	45,658	48,835	6.96
Redington Beach	1,539	1,583	2.86
Redington Shores	2,338	2,366	1.20
Safety Harbor	17,203	17,838	3.69
St. Pete Beach	9,929	10,050	1.22
St. Petersburg	248,232	254,225	2.41
Seminole	10,890	18,716	71.86
South Pasadena	5,778	5,758	-0.35
Tarpon Springs	21,003	24,161	15.04
Treasure Island	7,450	7,505	0.74
Unincorporated 1/	287,953	280,487	-2.59
Polk	483,924	565,049	16.76
Auburndale	11,032	12,512	13.42
Bartow	15,340	16,181	5.48
Davenport	1,924	2,344	21.83
Dundee	2,912	3,126	7.35
Eagle Lake	2,496	2,659	6.53
Ft. Meade	5,691	5,877	3.27
Frostproof	2,975	2,991	0.54
Haines City	13,174	17,973	36.43
Highland Park	244	246	0.82
Hillcrest Heights	266	262	-1.50
Lake Alfred	3,890	4,239	8.97
Lake Hamilton	1,304	1,409	8.05
Lake Wales	10,194	12,755	25.12
Lakeland	78,452	91,623	16.79
Mulberry	3,230	3,459	7.09
Polk City	1,516	1,831	20.78
Winter Haven	26,487	31,419	18.62
Unincorporated	302,797	354,143	16.96
Putnam	70,423	74,416	5.67
Crescent City	1,776	1,787	0.62
Interlachen	1,475	1,475	0.00
Palatka	10,033	11,417	13.79
Pomona Park	789	796	0.89
Welaka	586	624	6.48
Unincorporated	55,764	58,317	4.58

See footnotes at end of table.

Continued . . .

Table 1.25. COUNTIES AND CITIES: CENSUS COUNTS, APRIL 1, 2000, AND POPULATION ESTIMATES APRIL 1, 2006, IN THE STATE, COUNTIES, AND MUNICIPALITIES OF FLORIDA (Continued)

Area	Census 2000	Estimates 2006	Percentage change
St. Johns	123,135	165,291	34.24
Hastings	521	655	25.72
Marineland (part)	0	1	(X)
St. Augustine	11,592	13,702	18.20
St. Augustine Beach	4,683	5,908	26.16
Unincorporated	106,339	145,025	36.38
St. Lucie	192,695	259,315	34.57
Ft. Pierce	37,516	41,102	9.56
Port St. Lucie	88,769	144,159	62.40
St. Lucie Village	604	622	2.98
Unincorporated	65,806	73,432	11.59
Santa Rosa	117,743	141,428	20.12
Gulf Breeze	5,665	5,774	1.92
Jay	579	554	-4.32
Milton	7,045	7,689	9.14
Unincorporated	104,454	127,411	21.98
Sarasota 1/	325,961	379,386	16.39
Longboat Key (part)	5,012	5,067	1.10
North Port	22,797	47,770	109.55
Sarasota	52,715	55,364	5.03
Venice 1/	17,864	21,584	20.82
Unincorporated 1/	227,573	249,601	9.68
Seminole 1/	365,199	420,667	15.19
Altamonte Springs	41,200	43,054	4.50
Casselberry 1/	23,438	24,930	6.37
Lake Mary	11,458	14,020	22.36
Longwood	13,745	13,925	1.31
Oviedo	26,316	31,946	21.39
Sanford	38,291	51,227	33.78
Winter Springs 1/	30,860	33,971	10.08
Unincorporated 1/	179,891	207,594	15.40
Sumter	53,345	82,599	54.84
Bushnell	2,050	2,327	13.51
Center Hill	910	893	-1.87
Coleman	647	655	1.24
Webster	805	767	-4.72
Wildwood	3,924	4,564	16.31
Unincorporated	45,009	73,393	63.06
Suwannee	34,844	38,799	11.35
Branford	695	711	2.30
Live Oak	6,480	6,634	2.38
Unincorporated	27,669	31,454	13.68
Taylor	19,256	21,471	11.50
Perry	6,847	6,839	-0.12
Unincorporated	12,409	14,632	17.91
Union	13,442	15,028	11.80
Lake Butler	1,927	1,917	-0.52
Raiford 3/	187	251	34.22
Worthington Springs	193	494	155.96
Unincorporated	11,135	12,366	11.06
Volusia	443,343	503,844	13.65
Daytona Beach	64,112	64,977	1.35
Daytona Beach Shores	4,299	4,980	15.84
DeBary	15,559	18,620	19.67
DeLand	20,904	26,536	26.94
Deltona	69,543	85,484	22.92
Edgewater	18,668	21,572	15.56
Flagler Beach (part)	76	76	0.00
Holly Hill	12,119	12,614	4.08
Lake Helen	2,743	2,893	5.47
New Smyrna Beach	20,048	22,864	14.05
Oak Hill	1,378	2,042	48.19
Orange City	6,604	9,416	42.58
Ormond Beach	36,301	40,294	11.00
Pierson	2,596	2,645	1.89
Ponce Inlet	2,513	3,271	30.16
Port Orange	45,823	56,067	22.36
South Daytona	13,177	13,773	4.52
Unincorporated	106,880	115,720	8.27
Wakulla	22,863	28,393	24.19
St. Marks	272	315	15.81
Sopchoppy	426	415	-2.58
Unincorporated	22,165	27,663	24.80
Walton	40,601	55,786	37.40
DeFuniak Springs	5,089	5,387	5.86
Freeport	1,190	1,645	38.24
Paxton	656	720	9.76
Unincorporated	33,666	48,034	42.68
Washington	20,973	23,073	10.01
Caryville	218	365	67.43
Chipley	3,592	3,653	1.70
Ebro	250	259	3.60
Vernon	743	789	6.19
Wausau	398	436	9.55
Unincorporated	15,772	17,571	11.41

(X) Not applicable.
1/ Includes census corrections through October 10, 2004.
2/ Incorporated after April 1, 2000.
3/ Self-census.
Source: University of Florida, Bureau of Economic and Business Research, Population Program, *Florida Estimates of Population, April 1, 2006.* Census data from U.S. Census Bureau.

Table 1.30. AGE, RACE, AND SEX: CENSUS COUNTS, APRIL 1, 2000, AND ESTIMATES APRIL 1, 2006, BY AGE, SEX, RACE AND HISPANIC ORIGIN IN FLORIDA

Sex and race	Total	Age (years) 0-17	18-34	35-64	65-79	80 and over
			Census, 2000			
Total	15,982,378	3,646,342	3,414,702	6,113,723	2,068,883	738,728
Male	7,797,715	1,870,988	1,734,485	2,975,581	936,698	279,963
Female	8,184,663	1,775,354	1,680,217	3,138,142	1,132,185	458,765
Non-Hispanic white	10,591,456	2,065,205	1,950,685	4,239,257	1,700,335	635,974
Percentage of total	66.3	56.6	57.1	69.3	82.2	86.1
Male	5,159,630	1,062,406	990,482	2,082,991	778,213	245,538
Female	5,431,826	1,002,799	960,203	2,156,266	922,122	390,436
Non-Hispanic black	2,358,124	788,351	615,983	783,096	133,196	37,498
Percentage of total	14.8	21.6	18.0	12.8	6.4	5.1
Male	1,131,682	400,280	296,529	367,223	55,783	11,867
Female	1,226,442	388,071	319,454	415,873	77,413	25,631
Hispanic origin	2,682,746	706,748	747,357	949,987	216,803	61,851
Percentage of total	16.8	19.4	21.9	15.5	10.5	8.4
Male	1,340,140	364,786	398,031	461,361	94,776	21,186
Female	1,342,606	341,962	349,326	488,626	122,027	40,665
			Estimates, 2006			
Total	18,349,132	4,113,765	3,869,439	7,218,422	2,196,491	951,015
Male	8,979,098	2,102,760	1,973,335	3,529,653	998,126	375,224
Female	9,370,034	2,011,005	1,896,104	3,688,769	1,198,365	575,791
White	14,842,047	3,049,174	2,935,903	5,976,809	1,988,113	892,048
Percentage of total	80.9	74.1	75.9	82.8	90.5	93.8
Male	7,288,700	1,561,480	1,511,532	2,951,186	909,111	355,391
Female	7,553,347	1,487,694	1,424,371	3,025,623	1,079,002	536,657
Non-Hispanic white	11,427,917	2,138,869	2,042,923	4,714,406	1,725,295	806,424
Percentage of total	62.3	52.0	52.8	65.3	78.5	84.8
Male	5,579,730	1,095,514	1,040,395	2,325,399	794,231	324,191
Female	5,848,187	1,043,355	1,002,528	2,389,007	931,064	482,233
Black	3,004,854	912,184	800,437	1,063,088	178,537	50,608
Percentage of total	16.4	22.2	20.7	14.7	8.1	5.3
Male	1,448,182	463,777	395,929	495,235	76,245	16,996
Female	1,556,672	448,407	404,508	567,853	102,292	33,612
Non-Hispanic black	2,851,251	870,391	758,922	1,007,161	167,627	47,150
Percentage of total	15.5	21.2	19.6	14.0	7.6	5.0
Male	1,370,824	442,390	373,871	467,352	71,483	15,728
Female	1,480,427	428,001	385,051	539,809	96,144	31,422
Hispanic origin	3,613,482	965,102	947,290	1,334,460	276,666	89,964
Percentage of total	19.7	23.5	24.5	18.5	12.6	9.5
Male	1,809,708	494,008	500,117	661,850	120,939	32,794
Female	1,803,774	471,094	447,173	672,610	155,727	57,170

Note: Persons of Hispanic origin may be of any race. Includes persons of Latino or Spanish origin.

Source: University of Florida, Bureau of Economic and Business Research, Population Program, *Florida Population Studies,* June 2007, Volume 40, Bulletin No. 148, and unpublished data.

Table 1.31. RACE AND SEX: ESTIMATES BY RACE AND SEX IN THE STATE AND COUNTIES OF FLORIDA, APRIL 1, 2006

(rounded to thousands)

County	All races			Non-Hispanic white			Non-Hispanic black		
	Total	Male	Female	Total	Male	Female	Total	Male	Female
Florida	18,349.1	8,979.1	9,370.0	11,427.9	5,579.7	5,848.2	2,851.3	1,370.8	1,480.4
Alachua	243.8	119.3	124.5	164.1	80.8	83.2	50.4	24.0	26.4
Baker	25.0	13.4	11.6	20.8	10.7	10.1	3.3	2.1	1.2
Bay	165.5	81.7	83.8	135.8	67.4	68.4	18.6	8.8	9.8
Bradford	28.6	16.2	12.3	21.3	11.3	10.0	6.1	4.1	2.0
Brevard	543.1	265.6	277.4	446.0	218.9	227.1	50.2	23.7	26.5
Broward	1,753.2	851.5	901.6	908.3	444.5	463.9	422.9	201.5	221.3
Calhoun	14.1	7.6	6.6	10.9	5.5	5.4	2.3	1.4	0.9
Charlotte	160.3	76.6	83.7	142.6	68.0	74.6	8.7	4.1	4.6
Citrus	136.7	65.7	71.1	125.9	60.5	65.4	3.8	1.8	2.0
Clay	176.9	87.3	89.6	146.4	72.5	73.9	14.5	7.0	7.6
Collier	326.7	162.6	164.0	225.1	108.5	116.7	19.2	9.3	9.9
Columbia	63.5	32.6	31.0	49.7	25.0	24.7	10.6	5.8	4.9
DeSoto	33.2	18.4	14.7	19.9	9.9	10.1	3.9	2.4	1.5
Dixie	15.7	8.4	7.3	13.8	7.2	6.7	1.4	1.0	0.4
Duval	879.2	427.0	452.2	527.0	259.1	267.8	265.9	125.2	140.6
Escambia	309.6	152.5	157.1	219.2	109.0	110.2	68.7	32.6	36.1
Flagler	89.1	42.8	46.3	72.8	35.2	37.6	9.2	4.2	5.0
Franklin	11.9	6.3	5.6	10.0	5.1	4.8	1.6	1.0	0.6
Gadsden	48.2	23.1	25.1	16.4	8.0	8.4	27.2	12.6	14.6
Gilchrist	16.7	8.6	8.1	14.9	7.5	7.4	1.1	0.7	0.4
Glades	10.8	6.0	4.8	7.2	3.7	3.5	1.1	0.7	0.4
Gulf	16.5	9.6	6.9	12.4	6.6	5.8	3.3	2.3	0.9
Hamilton	14.5	8.5	6.0	7.8	4.3	3.4	5.3	3.2	2.1
Hardee	27.2	14.7	12.5	14.5	7.4	7.1	2.3	1.5	0.8
Hendry	38.7	20.8	17.9	15.9	8.0	7.9	5.3	2.8	2.5
Hernando	157.0	75.1	81.9	136.5	65.3	71.2	7.4	3.4	4.0
Highlands	96.7	47.0	49.7	70.9	33.6	37.3	9.0	4.3	4.7
Hillsborough	1,164.4	570.2	594.2	681.6	333.0	348.6	190.4	90.4	100.0
Holmes	19.5	10.3	9.2	17.3	8.8	8.5	1.5	1.0	0.4
Indian River	135.3	65.5	69.8	109.5	52.4	57.1	11.7	5.6	6.1
Jackson	50.2	27.4	22.9	34.3	17.8	16.5	13.6	7.9	5.7
Jefferson	14.4	7.5	6.8	8.6	4.4	4.2	5.0	2.6	2.4
Lafayette	8.1	4.9	3.1	6.0	3.2	2.8	1.1	1.0	0.2
Lake	276.8	134.7	142.1	225.4	109.2	116.2	23.2	11.0	12.2

See footnote at end of table.

Continued . . .

Table 1.31. RACE AND SEX: ESTIMATES BY RACE AND SEX IN THE STATE AND COUNTIES OF FLORIDA, APRIL 1, 2006

(rounded to thousands)

County	All races			Non-Hispanic white			Non-Hispanic black		
	Total	Male	Female	Total	Male	Female	Total	Male	Female
Lee	585.6	287.1	298.5	448.9	217.1	231.8	42.0	20.0	22.0
Leon	272.5	130.1	142.4	164.8	80.1	84.7	88.4	40.7	47.7
Levy	39.0	18.9	20.1	32.3	15.8	16.5	4.1	1.8	2.3
Liberty	7.8	4.7	3.0	5.6	3.1	2.5	1.6	1.2	0.4
Madison	19.8	10.4	9.4	11.0	5.6	5.4	7.7	4.1	3.6
Manatee	308.3	150.1	158.3	235.4	112.8	122.6	27.1	12.9	14.2
Marion	315.1	152.5	162.6	248.5	120.0	128.5	35.3	16.8	18.6
Martin	142.6	69.8	72.9	120.1	57.9	62.2	7.7	3.9	3.8
Miami-Dade	2,437.0	1,177.7	1,259.3	404.6	202.6	202.0	485.8	229.8	256.0
Monroe	80.5	42.4	38.1	60.4	31.9	28.5	4.0	2.1	1.9
Nassau	68.2	33.6	34.6	61.4	30.3	31.0	4.8	2.3	2.5
Okaloosa	192.7	96.3	96.3	154.4	77.5	76.9	19.6	9.4	10.2
Okeechobee	38.7	20.6	18.1	26.5	13.3	13.3	3.3	2.1	1.2
Orange	1,079.5	536.3	543.2	544.2	271.9	272.3	222.9	107.6	115.3
Osceola	255.9	127.1	128.8	124.0	61.4	62.6	20.9	10.0	10.9
Palm Beach	1,288.0	623.1	664.9	858.1	408.8	449.3	203.5	98.5	105.0
Pasco	424.4	205.5	218.8	370.2	178.4	191.8	11.6	5.5	6.0
Pinellas	948.1	456.7	491.5	761.6	366.0	395.6	98.3	46.7	51.7
Polk	565.0	278.0	287.1	395.7	192.0	203.6	80.9	39.2	41.7
Putnam	74.4	36.7	37.7	55.0	27.2	27.9	12.4	5.9	6.5
St. Johns	165.3	80.9	84.4	147.7	72.4	75.3	9.8	4.6	5.2
St. Lucie	259.3	126.8	132.5	182.0	88.2	93.8	41.6	19.9	21.7
Santa Rosa	141.4	70.9	70.5	125.4	62.6	62.8	6.6	3.4	3.2
Sarasota	379.4	180.8	198.6	334.9	158.8	176.1	16.3	7.6	8.7
Seminole	420.7	207.0	213.7	300.3	148.2	152.1	45.0	21.5	23.5
Sumter	82.6	44.0	38.6	66.0	32.7	33.3	8.4	5.6	2.9
Suwannee	38.8	19.2	19.6	31.3	15.2	16.1	4.3	2.0	2.3
Taylor	21.5	11.2	10.2	16.4	8.3	8.1	4.3	2.5	1.9
Union	15.0	9.9	5.1	10.8	6.5	4.3	3.4	2.7	0.7
Volusia	503.8	245.5	258.3	400.6	194.7	205.9	49.3	23.5	25.8
Wakulla	28.4	15.1	13.3	24.1	12.3	11.8	3.2	2.0	1.2
Walton	55.8	28.3	27.5	48.4	24.2	24.1	3.9	2.1	1.8
Washington	23.1	12.2	10.9	18.7	9.5	9.2	3.2	1.9	1.2

Note: Detail may not add to totals because of rounding.

Source: University of Florida, Bureau of Economic and Business Research, Population Program, *Florida Population Studies,* June 2007, Volume 40, Bulletin No. 148.

Table 1.32. HISPANIC ORIGIN POPULATION: ESTIMATES IN THE STATE AND COUNTIES OF FLORIDA, APRIL 1, 2006

County	Total population	Hispanic origin population 1/ Number	Hispanic origin population 1/ As a percentage of total	County	Total population	Hispanic origin population 1/ Number	Hispanic origin population 1/ As a percentage of total
Florida	18,349,132	3,613,482	19.7	Lake	276,783	24,478	8.8
				Lee	585,608	87,119	14.9
Alachua	243,779	18,476	7.6	Leon	272,497	11,520	4.2
Baker	25,004	619	2.5	Levy	38,981	2,214	5.7
Bay	165,515	6,068	3.7	Liberty	7,772	428	5.5
Bradford	28,551	808	2.8	Madison	19,814	903	4.6
Brevard	543,050	33,989	6.3	Manatee	308,325	41,514	13.5
Broward	1,753,162	363,108	20.7	Marion	315,074	27,266	8.7
Calhoun	14,113	605	4.3	Martin	142,645	13,456	9.4
Charlotte	160,315	6,536	4.1	Miami-Dade	2,437,022	1,501,541	61.6
Citrus	136,749	5,057	3.7	Monroe	80,510	14,904	18.5
Clay	176,901	10,110	5.7	Nassau	68,188	1,419	2.1
Collier	326,658	78,700	24.1	Okaloosa	192,672	11,137	5.8
Columbia	63,538	2,243	3.5	Okeechobee	38,666	8,338	21.6
DeSoto	33,164	9,072	27.4	Orange	1,079,524	261,155	24.2
Dixie	15,677	306	2.0	Osceola	255,903	102,300	40.0
Duval	879,235	52,765	6.0	Palm Beach	1,287,987	198,213	15.4
Escambia	309,647	10,030	3.2	Pasco	424,355	34,674	8.2
Flagler	89,075	5,429	6.1	Pinellas	948,102	59,266	6.3
Franklin	11,916	248	2.1	Polk	565,049	79,787	14.1
Gadsden	48,195	4,234	8.8	Putnam	74,416	6,209	8.3
Gilchrist	16,703	559	3.3	St. Johns	165,291	5,648	3.4
Glades	10,796	2,016	18.7	St. Lucie	259,315	31,909	12.3
Gulf	16,509	577	3.5	Santa Rosa	141,428	5,300	3.7
Hamilton	14,517	1,386	9.5	Sarasota	379,386	23,890	6.3
Hardee	27,186	10,197	37.5	Seminole	420,667	60,479	14.4
Hendry	38,678	17,065	44.1	Sumter	82,599	7,472	9.0
Hernando	157,006	11,121	7.1	Suwannee	38,799	2,809	7.2
Highlands	96,672	15,358	15.9	Taylor	21,471	418	1.9
Hillsborough	1,164,425	254,566	21.9	Union	15,028	668	4.4
Holmes	19,502	414	2.1	Volusia	503,844	45,909	9.1
Indian River	135,262	12,442	9.2	Wakulla	28,393	807	2.8
Jackson	50,246	1,668	3.3	Walton	55,786	2,328	4.2
Jefferson	14,353	667	4.6	Washington	23,073	705	3.1
Lafayette	8,060	860	10.7				

1/ Persons of Hispanic origin may be of any race. Includes persons of Latino or Spanish origin.

Source: University of Florida, Bureau of Economic and Business Research, Population Program, *Florida Population Studies,* June 2007, Volume 40, Bulletin No. 148.

Table 1.33. HISPANIC ORIGIN POPULATION: ESTIMATES BY SEX IN THE STATE AND COUNTIES OF FLORIDA, APRIL 1, 2006

County	Total	Male	Female	County	Total	Male	Female
Florida	3,613,482	1,809,708	1,803,774	Lake	24,478	12,698	11,780
Alachua	18,476	9,281	9,195	Lee	87,119	46,437	40,682
Baker	619	470	149	Leon	11,520	5,728	5,792
Bay	6,068	3,148	2,920	Levy	2,214	1,126	1,088
Bradford	808	564	244	Liberty	428	340	88
Brevard	33,989	16,936	17,053	Madison	903	637	266
Broward	363,108	177,482	185,626	Manatee	41,514	22,259	19,255
Calhoun	605	449	156	Marion	27,266	13,895	13,371
Charlotte	6,536	3,266	3,270	Martin	13,456	7,308	6,148
Citrus	5,057	2,417	2,640	Miami-Dade	1,501,541	724,042	777,499
Clay	10,110	5,090	5,020	Monroe	14,904	7,877	7,027
Collier	78,700	43,128	35,572	Nassau	1,419	739	680
Columbia	2,243	1,293	950	Okaloosa	11,137	5,814	5,323
DeSoto	9,072	6,027	3,045	Okeechobee	8,338	4,893	3,445
Dixie	306	195	111	Orange	261,155	132,022	129,133
Duval	52,765	26,834	25,931	Osceola	102,300	51,511	50,789
Escambia	10,030	5,342	4,688	Palm Beach	198,213	102,188	96,025
Flagler	5,429	2,607	2,822	Pasco	34,674	17,773	16,901
Franklin	248	152	96	Pinellas	59,266	30,264	29,002
Gadsden	4,234	2,384	1,850	Polk	79,787	42,503	37,284
Gilchrist	559	355	204	Putnam	6,209	3,257	2,952
Glades	2,016	1,243	773	St. Johns	5,648	2,867	2,781
Gulf	577	513	64	St. Lucie	31,909	16,823	15,086
Hamilton	1,386	952	434	Santa Rosa	5,300	2,780	2,520
Hardee	10,197	5,698	4,499	Sarasota	23,890	12,367	11,523
Hendry	17,065	9,738	7,327	Seminole	60,479	30,201	30,278
Hernando	11,121	5,504	5,617	Sumter	7,472	5,217	2,255
Highlands	15,358	8,390	6,968	Suwannee	2,809	1,790	1,019
Hillsborough	254,566	128,914	125,652	Taylor	418	277	141
Holmes	414	281	133	Union	668	548	120
Indian River	12,442	6,735	5,707	Volusia	45,909	23,500	22,409
Jackson	1,668	1,249	419	Wakulla	807	546	261
Jefferson	667	432	235	Walton	2,328	1,285	1,043
Lafayette	860	655	205	Washington	705	472	233

Note: Persons of Hispanic origin may be of any race. Includes persons of Latino or Spanish origin.

Source: University of Florida, Bureau of Economic and Business Research, Population Program, *Florida Population Studies,* June 2007, Volume 40, Bulletin No. 148.

Table 1.34. AGE: ESTIMATES BY AGE GROUP IN THE STATE AND COUNTIES OF FLORIDA, APRIL 1, 2006

County	Total	Age (years) 0-17	18-34	35-54	55-64	65-79	80 and over
Florida	18,349,132	4,113,765	3,869,439	5,137,009	2,081,413	2,196,491	951,015
Alachua	243,779	46,277	94,175	58,731	21,372	16,428	6,796
Baker	25,004	6,542	5,875	7,418	2,612	2,026	531
Bay	165,515	37,354	34,133	49,907	20,384	17,944	5,793
Bradford	28,551	5,839	7,329	8,480	3,087	2,752	1,064
Brevard	543,050	111,092	95,414	156,989	68,678	79,571	31,306
Broward	1,753,162	414,093	368,102	535,564	179,368	165,346	90,689
Calhoun	14,113	3,161	3,595	3,822	1,449	1,478	608
Charlotte	160,315	24,359	19,895	37,156	24,296	37,678	16,931
Citrus	136,749	21,908	17,123	31,632	21,915	31,336	12,835
Clay	176,901	46,994	36,955	53,949	19,750	14,362	4,891
Collier	326,658	66,408	57,649	81,782	43,878	56,731	20,210
Columbia	63,538	15,021	13,909	17,377	7,644	7,141	2,446
DeSoto	33,164	7,066	8,401	7,455	3,720	4,781	1,741
Dixie	15,677	3,292	3,239	4,108	2,089	2,253	696
Duval	879,235	222,170	214,869	261,440	88,109	66,349	26,298
Escambia	309,647	70,723	80,679	81,405	32,740	31,221	12,879
Flagler	89,075	16,066	12,272	22,789	13,752	18,245	5,951
Franklin	11,916	2,259	2,285	3,349	1,774	1,712	537
Gadsden	48,195	11,806	11,613	13,446	5,221	4,495	1,614
Gilchrist	16,703	3,771	3,839	4,522	2,019	1,947	605
Glades	10,796	2,225	2,322	2,852	1,382	1,586	429
Gulf	16,509	3,006	3,754	5,190	1,996	1,920	643
Hamilton	14,517	3,158	3,921	4,253	1,509	1,225	451
Hardee	27,186	7,132	7,348	6,583	2,354	2,684	1,085
Hendry	38,678	11,278	11,316	8,906	3,105	3,059	1,014
Hernando	157,006	29,653	22,485	37,275	22,117	31,855	13,621
Highlands	96,672	18,217	14,710	20,420	12,250	21,348	9,727
Hillsborough	1,164,425	293,783	279,319	337,558	116,161	97,498	40,106
Holmes	19,502	4,418	4,599	5,163	2,242	2,228	852
Indian River	135,262	25,317	21,006	33,731	18,230	24,767	12,211
Jackson	50,246	10,254	12,115	14,635	5,673	5,352	2,217
Jefferson	14,353	2,853	3,085	4,413	1,889	1,481	632
Lafayette	8,060	1,559	2,501	2,168	768	793	271
Lake	276,783	55,302	43,475	70,061	37,154	51,496	19,295

Continued . . .

Table 1.34. AGE: ESTIMATES BY AGE GROUP IN THE STATE AND COUNTIES OF FLORIDA, APRIL 1, 2006 (Continued)

County	Total	Age (years) 0-17	18-34	35-54	55-64	65-79	80 and over
Lee	585,608	118,043	99,616	147,872	80,826	99,233	40,018
Leon	272,497	55,190	101,038	69,015	24,418	16,147	6,689
Levy	38,981	8,813	7,035	10,307	5,440	5,501	1,885
Liberty	7,772	1,639	2,251	2,337	719	632	194
Madison	19,814	4,491	5,117	5,164	2,085	2,091	866
Manatee	308,325	63,602	55,757	79,725	38,567	47,822	22,852
Marion	315,074	64,643	52,530	80,803	41,172	54,279	21,647
Martin	142,645	25,690	19,775	37,648	20,070	26,828	12,634
Miami-Dade	2,437,022	595,293	558,780	706,903	246,377	237,379	92,290
Monroe	80,510	13,911	14,123	26,967	12,554	9,751	3,204
Nassau	68,188	15,728	12,599	20,480	9,492	7,833	2,056
Okaloosa	192,672	45,416	44,865	55,941	21,492	19,081	5,877
Okeechobee	38,666	9,781	8,460	10,006	3,867	4,808	1,744
Orange	1,079,524	278,272	295,925	311,968	93,882	73,192	26,285
Osceola	255,903	69,469	60,897	74,078	24,939	19,879	6,641
Palm Beach	1,287,987	275,973	235,444	350,459	146,812	180,773	98,526
Pasco	424,355	88,710	69,774	110,099	53,587	69,221	32,964
Pinellas	948,102	180,383	170,296	275,176	121,264	131,029	69,954
Polk	565,049	135,895	114,608	147,709	65,032	72,821	28,984
Putnam	74,416	17,720	13,886	19,202	9,586	10,584	3,438
St. Johns	165,291	35,594	31,580	51,155	21,604	18,391	6,967
St. Lucie	259,315	57,174	46,119	68,057	31,666	39,949	16,350
Santa Rosa	141,428	35,005	29,332	43,770	16,267	13,201	3,853
Sarasota	379,386	61,368	50,273	93,828	56,450	77,910	39,557
Seminole	420,667	100,628	96,076	133,186	45,348	33,312	12,117
Sumter	82,599	12,679	14,079	19,774	10,581	19,487	5,999
Suwannee	38,799	8,548	7,943	10,295	4,836	5,136	2,041
Taylor	21,471	4,841	4,749	6,179	2,658	2,292	752
Union	15,028	3,034	4,073	5,365	1,381	915	260
Volusia	503,844	99,200	97,213	136,597	64,307	73,261	33,266
Wakulla	28,393	6,328	6,060	9,166	3,568	2,577	694
Walton	55,786	11,318	10,777	16,697	7,101	7,459	2,434
Washington	23,073	5,030	5,082	6,552	2,778	2,629	1,002

Source: University of Florida, Bureau of Economic and Business Research, Population Program, *Florida Population Studies,* June 2007, Volume 40, Bulletin No. 148.

Table 1.35. NON-HISPANIC WHITE POPULATION: ESTIMATES BY AGE GROUP IN THE STATE AND COUNTIES OF FLORIDA, APRIL 1, 2006

County	Total	Age (years) 0-17	18-34	35-54	55-64	65-79	80 and over
Florida	11,427,917	2,138,869	2,042,923	3,193,298	1,521,108	1,725,295	806,424
Alachua	164,068	26,186	62,110	41,002	16,419	12,749	5,602
Baker	20,841	5,532	4,478	6,158	2,335	1,859	479
Bay	135,810	28,581	26,130	41,683	17,997	16,183	5,236
Bradford	21,276	4,421	4,774	6,088	2,676	2,393	924
Brevard	445,999	83,133	71,810	130,396	59,789	71,740	29,131
Broward	908,340	163,244	151,535	277,097	116,366	120,287	79,811
Calhoun	10,864	2,442	2,411	2,953	1,254	1,290	514
Charlotte	142,612	20,198	16,179	32,419	22,423	35,247	16,146
Citrus	125,916	19,206	14,765	28,845	20,795	29,918	12,387
Clay	146,394	37,078	29,343	44,874	17,483	13,076	4,540
Collier	225,142	33,027	26,806	55,447	37,865	52,628	19,369
Columbia	49,746	11,216	10,006	13,672	6,472	6,241	2,139
DeSoto	19,935	3,707	3,035	4,170	3,031	4,357	1,635
Dixie	13,845	2,921	2,573	3,565	1,968	2,153	665
Duval	526,950	112,675	119,481	163,282	62,296	48,666	20,550
Escambia	219,166	43,414	55,572	58,684	25,473	25,137	10,886
Flagler	72,774	12,191	9,479	19,000	11,722	15,284	5,098
Franklin	9,961	1,817	1,724	2,781	1,590	1,571	478
Gadsden	16,367	2,649	3,011	5,000	2,486	2,323	898
Gilchrist	14,943	3,302	3,089	4,198	1,914	1,857	583
Glades	7,167	1,199	1,145	1,814	1,179	1,426	404
Gulf	12,445	2,435	2,298	3,672	1,763	1,712	565
Hamilton	7,760	1,529	1,596	2,353	1,025	922	335
Hardee	14,479	2,936	2,884	3,687	1,759	2,233	980
Hendry	15,887	3,633	3,384	4,080	1,968	2,070	752
Hernando	136,480	23,847	17,966	32,164	20,021	29,548	12,934
Highlands	70,850	9,992	7,696	14,059	10,325	19,528	9,250
Hillsborough	681,609	145,437	146,140	208,188	80,173	70,084	31,587
Holmes	17,270	4,014	3,704	4,527	2,096	2,120	809
Indian River	109,496	17,192	13,823	27,105	16,369	23,267	11,740
Jackson	34,349	6,865	7,286	9,784	4,433	4,234	1,747
Jefferson	8,571	1,546	1,499	2,701	1,332	1,065	428
Lafayette	5,999	1,252	1,476	1,550	706	753	262
Lake	225,424	38,772	30,457	56,627	33,111	48,128	18,329

See footnote at end of table.

Continued . . .

Table 1.35. NON-HISPANIC WHITE POPULATION: ESTIMATES BY AGE GROUP IN THE STATE AND COUNTIES OF FLORIDA, APRIL 1, 2006 (Continued)

		Age (years)					
County	Total	0-17	18-34	35-54	55-64	65-79	80 and over
Lee	448,906	72,242	60,986	113,001	72,057	92,261	38,359
Leon	164,760	28,865	54,467	45,497	18,358	12,180	5,393
Levy	32,303	6,694	5,397	8,626	4,887	4,997	1,702
Liberty	5,577	1,296	1,316	1,631	623	544	167
Madison	11,006	2,115	2,359	2,939	1,440	1,544	609
Manatee	235,423	38,234	34,360	61,620	34,424	44,754	22,031
Marion	248,478	44,122	37,013	62,801	35,845	48,807	19,890
Martin	120,125	18,379	13,632	31,630	18,536	25,665	12,283
Miami-Dade	404,631	98,930	82,482	108,569	48,127	41,773	24,750
Monroe	60,410	8,954	8,933	20,912	10,690	8,168	2,753
Nassau	61,350	13,809	10,981	18,533	8,815	7,322	1,890
Okaloosa	154,363	34,223	33,152	45,214	18,710	17,533	5,531
Okeechobee	26,543	5,785	4,462	7,007	3,270	4,367	1,652
Orange	544,158	115,412	141,294	166,105	55,516	46,279	19,552
Osceola	123,995	28,555	25,852	37,382	14,569	12,604	5,033
Palm Beach	858,138	141,173	123,599	228,530	114,977	157,303	92,556
Pasco	370,164	71,912	56,493	95,127	49,205	65,548	31,879
Pinellas	761,610	124,209	121,114	223,341	106,217	120,025	66,704
Polk	395,650	78,465	68,646	104,613	53,676	63,803	26,447
Putnam	55,034	10,980	9,047	14,690	8,130	9,184	3,003
St. Johns	147,671	30,553	27,610	45,891	19,917	17,173	6,527
St. Lucie	182,001	31,491	26,876	48,477	25,653	34,694	14,810
Santa Rosa	125,443	30,554	24,971	38,862	15,006	12,422	3,628
Sarasota	334,901	47,950	38,894	81,970	52,885	74,627	38,575
Seminole	300,344	66,082	64,239	98,054	35,661	26,231	10,077
Sumter	65,989	9,386	8,587	14,450	9,450	18,377	5,739
Suwannee	31,327	6,387	5,711	8,485	4,242	4,637	1,865
Taylor	16,359	3,565	3,161	4,699	2,270	2,020	644
Union	10,788	2,459	2,634	3,570	1,126	775	224
Volusia	400,585	69,748	67,716	109,894	56,029	65,989	31,209
Wakulla	24,116	5,383	4,765	7,738	3,249	2,352	629
Walton	48,373	9,362	8,756	14,597	6,484	6,944	2,230
Washington	18,661	4,006	3,753	5,218	2,450	2,344	890

Note: Excludes persons of Hispanic origin.

Source: University of Florida, Bureau of Economic and Business Research, Population Program, *Florida Population Studies,* June 2007, Volume 40, Bulletin No. 148.

Table 1.36. NON-HISPANIC BLACK POPULATION: ESTIMATES BY AGE GROUP IN THE STATE AND COUNTIES OF FLORIDA, APRIL 1, 2006

County	Total	Age (years) 0-17	18-34	35-54	55-64	65-79	80 and over
Florida	2,851,251	870,391	758,922	780,542	226,619	167,627	47,150
Alachua	50,421	13,547	18,389	11,738	3,386	2,520	841
Baker	3,322	819	1,099	995	229	137	43
Bay	18,570	5,522	4,956	5,069	1,554	1,104	365
Bradford	6,108	1,180	2,143	2,017	342	301	125
Brevard	50,169	14,577	11,836	13,624	4,782	4,226	1,124
Broward	422,880	132,182	108,209	124,890	31,641	21,021	4,937
Calhoun	2,348	531	811	622	148	156	80
Charlotte	8,722	2,077	1,680	2,252	970	1,315	428
Citrus	3,821	958	839	1,063	412	446	103
Clay	14,544	4,683	3,349	4,499	1,214	637	162
Collier	19,226	6,446	4,633	5,103	1,766	1,078	200
Columbia	10,647	2,921	3,007	2,834	926	710	249
DeSoto	3,909	883	1,469	992	282	215	68
Dixie	1,403	266	511	445	85	73	23
Duval	265,869	83,779	70,317	73,777	19,755	13,796	4,445
Escambia	68,695	20,922	18,287	17,480	5,652	4,780	1,574
Flagler	9,200	2,184	1,577	1,965	1,136	1,796	542
Franklin	1,627	358	473	480	145	115	56
Gadsden	27,199	7,504	7,113	7,297	2,531	2,068	686
Gilchrist	1,116	287	511	185	60	58	15
Glades	1,102	271	353	326	77	65	10
Gulf	3,252	495	1,122	1,194	189	184	68
Hamilton	5,254	1,228	1,744	1,513	403	258	108
Hardee	2,297	418	812	735	156	137	39
Hendry	5,287	1,797	1,566	1,093	373	339	119
Hernando	7,406	2,102	1,685	1,894	743	768	214
Highlands	8,952	2,927	1,960	2,325	856	689	195
Hillsborough	190,410	59,480	51,870	51,669	14,736	9,941	2,714
Holmes	1,468	244	609	426	90	69	30
Indian River	11,726	3,516	2,969	3,012	1,069	893	267
Jackson	13,559	2,970	3,989	4,038	1,112	1,014	436
Jefferson	4,995	1,148	1,361	1,444	476	382	184
Lafayette	1,146	99	621	371	32	18	5
Lake	23,231	7,225	5,337	6,306	2,010	1,781	572

See footnote at end of table.

Continued . . .

Table 1.36. NON-HISPANIC BLACK POPULATION: ESTIMATES BY AGE GROUP IN THE STATE AND COUNTIES OF FLORIDA, APRIL 1, 2006 (Continued)

		Age (years)					
County	Total	0-17	18-34	35-54	55-64	65-79	80 and over
Lee	42,020	14,548	9,927	10,836	3,323	2,697	689
Leon	88,413	22,221	36,954	19,511	5,173	3,431	1,123
Levy	4,102	1,257	986	1,085	339	319	116
Liberty	1,591	242	663	519	72	73	22
Madison	7,732	2,136	2,338	1,931	579	506	242
Manatee	27,105	9,203	7,098	6,727	2,008	1,620	449
Marion	35,324	10,727	7,968	9,800	2,885	2,924	1,020
Martin	7,720	2,454	1,649	2,241	724	502	150
Miami-Dade	485,822	149,833	125,467	129,639	41,593	31,236	8,054
Monroe	4,017	985	900	1,284	447	307	94
Nassau	4,784	1,312	1,109	1,364	499	369	131
Okaloosa	19,582	5,642	5,747	5,607	1,576	822	188
Okeechobee	3,268	871	1,095	879	197	179	47
Orange	222,917	69,242	62,442	60,928	16,406	11,048	2,851
Osceola	20,889	6,294	5,229	6,049	1,772	1,251	294
Palm Beach	203,519	66,574	50,248	57,379	15,911	10,710	2,697
Pasco	11,563	3,442	2,576	3,413	979	887	266
Pinellas	98,337	30,149	24,404	27,763	8,432	5,906	1,683
Polk	80,877	26,245	19,517	21,648	6,475	5,365	1,627
Putnam	12,422	4,037	2,912	3,143	1,009	985	336
St. Johns	9,805	2,779	2,170	2,824	1,011	750	271
St. Lucie	41,627	13,912	9,322	10,809	3,688	3,048	848
Santa Rosa	6,621	1,779	1,748	2,080	603	328	83
Sarasota	16,263	5,096	3,538	4,292	1,543	1,379	415
Seminole	44,980	13,027	11,790	13,156	3,710	2,599	698
Sumter	8,448	1,747	2,919	2,613	472	540	157
Suwannee	4,297	1,261	1,074	1,057	398	369	138
Taylor	4,331	1,077	1,315	1,268	332	244	95
Union	3,402	464	1,143	1,449	208	107	31
Volusia	49,294	13,907	14,535	12,400	4,057	3,353	1,042
Wakulla	3,204	697	948	1,070	255	177	57
Walton	3,914	954	1,042	1,147	359	289	123
Washington	3,180	731	942	958	246	217	86

Note: Excludes persons of Hispanic origin.

Source: University of Florida, Bureau of Economic and Business Research, Population Program, *Florida Population Studies,* June 2007, Volume 40, Bulletin No. 148.

Table 1.37. HISPANIC ORIGIN POPULATION: ESTIMATES BY AGE GROUP IN THE STATE AND COUNTIES OF FLORIDA, APRIL 1, 2006

County	Total	Age (years) 0-17	18-34	35-54	55-64	65-79	80 and over
Florida	3,613,482	965,102	947,290	1,037,368	297,092	276,666	89,964
Alachua	18,476	3,638	9,733	3,473	841	619	172
Baker	619	136	223	200	33	20	7
Bay	6,068	1,744	1,695	1,773	409	355	92
Bradford	808	168	286	256	49	40	9
Brevard	33,989	9,635	8,727	9,466	2,877	2,521	763
Broward	363,108	100,278	93,302	116,203	26,959	21,113	5,253
Calhoun	605	119	273	168	28	13	4
Charlotte	6,536	1,501	1,567	1,853	630	748	237
Citrus	5,057	1,253	1,091	1,181	497	744	291
Clay	10,110	3,347	2,917	2,765	565	393	123
Collier	78,700	25,731	25,345	20,279	3,918	2,823	604
Columbia	2,243	636	641	632	168	130	36
DeSoto	9,072	2,419	3,803	2,230	390	196	34
Dixie	306	82	109	60	28	21	6
Duval	52,765	15,112	16,172	15,044	3,557	2,140	740
Escambia	10,030	2,804	3,693	2,250	648	486	149
Flagler	5,429	1,295	929	1,467	687	838	213
Franklin	248	65	66	64	32	20	1
Gadsden	4,234	1,544	1,387	1,043	167	74	19
Gilchrist	559	160	198	126	40	28	7
Glades	2,016	629	662	560	90	64	11
Gulf	577	41	253	238	31	10	4
Hamilton	1,386	375	540	355	71	39	6
Hardee	10,197	3,740	3,576	2,093	424	302	62
Hendry	17,065	5,697	6,238	3,642	733	622	133
Hernando	11,121	3,135	2,381	2,705	1,153	1,332	415
Highlands	15,358	4,805	4,720	3,643	925	1,015	250
Hillsborough	254,566	77,046	71,000	67,433	18,324	15,497	5,266
Holmes	414	101	142	109	33	23	6
Indian River	12,442	4,130	3,810	3,203	646	486	167
Jackson	1,668	271	642	615	73	54	13
Jefferson	667	132	192	234	70	24	15
Lafayette	860	203	374	228	29	22	4
Lake	24,478	8,168	6,844	6,138	1,717	1,307	304

See footnote at end of table.

Continued . . .

Table 1.37. HISPANIC ORIGIN POPULATION: ESTIMATES BY AGE GROUP IN THE STATE AND COUNTIES OF FLORIDA, APRIL 1, 2006 (Continued)

		Age (years)					
County	Total	0-17	18-34	35-54	55-64	65-79	80 and over
Lee	87,119	28,636	26,915	22,085	4,848	3,789	846
Leon	11,520	2,140	6,356	2,286	431	233	74
Levy	2,214	751	565	500	185	157	56
Liberty	428	75	199	129	16	7	2
Madison	903	192	367	252	53	30	9
Manatee	41,514	14,711	13,176	10,316	1,817	1,192	302
Marion	27,266	8,578	6,646	7,090	2,115	2,216	621
Martin	13,456	4,430	4,207	3,387	683	573	176
Miami-Dade	1,501,541	332,641	339,203	456,680	152,803	161,474	58,740
Monroe	14,904	3,684	4,024	4,394	1,286	1,186	330
Nassau	1,419	433	363	401	111	93	18
Okaloosa	11,137	3,364	3,738	2,946	596	407	86
Okeechobee	8,338	2,986	2,732	1,981	368	234	37
Orange	261,155	77,685	77,820	70,917	18,185	13,322	3,226
Osceola	102,300	31,995	27,632	28,120	7,858	5,503	1,192
Palm Beach	198,213	59,029	54,655	56,623	13,725	11,281	2,900
Pasco	34,674	10,987	8,935	9,209	2,729	2,178	636
Pinellas	59,266	17,169	17,608	15,914	4,138	3,364	1,073
Polk	79,787	28,350	24,337	19,110	4,182	3,074	734
Putnam	6,209	2,458	1,752	1,178	387	356	78
St. Johns	5,648	1,647	1,319	1,816	454	303	109
St. Lucie	31,909	10,510	9,075	7,790	1,990	1,929	615
Santa Rosa	5,300	1,580	1,542	1,551	287	249	91
Sarasota	23,890	6,966	6,897	6,423	1,610	1,538	456
Seminole	60,479	17,216	16,149	17,629	4,751	3,623	1,111
Sumter	7,472	1,406	2,333	2,497	620	526	90
Suwannee	2,809	796	1,064	663	162	98	26
Taylor	418	110	160	105	28	9	6
Union	668	89	237	274	37	27	4
Volusia	45,909	13,272	12,587	12,276	3,559	3,370	845
Wakulla	807	191	267	269	42	35	3
Walton	2,328	715	667	610	152	140	44
Washington	705	170	232	218	42	31	12

Note: Persons of Hispanic origin may be of any race. Includes persons of Latino or Spanish origin.

Source: University of Florida, Bureau of Economic and Business Research, Population Program, *Florida Population Studies,* June 2007, Volume 40, Bulletin No. 148.

Table 1.38. AGE: MEDIAN AGE BY SEX IN THE STATE AND COUNTIES OF FLORIDA, APRIL 1, 2006

County	Both sexes	Male	Female	County	Both sexes	Male	Female
Florida	39.9	38.4	41.3	Lake	46.4	44.9	47.9
				Lee	45.6	43.9	47.2
Alachua	29.3	28.6	30.0	Leon	29.4	28.8	30.1
Baker	35.2	34.5	36.2	Levy	42.7	41.5	43.7
Bay	40.1	38.9	41.1	Liberty	35.0	34.2	37.4
Bradford	37.6	36.1	40.7	Madison	36.2	33.8	39.6
Brevard	44.0	42.8	45.2	Manatee	44.1	42.3	45.8
Broward	38.5	37.4	39.7	Marion	45.4	43.8	46.9
Calhoun	36.5	34.6	39.5	Martin	49.2	47.6	50.9
Charlotte	54.4	52.8	55.8	Miami-Dade	36.8	35.4	38.2
Citrus	53.8	52.3	55.1	Monroe	45.0	44.9	45.1
Clay	36.8	35.8	37.8	Nassau	41.1	40.2	41.9
Collier	44.8	43.1	46.7	Okaloosa	37.3	36.3	38.3
Columbia	38.6	36.8	40.7	Okeechobee	37.3	35.6	39.8
DeSoto	37.6	35.3	41.8	Orange	33.0	32.1	33.8
Dixie	41.7	39.9	44.5	Osceola	34.3	33.2	35.4
Duval	35.2	33.9	36.5	Palm Beach	42.8	41.1	44.5
Escambia	35.9	34.1	37.8	Pasco	45.1	43.4	46.7
Flagler	50.1	48.7	51.2	Pinellas	44.5	42.8	46.1
Franklin	44.0	42.4	45.8	Polk	39.5	38.0	41.0
Gadsden	36.0	33.8	37.9	Putnam	41.7	40.3	43.1
Gilchrist	38.7	35.6	41.4	St. Johns	41.9	40.9	42.9
Glades	40.8	39.1	43.6	St. Lucie	43.3	41.9	44.7
Gulf	40.8	38.8	44.7	Santa Rosa	38.1	37.0	39.3
Hamilton	35.8	34.6	38.0	Sarasota	52.0	50.0	53.9
Hardee	32.7	32.2	33.6	Seminole	37.1	36.0	38.2
Hendry	29.4	28.8	30.4	Sumter	49.6	45.6	54.4
Hernando	49.8	48.2	51.2	Suwannee	41.3	39.5	43.1
Highlands	50.6	48.2	52.8	Taylor	38.9	37.4	41.0
Hillsborough	35.5	34.5	36.6	Union	36.3	36.8	34.1
Holmes	37.7	35.4	40.8	Volusia	43.8	42.1	45.5
Indian River	48.3	46.4	50.1	Wakulla	39.2	38.2	40.5
Jackson	38.9	37.0	41.9	Walton	42.6	41.4	44.0
Jefferson	40.9	39.1	43.3	Washington	39.5	37.7	41.7
Lafayette	34.8	33.2	39.1				

Source: University of Florida, Bureau of Economic and Business Research, Population Program, unpublished data.

Table. 1.39. PERSONS AGED 65 AND OVER: ESTIMATES, APRIL 1, 2006, BY AGE GROUP IN THE STATE AND COUNTIES OF FLORIDA

County	Persons aged 65 and over			Age group (years)				
	Total	Percentage of total population	Female (percentage)	65-69	70-74	75-79	80-84	85 and over
Florida	3,147,506	17.2	56.4	804,847	728,953	662,691	512,676	438,339
Alachua	23,224	9.5	57.8	6,652	5,276	4,500	3,549	3,247
Baker	2,557	10.2	54.2	896	651	479	287	244
Bay	23,737	14.3	55.7	7,184	5,897	4,863	3,292	2,501
Bradford	3,816	13.4	55.4	1,113	901	738	569	495
Brevard	110,877	20.4	55.4	28,489	27,527	23,555	18,049	13,257
Broward	256,035	14.6	58.5	60,375	53,841	51,130	43,690	46,999
Calhoun	2,086	14.8	57.7	595	470	413	301	307
Charlotte	54,609	34.1	54.5	12,509	12,956	12,213	9,403	7,528
Citrus	44,171	32.3	54.0	10,971	10,696	9,669	7,106	5,729
Clay	19,253	10.9	55.0	6,183	4,674	3,505	2,646	2,245
Collier	76,941	23.6	53.5	20,204	19,363	17,164	11,936	8,274
Columbia	9,587	15.1	53.9	2,826	2,402	1,913	1,347	1,099
DeSoto	6,522	19.7	53.4	1,712	1,636	1,433	1,039	702
Dixie	2,949	18.8	51.7	890	755	608	411	285
Duval	92,647	10.5	59.1	26,368	21,437	18,544	14,320	11,978
Escambia	44,100	14.2	57.8	12,070	10,374	8,777	6,912	5,967
Flagler	24,196	27.2	54.1	6,530	6,259	5,456	3,677	2,274
Franklin	2,249	18.9	50.2	729	558	425	274	263
Gadsden	6,109	12.7	58.6	1,800	1,486	1,209	826	788
Gilchrist	2,552	15.3	54.2	788	644	515	345	260
Glades	2,015	18.7	50.0	651	534	401	250	179
Gulf	2,563	15.5	53.8	773	647	500	350	293
Hamilton	1,676	11.5	54.7	501	407	317	223	228
Hardee	3,769	13.9	53.4	955	873	856	654	431
Hendry	4,073	10.5	51.4	1,218	1,018	823	578	436
Hernando	45,476	29.0	54.8	10,671	10,758	10,426	8,167	5,454
Highlands	31,075	32.1	54.8	6,958	7,248	7,142	5,591	4,136
Hillsborough	137,604	11.8	57.1	38,047	31,927	27,524	21,641	18,465
Holmes	3,080	15.8	56.0	909	735	584	426	426
Indian River	36,978	27.3	55.5	8,143	8,422	8,202	6,724	5,487
Jackson	7,569	15.1	57.2	2,054	1,781	1,517	1,119	1,098
Jefferson	2,113	14.7	56.1	554	487	440	339	293
Lafayette	1,064	13.2	53.2	316	275	202	145	126

Continued . . .

Table. 1.39. PERSONS AGED 65 AND OVER: ESTIMATES, APRIL 1, 2006, BY AGE GROUP IN THE STATE AND COUNTIES OF FLORIDA (Continued)

County	Persons aged 65 and over: Total	Percentage of total population	Female (percentage)	Age group (years): 65-69	70-74	75-79	80-84	85 and over
Lake	70,791	25.6	54.7	18,965	17,022	15,509	11,129	8,166
Lee	139,251	23.8	54.5	35,592	33,080	30,561	22,828	17,190
Leon	22,836	8.4	58.2	6,652	5,134	4,361	3,404	3,285
Levy	7,386	18.9	52.6	2,218	1,775	1,508	1,080	805
Liberty	826	10.6	54.1	260	204	168	114	80
Madison	2,957	14.9	57.7	842	677	572	435	431
Manatee	70,674	22.9	56.1	16,605	15,706	15,511	12,301	10,551
Marion	75,926	24.1	55.0	19,068	18,118	17,093	12,566	9,081
Martin	39,462	27.7	55.1	9,342	9,051	8,435	6,909	5,725
Miami-Dade	329,669	13.5	58.4	92,954	78,219	66,206	48,034	44,256
Monroe	12,955	16.1	49.0	4,030	3,126	2,595	1,840	1,364
Nassau	9,889	14.5	53.7	3,295	2,567	1,971	1,226	830
Okaloosa	24,958	13.0	55.3	7,861	6,397	4,823	3,388	2,489
Okeechobee	6,552	16.9	52.6	1,753	1,597	1,458	1,024	720
Orange	99,477	9.2	57.7	28,936	24,196	20,060	14,558	11,727
Osceola	26,520	10.4	55.5	8,177	6,578	5,124	3,657	2,984
Palm Beach	279,299	21.7	56.6	59,786	59,137	61,850	51,603	46,923
Pasco	102,185	24.1	55.9	23,828	23,098	22,295	17,925	15,039
Pinellas	200,983	21.2	57.6	46,245	43,239	41,545	35,080	34,874
Polk	101,805	18.0	55.5	26,707	24,265	21,849	16,382	12,602
Putnam	14,022	18.8	53.9	3,983	3,636	2,965	2,056	1,382
St. Johns	25,358	15.3	55.3	7,076	5,872	5,443	3,968	2,999
St. Lucie	56,299	21.7	54.9	13,768	13,373	12,808	9,760	6,590
Santa Rosa	17,054	12.1	53.8	5,651	4,466	3,084	2,203	1,650
Sarasota	117,467	31.0	56.2	26,191	25,923	25,796	20,656	18,901
Seminole	45,429	10.8	56.7	13,211	10,964	9,137	6,921	5,196
Sumter	25,486	30.9	53.0	6,745	7,067	5,675	3,638	2,361
Suwannee	7,177	18.5	55.5	2,009	1,676	1,451	1,070	971
Taylor	3,044	14.2	55.8	891	770	631	421	331
Union	1,175	7.8	50.2	389	303	223	146	114
Volusia	106,527	21.1	56.4	26,034	24,595	22,632	17,907	15,359
Wakulla	3,271	11.5	52.4	1,183	812	582	371	323
Walton	9,893	17.7	53.7	2,915	2,512	2,032	1,387	1,047
Washington	3,631	15.7	54.7	1,051	883	695	503	499

Source: University of Florida, Bureau of Economic and Business Research, Population Program, unpublished data.

Table 1.40. PLANNING DISTRICTS: ESTIMATES, APRIL 1, 2006, AND PROJECTIONS SPECIFIED YEARS, APRIL 1, 2010 THROUGH 2030, IN THE STATE AND COMPREHENSIVE PLANNING DISTRICTS OF FLORIDA

(rounded to thousands)

District	Estimates 2006	Projections 2010	2015	2020	2025	2030
Florida	18,349.1					
Low		19,144.2	20,409.9	21,692.5	22,948.4	24,132.3
Medium		19,974.2	21,831.5	23,552.1	25,086.0	26,513.3
High		20,384.2	22,634.6	24,876.0	27,054.2	29,119.3
District 1	907.6					
Low		940.4	976.8	1,002.9	1,019.4	1,027.8
Medium		980.6	1,060.7	1,135.2	1,202.1	1,264.6
High		1,019.2	1,148.7	1,281.9	1,417.9	1,558.6
District 2	464.0					
Low		477.8	489.3	495.8	498.9	498.2
Medium		497.8	531.0	560.1	586.6	611.1
High		517.3	573.8	630.2	687.6	746.3
District 3	485.9					
Low		497.9	509.1	514.4	515.1	512.5
Medium		519.9	555.3	586.0	613.4	638.9
High		541.7	603.0	663.7	725.2	788.3
District 4	1,478.1					
Low		1,556.7	1,647.8	1,714.9	1,758.0	1,782.6
Medium		1,631.8	1,807.9	1,971.1	2,117.5	2,254.9
High		1,703.6	1,976.7	2,259.5	2,549.7	2,852.4
District 5	730.4					
Low		778.2	833.4	875.1	902.0	917.7
Medium		819.2	921.5	1,017.0	1,102.1	1,181.7
High		858.1	1,014.8	1,177.9	1,344.6	1,518.3
District 6	3,079.8					
Low		3,256.1	3,459.4	3,610.1	3,707.4	3,760.5
Medium		3,421.1	3,812.1	4,175.6	4,501.6	4,805.7
High		3,578.6	4,184.4	4,813.1	5,458.2	6,128.2
District 7	760.7					
Low		792.7	831.8	861.2	880.6	892.6
Medium		825.6	900.9	969.1	1,029.7	1,085.2
High		857.2	973.4	1,090.9	1,208.7	1,328.7
District 8	2,845.2					
Low		2,934.5	3,044.5	3,125.0	3,174.1	3,198.8
Medium		3,053.8	3,293.2	3,514.7	3,711.0	3,892.9
High		3,168.8	3,554.0	3,948.3	4,345.9	4,752.8
District 9	1,501.4					
Low		1,612.8	1,741.5	1,839.9	1,906.4	1,948.0
Medium		1,697.1	1,923.6	2,134.5	2,323.4	2,500.3
High		1,777.1	2,117.0	2,471.2	2,834.4	3,213.7
District 10	1,825.2					
Low		1,921.1	2,035.9	2,125.4	2,187.7	2,228.3
Medium		2,007.8	2,218.8	2,415.5	2,591.1	2,754.5
High		2,090.5	2,412.2	2,744.5	3,082.0	3,429.5
District 11	4,270.7					
Low		4,336.8	4,430.5	4,490.0	4,510.5	4,501.5
Medium		4,519.4	4,806.7	5,073.1	5,307.5	5,523.3
High		4,696.6	5,197.4	5,709.0	6,221.1	6,742.0

Note: The medium projection is the one we believe is most likely to provide an accurate forecast of future population. The high and low projections indicate the range in which future populations are likely to fall. They do not represent absolute limits to growth; for any county, the future population may be above the high projection or below the low projection. See source for a detailed description of methodology.

Source: University of Florida, Bureau of Economic and Business Research, Population Program, *Florida Population Studies,* February 2007, Volume 40, Bulletin No. 147.

Table 1.41. PROJECTIONS: ESTIMATES, APRIL 1, 2006, AND PROJECTIONS SPECIFIED YEARS APRIL 1, 2010 THROUGH 2030, IN THE STATE AND COUNTIES OF FLORIDA

(in thousands, rounded to hundreds)

County	Estimates 2006	Projections 2010	2015	2020	2025	2030
Florida	18,349.1					
Low		19,144.2	20,409.9	21,692.5	22,948.4	24,132.3
Medium		19,974.2	21,831.5	23,552.1	25,086.0	26,513.3
High		20,384.2	22,634.6	24,876.0	27,054.2	29,119.3
Alachua	243.8					
Low		249.3	255.5	258.0	258.7	257.8
Medium		259.8	277.3	291.8	304.7	316.8
High		270.1	299.9	328.4	357.2	386.7
Baker	25.0					
Low		25.8	26.7	27.4	27.7	27.9
Medium		26.9	29.0	30.9	32.6	34.1
High		28.0	31.4	34.8	38.3	41.8
Bay	165.5					
Low		170.2	175.7	179.6	182.0	183.1
Medium		177.4	190.6	202.9	214.0	224.2
High		184.3	206.2	228.6	251.4	274.7
Bradford	28.6					
Low		28.9	29.3	29.7	29.9	29.9
Medium		29.8	31.2	32.5	33.7	34.7
High		30.7	33.1	35.6	38.0	40.5
Brevard	543.1					
Low		562.2	585.5	602.1	613.2	619.7
Medium		586.1	635.2	679.7	720.0	757.5
High		609.0	687.3	766.3	846.9	929.6
Broward	1,753.2					
Low		1,793.9	1,848.4	1,886.4	1,904.1	1,907.4
Medium		1,869.9	2,005.7	2,131.2	2,239.8	2,339.0
High		1,943.4	2,169.8	2,400.9	2,629.5	2,861.0
Calhoun	14.1					
Low		14.2	14.3	14.4	14.4	14.3
Medium		14.8	15.6	16.3	16.9	17.5
High		15.4	16.8	18.3	19.8	21.4
Charlotte	160.3					
Low		168.2	177.7	185.0	190.0	193.5
Medium		175.4	192.8	208.6	222.7	235.9
High		182.2	208.6	235.4	262.4	290.2
Citrus	136.7					
Low		143.2	150.7	156.5	160.4	163.1
Medium		149.3	163.5	176.6	188.1	198.9
High		155.1	177.0	199.2	221.5	244.6
Clay	176.9					
Low		190.8	207.0	219.5	227.9	233.1
Medium		201.1	229.4	255.6	279.1	300.9
High		210.9	253.1	296.9	341.9	388.6
Collier	326.7					
Low		355.9	388.7	412.6	427.1	434.7
Medium		379.2	440.1	497.5	549.2	598.5
High		401.4	494.7	593.8	696.9	807.3

See footnote at end of table.

Continued . . .

Table 1.41. PROJECTIONS: ESTIMATES, APRIL 1, 2006, AND PROJECTIONS SPECIFIED YEARS APRIL 1, 2010 THROUGH 2030, IN THE STATE AND COUNTIES OF FLORIDA (Continued)

(in thousands, rounded to hundreds)

County	Estimates 2006	Projections 2010	2015	2020	2025	2030
Columbia	63.5					
Low		66.0	68.4	70.1	71.1	71.5
Medium		68.8	74.2	79.2	83.5	87.6
High		71.5	80.3	89.2	98.2	107.3
DeSoto	33.2					
Low		34.3	36.7	37.8	38.4	38.6
Medium		35.7	39.9	42.6	45.1	47.3
High		37.1	43.1	48.1	53.0	58.0
Dixie	15.7					
Low		15.9	16.2	16.3	16.1	15.7
Medium		16.9	18.4	19.7	20.9	22.0
High		17.9	20.6	23.4	26.3	29.2
Duval	879.2					
Low		906.0	938.0	960.1	973.3	980.3
Medium		944.5	1,017.7	1,084.4	1,143.9	1,199.9
High		981.5	1,101.1	1,221.9	1,344.1	1,470.4
Escambia	309.6					
Low		313.9	320.4	325.0	328.0	329.6
Medium		323.8	340.4	355.7	369.3	382.0
High		333.4	361.3	389.3	417.4	445.9
Flagler	89.1					
Low		106.1	124.9	139.9	150.7	157.8
Medium		113.1	141.3	168.0	192.2	215.1
High		119.7	159.0	201.3	245.8	293.1
Franklin	11.9					
Low		11.9	12.0	12.1	12.1	12.0
Medium		12.4	13.1	13.7	14.2	14.7
High		12.9	14.1	15.4	16.6	17.9
Gadsden	48.2					
Low		48.8	49.1	49.2	49.2	48.9
Medium		50.3	52.2	53.9	55.5	56.9
High		51.8	55.4	59.0	62.6	66.2
Gilchrist	16.7					
Low		17.1	17.4	17.4	17.0	16.3
Medium		18.6	20.7	22.7	24.6	26.3
High		20.0	24.1	28.4	33.0	37.9
Glades	10.8					
Low		11.1	11.2	11.1	11.0	10.8
Medium		11.6	12.1	12.6	13.0	13.4
High		12.1	13.1	14.2	15.2	16.2
Gulf	16.5					
Low		16.3	16.0	15.6	15.1	14.5
Medium		17.3	18.2	19.0	19.7	20.4
High		18.3	20.4	22.5	24.6	26.9
Hamilton	14.5					
Low		14.4	14.2	14.1	13.8	13.6
Medium		15.0	15.5	16.0	16.4	16.8
High		15.6	16.7	17.9	19.1	20.3

See footnote at end of table.

Continued . . .

Table 1.41. PROJECTIONS: ESTIMATES, APRIL 1, 2006, AND PROJECTIONS SPECIFIED YEARS APRIL 1, 2010 THROUGH 2030, IN THE STATE AND COUNTIES OF FLORIDA (Continued)

(in thousands, rounded to hundreds)

County	Estimates 2006	Projections 2010	2015	2020	2025	2030
Hardee	27.2					
Low		27.5	27.9	28.3	28.5	28.7
Medium		28.4	29.7	30.9	32.1	33.2
High		29.2	31.5	33.9	36.3	38.8
Hendry	38.7					
Low		39.7	41.1	42.2	42.9	43.2
Medium		41.4	44.6	47.6	50.4	52.9
High		43.0	48.3	53.7	59.3	64.8
Hernando	157.0					
Low		165.1	174.9	182.0	186.0	188.0
Medium		174.0	193.8	212.3	228.5	243.7
High		182.5	213.8	246.3	279.0	313.3
Highlands	96.7					
Low		99.5	103.2	106.0	107.7	108.6
Medium		103.7	112.0	119.7	126.5	132.8
High		107.8	121.2	134.9	148.7	162.9
Hillsborough	1,164.4					
Low		1,220.3	1,285.9	1,336.5	1,370.7	1,392.3
Medium		1,272.3	1,394.6	1,507.6	1,607.0	1,698.6
High		1,322.0	1,509.5	1,701.0	1,892.9	2,088.5
Holmes	19.5					
Low		19.4	19.4	19.3	19.1	18.8
Medium		20.2	21.1	21.9	22.6	23.3
High		21.0	22.8	24.6	26.4	28.3
Indian River	135.3					
Low		142.3	150.5	156.3	159.7	161.1
Medium		150.0	166.8	182.4	196.2	209.0
High		157.3	183.9	211.5	239.6	268.5
Jackson	50.2					
Low		52.4	52.9	53.0	53.0	52.8
Medium		54.1	56.2	58.1	59.8	61.4
High		55.7	59.6	63.5	67.4	71.4
Jefferson	14.4					
Low		14.3	14.3	14.3	14.1	13.9
Medium		14.9	15.6	16.1	16.7	17.2
High		15.5	16.8	18.1	19.5	20.9
Lafayette	8.1					
Low		8.1	8.2	8.2	8.2	8.1
Medium		8.4	8.9	9.3	9.6	10.0
High		8.8	9.6	10.4	11.3	12.2
Lake	276.8					
Low		299.7	325.4	343.8	354.6	358.9
Medium		319.3	368.5	414.7	456.2	495.0
High		338.0	414.1	494.7	578.5	666.5
Lee	585.6					
Low		641.8	706.7	757.8	794.3	818.9
Medium		676.5	782.6	881.7	970.7	1,053.9
High		709.3	863.8	1,025.3	1,191.5	1,364.8

See footnote at end of table. Continued . . .

Table 1.41. PROJECTIONS: ESTIMATES, APRIL 1, 2006, AND PROJECTIONS SPECIFIED YEARS APRIL 1, 2010 THROUGH 2030, IN THE STATE AND COUNTIES OF FLORIDA (Continued)

(in thousands, rounded to hundreds)

County	Estimates 2006	Projections 2010	2015	2020	2025	2030
Leon	272.5					
Low		279.8	288.5	293.4	296.1	296.5
Medium		291.7	313.1	331.6	348.3	363.7
High		303.2	338.7	373.4	408.9	444.8
Levy	39.0					
Low		40.8	43.0	44.7	45.9	46.8
Medium		42.5	46.6	50.4	53.8	57.0
High		44.2	50.5	56.9	63.5	70.2
Liberty	7.8					
Low		7.7	7.6	7.4	7.2	6.9
Medium		8.2	8.6	9.0	9.4	9.7
High		8.7	9.7	10.7	11.7	12.8
Madison	19.8					
Low		19.7	19.6	19.5	19.2	18.9
Medium		20.5	21.3	22.0	22.7	23.3
High		21.3	23.0	24.8	26.5	28.3
Manatee	308.3					
Low		324.4	343.3	358.0	368.2	374.9
Medium		338.3	372.3	403.7	431.4	457.0
High		351.5	403.0	455.6	508.5	562.4
Marion	315.1					
Low		335.6	359.1	376.8	388.1	394.3
Medium		353.7	398.0	439.2	476.0	510.2
High		370.9	439.0	509.8	582.2	657.1
Martin	142.6					
Low		147.8	153.9	158.5	161.6	163.4
Medium		154.1	167.0	179.0	189.7	199.7
High		160.1	180.7	201.8	223.2	245.1
Miami-Dade	2,437.0					
Low		2,464.7	2,506.1	2,529.9	2,534.9	2,524.9
Medium		2,568.8	2,720.2	2,860.9	2,986.5	3,103.0
High		2,670.1	2,941.9	3,219.8	3,500.6	3,787.4
Monroe	80.5					
Low		78.2	76.0	73.7	71.5	69.2
Medium		80.7	80.8	81.0	81.2	81.3
High		83.1	85.7	88.3	91.0	93.6
Nassau	68.2					
Low		71.9	76.3	79.4	81.4	82.5
Medium		75.8	84.5	92.7	100.0	106.9
High		79.5	93.2	107.5	122.1	137.5
Okaloosa	192.7					
Low		199.4	207.4	213.2	216.8	219.0
Medium		207.9	225.0	240.7	254.6	267.7
High		216.1	243.5	271.3	299.4	328.4
Okeechobee	38.7					
Low		39.1	39.8	40.3	40.7	40.9
Medium		40.3	42.3	44.1	45.9	47.4
High		41.5	44.9	48.3	51.9	55.3

See footnote at end of table.

Continued . . .

Table 1.41. PROJECTIONS: ESTIMATES, APRIL 1, 2006, AND PROJECTIONS SPECIFIED YEARS APRIL 1, 2010 THROUGH 2030, IN THE STATE AND COUNTIES OF FLORIDA (Continued)

(in thousands, rounded to hundreds)

County	Estimates 2006	Projections 2010	2015	2020	2025	2030
Orange	1,079.5					
Low		1,143.0	1,216.2	1,270.4	1,304.1	1,321.1
Medium		1,204.5	1,347.8	1,481.4	1,600.5	1,711.1
High		1,263.3	1,486.5	1,718.8	1,956.1	2,201.9
Osceola	255.9					
Low		290.1	328.0	357.2	377.0	388.7
Medium		309.2	371.2	429.8	482.8	532.6
High		327.1	417.5	514.0	615.0	721.9
Palm Beach	1,288.0					
Low		1,347.5	1,418.8	1,475.0	1,514.8	1,541.4
Medium		1,404.9	1,538.8	1,663.7	1,775.5	1,879.4
High		1,459.8	1,665.5	1,877.2	2,091.8	2,312.0
Pasco	424.4					
Low		450.4	481.6	504.3	518.6	526.1
Medium		474.6	533.6	587.9	636.2	681.1
High		497.8	588.6	682.3	777.9	876.9
Pinellas	948.1					
Low		939.4	933.7	926.2	916.6	905.5
Medium		968.6	992.7	1,015.5	1,036.4	1,056.2
High		997.5	1,052.9	1,109.4	1,166.6	1,225.0
Polk	565.0					
Low		592.3	624.2	648.8	665.3	675.8
Medium		617.5	677.0	731.8	780.1	824.5
High		641.6	732.7	825.7	918.8	1,013.7
Putnam	74.4					
Low		74.6	75.2	75.5	75.5	75.3
Medium		77.0	79.9	82.7	85.2	87.5
High		79.3	84.8	90.5	96.1	101.9
St. Johns	165.3					
Low		181.5	199.7	213.1	221.5	225.7
Medium		193.4	226.1	256.8	284.5	310.5
High		204.7	254.1	306.6	361.4	419.1
St. Lucie	259.3					
Low		283.5	312.7	335.6	351.6	362.4
Medium		298.8	346.2	390.4	429.7	466.4
High		313.3	382.1	454.0	527.4	603.9
Santa Rosa	141.4					
Low		151.3	161.3	168.9	174.1	177.1
Medium		159.5	178.8	196.9	213.5	229.0
High		167.2	197.2	228.5	261.1	295.1
Sarasota	379.4					
Low		396.1	416.1	431.2	441.1	446.9
Medium		413.0	451.4	486.5	517.4	545.7
High		429.1	488.5	548.8	609.1	670.4
Seminole	420.7					
Low		439.3	461.3	478.3	490.4	498.2
Medium		458.0	500.3	539.6	575.0	607.8
High		475.9	541.5	608.7	677.2	747.4

See footnote at end of table.

Continued . . .

Table 1.41. PROJECTIONS: ESTIMATES, APRIL 1, 2006, AND PROJECTIONS SPECIFIED YEARS APRIL 1, 2010 THROUGH 2030, IN THE STATE AND COUNTIES OF FLORIDA (Continued)

(in thousands, rounded to hundreds)

County	Estimates 2006	Projections 2010	2015	2020	2025	2030
Sumter	82.6					
Low		93.5	105.7	115.1	121.6	125.5
Medium		99.7	119.6	138.5	155.7	171.9
High		105.4	134.5	165.7	198.4	233.1
Suwannee	38.8					
Low		41.8	43.7	44.8	45.5	45.9
Medium		43.5	47.4	50.6	53.5	56.2
High		45.3	51.3	57.1	62.9	68.8
Taylor	21.5					
Low		21.5	21.6	21.6	21.4	21.2
Medium		22.4	23.4	24.4	25.3	26.1
High		23.3	25.3	27.4	29.6	31.8
Union	15.0					
Low		15.2	15.0	14.7	14.2	13.6
Medium		16.2	17.0	17.8	18.5	19.1
High		17.2	19.1	21.1	23.1	25.3
Volusia	503.8					
Low		521.8	543.0	558.3	568.1	573.9
Medium		544.0	589.1	630.4	667.1	701.7
High		565.3	637.5	710.6	784.5	860.9
Wakulla	28.4					
Low		32.4	34.6	36.4	37.7	38.4
Medium		34.1	38.4	42.4	46.1	49.6
High		35.8	42.3	49.3	56.5	64.0
Walton	55.8					
Low		61.7	68.2	73.0	76.1	77.8
Medium		65.7	77.2	88.0	97.8	106.9
High		69.5	86.7	105.1	124.2	144.5
Washington	23.1					
Low		24.5	24.4	23.9	23.3	22.4
Medium		26.1	27.6	29.1	30.3	31.5
High		27.7	31.0	34.5	38.0	41.7

Note: The medium projection is the one we believe is most likely to provide an accurate forecast of future population. The high and low projections indicate the range in which future populations are likely to fall. They do not represent absolute limits to growth; for any county, the future population may be above the high projection or below the low projection. If future distributions of errors are similar to past distributions, however, future populations will fall between high and low projections in approximately two-thirds of Florida's counties. For a detailed description of projection methodology, see the source.

Source: University of Florida, Bureau of Economic and Business Research, Population Program, *Florida Population Studies,* February 2007, Volume 40, Bulletin No. 147.

Table 1.50. AGE AND SEX PROJECTIONS: TOTAL AND FEMALE POPULATION CENSUS COUNTS APRIL 1, 2000, ESTIMATES, APRIL 1, 2006, AND PROJECTIONS APRIL 1, 2010, 2020, AND 2030 IN FLORIDA

Age	Census 2000	Estimates 2006	Projections 2010	Projections 2020	Projections 2030
Total	15,982,378	18,349,132	19,974,199	23,552,136	26,513,332
0-4	945,823	1,092,995	1,179,974	1,325,673	1,383,989
5-9	1,031,718	1,124,542	1,211,349	1,384,351	1,463,362
10-14	1,057,024	1,174,398	1,212,895	1,395,323	1,513,394
15-19	1,014,070	1,192,460	1,279,764	1,391,420	1,538,375
15-17	611,777	721,830	775,584	843,626	933,269
18-19	402,293	470,630	504,180	547,794	605,106
20-24	928,329	1,176,112	1,290,947	1,360,953	1,522,321
25-29	995,296	1,092,752	1,252,786	1,419,847	1,481,379
30-34	1,088,784	1,129,945	1,179,327	1,431,754	1,436,581
35-39	1,261,015	1,216,834	1,240,885	1,430,122	1,552,441
40-44	1,224,164	1,352,216	1,311,165	1,357,671	1,568,381
45-49	1,085,389	1,340,857	1,448,361	1,380,292	1,541,323
50-54	984,116	1,227,102	1,413,630	1,453,724	1,473,837
55-59	821,534	1,128,515	1,292,455	1,633,251	1,523,461
60-64	737,505	952,898	1,179,390	1,622,291	1,621,042
65-69	727,505	804,847	950,262	1,458,022	1,786,728
70-74	724,684	728,953	776,129	1,255,378	1,698,597
75-79	616,694	662,691	669,734	902,715	1,387,388
80-84	407,441	512,676	553,008	623,871	1,031,111
85 and over	331,287	438,339	532,138	725,478	989,622
Female	8,184,663	9,370,034	10,190,548	12,028,698	13,556,963
0-4	461,056	536,771	579,484	650,923	679,440
5-9	502,682	549,510	594,651	679,467	718,140
10-14	515,297	572,471	591,975	684,088	741,832
15-19	492,593	583,415	625,977	684,121	756,084
15-17	296,319	352,253	378,440	413,814	457,729
18-19	196,274	231,162	247,537	270,307	298,355
20-24	453,132	573,510	632,350	667,311	748,660
25-29	491,147	533,665	611,308	698,823	732,295
30-34	539,664	557,767	577,763	708,432	712,232
35-39	629,930	603,147	614,104	704,630	770,908
40-44	617,628	677,600	653,218	671,536	782,223
45-49	555,337	680,764	732,799	693,745	770,192
50-54	508,938	632,654	725,559	738,625	742,642
55-59	433,375	588,173	672,844	842,493	779,435
60-64	392,934	506,431	622,064	849,575	839,344
65-69	388,051	432,749	510,967	774,961	940,559
70-74	395,568	396,009	423,759	678,240	909,572
75-79	348,566	369,607	371,653	501,963	759,641
80-84	239,638	297,575	317,911	357,015	579,555
85 and over	219,127	278,216	332,162	442,750	594,209

Note: Medium projections are shown. High and low projections for total population are available from the Bureau of Economic and Business Research, University of Florida.

Source: University of Florida, Bureau of Economic and Business Research, Population Program, unpublished data. Census data from U.S. Census Bureau.

Table 1.51. AGE: MEDIAN AGE ESTIMATES, APRIL 1, 2006, AND PROJECTIONS, APRIL 1, 2010 2020, AND 2030, IN THE STATE AND COUNTIES OF FLORIDA

County	Esti-mates 2006	Projections 2010	2020	2030	County	Esti-mates 2006	Projections 2010	2020	2030
Florida	39.9	40.5	42.3	44.4	Lake	46.4	47.5	51.2	54.1
					Lee	45.6	46.2	49.0	51.3
Alachua	29.3	29.5	31.4	33.1	Leon	29.4	29.1	30.6	31.9
Baker	35.2	35.9	37.6	39.8	Levy	42.7	43.6	45.5	47.2
Bay	40.1	41.5	44.9	47.5	Liberty	35.0	35.2	35.9	37.2
Bradford	37.6	37.8	38.6	40.2	Madison	36.2	36.2	37.2	40.0
Brevard	44.0	45.8	48.9	50.9	Manatee	44.1	44.4	46.0	47.9
Broward	38.5	38.8	39.7	41.1	Marion	45.4	46.5	49.6	51.8
Calhoun	36.5	36.8	37.3	39.4	Martin	49.2	50.8	55.1	57.7
Charlotte	54.4	55.0	58.0	60.9	Miami-Dade	36.8	37.6	39.2	40.6
Citrus	53.8	54.6	57.8	60.4	Monroe	45.0	46.9	50.2	50.5
Clay	36.8	37.3	39.0	41.4	Nassau	41.1	42.8	46.4	48.8
Collier	44.8	46.0	48.9	51.3	Okaloosa	37.3	38.1	40.2	42.7
Columbia	38.6	39.3	41.2	43.6	Okeechobee	37.3	38.0	39.0	40.6
DeSoto	37.6	38.2	38.9	40.7	Orange	33.0	33.1	34.6	36.4
Dixie	41.7	42.8	44.6	46.3	Osceola	34.3	34.8	37.1	39.5
Duval	35.2	35.9	37.9	40.3	Palm Beach	42.8	43.6	45.5	47.3
Escambia	35.9	36.1	37.3	39.2	Pasco	45.1	45.8	48.3	50.4
Flagler	50.1	51.1	55.2	57.8	Pinellas	44.5	45.6	47.3	48.2
Franklin	44.0	44.2	46.7	48.3	Polk	39.5	39.9	41.8	44.1
Gadsden	36.0	36.3	37.7	39.2	Putnam	41.7	42.3	43.6	45.2
Gilchrist	38.7	40.5	44.4	47.6	St. Johns	41.9	42.9	44.9	46.9
Glades	40.8	40.8	43.1	45.0	St. Lucie	43.3	44.2	46.8	49.5
Gulf	40.8	41.7	43.5	45.1	Santa Rosa	38.1	38.7	40.3	42.6
Hamilton	35.8	36.7	38.2	40.1	Sarasota	52.0	53.2	57.2	60.5
Hardee	32.7	32.0	32.7	33.5	Seminole	37.1	37.6	39.1	41.0
Hendry	29.4	29.1	29.9	30.5	Sumter	49.6	50.8	54.1	56.0
Hernando	49.8	50.8	54.5	57.2	Suwannee	41.3	41.9	44.3	47.3
Highlands	50.6	51.2	54.3	56.7	Taylor	38.9	39.6	41.5	43.6
Hillsborough	35.5	35.9	37.2	39.0	Union	36.3	36.5	36.8	37.6
Holmes	37.7	38.0	37.6	39.3	Volusia	43.8	45.0	47.5	49.3
Indian River	48.3	49.8	53.6	56.4	Wakulla	39.2	40.3	42.9	45.3
Jackson	38.9	39.6	41.5	43.7	Walton	42.6	43.9	46.4	48.6
Jefferson	40.9	41.8	44.0	46.1	Washington	39.5	39.3	39.9	41.7
Lafayette	34.8	34.8	36.0	37.2					

Note: Projections are based on U.S. Census Bureau modified age, race, and sex data.

Source: University of Florida, Bureau of Economic and Business Research, Population Program, unpublished data.

Table 1.52. MALE AND FEMALE PROJECTIONS: PROJECTIONS BY SEX IN THE STATE AND COUNTIES OF FLORIDA, APRIL 1, 2010 AND 2030

County	2010 Total	2010 Male	2010 Female	2030 Total	2030 Male	2030 Female
Florida	19,974,199	9,783,651	10,190,548	26,513,332	12,956,369	13,556,963
Alachua	259,838	127,257	132,581	316,783	154,982	161,801
Baker	26,904	14,322	12,582	34,146	17,884	16,262
Bay	177,372	87,480	89,892	224,235	109,771	114,464
Bradford	29,776	16,871	12,905	34,726	19,348	15,378
Brevard	586,060	286,461	299,599	757,544	369,482	388,062
Broward	1,869,913	909,867	960,046	2,338,998	1,133,693	1,205,305
Calhoun	14,770	7,886	6,884	17,542	9,262	8,280
Charlotte	175,389	83,870	91,519	235,855	113,424	122,431
Citrus	149,275	71,698	77,577	198,911	96,043	102,868
Clay	201,131	99,306	101,825	300,908	147,926	152,982
Collier	379,226	188,250	190,976	598,519	294,358	304,161
Columbia	68,838	35,761	33,077	87,562	44,873	42,689
DeSoto	35,707	19,406	16,301	47,291	25,441	21,850
Dixie	16,935	9,002	7,933	21,980	11,417	10,563
Duval	944,488	458,886	485,602	1,199,858	579,743	620,115
Escambia	323,801	159,132	164,669	381,961	186,697	195,264
Flagler	113,148	54,304	58,844	215,078	102,942	112,136
Franklin	12,446	6,770	5,676	14,720	7,819	6,901
Gadsden	50,324	24,277	26,047	56,925	27,517	29,408
Gilchrist	18,555	9,540	9,015	26,299	13,306	12,993
Glades	11,613	6,534	5,079	13,368	7,420	5,948
Gulf	17,317	10,053	7,264	20,368	11,512	8,856
Hamilton	14,961	8,763	6,198	16,776	9,643	7,133
Hardee	28,389	15,327	13,062	33,220	17,537	15,683
Hendry	41,410	22,046	19,364	52,885	27,228	25,657
Hernando	173,986	83,435	90,551	243,699	117,955	125,744
Highlands	103,735	50,382	53,353	132,842	64,796	68,046
Hillsborough	1,272,270	623,110	649,160	1,698,649	828,772	869,877
Holmes	20,236	10,706	9,530	23,261	12,183	11,078
Indian River	149,972	72,656	77,316	208,987	101,521	107,466
Jackson	54,054	30,023	24,031	61,356	33,608	27,748
Jefferson	14,932	7,846	7,086	17,156	8,960	8,196
Lafayette	8,440	5,170	3,270	9,992	5,930	4,062
Lake	319,321	155,673	163,648	495,005	241,756	253,249

Continued . . .

Table 1.52. MALE AND FEMALE PROJECTIONS: PROJECTIONS BY SEX IN THE STATE AND COUNTIES OF FLORIDA, APRIL 1, 2010 AND 2030 (Continued)

County	2010 Total	2010 Male	2010 Female	2030 Total	2030 Male	2030 Female
Lee	676,531	332,091	344,440	1,053,932	516,196	537,736
Leon	291,676	139,354	152,322	363,660	173,903	189,757
Levy	42,545	20,705	21,840	57,020	27,832	29,188
Liberty	8,203	4,946	3,257	9,709	5,691	4,018
Madison	20,525	10,856	9,669	23,321	12,304	11,017
Manatee	338,254	165,275	172,979	457,030	224,551	232,479
Marion	353,683	171,466	182,217	510,153	248,432	261,721
Martin	154,050	75,302	78,748	199,714	97,524	102,190
Miami-Dade	2,568,807	1,240,304	1,328,503	3,103,028	1,488,856	1,614,172
Monroe	80,663	42,195	38,468	81,323	41,123	40,200
Nassau	75,805	37,371	38,434	106,885	52,419	54,466
Okaloosa	207,905	103,564	104,341	267,731	131,962	135,769
Okeechobee	40,300	21,242	19,058	47,422	24,530	22,892
Orange	1,204,474	598,790	605,684	1,711,106	847,474	863,632
Osceola	309,202	153,817	155,385	532,621	264,068	268,553
Palm Beach	1,404,907	679,607	725,300	1,879,371	908,350	971,021
Pasco	474,600	230,811	243,789	681,092	333,251	347,841
Pinellas	968,631	468,924	499,707	1,056,224	516,445	539,779
Polk	617,492	304,343	313,149	824,476	405,810	418,666
Putnam	76,982	37,902	39,080	87,538	43,003	44,535
St. Johns	193,431	94,843	98,588	310,534	152,217	158,317
St. Lucie	298,841	146,155	152,686	466,421	227,442	238,979
Santa Rosa	159,450	80,419	79,031	228,996	114,479	114,517
Sarasota	412,970	197,533	215,437	545,724	263,415	282,309
Seminole	458,006	225,797	232,209	607,824	299,903	307,921
Sumter	99,654	52,183	47,471	171,915	86,755	85,160
Suwannee	43,547	21,698	21,849	56,160	28,219	27,941
Taylor	22,410	11,735	10,675	26,107	13,591	12,516
Union	16,207	10,633	5,574	19,133	12,057	7,076
Volusia	543,988	265,496	278,492	701,666	343,359	358,307
Wakulla	34,098	18,677	15,421	49,639	26,207	23,432
Walton	65,701	33,158	32,543	106,942	53,185	53,757
Washington	26,129	14,389	11,740	31,510	17,067	14,443

Source: University of Florida, Bureau of Economic and Business Research, Population Program, *Florida Population Studies*, June 2007, Volume 40, Bulletin No. 148.

Table 1.53. RACE: ESTIMATES, APRIL 1, 2006, AND PROJECTIONS, APRIL 1, 2010 AND 2030, IN THE STATE AND COUNTIES OF FLORIDA

(rounded to thousands)

	Estimates, 2006			Projections					
				2010			2030		
County	Total	Non-Hispanic white	Non-Hispanic black	Total	Non-Hispanic white	Non-Hispanic black	Total	Non-Hispanic white	Non-Hispanic black
Florida	18,349	11,428	2,851	19,974	11,893	3,159	26,513	14,198	4,359
Alachua	244	164	50	260	170	55	317	189	71
Baker	25	21	3	27	22	3	34	29	3
Bay	166	136	19	177	142	20	224	171	26
Bradford	29	21	6	30	22	6	35	26	7
Brevard	543	446	50	586	469	56	758	575	78
Broward	1,753	908	423	1,870	866	480	2,339	791	670
Calhoun	14	11	2	15	11	2	18	13	3
Charlotte	160	143	9	175	153	10	236	198	18
Citrus	137	126	4	149	135	4	199	174	7
Clay	177	146	15	201	162	18	301	230	31
Collier	327	225	19	379	253	23	599	370	38
Columbia	64	50	11	69	53	11	88	67	13
DeSoto	33	20	4	36	21	4	47	24	4
Dixie	16	14	1	17	15	1	22	20	2
Duval	879	527	266	944	538	292	1,200	591	404
Escambia	310	219	69	324	226	72	382	252	89
Flagler	89	73	9	113	91	12	215	168	23
Franklin	12	10	2	12	10	2	15	12	2
Gadsden	48	16	27	50	17	28	57	17	30
Gilchrist	17	15	1	19	17	1	26	23	2
Glades	11	7	1	12	7	1	13	8	1
Gulf	17	12	3	17	13	3	20	16	3
Hamilton	15	8	5	15	8	5	17	9	5
Hardee	27	14	2	28	14	2	33	13	3
Hendry	39	16	5	41	15	5	53	15	5
Hernando	157	136	7	174	148	9	244	198	14
Highlands	97	71	9	104	73	10	133	84	12
Hillsborough	1,164	682	190	1,272	700	215	1,699	788	314
Holmes	20	17	1	20	18	2	23	20	2
Indian River	135	109	12	150	119	13	209	158	19
Jackson	50	34	14	54	36	15	61	41	17
Jefferson	14	9	5	15	9	5	17	11	5
Lafayette	8	6	1	8	6	1	10	7	1

Continued . . .

Table 1.53. RACE: ESTIMATES, APRIL 1, 2006, AND PROJECTIONS, APRIL 1, 2010 AND 2030, IN THE STATE AND COUNTIES OF FLORIDA (Continued)

(rounded to thousands)

County	Estimates, 2006			Projections 2010			Projections 2030		
	Total	Non-Hispanic white	Non-Hispanic black	Total	Non-Hispanic white	Non-Hispanic black	Total	Non-Hispanic white	Non-Hispanic black
Lake	277	225	23	319	252	29	495	373	44
Lee	586	449	42	677	493	51	1,054	703	84
Leon	272	165	88	292	168	100	364	186	139
Levy	39	32	4	43	35	4	57	45	5
Liberty	8	6	2	8	6	2	10	7	2
Madison	20	11	8	21	11	8	23	12	8
Manatee	308	235	27	338	247	31	457	302	43
Marion	315	248	35	354	272	39	510	376	54
Martin	143	120	8	154	127	9	200	158	11
Miami-Dade	2,437	405	486	2,569	359	502	3,103	214	590
Monroe	81	60	4	81	60	4	81	59	4
Nassau	68	61	5	76	68	5	107	96	6
Okaloosa	193	154	20	208	162	21	268	197	29
Okeechobee	39	27	3	40	27	3	47	30	4
Orange	1,080	544	223	1,204	548	258	1,711	593	402
Osceola	256	124	21	309	130	28	533	175	53
Palm Beach	1,288	858	204	1,405	899	231	1,879	1,073	340
Pasco	424	370	12	475	402	15	681	544	27
Pinellas	948	762	98	969	755	108	1,056	744	144
Polk	565	396	81	617	406	90	824	474	124
Putnam	74	55	12	77	55	13	88	59	14
St. Johns	165	148	10	193	172	11	311	274	15
St. Lucie	259	182	42	299	200	49	466	292	74
Santa Rosa	141	125	7	159	139	8	229	194	11
Sarasota	379	335	16	413	357	18	546	451	24
Seminole	421	300	45	458	313	52	608	372	77
Sumter	83	66	8	100	81	9	172	143	10
Suwannee	39	31	4	44	34	4	56	42	5
Taylor	21	16	4	22	17	4	26	20	5
Union	15	11	3	16	12	3	19	14	4
Volusia	504	401	49	544	422	52	702	511	68
Wakulla	28	24	3	34	29	4	50	43	5
Walton	56	48	4	66	56	4	107	89	7
Washington	23	19	3	26	21	4	32	25	4

Source: University of Florida, Bureau of Economic and Business Research, Population Program, *Florida Population Studies*, June 2007, Volume 40, Bulletin No. 148.

Table 1.54. RACE AND SEX: NON-HISPANIC WHITE POPULATION PROJECTIONS BY SEX IN THE STATE AND COUNTIES OF FLORIDA, APRIL 1, 2010 AND 2030

	2010			2030		
County	Total	Male	Female	Total	Male	Female
Florida	11,893,250	5,810,820	6,082,430	14,198,118	6,937,472	7,260,646
Alachua	169,599	83,607	85,992	188,603	92,983	95,620
Baker	22,431	11,454	10,977	28,860	14,494	14,366
Bay	141,828	70,283	71,545	171,489	84,294	87,195
Bradford	22,286	11,764	10,522	25,853	13,371	12,482
Brevard	469,427	230,193	239,234	575,315	281,448	293,867
Broward	865,824	425,814	440,010	791,046	392,327	398,719
Calhoun	11,376	5,732	5,644	13,156	6,550	6,606
Charlotte	153,434	73,333	80,101	197,501	95,325	102,176
Citrus	134,793	64,832	69,961	173,997	84,214	89,783
Clay	161,819	80,127	81,692	229,829	113,419	116,410
Collier	252,715	121,745	130,970	370,295	178,872	191,423
Columbia	53,290	26,922	26,368	67,491	33,670	33,821
DeSoto	20,864	10,282	10,582	23,588	11,629	11,959
Dixie	15,033	7,704	7,329	19,702	9,885	9,817
Duval	537,631	263,817	273,814	590,727	286,563	304,164
Escambia	225,647	111,924	113,723	251,558	124,315	127,243
Flagler	90,818	43,909	46,909	168,357	81,280	87,077
Franklin	10,206	5,303	4,903	12,100	6,119	5,981
Gadsden	16,721	8,154	8,567	16,597	8,027	8,570
Gilchrist	16,561	8,296	8,265	23,187	11,475	11,712
Glades	7,278	3,777	3,501	7,682	3,921	3,761
Gulf	13,167	6,920	6,247	16,003	8,131	7,872
Hamilton	8,088	4,442	3,646	8,847	4,641	4,206
Hardee	13,668	6,947	6,721	12,986	6,544	6,442
Hendry	15,119	7,628	7,491	14,748	7,343	7,405
Hernando	147,865	70,916	76,949	197,603	95,804	101,799
Highlands	73,007	34,642	38,365	84,262	40,580	43,682
Hillsborough	699,516	340,982	358,534	788,201	381,186	407,015
Holmes	17,844	9,041	8,803	19,969	10,016	9,953
Indian River	119,122	57,079	62,043	158,154	76,393	81,761
Jackson	36,172	18,900	17,272	40,771	20,825	19,946
Jefferson	9,037	4,616	4,421	11,004	5,515	5,489
Lafayette	6,096	3,262	2,834	7,067	3,641	3,426
Lake	252,229	122,448	129,781	373,364	182,090	191,274

Continued . . .

Table 1.54. RACE AND SEX: NON-HISPANIC WHITE POPULATION PROJECTIONS BY SEX IN THE STATE AND COUNTIES OF FLORIDA, APRIL 1, 2010 AND 2030 (Continued)

	2010			2030		
County	Total	Male	Female	Total	Male	Female
Lee	492,746	238,332	254,414	703,449	340,628	362,821
Leon	168,296	81,825	86,471	186,118	90,680	95,438
Levy	34,574	16,921	17,653	44,693	21,863	22,830
Liberty	5,825	3,178	2,647	6,567	3,471	3,096
Madison	11,203	5,684	5,519	12,382	6,162	6,220
Manatee	246,870	118,771	128,099	302,104	146,953	155,151
Marion	272,174	131,522	140,652	375,820	182,644	193,176
Martin	127,126	61,315	65,811	157,829	76,594	81,235
Miami-Dade	358,995	180,180	178,815	214,082	108,583	105,499
Monroe	60,296	31,596	28,700	59,383	29,974	29,409
Nassau	67,985	33,569	34,416	95,890	47,025	48,865
Okaloosa	161,992	81,033	80,959	197,206	97,666	99,540
Okeechobee	27,373	13,601	13,772	29,662	14,596	15,066
Orange	548,277	274,213	274,064	593,393	296,895	296,498
Osceola	130,366	64,607	65,759	174,761	86,421	88,340
Palm Beach	899,303	427,960	471,343	1,073,255	510,933	562,322
Pasco	401,816	194,512	207,304	544,188	266,043	278,145
Pinellas	755,287	364,960	390,327	743,802	364,076	379,726
Polk	405,661	197,169	208,492	473,829	231,177	242,652
Putnam	55,372	27,294	28,078	58,617	28,817	29,800
St. Johns	171,746	84,336	87,410	273,662	134,341	139,321
St. Lucie	200,203	97,108	103,095	291,902	141,882	150,020
Santa Rosa	138,913	69,472	69,441	194,287	96,517	97,770
Sarasota	356,562	169,563	186,999	450,964	216,694	234,270
Seminole	312,610	154,543	158,067	372,454	184,554	187,900
Sumter	80,669	39,523	41,146	142,828	68,690	74,138
Suwannee	34,295	16,684	17,611	42,473	20,722	21,751
Taylor	17,075	8,631	8,444	19,854	9,919	9,935
Union	11,704	7,009	4,695	14,066	7,976	6,090
Volusia	421,954	205,300	216,654	511,025	249,554	261,471
Wakulla	28,687	14,890	13,797	43,076	21,714	21,362
Walton	56,089	27,983	28,106	89,231	43,888	45,343
Washington	20,695	10,741	9,954	25,354	12,930	12,424

Source: University of Florida, Bureau of Economic and Business Research, Population Program, *Florida Population Studies*, June 2007, Volume 40, Bulletin No. 148.

Table 1.55. RACE AND SEX: NON-HISPANIC BLACK POPULATION PROJECTIONS BY SEX IN THE STATE AND COUNTIES OF FLORIDA, APRIL 1, 2010 AND 2030

County	2010 Total	2010 Male	2010 Female	2030 Total	2030 Male	2030 Female
Florida	3,158,870	1,519,702	1,639,168	4,358,923	2,082,953	2,275,970
Alachua	54,697	26,072	28,625	71,369	33,892	37,477
Baker	3,372	2,118	1,254	3,455	2,222	1,233
Bay	20,236	9,533	10,703	26,353	12,315	14,038
Bradford	6,161	4,201	1,960	6,883	4,675	2,208
Brevard	55,920	26,355	29,565	77,889	36,486	41,403
Broward	480,109	229,418	250,691	670,487	321,344	349,143
Calhoun	2,374	1,453	921	2,871	1,726	1,145
Charlotte	10,496	4,901	5,595	17,551	7,964	9,587
Citrus	4,474	2,101	2,373	6,979	3,226	3,753
Clay	17,618	8,412	9,206	30,553	14,431	16,122
Collier	22,745	10,931	11,814	38,357	17,910	20,447
Columbia	11,438	6,472	4,966	13,079	7,328	5,751
DeSoto	3,922	2,489	1,433	4,113	3,028	1,085
Dixie	1,435	989	446	1,581	1,085	496
Duval	291,573	137,813	153,760	404,316	191,740	212,576
Escambia	72,065	34,189	37,876	89,126	42,073	47,053
Flagler	11,651	5,297	6,354	23,290	10,430	12,860
Franklin	1,812	1,184	628	1,934	1,280	654
Gadsden	27,687	12,867	14,820	29,838	13,931	15,907
Gilchrist	1,217	761	456	1,747	1,030	717
Glades	1,170	785	385	1,073	757	316
Gulf	3,273	2,385	888	3,262	2,449	813
Hamilton	5,281	3,238	2,043	5,379	3,383	1,996
Hardee	2,348	1,582	766	2,740	1,789	951
Hendry	5,047	2,684	2,363	5,046	2,728	2,318
Hernando	8,744	3,998	4,746	13,835	6,327	7,508
Highlands	9,710	4,636	5,074	12,130	5,694	6,436
Hillsborough	214,575	101,927	112,648	314,307	148,495	165,812
Holmes	1,553	1,093	460	2,075	1,377	698
Indian River	13,247	6,308	6,939	18,796	8,783	10,013
Jackson	14,972	8,989	5,983	16,693	10,001	6,692
Jefferson	4,952	2,643	2,309	4,586	2,528	2,058
Lafayette	1,243	1,086	157	1,248	1,123	125
Lake	28,553	13,543	15,010	44,358	20,794	23,564

Continued . . .

Table 1.55. RACE AND SEX: NON-HISPANIC BLACK POPULATION PROJECTIONS BY SEX IN THE STATE AND COUNTIES OF FLORIDA, APRIL 1, 2010 AND 2030 (Continued)

County	2010 Total	2010 Male	2010 Female	2030 Total	2030 Male	2030 Female
Lee	51,286	24,398	26,888	84,163	39,647	44,516
Leon	99,794	46,106	53,688	139,018	64,566	74,452
Levy	4,302	1,940	2,362	5,169	2,390	2,779
Liberty	1,724	1,260	464	2,222	1,539	683
Madison	7,770	4,165	3,605	8,127	4,437	3,690
Manatee	30,526	14,558	15,968	43,370	20,583	22,787
Marion	39,409	18,709	20,700	53,939	25,562	28,377
Martin	8,532	4,233	4,299	10,966	5,195	5,771
Miami-Dade	502,409	237,264	265,145	590,309	276,575	313,734
Monroe	4,129	2,129	2,000	4,147	2,103	2,044
Nassau	5,007	2,370	2,637	5,803	2,755	3,048
Okaloosa	21,224	10,087	11,137	29,305	13,776	15,529
Okeechobee	3,372	2,167	1,205	3,915	2,478	1,437
Orange	257,748	124,198	133,550	401,636	191,536	210,100
Osceola	27,681	13,215	14,466	53,046	24,711	28,335
Palm Beach	230,572	111,360	119,212	339,621	162,258	177,363
Pasco	14,863	7,065	7,798	26,805	12,373	14,432
Pinellas	107,608	51,149	56,459	143,934	68,509	75,425
Polk	90,220	43,567	46,653	123,978	59,089	64,889
Putnam	12,953	6,159	6,794	14,083	6,706	7,377
St. Johns	10,538	4,941	5,597	15,013	7,013	8,000
St. Lucie	48,709	23,240	25,469	74,397	35,097	39,300
Santa Rosa	7,670	4,107	3,563	11,302	5,850	5,452
Sarasota	17,822	8,340	9,482	23,823	11,104	12,719
Seminole	52,077	24,853	27,224	77,160	36,572	40,588
Sumter	8,734	5,810	2,924	9,933	6,544	3,389
Suwannee	4,473	2,075	2,398	4,809	2,281	2,528
Taylor	4,383	2,522	1,861	4,832	2,819	2,013
Union	3,487	2,818	669	3,597	2,966	631
Volusia	52,017	24,790	27,227	68,293	32,426	35,867
Wakulla	4,044	2,821	1,223	4,527	3,124	1,403
Walton	4,396	2,362	2,034	6,661	3,493	3,168
Washington	3,721	2,471	1,250	3,721	2,532	1,189

Source: University of Florida, Bureau of Economic and Business Research, Population Program, *Florida Population Studies*, June 2007, Volume 40, Bulletin No. 148.

Table 1.56. HISPANIC ORIGIN POPULATION: PROJECTIONS BY SEX IN THE STATE AND COUNTIES OF FLORIDA, APRIL 1, 2010 AND 2030

County	2010 Total	2010 Male	2010 Female	2030 Total	2030 Male	2030 Female
Florida	4,393,095	2,199,452	2,193,643	7,085,778	3,521,499	3,564,279
Alachua	23,491	11,835	11,656	38,910	19,609	19,301
Baker	864	602	262	1,499	954	545
Bay	9,651	4,997	4,654	18,151	9,310	8,841
Bradford	944	643	301	1,391	898	493
Brevard	45,992	22,974	23,018	81,284	40,749	40,535
Broward	454,684	221,524	233,160	762,711	365,021	397,690
Calhoun	707	507	200	1,063	714	349
Charlotte	8,448	4,228	4,220	15,170	7,579	7,591
Citrus	7,722	3,690	4,032	14,375	6,957	7,418
Clay	14,605	7,385	7,220	28,230	14,268	13,962
Collier	99,389	53,471	45,918	181,371	93,608	87,763
Columbia	3,085	1,787	1,298	5,503	3,041	2,462
DeSoto	10,657	6,470	4,187	19,213	10,506	8,707
Dixie	336	220	116	505	314	191
Duval	76,894	39,110	37,784	140,975	71,164	69,811
Escambia	13,358	6,980	6,378	23,010	11,688	11,322
Flagler	8,495	4,104	4,391	18,395	8,979	9,416
Franklin	331	219	112	543	326	217
Gadsden	5,395	3,011	2,384	9,302	5,004	4,298
Gilchrist	679	422	257	1,183	694	489
Glades	2,616	1,603	1,013	4,117	2,391	1,726
Gulf	622	560	62	780	689	91
Hamilton	1,459	1,002	457	2,299	1,462	837
Hardee	12,139	6,638	5,501	17,161	8,985	8,176
Hendry	20,798	11,495	9,303	32,526	16,852	15,674
Hernando	14,963	7,419	7,544	27,973	13,863	14,110
Highlands	19,325	10,296	9,029	33,990	17,367	16,623
Hillsborough	314,300	159,359	154,941	522,520	264,309	258,211
Holmes	462	308	154	648	415	233
Indian River	15,730	8,378	7,352	28,882	14,873	14,009
Jackson	2,105	1,651	454	2,619	2,021	598
Jefferson	801	510	291	1,338	793	545
Lafayette	1,029	759	270	1,572	1,072	500
Lake	33,902	17,483	16,419	68,859	34,923	33,936

See footnote at end of table.

Continued . . .

Table 1.56. HISPANIC ORIGIN POPULATION: PROJECTIONS BY SEX IN THE STATE AND COUNTIES OF FLORIDA, APRIL 1, 2010 AND 2030 (Continued)

County	2010			2030		
	Total	Male	Female	Total	Male	Female
Lee	122,980	64,833	58,147	248,281	127,425	120,856
Leon	14,299	7,133	7,166	22,188	11,067	11,121
Levy	3,265	1,660	1,605	6,545	3,291	3,254
Liberty	451	359	92	606	462	144
Madison	1,344	896	448	2,425	1,497	928
Manatee	55,868	29,566	26,302	103,260	53,076	50,184
Marion	37,439	19,024	18,415	72,625	36,544	36,081
Martin	16,861	8,994	7,867	28,646	14,658	13,988
Miami-Dade	1,658,424	799,729	858,695	2,226,543	1,069,918	1,156,625
Monroe	15,004	7,839	7,165	16,402	8,340	8,062
Nassau	2,121	1,104	1,017	4,236	2,185	2,051
Okaloosa	16,466	8,535	7,931	29,863	15,179	14,684
Okeechobee	9,002	5,119	3,883	13,098	6,982	6,116
Orange	337,575	171,045	166,530	608,631	307,802	300,829
Osceola	139,596	70,478	69,118	282,665	142,620	140,045
Palm Beach	241,979	124,327	117,652	408,721	207,555	201,166
Pasco	47,694	24,369	23,325	91,666	46,329	45,337
Pinellas	73,395	37,439	35,956	120,231	60,890	59,341
Polk	111,425	58,688	52,737	209,524	107,374	102,150
Putnam	7,818	4,053	3,765	13,593	6,887	6,706
St. Johns	8,753	4,445	4,308	17,986	9,053	8,933
St. Lucie	45,277	23,589	21,688	91,183	46,242	44,941
Santa Rosa	8,161	4,319	3,842	16,470	8,520	7,950
Sarasota	33,719	17,351	16,368	63,642	32,218	31,424
Seminole	75,746	38,017	37,729	129,338	65,095	64,243
Sumter	9,500	6,353	3,147	18,055	10,797	7,258
Suwannee	4,381	2,757	1,624	8,328	4,956	3,372
Taylor	560	356	204	873	533	340
Union	829	657	172	1,197	887	310
Volusia	61,232	31,218	30,014	108,902	54,993	53,909
Wakulla	1,010	718	292	1,522	1,014	508
Walton	3,871	2,090	1,781	8,781	4,618	4,163
Washington	1,072	752	320	1,684	1,094	590

Note: Persons of Hispanic origin may be of any race. Includes persons of Latino or Spanish origin.

Source: University of Florida, Bureau of Economic and Business Research, Population Program, *Florida Population Studies*, June 2007, Volume 40, Bulletin No. 148.

Table 1.60. AGE: PROJECTIONS BY AGE GROUP IN THE STATE AND COUNTIES OF FLORIDA, APRIL 1, 2010 AND 2030

County	2010 Less than 18	2010 18-64	2010 65 and over	2030 Less than 18	2030 18-64	2030 65 and over
Florida	4,379,802	12,113,126	3,481,271	5,294,014	14,325,872	6,893,446
Alachua	48,808	184,801	26,229	57,183	204,664	54,936
Baker	6,948	16,875	3,081	7,815	19,242	7,089
Bay	38,438	111,449	27,485	41,490	120,111	62,634
Bradford	5,955	19,640	4,181	6,518	20,711	7,497
Brevard	113,734	348,645	123,681	131,274	378,194	248,076
Broward	434,925	1,168,235	266,753	500,658	1,359,342	478,998
Calhoun	3,157	9,289	2,324	3,530	10,383	3,629
Charlotte	25,936	90,400	59,053	31,619	101,258	102,978
Citrus	22,917	78,099	48,259	27,840	86,003	85,068
Clay	51,658	125,558	23,915	70,153	165,241	65,514
Collier	76,732	212,137	90,357	109,783	286,917	201,819
Columbia	15,494	42,263	11,081	17,655	46,548	23,359
DeSoto	7,629	20,885	7,193	9,284	25,745	12,262
Dixie	3,481	10,001	3,453	4,243	10,912	6,825
Duval	231,207	607,400	105,881	263,058	692,332	244,468
Escambia	72,344	203,081	48,376	81,357	213,165	87,439
Flagler	19,709	61,932	31,507	34,315	94,290	86,473
Franklin	2,116	7,838	2,492	2,219	8,026	4,475
Gadsden	12,025	31,471	6,828	12,344	32,122	12,459
Gilchrist	3,950	11,462	3,143	4,709	13,874	7,716
Glades	2,262	7,254	2,097	2,343	7,774	3,251
Gulf	2,993	11,358	2,966	3,212	11,378	5,778
Hamilton	3,101	9,955	1,905	3,052	10,176	3,548
Hardee	7,489	17,071	3,829	8,339	19,610	5,271
Hendry	12,072	25,041	4,297	14,859	31,347	6,679
Hernando	31,819	91,979	50,188	39,018	108,567	96,114
Highlands	19,514	51,475	32,746	22,363	57,638	52,841
Hillsborough	315,397	800,434	156,439	388,384	976,045	334,220
Holmes	4,406	12,405	3,425	4,825	13,341	5,095
Indian River	27,271	81,772	40,929	33,568	94,363	81,056
Jackson	10,544	34,815	8,695	10,706	34,353	16,297
Jefferson	2,863	9,717	2,352	2,950	9,570	4,636
Lafayette	1,605	5,659	1,176	1,791	6,381	1,820
Lake	62,772	174,732	81,817	84,926	230,988	179,091

Continued . . .

Table 1.60. AGE: PROJECTIONS BY AGE GROUP IN THE STATE AND COUNTIES OF FLORIDA, APRIL 1, 2010 AND 2030 (Continued)

County	2010 Less than 18	2010 18-64	2010 65 and over	2030 Less than 18	2030 18-64	2030 65 and over
Lee	136,598	379,679	160,254	191,248	507,382	355,302
Leon	58,366	207,297	26,013	71,862	234,847	56,951
Levy	9,310	24,886	8,349	11,116	29,343	16,561
Liberty	1,707	5,558	938	1,918	6,036	1,755
Madison	4,427	12,913	3,185	4,676	13,729	4,916
Manatee	69,688	193,619	74,947	87,044	233,498	136,488
Marion	70,663	197,422	85,598	91,395	244,969	173,789
Martin	26,466	84,430	43,154	30,085	89,538	80,091
Miami-Dade	613,098	1,598,116	357,593	668,730	1,816,012	618,286
Monroe	13,659	52,114	14,890	13,348	40,822	27,153
Nassau	16,502	46,931	12,372	19,895	55,333	31,657
Okaloosa	47,971	130,990	28,944	56,283	146,672	64,776
Okeechobee	9,939	23,348	7,013	10,816	25,498	11,108
Orange	306,340	785,401	112,733	403,749	1,038,201	269,156
Osceola	82,295	194,412	32,495	126,204	309,064	97,353
Palm Beach	293,912	807,883	303,112	357,049	955,427	566,895
Pasco	97,230	266,341	111,029	125,353	333,947	221,792
Pinellas	180,039	582,175	206,417	184,015	555,662	316,547
Polk	147,203	359,237	111,052	175,277	434,585	214,614
Putnam	17,871	44,303	14,808	18,407	45,318	23,813
St. Johns	40,001	122,540	30,890	59,085	165,174	86,275
St. Lucie	64,769	169,336	64,736	90,813	225,160	150,448
Santa Rosa	37,667	101,512	20,271	49,369	128,366	51,261
Sarasota	64,833	219,724	128,413	74,429	234,916	236,379
Seminole	106,131	299,853	52,022	130,393	360,723	116,708
Sumter	15,391	52,337	31,926	26,721	77,420	67,774
Suwannee	9,315	25,852	8,380	10,590	29,805	15,765
Taylor	4,859	14,128	3,423	5,001	14,772	6,334
Union	3,196	11,595	1,416	3,745	12,234	3,154
Volusia	104,052	323,980	115,956	124,132	358,517	219,017
Wakulla	6,802	22,956	4,340	8,769	27,978	12,892
Walton	12,993	40,400	12,308	19,173	56,181	31,588
Washington	5,238	16,730	4,161	5,941	18,132	7,437

Source: University of Florida, Bureau of Economic and Business Research, Population Program, *Florida Population Studies*, June 2007, Volume 40, Bulletin No. 148.

Table 1.61. AGE: NON-HISPANIC WHITE POPULATION PROJECTIONS BY AGE GROUP IN THE STATE AND COUNTIES OF FLORIDA, APRIL 1, 2010 AND 2030

County	2010 Less than 18	2010 18-64	2010 65 and over	2030 Less than 18	2030 18-64	2030 65 and over
Florida	2,132,112	7,025,948	2,735,190	2,289,889	6,974,814	4,933,415
Alachua	26,747	122,414	20,438	28,573	121,115	38,915
Baker	5,871	13,742	2,818	6,685	15,644	6,531
Bay	28,434	88,833	24,561	28,998	88,946	53,545
Bradford	4,604	14,001	3,681	5,059	14,234	6,560
Brevard	81,796	276,792	110,839	89,094	274,653	211,568
Broward	148,264	522,958	194,602	122,046	410,425	258,575
Calhoun	2,416	6,921	2,039	2,652	7,369	3,135
Charlotte	21,045	77,389	55,000	24,631	81,201	91,669
Citrus	19,520	69,569	45,704	22,384	72,075	79,538
Clay	39,343	100,873	21,603	50,895	123,488	55,446
Collier	35,252	133,792	83,671	44,944	150,366	174,985
Columbia	11,536	32,059	9,695	13,113	34,107	20,271
DeSoto	3,851	10,470	6,543	3,769	9,543	10,276
Dixie	3,111	8,609	3,313	3,833	9,278	6,591
Duval	110,331	349,663	77,637	109,280	325,771	155,676
Escambia	43,828	142,611	39,208	47,773	137,704	66,081
Flagler	14,515	50,035	26,268	24,940	72,098	71,319
Franklin	1,717	6,198	2,291	1,787	6,191	4,122
Gadsden	2,715	10,402	3,604	2,856	8,426	5,315
Gilchrist	3,447	10,113	3,001	3,982	11,908	7,297
Glades	1,153	4,254	1,871	1,142	3,871	2,669
Gulf	2,454	8,030	2,683	2,743	7,890	5,370
Hamilton	1,554	5,060	1,474	1,469	4,650	2,728
Hardee	2,698	7,860	3,110	2,524	7,119	3,343
Hendry	3,335	8,942	2,842	3,225	7,992	3,531
Hernando	24,814	76,847	46,204	28,949	84,313	84,341
Highlands	10,004	33,088	29,915	9,627	30,092	44,543
Hillsborough	145,146	442,551	111,819	153,393	430,254	204,554
Holmes	3,997	10,600	3,247	4,247	11,038	4,684
Indian River	17,821	62,890	38,411	20,503	64,632	73,019
Jackson	6,957	22,327	6,888	7,141	20,763	12,867
Jefferson	1,571	5,769	1,697	1,726	5,717	3,561
Lafayette	1,263	3,722	1,111	1,405	4,008	1,654
Lake	41,839	134,516	75,874	53,480	161,752	158,132

Continued . . .

Table 1.61. AGE: NON-HISPANIC WHITE POPULATION PROJECTIONS BY AGE GROUP IN THE STATE OF FLORIDA, APRIL 1, 2010 AND 2030 (Continued)

County	2010 Less than 18	2010 18-64	2010 65 and over	2030 Less than 18	2030 18-64	2030 65 and over
Lee	76,338	268,378	148,030	95,140	299,264	309,045
Leon	28,662	119,861	19,773	30,817	116,301	39,000
Levy	6,828	20,240	7,506	7,857	22,225	14,611
Liberty	1,349	3,663	813	1,450	3,661	1,456
Madison	2,060	6,787	2,356	2,269	6,647	3,466
Manatee	38,665	138,263	69,942	42,372	140,903	118,829
Marion	46,539	149,004	76,631	57,740	168,616	149,464
Martin	18,071	67,903	41,152	19,060	64,821	73,948
Miami-Dade	82,852	216,274	59,869	45,506	124,099	44,477
Monroe	8,673	38,907	12,716	8,328	27,258	23,797
Nassau	14,394	41,973	11,618	17,179	48,736	29,975
Okaloosa	34,784	100,831	26,377	38,095	103,798	55,313
Okeechobee	5,794	15,192	6,387	5,760	14,471	9,431
Orange	113,915	365,981	68,381	120,841	356,188	116,364
Osceola	28,937	81,976	19,453	35,693	96,212	42,856
Palm Beach	141,057	492,557	265,689	149,335	475,720	448,200
Pasco	75,669	221,880	104,267	91,565	256,121	196,502
Pinellas	117,823	447,984	189,480	104,334	367,219	272,249
Polk	77,111	232,364	96,186	77,372	229,276	167,181
Putnam	10,621	31,982	12,769	10,087	29,106	19,424
St. Johns	34,025	108,887	28,834	50,598	143,945	79,119
St. Lucie	32,795	111,802	55,606	42,019	130,023	119,860
Santa Rosa	32,345	87,673	18,895	41,543	106,796	45,948
Sarasota	48,294	185,438	122,830	51,105	180,396	219,463
Seminole	65,953	206,381	40,276	73,905	217,779	80,770
Sumter	11,629	38,886	30,154	21,210	58,936	62,682
Suwannee	6,717	20,014	7,564	7,319	21,282	13,872
Taylor	3,608	10,447	3,020	3,685	10,599	5,570
Union	2,644	7,831	1,229	3,191	8,023	2,852
Volusia	70,443	246,920	104,591	78,075	245,393	187,557
Wakulla	5,913	18,757	4,017	7,753	23,100	12,223
Walton	10,449	34,269	11,371	14,917	45,499	28,815
Washington	4,206	12,743	3,746	4,901	13,768	6,685

Source: University of Florida, Bureau of Economic and Business Research, Population Program, *Florida Population Studies*, June 2007, Volume 40, Bulletin No. 148.

Table 1.62. AGE: NON-HISPANIC BLACK POPULATION PROJECTIONS BY AGE GROUP IN THE STATE AND COUNTIES OF FLORIDA, APRIL 1, 2010 AND 2030

County	2010 Less than 18	2010 18-64	2010 65 and over	2030 Less than 18	2030 18-64	2030 65 and over
Florida	924,455	1,979,524	254,891	1,106,918	2,575,588	676,417
Alachua	14,216	36,618	3,863	16,941	45,089	9,339
Baker	814	2,362	196	722	2,388	345
Bay	5,757	12,776	1,703	6,484	15,499	4,370
Bradford	1,089	4,663	409	1,120	5,058	705
Brevard	15,388	34,015	6,517	18,340	43,280	16,269
Broward	142,883	304,799	32,427	168,924	406,700	94,863
Calhoun	521	1,622	231	580	1,953	338
Charlotte	2,402	5,951	2,143	3,383	8,483	5,685
Citrus	1,063	2,751	660	1,391	3,964	1,624
Clay	5,468	11,069	1,081	8,173	17,664	4,716
Collier	7,487	13,490	1,768	10,170	20,647	7,540
Columbia	2,881	7,522	1,035	2,873	8,173	2,033
DeSoto	814	2,811	297	568	3,219	326
Dixie	265	1,067	103	259	1,165	157
Duval	88,273	182,474	20,826	106,059	241,181	57,076
Escambia	21,096	43,930	7,039	23,127	51,014	14,985
Flagler	2,743	5,938	2,970	5,130	10,710	7,450
Franklin	306	1,343	163	297	1,387	250
Gadsden	7,232	17,435	3,020	6,532	17,258	6,048
Gilchrist	297	833	87	409	1,110	228
Glades	241	851	78	164	823	86
Gulf	464	2,565	244	387	2,546	329
Hamilton	1,146	3,758	377	1,013	3,736	630
Hardee	403	1,751	194	457	1,959	324
Hendry	1,647	2,964	436	1,390	3,124	532
Hernando	2,382	5,161	1,201	3,202	7,397	3,236
Highlands	2,973	5,715	1,022	3,016	6,595	2,519
Hillsborough	64,007	135,015	15,553	80,972	186,304	47,031
Holmes	244	1,194	115	347	1,474	254
Indian River	3,778	8,050	1,419	4,542	10,554	3,700
Jackson	3,115	10,221	1,636	2,995	10,720	2,978
Jefferson	1,091	3,278	583	934	2,881	771
Lafayette	98	1,120	25	71	1,139	38
Lake	8,478	17,116	2,959	10,816	25,099	8,443

Continued . . .

Table 1.62. AGE: NON-HISPANIC BLACK POPULATION PROJECTIONS BY AGE GROUP IN THE STATE AND COUNTIES OF FLORIDA, APRIL 1, 2010 AND 2030 (Continued)

	2010			2030		
County	Less than 18	18-64	65 and over	Less than 18	18-64	65 and over
Lee	17,361	29,547	4,378	23,905	46,833	13,425
Leon	24,713	69,727	5,354	32,814	91,166	15,038
Levy	1,281	2,560	461	1,306	2,967	896
Liberty	252	1,370	102	328	1,662	232
Madison	2,004	5,036	730	1,811	5,194	1,122
Manatee	10,004	18,078	2,444	12,587	24,660	6,123
Marion	11,393	23,595	4,421	13,203	31,044	9,692
Martin	2,668	5,077	787	2,933	5,966	2,067
Miami-Dade	148,558	308,432	45,419	151,444	337,100	101,765
Monroe	972	2,686	471	881	2,331	935
Nassau	1,330	3,179	498	1,462	3,552	789
Okaloosa	5,993	13,963	1,268	7,486	17,813	4,006
Okeechobee	842	2,287	243	862	2,655	398
Orange	76,949	163,376	17,423	104,193	241,393	56,050
Osceola	8,000	17,504	2,177	13,415	30,838	8,793
Palm Beach	71,796	142,263	16,513	90,610	197,256	51,755
Pasco	4,231	9,052	1,580	6,401	14,471	5,933
Pinellas	31,636	67,277	8,695	36,848	86,202	20,884
Polk	28,136	53,886	8,198	32,648	70,584	20,746
Putnam	4,008	7,575	1,370	3,591	8,151	2,341
St. Johns	2,834	6,566	1,138	3,437	8,432	3,144
St. Lucie	15,756	28,180	4,773	21,033	40,466	12,898
Santa Rosa	1,890	5,270	510	2,472	7,128	1,702
Sarasota	5,450	10,301	2,071	6,355	12,842	4,626
Seminole	14,488	33,585	4,004	18,885	47,308	10,967
Sumter	1,688	6,337	709	1,756	6,931	1,246
Suwannee	1,249	2,672	552	1,224	2,756	829
Taylor	1,014	3,026	343	998	3,209	625
Union	405	2,943	139	346	3,051	200
Volusia	14,102	33,225	4,690	17,173	41,195	9,925
Wakulla	653	3,130	261	657	3,398	472
Walton	1,047	2,870	479	1,475	4,049	1,137
Washington	690	2,721	310	591	2,692	438

Source: University of Florida, Bureau of Economic and Business Research, Population Program, *Florida Population Studies*, June 2007, Volume 40, Bulletin No. 148.

Table 1.63. AGE: HISPANIC ORIGIN POPULATION PROJECTIONS BY AGE GROUP IN THE STATE AND COUNTIES OF FLORIDA, APRIL 1, 2010 AND 2030

County	2010			2030		
	Less than 18	18-64	65 and over	Less than 18	18-64	65 and over
Florida	1,168,376	2,776,245	448,474	1,676,285	4,262,245	1,147,248
Alachua	4,711	17,703	1,077	7,418	27,153	4,339
Baker	206	604	54	337	983	179
Bay	2,640	6,266	745	3,982	10,815	3,354
Bradford	190	687	67	240	980	171
Brevard	12,500	28,883	4,609	18,411	47,451	15,422
Broward	123,155	296,487	35,042	180,776	472,612	109,323
Calhoun	151	533	23	206	755	102
Charlotte	1,801	5,352	1,295	2,517	8,854	3,799
Citrus	1,790	4,374	1,558	3,355	7,942	3,078
Clay	4,646	9,162	797	7,794	16,982	3,454
Collier	32,554	62,257	4,578	52,419	111,328	17,624
Columbia	820	2,007	258	1,342	3,337	824
DeSoto	2,909	7,416	332	4,896	12,689	1,628
Dixie	82	226	28	122	325	58
Duval	20,980	51,237	4,677	30,974	87,297	22,704
Escambia	3,693	8,779	886	5,717	13,993	3,300
Flagler	1,938	4,845	1,712	3,137	9,165	6,093
Franklin	76	225	30	114	345	84
Gadsden	1,942	3,304	149	2,696	5,750	856
Gilchrist	181	448	50	274	742	167
Glades	756	1,749	111	964	2,695	458
Gulf	38	564	20	45	689	46
Hamilton	371	1,043	45	520	1,618	161
Hardee	4,348	7,286	505	5,302	10,295	1,564
Hendry	6,946	12,871	981	10,088	19,881	2,557
Hernando	3,967	8,548	2,448	5,875	14,565	7,533
Highlands	6,019	11,674	1,632	9,108	19,614	5,268
Hillsborough	93,154	195,261	25,885	135,053	315,847	71,620
Holmes	104	322	36	137	424	87
Indian River	5,139	9,694	897	7,760	17,406	3,716
Jackson	306	1,718	81	341	2,054	224
Jefferson	171	574	56	243	830	265
Lafayette	237	752	40	310	1,134	128
Lake	11,079	20,321	2,502	18,575	39,372	10,912

Continued . . .

Table 1.63. AGE: HISPANIC ORIGIN POPULATION PROJECTIONS BY AGE GROUP IN THE STATE AND COUNTIES OF FLORIDA, APRIL 1, 2010 AND 2030 (Continued)

	2010			2030		
County	Less than 18	18-64	65 and over	Less than 18	18-64	65 and over
Lee	39,676	76,271	7,033	67,080	151,245	29,956
Leon	2,691	11,220	388	4,374	16,668	1,146
Levy	1,082	1,845	338	1,799	3,797	949
Liberty	74	366	11	96	475	35
Madison	309	956	79	510	1,640	275
Manatee	19,385	34,321	2,162	29,679	63,216	10,365
Marion	11,383	22,034	4,022	18,552	40,835	13,238
Martin	5,247	10,539	1,075	7,484	17,514	3,648
Miami-Dade	367,207	1,043,338	247,879	453,286	1,313,640	459,617
Monroe	3,722	9,723	1,559	3,844	10,452	2,106
Nassau	596	1,338	187	1,014	2,458	764
Okaloosa	4,870	10,787	809	7,801	18,157	3,905
Okeechobee	3,169	5,490	343	4,027	7,868	1,203
Orange	97,301	217,458	22,816	150,841	376,043	81,747
Osceola	42,018	87,623	9,955	71,495	169,140	42,030
Palm Beach	70,766	152,671	18,542	101,690	248,894	58,137
Pasco	14,419	29,180	4,095	22,986	53,406	15,274
Pinellas	21,073	46,693	5,629	30,479	73,339	16,413
Polk	38,778	66,901	5,746	60,741	124,966	23,817
Putnam	2,983	4,256	579	4,413	7,339	1,841
St. Johns	2,500	5,596	657	4,163	10,622	3,201
St. Lucie	14,715	26,662	3,900	25,236	49,805	16,142
Santa Rosa	2,270	5,337	554	3,838	10,065	2,567
Sarasota	9,602	21,170	2,947	15,021	37,748	10,873
Seminole	20,801	48,554	6,391	30,536	77,935	20,867
Sumter	1,929	6,569	1,002	3,560	10,787	3,708
Suwannee	1,236	2,931	214	1,905	5,453	970
Taylor	147	385	28	206	598	69
Union	122	667	40	183	925	89
Volusia	17,125	38,223	5,884	25,504	63,817	19,581
Wakulla	179	792	39	285	1,092	145
Walton	1,178	2,381	312	2,278	5,256	1,247
Washington	223	796	53	331	1,128	225

Source: University of Florida, Bureau of Economic and Business Research, Population Program, *Florida Population Studies*, June 2007, Volume 40, Bulletin No. 148.

Table 1.64. PERSONS AGED 65 AND OVER: PROJECTIONS BY AGE GROUP IN THE STATE AND COUNTIES OF FLORIDA, APRIL 1, 2010 AND 2030

County	2010 65-74	2010 75-84	2010 85 and over	2030 65-74	2030 75-84	2030 85 and over
Florida	1,726,391	1,222,742	532,138	3,485,325	2,418,499	989,622
Alachua	14,077	8,279	3,873	28,269	19,268	7,399
Baker	1,867	917	297	3,810	2,435	844
Bay	15,207	9,024	3,254	33,484	21,200	7,950
Bradford	2,233	1,347	601	3,809	2,612	1,076
Brevard	61,506	45,010	17,165	125,284	87,828	34,964
Broward	127,622	89,461	49,670	254,157	159,846	64,995
Calhoun	1,219	755	350	1,684	1,267	678
Charlotte	26,717	22,659	9,677	47,166	37,830	17,982
Citrus	23,356	17,626	7,277	40,593	30,857	13,618
Clay	13,738	7,159	3,018	34,820	21,965	8,729
Collier	45,562	33,504	11,291	97,173	74,624	30,022
Columbia	6,040	3,623	1,418	11,820	8,230	3,309
DeSoto	3,665	2,641	887	6,049	4,586	1,627
Dixie	1,867	1,187	399	3,243	2,514	1,068
Duval	56,820	34,342	14,719	131,533	83,029	29,906
Escambia	24,538	16,360	7,478	42,888	30,447	14,104
Flagler	16,120	11,743	3,644	40,041	32,682	13,750
Franklin	1,443	762	287	2,165	1,616	694
Gadsden	3,699	2,234	895	6,117	4,524	1,818
Gilchrist	1,767	1,036	340	3,910	2,782	1,024
Glades	1,222	667	208	1,898	1,007	346
Gulf	1,617	968	381	2,788	2,024	966
Hamilton	1,005	622	278	1,659	1,290	599
Hardee	1,839	1,422	568	2,592	1,732	947
Hendry	2,309	1,456	532	3,350	2,267	1,062
Hernando	23,845	19,049	7,294	46,258	35,796	14,060
Highlands	14,875	12,614	5,257	24,786	19,544	8,511
Hillsborough	81,714	51,721	23,004	175,806	113,003	45,411
Holmes	1,827	1,111	487	2,334	1,794	967
Indian River	18,491	15,366	7,072	38,009	29,907	13,140
Jackson	4,419	2,956	1,320	7,545	5,953	2,799
Jefferson	1,187	809	356	2,223	1,747	666
Lafayette	625	397	154	823	645	352
Lake	42,104	29,204	10,509	88,476	66,080	24,535

Continued . . .

Table 1.64. PERSONS AGED 65 AND OVER: PROJECTIONS BY AGE GROUP IN THE STATE AND COUNTIES OF FLORIDA, APRIL 1, 2010 AND 2030 (Continued)

	2010			2030		
County	65-74	75-84	85 and over	65-74	75-84	85 and over
Lee	79,400	58,243	22,611	171,001	130,931	53,370
Leon	14,152	7,963	3,898	29,609	19,827	7,515
Levy	4,539	2,759	1,051	8,364	5,841	2,356
Liberty	517	314	107	900	602	253
Madison	1,661	1,033	491	2,247	1,775	894
Manatee	35,008	27,256	12,683	67,703	48,323	20,462
Marion	41,564	31,779	12,255	84,507	62,936	26,346
Martin	20,549	15,421	7,184	38,406	29,195	12,490
Miami-Dade	186,395	120,413	50,785	339,873	196,484	81,929
Monroe	8,452	4,702	1,736	12,607	10,404	4,142
Nassau	7,382	3,887	1,103	16,518	11,386	3,753
Okaloosa	16,205	9,384	3,355	34,636	21,860	8,280
Okeechobee	3,424	2,637	952	5,415	3,828	1,865
Orange	61,847	37,001	13,885	154,029	87,044	28,083
Osceola	18,508	10,179	3,808	55,981	30,813	10,559
Palm Beach	133,185	113,053	56,874	266,864	206,751	93,280
Pasco	52,697	40,357	17,975	110,130	80,510	31,152
Pinellas	96,123	71,966	38,328	155,857	112,284	48,406
Polk	55,844	39,545	15,663	108,792	75,603	30,219
Putnam	7,961	5,147	1,700	12,690	8,230	2,893
St. Johns	16,288	10,579	4,023	44,508	31,154	10,613
St. Lucie	31,097	24,717	8,922	73,438	55,488	21,522
Santa Rosa	11,898	6,127	2,246	28,931	16,554	5,776
Sarasota	57,786	47,366	23,261	106,531	88,327	41,521
Seminole	28,460	17,193	6,369	63,526	40,116	13,066
Sumter	15,088	13,062	3,776	28,618	24,175	14,981
Suwannee	4,242	2,881	1,257	7,456	5,689	2,620
Taylor	1,868	1,161	394	3,212	2,270	852
Union	829	439	148	1,687	1,093	374
Volusia	55,773	41,372	18,811	108,314	78,019	32,684
Wakulla	2,739	1,160	441	7,193	4,285	1,414
Walton	6,531	4,269	1,508	15,480	11,188	4,920
Washington	2,237	1,346	578	3,740	2,583	1,114

Source: University of Florida, Bureau of Economic and Business Research, Population Program, unpublished data.

Planning Districts

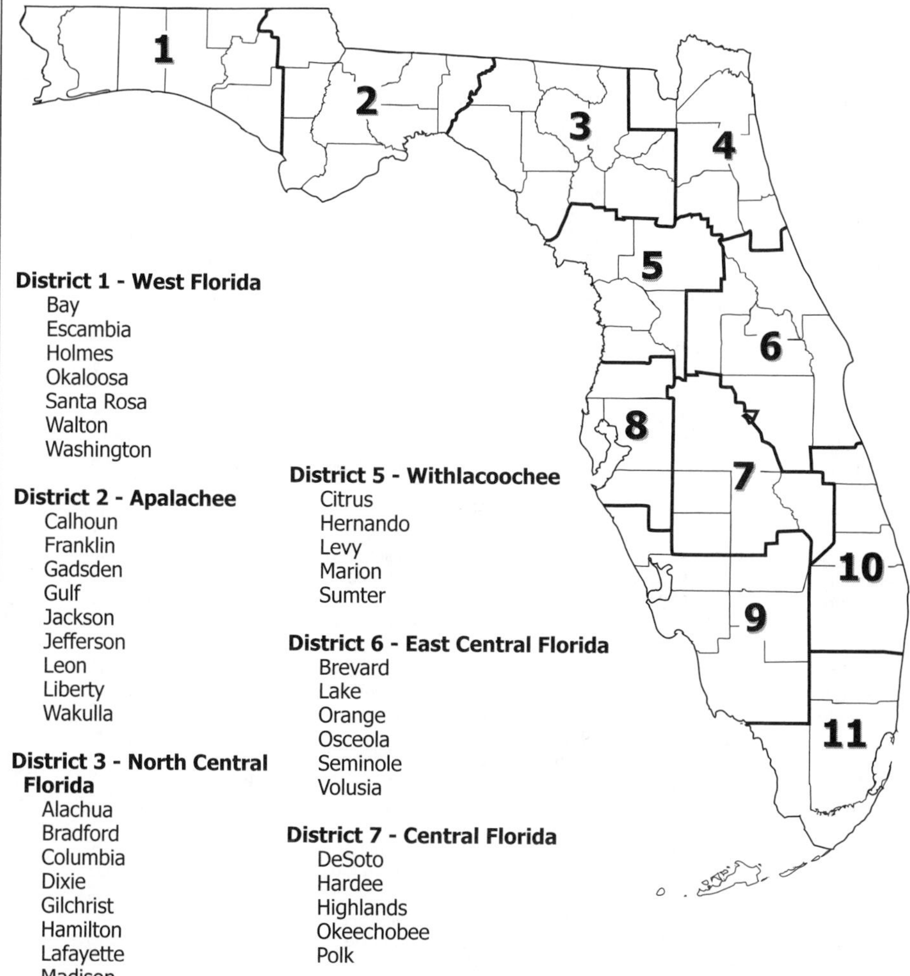

District 1 - West Florida
- Bay
- Escambia
- Holmes
- Okaloosa
- Santa Rosa
- Walton
- Washington

District 2 - Apalachee
- Calhoun
- Franklin
- Gadsden
- Gulf
- Jackson
- Jefferson
- Leon
- Liberty
- Wakulla

District 3 - North Central Florida
- Alachua
- Bradford
- Columbia
- Dixie
- Gilchrist
- Hamilton
- Lafayette
- Madison
- Suwannee
- Taylor
- Union

District 4 - Northeast Florida
- Baker
- Clay
- Duval
- Flagler
- Nassau
- Putnam
- St. Johns

District 5 - Withlacoochee
- Citrus
- Hernando
- Levy
- Marion
- Sumter

District 6 - East Central Florida
- Brevard
- Lake
- Orange
- Osceola
- Seminole
- Volusia

District 7 - Central Florida
- DeSoto
- Hardee
- Highlands
- Okeechobee
- Polk

District 8 - Tampa Bay
- Hillsborough
- Manatee
- Pasco
- Pinellas

District 9 - Southwest Florida
- Charlotte
- Collier
- Glades
- Hendry
- Lee
- Sarasota

District 10 - Treasure Coast
- Indian River
- Martin
- Palm Beach
- St. Lucie

District 11- South Florida
- Broward
- Miami-Dade
- Monroe

Table 1.66. PLANNING DISTRICTS: CENSUS COUNTS, APRIL 1, 2000, AND POPULATION ESTIMATES, APRIL 1, 2006, IN THE STATE, COMPREHENSIVE PLANNING DISTRICTS AND COUNTIES OF FLORIDA

District and county	Census 2000	Estimates 2006	Percentage change
Florida	15,982,824	18,349,132	14.8
District 1	811,006	907,623	11.9
Bay	148,217	165,515	11.7
Escambia	294,410	309,647	5.2
Holmes	18,564	19,502	5.1
Okaloosa	170,498	192,672	13.0
Santa Rosa	117,743	141,428	20.1
Walton	40,601	55,786	37.4
Washington	20,973	23,073	10.0
District 2	411,486	463,994	12.8
Calhoun	13,017	14,113	8.4
Franklin	9,829	11,916	21.2
Gadsden	45,087	48,195	6.9
Gulf	14,560	16,509	13.4
Jackson	46,755	50,246	7.5
Jefferson	12,902	14,353	11.2
Leon	239,452	272,497	13.8
Liberty	7,021	7,772	10.7
Wakulla	22,863	28,393	24.2
District 3	435,444	485,937	11.6
Alachua	217,955	243,779	11.8
Bradford	26,088	28,551	9.4
Columbia	56,513	63,538	12.4
Dixie	13,827	15,677	13.4
Gilchrist	14,437	16,703	15.7
Hamilton	13,327	14,517	8.9
Lafayette	7,022	8,060	14.8
Madison	18,733	19,814	5.8
Suwannee	34,844	38,799	11.4
Taylor	19,256	21,471	11.5
Union	13,442	15,028	11.8
District 4	1,243,005	1,478,110	18.9
Baker	22,259	25,004	12.3
Clay	140,814	176,901	25.6
Duval	778,879	879,235	12.9
Flagler	49,832	89,075	78.8
Nassau	57,663	68,188	18.3
Putnam	70,423	74,416	5.7
St. Johns	123,135	165,291	34.2
District 5	595,598	730,409	22.6
Citrus	118,085	136,749	15.8
District 5 (Continued)			
Hernando	130,802	157,006	20.0
Levy	34,450	38,981	13.2
Marion	258,916	315,074	21.7
Sumter	53,345	82,599	54.8
District 6	2,564,136	3,079,771	20.1
Brevard	476,230	543,050	14.0
Lake	210,527	276,783	31.5
Orange	896,344	1,079,524	20.4
Osceola	172,493	255,903	48.4
Seminole	365,199	420,667	15.2
Volusia	443,343	503,844	13.6
District 7	666,347	760,737	14.2
DeSoto	32,209	33,164	3.0
Hardee	26,938	27,186	0.9
Highlands	87,366	96,672	10.7
Okeechobee	35,910	38,666	7.7
Polk	483,924	565,049	16.8
District 8	2,529,213	2,845,207	12.5
Hillsborough	998,948	1,164,425	16.6
Manatee	264,002	308,325	16.8
Pasco	344,768	424,355	23.1
Pinellas	921,495	948,102	2.9
District 9	1,206,639	1,501,441	24.4
Charlotte	141,627	160,315	13.2
Collier	251,377	326,658	29.9
Glades	10,576	10,796	2.1
Hendry	36,210	38,678	6.8
Lee	440,888	585,608	32.8
Sarasota	325,961	379,386	16.4
District 10	1,563,564	1,825,209	16.7
Indian River	112,947	135,262	19.8
Martin	126,731	142,645	12.6
Palm Beach	1,131,191	1,287,987	13.9
St. Lucie	192,695	259,315	34.6
District 11	3,956,386	4,270,694	7.9
Broward	1,623,018	1,753,162	8.0
Miami-Dade	2,253,779	2,437,022	8.1
Monroe	79,589	80,510	1.2

Note: Data are for planning district boundaries as defined by the Florida Regional Planning Council, May 23 2005 (http://www.ncfrpc.org/state.html). See map.

Source: University of Florida, Bureau of Economic and Business Research, Population Program, *Florida Estimates of Population, April 1, 2006.* Census data from U.S. Census Bureau.

Table 1.67. CHILDREN AND FAMILIES DISTRICTS: CENSUS COUNTS, APRIL 1, 2000 AND POPULATION ESTIMATES, APRIL 1, 2006, IN THE STATE, DEPARTMENT OF CHILDREN AND FAMILIES DISTRICTS, AND COUNTIES OF FLORIDA

District or region and county	Census 2000	Estimates 2006	Percentage change
Florida	15,982,824	18,349,132	14.8
District 1	623,252	699,533	12.2
Escambia	294,410	309,647	5.2
Okaloosa	170,498	192,672	13.0
Santa Rosa	117,743	141,428	20.1
Walton	40,601	55,786	37.4
District 2	637,229	713,369	11.9
Bay	148,217	165,515	11.7
Calhoun	13,017	14,113	8.4
Franklin	9,829	11,916	21.2
Gadsden	45,087	48,195	6.9
Gulf	14,560	16,509	13.4
Holmes	18,564	19,502	5.1
Jackson	46,755	50,246	7.5
Jefferson	12,902	14,353	11.2
Leon	239,452	272,497	13.8
Liberty	7,021	7,772	10.7
Madison	18,733	19,814	5.8
Taylor	19,256	21,471	11.5
Wakulla	22,863	28,393	24.2
Washington	20,973	23,073	10.0
District 3	502,328	558,049	11.1
Alachua	217,955	243,779	11.8
Bradford	26,088	28,551	9.4
Columbia	56,513	63,538	12.4
Dixie	13,827	15,677	13.4
Gilchrist	14,437	16,703	15.7
Hamilton	13,327	14,517	8.9
Lafayette	7,022	8,060	14.8
Levy	34,450	38,981	13.2
Putnam	70,423	74,416	5.7
Suwannee	34,844	38,799	11.4
Union	13,442	15,028	11.8
District 4	1,122,750	1,314,619	17.1
Baker	22,259	25,004	12.3
Clay	140,814	176,901	25.6
Duval	778,879	879,235	12.9
Nassau	57,663	68,188	18.3
St. Johns	123,135	165,291	34.2
District 7	1,910,266	2,299,144	20.4
Brevard	476,230	543,050	14.0
Orange	896,344	1,079,524	20.4
Osceola	172,493	255,903	48.4
Seminole	365,199	420,667	15.2
District 8	880,678	1,122,055	27.4
Charlotte	141,627	160,315	13.2
Collier	251,377	326,658	29.9
Glades	10,576	10,796	2.1
Hendry	36,210	38,678	6.8
Lee	440,888	585,608	32.8
District 9	1,131,191	1,287,987	13.9
Palm Beach	1,131,191	1,287,987	13.9
District 10	1,623,018	1,753,162	8.0
Broward	1,623,018	1,753,162	8.0
District 11	2,333,368	2,517,532	7.9
Miami-Dade	2,253,779	2,437,022	8.1
Monroe	79,589	80,510	1.2
District 12	493,175	592,919	20.2
Flagler	49,832	89,075	78.8
Volusia	443,343	503,844	13.6
District 13	771,675	968,211	25.5
Citrus	118,085	136,749	15.8
Hernando	130,802	157,006	20.0
Lake	210,527	276,783	31.5
Marion	258,916	315,074	21.7
Sumter	53,345	82,599	54.8
District 14	598,228	688,907	15.2
Hardee	26,938	27,186	0.9
Highlands	87,366	96,672	10.7
Polk	483,924	565,049	16.8
District 15	468,283	575,888	23.0
Indian River	112,947	135,262	19.8
Martin	126,731	142,645	12.6
Okeechobee	35,910	38,666	7.7
St. Lucie	192,695	259,315	34.6
Suncoast Regior	2,887,383	3,257,757	12.8
DeSoto	32,209	33,164	3.0
Hillsborough	998,948	1,164,425	16.6
Manatee	264,002	308,325	16.8
Pasco	344,768	424,355	23.1
Pinellas	921,495	948,102	2.9
Sarasota	325,961	379,386	16.4

Note: See map of districts in Section 7.00.

Source: University of Florida, Bureau of Economic and Business Research, Population Program, *Florida Estimates of Population, April 1, 2006.* Census data from U.S. Census Bureau.

Table 1.69. POPULOUS CITIES: CENSUS COUNTS, APRIL 1, 1990 AND 2000, AND POPULATION ESTIMATES, APRIL 1, 2006, IN THE 35 MOST POPULOUS CITIES OF FLORIDA

City	Total population: Census counts 1990	Total population: Census counts 2000	Total population: Estimates 2006	Rank: Census counts 1990	Rank: Census counts 2000	Rank: Estimates 2006	Percentage change 2000 to 2006
Jacksonville	635,230	735,617	834,789	1	1	1	13.5
Miami	358,648	362,470	391,355	2	2	2	8.0
Tampa	280,015	303,447	330,886	3	3	3	9.0
St. Petersburg	240,318	248,232	254,225	4	4	4	2.4
Hialeah	188,008	226,419	228,344	5	5	5	0.9
Orlando	164,674	185,951	224,055	6	6	6	20.5
Tallahassee	124,773	150,624	176,336	8	8	7	17.1
Ft. Lauderdale	149,238	152,397	175,836	7	7	8	15.4
Cape Coral	74,991	102,286	154,499	14	13	9	51.0
Pembroke Pines	65,566	137,427	151,786	21	10	10	10.4
Port St. Lucie	55,761	88,769	144,159	27	15	11	62.4
Hollywood	121,720	139,368	143,287	9	9	12	2.8
Coral Springs	78,864	117,549	129,615	13	11	13	10.3
Gainesville	85,075	95,447	120,919	12	14	14	26.7
Clearwater	98,784	108,789	110,602	10	12	15	1.7
Miramar	40,663	72,739	110,322	41	25	16	51.7
West Palm Beach	67,764	82,103	107,617	17	19	17	31.1
Miami Gardens	(X)	(X)	107,579	(X)	(X)	18	(X)
Pompano Beach	72,411	78,191	101,103	15	22	19	29.3
Palm Bay	62,543	79,413	96,683	22	20	20	21.7
Miami Beach	92,639	87,933	92,145	11	16	21	4.8
Lakeland	70,576	78,452	91,623	16	21	22	16.8
Sunrise	65,683	85,787	89,669	20	17	23	4.5
Boca Raton	61,486	74,764	85,488	24	24	24	14.3
Deltona	(X)	69,543	85,484	(X)	27	25	22.9
Plantation	66,814	82,934	84,891	18	18	26	2.4
Davie	47,143	75,720	84,057	32	23	27	11.0
Melbourne	60,034	71,382	76,742	25	26	28	7.5
Largo	65,910	69,371	75,850	19	28	29	9.3
Deerfield Beach	46,997	64,585	75,603	33	29	30	17.1
Palm Coast	(X)	32,732	67,832	(X)	62	31	107.2
Boynton Beach	46,284	60,389	67,071	34	31	32	11.1
Ft. Myers	44,947	48,208	65,729	35	41	33	36.3
Daytona Beach	61,991	64,112	64,977	23	30	34	1.3
Delray Beach	47,184	60,020	64,095	31	32	35	6.8

(X) Not applicable.
1/ Incorporated after the 2000 census.
Note: Data are for the 35 most populous cities in the state. Changes in city populations include the effects of annexations.

Source: University of Florida, Bureau of Economic and Business Research, Population Program, *Florida Estimates of Population, April 1, 2006.* Census data from U.S. Census Bureau.

Table 1.72. COMPONENTS OF CHANGE: COMPONENTS OF POPULATION CHANGE IN THE STATE AND COUNTIES OF FLORIDA, APRIL 1, 2000 TO APRIL 1, 2006

County	Total population: Census counts 2000	Total population: Estimates 2006	Population change 2000 to 2006	Components of change 1/: Natural increase: Number	Natural increase: Percentage	Net migration: Number	Net migration: Percentage
Florida	15,982,824	18,349,132	2,366,308	267,220	11.3	2,099,088	88.7
Alachua	217,955	243,779	25,824	5,898	22.8	19,926	77.2
Baker	22,259	25,004	2,745	983	35.8	1,762	64.2
Bay	148,217	165,515	17,298	3,860	22.3	13,438	77.7
Bradford	26,088	28,551	2,463	289	11.7	2,174	88.3
Brevard	476,230	543,050	66,820	-2,475	0.0	69,295	100.0
Broward	1,623,018	1,753,162	130,144	40,207	30.9	89,937	69.1
Calhoun	13,017	14,113	1,096	55	5.0	1,041	95.0
Charlotte	141,627	160,315	18,688	-6,925	0.0	25,613	100.0
Citrus	118,085	136,749	18,664	-7,136	0.0	25,800	100.0
Clay	140,814	176,901	36,087	4,940	13.7	31,147	86.3
Collier	251,377	326,658	75,281	7,292	9.7	67,989	90.3
Columbia	56,513	63,538	7,025	922	13.1	6,103	86.9
DeSoto	32,209	33,164	955	912	95.5	43	4.5
Dixie	13,827	15,677	1,850	-59	0.0	1,909	100.0
Duval	778,879	879,235	100,356	32,003	31.9	68,353	68.1
Escambia	294,410	309,647	15,237	6,681	43.8	8,556	56.2
Flagler	49,832	89,075	39,243	-983	0.0	40,226	100.0
Franklin	9,829	11,916	2,087	-41	0.0	2,128	100.0
Gadsden	45,087	48,195	3,108	1,510	48.6	1,598	51.4
Gilchrist	14,437	16,703	2,266	197	8.7	2,069	91.3
Glades	10,576	10,796	220	-145	0.0	365	100.0
Gulf	14,560	16,509	1,949	-160	0.0	2,109	100.0
Hamilton	13,327	14,517	1,190	258	21.7	932	78.3
Hardee	26,938	27,186	248	1,582	100.0	-1,334	0.0
Hendry	36,210	38,678	2,468	2,372	96.1	96	3.9
Hernando	130,802	157,006	26,204	-5,266	0.0	31,470	100.0
Highlands	87,366	96,672	9,306	-2,526	0.0	11,832	100.0
Hillsborough	998,948	1,164,425	165,477	40,046	24.2	125,431	75.8
Holmes	18,564	19,502	938	84	9.0	854	91.0
Indian River	112,947	135,262	22,315	-2,827	0.0	25,142	100.0
Jackson	46,755	50,246	3,491	229	6.6	3,262	93.4
Jefferson	12,902	14,353	1,451	24	1.7	1,427	98.3
Lafayette	7,022	8,060	1,038	145	14.0	893	86.0
Lake	210,527	276,783	66,256	-1,695	0.0	67,951	100.0
Lee	440,888	585,608	144,720	1,864	1.3	142,856	98.7
Leon	239,452	272,497	33,045	9,045	27.4	24,000	72.6

See footnotes at end of table.

Continued . . .

Table 1.72. COMPONENTS OF CHANGE: COMPONENTS OF POPULATION CHANGE IN THE STATE AND COUNTIES OF FLORIDA, APRIL 1, 2000 TO APRIL 1, 2006 (Continued)

County	Total population: Census counts 2000	Total population: Estimates 2006	Population change 2000 to 2006	Components of change 1/: Natural increase: Number	Natural increase: Percentage	Net migration: Number	Net migration: Percentage
Levy	34,450	38,981	4,531	-177	0.0	4,708	100.0
Liberty	7,021	7,772	751	182	24.2	569	75.8
Madison	18,733	19,814	1,081	140	13.0	941	87.0
Manatee	264,002	308,325	44,323	500	1.1	43,823	98.9
Marion	258,916	315,074	56,158	-3,612	0.0	59,770	100.0
Martin	126,731	142,645	15,914	-2,374	0.0	18,288	100.0
Miami-Dade	2,253,779	2,437,022	183,243	83,084	45.3	100,159	54.7
Monroe	79,589	80,510	921	196	21.3	725	78.7
Nassau	57,663	68,188	10,525	981	9.3	9,544	90.7
Okaloosa	170,498	192,672	22,174	6,783	30.6	15,391	69.4
Okeechobee	35,910	38,666	2,756	992	36.0	1,764	64.0
Orange	896,344	1,079,524	183,180	50,573	27.6	132,607	72.4
Osceola	172,493	255,903	83,410	9,810	11.8	73,600	88.2
Palm Beach	1,131,191	1,287,987	156,796	5,455	3.5	151,341	96.5
Pasco	344,768	424,355	79,587	-7,278	0.0	86,865	100.0
Pinellas	921,495	948,102	26,607	-18,490	0.0	45,097	100.0
Polk	483,924	565,049	81,125	10,440	12.9	70,685	87.1
Putnam	70,423	74,416	3,993	207	5.2	3,786	94.8
St. Johns	123,135	165,291	42,156	1,627	3.9	40,529	96.1
St. Lucie	192,695	259,315	66,620	893	1.3	65,727	98.7
Santa Rosa	117,743	141,428	23,685	3,762	15.9	19,923	84.1
Sarasota	325,961	379,386	53,425	-11,218	0.0	64,643	100.0
Seminole	365,199	420,667	55,468	11,643	21.0	43,825	79.0
Sumter	53,345	82,599	29,254	-1,537	0.0	30,791	100.0
Suwannee	34,844	38,799	3,955	65	1.6	3,890	98.4
Taylor	19,256	21,471	2,215	120	5.4	2,095	94.6
Union	13,442	15,028	1,586	-83	0.0	1,669	100.0
Volusia	443,343	503,844	60,501	-7,445	0.0	67,946	100.0
Wakulla	22,863	28,393	5,530	537	9.7	4,993	90.3
Walton	40,601	55,786	15,185	370	2.4	14,815	97.6
Washington	20,973	23,073	2,100	-93	0.0	2,193	100.0

1/ Natural increase is calculated as the difference between the number of births and the number of deaths; net migration is calculated as the difference between total population change and natural increase.

Note: Vital statistics data for persons of unreported residence are included only in the entries for the state. For this reason, natural increase and net migration columns may not add to their state totals.

Source: University of Florida, Bureau of Economic and Business Research, Population Program, *Florida Estimates of Population, April 1, 2006.* Census data from U.S. Census Bureau.

Table 1.80. INSTITUTIONAL POPULATION: ESTIMATED NUMBER OF INMATES AND PATIENTS IN THE STATE, COUNTIES, AND MUNICIPALITIES OF FLORIDA, APRIL 1, 2006

County or city	Total
Florida	115,355
Incorporated	17,332
Unincorporated	98,023
Alachua	1,729
Gainesville	1,238
Unincorporated	491
Baker	1,952
Bay	956
Panama City	136
Unincorporated	820
Bradford	4,460
Starke	11
Unincorporated	4,449
Brevard	1,276
Rockledge	16
Titusville	33
Unincorporated	1,227
Broward	2,084
Cooper City	28
Davie	6
Ft. Lauderdale	318
Pembroke Pines	733
Pompano Beach	155
Unincorporated	844
Calhoun	1,415
Charlotte	1,091
Citrus	191
Collier	106
Columbia	3,336
Lake City	333
Unincorporated	3,003
DeSoto	2,073
Dixie	1,275
Duval	595
Jacksonville	595
Escambia	2,602
Pensacola	101
Unincorporated	2,501
Franklin	1,322
Gadsden	2,979
Chattahoochee	1,472
Quincy	375
Unincorporated	1,132
Gilchrist	808
Glades	740
Gulf	3,066
Hamilton	2,894
Hardee	1,662
Bowling Green	50
Unincorporated	1,612
Hendry	994
Hernando	512
Highlands	22
Hillsborough	1,295
Tampa	693
Unincorporated	602
Holmes	1,386
Indian River	447
Jackson	5,954
Malone	1,532
Marianna	287
Unincorporated	4,135
Jefferson	1,163
Monticello	20
Unincorporated	1,143
Lafayette	1,680
Mayo	9
Unincorporated	1,671
Lake	1,115
Umatilla	50
Unincorporated	1,065
Lee	557
Bonita Springs	6
Cape Coral	30
Ft. Myers	103
Unincorporated	418
Leon	1,858
Tallahassee	1,757
Unincorporated	101
Levy	325
Liberty	1,643
Bristol	64
Unincorporated	1,579
Madison	1,654
Greenville	17
Madison	40
Unincorporated	1,597

See footnote at end of table. Continued . . .

Table 1.80. INSTITUTIONAL POPULATION: ESTIMATED NUMBER OF INMATES AND PATIENTS IN THE STATE, COUNTIES, AND MUNICIPALITIES OF FLORIDA, APRIL 1, 2006 (Continued)

County or city	Total
Manatee	355
Bradenton	128
Palmetto	22
Unincorporated	205
Marion	3,885
Belleview	6
Ocala	182
Unincorporated	3,697
Martin	1,280
Stuart	22
Unincorporated	1,258
Miami-Dade	10,088
Homestead	18
Miami	2,653
Unincorporated	7,417
Monroe	71
Key West	7
Unincorporated	64
Nassau	103
Fernandina Beach	89
Unincorporated	14
Okaloosa	1,544
Okeechobee	2,042
Orange	2,946
Eatonville	63
Orlando	180
Winter Park	91
Unincorporated	2,612
Osceola	299
Kissimmee	45
Unincorporated	254
Palm Beach	4,080
Lantana	65
Pahokee	253
South Bay	1,854
West Palm Beach	236
Unincorporated	1,672
Pasco	917
Pinellas	1,050
Dunedin	6
Safety Harbor	6
St. Petersburg	369
Unincorporated	669
Polk	3,486
Bartow	236
Unincorporated	3,250
Putnam	458
St. Johns	325
St. Lucie	174
Ft. Pierce	85
Unincorporated	89
Santa Rosa	1,831
Milton	97
Unincorporated	1,734
Sarasota	23
Sarasota	23
Seminole	243
Casselberry	6
Sanford	110
Unincorporated	127
Sumter	8,220
Taylor	1,663
Union	4,650
Volusia	1,963
Daytona Beach	42
Ormond Beach	6
Unincorporated	1,915
Wakulla	1,594
Walton	1,451
DeFuniak Springs	38
Unincorporated	1,413
Washington	1,397
Chipley	123
Caryville	23
Vernon	40
Unincorporated	1,211

Note: Inmates and patients residing in federal and state government-operated institutions are considered nonresidents of the local area for revenue-sharing purposes. Unless city data are specified separately for a county, county data are for unincorporated areas.

Source: University of Florida, Bureau of Economic and Business Research, Population Program, *Florida Estimates of Population, April 1, 2006.*

Table 1.81. HOMELESS POPULATION: ESTIMATED DAILY HOMELESS POPULATION IN THE STATE, DEPARTMENT OF CHILDREN AND FAMILIES DISTRICTS, AND COUNTIES OF FLORIDA, 2006 AND 2007

Area	2006	2007	Percentage change
Florida	85,887	60,168	-29.9
District 1	7,619	4,618	-39.4
Escambia	2,911	1,247	-57.2
Okaloosa	2,026	2,110	4.1
Santa Rosa	2,527	1,192	-52.8
Walton	155	69	-55.5
District 2	1,929	1,313	-31.9
Bay	1,051	312	-70.3
Calhoun	0	0	(X)
Franklin	0	39	(X)
Gadsden	139	177	27.3
Gulf	0	0	(X)
Holmes	0	0	(X)
Jackson	0	3	(X)
Jefferson	0	56	(X)
Leon	739	430	-41.8
Liberty	0	30	(X)
Madison	0	73	(X)
Taylor	0	75	(X)
Wakulla	0	112	(X)
Washington	0	6	(X)
District 3	3,024	2,622	-13.3
Alachua	1,217	952	-21.8
Bradford	149	67	-55.0
Columbia	208	364	75.0
Dixie	77	0	-100.0
Gilchrist	86	0	-100.0
Hamilton	50	83	66.0
Lafayette	26	46	76.9
Levy	201	99	-50.7
Putnam	797	789	-1.0
Suwannee	134	222	65.7
Union	79	0	-100.0
District 4	3,874	4,025	3.9
Baker	0	0	(X)
Clay	0	103	(X)
Duval	2,877	2,613	-9.2
Nassau	0	71	(X)
St. Johns	997	1,238	24.2
District 7	10,900	3,842	-64.8
Brevard	1,600	1,287	-19.6
Orange	6,500	1,473	-77.3
Osceola	1,300	514	-60.5
Seminole	1,500	568	-62.1
District 8	7,047	4,672	-33.7
Charlotte	3,314	730	-78.0
Collier	513	414	-19.3
DeSoto	644	659	2.3
Glades	50	61	22.0
Hendry	448	426	-4.9
Lee	2,078	2,382	14.6
District 9	1,002	1,766	76.2
Palm Beach	1,002	1,766	76.2
District 10	3,314	5,218	57.5
Broward	3,314	5,218	57.5
District 11	5,690	5,513	-3.1
Miami-Dade	4,709	4,392	-6.7
Monroe	981	1,121	14.3
District 12	2,696	2,690	-0.2
Flagler	191	207	8.4
Volusia	2,505	2,483	-0.9
District 13	3,562	2,477	-30.5
Citrus	498	856	71.9
Hernando	452	241	-46.7
Lake	395	878	122.3
Marion	2,149	458	-78.7
Sumter	68	44	-35.3
District 14	1,986	2,015	1.5
Hardee	749	679	-9.3
Highlands	436	519	19.0
Polk	801	817	2.0
District 15	2,609	2,050	-21.4
Indian River	741	572	-22.8
Martin	759	521	-31.4
Okeechobee	296	316	6.8
St. Lucie	813	641	-21.2
SunCoast Region	30,635	17,347	-43.4
Hillsborough	8,598	9,532	10.9
Manatee	6,722	487	-92.8
Pasco	3,677	2,260	-38.5
Pinellas	4,385	4,680	6.7
Sarasota	7,253	388	-94.7

(X) Not applicable.

Note: Beginning in 2005, daily statewide point-in-time surveys were conducted during the last week of January. See map of districts in Section 7.00.

Source: State of Florida, Department of Children and Families, *Annual Report on Homeless Conditions in Florida*, Internet site <http://www.dcf.state.fl.us/> (accessed 29, June 2007).

Table 1.88. VETERANS: ESTIMATED NUMBER OF VETERANS IN CIVIL LIFE BY PERIOD OF SERVICE IN FLORIDA AND THE UNITED STATES, SEPTEMBER 30, 2006

(rounded to thousands)

		War veterans					Peacetime veterans		
Area	Total veterans	Total	World War II	Korean conflict 1/	Vietnam era 1/	Gulf war 1/	Between Korea and Vietnam	Between Vietnam and Gulf war	Other
Florida	1,747	1,315	268	210	461	285	180	239	13
United States	23,977	17,835	2,822	2,531	7,287	4,297	2,538	3,448	156

1/ No prior wartime service.

Source: U.S., Department of Veterans Affairs, Internet site <http://www.va.gov/vetdata/> (accessed 4, June 2007).

Table 1.89. IMMIGRANTS: ADMISSIONS BY INTENDED RESIDENCE IN FLORIDA AND IN THE UNITED STATES, FISCAL YEARS 1995 THROUGH 2006

Year	Florida	United States	Year	Florida	United States
1995	62,023	720,461	2001	104,148	1,058,902
1996	79,401	915,560	2002	90,460	1,059,356
1997	82,232	797,847	2003	52,770	703,542
1998	59,756	653,206	2004	76,178	957,883
1999	57,216	644,787	2005	122,918	1,122,373
2000	94,474	841,002	2006	155,996	1,266,264

Note: Data are for federal fiscal years ending September 30.

Table 1.90. NONIMMIGRANTS: NUMBER ADMITTED BY CATEGORY OF ADMISSION AND DESTINATION TO FLORIDA AND THE UNITED STATES, FISCAL YEAR 2005

		Tourists and business travelers						
Area	Total	Visa waiver	Other	Students and ex-change students	Temp-orary workers	Diplomats and other represent-tatives	All other classes	Unknown
Florida	5,061,923	2,462,196	2,226,365	57,888	171,412	14,562	96,134	33,366
Percentage of total	15.82	15.09	18.26	5.53	10.89	5.07	21.46	24.25
United States	32,003,435	16,319,170	12,191,204	1,046,421	1,573,631	287,484	447,940	137,585

Note: Data are for fiscal year ending September 30. Admissions refer to counts of arrivals rather than individuals since nonimmigrants may enter the United States multiple times during a year. Also, the majority of short-term admissions from Canada and Mexico are excluded.

Source for Tables 1.89 and 1.90: U.S., Department of Homeland Security, Bureau of U.S. Citizenship and Immigration Services, Office of Immigration Statistics, *2006 Yearbook of Immigration Statistics,* and previous edition, Internet site <http://www.dhs.gov/index.shtm> (accessed 4, June 2007).

Table 1.91. IMMIGRANTS: ARRIVALS BY COUNTRY OF ORIGIN TO THE STATE AND COUNTIES OF FLORIDA, 2006

County	Total	Cuba	Haiti	Ukraine	Vietnam	Other
Florida	14,290	13,696	24	70	84	416
Alachua	2	2	0	0	0	0
Bay	1	0	0	0	1	0
Brevard	4	4	0	0	0	0
Broward	367	338	7	0	0	22
Charlotte	10	10	0	0	0	0
Clay	10	10	0	0	0	0
Collier	293	292	1	0	0	0
Duval	358	108	0	6	26	218
Escambia	1	0	0	0	1	0
Flagler	23	5	0	18	0	0
Hendry	30	30	0	0	0	0
Hernando	4	4	0	0	0	0
Highlands	7	7	0	0	0	0
Hillsborough	581	524	0	0	9	48
Holmes	2	2	0	0	0	0
Indian River	5	5	0	0	0	0
Lake	78	77	1	0	0	0
Lee	162	162	0	0	0	0
Leon	9	6	0	0	0	3
Manatee	6	4	1	0	1	0
Marion	21	18	0	0	2	1
Miami-Dade	10,960	10,925	7	8	0	20
Monroe	101	101	0	0	0	0
Okeechobee	8	8	0	0	0	0
Orange	348	268	6	0	19	55
Osceola	36	35	0	0	0	1
PalmBeach	474	462	1	0	6	5
Pasco	38	21	0	0	10	7
Pinellas	88	72	0	0	6	10
Polk	58	58	0	0	0	0
St. Johns	3	3	0	0	0	0
St. Lucie	36	33	0	0	0	3
Sarasota	104	41	0	38	3	22
Seminole	26	25	0	0	0	1
Suwannee	16	16	0	0	0	0
Volusia	19	19	0	0	0	0
Walton	1	1	0	0	0	0

Note: Data are for federal fiscal year ending September 30, and are preliminary.

Source: State of Florida, Department of Children and Families, Refugee Services, *Florida's Refugee and Entrant Arrivals Statistical Report, October 1, 2005–September 30, 2006,* Internet site <http://www.state.fl.us/cf_web/> (accessed 22, February 2007).

Table 1.92. IMMIGRANTS: CUBAN AND HAITIAN REFUGEE AND ENTRANT ARRIVALS BY IMMIGRATION STATUS IN THE STATE AND COUNTIES OF FLORIDA, 2006

County	Total	Refugees	Entrants	Parolees	County	Total	Refugees	Entrants	Parolees
Total	14,290	2,324	2,921	9,045	Leon	9	3	1	5
					Manatee	6	1	3	2
Alachua	2	2	0	0	Marion	21	6	2	13
Bay	1	1	0	0	Miami-Dade	10,960	1,162	2,408	7,390
Brevard	4	0	2	2	Monroe	101	4	51	46
Broward	367	63	57	247	Okeechobee	8	0	0	8
Charlotte	10	7	0	3	Orange	348	164	29	155
Clay	10	0	0	10	Osceola	36	8	4	24
Collier	293	53	45	195	Palm Beach	474	73	118	283
Duval	358	322	2	34	Pasco	38	23	1	14
Escambia	1	1	0	0	Pinellas	88	51	1	36
Flagler	23	18	0	5	Polk	58	9	21	28
Hendry	30	0	2	28	St. Johns	3	0	0	3
Hernando	4	0	1	3	St. Lucie	36	19	2	15
Highlands	7	7	0	0	Sarasota	104	67	6	31
Hillsborough	581	208	99	274	Seminole	26	13	2	11
Holmes	2	0	0	2	Suwannee	16	14	1	1
Indian River	5	0	5	0	Volusia	19	11	2	6
Lake	78	0	25	53	Walton	1	0	1	0
Lee	162	14	30	118					

Note: Data are for federal fiscal year ending September 30, and are preliminary.

Table 1.93. REFUGEES: ARRIVALS BY COUNTRY OF ORIGIN AND BY AGE IN FLORIDA, 2006

Country	Total	0–4	5–18	19–39	40–59	60 and over
Total	14,290	751	2,148	5,386	2,561	198
Afghanistan	9	0	3	3	2	0
Belarus	7	2	0	0	2	0
Burma	52	8	0	11	1	0
Cameroon	5	0	1	3	0	1
Colombia	36	1	7	7	3	0
Costa Rica	2	0	1	1	0	0
Cuba	13,696	693	2,003	5,212	2,502	184
Eritrea	9	0	0	5	0	0
Ethiopia	7	1	2	3	1	0
Haiti	24	1	12	3	0	0
Iran	23	1	2	14	1	1
Liberia	41	4	14	9	4	0
Mauritania	2	0	1	0	1	0
Philippines	2	0	2	0	0	0
Russia	153	15	50	35	18	8
Rwanda	6	2	2	1	1	0
Sierra Leone	6	0	2	2	1	0
Somalia	17	0	6	4	2	0
Sudan	24	3	2	9	2	0
Ukraine	70	8	20	22	6	4
Vietnam	84	11	17	35	12	0
Zaire	6	0	1	4	1	0

Note: Data are for federal fiscal year ending September 30, and are preliminary.

Source for Tables 1.92 and 1.93: State of Florida, Department of Children and Families, Refugee Services, *Florida's Refugee and Entrant Arrivals Statistical Report, October 1, 2005–September 30, 2006,* Internet site <http://www.state.fl.us/cf_web/> (accessed 22, February 2007).

Table 1.94. IMMIGRANTS: REFUGEE AND ENTRANT ARRIVALS IN THE STATE AND COUNTIES OF FLORIDA, 2002 THROUGH 2006

County	Total arrivals 2002 to 2006	As a percent-age of state	2002	2003	2004	2005	2006
Florida	70,568	100.00	15,086	8,245	20,519	12,428	14,290
Alachua	16	0.02	0	4	6	4	2
Bay	6	0.01	0	0	3	2	1
Brevard	30	0.04	1	7	2	16	4
Broward	2,340	3.32	497	336	681	459	367
Charlotte	39	0.06	9	12	4	4	10
Citrus	3	0.00	0	1	2	0	0
Clay	32	0.05	1	15	5	1	10
Collier	1,502	2.13	297	177	511	224	293
Columbia	6	0.01	0	4	2	0	0
Duval	1,690	2.39	175	208	511	438	358
Escambia	9	0.01	2	1	5	0	1
Flagler	90	0.13	7	27	26	7	23
Hendry	131	0.19	19	9	38	35	30
Hernando	9	0.01	0	0	4	1	4
Highlands	26	0.04	0	0	8	11	7
Hillsborough	3,593	5.09	635	341	1,219	817	581
Holmes	2	0.00	0	0	0	0	2
Indian River	25	0.04	13	0	5	2	5
Lafayette	1	0.00	0	0	0	1	0
Lake	166	0.24	17	8	23	40	78
Lee	505	0.72	44	52	135	112	162
Leon	14	0.02	0	0	5	0	9
Levy	3	0.00	3	0	0	0	0
Manatee	68	0.10	10	5	36	11	6
Marion	34	0.05	0	0	13	0	21
Martin	12	0.02	8	0	1	3	0
Miami-Dade	53,412	75.69	12,158	5,988	15,252	9,054	10,960
Monroe	480	0.68	87	89	120	83	101
Okaloosa	3	0.00	0	0	3	0	0
Okeechobee	16	0.02	1	0	7	0	8
Orange	1,391	1.97	223	153	402	265	348
Osceola	157	0.22	15	11	58	37	36
Palm Beach	2,511	3.56	544	362	725	406	474
Pasco	285	0.40	51	31	117	48	38
Pinellas	920	1.30	133	232	329	138	88
Polk	189	0.27	24	29	44	34	58
St. Johns	5	0.01	0	0	2	0	3
St. Lucie	115	0.16	7	11	43	18	36
Sarasota	516	0.73	70	100	120	122	104
Seminole	132	0.19	31	25	36	14	26
Suwannee	21	0.03	0	1	0	4	16
Volusia	62	0.09	4	6	16	17	19
Walton	1	0.00	0	0	0	0	1

Note: Data are for federal fiscal years ending September 30. Data for 2006 are preliminary.

Source: State of Florida, Department of Children and Families, Refugee Services, *Florida's Refugee and Entrant Arrivals Statistical Report, October 1, 2005–September 30, 2006,* Internet site <http://www.state.fl.us/cf_web/> (accessed 22, February 2007).

HOUSING

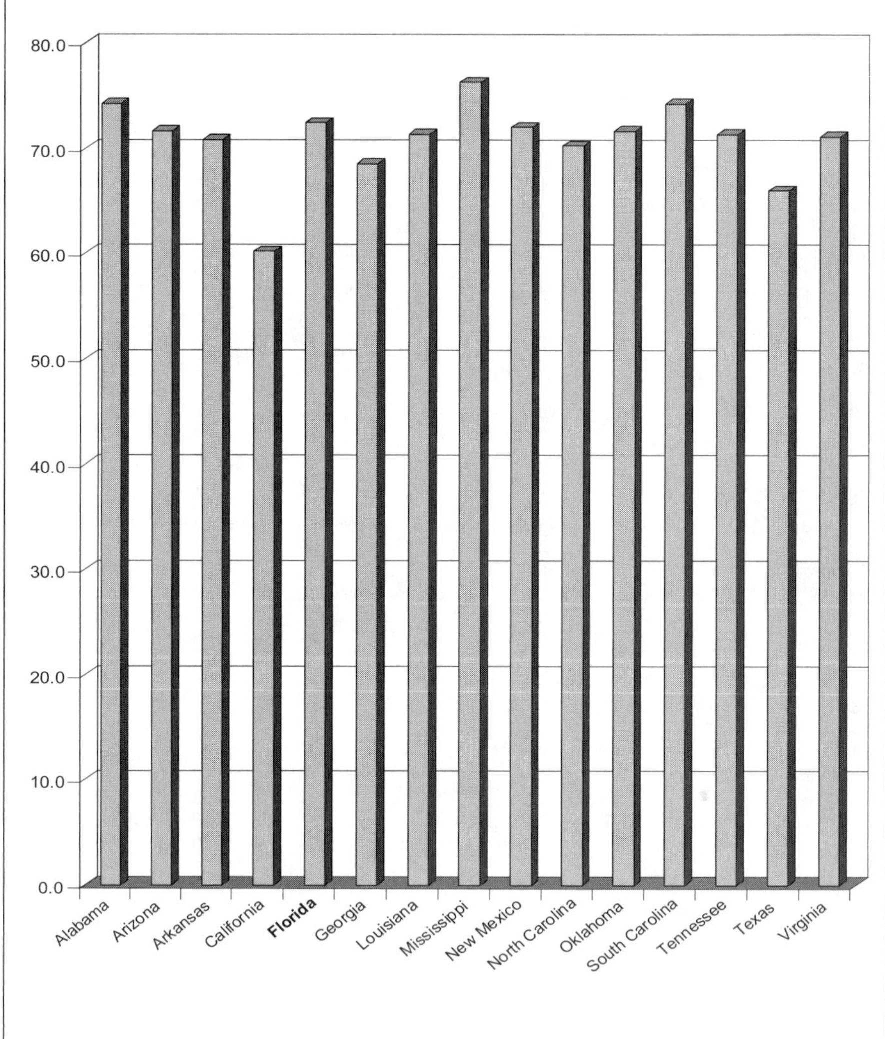

Source: Table 2.02

Section 2.00
Housing

This section presents data on housing Florida's residents and contains data on various housing characteristics: housing units, households, and household size; home sales and prices, mortgage status, and housing costs; homeownership rates; occupancy; medical, nursing home, and assisted living facilities; public lodgings; and mobile homes and recreational vehicles licensed in the state.

Sources. The decennial Census of Housing is conducted simultaneously with the Census of Population and provides basic information about people in their living arrangements. Census counts of housing units, households, and persons per household in every state appear in Table 2.01. The Population Program of the Bureau of Economic and Business Research (BEBR), University of Florida, makes annual estimates of the number of households and average household size for intercensal years. These are published in the series, *Florida Population Studies* and are presented on Table 2.05.

The Census Bureau also releases annual survey statistics from the *American Housing Survey*. Survey data on homeownership rates for Florida, large Florida metropolitan areas, other states, and the United States are presented in Table 2.02 and general housing characteristics for Florida from the survey appear in Table 2.03. New this year from the *Annual Housing Survey* are county-level data on the mortgage status of owner-occupied housing units and monthly housing costs (Tables 2.11 and 2.12).

BEBR's Economic Analysis Program provides average housing cost data, as measured by the Florida County Retail Price Index. The Florida Association of Realtors and the University of Florida's Media Center provide data on existing single-family home sales and median sales prices in metropolitan statistical areas throughout the state.

Various State of Florida agencies also provide information relating to housing. The Florida Agency for Health Care Administration provides county-level data on nursing home facilities and beds. The Department of Elder Affairs also provides medical facility beds and assisted living facilities data. Statistics on licensed public lodgings, including apartment buildings, rooming houses, rental condominiums, and transient apartment buildings may be found on the Florida Division of Hotels and Restaurants Web site within the state's Department of Business and Professional Regulation. The Department of Highway Safety and Motor Vehicles annually publishes the number of vehicle tags sold to owners of mobile homes, park trailers, and recreational vehicles in *Revenue Report*.

Section 2.00
Housing

Tables listed by major heading

Table 2.01. STATES: COUNTS OF HOUSING UNITS AND HOUSEHOLDS IN FLORIDA OTHER STATES, AND THE UNITED STATES, APRIL 1, 2005

State	Total housing units	Households Total	Households Persons per–	State	Total housing units	Households Total	Households Persons per–
Florida	8,256,847	7,048,800	2.47	Missouri	2,592,809	2,285,280	2.46
				Montana	428,357	368,268	2.47
Alabama	2,082,140	1,788,692	2.48	Nebraska	766,951	695,592	2.45
Alaska	274,246	233,252	2.75	Nevada	1,019,427	906,719	2.63
Arizona	2,544,806	2,204,013	2.65	New Hampshire	583,324	497,054	2.56
Arkansas	1,249,116	1,087,542	2.48	New Jersey	3,443,981	3,141,956	2.71
California	12,989,254	12,097,894	2.92	New Mexico	838,668	727,820	2.59
Colorado	2,053,178	1,819,037	2.51	New York	7,853,020	7,114,431	2.62
Connecticut	1,423,343	1,323,838	2.56	North Carolina	3,940,554	3,409,840	2.47
Delaware	374,872	317,640	2.58	North Dakota	304,458	270,437	2.25
District of				Ohio	5,007,091	4,507,821	2.47
Columbia	277,775	248,213	2.08	Oklahoma	1,588,749	1,380,595	2.49
Georgia	3,771,466	3,320,278	2.66	Oregon	1,558,421	1,425,340	2.50
Hawaii	491,071	430,007	2.88	Pennsylvania	5,422,362	4,860,140	2.46
Idaho	595,572	532,135	2.62	Rhode Island	447,810	406,089	2.54
Illinois	5,144,623	4,691,020	2.65	South Carolina	1,927,864	1,635,907	2.51
Indiana	2,724,429	2,443,010	2.49	South Dakota	347,931	310,331	2.40
Iowa	1,306,943	1,200,833	2.38	Tennessee	2,637,441	2,366,130	2.46
Kansas	1,196,211	1,071,938	2.48	Texas	9,026,011	7,978,095	2.79
Kentucky	1,865,516	1,653,898	2.45	Utah	873,097	791,929	3.07
Louisiana	1,940,399	1,676,599	2.62	Vermont	307,345	248,825	2.42
Maine	683,799	542,158	2.37	Virginia	3,174,708	2,889,688	2.54
Maryland	2,273,793	2,085,647	2.62	Washington	2,651,645	2,450,474	2.51
Massachusetts	2,688,014	2,448,032	2.53	West Virginia	872,203	740,702	2.39
Michigan	4,478,507	3,887,994	2.54	Wisconsin	2,498,500	2,219,571	2.42
Minnesota	2,252,022	2,020,144	2.47	Wyoming	235,721	204,935	2.42
Mississippi	1,235,496	1,084,034	2.61	United States	124,521,886	111,090,617	2.60

Note: Detail may not add to totals because of rounding. See Glossary for definition of household.

Source: U.S., Department of Commerce, Census Bureau, American FactFinder, 2005 American Community Survey, Internet site <http://factfinder.census.gov/> (accessed 26, February 2007).

Table 2.02. STATES: HOMEOWNERSHIP RATES IN THE STATE AND SPECIFIED METROPOLITAN STATISTICAL AREAS (MSAS) OF FLORIDA AND IN OTHER STATES AND THE UNITED STATES 2004, 2005, AND 2006

State and MSA	2004	2005	2006
Florida	72.2	72.4	72.4
Metropolitan Statistical Area 1/			
Jacksonville	69.1	67.9	70.0
Orlando	69.1	70.5	71.1
Tampa-St. Petersburg-Clearwater	71.5	71.7	71.6
Miami-Ft. Lauderdale-Miami Beach	(NA)	69.2	67.4
Other states			
Alabama	78.0	76.6	74.2
Alaska	67.2	66.0	67.2
Arizona	68.7	71.1	71.6
Arkansas	69.1	69.2	70.8
California	59.7	59.7	60.2
Colorado	71.1	71.0	70.1
Connecticut	71.7	70.5	71.1
Delaware	77.3	75.8	76.8
District of Columbia	45.6	45.8	45.9
Georgia	70.9	67.9	68.5
Hawaii	60.6	59.8	59.9
Idaho	73.7	74.2	75.1
Illinois	72.7	70.9	70.4
Indiana	75.8	75.0	74.2
Iowa	73.2	73.9	74.0
Kansas	69.9	69.5	70.0
Kentucky	73.3	71.6	71.7
Louisiana	70.6	72.5	71.3
Maine	74.7	73.9	75.3
Maryland	72.1	71.2	72.6
Massachusetts	63.8	63.4	65.2
Michigan	77.1	76.4	77.4
Minnesota	76.4	76.5	75.6
Mississippi	74.0	78.8	76.2
Missouri	72.4	72.3	71.9
Montana	72.4	70.4	69.5
Nebraska	71.2	70.2	67.6
Nevada	65.7	63.4	65.7
New Hampshire	73.3	74.0	74.2
New Jersey	68.8	70.1	69.0
New Mexico	71.5	71.4	72.0
New York	54.8	55.9	55.7
North Carolina	69.8	70.9	70.2
North Dakota	70.0	68.5	68.3
Ohio	73.1	73.3	72.1
Oklahoma	71.1	72.9	71.6
Oregon	69.0	68.2	68.1
Pennsylvania	74.9	73.3	73.2
Rhode Island	61.5	63.1	64.6
South Carolina	76.2	73.9	74.2
South Dakota	68.5	68.4	70.6
Tennessee	71.6	72.4	71.3
Texas	65.5	65.9	66.0
Utah	74.9	73.9	73.5
Vermont	72.0	74.2	74.0
Virginia	73.4	71.2	71.1
Washington	66.0	67.6	66.7
West Virginia	80.3	81.3	78.4
Wisconsin	73.3	71.1	70.2
Wyoming	72.8	72.8	73.7
United States	69.0	68.9	68.8

(NA) Not available.
1/ MSA data for 2004 are based on 1990 metropolitan/nonmetropolitan definitions. Data for 2005 and 2006 are based on 2000 metropolitan/nonmetropolitan definitions.
Note: Data are based on the American Housing Survey (AHS) conducted by the Census Bureau. Homeownership rates are computed by dividing the number of owner households by the total number of households.

Source: U.S., Department of Commerce, Census Bureau, *Housing Vacancies and Homeownership Annual Statistics: 2006,* Internet site <http://www.census.gov/> (accessed 20, March 2007).

Table 2.03. GENERAL HOUSING CHARACTERISTICS: ESTIMATES IN FLORIDA, 2005

Characteristic	Number	Percentage
Occupancy status and tenure		
Housing units, total	8,256,847	100.0
Occupied	7,048,800	85.4
Owner-occupied	4,903,949	69.6
Renter-occupied	2,144,851	30.4
Year structure built		
2000 or later	888,149	12.6
1990 to 1999	1,339,272	19.0
1980 to 1989	1,642,370	23.3
1960 to 1979	2,192,177	31.1
1940 to 1959	796,514	11.3
1939 or earlier	183,269	2.6
Vacant	1,208,047	14.6
For rent	183,623	15.2
Rented, not occupied	42,282	3.5
For sale only	83,355	6.9
Sold, not occupied	84,563	7.0
For seasonal, recreational, or occasional use	595,567	49.3
For migratory workers	4,832	0.4
Other	213,824	17.7
Occupancy characteristics		
Household size		
1-person household	1,959,566	27.8
2-person household	2,615,105	37.1
3-person household	1,078,466	15.3
4-or-more person household	1,395,662	19.8
Household type		
Family households	4,595,818	65.2
Married-couple family	3,376,375	47.9
Other family	1,212,394	17.2
Female householder, no husband present	895,198	12.7
Nonfamily households	2,452,982	34.8
Householder living alone	1,959,566	27.8
Family type and presence of children		
With related children under 18 years	2,114,640	30.0
No related children under 18 years	4,934,160	70.0
Householder characteristics		
Race or Hispanic origin		
One race		
White	5,674,284	80.5
Black or African American	930,442	13.2
American Indian and Alaska native	21,146	0.3
Asian	119,830	1.7
Native Hawaiian and other Pacific Islander	0	0.0
Other	211,464	3.0
Two or more races	77,537	1.1
Hispanic or Latino (of any race)	1,127,808	16.0
White alone	4,807,282	68.2
Age 1/ (years)		
Under 35 years	1,367,467	19.4
35 to 44	1,353,370	19.2
45 to 54	1,381,565	19.6
55 to 64	1,134,857	16.1
65 to 74	902,246	12.8
75 to 84	690,782	9.8
85 and over	218,513	3.1

See footnotes at end of table.

Continued . . .

Table 2.03. GENERAL HOUSING CHARACTERISTICS: ESTIMATES IN FLORIDA, 2005 (Continued)

Characteristic	Number	Percentage
Householder characteristics (Continued)		
Educational attainment		
Less than high school graduate	1,000,930	14.2
High school graduate 1/	2,015,957	28.6
Some college or associate's degree	2,163,982	30.7
Bachelor's degree or higher	1,874,981	26.6
Year moved into unit		
2000 or later	3,926,182	55.7
1990 to 1999	1,882,030	26.7
1980 to 1989	718,978	10.2
1970 to 1979	338,342	4.8
1969 or earlier	183,269	2.6
Financial characteristics		
Household income 2/		
Less than $5,000	239,659	3.4
$5,000 to $9,999	345,391	4.9
$10,000 to $14,999	451,123	6.4
$15,000 to $19,999	444,074	6.3
$20,000 to $24,999	486,367	6.9
$25,000 to $34,999	923,393	13.1
$35,000 to $49,999	1,163,052	16.5
$50,000 to $74,999	1,311,077	18.6
$75,000 to $99,999	718,978	10.2
$100,000 to $149,999	592,099	8.4
$150,000 or more	373,586	5.3
Median household income (dollars)	42,433	(X)
Monthly housing costs 2/		
Less than $100	42,293	0.6
$100 to $199	225,562	3.2
$200 to $299	394,733	5.6
$300 to $399	444,074	6.3
$400 to $499	451,123	6.4
$500 to $599	479,318	6.8
$600 to $699	521,611	7.4
$700 to $799	556,855	7.9
$800 to $899	542,758	7.7
$900 to $999	486,367	6.9
$1,000 to $1,499	1,494,346	21.2
$1,500 to $1,999	669,636	9.5
$2,000 or more	634,392	9.0
No cash rent	105,732	1.5
Median (dollars)	866	(X)
Monthly housing costs by household income		
Less than $20,000	1,346,321	19.1
$20,000 to $34,999	1,381,565	19.6
$35,000 to $49,999	1,148,954	16.3
$50,000 to $74,999	1,296,979	18.4
$75,000 or more	1,677,614	23.8
Zero or negative income	84,586	1.2
No cash rent	105,732	1.5

(X) Not applicable.
1/ Includes equivalency.
2/ Income or costs in the past 12 months. Income is in 2005 inflation-adjusted dollars.
Note: Data are for occupied housing units, unless otherwise specified.
Source: U.S., Department of Commerce, Census Bureau, *2005 American Community Survey,* Internet site <http://factfinder/census.gov/> (accessed 25, January 2007).

Table 2.05. HOUSEHOLDS AND AVERAGE HOUSEHOLD SIZE: ESTIMATES IN THE STATE AND COUNTIES OF FLORIDA, APRIL 1, 2006

County	Households Number	Households Percentage change 2000 to 2006	Average household size	County	Households Number	Households Percentage change 2000 to 2006	Average household size
Florida	7,291,013	15.0	2.46	Lake	116,400	31.7	2.34
				Lee	250,350	32.7	2.31
Alachua	99,173	13.3	2.31	Leon	110,825	14.8	2.32
Baker	7,971	13.2	2.84	Levy	15,900	14.7	2.41
Bay	67,856	13.9	2.39	Liberty	2,425	9.1	2.50
Bradford	9,140	7.6	2.56	Madison	7,040	6.2	2.54
Brevard	228,121	15.1	2.33	Manatee	133,050	18.3	2.27
Broward	698,139	6.7	2.48	Marion	131,660	23.3	2.32
Calhoun	4,929	10.3	2.50	Martin	62,425	12.9	2.22
Charlotte	72,972	14.3	2.16	Miami-Dade	846,750	9.0	2.82
Citrus	61,523	16.9	2.18	Monroe	36,290	3.4	2.18
Clay	64,277	27.9	2.72	Nassau	26,529	20.7	2.54
Collier	131,450	27.7	2.44	Okaloosa	75,150	13.4	2.49
Columbia	23,325	11.5	2.54	Okeechobee	13,300	5.6	2.71
DeSoto	11,035	2.7	2.70	Orange	400,292	19.0	2.64
Dixie	5,896	13.3	2.41	Osceola	90,119	47.8	2.80
Duval	342,308	12.7	2.52	Palm Beach	538,138	13.5	2.35
Escambia	117,568	5.9	2.44	Pasco	181,819	23.2	2.30
Flagler	37,522	76.2	2.35	Pinellas	428,925	3.4	2.16
Franklin	4,554	11.2	2.27	Polk	219,325	17.1	2.51
Gadsden	16,843	6.2	2.66	Putnam	29,450	5.8	2.48
Gilchrist	5,897	17.4	2.60	St. Johns	67,125	35.3	2.42
Glades	3,955	2.7	2.50	St. Lucie	103,345	34.3	2.47
Gulf	5,425	10.0	2.42	Santa Rosa	52,600	20.1	2.63
Hamilton	4,450	6.9	2.58	Sarasota	173,854	15.9	2.14
Hardee	8,084	-1.0	3.08	Seminole	161,000	15.4	2.59
Hendry	11,660	7.5	3.09	Sumter	33,735	62.4	2.18
Hernando	66,800	20.5	2.31	Suwannee	15,163	12.7	2.51
Highlands	41,485	10.7	2.30	Taylor	7,895	10.0	2.48
Hillsborough	457,157	16.8	2.50	Union	3,735	10.9	2.75
Holmes	7,280	5.2	2.43	Volusia	212,719	15.2	2.29
Indian River	59,250	20.6	2.24	Wakulla	10,363	22.6	2.55
Jackson	17,734	6.7	2.44	Walton	23,190	40.1	2.32
Jefferson	5,184	10.4	2.48	Washington	8,812	11.1	2.43
Lafayette	2,352	9.8	2.65				

Source: University of Florida, Bureau of Economic and Business Research, Population Program, *Florida Population Studies,* January 2007, Volume 40, Bulletin No. 146.

Table 2.10. HOUSE PURCHASE PRICE: COST OF A HOUSE IN THE STATE AND COUNTIES OF FLORIDA, 2004 AND 2005

County	House cost index 2004	House cost (dollars) 2004	House cost (dollars) 2005
Florida	(X)	188,700	246,500
Alachua	86.39	163,013	212,945
Baker	80.77	152,414	199,100
Bay	85.02	160,429	209,569
Bradford	78.85	148,794	194,371
Brevard	93.10	175,675	229,485
Broward	126.66	239,013	312,225
Calhoun	76.13	143,649	187,650
Charlotte	86.79	163,778	213,944
Citrus	79.64	150,288	196,322
Clay	83.73	157,992	206,386
Collier	97.66	184,291	240,740
Columbia	79.12	149,308	195,042
DeSoto	81.17	153,159	200,072
Dixie	76.05	143,505	187,462
Duval	91.97	173,549	226,708
Escambia	82.91	156,444	204,364
Flagler	82.66	155,978	203,756
Franklin	77.63	146,481	191,350
Gadsden	74.68	140,924	184,090
Gilchrist	77.07	145,429	189,974
Glades	78.14	147,458	192,625
Gulf	77.92	147,029	192,065
Hamilton	76.73	144,792	189,143
Hardee	79.20	149,445	195,221
Hendry	75.54	142,546	186,209
Hernando	82.98	156,575	204,535
Highlands	78.41	147,955	193,274
Hillsborough	93.00	175,493	229,248
Holmes	73.22	138,172	180,495
Indian River	89.35	168,612	220,260
Jackson	74.43	140,451	183,472
Jefferson	77.17	145,618	190,221
Lafayette	75.75	142,941	186,724
Lake	86.19	162,637	212,454
Lee	90.21	170,222	222,362
Leon	85.99	162,267	211,971
Levy	77.28	145,824	190,491
Liberty	76.20	143,782	187,824
Madison	76.05	143,503	187,458
Manatee	98.43	185,735	242,627
Marion	81.71	154,189	201,419
Martin	97.25	183,520	239,733
Miami-Dade	120.70	227,764	297,530
Monroe	132.65	250,319	326,994
Nassau	86.83	163,842	214,028
Okaloosa	86.15	162,566	212,361
Okeechobee	76.20	143,781	187,822
Orange	94.27	177,886	232,374
Osceola	87.97	165,999	216,846
Palm Beach	108.56	204,857	267,606
Pasco	91.05	171,803	224,427
Pinellas	110.07	207,695	271,313
Polk	84.45	159,361	208,174
Putnam	82.53	155,727	203,427
St. Johns	86.58	163,381	213,426
St. Lucie	88.25	166,532	217,542
Santa Rosa	78.70	148,510	194,000
Sarasota	107.06	202,020	263,901
Seminole	93.10	175,680	229,492
Sumter	84.30	159,074	207,800
Suwannee	77.09	145,464	190,021
Taylor	76.12	143,637	187,634
Union	77.60	146,427	191,279
Volusia	89.64	169,143	220,952
Wakulla	77.75	146,705	191,642
Walton	74.07	139,777	182,591
Washington	71.75	135,393	176,864

(X) Not applicable.

Note: House cost index from the Florida County Retail Price Index (FCRPI) published by the Bureau of Economic and Business Research. House cost estimated by multiplying the Florida median sales price by the house cost index. The median sales prices were obtained from the Florida Association of Realtors. See discussion of FCRPI on Table 24.80.

Source: University of Florida, Bureau of Economic and Business Research, Economic Analysis Program, unpublished data.

Table 2.11. MORTGAGE STATUS: OWNER-OCCUPIED HOUSING UNITS BY MORTGAGE STATUS IN THE STATE AND COUNTIES OF FLORIDA, 2005

County	Total units	Units with a mortgage 1/				Aggregate value ($1,000)	
		Total	Both second mortage and home equity loan	Second mortgage only	Home equity loan only	Total	Units with a mortgage
Florida	4,903,949	3,213,520	34,246	156,360	583,003	1,247,052,763	875,430,120
Alachua	48,047	31,831	688	1,108	4,752	8,732,438	6,013,420
Bay	44,810	27,933	344	1,522	3,710	9,577,730	5,874,503
Brevard	160,884	104,646	660	5,711	19,292	39,137,193	26,963,663
Broward	481,133	337,731	3,833	14,296	70,859	147,094,153	113,129,583
Charlotte	60,269	33,663	158	824	5,664	15,372,448	8,781,015
Citrus	46,530	24,723	117	842	3,799	7,598,453	4,298,770
Clay	45,908	34,678	560	2,938	7,618	8,469,358	6,631,840
Collier	89,520	55,690	303	1,820	12,322	42,163,033	26,228,965
Duval	214,309	161,132	2,590	10,744	27,068	41,425,140	32,721,475
Escambia	82,447	52,880	465	4,130	7,212	13,625,438	9,461,948
Flagler	25,369	16,101	80	557	4,336	7,417,448	4,893,253
Hernando	55,708	32,402	312	1,499	4,349	9,568,318	6,038,603
Highlands	30,194	12,993	63	714	2,309	4,078,243	2,265,430
Hillsborough	290,233	210,603	2,772	12,954	37,623	64,508,460	50,175,493
Indian River	44,296	25,379	367	705	5,119	13,005,975	7,374,445
Lake	91,184	49,233	1,089	3,041	10,322	16,445,745	10,763,808
Lee	172,404	105,643	1,202	3,372	23,636	49,968,048	32,626,270
Leon	63,375	45,789	262	2,625	7,388	13,100,598	9,930,943
Manatee	96,778	59,019	686	3,672	12,119	25,087,713	17,069,683
Marion	100,046	57,543	50	3,569	6,528	15,714,048	10,101,880
Martin	45,022	24,650	67	718	6,656	16,809,573	10,073,105
Miami-Dade	488,681	359,180	4,328	13,457	48,306	156,652,435	116,879,775
Monroe	23,621	12,444	0	137	3,664	16,900,628	9,654,098
Okaloosa	48,416	31,489	115	1,867	7,096	12,746,540	8,427,425
Orange	232,093	179,904	1,539	10,293	33,975	58,858,900	47,308,098
Osceola	57,443	43,240	312	3,902	6,282	12,660,600	10,139,505
Palm Beach	378,320	240,445	2,170	8,533	51,454	128,066,605	85,905,963
Pasco	140,008	81,851	767	3,748	15,124	24,861,085	16,954,303
Pinellas	297,069	183,288	2,155	7,660	38,410	66,131,890	44,985,633
Polk	156,813	93,620	553	4,947	12,295	21,580,493	14,794,155
Putnam	20,886	10,633	90	523	651	2,451,723	1,276,768
St. Johns	49,100	34,956	312	2,179	9,213	17,693,633	13,138,663
St. Lucie	72,266	44,943	1,349	2,812	6,305	16,105,633	11,244,530
Santa Rosa	36,325	24,205	56	833	3,717	7,577,383	5,048,890
Sarasota	126,223	73,337	1,102	4,779	15,618	40,781,718	25,166,238
Seminole	106,672	82,788	1,120	3,437	20,580	27,898,605	22,842,173
Volusia	150,240	91,507	736	5,033	15,100	31,115,923	20,292,730

1/ Includes contract to purchase or similar debt.

Note: Data are estimates and are limited to the household population and exclude the population living in institutions, college dormitories, and other group quarters.

Source: U.S. Department of Commerce, Census Bureau, *2005 American Community Survey*, Internet site <http://factfinder.census.gov/> (accessed 15, August 2007).

Table 2.12. HOUSING COSTS: MONTHLY HOUSING COSTS FOR OCCUPIED HOUSING UNITS IN THE STATE AND COUNTIES OF FLORIDA, 2005

County	Total	Less than $200	$200 to $399	$400 to $599	$600 to $799	$800 to $999	$1,000 to $1,499	$1,500 to $1,999	$2,000 or more	No cash rent
Florida	7,048,800	269,662	835,961	927,976	1,077,093	1,029,543	1,492,000	672,027	635,330	109,208
Alachua	94,960	2,357	9,529	19,749	18,827	16,762	16,411	4,968	4,327	2,030
Bay	69,342	3,347	11,823	11,887	11,923	10,762	12,240	2,551	2,862	1,947
Brevard	218,052	6,765	30,773	33,168	40,537	28,845	45,995	16,394	12,900	2,675
Broward	687,331	10,356	51,928	67,025	88,623	91,316	165,772	96,763	108,074	7,474
Charlotte	70,838	2,734	13,268	10,973	11,929	7,848	13,158	5,980	4,395	553
Citrus	57,831	6,688	12,379	10,617	10,027	6,558	7,440	1,792	1,365	965
Clay	61,670	2,437	6,015	5,951	8,010	9,504	17,284	6,923	4,962	584
Collier	121,171	2,251	9,522	12,259	13,282	16,123	28,849	17,952	19,308	1,625
Duval	333,132	13,257	37,830	38,573	62,653	56,163	71,873	28,110	18,426	6,247
Escambia	120,133	6,113	22,242	19,205	21,006	17,570	19,009	6,877	4,560	3,551
Flagler	33,009	1,481	5,810	2,939	2,347	6,319	8,102	3,113	1,764	1,134
Hernando	66,127	4,137	14,923	11,274	9,159	9,184	11,981	2,450	2,563	456
Highlands	39,437	5,615	10,237	8,613	5,348	4,206	2,878	821	1,120	599
Hillsborough	450,126	14,935	42,062	57,900	74,051	71,601	100,383	43,854	38,516	6,824
Indian River	57,315	1,383	8,520	8,003	8,275	9,783	10,134	3,775	6,894	548
Lake	114,416	8,071	22,531	18,530	16,938	10,842	20,643	9,404	5,148	2,309
Lee	235,033	8,448	21,924	32,120	35,937	38,861	52,385	22,850	18,475	4,033
Leon	106,426	2,766	10,858	15,107	20,279	16,701	21,293	8,978	8,204	2,240
Manatee	132,891	6,323	14,095	19,382	20,918	19,638	26,611	12,309	12,606	1,009
Marion	125,805	10,330	26,949	22,872	23,038	15,843	15,447	4,542	4,840	1,944
Martin	59,238	1,234	8,835	7,657	7,276	9,744	9,857	5,882	7,632	1,121
Miami-Dade	834,800	20,605	56,553	88,901	130,558	129,595	192,646	100,520	106,646	8,776
Monroe	33,961	1,188	2,365	4,080	2,552	3,406	6,900	4,649	7,526	1,295
Okaloosa	72,402	2,694	10,171	10,639	11,840	8,859	14,796	5,079	4,550	3,774
Orange	391,440	6,709	30,424	36,371	65,118	76,640	98,204	39,011	34,435	4,528
Osceola	83,737	1,727	7,966	8,309	10,207	14,886	24,994	9,164	5,736	748
Palm Beach	513,556	8,947	45,169	65,121	56,988	70,181	118,136	66,893	76,264	5,857
Pasco	172,639	14,573	32,785	28,199	21,984	19,261	32,864	12,978	7,523	2,472
Pinellas	418,019	16,818	52,677	63,874	69,653	59,711	88,090	31,047	31,666	4,483
Polk	214,835	12,483	35,701	37,464	39,518	30,493	38,881	12,108	5,601	2,586
Putnam	27,923	4,927	6,181	5,854	5,099	2,723	2,280	215	104	540
St. Johns	63,255	1,992	6,846	4,891	8,444	5,813	16,138	8,225	10,147	759
St. Lucie	95,112	3,266	12,863	13,266	13,326	12,002	21,257	13,074	5,064	994
Santa Rosa	49,296	1,779	7,221	7,215	5,907	7,972	10,918	3,879	1,946	2,459
Sarasota	165,367	3,778	21,513	22,326	22,254	23,412	34,750	17,325	17,313	2,696
Seminole	155,477	2,635	12,229	11,978	23,047	26,289	42,225	19,144	16,366	1,564
Volusia	201,793	9,777	30,923	29,103	34,923	30,836	39,310	14,117	8,906	3,898

Note: Data are estimates and are limited to the household population and exclude the population living in institutions, college dormitories, and other group quarters.

Source: U.S. Department of Commerce, Census Bureau, *2005 American Community Survey*, Internet site <http://factfinder.census.gov/> (accessed 15, August 2007).

Table 2.18. MEDICAL FACILITY BEDS: NUMBER IN THE STATE AND COUNTIES OF FLORIDA, 2007

County	Licensed hospital	Nursing home	Skilled nursing unit	Ambulatory surgical	County	Licensed hospital	Nursing home	Skilled nursing unit	Ambulatory surgical
Florida	62,482	82,407	394	1,026	Lake	657	1,407	0	11
Alachua	1,443	976	0	18	Lee	1,688	2,172	0	53
Baker	1,163	188	0	0	Leon	1,068	816	113	26
Bay	694	974	0	14	Levy	40	180	0	0
Bradford	25	240	0	0	Liberty	0	0	0	0
Brevard	1,582	2,629	0	30	Madison	25	238	0	0
Broward	6,831	4,552	16	71	Manatee	909	1,562	0	16
Calhoun	25	246	0	0	Marion	737	1,492	0	23
Charlotte	658	1,228	0	12	Martin	424	833	0	13
Citrus	326	1,081	0	9	Miami-Dade	9,537	7,928	0	68
Clay	310	1,033	0	10	Monroe	267	240	0	0
Collier	906	908	0	38	Nassau	54	240	0	0
Columbia	166	275	0	2	Okaloosa	446	996	0	13
DeSoto	49	41	0	0	Okeechobee	100	173	0	3
Dixie	0	60	0	0	Orange	3,267	4,263	0	50
Duval	3,104	4,014	40	53	Osceola	496	1,080	0	7
Escambia	1,440	1,747	0	23	Palm Beach	3,918	6,514	0	84
Flagler	83	240	0	0	Pasco	1,075	1,938	0	31
Franklin	25	0	0	0	Pinellas	4,130	8,120	78	75
Gadsden	2,032	120	0	0	Polk	1,730	2,865	0	20
Gilchrist	0	201	0	0	Putnam	141	337	10	0
Glades	0	0	0	0	St. Johns	316	698	14	19
Gulf	0	120	0	0	St. Lucie	610	1,050	0	12
Hamilton	42	60	0	0	Santa Rosa	349	410	0	12
Hardee	25	104	0	0	Sarasota	1,502	2,897	0	56
Hendry	25	248	0	0	Seminole	701	1,232	18	15
Hernando	574	660	0	10	Sumter	74	270	0	0
Highlands	335	598	0	6	Suwannee	15	401	0	0
Hillsborough	3,759	3,951	30	67	Taylor	48	120	0	3
Holmes	25	180	0	0	Union	178	0	0	2
Indian River	554	645	41	20	Volusia	1,495	3,379	0	29
Jackson	125	540	0	0	Wakulla	0	120	0	0
Jefferson	0	157	0	0	Walton	100	180	0	2
Lafayette	0	60	0	0	Washington	59	180	34	0

Source: State of Florida, Department of Elder Affairs, unpublished data.

Table 2.19. NURSING HOMES: NUMBER, DAYS, BEDS, AND RATES IN THE STATE AND COUNTIES OF FLORIDA, 2006

County	Free standing facilities 1/	Beds Total	Beds Com-munity	Beds Shel-ters	Beds Occu-pancy rate	Beds Medicaid (per-centage)	Days Community bed	Days Community patient	Days Medicaid patient
Florida	655	82,977	79,909	2,403	54.93	40.75	29,004,224	25,575,066	15,544,079
Alachua	7	976	934	42	87.25	64.48	340,910	297,434	191,791
Baker	2	188	188	0	86.32	76.60	68,620	59,236	45,377
Bay	8	974	854	0	90.09	62.30	311,710	280,809	174,943
Bradford	2	240	240	0	95.74	69.74	87,600	83,870	58,493
Brevard	20	2,629	2,629	0	90.98	55.83	959,585	873,011	487,429
Broward	34	4,672	4,349	167	82.28	61.09	1,575,145	1,296,067	791,709
Calhoun	2	246	246	0	84.58	78.29	89,790	75,942	59,454
Charlotte	8	1,228	1,108	0	82.35	54.90	404,420	333,024	182,835
Citrus	9	1,081	1,081	0	90.95	54.08	394,565	358,852	194,070
Clay	10	1,093	1,093	0	86.16	55.34	398,945	343,743	190,239
Collier	10	908	755	153	87.49	48.26	275,575	241,102	116,366
Columbia	3	305	305	0	92.68	65.03	101,695	94,248	61,290
DeSoto	1	41	41	0	40.31	44.89	22,049	8,887	3,989
Dixie	1	60	60	0	90.76	53.94	21,900	19,876	10,721
Duval	30	4,014	3,934	80	92.42	63.40	1,435,910	1,327,046	841,376
Escambia	13	1,747	1,712	35	87.17	61.22	624,880	544,703	333,470
Flagler	2	240	240	0	93.61	61.16	87,600	82,000	50,152
Franklin	0	0	0	0	(NA)	(NA)	0	0	0
Gadsden	1	120	120	0	93.96	86.99	43,800	41,153	35,797
Gilchrist	2	201	201	0	94.74	60.66	73,365	69,505	42,164
Glades	0	0	0	0	(NA)	(NA)	0	0	0
Gulf	1	120	120	0	76.69	83.69	43,800	33,592	28,113
Hamilton	1	60	60	0	98.80	84.74	21,900	21,638	18,336
Hardee	2	102	102	0	88.59	62.46	37,230	32,982	20,600
Hendry	2	248	248	0	80.70	78.63	90,520	73,049	57,436
Hernando	5	660	660	0	86.45	56.95	240,900	208,261	118,596
Highlands	5	598	598	0	88.28	54.23	218,270	192,699	104,508
Hillsborough	29	3,951	3,761	190	90.96	62.09	1,372,765	1,248,676	775,355
Holmes	1	180	180	0	92.01	76.30	65,700	60,449	46,120
Indian River	5	645	545	100	89.27	56.80	198,925	177,572	100,855
Jackson	4	540	540	0	87.66	77.36	189,300	165,939	128,364
Jefferson	2	157	157	0	89.97	76.56	57,305	51,557	39,472
Lafayette	1	60	60	0	88.50	79.39	21,900	19,381	15,386
Lake	12	1,407	1,397	10	85.79	48.97	509,905	437,437	214,220
Lee	17	2,172	2,018	154	86.51	58.84	736,570	637,197	374,950

See footnotes at end of table. Continued. . .

Table 2.19. NURSING HOMES: NUMBER, DAYS, BEDS, AND RATES IN THE STATE AND COUNTIES OF FLORIDA, 2006 (Continued)

County	Free standing facilities 1/	Beds: Total	Beds: Community	Beds: Shelters	Beds: Occupancy rate	Beds: Medicaid (percentage)	Days: Community bed	Days: Community patient	Days: Medicaid patient
Leon	6	816	744	72	95.21	60.24	271,560	258,546	155,749
Levy	1	180	180	0	60.66	71.72	65,700	39,853	28,584
Liberty	0	0	0	0	(NA)	(NA)	0	0	0
Madison	3	238	238	0	88.24	80.68	86,870	76,657	61,848
Manatee	12	1,562	1,360	202	84.21	55.28	496,400	418,017	231,067
Marion	9	1,372	1,372	0	90.49	54.08	500,780	453,137	245,078
Martin	7	833	795	38	88.61	59.68	290,175	257,126	153,451
Miami-Dade	53	8,282	8,232	50	91.47	65.49	2,917,722	2,668,778	1,747,833
Monroe	2	240	240	0	74.54	70.71	87,600	65,296	46,171
Nassau	2	240	240	0	91.61	65.43	87,600	80,252	52,510
Okaloosa	8	899	899	0	85.34	61.88	328,135	280,016	173,272
Okeechobee	1	173	173	0	93.00	78.97	63,145	58,727	46,376
Orange	33	4,263	4,074	189	88.46	59.59	1,487,010	1,315,422	783,904
Osceola	9	1,080	1,080	0	85.56	63.53	384,360	328,867	208,934
Palm Beach	54	6,514	6,197	317	85.10	56.84	2,261,905	1,924,938	1,094,051
Pasco	15	1,938	1,818	0	91.99	56.71	663,570	610,415	346,161
Pinellas	71	8,120	7,890	201	89.36	62.91	2,879,850	2,573,310	1,618,930
Polk	23	2,993	2,945	48	88.38	61.28	1,038,205	917,532	562,292
Putnam	3	337	337	0	93.13	74.82	123,005	114,550	85,712
St. Johns	6	698	605	93	90.53	53.05	220,825	199,910	106,059
St. Lucie	9	1,050	1,050	0	88.24	66.12	383,250	338,196	223,621
Santa Rosa	4	410	410	0	92.65	66.60	149,650	138,651	92,342
Sarasota	25	2,897	2,800	97	83.30	52.67	1,022,000	851,312	448,422
Seminole	9	1,232	1,172	60	93.49	60.68	427,780	399,942	242,679
Sumter	2	270	270	0	80.88	45.78	98,550	79,704	36,490
Suwannee	3	401	401	0	96.42	73.19	146,365	141,131	103,300
Taylor	1	120	120	0	91.78	78.87	43,800	40,200	31,705
Union	0	0	0	0	(NA)	(NA)	0	0	0
Volusia	28	3,379	3,154	105	85.99	58.80	1,151,210	989,868	582,068
Wakulla	1	120	120	0	85.10	71.52	43,800	37,272	26,657
Walton	2	277	277	0	76.22	66.40	94,648	72,145	47,903
Washington	1	180	180	0	82.74	86.34	65,700	54,359	46,934

(NA) Not available.

1/ Includes adult family care home facilities, hospitals with skilled nursing units, and adult day care facilities.

Source: State of Florida, Agency for Health Care Administration, Department of Elder Affairs, unpublished data.

Table 2.20. ASSISTED LIVING FACILITIES: NUMBER AND LICENSED BEDS IN THE STATE AND COUNTIES OF FLORIDA, JULY 2007

County	Facil-ities	Beds Total	Beds Private	Beds OSS	County	Facil-ities	Beds Total	Beds Private	Beds OSS
Florida	2,433	75,967	61,713	14,254	Lake	26	1,201	1,170	31
					Lee	36	2,286	2,259	27
Alachua	10	484	482	2	Leon	11	641	639	2
Baker	0	0	0	0	Levy	1	50	40	10
Bay	13	504	329	175	Liberty	3	57	14	43
Bradford	2	42	28	14	Madison	3	40	8	32
Brevard	44	1,549	1,489	60	Manatee	38	1,810	1,666	144
Broward	263	8,257	6,820	1,437	Marion	26	1,348	1,238	110
Calhoun	1	23	10	13	Martin	9	432	427	5
Charlotte	18	1,076	1,065	11	Miami-Dade	764	9,092	2,489	6,603
Citrus	18	813	790	23	Monroe	3	38	27	11
Clay	10	300	276	24	Nassau	4	220	130	90
Collier	21	1,701	1,701	0	Okaloosa	11	492	457	35
Columbia	8	340	259	81	Okeechobee	0	0	0	0
DeSoto	4	105	77	28	Orange	77	2,155	1,905	250
Dixie	1	25	6	19	Osceola	13	373	277	96
Duval	72	2,551	2,038	513	Palm Beach	99	5,124	4,731	393
Escambia	21	1,190	1,046	144	Pasco	52	2,308	1,964	344
Flagler	23	192	182	10	Pinellas	224	7,869	6,992	877
Franklin	1	30	30	0	Polk	31	1,920	1,691	229
Gadsden	4	116	62	54	Putnam	10	317	142	175
Gilchrist	0	0	0	0	St. Johns	12	461	461	0
Glades	0	0	0	0	St. Lucie	50	1,040	972	68
Gulf	2	49	49	0	Santa Rosa	8	414	354	60
Hamilton	2	28	14	14	Sarasota	66	3,479	3,417	62
Hardee	4	129	31	98	Seminole	45	2,040	1,919	121
Hendry	1	30	30	0	Sumter	3	82	82	0
Hernando	16	994	923	71	Suwannee	1	60	60	0
Highlands	11	544	467	77	Taylor	0	0	0	0
Hillsborough	121	4,939	3,957	982	Union	0	0	0	0
Holmes	3	94	33	61	Volusia	79	3,265	3,015	250
Indian River	19	817	788	29	Wakulla	0	0	0	0
Jackson	1	76	50	26	Walton	4	87	50	37
Jefferson	1	33	0	33	Washington	7	151	21	130
Lafayette	2	84	64	20					

OSS Optional State Supplement.

Source: State of Florida, Department of Elder Affairs, unpublished data.

Table 2.21. HOME SALES: SALES AND MEDIAN SALES PRICE OF EXISTING SINGLE-FAMILY HOMES IN THE STATE AND METROPOLITAN STATISTICAL AREAS (MSAS) OF FLORIDA, 2005 AND 2006

MSA	Number of homes sold 2005 A/	Number of homes sold 2006	Number of homes sold Percentage change	Median sales price 2005 A/ (dollars)	Median sales price 2006 (dollars)	Median sales price Percentage change
Florida	248,575	180,037	-27.6	235,200	248,300	5.6
Daytona Beach 1/	14,069	9,121	-35.2	205,500	219,900	7.0
Ft. Lauderdale	11,331	8,373	-26.1	361,100	367,800	1.9
Ft. Myers-Cape Coral	12,273	9,189	-25.1	281,900	272,300	-3.4
Ft. Pierce-Port St. Lucie	6,923	4,965	-28.3	254,000	253,200	-0.3
Ft. Walton Beach	3,976	2,861	-28.0	240,500	231,400	-3.8
Gainesville	3,993	3,174	-20.5	179,200	213,200	19.0
Jacksonville	18,317	16,405	-10.4	187,300	200,600	7.1
Lakeland-Winter Haven	6,417	5,160	-19.6	148,700	176,200	18.5
Melbourne-Titusville-Palm Bay	8,098	5,830	-28.0	226,200	219,400	-3.0
Miami	11,016	8,692	-21.1	351,200	375,800	7.0
Naples 2/	4,846	2,863	-40.9	486,500	486,500	0.0
Ocala	6,118	5,347	-12.6	142,000	167,800	18.2
Orlando	36,727	27,212	-25.9	231,400	262,900	13.6
Panama City	2,254	1,700	-24.6	216,800	217,400	0.3
Pensacola	6,340	5,196	-18.0	161,300	165,600	2.7
Punta Gorda	4,029	3,050	-24.3	219,700	218,000	-0.8
Sarasota-Bradenton	12,059	7,941	-34.1	322,700	305,200	-5.4
Tallahassee	5,258	4,929	-6.3	167,600	177,600	6.0
Tampa-St. Petersburg-Clearwater	53,183	34,322	-35.5	201,700	229,100	13.6
West Palm Beach-Boca Raton	13,679	8,640	-36.8	390,100	384,700	-1.4

A/ Revised.
1/ Data from the New Smyrna Beach Board of Realtors for December 2006 were not available.
2/ Data from the Marco Island Association of Realtors for the months of April and November 2006 were not available; also, data from the Naples Area Board of Realtors and Association of Real Estate Professionals for December 2006 were not available.
Note: Data are for Metropolitan Statistical Areas (MSAs) and Primary Metropolitan Statistical Areas (PMSAs) based on 1999 designations as defined by the U.S. Census Bureau. See Glossary for definitions.
Data are for Realtor sales only.

Source: Florida Association of Realtors and University of Florida, Media Center, *Existing Home Sales Statistics,* Year-End 2006, Internet site <http://media.living.net/> (accessed 19, March 2007).

Table 2.30. PUBLIC LODGINGS: LICENSED LODGINGS IN THE STATE AND COUNTIES OF FLORIDA, JULY 2, 2007

County	Total licensed lodgings		County	Total licensed lodgings	
	Number	Units		Number	Units
Florida	36,950	1,482,142	Lake	1,090	13,172
			Lee	731	33,512
Alachua	458	31,771	Leon	484	32,974
Baker	5	206	Levy	54	936
Bay	629	21,793	Liberty	1	13
Bradford	28	860	Madison	14	492
Brevard	649	33,354	Manatee	369	19,324
Broward	3,382	137,585	Marion	240	12,851
Calhoun	6	126	Martin	121	5,179
Charlotte	141	4,494	Miami-Dade	6,266	203,467
Citrus	76	2,269	Monroe	1,060	15,693
Clay	63	7,309	Nassau	119	3,755
Collier	280	22,025	Okaloosa	325	15,223
Columbia	89	3,466	Okeechobee	24	654
DeSoto	19	655	Orange	1,411	203,950
Dixie	11	187	Osceola	5,936	55,753
Duval	787	88,005	Palm Beach	1,603	80,763
Escambia	346	21,538	Pasco	277	13,547
Flagler	52	1,624	Pinellas	1,990	86,180
Franklin	314	1,490	Polk	2,919	31,265
Gadsden	35	1,310	Putnam	66	2,033
Gilchrist	8	130	St. Johns	218	10,583
Glades	13	218	St. Lucie	162	8,803
Gulf	188	884	Santa Rosa	133	3,091
Hamilton	20	568	Sarasota	494	20,352
Hardee	19	573	Seminole	224	36,673
Hendry	35	823	Sumter	46	1,859
Hernando	75	2,968	Suwannee	25	571
Highlands	122	3,687	Taylor	46	872
Hillsborough	1,056	121,991	Union	2	80
Holmes	15	321	Volusia	882	39,661
Indian River	140	6,062	Wakulla	7	248
Jackson	48	1,830	Walton	460	7,560
Jefferson	19	422	Washington	19	434
Lafayette	4	75			

Caution: Data were collected from unaudited, raw data files as reported by the Department of Business and Professional Regulation and may contain reporting errors.

Note: Includes apartment buildings, rooming houses, resort condominiums, resort dwellings, and transient apartment buildings shown separately in Table 2.31 and hotels and motels shown separately in Table 19.60.

Source: State of Florida, Department of Business and Professional Regulation, Divison of Hotels and Restaurants, Licensee Information Download files: Lodging, Internet site <http://www.myflorida.com/dbpr/> (accessed 2, July 2007).

Table 2.31. PUBLIC LODGINGS: APARTMENTS, ROOMING HOUSES, RENTAL CONDOMINIUMS, AND TRANSIENT APARTMENTS IN THE STATE AND COUNTIES OF FLORIDA, JULY 2, 2007

County	Apartment buildings		Rooming houses		Rental condominiums 1/		Transient apartment buildings 2/	
	Number	Units	Number	Units	Number	Units	Number	Units
Florida	19,019	978,743	360	6,015	12,986	114,635	1,032	12,902
Alachua	391	27,177	3	71	0	0	6	134
Baker	2	59	0	0	0	0	0	0
Bay	156	6,960	0	0	348	7,647	6	105
Bradford	14	489	1	2	1	12	2	10
Brevard	416	22,662	8	112	110	1,809	36	392
Broward	2,844	104,852	24	263	83	3,555	235	2,871
Calhoun	4	102	0	0	0	0	0	0
Charlotte	51	2,307	0	0	68	1,173	21	155
Citrus	43	1,124	2	9	5	15	11	116
Clay	46	5,987	0	0	1	17	0	0
Collier	117	11,707	4	128	84	3,431	3	39
Columbia	56	1,619	0	0	0	0	2	21
DeSoto	13	455	0	0	0	0	1	3
Dixie	2	44	1	16	0	0	1	12
Duval	622	71,940	15	180	4	11	0	0
Escambia	188	13,153	2	13	76	2,112	1	24
Flagler	12	367	2	34	20	590	1	3
Franklin	5	125	2	13	292	1,004	1	4
Gadsden	18	893	0	0	2	8	2	65
Gilchrist	2	60	0	0	1	1	0	0
Glades	3	48	0	0	1	5	1	8
Gulf	4	119	0	0	173	596	1	6
Hamilton	6	155	0	0	0	0	0	0
Hardee	13	456	1	5	0	0	0	0
Hendry	16	338	1	8	2	31	0	0
Hernando	59	2,295	0	0	0	0	4	25
Highlands	89	2,254	2	10	5	222	16	291
Hillsborough	840	101,099	18	260	9	252	21	266
Holmes	10	139	0	0	1	1	0	0
Indian River	91	3,990	4	32	11	398	5	52
Jackson	29	918	0	0	1	10	0	0
Jefferson	9	218	1	5	0	0	1	1
Lafayette	1	36	0	0	0	0	0	0
Lake	180	8,747	5	45	835	1,494	7	72

See footnotes at end of table

Continued . . .

Table 2.31. PUBLIC LODGINGS: APARTMENTS, ROOMING HOUSES, RENTAL CONDOMINIUMS, AND TRANSIENT APARTMENTS IN THE STATE AND COUNTIES OF FLORIDA, JULY 2, 2007 (Continued)

County	Apartment buildings		Rooming houses		Rental condominiums 1/		Transient apartment buildings 2/	
	Number	Units	Number	Units	Number	Units	Number	Units
Lee	308	16,735	9	93	239	6,608	40	227
Leon	412	26,721	6	403	2	103	4	661
Levy	22	420	1	3	8	117	6	36
Liberty	0	0	0	0	0	0	0	0
Madison	8	285	0	0	0	0	0	0
Manatee	178	13,781	4	57	118	2,200	35	351
Marion	151	8,557	0	0	7	43	10	50
Martin	83	3,658	3	57	8	419	7	250
Miami-Dade	5,699	156,103	96	1,678	48	3,285	20	809
Monroe	250	2,843	19	194	562	4,529	128	812
Nassau	32	1,070	2	15	57	1,049	3	6
Okaloosa	132	5,349	1	10	133	5,483	3	169
Okeechobee	12	205	2	24	0	0	4	39
Orange	727	107,096	23	304	391	16,974	11	385
Osceola	139	14,195	6	367	5,661	14,596	12	413
Palm Beach	1,298	61,440	34	653	73	2,565	63	937
Pasco	156	10,472	1	25	77	934	9	103
Pinellas	1,467	61,229	11	147	174	6,058	145	1,292
Polk	398	19,004	19	412	2,387	5,363	26	278
Putnam	35	1,435	2	22	1	23	1	11
St. Johns	52	2,915	3	36	48	2,017	3	14
St. Lucie	103	5,185	5	63	11	567	16	139
Santa Rosa	54	1,896	0	0	67	535	0	0
Sarasota	285	11,633	3	62	121	3,674	67	612
Seminole	170	31,943	5	43	5	27	4	435
Sumter	20	491	0	0	12	702	4	24
Suwannee	13	260	0	0	2	2	4	16
Taylor	9	287	1	7	16	84	2	5
Union	2	80	0	0	0	0	0	0
Volusia	430	20,014	6	116	199	6,864	19	149
Wakulla	0	0	0	0	1	24	0	0
Walton	12	382	2	18	424	5,395	1	4
Washington	10	165	0	0	1	1	0	0

1/ Rental condominiums include resort condominiums and resort dwellings.
2/ Apartments which rent for six months or less.
Caution: Data were collected from unaudited, raw data files as reported by the Department of Business and Professional Regulation and may contain reporting errors.

Source: State of Florida, Department of Business and Professional Regulation, Divison of Hotels and Restaurants, Licensee Information Download files: Lodging, Internet site <http://www.myflorida.com/dbpr/> (accessed 2, July 2007).

Table 2.36. MOBILE HOME AND RECREATIONAL VEHICLE TAGS: NUMBER SOLD IN THE STATE AND COUNTIES OF FLORIDA, FISCAL YEAR 2005–06

County	Mobile homes 1/	Park trailers 2/	Recrea- tional vehicles 3/	County	Mobile homes 1/	Park trailers 2/	Recrea- tional vehicles 3/
Florida	500,402	656,419	129,608	Lake	19,085	26,324	4,337
				Lee	32,109	38,262	5,717
Alachua	3,545	4,854	1,410	Leon	4,848	6,531	1,396
Baker	430	956	277	Levy	1,303	2,061	569
Bay	2,507	5,155	1,960	Liberty	102	194	52
Bradford	489	917	280	Madison	952	1,187	178
Brevard	12,323	17,482	6,733	Manatee	22,134	26,581	2,522
Broward	16,258	19,651	4,186	Marion	15,637	21,546	4,467
Calhoun	176	341	87	Martin	4,902	6,255	1,591
Charlotte	5,369	7,980	2,224	Miami-Dade	11,164	13,841	3,670
Citrus	5,829	8,593	2,461	Monroe	1,603	3,218	1,088
Clay	1,634	4,251	2,038	Nassau	1,008	1,958	772
Collier	5,792	8,025	2,055	Okaloosa	2,170	3,907	1,706
Columbia	2,594	3,717	774	Okeechobee	1,593	4,533	823
DeSoto	2,315	4,262	400	Orange	15,734	19,087	4,264
Dixie	239	516	195	Osceola	7,353	9,342	1,408
Duval	9,587	14,116	4,954	Palm Beach	16,466	20,508	4,357
Escambia	2,375	5,366	3,009	Pasco	22,075	35,958	5,241
Flagler	2,248	2,956	719	Pinellas	45,853	51,891	7,463
Franklin	103	266	158	Polk	49,977	58,788	6,568
Gadsden	708	957	226	Putnam	2,339	3,581	980
Gilchrist	741	1,071	181	St. Johns	3,624	5,550	1,484
Glades	357	810	167	St. Lucie	13,567	15,831	2,332
Gulf	124	344	162	Santa Rosa	1,383	3,513	1,713
Hamilton	343	498	112	Sarasota	15,686	20,436	4,017
Hardee	872	1,649	302	Seminole	4,304	5,877	2,127
Hendry	3,249	4,178	380	Sumter	2,577	4,500	1,199
Hernando	5,823	8,086	2,043	Suwannee	2,469	3,238	530
Highlands	13,019	16,036	1,509	Taylor	2,410	2,791	190
Hillsborough	30,093	39,603	9,307	Union	438	600	78
Holmes	582	838	117	Volusia	31,516	36,145	4,566
Indian River	8,908	10,268	1,621	Wakulla	375	816	300
Jackson	1,326	2,273	439	Walton	1,275	1,924	520
Jefferson	372	590	167	Washington	570	976	189
Lafayette	117	251	65	Agency office	1,354	1,813	476

1/ Includes military mobile homes.
2/ Includes park trailers and 5th-wheel travel trailers.
3/ Includes auto-motorcoaches and camp trailers. Due to changes in the revenue system, these data are not comparable to those published in previous years.

Source: State of Florida, Department of Highway Safety and Motor Vehicles, *Revenue Report, July 1, 2005 through June 30, 2006,* Internet site <http://www.hsmv.state.fl.us/> (accessed 23, February 2007).

VITAL STATISTICS AND HEALTH

Resident Live Births by Age of Mother, 2005 (%)

Less than 19 years 7%
Age 19 4%
Age 20–24 26%
Age 25–29 26%
Age 30–34 22%
35 years and over 14%

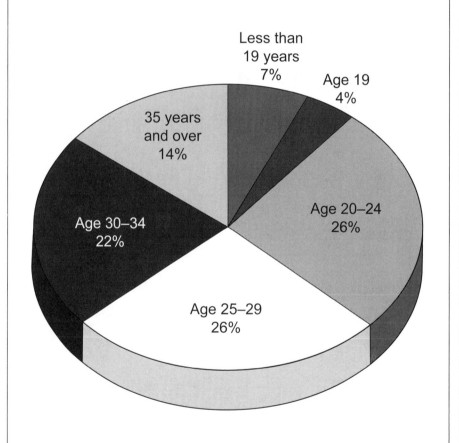

Source: Table 3.02

Section 3.00
Vital Statistics and Health

This section presents vital statistics data on births, deaths, abortions, marriages, and marriage dissolutions. It also reports statistics pertaining to general health and well-being issues, such as child well-being indicators; reported cases of child and elder abuse; community-based care agencies assisting maltreated youth; elder care and elder persons with disabilities; adverse incidents occurring in nursing home and assisted living facilities; HIV and AIDS cases; and sexually transmitted diseases.

Explanatory notes. Vital statistics usually include data on births, infant deaths, abortions, teenage pregnancies, illegitimate births, marriages, divorces, annulments, and deaths by cause. "Resident" is the term indicating births or deaths among residents of a specified area regardless of where the event occurred. "Recorded" is the term used to identify births or deaths occurring in a specified area regardless of the usual residence of the person counted. The birth and death figures depicted in this section are resident data. Marriages and dissolutions of marriage are reported by place of occurrence rather than by residence.

Cases of Human Immunodeficiency Virus (HIV) and Acquired Immunodeficiency Syndrome (AIDS) in Table 3.28 are reported cases. There is a time lag, occasionally as much as several years, between diagnosis of a case according to national Centers for Disease Control criteria and the case's entry into the Florida Department of Health's AIDS Reporting System.

Sources. The Public Health Statistics Section of the Florida Department of Health is the principal source of vital statistics data for the state and counties. Data are released monthly in *Vital News* and later accumulated in an annual report, *Florida Vital Statistics Annual Report.*

Child well-being. The Louis de la Parte Florida Mental Health Institute's Center for the Study of Children's Futures at the University of South Florida (USF) permits publication of unpublished data on child and teen deaths and children affected by divorce. USF and the Florida Department of Children and Families jointly produce a report for the Florida Legislature providing data on community-based care agencies that assist maltreated youths and includes the counties covered by each agency. Data from the *Report to the Legislature: Evaluation of the Department of Children and Families Community-Based Care Initiative* can be found on Table 3.22.

The Florida Department of Children and Families (DCF) presents fiscal year reported cases of child abuse and monthly abuse rates as shown on Table 3.21 in their *Child Welfare Annual Statistical Data Tables.*

Elder care and abuse. Last year, the Department of Elder Affairs reported results from a 2003 statewide survey on the number of caregivers throughout the state in their report, *Assessing the Needs of Elder Floridians.* Updates of these data were not available in time to appear in this *Abstract* and were repeated in the first column of Table 3.24. The Department of Elder Affairs published current data about elders with disabilities in their series, *Florida County Profiles* on their Web site.

County-level adverse incident data reported in nursing homes and assisted living facilities are provided by the Florida Agency for Health Care Administration in their current status report to the Florida Legislature, *Nursing Home and Assisted Living Facility Adverse Incidents and Notices of Intent Filed.*

Other health issues. Statistics on HIV, AIDS, and sexually transmitted diseases are available online from the Department of Health's Division of Disease Control in *The Florida Division of Disease Control Surveillance Report.*

Section 3.00
Vital Statistics and Health

Tables listed by major heading

Tables listed by major heading

Table 3.01. BIRTH AND DEATH RATES: RESIDENT LIVE BIRTH AND DEATH RATES BY RACE IN FLORIDA AND THE UNITED STATES, 1994 THROUGH 2005

	Birth rates						Death rates					
	Total		White		Nonwhite		Total		White		Nonwhite	
Year	Florida	U.S.	Florida	U.S.	Florida	U.S.	Florida	U.S.	Florida	U.S.	Florida	U.S.
1994	13.5	15.0	12.1	14.3	20.3	18.4	10.4	8.7	11.2	9.0	6.5	7.1
1995	13.1	14.6	11.8	14.1	19.3	16.9	10.5	8.7	11.5	9.0	6.4	7.1
1996	12.9	14.4	11.7	13.9	18.8	16.7	10.4	8.6	11.5	9.0	5.8	6.8
1997	12.8	14.2	11.6	13.7	18.7	16.5	10.2	8.5	11.5	8.9	5.4	6.6
1998	12.8	14.3	11.5	13.8	18.5	16.6	10.3	8.5	11.6	8.9	5.2	6.5
1999	12.6	14.2	11.3	13.7	18.2	16.5	10.3	8.6	11.8	9.0	5.2	6.6
2000	12.7	14.4	11.4	13.9	18.7	16.6	10.1	8.5	11.6	9.0	5.0	6.5
2001	12.5	14.1	11.3	13.7	18.2	15.8	10.2	8.5	11.6	9.0	5.1	6.4
2002	12.3	13.9	11.1	13.5	17.4	15.6	10.0	8.5	11.4	9.0	5.1	6.1
2003	12.3	14.1	11.1	13.6	17.5	16.3	9.8	8.4	10.6	8.9	6.1	6.0
2004	12.4	14.0	11.1	13.5	17.8	16.2	9.6	8.2	10.4	8.6	5.9	6.1
2005	12.6	(NA)	11.4	(NA)	17.3	(NA)	9.5	(NA)	10.3	(NA)	5.8	(NA)

(NA) Not available.

Note: Rates per 1,000 population based on July 1 population estimates for noncensus years. Some data are revised; some 2004 data are preliminary. Some U.S. white and nonwhite birth and death rates are calculated by BEBR.

Source: U.S., Department of Health and Human Services, Centers for Disease Control and Prevention, National Center for Health Statistics, *National Vital Statistics Reports,* Internet site <http://www.cdc.gov/nchs/>, and State of Florida, Department of Health, Office of Vital Statistics, *Florida Vital Statistics Annual Report, 2005,* and previous editions, Internet site <http://doh.state.fl.us/> (both sites accessed 19, March 2007).

Table 3.02. BIRTHS: NUMBER OF RESIDENT LIVE BIRTHS BY AGE OF MOTHER IN FLORIDA 2000 THROUGH 2005

Age of mother	2000	2001	2002	2003	2004	2005
All ages	204,030	205,800	205,580	212,243	218,045	226,219
Less than 13	24	17	10	10	10	15
13	95	96	87	65	65	59
14	412	394	323	287	329	341
15	1,213	1,111	1,034	947	1,014	1,036
16	2,702	2,514	2,316	2,290	2,314	2,428
17	4,730	4,388	4,078	3,990	4,108	4,126
18	7,094	6,891	6,582	6,514	6,661	6,797
19	9,414	9,315	9,150	9,027	9,303	9,780
20-24	51,408	52,615	52,419	54,469	56,398	58,968
25-29	53,421	52,865	53,018	54,804	56,378	59,838
30-34	45,019	46,338	47,137	49,109	49,693	50,177
35-44	28,247	28,978	29,079	30,423	31,419	32,282
45 years and over	200	261	297	283	335	354
Age not stated	51	17	50	25	18	18
Less than 19 years, number	16,270	15,411	14,430	14,103	14,501	14,802
Percentage of total	8.0	7.5	7.0	6.6	6.7	6.5

Source: State of Florida, Department of Health, Office of Vital Statistics, Public Health Statistics Section, *Florida Vital Statistics Annual Report, 2005,* and previous editions, Internet site <http://doh.state.fl.us/> (accessed 19, March 2007).

Table 3.03. BIRTHS: NUMBER AND RATES OF RESIDENT LIVE BIRTHS BY RACE IN THE STATE AND COUNTIES OF FLORIDA, 2005

County	Number of births					Birth rate 1/		
			Nonwhite					
	Total 2/	White 3/	Total	Black	Other	Total 2/	White 3/	Non-white
Florida	226,219	166,181	59,608	47,957	11,651	12.6	11.4	17.3
Alachua	2,690	1,646	1,044	814	230	11.1	9.2	16.8
Baker	369	315	54	48	6	15.4	15.4	15.1
Bay	2,391	1,829	523	334	189	14.7	13.2	21.9
Bradford	332	277	55	50	5	11.8	12.8	8.3
Brevard	5,387	4,348	1,018	727	291	10.1	9.3	15.7
Broward	23,127	13,576	9,467	7,868	1,599	13.2	10.8	19.2
Calhoun	158	140	18	16	2	11.3	12.4	6.6
Charlotte	1,084	973	110	66	44	7.0	6.8	9.9
Citrus	1,021	945	76	32	44	7.6	7.4	13.0
Clay	2,238	1,897	339	213	126	13.1	12.6	16.6
Collier	4,069	3,514	553	458	95	12.7	11.9	22.4
Columbia	851	672	178	158	20	13.8	13.4	15.5
DeSoto	505	450	54	50	4	15.6	16.4	11.1
Dixie	170	164	6	5	1	11.0	11.8	3.9
Duval	12,974	7,597	5,368	4,449	919	15.0	13.5	17.8
Escambia	4,237	2,745	1,490	1,241	249	14.0	12.3	18.6
Flagler	689	587	102	79	23	8.6	8.4	9.9
Franklin	119	108	10	5	5	10.9	11.2	7.7
Gadsden	741	278	462	450	12	15.5	13.9	16.5
Gilchrist	194	178	16	13	3	11.9	11.8	13.1
Glades	77	58	19	12	7	7.2	6.4	11.1
Gulf	130	110	20	20	0	7.9	8.5	5.5
Hamilton	191	123	68	64	4	13.3	14.0	12.3
Hardee	456	425	31	25	6	16.7	17.4	10.8
Hendry	757	643	114	95	19	19.6	19.8	18.5
Hernando	1,496	1,313	181	116	65	9.8	9.2	18.7
Highlands	939	754	184	145	39	10.0	9.1	16.9
Hillsborough	16,753	12,602	4,134	3,132	1,002	14.7	14.0	17.4
Holmes	247	233	14	9	5	12.9	13.4	7.6
Indian River	1,360	1,138	222	191	31	10.4	9.7	16.7
Jackson	567	389	176	161	15	11.4	10.9	12.3
Jefferson	167	96	71	70	1	11.7	10.7	13.5
Lafayette	114	100	14	14	0	14.1	14.7	11.0
Lake	3,223	2,679	541	396	145	12.1	11.2	20.4
Lee	6,704	5,685	1,017	844	173	12.1	11.3	19.9

See footnotes at end of table. Continued . . .

Table 3.03. BIRTHS: NUMBER AND RATES OF RESIDENT LIVE BIRTHS BY RACE IN THE STATE AND COUNTIES OF FLORIDA, 2005 (Continued)

County	Number of births					Birth rate 1/		
			Nonwhite					
	Total 2/	White 3/	Total	Black	Other	Total 2/	White 3/	Non-white
Leon	3,105	1,676	1,426	1,222	204	11.4	9.5	14.7
Levy	462	403	59	50	9	12.1	12.0	13.0
Liberty	108	95	13	11	2	14.2	16.3	7.3
Madison	253	130	123	123	0	12.8	11.1	15.2
Manatee	3,809	3,098	710	470	240	12.4	11.3	21.5
Marion	3,449	2,651	798	616	182	11.2	9.9	19.8
Martin	1,340	1,010	329	111	218	9.4	7.7	32.9
Miami-Dade	32,365	23,334	8,865	8,107	758	13.3	12.7	15.1
Monroe	768	663	103	70	33	9.3	8.6	17.8
Nassau	812	751	60	47	13	12.3	12.4	11.0
Okaloosa	2,738	2,182	553	300	253	14.4	13.5	19.7
Okeechobee	587	535	52	36	16	15.5	15.8	13.1
Orange	16,556	11,175	5,371	4,162	1,209	15.8	14.6	18.9
Osceola	3,593	3,068	522	353	169	15.1	15.0	15.5
Palm Beach	15,160	10,562	4,583	3,788	795	11.9	10.2	19.2
Pasco	4,753	4,341	409	189	220	11.6	11.1	20.6
Pinellas	9,065	6,999	2,060	1,402	658	9.6	8.6	15.8
Polk	7,786	6,088	1,693	1,406	287	14.3	13.4	18.7
Putnam	1,034	766	268	252	16	14.0	12.7	20.0
St. Johns	1,761	1,547	214	130	84	11.1	10.5	17.6
St. Lucie	3,003	2,132	869	741	128	12.4	10.7	19.6
Santa Rosa	1,746	1,594	151	64	87	12.7	12.6	13.9
Sarasota	2,997	2,632	365	236	129	8.1	7.5	17.2
Seminole	4,786	3,787	995	659	336	11.6	10.8	16.0
Sumter	501	398	103	89	14	6.6	6.1	9.7
Suwannee	470	387	82	73	9	12.3	11.5	17.1
Taylor	244	183	60	56	4	11.4	11.0	12.5
Union	166	141	25	24	1	11.0	12.4	6.7
Volusia	5,093	4,228	861	699	162	10.2	9.7	14.4
Wakulla	288	256	32	27	5	10.6	10.8	9.1
Walton	604	545	59	36	23	11.1	11.1	11.3
Washington	249	208	41	35	6	10.7	10.7	10.8

1/ Rates per 1,000 midyear 2005 population estimates based on 2000 Census data.
2/ Unknown race included in total only.
3/ Persons designating "Hispanic" as a race were counted as white.
Note: Data are for births occurring to residents of the specified area regardless of place of occurrence.
Source: State of Florida, Department of Health, Office of Vital Statistics, Public Health Statistics Section, *Florida Vital Statistics Annual Report, 2005,* Internet site <http://doh.state.fl.us/> (accessed 19, March 2007).

Table 3.04. BIRTHS: RESIDENT LIVE BIRTHS BY HISPANIC OR HAITIAN ORIGIN OF MOTHER IN THE STATE AND COUNTIES OF FLORIDA, 2005

		Hispanic origin						Non-Hispanic/ Haitian origin	
			As a percent-age of total births	Percentage					As a percent-age of total births
County	Total births 1/	Total 2/		Mexican	Central/ South American	Cuban	Haitian origin	Total	
Florida	226,219	63,757	28.2	26.4	32.2	17.9	7,229	154,411	68.3
Alachua	2,690	192	7.1	22.4	34.9	12.5	7	2,489	92.5
Baker	369	5	1.4	80.0	0.0	20.0	0	362	98.1
Bay	2,391	157	6.6	51.6	14.6	5.7	3	2,218	92.8
Bradford	332	11	3.3	63.6	9.1	18.2	0	321	96.7
Brevard	5,387	509	9.4	26.1	27.1	8.3	32	4,827	89.6
Broward	23,127	6,847	29.6	10.4	52.9	13.1	1,939	14,270	61.7
Calhoun	158	7	4.4	71.4	0.0	0.0	0	150	94.9
Charlotte	1,084	107	9.9	30.8	18.7	9.3	16	960	88.6
Citrus	1,021	52	5.1	28.8	15.4	11.5	1	968	94.8
Clay	2,238	167	7.5	32.3	18.6	4.2	7	2,060	92.0
Collier	4,069	2,139	52.6	61.2	21.0	10.3	331	1,592	39.1
Columbia	851	38	4.5	42.1	18.4	10.5	0	813	95.5
DeSoto	505	229	45.3	92.1	4.8	0.4	0	276	54.7
Dixie	170	4	2.4	50.0	25.0	0.0	0	166	97.6
Duval	12,974	1,146	8.8	28.1	28.0	8.6	68	11,720	90.3
Escambia	4,237	202	4.8	51.0	20.8	3.0	1	4,033	95.2
Flagler	689	73	10.6	13.7	31.5	5.5	5	609	88.4
Franklin	119	9	7.6	55.6	22.2	0.0	0	109	91.6
Gadsden	741	119	16.1	75.6	19.3	0.0	0	621	83.8
Gilchrist	194	18	9.3	27.8	33.3	5.6	0	176	90.7
Glades	77	21	27.3	76.2	4.8	0.0	1	54	70.1
Gulf	130	0	0.0	0.0	0.0	0.0	0	129	99.2
Hamilton	191	35	18.3	88.6	5.7	2.9	1	154	80.6
Hardee	456	280	61.4	96.4	0.4	0.4	1	175	38.4
Hendry	757	448	59.2	75.2	4.5	5.4	0	304	40.2
Hernando	1,496	146	9.8	14.4	13.7	10.3	2	1,340	89.6
Highlands	939	264	28.1	70.5	3.4	2.7	3	670	71.4
Hillsborough	16,753	5,141	30.7	37.9	17.6	12.4	132	11,197	66.8
Holmes	247	6	2.4	50.0	0.0	16.7	0	241	97.6
Indian River	1,360	320	23.5	79.1	11.9	4.1	22	1,018	74.9
Jackson	567	21	3.7	61.9	4.8	9.5	0	545	96.1
Jefferson	167	8	4.8	75.0	0.0	25.0	0	159	95.2
Lafayette	114	13	11.4	100.0	0.0	0.0	0	101	88.6
Lake	3,223	684	21.2	55.1	14.0	4.5	13	2,524	78.3
Lee	6,704	2,157	32.2	45.1	23.1	8.3	218	4,323	64.5

See footnotes at end of table. Continued . . .

Table 3.04. BIRTHS: RESIDENT LIVE BIRTHS BY HISPANIC OR HAITIAN ORIGIN OF MOTHER IN THE STATE AND COUNTIES OF FLORIDA, 2005 (Continued)

		Hispanic origin						Non-Hispanic/ Haitian origin	
			As a percent-age of total births	Percentage					As a percent-age of total births
County	Total births 1/	Total 2/		Mexican	Central/ South American	Cuban	Haitian origin	Total	
Leon	3,105	134	4.3	32.8	22.4	9.7	17	2,954	95.1
Levy	462	39	8.4	53.8	15.4	12.8	1	422	91.3
Liberty	108	5	4.6	80.0	0.0	0.0	0	103	95.4
Madison	253	19	7.5	42.1	31.6	15.8	2	232	91.7
Manatee	3,809	1,276	33.5	73.8	15.7	2.4	53	2,479	65.1
Marion	3,449	503	14.6	40.0	7.8	3.6	7	2,936	85.1
Martin	1,340	282	21.0	61.7	22.0	1.8	13	1,045	78.0
Miami-Dade	32,365	20,433	63.1	6.1	42.1	38.8	1,740	10,081	31.1
Monroe	768	227	29.6	18.1	31.3	40.1	26	509	66.3
Nassau	812	26	3.2	53.8	11.5	3.8	0	783	96.4
Okaloosa	2,738	335	12.2	53.7	18.8	3.3	0	2,399	87.6
Okeechobee	587	200	34.1	89.0	4.0	1.0	1	386	65.8
Orange	16,556	5,086	30.7	19.9	26.7	4.2	763	10,673	64.5
Osceola	3,593	1,750	48.7	11.8	22.9	3.3	41	1,801	50.1
Palm Beach	15,160	4,552	30.0	27.7	48.4	9.6	1,406	9,170	60.5
Pasco	4,753	701	14.7	41.5	15.4	7.7	6	3,954	83.2
Pinellas	9,065	1,182	13.0	52.3	9.6	5.2	10	7,855	86.7
Polk	7,786	1,947	25.0	67.9	6.7	2.3	119	5,712	73.4
Putnam	1,034	169	16.3	69.8	3.6	1.8	1	864	83.6
St. Johns	1,761	100	5.7	26.0	22.0	10.0	3	1,655	94.0
St. Lucie	3,003	704	23.4	54.4	25.6	4.4	165	2,133	71.0
Santa Rosa	1,746	93	5.3	57.0	17.2	4.3	0	1,653	94.7
Sarasota	2,997	497	16.6	56.7	22.1	6.8	17	2,481	82.8
Seminole	4,786	894	18.7	17.3	27.5	4.6	19	3,867	80.8
Sumter	501	72	14.4	90.3	0.0	1.4	1	428	85.4
Suwannee	470	64	13.6	70.3	21.9	4.7	0	406	86.4
Taylor	244	4	1.6	0.0	50.0	25.0	0	239	98.0
Union	166	5	3.0	80.0	0.0	0.0	0	161	97.0
Volusia	5,093	820	16.1	39.9	14.0	4.1	15	4,245	83.3
Wakulla	288	3	1.0	0.0	0.0	0.0	0	285	99.0
Walton	604	46	7.6	76.1	8.7	4.3	0	556	92.1
Washington	249	4	1.6	25.0	0.0	0.0	0	245	98.4

1/ Unknown origin included in total only.
2/ Includes Puerto Rican, other, and unknown Hispanic origin.
Note: Data are for births occurring to residents of the specified area regardless of place of occurrence.

Source: State of Florida, Department of Health, Office of Vital Statistics, Public Health Statistics Section, *Florida Vital Statistics Annual Report, 2005,* Internet site <http://doh.state.fl.us/> (accessed 19, March 2007).

Table 3.05. BIRTHS: RESIDENT LIVE BIRTHS BY RACE AND BY MOTHER'S HIGHEST LEVEL OR DEGREE OF EDUCATION COMPLETED IN THE STATE AND COUNTIES OF FLORIDA, 2005

County	White births 1/				Nonwhite births			
		Education of mother (percentage)				Education of mother (percentage)		
	Total 2/	High school or less	Undergraduate college	Graduate school	Total 2/	High school or less	Undergraduate college	Graduate school
Florida	166,181	49.8	42.8	6.7	60,038	59.6	34.2	4.2
Alachua	1,646	23.1	55.8	21.0	1,044	52.8	37.5	9.8
Baker	315	62.2	37.5	0.3	54	77.8	20.4	0.0
Bay	1,829	50.5	44.0	4.8	562	56.6	39.0	2.8
Bradford	277	65.7	32.9	1.4	55	70.9	29.1	0.0
Brevard	4,348	39.7	54.1	5.7	1,039	54.7	40.5	4.3
Broward	13,576	36.4	50.0	10.4	9,551	49.8	36.9	5.2
Calhoun	140	64.3	32.9	2.9	18	72.2	27.8	0.0
Charlotte	973	54.7	42.3	2.9	111	55.9	41.4	2.7
Citrus	945	65.3	32.1	2.3	76	50.0	47.4	1.3
Clay	1,897	48.6	45.6	5.4	341	47.8	43.4	7.9
Collier	3,514	68.0	27.6	4.3	555	75.0	21.8	3.1
Columbia	672	58.3	37.5	4.0	179	66.5	32.4	1.1
DeSoto	450	87.3	10.9	1.6	55	74.5	25.5	0.0
Dixie	164	67.7	31.1	0.6	6	100.0	0.0	0.0
Duval	7,597	46.0	46.2	6.9	5,377	58.8	35.7	3.8
Escambia	2,745	52.2	42.2	5.5	1,492	73.8	23.6	2.4
Flagler	587	42.4	51.6	6.0	102	56.9	39.2	3.9
Franklin	108	77.8	19.4	1.9	11	72.7	27.3	0.0
Gadsden	278	65.5	30.2	4.3	463	68.0	29.4	1.9
Gilchrist	178	65.2	32.6	2.2	16	62.5	37.5	0.0
Glades	58	75.9	24.1	0.0	19	78.9	21.1	0.0
Gulf	110	52.7	42.7	3.6	20	55.0	45.0	0.0
Hamilton	123	70.7	27.6	0.8	68	86.8	13.2	0.0
Hardee	425	78.4	20.0	1.6	31	87.1	12.9	0.0
Hendry	643	85.2	13.5	0.9	114	78.1	21.9	0.0
Hernando	1,313	56.9	34.1	2.5	183	65.0	25.7	3.8
Highlands	754	66.8	29.6	3.4	185	71.9	27.6	0.5
Hillsborough	12,602	49.3	42.6	7.3	4,151	53.1	39.7	6.2
Holmes	233	64.8	32.2	2.6	14	64.3	35.7	0.0
Indian River	1,138	57.5	37.2	5.4	222	73.0	24.8	2.3
Jackson	389	57.3	39.3	3.1	178	61.2	37.6	1.1
Jefferson	96	50.0	44.8	4.2	71	69.0	29.6	0.0
Lafayette	100	70.0	30.0	0.0	14	78.6	21.4	0.0
Lake	2,679	54.7	41.5	3.6	544	64.5	32.0	3.1
Lee	5,685	60.7	35.5	3.7	1,019	74.9	23.7	1.0

See footnotes at end of table.

Continued . . .

Table 3.05. BIRTHS: RESIDENT LIVE BIRTHS BY RACE AND BY MOTHER'S HIGHEST LEVEL OR DEGREE OF EDUCATION COMPLETED IN THE STATE AND COUNTIES OF FLORIDA, 2005 (Continued)

	White births 1/				Nonwhite births			
		Education of mother (percentage)				Education of mother (percentage)		
County	Total 2/	High school or less	Undergraduate college	Graduate school	Total 2/	High school or less	Undergraduate college	Graduate school
Leon	1,676	25.4	58.1	16.2	1,429	40.8	50.3	8.4
Levy	403	65.3	33.0	1.7	59	71.2	28.8	0.0
Liberty	95	54.7	41.1	4.2	13	69.2	30.8	0.0
Madison	130	56.2	39.2	4.6	123	73.2	26.8	0.0
Manatee	3,098	61.9	33.3	4.6	711	71.3	26.7	1.8
Marion	2,651	60.8	35.9	3.1	798	66.3	32.2	1.5
Martin	1,010	45.8	45.8	8.1	330	80.6	16.7	2.7
Miami-Dade	23,334	49.8	41.2	8.6	9,031	66.1	29.7	3.4
Monroe	663	45.4	49.5	4.7	105	57.1	39.0	1.0
Nassau	751	54.3	40.5	4.8	61	77.0	19.7	3.3
Okaloosa	2,182	48.6	46.6	4.6	556	55.6	42.1	2.2
Okeechobee	535	74.8	23.6	1.5	52	75.0	23.1	0.0
Orange	11,175	46.7	46.2	6.9	5,381	58.5	36.5	4.5
Osceola	3,068	58.8	38.4	2.7	525	52.2	44.6	3.2
Palm Beach	10,562	44.2	46.1	8.9	4,598	200.6	32.4	4.3
Pasco	4,341	48.6	45.1	5.4	412	44.4	46.8	8.3
Pinellas	6,999	45.5	46.4	7.2	2,066	61.3	32.5	3.7
Polk	6,088	65.6	32.3	2.0	1,698	70.3	27.3	2.2
Putnam	766	74.0	23.8	1.6	268	80.2	19.4	0.4
St. Johns	1,547	30.0	58.1	11.6	214	48.6	39.7	11.2
St. Lucie	2,132	62.2	35.2	2.6	871	72.3	24.1	3.3
Santa Rosa	1,594	45.0	48.6	6.4	152	49.3	46.1	4.6
Sarasota	2,632	48.2	44.6	7.1	365	60.0	37.5	2.5
Seminole	3,787	36.0	54.8	8.9	999	47.1	44.2	8.1
Sumter	398	69.8	27.6	1.8	103	77.7	20.4	1.9
Suwannee	387	73.4	25.1	1.6	83	91.6	8.4	0.0
Taylor	183	65.0	31.7	2.7	61	85.2	14.8	0.0
Union	141	58.2	38.3	3.5	25	76.0	20.0	0.0
Volusia	4,228	51.3	44.2	4.3	865	56.3	40.7	2.5
Wakulla	256	55.1	42.2	2.3	32	53.1	40.6	6.3
Walton	545	57.2	38.3	3.9	59	72.9	22.0	3.4
Washington	208	62.0	33.2	4.3	41	68.3	29.3	0.0

1/ Persons designating "Hispanic" as a race were counted as white.
2/ Unknown race included in total only.
Note: Data are for births occurring to residents of the specified area regardless of place of occurrence.

Source: State of Florida, Department of Health, Office of Vital Statistics, Public Health Statistics Section, *Florida Vital Statistics Annual Report, 2005,* Internet site <http://doh.state.fl.us/> (accessed 19, March 2007).

Table 3.06. TEENAGE BIRTHS: RESIDENT LIVE BIRTHS TO MOTHERS UNDER AGE 20 BY RACE IN THE STATE AND COUNTIES OF FLORIDA, 2005

County	Total 1/	White			Nonwhite		
		Number	Percent-age of total teenage births	As a per-centage of all white births	Number	Percent-age of total teenage births	As a per-centage of all nonwhite births
Florida	24,582	15,816	64.3	9.5	8,766	35.7	14.6
Alachua	239	91	38.1	5.5	148	61.9	14.2
Baker	62	48	77.4	15.2	14	22.6	25.9
Bay	317	220	69.4	12.0	97	30.6	17.3
Bradford	60	48	80.0	17.3	12	20.0	21.8
Brevard	568	414	72.9	9.5	154	27.1	14.8
Broward	1,767	667	37.7	4.9	1,100	62.3	11.5
Calhoun	35	30	85.7	21.4	5	14.3	27.8
Charlotte	123	114	92.7	11.7	9	7.3	8.1
Citrus	152	141	92.8	14.9	11	7.2	14.5
Clay	252	214	84.9	11.3	38	15.1	11.1
Collier	454	394	86.8	11.2	60	13.2	10.8
Columbia	124	85	68.5	12.6	39	31.5	21.8
DeSoto	98	85	86.7	18.9	13	13.3	23.6
Dixie	29	27	93.1	16.5	2	6.9	33.3
Duval	1,502	640	42.6	8.4	862	57.4	16.0
Escambia	597	295	49.4	10.7	302	50.6	20.2
Flagler	57	38	66.7	6.5	19	33.3	18.6
Franklin	25	24	96.0	22.2	1	4.0	9.1
Gadsden	123	32	26.0	11.5	91	74.0	19.7
Gilchrist	39	36	92.3	20.2	3	7.7	18.8
Glades	15	13	86.7	22.4	2	13.3	10.5
Gulf	13	9	69.2	8.2	4	30.8	20.0
Hamilton	42	23	54.8	18.7	19	45.2	27.9
Hardee	86	79	91.9	18.6	7	8.1	22.6
Hendry	128	111	86.7	17.3	17	13.3	14.9
Hernando	177	160	90.4	12.2	17	9.6	9.3
Highlands	143	104	72.7	13.8	39	27.3	21.1
Hillsborough	1,889	1,312	69.5	10.4	577	30.5	13.9
Holmes	49	43	87.8	18.5	6	12.2	42.9
Indian River	161	118	73.3	10.4	43	26.7	19.4
Jackson	75	48	64.0	12.3	27	36.0	15.2
Jefferson	24	12	50.0	12.5	12	50.0	16.9
Lafayette	16	14	87.5	14.0	2	12.5	14.3
Lake	410	318	77.6	11.9	92	22.4	16.9
Lee	833	660	79.2	11.6	173	20.8	17.0

See footnotes at end of table.

Continued . . .

Table 3.06. TEENAGE BIRTHS: RESIDENT LIVE BIRTHS TO MOTHERS UNDER AGE 20 BY RACE IN THE STATE AND COUNTIES OF FLORIDA, 2005 (Continued)

		White			Nonwhite		
County	Total 1/	Number	Percent-age of total teenage births	As a per-centage of all white births	Number	Percent-age of total teenage births	As a per-centage of all nonwhite births
Leon	293	104	35.5	6.2	189	64.5	13.2
Levy	74	63	85.1	15.6	11	14.9	18.6
Liberty	20	17	85.0	17.9	3	15.0	23.1
Madison	49	20	40.8	15.4	29	59.2	23.6
Manatee	497	380	76.5	12.3	117	23.5	16.5
Marion	555	389	70.1	14.7	166	29.9	20.8
Martin	154	89	57.8	8.8	65	42.2	19.7
Miami-Dade	3,002	1,704	56.8	7.3	1,298	43.2	14.4
Monroe	53	47	88.7	7.1	6	11.3	5.7
Nassau	122	107	87.7	14.2	15	12.3	24.6
Okaloosa	277	201	72.6	9.2	76	27.4	13.7
Okeechobee	106	96	90.6	17.9	10	9.4	19.2
Orange	1,709	997	58.3	8.9	712	41.7	13.2
Osceola	422	363	86.0	11.8	59	14.0	11.2
Palm Beach	1,379	777	56.3	7.4	602	43.7	13.1
Pasco	478	438	91.6	10.1	40	8.4	9.7
Pinellas	973	593	60.9	8.5	380	39.1	18.4
Polk	1,163	859	73.9	14.1	304	26.1	17.9
Putnam	195	139	71.3	18.1	56	28.7	20.9
St. Johns	143	113	79.0	7.3	30	21.0	14.0
St. Lucie	397	242	61.0	11.4	155	39.0	17.8
Santa Rosa	181	166	91.7	10.4	15	8.3	9.9
Sarasota	287	213	74.2	8.1	74	25.8	20.3
Seminole	378	256	67.7	6.8	122	32.3	12.2
Sumter	71	55	77.5	13.8	16	22.5	15.5
Suwannee	87	71	81.6	18.3	16	18.4	19.3
Taylor	50	33	66.0	18.0	17	34.0	27.9
Union	18	9	50.0	6.4	9	50.0	36.0
Volusia	607	478	78.7	11.3	129	21.3	14.9
Wakulla	43	33	76.7	12.9	10	23.3	31.3
Walton	76	71	93.4	13.0	5	6.6	8.5
Washington	35	24	68.6	11.5	11	31.4	26.8

1/ Unknown race included in total only.
Note: Persons designating "Hispanic" as a race were counted as white.

Source: State of Florida, Department of Health, Office of Vital Statistics, Public Health Statistics Section, *Florida Vital Statistics Annual Report, 2005,* Internet site <http://doh.state.fl.us/> (accessed 19, March 2007).

Table 3.07. TEENAGE BIRTHS: RESIDENT LIVE BIRTHS TO MOTHERS AGED 15 THROUGH 19 BY SPECIFIED CHARACTERISTIC IN THE STATE AND COUNTIES OF FLORIDA, 2005

		Percentage–					
			Birthweight				
County	Total	Unwed	Under 1,500 grams	Under 2,500 grams	No prenatal care 1/	One or more previous births	Birth rate 2/
Florida	24,167	85.9	1.9	10.7	7.6	18.6	41.9
Alachua	236	89.4	3.0	14.0	3.0	19.1	19.4
Baker	62	69.4	6.5	16.1	3.2	25.8	72.1
Bay	310	80.0	2.6	10.0	9.0	21.0	64.4
Bradford	60	75.0	0.0	18.3	1.7	26.7	73.1
Brevard	560	87.5	1.1	13.6	5.4	16.3	32.8
Broward	1,741	90.3	2.1	12.3	10.3	15.7	32.5
Calhoun	35	77.1	2.9	22.9	5.7	20.0	78.3
Charlotte	122	86.9	1.6	6.6	13.1	15.6	33.9
Citrus	152	81.6	0.7	9.2	4.6	15.8	45.6
Clay	251	75.7	1.2	7.6	5.2	12.0	37.5
Collier	445	80.9	1.3	9.2	9.9	21.8	53.0
Columbia	122	80.3	1.6	8.2	7.4	23.0	59.3
DeSoto	95	72.6	0.0	7.4	9.5	16.8	95.8
Dixie	28	67.9	3.6	7.1	7.1	14.3	59.1
Duval	1,479	85.9	2.1	10.5	5.5	19.5	49.5
Escambia	586	88.2	2.7	12.8	10.8	21.3	48.4
Flagler	55	76.4	1.8	5.5	0.0	9.1	24.4
Franklin	25	68.0	12.0	16.0	8.0	32.0	76.2
Gadsden	117	90.6	2.6	13.7	2.6	19.7	69.5
Gilchrist	38	84.2	0.0	2.6	5.3	31.6	70.4
Glades	15	86.7	0.0	0.0	13.3	20.0	47.5
Gulf	13	76.9	15.4	15.4	0.0	0.0	27.3
Hamilton	41	80.5	0.0	14.6	4.9	9.8	96.7
Hardee	85	71.8	0.0	8.2	16.5	25.9	91.6
Hendry	125	76.8	0.8	4.8	15.2	20.0	81.4
Hernando	175	85.1	1.1	6.9	7.4	18.9	42.6
Highlands	139	89.9	2.9	10.1	5.8	19.4	58.1
Hillsborough	1,856	88.0	2.0	11.3	6.1	20.6	47.4
Holmes	49	75.5	0.0	10.2	16.3	24.5	78.7
Indian River	153	79.1	0.7	11.1	12.4	16.3	43.0
Jackson	75	88.0	1.3	9.3	2.7	16.0	53.9
Jefferson	23	82.6	0.0	13.0	0.0	26.1	49.1
Lafayette	16	81.3	0.0	6.3	6.3	18.8	78.4
Lake	408	84.6	1.5	9.6	6.1	17.6	57.2

See footnotes at end of table.

Continued . . .

Table 3.07. TEENAGE BIRTHS: RESIDENT LIVE BIRTHS TO MOTHERS AGED 15 THROUGH 19 BY SPECIFIED CHARACTERISTIC IN THE STATE AND COUNTIES OF FLORIDA, 2005 (Continued)

		Percentage–					
			Birthweight				
County	Total	Unwed	Under 1,500 grams	Under 2,500 grams	No prenatal care 1/	One or more previous births	Birth rate 2/
Lee	819	84.7	1.5	10.1	8.5	22.7	54.9
Leon	290	88.6	4.1	10.7	3.8	16.9	19.9
Levy	73	78.1	1.4	6.8	5.5	19.2	56.1
Liberty	20	80.0	0.0	15.0	0.0	30.0	88.1
Madison	45	86.7	6.7	11.1	2.2	15.6	61.3
Manatee	489	86.3	2.5	10.4	10.8	24.3	58.0
Marion	545	85.5	2.0	11.0	7.0	16.1	58.3
Martin	153	84.3	0.7	8.5	21.6	17.0	42.8
Miami-Dade	2,945	88.4	2.2	11.8	6.0	16.7	35.0
Monroe	52	88.5	1.9	5.8	7.7	5.8	25.3
Nassau	122	79.5	0.8	9.0	1.6	18.0	53.2
Okaloosa	273	73.3	1.5	7.7	11.7	15.4	44.6
Okeechobee	100	90.0	0.0	6.0	4.0	20.0	80.9
Orange	1,672	87.0	1.7	11.7	5.4	18.1	44.9
Osceola	419	85.2	2.1	8.1	6.2	16.0	47.6
Palm Beach	1,351	88.8	1.8	11.0	13.0	21.7	36.4
Pasco	473	87.3	3.0	10.4	6.8	16.7	41.7
Pinellas	959	90.2	1.6	10.2	5.4	17.2	37.6
Polk	1,140	82.7	2.0	10.1	11.3	22.3	65.4
Putnam	188	82.4	2.7	11.7	3.2	21.8	75.9
St. Johns	141	80.1	0.0	1.4	7.1	18.4	27.5
St. Lucie	387	86.8	1.3	8.8	8.0	21.4	50.1
Santa Rosa	180	71.7	1.1	11.1	6.1	15.6	36.7
Sarasota	282	86.9	1.1	6.0	6.7	14.9	34.2
Seminole	376	87.8	2.9	9.3	7.7	15.2	27.4
Sumter	70	80.0	0.0	10.0	2.9	27.1	43.8
Suwannee	86	69.8	0.0	7.0	9.3	23.3	73.3
Taylor	49	75.5	4.1	22.4	4.1	24.5	71.0
Union	18	77.8	0.0	16.7	16.7	5.6	42.4
Volusia	602	84.2	1.5	9.1	6.5	15.3	38.6
Wakulla	42	78.6	4.8	7.1	2.4	14.3	45.0
Walton	76	69.7	2.6	10.5	14.5	9.2	46.8
Washington	34	73.5	5.9	14.7	8.8	14.7	46.8

1/ Third trimester or no prenatal care.
2/ Births to females aged 15-19 per 1,000 population.

Source: State of Florida, Department of Health, Office of Vital Statistics, Public Health Statistics Section, *Florida Vital Statistics Annual Report, 2005,* Internet site <http://doh.state.fl.us/> (accessed 19, March 2007).

Table 3.08. INFANT DEATHS: NUMBER AND RATE OF RESIDENT INFANT DEATHS BY RACE IN FLORIDA, 1991 THROUGH 2005

Year	Number of deaths			Mortality rate per 1,000 live births			
	Total 1/	White 2/	Non-white	Total 1/	White 2/	Non-white	United States
1991	1,726	966	758	8.9	6.7	15.6	8.9
1992	1,685	987	695	8.8	6.9	14.4	8.5
1993	1,654	951	699	8.6	6.6	14.5	8.4
1994	1,540	927	611	8.1	6.5	12.9	8.0
1995	1,402	840	562	7.4	5.9	12.1	7.6
1996	1,405	821	583	7.4	5.8	12.4	7.3
1997	1,358	805	552	7.1	5.6	11.4	7.2
1998	1,415	850	562	7.2	5.8	11.4	7.2
1999	1,442	815	625	7.3	5.6	12.4	7.1
2000	1,423	810	611	7.0	5.4	11.4	6.9
2001	1,495	839	655	7.3	5.5	12.3	6.8
2002	1,548	892	656	7.5	5.9	12.4	7.0
2003	1,584	907	674	7.5	5.8	12.4	6.9
2004	1,536	876	659	7.0	5.5	11.5	6.8
2005	1,626	882	743	7.2	5.3	12.5	6.8

1/ Unknown race included in total only.
2/ Persons designating "Hispanic" as a race were counted as white.
Note: Infants are considered to be less than one year. Some data may be revised.

Table 3.09. ABORTIONS: REPORTED TERMINATIONS OF PREGNANCY IN FLORIDA 1991 THROUGH 2005

Year	Induced abortions 2/	Resident live births	Total known pregnancies 1/		Abortion rate per 100 pregnancies
			Number	Rate per 100 women aged 15-44	
1991	71,254	193,717	266,663	9.6	26.7
1992	69,285	191,530	262,313	9.3	26.4
1993	70,069	192,453	263,969	9.3	26.5
1994	73,394	190,546	265,459	9.3	27.6
1995	74,749	188,535	264,815	9.0	28.2
1996	80,040	189,338	270,856	9.3	29.6
1997	81,692	192,304	275,519	9.3	29.7
1998	82,335	195,564	279,419	9.4	29.5
1999	83,971	196,963	282,513	9.4	29.7
2000	88,563	204,030	294,268	9.1	30.1
2001	85,589	205,800	293,057	9.1	29.2
2002	87,964	205,580	295,135	8.8	29.8
2003	88,247	212,243	302,094	9.0	29.2
2004	91,710	218,045	309,755	9.1	29.6
2005	92,513	226,219	320,382	9.2	28.9

1/ Includes induced abortions, total resident births, and total reported resident fetal deaths.
2/ Abortions have been legal in Florida since April 1972.
Note: Some data may be revised.

Source for Tables 3.08 and 3.09: State of Florida, Department of Health, Office of Vital Statistics, Public Health Statistics Section, *Florida Vital Statistics Annual Report, 2005,* and previous editions, Internet site <http://doh.state.fl.us/> (accessed 19, March 2007).

Table 3.10. ABORTIONS: REPORTED TERMINATIONS OF PREGNANCY IN THE STATE AND COUNTIES OF FLORIDA, 1999 THROUGH 2005

County	1999	2000	2001	2002	2003	2004	2005 Number	2005 Rate 1/
Florida	83,971	88,563	85,589	87,964	88,247	91,710	92,513	265.8
Alachua	2,161	2,215	2,090	1,998	2,151	2,075	1,945	298.9
Brevard	1,115	1,243	1,135	910	937	885	534	57.0
Broward	11,207	13,190	13,193	14,017	14,636	15,469	14,623	407.4
Charlotte	262	275	246	265	298	342	355	180.2
Citrus	0	0	0	5	1	11	10	5.7
Duval	6,269	7,069	5,200	7,812	7,989	8,391	8,021	418.9
Escambia	2,470	2,456	2,486	2,503	2,673	2,501	2,608	410.8
Hillsborough	6,544	7,459	7,360	7,376	8,028	7,958	7,920	321.6
Jackson	0	2	2	3	3	1	0	0.0
Lee	2,063	2,228	2,187	2,308	2,404	2,640	2,629	300.0
Leon	2,682	2,492	2,303	2,098	1,713	2,041	2,292	304.4
Marion	573	528	530	524	489	518	564	111.5
Martin	0	2	6	1	4	8	0	0.0
Miami-Dade	22,343	23,061	22,272	22,240	21,341	21,505	22,939	438.5
Orange	9,341	9,303	8,554	8,366	8,873	8,627	9,507	393.0
Palm Beach	6,341	6,268	6,460	6,113	5,662	5,859	5,334	238.1
Pinellas	3,954	4,105	4,353	4,186	4,403	4,962	4,683	279.7
Polk	1,244	1,200	1,150	1,089	1,025	1,376	1,482	147.9
St. Lucie	835	576	503	724	782	920	1,047	254.6
Sarasota	1,914	1,969	2,244	2,181	1,262	2,023	2,343	467.8
Seminole	735	919	1,413	1,329	1,688	1,718	2,061	231.5
Volusia	1,918	2,003	1,902	1,916	1,885	1,880	1,616	185.3

1/ Rate per 10,000 female population aged 15-44, April 1, 2005.
Note: Only counties reporting induced terminations of pregnancy are shown.

Source: State of Florida, Department of Health, Office of Vital Statistics, Public Health Statistics Section, *Florida Vital Statistics Annual Report, 2005,* and previous editions, Internet site <http://doh.state.fl.us/> (accessed 19, March 2007).

Table 3.11. BIRTHS TO UNWED MOTHERS: RESIDENT LIVE BIRTHS AND BIRTHS TO UNWED MOTHERS BY AGE AND RACE OF THE MOTHER IN THE STATE AND COUNTIES OF FLORIDA, 2005

		Births to unwed mothers					
			Percent-	Age of mother		Race of mother	
County	Total births	Number 1/	age of total	Under 20	20 and over	White 2/	Non-white
Florida	226,219	96,895	42.8	21,159	75,729	60,665	36,230
Alachua	2,690	1,085	40.3	214	871	408	677
Baker	369	151	40.9	43	108	107	44
Bay	2,391	1,004	42.0	255	749	687	317
Bradford	332	154	46.4	45	109	114	40
Brevard	5,387	2,195	40.7	498	1,697	1,558	637
Broward	23,127	8,986	38.9	1,598	7,386	3,766	5,220
Calhoun	158	70	44.3	27	43	58	12
Charlotte	1,084	458	42.3	107	351	399	59
Citrus	1,021	481	47.1	124	357	440	41
Clay	2,238	689	30.8	191	498	553	136
Collier	4,069	1,776	43.6	369	1,407	1,507	269
Columbia	851	380	44.7	99	281	250	130
DeSoto	505	269	53.3	72	197	227	42
Dixie	170	74	43.5	20	54	70	4
Duval	12,974	5,746	44.3	1,293	4,452	2,375	3,371
Escambia	4,237	1,979	46.7	527	1,452	938	1,041
Flagler	689	245	35.6	44	201	184	61
Franklin	119	58	48.7	17	41	48	10
Gadsden	741	480	64.8	112	368	104	376
Gilchrist	194	85	43.8	33	52	77	8
Glades	77	41	53.2	13	28	26	15
Gulf	130	52	40.0	10	42	36	16
Hamilton	191	96	50.3	34	62	41	55
Hardee	456	230	50.4	62	168	208	22
Hendry	757	440	58.1	99	341	353	87
Hernando	1,496	626	41.8	151	475	529	97
Highlands	939	480	51.1	129	351	347	133
Hillsborough	16,753	7,276	43.4	1,666	5,610	4,806	2,470
Holmes	247	98	39.7	37	61	90	8
Indian River	1,360	561	41.3	129	432	406	155
Jackson	567	276	48.7	66	210	145	131
Jefferson	167	80	47.9	20	60	21	59
Lafayette	114	49	43.0	13	36	40	9
Lake	3,223	1,314	40.8	347	967	987	327

See footnotes at end of table.

Continued . . .

Table 3.11. BIRTHS TO UNWED MOTHERS: RESIDENT LIVE BIRTHS AND BIRTHS TO UNWED MOTHERS BY AGE AND RACE OF THE MOTHER IN THE STATE AND COUNTIES OF FLORIDA, 2005 (Continued)

		Births to unwed mothers					
			Percent-	Age of mother		Race of mother	
	Total	Num-	age of	Under	20 and	White	Non-
County	births	ber 1/	total	20	over	2/	white
Lee	6,704	3,067	45.7	708	2,359	2,419	648
Leon	3,105	1,301	41.9	260	1,041	370	931
Levy	462	205	44.4	58	147	161	44
Liberty	108	54	50.0	16	38	42	12
Madison	253	149	58.9	43	106	48	101
Manatee	3,809	1,856	48.7	430	1,426	1,385	471
Marion	3,449	1,762	51.1	476	1,285	1,215	547
Martin	1,340	554	41.3	130	424	355	199
Miami-Dade	32,365	14,691	45.4	2,657	12,033	8,781	5,910
Monroe	768	279	36.3	47	232	225	54
Nassau	812	292	36.0	97	195	252	40
Okaloosa	2,738	925	33.8	204	721	670	255
Okeechobee	587	301	51.3	95	206	267	34
Orange	16,556	7,113	43.0	1,492	5,620	4,124	2,989
Osceola	3,593	1,587	44.2	360	1,227	1,338	249
Palm Beach	15,160	6,154	40.6	1,228	4,925	3,608	2,546
Pasco	4,753	1,737	36.5	417	1,320	1,584	153
Pinellas	9,065	4,005	44.2	879	3,126	2,658	1,347
Polk	7,786	3,792	48.7	965	2,827	2,640	1,152
Putnam	1,034	596	57.6	162	434	383	213
St. Johns	1,761	459	26.1	115	344	349	110
St. Lucie	3,003	1,341	44.7	346	995	838	503
Santa Rosa	1,746	496	28.4	130	366	445	51
Sarasota	2,997	1,153	38.5	250	903	928	225
Seminole	4,786	1,630	34.1	332	1,298	1,130	500
Sumter	501	244	48.7	57	187	167	77
Suwannee	470	229	48.7	61	168	169	60
Taylor	244	136	55.7	38	98	82	54
Union	166	69	41.6	14	55	51	18
Volusia	5,093	2,268	44.5	512	1,756	1,705	563
Wakulla	288	121	42.0	34	87	97	24
Walton	604	228	37.7	53	175	190	38
Washington	249	102	41.0	26	76	73	29

1/ Includes data for mothers whose age was not stated.
2/ Persons designating "Hispanic" as a race were counted as white.
Note: Totals may include "unknown."

Source: State of Florida, Department of Health, Office of Vital Statistics, Public Health Statistics Section, *Florida Vital Statistics Annual Report, 2005,* Internet site <http://doh.state.fl.us/> (accessed 19, March 2007).

Table 3.15. DEATHS: RESIDENT DEATH RATES BY RACE IN THE STATE AND COUNTIES OF FLORIDA, 2005

County	Number of deaths					Death rate 1/		
			Nonwhite					
	Total 2/	White 3/	Total	Black	Other	Total 2/	White 3/	Non-white
Florida	170,300	150,102	20,103	18,004	2,099	9.5	10.3	5.8
Alachua	1,554	1,222	331	308	23	6.4	6.8	5.3
Baker	197	176	21	18	3	8.2	8.6	5.9
Bay	1,514	1,365	149	125	24	9.3	9.8	6.2
Bradford	267	225	42	42	0	9.5	10.4	6.4
Brevard	5,685	5,253	431	366	65	10.6	11.2	6.6
Broward	15,711	13,394	2,312	2,051	261	9.0	10.7	4.7
Calhoun	147	130	17	16	1	10.5	11.5	6.2
Charlotte	2,155	2,081	73	63	10	14.0	14.6	6.6
Citrus	2,184	2,141	41	28	13	16.4	16.8	7.0
Clay	1,335	1,246	89	65	24	7.8	8.3	4.4
Collier	2,618	2,547	68	56	12	8.2	8.6	2.8
Columbia	603	510	93	89	4	9.8	10.1	8.1
DeSoto	291	244	46	43	3	9.0	8.9	9.4
Dixie	170	159	11	8	3	11.0	11.4	7.1
Duval	6,969	5,066	1,901	1,763	138	8.0	9.0	6.3
Escambia	2,890	2,301	586	522	64	9.5	10.3	7.3
Flagler	765	694	71	57	14	9.5	9.9	6.9
Franklin	115	108	7	7	0	10.5	11.2	5.4
Gadsden	437	207	230	221	9	9.1	10.4	8.2
Gilchrist	155	148	7	6	1	9.5	9.8	5.8
Glades	110	100	10	8	2	10.2	11.1	5.8
Gulf	125	100	25	23	2	7.6	7.8	6.8
Hamilton	131	93	38	38	0	9.1	10.6	6.9
Hardee	199	181	16	15	1	7.3	7.4	5.6
Hendry	299	249	50	45	5	7.7	7.7	8.1
Hernando	2,192	2,128	64	57	7	14.4	14.9	6.6
Highlands	1,417	1,321	95	73	22	15.1	15.9	8.7
Hillsborough	8,944	7,600	1,340	1,224	116	7.9	8.4	5.6
Holmes	215	209	6	5	1	11.2	12.0	3.3
Indian River	1,616	1,513	100	95	5	12.4	12.9	7.5
Jackson	504	375	129	125	4	10.1	10.5	9.0
Jefferson	135	80	53	52	1	9.5	8.9	10.1
Lafayette	65	64	1	1	0	8.1	9.4	0.8
Lake	3,252	3,017	232	204	28	12.2	12.6	8.7
Lee	5,736	5,430	302	262	40	10.3	10.8	5.9

See footnotes at end of table.

Continued . . .

Table 3.15. DEATHS: RESIDENT DEATH RATES BY RACE IN THE STATE AND COUNTIES OF FLORIDA, 2005 (Continued)

County	Number of deaths					Death rate 1/		
			Nonwhite					
	Total 2/	White 3/	Total	Black	Other	Total 2/	White 3/	Non-white
Leon	1,535	1,150	385	373	12	5.6	6.5	4.0
Levy	473	427	46	42	4	12.4	12.7	10.2
Liberty	66	52	14	13	1	8.7	8.9	7.8
Madison	221	137	84	81	3	11.2	11.7	10.4
Manatee	3,335	3,126	207	190	17	10.9	11.4	6.3
Marion	3,897	3,575	321	277	44	12.7	13.4	8.0
Martin	1,656	1,591	64	60	4	11.7	12.1	6.4
Miami-Dade	18,364	14,790	3,566	3,332	234	7.6	8.0	6.1
Monroe	723	670	52	48	4	8.8	8.7	9.0
Nassau	617	568	49	44	5	9.3	9.4	9.0
Okaloosa	1,439	1,347	92	55	37	7.6	8.3	3.3
Okeechobee	426	395	31	24	7	11.3	11.7	7.8
Orange	6,576	5,310	1,262	1,068	194	6.3	6.9	4.4
Osceola	1,497	1,344	153	101	52	6.3	6.6	4.5
Palm Beach	13,652	12,357	1,284	1,127	157	10.7	12.0	5.4
Pasco	5,336	5,216	115	81	34	13.0	13.3	5.8
Pinellas	11,823	10,897	919	784	135	12.5	13.3	7.0
Polk	5,603	4,945	655	602	53	10.3	10.9	7.2
Putnam	901	748	153	150	3	12.2	12.4	11.4
St. Johns	1,292	1,204	87	85	2	8.1	8.2	7.2
St. Lucie	2,407	2,090	315	290	25	9.9	10.5	7.1
Santa Rosa	1,069	1,019	49	33	16	7.8	8.1	4.5
Sarasota	4,834	4,654	178	147	31	13.1	13.3	8.4
Seminole	2,755	2,425	329	278	51	6.7	6.9	5.3
Sumter	825	765	60	54	6	10.9	11.8	5.7
Suwannee	485	437	48	44	4	12.7	13.0	10.0
Taylor	190	157	33	32	1	8.9	9.5	6.9
Union	194	136	58	54	4	12.8	11.9	15.5
Volusia	6,152	5,737	410	365	45	12.4	13.1	6.8
Wakulla	254	234	20	20	0	9.3	9.9	5.7
Walton	475	434	41	36	5	8.8	8.9	7.8
Washington	249	223	26	24	2	10.7	11.5	6.8

1/ Rate per 1,000 computed from midyear 2005 population estimates based upon 2000 Census data.
2/ Unknown race included in total only.
3/ Persons designating "Hispanic" as a race were counted as white.
Note: Data are for deaths occurring to residents of the specified area regardless of place of occurrence.

Source: State of Florida, Department of Health, Office of Vital Statistics, Public Health Statistics Section, *Florida Vital Statistics Annual Report, 2005,* Internet site <http://doh.state.fl.us/> (accessed 19, March 2007).

Table 3.17. CAUSE OF DEATH: NUMBER OF RESIDENT DEATHS BY CAUSE IN FLORIDA 2003, 2004, AND 2005

Cause of death and international list number	2003	2004	2005
All causes	168,459	168,364	170,300
Salmonella infections (A01-A02)	2	3	5
Shigellosis and ambeiasis (A03, A06)	0	0	0
Certain other intestinal infections (A04, A07-A09)	337	451	496
Tuberculosis (A16-A19)	49	39	45
Whooping cough (A37)	0	0	1
Scarlet fever and erysipelas (A38, A46)	0	0	0
Meningococcal infection (A39)	11	11	7
Septicemia (A40-A41)	1,902	1,965	1,837
Syphilis (A50-A53)	2	7	8
Acute poliomyelitis (A80)	0	0	0
Arthropod-borne viral encephalitis (A83-A84, A85.2)	2	0	2
Measles (B05)	0	0	0
Viral hepatitis (B15-B19)	503	481	496
Human immunodeficiency virus (HIV) disease (B20-B24)	1,742	1,714	1,706
Malaria (B50-B54)	0	1	0
Other and unspecific infectious/parasitic disease and sequelae	413	430	429
Malignant neoplasm (C00-C97)	39,238	39,502	40,321
Lip, oral cavity, pharynx (C00-C14)	606	610	603
Esophagus (C15)	875	909	943
Stomach (C16)	813	809	821
Colon, rectum, anus (C18-C21)	3,698	3,701	3,751
Liver and intrahepatic bile ducts (C22)	1,045	1,027	1,156
Pancreas (C25)	2,233	2,203	2,347
Larynx (C32)	328	299	327
Trachea, bronchus, lung (C33-C34)	11,866	11,969	12,033
Skin (C43)	628	626	621
Breast (C50)	2,613	2,766	2,699
Cervix uteri (C53)	276	249	293
Corpus uteri and uterus, part unspecified (C54-C55)	434	420	458
Ovary (C56)	975	950	981
Prostate (C61)	2,128	2,117	2,193
Kidney and renal pelvis (C64-c65)	806	793	817
Bladder (C67)	947	1,055	1,054
Meninges, brain, and other part central nervous system (C70-C72)	814	833	883
Lymphoid, hematopoietic and related tissue (C81-C96)	3,945	3,884	3,962
Hodgkin's disease (C81)	64	82	83
Nonhodgkin's lymphoma (C82-C85)	1,542	1,528	1,552
Leukemia (C91-C95)	1,574	1,502	1,589
Multiple myeloma and immunoprolifera neoplasm (C88, C90)	763	769	735
Other and unspecified–lymphoid, hematopoietic, related tissue (C96)	2	3	3
All other and unspecified	4,208	4,282	4,379
In situ, benign, uncertain/unknown behavior neoplasms (D00-D48)	1,009	1,010	997
Anemias (D50-D64)	306	337	312
Diabetes mellitus (E10-E14)	4,754	4,790	5,181
Nutritional deficiencies (E40-E64)	200	125	148
Meningitis (G00,G03)	50	31	29
Parkinson's disease (G20-G21)	1,381	1,335	1,463
Alzheimer's disease (G30)	4,311	4,294	4,600
Major cardiovascular diseases (I00-I78)	62,272	60,623	59,613
Heart diseases (I00-I09, I11, I13, I20-I51)	48,129	46,839	45,992
Acute rheumatic fever and chronic rheumatic heart disease (I00-I09)	225	217	215
Hypertensive heart disease (I11)	2,318	2,177	2,311
Hypertensive heart and renal disease (I13)	222	190	218
Ischemic heart disease (I20-I25)	36,659	35,430	34,310
Other heart diseases (I26-I51)	8,705	8,825	8,938
Essential hypertension and hypertensive renal disease (I10, I12)	1,556	1,696	1,807

Continued . . .

Table 3.17. CAUSE OF DEATH: NUMBER OF RESIDENT DEATHS BY CAUSE IN FLORIDA 2003, 2004, AND 2005 (Continued)

Cause of death and international list number	2003	2004	2005
All causes (Continued)			
Major cardiovascular diseases (I00-I78) (Continued)			
Cerebrovascular diseases (I60-I69)	9,873	9,661	9,321
Atherosclerosis (I70)	965	874	851
Other disease of circulatory system (I71-I78)	1,749	1,553	1,642
Other circulatory system disorders (I80-I99)	304	301	298
Influenza and pneumonia (J11-J18)	2,985	3,025	2,787
Influenza (J10-J11)	25	42	20
Pneumonia (J12-J18)	2,960	2,983	2,767
Other acute lower respiratory infections (J20-J22)	20	16	23
Chronic lower respiratory diseases (J40-J47)	9,030	8,931	9,454
Bronchitis, chronic and unspecified (J40-J42)	61	56	67
Emphysema (J43)	1,044	965	991
Asthma (J45-J46)	218	190	220
Other chronic lower respiratory diseases (J44, J47)	7,707	7,720	8,176
Pneumoconiosis and chemical effects (J60-J66, J68)	68	44	49
Pneumonitis due to solids and liquids (J69)	1,120	1,016	923
Other respiratory system disease (J00-J06, J30-J39, J67, J70-J98)	1,616	1,781	1,619
Peptic ulcer (K25-K28)	252	229	219
Appendix diseases (K35-K38)	23	29	22
Hernia (K40-K46)	86	82	78
Chronic liver disease and cirrhosis (K70, K73-K74)	2,238	2,077	2,134
Cholelithiasis and other gallbladder disorders (K80-K82)	161	179	198
Nephritis, nephrotic syndrome and nephrosis (N00-N07, N17-N19, N25-N27)	2,290	2,238	2,386
Acute/progressive nephritic/nephrotic syndrome (N00-N01, N04)	20	10	6
Glomeruloneph, nephri/nephro, renal sclerosis	41	31	38
Renal failure (N17-N19)	2,194	2,194	2,340
Other kidney disorders (N25, N27)	35	3	2
Kidney infections (N10-N12, N13.6, N15.1)	0	37	34
Hyperplasia of prostate (N40)	22	21	20
Female pelvic organs–inflammatory diseases (N70-N76)	6	8	7
Pregnancy, childbirth, and the puerperium (O00-O99)	24	36	55
Perinatal period conditions (P00-P96)	789	782	805
Congenital and chromosomal anomalies (Q00-Q99)	551	540	590
Symptoms, signs, abnormal, clinical/lab findings (R00-R99)	4,094	4,440	4,006
All other diseases (residual)	12,855	13,511	14,537
Unintentional injury (accident) (V01-X59, Y85-Y86)	7,901	8,176	8,744
Transport accident (V01-V99, Y85)	3,484	3,519	3,754
Motor vehicle	3,237	3,282	3,491
Other land transport	77	57	97
Water/air/space/other-unspecified transport and sequelae (V90-V99,V85)	170	180	166
Nontransport accident (W00-X59, Y86)	4,417	4,657	4,990
Falls (W00-W19)	1,379	1,497	1,685
Firearms discharge (W32-W34)	26	22	23
Drowning and submersion (W65-W74)	381	355	353
Smoke, fire, flames exposure (X00-X09)	129	139	133
Poisoning and noxious substance exposure (X40-X49)	1,733	1,824	1,943
Other and unspecified nontransport and sequelae	769	820	853
Suicide (X60-X84, Y87.0)	2,294	2,382	2,308
Homicide (X85-Y09, Y87.1)	1,004	1,030	988
Legal intervention (Y35, Y89.0)	12	13	14
Undetermined injury (Y10-Y34, Y87.2, Y89.9)	102	149	145
War operations and sequelae (Y36, Y89.1)	1	2	1
Medical and surgical care complications (Y40-Y84, Y88)	127	140	136

Source: State of Florida, Department of Health, Office of Vital Statistics, Public Health Statistics Section, *Florida Vital Statistics Annual Report, 2005,* and previous editions, Internet site <http://doh.state.fl.us/> (accessed 19, March 2007).

Table 3.18. DEATHS: NUMBER OF RESIDENT DEATHS AND DEATH RATES BY LEADING CAUSE AND BY RACE IN FLORIDA, 2005

Cause in 2005 rank order	Number of deaths Total 2/	White 3/	Nonwhite	Death rate 1/ Total 2/	White 3/	Nonwhite
Heart disease	45,992	41,353	4,618	255.2	283.6	134.4
Malignant neoplasm (cancer)	40,321	36,018	4,274	223.8	247.0	124.4
Chronic lower respiratory disease (CLRD)	9,454	8,919	529	52.5	61.2	15.4
Cerebrovascular disease (stroke)	9,321	7,959	1,358	51.7	54.6	39.5
Unintentional injury (accident)	8,744	7,650	1,086	48.5	52.5	31.6
Diabetes mellitus	5,181	4,197	984	28.8	28.8	28.6
Alzheimer's disease	4,600	4,334	265	25.5	29.7	7.7
Influenza and pneumonia	2,787	2,489	297	15.5	17.1	8.6
Nephritis, nephrotic syndrome, and nephrosis	2,386	1,960	425	13.2	13.4	12.4
Suicide	2,308	2,140	168	12.8	14.7	4.9
Chronic liver disease and cirrhosis	2,134	1,975	159	11.8	13.5	4.6
Septicemia	1,837	1,553	284	10.2	10.7	8.3
Hypertension	1,807	1,420	387	10.0	9.7	11.3
Human Immunodeficiency Virus (HIV)	1,706	669	1,036	9.5	4.6	30.1
Parkinson's Disease	1,463	1,399	60	8.1	9.6	1.7
Aortic Aneurysm and Dissection	998	892	106	5.5	6.1	3.1

1/ Rate per 100,000 population, mid-year 2005 estimates based on 2000 Census data.
2/ Unknown race included in total only.
3/ Persons designating "Hispanic" as a race were counted as white.
Note: Data are for deaths occurring to residents of Florida regardless of the state of occurrence.

Table 3.19. DEATHS: RESIDENT ACCIDENT AND SUICIDE DEATHS AND DEATH RATES BY RACE AND SEX IN FLORIDA, 2001 THROUGH 2005

Year	Number of deaths Total 3/	White 2/ Male	White 2/ Female	Nonwhite Male	Nonwhite Female	Death rate 1/ Total 3/	White 2/ Male	White 2/ Female	Nonwhite Male	Nonwhite Female
	Unintentional injury (accident)									
2001	6,872	4,036	1,952	610	266	41.9	61.3	28.4	42.8	17.3
2002	7,361	4,210	2,215	653	271	43.9	62.7	31.6	44.6	17.2
2003	7,901	4,556	2,389	657	295	46.0	66.3	33.3	43.9	18.3
2004	8,176	4,720	2,422	722	306	46.4	66.8	33.1	46.4	18.4
2005	8,744	5,126	2,523	745	341	48.5	71.6	34.0	45.0	19.1
	Suicide									
2001	2,290	1,666	482	118	23	14.0	25.3	7.0	8.3	1.5
2002	2,332	1,710	494	103	24	13.9	25.5	7.0	7.0	1.5
2003	2,294	1,677	474	120	22	13.4	24.4	6.6	8.0	1.4
2004	2,382	1,686	560	104	30	13.5	23.9	7.6	6.7	1.8
2005	2,308	1,620	520	130	38	12.8	22.6	7.0	7.8	2.1

1/ Rate per 100,000 population, mid-year 2005 estimates based on 2000 Census data.
2/ Persons designating "Hispanic" as a race were counted as white.
3/ Unknown race included in total only.

Source for Tables 3.18 and 3.19: State of Florida, Department of Health, Office of Vital Statistics, Public Health Statistics Section, *Florida Vital Statistics Annual Report, 2005,* and previous editions, Internet site <http://doh.state.fl.us/> (accessed 19, March 2007).

Table 3.20. CHILD WELL-BEING: INDICATORS OF CHILD WELL-BEING IN THE STATE AND COUNTIES OF FLORIDA, 2005

County	Child deaths 3/	Teen violent deaths 1/ Number	Teen violent deaths 1/ Rate 4/	Marriage dissolutions 2/ Number	Marriage dissolutions 2/ Children 5/
Florida	688	693	5.9	31,118	50,641
Alachua	9	2	0.9	328	515
Baker	1	2	10.7	49	82
Bay	9	13	13.2	359	573
Bradford	4	1	5.6	38	63
Brevard	24	20	5.7	30	39
Broward	66	55	5.0	3,216	5,158
Calhoun	0	1	9.9	29	49
Charlotte	3	4	5.5	241	407
Citrus	5	8	11.6	202	314
Clay	7	8	5.8	372	614
Collier	8	7	4.1	549	886
Columbia	3	3	6.9	137	232
DeSoto	2	1	4.7	68	133
Dixie	1	1	10.0	18	30
Duval	39	39	6.4	1,859	3,035
Escambia	8	17	6.9	541	867
Flagler	2	0	0.0	103	182
Franklin	1	0	0.0	8	14
Gadsden	1	5	14.3	40	71
Gilchrist	0	0	0.0	28	46
Glades	3	0	0.0	5	11
Gulf	0	0	0.0	19	42
Hamilton	2	1	10.8	16	26
Hardee	1	1	5.0	42	66
Hendry	1	3	8.9	15	27
Hernando	8	5	6.0	142	247
Highlands	6	6	12.1	120	197
Hillsborough	53	45	5.7	2,404	3,917
Holmes	0	2	15.1	41	74
Indian River	4	6	8.2	224	362
Jackson	4	3	10.0	20	31
Jefferson	0	1	10.8	2	3
Lafayette	0	1	22.8	13	27
Lake	9	12	8.3	348	617
Lee	22	32	10.5	897	1,518
Leon	4	6	2.2	428	689
Levy	4	5	18.9	66	115
Liberty	1	1	22.0	17	27
Madison	1	2	13.0	18	24
Manatee	11	10	5.8	476	791
Marion	11	12	6.3	497	833
Martin	2	5	6.7	227	362
Miami-Dade	75	68	4.0	4,971	7,801
Monroe	1	1	2.4	155	232
Nassau	2	4	8.5	166	284
Okaloosa	4	8	6.4	568	904
Okeechobee	6	3	10.6	47	79
Orange	43	39	5.2	1,929	3,177
Osceola	8	9	5.0	500	812
Palm Beach	36	52	6.8	1,793	2,979
Pasco	18	11	4.7	763	1,237
Pinellas	26	26	5.0	1,440	2,272
Polk	30	29	8.1	962	1,659
Putnam	2	7	13.6	144	223
St. Johns	5	5	4.8	302	520
St. Lucie	7	21	13.2	369	589
Santa Rosa	9	3	2.9	153	252
Sarasota	12	10	5.9	627	1,067
Seminole	24	17	6.0	792	1,300
Sumter	2	3	8.3	71	112
Suwannee	4	6	24.7	72	110
Taylor	1	2	13.9	40	69
Union	2	0	0.0	20	28
Volusia	20	15	4.7	883	1,467
Wakulla	3	1	5.1	30	49
Walton	4	6	18.4	27	43
Washington	1	1	6.4	42	60

1/ Deaths from homicides, suicides, and accidents to teens aged 15-19 years.
2/ Dissolutions of marriage with minor children affected.
3/ Deaths from all causes to children aged 1-14 years.
4/ Per 10,000 population aged 15-19 years.
5/ Minimum number of children affected.

Source: University of South Florida, Louis de la Parte Florida Mental Health Institute, Center for the Study of Children's Futures, unpublished data.

Table 3.21. CHILD ABUSE: REPORTED CASES IN THE STATE, DEPARTMENT OF CHILDREN AND FAMILIES DISTRICTS, AND COUNTIES OF FLORIDA, FISCAL YEAR 2005–06

District or region and county	Child population	Cases reported 1/	Abuse rate per month 2/
Florida	4,043,666	178,397	3.7
District 1	160,745	9,383	4.9
Escambia	70,011	4,150	4.9
Okaloosa	44,820	2,669	5.0
Santa Rosa	34,904	1,881	4.5
Walton	11,010	683	5.2
District 2	149,483	8,894	5.0
Bay	36,187	2,713	6.2
Calhoun	3,060	221	6.0
Franklin	2,039	141	5.8
Gadsden	11,850	517	3.6
Gulf	2,979	145	4.1
Holmes	4,162	626	12.5
Jackson	10,120	772	6.4
Jefferson	2,912	156	4.5
Leon	54,249	2,278	3.5
Liberty	1,589	166	8.7
Madison	4,440	313	5.9
Taylor	4,775	330	5.8
Wakulla	6,061	372	5.1
Washington	5,060	144	2.4
District 3	115,791	7,573	5.5
Alachua	45,907	2,558	4.6
Bradford	5,734	485	7.0
Columbia	14,840	1,014	5.7
Dixie	3,288	227	5.8
Gilchrist	3,785	291	6.4
Hamilton	3,060	148	4.0
Lafayette	1,537	59	3.2
Levy	8,615	654	6.3
Putnam	17,407	1,454	7.0
Suwannee	8,563	511	5.0
Union	3,055	172	4.7
District 4	319,477	15,254	4.0
Baker	6,251	531	7.1
Clay	45,741	2,215	4.0
Duval	217,421	10,453	4.0
Nassau	15,766	593	3.1
St. Johns	34,298	1,462	3.6
District 7	545,677	27,073	4.1
Brevard	109,815	6,422	4.9
Orange	270,005	13,779	4.3
Osceola	65,604	3,020	3.8
Seminole	100,253	3,852	3.2
District 8	213,163	8,185	3.2
Charlotte	24,739	1,091	3.7
Collier	65,783	1,849	2.3
Glades	2,343	90	3.2
Hendry	11,481	448	3.3
Lee	108,817	4,707	3.6
District 9	276,201	10,181	3.1
Palm Beach	276,201	10,181	3.1
District 10	416,789	12,552	2.5
Broward	416,789	12,552	2.5
District 11	610,096	13,217	1.8
Miami-Dade	595,986	12,530	1.8
Monroe	14,110	687	4.1
District 12	110,590	7,658	5.8
Flagler	13,566	809	5.0
Volusia	97,024	6,849	5.9
District 13	176,966	11,434	5.4
Citrus	21,533	1,664	6.4
Hernando	28,409	1,924	5.6
Lake	53,260	2,967	4.6
Marion	62,557	4,276	5.7
Sumter	11,207	603	4.5
District 14	154,018	9,188	5.0
Hardee	7,181	143	1.7
Highlands	17,634	1,095	5.2
Polk	129,203	7,950	5.1
District 15	110,716	4,947	3.7
Indian River	24,528	777	2.6
Martin	25,117	684	2.3
Okeechobee	9,403	679	6.0
St. Lucie	51,668	2,807	4.5
Suncoast Region	683,954	32,858	4.0
DeSoto	7,551	493	5.4
Hillsborough	288,902	11,277	3.3
Manatee	62,835	3,845	5.1
Pasco	84,778	4,857	4.8
Pinellas	180,319	9,867	4.6
Sarasota	59,569	2,519	3.5

1/ Unduplicated total.
2/ Rate of initial and additional reports received during the fiscal year per 1,000 child population.
Note: See map of districts in Section 7.00.
Source: State of Florida, Department of Children and Families, *Child Welfare Annual Statistical Data Tables, Fiscal Year 2005-2006,* Internet site <http://www.dcf.state.fl.us> (accessed 15, August 2007).

Table 3.22. COMMUNITY-BASED CARE: YOUTHS SERVED AND RECURRENT MALTREATMENT CASES BY LEAD AGENCY IN FLORIDA, FISCAL YEAR 2005–06

Lead agency and counties served	Number of youths served 1/	Maltreatment cases Number	Maltreatment cases Proportion with recurrence 2/ (percentage)
Big Bend Community Based Care 2A	2,348	2,804	21.05
Holmes, Washington, Bay, Jackson, Calhoun, Gulf			
Big Bend Community Based Care 2B	1,873	1,901	15.37
Gadsden, Liberty, Franklin, Leon, Wakulla, Jefferson, Madison, Taylor			
Child and Family Connections, Inc.	3,469	5,876	13.04
Palm Beach			
ChildNet, Inc.	6,414	7,343	12.18
Broward			
Children's Network of Southwest Florida	2,602	3,025	11.21
Charlotte, Lee, Glades, Hendry, Collier			
Clay and Baker Kids Net, Inc.	966	1,373	16.25
Clay, Baker			
Community Based Care of Seminole, Inc.	1,276	1,711	14.79
Seminole			
Community-Based Care of Brevard	2,566	3,693	18.36
Brevard			
Community-Based Care of Volusia and Flagler Counties	2,460	3,473	17.51
Volusia, Flagler			
Family First Network	5,229	4,827	15.98
Escambia, Santa Rosa, Okaloosa, Walton			
Family Services of Metro-Orlando, Inc.	6,555	8,136	13.45
Orange, Osceola			
Family Support Services of North Florida, Inc.	4,901	5,919	12.88
Duval			
Heartland for Children	5,687	5,155	17.33
Polk, Hardee, Highlands			
Hillsborough Kids, Inc.	7,437	6,912	15.41
Hillsborough			
Kids Central, Inc.	8,088	6,713	16.85
Marion, Citrus, Sumter, Lake, Hernando			
Nassau County Board of County Commissioners	358	331	16.32
Nassau			
Our Kids of Miami-Dade and Monroe, Inc.	7,228	7,273	10.06
Miami-Dade, Monroe			
Partnership for Strong Families	3,638	3,757	15.85
Alachua, Bradford, Columbia, Dixie, Gilchrist, Hamilton, Lafayette, Putnam, Suwannee, Levy, Union			
Sarasota Family YMCA, Inc. North	6,422	7,904	17.03
Pasco, Pinellas			
Sarasota Family YMCA, Inc. South	1,860	3,589	14.83
Manatee, DeSoto, Sarasota			
St. Johns County Board of County Commissioners	552	836	17.83
St. Johns			
United for Families	3,433	2,343	13.07
Okeechobee, St. Lucie, Indian River, Martin			

1/ Unduplicated count.

2/ Percentage of fiscal year 2004–05 cohort children with recurrence of maltreatment within 12 months after the first incident.

Source: University of South Florida and Florida Department of Children and Families, *Report to the Legislature: Evaluation of the Department of Children and Families Community-Based Care Initiative, Fiscal Year 2005–2006,* Internet site <http://www.dcf.state.fl.us> (accessed 15, February 2007).

Table 3.24. ELDER CARE: CAREGIVERS AND PERSONS AGED 65 AND OVER WITH DISABILITIES IN THE STATE AND COUNTIES OF FLORIDA, 2003 AND 2006

PSA and County	Care-givers 2003 A/	Elders with disabilities, 2006			
		Medically needy	Alzheimer's	With more than one disability	Self-care limitations 1/
Florida	901,796	695,752	479,875	611,950	249,627
PSA 1	34,502	22,332	13,169	22,059	9,445
Escambia	16,110	11,314	6,547	10,846	4,941
Okaloosa	8,955	113	3,292	5,036	2,002
Santa Rosa	6,221	7,474	2,064	3,567	1,487
Walton	3,216	3,431	1,266	2,610	1,015
PSA 2	31,496	44,291	12,300	22,851	9,669
Bay	8,461	7,431	3,171	5,785	2,312
Calhoun	761	962	312	668	334
Franklin	799	998	299	555	254
Gadsden	2,295	6,237	871	1,791	689
Gulf	934	1,009	365	689	285
Holmes	1,166	3,172	453	1,009	336
Jackson	2,731	3,809	1,170	2,547	1,112
Jefferson	769	888	312	716	387
Leon	8,501	5,734	3,444	5,094	2,252
Liberty	310	835	106	325	138
Madison	1,097	3,067	455	782	384
Taylor	1,148	3,114	413	848	367
Wakulla	1,127	3,283	393	704	298
Washington	1,397	3,752	536	1,338	521
PSA 3	94,991	122,282	47,027	63,481	24,314
Alachua	7,376	7,047	3,579	5,616	2,306
Bradford	1,195	3,802	537	1,107	346
Citrus	12,547	12,725	6,356	7,457	2,544
Columbia	2,782	4,121	1,310	2,656	1,001
Dixie	888	3,063	388	917	348
Gilchrist	712	1,205	343	702	277
Hamilton	540	1,771	250	456	144
Hernando	12,866	12,111	6,595	8,182	3,016
Lafayette	309	1,046	139	207	81
Lake	19,536	12,118	9,707	11,592	4,653
Levy	2,312	3,128	998	1,950	704
Marion	21,264	23,531	10,964	13,340	5,061
Putnam	4,433	6,126	1,842	3,415	1,531
Sumter	5,737	21,811	2,788	3,600	1,402
Suwannee	2,106	7,443	1,079	1,889	705
Union	388	1,234	152	395	195
PSA 4	70,425	66,670	40,768	56,180	23,223
Baker	675	2,616	313	781	265
Clay	4,722	638	2,512	4,162	1,687
Duval	24,634	16,968	13,580	22,584	9,866
Flagler	4,591	4,033	2,871	2,661	1,248
Nassau	2,384	10,079	1,188	2,230	993
St. Johns	6,158	2,085	3,537	3,786	1,495
Volusia	27,261	30,251	16,767	19,976	7,669

See footnotes at end of table. Continued . . .

Table 3.24. ELDER CARE: CAREGIVERS AND PERSONS AGED 65 AND OVER WITH DISABILITIES IN THE STATE AND COUNTIES OF FLORIDA, 2003 AND 2006 (Continued)

PSA and County	Care-givers 2003 A/	Elders with disabilities, 2006			
		Medically needy	Alzheimer's	With more than one disability	Self-care limitations 1/
PSA 5	76,435	49,462	50,325	57,348	21,537
Pasco	24,166	31,213	15,601	18,420	6,290
Pinellas	52,269	18,249	34,724	38,928	15,247
PSA 6	81,129	80,374	51,700	70,634	28,081
Hardee	975	4,077	586	1,197	505
Highlands	6,979	9,167	4,755	5,655	2,036
Hillsborough	33,199	19,725	20,510	31,918	13,110
Manatee	16,538	16,774	11,276	11,291	4,215
Polk	23,438	30,631	14,573	20,573	8,215
PSA 7	86,865	68,759	39,662	58,659	23,228
Brevard	31,680	27,253	15,887	20,634	7,590
Orange	32,939	10,840	14,056	22,606	9,772
Osceola	7,854	26,478	3,511	5,671	1,810
Seminole	14,392	4,188	6,208	9,748	4,056
PSA 8	109,516	63,728	60,092	57,828	22,384
Charlotte	15,259	12,928	8,573	8,524	3,670
Collier	21,468	11,466	10,979	9,338	3,207
De Soto	1,971	2,024	926	1,222	455
Glades	678	2,120	255	475	191
Hendry	1,237	1,524	567	982	388
Lee	36,969	28,932	19,933	20,417	7,740
Sarasota	31,934	4,734	18,859	16,870	6,733
PSA 9	151,658	35,524	69,020	66,269	26,671
Indian River	13,052	7,928	5,921	5,385	2,019
Martin	14,174	1,019	6,240	4,639	1,793
Okeechobee	2,594	2,565	916	1,424	470
Palm Beach	103,717	10,278	48,184	46,068	19,078
St. Lucie	18,121	13,734	7,759	8,753	3,311
PSA 10	69,796	39,670	45,606	54,673	23,561
Broward	69,796	39,670	45,606	54,673	23,561
PSA 11	94,983	102,660	50,206	81,968	37,514
Miami-Dade	91,309	88,861	48,401	79,996	36,799
Monroe	3,674	13,799	1,805	1,972	715

PSA Planning and Service Area.
A/ Estimates based on a 2003 Florida Department of Elder Affairs statewide survey applied to persons aged 60 and over measuring elder Floridian's needs.
1/ Self-care limitation is defined as a person with two or more disabilities, including self-care limitations.

Source: State of Florida, Department of Elder Affairs, *Assessing the Needs of Elder Floridians, 2004,* and *2006 Florida County Profiles,* Internet site <http://elderaffairs.state.fl.us/> (accessed 13, August 2007).

Table 3.26. NURSING HOMES AND ASSISTED LIVING FACILITIES: ADVERSE INCIDENTS IN THE STATE AND COUNTIES OF FLORIDA, 2006

County	Total incidents	Percentage– Nursing home incidents	Percentage– Assisted living incidents	County	Total incidents	Percentage– Nursing home incidents	Percentage– Assisted living incidents
Florida	4,672	56.3	43.7	Lake	75	50.7	49.3
				Lee	303	40.9	59.1
Alachua	40	90.0	10.0	Leon	77	24.7	75.3
Baker	4	100.0	0.0	Levy	11	90.9	9.1
Bay	127	63.8	36.2	Liberty	1	0.0	100.0
Bradford	2	100.0	0.0	Madison	13	100.0	0.0
Brevard	146	56.8	43.2	Manatee	84	50.0	50.0
Broward	226	49.1	50.9	Marion	111	54.1	45.9
Calhoun	6	83.3	16.7	Martin	37	83.8	16.2
Charlotte	142	45.1	54.9	Miami-Dade	195	67.7	32.3
Citrus	99	51.5	48.5	Monroe	15	86.7	13.3
Clay	30	80.0	20.0	Nassau	9	77.8	22.2
Collier	49	32.7	67.3	Okaloosa	37	59.5	40.5
Columbia	23	73.9	26.1	Okeechobee	0	0.0	0.0
DeSoto	0	0.0	0.0	Orange	292	52.4	47.6
Dixie	2	50.0	50.0	Osceola	71	84.5	15.5
Duval	155	71.0	29.0	Palm Beach	265	66.8	33.2
Escambia	81	65.4	34.6	Pasco	144	36.1	63.9
Flagler	14	78.6	21.4	Pinellas	541	60.4	39.6
Franklin	1	0.0	0.0	Polk	172	64.5	35.5
Gadsden	3	33.3	66.7	Putnam	27	81.5	18.5
Gilchrist	2	100.0	0.0	St. Johns	45	82.2	17.8
Glades	0	0.0	0.0	St. Lucie	68	73.5	26.5
Gulf	9	100.0	0.0	Santa Rosa	31	61.3	38.7
Hamilton	6	33.3	66.7	Sarasota	194	31.4	68.6
Hardee	11	45.5	54.5	Seminole	75	34.7	65.3
Hendry	10	100.0	0.0	Sumter	1	100.0	0.0
Hernando	30	63.3	36.7	Suwannee	12	66.7	33.3
Highlands	45	60.0	40.0	Taylor	2	100.0	0.0
Hillsborough	222	45.0	55.0	Union	0	0.0	0.0
Holmes	15	86.7	13.3	Volusia	145	66.9	33.1
Indian River	44	31.8	68.2	Wakulla	1	100.0	0.0
Jackson	16	93.8	6.3	Walton	6	33.3	66.7
Jefferson	11	81.8	18.2	Washington	28	25.0	75.0
Lafayette	13	100.0	0.0				

Note: Adverse incidents as reported July 1, 2005 through June 30, 2006.

Source: State of Florida, Agency for Health Care Administration, *Nursing Home and Assisted Living Facility Adverse Incidents and Notices of Intent Filed, Report to the Legislature July 2006—Status Report,* July 31, 2006, Internet site <http://www.fdhc.state.fl.us/> (accessed 30, January 2007).

Table 3.28. HIV AND AIDS: CASES, 2006, AND CUMULATIVE CASES OF AIDS JANUARY 1, 1981 THROUGH DECEMBER 31, 2006, IN THE STATE AND COUNTIES OF FLORIDA

County	Number of cases reported 1/		Cumulative cases 1981-2006	
	HIV 2/	AIDS	Number 3/	Rate per 100,000 population 4/
Florida	5,225	4,960	105,551	575.2
Alachua	44	58	858	352.0
Baker	3	3	41	164.0
Bay	27	23	403	243.5
Bradford	9	4	51	178.6
Brevard	62	54	1,521	280.1
Broward	880	765	16,552	944.1
Calhoun	2	0	10	70.9
Charlotte	8	13	209	130.4
Citrus	12	18	136	99.5
Clay	15	17	209	118.1
Collier	54	63	957	293.0
Columbia	12	9	160	251.8
DeSoto	6	4	100	301.5
Dixie	1	3	22	140.3
Duval	320	276	5,397	613.8
Escambia	67	61	1,277	412.4
Flagler	3	7	90	101.0
Franklin	0	0	17	142.7
Gadsden	22	21	178	369.3
Gilchrist	0	0	14	83.8
Glades	1	1	25	231.6
Gulf	2	0	13	78.7
Hamilton	9	1	26	179.1
Hardee	2	3	79	290.6
Hendry	5	14	157	405.9
Hernando	11	5	200	127.4
Highlands	11	9	187	193.4
Hillsborough	333	323	6,229	534.9
Holmes	0	0	16	82.0
Indian River	12	18	337	249.1
Jackson	10	4	93	185.1
Jefferson	1	1	30	209.0
Lafayette	0	0	5	62.0
Lake	34	44	430	155.4
Lee	105	92	1,716	293.0
Leon	60	60	814	298.7
Levy	3	3	70	179.6
Liberty	2	1	8	102.9
Madison	7	6	47	237.2
Manatee	40	53	989	320.8
Marion	43	47	676	214.6
Martin	22	31	392	274.8
Miami-Dade	1,203	1,140	29,640	1,216.2
Monroe	25	20	1,199	1,489.3
Nassau	3	4	91	133.5
Okaloosa	21	14	251	130.3
Okeechobee	5	5	111	287.1
Orange	385	345	6,312	584.7
Osceola	53	55	648	253.2
Palm Beach	361	370	9,860	765.5
Pasco	39	51	700	165.0
Pinellas	185	221	4,106	433.1
Polk	99	107	1,773	313.8
Putnam	13	10	221	297.0
St. Johns	14	17	313	189.4
St. Lucie	71	94	1,776	684.9
Santa Rosa	6	7	139	98.3
Sarasota	49	54	1,016	267.8
Seminole	37	45	960	228.2
Sumter	3	3	89	107.7
Suwannee	7	6	91	234.5
Taylor	0	2	39	181.6
Union	5	4	21	139.7
Volusia	78	89	1,423	282.4
Wakulla	4	1	44	155.0
Walton	3	3	53	95.0
Washington	3	3	32	138.7
Unknown	0	0	3	(X)
DC	293	175	3,899	(X)

HIV Human Immunodeficiency Virus.
AIDS Acquired Immunodeficiency Syndrome.
DC Department of Corrections.
(X) Not applicable.
1/ Includes diagnosed cases from earlier years not previously reported. See the introduction to this section for further discussion.
2/ Includes only persons reported with HIV infection who have not developed AIDS.
3/ Includes 1,515 diagnosed and reported pediatric (under age 13) cases of AIDS.
4/ Based on April 1, 2006 BEBR population estimates.

Source: State of Florida, Department of Health, Division of Disease Control, *The Florida Division of Disease Control Surveillance Report,* January 2007, Number 268, Internet site <http://www.doh.state. fl.us/> (accessed 5, April 2007).

Table 3.29. SEXUALLY TRANSMITTED DISEASES: CASES OF SPECIFIED DISEASES IN THE STATE AND COUNTIES OF FLORIDA, 2005 AND 2006

County	Gonorrhea				Chlamydia				Infectious syphilis		
	2005	2006 Total	2006 Rank	Percentage change	2005	2006 Total	2006 Rank	Percentage change	2005	2006	Percentage change
Florida	20,225	23,247	(X)	14.9	43,372	49,198	(X)	13.4	724	722	-0.3
Alachua	592	703	10	18.8	1,263	1,375	11	8.9	5	7	40.0
Baker	33	20	53	-39.4	81	73	49	-9.9	1	1	0.0
Bay	163	137	27	-16.0	359	330	26	-8.1	1	0	-100.0
Bradford	43	46	44	7.0	92	85	47	-7.6	1	0	-100.0
Brevard	495	521	13	5.3	937	1,176	13	25.5	5	0	-100.0
Broward	1,981	2,342	2	18.2	4,313	4,870	2	12.9	196	154	-21.4
Calhoun	14	14	60	0.0	30	28	59	-6.7	0	0	(X)
Charlotte	52	62	38	19.2	164	151	37	-7.9	1	2	100.0
Citrus	53	55	40	3.8	131	184	33	40.5	0	2	(X)
Clay	122	146	24	19.7	299	332	25	11.0	0	2	(X)
Collier	108	136	28	25.9	585	666	18	13.8	2	27	1250.0
Columbia	75	89	30	18.7	157	151	38	-3.8	0	0	(X)
DeSoto	45	29	49	-35.6	77	103	45	33.8	0	0	(X)
Dixie	12	14	61	16.7	40	18	64	-55.0	0	0	(X)
Duval	2,343	2,417	1	3.2	4,625	4,831	3	4.5	49	36	-26.5
Escambia	642	944	8	47.0	1,256	1,353	12	7.7	10	4	-60.0
Flagler	35	40	46	14.3	58	149	39	156.9	0	0	(X)
Franklin	9	10	62	11.1	30	23	62	-23.3	0	0	(X)
Gadsden	129	146	25	13.2	264	271	28	2.7	0	2	(X)
Gilchrist	7	16	56	128.6	26	27	60	3.8	0	0	(X)
Glades	2	3	66	50.0	18	22	63	22.2	0	0	(X)
Gulf	12	10	63	-16.7	25	14	65	-44.0	0	1	(X)
Hamilton	19	17	55	-10.5	53	49	53	-7.5	0	0	(X)
Hardee	10	36	47	260.0	74	104	44	40.5	0	0	(X)
Hendry	28	52	41	85.7	105	117	42	11.4	0	0	(X)
Hernando	64	78	32	21.9	148	163	35	10.1	0	1	(X)
Highlands	67	48	43	-28.4	195	286	27	46.7	2	0	-100.0
Hillsborough	1,263	1,685	5	33.4	3,211	3,800	5	18.3	41	65	58.5
Holmes	11	10	64	-9.1	29	25	61	-13.8	0	0	(X)
Indian River	139	108	29	-22.3	221	241	29	9.0	1	1	0.0
Jackson	62	75	33	21.0	123	119	41	-3.3	0	1	(X)
Jefferson	8	15	59	87.5	22	31	57	40.9	0	0	(X)
Lafayette	0	5	65	(X)	8	10	67	25.0	0	0	(X)
Lake	269	285	18	5.9	491	530	21	7.9	4	3	-25.0

See footnotes at end of table.

Continued . . .

Table 3.29. SEXUALLY TRANSMITTED DISEASES: CASES OF SPECIFIED DISEASES IN THE STATE AND COUNTIES OF FLORIDA, 2005 AND 2006 (Continued)

County	Gonorrhea				Chlamydia				Infectious syphilis		
	2005	2006 Total	2006 Rank	Percentage change	2005	2006 Total	2006 Rank	Percentage change	2005	2006	Percentage change
Lee	528	627	12	18.8	1,287	1,423	10	10.6	7	9	28.6
Leon	648	682	11	5.2	1,626	1,561	9	-4.0	4	3	-25.0
Levy	43	73	35	69.8	116	120	40	3.4	0	0	(X)
Liberty	1	3	67	200.0	9	12	66	33.3	0	0	(X)
Madison	21	16	57	-23.8	56	44	54	-21.4	0	0	(X)
Manatee	314	333	17	6.1	646	727	17	12.5	2	2	0.0
Marion	367	468	15	27.5	676	967	14	43.0	5	4	-20.0
Martin	90	58	39	-35.6	199	169	34	-15.1	1	1	0.0
Miami-Dade	1,661	1,923	4	15.8	3,892	5,245	1	34.8	168	202	20.2
Monroe	23	27	51	17.4	67	58	52	-13.4	3	1	-66.7
Nassau	42	73	36	73.8	107	158	36	47.7	0	2	(X)
Okaloosa	174	207	21	19.0	411	460	23	11.9	1	1	0.0
Okeechobee	25	16	58	-36.0	114	108	43	-5.3	1	0	-100.0
Orange	1,990	2,341	3	17.6	4,160	4,597	4	10.5	98	82	-16.3
Osceola	145	180	23	24.1	463	665	19	43.6	0	2	(X)
Palm Beach	856	1,045	7	22.1	2,198	2,227	7	1.3	31	13	-58.1
Pasco	160	184	22	15.0	461	508	22	10.2	2	4	100.0
Pinellas	1,423	1,647	6	15.7	2,495	2,946	6	18.1	42	41	-2.4
Polk	797	944	9	18.4	1,551	1,693	8	9.2	20	22	10.0
Putnam	182	139	26	-23.6	226	229	30	1.3	2	4	100.0
St. Johns	38	65	37	71.1	134	199	32	48.5	0	1	(X)
St. Lucie	247	280	20	13.4	479	658	20	37.4	3	1	-66.7
Santa Rosa	44	74	34	68.2	182	207	31	13.7	0	0	(X)
Sarasota	281	285	19	1.4	489	443	24	-9.4	7	6	-14.3
Seminole	444	446	16	0.5	748	819	16	9.5	4	8	100.0
Sumter	83	81	31	-2.4	111	87	46	-21.6	0	0	(X)
Suwannee	36	49	42	36.1	73	81	48	11.0	0	0	(X)
Taylor	38	36	48	-5.3	57	66	51	15.8	0	0	(X)
Union	12	18	54	50.0	33	31	58	-6.1	0	0	(X)
Volusia	535	518	14	-3.2	642	841	15	31.0	2	4	100.0
Wakulla	20	29	50	45.0	46	41	55	-10.9	0	0	(X)
Walton	39	44	45	12.8	82	67	50	-18.3	2	0	-100.0
Washington	11	22	52	100.0	26	34	56	30.8	0	0	(X)

(X) Not applicable.
Note: Data for 2005 have been revised.
Source: State of Florida, Department of Health, Division of Disease Control, *The Florida Division of Disease Control Surveillance Report,* January 2007, Number 268, Internet site <http://www.doh.state.fl.us/> (accessed 5, April 2007).

Table 3.32. MARRIAGES AND DISSOLUTIONS OF MARRIAGE: NUMBER PERFORMED OR GRANTED IN THE STATE AND COUNTIES OF FLORIDA, 2004 AND 2005

County	Marriages 1/		Dissolutions of marriage 2/		County	Marriages 1/		Dissolutions of marriage 2/	
	2004	2005	2004	2005		2004	2005	2004	2005
Florida	154,453	158,192	83,306	81,287	Lake	1,951	2,087	994	953
					Lee	4,012	4,493	2,062	2,127
Alachua	1,920	1,874	763	835	Leon	1,933	1,822	954	989
Baker	241	255	141	101	Levy	222	237	191	166
Bay	2,311	2,343	961	822	Liberty	64	69	32	34
Bradford	254	239	106	93	Madison	157	131	102	56
Brevard	4,068	4,185	1,356	1,360	Manatee	1,986	2,028	1,164	1,062
Broward	14,411	15,479	9,491	8,596	Marion	2,096	2,177	1,281	1,330
Calhoun	137	115	54	64	Martin	947	996	511	550
Charlotte	1,100	1,057	522	599	Miami-Dade	26,050	26,105	14,278	14,052
Citrus	825	849	506	544	Monroe	3,126	3,002	482	456
Clay	1,436	1,466	826	755	Nassau	672	664	266	311
Collier	2,975	3,201	1,241	1,306	Okaloosa	2,743	2,928	1,301	1,351
Columbia	592	549	366	327	Okeechobee	271	304	166	125
DeSoto	244	263	136	174	Orange	9,945	10,714	4,895	4,814
Dixie	133	140	85	54	Osceola	4,767	4,705	1,602	1,373
Duval	6,429	6,378	4,475	4,350	Palm Beach	9,182	9,038	5,428	5,297
Escambia	2,950	2,785	1,438	1,361	Pasco	2,540	2,474	1,583	1,753
Flagler	454	525	264	263	Pinellas	7,427	7,563	4,132	3,827
Franklin	191	147	49	31	Polk	3,772	3,937	2,416	2,218
Gadsden	307	268	160	114	Putnam	542	531	459	336
Gilchrist	138	143	86	79	St. Johns	1,502	1,456	633	635
Glades	51	53	20	21	St. Lucie	1,400	1,516	908	872
Gulf	162	163	65	53	Santa Rosa	871	878	576	563
Hamilton	116	133	56	46	Sarasota	2,982	2,956	1,567	1,610
Hardee	191	209	130	80	Seminole	3,023	3,117	1,391	1,681
Hendry	280	265	128	144	Sumter	301	292	197	189
Hernando	915	957	427	387	Suwannee	260	260	152	145
Highlands	604	628	331	327	Taylor	142	178	128	102
Hillsborough	9,344	9,979	5,539	5,830	Union	110	101	67	41
Holmes	189	186	105	81	Volusia	3,607	3,652	2,313	2,231
Indian River	942	925	506	546	Wakulla	220	217	165	100
Jackson	367	345	140	179	Walton	998	1,142	219	246
Jefferson	128	94	75	48	Washington	165	159	111	91
Lafayette	62	65	32	31					

1/ State total may include a few marriages performed out of state but recorded in Florida.
2/ Includes divorces and annulments.

Source: State of Florida, Department of Health, Office of Vital Statistics, Public Health Statistics Section, *Florida Vital Statistics Annual Report, 2005,* and previous edition, Internet site <http://doh.state.fl.us/> (accessed 19, March 2007).

EDUCATION

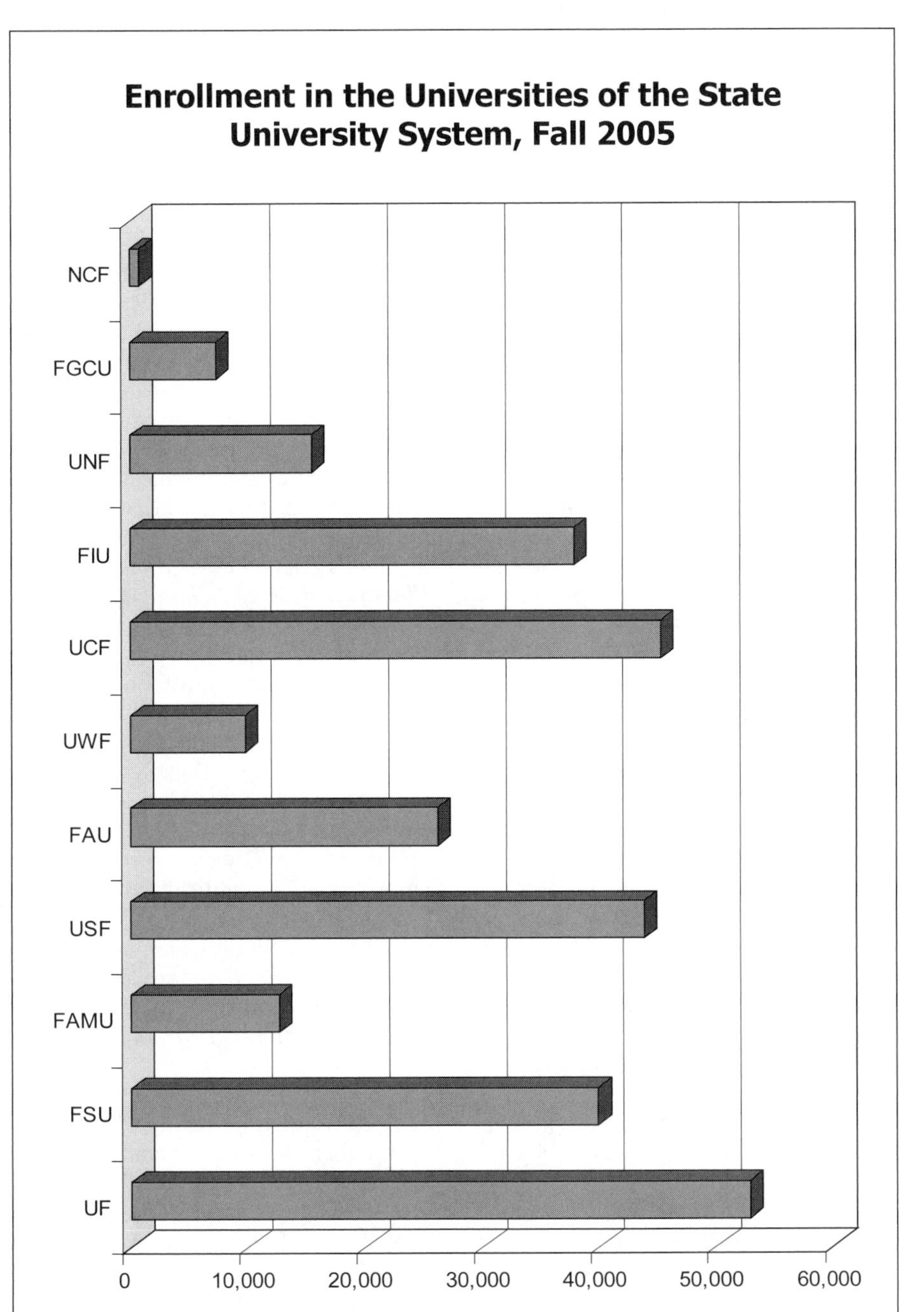

Source: Table 4.55

Section 4.00
Education

This section presents formal education data at various levels. Public school data are the primary focus, however, nonpublic and home school data are also presented. This section first presents enrollment and characteristics of elementary and secondary schools followed by higher education. Public high school testing data, information pertaining to high school graduates and dropouts, and readiness for college data appear at the end of this section.

Data on the extent of public and private education, exceptional programs, the level achieved by the pupils, home school programs, and the availability and enrollments of schools, colleges, and universities are all included in Section 4.00. Employment and finances of educational institutions and data on educational services are found in Section 20.00. Additional information on the public funding of education is in Section 23.00.

Explanatory notes. Generally, when discussing race characteristics, persons of Hispanic origin are considered to be of any race since "Hispanic origin" is widely considered an ethnic rather than racial categorization. The Florida Department of Education reports Hispanic origin as a separate racial category. Some duplication of data results when persons of Hispanic origin are summed with race data.Therefore, totals are not complete unless persons of Hispanic origin are included. Every effort has been made to note the differences on the education tables where this occurs.

Sources. This sections begins with school-age population (aged 5-17) as published by the Bureau of Economic and Business Research in the *Florida Population Studies* series, *Population Projections by Age, Sex, Race, and Hispanic Origin for Florida and Its Counties*. Tables 4.01 and 4.02 depict school-age population by race and by Hispanic origin respectively.

The principal sources of information about public, private, and home school elementary and secondary education in Florida are provided by the various offices of the Florida Department of Education (FLDOE). The Education Information and Accountability Services (EIAS) office of the FLDOE is the primary source of published public elementary and secondary education data. EIAS publications are available on the Internet. New to this section this year are county-level statistics about student discipline, depicted on Table 4.04, as provided by EIAS. Home and nonpublic school education information is provided by the FLDOE Office of Independent Education and Parental Choice in *Home Education Program Statistics* and *Florida's Private Schools* respectively.

The National Center for Education Statistics, U.S. Department of Education publishes accredited colleges and universities enrollment data from their Integrated Postsecondary Education Data System (IPEDS) available online.State University System enrollment is from the state Department of Education's Division of Colleges and Universities, as published in *Fact Book.* Data on public community colleges are from the FLDOE Florida Community College System, *The Fact Book: Report for the Florida Community College System* and *Articulation Report for the Fall Data.*

The Student Assessment Services Section of FLDOE provides public school Florida Comprehensive Assessment Test (FCAT) results. Data on high school graduates, dropouts, and readiness for college are published by EIAS in the *Statistical Brief* series and *College Readiness,* respectively. Both are available on the Internet.

Section 4.00
Education

Tables listed by major heading

Heading | Page

Section 4.00
Education—Continued

Tables listed by major heading

Heading | Page

Table 4.01. SCHOOL-AGE POPULATION: ESTIMATES OF THE POPULATION AGED 5 TO 17 YEARS BY SEX AND RACE IN THE STATE AND COUNTIES OF FLORIDA, APRIL 1, 2006

County	Total school-age population	Percentage– Female	Non-Hispanic White	Non-Hispanic Black	County	Total school-age population	Percentage– Female	Non-Hispanic White	Non-Hispanic Black
Florida	3,020,770	48.8	53.0	20.9	Lake	41,033	48.9	71.5	12.6
					Lee	85,410	48.7	62.8	12.1
Alachua	32,933	48.7	56.7	29.0	Leon	39,890	48.9	52.3	40.3
Baker	4,712	47.9	84.8	12.1	Levy	6,580	48.5	76.7	13.8
Bay	27,220	48.6	76.6	14.7	Liberty	1,220	49.0	78.5	15.0
Bradford	4,190	47.6	74.8	21.1	Madison	3,318	48.4	47.7	47.1
Brevard	85,014	48.9	75.2	12.8	Manatee	46,178	49.0	61.4	14.7
Broward	304,711	48.7	40.1	31.6	Marion	48,115	48.4	68.3	16.3
Calhoun	2,373	49.2	77.7	16.6	Martin	19,718	48.9	73.7	8.7
Charlotte	18,788	49.1	83.5	8.4	Miami-Dade	428,229	48.8	18.2	25.0
Citrus	17,086	48.7	88.0	4.2	Monroe	9,999	48.1	65.0	7.1
Clay	36,421	49.0	78.6	10.0	Nassau	11,749	49.1	87.8	8.3
Collier	47,885	49.4	53.1	9.4	Okaloosa	32,891	49.1	75.6	12.1
Columbia	11,056	48.4	74.4	19.6	Okeechobee	7,223	47.3	59.5	9.6
DeSoto	4,980	48.8	53.8	13.0	Orange	199,218	48.8	41.0	24.9
Dixie	2,424	49.3	88.4	8.2	Osceola	52,718	48.8	40.9	8.9
Duval	158,412	49.1	49.8	38.4	Palm Beach	204,753	48.8	52.9	23.6
Escambia	50,797	49.7	61.4	29.5	Pasco	67,448	48.7	81.3	3.8
Flagler	12,683	49.5	76.4	13.2	Pinellas	132,870	48.6	69.3	16.7
Franklin	1,651	46.3	80.7	15.7	Polk	98,593	48.5	58.1	19.6
Gadsden	8,290	49.2	22.4	63.9	Putnam	13,128	47.8	62.3	22.6
Gilchrist	2,834	49.3	87.0	8.0	St. Johns	27,716	48.6	86.4	7.3
Glades	1,716	47.7	55.0	11.8	St. Lucie	42,822	49.0	56.1	23.8
Gulf	2,331	48.3	81.6	16.0	Santa Rosa	26,565	48.4	87.1	5.1
Hamilton	2,334	49.1	47.9	39.2	Sarasota	46,776	48.8	79.6	8.0
Hardee	4,960	48.9	44.3	6.0	Seminole	75,955	48.7	65.8	12.7
Hendry	7,886	48.9	33.2	16.3	Sumter	9,432	47.3	74.6	13.6
Hernando	22,857	49.0	80.5	6.7	Suwannee	6,198	49.3	74.8	14.8
Highlands	13,335	48.8	55.9	16.6	Taylor	3,552	49.4	73.5	22.3
Hillsborough	214,652	48.9	50.1	20.2	Union	2,294	48.3	81.0	15.3
Holmes	3,306	47.7	90.6	5.7	Volusia	74,786	49.0	70.8	13.7
Indian River	18,990	49.2	69.8	13.5	Wakulla	4,728	48.0	85.5	10.8
Jackson	7,397	48.7	67.4	28.6	Walton	8,355	48.5	82.8	8.3
Jefferson	2,062	49.1	55.8	39.0	Washington	3,865	48.7	80.3	14.1
Lafayette	1,159	47.9	79.0	6.6					

Source: University of Florida, Bureau of Economic and Business Research, Population Program, *Florida Population Studies,* June 2007, Volume 40, Bulletin No. 148.

Table 4.02. HISPANIC ORIGIN SCHOOL-AGE POPULATION: ESTIMATES OF THE HISPANIC ORIGIN POPULATION AGED 5 TO 17 YEARS BY SEX IN THE STATE AND COUNTIES OF FLORIDA, APRIL 1, 2006

County	Total school-age population	Hispanic origin (percentage)		
		Total	Male	Female
Florida	3,020,770	22.8	11.7	11.1
Alachua	32,933	8.0	4.0	4.0
Baker	4,712	2.2	1.4	0.8
Bay	27,220	4.7	2.4	2.3
Bradford	4,190	2.8	1.8	1.1
Brevard	85,014	8.7	4.4	4.3
Broward	304,711	23.9	12.3	11.6
Calhoun	2,373	3.6	2.0	1.6
Charlotte	18,788	5.8	2.9	2.8
Citrus	17,086	5.6	2.6	2.9
Clay	36,421	7.3	3.7	3.6
Collier	47,885	35.7	18.2	17.5
Columbia	11,056	4.2	2.2	2.1
DeSoto	4,980	32.3	17.0	15.4
Dixie	2,424	2.7	1.3	1.4
Duval	158,412	7.0	3.6	3.4
Escambia	50,797	4.0	2.0	2.0
Flagler	12,683	8.0	4.1	3.9
Franklin	1,651	2.7	1.6	1.1
Gadsden	8,290	12.8	6.6	6.1
Gilchrist	2,834	4.3	2.5	1.9
Glades	1,716	27.7	14.8	12.9
Gulf	2,331	1.2	0.8	0.4
Hamilton	2,334	12.1	5.7	6.4
Hardee	4,960	49.1	24.9	24.2
Hendry	7,886	49.1	24.9	24.3
Hernando	22,857	11.0	5.7	5.3
Highlands	13,335	24.7	12.8	12.0
Hillsborough	214,652	25.8	13.2	12.6
Holmes	3,306	2.3	1.3	1.0
Indian River	18,990	14.8	7.5	7.3
Jackson	7,397	2.6	1.3	1.4
Jefferson	2,062	4.2	2.4	1.8
Lafayette	1,159	14.0	7.8	6.2
Lake	41,033	13.9	7.0	6.9
Lee	85,410	22.9	11.8	11.1
Leon	39,890	3.9	2.0	1.9
Levy	6,580	8.3	4.2	4.1
Liberty	1,220	4.8	2.0	2.8
Madison	3,318	4.1	2.2	1.9
Manatee	46,178	21.6	11.1	10.5
Marion	48,115	13.6	7.0	6.6
Martin	19,718	16.1	8.4	7.7
Miami-Dade	428,229	54.5	28.0	26.5
Monroe	9,999	25.9	13.6	12.4
Nassau	11,749	2.8	1.4	1.4
Okaloosa	32,891	7.6	3.9	3.7
Okeechobee	7,223	29.4	15.3	14.1
Orange	199,218	28.4	14.6	13.9
Osceola	52,718	46.5	23.8	22.7
Palm Beach	204,753	20.2	10.3	9.9
Pasco	67,448	12.3	6.4	5.9
Pinellas	132,870	9.1	4.6	4.5
Polk	98,593	20.1	10.4	9.7
Putnam	13,128	13.7	7.3	6.4
St. Johns	27,716	4.6	2.4	2.2
St. Lucie	42,822	18.0	9.2	8.7
Santa Rosa	26,565	4.7	2.4	2.3
Sarasota	46,776	10.2	5.2	5.0
Seminole	75,955	17.3	8.8	8.5
Sumter	9,432	10.7	5.6	5.1
Suwannee	6,198	9.1	4.8	4.3
Taylor	3,552	2.4	1.2	1.2
Union	2,294	2.9	1.5	1.4
Volusia	74,786	13.2	6.8	6.4
Wakulla	4,728	2.8	1.4	1.5
Walton	8,355	6.3	3.2	3.1
Washington	3,865	3.2	1.8	1.5

Note: Persons of Hispanic origin may be of any race. Includes persons of Latino or Spanish origin.

Source: University of Florida, Bureau of Economic and Business Research, Population Program, *Florida Population Studies,* June 2007, Volume 40, Bulletin No. 148.

Table 4.03. ELEMENTARY AND SECONDARY SCHOOLS: SPECIFIED STUDENT DATA IN FLORIDA, 2002–03 THROUGH 2005–06

Item	2002–03	2003–04	2004–05	2005–06	Percentage change since 2002–03
Student membership 1/	2,476,244	2,598,772	2,639,927	2,669,565	7.8
Prekindergarten	49,502	49,534	48,086	47,186	-4.7
Kindergarten	178,802	192,017	197,198	203,324	13.7
Grade 1	181,953	194,883	201,509	205,408	12.9
Grade 2	183,494	189,184	195,352	200,709	9.4
Grade 3	188,095	211,223	206,734	208,559	10.9
Grade 4	192,845	179,303	197,284	195,233	1.2
Grade 5	192,323	200,135	184,064	200,751	4.4
Grade 6	200,006	207,402	208,255	193,636	-3.2
Grade 7	201,436	210,529	209,874	210,046	4.3
Grade 8	195,954	206,690	209,593	208,295	6.3
Grade 9	244,111	254,710	250,304	245,023	0.4
Grade 10	179,424	192,450	202,485	211,419	17.8
Grade 11	154,165	165,709	179,087	184,497	19.7
Grade 12	134,134	145,003	150,102	155,479	15.9
Graduates (standard diplomas)	120,670	125,046	126,713	130,019	7.7
Exceptional student membership	499,145	513,733	517,536	521,385	4.5
Educable mentally handicapped	29,394	28,830	27,717	26,207	-10.8
Trainable mentally handicapped	8,895	8,960	9,062	9,131	2.7
Orthopedically impaired	4,896	4,800	4,711	4,569	-6.7
Speech impaired	55,423	56,084	56,165	56,902	2.7
Language impaired	35,184	36,140	35,933	35,596	1.2
Deaf/hard of hearing	3,774	3,920	4,020	4,121	9.2
Visually impaired	1,346	1,336	1,320	1,320	-1.9
Emotionally handicapped	30,813	30,685	29,896	28,933	-6.1
Specific learning disability	176,630	182,014	182,254	181,480	2.7
Gifted	111,624	115,002	116,798	119,385	7.0
Hospital/homebound	2,907	3,026	2,767	2,863	-1.5
Profoundly mentally handicapped	3,009	2,936	2,818	2,824	-6.1
Dual sensory impaired	68	66	67	68	0.0
Autistic	6,230	7,235	8,429	9,621	54.4
Severely emotionally disturbed	7,027	6,830	6,531	6,204	-11.7
Traumatic brain injured	532	572	613	645	21.2
Developmentally delayed	11,161	12,638	13,554	14,244	27.6
Established conditions	132	115	99	139	5.3
Other health impaired	10,100	12,544	14,782	17,133	69.6
Disciplinary actions					
Out-of-school suspensions	239,696	241,639	178,950	237,990	-0.7
In-school suspensions	258,320	266,196	224,118	269,648	4.4
Corporal punishment	10,039	9,472	7,819	5,485	-45.4
Expulsions	1,242	983	1,059	1,329	7.0
Non-promotions	208,103	201,274	191,629	175,336	-15.7
Dropouts	44,597	43,334	47,352	32,576	-27.0

1/ Based on fall membership survey.
Note: Data are for public schools only.

Source: State of Florida, Department of Education, Education Information and Accountability Services, (EIAS), *Profiles of Florida School Districts, 2005-2006, Student and Staff Data,* Internet site <http://www.fldoe.org/eias/> (accessed 19, June 2007).

Table 4.04. ELEMENTARY AND SECONDARY SCHOOLS: STUDENT DISCIPLINE DATA IN THE STATE AND COUNTIES OF FLORIDA, 2005–06

County	Total disciplinary actions	Suspensions Out-of-school	Suspensions In-school	Corporal punishment 1/	Expulsions
Florida 2/	514,442	237,984	269,644	5,485	1,329
Alachua	1,226	1,086	140	0	0
Baker	1,088	517	215	330	26
Bay	4,909	2,476	2,327	28	78
Bradford	1,453	476	976	0	1
Brevard	11,675	8,161	3,385	0	129
Broward	30,291	11,776	18,500	0	15
Calhoun	477	85	229	163	0
Charlotte	3,671	1,539	2,131	0	1
Citrus	3,454	1,581	1,837	1	35
Clay	8,766	2,694	5,776	255	41
Collier	7,765	1,622	6,143	0	0
Columbia	2,334	1,197	1,135	0	2
DeSoto	394	288	82	24	0
Dixie	412	232	174	6	0
Duval	40,354	21,891	18,459	0	4
Escambia	9,545	6,949	2,449	0	147
Flagler	3,601	873	2,728	0	0
Franklin	597	218	320	48	11
Gadsden	2,413	1,358	1,009	0	46
Gilchrist	975	294	485	193	3
Glades	530	150	364	13	3
Gulf	917	215	535	167	0
Hamilton	1,115	458	369	271	17
Hardee	768	401	157	195	15
Hendry	2,047	1,123	785	139	0
Hernando	5,943	2,423	3,520	0	0
Highlands	4,428	1,261	3,063	98	6
Hillsborough	45,508	15,132	30,296	0	80
Holmes	686	196	190	300	0
Indian River	3,450	1,733	1,714	0	3
Jackson	1,584	839	735	0	10
Jefferson	266	194	10	62	0
Lafayette	346	77	213	56	0
Lake	6,229	3,923	2,248	30	28
Lee	15,416	7,075	8,303	0	38

See footnotes at end of table.

Continued . . .

Table 4.04. ELEMENTARY AND SECONDARY SCHOOLS: STUDENT DISCIPLINE DATA IN THE STATE AND COUNTIES OF FLORIDA, 2005–06 (Continued)

County	Total disciplinary actions	Suspensions Out-of-school	In-school	Corporal punish-ment 1/	Expulsions
Leon	5,269	2,663	2,520	0	86
Levy	2,409	620	1,654	116	19
Liberty	315	53	82	180	0
Madison	1,249	478	714	57	0
Manatee	9,137	4,862	4,275	0	0
Marion	12,466	7,148	5,071	213	34
Martin	2,484	1,607	875	0	2
Miami-Dade	65,713	27,662	38,051	0	0
Monroe	996	536	460	0	0
Nassau	2,765	1,007	1,689	69	0
Okaloosa	3,925	2,553	1,234	118	20
Okeechobee	1,688	1,188	459	1	40
Orange	20,538	11,148	9,375	0	15
Osceola	10,894	7,523	3,267	0	104
Palm Beach	26,413	16,099	10,296	0	18
Pasco	14,617	5,441	9,172	0	4
Pinellas	21,439	6,794	14,630	0	15
Polk	18,717	10,688	7,993	33	3
Putnam	3,548	1,656	1,768	99	25
St. Johns	3,347	1,981	1,366	0	0
St. Lucie	10,642	5,509	5,106	0	27
Santa Rosa	3,557	1,109	1,893	529	26
Sarasota	5,793	2,968	2,774	0	51
Seminole	11,308	4,769	6,491	0	48
Sumter	2,176	975	1,175	0	26
Suwannee	2,291	662	1,083	545	1
Taylor	1,651	705	942	2	2
Union	723	255	340	128	0
Volusia	19,100	7,550	11,538	0	12
Wakulla	1,467	289	924	247	7
Walton	1,688	474	719	494	1
Washington	1,050	253	522	275	0

1/ Corporal punishment is defined by Florida Statutes as the moderate use of physical force or physical contact by a teacher or principal to maintain discipline or to enforce school rules.
2/ Includes special districts not shown separately.

Source: State of Florida, Department of Education, Education Information and Accountability Services (EIAS), *Florida Information Note: Trends in Discipline and the Decline in the Use of Corporal Punishment,* February 2007, Series 2007-11F, Internet site <http:/www.fldoe.org/eias/> (accessed 19, June 2007).

Table 4.05. ELEMENTARY AND SECONDARY SCHOOLS: SPECIFIED CHARACTERISTICS IN FLORIDA, 1990–91 THROUGH 2005–06

School year	Resident population 1/ Total	Resident population 1/ Aged 5-17	Fall membership 2/	High school graduates 3/	Instructional personnel
1990–91	12,937,926	2,016,641	1,861,592	89,494	119,123
1991–92	13,195,952	2,057,688	1,932,131	93,368	121,185
1992–93	13,424,416	2,100,608	1,979,933	91,423	118,713
1993–94	13,608,627	2,135,410	2,040,763	90,034	124,027
1994–95	14,149,317	2,207,525	2,107,514	91,899	129,223
1995–96	14,411,563	2,297,513	2,175,233	91,495	132,079
1996–97	14,712,922	2,356,578	2,240,283	95,082	135,527
1997–98	15,000,475	2,412,497	2,294,160	98,435	140,163
1998–99	15,322,040	2,475,372	2,335,124	102,382	144,324
1999–00	15,982,378	2,700,517	2,380,451	106,381	147,745
2000–01	16,330,601	2,735,936	2,434,403	110,801	150,551
2001–02	16,674,608	2,759,767	2,500,161	119,233	153,390
2002–03	17,071,508	2,838,144	2,539,932	126,830	158,237
2003–04	17,516,732	2,898,006	2,598,231	131,303	165,607
2004-05	17,918,227	2,972,227	2,638,127	133,231	177,077
2005-06	18,349,132	3,020,770	2,673,563	136,476	182,988

School year	Average teacher salary 4/ (dollars)	Number of schools	Assessed valuation of property ($1,000)	Total expenditure all purposes ($1,000)	Current expense per pupil 5/ (dollars)
1990–91	30,555	2,694	449,979,199	11,308,952	4,475
1991–92	31,067	2,730	475,960,538	11,745,293	4,439
1992–93	31,174	2,784	479,892,429	11,750,331	4,525
1993–94	31,948	2,867	488,458,004	12,780,952	4,724
1994–95	32,600	2,946	511,789,104	13,801,787	4,879
1995–96	33,330	3,003	535,588,385	14,455,035	5,026
1996–97	33,887	3,156	559,519,989	12,144,938	5,120
1997–98	34,473	3,178	592,847,936	12,846,999	5,317
1998–99	35,915	3,179	630,165,205	13,141,469	A/ 5,262
1999–00	36,722	3,531	674,898,325	13,532,165	5,820
2000–01	38,717	3,615	729,584,488	14,640,211	6,138
2001–02	38,718	3,683	805,911,056	15,153,687	6,187
2002–03	39,896	3,758	888,308,974	15,916,065	6,381
2003–04	40,159	3,971	989,504,170	17,132,207	6,715
2004–05	41,155	4,096	(NA)	(NA)	(NA)
2005-06	42,702	4,193	(NA)	(NA)	(NA)

(NA) Not available.
A/ Beginning in 1998–99 data are for students in kindergarten through grade 12 only.
1/ Population figures are as of April 1 of the school year.
2/ Based on a pre-kindergarten through grade 12 membership survey conducted during the school year.
3/ Regular day school only; excludes state/university schools and adult programs. Includes standard and special diplomas.
4/ A professional paid on the instructional salary schedule negotiated by a Florida school district.
5/ Based on full-time equivalent student count.
Note: Data are for public schools only.

Source: Columns 1, 2, University of Florida, Bureau of Economic and Business Research, Population Program, *Florida Population Studies.* State of Florida, Department of Education, Education Information and Accountability Services (EIAS), Column 3, *Membership in Florida's Public Schools, Fall 2005;* Columns 4-7, *Profiles of Florida School Districts: 2005-06 Student and Staff Data; Columns 8-10, Profiles of Florida School Districts: 2003-04 Financial Data Statistical Report*. EIAS data accessed from Internet site <http://www.fldoe.org/eias/> on June 19, 2007.

Table 4.06. ELEMENTARY AND SECONDARY SCHOOLS: ENROLLMENT IN KINDERGARTEN THROUGH GRADE TWELVE IN THE STATE OF FLORIDA
1996–97 THROUGH 2005–06

School year	Total enrollment	Public schools		Nonpublic schools 1/	
		Enrollment	Percentage of total	Enrollment	Percentage of total
1996–97	2,446,044	2,188,239	89.46	257,805	10.54
1997–98	2,563,647	2,293,093	89.45	270,554	10.55
1998–99	2,610,392	2,335,681	89.48	274,711	10.52
1999–00	2,670,108	2,381,860	89.20	288,248	10.80
2000–01	2,784,625	2,435,889	87.48	348,736	12.52
2001–02	2,856,925	2,502,384	87.59	354,541	12.41
2002–03	2,919,515	2,541,814	87.06	377,701	12.94
2003–04	2,981,867	2,600,521	87.21	381,346	12.79
2004–05	3,040,305	2,673,563	87.94	366,742	12.06
2005–06	3,012,945	2,662,658	88.37	350,287	11.63

1/ Private (nonpublic) elementary and secondary schools in Florida are not licensed, accredited, approved, or regulated by the state but they are required to make their existence known to the Department of Education and respond to an annual survey. See Glossary under Private school for definition.

Note: Based on DOE survey taken during the school year. Data may differ slightly from data based on fall surveys as shown in other *Abstract* tables.

Source: State of Florida, Department of Education, Office of Independent Education and Parental Choice, *Florida's Private Schools, 2005–2006,* August 2006, Internet site <http:/www.floridaschoolchoice.org/> (accessed 18, February 2007).

Table 4.07. ELEMENTARY AND SECONDARY SCHOOLS: NET CHANGE IN MEMBERSHIP IN THE STATE AND COUNTIES OF FLORIDA, FALL 2002 TO FALL 2006

County	Number	Percentage	County	Number	Percentage	County	Number	Percentage
Florida	120,627	4.76	Gulf	29	1.34	Nassau	417	3.96
			Hamilton	-31	-1.50	Okaloosa	-695	-2.25
Alachua	-311	-1.06	Hardee	-138	-2.67	Okeechobee	205	2.89
Baker	449	9.92	Hendry	-210	-2.74	Orange	16,512	10.41
Bay	574	2.17	Hernando	3,846	20.68	Osceola	11,399	28.16
Bradford	-346	-8.59	Highlands	1,025	8.97	Palm Beach	6,633	4.02
Brevard	2,262	3.12	Hillsborough	18,175	10.37	Pasco	9,731	17.71
Broward	-5,158	-1.93	Holmes	-30	-0.88	Pinellas	-4,874	-4.25
Calhoun	54	2.49	Indian River	1,631	10.21	Polk	10,725	13.06
Charlotte	218	1.23	Jackson	154	2.13	Putnam	-382	-3.06
Citrus	733	4.78	Jefferson	-355	-22.54	St. Johns	4,982	22.71
Clay	5,850	19.59	Lafayette	25	2.38	St. Lucie	7,236	22.94
Collier	5,060	13.28	Lake	7,793	24.53	Santa Rosa	1,749	7.40
Columbia	478	4.93	Lee	15,832	25.07	Sarasota	4,164	10.95
DeSoto	68	1.38	Leon	528	1.66	Seminole	2,937	4.63
Dixie	12	0.54	Levy	144	2.36	Sumter	874	13.33
Duval	-2,947	-2.30	Liberty	92	6.65	Suwannee	179	3.09
Escambia	-1,163	-2.65	Madison	-376	-11.36	Taylor	-170	-4.74
Flagler	4,562	60.13	Manatee	3,136	8.02	Union	91	4.19
Franklin	-26	-1.94	Marion	2,881	7.26	Volusia	3,013	4.79
Gadsden	-545	-7.57	Martin	984	5.70	Wakulla	389	8.35
Gilchrist	153	5.60	Miami-Dade	-19,592	-5.25	Walton	400	6.35
Glades	258	25.85	Monroe	-820	-8.92	Washington	154	4.51

Note: Data are for public schools grades prekinderdgarten through twelve.

Source: State of Florida, Department of Education, Education Information and Accountability Services (EIAS), *Statistical Brief: Membership in Florida's Public Schools, Fall 2006,* January 2007, Series 2007-06B, Internet site <http://www.fldoe.org/eias/> (accessed 2, February 2007).

Table 4.20. ELEMENTARY AND SECONDARY SCHOOLS: MEMBERSHIP BY RACE OR HISPANIC ORIGIN IN THE STATE AND COUNTIES OF FLORIDA, FALL 2006

			Percentage of membership					
			Race					
County	Total membership	Total minority	White Non-Hispanic	Black Non-Hispanic	Asian/ Pacific Islander	American Indian/ Alaskan native	Multi-racial	Hispanic origin 1/
Florida	2,655,782	1,415,524	46.70	23.14	2.31	0.30	3.29	24.27
Alachua	28,998	14,697	49.32	36.71	3.81	0.23	4.35	5.59
Baker	4,974	769	84.54	12.48	0.36	0.18	1.41	1.03
Bay	27,005	6,803	74.81	15.17	2.02	0.44	3.77	3.78
Bradford	3,683	1,048	71.54	23.62	0.79	0.08	1.93	2.04
Brevard	74,791	21,679	71.01	14.30	1.94	0.32	4.77	7.65
Broward	262,726	180,219	31.40	37.21	3.26	0.19	2.58	25.35
Calhoun	2,227	414	81.41	13.34	0.49	0.31	2.42	2.02
Charlotte	17,888	3,875	78.34	8.42	1.64	0.26	4.05	7.29
Citrus	16,077	2,267	85.90	4.33	1.39	0.38	3.57	4.43
Clay	35,711	8,501	76.20	12.21	2.64	0.18	2.28	6.49
Collier	43,164	24,247	43.83	11.17	1.07	0.31	2.41	41.22
Columbia	10,179	3,092	69.62	21.83	0.87	0.37	3.34	3.96
DeSoto	4,984	2,493	49.98	16.03	0.54	0.06	1.48	31.90
Dixie	2,241	275	87.73	8.57	0.31	0.13	1.38	1.87
Duval	125,171	72,239	42.29	43.64	3.68	0.19	3.82	6.38
Escambia	42,708	19,670	53.94	36.31	2.65	0.73	3.32	3.05
Flagler	12,149	3,594	70.42	13.74	2.19	0.36	4.02	9.28
Franklin	1,317	229	82.61	13.82	0.08	0.08	1.37	2.05
Gadsden	6,650	6,390	3.91	80.44	0.14	0.03	1.04	14.45
Gilchrist	2,887	230	92.03	3.74	0.14	0.24	0.94	2.91
Glades	1,256	671	46.58	17.83	0.24	0.80	1.51	33.04
Gulf	2,193	434	80.21	16.60	0.50	0.18	1.50	1.00
Hamilton	2,036	1,131	44.45	44.45	0.54	0.20	1.13	9.23
Hardee	5,037	3,066	39.13	7.62	1.55	0.08	0.89	50.72
Hendry	7,463	5,279	29.26	15.76	0.29	0.47	2.96	51.25
Hernando	22,447	5,199	76.84	6.78	1.13	0.30	3.93	11.02
Highlands	12,453	5,820	53.26	18.21	1.24	0.63	2.63	24.03
Hillsborough	193,480	110,521	42.88	22.00	2.79	0.29	5.08	26.96
Holmes	3,384	217	93.59	3.58	0.65	0.27	0.62	1.30
Indian River	17,611	6,189	64.86	14.82	1.18	0.22	2.99	15.93
Jackson	7,382	2,747	62.79	30.79	0.58	0.60	2.95	2.29
Jefferson	1,220	928	23.93	70.57	0.33	0.49	1.15	3.52
Lafayette	1,074	289	73.09	10.71	0.09	0.09	2.70	13.31
Lake	39,566	14,322	63.80	15.65	2.08	0.48	2.10	15.89
Lee	78,980	37,235	52.86	13.71	1.50	0.33	3.75	27.85
Leon	32,383	16,092	50.31	40.59	2.83	0.16	3.10	3.01
Levy	6,257	1,506	75.93	15.23	0.50	0.10	1.57	6.68

See footnotes at end of table.

Continued . . .

Table 4.20. ELEMENTARY AND SECONDARY SCHOOLS: MEMBERSHIP BY RACE OR HISPANIC ORIGIN IN THE STATE AND COUNTIES OF FLORIDA, FALL 2006 (Continued)

			Percentage of membership					
			Race					
County	Total membership	Total minority	White Non-Hispanic	Black Non-Hispanic	Asian/ Pacific Islander	American Indian/ Alaskan native	Multi-racial	Hispanic origin 1/
Liberty	1,475	313	78.78	14.85	0.00	0.27	1.90	4.20
Madison	2,935	1,743	40.61	55.40	0.14	0.55	0.48	2.83
Manatee	42,242	17,703	58.09	15.03	1.44	0.12	3.50	21.82
Marion	42,570	16,625	60.95	19.52	1.37	0.57	3.96	13.63
Martin	18,239	5,770	68.36	8.44	1.18	0.23	3.45	18.34
Miami-Dade	353,783	320,511	9.40	26.87	1.15	0.09	1.28	61.20
Monroe	8,375	3,306	60.53	9.89	1.22	0.33	3.92	24.12
Nassau	10,938	1,468	86.58	8.68	0.81	0.23	1.68	2.02
Okaloosa	30,254	8,009	73.53	12.08	2.58	0.47	5.86	5.49
Okeechobee	7,289	3,012	58.68	8.59	0.51	2.99	1.58	27.66
Orange	175,155	114,129	34.84	27.63	4.22	0.43	2.32	30.55
Osceola	51,881	35,095	32.35	10.33	2.49	0.28	5.08	49.47
Palm Beach	171,429	101,333	40.89	28.35	2.61	0.54	4.45	23.15
Pasco	64,688	15,170	76.55	4.98	1.93	0.30	3.77	12.47
Pinellas	109,880	39,663	63.90	19.07	3.65	0.30	4.43	8.65
Polk	92,873	43,606	53.05	21.42	1.37	0.24	2.91	21.02
Putnam	12,101	4,928	59.28	25.58	0.56	0.14	2.80	11.64
St. Johns	26,922	4,531	83.17	8.70	2.14	0.17	1.86	3.96
St. Lucie	38,786	21,643	44.20	28.39	1.69	0.32	4.37	21.03
Santa Rosa	25,392	3,506	86.19	5.37	1.89	0.61	3.00	2.94
Sarasota	42,190	11,446	72.87	9.32	1.74	0.23	4.25	11.59
Seminole	66,349	26,693	59.77	13.44	3.58	0.24	5.46	17.50
Sumter	7,432	2,208	70.29	16.56	0.86	0.23	1.57	10.48
Suwannee	5,981	1,500	74.92	15.06	0.84	0.25	1.47	7.46
Taylor	3,420	1,012	70.41	24.42	0.99	0.50	2.25	1.43
Union	2,265	483	78.68	16.29	0.13	0.00	1.32	3.58
Volusia	65,867	23,122	64.90	14.80	1.47	0.21	3.87	14.75
Wakulla	5,050	765	84.85	11.01	0.53	0.26	2.22	1.13
Walton	6,704	1,022	84.76	7.97	0.63	0.57	1.80	4.28
Washington	3,565	832	76.66	16.83	0.67	1.01	3.06	1.77
Other 2/	6,919	3,367	51.34	27.26	2.17	0.49	4.08	14.67

1/ Persons of Hispanic origin may be of any race. However, these data are not distributed by race.
2/ Includes Florida School for the Deaf and Blind, Dozier School, Florida Virtual School, and University Developmental Research schools.
Note: Data are for public schools grades pre-kindergarten through twelve. Data were obtained from the Florida DOE Student Information Data Base, Survey 2, as of December 14, 2006, and are for public schools that responded to the survey only.

Source: State of Florida, Department of Education, Education Information and Accountability Services (EIAS), *Statistical Brief: Membership in Florida's Public Schools, Fall 2006,* January 2007, Series 2007-06B, Internet site <http:/www.fldoe.org/eias/> (accessed 2, February 2007).

Table 4.21. ELEMENTARY AND SECONDARY SCHOOLS: MEMBERSHIP IN EXCEPTIONAL STUDENT PROGRAMS IN THE STATE AND COUNTIES OF FLORIDA, FALL 2006

County	Total	Students in specified programs (percentage)				
		Specific learning disabilities	Speech language and hearing	Gifted	Educable mentally handicapped	Emotionally handicapped
Florida	517,602	33.71	18.34	24.49	4.64	5.25
Alachua	9,375	33.86	9.50	39.95	2.36	3.50
Baker	587	29.98	29.98	11.07	10.22	4.60
Bay	5,181	35.24	31.91	6.54	3.82	7.37
Bradford	900	46.00	13.11	9.44	6.44	11.33
Brevard	17,393	33.40	21.12	26.69	2.79	4.48
Broward	41,426	19.93	25.51	25.72	3.85	3.51
Calhoun	558	36.20	22.76	12.72	7.17	6.27
Charlotte	3,707	50.26	17.18	7.93	3.43	7.04
Citrus	4,094	31.95	23.16	24.06	5.50	5.86
Clay	7,484	34.05	24.16	15.65	3.59	10.53
Collier	8,301	35.14	18.50	26.73	2.65	2.30
Columbia	1,985	31.03	21.31	3.48	10.83	8.21
DeSoto	927	33.33	27.51	10.68	5.83	10.90
Dixie	504	33.53	31.75	1.98	8.93	7.94
Duval	22,069	35.04	17.61	15.85	7.30	5.38
Escambia	9,414	37.32	18.05	22.25	4.22	6.56
Flagler	2,058	38.19	21.23	15.84	4.08	5.00
Franklin	244	35.66	25.82	5.33	7.38	10.25
Gadsden	1,130	25.22	30.44	8.05	12.39	5.40
Gilchrist	928	49.14	10.99	19.29	2.91	2.91
Glades	226	49.56	20.80	13.72	3.98	3.54
Gulf	561	45.45	14.80	21.75	2.50	4.81
Hamilton	306	23.53	31.70	0.98	11.76	4.25
Hardee	1,043	51.20	15.44	12.27	8.05	5.75
Hendry	1,380	53.26	17.46	9.71	7.46	4.20
Hernando	4,066	40.29	24.23	13.90	3.94	8.04
Highlands	2,238	40.53	13.76	14.92	8.04	10.72
Hillsborough	36,180	34.20	24.37	19.02	5.34	6.21
Holmes	482	36.72	31.95	1.24	14.94	5.39
Indian River	3,353	34.69	17.48	30.45	3.79	3.04
Jackson	1,469	18.65	26.07	11.50	11.78	16.68
Jefferson	272	11.76	26.47	0.74	16.91	22.43
Lafayette	161	38.51	24.22	6.21	15.53	6.83
Lake	6,710	32.46	27.38	12.58	7.93	7.93
Lee	16,369	33.63	14.33	32.56	2.91	4.94
Leon	7,174	18.66	34.39	21.69	4.75	3.90

See footnotes at end of table. Continued . . .

Table 4.21. ELEMENTARY AND SECONDARY SCHOOLS: MEMBERSHIP IN EXCEPTIONAL STUDENT PROGRAMS IN THE STATE AND COUNTIES OF FLORIDA, FALL 2006 (Continued)

		Students in specified programs (percentage)				
County	Total	Specific learning disabilities	Speech language and hearing	Gifted	Educable mentally handicapped	Emotionally handicapped
Levy	1,771	45.85	19.93	17.22	5.93	5.25
Liberty	349	31.23	25.21	0.29	19.48	8.31
Madison	740	28.11	19.32	10.14	19.46	7.16
Manatee	9,241	35.94	24.51	19.10	3.98	6.76
Marion	8,525	37.00	20.01	15.92	7.23	8.00
Martin	3,586	39.10	22.42	17.04	3.76	4.91
Miami-Dade	71,465	30.68	6.07	42.66	2.83	4.40
Monroe	1,772	50.68	9.31	16.48	3.67	6.94
Nassau	1,925	30.86	20.16	15.84	5.51	9.30
Okaloosa	5,904	30.45	27.64	19.09	4.89	5.08
Okeechobee	1,649	50.76	11.16	10.67	5.52	5.94
Orange	33,558	39.81	12.06	24.82	6.56	3.26
Osceola	7,675	43.14	21.20	4.17	7.50	8.52
Palm Beach	32,588	37.14	23.27	22.71	3.93	3.02
Pasco	13,467	39.55	22.73	15.24	4.17	6.71
Pinellas	22,927	30.70	18.21	23.86	3.57	8.31
Polk	15,687	37.48	12.70	20.06	9.54	5.09
Putnam	2,621	43.15	16.02	15.45	6.87	4.01
St. Johns	4,775	45.30	14.93	19.31	3.06	4.23
St. Lucie	6,309	32.27	25.66	20.65	5.91	3.41
Santa Rosa	4,791	30.41	29.56	18.43	5.16	3.26
Sarasota	11,324	32.91	10.91	40.43	1.87	7.28
Seminole	12,569	30.65	22.36	30.07	2.36	4.10
Sumter	1,286	26.83	31.65	14.77	6.14	10.34
Suwannee	816	27.45	21.94	7.23	20.71	7.60
Taylor	729	34.98	22.09	16.46	6.45	8.37
Union	465	38.28	22.80	14.19	7.31	7.96
Volusia	14,279	42.27	12.14	19.33	5.01	5.66
Wakulla	1,167	27.51	25.02	11.14	5.40	5.48
Walton	1,116	33.78	22.85	22.85	6.72	4.75
Washington	630	35.87	27.62	11.43	5.08	8.57
Other schools 1/	1,641	16.09	45.95	14.87	0.91	5.00

1/ Includes Florida School for the Deaf and Blind, Dozier School, Florida Virtual School, and University Developmental Research schools.

Note: Data were obtained from the Fall 2006 Florida DOE Student Information Data Base, Survey 2, as of December 14, 2006, and are for public schools only.

Source: State of Florida, Department of Education, Education Information and Accountability Services (EIAS), *Statistical Brief: Membership in Programs for Exceptional Students, Fall 2006,* January 2007, Series 2007-07B, Internet site <http://www.fldoe.org/eias/> (accessed 2, February 2007).

Table 4.22. ELEMENTARY AND SECONDARY SCHOOLS: NONPROMOTIONS BY SEX AND BY RACE OR HISPANIC ORIGIN IN THE STATE AND COUNTIES OF FLORIDA, 2005–06

		Female		Race (percentage)			Hispanic origin 1/	
County	Total	Number	Percentage	White Non-Hispanic	Black Non-Hispanic	Other 2/	Number	Percentage
Florida	175,494	67,832	5.4	36.4	34.7	3.8	44,070	25.1
Alachua	2,680	1,126	7.5	32.4	58.3	4.1	139	5.2
Baker	348	121	5.5	79.0	18.4	1.1	5	1.4
Bay	1,747	695	5.4	67.3	23.6	4.8	74	4.2
Bradford	251	86	5.1	61.0	34.3	2.4	6	2.4
Brevard	4,764	1,891	5.3	64.1	21.2	5.4	445	9.3
Broward	15,448	5,661	4.4	20.0	53.7	3.4	3,533	22.9
Calhoun	107	45	4.3	81.3	14.0	1.9	3	2.8
Charlotte	465	182	2.2	73.3	10.8	8.4	35	7.5
Citrus	698	282	3.5	85.4	5.9	4.7	28	4.0
Clay	1,423	561	3.4	71.2	17.3	4.4	101	7.1
Collier	2,401	917	4.5	29.8	14.7	2.3	1,278	53.2
Columbia	880	337	7.1	61.9	27.5	5.5	45	5.1
DeSoto	320	107	4.2	39.7	19.4	2.8	122	38.1
Dixie	189	79	8.3	84.1	13.2	0.5	4	2.1
Duval	15,641	6,307	10.5	34.4	54.7	4.4	1,015	6.5
Escambia	2,542	978	4.9	40.2	52.5	4.2	79	3.1
Flagler	441	168	3.4	63.5	20.9	5.4	45	10.2
Franklin	122	48	7.8	62.3	32.0	4.1	2	1.6
Gadsden	717	294	10.1	5.2	78.9	0.8	108	15.1
Gilchrist	189	83	6.3	87.3	9.0	1.1	5	2.6
Glades	142	52	7.1	38.7	16.9	5.6	55	38.7
Gulf	86	27	2.7	75.6	22.1	1.2	1	1.2
Hamilton	88	29	3.4	27.3	51.1	1.1	18	20.5
Hardee	440	175	7.2	28.0	9.8	2.0	265	60.2
Hendry	353	144	4.0	19.0	17.8	4.2	208	58.9
Hernando	2,031	834	8.0	75.9	8.1	3.9	245	12.1
Highlands	1,231	461	7.9	43.5	24.5	3.1	355	28.8
Hillsborough	13,372	5,228	5.7	29.6	31.8	4.8	4,521	33.8
Holmes	171	61	3.9	95.9	1.2	1.2	3	1.8
Indian River	376	136	1.7	47.9	21.8	5.1	95	25.3
Jackson	420	145	4.2	51.7	39.8	6.2	10	2.4
Jefferson	91	27	4.8	36.3	60.4	2.2	1	1.1
Lafayette	40	11	2.3	65.0	10.0	7.5	7	17.5
Lake	1,755	707	3.9	54.1	22.1	3.6	354	20.2
Lee	5,493	2,128	5.9	41.3	21.0	4.3	1,830	33.3
Leon	2,074	824	5.7	34.4	59.2	3.5	60	2.9
Levy	440	154	5.6	72.7	18.4	0.9	35	8.0
Liberty	134	45	7.9	73.1	17.2	3.0	9	6.7

See footnotes at end of table. Continued . . .

Table 4.22. ELEMENTARY AND SECONDARY SCHOOLS: NONPROMOTIONS BY SEX AND BY RACE OR HISPANIC ORIGIN IN THE STATE AND COUNTIES OF FLORIDA, 2005–06 (Continued)

County	Total	Female Num-ber	Female Percent-age	Race (percentage) White Non-Hispanic	Race (percentage) Black Non-Hispanic	Race (percentage) Other 2/	Hispanic origin 1/ Num-ber	Hispanic origin 1/ Percent-age
Madison	325	137	10.3	34.2	63.1	0.6	7	2.2
Manatee	3,271	1,346	6.7	44.1	23.4	3.9	932	28.5
Marion	3,264	1,261	6.3	55.7	26.7	3.6	453	13.9
Martin	463	172	2.0	45.4	19.0	6.5	135	29.2
Miami-Dade	20,805	7,773	4.6	5.8	34.9	1.3	12,084	58.1
Monroe	535	190	4.8	51.2	14.6	3.2	166	31.0
Nassau	625	237	4.6	84.5	9.4	2.9	20	3.2
Okaloosa	2,064	740	5.2	61.0	24.4	7.0	157	7.6
Okeechobee	577	218	6.4	52.5	14.4	3.6	170	29.5
Orange	15,432	5,937	6.6	25.2	40.8	3.4	4,721	30.6
Osceola	3,327	1,320	5.6	25.1	11.2	5.9	1,923	57.8
Palm Beach	10,959	4,192	5.1	25.8	44.4	4.4	2,786	25.4
Pasco	3,885	1,563	5.3	76.1	6.4	3.5	544	14.0
Pinellas	5,681	2,301	4.3	55.6	28.2	6.1	571	10.1
Polk	6,407	2,454	5.8	46.2	28.9	3.2	1,391	21.7
Putnam	914	343	6.4	50.4	32.5	3.6	123	13.5
St. Johns	633	242	2.0	72.8	18.8	3.6	30	4.7
St. Lucie	2,627	1,031	5.8	36.6	39.1	3.5	546	20.8
Santa Rosa	912	333	2.8	83.8	8.0	4.6	33	3.6
Sarasota	1,924	782	3.9	63.2	16.0	4.0	325	16.9
Seminole	3,549	1,463	4.6	44.0	26.9	6.8	792	22.3
Sumter	446	160	5.9	60.3	23.5	2.0	63	14.1
Suwannee	366	124	4.6	63.4	23.5	1.9	41	11.2
Taylor	260	110	7.5	64.6	28.5	4.2	7	2.7
Union	199	82	8.1	70.4	23.1	2.5	8	4.0
Volusia	4,555	1,783	5.7	55.1	22.4	4.3	824	18.1
Wakulla	264	94	4.3	81.8	14.0	3.8	1	0.4
Walton	436	150	4.9	77.5	13.5	2.1	30	6.9
Washington	201	87	5.2	68.7	21.9	7.0	5	2.5
Deaf and Blind	20	6	2.0	35.0	10.0	0.0	11	55.0
Dozier	351	0	0.0	36.5	58.1	0.0	19	5.4
FAU Lab	8	3	0.9	50.0	37.5	0.0	1	12.5
FSU Lab	53	22	2.0	50.9	30.2	5.7	7	13.2
FAMU Lab	38	15	6.1	0.0	97.4	2.6	0	0.0
UF Lab	8	5	1.0	25.0	75.0	0.0	0	0.0

1/ Persons of Hispanic origin may be of any race. However, these data are not distributed by race.
2/ Includes Asian, American Indian, and multiracial.
Note: Data are for public schools students in kindergarten through grade 12 and were obtained from the Florida DOE Student Information Data Base, Survey 5, as of December 20, 2006.

Source: State of Florida, Department of Education, Education Information and Accountability Services (EIAS), *Statistical Brief: Non-promotions in Florida's Public Schools, 2005–06,* January 2007, Series 2007-10B, Internet site <http:/www.fldoe.org/eias/> (accessed 22, March 2007).

Table 4.25. HOME EDUCATION PROGRAMS: ENROLLMENT IN THE STATE AND COUNTIES OF FLORIDA, 2005–06

County	Families		Students		County	Families		Students	
	Number	Percent-age of growth	Number	Percent-age of growth		Number	Percent-age of growth	Number	Percent-age of growth
Florida	36,149	2.2	52,613	2.9	Lake	763	8.8	1,081	2.9
					Lee	1,189	3.0	1,763	3.8
Alachua	671	15.7	919	1.7	Leon	649	11.9	1,046	13.3
Baker	62	55.0	90	38.5	Levy	146	0.7	204	6.3
Bay	460	9.0	636	1.1	Liberty	7	0.0	7	-30.0
Bradford	89	-8.2	135	-9.4	Madison	58	7.4	81	11.0
Brevard	1,664	20.1	2,380	6.3	Manatee	423	-22.2	641	7.4
Broward	2,016	4.1	2,752	4.3	Marion	913	4.3	1,531	37.6
Calhoun	43	10.3	67	15.5	Martin	351	-8.8	463	-6.8
Charlotte	215	-15.0	309	-3.4	Miami-Dade	1,829	-1.5	2,524	-1.6
Citrus	432	12.8	634	15.1	Monroe	142	9.2	194	-24.2
Clay	270	-36.6	841	21.2	Nassau	165	-56.8	208	-64.7
Collier	471	17.5	749	20.6	Okaloosa	411	-7.6	608	-16.4
Columbia	287	-26.0	547	-2.5	Okeechobee	170	38.2	226	29.9
DeSoto	133	31.7	189	31.3	Orange	1,774	20.0	2,607	-9.9
Dixie	77	26.2	106	16.5	Osceola	660	43.2	870	31.8
Duval	2,071	6.3	3,116	9.8	Palm Beach	2,675	1.3	3,737	3.5
Escambia	988	13.6	1,273	2.8	Pasco	1,089	-16.9	1,599	2.0
Flagler	260	18.7	395	24.6	Pinellas	1,673	-0.2	2,504	-1.2
Franklin	25	-13.8	37	0.0	Polk	1,937	-21.7	2,572	-17.2
Gadsden	233	9.4	361	12.1	Putnam	195	19.6	234	-7.5
Gilchrist	105	19.3	144	2.9	St. Johns	520	36.8	667	17.4
Glades	35	2.9	43	-2.3	St. Lucie	504	-4.0	729	19.9
Gulf	21	75.0	27	58.8	Santa Rosa	481	-0.2	720	-3.0
Hamilton	47	30.6	80	29.0	Sarasota	550	0.0	783	2.6
Hardee	31	10.7	45	7.1	Seminole	746	-25.4	1,155	2.4
Hendry	72	12.5	106	10.4	Sumter	136	9.7	204	11.5
Hernando	514	70.2	695	7.1	Suwannee	288	62.7	421	66.4
Highlands	172	2.4	286	5.9	Taylor	112	-18.8	205	5.1
Hillsborough	1,973	0.6	3,179	2.8	Union	39	-11.4	51	-13.6
Holmes	60	5.3	84	9.1	Volusia	1,204	31.4	1,409	2.1
Indian River	337	-16.0	493	2.3	Wakulla	74	23.3	95	26.7
Jackson	137	-1.4	195	-3.9	Walton	107	-29.6	248	17.0
Jefferson	66	88.6	112	67.2	Washington	107	0.9	164	2.5
Lafayette	25	25.0	37	12.1					

Note: Home education is defined by Florida Statutes as the "sequentially progressive instruction of a student in his or her home by his or her parent or guardian." No curriculum is prescribed. See Glossary under Private school for definition of private schools.

Source: State of Florida, Department of Education, Office of Independent Education and Parental Choice, *Home Education Program Statistics, 2005-06,* July 2006, Internet site <http:/www.floridaschoolchoice.org/> (accessed 2, February 2007).

Table 4.26. NONPUBLIC ELEMENTARY AND SECONDARY SCHOOLS: SCHOOLS AND PUPIL MEMBERSHIP IN THE STATE AND COUNTIES OF FLORIDA, 2005–06

County	Number of schools	Membership PK-12	Percentage of total membership	County	Number of schools	Membership PK-12	Percentage of total membership
Florida	2,078	350,287	11.63	Lake	38	4,486	10.55
				Lee	61	9,043	10.69
Alachua	36	4,236	12.70	Leon	42	6,146	15.98
Baker	1	15	0.31	Levy	5	173	2.69
Bay	9	1,641	5.61	Liberty	0	0	0.00
Bradford	7	360	8.70	Madison	4	287	8.65
Brevard	83	10,721	12.48	Manatee	27	3,360	7.35
Broward	144	39,024	12.57	Marion	37	5,266	11.14
Calhoun	0	0	0.00	Martin	14	2,468	11.98
Charlotte	14	994	5.27	Miami-Dade	372	62,665	14.76
Citrus	9	1,098	6.48	Monroe	5	515	5.66
Clay	26	3,016	8.11	Nassau	8	856	7.31
Collier	23	4,345	9.12	Okaloosa	13	2,529	7.55
Columbia	9	492	4.61	Okeechobee	2	156	2.08
DeSoto	4	209	4.00	Orange	152	28,389	13.94
Dixie	1	13	0.58	Osceola	34	4,620	8.49
Duval	155	28,068	18.15	Palm Beach	108	26,128	13.00
Escambia	31	7,118	14.08	Pasco	31	3,033	4.61
Flagler	5	631	5.41	Pinellas	111	18,766	14.34
Franklin	1	95	6.57	Polk	49	8,849	9.00
Gadsden	5	639	8.93	Putnam	15	774	5.93
Gilchrist	2	131	4.33	St. Johns	17	2,630	9.27
Glades	0	0	0.00	St. Lucie	23	4,542	11.15
Gulf	1	139	6.00	Santa Rosa	5	731	2.82
Hamilton	2	117	5.51	Sarasota	37	5,955	12.45
Hardee	1	25	0.50	Seminole	55	9,682	12.55
Hendry	2	239	3.06	Sumter	1	52	0.70
Hernando	11	1,732	7.39	Suwannee	4	407	6.40
Highlands	11	903	6.93	Taylor	3	86	2.48
Hillsborough	137	22,446	10.39	Union	1	36	1.55
Holmes	2	78	2.22	Volusia	48	6,065	8.46
Indian River	12	2,018	10.48	Wakulla	2	66	1.33
Jackson	3	242	3.14	Walton	3	129	1.84
Jefferson	2	410	25.08	Washington	1	112	3.05
Lafayette	1	90	7.79				

PK-12 Prekindergarten through grade 12.
Note: Data are revised. See Glossary under Private school for definition of nonpublic schools.

Source: State of Florida, Department of Education, Office of Independent Education and Parental Choice, *Florida's Private Schools, 2005–2006,* August 2006, Internet site <http:/www.floridaschoolchoice.org/> (accessed 2, February 2007).

Table 4.27. ELEMENTARY AND SECONDARY SCHOOLS: NUMBER AND PUPIL MEMBERSHIP IN THE STATE AND COUNTIES OF FLORIDA, SCHOOL YEAR 2005–06

County	Number of schools	Membership 1/ Total	Membership 1/ Percentage change from 2004–05	County	Number of schools	Membership 1/ Total	Membership 1/ Percentage change from 2004–05
Florida	4,193	2,622,379	1.2	Lake	59	37,324	5.7
				Lee	105	73,996	6.6
Alachua	72	28,149	0.1	Leon	61	31,316	1.0
Baker	12	4,743	1.8	Levy	20	6,140	0.9
Bay	52	26,950	2.4	Liberty	14	1,372	5.3
Bradford	16	3,612	-1.3	Madison	13	2,905	-3.6
Brevard	129	73,507	0.8	Manatee	76	41,701	3.1
Broward	287	266,468	-0.3	Marion	65	41,339	2.3
Calhoun	11	2,189	-1.6	Martin	43	17,685	1.3
Charlotte	28	17,418	2.1	Miami-Dade	438	354,753	-1.1
Citrus	29	15,551	1.2	Monroe	26	8,281	-1.7
Clay	41	33,847	6.0	Nassau	24	10,692	1.6
Collier	67	42,339	3.1	Okaloosa	64	30,685	0.4
Columbia	20	9,984	2.9	Okeechobee	22	7,147	0.5
DeSoto	18	4,897	1.5	Orange	222	173,208	1.7
Dixie	10	2,077	2.1	Osceola	68	48,955	4.9
Duval	182	125,214	-0.6	Palm Beach	265	171,959	0.2
Escambia	84	42,676	-0.5	Pasco	93	61,645	4.2
Flagler	19	10,969	14.3	Pinellas	180	110,896	-0.6
Franklin	12	1,287	-0.6	Polk	156	88,262	3.6
Gadsden	28	6,039	-0.2	Putnam	27	11,883	-1.3
Gilchrist	10	2,720	1.3	St. Johns	41	25,401	5.8
Glades	11	1,258	3.0	St. Lucie	49	35,946	4.4
Gulf	12	2,112	-0.3	Santa Rosa	42	24,626	0.7
Hamilton	12	1,917	0.5	Sarasota	65	41,528	1.7
Hardee	14	4,908	-2.8	Seminole	81	66,748	1.7
Hendry	21	7,485	-0.3	Sumter	20	7,221	3.3
Hernando	32	21,551	6.5	Suwannee	14	5,783	3.0
Highlands	22	11,999	0.8	Taylor	13	3,053	-4.4
Hillsborough	279	189,898	2.8	Union	11	2,239	4.1
Holmes	13	3,351	1.2	Volusia	98	65,145	0.9
Indian River	32	16,919	1.2	Wakulla	16	4,643	1.7
Jackson	26	7,135	1.9	Walton	22	6,842	6.5
Jefferson	14	1,157	-10.3	Washington	13	3,523	2.7
Lafayette	8	1,053	0.3	Other schools 2/	44	6,158	-36.4

1/ Based on kindergarten through grade 12 fall membership survey.
2/ Includes Florida School for the Deaf and Blind, Dozier School, Florida Virtual School, and University Developmental Research schools.
Note: Data are for public schools only.

Source: State of Florida, Department of Education, Education Information and Accountability Services, (EIAS), *Profiles of Florida School Districts, 2005-2006, Student and Staff Data,* Internet site <http://www.fldoe.org/eias/> (accessed 19, June 2007).

Table 4.28. ELEMENTARY AND SECONDARY SCHOOLS: STUDENTS ELIGIBLE FOR FREE/REDUCED-PRICE LUNCH, 2005–06

County	Total membership	Eligible		Change since 1996–97 A/
		Number	Percentage	
Florida 1/	2,669,565	1,223,442	45.8	2.3
Alachua	29,109	13,518	46.4	0.9
Baker	4,903	2,096	42.8	0.9
Bay	27,614	12,630	45.7	0.2
Bradford	3,779	2,000	52.9	-0.6
Brevard	75,207	22,584	30.0	0.2
Broward	271,564	112,599	41.5	4.7
Calhoun	2,274	1,178	51.8	4.2
Charlotte	17,901	7,065	39.5	-2.5
Citrus	15,812	6,707	42.4	0.2
Clay	34,167	8,427	24.7	2.5
Collier	43,288	17,858	41.3	-1.3
Columbia	10,188	5,488	53.9	6.2
DeSoto	5,019	2,979	59.4	-3.1
Dixie	2,238	1,535	68.6	8.3
Duval	126,648	52,709	41.6	-4.8
Escambia	43,458	26,846	61.8	6.9
Flagler	11,049	3,864	35.0	-3.0
Franklin	1,350	826	61.2	6.8
Gadsden	6,515	5,225	80.2	-3.2
Gilchrist	2,892	1,445	50.0	-0.3
Glades	1,272	775	60.9	3.3
Gulf	2,179	980	45.0	-2.6
Hamilton	2,006	1,124	56.0	-6.0
Hardee	4,967	3,177	64.0	7.1
Hendry	7,572	5,277	69.7	14.8
Hernando	21,707	9,490	43.7	-2.2
Highlands	12,128	6,950	57.3	5.3
Hillsborough	193,669	95,726	49.4	0.8
Holmes	3,439	1,958	56.9	-2.4
Indian River	17,233	6,788	39.4	-1.0
Jackson	7,455	3,931	52.7	0.1
Jefferson	1,230	855	69.5	2.5
Lafayette	1,080	560	51.9	-0.8
Lake	38,058	15,932	41.9	1.3
Lee	75,610	33,503	44.3	0.4
Leon	32,319	11,838	36.6	6.7
Levy	6,256	3,490	55.8	0.2
Liberty	1,471	700	47.6	3.2
Madison	3,032	2,231	73.6	10.6
Manatee	42,348	18,433	43.5	0.5
Marion	42,017	22,059	52.5	1.6
Martin	18,150	4,815	26.5	-4.1
Miami-Dade	362,050	221,229	61.1	1.9
Monroe	8,594	3,383	39.4	4.4
Nassau	10,866	3,652	33.6	2.3
Okaloosa	30,999	8,743	28.2	-1.6
Okeechobee	7,329	3,826	52.2	-1.8
Orange	175,593	81,245	46.3	1.9
Osceola 2/	49,772	27,340	54.9	(X)
Palm Beach	174,861	72,947	41.7	12.3
Pasco	62,766	27,283	43.5	-0.6
Pinellas	112,150	45,217	40.3	2.5
Polk	89,423	51,575	57.7	4.7
Putnam	12,268	8,055	65.7	3.8
St. Johns	25,757	4,592	17.8	-9.1
St. Lucie	36,189	19,022	52.6	-0.6
Santa Rosa	25,188	8,144	32.3	1.3
Sarasota	41,884	12,081	28.8	-4.7
Seminole	67,508	20,566	30.5	5.2
Sumter	7,416	3,919	52.9	-10.0
Suwannee	5,954	3,147	52.9	8.0
Taylor	3,378	1,930	57.1	10.4
Union	2,290	1,013	44.2	2.0
Volusia	65,599	27,459	41.9	2.2
Wakulla	4,914	1,741	35.4	-0.7
Walton	6,896	3,276	47.5	-3.3
Washington	3,560	1,937	54.4	2.4

(X) Not applicable.
A/ Percentage change 1996–97 to 2005–06.
1/ Includes special school districts not reported elsewhere.
2/ No data was reported for Osceola in 1996–97.
Note: Data are for public schools only.

Source: State of Florida, Department of Education, Education Information and Accountability Services (EIAS), *Florida Information Note: Free/Reduced-Price Lunch Eligibility,* Series 2007-04F, April 2007, Internet site <http://www.fldoe.org/eias/> (accessed 27, July 2007).

Table 4.50. HIGHER EDUCATION: ENROLLMENT IN SELECTED COLLEGES AND UNIVERSITIES IN SPECIFIED CITIES AND COUNTIES OF FLORIDA, FALL 2003

School 1/	City	County	Enroll-ment 2/
AI Miami International University of Art and Design	Miami	Miami-Dade	1,311
American Intercontinental University	Weston	Broward	1,939
Angley College	Deland	Volusia	113
Argosy University	Sarasota	Sarasota	1,965
Argosy University	Tampa	Hillsborough	538
ATI Career Training Center	Miami	Miami-Dade	616
ATI Career Training Center	Ft. Lauderdale	Broward	627
ATI Health Education Center	Miami	Miami-Dade	345
Atlantic Institute of Oriental Medicine	Ft. Lauderdale	Broward	92
Atlantic Technical Center	Coconut Creek	Broward	896
Barry University	Miami	Miami-Dade	9,298
Bethune Cookman College	Daytona Beach	Volusia	2,895
Brevard Community College	Cocoa	Brevard	14,616
Broward Community College	Ft. Lauderdale	Broward	32,948
Carlos Albizu University	Miami	Miami-Dade	1,010
Central Florida College	Winter Park	Orange	349
Central Florida Community College	Ocala	Marion	5,999
Chipola College	Marianna	Jackson	2,253
City College	Ft. Lauderdale	Broward	651
City College	Casselberry	Seminole	270
City College	Miami	Miami-Dade	279
City College	Gainesville	Alachua	321
Clearwater Christian College	Clearwater	Pinellas	628
College of Business and Technology	Miami	Miami-Dade	154
Daytona Beach Community College	Daytona Beach	Volusia	12,083
Devry University	Orlando	Orange	3,317
East West College of Natural Medicine	Sarasota	Sarasota	104
Eckerd College	St. Petersburg	Pinellas	1,684
Edison Community College	Ft. Myers	Lee	10,116
Edward Waters College	Jacksonville	Duval	1,206
Embry Riddle Aeronautical University Extended Campus	Daytona Beach	Volusia	13,292
Embry Riddle Aeronautical University	Daytona Beach	Volusia	4,788
Flagler College	St. Augustine	St. Johns	2,103
Florida Agricultural and Mechanical University	Tallahassee	Leon	13,067
Florida Atlantic University	Boca Raton	Palm Beach	25,319
Florida Career College	Miami	Miami-Dade	2,461
Florida Christian College, Inc.	Kissimmee	Osceola	299
Florida Coastal School of Law	Jacksonville	Duval	904
Florida College	Temple Terrace	Hillsborough	503
Florida College of Natural Health	Pompano Beach	Broward	340
Florida College of Natural Health	Miami	Miami-Dade	209
Florida College of Natural Health	Maitland	Seminole	366
Florida College of Natural Health	Bradenton	Sarasota	168
Florida Community College at Jacksonville	Jacksonville	Duval	24,769
Florida Gulf Coast University	Ft. Myers	Lee	5,955
Florida Hospital College of Health Sciences	Orlando	Orange	1,796
Florida Institute of Technology	Melbourne	Brevard	4,683
Florida International University	Miami	Miami-Dade	34,865
Florida Keys Community College	Key West	Monroe	1,131

See footnotes at end of table. Continued . . .

Table 4.50. HIGHER EDUCATION: ENROLLMENT IN SELECTED COLLEGES AND UNIVERSITIES IN SPECIFIED CITIES AND COUNTIES OF FLORIDA, FALL 2003 (Continued)

School 1/	City	County	Enroll-ment 2/
Florida Memorial College	Miami	Miami-Dade	2,219
Florida Metropolitan University-Brandon	Tampa	Hillsborough	1,332
Florida Metropolitan University-Ft. Lauderdale	Pompano Beach	Broward	1,594
Florida Metropolitan University	Jacksonville	Duval	1,305
Florida Metropolitan University	Lakeland	Polk	1,121
Florida Metropolitan University	Melbourne	Brevard	1,014
Florida Metropolitan University-North Orlando	Orlando	Orange	1,612
Florida Metropolitan University-Pinellas	Clearwater	Pinellas	1,085
Florida Metropolitan University-South Orlando	Orlando	Orange	2,163
Florida Metropolitan University	Tampa	Hillsborough	1,903
Florida National College	Hialeah	Miami-Dade	1,739
Florida Southern College	Lakeland	Polk	2,546
Florida State University	Tallahassee	Leon	38,431
Florida Technical College	Orlando	Orange	789
Florida Technical College of Jacksonville, Inc.	Jacksonville	Duval	177
Full Sail Real World Education	Winter Park	Orange	5,034
Golf Academy of the South	Altamonte Springs	Seminole	219
Gooding Institute of Nurse Anesthesia	Panama City	Bay	38
Gulf Coast Community College	Panama City	Bay	6,737
Herzing College	Winter Park	Orange	158
High-Tech Institute	Orlando	Orange	1,046
Hillsborough Community College	Tampa	Hillsborough	22,123
Hobe Sound Bible College	Hobe Sound	Martin	123
Indian River Community College	Ft. Pierce	St. Lucie	12,912
International Academy of Design and Technology	Tampa	Hillsborough	2,405
International Academy of Design and Technology	Orlando	Orange	863
International College	Naples	Collier	1,544
ITT Technical Institute	Tampa	Hillsborough	649
ITT Technical Institute	Lake Mary	Seminole	474
ITT Technical Institute	Jacksonville	Duval	747
ITT Technical Institute	Ft. Lauderdale	Broward	656
ITT Technical Institute	Miami	Miami-Dade	536
Jacksonville University	Jacksonville	Duval	2,946
Johnson and Wales University-Florida Campus	North Miami	Miami-Dade	2,389
Jones College	Jacksonville	Duval	623
Jones College	Miami	Miami-Dade	154
Keiser College	Ft. Lauderdale	Broward	6,121
Lake City Community College	Lake City	Columbia	2,777
Lake-Sumter Community College	Leesburg	Lake	3,576
Lynn University	Boca Raton	Palm Beach	2,510
Manatee Community College	Bradenton	Manatee	9,582
Miami Dade College	Miami	Miami-Dade	57,026
New College of Florida	Sarasota	Sarasota	692
North Florida Community College	Madison	Madison	1,262
North Florida Institute	Orange Park	Clay	347
Northwood University-Florida Education Center	West Palm Beach	Palm Beach	956
Nova Southeastern University	Ft. Lauderdale	Broward	25,430
Okaloosa-Walton Community College	Niceville	Okaloosa	7,079
Orlando Culinary Academy	Orlando	Orange	1,171
Palm Beach Atlantic College	West Palm Beach	Palm Beach	3,066
Palm Beach Community College	Lake Worth	Palm Beach	22,554

See footnotes at end of table. Continued . . .

Table 4.50. HIGHER EDUCATION: ENROLLMENT IN SELECTED COLLEGES AND UNIVERSITIES IN SPECIFIED CITIES AND COUNTIES OF FLORIDA, FALL 2003 (Continued)

School 1/	City	County	Enroll-ment 2/
Pasco-Hernando Community College	New Port Richey	Pasco	7,213
Pensacola Junior College	Pensacola	Escambia	10,879
Polk Community College	Winter Haven	Polk	7,057
Remington College	Jacksonville	Duval	336
Remington College	Largo	Pinellas	805
Remington College	Tampa	Hillsborough	685
Ringling School of Art And Design	Sarasota	Sarasota	1,008
Rollins College	Winter Park	Orange	3,726
St. John Vianney College Seminary	Miami	Miami-Dade	62
St. Johns River Community College	Palatka	Putnam	4,982
St. Leo University	St. Leo	Pasco	12,677
St. Petersburg College	Pinellas Park	Pinellas	24,102
St. Petersburg Theological Seminary	St. Petersburg	Pinellas	69
St. Thomas University	Miami Gardens	Miami-Dade	2,630
St. Vincent de Paul Regional Seminary	Boynton Beach	Palm Beach	87
Santa Fe Community College	Gainesville	Alachua	13,888
Schiller International University	Dunedin	Pinellas	190
Seminole Community College	Sanford	Seminole	12,202
South Florida Community College	Avon Park	Highlands	2,546
South University	West Palm Beach	Palm Beach	502
Southeastern College Assemblies of God	Lakeland	Polk	1,964
Southwest Florida College	Ft. Myers	Lee	1,961
Stetson University	Deland	Volusia	3,577
Tallahassee Community College	Tallahassee	Leon	12,775
Talmudic College of Florida	Miami Beach	Miami-Dade	44
The Baptist College of Florida	Graceville	Alachua	652
The University of West Florida	Pensacola	Escambia	9,518
Trinity Baptist College	Jacksonville	Duval	434
Trinity College of Florida	Trinity	Pasco	202
Trinity International University	Miami	Miami-Dade	236
University of Central Florida	Orlando	Orange	42,465
University of Florida	Gainesville	Alachua	47,993
University of Miami	Coral Gables	Miami-Dade	15,250
University of North Florida	Jacksonville	Duval	14,533
University of Phoenix-Ft. Lauderdale	Plantation	Broward	2,586
University of Phoenix	Jacksonville	Duval	2,122
University of Phoenix-Orlando	Maitland	Orange	2,142
University of Phoenix-Tampa	Temple Terrace	Hillsborough	2,570
University of South Florida	Tampa	Hillsborough	42,238
Valencia Community College	Orlando	Orange	29,556
Warner Southern College	Lake Wales	Polk	1,023
Webber International	Babson Park	Polk	641
Webster College	Ocala	Marion	395
Webster College, Inc.	Holiday	Pasco	258
Yeshivah Gedolah Rabbinical College	Miami Beach	Miami-Dade	56

1/ Includes institutions accredited at the college level by an agency recognized by the U.S. Secretary of Education.

2/ Includes undergraduate, graduate, first-professional, and unclassified students, both full- and part-time.

Note: Only accredited, degree-granting schools with reported fall enrollment are listed.

Source: U.S., Department of Education, National Center for Education Statistics, Integrated Postsecondary Education Data System (IPEDS), Internet site <http://nces.ed.gov/> (accessed 18, August 2006).

Table 4.53. HIGHER EDUCATION: ENROLLMENT IN THE UNIVERSITIES OF THE STATE UNIVERSITY SYSTEM OF FLORIDA BY LEVEL, SEX, RACE OR HISPANIC ORIGIN AND STATUS, 2002, 2003, AND 2004

Sex and race	Educational and general 1/ 2002	Educational and general 1/ 2003	Educational and general 1/ 2004 Total	Educational and general 1/ 2004 Undergraduates (percentage)	Health or medical center 2002	Health or medical center 2003	Health or medical center 2004 Total	Health or medical center 2004 Undergraduates (percentage)
Part-time 2/								
Total	81,690	79,509	80,654	75.1	1,002	591	583	42.7
Sex								
Female	47,249	46,324	47,387	74.3	663	448	463	48.4
Male	34,112	33,090	33,197	76.3	334	141	118	19.5
Not reported	329	95	70	91.4	5	2	2	100.0
Race								
Asian	3,471	3,374	3,360	76.1	60	30	24	29.2
African-American	10,167	10,029	10,371	81.9	77	60	53	49.1
American Indian or Alaskan native	365	369	351	78.3	13	3	3	66.7
White	49,321	47,722	47,326	71.7	755	426	423	45.4
Other	2,254	2,029	2,626	51.2	5	10	30	3.3
Not reported	1,720	1,616	1,668	79.4	18	13	8	37.5
Hispanic origin 3/	14,392	14,370	14,952	84.8	74	49	42	42.9
Full-time 4/								
Total	179,977	186,934	195,529	85.2	1,791	2,272	2,464	10.3
Sex								
Female	101,122	105,264	110,409	85.7	1,092	1,332	1,493	15.2
Male	78,771	81,583	85,043	84.6	699	924	952	2.7
Not reported	84	87	77	67.5	0	16	19	0.0
Race								
Asian	8,333	8,605	9,066	85.4	170	244	263	3.8
African-American	27,725	28,902	29,438	90.2	120	162	192	20.3
American Indian or Alaskan native	750	740	718	87.7	8	19	17	0.0
White	107,469	111,112	116,053	86.0	1,244	1,558	1,606	9.4
Other	9,321	8,830	9,486	44.9	54	42	91	6.6
Not reported	2,561	3,053	2,967	84.3	18	24	47	23.4
Hispanic origin 3/	23,818	25,692	27,801	90.5	177	223	248	14.5

1/ Includes University of Florida Institute of Food and Agricultural Sciences and nonmedical professional headcounts from the Medical Center.

2/ Includes undergraduates enrolled for fewer than 12 hours and graduate students enrolled for fewer than 9 hours.

3/ Persons of Hispanic origin may be of any race. However, these data are not distributed by race.

4/ Includes undergraduates enrolled for 12 or more hours and graduate students enrolled for 9 or more hours.

Note: Unclassified students are counted as undergraduates. Data are from the student data course file enrollment report. Staff and senior citizen waivers are excluded.

Source: State of Florida, Department of Education, Division of Colleges and Universities, State University System, *Fact Book, 2004–2005,* Internet site <http://www.fldcu.org/> (accessed 18, September 2007).

Table 4.54. HIGHER EDUCATION: ENROLLMENT IN THE UNIVERSITIES OF THE STATE UNIVERSITY SYSTEM OF FLORIDA, FALL 1997 THROUGH 2004

University	1997	1998	1999	2000
Total	213,066	218,770	227,609	235,597
Educational and general, total	203,719	216,221	224,981	232,967
University of Florida	33,524	41,652	42,612	44,480
Florida State University	29,629	30,389	32,405	33,587
Florida A & M University	10,477	11,324	11,639	11,723
University of South Florida	31,906	31,555	32,887	33,924
Florida Atlantic University	19,107	19,153	20,032	20,944
University of West Florida	7,855	7,790	7,924	8,218
University of Central Florida	28,302	30,009	31,472	33,453
Florida International University	29,357	30,096	30,979	30,725
University of North Florida	11,116	11,360	11,897	12,417
Florida Gulf Coast University	2,446	2,893	3,134	3,496
New College of Florida	(X)	(X)	(NA)	(NA)
Special units, total 1/	9,347	2,549	2,628	2,630
University of Florida				
Institute of Food and Agriculture Science 2/ (IFAS)	3,981	(X)	(X)	(X)
Health and Medical Center	3,924	1,072	1,074	1,081
Florida State University - Health	(X)	(X)	(X)	(X)
University of South Florida				
Medical Center	1,442	1,477	1,554	1,549
	2001	**2002**	**2003**	**2004**
Total	251,196	261,667	269,306	275,600
Educational and general, total	248,471	258,874	266,443	272,553
University of Florida	45,521	46,850	47,280	47,401
Florida State University	35,442	36,651	37,072	38,316
Florida A & M University	12,347	12,467	12,907	12,940
University of South Florida	35,971	37,764	39,563	40,425
Florida Atlantic University	23,643	23,996	25,139	25,474
University of West Florida	9,063	9,206	9,412	9,485
University of Central Florida	36,013	38,795	41,185	42,391
Florida International University	32,614	33,799	33,601	34,817
University of North Florida	13,007	13,460	13,837	14,446
Florida Gulf Coast University	4,216	5,236	5,776	6,167
New College of Florida	634	650	671	691
Special units, total 1/	2,725	2,793	2,863	3,047
University of Florida				
Institute of Food and Agriculture Science 2/ (IFAS)	(X)	(X)	(X)	(X)
Health and Medical Center	1,105	1,113	1,115	1,130
Florida State University - Health	30	69	115	172
University of South Florida				
Medical Center	1,590	1,611	1,633	1,745

(X) Not applicable.
(NA) Not available.
1/ Includes medical professionals.
2/ Beginning in 1998, the headcount enrollment for IFAS and nonmedical professional students at the University of Florida is included in the University of Florida educational and general headcount total.
Note: Data are from the student data course file enrollment reports. Staff and senior citizen waivers are excluded.
Source: State of Florida, Department of Education, Division of Colleges and Universities, State University System, *Fact Book, 2004–2005,* Internet site <http://www.fldcu.org/> (accessed 18, September 2007).

Table 4.55. HIGHER EDUCATION: ENROLLMENT IN THE UNIVERSITIES OF THE STATE UNIVERSITY SYSTEM BY RESIDENCE AT TIME OF ADMISSION OR READMISSION IN THE STATE AND COUNTIES OF FLORIDA, FALL 2005

County	Total	UF	FSU	FAMU	USF	FAU	UWF	UCF	FIU	UNF	FGCU	NCF
Florida	289,011	50,512	39,826	12,594	43,775	26,108	9,749	45,153	37,788	15,464	7,279	763
Alachua	6,143	4,499	412	122	276	97	48	341	92	199	34	23
Baker	136	30	21	3	2	1	1	12	1	65	0	0
Bay	2,058	290	1,217	64	62	9	260	111	3	32	4	6
Bradford	170	69	11	7	15	0	4	15	1	46	1	1
Brevard	7,684	1,432	866	144	657	137	28	3,880	85	422	25	8
Broward	31,196	4,860	3,087	1,185	1,202	10,810	108	3,823	5,354	369	352	46
Calhoun	106	13	57	11	1	1	21	0	1	1	0	0
Charlotte	1,256	194	144	3	334	32	10	149	16	28	337	9
Citrus	848	204	113	11	239	13	15	179	6	44	19	5
Clay	2,497	574	388	40	64	11	13	242	11	1,144	8	2
Collier	3,280	479	312	21	295	113	16	395	72	48	1,508	21
Columbia	358	160	62	44	18	0	5	19	1	46	1	2
DeSoto	158	22	6	5	44	1	2	23	2	0	52	1
Dixie	48	15	17	1	5	1	5	3	0	0	1	0
Duval	12,968	2,143	1,535	773	296	77	70	935	75	7,022	29	13
Escambia	4,883	425	491	198	102	16	3,351	197	14	77	5	7
Flagler	657	124	75	22	41	8	12	209	4	160	1	1
Franklin	47	2	25	7	1	1	9	0	0	1	0	1
Gadsden	542	31	236	237	15	0	9	8	1	3	2	0
Gilchrist	97	68	6	1	4	1	5	2	0	10	0	0
Glades	44	8	3	4	0	3	0	4	0	0	22	0
Gulf	131	14	77	10	4	0	13	3	0	10	0	0
Hamilton	55	13	10	18	2	0	1	7	0	4	0	0
Hardee	134	21	21	2	66	2	1	11	1	4	5	0
Hendry	238	47	12	14	20	26	1	32	12	3	71	0
Hernando	1,178	135	98	21	691	12	10	147	6	31	21	6
Highlands	538	111	49	22	159	17	3	101	6	11	55	4
Hillsborough	20,829	2,632	1,719	408	14,313	164	75	1,040	130	187	110	51
Holmes	130	14	42	6	5	0	60	1	1	1	0	0
Indian River	1,188	262	195	34	97	212	5	251	34	86	9	3
Jackson	440	45	177	48	5	0	147	13	0	5	0	0
Jefferson	172	12	76	62	6	0	9	4	1	2	0	0
Lafayette	23	6	8	4	3	0	0	1	0	1	0	0
Lake	1,939	372	225	56	286	31	17	843	10	82	15	2
Lee	5,450	692	512	58	580	147	16	622	77	36	2,697	13
Leon	8,786	733	4,955	2,163	184	116	102	292	73	127	20	21

See footnotes at end of table.

Continued . . .

Table 4.55. HIGHER EDUCATION: ENROLLMENT IN THE UNIVERSITIES OF THE STATE UNIVERSITY SYSTEM BY RESIDENCE AT TIME OF ADMISSION OR READMISSION IN THE STATE AND COUNTIES OF FLORIDA, FALL 2005 (Continued)

County	Total	UF	FSU	FAMU	USF	FAU	UWF	UCF	FIU	UNF	FGCU	NCF
Levy	162	102	23	5	7	3	3	16	1	2	0	0
Liberty	50	2	30	6	1	1	8	0	0	1	1	0
Madison	181	22	82	54	4	3	2	6	2	6	0	0
Manatee	3,022	437	319	62	1,637	41	12	303	29	83	75	24
Marion	2,102	774	291	46	273	21	28	473	18	146	18	14
Martin	1,704	419	241	9	126	485	16	232	27	128	17	4
Miami-Dade	39,969	4,100	2,476	1,515	864	1,340	86	1,367	27,944	115	105	57
Monroe	705	129	123	13	75	48	12	140	106	9	40	10
Nassau	707	115	97	24	24	10	15	60	8	350	3	1
Okaloosa	3,039	452	668	56	107	7	1,447	243	6	45	7	1
Okeechobee	215	44	24	3	24	70	2	35	4	2	7	0
Orange	17,069	2,512	1,612	684	1,156	201	68	10,330	179	254	57	16
Osceola	1,947	267	160	41	319	27	6	1,021	50	32	20	4
Palm Beach	18,441	2,864	1,922	461	686	9,016	63	2,312	570	329	197	21
Pasco	3,984	477	352	31	2,582	31	25	342	16	54	64	10
Pinellas	13,474	2,254	1,477	234	7,126	92	78	1,640	74	304	144	51
Polk	4,515	677	572	224	2,096	47	27	646	37	135	45	9
Putnam	400	138	61	13	28	3	2	44	1	109	1	0
St. Johns	2,477	517	446	24	76	27	8	169	15	1,174	9	12
St. Lucie	1,892	307	161	68	138	693	10	399	32	72	11	1
Santa Rosa	2,538	184	347	23	52	12	1,681	153	7	72	4	3
Sarasota	4,300	856	579	32	1,674	64	31	643	58	72	243	48
Seminole	8,535	1,434	963	154	432	72	36	5,107	63	235	22	17
Sumter	190	48	24	18	63	1	2	28	0	5	1	0
Suwannee	204	86	53	30	7	0	1	6	1	17	2	1
Taylor	158	20	84	38	4	1	2	2	0	6	0	1
Union	45	30	4	1	1	0	0	1	0	7	1	0
Volusia	4,821	896	549	122	348	47	26	2,314	43	438	26	12
Wakulla	247	8	182	34	10	0	8	2	0	2	1	0
Walton	314	33	107	5	11	1	138	11	2	4	1	1
Washington	137	14	73	12	3	1	26	6	0	2	0	0
County not reported 1/	35,060	9,543	8,464	2,723	3,727	1,684	1,428	3,187	2,405	947	753	199

1/ Includes two previously reported categories, "NonFlorida" and "NonUSA."

Note: County of residence shown as self-reported by students. Headcounts include nonfee-paying students. See Table 4.54 for a complete list of university names.

Source: State of Florida, Department of Education, Division of Colleges and Universities, State University System, *Fact Book, 2005–2006,* Internet site <http://www.fldcu.org/> (accessed 21, March 2007).

Table 4.60. PUBLIC COMMUNITY COLLEGES: COLLEGE LEVEL HEADCOUNT ENROLLMENT BY PROGRAM AND INSTITUTION IN FLORIDA, 2005–06

Community college	Total		Associate in arts 1/	Workforce development	Other objectives		
	Unduplicated	Duplicated			Preparatory and adult education	Community instructional services 2/	Lifelong learning
Total	793,517	1,013,608	242,368	277,342	179,698	309,272	4,928
Brevard	25,713	31,063	9,884	9,712	3,329	7,759	379
Broward	52,684	68,796	16,409	11,571	13,202	27,204	410
Central Florida	18,520	19,741	4,620	9,044	2,880	795	2,402
Chipola	5,209	5,812	1,994	3,058	498	262	0
Daytona Beach	27,911	32,436	5,607	10,772	11,228	4,802	27
Edison	17,111	17,914	7,820	4,989	2,645	2,460	0
Florida Community College at Jacksonville	64,493	64,692	13,353	21,960	15,085	14,294	0
Florida Keys	2,814	3,628	356	1,097	281	1,894	0
Gulf Coast	22,140	26,478	4,634	15,035	1,917	4,892	0
Hillsborough	43,915	44,982	17,719	13,517	8,240	5,506	0
Indian River	35,928	41,109	4,437	5,477	13,537	17,658	0
Lake City	7,198	9,069	1,900	5,194	940	1,035	0
Lake-Sumter	6,581	9,796	2,761	2,537	1,031	3,431	36
Manatee	20,036	24,686	8,586	9,233	3,036	3,356	475
Miami-Dade	132,060	197,530	30,555	40,829	35,756	90,390	0
North Florida	3,175	4,110	1,232	1,461	707	710	0
Okaloosa-Walton	12,841	16,466	3,747	2,572	3,129	7,018	0
Palm Beach	47,572	59,312	11,572	17,684	7,677	21,696	683
Pasco-Hernando	13,209	15,737	5,373	4,418	2,976	2,748	222
Pensacola	20,288	28,049	5,878	4,470	6,111	11,590	0
Polk	18,471	24,794	3,305	10,152	2,352	8,985	0
St. Johns River	9,296	11,150	3,991	4,203	1,807	1,149	0
St. Petersburg	47,694	73,699	17,778	22,166	7,862	25,893	0
Santa Fe	22,897	32,226	12,684	5,071	5,430	9,041	0
Seminole	30,374	34,114	9,592	9,169	9,733	5,501	119
South Florida	7,624	13,354	2,150	3,607	2,385	5,212	0
Tallahassee	27,381	33,845	9,221	10,954	5,951	7,719	0
Valencia	50,382	69,020	25,210	17,390	9,973	16,272	175

1/ Formerly advanced and professional.
2/ Includes students awaiting enrollment in limited access programs, students enrolled in apprenticeship courses, students who are enrolled in courses related to employment, as general freshmen or for other personal objectives.
Note: There may be some duplication between major program areas.

Source: State of Florida, Department of Education, Florida Community College System, *The Fact Book: Report for the Florida Community College System,* January 2007, Internet site <http://www.firn.edu/> (accessed 2, February 2007).

Table 4.61. PUBLIC COMMUNITY COLLEGES: TRANSFER STUDENTS FROM FLORIDA COMMUNITY COLLEGES TO FLORIDA UNIVERSITIES BY SEX AND UNIVERSITY FALL 2003 AND 2004

Institution	2003			2004		
	Total	Male	Female	Total	Male	Female
State University System, total	77,422	31,752	45,670	79,897	32,472	47,386
Florida Agricultural and Mechanical University	844	380	464	955	416	539
Florida Atlantic University	9,320	3,233	6,087	9,611	3,380	6,231
Florida Gulf Coast University	1,390	450	940	1,416	482	934
Florida International University	9,368	3,936	5,432	11,011	4,543	6,468
Florida State University	10,882	4,640	6,242	11,028	4,692	6,336
University of Central Florida	17,258	7,246	10,012	16,957	7,061	9,896
University of Florida	6,116	3,226	2,890	5,788	3,058	2,730
University of North Florida	5,297	2,142	3,155	5,420	2,129	3,291
University of South Florida	13,725	5,212	8,513	14,569	5,465	9,065
University of West Florida	3,132	1,251	1,881	3,054	1,212	1,842
New College of Florida	90	36	54	88	34	54

Table 4.62. PUBLIC COMMUNITY COLLEGES: TRANSFER STUDENTS FROM FLORIDA COMMUNITY COLLEGES TO FLORIDA UNIVERSITIES BY RACE OR HISPANIC ORIGIN AND UNIVERSITY, FALL 2004

Institution	Total	Race					Hispanic origin 2/
		White	Black	American Indian	Asian	Other 1/	
State University System, total	79,897	49,462	9,835	363	3,174	3,374	13,689
Florida Agricultural and Mechanical University	955	120	771	0	12	32	20
Florida Atlantic University	9,611	5,295	1,924	39	393	328	1,632
Florida Gulf Coast University	1416	1109	98	5	22	40	142
Florida International University	11,011	1,903	1,629	16	337	733	6,393
Florida State University	11,028	8,436	1,198	49	281	201	863
University of Central Florida	16,957	11,766	1,287	93	804	991	2,016
University of Florida	5,788	4,312	258	33	263	227	695
University of North Florida	5,420	4,195	544	32	253	91	305
University of South Florida	14,569	9,863	1,837	62	694	613	1,500
University of West Florida	3054	2390	289	34	113	115	113
New College of Florida	88	73	0	0	2	3	10

1/ Includes students classified as nonresident aliens and unclassified students.
2/ Persons of Hispanic origin may be of any race. However, these data are not distributed by race.

Source for Tables 4.61 and 4.62: State of Florida, Department of Education, Division of Community Colleges, *Articulation Report for the Fall Data 2002, 2003, 2004,* Internet site <http://www.fldoe.org/cc/> (accessed 2, February 2007).

Table 4.70. PUBLIC HIGH SCHOOL TESTING: RESULTS OF THE FLORIDA COMPREHENSIVE ASSESSMENT TEST (FCAT) FOR READING ACROSS ALL CURRICULUM GROUPS IN THE STATE AND COUNTIES OF FLORIDA, 2007

County	Number of students tested	Mean scale score	Percentage passing	Percentage in each achievement level 1	2	3	4	5	Achieving level 3 and above
Florida	186,048	300	52	39	28	16	7	11	34
Alachua	2,081	307	56	38	21	16	8	17	41
Baker	314	297	54	39	31	17	7	7	31
Bay	1,904	311	58	32	29	19	8	13	39
Bradford	238	290	42	47	27	13	5	8	26
Brevard	5,407	322	68	24	29	20	10	17	47
Broward	18,598	302	53	38	28	17	7	10	34
Calhoun	149	307	56	36	32	16	6	9	32
Charlotte	1,478	310	60	32	29	19	9	12	40
Citrus	1,221	299	51	38	31	17	5	9	31
Clay	2,786	308	57	33	31	18	7	11	36
Collier	2,722	301	54	38	28	16	7	11	34
Columbia	604	298	52	39	29	17	6	9	32
DeSoto	301	278	38	53	28	11	2	6	19
Dixie	154	294	47	42	31	17	3	7	27
Duval	7,434	298	50	40	28	15	6	10	31
Escambia	2,965	297	50	40	29	15	6	10	31
Flagler	921	300	53	38	31	15	6	10	32
Franklin	82	287	37	44	33	10	9	5	23
Gadsden	381	257	19	71	21	6	1	1	8
Gilchrist	199	314	66	27	31	18	13	11	42
Glades	80	278	34	58	24	11	4	4	19
Gulf	174	290	46	43	37	11	3	6	20
Hamilton	111	264	28	67	24	4	2	4	9
Hardee	305	282	42	50	28	11	4	7	22
Hendry	532	272	33	59	23	10	4	5	18
Hernando	1,632	300	50	39	29	15	7	10	32
Highlands	730	299	53	37	30	18	7	9	33
Hillsborough	12,563	304	56	36	28	17	7	12	36
Holmes	238	306	59	31	31	23	8	8	38
Indian River	1,300	308	57	35	27	19	7	12	38
Jackson	495	291	47	41	33	12	7	7	26
Jefferson	73	270	37	59	25	7	7	3	16
Lafayette	69	275	41	54	29	10	3	4	17
Lake	2,788	295	49	42	28	16	6	9	30
Lee	5,339	296	51	41	28	16	6	9	32
Leon	2,086	320	63	27	29	19	8	17	45
Levy	397	286	43	46	31	10	5	7	22
Liberty	62	323	68	21	27	19	10	23	52

See footnote at end of table. Continued . . .

Table 4.70. PUBLIC HIGH SCHOOL TESTING: RESULTS OF THE FLORIDA COMPREHENSIVE ASSESSMENT TEST (FCAT) FOR READING ACROSS ALL CURRICULUM GROUPS IN THE STATE AND COUNTIES OF FLORIDA, 2007 (Continued)

County	Number of students tested	Mean scale score	Percentage passing	Percentage in each achievement level: 1	2	3	4	5	Achieving level 3 and above
Madison	158	290	45	42	27	17	3	11	31
Manatee	2,848	293	50	41	28	16	7	8	31
Marion	3,054	301	53	36	32	16	6	10	32
Martin	1,481	317	65	28	27	18	9	18	46
Miami-Dade	25,637	288	44	47	26	13	5	8	27
Monroe	592	309	59	31	29	18	8	14	40
Nassau	834	306	55	34	33	15	7	12	34
Okaloosa	2,181	327	72	20	27	23	11	18	52
Okeechobee	439	291	46	44	31	13	6	6	24
Orange	12,270	296	49	42	26	14	6	11	31
Osceola	3,630	286	43	47	26	14	6	6	26
Palm Beach	12,365	302	53	38	27	16	7	12	35
Pasco	4,419	300	52	38	30	16	7	9	32
Pinellas	8,374	305	56	36	27	17	7	13	37
Polk	6,232	288	45	47	25	14	6	8	28
Putnam	766	288	42	47	27	15	5	5	26
St. Johns	2,024	324	69	23	28	21	10	18	49
St. Lucie	2,649	289	44	46	29	13	5	7	25
Santa Rosa	1,864	320	67	24	31	19	10	16	45
Sarasota	3,084	310	59	33	27	18	7	15	41
Seminole	4,949	319	67	26	28	21	9	16	47
Sumter	512	295	50	42	29	17	4	7	29
Suwannee	404	301	54	36	33	18	5	8	31
Taylor	195	293	52	39	35	15	4	7	26
Union	134	297	50	39	33	15	5	8	28
Volusia	4,680	300	53	38	29	16	6	11	33
Wakulla	277	314	58	30	30	17	8	15	40
Walton	461	304	57	33	30	22	8	8	37
Washington	241	312	60	28	33	19	9	11	39
Deaf/Blind	63	225	21	79	10	5	5	2	11
FAU Henderson	18	381	100	0	0	28	17	56	100
FSU Developmental	152	319	68	23	40	13	9	15	37
FAMU Developmental	30	294	37	50	37	3	7	3	13
UF P.K.Yonge	118	330	70	21	28	21	10	19	51

Note: Scores are for students in grade 10. The Florida Comprehensive Assessment Test (FCAT) measures student performance on selected benchmarks in reading that are defined by Sunshine State Standards articulating challenging content that Florida students are expected to know and be able to do. Achievement levels range from 1, indicating little success with the challenging content, to 5, indicating success with the most challenging content of the Sunshine State Standards.

Source: State of Florida, Department of Education, Student Assessment Services Section, Internet site <http://www.fcat.fldoe.org> (accessed 4, June 2007).

Table 4.71. PUBLIC HIGH SCHOOL TESTING: RESULTS OF THE FLORIDA COMPREHENSIVE ASSESSMENT TEST (FCAT) FOR MATHEMATICS ACROSS ALL CURRICULUM GROUPS IN THE STATE AND COUNTIES OF FLORIDA, 2007

County	Number of students tested	Mean scale score	Percentage passing	Percentage in each achievement level 1	2	3	4	5	Achieving level 3 and above
Florida	185,346	323	78	14	20	28	30	7	65
Alachua	2,061	325	75	17	19	22	30	12	64
Baker	317	322	76	15	20	28	35	3	65
Bay	1,896	330	83	10	18	31	33	8	72
Bradford	238	315	73	17	25	30	26	3	58
Brevard	5,403	337	88	7	14	27	40	12	79
Broward	18,560	326	80	13	19	28	33	8	68
Calhoun	148	327	83	7	24	34	30	5	69
Charlotte	1,488	328	82	11	19	30	35	6	70
Citrus	1,214	323	79	12	24	30	31	4	65
Clay	2,786	329	84	9	21	30	33	7	70
Collier	2,708	324	80	13	20	28	32	7	67
Columbia	606	319	76	15	23	31	27	4	62
DeSoto	299	314	70	17	30	29	20	3	53
Dixie	152	323	83	12	23	35	26	5	65
Duval	7,373	322	77	15	21	27	30	7	64
Escambia	2,960	314	71	19	26	27	23	4	55
Flagler	911	323	79	14	20	28	33	5	67
Franklin	81	309	72	16	32	33	17	1	52
Gadsden	379	291	51	33	36	21	10	0	31
Gilchrist	196	331	84	10	13	29	38	10	77
Glades	80	304	60	25	24	35	15	1	51
Gulf	170	316	76	15	27	34	24	1	58
Hamilton	109	299	57	28	33	29	9	1	39
Hardee	304	316	75	17	23	30	26	4	60
Hendry	529	305	65	23	29	30	17	2	49
Hernando	1,623	320	77	14	24	31	27	4	63
Highlands	726	323	79	13	19	31	31	5	68
Hillsborough	12,501	326	79	13	20	27	31	8	67
Holmes	239	326	81	10	20	31	33	5	70
Indian River	1,295	329	82	11	19	28	36	7	71
Jackson	495	319	78	16	21	34	26	3	63
Jefferson	72	300	64	26	24	29	21	0	50
Lafayette	70	309	70	21	20	40	14	4	59
Lake	2,779	318	76	16	22	32	27	4	63
Lee	5,341	320	77	16	21	31	29	4	64
Leon	2,084	335	88	6	17	29	36	11	76
Levy	397	317	72	16	22	30	29	3	61
Liberty	62	335	87	8	13	27	50	2	79

See footnote at end of table.

Continued . . .

Table 4.71. PUBLIC HIGH SCHOOL TESTING: RESULTS OF THE FLORIDA COMPREHENSIVE ASSESSMENT TEST (FCAT) FOR MATHEMATICS ACROSS ALL CURRICULUM GROUPS IN THE STATE AND COUNTIES OF FLORIDA, 2007 (Continued)

County	Number of students tested	Mean scale score	Percentage passing	Percentage in each achievement level 1	2	3	4	5	Achieving level 3 and above
Madison	208	305	65	23	26	23	26	2	51
Manatee	2,837	320	76	16	22	28	29	5	62
Marion	3,051	325	80	12	21	28	33	6	67
Martin	1,481	333	85	10	14	27	39	10	76
Miami-Dade	25,518	315	71	19	24	28	24	5	57
Monroe	587	329	85	10	17	31	37	5	73
Nassau	836	327	83	10	19	33	32	5	71
Okaloosa	2,173	341	91	4	13	26	43	13	82
Okeechobee	435	321	76	14	24	29	29	4	62
Orange	12,158	321	75	17	20	26	30	7	63
Osceola	3,606	315	72	19	22	31	25	3	59
Palm Beach	12,330	326	80	12	19	28	32	9	68
Pasco	4,359	322	78	13	24	30	28	5	63
Pinellas	8,324	324	78	14	20	27	32	7	66
Polk	6,227	314	70	20	23	27	25	4	56
Putnam	769	317	73	16	25	28	28	3	59
St. Johns	2,017	338	89	6	14	29	39	12	80
St. Lucie	2,646	314	71	19	25	30	23	3	56
Santa Rosa	1,870	333	88	8	15	30	39	8	77
Sarasota	3,069	331	83	11	16	27	35	10	72
Seminole	4,944	337	87	8	14	26	40	13	78
Sumter	512	321	76	17	18	31	30	4	65
Suwannee	403	318	77	12	24	33	27	3	64
Taylor	196	316	79	14	27	34	22	4	60
Union	133	318	74	15	26	34	23	3	59
Volusia	4,651	320	77	15	23	31	28	4	63
Wakulla	276	334	87	9	17	28	37	10	74
Walton	460	326	86	8	22	35	33	2	70
Washington	242	329	86	9	16	36	34	5	75
Deaf/Blind	63	271	30	54	27	8	11	0	19
FAU Henderson	18	371	100	0	0	0	67	33	100
FSU Developmental	151	335	92	4	17	32	40	6	79
FAMU Developmental	26	311	77	15	42	27	15	0	42
UF P.K.Yonge	118	340	92	3	17	28	42	11	81

Note: Scores are for students in grade 10. The Florida Comprehensive Assessment Test (FCAT) measures student performance on selected benchmarks in mathematics that are defined by Sunshine State Standards articulating challenging content that Florida students are expected to know and be able to do. Achievement levels range from 1, indicating little success with the challenging content, to 5, indicating success with the most challenging content of the Sunshine State Standards.

Source: State of Florida, Department of Education, Student Assessment Services Section, Internet site <http://www.fcat.fldoe.org> (accessed 4, June 2007).

Table 4.72. PUBLIC HIGH SCHOOL TESTING: RESULTS OF THE FLORIDA COMPREHENSIVE ASSESSMENT TEST (FCAT) FOR SCIENCE ACROSS ALL CURRICULUM GROUPS IN THE STATE AND COUNTIES OF FLORIDA, 2007

County	Number of students tested	Mean scale score	Percentage in each achievement level					
			1	2	3	4	5	Achieving level 3 and above
Florida	164,580	302	30	33	31	5	1	37
Alachua	1,909	312	26	31	33	9	1	43
Baker	263	306	25	37	35	3	0	38
Bay	1,708	308	24	36	35	5	0	40
Bradford	209	297	32	41	26	1	0	27
Brevard	5,198	326	15	29	45	10	2	56
Broward	16,446	302	30	35	29	5	1	34
Calhoun	135	311	26	33	36	5	0	41
Charlotte	1,393	305	25	39	31	4	0	36
Citrus	1,008	318	16	37	40	7	1	47
Clay	2,327	311	24	35	33	7	1	41
Collier	2,440	301	33	30	30	6	1	36
Columbia	525	300	31	36	30	4	0	34
DeSoto	221	280	46	31	22	1	0	24
Dixie	124	297	31	40	27	1	1	29
Duval	6,371	301	32	33	29	5	1	35
Escambia	2,407	310	24	34	35	6	1	42
Flagler	821	306	24	40	33	3	0	36
Franklin	51	283	41	33	25	0	0	25
Gadsden	288	269	57	36	7	0	0	7
Gilchrist	172	319	16	38	41	5	0	46
Glades	42	272	55	36	10	0	0	10
Gulf	176	302	32	31	32	5	0	37
Hamilton	122	252	66	22	11	0	0	11
Hardee	254	289	37	37	24	2	0	26
Hendry	481	281	48	31	19	2	0	21
Hernando	1,394	303	27	39	31	3	0	34
Highlands	731	300	31	34	31	3	0	35
Hillsborough	11,504	307	29	31	33	6	1	41
Holmes	215	301	30	37	29	3	0	33
Indian River	1,119	308	27	32	34	6	1	41
Jackson	443	304	28	37	31	4	0	35
Jefferson	37	285	49	32	19	0	0	19
Lafayette	79	289	42	32	27	0	0	27
Lake	2,473	301	30	35	30	5	0	35
Lee	4,621	296	34	35	28	3	0	31
Leon	1,966	318	23	28	38	9	2	49
Levy	352	307	23	40	34	3	0	37
Liberty	61	307	20	36	43	2	0	44

See footnote at end of table. Continued . . .

Table 4.72. PUBLIC HIGH SCHOOL TESTING: RESULTS OF THE FLORIDA COMPREHENSIVE ASSESSMENT TEST (FCAT) FOR SCIENCE ACROSS ALL CURRICULUM GROUPS IN THE STATE AND COUNTIES OF FLORIDA, 2007 (Continued)

County	Number of students tested	Mean scale score	Percentage in each achievement level 1	2	3	4	5	Achieving level 3 and above
Madison	158	282	44	30	23	3	0	26
Manatee	2,242	306	27	35	33	5	1	39
Marion	2,557	306	27	35	33	5	1	39
Martin	1,272	323	17	28	43	10	1	54
Miami-Dade	22,136	286	42	32	23	3	0	26
Monroe	530	308	26	33	35	6	0	41
Nassau	656	304	26	37	33	3	0	37
Okaloosa	2,097	326	14	30	45	10	1	56
Okeechobee	369	305	31	30	31	7	1	39
Orange	10,947	301	32	32	30	6	1	36
Osceola	3,349	290	38	35	24	3	0	27
Palm Beach	11,324	309	27	31	34	7	1	42
Pasco	3,717	302	29	37	30	4	0	35
Pinellas	7,758	294	36	32	27	4	0	32
Polk	5,365	288	42	32	22	4	0	26
Putnam	605	293	35	35	26	3	0	30
St. Johns	1,835	325	15	28	45	9	1	56
St. Lucie	2,257	295	36	33	26	4	0	31
Santa Rosa	1,842	321	15	35	42	7	1	50
Sarasota	2,888	311	25	31	35	9	1	44
Seminole	4,371	320	17	33	40	8	1	50
Sumter	441	302	30	35	29	5	0	35
Suwannee	321	303	29	32	34	5	0	39
Taylor	141	290	38	37	23	2	0	25
Union	113	304	25	38	35	3	0	37
Volusia	3,908	306	27	33	34	5	0	40
Wakulla	286	310	26	36	33	4	1	38
Walton	412	310	21	37	39	3	0	42
Washington	243	307	24	38	34	4	0	38
Deaf/Blind	50	239	82	12	4	2	0	6
FSU Developmental	138	322	13	37	43	7	0	50
FAMU Developmental	33	265	67	27	6	0	0	6
UF P.K.Yonge	128	323	11	39	45	3	2	50

Note: Scores are for students in grade 11. The Florida Comprehensive Assessment Test (FCAT) measures student performance on selected benchmarks in science that are defined by Sunshine State Standards articulating challenging content that Florida students are expected to know and be able to do. Achievement levels range from 1, indicating little success with the challenging content, to 5, indicating success with the most challenging content of the Sunshine State Standards.

Source: State of Florida, Department of Education, Student Assessment Services Section, Internet site <http://www.fcat.fldoe.org> (accessed 4, June 2007).

Table 4.80. HIGH SCHOOL GRADUATES AND DROPOUTS: GRADUATION AND DROPOUT RATES IN THE STATE AND COUNTIES OF FLORIDA, 2005–06

County	Four-year graduation rate	Dropout rate 2005–06	County	Four-year graduation rate	Dropout rate 2005–06
Florida	71.0	3.5	Lake	70.1	4.7
			Lee	71.5	3.5
Alachua	69.8	6.1	Leon	76.2	2.3
Baker	73.1	3.7	Levy	65.6	4.8
Bay	77.5	2.0	Liberty	89.7	0.9
Bradford	69.5	5.4	Madison	58.5	5.5
Brevard	90.7	0.8	Manatee	76.9	3.1
Broward	67.8	2.7	Marion	71.8	4.2
Calhoun	89.6	3.0	Martin	93.2	0.4
Charlotte	78.0	2.5	Miami-Dade	59.2	6.7
Citrus	73.2	4.7	Monroe	75.5	1.5
Clay	73.8	1.9	Nassau	81.8	3.4
Collier	74.7	2.0	Okaloosa	86.0	2.2
Columbia	67.4	2.1	Okeechobee	62.8	6.0
DeSoto	70.0	6.1	Orange	72.2	1.9
Dixie	70.4	5.6	Osceola	64.5	4.1
Duval	60.5	6.6	Palm Beach	69.3	3.0
Escambia	74.8	3.1	Pasco	74.4	4.2
Flagler	78.4	1.9	Pinellas	67.0	3.0
Franklin	60.7	13.3	Polk	68.8	4.4
Gadsden	43.9	4.9	Putnam	76.4	4.0
Gilchrist	78.7	2.3	St. Johns	76.7	2.0
Glades	63.4	6.9	St. Lucie	72.7	2.2
Gulf	83.8	2.9	Santa Rosa	85.5	2.3
Hamilton	63.2	5.4	Sarasota	79.9	2.5
Hardee	70.3	5.7	Seminole	83.4	1.2
Hendry	72.1	4.2	Sumter	76.3	2.6
Hernando	74.1	4.9	Suwannee	65.1	4.8
Highlands	69.6	5.7	Taylor	78.3	3.5
Hillsborough	77.3	2.1	Union	76.7	2.6
Holmes	71.3	3.8	Volusia	81.9	1.4
Indian River	84.7	1.0	Wakulla	77.6	5.7
Jackson	87.8	1.2	Walton	76.1	2.6
Jefferson	53.5	7.7	Washington	69.8	3.4
Lafayette	81.7	2.8			

Note: Data are for public schools only. Graduation rates track individuals by student I.D. numbers, beginning with their first-time enrollment in grades 9-12. The reported dropout rate is for all dropouts in grades 9-12.

Source: State of Florida, Department of Education, Education Information and Accountability Services *(EIAS), Graduation and Dropout Rates by District, 2005–06 School Year,* Internet site <http://www.fldoe.org/eias/> (accessed 21, March 2007).

Table 4.83. HIGH SCHOOL GRADUATES: GRADUATES RECEIVING STANDARD DIPLOMAS BY SEX AND BY RACE OR HISPANIC ORIGIN IN THE STATE AND COUNTIES OF FLORIDA, 2005–06

County	Total 1/		Race				Hispanic origin 2/	
			White Non-Hispanic		Black Non-Hispanic			
	Male	Female	Male	Female	Male	Female	Male	Female
Florida	61,847	68,172	36,138	37,998	10,670	13,581	12,033	13,333
Alachua	735	919	472	590	174	226	46	49
Baker	113	118	102	104	7	12	2	1
Bay	674	756	548	598	72	91	13	27
Bradford	72	85	54	61	14	23	1	0
Brevard	2,168	2,280	1,736	1,733	211	277	112	154
Broward	6,357	7,118	2,601	2,696	1,879	2,390	1,499	1,607
Calhoun	61	55	53	47	6	7	0	1
Charlotte	650	633	548	548	49	43	29	27
Citrus	439	484	399	429	9	16	16	17
Clay	999	982	784	764	108	124	57	46
Collier	1,021	1,128	662	696	88	118	250	299
Columbia	202	226	148	175	41	35	9	9
DeSoto	100	120	68	68	16	27	16	25
Dixie	51	56	47	52	2	4	1	0
Duval	2,528	2,911	1,383	1,522	857	1,104	135	124
Escambia	915	1,014	617	631	210	292	26	30
Flagler	244	254	187	194	28	25	20	20
Franklin	32	29	22	20	10	7	0	1
Gadsden	74	89	3	4	67	81	4	4
Gilchrist	66	71	59	69	4	0	2	2
Glades	24	20	14	12	6	4	3	4
Gulf	51	59	41	52	10	7	0	0
Hamilton	23	43	10	25	9	13	2	5
Hardee	86	95	47	39	6	16	32	39
Hendry	191	167	93	63	31	24	62	75
Hernando	538	539	440	433	31	38	55	55
Highlands	271	292	180	194	45	44	40	46
Hillsborough	4,527	4,982	2,435	2,584	762	961	1,009	1,102
Holmes	80	79	74	74	5	1	0	0
Indian River	451	448	363	342	45	55	32	40
Jackson	178	178	126	121	46	53	2	2
Jefferson	21	38	10	11	10	27	0	0
Lafayette	30	28	26	25	2	2	1	1
Lake	856	929	620	693	118	117	79	85
Lee	1,578	1,783	1,102	1,233	165	186	260	284
Leon	780	921	554	579	168	285	23	29
Levy	122	127	98	107	17	14	5	3
Liberty	37	24	30	21	7	2	0	1
Madison	67	77	35	42	30	32	1	0
Manatee	979	979	780	740	102	122	71	94

See footnotes at end of table. Continued . . .

Table 4.83. HIGH SCHOOL GRADUATES: GRADUATES RECEIVING STANDARD DIPLOMAS BY SEX AND BY RACE OR HISPANIC ORIGIN IN THE STATE AND COUNTIES OF FLORIDA, 2005–06 (Continued)

			Race					
	Total 1/		White Non-Hispanic		Black Non-Hispanic		Hispanic origin 2/	
County	Male	Female	Male	Female	Male	Female	Male	Female
Marion	986	1,062	686	753	156	170	102	99
Martin	542	518	448	425	29	36	51	40
Miami-Dade	7,756	8,790	1,050	1,048	1,715	2,206	4,779	5,298
Monroe	232	273	186	183	8	20	30	58
Nassau	337	291	287	267	33	20	13	0
Okaloosa	971	1,001	789	786	76	92	31	40
Okeechobee	157	150	114	105	11	10	29	32
Orange	3,838	4,414	1,852	2,008	798	1,092	870	995
Osceola	1,076	1,210	464	506	114	135	443	485
Palm Beach	3,969	4,415	2,255	2,320	786	1,096	680	725
Pasco	1,331	1,530	1,107	1,271	57	59	111	135
Pinellas	2,498	2,954	1,955	2,240	261	386	129	171
Polk	1,740	1,953	1,194	1,322	296	354	186	224
Putnam	257	264	186	186	55	56	14	15
St. Johns	728	739	645	639	41	41	21	31
St. Lucie	663	825	397	462	165	219	78	108
Santa Rosa	746	780	661	683	33	42	25	12
Sarasota	1,136	1,197	924	992	66	64	84	84
Seminole	1,903	1,918	1,346	1,301	185	206	268	285
Sumter	162	153	136	116	21	25	4	8
Suwannee	138	140	106	111	22	24	6	4
Taylor	72	81	63	51	8	28	0	0
Union	63	55	54	52	9	3	0	0
Volusia	1,620	1,800	1,239	1,367	177	209	149	162
Wakulla	88	115	80	101	6	12	1	1
Walton	170	170	156	155	6	9	2	3
Washington	88	86	70	70	17	12	0	0
Deaf/Blind	22	19	20	13	0	3	2	3
Dozier	33	0	25	0	7	0	1	0
FAU Developmental	1	3	1	2	0	1	0	0
FSU Developmental	65	67	37	39	17	21	5	4
FAMU Developmental	18	17	0	0	18	17	0	0
UF P.K.Yonge Developmental	50	46	34	33	10	8	4	3

1/ Includes other races and multiracial not shown separately.
2/ Persons of Hispanic origin may be of any race. However, these data are not distributed by race.
Note: Data were obtained from the Florida DOE Student Information Data Base, Survey 5, as of December 20, 2006, and are for public schools only. Standard diplomas are awarded to students who have mastered eleventh grade minimum student performance standards, passed both sections of the High School Competency Test (HSCT or SSAT II), successfully completed the minimum number of academic credits, and successfully completed any other requirements prescribed by state or the local school board. Also includes differentiated diplomas awarded in lieu of the standard diplomas to those students exceeding the prescribed minimums.
Source: State of Florida, Department of Education, Education Information and Accountability Services (EIAS), *Statistical Brief: Florida Public High School Graduates, 2005–06 School Year,* January 2007, Series 2007-08B, Internet site <http://www.fldoe.org/eias/> (accessed 19, April 2007).

Table 4.84. HIGH SCHOOL COMPLETERS: STUDENTS COMPLETING HIGH SCHOOL BY SEX AND BY RACE OR HISPANIC ORIGIN IN THE STATE AND COUNTIES OF FLORIDA 2005–06

County	Total	Sex		Race					
		Male	Female	White Non-Hispanic	Black Non-Hispanic	Asian or Pacific Islander	American Indian Eskimo or Aleut	Multi-racial	Hispanic origin 1/
Florida	147,412	71,000	76,412	79,527	31,284	4,249	451	2,017	29,884
Alachua	1,748	801	947	1,094	456	63	3	31	101
Baker	269	135	134	230	33	0	0	3	3
Bay	1,567	739	828	1,228	208	44	8	36	43
Bradford	211	103	108	147	58	4	0	1	1
Brevard	4,728	2,327	2,401	3,620	579	132	13	86	298
Broward	15,039	7,140	7,899	5,530	5,188	627	29	182	3,483
Calhoun	127	65	62	105	19	2	0	0	1
Charlotte	1,368	701	667	1,151	113	17	5	19	63
Citrus	987	472	515	882	30	19	2	17	37
Clay	2,256	1,165	1,091	1,680	325	66	5	44	136
Collier	2,493	1,210	1,283	1,451	300	23	2	13	704
Columbia	545	265	280	372	135	11	1	2	24
DeSoto	266	130	136	160	52	0	0	0	54
Dixie	116	55	61	104	9	0	0	1	2
Duval	6,320	2,965	3,355	3,179	2,475	261	13	75	317
Escambia	2,285	1,119	1,166	1,379	708	91	14	30	63
Flagler	553	272	281	413	64	19	1	8	48
Franklin	69	37	32	47	19	0	0	1	2
Gadsden	209	92	117	9	184	0	0	0	16
Gilchrist	149	71	78	138	5	1	0	1	4
Glades	56	32	24	29	14	1	0	0	12
Gulf	123	60	63	97	26	0	0	0	0
Hamilton	85	33	52	39	36	2	0	0	8
Hardee	199	97	102	89	29	3	1	0	77
Hendry	451	226	225	182	74	6	3	3	183
Hernando	1,197	603	594	947	91	14	2	12	131
Highlands	662	323	339	408	141	7	4	3	99
Hillsborough	10,516	5,055	5,461	5,307	2,119	363	44	283	2,400
Holmes	205	113	92	184	14	3	2	1	1
Indian River	1,006	511	495	754	130	15	1	8	98
Jackson	396	202	194	265	121	2	0	4	4
Jefferson	70	25	45	23	46	1	0	0	0
Lafayette	64	32	32	54	7	1	0	0	2
Lake	2,077	1,017	1,060	1,443	340	39	13	32	210
Lee	3,930	1,892	2,038	2,561	513	63	16	56	721
Leon	1,862	867	995	1,178	564	50	1	14	55
Levy	285	143	142	224	45	4	0	2	10
Liberty	97	72	25	72	22	0	0	0	3

See footnotes at end of table. Continued . . .

Table 4.84. HIGH SCHOOL COMPLETERS: STUDENTS COMPLETING HIGH SCHOOL BY SEX AND BY RACE OR HISPANIC ORIGIN IN THE STATE AND COUNTIES OF FLORIDA 2005–06 (Continued)

County	Total	Sex		Race					
		Male	Female	White Non-Hispanic	Black Non-Hispanic	Asian or Pacific Islander	American Indian Eskimo or Aleut	Multi-racial	Hispanic origin 1/
Madison	213	109	104	98	108	2	0	3	2
Manatee	2,250	1,151	1,099	1,657	306	35	2	18	232
Marion	2,422	1,202	1,220	1,602	465	37	12	44	262
Martin	1,152	607	545	911	96	18	6	8	113
Miami-Dade	19,014	8,884	10,130	2,214	4,865	329	24	127	11,455
Monroe	558	256	302	387	42	9	3	11	106
Nassau	686	379	307	598	62	4	1	6	15
Okaloosa	2,161	1,093	1,068	1,694	217	80	10	78	82
Okeechobee	375	192	183	254	33	2	4	0	82
Orange	9,739	4,637	5,102	4,182	2,502	561	55	76	2,363
Osceola	2,839	1,360	1,479	1,093	339	92	10	54	1,251
Palm Beach	9,497	4,515	4,982	4,746	2,537	303	35	207	1,669
Pasco	3,294	1,563	1,731	2,698	142	70	9	56	319
Pinellas	6,015	2,780	3,235	4,462	873	260	17	57	346
Polk	4,503	2,223	2,280	2,834	990	93	10	31	545
Putnam	628	323	305	423	152	4	0	7	42
St. Johns	1,530	768	762	1,330	96	30	4	16	54
St. Lucie	1,671	746	925	905	473	34	6	27	226
Santa Rosa	1,603	789	814	1,404	84	40	14	20	41
Sarasota	2,590	1,281	1,309	2,057	199	69	6	52	207
Seminole	4,107	2,036	2,071	2,752	488	141	13	88	625
Sumter	369	192	177	280	71	1	2	2	13
Suwannee	306	153	153	235	54	2	3	0	12
Taylor	172	80	92	125	43	3	1	0	0
Union	127	66	61	108	17	0	0	0	2
Volusia	3,807	1,826	1,981	2,789	528	69	14	44	363
Wakulla	223	99	124	194	25	1	0	1	2
Walton	375	191	184	334	26	3	4	3	5
Washington	189	92	97	152	32	1	2	2	0
Deaf/Blind	89	52	37	56	15	0	0	1	17
Dozier School	52	52	0	31	18	0	0	0	3
FAU Developmental	4	1	3	3	1	0	0	0	0
FSU Developmental	133	65	68	77	38	2	1	6	9
FAMU Developmental	37	20	17	0	37	0	0	0	0
UF P.K. Yonge Developmental	96	50	46	67	18	0	0	4	7

1/ Persons of Hispanic origin may be of any race. However, these data are not distributed by race.

Note: High school completers are those students receiving standard diplomas, special diplomas, certificates of completion, and special certificates of completion. Data were obtained from the Florida DOE Student Information Data Base, Survey 5, as of December 20, 2006, and are for public schools only.

Source: State of Florida, Department of Education, Education Information and Accountability Services (EIAS), *Statistical Brief: Florida Public High School Graduates, 2005–06 School Year,* January 2007, Series 2007-08B, Internet site <http://www.fldoe.org/eias/> (accessed 19, April 2007).

Table 4.85. READINESS FOR COLLEGE: PERCENTAGE OF STUDENTS ENTERING COLLEGE WHO TESTED COMPETENT IN READING, WRITING, AND MATHEMATIC SKILLS IN THE STATE AND COUNTIES OF FLORIDA, 2004–05

County	Number of degree-seeking students 1/	Number tested in all areas	Ready in all areas: Number	Ready in all areas: Percentage change from 2002-03 A/	Ready in all areas: Percentage	Percentage ready in– Reading	Percentage ready in– Writing	Percentage ready in– Mathematics
Florida 2/	69,938	68,086	40,430	19.1	59.4	74.1	82.9	67.0
Alachua	1,145	1,135	587	-4.1	51.7	70.3	80.9	60.4
Baker	102	99	51	54.5	51.5	77.2	85.1	59.6
Bay	781	774	387	6.0	50.0	65.9	83.7	67.8
Bradford	93	93	30	11.1	32.3	67.7	80.6	39.8
Brevard	2,587	2,563	1,555	16.7	60.7	74.3	85.3	68.3
Broward	7,472	7,384	4,443	21.6	60.2	73.4	81.0	68.4
Calhoun	62	61	28	-3.4	45.9	77.0	88.5	52.5
Charlotte	549	542	353	16.1	65.1	81.5	86.9	69.6
Citrus	357	354	225	3.7	63.6	77.1	85.9	74.9
Clay	1,063	996	577	27.4	57.9	75.0	85.8	62.3
Collier	900	883	611	27.3	69.2	80.7	88.0	76.6
Columbia	211	209	95	14.5	45.5	65.9	79.6	53.1
DeSoto	65	64	30	-33.3	46.9	71.9	71.9	50.8
Dixie	36	36	12	0.0	33.3	69.4	63.9	44.4
Duval	3,140	2,749	1,735	17.5	63.1	73.6	84.3	69.9
Escambia	1,054	1,051	616	0.8	58.6	78.3	86.1	66.1
Flagler	275	273	170	68.3	62.3	73.6	82.1	73.0
Franklin	27	27	9	125.0	33.3	51.9	66.7	33.3
Gadsden	100	99	22	22.2	22.2	38.0	51.0	26.3
Gilchrist	85	84	44	51.7	52.4	74.1	82.4	58.3
Glades	14	14	7	14	50.0	64.3	78.6	64.3
Gulf	88	86	40	81.8	46.5	72.4	81.6	54.7
Hamilton	37	35	18	9	51.4	69.4	75.0	54.3
Hardee	73	73	35	16.7	47.9	58.9	71.2	58.9
Hendry	154	153	73	28.1	47.7	66.9	76.0	54.9
Hernando	503	496	279	26.8	56.2	80.1	88.4	60.9
Highlands	280	277	160	27.0	57.8	68.8	82.1	70.8
Hillsborough	4,689	4,559	3,078	22.8	67.5	78.1	84.8	74.9
Holmes	79	79	47	27.0	59.5	81.0	83.5	69.6
Indian River	490	478	266	24.3	55.6	75.4	85.0	63.8
Jackson	211	210	83	-23.1	39.5	71.9	79.0	44.3
Jefferson	26	26	11	22.2	42.3	57.7	73.1	46.2
Lafayette	27	26	10	-23.1	38.5	65.4	76.9	42.3
Lake	856	851	523	25.7	61.5	75.7	84.9	68.4
Lee	1,524	1,515	977	33.5	64.5	80.4	86.1	71.1
Leon	1,204	1,195	821	20.2	68.7	80.6	85.4	76.1

See footnotes at end of table.

Continued . . .

Table 4.85. READINESS FOR COLLEGE: PERCENTAGE OF STUDENTS ENTERING COLLEGE WHO TESTED COMPETENT IN READING, WRITING, AND MATHEMATIC SKILLS IN THE STATE AND COUNTIES OF FLORIDA, 2004–05 (Continued)

County	Number of degree-seeking students 1/	Number tested in all areas	Ready in all areas			Percentage ready in–		
			Number	Percentage change from 2002-03 A/	Percent-age	Reading	Writing	Mathe-matics
Levy	105	103	65	-4.4	63.1	76.9	79.8	67.0
Liberty	31	31	21	31.3	67.7	87.1	90.3	74.2
Madison	94	89	32	3.2	36.0	61.1	66.7	46.1
Manatee	1,018	984	570	26.7	57.9	72.2	76.5	64.5
Marion	956	938	543	6.7	57.9	75.7	86.4	65.9
Martin	614	599	420	31.3	70.1	84.2	89.4	74.5
Miami-Dade	10,000	9,859	4,954	17.8	50.2	67.2	78.3	59.1
Monroe	271	265	179	55.7	67.5	78.9	85.3	77.0
Nassau	302	260	156	34.5	60.0	74.0	87.7	64.6
Okaloosa	1,046	1,041	747	23.1	71.8	84.2	91.2	77.4
Okeechobee	130	125	46	-30.3	36.8	62.0	73.6	40.8
Orange	4,220	4,160	2,402	38.0	57.7	69.7	79.7	67.5
Osceola	951	940	397	14.1	42.2	61.2	75.9	52.2
Palm Beach	4,461	4,221	2,676	4.2	63.4	76.8	82.7	69.1
Pasco	1,474	1,423	872	31.9	61.3	79.2	86.6	66.8
Pinellas	3,411	3,326	2,134	-0.9	64.2	76.1	84.6	71.6
Polk	1,725	1,701	857	2.3	50.4	70.7	82.4	57.8
Putnam	220	218	98	4.3	45.0	68.0	76.7	52.3
St. Johns	839	801	549	23.4	68.5	80.6	89.4	73.8
St. Lucie	699	653	328	20.1	50.2	71.3	81.2	57.9
Santa Rosa	884	884	613	25.1	69.3	86.2	92.0	75.7
Sarasota	1,151	1,132	791	32.5	69.9	80.5	84.6	75.5
Seminole	2,295	2,138	1,480	6.5	69.2	79.6	87.1	76.0
Sumter	119	117	62	8.8	53.0	69.2	85.5	59.8
Suwannee	119	117	67	-6.9	57.3	76.9	77.8	60.7
Taylor	75	74	33	-32.7	44.6	68.9	75.7	45.9
Union	50	48	19	-13.6	39.6	76.0	76.0	47.9
Volusia	1,755	1,736	1,022	7.9	58.9	75.8	86.0	63.9
Wakulla	131	127	58	1.8	45.7	72.7	80.5	48.4
Walton	140	137	64	33.3	46.7	69.3	83.9	57.7
Washington	85	85	44	-2.2	51.8	74.1	76.5	64.7

A/ Change in overall readiness.
1/ High school graduates, 2005, who enrolled as degree-seeking students in Florida public community colleges and state universities during the 2005–06 academic year.
2/ Includes special district schools not shown separately. Detail may not add to totals.

Source: State of Florida, Department of Education, Education Information and Accountability Services (EIAS), *Florida Informantion Note: Performance on the Common Placement Test for Graduates Entering College, 2004-05,* Series 2007-20F, Internet site <http://www.fldoe.org/eias/> (accessed 27, June 2007).

INCOME AND WEALTH

Per Capita Personal Income, 2005

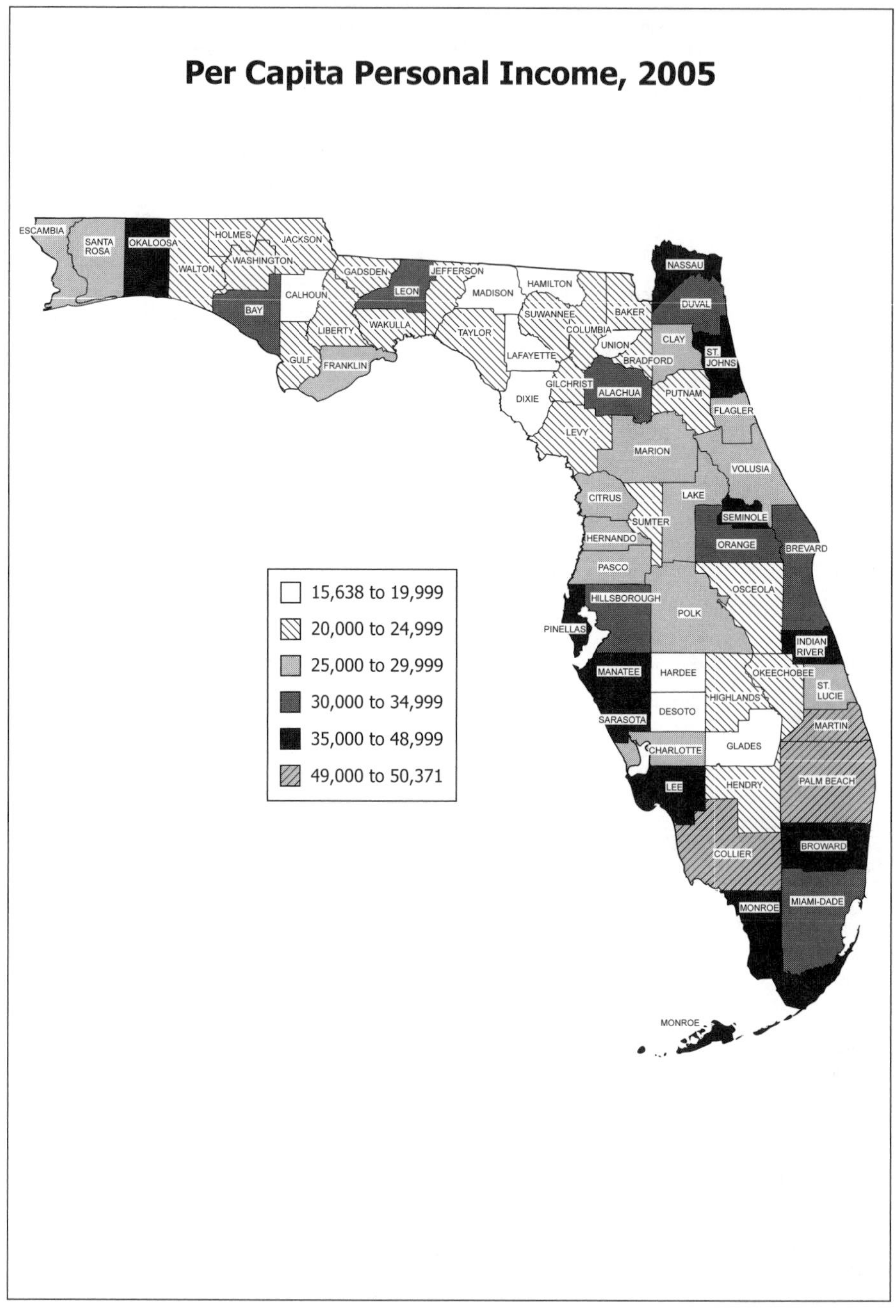

ESCAMBIA
SANTA ROSA
OKALOOSA
WALTON
HOLMES
WASHINGTON
JACKSON
BAY
CALHOUN
GADSDEN
LIBERTY
GULF
FRANKLIN
LEON
WAKULLA
JEFFERSON
MADISON
TAYLOR
HAMILTON
SUWANNEE
LAFAYETTE
DIXIE
COLUMBIA
BAKER
UNION
BRADFORD
GILCHRIST
ALACHUA
LEVY
NASSAU
DUVAL
CLAY
ST. JOHNS
PUTNAM
FLAGLER
MARION
VOLUSIA
CITRUS
LAKE
SUMTER
SEMINOLE
HERNANDO
ORANGE
BREVARD
PASCO
OSCEOLA
HILLSBOROUGH
POLK
PINELLAS
INDIAN RIVER
MANATEE
HARDEE
OKEECHOBEE
ST. LUCIE
HIGHLANDS
SARASOTA
DESOTO
MARTIN
CHARLOTTE
GLADES
PALM BEACH
LEE
HENDRY
COLLIER
BROWARD
MONROE
MIAMI-DADE
MONROE
15,638 to 19,999
20,000 to 24,999
25,000 to 29,999
30,000 to 34,999
35,000 to 48,999
49,000 to 50,371

Source: Table 5.10

Section 5.00
Income and Wealth

This section presents data pertaining to the personal income and wealth of Floridians. Personal income, earned income, transfer payments, military retirement income, and poverty thresholds and income are depicted throughout this section.

Explanatory notes. The earnings components of personal income are allocated on a place-of-work basis. These earnings are converted to a place-of-residence basis by means of a residence adjustment factor. Property income and transfer payments are then added to earnings, resulting in total income on a place-of-residence basis. This conversion is illustrated in Table 5.14. The first basis, earnings by place of work, is useful in the analysis of the income structure of a given area in terms of industrial markets and purchasing power. Expressed per capita, the latter basis, earnings by place of residence, is an indicator of living standards and welfare level. See Section 9.00 for estimates of farm income.

The *Statistics of Income* series data published by the U.S. Internal Revenue Service are based on the tax-defined concept, adjusted gross income (AGI), which excludes certain types of income. Caution should be exercised in comparing these data over time, as annual changes in tax law will continue to affect the definition of AGI.

Retirement income. In June 2000, the Bureau of Economic Analysis (BEA) reclassified government employee retirement plans covering federal civilian, military, and state and local government employees, which resulted in a raise in the amount of employer contributions (added to other labor income), dividend and interest received by these plans (added to personal dividend income and personal interest income), and personal contributions (no longer included in personal contributions for social insurance).

Poverty status. Families and unrelated individuals are classified as being above or below the poverty level by comparing their calendar-year money income to an income cutoff or "poverty threshold." The income cutoffs vary by family size, number of children, and age of the family householder or unrelated individual. Poverty status is determined for all families (and, by implication, all family members). Poverty status is also determined for persons not in families, except for inmates of institutions, members of the Armed Forces living in barracks, college students living in dormitories, and unrelated individuals under 15 years old.

The poverty thresholds are revised annually to reflect changes in the Consumer Price Index (CPI). The poverty threshold for a family of four in 2006 was $20,794 as shown on Table 5.46. Poverty thresholds are computed on a national basis only. No attempt has been made to adjust these thresholds for regional, state, or other local variations in the cost of living.

Sources. Data on income sources, tax deductions, and credits are from statistical samplings of individual tax returns and are reported in the series *Statistics of Income: SOI Bulletin* published by the U.S. Treasury Department's Internal Revenue Service.

Florida household income data by household size and income class are based on results from the Florida Consumer Confidence Survey, conducted monthly by the Bureau of Economic and Business Research's UF Survey Research Center.

Statistics pertaining to personal income in Florida are provided by the U.S. Bureau of Economic Analysis (BEA). Annual estimates for states are published in the *Annual State Personal Income* and are available on the Internet. State and county data shown in this *Abstract* are from the BEA's Regional Economic Information System (REIS), and are also available on the Internet.

Federal fiscal year retirement income of military retirees and surviving families broken down by branch of service published in the U.S. Department of Defense publication, *DoD Statistical Report on the Military Retirement System* produced by the Office of the Actuary, and available on the Internet. National poverty thresholds based on money income and county-level data on median household income, the number of poor persons, and related children living in poverty are produced annually by the U.S. Census Bureau and are available on the Internet. The annual Consumer Price Index for the United States are provided by the U.S. Department of Labor, Bureau of Labor Statistics.

County-level poverty status statistics for all races and minorities aged 60 and over within the state's 11 Planning and Service Areas are provided by the Florida Department of Elder Affairs in their *Florida County Profiles,* available on the Internet.

Section 5.00
Income and Wealth

Tables listed by major heading

Heading | Page

Tables listed by major heading

Table 5.01. INDIVIDUAL INCOME TAX RETURNS: SPECIFIED INCOME, DEDUCTION, AND TAX ITEMS IN FLORIDA AND THE UNITED STATES, 2005

(numbers in thousands; amounts in millions of dollars)

Item	Florida		United States	
	Number	Amount	Number	Amount
All returns	8,411	(X)	135,258	(X)
Adjusted gross income (AGI)	(X)	481,888	(X)	7,364,640
Salaries and wages in AGI	6,841	282,439	114,061	5,161,583
Taxable interest	3,407	14,441	59,554	161,325
Dividends	1,837	14,323	31,159	164,247
Business or profession net income (less loss)	1,393	16,013	21,288	269,595
Number of farm returns	38	(X)	2,008	(X)
Net capital gain (less loss) in AGI	1,635	72,956	26,124	625,706
Taxable Individual Retirement Arrangements (IRA) distributions	672	9,516	9,502	114,518
Pensions and annuities in AGI	1,528	29,439	23,184	417,390
Unemployment compensation	273	830	7,888	27,914
Social Security benefits in AGI	962	9,953	12,476	123,704
Self-employment retirement plans	46	746	1,236	20,614
Total itemized deductions 1/	2,777	66,737	48,164	1,136,072
Average (whole dollars)	(X)	24,034	(X)	23,588
State and local income taxes	200	2,066	35,261	230,092
State and local general sales taxes	2,201	3,062	11,168	17,627
Real estate taxes	2,367	9,437	41,496	145,630
Taxes paid	2,696	14,806	47,940	420,163
Interest paid	2,286	25,757	39,314	413,969
Contributions	2,322	11,346	41,395	181,644
Taxable income	6,404	349,403	104,619	5,102,017
Total tax credits	2,374	2,763	40,532	54,074
Child tax credit	1,420	1,597	25,961	31,897
Child care credit	416	220	6,387	3,360
Earned income credit	1,632	3,054	22,748	42,636
Excess earned income credit (refundable) 2/	1,419	2,649	19,977	37,638
Alternative minimum tax	161	788	4,068	17,270
Income tax	5,619	67,204	92,646	938,184
Total tax liability	6,186	69,938	100,222	989,191
Tax due at time of filing	1,591	10,202	25,496	117,979
Overpayments	6,318	15,273	102,298	235,357

(X) Not applicable.

1/ Includes any amounts reported by the taxpayer, even if they could not be used in computing "taxable income," the base on which tax was computed.

2/ Represents the refundable portion of the credit and equals the amount in excess of total tax liability, including any advance earned income credit payments for those returns which had such an excess.

Note: Data are estimates based on samples and are preliminary.

Source: U.S., Department of the Treasury, Internal Revenue Service, *Statistics of Income: SOI Bulletin*, Spring 2007.

Table 5.02. INDIVIDUAL INCOME TAXES: RETURNS, ADJUSTED GROSS INCOME EXEMPTIONS, AND INCOME TAX IN FLORIDA AND THE UNITED STATES 1990 THROUGH 2005

Year	Number (1,000)				Amount ($1,000,000)			
	Returns		Exemptions 1/		Adjusted gross income 2/		Total income tax	
	Florida	United States	Florida	United States	Florida	United States	Florida	United States
1990	6,141	113,717	13,390	227,549	176,297	3,405,427	25,643	447,127
1991	6,250	114,730	13,721	231,297	177,889	3,464,534	25,504	448,430
1992	6,239	113,605	13,702	230,547	187,754	3,629,130	27,732	476,239
1993	6,282	115,061	13,840	253,489	193,995	3,720,611	29,539	532,213
1994	6,381	116,466	13,945	253,599	203,882	3,898,340	31,427	564,526
1995	6,553	118,784	14,281	257,737	221,515	4,182,770	34,968	620,972
1996	6,749	120,787	12,979	239,908	245,122	4,520,289	40,152	693,529
1997	6,898	123,057	14,993	267,906	273,066	4,950,214	45,054	770,465
1998	7,076	125,394	13,661	251,220	298,976	5,381,508	46,836	792,296
1999	7,264	127,075	(NA)	248,657	320,843	5,855,468	50,952	880,324
2000	7,499	130,122	14,331	258,895	348,609	6,307,009	56,618	980,064
2001	7,630	130,977	(NA)	(NA)	339,034	6,144,619	52,221	891,653
2002	7,738	130,836	14,948	263,875	339,492	6,015,047	48,460	798,634
2003	7,850	131,357	15,181	266,531	350,664	6,199,925	44,497	751,617
2004	8,173	133,093	15,782	269,663	415,063	6,745,102	55,276	832,385
2005	8,411	135,258	16,121	273,738	481,888	7,364,640	67,204	938,184

(NA) Not available.
1/ Includes exemptions for age and blindness.
2/ Less deficit.
Note: Includes taxable and nontaxable returns. All figures are estimates based on samples. Some data are revised; 2005 data are preliminary.

Source: U.S., Department of the Treasury, Internal Revenue Service, *Statistics of Income: SOI Bulletin,* Spring 2007, and previous editions.

Table 5.03. HOUSEHOLD INCOME: PERCENTAGE DISTRIBUTION OF ANNUAL INCOME BY INCOME CATEGORY AND HOUSEHOLD SIZE IN FLORIDA, 2006

Income category	All households	Household size					
		1	2	3	4	5	6 or more
Total	100.0	20.4	38.8	16.4	15.0	6.2	3.2
Less than $10,000	5.8	49.2	20.0	10.9	8.1	6.4	5.4
$10,000 to $19,999	9.4	35.2	33.3	13.3	9.6	5.2	3.3
$20,000 to $39,999	25.3	27.1	38.2	14.8	11.4	5.5	3.0
$40,000 to $59,999	20.7	20.5	40.9	18.2	13.4	4.5	2.4
$60,000 to $79,999	12.8	11.5	43.7	16.4	17.5	7.7	3.2
$80,000 to $99,999	9.5	6.2	43.1	18.6	22.3	7.0	2.9
More than $100,000	16.5	6.6	40.6	18.9	21.8	8.3	3.8

Note: Distribution of household income is based on telephone surveys with sample size of approximately 500 Florida households. The surveys are conducted throughout the year and the monthly results have been pooled to develop the annual frequency distributions.

Source: University of Florida, Bureau of Economic and Business Research, UF Survey Research Center, unpublished data.

Table 5.05. PERSONAL INCOME: TOTAL AND PER CAPITA AMOUNTS IN FLORIDA, OTHER SUNBELT STATES, OTHER POPULOUS STATES, AND THE UNITED STATES 2004 THROUGH 2006

State	Total personal income ($1,000,000) 2004	2005	2006	Percentage change 2005 to 2006	Per capita personal income (amounts in dollars) 2004	2005	2006 Amount	2006 Rank among states
				Sunbelt states				
Florida	564,997	604,131	647,583	7.2	32,534	34,001	35,798	20
Alabama	126,655	134,736	143,925	6.8	28,037	29,623	31,295	40
Arizona	164,122	178,706	193,983	8.5	28,564	30,019	31,458	39
Arkansas	70,853	74,059	78,521	6.0	25,794	26,681	27,935	48
California	1,268,049	1,335,386	1,420,245	6.4	35,380	36,936	38,956	11
Georgia	264,728	282,322	298,627	5.8	29,628	30,914	31,891	38
Louisiana	121,781	111,167	132,715	19.4	27,088	24,664	30,952	41
Mississippi	69,450	72,862	77,232	6.0	24,009	25,051	26,535	50
New Mexico	50,707	53,714	57,998	8.0	26,679	27,889	29,673	44
North Carolina	252,253	269,203	285,477	6.0	29,569	31,041	32,234	36
Oklahoma	100,027	106,119	115,288	8.6	28,394	29,948	32,210	37
South Carolina	113,632	120,123	127,543	6.2	27,090	28,285	29,515	45
Tennessee	174,452	184,443	195,078	5.8	29,641	30,969	32,304	35
Texas	690,480	744,270	805,307	8.2	30,664	32,460	34,257	25
Virginia	266,751	283,685	299,393	5.5	35,698	37,503	39,173	9
				Other populous states				
Illinois	442,349	462,928	490,374	5.9	34,794	36,264	38,215	13
Indiana	187,533	195,332	205,355	5.1	30,134	31,173	32,526	33
Massachusetts	267,972	279,860	295,320	5.5	41,636	43,501	45,877	3
Michigan	320,261	331,349	341,710	3.1	31,730	32,804	33,847	27
New Jersey	363,158	381,466	404,331	6.0	41,858	43,831	46,344	2
New York	742,209	771,990	818,426	6.0	38,473	39,967	42,392	5
Ohio	352,588	365,453	382,658	4.7	30,763	31,860	33,338	29
Pennsylvania	413,589	433,400	456,316	5.3	33,415	34,937	36,680	18
United States	9,716,351	10,220,942	10,860,917	6.3	33,090	34,471	36,276	(X)

(X) Not applicable.
Note: Data for 2004 and 2005 are revised; 2006 are preliminary.

Source: U.S., Department of Commerce, Bureau of Economic Analysis, *Annual State Personal Income,* released March 27, 2007, Internet site <http://www.bea.doc.gov/> (accessed 5, April 2007).

Table 5.08. DISPOSABLE PERSONAL INCOME: TOTAL AND PER CAPITA AMOUNTS IN FLORIDA OTHER SUNBELT STATES, OTHER POPULOUS STATES, AND THE UNITED STATES 2004 THROUGH 2006

State	Total disposable personal income ($1,000,000)			Percentage change 2005 to 2006	Per capita disposable personal income (amounts in dollars)			
							2006	
	2004	2005	2006		2004	2005	Amount	Rank among states
				Sunbelt states				
Florida	509,980	538,621	572,272	6.2	29,366	30,314	31,635	21
Alabama	115,693	122,102	129,622	6.2	25,610	26,845	28,185	41
Arizona	148,003	159,355	171,195	7.4	25,759	26,769	27,763	37
Arkansas	64,598	66,918	70,585	5.5	23,517	24,108	25,112	48
California	1,116,527	1,159,068	1,216,692	5.0	31,152	32,059	33,373	13
Georgia	236,945	250,692	263,213	5.0	26,518	27,450	28,109	36
Louisiana	112,036	101,880	122,427	20.2	24,921	22,603	28,553	50
Mississippi	64,517	67,193	70,901	5.5	22,304	23,102	24,360	49
New Mexico	46,377	48,831	52,459	7.4	24,401	25,354	26,839	46
North Carolina	226,119	238,972	250,982	5.0	26,505	27,555	28,339	38
Oklahoma	90,911	95,721	103,422	8.0	25,806	27,014	28,895	39
South Carolina	103,146	108,214	114,105	5.4	24,590	25,481	26,406	42
Tennessee	161,232	169,278	177,880	5.1	27,394	28,423	29,456	32
Texas	634,778	678,742	729,012	7.4	28,190	29,603	31,012	23
Virginia	234,325	246,044	257,017	4.5	31,359	32,527	33,628	8
				Other populous states				
Illinois	394,318	408,152	428,828	5.1	31,016	31,973	33,419	17
Indiana	169,280	174,920	182,959	4.6	27,201	27,916	28,979	34
Massachusetts	232,021	239,505	249,722	4.3	36,050	37,229	38,794	3
Michigan	288,533	296,335	304,046	2.6	28,586	29,338	30,117	24
New Jersey	319,020	330,867	347,587	5.1	36,771	38,017	39,840	2
New York	637,667	652,696	683,569	4.7	33,054	33,791	35,407	6
Ohio	313,282	321,777	335,421	4.2	27,334	28,052	29,223	30
Pennsylvania	369,655	383,716	400,865	4.5	29,865	30,932	32,222	18
United States	8,667,643	9,019,122	9,501,462	5.3	29,518	30,418	31,735	(X)

(X) Not applicable.
Note: Data for 2004 and 2005 are revised; 2006 are preliminary.

Source: U.S., Department of Commerce, Bureau of Economic Analysis, *Annual State Personal Income,* released March 27, 2007, Internet site <http://www.bea.doc.gov/> (accessed 5, April 2007).

Table 5.09. PERSONAL INCOME: TOTAL AMOUNTS ON A PLACE-OF-RESIDENCE BASIS IN THE UNITED STATES AND IN THE STATE AND COUNTIES OF FLORIDA, 1996 THROUGH 2005

(in thousands of dollars)

County	1996	1997	1998	1999	2000
United States	6,512,485,000	6,907,332,000	7,415,709,000	7,796,137,000	8,422,074,000
Florida	351,355,341	372,093,817	402,454,015	423,833,681	457,539,355
Alachua	4,156,226	4,396,469	4,723,572	4,925,739	5,238,274
Baker	331,442	353,269	373,303	405,324	431,141
Bay	2,896,933	3,062,313	3,234,088	3,353,267	3,521,822
Bradford	391,751	428,184	469,256	456,191	483,922
Brevard	9,791,094	10,510,161	11,143,606	11,613,186	12,865,456
Broward	39,350,853	40,927,624	44,487,335	46,481,179	50,137,561
Calhoun	171,246	180,430	187,791	206,909	207,452
Charlotte	2,801,781	3,016,960	3,241,421	3,398,226	3,649,552
Citrus	1,972,294	2,138,173	2,287,302	2,444,376	2,635,444
Clay	2,840,871	3,028,117	3,284,632	3,419,309	3,730,190
Collier	6,970,600	7,796,743	8,622,584	9,338,997	10,011,970
Columbia	858,348	913,474	975,949	1,008,262	1,063,363
DeSoto	462,478	485,573	531,243	547,665	531,470
Dixie	171,551	180,427	194,082	202,657	211,498
Duval	17,428,690	18,299,740	19,822,257	20,616,898	22,548,896
Escambia	5,556,224	5,847,820	6,260,541	6,467,395	6,852,083
Flagler	862,360	955,563	1,046,759	1,123,039	1,194,237
Franklin	165,625	169,736	178,075	189,760	205,232
Gadsden	712,361	754,981	805,911	845,457	882,543
Gilchrist	202,151	221,331	249,293	271,823	282,838
Glades	131,458	138,906	153,436	161,487	163,237
Gulf	219,155	228,731	231,210	230,520	242,455
Hamilton	165,882	171,759	178,363	184,180	194,216
Hardee	370,902	393,794	429,087	458,219	447,258
Hendry	554,253	591,910	657,057	698,163	657,825
Hernando	2,337,749	2,534,308	2,713,353	2,823,363	3,087,275
Highlands	1,496,157	1,575,800	1,679,875	1,743,225	1,770,538
Hillsborough	21,267,796	22,730,424	24,754,135	26,483,397	28,645,545
Holmes	263,298	278,924	299,443	313,528	326,422
Indian River	3,260,652	3,494,975	3,770,896	3,983,019	4,207,683
Jackson	706,975	726,399	766,002	809,900	842,466
Jefferson	230,855	244,212	265,374	279,862	307,716
Lafayette	91,712	97,787	102,709	109,333	105,690

See footnote at end of table. Continued . . .

Table 5.09. PERSONAL INCOME: TOTAL AMOUNTS ON A PLACE-OF-RESIDENCE BASIS IN THE UNITED STATES AND IN THE STATE AND COUNTIES OF FLORIDA, 1996 THROUGH 2005 (Continued)

(in thousands of dollars)

County	1996	1997	1998	1999	2000
Lake	3,924,768	4,277,338	4,714,335	5,048,075	5,459,638
Lee	9,577,927	10,187,142	11,132,965	11,777,818	12,874,770
Leon	4,932,596	5,170,978	5,628,493	5,978,233	6,255,318
Levy	490,514	531,160	571,913	607,256	628,130
Liberty	98,471	105,145	106,678	114,946	118,658
Madison	257,081	269,726	282,231	299,081	312,154
Manatee	6,023,631	6,424,554	7,099,278	7,556,478	8,088,102
Marion	4,444,979	4,742,676	5,182,725	5,497,544	5,893,863
Martin	4,105,534	4,405,623	4,800,649	5,092,917	5,347,264
Miami-Dade	45,517,645	47,241,852	50,612,433	53,414,335	57,922,341
Monroe	2,283,617	2,400,882	2,635,045	2,672,638	2,941,452
Nassau	1,247,274	1,354,521	1,479,091	1,585,030	1,747,202
Okaloosa	3,636,776	3,900,963	4,123,073	4,389,141	4,610,536
Okeechobee	516,626	549,266	576,227	606,955	610,495
Orange	17,585,835	18,869,846	20,684,847	22,323,667	24,437,484
Osceola	2,427,002	2,648,609	2,930,561	3,233,548	3,502,985
Palm Beach	37,580,308	39,519,095	42,798,012	44,811,378	48,954,794
Pasco	5,966,735	6,410,706	6,831,464	7,212,317	7,844,336
Pinellas	23,284,283	24,699,324	26,306,816	27,199,287	29,313,800
Polk	9,198,498	9,539,839	10,472,253	11,061,993	11,516,995
Putnam	1,080,755	1,118,436	1,170,711	1,219,627	1,281,562
St. Johns	3,118,634	3,531,882	3,994,916	4,279,815	4,693,235
St. Lucie	3,351,908	3,550,948	3,808,538	3,983,982	4,302,495
Santa Rosa	2,136,603	2,325,180	2,486,093	2,606,261	2,850,569
Sarasota	9,935,489	10,640,081	11,555,905	11,980,865	12,938,930
Seminole	8,423,541	9,088,999	9,888,386	10,594,809	11,350,658
Sumter	596,461	657,190	717,576	777,088	826,434
Suwannee	560,695	581,201	625,874	648,913	665,680
Taylor	307,479	318,553	337,350	347,696	369,523
Union	140,912	154,679	163,226	172,200	178,274
Volusia	8,202,122	8,692,190	9,206,431	9,638,706	10,380,740
Wakulla	360,556	398,648	428,148	458,993	511,961
Walton	552,796	595,258	644,470	693,741	755,244
Washington	295,567	316,310	337,362	354,493	370,463

See footnote at end of table. Continued . . .

Table 5.09. PERSONAL INCOME: TOTAL AMOUNTS ON A PLACE-OF-RESIDENCE BASIS IN THE UNITED STATES AND IN THE STATE AND COUNTIES OF FLORIDA, 1996 THROUGH 2005 (Continued)

(in thousands of dollars)

County	2001	2002	2003	2004	2005
United States	8,716,992,000	8,872,871,000	9,150,320,000	9,716,351,000	10,220,942,000
Florida	478,637,023	495,489,345	514,377,645	564,997,468	604,131,000
Alachua	5,418,264	5,519,952	5,672,386	6,287,229	6,808,684
Baker	447,185	468,757	502,708	549,003	574,348
Bay	3,675,638	3,870,336	4,119,403	4,545,721	4,887,759
Bradford	493,034	510,992	543,509	585,679	620,858
Brevard	13,327,716	13,853,189	14,586,155	15,779,826	16,810,526
Broward	52,614,372	54,850,632	56,254,396	60,265,418	65,213,329
Calhoun	215,147	215,475	226,028	232,657	251,103
Charlotte	3,794,983	3,819,661	3,914,577	4,333,898	4,613,154
Citrus	2,765,684	2,875,327	3,003,263	3,232,634	3,495,021
Clay	3,838,983	4,044,521	4,312,269	4,667,049	5,017,632
Collier	11,061,849	11,607,197	12,288,703	14,550,101	15,236,905
Columbia	1,094,516	1,129,706	1,179,366	1,306,214	1,414,160
DeSoto	552,702	544,993	557,197	601,133	635,027
Dixie	224,664	227,058	228,999	252,722	277,165
Duval	22,828,124	23,651,670	25,016,241	26,515,178	27,881,752
Escambia	7,174,856	7,349,882	7,593,294	7,964,696	8,387,199
Flagler	1,282,887	1,391,448	1,555,403	1,849,888	2,075,802
Franklin	211,943	219,289	223,875	253,517	265,694
Gadsden	896,439	919,897	959,438	1,029,185	1,068,743
Gilchrist	310,626	314,548	328,442	361,259	385,113
Glades	183,535	183,738	181,973	194,985	208,554
Gulf	258,906	264,335	280,770	316,131	332,995
Hamilton	184,631	182,288	193,224	210,095	219,123
Hardee	482,982	473,716	485,653	492,832	530,198
Hendry	718,268	726,471	732,017	783,553	839,419
Hernando	3,234,829	3,387,896	3,538,276	3,809,865	4,107,604
Highlands	1,875,362	1,959,546	2,014,682	2,123,732	2,249,711
Hillsborough	29,977,256	31,070,635	32,485,969	35,135,371	37,379,401
Holmes	342,975	341,860	358,115	389,062	410,544
Indian River	4,552,238	4,680,414	4,886,086	5,643,408	5,886,319
Jackson	883,777	913,933	977,877	985,604	1,066,183
Jefferson	308,811	311,230	325,348	339,795	352,308
Lafayette	115,107	107,690	108,470	118,343	123,836

See footnote at end of table.

Continued . . .

Table 5.09. PERSONAL INCOME: TOTAL AMOUNTS ON A PLACE-OF-RESIDENCE BASIS IN THE UNITED STATES AND IN THE STATE AND COUNTIES OF FLORIDA, 1996 THROUGH 2005 (Continued)

(in thousands of dollars)

County	2001	2002	2003	2004	2005
Lake	5,839,137	6,093,467	6,547,582	7,306,625	8,011,686
Lee	14,304,478	14,798,568	15,743,763	18,381,025	19,905,093
Leon	6,517,209	6,659,704	6,882,479	7,513,507	7,861,004
Levy	678,392	678,345	711,556	779,030	838,037
Liberty	127,924	131,342	137,097	149,476	154,881
Madison	324,969	323,056	331,238	362,472	377,510
Manatee	8,762,299	8,920,616	8,941,453	10,002,623	10,766,001
Marion	6,157,977	6,294,557	6,729,211	7,494,886	8,160,559
Martin	5,654,262	5,657,926	5,868,733	6,549,860	6,962,997
Miami-Dade	60,401,717	62,664,565	64,764,869	70,514,064	74,533,598
Monroe	2,940,428	2,925,881	3,021,939	3,365,337	3,498,309
Nassau	1,823,215	1,890,698	2,001,950	2,252,088	2,365,779
Okaloosa	4,757,566	5,166,167	5,532,745	5,968,451	6,392,599
Okeechobee	670,264	685,911	713,397	782,547	833,374
Orange	24,900,089	25,879,570	27,348,842	29,726,474	32,259,655
Osceola	3,646,332	3,871,702	4,175,478	4,602,693	5,094,559
Palm Beach	50,843,978	52,287,552	52,980,627	59,650,738	63,717,587
Pasco	8,401,592	8,853,085	9,383,876	10,297,721	11,214,084
Pinellas	30,098,956	30,840,120	31,078,837	33,449,376	35,297,595
Polk	12,211,632	12,462,296	13,051,067	14,375,686	15,659,093
Putnam	1,333,567	1,377,309	1,469,453	1,503,115	1,599,879
St. Johns	4,866,985	5,067,670	5,352,223	6,364,643	6,945,963
St. Lucie	4,537,494	4,712,133	4,978,593	5,745,212	6,205,838
Santa Rosa	2,990,543	3,140,971	3,327,655	3,664,694	3,973,767
Sarasota	13,645,790	14,177,419	14,420,988	16,283,115	17,147,801
Seminole	11,964,062	12,474,401	13,038,453	14,330,294	15,585,485
Sumter	921,079	994,715	1,101,158	1,251,288	1,398,183
Suwannee	720,759	724,372	751,077	819,659	864,835
Taylor	372,747	382,481	389,010	419,449	450,764
Union	187,246	184,978	199,025	218,991	232,455
Volusia	10,949,705	11,356,533	11,812,530	12,971,188	13,829,988
Wakulla	532,647	538,118	565,412	618,809	661,938
Walton	828,815	901,161	986,869	1,139,237	1,230,461
Washington	374,879	383,674	404,348	437,312	473,474

Note: Data for 2003 and 2004 are revised.

Source: U.S., Department of Commerce, Bureau of Economic Analysis, Regional Economic Information System (REIS), 1969–2005, Internet site <http://www.bea.gov/> (accessed 30, May 2007).

Table 5.10. PERSONAL INCOME: PER CAPITA AMOUNTS ON A PLACE-OF-RESIDENCE BASIS IN THE UNITED STATES AND IN THE STATE AND COUNTIES OF FLORIDA, 1996 THROUGH 2005

(rounded to dollars)

County	1996	1997	1998	1999	2000
United States	24,175	25,334	26,883	27,939	29,843
Florida	23,655	24,502	25,987	26,894	28,507
Alachua	20,117	20,926	22,207	22,821	24,008
Baker	15,809	16,590	17,582	18,787	19,255
Bay	20,003	20,882	21,999	22,634	23,754
Bradford	15,644	16,767	18,124	17,622	18,550
Brevard	21,477	22,765	23,830	24,597	26,922
Broward	26,564	26,888	28,506	29,158	30,706
Calhoun	13,537	14,340	14,947	16,171	15,904
Charlotte	21,132	22,355	23,557	24,232	25,647
Citrus	17,937	19,096	20,004	20,958	22,210
Clay	22,289	22,943	24,235	24,652	26,326
Collier	33,319	35,292	36,948	38,104	39,393
Columbia	16,601	17,260	17,982	18,185	18,734
DeSoto	15,962	16,278	17,473	17,468	16,449
Dixie	13,414	13,605	14,380	14,790	15,295
Duval	23,404	24,147	25,869	26,666	28,920
Escambia	19,661	20,199	21,205	22,001	23,278
Flagler	20,493	21,454	22,450	23,240	23,608
Franklin	15,525	15,834	16,414	17,494	20,859
Gadsden	15,935	16,860	18,012	18,739	19,588
Gilchrist	15,487	16,588	17,849	19,330	19,447
Glades	13,731	14,190	15,144	15,552	15,391
Gulf	17,048	17,913	18,234	18,143	16,605
Hamilton	13,462	14,041	14,207	14,381	14,565
Hardee	15,068	15,575	16,378	17,293	16,612
Hendry	16,964	17,429	19,005	19,590	18,083
Hernando	19,182	20,289	21,259	21,842	23,475
Highlands	18,089	18,685	19,636	20,129	20,245
Hillsborough	23,062	24,081	25,648	26,889	28,554
Holmes	14,682	15,145	16,197	16,797	17,611
Indian River	31,479	32,881	34,608	35,788	37,106
Jackson	15,536	15,894	16,661	17,592	18,014
Jefferson	17,514	18,202	19,519	20,672	23,817
Lafayette	13,951	15,443	16,058	16,787	14,972
Lake	21,255	22,295	23,698	24,610	25,650

See footnote at end of table.

Continued . . .

Table 5.10. PERSONAL INCOME: PER CAPITA AMOUNTS ON A PLACE-OF-RESIDENCE BASIS IN THE UNITED STATES AND IN THE STATE AND COUNTIES OF FLORIDA, 1996 THROUGH 2005 (Continued)

(rounded to dollars)

County	1996	1997	1998	1999	2000
Lee	23,902	24,796	26,388	27,265	29,003
Leon	21,909	22,536	24,153	25,345	26,067
Levy	15,726	16,506	17,357	17,917	18,143
Liberty	14,415	14,864	15,389	16,158	16,975
Madison	14,211	14,883	15,422	16,072	16,653
Manatee	24,833	25,958	27,932	29,170	30,436
Marion	18,784	19,496	20,724	21,562	22,639
Martin	34,956	36,628	38,811	40,428	42,060
Miami-Dade	21,360	21,888	23,216	24,050	25,622
Monroe	28,069	29,668	32,596	33,419	37,005
Nassau	23,847	25,025	26,609	27,868	30,141
Okaloosa	22,022	23,353	24,545	25,963	26,976
Okeechobee	15,779	16,141	16,536	17,073	16,998
Orange	21,951	22,760	24,173	25,493	27,082
Osceola	16,627	17,302	18,308	19,360	20,109
Palm Beach	36,130	36,943	39,045	40,121	43,101
Pasco	18,861	19,795	20,637	21,368	22,580
Pinellas	25,986	27,305	28,813	29,649	31,783
Polk	20,238	20,581	22,213	23,140	23,721
Putnam	15,430	15,890	16,565	17,300	18,196
St. Johns	29,159	31,585	34,353	35,771	37,701
St. Lucie	18,570	19,232	20,313	20,930	22,236
Santa Rosa	20,181	21,058	21,868	22,454	24,063
Sarasota	32,213	33,906	36,244	37,111	39,562
Seminole	24,932	26,258	27,996	29,416	30,922
Sumter	13,913	14,099	14,714	15,023	15,421
Suwannee	17,704	17,780	18,674	18,963	18,993
Taylor	16,310	16,896	17,637	17,861	19,239
Union	11,058	12,033	12,470	12,814	13,249
Volusia	19,600	20,387	21,293	21,988	23,326
Wakulla	18,104	19,198	20,088	20,584	22,264
Walton	15,342	15,761	16,641	17,403	18,502
Washington	14,895	15,522	16,459	16,986	17,626

See footnote at end of table.

Continued . . .

Table 5.10. PERSONAL INCOME: PER CAPITA AMOUNTS ON A PLACE-OF-RESIDENCE BASIS IN THE UNITED STATES AND IN THE STATE AND COUNTIES OF FLORIDA, 1996 THROUGH 2005 (Continued)

(rounded to dollars)

County	2001	2002	2003	2004	2005
United States	30,562	30,795	31,466	33,090	34,471
Florida	29,266	29,702	30,290	32,534	34,001
Alachua	24,757	25,039	25,661	28,300	30,435
Baker	19,736	20,189	21,499	22,955	23,396
Bay	24,526	25,438	26,623	28,836	30,298
Bradford	19,022	19,522	20,206	21,239	22,141
Brevard	27,402	27,960	28,895	30,455	31,800
Broward	31,464	32,137	32,512	34,340	36,595
Calhoun	16,926	16,880	17,470	17,846	18,859
Charlotte	25,957	25,493	25,643	27,588	29,890
Citrus	22,803	23,248	23,737	24,831	26,072
Clay	26,301	26,680	27,484	28,414	29,410
Collier	41,808	42,048	42,942	49,043	49,492
Columbia	19,036	19,343	19,612	21,209	22,076
DeSoto	16,833	16,499	16,386	17,247	18,113
Dixie	16,148	16,259	16,448	17,724	18,945
Duval	28,884	29,515	30,876	32,400	33,723
Escambia	24,144	24,717	25,556	26,913	28,371
Flagler	23,888	24,181	24,909	26,913	27,297
Franklin	21,408	21,907	22,250	25,163	26,133
Gadsden	19,668	20,254	21,273	22,443	23,129
Gilchrist	21,231	20,896	21,059	22,719	23,369
Glades	17,000	16,810	16,560	17,495	18,513
Gulf	16,489	20,069	20,720	23,095	23,836
Hamilton	13,442	13,266	13,846	14,946	15,721
Hardee	17,962	17,179	17,517	17,595	18,752
Hendry	19,674	19,719	19,709	20,579	21,205
Hernando	24,075	24,503	24,684	25,330	25,975
Highlands	21,158	21,755	22,152	22,812	23,511
Hillsborough	29,209	29,562	30,311	31,960	33,034
Holmes	18,353	18,272	18,858	20,501	21,500
Indian River	39,466	39,682	40,648	45,336	46,219
Jackson	19,068	19,670	20,904	20,709	21,837
Jefferson	23,046	22,637	23,223	23,659	24,368
Lafayette	16,016	14,776	14,806	15,781	15,638
Lake	26,048	25,939	26,552	27,924	28,942

See footnote at end of table.

Continued . . .

Table 5.10. PERSONAL INCOME: PER CAPITA AMOUNTS ON A PLACE-OF-RESIDENCE BASIS IN THE UNITED STATES AND IN THE STATE AND COUNTIES OF FLORIDA, 1996 THROUGH 2005 (Continued)

(rounded to dollars)

County	2001	2002	2003	2004	2005
Lee	31,157	31,123	32,001	35,728	36,577
Leon	27,252	27,798	28,405	30,931	32,188
Levy	19,348	18,932	19,623	20,938	22,036
Liberty	18,212	18,277	18,742	20,148	20,044
Madison	17,251	17,299	17,666	19,076	19,889
Manatee	32,170	31,836	31,143	33,807	35,154
Marion	23,236	23,113	23,983	25,721	26,893
Martin	43,751	42,931	43,498	47,603	49,992
Miami-Dade	26,398	27,050	27,744	29,955	31,347
Monroe	37,149	37,022	38,336	43,174	45,946
Nassau	30,836	31,241	32,543	35,745	36,583
Okaloosa	27,705	29,492	31,153	33,034	35,275
Okeechobee	18,422	18,531	19,008	20,064	20,980
Orange	26,885	27,394	28,405	30,068	31,569
Osceola	19,877	19,928	20,260	20,901	22,008
Palm Beach	43,885	44,042	43,755	48,034	50,371
Pasco	23,379	23,740	24,198	25,240	26,076
Pinellas	32,585	33,357	33,602	36,109	38,085
Polk	24,822	24,931	25,584	27,459	28,896
Putnam	18,927	19,365	20,518	20,744	21,814
St. Johns	37,415	37,182	37,489	41,713	43,086
St. Lucie	22,897	22,957	23,293	25,319	25,861
Santa Rosa	24,538	24,675	25,189	26,558	27,897
Sarasota	40,936	41,700	41,618	45,808	46,965
Seminole	32,044	32,747	33,871	36,668	38,838
Sumter	16,801	17,228	18,610	20,677	21,878
Suwannee	20,256	20,016	20,437	21,821	22,415
Taylor	19,266	19,785	20,139	21,787	22,971
Union	13,505	13,307	14,290	14,988	15,641
Volusia	24,253	24,732	25,286	27,117	28,347
Wakulla	22,008	21,384	21,733	22,862	23,451
Walton	19,342	20,265	21,312	23,574	24,412
Washington	17,495	17,951	18,742	19,929	21,297

Note: These data were derived by dividing each type of income by the total population of the area, not just the segment of the population receiving that type of income. All per capita figures are prepared by the Bureau of Economic Analysis using U.S. Census Bureau population data. Data from 2000 to 2004 are revised.

Source: U.S., Department of Commerce, Bureau of Economic Analysis, Regional Economic Information System (REIS), 1969–2005, Internet site <http://www.bea.gov/> (accessed 30, May 2007).

Table 5.11. PERSONAL INCOME: TOTAL AND PER CAPITA AMOUNTS ON A PLACE-OF-RESIDENCE BASIS IN THE STATE AND METROPOLITAN AREAS OF FLORIDA 2003, 2004 AND 2005

Metropolitan area	Total personal income ($1,000,000) 2003	2004	2005	Per capita personal income (dollars) 2003	2004	2005
Florida	514,378	564,997	604,131	30,290	32,534	34,001
Cape Coral-Ft. Myers	15,744	18,381	19,905	32,001	35,728	36,577
Deltona-Daytona Beach-Ormond Beach	11,813	12,971	13,830	25,286	27,117	28,347
Ft. Walton Beach-Crestview-Destin	5,533	5,968	6,393	31,153	33,034	35,275
Gainesville	6,001	6,648	7,194	25,358	27,927	29,951
Alachua County	5,672	6,287	6,809	25,661	28,300	30,435
Gilchrist County	328	361	385	21,059	22,719	23,369
Jacksonville	37,185	40,348	42,785	31,123	33,014	34,288
Baker County	503	549	574	21,499	22,955	23,396
Clay County	4,312	4,667	5,018	27,484	28,414	29,410
Duval County	25,016	26,515	27,882	30,876	32,400	33,723
Nassau County	2,002	2,252	2,366	32,543	35,745	36,583
St. Johns County	5,352	6,365	6,946	37,489	41,713	43,086
Lakeland	13,051	14,376	15,659	25,584	27,459	28,896
Miami-Ft. Lauderdale-Pompano Beach	174,000	190,430	203,465	32,983	35,589	37,507
Broward County	56,254	60,265	65,213	32,512	34,340	36,595
Miami-Dade County	64,765	70,514	74,534	27,744	29,955	31,347
Palm Beach County	52,981	59,651	63,718	43,755	48,034	50,371
Naples-Marco Island	12,289	14,550	15,237	42,942	49,043	49,492
Ocala	6,729	7,495	8,161	23,983	25,721	26,893
Orlando-Kissimmee	51,110	55,966	60,951	28,387	30,068	31,557
Lake County	6,548	7,307	8,012	26,552	27,924	28,942
Orange County	27,349	29,726	32,260	28,405	30,068	31,569
Osceola County	4,175	4,603	5,095	20,260	20,901	22,008
Seminole County	13,038	14,330	15,585	33,871	36,668	38,838
Palm Bay-Melbourne-Titusville	14,586	15,780	16,811	28,895	30,455	31,800
Palm Coast	1,555	1,850	2,076	24,909	26,913	27,297
Panama City-Lynn Haven	4,119	4,546	4,888	26,623	28,836	30,298
Pensacola-Ferry Pass-Brent	10,921	11,629	12,361	25,443	26,800	28,217
Escambia County	7,593	7,965	8,387	25,556	26,913	28,371
Santa Rosa County	3,328	3,665	3,974	25,189	26,558	27,897
Port St. Lucie	10,847	12,295	13,169	31,111	33,731	34,723
Martin County	5,869	6,550	6,963	43,498	47,603	49,992
St. Lucie County	4,979	5,745	6,206	23,293	25,319	25,861
Punta Gorda	3,915	4,334	4,613	25,643	27,588	29,890
Sarasota-Bradenton-Venice	23,362	26,286	27,914	36,872	40,356	41,577
Manatee County	8,941	10,003	10,766	31,143	33,807	35,154
Sarasota County	14,421	16,283	17,148	41,618	45,808	46,965
Sebastian-Vero Beach	4,886	5,643	5,886	40,648	45,336	46,219
Tallahassee	8,733	9,501	9,944	26,671	28,775	29,852
Gadsden County	959	1,029	1,069	21,273	22,443	23,129
Jefferson County	325	340	352	23,223	23,659	24,368
Leon County	6,882	7,514	7,861	28,405	30,931	32,188
Wakulla County	565	619	662	21,733	22,862	23,451
Tampa-St. Petersburg-Clearwater	76,487	82,692	87,999	30,258	32,000	33,250
Hernando County	3,538	3,810	4,108	24,684	25,330	25,975
Hillsborough County	32,486	35,135	37,379	30,311	31,960	33,034
Pasco County	9,384	10,298	11,214	24,198	25,240	26,076
Pinellas County	31,079	33,449	35,298	33,602	36,109	38,085

Note: Data are for Metropolitan Statistical Areas (MSAs) defined as of December 18, 2006. See Glossary for definitions and map at the front of the book for area boundaries. Data for 2003 and 2004 are revised.

Source: U.S., Department of Commerce, Bureau of Economic Analysis, Regional Economic Information System (REIS), 1969–2005, Internet site <http://www.bea.gov/> (accessed 30, May 2007).

Table 5.12. PERSONAL INCOME: PER CAPITA AMOUNTS BY TYPE IN THE UNITED STATES AND IN THE STATE AND COUNTIES OF FLORIDA, 2004 AND 2005

(rounded to dollars)

County	Total personal income	Dividends interest and rent	Transfer payments: Total	Payments to individuals: Income-maintenance 1/	Payments to individuals: Medical payments	Payments to individuals: Unemployment insurance	Payments to individuals: Retirement 2/	Other 3/
				2004				
United States	33,090	5,292	4,859	488	2,084	126	1,760	401
Florida	32,534	7,893	5,460	483	2,248	68	2,070	591
Alachua	28,300	5,428	4,312	451	1,791	53	1,421	595
Baker	22,955	2,281	4,875	555	2,040	51	1,586	641
Bay	28,836	5,252	5,472	502	2,313	62	1,921	674
Bradford	21,239	2,008	5,049	590	2,162	56	1,556	685
Brevard	30,455	5,796	6,101	387	2,214	71	2,548	881
Broward	34,340	7,383	4,591	378	2,067	91	1,688	367
Calhoun	17,846	2,152	5,647	611	2,694	60	1,779	501
Charlotte	27,588	8,085	8,911	476	2,644	43	3,635	2,115
Citrus	24,831	7,593	7,587	392	2,813	69	3,931	383
Clay	28,414	3,969	3,801	263	1,381	53	1,617	488
Collier	49,043	25,532	4,740	236	1,669	43	2,530	262
Columbia	21,209	3,297	5,643	587	2,462	48	1,890	656
DeSoto	17,247	1,743	6,460	708	2,151	65	1,717	1,819
Dixie	17,724	2,727	6,718	800	2,610	55	2,302	950
Duval	32,400	4,906	4,483	566	1,855	74	1,520	467
Escambia	26,913	3,757	6,377	713	2,223	48	1,871	1,522
Flagler	26,913	8,983	6,084	181	1,849	49	3,651	354
Franklin	25,163	6,456	6,624	603	2,974	57	2,294	694
Gadsden	22,443	3,267	5,384	1,003	2,270	58	1,679	375
Gilchrist	22,719	2,809	4,970	521	1,963	32	1,890	562
Glades	17,495	3,688	4,069	358	1,044	58	1,986	622
Gulf	23,095	4,291	6,843	506	3,336	52	2,417	530
Hamilton	14,946	1,805	5,018	758	2,168	31	1,570	489
Hardee	17,595	1,215	6,034	940	2,007	55	1,331	1,701
Hendry	20,579	2,807	4,374	698	1,863	90	1,273	451
Hernando	25,330	5,932	7,424	357	2,857	55	3,578	578
Highlands	22,812	5,809	7,558	512	2,764	49	3,373	861
Hillsborough	31,960	4,901	4,494	511	1,830	75	1,589	489
Holmes	20,501	2,493	6,700	729	3,103	35	2,117	714
Indian River	45,336	22,308	8,067	477	2,563	77	3,308	1,644
Jackson	20,709	3,092	6,067	574	2,868	45	2,013	567
Jefferson	23,659	3,790	5,122	659	2,187	34	1,765	474

See footnotes at end of table. Continued . . .

Table 5.12. PERSONAL INCOME: PER CAPITA AMOUNTS BY TYPE IN THE UNITED STATES AND IN THE STATE AND COUNTIES OF FLORIDA, 2004 AND 2005 (Continued)

(rounded to dollars)

			Transfer payments					
				Payments to individuals				
County	Total personal income	Dividends interest and rent	Total	Income-mainte-nance 1/	Medical payments	Unemploy-ment insurance	Retire-ment 2/	Other 3/
				2004 (Continued)				
Lafayette	15,781	2,212	4,020	479	1,677	34	1,317	507
Lake	27,924	7,128	6,603	348	2,622	50	3,093	490
Lee	35,728	11,910	5,841	321	2,125	51	2,733	611
Leon	30,931	5,112	3,487	416	1,252	46	1,241	532
Levy	20,938	3,630	6,108	590	2,306	51	2,526	635
Liberty	20,148	1,983	4,471	541	1,975	26	1,482	440
Madison	19,076	2,767	6,019	857	2,625	42	1,849	643
Manatee	33,807	9,963	5,396	355	1,884	55	2,661	441
Marion	25,721	5,862	6,451	473	2,303	48	3,178	449
Martin	47,603	22,654	7,216	333	2,368	64	3,392	1,060
Miami-Dade	29,955	5,346	5,598	795	3,054	75	1,311	363
Monroe	43,174	17,910	4,515	318	1,916	51	1,823	407
Nassau	35,745	8,635	4,758	337	1,799	52	2,194	375
Okaloosa	33,034	6,395	4,937	355	1,890	45	1,676	971
Okeechobee	20,064	2,585	6,963	662	2,856	56	2,042	1,347
Orange	30,068	3,760	4,347	540	1,780	62	1,318	646
Osceola	20,901	1,918	4,662	471	1,842	57	1,470	822
Palm Beach	48,034	19,624	5,993	348	2,369	83	2,591	602
Pasco	25,240	5,087	6,214	338	2,528	58	2,760	529
Pinellas	36,109	9,489	6,100	405	2,661	76	2,512	446
Polk	27,459	4,938	5,733	612	1,958	61	2,301	801
Putnam	20,744	3,126	6,468	633	2,737	66	2,434	598
St. Johns	41,713	12,209	4,492	219	1,704	43	2,134	392
St. Lucie	25,319	5,584	7,220	601	2,553	84	2,572	1,409
Santa Rosa	26,558	3,422	5,350	428	1,683	44	1,757	1,438
Sarasota	45,808	19,229	6,876	239	2,723	56	3,457	402
Seminole	36,668	5,279	3,929	317	1,291	68	1,545	708
Sumter	20,677	5,338	7,229	429	1,695	39	4,360	707
Suwannee	21,821	3,468	6,535	732	2,734	39	2,442	588
Taylor	21,787	3,142	6,143	754	2,678	63	2,176	470
Union	14,988	1,847	3,532	495	1,493	25	1,052	465
Volusia	27,117	7,098	6,185	401	2,326	70	2,676	713
Wakulla	22,862	3,027	3,891	446	1,656	25	1,371	392
Walton	23,574	5,580	4,908	412	1,780	43	1,929	744
Washington	19,929	2,757	6,525	624	3,017	60	2,113	709

See footnotes at end of table.

Continued . . .

Table 5.12. PERSONAL INCOME: PER CAPITA AMOUNTS BY TYPE IN THE UNITED STATES AND IN THE STATE AND COUNTIES OF FLORIDA, 2004 AND 2005 (Continued)

(rounded to dollars)

			Transfer payments					
				Payments to individuals				
County	Total personal income	Dividends interest and rent	Total	Income-maintenance 1/	Medical payments	Unemployment insurance	Retirement 2/	Other 3/
				2005				
United States	34,471	5,366	5,149	532	2,205	109	1,839	463
Florida	34,001	8,041	5,553	504	2,348	52	2,134	515
Alachua	30,435	5,595	4,680	487	2,046	44	1,523	578
Baker	23,396	2,289	4,711	583	1,984	39	1,684	421
Bay	30,298	5,334	5,634	570	2,384	48	1,973	658
Bradford	22,141	2,228	5,182	609	2,373	45	1,688	466
Brevard	31,800	6,208	5,885	362	2,307	55	2,624	538
Broward	36,595	7,454	5,018	452	2,181	69	1,709	606
Calhoun	18,859	2,118	6,009	644	3,017	44	1,853	450
Charlotte	29,890	10,120	7,278	256	2,721	33	3,781	487
Citrus	26,072	7,616	7,953	419	2,902	51	4,093	488
Clay	29,410	4,008	3,994	289	1,391	41	1,729	543
Collier	49,492	24,635	5,140	277	1,741	33	2,602	488
Columbia	22,076	3,365	5,756	593	2,546	37	1,968	611
DeSoto	18,113	3,248	4,754	528	2,063	48	1,763	352
Dixie	18,945	2,960	6,766	828	2,746	40	2,461	689
Duval	33,723	5,014	4,754	630	1,981	57	1,601	486
Escambia	28,371	4,793	5,715	658	2,354	38	1,973	692
Flagler	27,297	8,529	6,145	199	1,825	36	3,646	440
Franklin	26,133	6,709	6,414	651	2,889	53	2,371	448
Gadsden	23,129	3,266	5,600	1,111	2,254	47	1,789	398
Gilchrist	23,369	2,796	5,047	537	2,072	24	1,903	510
Glades	18,513	3,829	4,137	408	1,089	46	2,071	523
Gulf	23,836	4,248	6,771	570	3,234	43	2,463	459
Hamilton	15,721	1,830	5,400	859	2,285	25	1,785	444
Hardee	18,752	2,486	4,554	807	2,011	42	1,367	326
Hendry	21,205	2,710	4,594	815	1,856	73	1,293	558
Hernando	25,975	5,846	7,525	378	2,891	42	3,621	593
Highlands	23,511	6,166	7,342	482	2,856	37	3,465	502
Hillsborough	33,034	4,889	4,649	542	1,913	58	1,640	495
Holmes	21,500	2,619	6,923	788	3,266	28	2,244	596
Indian River	46,219	23,217	6,764	324	2,605	51	3,365	420
Jackson	21,837	3,078	6,498	601	3,226	36	2,100	535
Jefferson	24,368	3,866	5,259	714	2,139	28	1,911	465
Lafayette	15,638	2,083	3,958	495	1,661	27	1,237	537
Lake	28,942	7,120	6,772	347	2,774	38	3,172	441
Lee	36,577	11,503	5,729	310	2,179	38	2,748	454

See footnotes at end of table. Continued . . .

Table 5.12. PERSONAL INCOME: PER CAPITA AMOUNTS BY TYPE IN THE UNITED STATES AND IN THE STATE AND COUNTIES OF FLORIDA, 2004 AND 2005 (Continued)

(rounded to dollars)

County	Total personal income	Dividends interest and rent	Transfer payments: Total	Payments to individuals: Income-mainte-nance 1/	Payments to individuals: Medical payments	Payments to individuals: Unemploy-ment insurance	Payments to individuals: Retire-ment 2/	Other 3/
				2005 (Continued)				
Leon	32,188	5,174	3,775	459	1,380	38	1,328	570
Levy	22,036	3,717	6,240	622	2,372	40	2,661	545
Liberty	20,044	1,911	4,143	572	1,653	19	1,497	400
Madison	19,889	2,877	6,286	921	2,868	38	1,937	520
Manatee	35,154	9,957	5,503	371	1,948	41	2,711	432
Marion	26,893	5,899	6,719	483	2,396	37	3,321	482
Martin	49,992	23,709	6,750	272	2,442	48	3,466	521
Miami-Dade	31,347	5,366	6,016	870	3,226	56	1,356	508
Monroe	45,946	18,306	5,258	459	2,026	43	1,933	797
Nassau	36,583	8,387	4,941	378	1,782	41	2,332	409
Okaloosa	35,275	6,868	4,933	388	2,006	37	1,754	748
Okeechobee	20,980	3,237	6,152	605	2,919	42	2,073	512
Orange	31,569	3,938	4,247	535	1,854	47	1,346	465
Osceola	22,008	2,419	4,330	426	1,962	43	1,504	396
Palm Beach	50,371	19,986	6,082	371	2,451	63	2,638	558
Pasco	26,076	4,956	6,250	343	2,557	45	2,775	531
Pinellas	38,085	9,763	6,419	440	2,816	61	2,602	501
Polk	28,896	5,300	5,439	592	2,000	46	2,368	434
Putnam	21,814	3,340	6,579	645	2,821	51	2,549	512
St. Johns	43,086	11,570	4,607	220	1,747	33	2,207	399
St. Lucie	25,861	6,126	6,175	500	2,556	60	2,551	509
Santa Rosa	27,897	4,326	4,516	335	1,717	35	1,824	606
Sarasota	46,965	19,050	7,071	254	2,836	42	3,527	412
Seminole	38,838	5,471	3,755	320	1,338	51	1,605	441
Sumter	21,878	5,169	7,651	448	1,741	30	4,965	467
Suwannee	22,415	3,447	6,899	799	2,957	31	2,584	529
Taylor	22,971	3,111	6,323	803	2,718	47	2,293	460
Union	15,641	1,924	3,569	528	1,507	20	1,136	377
Volusia	28,347	7,421	6,170	383	2,469	53	2,746	518
Wakulla	23,451	2,877	4,109	523	1,686	19	1,438	443
Walton	24,412	5,400	4,777	415	1,767	35	1,966	593
Washington	21,297	2,866	6,757	668	3,100	47	2,232	708

1/ Includes supplemental security income payments, family assistance, food stamp payments, and other assistance payments, including general assistance.
2/ Retirement and disability insurance benefit payments.
3/ Includes veterans' benefits, federal education and training assistance (excluding veterans), business and other payments to individuals, and payments to nonprofit institutions.
Note: These data were derived by dividing each type of income by the total population of the area, not just the segment of the population receiving that particular type of income. All data are revised.

Source: U.S., Department of Commerce, Bureau of Economic Analysis, Regional Economic Information System (REIS), 1969–2005, Internet site <http://www.bea.gov/> (accessed 30, May 2007).

Table 5.13. PERSONAL INCOME: DERIVATION ON A PLACE-OF-RESIDENCE BASIS IN THE STATE AND METROPOLITAN AREAS OF FLORIDA, 2005

(in millions of dollars)

Metropolitan area	Total earnings by place of work	Less personal contributions for social insurance	Plus residence adjust- ment	Plus dividends interest and rent	Plus transfer payments	Personal income by place of residence
Florida	407,351	46,402	1,638	142,877	98,667	604,131
Cape Coral-Ft. Myers	11,441	1,314	401	6,260	3,117	19,905
Deltona-Daytona Beach-Ormond Beach	6,952	850	1,098	3,620	3,010	13,830
Ft. Walton Beach-Crestview-Destin	6,393	5,350	552	-543	1,245	894
Gainesville	5,821	644	-412	1,298	1,130	7,194
Alachua County	5,692	629	-553	1,252	1,047	6,809
Gilchrist County	129	15	142	46	83	385
Jacksonville	33,528	3,768	-57	7,293	5,790	42,785
Baker County	279	31	155	56	116	574
Clay County	1,792	209	2,069	684	681	5,018
Duval County	28,096	3,144	-5,146	4,146	3,930	27,882
Nassau County	914	101	691	542	320	2,366
St. Johns County	2,446	282	2,174	1,865	743	6,946
Lakeland	9,787	1,135	1,187	2,872	2,948	15,659
Miami-Ft. Lauderdale-Pompano Beach	136,906	15,412	-293	51,325	30,938	203,465
Broward County	42,099	4,806	5,695	13,283	8,942	65,213
Miami-Dade County	61,447	6,820	-7,156	12,760	14,303	74,534
Palm Beach County	33,360	3,786	1,168	25,282	7,693	63,718
Naples-Marco Island	7,352	827	-455	7,584	1,582	15,237
Ocala	4,277	526	581	1,790	2,039	8,161
Orlando-Kissimmee	51,825	5,872	-2,476	8,750	8,724	60,951
Lake County	3,591	451	1,026	1,971	1,875	8,012
Orange County	35,806	4,029	-7,882	4,024	4,340	32,260
Osceola County	2,754	327	1,105	560	1,002	5,095
Seminole County	9,674	1,065	3,274	2,195	1,507	15,585
Palm Bay-Melbourne-Titusville	11,467	1,342	292	3,282	3,111	16,811
Palm Coast	820	106	246	649	467	2,076
Panama City-Lynn Haven	3,620	400	-102	861	909	4,888
Pensacola-Ferry Pass-Brent	8,235	922	681	2,033	2,333	12,361
Escambia County	6,693	743	-669	1,417	1,689	8,387
Santa Rosa County	1,542	178	1,350	616	643	3,974
Port St. Lucie	6,101	730	604	4,772	2,422	13,169
Martin County	3,100	363	-17	3,302	940	6,963
St. Lucie County	3,000	367	621	1,470	1,482	6,206
Punta Gorda	1,928	243	243	1,562	1,123	4,613
Sarasota-Bradenton-Venice	14,565	1,700	777	10,005	4,267	27,914
Manatee County	6,260	707	479	3,049	1,685	10,766
Sarasota County	8,305	993	298	6,955	2,582	17,148
Sebastian-Vero Beach	2,326	280	22	2,957	861	5,886
Tallahassee	8,084	883	-181	1,552	1,373	9,944
Gadsden County	617	68	110	151	259	1,069
Jefferson County	137	15	99	56	76	352
Leon County	7,108	775	-657	1,263	922	7,861
Wakulla County	223	26	267	81	116	662
Tampa-St. Petersburg-Clearwater	64,019	7,385	-1,359	17,637	15,087	87,999
Hernando County	1,623	212	582	924	1,190	4,108
Hillsborough County	35,815	4,001	-5,226	5,532	5,260	37,379
Pasco County	3,860	500	3,036	2,131	2,688	11,214
Pinellas County	22,721	2,671	250	9,049	5,949	35,298

Note: Data are for Metropolitan Statistical Areas (MSAs) defined as of December 18, 2006. See Table 5.14 for derivation of personal income notes. See Glossary for MSA definitions and map at the front of the book for area boundaries.

Source: U.S., Department of Commerce, Bureau of Economic Analysis, Regional Economic Information System (REIS), 1969–2005, Internet site <http://www.bea.gov/> (accessed 30, May 2007).

Table 5.14. PERSONAL INCOME: DERIVATION ON A PLACE-OF-RESIDENCE BASIS IN THE UNITED STATES AND IN THE STATE AND COUNTIES OF FLORIDA, 2004 AND 2005

(rounded to millions of dollars)

County	Total earnings by place of work 1/	Less personal contributions for social insurance	Plus residence adjust- ment 2/	Plus dividends interest and rent 3/	Plus transfer payments	Personal income by place of residence
			2004 A/			
United States	7,561,778	824,946	-1,228	1,553,960	1,426,787	9,716,351
Florida	373,719	42,221	1,591	137,080	94,828	564,997
Alachua	5,213	573	-517	1,206	958	6,287
Baker	256	29	151	55	117	549
Bay	3,305	362	-88	828	863	4,546
Bradford	300	34	125	55	139	586
Brevard	10,569	1,225	272	3,003	3,161	15,780
Broward	38,363	4,339	5,227	12,958	8,056	60,265
Calhoun	104	12	39	28	74	233
Charlotte	1,661	212	215	1,270	1,400	4,334
Citrus	1,255	163	164	989	988	3,233
Clay	1,594	185	1,981	652	624	4,667
Collier	6,600	740	-291	7,575	1,406	14,550
Columbia	818	94	31	203	348	1,306
DeSoto	329	37	22	61	225	601
Dixie	105	12	26	39	96	253
Duval	26,488	2,937	-4,720	4,015	3,668	26,515
Escambia	6,295	696	-634	1,112	1,887	7,965
Flagler	687	89	215	617	418	1,850
Franklin	139	15	-2	65	67	254
Gadsden	583	63	113	150	247	1,029
Gilchrist	119	14	132	45	79	361
Glades	62	6	53	41	45	195
Gulf	163	19	20	59	94	316
Hamilton	181	20	-46	25	71	210
Hardee	280	31	40	34	169	493
Hendry	496	52	66	107	167	784
Hernando	1,429	185	557	892	1,117	3,810
Highlands	987	124	16	541	704	2,124
Hillsborough	33,146	3,676	-4,664	5,388	4,941	35,135
Holmes	149	16	82	47	127	389
Indian River	2,102	252	13	2,777	1,004	5,643
Jackson	562	63	51	147	289	986
Jefferson	128	14	98	54	74	340
Lafayette	64	6	14	17	30	118
Lake	3,211	398	901	1,865	1,728	7,307
Lee	10,137	1,156	267	6,128	3,005	18,381
Leon	6,808	739	-644	1,242	847	7,514

See footnotes at end of table.

Continued . . .

Table 5.14. PERSONAL INCOME: DERIVATION ON A PLACE-OF-RESIDENCE BASIS IN THE UNITED STATES AND IN THE STATE AND COUNTIES OF FLORIDA, 2004 AND 2005 (Continued)

(rounded to millions of dollars)

County	Total earnings by place of work 1/	Less personal contributions for social insurance	Plus residence adjust- ment 2/	Plus dividends interest and rent 3/	Plus transfer payments	Personal income by place of residence
			2004 A/ (Continued)			
Levy	332	38	122	135	227	779
Liberty	90	10	22	15	33	149
Madison	182	21	35	53	114	362
Manatee	5,537	619	540	2,948	1,597	10,003
Marion	3,856	468	519	1,708	1,880	7,495
Martin	2,673	312	79	3,117	993	6,550
Miami-Dade	57,517	6,340	-6,423	12,583	13,177	70,514
Monroe	1,785	194	26	1,396	352	3,365
Nassau	854	93	648	544	300	2,252
Okaloosa	4,976	512	-542	1,155	892	5,968
Okeechobee	401	47	56	101	272	783
Orange	32,786	3,660	-7,414	3,717	4,298	29,726
Osceola	2,411	283	1,026	422	1,027	4,603
Palm Beach	30,324	3,421	935	24,370	7,443	59,651
Pasco	3,473	443	2,658	2,075	2,535	10,298
Pinellas	21,413	2,488	84	8,790	5,651	33,449
Polk	8,789	1,011	1,011	2,585	3,001	14,376
Putnam	745	90	154	227	469	1,503
St. Johns	2,173	248	1,892	1,863	685	6,365
St. Lucie	2,667	326	499	1,267	1,638	5,745
Santa Rosa	1,318	152	1,289	472	738	3,665
Sarasota	7,535	891	359	6,835	2,444	16,283
Seminole	8,355	915	3,292	2,063	1,535	14,330
Sumter	540	63	13	323	437	1,251
Suwannee	405	45	84	130	245	820
Taylor	276	31	-4	60	118	419
Union	168	19	-9	27	52	219
Volusia	6,409	776	985	3,395	2,958	12,971
Wakulla	200	23	254	82	105	619
Walton	624	70	78	270	237	1,139
Washington	220	26	40	61	143	437

See footnotes at end of table.

Continued . . .

Table 5.14. PERSONAL INCOME: DERIVATION ON A PLACE-OF-RESIDENCE BASIS IN THE UNITED STATES AND IN THE STATE AND COUNTIES OF FLORIDA, 2004 AND 2005 (Continued)

(rounded to millions of dollars)

County	Total earnings by place of work 1/	Less personal contributions for social insurance	Plus residence adjust- ment 2/	Plus dividends interest and rent 3/	Plus transfer payments	Personal income by place of residence
			2005			
United States	7,983,652	879,189	-1,264	1,591,151	1,526,592	10,220,942
Florida	407,351	46,402	1,638	142,877	98,667	604,131
Alachua	5,692	629	-553	1,252	1,047	6,809
Baker	279	31	155	56	116	574
Bay	3,620	400	-102	861	909	4,888
Bradford	313	35	136	62	145	621
Brevard	11,467	1,342	292	3,282	3,111	16,811
Broward	42,099	4,806	5,695	13,283	8,942	65,213
Calhoun	110	13	45	28	80	251
Charlotte	1,928	243	243	1,562	1,123	4,613
Citrus	1,409	186	185	1,021	1,066	3,495
Clay	1,792	209	2,069	684	681	5,018
Collier	7,352	827	-455	7,584	1,582	15,237
Columbia	910	106	26	216	369	1,414
DeSoto	373	42	24	114	167	635
Dixie	122	15	27	43	99	277
Duval	28,096	3,144	-5,146	4,146	3,930	27,882
Escambia	6,693	743	-669	1,417	1,689	8,387
Flagler	820	106	246	649	467	2,076
Franklin	151	17	-2	68	65	266
Gadsden	617	68	110	151	259	1,069
Gilchrist	129	15	142	46	83	385
Glades	68	7	57	43	47	209
Gulf	177	21	23	59	95	333
Hamilton	189	22	-49	26	75	219
Hardee	327	36	40	70	129	530
Hendry	535	57	72	107	182	839
Hernando	1,623	212	582	924	1,190	4,108
Highlands	1,075	137	19	590	703	2,250
Hillsborough	35,815	4,001	-5,226	5,532	5,260	37,379
Holmes	155	18	91	50	132	411
Indian River	2,326	280	22	2,957	861	5,886
Jackson	619	71	51	150	317	1,066
Jefferson	137	15	99	56	76	352
Lafayette	68	7	15	16	31	124
Lake	3,591	451	1,026	1,971	1,875	8,012
Lee	11,441	1,314	401	6,260	3,117	19,905
Leon	7,108	775	-657	1,263	922	7,861

See footnotes at end of table.

Continued . . .

Table 5.14. PERSONAL INCOME: DERIVATION ON A PLACE-OF-RESIDENCE BASIS IN THE UNITED STATES AND IN THE STATE AND COUNTIES OF FLORIDA, 2004 AND 2005 (Continued)

(rounded to millions of dollars)

County	Total earnings by place of work 1/	Less personal contributions for social insurance	Plus residence adjust-ment 2/	Plus dividends interest and rent 3/	Plus transfer payments	Personal income by place of residence
			2005 (Continued)			
Levy	371	43	132	141	237	838
Liberty	100	11	20	15	32	155
Madison	190	23	36	55	119	378
Manatee	6,260	707	479	3,049	1,685	10,766
Marion	4,277	526	581	1,790	2,039	8,161
Martin	3,100	363	-17	3,302	940	6,963
Miami-Dade	61,447	6,820	-7,156	12,760	14,303	74,534
Monroe	1,880	206	30	1,394	400	3,498
Nassau	914	101	691	542	320	2,366
Okaloosa	5,350	552	-543	1,245	894	6,393
Okeechobee	454	52	59	129	244	833
Orange	35,806	4,029	-7,882	4,024	4,340	32,260
Osceola	2,754	327	1,105	560	1,002	5,095
Palm Beach	33,360	3,786	1,168	25,282	7,693	63,718
Pasco	3,860	500	3,036	2,131	2,688	11,214
Pinellas	22,721	2,671	250	9,049	5,949	35,298
Polk	9,787	1,135	1,187	2,872	2,948	15,659
Putnam	797	98	174	245	483	1,600
St. Johns	2,446	282	2,174	1,865	743	6,946
St. Lucie	3,000	367	621	1,470	1,482	6,206
Santa Rosa	1,542	178	1,350	616	643	3,974
Sarasota	8,305	993	298	6,955	2,582	17,148
Seminole	9,674	1,065	3,274	2,195	1,507	15,585
Sumter	672	78	-15	330	489	1,398
Suwannee	419	48	95	133	266	865
Taylor	306	35	-5	61	124	451
Union	181	20	-10	29	53	232
Volusia	6,952	850	1,098	3,620	3,010	13,830
Wakulla	223	26	267	81	116	662
Walton	738	83	63	272	241	1,230
Washington	241	29	47	64	150	473

A/ Revised.
1/ Consists of wage and salary disbursements, other labor income, and proprietors' income.
2/ An estimate of the net gain or loss to an area because of commuting from place of residence to place of work. Some persons earn income in the area in which they live; others earn income outside that area. United States includes adjustments for border workers, U.S. residents commuting outside U.S. borders less income of foreign residents commuting inside U.S. borders, plus certain Caribbean seasonal workers.
3/ Includes the capital consumption adjustment for rental income of persons.

Source: U.S., Department of Commerce, Bureau of Economic Analysis, Regional Economic Information System (REIS), 1969–2005, Internet site <http://www.bea.gov/> (accessed 30, May 2007).

Table 5.19. EARNED INCOME: TOTAL EARNINGS ON A PLACE-OF-WORK BASIS AND PERCENTAGE DISTRIBUTION BY TYPE IN FLORIDA, OTHER SUNBELT STATES, OTHER POPULOUS STATES, AND THE UNITED STATES, 2005

State	Earnings by place of work ($1,000)	Percentage distribution by type of income: Wage and salary disburse- ments	Other labor income	Proprietors' income 1/: Total	Farm	Non- farm
			Sunbelt states			
Florida	407,350,735	74.20	16.55	9.25	0.08	9.17
Alabama	98,671,955	70.83	17.89	11.28	1.16	10.12
Arizona	137,109,358	72.79	16.00	11.21	0.23	10.98
Arkansas	54,560,540	70.18	18.14	11.68	1.32	10.37
California	1,065,279,659	69.11	16.99	13.90	0.30	13.60
Georgia	229,413,268	71.56	17.16	11.28	0.59	10.69
Louisiana	88,982,373	74.51	18.62	6.87	0.31	6.56
Mississippi	51,278,077	69.85	18.85	11.30	2.04	9.27
New Mexico	39,793,255	70.75	17.59	11.66	0.96	10.70
North Carolina	206,622,778	72.33	17.97	9.70	0.86	8.84
Oklahoma	79,336,326	63.13	17.09	19.78	0.59	19.19
South Carolina	89,010,656	72.48	18.48	9.04	0.37	8.67
Tennessee	147,894,261	68.52	16.33	15.15	0.09	15.06
Texas	618,504,440	65.81	15.37	18.82	0.32	18.49
Virginia	228,460,597	72.71	18.46	8.83	0.13	8.70
			Other populous states			
Illinois	367,173,196	71.85	17.13	11.02	0.05	10.97
Indiana	149,310,505	71.36	18.91	9.73	0.24	9.49
Massachusetts	224,878,696	73.37	16.01	10.63	0.00	10.62
Michigan	257,610,003	71.30	17.82	10.89	0.12	10.76
New Jersey	278,468,425	72.40	15.62	11.99	0.02	11.97
New York	630,690,362	71.77	15.30	12.93	0.08	12.85
Ohio	282,834,621	73.05	17.71	9.24	0.11	9.12
Pennsylvania	323,799,141	71.17	16.82	12.01	0.24	11.77
United States	7,983,652,000	70.89	17.00	12.11	0.33	11.78

1/ Includes the inventory valuation adjustment and capital consumption adjustment.

Source: U.S., Department of Commerce, Bureau of Economic Analysis, Regional Economic Information System (REIS), 1969–2005, Internet site <http://www.bea.gov/> (accessed 30, May 2007).

Table 5.20. EARNED INCOME: TOTAL EARNINGS ON A PLACE-OF-WORK BASIS AND PERCENTAGE DISTRIBUTION BY INDUSTRY IN FLORIDA, OTHER SUNBELT STATES, OTHER POPULOUS STATES, AND THE UNITED STATES, 2005

State	Earnings by place of work ($1,000,000)	Percentage distribution by industry									
		Forestry and fishing 1/	Mining	Utilities	Con-struc-tion	Manu-factur-ing	Whole-sale trade	Retail trade	Trans-porta-tion 2/	Infor-mation	Finance 3/
	Sunbelt states										
Florida	407,351	0.4	0.2	0.7	8.3	6.2	5.6	8.1	3.1	3.2	6.9
Alabama	98,672	0.6	1.0	1.4	6.4	17.6	5.0	7.3	3.1	1.9	5.0
Arizona	137,109	0.3	0.6	0.8	9.6	10.0	5.2	8.3	3.0	2.3	6.9
Arkansas	54,561	0.9	1.0	1.1	5.6	17.4	5.0	6.8	5.8	3.0	3.8
California	1,065,280	0.6	0.3	0.9	6.9	11.9	4.9	6.6	2.7	5.2	7.1
Georgia	229,413	0.3	0.3	1.3	6.1	11.6	6.9	6.5	4.2	5.4	6.0
Louisiana	88,982	0.5	5.8	1.1	7.2	11.7	4.7	7.1	4.9	2.1	4.3
Mississippi	51,278	1.0	1.3	1.2	5.7	16.6	4.0	7.6	3.9	1.7	3.6
New Mexico	39,793	0.3	4.5	0.8	7.1	5.8	3.1	7.5	2.7	2.0	3.6
North Carolina	206,623	0.3	0.2	0.7	6.5	16.6	5.4	6.9	2.9	2.8	6.0
Oklahoma	79,336	0.2	8.1	1.6	4.8	15.4	4.0	6.7	3.6	2.5	3.9
South Carolina	89,011	0.4	0.1	1.2	7.2	17.7	4.6	8.0	2.8	1.9	4.8
Tennessee	147,894	0.2	0.2	0.2	5.8	17.4	5.7	7.6	5.7	2.1	5.6
Texas	618,504	0.2	6.2	1.8	6.5	12.7	6.0	6.3	4.4	3.3	6.2
Virginia	228,461	0.1	0.4	0.7	6.8	7.8	3.7	5.7	2.6	4.3	5.6
	Other populous states										
Illinois	367,173	0.1	0.9	0.8	6.0	13.7	6.3	5.6	3.9	2.9	8.9
Indiana	149,311	0.1	0.5	1.0	6.5	26.3	5.0	6.4	3.9	1.6	4.4
Massachusetts	224,879	0.2	0.3	0.6	5.8	11.6	5.1	5.7	1.8	3.9	10.9
Michigan	257,610	0.1	0.4	1.1	5.7	21.9	4.9	6.1	2.8	1.9	4.8
New Jersey	278,468	0.0	0.1	0.8	5.4	10.9	7.2	6.7	3.5	4.0	9.0
New York	630,690	0.2	0.3	0.9	4.1	7.1	4.6	5.0	2.0	5.6	17.1
Ohio	282,835	0.1	0.5	0.8	5.5	19.4	5.5	6.6	3.5	2.1	6.0
Pennsylvania	323,799	0.1	0.7	1.1	6.1	14.8	5.2	6.5	3.6	2.7	6.8
United States	7,983,652	0.3	1.1	1.0	6.4	12.7	5.2	6.5	3.3	3.6	7.5

See footnotes at end of table.

Continued . . .

Table 5.20. EARNED INCOME: TOTAL EARNINGS ON A PLACE-OF-WORK BASIS AND PERCENTAGE DISTRIBUTION BY INDUSTRY IN FLORIDA, OTHER SUNBELT STATES, OTHER POPULOUS STATES, AND THE UNITED STATES, 2005 (Continued)

State	Percentage distribution by industry (Continued)									
	Real estate 4/	Profes- sional ser- vices 5/	Manage- ment 6/	Adminis- trative ser- vices 7/	Educa- tional services	Health care 8/	Arts 9/	Accom- moda- tion 10/	Other services 11/	Govern- ment 12/
					Sunbelt states					
Florida	3.4	8.8	1.7	6.8	1.0	10.2	1.8	3.9	3.3	16.0
Alabama	1.7	7.6	1.0	3.0	0.7	9.4	0.4	2.3	3.2	20.2
Arizona	4.1	7.6	1.2	5.8	1.1	9.3	1.0	3.3	2.5	16.5
Arkansas	1.6	5.1	3.4	2.6	0.6	10.5	0.5	2.3	2.9	18.6
California	3.3	11.1	2.0	3.8	1.1	7.8	1.5	2.7	2.8	15.8
Georgia	2.6	8.7	2.4	4.4	1.2	7.9	0.7	2.8	2.7	17.1
Louisiana	-1.9	6.6	1.6	3.3	1.2	10.2	1.5	3.0	3.2	21.4
Mississippi	0.5	4.6	1.2	2.4	0.8	9.6	0.8	4.1	3.0	24.1
New Mexico	1.7	9.0	0.8	3.7	0.8	9.5	0.7	3.3	2.8	28.6
North Carolina	2.1	6.6	3.0	3.4	1.2	8.9	0.8	2.5	2.8	19.4
Oklahoma	1.8	5.6	1.1	3.7	0.7	8.8	0.5	2.3	2.8	20.9
South Carolina	2.3	6.0	0.8	4.7	0.8	7.9	0.8	3.5	3.1	20.9
Tennessee	2.5	6.7	1.1	4.8	1.4	11.7	1.1	3.0	3.1	13.9
Texas	2.9	8.7	0.9	3.8	0.8	8.2	0.6	2.6	2.6	14.8
Virginia	2.6	15.0	3.3	3.1	1.0	6.9	0.6	2.4	3.1	23.7
					Other populous states					
Illinois	2.6	11.2	2.9	3.9	1.4	8.6	0.9	2.4	3.0	13.8
Indiana	1.9	5.0	1.5	3.3	1.1	10.0	1.1	2.4	3.0	14.3
Massachusetts	2.5	13.5	2.8	3.3	3.3	11.2	0.9	2.5	2.5	11.5
Michigan	2.9	9.9	2.8	4.2	0.9	9.6	0.9	2.2	2.7	14.0
New Jersey	2.5	11.2	3.2	4.0	1.2	9.5	0.8	2.6	2.6	14.7
New York	2.7	11.3	2.7	3.2	2.2	10.2	1.3	2.2	2.6	14.5
Ohio	1.9	7.4	3.4	3.6	1.1	10.9	0.8	2.4	2.9	15.4
Pennsylvania	2.1	9.6	2.7	3.1	2.6	12.4	0.9	2.3	3.0	13.3
United States	2.5	9.4	2.2	3.7	1.3	9.4	1.0	2.8	2.9	16.5

1/ Includes related activities and other.
2/ Includes warehousing.
3/ Includes insurance.
4/ Includes rental and leasing.
5/ Includes technical services.
6/ Management of companies and enterprises.
7/ Includes waste services.
8/ Includes social assistance.
9/ Includes entertainment and recreation.
10/ Includes food services.
11/ Except public administration.
12/ Includes government enterprises.

Source: U.S., Department of Commerce, Bureau of Economic Analysis, Regional Economic Information System (REIS), 1969-2005, Internet site <http://ww.bea.gov/> (accessed 30, May 2007).

Table 5.21. PERSONAL INCOME: AMOUNTS BY MAJOR SOURCE IN THE METROPOLITAN AREAS OF FLORIDA, THE SOUTHEAST, AND THE UNITED STATES, 2004 AND 2005

(rounded to millions of dollars)

Item	Florida		Southeast		United States	
	Total	Metro areas	Total	Metro areas	Total	Metro areas
			2004 A/			
Total personal income	564,997	541,691	2,183,245	1,788,765	9,716,351	8,476,476
Derivation of personal income						
Total earnings by place of work	373,719	361,957	1,624,755	1,381,291	7,561,778	6,771,100
Less: Personal contributions for social insurance	42,221	40,863	178,975	151,559	824,946	737,914
Plus: Adjustment for residence	1,591	273	10,208	-11,883	-1,228	-65,877
Equals: Net earnings by place of residence	333,089	321,368	1,455,988	1,217,849	6,735,604	5,967,309
Plus: Dividends, interest, and rent	137,080	131,825	366,619	309,147	1,553,960	1,351,217
Plus: Transfer payments	94,828	88,498	360,638	261,769	1,426,787	1,157,950
Components of earnings						
Wages and salaries	279,096	270,493	1,175,183	1,004,442	5,386,149	4,840,154
Other labor income	61,510	59,448	281,518	237,540	1,265,351	1,124,911
Proprietors' income 1/	33,113	32,016	168,054	139,308	910,278	806,036
Farm	409	255	8,734	3,037	35,402	13,825
Nonfarm	32,704	31,761	159,319	136,271	874,876	792,211
Earnings by industry						
Farm	1,683	1,345	12,962	5,353	57,936	27,427
Nonfarm	372,036	360,612	1,611,793	1,375,938	7,503,842	6,743,674
Private	310,152	301,911	1,305,339	1,122,500	6,245,602	5,660,293
Forestry and fishing 2/	1,592	(D)	6,264	(D)	25,162	16,420
Mining	579	(D)	13,195	(D)	77,456	59,052
Utilities	2,755	(D)	14,677	(D)	76,062	65,806
Construction	28,400	27,548	104,931	89,101	466,087	418,362
Manufacturing	23,677	22,688	204,058	149,171	978,550	828,045
Wholesale trade	20,950	20,680	84,681	69,210	391,041	364,798
Retail trade	30,485	29,360	116,850	97,202	497,315	434,883
Transportation and warehousing	11,648	(D)	61,133	(D)	250,006	219,906
Information	12,650	12,483	52,453	48,981	283,743	273,053
Finance and insurance	25,669	25,335	91,217	84,089	564,214	540,839
Real estate and rental and leasing	11,289	11,096	37,705	34,307	187,791	176,192
Professional and technical services	32,321	31,797	132,031	122,550	691,601	665,161
Management of companies and enterprises	5,852	5,813	31,218	28,676	161,828	155,949
Administrative and waste services	24,246	23,914	68,476	62,756	276,598	260,318
Educational services	3,955	3,913	16,721	14,589	100,414	93,859
Health care and social services	39,334	38,073	152,170	125,967	706,640	632,623
Arts, entertainment, and recreation	7,165	7,039	17,289	15,451	78,959	73,286
Accommodation and food services	14,638	13,971	49,354	41,810	209,804	185,981
Other services 3/	12,947	12,430	50,915	42,320	222,331	195,759
Government	61,884	58,701	306,453	253,438	1,258,240	1,083,381
Federal, civilian	10,760	10,334	61,393	54,323	242,141	218,383
Federal, military	6,972	6,773	47,481	42,081	121,773	106,702
State and local	44,152	41,595	197,579	157,034	894,326	758,295

See footnotes at end of table.

Continued . . .

Table 5.21. PERSONAL INCOME: AMOUNTS BY MAJOR SOURCE IN THE METROPOLITAN AREAS OF FLORIDA, THE SOUTHEAST, AND THE UNITED STATES, 2004 AND 2005 (Continued)

(rounded to millions of dollars)

Item	Florida		Southeast		United States	
	Total	Metro areas	Total	Metro areas	Total	Metro areas
			2005			
Total personal income	604,131	579,239	2,302,623	1,887,492	10,220,942	8,924,022
Derivation of personal income						
Total earnings by place of work	407,351	394,404	1,726,340	1,470,185	7,983,652	7,157,081
Less: Personal contributions for social insurance	46,402	44,889	192,345	163,088	879,189	786,458
Plus: Adjustment for residence	1,638	253	10,492	-13,112	-1,264	-69,518
Equals: Net earnings by place of residence	362,587	349,768	1,544,487	1,293,986	7,103,199	6,301,105
Plus: Dividends, interest, and rent	142,877	137,345	360,005	301,632	1,591,151	1,383,664
Plus: Transfer payments	98,667	92,127	398,130	291,875	1,526,592	1,239,253
Components of earnings						
Wages and salaries	302,238	292,823	1,245,688	1,066,925	5,659,282	5,089,306
Other labor income	67,437	65,150	304,451	257,215	1,357,328	1,206,677
Proprietors' income 1/	37,676	36,431	176,201	146,045	967,042	861,098
Farm	329	222	8,500	2,868	26,609	9,554
Nonfarm	37,346	36,209	167,701	143,177	940,433	851,544
Earnings by industry						
Farm	1,605	1,313	12,733	5,166	50,903	24,128
Nonfarm	405,746	393,091	1,713,608	1,465,020	7,932,749	7,132,953
Private	340,465	331,179	1,389,293	1,196,709	6,613,603	5,997,341
Forestry and fishing 2/	1,664	(D)	6,473	(D)	26,325	17,195
Mining	646	(D)	14,608	(D)	91,806	70,655
Utilities	2,831	2,418	14,897	(D)	77,668	67,136
Construction	33,632	32,530	117,596	99,399	512,144	459,517
Manufacturing	25,242	24,147	211,634	154,953	1,015,266	859,899
Wholesale trade	22,859	22,542	90,693	76,607	415,578	387,665
Retail trade	32,916	31,647	123,307	102,671	517,938	453,089
Transportation and warehousing	12,487	11,835	63,576	(D)	260,028	228,298
Information	13,097	12,959	54,093	50,590	288,777	278,022
Finance and insurance	27,989	27,635	97,597	90,213	597,567	573,166
Real estate and rental and leasing	13,925	13,620	38,766	35,162	202,514	189,827
Professional and technical services	35,986	35,449	144,271	133,276	750,224	721,708
Management of companies and enterprises	6,822	6,771	35,113	32,235	175,750	169,349
Administrative and waste services	27,680	27,280	75,373	68,833	297,957	280,288
Educational services	4,226	4,186	17,844	15,651	106,628	99,676
Health care and social services	41,592	40,249	161,192	134,031	747,106	669,321
Arts, entertainment, and recreation	7,467	7,345	17,825	15,682	81,096	75,204
Accommodation and food services	15,936	15,244	52,111	43,356	220,500	195,803
Other services 3/	13,468	12,925	52,325	43,509	228,731	201,521
Government	65,282	61,912	324,314	268,310	1,319,146	1,135,612
Federal, civilian	11,169	10,731	64,030	56,679	250,309	225,741
Federal, military	7,170	6,953	51,713	45,691	132,077	115,369
State and local	46,942	44,229	208,571	165,941	936,760	794,502

(D) Data withheld to avoid disclosure of information about individual firms.

A/ Revised. 1/ Includes inventory valuation and capital consumption adjustments. 2/ Includes related activities and other. 3/ Except public administration.

Note: Income by place of residence; earnings by place of work. Some Florida and Southeast metro area estimates constitute the major portion of the true estimate. See source. See Table 5.14 for additional notes.

Source: U.S., Department of Commerce, Bureau of Economic Analysis, Regional Economic Information System (REIS), 1969–2005, Internet site <http://www.bea.gov/> (accessed 30, May 2007).

Table 5.23. PERSONAL INCOME: AMOUNTS BY MAJOR SOURCE IN FLORIDA
FOURTH QUARTER 2005 THROUGH FOURTH QUARTER 2006

(in millions of dollars)

Item	Fourth quarter 2005	2006 First quarter	2006 Second quarter	2006 Third quarter	2006 Fourth quarter
Total personal income 1/	619,890	634,956	641,933	652,101	661,341
Derivation of total personal income					
Total earnings by place of work	416,790	431,127	433,076	437,952	444,971
Less contributions for social insurance	47,550	49,793	49,949	50,497	51,286
Plus adjustment for residence	1,675	1,720	1,714	1,722	1,744
Equals net earnings by place of residence	370,916	383,054	384,840	389,177	395,430
Plus dividends, interest, and rent 2/	145,747	150,307	153,957	157,706	159,795
Plus transfer payments	103,227	101,595	103,136	105,217	106,116
State unemployment benefits	850	711	742	758	816
Other transfer payments	102,377	100,884	102,394	104,459	105,300
Components of earnings 1/					
Wages and salary disbursements	309,747	321,195	322,062	325,890	331,355
Supplements to wages and salaries	69,023	70,940	71,656	72,912	74,105
Proprietors' income 3/	38,020	38,993	39,358	39,150	39,511
Farm	93	65	-8	-67	241
Nonfarm	37,927	38,928	39,366	39,217	39,270
Earnings by industry 1/					
Farm	1,373	1,353	1,292	1,245	1,563
Nonfarm	415,417	429,774	431,784	436,707	443,409
Private	350,293	363,005	366,219	368,155	373,727
Forestry, fishing, related activities, and other 4/	1,751	1,779	1,825	1,939	2,039
Mining	654	641	666	703	728
Utilities	2,935	2,701	2,851	2,641	2,684
Construction	35,786	37,530	38,796	39,081	38,924
Manufacturing	25,902	26,645	26,735	26,844	26,816
Durable goods	17,855	18,518	18,644	18,705	18,671
Nondurable goods	8,048	8,127	8,091	8,139	8,145
Wholesale trade	23,737	24,317	24,899	25,228	25,644
Retail trade	33,468	34,717	35,052	35,073	35,273
Transportation and warehousing	12,862	13,101	13,373	13,340	13,480
Information	13,554	13,656	13,820	13,620	13,933
Finance and insurance	28,864	29,367	29,052	29,260	30,117
Real estate and rental leasing	14,139	14,370	14,282	13,844	14,017
Professional and technical services	37,352	38,772	39,042	39,567	40,485
Management of companies and enterprises	7,058	7,253	7,674	7,266	7,550
Administrative and waste services	28,156	30,997	30,407	30,993	31,592
Educational services	4,317	4,532	4,547	4,653	4,725
Health care and social assistance	42,316	43,784	44,471	45,016	45,827
Arts, entertainment, and recreation	7,478	8,030	7,858	7,815	7,881
Accommodation and food services	16,231	16,744	16,742	16,985	17,455
Other services, except public administration	13,730	14,069	14,126	14,288	14,557
Government and government enterprises	65,124	66,769	65,565	68,552	69,682
Federal, civilian	11,096	11,278	11,347	11,455	11,556
Federal, military	7,030	7,187	7,218	7,310	7,277
State and local	46,998	48,304	47,000	49,787	50,849

1/ Income by place of residence; earnings by place of work. 2/ Includes capital consumption adjustment for rental income of persons. 3/ Includes the inventory valuation and capital consumption adjustments. 4/ Includes wages and salaries of U.S. residents employed by foreign embassies, consulates, and international organizations in the United States.

Note: Reported in March 2007, data are for North America Industry Classification System (NAICS) industries and are seasonally adjusted at annual rates. See Table 5.14 for derivation of personal income notes.

Source: U.S., Department of Commerce, Bureau of Economic Analysis, Internet site <http://www.bea.doc.gov/> (accessed 5, April 2007).

Table 5.26. EARNED INCOME: TOTAL EARNINGS ON A PLACE-OF-WORK BASIS BY MAJOR TYPE OF INCOME IN THE UNITED STATES AND IN THE STATE AND COUNTIES OF FLORIDA, 2004 AND 2005

(in thousands of dollars, except where indicated)

County	Total earnings	Wage and salary disbursements	Other labor income	Proprietors' income Total 1/	Proprietors' income Farm	Proprietors' income Nonfarm
			2004 A/			
United States 2/	7,561,778	5,386,149	1,265,351	910,278	35,402	874,876
Florida	373,719,075	279,096,162	61,509,953	33,112,960	408,822	32,704,138
Alachua	5,213,342	3,965,395	998,234	249,713	6,922	242,791
Baker	255,670	186,071	47,755	21,844	3,455	18,389
Bay	3,304,781	2,426,501	662,193	216,087	1,492	214,595
Bradford	300,148	218,278	56,807	25,063	3,257	21,806
Brevard	10,568,775	8,088,708	1,867,124	612,943	224	612,719
Broward	38,362,800	28,970,382	6,058,835	3,333,583	1,691	3,331,892
Calhoun	103,686	73,326	18,182	12,178	1,342	10,836
Charlotte	1,660,893	1,275,699	265,503	119,691	2,647	117,044
Citrus	1,255,347	933,510	210,342	111,495	565	110,930
Clay	1,594,165	1,195,645	258,909	139,611	306	139,305
Collier	6,600,385	4,865,494	958,053	776,838	15,342	761,496
Columbia	818,474	617,201	160,528	40,745	609	40,136
DeSoto	329,475	253,787	53,324	22,364	10,529	11,835
Dixie	105,000	69,277	18,124	17,599	850	16,749
Duval	26,488,198	19,778,519	4,863,014	1,846,665	3,213	1,843,452
Escambia	6,294,682	4,749,587	1,338,871	206,224	1,735	204,489
Flagler	687,486	551,373	119,876	16,237	6,185	10,052
Franklin	139,361	90,377	21,021	27,963	0	27,963
Gadsden	582,966	424,996	109,465	48,505	14,264	34,241
Gilchrist	119,472	79,145	20,240	20,087	592	19,495
Glades	62,263	38,734	8,994	14,535	955	13,580
Gulf	162,673	117,492	29,256	15,925	0	15,925
Hamilton	180,501	131,427	41,588	7,486	1,053	6,433
Hardee	279,874	213,767	46,697	19,410	14,932	4,478
Hendry	496,049	369,344	76,288	50,417	7,087	43,330
Hernando	1,429,184	1,053,547	229,805	145,832	3,469	142,363
Highlands	986,660	747,401	157,739	81,520	12,453	69,067
Hillsborough	33,146,448	24,924,191	5,506,089	2,716,168	35,552	2,680,616
Holmes	148,735	88,289	23,403	37,043	11,081	25,962
Indian River	2,101,673	1,621,971	323,663	156,039	1,616	154,423
Jackson	562,042	399,055	110,329	52,658	9,410	43,248
Jefferson	127,525	87,865	21,064	18,596	4,727	13,869
Lafayette	64,387	43,049	11,110	10,228	6,894	3,334

See footnotes at end of table.

Continued . . .

Table 5.26. EARNED INCOME: TOTAL EARNINGS ON A PLACE-OF-WORK BASIS BY MAJOR TYPE OF INCOME IN THE UNITED STATES AND IN THE STATE AND COUNTIES OF FLORIDA, 2004 AND 2005 (Continued)

(in thousands of dollars, except where indicated)

County	Total earnings	Wage and salary disbursements	Other labor income	Proprietors' income Total 1/	Proprietors' income Farm	Proprietors' income Nonfarm
			2004 A/ (Continued)			
Lake	3,211,016	2,420,423	521,530	269,063	15,961	253,102
Lee	10,137,214	7,389,988	1,558,826	1,188,400	4,853	1,183,547
Leon	6,807,802	5,166,145	1,246,995	394,662	(L)	394,640
Levy	332,433	232,507	54,424	45,502	15,618	29,884
Liberty	89,748	65,537	16,867	7,344	76	7,268
Madison	181,984	131,306	32,675	18,003	6,854	11,149
Manatee	5,536,721	3,876,741	813,847	846,133	16,123	830,010
Marion	3,856,118	2,907,068	660,303	288,747	6,054	282,693
Martin	2,673,158	1,991,905	411,512	269,741	1,246	268,495
Miami-Dade	57,516,675	42,063,063	9,056,774	6,396,838	1,461	6,395,377
Monroe	1,784,610	1,295,910	304,942	183,758	0	183,758
Nassau	853,570	598,506	148,528	106,536	5,415	101,121
Okaloosa	4,975,748	3,491,506	1,164,318	319,924	528	319,396
Okeechobee	400,529	299,220	63,795	37,514	6,276	31,238
Orange	32,785,823	25,304,949	5,221,688	2,259,186	9,266	2,249,920
Osceola	2,410,807	1,892,285	392,995	125,527	3,207	122,320
Palm Beach	30,323,593	22,367,847	4,528,810	3,426,936	12,493	3,414,443
Pasco	3,472,909	2,693,317	581,713	197,879	5,385	192,494
Pinellas	21,412,630	16,260,834	3,501,900	1,649,896	1,499	1,648,397
Polk	8,788,618	6,500,538	1,440,442	847,638	31,650	815,988
Putnam	744,745	577,348	145,686	21,711	5,922	15,789
St. Johns	2,173,113	1,618,872	346,644	207,597	3,630	203,967
St. Lucie	2,666,630	2,109,629	449,171	107,830	1,463	106,367
Santa Rosa	1,318,000	991,309	258,476	68,215	5,184	63,031
Sarasota	7,535,459	5,582,216	1,134,517	818,726	1,897	816,829
Seminole	8,354,627	5,929,245	1,258,181	1,167,201	2,616	1,164,585
Sumter	540,318	390,844	110,478	38,996	5,874	33,122
Suwannee	404,739	262,677	61,697	80,365	23,091	57,274
Taylor	275,998	205,757	53,585	16,656	1,390	15,266
Union	167,544	124,792	34,871	7,881	1,107	6,774
Volusia	6,408,749	4,954,515	1,064,484	389,750	21,377	368,373
Wakulla	199,861	137,499	37,455	24,907	716	24,191
Walton	624,287	448,509	98,667	77,111	4,958	72,153
Washington	220,179	163,952	40,732	15,495	1,161	14,334

See footnotes at end of table.

Continued . . .

Table 5.26. EARNED INCOME: TOTAL EARNINGS ON A PLACE-OF-WORK BASIS BY MAJOR TYPE OF INCOME IN THE UNITED STATES AND IN THE STATE AND COUNTIES OF FLORIDA, 2004 AND 2005 (Continued)

(in thousands of dollars, except where indicated)

County	Total earnings	Wage and salary disbursements	Other labor income	Proprietors' income Total 1/	Proprietors' income Farm	Proprietors' income Nonfarm
			2005			
United States 2/	7,983,652	5,659,282	1,357,328	967,042	26,609	940,433
Florida	407,350,735	302,238,459	67,436,628	37,675,648	329,243	37,346,405
Alachua	5,692,424	4,313,354	1,096,068	283,002	8,079	274,923
Baker	279,262	203,266	53,098	22,898	1,933	20,965
Bay	3,620,066	2,649,014	728,209	242,843	1,714	241,129
Bradford	312,503	224,825	60,295	27,383	882	26,501
Brevard	11,466,868	8,683,869	2,027,611	755,388	520	754,868
Broward	42,098,663	31,654,144	6,755,211	3,689,308	2,356	3,686,952
Calhoun	110,114	75,700	19,155	15,259	2,854	12,405
Charlotte	1,928,354	1,401,468	295,939	230,947	3,660	227,287
Citrus	1,408,781	1,045,334	235,978	127,469	880	126,589
Clay	1,792,485	1,338,855	296,342	157,288	313	156,975
Collier	7,352,256	5,410,857	1,079,735	861,664	8,706	852,958
Columbia	909,837	683,469	180,281	46,087	-3,310	49,397
DeSoto	372,963	282,209	60,468	30,286	8,627	21,659
Dixie	121,898	79,405	20,803	21,690	799	20,891
Duval	28,095,719	20,917,456	5,192,202	1,986,061	1,912	1,984,149
Escambia	6,693,031	4,963,903	1,396,190	332,938	1,852	331,086
Flagler	820,058	658,051	142,260	19,747	6,219	13,528
Franklin	150,726	95,798	22,139	32,789	0	32,789
Gadsden	616,710	449,404	116,313	50,993	13,045	37,948
Gilchrist	129,026	84,727	21,745	22,554	268	22,286
Glades	68,493	41,849	9,961	16,683	847	15,836
Gulf	177,386	126,611	32,563	18,212	0	18,212
Hamilton	188,762	138,933	44,982	4,847	-2,493	7,340
Hardee	326,599	243,525	52,904	30,170	11,468	18,702
Hendry	534,749	400,006	83,680	51,063	2,380	48,683
Hernando	1,623,370	1,194,232	265,323	163,815	2,753	161,062
Highlands	1,075,014	803,064	170,606	101,344	9,799	91,545
Hillsborough	35,814,881	26,789,577	6,017,564	3,007,740	32,355	2,975,385
Holmes	155,354	93,996	25,552	35,806	6,405	29,401
Indian River	2,326,011	1,733,927	355,506	236,578	1,256	235,322
Jackson	618,633	438,031	121,981	58,621	8,527	50,094
Jefferson	136,538	92,785	22,741	21,012	5,315	15,697
Lafayette	67,507	44,859	12,221	10,427	6,727	3,700
Lake	3,590,519	2,692,036	586,603	311,880	17,384	294,496

See footnotes at end of table.

Continued . . .

Table 5.26. EARNED INCOME: TOTAL EARNINGS ON A PLACE-OF-WORK BASIS BY MAJOR TYPE OF INCOME IN THE UNITED STATES AND IN THE STATE AND COUNTIES OF FLORIDA, 2004 AND 2005 (Continued)

(in thousands of dollars, except where indicated)

County	Total earnings	Wage and salary disbursements	Other labor income	Proprietors' income Total 1/	Proprietors' income Farm	Proprietors' income Nonfarm
			2005 (Continued)			
Lee	11,440,658	8,314,725	1,775,839	1,350,094	4,062	1,346,032
Leon	7,107,820	5,364,181	1,315,501	428,138	-546	428,684
Levy	370,863	257,267	61,440	52,156	16,740	35,416
Liberty	99,620	72,211	19,600	7,809	(L)	7,792
Madison	190,169	138,118	36,662	15,389	2,109	13,280
Manatee	6,259,982	4,399,727	919,331	940,924	16,290	924,634
Marion	4,277,134	3,206,426	740,475	330,233	2,510	327,723
Martin	3,100,298	2,285,983	478,402	335,913	1,658	334,255
Miami-Dade	61,447,272	44,665,363	9,745,251	7,036,658	4,024	7,032,634
Monroe	1,879,828	1,356,328	324,356	199,144	0	199,144
Nassau	914,391	639,265	160,758	114,368	-166	114,534
Okaloosa	5,349,882	3,726,826	1,243,548	379,508	398	379,110
Okeechobee	453,623	326,530	70,579	56,514	4,647	51,867
Orange	35,806,414	27,435,380	5,754,918	2,616,116	980	2,615,136
Osceola	2,753,885	2,149,677	455,518	148,690	1,742	146,948
Palm Beach	33,360,177	24,455,777	4,984,254	3,920,146	8,236	3,911,910
Pasco	3,859,605	2,976,945	655,816	226,844	3,156	223,688
Pinellas	22,720,672	17,116,909	3,738,873	1,864,890	2,356	1,862,534
Polk	9,787,062	7,159,002	1,608,564	1,019,496	28,962	990,534
Putnam	797,081	610,049	157,175	29,857	5,417	24,440
St. Johns	2,445,778	1,818,503	392,777	234,498	2,764	231,734
St. Lucie	3,000,343	2,310,284	503,361	186,698	478	186,220
Santa Rosa	1,542,334	1,131,992	289,850	120,492	3,262	117,230
Sarasota	8,305,091	6,124,534	1,261,994	918,563	2,783	915,780
Seminole	9,674,002	6,862,996	1,471,756	1,339,250	3,881	1,335,369
Sumter	671,719	488,410	136,061	47,248	6,249	40,999
Suwannee	418,750	274,638	65,850	78,262	14,889	63,373
Taylor	306,321	228,566	60,555	17,200	254	16,946
Union	180,690	133,793	38,598	8,299	120	8,179
Volusia	6,951,724	5,294,221	1,162,005	495,498	25,012	470,486
Wakulla	222,999	153,554	42,198	27,247	327	26,920
Walton	737,758	533,071	116,959	87,728	1,939	85,789
Washington	241,230	178,669	45,575	16,986	661	16,325

(L) Less than $50,000.
A/ Revised.
1/ Includes the inventory valuation and capital consumption adjustments.
2/ United States amounts are rounded to millions of dollars.

Source: U.S., Department of Commerce, Bureau of Economic Analysis, Regional Economic Information System (REIS), 1969–2005, Internet site <http://www.bea.gov/> (accessed 30, May 2007).

Table 5.30. EARNED INCOME: TOTAL, FARM, AND NONFARM EARNINGS ON A PLACE-OF-WORK BASIS IN THE UNITED STATES AND IN THE STATE AND COUNTIES OF FLORIDA, 2004 AND 2005

(in thousands of dollars)

County	Total earnings	Farm income	Nonfarm Total	Nonfarm Private 1/
		2004 A/		
United States	7,561,778,000	57,936,000	7,503,842,000	6,245,602,000
Florida	373,719,075	1,683,296	372,035,779	310,152,109
Alachua	5,213,342	16,924	5,196,418	3,249,744
Baker	255,670	5,569	250,101	139,747
Bay	3,304,781	2,037	3,302,744	2,267,862
Bradford	300,148	3,633	296,515	181,260
Brevard	10,568,775	6,104	10,562,671	8,720,831
Broward	38,362,800	18,446	38,344,354	32,742,745
Calhoun	103,686	4,568	99,118	60,428
Charlotte	1,660,893	10,272	1,650,621	1,364,632
Citrus	1,255,347	2,125	1,253,222	1,060,593
Clay	1,594,165	2,994	1,591,171	1,300,528
Collier	6,600,385	106,415	6,493,970	5,833,266
Columbia	818,474	1,295	817,179	550,957
DeSoto	329,475	26,376	303,099	204,579
Dixie	105,000	1,363	103,637	63,512
Duval	26,488,198	17,611	26,470,587	21,357,168
Escambia	6,294,682	3,763	6,290,919	4,242,558
Flagler	687,486	8,883	678,603	564,269
Franklin	139,361	0	139,361	109,434
Gadsden	582,966	49,132	533,834	310,163
Gilchrist	119,472	5,029	114,443	67,690
Glades	62,263	4,809	57,454	41,194
Gulf	162,673	0	162,673	104,099
Hamilton	180,501	1,490	179,011	123,083
Hardee	279,874	30,216	249,658	174,163
Hendry	496,049	55,917	440,132	337,289
Hernando	1,429,184	6,903	1,422,281	1,150,262
Highlands	986,660	40,021	946,639	767,820
Hillsborough	33,146,448	185,981	32,960,467	28,378,854
Holmes	148,735	11,295	137,440	83,861
Indian River	2,101,673	26,493	2,075,180	1,790,340
Jackson	562,042	11,163	550,879	291,808
Jefferson	127,525	9,370	118,155	82,005
Lafayette	64,387	10,701	53,686	27,037
Lake	3,211,016	49,482	3,161,534	2,652,753

See footnotes at end of table. Continued . . .

Table 5.30. EARNED INCOME: TOTAL, FARM, AND NONFARM EARNINGS ON A PLACE-OF-WORK BASIS IN THE UNITED STATES AND IN THE STATE AND COUNTIES OF FLORIDA, 2004 AND 2005 (Continued)

(in thousands of dollars)

County	Total earnings	Farm income	Nonfarm Total	Nonfarm Private 1/
		2004 A/ (Continued)		
Lee	10,137,214	37,700	10,099,514	8,527,039
Leon	6,807,802	2,529	6,805,273	4,049,539
Levy	332,433	25,694	306,739	223,319
Liberty	89,748	100	89,648	58,137
Madison	181,984	8,972	173,012	117,383
Manatee	5,536,721	90,060	5,446,661	4,815,527
Marion	3,856,118	35,790	3,820,328	3,149,953
Martin	2,673,158	13,387	2,659,771	2,367,148
Miami-Dade	57,516,675	142,028	57,374,647	47,982,841
Monroe	1,784,610	0	1,784,610	1,330,375
Nassau	853,570	15,010	838,560	613,420
Okaloosa	4,975,748	817	4,974,931	2,798,556
Okeechobee	400,529	32,906	367,623	278,488
Orange	32,785,823	84,003	32,701,820	29,222,563
Osceola	2,410,807	15,564	2,395,243	1,951,934
Palm Beach	30,323,593	172,162	30,151,431	26,599,614
Pasco	3,472,909	21,871	3,451,038	2,768,033
Pinellas	21,412,630	4,381	21,408,249	18,870,867
Polk	8,788,618	71,348	8,717,270	7,474,759
Putnam	744,745	13,632	731,113	531,148
St. Johns	2,173,113	12,561	2,160,552	1,814,868
St. Lucie	2,666,630	12,553	2,654,077	2,103,282
Santa Rosa	1,318,000	7,298	1,310,702	901,498
Sarasota	7,535,459	9,179	7,526,280	6,779,771
Seminole	8,354,627	8,961	8,345,666	7,514,625
Sumter	540,318	11,976	528,342	330,162
Suwannee	404,739	28,879	375,860	294,989
Taylor	275,998	1,577	274,421	210,757
Union	167,544	1,385	166,159	61,014
Volusia	6,408,749	55,997	6,352,752	5,253,199
Wakulla	199,861	765	199,096	136,294
Walton	624,287	5,882	618,405	497,421
Washington	220,179	1,949	218,230	127,052

See footnotes at end of table. Continued . . .

Table 5.30. EARNED INCOME: TOTAL, FARM, AND NONFARM EARNINGS ON A PLACE-OF-WORK BASIS IN THE UNITED STATES AND IN THE STATE AND COUNTIES OF FLORIDA, 2004 AND 2005 (Continued)

(in thousands of dollars)

County	Total earnings	Farm income	Nonfarm Total	Nonfarm Private 1/
		2005		
United States	7,983,652,000	50,903,000	7,932,749,000	6,613,603,000
Florida	407,350,735	1,604,522	405,746,213	340,464,523
Alachua	5,692,424	18,668	5,673,756	3,492,407
Baker	279,262	3,980	275,282	161,564
Bay	3,620,066	2,376	3,617,690	2,536,455
Bradford	312,503	1,495	311,008	187,577
Brevard	11,466,868	6,270	11,460,598	9,622,038
Broward	42,098,663	16,924	42,081,739	35,933,862
Calhoun	110,114	6,176	103,938	63,486
Charlotte	1,928,354	13,658	1,914,696	1,607,763
Citrus	1,408,781	2,303	1,406,478	1,201,304
Clay	1,792,485	2,816	1,789,669	1,471,231
Collier	7,352,256	97,089	7,255,167	6,541,983
Columbia	909,837	-2,352	912,189	628,875
DeSoto	372,963	23,292	349,671	248,093
Dixie	121,898	1,374	120,524	77,957
Duval	28,095,719	11,234	28,084,485	22,964,947
Escambia	6,693,031	4,007	6,689,024	4,653,162
Flagler	820,058	12,695	807,363	668,315
Franklin	150,726	0	150,726	116,429
Gadsden	616,710	48,602	568,108	342,151
Gilchrist	129,026	5,163	123,863	75,124
Glades	68,493	4,967	63,526	45,425
Gulf	177,386	0	177,386	116,102
Hamilton	188,762	-1,876	190,638	131,414
Hardee	326,599	27,551	299,048	222,811
Hendry	534,749	45,609	489,140	381,053
Hernando	1,623,370	6,978	1,616,392	1,320,442
Highlands	1,075,014	42,940	1,032,074	846,820
Hillsborough	35,814,881	196,884	35,617,997	30,784,466
Holmes	155,354	6,622	148,732	92,303
Indian River	2,326,011	19,336	2,306,675	2,009,692
Jackson	618,633	10,180	608,453	336,959
Jefferson	136,538	9,754	126,784	89,560
Lafayette	67,507	10,578	56,929	27,236
Lake	3,590,519	51,209	3,539,310	2,985,594

See footnotes at end of table.

Continued . . .

Table 5.30. EARNED INCOME: TOTAL, FARM, AND NONFARM EARNINGS ON A PLACE-OF-WORK BASIS IN THE UNITED STATES AND IN THE STATE AND COUNTIES OF FLORIDA, 2004 AND 2005 (Continued)

(in thousands of dollars)

County	Total earnings	Farm income	Nonfarm Total	Nonfarm Private 1/
		2005 (Continued)		
Lee	11,440,658	36,449	11,404,209	9,674,648
Leon	7,107,820	2,359	7,105,461	4,374,624
Levy	370,863	24,294	346,569	259,148
Liberty	99,620	(L)	99,603	65,635
Madison	190,169	4,344	185,825	128,721
Manatee	6,259,982	92,123	6,167,859	5,496,449
Marion	4,277,134	33,743	4,243,391	3,536,280
Martin	3,100,298	15,524	3,084,774	2,774,587
Miami-Dade	61,447,272	149,710	61,297,562	51,318,743
Monroe	1,879,828	0	1,879,828	1,398,043
Nassau	914,391	1,465	912,926	678,774
Okaloosa	5,349,882	813	5,349,069	3,124,468
Okeechobee	453,623	32,396	421,227	326,167
Orange	35,806,414	75,769	35,730,645	32,012,336
Osceola	2,753,885	12,210	2,741,675	2,195,488
Palm Beach	33,360,177	160,183	33,199,994	29,448,597
Pasco	3,859,605	19,740	3,839,865	3,097,319
Pinellas	22,720,672	4,949	22,715,723	20,062,541
Polk	9,787,062	66,794	9,720,268	8,414,264
Putnam	797,081	13,062	784,019	575,970
St. Johns	2,445,778	13,715	2,432,063	2,062,522
St. Lucie	3,000,343	16,642	2,983,701	2,375,398
Santa Rosa	1,542,334	5,100	1,537,234	1,117,751
Sarasota	8,305,091	8,285	8,296,806	7,493,581
Seminole	9,674,002	10,649	9,663,353	8,772,590
Sumter	671,719	12,678	659,041	438,428
Suwannee	418,750	20,228	398,522	313,904
Taylor	306,321	472	305,849	238,891
Union	180,690	425	180,265	66,178
Volusia	6,951,724	58,893	6,892,831	5,732,345
Wakulla	222,999	463	222,536	154,447
Walton	737,758	3,051	734,707	605,319
Washington	241,230	1,475	239,755	145,767

(L) Less than $50,000.
A/ Revised.
1/ See Table 5.34 for private nonfarm income by industrial source.

Source: U.S., Department of Commerce, Bureau of Economic Analysis, Regional Economic Information System (REIS), 1969–2005, Internet site <http://www.bea.gov/> (accessed 30, May 2007).

Table 5.31. EARNED INCOME: NONFARM GOVERNMENT AND GOVERNMENT ENTERPRISES EARNINGS ON A PLACE-OF-WORK BASIS IN THE UNITED STATES AND IN THE STATE AND COUNTIES OF FLORIDA, 2004 AND 2005

(in thousands of dollars)

County	Total government earnings	Federal Civilian	Federal Military	State and local
		2004 A/		
United States	1,258,240,000	242,141,000	121,773,000	894,326,000
Florida	61,883,670	10,760,243	6,971,849	44,151,578
Alachua	1,946,674	306,039	24,005	1,616,630
Baker	110,354	4,831	1,521	104,002
Bay	1,034,882	266,303	369,371	399,208
Bradford	115,255	2,244	9,839	103,172
Brevard	1,841,840	541,749	236,546	1,063,545
Broward	5,601,609	693,102	132,529	4,775,978
Calhoun	38,690	1,566	829	36,295
Charlotte	285,989	20,130	10,225	255,634
Citrus	192,629	14,751	8,358	169,520
Clay	290,643	22,852	10,769	257,022
Collier	660,704	53,088	18,894	588,722
Columbia	266,222	81,450	4,082	180,690
DeSoto	98,520	3,549	2,214	92,757
Dixie	40,125	1,255	907	37,963
Duval	5,113,419	1,306,196	1,869,125	1,938,098
Escambia	2,048,361	425,100	939,747	683,514
Flagler	114,334	9,297	4,389	100,648
Franklin	29,927	1,288	1,434	27,205
Gadsden	223,671	8,950	2,929	211,792
Gilchrist	46,753	1,874	1,013	43,866
Glades	16,260	733	709	14,818
Gulf	58,574	1,205	871	56,498
Hamilton	55,928	1,932	894	53,102
Hardee	75,495	3,612	1,781	70,102
Hendry	102,843	7,620	2,423	92,800
Hernando	272,019	23,558	9,654	238,807
Highlands	178,819	21,913	5,987	150,919
Hillsborough	4,581,613	1,054,248	614,516	2,912,849
Holmes	53,579	3,274	1,208	49,097
Indian River	284,840	32,761	7,925	244,154
Jackson	259,071	40,727	3,336	215,008
Jefferson	36,150	2,442	915	32,793
Lafayette	26,649	1,045	478	25,126

See footnote at end of table. Continued . . .

Table 5.31. EARNED INCOME: NONFARM GOVERNMENT AND GOVERNMENT ENTERPRISES EARNINGS ON A PLACE-OF-WORK BASIS IN THE UNITED STATES AND IN THE STATE AND COUNTIES OF FLORIDA, 2004 AND 2005 (Continued)

(in thousands of dollars)

County	Total government earnings	Federal Civilian	Federal Military	State and local
		2004 A/ (Continued)		
Lake	508,781	39,810	16,814	452,157
Lee	1,572,475	185,126	36,369	1,350,980
Leon	2,755,734	149,873	34,886	2,570,975
Levy	83,420	5,076	3,959	74,385
Liberty	31,511	2,416	472	28,623
Madison	55,629	2,977	1,213	51,439
Manatee	631,134	85,682	20,672	524,780
Marion	670,375	48,527	18,828	603,020
Martin	292,623	20,701	9,251	262,671
Miami-Dade	9,391,806	1,916,944	388,066	7,086,796
Monroe	454,235	87,862	124,264	242,109
Nassau	225,140	88,924	4,010	132,206
Okaloosa	2,176,375	505,678	1,325,293	345,404
Okeechobee	89,135	4,990	2,480	81,665
Orange	3,479,257	800,276	112,077	2,566,904
Osceola	443,309	24,734	14,077	404,498
Palm Beach	3,551,817	542,783	87,892	2,921,142
Pasco	683,005	60,094	26,077	596,834
Pinellas	2,537,382	532,203	137,763	1,867,416
Polk	1,242,511	100,531	34,190	1,107,790
Putnam	199,965	9,724	4,613	185,628
St. Johns	345,684	37,309	10,944	297,431
St. Lucie	550,795	54,665	18,927	477,203
Santa Rosa	409,204	52,161	138,320	218,723
Sarasota	746,509	76,939	22,654	646,916
Seminole	831,041	111,576	25,008	694,457
Sumter	198,180	98,600	3,852	95,728
Suwannee	80,871	7,882	2,391	70,598
Taylor	63,664	2,636	1,226	59,802
Union	105,145	1,164	931	103,050
Volusia	1,099,553	120,948	34,928	943,677
Wakulla	62,802	5,788	1,721	55,293
Walton	120,984	11,512	6,861	102,611
Washington	91,178	3,448	1,397	86,333

See footnote at end of table.

Continued . . .

Table 5.31. EARNED INCOME: NONFARM GOVERNMENT AND GOVERNMENT ENTERPRISES EARNINGS ON A PLACE-OF-WORK BASIS IN THE UNITED STATES AND IN THE STATE AND COUNTIES OF FLORIDA, 2004 AND 2005 (Continued)

(in thousands of dollars)

County	Total government earnings	Federal Civilian	Federal Military	State and local
		2005		
United States	1,319,146,000	250,309,000	132,077,000	936,760,000
Florida	65,281,690	11,168,750	7,170,494	46,942,446
Alachua	2,181,349	329,037	25,599	1,826,713
Baker	113,718	4,858	1,852	107,008
Bay	1,081,235	276,436	383,323	421,476
Bradford	123,431	2,130	11,283	110,018
Brevard	1,838,560	576,526	244,840	1,017,194
Broward	6,147,877	723,971	157,168	5,266,738
Calhoun	40,452	1,479	1,002	37,971
Charlotte	306,933	21,429	12,077	273,427
Citrus	205,174	14,596	10,237	180,341
Clay	318,438	23,603	13,068	281,767
Collier	713,184	53,930	23,233	636,021
Columbia	283,314	84,166	4,923	194,225
DeSoto	101,578	3,563	2,670	95,345
Dixie	42,567	1,144	1,105	40,318
Duval	5,119,538	1,320,450	1,811,456	1,987,632
Escambia	2,035,862	438,648	890,203	707,011
Flagler	139,048	9,983	5,764	123,301
Franklin	34,297	1,254	1,490	31,553
Gadsden	225,957	9,065	3,503	213,389
Gilchrist	48,739	1,936	1,237	45,566
Glades	18,101	879	850	16,372
Gulf	61,284	1,189	1,055	59,040
Hamilton	59,224	1,888	1,055	56,281
Hardee	76,237	3,447	2,133	70,657
Hendry	108,087	7,148	2,982	97,957
Hernando	295,950	25,690	12,002	258,258
Highlands	185,254	18,820	7,271	159,163
Hillsborough	4,833,531	1,107,277	685,489	3,040,765
Holmes	56,429	3,419	1,453	51,557
Indian River	296,983	32,015	9,699	255,269
Jackson	271,494	41,793	4,050	225,651
Jefferson	37,224	2,454	1,094	33,676
Lafayette	29,693	1,006	599	28,088

See footnote at end of table. Continued . . .

Table 5.31. EARNED INCOME: NONFARM GOVERNMENT AND GOVERNMENT ENTERPRISES EARNINGS ON A PLACE-OF-WORK BASIS IN THE UNITED STATES AND IN THE STATE AND COUNTIES OF FLORIDA, 2004 AND 2005 (Continued)

(in thousands of dollars)

County	Total government earnings	Federal Civilian	Federal Military	State and local
		2005 (Continued)		
Lake	553,716	40,926	20,982	491,808
Lee	1,729,561	192,130	44,842	1,492,589
Leon	2,730,837	153,857	36,835	2,540,145
Levy	87,421	5,107	4,632	77,682
Liberty	33,968	2,964	586	30,418
Madison	57,104	3,092	1,440	52,572
Manatee	671,410	81,202	25,136	565,072
Marion	707,111	48,371	23,167	635,573
Martin	310,187	20,952	10,927	278,308
Miami-Dade	9,978,819	1,983,582	441,107	7,554,130
Monroe	481,785	88,463	129,597	263,725
Nassau	234,152	89,898	4,885	139,369
Okaloosa	2,224,601	533,759	1,321,520	369,322
Okeechobee	95,060	5,282	3,006	86,772
Orange	3,718,309	866,526	121,657	2,730,126
Osceola	546,187	27,951	17,557	500,679
Palm Beach	3,751,397	572,554	103,839	3,075,004
Pasco	742,546	62,017	32,513	648,016
Pinellas	2,653,182	531,988	150,748	1,970,446
Polk	1,306,004	100,611	41,643	1,163,750
Putnam	208,049	9,653	5,549	192,847
St. Johns	369,541	38,461	13,890	317,190
St. Lucie	608,303	60,378	22,851	525,074
Santa Rosa	419,483	48,385	134,818	236,280
Sarasota	803,225	78,029	27,825	697,371
Seminole	890,763	114,300	30,396	746,067
Sumter	220,613	109,650	4,841	106,122
Suwannee	84,618	7,987	2,913	73,718
Taylor	66,958	2,586	1,480	62,892
Union	114,087	1,131	1,125	111,831
Volusia	1,160,486	121,440	41,694	997,352
Wakulla	68,089	6,001	2,128	59,960
Walton	129,388	11,048	6,917	111,423
Washington	93,988	3,240	1,683	89,065

A/ Revised.

Source: U.S., Department of Commerce, Bureau of Economic Analysis, Regional Economic Information System (REIS), 1969–2005, Internet site <http://www.bea.gov/> (accessed 30, May 2007).

Table 5.33. EARNED INCOME: PRIVATE NONFARM EARNINGS ON A PLACE-OF-WORK BASIS BY INDUSTRIAL SOURCE IN FLORIDA, 2004 AND 2005

(amounts in thousands of dollars)

NAICS industry	2004	2005	Percentage change
Private nonfarm earnings, total	310,152,109	340,464,523	9.77
Forestry, fishing, related activities, and other 1/	1,592,157	1,663,672	4.49
Forestry and logging	161,766	182,956	13.10
Fishing, hunting, and trapping	82,270	81,893	-0.46
Agriculture and forestry support activities	1,338,856	1,389,480	3.78
Other 1/	9,265	9,343	0.84
Mining	578,528	645,599	11.59
Oil and gas extraction	164,346	195,310	18.84
Mining (except oil and gas)	394,015	417,007	5.84
Support activities for mining	20,167	33,282	65.03
Utilities	2,755,121	2,831,163	2.76
Construction	28,400,278	33,632,045	18.42
Construction of buildings	9,268,412	11,254,246	21.43
Heavy and civil engineering construction	3,771,281	4,146,576	9.95
Specialty trade contractors	15,360,585	18,231,223	18.69
Manufacturing	23,677,379	25,241,963	6.61
Durable goods manufacturing	16,237,813	17,332,340	6.74
Wood product manufacturing	888,615	1,046,602	17.78
Nonmetallic mineral product manufacturing	1,208,870	1,352,430	11.88
Primary metal manufacturing	266,833	298,018	11.69
Fabricated metal product manufacturing	1,729,860	1,869,107	8.05
Machinery manufacturing	1,536,954	1,594,067	3.72
Computer and electronic product manufacturing	4,006,431	4,225,435	5.47
Electrical equipment and appliance manufacturing	436,095	464,266	6.46
Motor vehicle manufacturing	760,305	832,091	9.44
Transportation equipment manufacturing, excluding motor vehicles	2,174,177	2,272,901	4.54
Furniture and related product manufacturing	885,658	882,920	-0.31
Miscellaneous manufacturing	2,344,015	2,494,503	6.42
Nondurable goods manufacturing	7,439,566	7,909,623	6.32
Food manufacturing	1,570,702	1,541,196	-1.88
Beverage and tobacco product manufacturing	663,205	751,361	13.29
Textile mills	95,461	82,956	-13.10
Textile product mills	225,350	211,925	-5.96
Apparel manufacturing	264,495	270,419	2.24
Leather and allied product manufacturing	73,860	82,563	11.78
Paper manufacturing	811,649	859,954	5.95
Printing and related support activities	1,139,114	1,164,699	2.25
Petroleum and coal products manufacturing	284,790	329,234	15.61
Chemical manufacturing	1,647,938	1,895,235	15.01
Plastics and rubber products manufacturing	663,002	720,081	8.61
Wholesale trade	20,949,937	22,859,161	9.11
Retail trade	30,484,515	32,915,521	7.97
Motor vehicle and parts dealers	6,903,250	7,641,651	10.70
Furniture and home furnishings stores	1,598,488	1,763,778	10.34

See footnotes at end of table. Continued . . .

Table 5.33. EARNED INCOME: PRIVATE NONFARM EARNINGS ON A PLACE-OF-WORK BASIS BY INDUSTRIAL SOURCE IN FLORIDA, 2004 AND 2005 (Continued)

(amounts in thousands of dollars)

NAICS industry	2004	2005	Percentage change
Retail trade (Continued)			
Electronics and appliance stores	1,471,238	1,579,086	7.33
Building material and garden supply stores	2,695,768	3,169,798	17.58
Food and beverage stores	4,526,490	4,709,025	4.03
Health and personal care stores	2,316,230	2,483,968	7.24
Gasoline stations	986,784	1,045,766	5.98
Clothing and clothing accessories stores	2,263,889	2,307,052	1.91
Sporting goods, hobby, book and music stores	758,054	769,678	1.53
General merchandise stores	3,928,906	4,244,318	8.03
Miscellaneous store retailers	1,804,891	1,930,352	6.95
Nonstore retailers	1,230,527	1,271,049	3.29
Transportation and warehousing	11,648,044	12,487,144	7.20
Air transportation	1,966,160	2,005,600	2.01
Rail transportation	579,083	587,725	1.49
Water transportation	932,345	916,392	-1.71
Truck transportation	2,660,143	2,895,374	8.84
Transit and ground passenger transportation	449,148	507,762	13.05
Pipeline transportation	26,087	23,098	-11.46
Scenic and sightseeing transportation	85,379	88,304	3.43
Support activities for transportation	2,639,691	2,903,135	9.98
Couriers and messengers	1,305,212	1,371,496	5.08
Warehousing and storage	1,004,796	1,188,258	18.26
Information	12,650,206	13,096,997	3.53
Publishing industries, except Internet	2,650,321	2,922,857	10.28
Motion picture and sound recording industries	490,462	578,002	17.85
Broadcasting, except Internet	3,079,284	3,075,775	-0.11
Internet publishing and broadcasts	169,895	140,842	-17.10
Telecommunications	4,460,328	4,507,420	1.06
ISPs, search portals, and data processing	1,717,107	1,790,966	4.30
Other information services	82,809	81,135	-2.02
Finance and insurance	25,668,822	27,989,013	9.04
Monetary authorities—central bank	(D)	(D)	(NA)
Credit intermediation and related activities	10,773,428	12,031,661	11.68
Securities, commodity contracts, investments	5,105,426	5,495,679	7.64
Insurance carriers and related activities	9,232,412	9,900,415	7.24
Funds, trusts, and other financial vehicles	(D)	(D)	(NA)
Real estate and rental and leasing	11,288,973	13,924,519	23.35
Real estate	9,757,174	11,753,285	20.46
Rental and leasing services	1,200,265	1,896,140	57.98
Lessors of nonfinancial intangible assets	331,534	275,094	-17.02
Professional and technical services	32,320,653	35,986,306	11.34
Management of companies and enterprises	5,852,355	6,821,738	16.56
Administrative and waste services	24,246,397	27,679,861	14.16
Administrative and support services	23,399,752	26,732,396	14.24
Waste management and remediation services	846,645	947,465	11.91

See footnotes at end of table.

Continued . . .

Table 5.33. EARNED INCOME: PRIVATE NONFARM EARNINGS ON A PLACE-OF-WORK BASIS BY INDUSTRIAL SOURCE IN FLORIDA, 2004 AND 2005 (Continued)

(amounts in thousands of dollars)

NAICS industry	2004	2005	Percentage change
Educational services	3,954,782	4,226,333	6.87
Health care and social assistance	39,333,735	41,591,736	5.74
Ambulatory health care services	21,339,609	22,953,519	7.56
Hospitals	10,809,842	11,217,085	3.77
Nursing and residential care facilities	4,547,861	4,656,097	2.38
Social assistance	2,636,423	2,765,035	4.88
Arts, entertainment, and recreation	7,164,901	7,467,340	4.22
Performing arts and spectator sports	2,392,425	2,562,027	7.09
Museums, historical sites, zoos, and parks	203,959	219,265	7.50
Amusement, gambling, and recreation	4,568,517	4,686,048	2.57
Accommodation and food services	14,638,066	15,936,011	8.87
Accommodation	4,770,961	5,129,361	7.51
Food services and drinking places	9,867,105	10,806,650	9.52
Other services, except public administration	12,947,260	13,468,401	4.03
Repair and maintenance	3,438,576	3,627,593	5.50
Personal and laundry services	2,604,737	2,708,950	4.00
Membership associations and organizations	5,304,647	5,493,751	3.56
Private households	1,599,300	1,638,107	2.43
Government and government enterprises	61,883,670	65,281,690	5.49
Federal, civilian	10,760,243	11,168,750	3.80
Military	6,971,849	7,170,494	2.85
State and local	44,151,578	46,942,446	6.32
State government	9,485,926	9,841,200	3.75
Local government	34,665,652	37,101,246	7.03

(D) Data withheld to avoid disclosure of confidential information, but the estimates for this item are included in the totals.

(NA) Not available.

1/ Includes wages and salaries of U.S. residents employed by foreign embassies, consulates and international organizations in the United States.

Note: Data are for North American Industry Classification System (NAICS) industries. See Glossary for definition.

Source: U.S., Department of Commerce, Bureau of Economic Analysis, Regional Economic Information System (REIS), 1969–2005, Internet site <http://www.bea.gov/> (accessed 30, May 2007).

Table 5.34. EARNED INCOME: PRIVATE NONFARM EARNINGS ON A PLACE-OF-WORK BASIS BY MAJOR INDUSTRIAL SOURCE IN THE UNITED STATES AND IN THE STATE AND COUNTIES OF FLORIDA, 2005

(in thousands of dollars)

County	Total private nonfarm earnings	Forestry and fishing 1/	Mining	Utilities	Construction
United States	6,613,603,000	26,325,000	91,806,000	77,668,000	512,144,000
Florida	340,464,523	1,663,672	645,599	2,831,163	33,632,045
Alachua	3,492,407	(D)	(D)	(D)	299,168
Baker	161,564	1,197	0	(D)	28,824
Bay	2,536,455	(D)	(D)	15,391	308,358
Bradford	187,577	(D)	(D)	(D)	17,152
Brevard	9,622,038	9,038	3,525	48,529	1,029,804
Broward	35,933,862	12,282	15,626	105,216	3,378,550
Calhoun	63,486	(D)	(D)	199	10,450
Charlotte	1,607,763	(D)	(D)	2,989	292,709
Citrus	1,201,304	4,338	2,296	(D)	170,098
Clay	1,471,231	(D)	(D)	(D)	242,773
Collier	6,541,983	76,536	16,789	22,815	1,159,923
Columbia	628,875	6,176	74	(D)	51,974
DeSoto	248,093	(D)	(D)	(D)	20,624
Dixie	77,957	8,996	74	(D)	7,292
Duval	22,964,947	12,503	6,266	188,459	2,098,359
Escambia	4,653,162	8,470	6,262	23,333	427,314
Flagler	668,315	4,721	2,605	(D)	84,962
Franklin	116,429	3,216	(D)	1,193	15,694
Gadsden	342,151	12,485	9,846	(D)	51,993
Gilchrist	75,124	4,741	74	(D)	7,685
Glades	45,425	(D)	(D)	(D)	(D)
Gulf	116,102	5,466	74	8,597	19,327
Hamilton	131,414	(D)	0	(D)	3,620
Hardee	222,811	(D)	(D)	(D)	21,879
Hendry	381,053	(D)	(D)	(D)	32,347
Hernando	1,320,442	2,338	23,413	10,808	188,568
Highlands	846,820	(D)	(D)	8,127	81,490
Hillsborough	30,784,466	93,955	7,707	578,327	2,403,391
Holmes	92,303	(D)	(D)	(D)	12,381
Indian River	2,009,692	(D)	(D)	788	276,174
Jackson	336,959	(D)	(D)	10,543	45,459
Jefferson	89,560	(D)	(D)	(D)	14,411

See footnotes at end of table.

Continued . . .

Table 5.34. EARNED INCOME: PRIVATE NONFARM EARNINGS ON A PLACE-OF-WORK BASIS BY MAJOR INDUSTRIAL SOURCE IN THE UNITED STATES AND IN THE STATE AND COUNTIES OF FLORIDA, 2005 (Continued)

(in thousands of dollars)

County	Total private nonfarm earnings	Forestry and fishing 1/	Mining	Utilities	Construction
Lafayette	27,236	(D)	(D)	73	1,783
Lake	2,985,594	18,491	12,909	12,754	529,466
Lee	9,674,648	18,370	20,052	67,188	1,909,815
Leon	4,374,624	(D)	(D)	(D)	380,731
Levy	259,148	(D)	(D)	(D)	36,329
Liberty	65,635	(D)	0	(D)	(D)
Madison	128,721	5,690	74	(D)	5,678
Manatee	5,496,449	(D)	(D)	22,122	528,067
Marion	3,536,280	58,580	11,226	24,370	439,855
Martin	2,774,587	(D)	(D)	150,152	339,470
Miami-Dade	51,318,743	98,100	44,055	322,610	3,776,924
Monroe	1,398,043	16,402	1,761	14,486	113,345
Nassau	678,774	(D)	(D)	5,733	53,897
Okaloosa	3,124,468	3,835	3,259	10,456	289,089
Okeechobee	326,167	(D)	(D)	2,216	36,438
Orange	32,012,336	56,421	8,928	47,544	2,645,913
Osceola	2,195,488	(D)	(D)	5,925	277,162
Palm Beach	29,448,597	141,838	15,261	312,281	2,911,454
Pasco	3,097,319	10,933	2,721	47,738	452,665
Pinellas	20,062,541	(D)	(D)	152,074	1,353,949
Polk	8,414,264	(D)	(D)	47,911	742,776
Putnam	575,970	10,223	4,175	36,952	53,574
St. Johns	2,062,522	(D)	(D)	8,715	208,280
St. Lucie	2,375,398	96,769	3,872	(D)	321,409
Santa Rosa	1,117,751	6,435	9,274	12,503	213,353
Sarasota	7,493,581	5,786	9,005	53,546	1,005,953
Seminole	8,772,590	2,817	474	78,053	1,184,529
Sumter	438,428	(D)	(D)	(D)	106,197
Suwannee	313,904	28,163	797	(D)	27,451
Taylor	238,891	(D)	(D)	1,737	23,142
Union	66,178	(D)	(D)	(L)	6,234
Volusia	5,732,345	(D)	(D)	36,344	648,773
Wakulla	154,447	(D)	(L)	2,921	23,193
Walton	605,319	(D)	(D)	15,001	133,930
Washington	145,767	(D)	(D)	(D)	19,919

See footnotes at end of table.

Continued . . .

Table 5.34. EARNED INCOME: PRIVATE NONFARM EARNINGS ON A PLACE-OF-WORK BASIS BY MAJOR INDUSTRIAL SOURCE IN THE UNITED STATES AND IN THE STATE AND COUNTIES OF FLORIDA, 2005 (Continued)

(in thousands of dollars)

County	Manufacturing	Wholesale trade	Retail trade	Transportation 2/	Information
United States	1,015,266,000	415,578,000	517,938,000	260,028,000	288,777,000
Florida	25,241,963	22,859,161	32,915,521	12,487,144	13,096,997
Alachua	210,551	159,056	371,937	(D)	112,447
Baker	13,350	5,771	18,120	(D)	3,945
Bay	182,571	134,018	288,712	81,220	85,371
Bradford	20,548	(D)	22,281	15,577	1,827
Brevard	1,802,737	313,304	866,045	172,761	194,087
Broward	2,266,085	3,299,623	3,636,631	1,267,870	1,670,417
Calhoun	1,912	(D)	10,464	(D)	(D)
Charlotte	41,300	41,165	238,695	22,131	28,789
Citrus	25,312	30,648	166,682	(D)	20,923
Clay	91,157	41,555	226,609	(D)	34,515
Collier	205,064	260,087	680,435	144,245	120,228
Columbia	125,723	44,710	95,266	(D)	14,652
DeSoto	18,496	8,835	50,257	(D)	2,118
Dixie	25,493	(D)	10,371	5,259	452
Duval	1,671,790	1,747,760	1,971,334	1,655,554	742,091
Escambia	372,622	297,765	522,856	165,628	172,235
Flagler	51,674	10,887	75,062	(D)	38,662
Franklin	(D)	9,509	18,952	1,287	1,040
Gadsden	62,350	25,345	35,497	(D)	3,528
Gilchrist	7,634	2,709	9,199	(D)	444
Glades	(D)	2,761	4,746	(D)	133
Gulf	8,481	12,484	10,079	1,851	6,004
Hamilton	(D)	(D)	6,195	7,735	(D)
Hardee	10,367	10,625	21,092	(D)	2,110
Hendry	79,247	10,898	45,431	(D)	5,604
Hernando	56,074	46,832	186,052	113,155	12,690
Highlands	53,887	27,587	123,262	21,309	11,183
Hillsborough	2,283,580	2,193,763	2,532,953	1,010,772	1,745,601
Holmes	6,556	(D)	9,719	10,664	976
Indian River	98,797	52,321	261,428	26,388	39,337
Jackson	48,248	16,074	59,240	22,657	6,366
Jefferson	2,805	(D)	9,371	6,022	1,176

See footnotes at end of table.

Continued . . .

Table 5.34. EARNED INCOME: PRIVATE NONFARM EARNINGS ON A PLACE-OF-WORK BASIS BY MAJOR INDUSTRIAL SOURCE IN THE UNITED STATES AND IN THE STATE AND COUNTIES OF FLORIDA, 2005 (Continued)

(in thousands of dollars)

County	Manufacturing	Wholesale trade	Retail trade	Transportation 2/	Information
Lafayette	3,494	(D)	4,050	(D)	(D)
Lake	202,882	119,902	385,009	128,900	68,363
Lee	373,768	443,538	1,261,394	230,509	505,409
Leon	113,128	194,894	455,599	(D)	255,236
Levy	29,938	10,292	38,880	(D)	3,328
Liberty	14,494	1,397	2,693	(D)	477
Madison	32,776	(D)	13,771	8,758	1,282
Manatee	565,713	236,750	578,276	68,648	92,470
Marion	486,880	196,915	498,141	119,525	90,149
Martin	172,744	108,235	359,998	52,587	56,870
Miami-Dade	2,867,698	5,022,596	4,225,663	3,630,361	2,706,204
Monroe	12,817	34,896	202,588	37,052	30,468
Nassau	119,737	23,838	74,319	31,902	7,186
Okaloosa	261,948	71,630	371,412	47,886	167,253
Okeechobee	40,418	9,503	46,149	20,195	4,774
Orange	2,184,886	2,170,764	2,217,812	1,027,819	1,380,138
Osceola	95,789	119,919	318,646	32,293	24,229
Palm Beach	1,650,634	1,776,680	2,495,916	490,460	916,919
Pasco	180,226	95,927	475,849	75,464	44,556
Pinellas	2,392,853	1,090,208	1,900,626	257,115	532,501
Polk	1,216,476	544,171	787,275	586,575	125,209
Putnam	171,993	17,950	76,121	14,702	4,256
St. Johns	188,198	117,611	238,238	29,715	34,105
St. Lucie	136,837	186,245	324,848	(D)	41,440
Santa Rosa	54,076	32,329	127,744	32,081	25,741
Sarasota	506,842	312,583	831,540	86,896	232,720
Seminole	421,974	790,349	1,016,426	130,883	481,667
Sumter	50,502	16,796	59,674	(D)	2,312
Suwannee	65,398	12,851	46,879	(D)	4,502
Taylor	92,436	2,292	25,489	3,826	2,018
Union	7,830	482	5,884	18,857	(D)
Volusia	501,171	245,720	759,704	103,554	163,746
Wakulla	32,305	9,175	11,715	5,683	1,148
Walton	25,055	13,629	73,990	5,461	6,171
Washington	30,652	(D)	18,230	8,126	2,505

See footnotes at end of table.

Continued . . .

Table 5.34. EARNED INCOME: PRIVATE NONFARM EARNINGS ON A PLACE-OF-WORK BASIS BY MAJOR INDUSTRIAL SOURCE IN THE UNITED STATES AND IN THE STATE AND COUNTIES OF FLORIDA, 2005 (Continued)

(in thousands of dollars)

County	Finance and insurance	Real estate 3/	Professional services 4/	Management 5/	Administrative services 6/
United States	597,567,000	202,514,000	750,224,000	175,750,000	297,957,000
Florida	27,989,013	13,924,519	35,986,306	6,821,738	27,679,861
Alachua	248,470	91,466	375,090	11,054	170,320
Baker	5,247	3,496	5,607	(D)	(D)
Bay	199,993	93,529	267,266	12,231	150,624
Bradford	4,469	3,269	12,585	0	4,027
Brevard	388,525	186,021	1,009,331	84,334	1,434,185
Broward	3,416,067	1,748,694	3,898,071	551,401	2,675,416
Calhoun	(D)	(D)	1,682	(D)	(D)
Charlotte	86,942	85,147	125,679	8,512	67,935
Citrus	48,604	33,941	77,885	1,787	69,179
Clay	58,282	44,365	99,490	10,831	80,255
Collier	537,315	430,782	528,216	182,009	375,178
Columbia	24,694	14,911	30,259	(D)	(D)
DeSoto	8,774	4,933	4,955	671	6,899
Dixie	1,096	1,629	2,482	0	401
Duval	3,380,311	611,256	2,184,653	541,204	1,606,606
Escambia	259,480	122,974	440,710	86,793	300,571
Flagler	36,615	147,356	36,949	1,062	36,381
Franklin	6,085	17,299	6,929	0	1,825
Gadsden	8,763	4,095	9,710	-57	40,819
Gilchrist	2,658	3,643	3,725	(D)	(D)
Glades	(D)	(D)	(D)	0	1,699
Gulf	6,614	6,857	6,008	(D)	(D)
Hamilton	708	284	1,252	0	3,881
Hardee	9,517	3,635	4,665	675	12,954
Hendry	9,952	5,994	7,417	(L)	9,943
Hernando	60,089	37,198	60,957	835	65,712
Highlands	29,615	28,132	39,048	3,368	67,563
Hillsborough	3,542,801	924,056	3,642,385	398,730	3,267,971
Holmes	8,654	1,628	3,619	0	3,357
Indian River	125,909	102,667	179,914	19,064	90,518
Jackson	14,655	3,015	12,424	(D)	(D)
Jefferson	7,193	863	5,845	0	6,303

See footnotes at end of table.

Continued . . .

Table 5.34. EARNED INCOME: PRIVATE NONFARM EARNINGS ON A PLACE-OF-WORK BASIS BY MAJOR INDUSTRIAL SOURCE IN THE UNITED STATES AND IN THE STATE AND COUNTIES OF FLORIDA, 2005 (Continued)

(in thousands of dollars)

County	Finance and insurance	Real estate 3/	Professional services 4/	Management 5/	Administrative services 6/
Lafayette	(D)	(D)	(D)	0	(D)
Lake	116,947	111,824	227,281	13,275	172,998
Lee	497,355	561,254	730,768	210,548	636,360
Leon	366,453	100,151	878,752	37,835	202,005
Levy	11,443	6,174	18,552	(D)	(D)
Liberty	(D)	(D)	(D)	0	(D)
Madison	3,461	1,447	6,795	(D)	(D)
Manatee	187,354	147,225	711,805	128,538	1,123,374
Marion	215,853	96,322	200,140	17,991	171,418
Martin	182,348	115,893	290,462	17,406	134,081
Miami-Dade	4,284,178	2,346,630	6,047,988	850,739	3,577,741
Monroe	81,893	84,371	105,941	10,114	72,428
Nassau	25,831	35,222	48,081	1,159	29,216
Okaloosa	180,614	300,455	469,427	26,416	204,472
Okeechobee	10,666	5,809	(D)	(D)	22,593
Orange	2,033,310	1,684,483	3,845,238	925,745	2,860,209
Osceola	55,156	158,171	(D)	(D)	131,633
Palm Beach	2,681,075	1,378,396	3,446,623	1,339,546	2,759,253
Pasco	131,073	72,571	198,327	16,245	184,733
Pinellas	1,809,854	567,929	1,959,720	760,164	2,029,913
Polk	521,694	148,995	632,065	320,534	727,834
Putnam	18,134	7,598	16,594	0	17,135
St. Johns	124,655	112,316	177,400	9,241	83,616
St. Lucie	150,106	61,192	146,985	8,144	155,795
Santa Rosa	34,824	30,223	91,788	15,433	142,874
Sarasota	685,838	267,133	755,365	47,267	554,245
Seminole	737,784	463,728	1,298,625	55,039	699,335
Sumter	6,080	7,169	12,022	0	13,500
Suwannee	15,805	3,217	12,373	(D)	(D)
Taylor	6,901	2,845	6,830	(D)	(D)
Union	(D)	(D)	(D)	(D)	1,640
Volusia	239,603	218,479	401,557	62,218	330,067
Wakulla	8,871	3,722	17,101	(D)	(D)
Walton	15,402	55,818	31,909	2,164	32,775
Washington	4,748	1,726	3,455	(D)	(D)

See footnotes at end of table.

Continued . . .

Table 5.34. EARNED INCOME: PRIVATE NONFARM EARNINGS ON A PLACE-OF-WORK BASIS BY MAJOR INDUSTRIAL SOURCE IN THE UNITED STATES AND IN THE STATE AND COUNTIES OF FLORIDA, 2005 (Continued)

(in thousands of dollars)

County	Educational services	Health care 7/	Arts 8/	Accommo- dation 9/	Other services 10/
United States	106,628,000	747,106,000	81,096,000	220,500,000	228,731,000
Florida	4,226,333	41,591,736	7,467,340	15,936,011	13,468,401
Alachua	45,289	921,740	58,194	178,874	151,943
Baker	(D)	(D)	189	6,481	9,280
Bay	7,511	352,024	31,434	182,614	132,774
Bradford	(D)	(D)	236	7,305	25,547
Brevard	101,445	1,233,747	106,579	299,938	338,103
Broward	652,482	3,707,303	476,196	1,651,003	1,504,929
Calhoun	(D)	(D)	(D)	(D)	(D)
Charlotte	5,469	366,261	22,501	63,550	90,519
Citrus	4,536	267,444	9,072	42,218	76,359
Clay	16,880	245,221	18,566	80,689	91,986
Collier	45,312	754,686	311,555	420,853	269,955
Columbia	2,212	107,019	2,209	32,515	29,054
DeSoto	(D)	(D)	1,388	7,101	13,025
Dixie	(D)	(D)	324	2,636	5,713
Duval	184,416	2,702,582	294,224	653,982	711,597
Escambia	66,855	924,081	29,405	205,992	219,816
Flagler	334	60,550	6,440	36,451	29,597
Franklin	(D)	(D)	1,672	10,418	5,240
Gadsden	2,769	26,683	2,703	6,896	17,423
Gilchrist	(D)	(D)	(D)	(D)	6,476
Glades	(D)	(D)	(D)	(D)	5,321
Gulf	79	12,573	1,149	3,399	5,112
Hamilton	71	9,598	(D)	(D)	4,617
Hardee	71	35,087	(D)	(D)	10,199
Hendry	112	30,674	1,155	12,166	17,473
Hernando	4,845	298,008	17,282	63,873	71,713
Highlands	2,338	184,508	7,396	35,071	47,450
Hillsborough	270,050	3,204,772	579,124	1,193,502	911,026
Holmes	(D)	(D)	438	2,582	9,554
Indian River	22,757	374,786	70,006	77,727	88,372
Jackson	441	45,479	2,534	14,384	22,503
Jefferson	(D)	(D)	(D)	(D)	4,955
Lafayette	(D)	(D)	(D)	(D)	(D)
Lake	34,785	539,800	21,163	122,213	146,632
Lee	78,432	1,011,529	207,112	457,527	453,720
Leon	36,156	735,105	21,102	197,657	317,302
Levy	1,530	23,490	4,892	11,734	14,983

See footnotes at end of table.

Continued . . .

Table 5.34. EARNED INCOME: PRIVATE NONFARM EARNINGS ON A PLACE-OF-WORK BASIS BY MAJOR INDUSTRIAL SOURCE IN THE UNITED STATES AND IN THE STATE AND COUNTIES OF FLORIDA, 2005 (Continued)

(in thousands of dollars)

County	Educational services	Health care 7/	Arts 8/	Accommo- dation 9/	Other services 10/
Liberty	71	6,829	(L)	(D)	2,576
Madison	1,724	22,822	554	3,782	8,849
Manatee	25,845	560,838	99,244	175,735	188,860
Marion	16,579	545,493	40,393	137,820	168,630
Martin	16,337	413,867	67,121	107,437	154,074
Miami-Dade	1,113,138	5,476,763	856,275	2,166,447	1,904,633
Monroe	11,078	114,130	63,661	312,244	78,368
Nassau	2,702	38,178	7,715	98,187	38,444
Okaloosa	28,473	305,416	26,478	212,486	143,463
Okeechobee	(L)	66,306	6,762	16,796	20,938
Orange	405,113	2,879,946	2,436,007	2,329,480	872,580
Osceola	7,617	334,098	30,438	356,973	109,313
Palm Beach	303,956	3,668,307	606,626	1,291,968	1,261,404
Pasco	38,431	677,826	33,022	158,724	200,288
Pinellas	186,655	3,040,230	288,720	783,968	713,758
Polk	88,897	1,075,253	83,851	215,881	328,587
Putnam	1,133	75,326	752	17,318	32,034
St. Johns	31,418	245,123	71,646	197,498	179,961
St. Lucie	13,429	375,416	27,106	93,799	123,139
Santa Rosa	14,104	134,488	11,351	60,713	68,417
Sarasota	58,610	1,240,244	151,429	355,094	333,485
Seminole	82,310	737,333	65,505	265,820	259,939
Sumter	(D)	(D)	2,770	18,089	23,264
Suwannee	(D)	(D)	578	8,239	19,289
Taylor	(D)	(D)	918	6,814	11,089
Union	(D)	(D)	(L)	(D)	3,989
Volusia	176,318	1,041,766	166,694	328,689	296,924
Wakulla	(D)	(D)	1,907	7,177	10,573
Walton	1,377	53,064	4,282	100,679	32,544
Washington	(D)	(D)	3,388	4,775	11,367

(D) Data withheld to avoid disclosure of information about individual firms.
(L) Less than $50,000.
1/ Includes related activities and other.
2/ Includes warehousing.
3/ Includes rental and leasing.
4/ Includes technical services.
5/ Management of companies and enterprises.
6/ Includes waste services.
7/ Includes social assistance.
8/ Includes entertainment and recreation.
9/ Includes food services.
10/ Except public administration.

Source: U.S., Department of Commerce, Bureau of Economic Analysis, Regional Economic Information System (REIS), 1969–2005, Internet site <http://www.bea.gov/> (accessed 30, May 2007).

Table 5.38. TRANSFER PAYMENTS: AMOUNTS BY TYPE IN FLORIDA, 2004 AND 2005

(in thousands of dollars)

Type of transfer payment	2004 A/	2005
Total personal income by place of residence	564,997,468	604,131,000
Total transfer payments	94,828,431	98,667,268
Percentage of personal income	16.78	16.33
Government payments to individuals	88,042,515	93,458,340
Retirement and disability insurance benefit	35,954,598	37,915,531
Old age, survivors, and disability insurance	34,982,759	36,896,306
Railroad retirement and disability	482,738	492,634
Workers' compensation (federal and state)	293,610	317,216
Other government disability insurance and retirement 1/	195,491	209,375
Medical payments	39,041,012	41,718,829
Medicare	25,257,482	27,551,822
Public assistance medical care	13,155,035	13,493,807
Military medical insurance	628,495	673,200
Income maintenance benefit payments	8,385,252	8,956,379
Supplemental Security Income (SSI)	2,015,588	2,065,925
Family assistance 2/	638,687	617,553
Food stamps	1,495,098	1,759,853
Other income maintenance 3/	4,235,879	4,513,048
Unemployment insurance benefit payments	1,176,540	918,857
State unemployment insurance compensation	1,141,971	885,281
Unemployment Compensation for Federal Civilian Employees (UCFE)	6,428	4,645
Unemployment Compensation for Railroad Employees	1,738	1,585
Unemployment Compensation for Veterans (UCX)	18,372	16,111
Other unemployment compensation 4/	8,031	11,235
Veterans' benefit payments	2,584,308	2,923,532
Veterans' pensions and disability	2,279,940	2,608,407
Veterans' readjustment 5/	147,684	166,522
Veterans' life insurance benefit	155,763	147,514
Other assistance to veterans, state and local government payments 5/	921	1,089
Federal education and training assistance payments, excluding veterans 6/	859,741	893,070
Other payments to individuals 7/	41,064	132,142
Payments to nonprofit institutions	2,789,597	3,011,170
Federal government	649,396	663,205
State and local government 8/	1,452,793	1,551,185
Business	687,408	796,780
Business payments to individuals 9/	3,996,319	2,197,758

A/ Revised.

1/ Largely temporary disability and black lung payments. 2/ Consists of benefits—generally known as Temporary Assistance for Needy Families—provided under the Personal Responsibility and Work Opportunity Reconciliation Act of 1996. 3/ Includes general, refugee, and energy assistance, foster home care payments and earned-income tax credits. 4/ Includes trade readjustment, public service employment benefit, and transitional benefit payments. 5/ Includes payments to paraplegics, transportation payments for disabled veterans, and veterans' aid and bonuses. 6/ Includes federal fellowship and Job Corps payments, basic educational opportunity grants, and loan interest subsidies. 7/ Includes Bureau of Indian Affairs and education exchange payments, compensation of survivors of public safety officers, crime victims, Japanese interment, natural disasters, and other special payments. 8/ State and local government educational assistance payments to nonprofit institutions and other payments to nonprofit institutions.

9/ Personal injury payments to individuals other than employees and other business transfer payments.

Note: See the introduction to this section for discussion.

Source: U.S., Department of Commerce, Bureau of Economic Analysis, Regional Economic Information System (REIS), 1969–2005, Internet site <http://www.bea.gov/> (accessed 30, May 2007).

Table 5.39. TRANSFER PAYMENTS: TOTAL AMOUNTS IN THE UNITED STATES AND IN THE STATE AND COUNTIES OF FLORIDA, 2003, 2004, AND 2005

(amounts in thousands of dollars, except where indicated)

County	2003 A/ Amount	2003 A/ As a percentage of total personal income	2004 A/ Amount	2004 A/ As a percentage of total personal income	2005 Amount	2005 As a percentage of total personal income
United States	1,351,499,000	14.8	1,426,787,000	14.7	1,526,592,000	14.9
Florida	85,471,409	16.6	94,828,431	16.8	98,667,268	16.3
Alachua	940,653	16.6	957,864	15.2	1,046,864	15.4
Baker	104,784	20.8	116,584	21.2	115,652	20.1
Bay	792,289	19.2	862,564	19.0	908,929	18.6
Bradford	126,579	23.3	139,234	23.8	145,304	23.4
Brevard	2,732,061	18.7	3,160,898	20.0	3,111,006	18.5
Broward	7,669,389	13.6	8,056,481	13.4	8,941,569	13.7
Calhoun	72,631	32.1	73,621	31.6	80,012	31.9
Charlotte	1,045,034	26.7	1,399,910	32.3	1,123,355	24.4
Citrus	901,234	30.0	987,764	30.6	1,066,144	30.5
Clay	536,220	12.4	624,398	13.4	681,368	13.6
Collier	1,293,054	10.5	1,406,194	9.7	1,582,332	10.4
Columbia	307,459	26.1	347,562	26.6	368,707	26.1
DeSoto	150,215	27.0	225,173	37.5	166,689	26.2
Dixie	80,795	35.3	95,785	37.9	98,981	35.7
Duval	3,465,339	13.9	3,668,366	13.8	3,930,365	14.1
Escambia	1,489,341	19.6	1,887,326	23.7	1,689,485	20.1
Flagler	357,379	23.0	418,166	22.6	467,331	22.5
Franklin	58,063	25.9	66,735	26.3	65,209	24.5
Gadsden	227,829	23.7	246,919	24.0	258,744	24.2
Gilchrist	76,160	23.2	79,026	21.9	83,175	21.6
Glades	38,711	21.3	45,352	23.3	46,603	22.3
Gulf	85,000	30.3	93,671	29.6	94,588	28.4
Hamilton	63,835	33.0	70,539	33.6	75,271	34.4
Hardee	119,189	24.5	169,019	34.3	128,763	24.3
Hendry	155,295	21.2	166,563	21.3	181,870	21.7
Hernando	1,020,469	28.8	1,116,723	29.3	1,189,950	29.0
Highlands	617,962	30.7	703,605	33.1	702,574	31.2
Hillsborough	4,536,801	14.0	4,941,017	14.1	5,260,036	14.1
Holmes	111,947	31.3	127,144	32.7	132,200	32.2
Indian River	774,699	15.9	1,004,231	17.8	861,392	14.6
Jackson	293,945	30.1	288,746	29.3	317,265	29.8
Jefferson	70,016	21.5	73,557	21.6	76,030	21.6
Lafayette	26,916	24.8	30,149	25.5	31,346	25.3

See footnotes at end of table.

Continued . . .

Table 5.39. TRANSFER PAYMENTS: TOTAL AMOUNTS IN THE UNITED STATES AND IN THE STATE AND COUNTIES OF FLORIDA, 2003, 2004, AND 2005 (Continued)

(amounts in thousands of dollars, except where indicated)

County	2003 A/ Amount	2003 A/ As a percentage of total personal income	2004 A/ Amount	2004 A/ As a percentage of total personal income	2005 Amount	2005 As a percentage of total personal income
Lake	1,527,982	23.3	1,727,710	23.6	1,874,775	23.4
Lee	2,662,289	16.9	3,004,924	16.3	3,117,493	15.7
Leon	812,135	11.8	847,091	11.3	921,886	11.7
Levy	197,499	27.8	227,244	29.2	237,307	28.3
Liberty	27,757	20.2	33,173	22.2	32,015	20.7
Madison	102,893	31.1	114,370	31.6	119,312	31.6
Manatee	1,483,064	16.6	1,596,692	16.0	1,685,396	15.7
Marion	1,670,123	24.8	1,879,701	25.1	2,038,840	25.0
Martin	845,314	14.4	992,911	15.2	940,129	13.5
Miami-Dade	12,353,572	19.1	13,177,016	18.7	14,303,272	19.2
Monroe	337,559	11.2	351,963	10.5	400,374	11.4
Nassau	261,641	13.1	299,779	13.3	319,521	13.5
Okaloosa	790,502	14.3	892,050	14.9	893,988	14.0
Okeechobee	210,931	29.6	271,582	34.7	244,357	29.3
Orange	3,796,450	13.9	4,297,693	14.5	4,340,414	13.5
Osceola	780,065	18.7	1,026,551	22.3	1,002,323	19.7
Palm Beach	6,709,818	12.7	7,442,943	12.5	7,693,487	12.1
Pasco	2,329,998	24.8	2,535,177	24.6	2,687,885	24.0
Pinellas	5,387,243	17.3	5,650,588	16.9	5,949,441	16.9
Polk	2,549,457	19.5	3,001,267	20.9	2,947,601	18.8
Putnam	412,573	28.1	468,663	31.2	482,512	30.2
St. Johns	615,407	11.5	685,332	10.8	742,621	10.7
St. Lucie	1,268,744	25.5	1,638,221	28.5	1,481,881	23.9
Santa Rosa	540,352	16.2	738,225	20.1	643,274	16.2
Sarasota	2,271,938	15.8	2,444,309	15.0	2,581,918	15.1
Seminole	1,366,339	10.5	1,535,353	10.7	1,506,921	9.7
Sumter	396,758	36.0	437,496	35.0	488,958	35.0
Suwannee	225,708	30.1	245,467	29.9	266,192	30.8
Taylor	108,936	28.0	118,265	28.2	124,068	27.5
Union	43,107	21.7	51,601	23.6	53,037	22.8
Volusia	2,610,165	22.1	2,958,497	22.8	3,010,015	21.8
Wakulla	96,375	17.0	105,319	17.0	115,974	17.5
Walton	207,103	21.0	237,183	20.8	240,751	19.6
Washington	130,319	32.2	143,189	32.7	150,221	31.7

A/ Revised.
Note: See the introduction to this section for discussion of government employee retirement plans.

Source: U.S., Department of Commerce, Bureau of Economic Analysis, Regional Economic Information System (REIS), 1969–2005, Internet site <http://www.bea.gov/> (accessed 30, May 2007).

Table 5.41. MILITARY RETIREES: PERSONS RECEIVING MILITARY RETIREMENT INCOME AND AMOUNT OF MONTHLY PAYMENT IN FLORIDA, SEPTEMBER 30, 2004, 2005, AND 2006

Branch and type of service	Total 1/			Paid by Department of Defense			Monthly payment 2/ ($1,000)		
	2004	2005	2006	2004	2005	2006	2004	2005	2006
Total	186,330	187,397	186,224	174,547	175,701	175,284	306,118	319,070	331,604
Army	46,126	46,484	46,379	42,073	42,445	42,426	71,035	74,665	77,606
Navy	62,131	62,628	62,199	58,871	59,399	59,403	100,696	104,765	109,188
Marine Corps	8,698	8,793	8,808	7,483	7,553	7,575	14,325	15,064	15,730
Air Force	69,375	69,492	68,838	66,120	66,304	65,880	120,062	124,576	129,079
Coast Guard 3/	4,525	4,595	4,615	4,346	4,398	4,426	6,771	7,081	7,453
Officers	52,787	52,506	51,863	51,961	51,693	51,157	144,248	148,944	153,798
Non-disabled and reserve	49,828	49,706	49,246	49,327	49,219	48,847	138,093	142,827	147,893
Disabled	2,959	2,800	2,617	2,634	2,474	2,310	6,155	6,117	5,905
Enlisted	133,543	134,891	134,361	122,586	124,008	124,127	161,870	170,126	177,806
Non-disabled and reserve	120,167	121,584	121,224	116,355	117,891	118,147	156,781	164,725	172,364
Disabled	13,376	13,307	13,137	6,231	6,117	5,980	5,089	5,401	5,442

1/ Includes retirees whose monthly payment is zero or less after survivor benefit deductions and/or other offsets such as Veterans Administration payments, dual compensation, pay cap limitations from civil service employment, and refusal of retired pay.

2/ Monthly payment prior to deductions for withholding taxes and allotments, but after deductions for survivor benefits, waivers to obtain benefits from the Veterans Administration, dual compensation, and other adjustments.

3/ Coast Guard members and their survivors are paid by the Department of Homeland Security. These data are included for informational purposes.

Note: These data reflect mailing, not necessarily residence, addresses. The 2006 data are preliminary due to reporting delays. Members who retired or died within one month of September 30, 2006 are not included.

Table 5.42. MILITARY RETIREES: SURVIVING FAMILIES RECEIVING RETIREMENT PAYMENTS AND AMOUNT OF MONTHLY PAYMENT IN FLORIDA, SEPTEMBER 30, 2004, 2005, AND 2006

Branch of service	Number of survivors			Monthly payment received (dollars)		
	2004	2005	2006	2004	2005	2006
Total	27,059	27,217	27,440	20,019,000	20,501,000	24,147,000
Army	8,888	8,863	8,892	6,616,000	6,642,000	7,662,000
Navy	7,946	8,012	8,134	5,443,000	5,608,000	6,691,000
Marine Corps	963	967	991	748,000	768,000	923,000
Air Force	9,262	9,375	9,423	7,212,000	7,483,000	8,871,000

Note: Data are for families receiving payments under the Retired Servicemen's Family Protection Plan or the Survivor Benefit Plan. These data reflect mailing, not necessarily residence, addresses. The 2006 data are preliminary due to reporting delays. Members who retired or died within one month of September 30, 2006 are not included.

Source for Tables 5.41 and 5.42: U.S., Department of Defense, Office of the Actuary, *FY 2006 DoD Statistical Report on the Military Retirement System,* and previous editions, Internet site <http://www.dod.mil/actuary/> (accessed 11, June 2007).

Table 5.46. POVERTY THRESHOLDS: AVERAGE POVERTY THRESHOLDS FOR A FAMILY OF FOUR AND THE ANNUAL CONSUMER PRICE INDEX IN THE UNITED STATES 1993 THROUGH 2006

Year	Average threshold (dollars)	Consumer Price Index (1982-84=100)	Year	Average threshold (dollars)	Consumer Price Index (1982-84=100)
1993	14,904	144.5	2000	17,761	172.2
1994	15,286	148.2	2001	18,267	177.1
1995	15,719	152.4	2002	18,556	179.9
1996	16,183	156.9	2003	18,979	184.0
1997	16,555	160.5	2004	19,484	188.9
1998	16,813	163.0	2005	20,144	195.3
1999	17,184	166.6	2006	20,794	201.6

Note: Poverty thresholds for a family of four with no related children under 18 years. See Glossary under Poverty status for definition of poverty thresholds. Average threshold data are revised.

Source: U.S., Department of Commerce, Census Bureau, *Poverty Thresholds,* Internet site <http://www.census.gov/>, and U.S., Department of Commerce, Bureau of Labor Statistics, Internet site <http://www.bls.gov/> (both accessed 9, May 2007).

Table 5.47. POVERTY THRESHOLDS: POVERTY LEVEL BASED ON MONEY INCOME BY SIZE OF FAMILY IN THE UNITED STATES, 2003 THROUGH 2006

(in dollars)

Size of family unit	2003	2004	2005	2006
1 person under 65 years	9,573	9,827	10,160	10,488
1 person 65 years and over	8,825	9,060	9,367	9,669
2 persons				
Householder under 65 years	12,321	12,649	13,078	13,500
Householder 65 years and over	11,122	11,418	11,805	12,186
3 persons	14,393	14,776	15,277	15,769
4 persons	18,979	19,484	20,144	20,794
5 persons	22,887	23,497	24,293	25,076
6 persons	26,324	27,025	27,941	28,842
7 persons	30,289	31,096	32,150	33,187
8 persons	33,876	34,778	35,957	37,117
9 persons or more	40,751	41,836	43,254	44,649

Note: Poverty thresholds for a family of four with no related children under 18 years. See Glossary under Poverty status for definition of poverty thresholds. Some data may be revised.

Source: U.S., Department of Commerce, Census Bureau, *Poverty Thresholds,* Internet site <http://www.census.gov/> (accessed 9, May 2007).

Table 5.48. INCOME AND POVERTY ESTIMATES: MEDIAN HOUSEHOLD INCOME POOR PERSONS, AND CHILDREN LIVING IN POVERTY IN THE STATE AND COUNTIES OF FLORIDA, 2004

County	Median household income (dollars)	Percentage change from 2000	Poor persons Total	Poor persons Percentage	Persons under age 18 in poverty Total	Persons under age 18 in poverty Percentage	Related children living in poverty 1/ Total	Related children living in poverty 1/ Percentage
Florida	40,900	5.5	2,074,997	11.9	699,280	17.3	447,172	15.6
Alachua	34,696	6.0	30,836	14.5	7,296	16.9	4,688	15.7
Baker	41,589	6.4	2,839	12.7	1,058	16.7	728	16.6
Bay	38,972	9.6	18,777	11.9	6,792	18.0	4,428	16.6
Bradford	34,104	3.7	3,457	14.8	1,057	18.2	741	17.9
Brevard	44,248	8.8	48,247	9.2	14,896	13.6	9,184	11.3
Broward	43,136	1.0	203,799	11.6	70,004	16.1	45,463	14.7
Calhoun	27,521	1.8	1,997	17.2	632	21.6	424	20.2
Charlotte	37,820	4.8	12,485	8.1	3,339	13.8	2,248	12.3
Citrus	33,576	7.1	14,808	11.2	4,151	18.9	2,750	16.5
Clay	53,201	8.6	12,080	7.1	4,271	9.9	2,662	8.4
Collier	48,812	2.1	26,829	8.8	8,771	13.8	5,679	13.3
Columbia	32,455	3.7	8,558	14.1	3,008	19.7	2,017	18.5
DeSoto	28,638	-4.4	5,542	16.7	1,811	23.8	1,241	24.5
Dixie	26,999	2.4	2,384	18.0	748	24.7	529	24.8
Duval	41,736	1.0	95,190	11.7	36,171	16.4	23,013	15.0
Escambia	36,743	7.0	39,036	14.2	13,680	19.6	8,848	18.3
Flagler	45,374	12.2	5,936	7.8	1,805	13.4	1,173	11.8
Franklin	30,678	10.6	1,299	13.5	419	19.9	288	19.5
Gadsden	31,070	1.4	6,878	15.8	2,724	22.7	1,801	22.0
Gilchrist	32,644	6.3	1,954	13.0	642	17.6	458	17.2
Glades	31,973	5.2	1,269	12.1	362	16.8	265	15.4
Gulf	32,893	9.6	1,777	14.5	517	19.3	361	17.7
Hamilton	26,411	1.5	2,295	20.9	749	24.7	522	24.8
Hardee	28,669	-3.4	5,122	19.5	1,939	25.1	1,340	26.2
Hendry	32,197	-2.5	6,374	16.7	2,606	22.5	1,738	22.4
Hernando	35,577	7.9	16,671	10.6	5,180	17.5	3,302	15.0
Highlands	30,343	1.6	12,355	13.1	3,846	21.2	2,516	19.5
Hillsborough	44,850	9.4	132,075	11.8	50,195	17.5	32,431	16.1
Holmes	28,694	3.1	3,078	17.6	1,013	24.4	703	23.9
Indian River	41,522	3.6	11,660	9.2	3,351	14.0	2,187	12.7
Jackson	31,022	4.5	6,647	15.7	2,107	20.6	1,401	19.4
Jefferson	33,962	3.2	1,821	14.5	542	18.9	366	18.0
Lafayette	27,896	-7.0	1,139	18.6	348	21.5	257	23.5
Lake	40,745	9.1	25,864	9.5	8,249	15.1	5,081	13.1
Lee	43,476	10.7	48,256	8.9	15,555	14.0	10,159	13.0
Leon	39,562	2.0	29,772	12.7	7,806	14.8	4,825	13.4

See footnotes at end of table. Continued . . .

Table 5.48. INCOME AND POVERTY ESTIMATES: MEDIAN HOUSEHOLD INCOME POOR PERSONS, AND CHILDREN LIVING IN POVERTY IN THE STATE AND COUNTIES OF FLORIDA, 2004 (Continued)

County	Median household income (dollars)	Percentage change from 2000	Poor persons		Persons under age 18 in poverty		Related children living in poverty 1/	
			Total	Percentage	Total	Percentage	Total	Percentage
Levy	29,314	5.7	5,589	15.0	1,943	22.9	1,300	21.0
Liberty	30,451	4.0	1,037	16.9	316	20.1	217	20.1
Madison	28,230	4.6	3,051	17.7	1,020	23.2	713	22.8
Manatee	41,419	6.9	29,352	9.7	9,497	14.7	6,112	13.5
Marion	34,948	7.4	36,194	12.2	12,081	19.5	7,805	17.4
Martin	45,341	3.9	11,100	8.1	3,240	12.6	2,163	11.5
Miami-Dade	34,682	4.4	400,339	17.1	137,497	23.4	85,384	20.8
Monroe	42,195	-0.6	6,903	9.2	1,738	13.5	1,188	13.2
Nassau	50,301	7.4	5,328	8.3	1,812	12.3	1,213	11.2
Okaloosa	45,424	8.9	15,958	9.0	6,017	13.5	3,870	12.5
Okeechobee	31,332	4.8	5,112	13.7	1,852	19.2	1,260	19.4
Orange	41,725	-2.2	126,348	12.6	46,612	17.6	28,753	15.8
Osceola	39,770	3.8	27,929	12.2	10,900	18.0	7,063	16.6
Palm Beach	44,186	5.2	125,884	10.1	40,886	14.8	26,354	13.5
Pasco	38,065	11.2	45,797	10.8	14,343	16.2	9,428	14.6
Pinellas	38,547	3.7	101,080	11.1	28,862	15.8	18,393	14.0
Polk	36,339	2.5	69,999	13.2	25,708	19.5	16,447	17.8
Putnam	30,098	8.1	12,544	17.3	4,645	26.0	3,106	24.3
St. Johns	55,712	6.6	11,976	7.5	3,400	10.0	2,268	8.9
St. Lucie	39,377	8.9	27,082	11.3	9,475	18.0	6,032	15.8
Santa Rosa	46,298	8.6	13,459	9.6	4,583	13.5	2,934	11.7
Sarasota	44,023	4.2	27,571	7.6	7,467	12.3	4,773	10.8
Seminole	50,842	1.4	33,878	8.5	11,570	11.9	7,555	10.6
Sumter	37,523	18.3	6,913	12.5	2,161	21.1	1,547	20.6
Suwannee	31,744	5.7	5,805	15.3	1,883	21.3	1,263	20.3
Taylor	31,784	3.5	2,872	15.9	963	21.7	642	20.1
Union	33,821	0.1	1,770	18.2	490	17.6	335	16.8
Volusia	37,247	5.6	53,524	11.2	16,796	17.2	10,588	15.0
Wakulla	39,849	5.5	2,743	10.4	896	14.3	607	13.1
Walton	37,350	15.4	5,537	11.5	1,898	17.9	1,321	17.3
Washington	30,138	5.7	3,216	15.5	1,092	22.3	721	19.8

1/ Related children aged 5 to 17 living in families in poverty.
Note: Released in November 2006, these estimates model a 3-year average income reported in the Annual Social and Economic Supplement of the Current Population Survey.

Source: U.S., Department of Commerce, Census Bureau, Internet site <http://www.census.gov/> (accessed 2, February 2007).

Table 5.49. ELDER POVERTY STATUS: ALL RACES AND MINORITIES AGED 60 AND OVER LIVING IN POVERTY BY INCOME STATUS IN THE STATE AND COUNTIES OF FLORIDA, 2006

PSA and County	All races		Minorities	
	Poor 1/	Low income 2/	Poor 1/	Low income 2/
Florida	382,828	559,220	171,170	232,095
PSA 1	11,216	16,749	3,288	4,480
Escambia	5,625	8,349	2,454	3,276
Okaloosa	2,347	3,387	368	540
Santa Rosa	1,833	2,876	286	400
Walton	1,411	2,137	180	264
PSA 2	15,767	22,277	5,934	7,668
Bay	3,603	5,115	864	1,093
Calhoun	532	697	133	161
Franklin	478	729	45	85
Gadsden	1,403	1,991	995	1,391
Gulf	489	689	153	183
Holmes	714	976	64	77
Jackson	1,991	2,782	750	889
Jefferson	499	597	303	348
Leon	2,673	3,964	1,701	2,171
Liberty	247	379	30	47
Madison	901	1,232	387	552
Taylor	709	1,076	246	313
Wakulla	613	763	139	196
Washington	915	1,287	124	162
PSA 3	36,836	56,627	8,227	11,418
Alachua	3,357	5,070	1,435	2,104
Bradford	878	1,197	210	293
Citrus	4,051	6,509	274	405
Columbia	1,908	2,844	568	713
Dixie	716	1,107	72	112
Gilchrist	501	783	24	31
Hamilton	408	580	226	292
Hernando	3,619	5,161	525	672
Lafayette	213	309	36	47
Lake	5,808	9,109	1,574	2,032
Levy	1,313	2,123	203	299
Marion	7,764	12,438	1,442	2,237
Putnam	2,547	3,922	769	1,145
Sumter	2,237	3,201	509	607
Suwannee	1,211	1,872	244	300
Union	305	402	116	129
PSA 4	32,066	47,074	10,846	14,280
Baker	381	564	52	104
Clay	1,915	2,942	281	360
Duval	14,757	21,010	7,439	9,565
PSA 4				
Flagler	1,257	1,900	283	456
Nassau	1,252	1,920	201	269
St. Johns	2,094	2,937	464	587
Volusia	10,410	15,801	2,126	2,939
PSA 5	32,192	49,848	4,777	6,530
Pasco	9,971	15,565	660	959
Pinellas	22,221	34,283	4,117	5,571
PSA 6	40,633	60,341	15,634	20,995
Hardee	891	1,186	337	415
Highlands	3,033	4,652	851	1,135
Hillsborough	19,189	28,216	9,644	12,948
Manatee	5,989	9,059	1,306	1,732
Polk	11,531	17,228	3,496	4,765
PSA 7	30,766	46,489	15,006	21,718
Brevard	9,983	15,127	2,288	3,348
Orange	12,973	19,267	8,696	12,344
Osceola	3,384	5,103	1,857	2,868
Seminole	4,426	6,992	2,165	3,158
PSA 8	28,275	42,138	5,630	7,745
Charlotte	3,696	5,808	491	736
Collier	5,052	7,126	1,205	1,760
DeSoto	698	1,044	217	280
Glades	345	533	61	72
Hendry	847	1,087	486	627
Lee	10,759	15,989	2,401	3,233
Sarasota	6,878	10,551	769	1,037
PSA 9	36,099	52,365	11,481	15,457
Indian River	2,771	4,103	568	812
Martin	2,626	3,989	354	474
Okeechobee	983	1,378	192	333
Palm Beach	24,240	35,147	8,380	11,299
St. Lucie	5,479	7,748	1,987	2,539
PSA 10	36,186	52,308	14,816	19,867
Broward	36,186	52,308	14,816	19,867
PSA 11	82,792	113,004	75,531	101,937
Miami-Dade	80,938	110,286	75,130	101,355
Monroe	1,854	2,718	401	582

PSA Planning and Service Area.
1/ Total persons and minorities whose income is below poverty level.
2/ Total persons and minorities whose income is below 125 percent of the poverty level.

Source: State of Florida, Department of Elder Affairs, *2006 Florida County Profiles,* Internet site <http://elderaffairs.state.fl.us/> (accessed 13, August 2007).

LABOR FORCE, EMPLOYMENT, AND EARNINGS

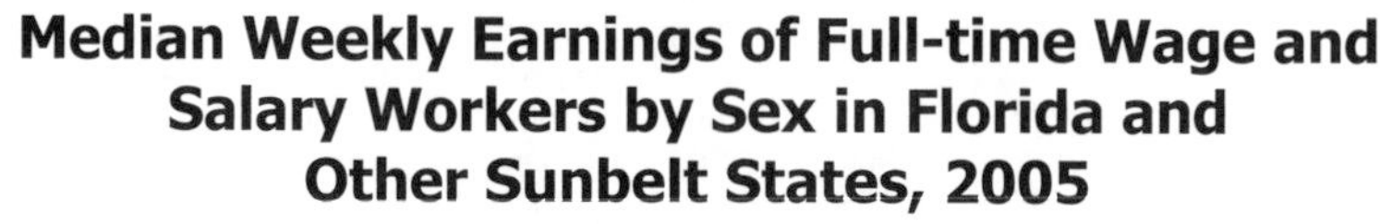

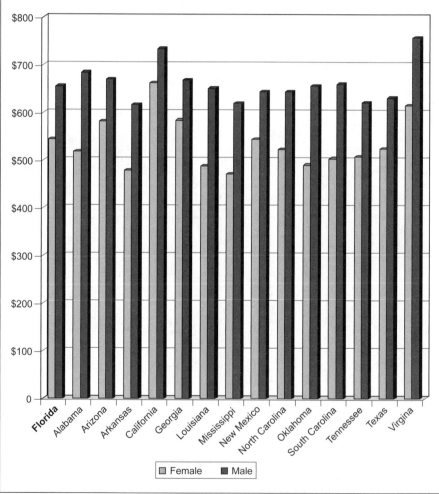

Source: Table 6.13

Section 6.00
Labor Force, Employment, and Earnings

This section presents statistics on Florida's labor force; nonagricultural private employment in Florida's industrial sectors; earnings; women- and black-owned businesses; estimates and projections of occupations in the state; and industry growth trends.

Explanatory notes. Tables of employment and payroll devoted to individual industries and nonprofit organizations are presented in this section and in other sections of the *Florida Statistical Abstract*. Data are defined by the State Unemployment Insurance Program and are often termed "covered employment" or "ES-202" data. Any firm or nonprofit establishment whose employees are covered by state and federal unemployment laws must submit monthly reports on the number of persons on its payroll and the amount employees were paid. The data generated from these reports compiled by the Labor Market Statistics section of the Florida Agency for Workforce Innovation (AWI), provide useful measures of the impact of various industries, firms, or other organizations on the economies of the state and its counties.

Annual covered employment data are reported using the North American Industry Classification System (NAICS) and are not comparable to the former Standard Industrial Classification or SIC code. However, plans are in process to provide NAICS-based data back to 1997 for future historical comparisons. All 2006 NAICS data are preliminary, with revised 2005 data presented for selected industries. See the Glossary for further discussion about NAICS and its categories.

Covered employment data include most employed persons in Florida, but certain workers are specifically excluded from coverage. These are some agricultural and domestic employees, self-employed workers, and elected officials. Among the excluded self-employed are such occupations as insurance or real estate agents whose earnings are from commissions. Certain nonprofit organizations such as churches may elect to participate in the program.

Also missing from the tables are data for the state or counties in which there were so few units that the information for an individual establishment might be made public or estimated by competitors. In these instances, and when one firm in a specific category or county has 80 percent of the employment of all the business in that category or county, no data are reported. Often data may be undisclosed at the level of the county or 4-digit NAICS industry group but are reported in aggregate at the state level. Disclosure guidelines adopted by AWI in keeping with federal rules prevent publication of reporting units and employment ranges for undisclosed establishments.

The derivation and meaning of NAICS codes are briefly discussed in the Glossary, which lists the major industrial groups and codes. Tables in various sections throughout the *Abstract* present state and county data by major industries and industry subgroupings. Detailed public government employment data appear in Section 23.00.

Sources. The basis of statistics on the employment status of the population is a monthly Current Population Survey (CPS) conducted by the U.S. Census Bureau and detailed data (e.g., employment by occupation, labor force status by age, race, and sex) are available from the decennial censuses.

Bureau of Labor Statistics. Much of the data appearing in this section is provided in downloadable format from the U.S. Bureau of Labor Statistics (BLS). Nonagricultural employment by industry and metropolitan area are provided by the BLS, Current Employment Statistics (CES), State and Area Employment, Hours, and Earnings on the Internet.

The BLS also publishes labor force participation statistics from the CPS on the Internet. Data for Florida and the United States by sex, race, and Hispanic origin appear on Table 6.09 and are provided by BLS on the Internet in "Employment Status of the Civilian Noninstitutional Population in States by Sex, Race, Hispanic or Latino Ethnicity, and Detailed Age."

Median weekly earnings of full-time wage and salary workers as reported in the CPS are published by the BLS in *Highlights of Women's Earnings in 2005,* and average annual pay by industry and metropolitan statistical area are produced by BLS in their Quarterly Census of Employment and Wages.

BLS also compiles statistics and publishes data on nonagricultural employment in Florida and its metropolitan areas. Longstanding BLS publications such as the monthly *Employment and Earnings* and annual *Geographic Profile of Employment and Unemployment,* and the series of bulletins or releases entitled *News* are now available on the Internet.

Bureau of Economic Analysis. Data on the number of jobs and propietors and average earnings per job are from the U.S. Bureau of Economic Analysis. Farm employment data appear in Section 9.00.

Florida Agency for Workforce Innovation. The Agency for Workforce Innovation (AWI) within the Florida Bureau of Labor Market Statistics (LMS) has the responsibility of preparing estimates of employment status following procedures developed in cooperation with the U.S. Bureau of Labor Statistics. LMS publishes information about Florida, its counties, metropolitan areas, and cities in *Florida Labor Force Summary*, and releases special reports on small counties. Different samples are used to prepare these sets of employment and unemployment estimates. Occupational employment estimates and projections and industry growth trends are published annually by the AWI Bureau of Labor Market Information in the report *Occupational Employment Statistics Projections.*

Equal Opportunity Commission. The U.S. Equal Opportunity Commission provides state summary occupational data in *Job Patterns for Minorities and Women in Private Industry.*

Census Bureau. The U.S. Census Bureau released final results from the 2002 Survey of Business Owners in a publication titled *Final Estimates of Business Ownership by Gender, Hispanic or Latino Origin, and Race, 2002,* available on the Internet. The Census Bureau also published data on women- and black-owned businesses in the state and counties from the 5-year Economic Census conducted in years ending in 5 and 7. Results from the 2002 census appear in Tables 6.15 and 6.16.

Section 6.00
Labor Force, Employment, and Earnings

Tables listed by major heading

Tables listed by major heading

Table 6.01. NONAGRICULTURAL EMPLOYMENT: EMPLOYMENT BY NORTH AMERICAN INDUSTRY CLASSIFICATION SYSTEM (NAICS) IN FLORIDA, 1997 THROUGH 2006

(in thousands)

NAICS industry	1997	1998	1999	2000	2001
All industries, total	6,403.4	6,625.4	6,816.0	7,069.5	7,159.7
Natural resources and mining	9.6	9.5	8.9	8.7	8.0
Construction	382.6	398.4	412.4	435.8	451.6
Manufacturing	471.7	467.9	463.9	463.4	440.8
Wholesale trade	289.8	300.3	303.4	313.6	312.8
Retail trade	856.2	884.4	908.5	937.9	934.3
Transportation and utilities	228.2	238.0	241.6	246.0	243.7
Information	152.4	164.6	178.6	187.9	188.3
Financial activities	418.9	440.1	451.8	463.0	469.4
Professional and business services	872.2	943.0	1,031.6	1,107.1	1,138.0
Educational and health services	768.5	787.4	793.3	815.5	840.6
Leisure and hospitality	747.3	762.4	776.5	794.9	809.2
Other services	269.2	274.7	279.8	293.9	299.4
Government	942.1	954.8	965.6	1,001.7	1,023.4
	2002	2003	2004	2005	2006
All industries, total	7,168.7	7,250.1	7,499.1	7,799.9	8,007.1
Natural resources and mining	7.2	7.1	7.1	7.1	6.5
Construction	457.0	476.2	525.0	589.7	636.6
Manufacturing	414.0	395.9	396.8	401.6	402.7
Wholesale trade	312.2	313.8	324.5	337.9	347.2
Retail trade	923.0	920.7	946.0	985.4	1,004.7
Transportation and utilities	236.8	229.2	232.8	241.8	244.5
Information	177.8	171.3	167.9	168.2	167.2
Financial activities	474.9	485.6	504.2	529.6	545.9
Professional and business services	1,140.2	1,155.6	1,214.9	1,291.0	1,341.3
Educational and health services	863.7	896.3	923.5	946.6	970.6
Leisure and hospitality	812.5	828.1	866.0	890.3	905.1
Other services	310.1	317.2	324.3	329.8	337.0
Government	1,039.2	1,053.0	1,066.2	1,081.2	1,097.7

Note: Benchmark 2006, not seasonally adjusted.

Source: U.S., Department of Labor, Bureau of Labor Statistics, Current Employment Statistics (CES), State and Area Employment, Hours, and Earnings, Internet site <http://stats.bls.gov/> (accessed 6, April 2007).

Table 6.02. NONAGRICULTURAL EMPLOYMENT: EMPLOYMENT BY NORTH AMERICAN INDUSTRY CLASSIFICATION SYSTEM (NAICS), 2004 THROUGH 2006, AND SPECIFIED METROPOLITAN STATISTICAL AREAS (MSAS), 2006, IN FLORIDA

(in thousands)

Year and MSA	Total	Construction 1/	Manufacturing	Trade 2/	Information	Financial activities
Year						
2004	7,499.1	532.1	396.8	1,503.3	167.9	504.2
2005	7,799.9	596.8	401.6	1,565.0	168.2	529.6
2006	8,007.1	643.1	402.7	1,596.5	167.2	545.9
MSA						
Cape Coral-Ft. Myers	232.2	37.3	7.7	48.8	4.0	14.0
Deltona-Daytona Beach-Ormond Beach	175.5	14.7	10.6	33.0	2.9	7.8
Ft. Walton Beach-Crestview-Destin	88.2	6.5	4.7	15.1	2.2	6.7
Gainesville	132.6	6.4	4.7	18.5	1.9	6.5
Jacksonville	624.4	50.0	33.2	136.2	11.4	60.3
Lakeland	219.9	16.7	17.9	49.0	2.5	11.4
Miami-Ft. Lauderdale-Pompano Beach	2,417.0	160.7	100.4	541.0	54.0	182.8
Ft. Lauderdale-Pompano Beach-Deerfield Beach	784.0	60.0	32.0	173.5	20.3	67.7
Miami-Miami Beach-Kendall	1,047.4	53.4	48.0	261.1	22.3	74.5
West Palm Beach-Boca Raton-Boynton Beach	585.7	47.1	20.4	106.3	11.5	40.6
Naples-Marco Island	135.2	24.2	3.3	24.5	1.9	8.0
Ocala	105.6	11.5	10.0	23.3	2.2	5.7
Orlando-Kissimmee	1,077.3	87.0	43.6	198.4	28.0	66.3
Palm Bay-Melbourne-Titusville	216.7	18.1	24.5	37.5	3.0	8.5
Panama City-Lynn Haven	76.6	7.5	3.8	14.0	1.5	5.5
Pensacola-Ferry Pass-Brent	172.6	15.2	7.4	32.4	3.8	8.7
Port St. Lucie	132.8	15.1	6.5	31.1	1.8	7.6
Punta Gorda	44.6	6.2	1.0	9.9	0.6	2.7
Sarasota-Bradenton-Venice	307.1	29.7	19.1	51.1	4.4	16.2
Sebastian-Vero Beach	48.7	6.0	2.4	10.1	0.6	2.8
Tallahassee	176.9	10.0	4.4	26.0	3.9	8.3
Tampa-St. Petersburg-Clearwater	1,308.6	89.4	76.1	233.4	32.9	102.6

Year and MSA	Professional and business services	Education and health services	Leisure and hospitality	Other services	Government
Year					
2004	1,214.9	923.5	866.0	324.3	1,066.2
2005	1,291.0	946.6	890.3	329.8	1,081.2
2006	1,341.3	970.6	905.1	337.0	1,097.7
MSA					
Cape Coral-Ft. Myers	28.4	21.2	28.4	9.3	33.1
Deltona-Daytona Beach-Ormond Beach	21.1	31.2	21.5	8.5	24.3
Ft. Walton Beach-Crestview-Destin	13.1	8.2	12.5	4.1	15.3
Gainesville	12.4	22.2	13.7	4.7	41.6
Jacksonville	95.5	74.4	62.3	27.2	74.0

See footnotes at end of table.

Continued . . .

Table 6.02. NONAGRICULTURAL EMPLOYMENT: EMPLOYMENT BY NORTH AMERICAN INDUSTRY CLASSIFICATION SYSTEM (NAICS), 2004 THROUGH 2006, AND SPECIFIED METROPOLITAN STATISTICAL AREAS (MSAS), 2006, IN FLORIDA (Continued)

(in thousands)

Year and MSA	Professional and business services	Education and health services	Leisure and hospitality	Other services	Govern-ment
MSA (Continued)					
Lakeland	40.6	26.6	17.1	9.9	28.3
Miami-Ft. Lauderdale-Pompano Beach	400.0	304.8	251.1	101.5	320.9
Ft. Lauderdale-Pompano Beach-Deerfield Beach	125.4	89.0	78.3	34.3	103.4
Miami-Miami Beach-Kendall	153.7	139.9	101.1	41.7	151.8
West Palm Beach-Boca Raton-Boynton Beach	120.9	75.9	71.7	25.5	65.7
Naples-Marco Island	17.0	15.2	21.9	5.8	13.4
Ocala	9.9	12.7	9.5	4.1	16.7
Orlando-Kissimmee	191.8	107.0	188.2	49.9	114.5
Palm Bay-Melbourne-Titusville	39.0	28.2	21.1	8.1	28.8
Panama City-Lynn Haven	8.6	7.9	10.8	3.5	13.6
Pensacola-Ferry Pass-Brent	23.2	27.0	17.8	7.8	29.3
Port St. Lucie	14.6	17.9	13.9	5.8	18.5
Punta Gorda	3.5	7.7	4.9	1.9	6.2
Sarasota-Bradenton-Venice	74.3	39.2	32.0	13.4	27.8
Sebastian-Vero Beach	5.1	8.1	5.9	1.8	5.9
Tallahassee	20.1	17.3	16.0	8.5	62.5
Tampa-St. Petersburg-Clearwater	303.5	155.1	119.2	47.4	149.0

1/ Includes natural resources and mining.
2/ Includes transportation and utilities.
Note: Data are for NAICS industries and are not comparable to data in *Abstracts* previous to 2003. See Glossary for definition. MSAs as defined December 2006. Data for the Palm Coast MSA are not available. See map at front of book.

Source: U.S., Department of Labor, Bureau of Labor Statistics, Current Employment Statistics (CES), State and Area Employment, Hours, and Earnings, Internet site <http://stats.bls.gov/> (accessed 5, April 2007).

Table 6.03. EMPLOYMENT AND EARNINGS: NUMBER OF JOBS AND PROPRIETORS AND AVERAGE EARNINGS PER JOB IN THE UNITED STATES AND IN THE STATE AND COUNTIES OF FLORIDA, 2004 AND 2005

County	Total employment 1/			Average earnings per job (dollars)		
	Wage and salary jobs	Number of proprietors				
		Nonfarm 2/	Farm	Total 3/	Wage and salary	Per nonfarm proprietor
			2004 A/			
United States	138,847,000	29,541,700	2,124,000	44,347	38,792	29,615
Florida	7,978,430	1,719,954	39,245	38,379	34,981	19,015
Alachua	130,624	20,119	1,316	34,285	30,357	12,068
Baker	6,974	1,413	194	29,795	26,681	13,014
Bay	77,857	17,042	80	34,795	31,166	12,592
Bradford	7,464	2,678	329	28,665	29,244	8,143
Brevard	218,638	50,500	551	39,189	36,996	12,133
Broward	774,551	178,852	256	40,227	37,403	18,629
Calhoun	3,157	1,034	156	23,852	23,226	10,480
Charlotte	43,181	18,729	241	26,724	29,543	6,249
Citrus	33,062	13,691	344	26,655	28,235	8,102
Clay	42,998	13,114	249	28,285	27,807	10,623
Collier	141,813	38,938	244	36,467	34,309	19,557
Columbia	21,647	2,605	728	32,765	28,512	15,407
DeSoto	11,484	1,737	890	23,349	22,099	6,813
Dixie	2,697	1,373	192	24,636	25,687	12,199
Duval	507,236	98,808	356	43,681	38,993	18,657
Escambia	147,163	27,826	564	35,856	32,274	7,349
Flagler	18,088	3,283	108	32,007	30,483	3,062
Franklin	3,650	2,361	0	23,184	24,761	11,844
Gadsden	16,183	2,737	340	30,268	26,262	12,510
Gilchrist	3,087	1,569	450	23,398	25,638	12,425
Glades	1,633	1,879	220	16,684	23,720	7,227
Gulf	4,189	1,461	0	28,792	28,048	10,900
Hamilton	3,854	591	312	37,944	34,101	10,885
Hardee	9,430	1,642	1,241	22,730	22,669	2,727
Hendry	16,003	3,168	459	25,270	23,080	13,677
Hernando	39,143	13,605	490	26,845	26,915	10,464
Highlands	31,500	6,929	828	25,133	23,727	9,968
Hillsborough	671,324	98,728	3,012	42,877	37,127	27,152
Holmes	3,706	2,471	705	21,612	23,823	10,507
Indian River	52,219	11,576	467	32,705	31,061	13,340
Jackson	15,432	2,664	1,056	29,346	25,859	16,234
Jefferson	3,479	1,171	444	25,034	25,256	11,844

See footnotes at end of table.

Continued . . .

Table 6.03. EMPLOYMENT AND EARNINGS: NUMBER OF JOBS AND PROPRIETORS AND AVERAGE EARNINGS PER JOB IN THE UNITED STATES AND IN THE STATE AND COUNTIES OF FLORIDA, 2004 AND 2005 (Continued)

County	Total employment 1/			Average earnings per job (dollars)		
	Wage and salary jobs	Number of proprietors				
		Nonfarm 2/	Farm	Total 3/	Wage and salary	Per nonfarm proprietor
			2004 A/ (Continued)			
Lafayette	1,810	385	256	26,270	23,784	8,660
Lake	84,174	21,359	1,514	29,996	28,755	11,850
Lee	218,742	55,763	575	36,852	33,784	21,225
Leon	152,377	24,198	292	38,491	33,904	16,309
Levy	9,538	3,079	664	25,031	24,377	9,706
Liberty	2,350	485	55	31,055	27,888	14,986
Madison	5,544	1,155	599	24,936	23,684	9,653
Manatee	129,002	34,048	753	33,801	30,052	24,378
Marion	101,335	24,690	1,901	30,143	28,688	11,450
Martin	62,308	19,382	286	32,609	31,969	13,853
Miami-Dade	1,098,546	255,597	1,415	42,430	38,290	25,021
Monroe	41,327	15,022	0	31,671	31,357	12,233
Nassau	18,958	5,731	284	34,180	31,570	17,645
Okaloosa	103,180	20,932	427	39,953	33,839	15,259
Okeechobee	11,046	1,456	507	30,789	27,089	21,455
Orange	689,217	94,336	812	41,799	36,716	23,850
Osceola	67,487	10,293	551	30,777	28,039	11,884
Palm Beach	589,453	144,027	660	41,305	37,947	23,707
Pasco	95,291	21,111	1,080	29,561	28,264	9,118
Pinellas	473,681	105,256	145	36,977	34,329	15,661
Polk	211,305	40,089	2,815	34,572	30,764	20,354
Putnam	20,178	2,187	449	32,644	28,613	7,219
St. Johns	51,895	11,231	174	34,330	31,195	18,161
St. Lucie	72,069	18,339	536	29,322	29,272	5,800
Santa Rosa	34,177	11,041	526	28,813	29,005	5,709
Sarasota	166,071	46,120	348	35,454	33,613	17,711
Seminole	169,827	39,922	342	39,767	34,913	29,172
Sumter	13,157	2,941	855	31,872	29,706	11,262
Suwannee	10,561	2,857	1,019	28,035	24,872	20,047
Taylor	7,156	1,131	156	32,690	28,753	13,498
Union	4,296	614	265	32,376	29,048	11,033
Volusia	170,635	32,083	1,059	31,450	29,036	11,482
Wakulla	5,086	2,484	106	26,037	27,035	9,739
Walton	16,696	4,775	581	28,310	26,863	15,111
Washington	6,489	1,541	416	26,069	25,266	9,302

See footnotes at end of table.

Continued . . .

Table 6.03. EMPLOYMENT AND EARNINGS: NUMBER OF JOBS AND PROPRIETORS AND AVERAGE EARNINGS PER JOB IN THE UNITED STATES AND IN THE STATE AND COUNTIES OF FLORIDA, 2004 AND 2005 (Continued)

	Total employment 1/			Average earnings per job (dollars)		
	Wage and	Number of proprietors			Wage	Per
					and	nonfarm
County	salary jobs	Nonfarm 2/	Farm	Total 3/	salary	proprietor
			2005			
United States	140,967,000	31,147,600	2,135,000	45,817	40,146	30,193
Florida	8,261,662	1,820,984	39,029	40,245	36,583	20,509
Alachua	130,936	21,283	1,308	37,078	32,942	12,917
Baker	7,378	1,489	193	30,824	27,550	14,080
Bay	80,516	18,032	80	36,704	32,900	13,372
Bradford	7,487	2,832	327	29,354	30,029	9,358
Brevard	226,102	53,497	548	40,932	38,407	14,110
Broward	808,202	189,459	255	42,187	39,166	19,460
Calhoun	3,073	1,091	155	25,495	24,634	11,370
Charlotte	44,482	19,912	240	29,835	31,506	11,415
Citrus	34,643	14,486	342	28,477	30,174	8,739
Clay	45,739	13,871	248	29,946	29,272	11,317
Collier	142,159	41,405	243	40,000	38,062	20,600
Columbia	22,736	2,753	724	34,709	30,061	17,943
DeSoto	12,549	1,827	885	24,439	22,489	11,855
Dixie	2,934	1,439	191	26,709	27,064	14,518
Duval	515,780	104,489	354	45,270	40,555	18,989
Escambia	147,079	29,433	561	37,798	33,750	11,249
Flagler	20,641	3,456	107	33,881	31,881	3,914
Franklin	3,629	2,463	0	24,742	26,398	13,313
Gadsden	16,122	2,892	338	31,868	27,875	13,122
Gilchrist	3,179	1,652	448	24,441	26,652	13,490
Glades	1,632	1,978	219	17,888	25,643	8,006
Gulf	4,309	1,547	0	30,291	29,383	11,772
Hamilton	3,897	619	310	39,114	35,651	11,858
Hardee	10,194	1,719	1,233	24,844	23,889	10,880
Hendry	16,860	3,320	457	25,912	23,725	14,664
Hernando	42,132	14,410	488	28,465	28,345	11,177
Highlands	32,006	7,317	823	26,778	25,091	12,511
Hillsborough	696,708	104,392	2,995	44,541	38,452	28,502
Holmes	3,813	2,597	702	21,844	24,651	11,321
Indian River	54,021	12,257	465	34,850	32,097	19,199
Jackson	15,859	2,805	1,050	31,380	27,620	17,859
Jefferson	3,473	1,235	442	26,512	26,716	12,710
Lafayette	1,801	410	255	27,375	24,908	9,024
Lake	87,174	22,644	1,505	32,253	30,881	13,005

See footnotes at end of table.   Continued . . .

Table 6.03. EMPLOYMENT AND EARNINGS: NUMBER OF JOBS AND PROPRIETORS AND AVERAGE EARNINGS PER JOB IN THE UNITED STATES AND IN THE STATE AND COUNTIES OF FLORIDA, 2004 AND 2005 (Continued)

County	Total employment 1/			Average earnings per job (dollars)		
	Wage and salary jobs	Number of proprietors: Nonfarm 2/	Number of proprietors: Farm	Total 3/	Wage and salary	Per nonfarm proprietor
			2005 (Continued)			
Lee	232,859	59,211	572	39,094	35,707	22,733
Leon	154,873	25,628	291	39,315	34,636	16,727
Levy	10,282	3,242	661	26,145	25,021	10,924
Liberty	2,372	511	55	33,907	30,443	15,249
Madison	5,663	1,212	596	25,454	24,390	10,957
Manatee	138,567	36,087	749	35,689	31,752	25,622
Marion	107,051	26,113	1,890	31,670	29,952	12,550
Martin	66,912	20,550	285	35,332	34,164	16,265
Miami-Dade	1,108,817	270,433	1,406	44,506	40,282	26,005
Monroe	40,331	15,827	0	33,474	33,630	12,583
Nassau	19,325	6,063	283	35,620	33,080	18,891
Okaloosa	104,510	22,203	425	42,079	35,660	17,075
Okeechobee	11,608	1,525	505	33,262	28,130	34,011
Orange	719,931	99,958	807	43,629	38,108	26,162
Osceola	73,142	10,945	548	32,538	29,390	13,426
Palm Beach	613,935	152,595	657	43,484	39,834	25,636
Pasco	101,445	22,363	1,073	30,906	29,345	10,003
Pinellas	484,436	111,358	144	38,126	35,334	16,726
Polk	223,539	42,331	2,798	36,428	32,026	23,400
Putnam	20,252	2,314	447	34,636	30,123	10,562
St. Johns	55,481	11,906	173	36,202	32,777	19,464
St. Lucie	75,880	19,409	533	31,312	30,447	9,595
Santa Rosa	36,276	11,700	523	31,801	31,205	10,020
Sarasota	173,843	48,935	346	37,222	35,230	18,714
Seminole	184,266	42,277	340	42,639	37,245	31,586
Sumter	16,187	3,105	850	33,349	30,173	13,204
Suwannee	10,655	3,004	1,013	28,541	25,776	21,096
Taylor	7,565	1,183	155	34,406	30,214	14,325
Union	4,386	644	264	34,131	30,505	12,700
Volusia	177,565	34,003	1,052	32,696	29,816	13,837
Wakulla	5,487	2,627	105	27,132	27,985	10,247
Walton	18,377	5,079	578	30,696	29,008	16,891
Washington	6,599	1,632	414	27,904	27,075	10,003

A/ Revised.
1/ Full- and part-time jobs.
2/ Excludes limited partners.
3/ Includes nonfarm proprietors', wage and salary, and other labor income.

Source: U.S., Department of Commerce, Bureau of Economic Analysis, Regional Economic Information System (REIS), 1969–2005, Internet site <http://www.bea.gov/> (accessed 30, May 2006).

Table 6.04. EMPLOYMENT: AVERAGE MONTHLY PRIVATE EMPLOYMENT COVERED BY UNEMPLOYMENT COMPENSATION LAW BY INDUSTRY IN FLORIDA, 2005 AND 2006

NAICS code	Industry	2005 A/	2006 B/
10	All industries	6,691,499	6,885,511
101	Goods, producing	1,077,203	1,134,364
102	Services, providing	5,614,296	5,751,147
11	Agriculture, forestry, fishing, and hunting	92,698	92,634
111	Crop production	56,304	55,913
112	Animal production	5,909	5,890
113	Forestry and logging	2,888	2,889
114	Fishing, hunting and trapping	517	512
115	Agriculture and forestry support activities	27,080	27,431
21	Mining	5,295	4,532
211	Oil and gas extraction	125	111
212	Mining, except oil and gas	4,733	3,961
213	Support activities for mining	437	460
22	Utilities	24,220	24,421
23	Construction	580,075	634,897
236	Construction of buildings	125,364	136,393
237	Heavy and civil engineering construction	70,262	76,747
238	Specialty trade contractors	384,449	421,757
31-33	Manufacturing	399,135	402,301
311	Food	31,698	30,556
312	Beverage and tobacco product	10,656	10,769
313	Textile mills	1,906	1,378
314	Textile product mills	5,670	5,694
315	Apparel	5,789	5,126
316	Leather and allied product	1,264	1,390
321	Wood product	22,418	21,589
322	Paper	10,495	10,376
323	Printing and related support activities	23,611	23,296
324	Petroleum and coal products	2,879	2,973
325	Chemical	20,440	19,662
326	Plastics and rubber products	15,368	15,997
327	Nonmetallic mineral product	25,674	29,533
331	Primary metal	5,378	5,755
332	Fabricated metal product	39,723	40,945
333	Machinery	26,027	26,213
334	Computer and electronic product	51,066	49,824
335	Electrical equipment and appliance	8,290	9,027
336	Transportation equipment	42,117	43,466
337	Furniture and related product	19,164	18,816
339	Miscellaneous	29,502	29,916
42	Wholesale trade	338,058	347,754
423	Merchant wholesalers, durable goods	181,067	186,618
424	Merchant wholesalers, nondurable goods	121,307	121,526
425	Electronic markets and agents and brokers	35,684	39,609

See footnotes at end of table. Continued . . .

Table 6.04. EMPLOYMENT: AVERAGE MONTHLY PRIVATE EMPLOYMENT COVERED BY BY UNEMPLOYMENT COMPENSATION LAW BY INDUSTRY IN FLORIDA, 2005 AND 2006 (Continued)

NAICS code	Industry	2005 A/	2006 B/
44-45	Retail trade	985,094	1,006,239
441	Motor vehicle and parts dealers	132,232	135,300
442	Furniture and home furnishings stores	42,987	45,296
443	Electronics and appliance stores	35,592	36,896
444	Building material and garden supply stores	86,105	90,409
445	Food and beverage stores	194,737	194,018
446	Health and personal care stores	65,521	68,192
447	Gasoline stations	39,302	40,068
448	Clothing and clothing accessories stores	98,757	103,286
451	Sporting goods, hobby, book and music stores	30,857	32,939
452	General merchandise stores	176,923	179,031
453	Miscellaneous store retailers	59,356	58,226
454	Nonstore retailers	22,725	22,578
48-49	Transportation and warehousing	209,620	214,140
481	Air transportation	31,208	29,810
482	Rail transportation	56	32
483	Water transportation	12,462	12,356
484	Truck transportation	49,038	49,610
485	Transit and ground passenger transportation	12,782	13,134
486	Pipeline transportation	229	242
487	Scenic and sightseeing transportation	2,386	2,362
488	Support activities for transportation	44,744	47,320
491	Postal service	252	206
492	Couriers and messengers	30,595	31,289
493	Warehousing and storage	25,869	27,779
51	Information	168,573	167,394
511	Publishing industries, except Internet	41,988	42,965
512	Motion picture and sound recording industries	14,442	14,141
515	Broadcasting, except Internet	18,866	18,960
516	Internet publishing and broadcasting	1,308	1,484
517	Telecommunications	64,864	63,367
518	ISPs, search portals, and data processing	25,736	25,124
519	Other information services	1,368	1,353
52	Finance and insurance	354,344	365,645
521	Monetary authorities - central bank	643	611
522	Credit intermediation and related activities	182,177	190,586
523	Securities, commodity contracts, investments	37,481	38,581
524	Insurance carriers and related activities	130,836	132,939
525	Funds, trusts, and other financial vehicles	3,206	2,928
53	Real estate and rental and leasing	171,925	178,294
531	Real estate	123,933	130,261
532	Rental and leasing services	46,715	46,769
533	Lessors of nonfinancial intangible assets	1,277	1,264
54	Professional, scientific, and technological services	429,568	451,078
55	Management of companies and enterprises	72,467	73,935

See footnotes at end of table.

Continued . . .

Table 6.04. EMPLOYMENT: AVERAGE MONTHLY PRIVATE EMPLOYMENT COVERED BY UNEMPLOYMENT COMPENSATION LAW BY INDUSTRY IN FLORIDA, 2005 AND 2006 (Continued)

NAICS code	Industry	2005 A/	2006 B/
56	Administrative and support and waste management and remediation services	819,171	822,284
561	Administrative and support services	801,294	802,996
562	Waste management and remediation services	17,877	19,288
61	Educational services	95,299	99,920
62	Health care and social assistance	809,945	840,134
621	Ambulatory health care services	333,605	348,577
622	Hospitals	235,825	238,930
623	Nursing and residential care facilities	148,533	154,152
624	Social assistance	91,981	98,476
71	Arts, entertainment, and recreation	169,516	174,005
711	Performing arts and spectator sports	28,827	29,959
712	Museums, historical sites, zoos, and parks	5,796	5,873
713	Amusements, gambling, and recreation	134,893	138,173
72	Accommodation and food services	715,564	730,386
721	Accommodation	156,147	154,956
722	Food services and drinking places	559,417	575,429
81	Other services (except public administration)	243,559	248,161
811	Repair and maintenance	75,984	76,895
812	Personal and laundry services	77,451	78,959
813	Membership associations and organizations	76,301	78,502
814	Private households	13,823	13,805
99	Unclassified	7,376	7,360

NAICS North American Industry Classification System. See Glossary for definition.

A/ Revised.

B/ Preliminary.

Note: Private employment for NAICS industries and are not comparable to data in *Abstracts* previous to 2003. Detail may not add to totals due to disclosure editing and/or rounding. See Tables 23.70, 23.72, 23.73, and 23.74 for public employment data.

Source: State of Florida, Agency for Workforce Innovation, Labor Market Statistics, "Quarterly Census of Employment and Wages" (ES-202), Annual NAICS files, Internet site <http://www.labormarketinfo.com/index.htm> (accessed 17, July 2007).

Table 6.05. EMPLOYMENT AND PAYROLL: AVERAGE MONTHLY PRIVATE REPORTING UNITS EMPLOYMENT, AND PAYROLL COVERED BY UNEMPLOYMENT COMPENSATION LAW FOR ALL INDUSTRIES IN THE STATE AND COUNTIES OF FLORIDA, 2005 AND 2006

County	Number of reporting units	Number of employees	Payroll ($1,000)	County	Number of reporting units	Number of employees	Payroll ($1,000)
			All industries, 2005 A/				
Florida	562,687	6,691,499	20,131,058	Lee	17,623	182,505	528,031
				Leon	7,489	92,531	251,026
Alachua	6,143	82,652	206,655	Levy	844	7,159	14,100
Baker	385	4,448	9,110	Liberty	83	1,418	3,624
Bay	4,875	57,282	145,132	Madison	317	3,705	7,016
Bradford	472	4,317	10,028	Manatee	8,191	110,451	284,425
Brevard	13,835	175,382	553,206	Marion	7,406	82,166	202,679
Broward	61,510	630,209	2,019,534	Martin	5,561	52,877	147,196
Calhoun	220	1,858	3,352	Miami-Dade	83,647	848,288	2,773,605
Charlotte	3,989	34,175	87,620	Monroe	4,063	29,933	77,169
Citrus	2,996	27,001	67,476	Nassau	1,631	14,069	34,637
Clay	3,760	35,435	82,856	Okaloosa	5,918	67,559	173,609
Collier	11,873	116,930	367,218	Okeechobee	922	8,741	19,146
Columbia	1,376	15,584	36,429	Orange	32,999	594,423	1,851,570
DeSoto	586	6,375	12,728	Osceola	5,010	55,822	128,856
Dixie	217	1,678	3,538	Palm Beach	47,324	482,988	1,612,954
Duval	24,471	397,606	1,302,267	Pasco	8,614	77,665	181,696
Escambia	7,448	103,705	273,209	Pinellas	30,524	392,555	1,144,397
Flagler	1,909	15,618	41,896	Polk	11,793	175,521	464,944
Franklin	382	2,560	5,278	Putnam	1,420	14,355	34,576
Gadsden	732	9,939	21,229	St. Johns	4,795	43,820	116,558
Gilchrist	264	1,838	3,712	St. Lucie	5,254	55,389	143,441
Glades	123	759	1,782	Santa Rosa	2,943	25,972	61,788
Gulf	355	2,606	6,024	Sarasota	14,676	143,905	417,910
Hamilton	192	2,325	7,384	Seminole	13,699	150,624	463,927
Hardee	533	5,966	12,283	Sumter	888	11,132	24,692
Hendry	702	10,088	21,554	Suwannee	708	7,938	15,885
Hernando	3,409	32,591	73,742	Taylor	401	5,397	13,556
Highlands	2,286	24,088	49,358	Union	169	1,654	3,456
Hillsborough	34,515	552,509	1,750,422	Volusia	13,229	139,756	335,272
Holmes	321	2,086	3,842	Wakulla	451	3,517	7,738
Indian River	4,505	42,273	111,773	Walton	1,644	14,133	32,832
Jackson	828	8,715	17,969	Washington	387	4,159	8,041
Jefferson	285	2,245	4,815	Statewide 1/	6,391	277,581	870,327
Lafayette	117	998	1,686	Out-of-state 2/	443	2,947	19,994
Lake	6,318	68,284	172,865	Unknown 1/	13,297	28,716	172,381

See footnotes at end of table. Continued . . .

Table 6.05. EMPLOYMENT AND PAYROLL: AVERAGE MONTHLY PRIVATE REPORTING UNITS EMPLOYMENT, AND PAYROLL COVERED BY UNEMPLOYMENT COMPENSATION LAW FOR ALL INDUSTRIES IN THE STATE AND COUNTIES OF FLORIDA, 2005 AND 2006 (Continued)

County	Number of reporting units	Number of employees	Payroll ($1,000)	County	Number of reporting units	Number of employees	Payroll ($1,000)
			All industries, 2006 B/				
Florida	583,679	6,885,511	21,692,352	Lee	18,552	191,487	575,560
				Leon	7,733	95,903	267,453
Alachua	6,322	84,795	220,959	Levy	883	6,969	14,321
Baker	428	4,560	9,347	Liberty	91	1,760	4,740
Bay	5,014	59,804	158,728	Madison	321	3,459	6,904
Bradford	507	4,679	10,640	Manatee	8,755	115,587	316,245
Brevard	14,308	179,152	585,453	Marion	7,936	86,942	223,884
Broward	63,134	643,578	2,171,333	Martin	5,882	54,647	156,472
Calhoun	232	1,941	3,822	Miami-Dade	83,951	860,280	2,989,443
Charlotte	4,223	37,620	97,435	Monroe	3,976	29,398	79,641
Citrus	3,165	29,127	75,869	Nassau	1,732	14,399	36,823
Clay	3,997	37,904	92,453	Okaloosa	5,868	68,949	185,405
Collier	12,235	122,126	394,465	Okeechobee	945	8,783	19,935
Columbia	1,446	16,117	38,827	Orange	34,548	612,076	1,993,938
DeSoto	601	6,737	14,425	Osceola	5,507	57,108	136,107
Dixie	217	1,781	3,704	Palm Beach	48,934	497,189	1,719,752
Duval	25,252	410,615	1,420,958	Pasco	9,332	84,034	208,531
Escambia	7,700	107,564	294,543	Pinellas	30,701	398,592	1,207,359
Flagler	2,072	15,183	37,385	Polk	12,274	180,194	495,765
Franklin	371	2,338	4,867	Putnam	1,513	14,448	35,476
Gadsden	749	9,694	21,620	St. Johns	5,171	47,329	134,519
Gilchrist	284	1,880	3,885	St. Lucie	5,579	57,934	156,975
Glades	150	906	2,345	Santa Rosa	3,041	26,324	69,788
Gulf	367	2,756	6,564	Sarasota	14,905	144,488	441,765
Hamilton	192	2,304	7,461	Seminole	14,538	159,963	501,350
Hardee	557	6,513	13,160	Sumter	997	13,304	30,957
Hendry	755	9,851	22,617	Suwannee	763	8,211	17,385
Hernando	3,552	33,546	77,297	Taylor	399	5,318	13,792
Highlands	2,398	24,643	53,967	Union	174	1,626	3,639
Hillsborough	35,820	566,417	1,881,337	Volusia	13,648	143,878	360,458
Holmes	338	2,150	4,084	Wakulla	460	3,854	8,919
Indian River	4,629	44,165	121,796	Walton	1,927	17,253	41,964
Jackson	852	8,874	18,144	Washington	411	4,393	8,462
Jefferson	303	2,362	5,294	Statewide 1/	6,358	269,595	922,394
Lafayette	117	1,002	1,781	Out-of-state 2/	535	3,699	19,549
Lake	6,778	71,406	188,811	Unknown 1/	16,271	42,021	221,159

NAICS North American Industry Classification System. See Glossary for details.
A/ Revised. B/ Preliminary.
1/ Reporting units without a fixed location within the state or of unknown county location.
2/ Employment based in Florida, but working out of the state or country.
Note: Private employment. Detail may not add to totals due to disclosure editing and/or rounding. See Tables 23.70, 23.72, 23.73, and 23.74 for public employment data.
Source: State of Florida, Agency for Workforce Innovation, Labor Market Statistics, "Quarterly Census of Employment and Wages" (ES-202), Annual NAICS files, Internet site <http://www.labormarketinfo.com/index.htm> (accessed 17, July 2007).

Table 6.06. EMPLOYMENT: AVERAGE MONTHLY PRIVATE EMPLOYMENT COVERED BY UNEMPLOYMENT COMPENSATION LAW BY MAJOR INDUSTRY GROUP IN THE STATE AND COUNTIES OF FLORIDA, 2005 AND 2006

County	All industries	Agriculture forestry fishing and hunting (11)	Mining (21)	Utilities (22)	Construction (23)	Manufacturing (31-33)	Wholesale trade (42)
				2005 A/			
Florida	6,691,499	92,698	5,295	24,220	580,075	399,135	338,058
Alachua	82,652	576	(NA)	(NA)	5,905	3,943	2,493
Baker	4,448	129	(NA)	(NA)	629	249	144
Bay	57,282	127	(NA)	(NA)	6,696	3,315	2,572
Bradford	4,317	72	(NA)	(NA)	348	463	99
Brevard	175,382	290	61	580	16,730	23,399	4,869
Broward	630,209	878	72	1,130	53,215	31,370	41,356
Calhoun	1,858	242	(NA)	(NA)	190	53	124
Charlotte	34,175	576	(NA)	48	5,470	887	641
Citrus	27,001	126	48	(NA)	4,070	662	603
Clay	35,435	127	(NA)	(NA)	4,770	1,748	701
Collier	116,930	6,298	55	238	19,724	3,226	3,221
Columbia	15,584	130	(NA)	(NA)	1,203	2,455	859
DeSoto	6,375	1,716	(NA)	(NA)	466	363	239
Dixie	1,678	126	(NA)	(NA)	153	466	18
Duval	397,606	395	26	350	33,720	27,114	22,818
Escambia	103,705	152	71	295	8,895	6,379	5,269
Flagler	15,618	305	(NA)	(NA)	2,102	1,195	178
Franklin	2,560	(NA)	(NA)	16	264	(NA)	151
Gadsden	9,939	2,062	(NA)	(NA)	883	1,472	410
Gilchrist	1,838	261	(NA)	(NA)	131	114	54
Glades	759	171	(NA)	(NA)	62	(NA)	64
Gulf	2,606	65	(NA)	126	375	219	155
Hamilton	2,325	86	(NA)	(NA)	119	(NA)	6
Hardee	5,966	1,706	(NA)	(NA)	374	220	200
Hendry	10,088	3,713	(NA)	(NA)	580	1,175	200
Hernando	32,591	190	448	144	4,299	1,134	892
Highlands	24,088	4,238	(NA)	127	1,952	1,065	592
Hillsborough	552,509	12,520	95	(NA)	42,067	31,743	29,798
Holmes	2,086	40	(NA)	(NA)	238	144	79
Indian River	42,273	2,119	(NA)	14	5,603	2,143	771
Jackson	8,715	146	(NA)	142	745	718	331
Jefferson	2,245	286	(NA)	(NA)	257	73	38
Lafayette	998	280	(NA)	(NA)	57	134	(NA)
Lake	68,284	1,887	204	167	10,487	4,603	2,069

See footnotes at end of table.

Continued . . .

Table 6.06. EMPLOYMENT: AVERAGE MONTHLY PRIVATE EMPLOYMENT COVERED BY UNEMPLOYMENT COMPENSATION LAW BY MAJOR INDUSTRY GROUP IN THE STATE AND COUNTIES OF FLORIDA, 2005 AND 2006 (Continued)

County	All industries	Agriculture forestry fishing and hunting (11)	Mining (21)	Utilities (22)	Con- struction (23)	Manu- facturing (31-33)	Wholesale trade (42)
			2005 A/ (Continued)				
Lee	182,505	1,582	225	825	32,767	6,783	6,312
Leon	92,531	174	(NA)	(NA)	7,392	2,178	2,859
Levy	7,159	655	(NA)	(NA)	884	761	252
Liberty	1,418	129	(NA)	(NA)	(NA)	290	36
Madison	3,705	228	(NA)	(NA)	111	794	74
Manatee	110,451	5,046	(NA)	(NA)	9,083	10,084	3,182
Marion	82,166	2,399	210	314	9,416	9,922	3,687
Martin	52,877	731	(NA)	441	6,679	3,153	1,459
Miami-Dade	848,288	8,886	578	(NA)	45,696	48,672	67,222
Monroe	29,933	100	(NA)	187	2,216	286	520
Nassau	14,069	434	(NA)	75	1,093	1,194	326
Okaloosa	67,559	65	(NA)	193	5,720	4,588	1,381
Okeechobee	8,741	1,264	(NA)	(NA)	914	235	219
Orange	594,423	4,354	55	494	40,971	30,264	28,421
Osceola	55,822	435	(NA)	92	5,825	1,670	2,153
Palm Beach	482,988	7,740	44	1,732	41,968	19,431	20,564
Pasco	77,665	925	56	662	10,838	3,659	1,857
Pinellas	392,555	202	(NA)	1,684	24,743	37,989	14,988
Polk	175,521	5,322	(NA)	504	14,744	18,157	9,415
Putnam	14,355	652	78	411	1,518	2,578	335
St. Johns	43,820	594	(NA)	106	3,841	3,152	1,447
St. Lucie	55,389	2,125	51	(NA)	6,929	2,932	3,863
Santa Rosa	25,972	175	97	234	4,182	1,041	563
Sarasota	143,905	311	65	559	17,381	8,745	4,523
Seminole	150,624	375	3	1,004	20,416	8,231	8,651
Sumter	11,132	359	(NA)	427	2,877	1,052	362
Suwannee	7,938	403	22	136	496	(NA)	303
Taylor	5,397	239	(NA)	23	510	1,626	62
Union	1,654	62	(NA)	(NA)	135	207	18
Volusia	139,756	2,188	(NA)	389	13,419	10,136	4,419
Wakulla	3,517	14	(NA)	56	474	(NA)	166
Walton	14,133	46	(NA)	267	2,519	594	273
Washington	4,159	82	(NA)	(NA)	451	(NA)	119
Statewide 1/	277,581	2,277	(NA)	87	7,314	1,378	21,100
Out-of-state 2/	2,947	(NA)	(NA)	(NA)	284	134	178
Unknown 1/	28,716	68	31	16	3,043	610	4,725

See footnotes at end of table.

Continued . . .

Table 6.06. EMPLOYMENT: AVERAGE MONTHLY PRIVATE EMPLOYMENT COVERED BY UNEMPLOYMENT COMPENSATION LAW BY MAJOR INDUSTRY GROUP IN THE STATE AND COUNTIES OF FLORIDA, 2005 AND 2006 (Continued)

County	Retail trade (44-45)	Transportation and warehousing (48-49)	Information (51)	Finance and insurance (52)	Real estate and rental and leasing (53)	Professional scientific and technical services (54)	Management companies and enterprises (55)
				2005 A/ (Continued)			
Florida	985,094	209,620	168,573	354,344	171,925	429,568	72,467
Alachua	13,194	1,274	1,995	4,122	1,821	5,353	156
Baker	800	(NA)	104	134	31	105	(NA)
Bay	9,800	1,085	1,685	3,761	1,596	3,251	181
Bradford	815	206	45	101	56	289	(NA)
Brevard	27,478	3,143	2,828	5,178	3,040	11,548	1,140
Broward	97,033	21,432	21,149	42,611	22,444	48,074	5,839
Calhoun	399	(NA)	21	66	(NA)	28	(NA)
Charlotte	7,707	390	591	1,260	1,043	1,508	72
Citrus	5,517	126	523	754	566	1,194	32
Clay	8,111	476	684	895	663	1,568	240
Collier	18,551	1,447	1,796	4,171	3,335	5,128	760
Columbia	3,099	346	314	342	248	509	(NA)
DeSoto	1,605	50	49	177	146	93	(NA)
Dixie	337	51	12	27	8	61	(NA)
Duval	53,402	22,631	10,070	44,633	8,018	24,859	6,958
Escambia	16,803	2,794	3,027	4,140	2,265	5,654	1,054
Flagler	2,711	71	(NA)	584	1,845	700	(NA)
Franklin	567	32	21	101	267	63	(NA)
Gadsden	1,386	407	59	184	85	161	(NA)
Gilchrist	277	9	(NA)	54	(NA)	64	(NA)
Glades	99	(NA)	(NA)	11	(NA)	16	(NA)
Gulf	398	18	(NA)	154	135	78	(NA)
Hamilton	281	100	(NA)	21	(NA)	19	(NA)
Hardee	696	116	52	220	57	103	8
Hendry	1,605	(NA)	108	204	149	123	(NA)
Hernando	6,466	2,120	242	1,014	495	1,086	(NA)
Highlands	4,068	291	233	518	455	875	36
Hillsborough	68,181	16,635	22,046	46,385	11,961	40,792	4,155
Holmes	400	93	18	171	22	103	(NA)
Indian River	8,240	451	652	1,549	1,117	2,045	154
Jackson	2,189	538	111	312	94	250	(NA)
Jefferson	382	84	26	126	12	97	(NA)
Lafayette	144	56	(NA)	(NA)	(NA)	39	(NA)
Lake	12,633	2,199	1,378	1,862	1,482	3,065	175
Lee	34,330	3,194	4,091	6,647	6,442	9,587	1,554

See footnotes at end of table.

Continued . . .

Table 6.06. EMPLOYMENT: AVERAGE MONTHLY PRIVATE EMPLOYMENT COVERED BY UNEMPLOYMENT COMPENSATION LAW BY MAJOR INDUSTRY GROUP IN THE STATE AND COUNTIES OF FLORIDA, 2005 AND 2006 (Continued)

County	Retail trade (44-45)	Transportation and warehousing (48-49)	Information (51)	Finance and insurance (52)	Real estate and rental and leasing (53)	Professional scientific and technical services (54)	Management companies and enterprises (55)
			2005 A/ (Continued)				
Leon	16,552	1,463	3,771	4,979	2,101	10,002	472
Levy	1,406	97	65	264	146	370	(NA)
Liberty	96	22	18	(NA)	(NA)	(NA)	(NA)
Madison	608	103	34	78	30	153	(NA)
Manatee	16,932	1,174	1,237	2,586	2,229	3,534	2,727
Marion	16,087	1,756	2,109	3,602	1,618	2,932	319
Martin	10,446	801	965	1,817	1,266	2,798	108
Miami-Dade	119,707	55,168	23,135	45,998	23,428	61,943	7,190
Monroe	5,461	775	456	1,220	1,084	1,055	102
Nassau	2,801	485	123	451	199	461	(NA)
Okaloosa	12,611	955	2,198	3,036	3,621	5,826	376
Okeechobee	1,634	360	116	230	135	164	(NA)
Orange	66,798	19,832	17,533	23,487	17,792	43,944	9,923
Osceola	11,149	374	367	1,061	2,607	1,845	(NA)
Palm Beach	69,768	7,722	10,931	24,460	14,131	34,621	8,413
Pasco	16,566	1,131	702	2,386	1,697	3,476	328
Pinellas	53,713	4,668	8,925	23,194	8,747	27,112	8,822
Polk	24,728	11,083	2,207	8,130	2,731	6,102	5,076
Putnam	2,924	205	82	452	176	362	(NA)
St. Johns	8,055	430	459	1,395	1,074	2,180	100
St. Lucie	9,514	1,654	643	2,778	1,200	2,531	71
Santa Rosa	4,689	438	624	572	628	1,280	(NA)
Sarasota	22,335	1,782	3,088	7,273	3,390	9,942	626
Seminole	27,690	1,882	6,540	10,187	3,492	9,491	624
Sumter	2,138	277	34	118	168	229	(NA)
Suwannee	1,565	132	91	327	57	200	(NA)
Taylor	987	55	49	132	85	118	(NA)
Union	225	380	14	16	15	18	(NA)
Volusia	25,463	1,657	2,680	4,029	3,092	6,854	804
Wakulla	504	71	24	208	57	356	(NA)
Walton	2,418	95	110	296	715	434	13
Washington	708	132	36	83	48	81	(NA)
Statewide 1/	16,778	8,663	2,962	5,233	3,055	14,889	2,138
Out-of-state 2/	243	25	41	136	96	264	198
Unknown 1/	2,090	677	1,144	1,601	1,008	5,515	382

See footnotes at end of table.

Continued . . .

Table 6.06. EMPLOYMENT: AVERAGE MONTHLY PRIVATE EMPLOYMENT COVERED BY UNEMPLOYMENT COMPENSATION LAW BY MAJOR INDUSTRY GROUP IN THE STATE AND COUNTIES OF FLORIDA, 2005 AND 2006 (Continued)

County	Adminis-tration and support 3/ (56)	Educational services (61)	Health care and social assistance (62)	Arts enter-tainment and recreation (71)	Accom-modation and food services (72)	Other services 4/ (81)	Unclassified (99)
				2005 A/ (Continued)			
Florida	819,171	95,299	809,945	169,516	715,564	243,559	7,376
Alachua	4,864	1,553	18,329	1,691	11,624	3,407	37
Baker	49	(NA)	487	(NA)	489	89	(NA)
Bay	3,558	285	6,814	1,123	8,777	2,466	16
Bradford	59	(NA)	764	(NA)	500	293	(NA)
Brevard	22,057	2,671	23,870	2,908	17,165	6,164	263
Broward	55,599	13,665	69,252	11,815	65,405	26,587	1,284
Calhoun	14	(NA)	359	(NA)	140	38	(NA)
Charlotte	1,465	136	7,002	675	3,324	1,259	68
Citrus	1,050	125	5,984	425	2,643	1,343	13
Clay	1,660	524	5,550	615	4,808	1,720	29
Collier	8,524	993	12,989	6,000	15,400	4,890	183
Columbia	368	92	2,629	111	2,181	595	(NA)
DeSoto	176	(NA)	617	70	436	138	9
Dixie	12	(NA)	118	15	200	62	7
Duval	36,757	4,649	49,046	4,457	34,663	12,841	202
Escambia	9,130	2,159	18,361	1,124	11,599	4,499	36
Flagler	913	14	1,278	208	1,882	520	28
Franklin	40	(NA)	245	55	581	56	(NA)
Gadsden	1,009	85	625	53	501	306	(NA)
Gilchrist	45	(NA)	379	(NA)	213	117	(NA)
Glades	29	(NA)	46	(NA)	105	26	(NA)
Gulf	43	(NA)	394	47	232	43	(NA)
Hamilton	(NA)	(NA)	265	(NA)	145	58	(NA)
Hardee	(NA)	(NA)	995	28	275	125	(NA)
Hendry	259	(NA)	891	47	747	178	(NA)
Hernando	1,668	183	6,149	679	4,199	1,151	16
Highlands	2,088	104	4,254	339	2,110	676	(NA)
Hillsborough	85,748	7,017	57,058	10,671	45,637	16,510	722
Holmes	45	(NA)	375	22	179	106	(NA)
Indian River	2,099	582	7,254	2,065	3,690	1,701	(NA)
Jackson	179	(NA)	1,440	112	1,031	326	(NA)
Jefferson	135	(NA)	267	(NA)	113	66	(NA)
Lafayette	(NA)	(NA)	122	(NA)	62	16	(NA)
Lake	3,944	876	11,015	811	6,991	2,374	62

See footnotes at end of table.

Continued . . .

Table 6.06. EMPLOYMENT: AVERAGE MONTHLY PRIVATE EMPLOYMENT COVERED BY UNEMPLOYMENT COMPENSATION LAW BY MAJOR INDUSTRY GROUP IN THE STATE AND COUNTIES OF FLORIDA, 2005 AND 2006 (Continued)

County	Adminis- tration and support 3/ (56)	Educational services (61)	Health care and social assistance (62)	Arts enter- tainment and recreation (71)	Accom- modation and food services (72)	Other services 4/ (81)	Unclassified (99)
			2005 A/ (Continued)				
Lee	14,735	1,801	18,089	5,804	20,605	6,915	217
Leon	5,539	935	14,032	1,012	12,978	5,920	23
Levy	84	53	686	161	928	164	(NA)
Liberty	(NA)	(NA)	240	(NA)	57	22	(NA)
Madison	53	90	871	21	295	80	(NA)
Manatee	25,196	652	11,762	2,246	9,392	3,058	94
Marion	4,382	608	10,878	1,608	7,699	2,585	37
Martin	3,536	426	7,823	1,760	5,600	3,061	(NA)
Miami-Dade	75,369	18,346	108,962	12,388	86,075	34,958	1,571
Monroe	1,317	282	2,213	1,121	10,041	1,472	25
Nassau	674	87	902	203	3,847	664	18
Okaloosa	4,709	406	6,908	1,067	11,090	2,780	15
Okeechobee	413	(NA)	1,582	190	963	284	(NA)
Orange	64,956	8,978	52,925	54,176	90,490	18,651	383
Osceola	3,697	246	7,137	1,224	13,770	1,477	99
Palm Beach	58,985	7,152	65,214	15,272	52,839	21,383	620
Pasco	4,675	1,021	13,823	1,341	9,165	3,301	56
Pinellas	56,115	4,583	58,987	6,714	37,462	13,519	371
Polk	19,904	2,842	21,656	2,922	13,361	5,155	102
Putnam	506	43	2,106	41	1,221	651	(NA)
St. Johns	1,831	996	5,280	1,659	8,581	2,578	60
St. Lucie	4,195	397	7,861	680	5,229	1,751	(NA)
Santa Rosa	2,494	204	3,200	573	3,545	1,091	14
Sarasota	13,264	1,314	22,604	4,454	15,556	6,554	140
Seminole	15,800	2,114	13,805	1,776	14,060	4,392	92
Sumter	353	(NA)	1,004	133	1,067	216	(NA)
Suwannee	151	(NA)	1,213	20	622	192	(NA)
Taylor	63	(NA)	722	36	502	91	(NA)
Union	(NA)	(NA)	292	(NA)	196	23	(NA)
Volusia	9,786	4,249	23,114	3,456	17,981	5,952	78
Wakulla	91	(NA)	280	76	558	102	(NA)
Walton	687	(NA)	1,527	132	3,395	575	13
Washington	53	(NA)	745	(NA)	398	136	(NA)
Statewide 1/	176,935	742	5,415	294	6,653	1,636	(NA)
Out-of-state 2/	585	(NA)	94	(NA)	569	9	(NA)
Unknown 1/	3,840	387	777	368	729	1,419	288

See footnotes at end of table.

Continued . . .

Table 6.06. EMPLOYMENT: AVERAGE MONTHLY PRIVATE EMPLOYMENT COVERED BY UNEMPLOYMENT COMPENSATION LAW BY MAJOR INDUSTRY GROUP IN THE STATE AND COUNTIES OF FLORIDA, 2005 AND 2006 (Continued)

County	All industries	Agriculture forestry fishing and hunting (11)	Mining (21)	Utilities (22)	Con-struction (23)	Manu-facturing (31-33)	Wholesale trade (42)
				2006 B/			
Florida	6,885,511	92,634	4,532	24,421	634,897	402,301	347,754
Alachua	84,795	599	(NA)	(NA)	5,916	4,517	2,433
Baker	4,560	118	(NA)	(NA)	643	276	133
Bay	59,804	138	21	193	7,253	3,706	2,384
Bradford	4,679	69	(NA)	(NA)	354	447	203
Brevard	179,152	298	80	491	17,375	24,197	5,084
Broward	643,578	911	119	1,179	58,413	31,809	42,188
Calhoun	1,941	263	(NA)	(NA)	221	57	140
Charlotte	37,620	629	63	46	5,936	952	662
Citrus	29,127	123	55	(NA)	4,329	928	603
Clay	37,904	136	(NA)	(NA)	5,120	1,899	784
Collier	122,126	5,526	50	235	23,334	3,260	2,998
Columbia	16,117	121	(NA)	(NA)	1,347	2,423	809
DeSoto	6,737	1,793	(NA)	(NA)	474	387	238
Dixie	1,781	126	(NA)	(NA)	136	481	22
Duval	410,615	389	23	441	36,747	26,542	23,429
Escambia	107,564	130	86	295	10,151	6,280	5,185
Flagler	15,183	327	29	(NA)	2,137	1,224	223
Franklin	2,338	(NA)	(NA)	(NA)	254	0	124
Gadsden	9,694	2,025	(NA)	(NA)	876	1,527	518
Gilchrist	1,880	250	(NA)	14	212	130	61
Glades	906	176	(NA)	(NA)	155	34	76
Gulf	2,756	63	(NA)	136	460	261	59
Hamilton	2,304	91	(NA)	(NA)	122	0	10
Hardee	6,513	1,841	(NA)	(NA)	287	222	244
Hendry	9,851	3,340	(NA)	(NA)	633	1,053	259
Hernando	33,546	181	139	141	4,603	1,424	848
Highlands	24,643	3,798	(NA)	111	2,140	1,101	596
Hillsborough	566,417	12,035	493	(NA)	43,427	32,180	30,396
Holmes	2,150	34	(NA)	(NA)	265	148	94
Indian River	44,165	2,662	(NA)	31	5,778	2,323	914
Jackson	8,874	172	(NA)	143	836	609	316
Jefferson	2,362	353	(NA)	(NA)	293	62	64
Lafayette	1,002	267	(NA)	(NA)	61	122	33
Lake	71,406	1,976	188	229	11,292	4,481	2,091

See footnotes at end of table.

Continued . . .

Table 6.06. EMPLOYMENT: AVERAGE MONTHLY PRIVATE EMPLOYMENT COVERED BY UNEMPLOYMENT COMPENSATION LAW BY MAJOR INDUSTRY GROUP IN THE STATE AND COUNTIES OF FLORIDA, 2005 AND 2006 (Continued)

County	All industries	Agriculture forestry fishing and hunting (11)	Mining (21)	Utilities (22)	Con-struction (23)	Manu-facturing (31-33)	Wholesale trade (42)
			2006 B/ (Continued)				
Lee	191,487	1,551	175	867	35,917	7,535	6,632
Leon	95,903	183	(NA)	136	7,778	2,216	2,714
Levy	6,969	555	(NA)	(NA)	972	744	242
Liberty	1,760	113	(NA)	(NA)	(NA)	308	31
Madison	3,459	159	(NA)	(NA)	92	706	67
Manatee	115,587	5,255	(NA)	(NA)	10,703	10,027	3,702
Marion	86,942	2,646	167	325	10,927	9,873	3,849
Martin	54,647	692	(NA)	476	7,100	3,038	1,676
Miami-Dade	860,280	9,356	350	(NA)	51,986	47,724	67,218
Monroe	29,398	156	(NA)	199	2,457	293	522
Nassau	14,399	417	(NA)	76	1,247	1,164	363
Okaloosa	68,949	64	(NA)	199	6,310	4,650	1,333
Okeechobee	8,783	1,106	(NA)	(NA)	900	278	230
Orange	612,076	4,192	53	526	44,547	28,462	28,779
Osceola	57,108	466	(NA)	104	6,194	1,602	2,379
Palm Beach	497,189	8,085	60	1,744	45,786	20,147	21,110
Pasco	84,034	971	58	705	11,939	4,127	2,142
Pinellas	398,592	142	(NA)	1,617	26,622	37,665	14,827
Polk	180,194	5,228	(NA)	466	15,447	17,814	9,739
Putnam	14,448	580	(NA)	419	1,606	2,484	381
St. Johns	47,329	563	(NA)	112	4,316	3,192	2,109
St. Lucie	57,934	2,146	56	(NA)	7,267	3,397	4,422
Santa Rosa	26,324	174	88	247	4,484	1,031	550
Sarasota	144,488	337	89	568	17,925	8,799	4,324
Seminole	159,963	341	8	980	22,090	8,585	8,966
Sumter	13,304	398	48	397	3,409	1,442	412
Suwannee	8,211	444	26	138	514	0	320
Taylor	5,318	281	(NA)	23	494	1,589	51
Union	1,626	62	(NA)	(NA)	197	186	12
Volusia	143,878	2,075	18	374	14,339	10,567	4,545
Wakulla	3,854	21	(NA)	60	533	576	74
Walton	17,253	38	(NA)	264	2,998	663	457
Washington	4,393	73	(NA)	(NA)	560	0	96
Statewide 1/	269,595	2,576	16	(NA)	10,181	1,757	23,049
Out-of-state 2/	3,699	(NA)	(NA)	(NA)	171	139	229
Unknown 1/	42,021	210	39	(NA)	4,818	599	5,988

See footnotes at end of table.

Continued . . .

Table 6.06. EMPLOYMENT: AVERAGE MONTHLY PRIVATE EMPLOYMENT COVERED BY UNEMPLOYMENT COMPENSATION LAW BY MAJOR INDUSTRY GROUP IN THE STATE AND COUNTIES OF FLORIDA, 2005 AND 2006 (Continued)

County	Retail trade (44-45)	Transportation and warehousing (48-49)	Information (51)	Finance and insurance (52)	Real estate and rental and leasing (53)	Professional scientific and technical services (54)	Management companies and enterprises (55)
			2006 B/ (Continued)				
Florida	1,006,239	214,140	167,394	365,645	178,294	451,078	73,935
Alachua	13,645	1,402	1,891	4,288	1,913	5,860	152
Baker	768	(NA)	106	147	38	102	(NA)
Bay	9,828	1,099	1,404	3,683	1,606	3,608	189
Bradford	991	237	53	118	58	318	(NA)
Brevard	27,978	2,918	2,921	5,330	3,025	11,764	1,244
Broward	100,710	21,771	19,602	43,995	22,395	48,990	6,116
Calhoun	354	(NA)	(NA)	63	(NA)	20	(NA)
Charlotte	8,634	367	615	1,551	1,061	1,702	83
Citrus	5,530	174	536	786	558	1,087	36
Clay	8,868	716	562	1,055	807	1,792	265
Collier	19,325	1,453	1,835	4,250	3,605	5,173	866
Columbia	3,108	377	306	351	244	519	(NA)
DeSoto	1,760	71	83	177	145	126	17
Dixie	394	60	12	31	9	91	(NA)
Duval	52,878	23,530	9,675	44,612	8,609	27,184	6,560
Escambia	16,854	3,007	3,093	5,064	2,225	6,079	997
Flagler	2,844	66	(NA)	594	533	696	6
Franklin	540	36	22	98	239	57	(NA)
Gadsden	1,349	483	114	181	93	157	(NA)
Gilchrist	263	13	(NA)	49	(NA)	75	(NA)
Glades	94	20	(NA)	(NA)	15	17	(NA)
Gulf	422	17	(NA)	167	156	80	(NA)
Hamilton	285	95	(NA)	32	10	19	(NA)
Hardee	721	138	72	243	47	111	10
Hendry	1,665	57	107	218	142	135	(NA)
Hernando	6,670	2,066	207	1,015	515	1,055	23
Highlands	4,229	352	257	587	445	937	46
Hillsborough	71,087	15,963	21,405	47,249	12,178	43,826	5,215
Holmes	366	99	15	150	31	107	(NA)
Indian River	8,270	595	629	1,604	1,103	2,215	121
Jackson	2,161	584	118	302	164	276	(NA)
Jefferson	368	83	24	127	16	98	(NA)
Lafayette	151	53	(NA)	(NA)	(NA)	40	(NA)
Lake	13,470	2,289	1,343	1,862	1,748	3,097	138
Lee	36,262	3,569	3,962	6,794	6,630	10,098	1,528

See footnotes at end of table. Continued . . .

Table 6.06. EMPLOYMENT: AVERAGE MONTHLY PRIVATE EMPLOYMENT COVERED BY UNEMPLOYMENT COMPENSATION LAW BY MAJOR INDUSTRY GROUP IN THE STATE AND COUNTIES OF FLORIDA, 2005 AND 2006 (Continued)

County	Retail trade (44-45)	Transportation and warehousing (48-49)	Information (51)	Finance and insurance (52)	Real estate and rental and leasing (53)	Professional scientific and technical services (54)	Management companies and enterprises (55)
			2006 B/ (Continued)				
Leon	16,966	1,361	3,568	5,151	2,210	10,562	426
Levy	1,418	117	72	277	148	243	(NA)
Liberty	88	16	18	(NA)	(NA)	0	(NA)
Madison	553	116	33	83	38	115	(NA)
Manatee	15,916	1,342	1,390	2,909	2,299	3,919	2,611
Marion	16,206	2,303	2,059	3,899	1,728	3,162	325
Martin	10,438	765	1,073	1,937	1,279	2,984	180
Miami-Dade	124,551	55,210	21,650	47,461	23,990	62,938	7,482
Monroe	5,411	775	472	1,227	1,067	1,074	177
Nassau	2,982	457	125	361	252	521	36
Okaloosa	12,117	1,002	2,135	3,131	3,384	6,276	363
Okeechobee	1,557	335	109	260	126	227	(NA)
Orange	67,276	21,522	19,185	23,013	18,930	45,829	9,929
Osceola	11,506	349	527	1,197	2,538	1,752	(NA)
Palm Beach	72,368	7,979	11,135	24,845	14,802	35,369	7,535
Pasco	17,237	1,223	925	2,670	1,869	3,559	297
Pinellas	52,983	4,855	9,233	25,235	9,141	28,430	9,326
Polk	25,818	11,407	2,382	8,291	2,933	6,380	5,367
Putnam	2,868	221	92	488	170	395	(NA)
St. Johns	8,236	580	475	1,545	1,168	2,443	47
St. Lucie	9,455	1,823	653	2,909	1,318	2,715	76
Santa Rosa	4,729	342	682	603	611	1,385	252
Sarasota	22,120	1,566	2,931	7,117	3,541	10,020	711
Seminole	28,387	2,436	6,049	10,854	3,978	10,404	563
Sumter	2,271	231	30	377	202	298	(NA)
Suwannee	1,632	199	84	320	70	215	(NA)
Taylor	940	62	58	136	106	126	(NA)
Union	217	380	(NA)	13	16	24	(NA)
Volusia	25,349	1,596	2,814	4,146	3,445	7,106	887
Wakulla	736	65	31	(NA)	51	328	(NA)
Walton	3,101	103	119	392	1,069	567	11
Washington	730	111	44	88	45	84	(NA)
Statewide 1/	14,696	7,467	3,466	5,108	3,691	15,472	1,976
Out-of-state 2/	266	18	44	143	122	248	266
Unknown 1/	2,280	976	1,584	2,392	1,500	8,399	604

See footnotes at end of table.

Continued . . .

Table 6.06. EMPLOYMENT: AVERAGE MONTHLY PRIVATE EMPLOYMENT COVERED BY UNEMPLOYMENT COMPENSATION LAW BY MAJOR INDUSTRY GROUP IN THE STATE AND COUNTIES OF FLORIDA, 2005 AND 2006 (Continued)

County	Adminis-tration and support 3/ (56)	Educational services (61)	Health care and social assistance (62)	Arts enter-tainment and recreation (71)	Accom-modation and food services (72)	Other services 4/ (81)	Unclassified (99)
				2006 B/ (Continued)			
Florida	822,284	99,920	840,134	174,005	730,386	248,161	7,360
Alachua	4,721	1,506	18,789	1,663	11,442	3,659	28
Baker	157	(NA)	516	6	444	106	(NA)
Bay	3,932	316	7,304	1,100	9,472	2,545	23
Bradford	87	18	763	29	618	159	(NA)
Brevard	22,359	2,785	24,560	2,989	17,970	5,600	183
Broward	55,680	14,077	70,820	12,766	64,723	26,417	899
Calhoun	20	(NA)	471	(NA)	135	34	(NA)
Charlotte	1,496	158	7,427	905	4,027	1,246	60
Citrus	2,103	122	6,321	495	2,791	1,393	16
Clay	1,626	596	5,886	481	5,036	1,739	22
Collier	8,956	1,027	13,449	6,630	15,064	4,851	242
Columbia	646	113	2,863	111	2,299	367	(NA)
DeSoto	235	(NA)	621	50	422	128	6
Dixie	(NA)	(NA)	128	12	212	50	(NA)
Duval	39,560	4,685	52,315	4,527	36,001	12,788	120
Escambia	9,153	2,155	19,016	1,206	12,170	4,378	42
Flagler	1,139	19	1,396	293	2,015	561	23
Franklin	69	(NA)	80	60	554	75	(NA)
Gadsden	685	120	511	66	497	251	(NA)
Gilchrist	68	(NA)	389	21	170	50	(NA)
Glades	59	(NA)	48	(NA)	76	28	(NA)
Gulf	56	(NA)	369	(NA)	306	39	(NA)
Hamilton	15	(NA)	291	(NA)	69	72	(NA)
Hardee	(NA)	(NA)	1,162	(NA)	321	148	(NA)
Hendry	297	(NA)	840	39	849	174	(NA)
Hernando	1,726	191	6,173	756	4,546	1,247	22
Highlands	1,989	104	4,599	490	2,082	710	(NA)
Hillsborough	86,131	7,867	58,544	10,863	47,068	17,301	537
Holmes	60	(NA)	407	27	209	84	(NA)
Indian River	2,276	629	7,333	2,208	3,719	1,731	8
Jackson	232	(NA)	1,467	122	1,010	297	(NA)
Jefferson	125	(NA)	292	(NA)	111	70	(NA)
Lafayette	(NA)	(NA)	126	(NA)	51	20	(NA)
Lake	4,111	904	11,589	870	7,245	2,437	49
Lee	13,628	1,951	18,574	5,986	22,001	7,470	359
Leon	6,318	955	14,599	1,050	13,397	6,222	38
Levy	80	48	811	98	786	191	(NA)
Liberty	(NA)	(NA)	(NA)	(NA)	60	12	(NA)
Madison	39	(NA)	916	13	328	78	(NA)

See footnotes at end of table.

Continued . . .

Table 6.06. EMPLOYMENT: AVERAGE MONTHLY PRIVATE EMPLOYMENT COVERED BY UNEMPLOYMENT COMPENSATION LAW BY MAJOR INDUSTRY GROUP IN THE STATE AND COUNTIES OF FLORIDA, 2005 AND 2006 (Continued)

County	Adminis-tration and support 3/ (56)	Educational services (61)	Health care and social assistance (62)	Arts enter-tainment and recreation (71)	Accom-modation and food services (72)	Other services 4/ (81)	Unclassified (99)
				2006 B/ (Continued)			
Manatee	26,468	676	12,748	2,310	9,571	3,358	144
Marion	5,048	709	11,538	1,726	7,733	2,639	82
Martin	3,579	446	8,415	1,867	5,890	2,805	(NA)
Miami-Dade	68,475	19,230	112,959	12,695	87,226	34,773	1,924
Monroe	1,372	322	2,236	956	9,225	1,422	32
Nassau	655	93	977	209	3,694	753	13
Okaloosa	5,107	463	7,312	1,098	11,229	2,750	19
Okeechobee	426	(NA)	1,766	177	971	280	(NA)
Orange	69,645	8,895	55,241	53,679	92,530	19,435	408
Osceola	3,720	324	7,304	1,263	13,548	1,552	71
Palm Beach	59,223	7,104	67,030	16,087	54,579	21,528	674
Pasco	5,917	1,165	14,675	1,732	9,403	3,364	57
Pinellas	58,248	4,528	58,748	6,483	36,800	13,306	395
Polk	20,749	3,028	22,379	3,194	13,580	5,067	118
Putnam	544	48	2,190	50	1,166	679	9
St. Johns	2,146	1,080	5,703	1,579	9,277	2,718	38
St. Lucie	4,009	360	8,200	862	5,341	1,950	10
Santa Rosa	2,299	235	3,462	551	3,537	1,043	20
Sarasota	13,366	1,417	22,936	4,464	15,201	6,886	170
Seminole	16,874	2,626	14,931	1,860	14,917	4,990	123
Sumter	504	(NA)	1,227	171	1,395	229	(NA)
Suwannee	149	(NA)	1,220	30	708	209	(NA)
Taylor	49	(NA)	727	35	448	96	(NA)
Union	(NA)	(NA)	264	(NA)	201	28	(NA)
Volusia	10,145	4,208	24,432	3,360	18,054	6,357	63
Wakulla	83	38	278	73	594	98	(NA)
Walton	749	44	1,604	172	4,193	688	23
Washington	39	(NA)	797	(NA)	414	154	(NA)
Statewide 1/	164,377	1,222	4,768	360	7,046	2,347	(NA)
Out-of-state 2/	1,457	(NA)	81	(NA)	384	11	(NA)
Unknown 1/	6,387	620	1,660	548	1,238	1,925	213

(NA) Not available.
A/ Revised. B/ Preliminary.
1/ Reporting units without a fixed or known location within the state.
2/ Employment based in Florida, but working out of the state or country.
3/ Includes waste management and remediation services.
4/ Except public administration.
Note: Private employment. Detail may not add to totals due to disclosure editing and/or rounding. See Tables 23.70, 23.72, 23.73, and 23.74 for public employment data. See Table 6.05 for total private employment by county.
Source: State of Florida, Agency for Workforce Innovation, Labor Market Statistics, "Quarterly Census of Employment and Wages" (ES-202), Annual NAICS files, Internet site <http://www.labormarketinfo.com/index.htm> (accessed 17, July 2007).

Table 6.07. EMPLOYMENT: AVERAGE MONTHLY EMPLOYMENT COVERED BY UNEMPLOYMENT COMPENSATION LAW IN THE STATE AND METROPOLITAN STATISTICAL AREAS (MSAS) OF FLORIDA, 2006

			Government		
Metropolitan area	Total 1/	Private	Federal	State	Local
Florida	7,950,497	6,885,511	127,743	192,373	744,870
MSA, total	7,308,682	6,318,345	121,896	169,756	698,687
Cape Coral-Ft. Myers	223,990	191,487	2,329	3,861	26,314
Deltona-Daytona Beach-Ormond Beach	167,222	143,878	1,425	3,149	18,771
Ft. Walton Bech-Crestview-Destin	83,911	68,949	6,780	1,090	7,091
Gainesville	127,827	86,675	3,712	25,791	11,649
Jacksonville	587,098	514,806	16,922	12,038	43,332
Lakeland	207,753	180,194	1,369	4,008	22,182
Miami-Ft. Lauderdale-Miami Beach	2,316,526	2,001,047	34,025	28,599	252,856
Ft. Lauderdale-Pompano Beach-Deerfield Beach 2/	746,612	643,578	7,866	6,385	88,784
Miami-Miami Beach-Kendall 3/	1,007,675	860,280	19,979	14,356	113,060
West Palm Beach-Boca Raton-Boynton Beach 4/	562,239	497,189	6,180	7,858	51,012
Naples-Marco Island	134,859	122,126	675	841	11,216
Ocala	103,383	86,942	714	2,397	13,331
Orlando-Kissimmee	1,008,561	900,553	11,403	13,697	82,909
Palm Bay-Melbourne-Titusville	207,795	179,152	6,146	2,279	20,217
Palm Coast	(NA)	(NA)	(NA)	(NA)	(NA)
Panama City-Lynn Haven	73,056	59,804	3,175	1,253	8,825
Pensacola-Ferry Pass-Brent	162,079	133,888	6,723	5,192	16,275
Port St. Lucie	130,526	112,581	944	2,168	14,833
Punta Gorda	43,661	37,620	313	850	4,878
Sarasota-Bradenton-Venice	286,906	260,075	1,944	2,772	22,115
Sebastian-Vero Beach	49,922	44,165	380	566	4,811
Tallahassee	169,834	111,813	1,926	40,667	15,428
Tampa-St. Petersburg-Clearwater	1,223,773	1,082,590	20,991	18,538	101,654

(NA) Not available.
1/ Total private and public employment. See Section 23.00 and the Glossary.
2/ Metropolitan Division (Broward County).
3/ Metropolitan Division (Miami-Dade County).
4/ Metropolitan Division (Palm Beach County).
Note: Data are for North American Industry Classification System (NAICS) industries and are preliminary. Based on 2006 MSA designations. See map at front of book. Detail may not add to totals due to disclosure editing and/or rounding.

Source: State of Florida, Agency for Workforce Innovation, Labor Market Statistics, "Quarterly Census of Employment and Wages" (ES-202), Annual NAICS files, Internet site <http://www.labormarketinfo.com/index.htm> (accessed 17, July 2007).

Table 6.09. LABOR FORCE PARTICIPATION: LABOR FORCE STATUS OF THE POPULATION 16 YEARS OLD AND OVER BY SEX, RACE, AND HISPANIC ORIGIN IN FLORIDA AND THE UNITED STATES, ANNUAL AVERAGES 2005 AND 2006

Area and population group	Civilian noninsti- tutional population (1,000)	Civilian labor force		Employment		Unemployment		
		Number (1,000)	Percent- age of popu- lation	Number (1,000)	Percent- age of popu- lation	Number (1,000)	Rate	Not in Labor force
				2005				
Florida								
Total	13,885	8,715	62.8	8,401	60.5	314	3.6	5,170
Men	6,664	4,669	70.1	4,513	67.7	156	3.3	1,995
Women	7,221	4,046	56.0	3,888	53.8	158	3.9	3,175
16 to 19 years	870	337	38.7	295	34.0	41	12.3	533
White	11,524	7,162	62.2	6,954	60.3	208	2.9	4,362
Men	5,597	3,924	70.1	3,817	68.2	108	2.7	1,673
Women	5,927	3,238	54.6	3,137	52.9	101	3.1	2,689
Black	1,921	1,249	65.0	1,158	60.3	91	7.3	672
Men	872	593	68.1	551	63.2	42	7.1	279
Women	1,049	655	62.5	606	57.8	49	7.5	394
Hispanic origin 1/	2,662	1,761	66.2	1,685	63.3	76	4.3	901
Men	1,344	1,045	77.7	1,004	74.7	40	3.9	299
Women	1,318	717	54.4	681	51.7	36	5.0	601
United States								
Total	226,082	149,320	66.0	141,730	62.7	7,591	5.1	76,762
Men	109,151	80,033	73.3	75,973	69.6	4,059	5.1	29,118
Women	116,931	69,288	59.3	65,757	56.2	3,531	5.1	47,643
16 to 19 years	16,398	7,164	43.7	5,978	36.5	1,186	16.6	9,234
White	184,446	122,299	66.3	116,949	63.4	5,350	4.4	62,147
Men	90,027	66,694	74.1	63,763	70.8	2,931	4.4	23,333
Women	94,419	55,605	58.9	53,186	56.3	2,419	4.4	38,814
Black	26,517	17,013	64.2	15,313	57.7	1,700	10.0	9,504
Men	11,882	7,998	67.3	7,155	60.2	844	10.5	3,884
Women	14,635	9,014	61.6	8,158	55.7	856	9.5	5,621
Hispanic origin 1/	29,133	19,824	68.0	18,632	64.0	1,191	6.0	9,309
Men	14,962	11,985	80.1	11,337	75.8	647	5.4	2,977
Women	14,172	7,839	55.3	7,295	51.5	544	6.9	6,333

See footnotes at end of table.

Continued . . .

Table 6.09. LABOR FORCE PARTICIPATION: LABOR FORCE STATUS OF THE POPULATION 16 YEARS OLD AND OVER BY SEX, RACE, AND HISPANIC ORIGIN IN FLORIDA AND THE UNITED STATES, ANNUAL AVERAGES 2005 AND 2006 (Continued)

Area and population group	Civilian noninsti-tutional population (1,000)	Civilian labor force		Employment		Unemployment		Not in Labor force
		Number (1,000)	Percent-age of popu-lation	Number (1,000)	Percent-age of popu-lation	Number (1,000)	Rate	
				2006				
Florida								
Total	14,285	9,074	63.5	8,782	61.5	292	3.2	5,211
Men	6,866	4,810	70.1	4,657	67.8	153	3.2	2,056
Women	7,419	4,264	57.5	4,125	55.6	139	3.3	3,155
16 to 19 years	886	356	40.2	315	35.6	41	11.6	530
White	11,804	7,429	62.9	7,222	61.2	207	2.8	4,375
Men	5,729	4,010	70.0	3,900	68.1	110	2.7	1,719
Women	6,075	3,419	56.3	3,322	54.7	97	2.8	2,656
Black	1,998	1,312	65.7	1,234	61.8	78	5.9	686
Men	906	622	68.7	584	64.5	38	6.1	284
Women	1,092	690	63.2	650	59.5	40	5.8	402
Hispanic origin 1/	2,898	1,955	67.5	1,889	65.2	67	3.4	943
Men	1,439	1,140	79.2	1,107	76.9	33	2.9	299
Women	1,459	815	55.9	782	53.6	34	4.2	644
United States								
Total	228,815	151,428	66.2	144,427	63.1	7,001	4.6	77,387
Men	110,605	81,255	73.5	77,502	70.1	3,753	4.6	29,350
Women	118,210	70,173	59.4	66,925	56.6	3,247	4.6	48,037
16 to 19 years	16,678	7,281	43.7	6,162	36.9	1,119	15.4	9,397
White	186,264	123,834	66.5	118,833	63.8	5,002	4.0	62,430
Men	91,021	67,613	74.3	64,883	71.3	2,730	4.0	23,408
Women	95,242	56,221	59.0	53,950	56.6	2,271	4.0	39,021
Black	27,007	17,314	64.1	15,765	58.4	1,549	8.9	9,693
Men	12,130	8,128	67.0	7,354	60.6	774	9.5	4,002
Women	14,877	9,186	61.7	8,410	56.5	775	8.4	5,691
Hispanic origin 1/	30,103	20,694	68.7	19,613	65.2	1,081	5.2	9,409
Men	15,473	12,488	80.7	11,887	76.8	601	4.8	2,985
Women	14,630	8,206	56.1	7,725	52.8	480	5.9	6,424

1/ Persons of Hispanic origin may be of any race. Includes persons of Latino or Spanish origin.
Note: Data are preliminary.

Source: U.S., Department of Labor, Bureau of Labor Statistics, Local Area Unemployment Statistics, Annual Average Tables: Statewide Data, "Employment Status of the Civilian Noninstitutional Population in States by Sex, Race, Hispanic or Latino Ethnicity, and Detailed Age," 2005 and 2006, Internet site <http://www.bls.gov/> (accessed 18, September 2007).

Table 6.11. LABOR FORCE: ESTIMATES BY EMPLOYMENT STATUS IN THE UNITED STATES AND IN THE STATE AND COUNTIES OF FLORIDA, 2005 AND 2006

County	2005 Labor force	2005 Employ-ment	2005 Unemployment Number	2005 Unemployment Rate	2006 Labor force	2006 Employ-ment	2006 Unemployment Number	2006 Unemployment Rate
United States 1/	149,320	141,730	7,591	5.5	151,428	144,427	7,001	4.6
Florida	8,711,000	8,376,000	335,000	3.8	8,989,000	8,693,000	296,000	3.3
Alachua	120,472	116,863	3,609	3.0	123,748	120,473	3,275	2.6
Baker	10,963	10,604	359	3.3	11,360	11,035	325	2.9
Bay	81,143	78,227	2,916	3.6	84,810	82,178	2,632	3.1
Bradford	11,508	11,135	373	3.2	12,022	11,680	342	2.8
Brevard	255,069	245,648	9,421	3.7	261,417	252,864	8,553	3.3
Broward	954,047	918,901	35,146	3.7	974,486	944,381	30,105	3.1
Calhoun	5,167	4,971	196	3.8	5,384	5,217	167	3.1
Charlotte	64,760	62,116	2,644	4.1	68,085	65,740	2,345	3.4
Citrus	50,646	48,458	2,188	4.3	54,339	52,300	2,039	3.8
Clay	85,486	82,520	2,966	3.5	88,534	85,872	2,662	3.0
Collier	145,347	140,324	5,023	3.5	153,365	148,713	4,652	3.0
Columbia	28,279	27,301	978	3.5	29,520	28,595	925	3.1
DeSoto	13,387	12,772	615	4.6	14,412	13,901	511	3.5
Dixie	5,455	5,245	210	3.8	5,774	5,580	194	3.4
Duval	415,946	399,159	16,787	4.0	430,322	415,377	14,945	3.5
Escambia	133,041	127,827	5,214	3.9	136,211	131,882	4,329	3.2
Flagler	29,514	28,208	1,306	4.4	31,480	30,167	1,313	4.2
Franklin	5,056	4,871	185	3.7	5,159	5,009	150	2.9
Gadsden	20,172	19,380	792	3.9	20,728	20,012	716	3.5
Gilchrist	7,303	7,066	237	3.2	7,504	7,285	219	2.9
Glades	4,237	4,028	209	4.9	4,549	4,369	180	4.0
Gulf	6,223	6,013	210	3.4	6,619	6,425	194	2.9
Hamilton	4,541	4,355	186	4.1	4,660	4,485	175	3.8
Hardee	11,273	10,731	542	4.8	12,091	11,625	466	3.9
Hendry	17,164	15,884	1,280	7.5	17,706	16,615	1,091	6.2
Hernando	58,734	55,949	2,785	4.7	60,263	57,655	2,608	4.3
Highlands	39,420	37,739	1,681	4.3	41,684	40,194	1,490	3.6
Hillsborough	586,876	565,533	21,343	3.6	601,719	582,784	18,935	3.1
Holmes	8,235	7,935	300	3.6	8,689	8,428	261	3.0
Indian River	57,671	54,839	2,832	4.9	59,596	57,102	2,494	4.2
Jackson	20,735	19,994	741	3.6	21,502	20,755	747	3.5
Jefferson	6,708	6,494	214	3.2	6,906	6,706	200	2.9
Lafayette	2,753	2,669	84	3.1	2,857	2,779	78	2.7
Lake	117,941	113,470	4,471	3.8	123,126	119,036	4,090	3.3
Lee	268,910	260,173	8,737	3.2	283,015	274,933	8,082	2.9
Leon	135,575	131,255	4,320	3.2	139,341	135,536	3,805	2.7

See footnotes at end of table.

Continued . . .

Table 6.11. LABOR FORCE: ESTIMATES BY EMPLOYMENT STATUS IN THE UNITED STATES AND IN THE STATE AND COUNTIES OF FLORIDA, 2005 AND 2006 (Continued)

County	2005 Labor force	2005 Employment	2005 Unemployment Number	2005 Unemployment Rate	2006 Labor force	2006 Employment	2006 Unemployment Number	2006 Unemployment Rate
Levy	16,272	15,644	628	3.9	16,791	16,222	569	3.4
Liberty	3,247	3,154	93	2.9	3,561	3,469	92	2.6
Madison	7,314	6,968	346	4.7	7,431	7,061	370	5.0
Manatee	148,677	143,680	4,997	3.4	154,265	149,801	4,464	2.9
Marion	124,977	120,150	4,827	3.9	131,653	127,200	4,453	3.4
Martin	63,295	60,741	2,554	4.0	65,866	63,601	2,265	3.4
Miami-Dade	1,136,285	1,085,668	50,617	4.5	1,158,801	1,115,164	43,637	3.8
Monroe	44,829	43,598	1,231	2.7	44,520	43,413	1,107	2.5
Nassau	32,283	31,200	1,083	3.4	33,424	32,467	957	2.9
Okaloosa	95,866	93,158	2,708	2.8	98,757	96,371	2,386	2.4
Okeechobee	16,963	16,134	829	4.9	17,497	16,786	711	4.1
Orange	552,091	532,206	19,885	3.6	575,990	558,312	17,678	3.1
Osceola	116,064	111,629	4,435	3.8	121,189	117,105	4,084	3.4
Palm Beach	616,401	590,441	25,960	4.2	631,038	608,515	22,523	3.6
Pasco	182,876	175,053	7,823	4.3	187,391	180,393	6,998	3.7
Pinellas	466,730	449,045	17,685	3.8	477,891	462,742	15,149	3.2
Polk	259,783	249,357	10,426	4.0	269,119	259,755	9,364	3.5
Putnam	30,840	29,489	1,351	4.4	31,508	30,340	1,168	3.7
St. Johns	82,391	79,848	2,543	3.1	85,415	83,092	2,323	2.7
St. Lucie	110,595	105,187	5,408	4.9	114,980	110,140	4,840	4.2
Santa Rosa	66,139	63,703	2,436	3.7	67,796	65,724	2,072	3.1
Sarasota	174,060	168,293	5,767	3.3	180,823	175,463	5,360	3.0
Seminole	226,271	218,669	7,602	3.4	236,170	229,395	6,775	2.9
Sumter	25,270	24,404	866	3.4	29,152	28,364	788	2.7
Suwannee	16,376	15,772	604	3.7	17,013	16,472	541	3.2
Taylor	8,681	8,326	355	4.1	8,736	8,394	342	3.9
Union	4,960	4,809	151	3.0	5,117	4,982	135	2.6
Volusia	240,661	231,645	9,016	3.7	248,026	239,965	8,061	3.3
Wakulla	14,176	13,776	400	2.8	14,596	14,225	371	2.5
Walton	27,555	26,789	766	2.8	31,513	30,851	662	2.1
Washington	9,146	8,803	343	3.8	9,604	9,291	313	3.3

1/ United States numbers are rounded to thousands. Data are from U.S., Department of Labor, Bureau of Labor Statistics.

Note: Data are for civilian labor force, benchmark 2006. Data are for federal fund allocations. Caution is urged when using these data for short-term economic analysis. Detail may not add to totals because of rounding.

Source: State of Florida, Agency for Workforce Innovation, Bureau of Labor Market Information, *Labor Force Summary: 2006 Annual Averages,* and previous editions, Internet site <http://www.labormarketinfo.com/> (accessed 5, April 2007).

Table 6.12. LABOR FORCE: ESTIMATES BY EMPLOYMENT STATUS IN THE STATE, METROPOLITAN STATISTICAL AREAS (MSAS), AND SELECTED CITIES OF FLORIDA, 2005 AND 2006

MSA or city 1/	2005 Labor force	2005 Employ-ment	2005 Unemployment Number	2005 Unemployment Rate	2006 Labor force	2006 Employ-ment	2006 Unemployment Number	2006 Unemployment Rate
Florida	8,711,000	8,376,000	335,000	3.8	8,989,000	8,693,000	296,000	3.3
MSA								
Cape Coral-Ft. Myers	268,910	260,173	8,737	3.2	283,015	274,933	8,082	2.9
Deltona-Daytona Beach-Ormond Beach	240,661	231,645	9,016	3.7	248,026	239,965	8,061	3.3
Ft. Walton Beach-Crestview-Destin	95,866	93,158	2,708	2.8	98,757	96,371	2,386	2.4
Gainesville	127,775	123,929	3,846	3.0	131,252	127,758	3,494	2.7
Jacksonville	627,068	603,330	23,738	3.8	649,056	627,844	21,212	3.3
Lakeland	259,783	249,357	10,426	4.0	269,119	259,755	9,364	3.5
Miami-Ft. Lauderdale-Miami Beach	2,706,733	2,595,009	111,724	4.1	2,764,325	2,668,060	96,265	3.5
Naples-Marco Island	145,347	140,324	5,023	3.5	153,365	148,713	4,652	3.0
Ocala	124,977	120,150	4,827	3.9	131,653	127,200	4,453	3.4
Orlando-Kissimmee	1,012,365	975,973	36,392	3.6	1,056,473	1,023,846	32,627	3.1
Palm Bay-Melbourne-Titusville	255,069	245,648	9,421	3.7	261,417	252,864	8,553	3.3
Palm Coast	29,514	28,208	1,306	4.4	31,480	30,167	1,313	4.2
Panama City-Lynn Haven	81,143	78,227	2,916	3.6	84,810	82,178	2,632	3.1
Pensacola-Ferry Pass-Brent	199,179	191,530	7,649	3.8	204,007	197,606	6,401	3.1
Port St. Lucie-Ft. Pierce	173,890	165,928	7,962	4.6	180,847	173,742	7,105	3.9
Punta Gorda	64,760	62,116	2,644	4.1	68,085	65,740	2,345	3.4
Sarasota-Bradenton-Venice	322,737	311,972	10,765	3.3	335,088	325,265	9,823	2.9
Sebastian-Vero Beach	57,671	54,839	2,832	4.9	59,596	57,102	2,494	4.2
Tallahassee	176,632	170,906	5,726	3.2	181,571	176,479	5,092	2.8
Tampa-St. Petersburg-Clearwater	1,295,216	1,245,580	49,636	3.8	1,327,263	1,283,573	43,690	3.3
City								
Altamonte Springs	26,158	25,285	873	3.3	27,253	26,526	727	2.7
Apopka	18,467	17,885	582	3.2	19,293	18,762	531	2.8
Boca Raton	45,333	43,911	1,422	3.1	46,496	45,255	1,241	2.7
Bonita Springs	18,196	17,654	542	3.0	19,162	18,655	507	2.6
Boynton Beach	33,110	31,914	1,196	3.6	33,916	32,891	1,025	3.0
Bradenton	26,047	25,204	843	3.2	27,052	26,278	774	2.9
Cape Coral	75,709	73,387	2,322	3.1	79,751	77,551	2,200	2.8
Clearwater	56,024	54,118	1,906	3.4	57,444	55,769	1,675	2.9
Coconut Creek	26,171	25,236	935	3.6	26,711	25,936	775	2.9
Coral Gables	24,215	23,520	695	2.9	24,784	24,159	625	2.5
Coral Springs	74,437	72,015	2,422	3.3	76,100	74,012	2,088	2.7
Davie	48,699	47,174	1,525	3.1	49,763	48,482	1,281	2.6
Daytona Beach	31,855	30,605	1,250	3.9	32,815	31,704	1,111	3.4
Deerfield Beach	38,186	36,831	1,355	3.5	38,993	37,852	1,141	2.9
Delray Beach	31,153	29,924	1,229	3.9	31,907	30,840	1,067	3.3
Deltona	43,075	41,390	1,685	3.9	44,369	42,877	1,492	3.4
Dunedin	17,901	17,254	647	3.6	18,327	17,780	547	3.0
Ft. Lauderdale	91,216	87,987	3,229	3.5	93,269	90,427	2,842	3.0
Ft. Myers	28,786	27,931	855	3.0	30,270	29,516	754	2.5
Ft. Pierce	16,692	15,610	1,082	6.5	17,379	16,345	1,034	5.9
Gainesville	56,077	54,375	1,702	3.0	57,604	56,055	1,549	2.7
Hallandale Beach	16,681	15,944	737	4.4	17,062	16,386	676	4.0
Hialeah	94,897	89,454	5,443	5.7	96,317	91,885	4,432	4.6
Hollywood	78,431	75,491	2,940	3.7	80,130	77,585	2,545	3.2
Homestead	20,264	19,514	750	3.7	20,703	20,044	659	3.2

See footnotes at end of table.

Continued . . .

Table 6.12. LABOR FORCE: ESTIMATES BY EMPLOYMENT STATUS IN THE STATE, METROPOLITAN STATISTICAL AREAS (MSAS), AND SELECTED CITIES OF FLORIDA, 2005 AND 2006 (Continued)

MSA or city 1/	2005 Labor force	2005 Employment	2005 Unemployment Number	2005 Unemployment Rate	2006 Labor force	2006 Employment	2006 Unemployment Number	2006 Unemployment Rate
City (Continued)								
Jacksonville	389,835	374,502	15,333	3.9	403,482	389,719	13,763	3.4
Jupiter	25,937	25,206	731	2.8	26,639	25,978	661	2.5
Kissimmee	31,410	30,340	1,070	3.4	32,807	31,829	978	3.0
Lake Worth	18,912	18,206	706	3.7	19,342	18,764	578	3.0
Lakeland	41,636	40,172	1,464	3.5	43,171	41,847	1,324	3.1
Largo	35,743	34,395	1,348	3.8	36,621	35,444	1,177	3.2
Lauderdale Lakes	14,213	13,567	646	4.5	14,509	13,943	566	3.9
Lauderhill	29,727	28,500	1,227	4.1	30,352	29,290	1,062	3.5
Margate	29,456	28,334	1,122	3.8	30,072	29,120	952	3.2
Melbourne	38,434	37,067	1,367	3.6	39,402	38,155	1,247	3.2
Miami	162,497	154,761	7,736	4.8	165,651	158,965	6,686	4.0
Miami Beach	47,264	45,501	1,763	3.7	48,270	46,737	1,533	3.2
Miami Gardens	46,513	43,674	2,839	6.1	47,231	44,860	2,371	5.0
Miramar	56,765	54,681	2,084	3.7	58,013	56,198	1,815	3.1
North Lauderdale	23,210	22,461	749	3.2	23,740	23,084	656	2.8
North Miami	26,595	25,334	1,261	4.7	27,180	26,022	1,158	4.3
North Miami Beach	18,226	17,332	894	4.9	18,568	17,803	765	4.1
North Port	20,477	19,837	640	3.1	21,335	20,682	653	3.1
Oakland Park	19,713	19,069	644	3.3	20,159	19,598	561	2.8
Ocala	22,058	21,304	754	3.4	23,280	22,554	726	3.1
Ocoee	16,939	16,431	508	3.0	17,689	17,237	452	2.6
Orlando	119,639	115,564	4,075	3.4	124,950	121,233	3,717	3.0
Ormond Beach	19,050	18,457	593	3.1	19,641	19,120	521	2.7
Palm Bay	46,279	44,567	1,712	3.7	47,501	45,876	1,625	3.4
Palm Beach Gardens	26,174	25,489	685	2.6	26,874	26,270	604	2.2
Palm Coast	23,601	22,592	1,009	4.3	25,191	24,161	1,030	4.1
Panama City	17,204	16,579	625	3.6	17,975	17,417	558	3.1
Pembroke Pines	81,664	78,944	2,720	3.3	83,462	81,133	2,329	2.8
Pensacola	25,632	24,735	897	3.5	26,253	25,520	733	2.8
Pinellas Park	24,042	23,122	920	3.8	24,583	23,827	756	3.1
Plant City	14,473	14,116	357	2.5	15,059	14,546	513	3.4
Plantation	51,778	50,161	1,617	3.1	52,895	51,552	1,343	2.5
Pompano Beach	50,584	48,773	1,811	3.6	51,707	50,126	1,581	3.1
Port Orange	27,843	27,035	808	2.9	28,770	28,006	764	2.7
Port St. Lucie	64,705	62,240	2,465	3.8	67,518	65,171	2,347	3.5
Riviera Beach	14,891	14,242	649	4.4	15,254	14,677	577	3.8
St. Petersburg	128,740	124,029	4,711	3.7	131,883	127,812	4,071	3.1
Sanford	22,667	21,815	852	3.8	23,710	22,886	824	3.5
Sarasota	27,081	26,241	840	3.1	28,124	27,359	765	2.7
Sunrise	48,584	46,800	1,784	3.7	49,648	48,098	1,550	3.1
Tallahassee	85,739	82,913	2,826	3.3	88,094	85,617	2,477	2.8
Tamarac	28,168	26,964	1,204	4.3	28,739	27,712	1,027	3.6
Tampa	159,380	153,456	5,924	3.7	163,382	158,137	5,245	3.2
Titusville	20,262	19,506	756	3.7	20,709	20,079	630	3.0
Wellington	29,047	28,171	876	3.0	29,811	29,033	778	2.6
West Palm Beach	50,328	48,512	1,816	3.6	51,669	49,997	1,672	3.2
Weston	34,423	33,455	968	2.8	35,222	34,383	839	2.4
Winter Springs	17,979	17,401	578	3.2	18,765	18,255	510	2.7

1/ Metropolitan Statistical Areas (MSAs) based on 2006 MSA designations and cities with a population of 32,000 or more in 2006.

Note: Civilian labor force.

Source: State of Florida, Agency for Workforce Innovation, Bureau of Labor Market Information, *Labor Force Summary: 2006 Annual Averages,* and previous editions, Internet site <http://www.labormarketinfo.com/> (accessed 5, April 2007).

Table 6.13. WAGES: MEDIAN WEEKLY EARNINGS OF FULL-TIME WAGE AND SALARY WORKERS BY SEX IN FLORIDA, OTHER SUNBELT STATES, AND THE UNITED STATES, 2006

State	Both sexes		Female		Male		Women's earnings as a percentage of men's 1/
	Number of workers (1,000)	Median weekly earnings (dollars)	Number of workers (1,000)	Median weekly earnings (dollars)	Number of workers (1,000)	Median weekly earnings (dollars)	
Florida	6,605	629	3,051	579	3,555	688	84.2
Alabama	1,657	614	736	535	922	710	75.4
Arizona	2,225	641	938	604	1,288	681	88.7
Arkansas	952	591	433	522	519	624	83.7
California	11,978	713	4,962	670	7,016	751	89.1
Georgia	3,508	626	1,586	586	1,922	694	84.4
Louisiana	1,415	621	632	499	783	722	69.1
Mississippi	908	564	415	497	493	615	80.8
New Mexico	655	615	284	506	372	698	72.5
North Carolina	3,242	599	1,455	544	1,787	637	85.3
Oklahoma	1,234	599	562	509	673	703	72.3
South Carolina	1,485	602	670	525	815	673	78.0
Tennessee	2,165	582	965	512	1,200	643	79.6
Texas	8,331	610	3,515	546	4,815	667	82.0
Virginia	2,914	714	1,311	608	1,603	824	73.8
United States	106,106	671	46,358	600	59,747	743	80.8

1/ Computed using unrounded medians and may differ slightly from percentages computed using the rounded medians displayed.

Source: U.S., Department of Labor, Bureau of Labor Statistics, Current Population Survey, *Highlights of Women's Earnings in 2006,* Report 1000, issued September 2007, Internet site <http://stats.bls.gov/> (accessed 12, September 2007).

Table 6.14. SURVEY OF BUSINESS OWNERS: ESTIMATES OF BUSINESS OWNERSHIP BY SEX, RACE AND HISPANIC ORIGIN, 2002

Characteristic	All firms		Firms with paid employment			
	Firms (number)	Sales and receipts ($1,000)	Firms (number)	Sales and receipts ($1,000)	Employ-ment (number)	Annual payroll ($1,000)
Florida	1,539,207	1,075,802,198	360,179	1,022,017,541	6,205,482	185,846,799
Male	884,919	371,480,391	221,677	336,265,725	2,233,504	65,948,322
Female	437,355	61,275,106	65,154	51,178,294	432,071	9,813,263
Equally male-/ female-owned	181,246	42,304,361	50,668	34,402,336	292,455	6,628,965
White	1,354,382	456,967,532	315,821	407,119,193	2,805,842	79,314,299
Black	102,053	5,721,314	7,025	3,719,790	54,742	906,163
American Indian and Alaska Native	9,923	640,810	832	375,819	3,898	94,976
Asian	41,258	11,221,605	13,610	10,085,422	91,422	1,972,616
Native Hawaiian and other Pacific Islander	1,480	71,540	133	50,618	832	21,702
Hispanic	266,688	40,891,975	39,955	33,380,312	222,516	5,869,062
Non-Hispanic	1,236,833	434,170,821	297,545	388,468,980	2,735,528	76,522,264
Publicly-held, foreign owned, and not-for-profit	31,971	596,693,081	22,323	595,064,540	3,209,309	103,385,143

Source: U.S., Department of Commerce, Census Bureau, Survey of Business Owners, *Final Estimates of Business Ownership by Gender, Hispanic or Latino Origin, and Race, 2002,* released September 14, 2006, Internet site <http://www.census.gov/> (accessed 19, April 2007).

Table 6.15. WOMEN-OWNED BUSINESSES: NUMBER, SALES, EMPLOYMENT, AND PAYROLL IN THE STATE AND SELECTED COUNTIES OF FLORIDA, 2002

County	All firms	Sales and receipts ($1,000)	Firms with paid employment: Number	Sales and receipts ($1,000)	Employ- ment	Annual payroll ($1,000)
Florida	437,355	61,275,106	65,154	51,178,294	432,071	9,813,263
Alachua	5,068	748,223	780	657,849	7,060	194,911
Baker	197	38,306	77	36,667	276	3,101
Bay	3,071	297,798	473	234,764	2,911	59,760
Bradford	406	20,934	(S)	(S)	(S)	(S)
Brevard	12,501	1,143,023	1,755	873,328	9,866	209,096
Broward	54,889	7,396,816	8,227	6,197,178	42,739	1,196,987
Charlotte	3,539	244,888	385	135,217	1,673	42,981
Citrus	2,840	213,186	350	139,221	1,693	33,730
Clay	3,155	306,827	543	232,171	2,667	53,205
Collier	8,279	1,114,995	1,534	840,141	9,349	230,519
Columbia	1,107	104,261	156	76,785	1,176	18,119
DeSoto	(S)	(S)	(S)	(S)	(S)	(S)
Dixie	142	15,212	(S)	(S)	(S)	(S)
Duval	17,733	2,689,856	2,961	2,308,234	19,323	499,898
Escambia	6,120	1,309,961	1,010	1,137,436	6,757	153,752
Flagler	1,701	95,151	(S)	(S)	(S)	(S)
Franklin	(S)	(S)	(S)	(S)	(S)	(S)
Gadsden	424	74,492	(S)	(S)	(S)	(S)
Gilchrist	(S)	(S)	(S)	(S)	(S)	(S)
Gulf	409	27,457	(S)	(S)	(S)	(S)
Hamilton	(S)	(S)	(S)	(S)	(S)	(S)
Hardee	510	64,605	50	57,462	297	4,165
Hendry	290	60,983	(S)	(S)	(S)	(S)
Hernando	2,190	189,696	330	151,974	1,731	34,335
Highlands	1,596	192,573	221	158,360	1,184	22,003
Hillsborough	22,076	5,003,741	3,736	4,338,130	29,794	684,688
Holmes	224	26,545	(S)	(S)	(S)	(S)
Indian River	2,649	314,510	463	261,024	3,531	71,244
Jackson	660	34,936	(S)	(S)	(S)	(S)
Jefferson	(S)	(S)	(S)	(S)	(S)	(S)
Lafayette	(S)	(S)	(S)	(S)	(S)	(S)
Lake	5,238	463,912	663	307,976	3,345	56,247
Lee	12,360	1,355,405	1,678	1,046,583	8,805	218,674
Leon	5,414	795,593	908	616,423	12,875	206,123

See footnotes at end of table.

Continued . . .

Table 6.15. WOMEN-OWNED BUSINESSES: NUMBER, SALES, EMPLOYMENT, AND PAYROLL IN THE STATE AND SELECTED COUNTIES OF FLORIDA, 2002 (Continued)

County	All firms	Sales and receipts ($1,000)	Firms with paid employment: Number	Sales and receipts ($1,000)	Employ-ment	Annual payroll ($1,000)
Levy	635	90,635	(S)	(S)	(S)	(S)
Liberty	(S)	(S)	(S)	(S)	(S)	(S)
Madison	(S)	(S)	(S)	(S)	(S)	(S)
Manatee	6,302	834,137	1,007	702,799	9,883	317,245
Marion	5,390	687,213	(S)	(S)	(S)	(S)
Martin	3,923	456,064	834	316,587	3,269	74,148
Miami-Dade	88,168	8,618,331	10,621	6,882,059	70,214	1,478,488
Monroe	2,681	516,052	621	433,944	3,363	77,802
Nassau	1,431	112,364	208	77,371	827	12,461
Okaloosa	4,207	528,435	716	399,271	5,270	87,830
Okeechobee	508	45,635	(S)	(S)	(S)	(S)
Orange	22,286	7,954,033	3,809	7,522,883	26,590	671,991
Osceola	3,974	263,639	495	163,031	2,429	41,017
Palm Beach	37,808	5,630,393	5,896	4,669,786	40,633	1,029,206
Pasco	6,626	474,655	874	328,437	8,407	77,947
Pinellas	23,631	2,790,367	3,821	2,249,446	20,368	543,903
Polk	7,874	1,895,884	1,286	1,734,371	17,849	287,838
Putnam	1,077	39,833	106	25,930	379	6,534
St. Johns	3,628	357,680	568	267,274	3,456	64,258
St. Lucie	4,475	688,160	707	620,796	5,107	104,061
Santa Rosa	3,343	168,849	257	115,683	1,319	32,252
Sarasota	9,948	1,085,552	1,794	812,565	10,033	225,864
Seminole	8,803	1,270,307	1,586	1,057,341	10,067	231,582
Sumter	932	523,600	(S)	(S)	(S)	(S)
Suwannee	468	59,053	53	45,877	215	5,632
Taylor	(S)	(S)	(S)	(S)	(S)	(S)
Volusia	10,202	1,378,521	1,501	1,144,582	7,362	136,732
Wakulla	633	42,882	(S)	(S)	(S)	(S)
Walton	1,371	71,763	(S)	(S)	(S)	(S)
Washington	424	22,558	(S)	(S)	(S)	(S)

(S) Firm count is less than 3, or the relative standard error of the sales and receipts is 50 percent or more.

Note: Only counties with 100 or more women-owned firms are shown. Some data are revised.

Source: U.S., Department of Commerce, Census Bureau, *2002 Economic Census: Survey of Business Owners, Women-Owned Firms*, Company Statistics Series, SB02-00CS-WMN (RV), Issued August 2006, Internet site <http://www.census.gov/> (accessed 11, May 2007)

Table 6.16. BLACK-OWNED BUSINESSES: NUMBER, SALES, EMPLOYMENT, AND PAYROLL IN THE STATE AND SELECTED COUNTIES OF FLORIDA, 2002

County	All firms	Sales and receipts ($1,000)	Firms with paid employment Number	Sales and receipts ($1,000)	Employ- ment	Annual payroll ($1,000)
Florida	102,053	5,721,314	7,025	3,719,790	54,742	906,163
Alachua	866	64,326	(S)	(S)	(S)	(S)
Bay	377	25,982	50	19,447	423	7,992
Bradford	(S)	(S)	(S)	(S)	(S)	(S)
Brevard	1,474	161,268	164	124,911	948	19,405
Broward	22,065	975,503	1,186	572,034	10,538	119,188
Charlotte	229	14,776	(S)	(S)	(S)	(S)
Clay	433	14,521	(S)	(S)	(S)	(S)
Collier	565	26,757	(S)	(S)	(S)	(S)
Columbia 1/	136	25,003	(S)	(D)	(NA)	(D)
DeSoto 1/	(S)	(S)	(S)	(D)	(NA)	(D)
Duval	6,164	349,529	598	257,149	6,044	74,399
Escambia	(S)	(S)	(S)	(S)	(S)	(S)
Flagler	164	15,894	(S)	(S)	(S)	(S)
Gadsden	328	10,237	(S)	(S)	(S)	(S)
Hernando	(S)	(S)	(S)	(S)	(S)	(S)
Highlands	(S)	(S)	(S)	(S)	(S)	(S)
Hillsborough	4,330	264,223	407	160,601	1,627	34,121
Indian River	346	11,107	(S)	(S)	(S)	(S)
Jackson	(S)	(S)	(S)	(S)	(S)	(S)
Jefferson 1/	(S)	(S)	(S)	(D)	(NA)	(D)
Lake 2/	797	(D)	39	(D)	(NA)	(D)
Lee	1,300	64,828	150	45,975	815	10,485
Leon	1,777	80,026	180	43,457	837	13,422
Madison	(S)	(S)	(S)	(S)	(S)	(S)
Manatee	503	23,333	(S)	(S)	(S)	(S)
Marion	1,201	40,216	(S)	(S)	(S)	(S)
Martin	304	93,529	(S)	(S)	(S)	(S)
Miami-Dade	28,335	1,634,395	1,532	1,149,018	16,783	276,313
Monroe	347	6,273	28	3,511	49	830
Okaloosa	399	66,310	(S)	(S)	(S)	(S)
Orange	7,835	450,272	541	302,388	3,375	79,238
Osceola	1,082	26,344	64	11,060	372	2,725
Palm Beach	8,169	431,852	500	151,894	2,138	49,342
Pasco	(S)	(S)	(S)	(S)	(S)	(S)
Pinellas	3,085	171,216	242	103,525	1,073	30,190
Polk	1,609	92,153	134	32,408	391	9,022
Putnam	439	17,022	24	7,355	96	2,656
St. Lucie	856	46,600	95	37,744	483	7,447
Santa Rosa	208	3,425	8	1,244	37	441
Sarasota	(S)	(S)	(S)	(S)	(S)	(S)
Seminole	1,340	96,155	95	69,944	753	22,401
Sumter 3/	(S)	(D)	(S)	(D)	(NA)	(D)
Volusia	868	151,806	80	139,214	818	21,394
Washington	(S)	(S)	(S)	(S)	(S)	(S)

(D) Data withheld to avoid disclosure of information about individual firms.
(S) Firm count is less than 3, or the relative standard error of sales and receipts is 50 percent or more.
Employment ranges: 1/ 20-99. 2/ 250-499. 3/ 0-19.
Note: Only counties with 100 or more black-owned firms are shown. Some data are revised.

Source: U.S., Department of Commerce, Census Bureau, *2002 Economic Census: Survey of Business Owners, Black-Owned Firms,* Company Statistics Series, SB02-00CS-BLK (RV), issued August 2006, Internet site <http://www.census.gov/> (accessed 11, May 2007).

Table 6.20. OCCUPATIONS: PRIVATE INDUSTRY EMPLOYMENT, PARTICIPATION RATE AND OCCUPATIONAL DISTRIBUTION OF WHITE AND MINORITY EMPLOYEES BY SEX AND BY OCCUPATION IN FLORIDA, 2005

Occupation	All		White		Minority 1/	
	Male	Female	Male	Female	Male	Female
	Number employed					
Total	1,234,391	1,241,050	741,697	727,215	492,694	513,835
Officials and managers	154,654	93,628	121,613	69,901	33,041	23,727
Professionals	152,684	202,528	114,667	143,837	38,017	58,691
Technicians	80,538	74,198	51,959	44,169	28,579	30,029
Sales workers	177,674	229,340	114,240	135,262	63,434	94,078
Office and clerical workers	90,403	305,383	50,581	179,210	39,822	126,173
Craft workers	123,484	16,291	77,706	8,987	45,778	7,304
Operatives	151,974	44,939	74,576	19,141	77,398	25,798
Laborers	120,005	46,862	47,243	18,722	72,762	28,140
Service workers	182,975	227,881	89,112	107,986	93,863	119,895
	Participation rate (percentage)					
Total	49.9	50.1	30.0	29.4	19.9	20.8
Officials and managers	62.3	37.7	49.0	28.2	13.3	9.6
Professionals	43.0	57.0	32.3	40.5	10.7	16.5
Technicians	52.0	48.0	33.6	28.5	18.5	19.4
Sales workers	43.7	56.3	28.1	33.2	15.6	23.1
Office and clerical workers	22.8	77.2	12.8	45.3	10.1	31.9
Craft workers	88.3	11.7	55.6	6.4	32.8	5.2
Operatives	77.2	22.8	37.9	9.7	39.3	13.1
Laborers	71.9	28.1	28.3	11.2	43.6	16.9
Service workers	44.5	55.5	21.7	26.3	22.8	29.2
	Occupational distribution (percentage)					
Total	100.0	100.0	100.0	100.0	100.0	100.0
Officials and managers	12.5	7.5	16.4	9.6	6.7	4.6
Professionals	12.4	16.3	15.5	19.8	7.7	11.4
Technicians	6.5	6.0	7.0	6.1	5.8	5.8
Sales workers	14.4	18.5	15.4	18.6	12.9	18.3
Office and clerical workers	7.3	24.6	6.8	24.6	8.1	24.6
Craft workers	10.0	1.3	10.5	1.2	9.3	1.4
Operatives	12.3	3.6	10.1	2.6	15.7	5.0
Laborers	9.7	3.8	6.4	2.6	14.8	5.5
Service workers	14.8	18.4	12.0	14.8	19.1	23.3

1/ Includes Black, Hispanic, Asian-American, and American Indian.

Note: Private industry data, based on 1997 North American Industry Classification System (NAICS) codes, from the 2005 Equal Employment Opportunity employer information report (EEO-1). Includes private employers with 100 or more employees, or 50 or more employees and: 1) have a federal contract or first-tier subcontract worth $50,000 or more; or 2) act as depositories of federal funds in any amount; or 3) act as issuing and paying agents for U.S. Savings Bonds and Notes.

Source: U.S., Equal Employment Opportunity Commission, *Job Patterns for Minorities and Women in Private Industry, 2005,* Internet site <http://www.eeoc.gov/> (accessed 4, June 2007).

Table 6.25. OCCUPATIONS: EMPLOYMENT ESTIMATES, 2006, PROJECTIONS, 2014, AND AVERAGE ANNUAL JOB OPENINGS BY OCCUPATIONAL CATEGORY IN FLORIDA

Major occupational category	Employment 2006	Employment Projections 2014	Annual percentage change	Average annual openings Total	Average annual openings Due to growth	Average annual openings Due to separations
All occupations, total 1/	8,807,799	10,207,095	1.99	380,908	178,011	202,897
Management 1/	372,667	425,402	1.77	12,910	6,713	6,197
Top executives	89,199	105,685	2.31	3,655	2,061	1,594
Marketing, public relations, and sales managers	25,562	31,112	2.71	1,137	694	444
Operations specialties managers	51,344	60,711	2.28	2,009	1,171	838
Business and financial operations	379,302	451,910	2.39	15,439	9,112	6,327
Business operations specialists	213,290	257,897	2.61	9,095	5,577	3,518
Financial specialists	166,012	194,013	2.11	6,344	3,535	2,809
Computer and mathematical	165,035	207,509	3.22	7,393	5,310	2,083
Computer specialists	158,836	200,754	3.30	7,175	5,240	1,935
Mathematical scientists	6,199	6,755	1.12	217	70	147
Architecture and engineering	129,731	151,045	2.05	5,441	2,665	2,776
Architects, surveyors, and cartographers	15,807	19,410	2.85	732	450	282
Engineers	64,119	74,673	2.06	2,577	1,320	1,257
Drafters, engineering, and mapping technicians	49,806	56,962	1.80	2,132	895	1,238
Life, physical, and social science	60,049	70,565	2.19	2,695	1,316	1,379
Life scientists	8,843	10,550	2.41	425	213	212
Physical scientists	11,434	13,124	1.85	458	211	247
Social scientists and related workers	25,380	30,073	2.31	1,192	587	605
Life, physical, and social science technicians	14,392	16,818	2.11	620	305	315
Community and social services	105,363	127,057	2.57	4,578	2,712	1,866
Social workers and community and social service specialists	86,371	103,781	2.52	3,749	2,176	1,573
Religious workers	18,992	23,276	2.82	829	536	294
Legal	89,829	108,614	2.61	3,327	2,348	979
Lawyers, judges, and related workers	55,326	65,744	2.35	1,980	1,302	678
Legal support workers	34,504	42,870	3.03	1,348	1,046	302
Education, training, and library 1/	415,583	505,133	2.69	18,971	11,194	7,778
Postsecondary teachers	74,141	93,858	3.32	4,028	2,465	1,563
Primary, secondary, and special education teachers	185,699	224,193	2.59	8,667	4,812	3,855
Other teachers and instructors	78,835	95,565	2.65	3,010	2,091	919
Librarians, curators, and archivists	11,548	13,038	1.61	492	186	306
Arts, entertainment, sports, and media	146,493	167,251	1.77	5,189	2,617	2,572
Art and design workers	45,063	50,378	1.47	1,342	666	676
Entertainers, athletes, and related workers	39,850	45,730	1.84	1,522	755	767
Media and communications workers	42,748	49,735	2.04	1,608	874	734
Media and communications equipment workers	18,833	21,408	1.71	718	322	396
Healthcare practitioners and technical	431,678	529,880	2.84	19,970	12,275	7,694
Health diagnosing and treating practitioners	265,860	326,874	2.87	12,512	7,627	4,886
Health technologists and technicians	161,169	197,633	2.83	7,277	4,558	2,719
Healthcare support 1/	210,864	266,801	3.32	10,146	6,992	3,153
Nursing, Psychiatric, and home health aides	120,257	150,467	3.14	5,253	3,776	1,477
Occupational and physical therapist assistants	7,313	9,547	3.82	387	279	107
Protective service 1/	225,156	257,433	1.79	10,392	4,036	6,356
First-line supervisors, protective service workers	11,666	13,250	1.70	567	198	369
Fire fighting and prevention workers	22,895	27,851	2.71	1,249	621	628
Law enforcement workers	83,111	92,815	1.46	3,123	1,213	1,910
Food preparation and serving related 1/	749,705	886,475	2.28	46,503	17,096	29,407
Supervisors, food preparation and serving	51,692	60,815	2.21	2,363	1,140	1,223
Cooks and food preparation workers	166,943	198,021	2.33	9,019	3,885	5,134
Food and beverage serving workers	433,341	511,335	2.25	29,730	9,749	19,980

See footnote at end of table.   Continued . . .

Table 6.25. OCCUPATIONS: EMPLOYMENT ESTIMATES, 2006, PROJECTIONS, 2014, AND AVERAGE ANNUAL JOB OPENINGS BY OCCUPATIONAL CATEGORY IN FLORIDA (Continued)

Major occupational category	Employment 2006	Employment Projections 2014	Annual percentage change	Average annual openings Total	Due to growth	Due to separations
Building and grounds cleaning and maintenance	376,085	453,888	2.59	16,854	9,725	7,129
Building cleaning and pest control workers	227,686	273,156	2.50	9,914	5,684	4,230
Grounds maintenance workers	121,090	147,908	2.77	5,841	3,352	2,488
Personal care and service 1/	277,230	328,978	2.33	12,980	6,469	6,512
Supervisors, personal care, and service workers	14,474	17,056	2.23	668	323	345
Animal care and service workers	14,872	17,860	2.51	710	374	336
Entertainment attendants and related workers	47,403	57,705	2.72	2,784	1,288	1,496
Funeral service workers	2,486	2,556	0.35	60	9	52
Personal appearance workers	53,292	61,570	1.94	2,050	1,035	1,015
Transportation, tourism, & lodging attendants	20,455	22,786	1.42	672	291	380
Sales and related 1/	1,104,510	1,247,704	1.62	51,126	17,938	33,188
Supervisors, sales workers	118,970	127,777	0.93	3,228	1,101	2,127
Retail sales workers	562,062	640,002	1.73	32,013	9,781	22,231
Sales representatives, services	117,109	133,881	1.79	4,276	2,097	2,179
Sales representatives, wholesale and manufacturing	141,482	162,241	1.83	6,174	2,595	3,579
Office and administrative support 1/	1,567,544	1,728,140	1.28	57,164	22,327	34,837
Communications equipment operators	18,066	17,436	-0.44	467	1	466
Financial clerks	255,393	288,635	1.63	9,847	4,155	5,692
Information and record clerks	396,159	456,467	1.90	16,665	8,664	8,001
Material recording, scheduling, and distributing	245,772	249,091	0.17	8,348	880	7,468
Secretaries and administrative assistants	279,713	307,887	1.26	8,744	3,522	5,222
Farming, fishing, and forestry	93,858	99,817	0.79	3,298	758	2,540
Supervisors, farming, fishing, and forestry	5,221	5,343	0.29	139	20	119
Agricultural workers	85,016	90,838	0.86	3,071	728	2,344
Fishing and hunting workers	696	674	-0.40	21	0	21
Forest, conservation, and logging workers	2,924	2,962	0.16	67	10	57
Construction and extraction 1/	617,201	733,495	2.36	25,920	14,540	11,380
Construction trades workers	460,917	548,068	2.36	18,829	10,894	7,935
Helpers, construction trades	36,680	42,822	2.09	2,227	768	1,459
Extraction workers	1,482	1,617	1.14	57	20	37
Installation, maintenance, and repair 1/	352,349	407,654	1.96	14,611	6,913	7,698
Electrical and electronic equipment installers, and repairers	42,305	47,332	1.49	1,414	628	785
Vehicle and mobile equipment mechanics	107,292	124,077	1.96	4,818	2,098	2,720
Production 1/	360,346	387,953	0.96	12,448	3,955	8,493
Assemblers and fabricators	76,077	82,165	1.00	2,765	879	1,887
Food processing workers	28,474	31,688	1.41	1,036	408	628
Metal workers and plastic workers	48,191	50,344	0.56	1,556	364	1,192
Printing workers	16,971	17,557	0.43	510	110	400
Textile, apparel, and furnishing workers	41,711	45,167	1.04	1,367	511	856
Woodworkers	13,089	13,039	-0.05	362	29	333
Plant and system operators	11,699	12,377	0.72	462	117	345
Transportation and material-moving 1/	577,221	664,391	1.89	23,554	10,999	12,555
Supervisors, transportation, & material-moving	18,932	21,796	1.89	787	358	429
Air transportation workers	8,362	9,072	1.06	305	89	217
Motor vehicle operators	236,432	279,431	2.27	8,618	5,375	3,244
Water transportation workers	9,760	11,365	2.06	532	202	330
Material moving workers	282,551	320,185	1.66	12,467	4,788	7,679

1/ Includes other occupations within categories not shown separately.

Source: State of Florida, Agency for Workforce Innovation, Bureau of Labor Market Information, *Employment Statistics Projections to 2014,* Internet site <http://www.labormarketinfo.com/> (accessed 5, February 2007).

Table 6.26. OCCUPATIONS: EMPLOYMENT ESTIMATES, 2006, AND PROJECTIONS, 2014 OF THE FASTEST-GROWING OCCUPATIONS IN THE STATE OF FLORIDA

Occupation	Estimates 2006	Projections 2014	Annual percentage change
Network systems and data communications analysts	18,878	26,722	5.19
Physician assistants	4,641	6,511	5.04
Medical assistants	28,667	39,446	4.70
Computer software engineers, applications	17,555	23,809	4.45
Computer software engineers, systems software	17,229	23,009	4.19
Network and computer systems administrators	13,793	18,384	4.16
Database administrators	5,450	7,253	4.14
Tile and marble setters	9,024	11,978	4.09
Home health aides	30,303	40,191	4.08
Dental hygienists	9,911	13,017	3.92
Paralegals and legal assistants	19,667	25,749	3.87
Dental assistants	14,678	19,200	3.85
Special education teachers, preschool—elementary	8,767	11,324	3.65
Health specialties teachers, postsecondary	8,289	10,706	3.64
Occupational therapists	5,491	7,074	3.60
Farm workers, farm and ranch animals	12,155	15,621	3.56
Pharmacy technicians	19,524	25,074	3.55
Personal and home care aides	11,022	14,127	3.52
Vocational education teachers, postsecondary	5,957	7,614	3.48
Highway maintenance workers	4,001	5,106	3.45
Veterinary technologists and technicians	5,004	6,366	3.40
Physical therapists	10,326	13,088	3.34
Computer systems analysts	26,400	33,438	3.33
Bill and account collectors	28,657	36,235	3.31
Employment, recruitment, and placement specialists	13,076	16,524	3.30
Social and community service managers	4,704	5,932	3.26
Directors, religious activities and education	7,829	9,872	3.26
Special education teachers, middle school	5,080	6,394	3.23
Security and fire alarm systems installers	6,268	7,889	3.23
Medical transcriptionists	4,939	6,210	3.22
Fitness trainers and aerobics instructors	11,779	14,778	3.18
Preschool teachers, except special education	20,569	25,739	3.14
Personal financial advisors	15,545	19,419	3.12
Customer service representatives	155,861	194,576	3.10
Medical and public health social workers	5,854	7,308	3.10
Registered nurses	147,050	183,478	3.10
Self-enrichment education teachers	16,908	21,093	3.09

See footnote at end of table. Continued . . .

Table 6.26. OCCUPATIONS: EMPLOYMENT ESTIMATES, 2006, AND PROJECTIONS, 2014 OF THE FASTEST-GROWING OCCUPATIONS IN THE STATE OF FLORIDA (Continued)

Occupation	Estimates 2006	Projections 2014	Annual percentage change
Pharmacists	16,065	19,938	3.01
Child, family, and school social workers	10,973	13,615	3.01
Medical records and health information technicians	9,539	11,813	2.98
Amusement and recreation attendants	33,093	40,904	2.95
Computer and information systems managers	8,680	10,714	2.93
Medical and clinical laboratory technicians	6,536	8,060	2.91
Architects, except landscape and naval	8,457	10,424	2.91
Special education teachers, secondary school	4,327	5,332	2.90
Construction and building inspectors	7,011	8,639	2.90
Compensation, benefits, and job analysis specialists	5,245	6,452	2.88
Instructional coordinators	7,134	8,774	2.87
Kindergarten teachers, except special education	11,404	14,018	2.87
Nursing aides, orderlies, and attendants	87,418	107,433	2.86
Radiologic technologists and technicians	12,917	15,857	2.85
Public relations specialists	19,764	24,234	2.83
Payroll and timekeeping clerks	11,785	14,439	2.82
Heating, A.C., and refrigeration mechanics and installers	25,296	30,990	2.81
Cost estimators	16,872	20,664	2.81
Fire fighters	22,120	27,086	2.81
Landscaping and groundskeeping workers	113,764	139,152	2.79
Sales managers	15,259	18,657	2.78
Painters, construction and maintenance	41,416	50,612	2.78
Interviewers, except eligibility and loan	13,102	15,989	2.75
Food preparation workers	49,297	60,150	2.75
Licensed practical and licensed vocational nurses	50,501	61,436	2.71
Computer support specialists	33,080	40,230	2.70
Training and development specialists	12,141	14,748	2.68
Marketing managers	6,635	8,057	2.68
Massage therapists	10,981	13,334	2.68
Social and human service assistants	15,314	18,587	2.67
Surgeons	4,688	5,684	2.66
Respiratory therapists	6,139	7,442	2.65
Financial analysts	7,216	8,746	2.65

Note: Occupations are ranked based on the anticipated rate of growth between 2006 and 2014. Only the top 70 occupations out of 100 are included.

Source: State of Florida, Agency for Workforce Innovation, Bureau of Labor Market Information, *Occupational Employment Statistics Projections to 2014,* Internet site <http://www.labormarketinfo.com/> (accessed 5, February 2007).

Table 6.40. INDUSTRY GROWTH TRENDS: EMPLOYMENT ESTIMATES, 2006, AND PROJECTIONS 2014, OF THE FASTEST-GROWING INDUSTRIES AND INDUSTRIES GAINING THE MOST NEW GROWTH IN THE STATE OF FLORIDA

Industry	Estimates 2006	Projections 2014	Annual change Total	Annual change Percentage
	Fastest-growing industries 1/			
Administrative and support services	837,898	1,101,428	32,941	3.93
Educational services	128,308	164,187	4,485	3.50
Water transportation	12,915	16,480	446	3.45
Ambulatory health care services	344,446	437,951	11,688	3.39
Social assistance	101,756	129,052	3,412	3.35
Museums, historical sites, and similar institutions	6,122	7,660	192	3.14
Furniture and home furnishings stores	44,294	55,341	1,381	3.12
Motion picture and sound recording industries	14,839	18,192	419	2.82
Nursing and residential care facilities	155,761	190,101	4,292	2.76
Management of companies and enterprises	73,932	90,153	2,028	2.74
Professional, scientific, and technical services	439,621	534,618	11,875	2.70
Amusement, gambling, and recreation industries	138,450	165,156	3,338	2.41
Specialty trade contractors	394,104	469,441	9,417	2.39
ISPs, web search portals, and data processing services	26,303	31,029	591	2.25
Membership associations and organizations	172,346	203,127	3,848	2.23
Food services and drinking places	572,252	673,737	12,686	2.22
Electronics and appliance stores	36,369	42,730	795	2.19
General merchandise stores	180,497	211,768	3,909	2.17
Building material and garden supply stores	86,728	101,371	1,830	2.11
Repair and maintenance	77,568	90,052	1,560	2.01
	Industries gaining the most new jobs 2/			
Administrative and support services	837,898	1,101,428	32,941	3.93
Local government	747,349	860,567	14,152	1.89
Food services and drinking places	572,252	673,737	12,686	2.22
Professional, scientific, and technical services	439,621	534,618	11,875	2.70
Ambulatory health care services	344,446	437,951	11,688	3.39
Specialty trade contractors	394,104	469,441	9,417	2.39
Educational services	128,308	164,187	4,485	3.50
Nursing and residential care facilities	155,761	190,101	4,292	2.76
Hospitals	239,595	271,497	3,988	1.66
General merchandise stores	180,497	211,768	3,909	2.17
Membership associations and organizations	172,346	203,127	3,848	2.23
Credit intermediation and related activities	185,489	214,772	3,660	1.97
State government	212,132	239,629	3,437	1.62
Social assistance	101,756	129,052	3,412	3.35
Amusement, gambling, and recreation industries	138,450	165,156	3,338	2.41
Merchant wholesalers, durable goods	184,019	208,819	3,100	1.68
Accommodation	158,858	179,083	2,528	1.59
Motor vehicle and parts dealers	134,672	153,869	2,400	1.78
Insurance carriers and related activities	135,156	154,019	2,358	1.74
Construction of buildings	127,518	145,823	2,288	1.79

1/ Ranked by annual percentage change. Industries with a minimum employment of 3,500 jobs in 2006.
2/ Ranked by number of new jobs.

Source: State of Florida, Agency for Workforce Innovation, Bureau of Labor Market Information, *Occupational Employment Statistics Projections to 2014,* Internet site <http://www.labormarketinfo.com/> (accessed 5, February 2007).

Table 6.41. OCCUPATION GROWTH TRENDS: EMPLOYMENT ESTIMATES, 2006, AND PROJECTIONS 2014, OF THE OCCUPATIONS GAINING THE MOST NEW JOBS AND DECLINING OR SLOW-GROWTH OCCUPATIONS IN THE STATE OF FLORIDA

Industry 1/	Estimates 2006	Projections 2014	Annual percentage change	Average annual openings Total	Average annual openings Due to growth
		Occupations gaining the most new jobs			
Network systems and data communications analysts	18,878	26,722	5.19	1,180	980
Medical assistants	28,667	39,446	4.70	1,828	1,347
Computer software engineers, applications	17,555	23,809	4.45	940	782
Computer software engineers, systems software	17,229	23,009	4.19	879	722
Network and computer systems administrators	13,793	18,384	4.16	714	574
Home health aides	30,303	40,191	4.08	1,601	1,236
Paralegals and legal assistants	19,667	25,749	3.87	906	760
Dental assistants	14,678	19,200	3.85	944	565
Farmworkers, farm and ranch animals	12,155	15,621	3.56	753	433
Pharmacy technicians	19,524	25,074	3.55	930	694
Computer systems analysts	26,400	33,438	3.33	1,159	880
Bill and account collectors	28,657	36,235	3.31	1,452	947
Employment, recruitment, and placement specialists	13,076	16,524	3.30	618	431
Preschool teachers, except special education	20,569	25,739	3.14	876	646
Personal financial advisors	15,545	19,419	3.12	673	484
Customer service representatives	155,861	194,576	3.10	7,013	4,839
Registered nurses	147,050	183,478	3.10	7,440	4,554
Self-enrichment education teachers	16,908	21,093	3.09	718	523
Pharmacists	16,065	19,938	3.01	777	484
Amusement and recreation attendants	33,093	40,904	2.95	1,873	976
		Declining or slow-growth occupations 2/			
Meter readers, utilities	1,512	932	-4.79	52	-72
Textile knitting and weaving machine setters and operators	254	161	-4.58	3	-12
Credit authorizers, checkers, and clerks	3,997	2,791	-3.77	83	-151
File clerks	19,997	14,322	-3.55	635	-709
Mail clerks and machine operators, excluding postal service	7,355	5,460	-3.22	234	-237
Telephone operators	2,523	1,912	-3.03	69	-76
Computer operators	6,223	4,719	-3.02	140	-188
Photographic processing machine operators	3,268	2,617	-2.49	85	-81
Coil winders, tapers, and finishers	716	577	-2.43	18	-17
Order clerks	12,276	10,336	-1.98	287	-242
Electromechanical equipment assemblers	3,041	2,636	-1.66	74	-51
Machine feeders and offbearers	5,182	4,615	-1.37	145	-71
Word processors and typists	8,855	7,960	-1.26	200	-112
Farm labor contractors	440	403	-1.05	10	-5
Chemical plant and system operators	1,244	1,141	-1.03	39	-13
Fallers	225	207	-1.00	4	-2
Tank car, truck, and ship loaders	691	637	-0.98	20	-7
Cutting, punching and press machine operator	5,392	4,978	-0.96	127	-52
Plating and coating machine setters and operators	733	679	-0.92	16	-7
Actors	2,217	2,059	-0.89	29	-20

1/ Rank based on annual percentage change.
2/ Includes occupations with a minimum of 200 jobs in 2006.
Source: State of Florida, Agency for Workforce Innovation, Bureau of Labor Market Information, *Occupational Employment Statistics Projections to 2014,* Internet site <http://www.labormarketinfo.com/> (accessed 5, February 2007).

Table 6.57. AVERAGE ANNUAL PAY: PAY OF EMPLOYEES COVERED BY STATE AND FEDERAL UNEMPLOYMENT INSURANCE PROGRAMS IN THE UNITED STATES AND IN THE STATE AND METROPOLITAN AREAS OF FLORIDA, 2004, 2005, AND 2006

Industry or metropolitan area	2004 (dollars)	2005 (dollars)	2006 A/ (dollars)	Percentage change 2004 to 2006
United States	38,955	40,270	42,114	8.1
United States, private industry	39,134	40,505	42,405	8.4
Florida	35,186	36,800	38,484	9.4
Private industry	34,438	36,096	37,806	9.8
Agriculture, forestry, fishing and hunting	20,479	21,254	22,744	11.1
Mining	46,907	49,229	53,964	15.0
Construction	36,653	38,297	40,743	11.2
Manufacturing	42,473	43,423	45,735	7.7
Wholesale trade	50,388	52,752	55,918	11.0
Retail trade	24,825	25,826	26,533	6.9
Transportation and warehousing	37,013	38,023	39,681	7.2
Utilities	65,715	66,927	64,847	-1.3
Information	51,017	52,856	55,002	7.8
Finance and insurance	56,145	59,212	61,694	9.9
Real estate and rental and leasing	35,820	39,056	39,691	10.8
Professional and technical services	52,999	55,705	58,824	11.0
Management of companies and enterprises	71,303	80,420	83,496	17.1
Administrative and waste services	25,802	27,244	28,513	10.5
Educational services	31,149	32,099	33,696	8.2
Health care and social assistance	37,897	39,066	40,533	7.0
Arts, entertainment, and recreation	28,940	29,462	30,542	5.5
Accommodation and food services	15,933	16,892	17,549	10.1
Other services, except public administration	24,680	25,781	26,986	9.3
Government	39,810	41,273	42,871	7.7
MSA, private industry				
Cape Coral-Ft. Myers	32,993	34,722	36,076	9.3
Deltona-Daytona Beach-Ormond Beach	28,102	28,770	30,046	6.9
Ft. Walton Beach-Crestview-Destin	28,946	30,841	32,263	11.5
Gainesville	28,679	29,892	31,114	8.5
Jacksonville	36,066	37,458	39,477	9.5
Lakeland	30,666	31,825	32,985	7.6
Miami-Ft. Lauderdale-Miami Beach	37,607	39,177	41,274	9.8
Naples-Marco Island	34,190	37,724	38,761	13.4
Ocala	28,568	29,665	30,943	8.3
Orlando	34,764	36,151	37,580	8.1
Palm Bay-Melbourne-Titusville	36,411	37,845	39,221	7.7
Panama City-Lynn Haven	28,687	30,400	31,841	11.0
Pensacola-Ferry Pass-Brent	29,361	31,009	32,623	11.1
Port St. Lucie	30,553	32,229	33,331	9.1
Punta Gorda	28,707	30,808	31,069	8.2
Sarasota-Bradenton-Venice	31,365	33,129	34,941	11.4
Sebastian-Vero Beach	30,625	31,716	33,007	7.8
Tallahassee	30,585	31,548	32,552	6.4
Tampa-St. Petersburg-Clearwater	34,736	35,802	37,407	7.7

A/ Data are preliminary.

Note: Data are reported using the North Americal Industry Classification System (NAICS) and are not comparable to earlier years. See Glossary for definition. Metropolitan Statistical Areas (MSAs) as defined December 2006. Data for Palm Coast are not available. See map at front of book.

Source: U.S., Department of Labor, Bureau of Labor Statistics, Quarterly Census of Employment and Wages, Internet site <http://www.bls.gov/> (accessed 15, August 2007).

SOCIAL INSURANCE AND WELFARE

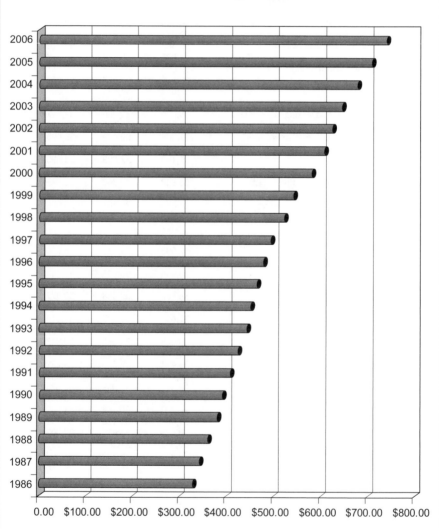

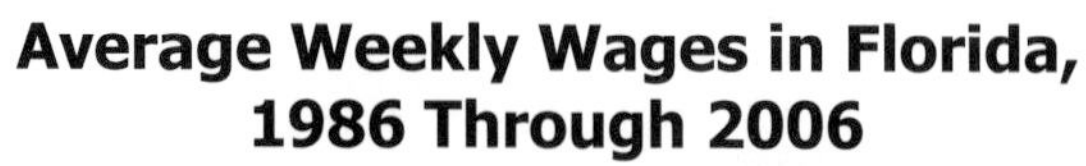

Source: Table 7.56

Section 7.00
Social Insurance and Welfare

This section presents statistics on enrollment and expenditure of the various government social programs such as Medicare, Social Security, Aid to Families with Dependent Children (AFDC), Supplemental Security Income (SSI), Medicaid, and Temporary Assistance for Needy Families (TANF). Also included in this section are data on food stamp recipients, elder assistance, elderly who are raising grandchildren, average weekly wages for persons covered by unemployment compensation law, and contributions and disbursements for unemployment insurance.

Explanatory notes. For purposes of managing state-administered public assistance programs, the state was divided into Department of Children and Families districts; a map showing these districts appears on page 303.

Sources. Four public assistance programs—for the aged, the blind, the permanently and totally disabled, and dependent children—are administered by the state but are financed, in part, by the federal government in grants to states under the Social Security Act. The principal source of state and national data on these programs is the U.S. Department of Health and Human Services, Social Security Administration through these published reports: *Social Security Bulletin, OASDI Beneficiaries by State and County,* and *SSI Recipients by State and County.* Related unpublished data are on the agency Web site. Medicare data are from the information services office of the Centers for Medicare and Medicaid Services in the U.S. Department of Health and Human Services (HHS). Enrollment data and county Medicare data may be located on the Internet. The principal source of Medicaid eligibility, recipient, and expenditure data for the state and counties is Florida's Agency for Health Care Administration.

Temporary Assistance for Needy Families (TANF) and food stamp recipient and benefit data are provided by the Economic Self-Sufficiency office of the Florida Department of Children and Families.

The Florida Department of Elder Affairs reports on the living situation, hurricane assistance, and food stamp recipient data for Florida's elderly in *Florida County Profiles* and *Assessing the Needs of Elder Floridians.* The former publication also reports on the circumstance of grandparents throughout the state who are responsible for the care of grandchildren.

The Florida Agency for Workforce Innovation (AWI) provides historical average weekly wages and unemployment insurance contribution and disbursement data. Current data are from the Florida Department of Financial Services and are published in *Florida's Comprehensive Annual Financial Report* on the Internet.

Section 7.00
Social Insurance and Welfare

Tables listed by major heading

Table 7.03. MEDICARE: ENROLLMENT IN HOSPITAL AND/OR MEDICAL INSURANCE BY METROPOLITAN/NONMETROPOLITAN RESIDENCE IN FLORIDA, 2003 AND 2004

Item	Total enrollment		Persons aged 65 and over		Disability beneficiaries 1/	
	2003	2004	2003	2004	2003	2004
Florida, total	2,920,971	2,980,077	2,558,145	2,596,515	362,826	383,562
Metropolitan counties 2/	2,686,924	2,722,799	2,359,823	2,378,287	327,101	344,512
With central city	2,114,201	2,123,041	1,853,719	1,851,655	260,482	271,386
Without central city	572,723	599,758	506,104	526,632	66,619	73,126
Nonmetropolitan counties	233,454	255,355	197,853	216,431	35,601	38,924

1/ Persons under age 65 entitled to cash disability benefits for at least 24 consecutive months and also those eligible solely on the basis of end-stage renal disease.
2/ Counties included in Metropolitan Statistical Areas (MSAs).
Note: Geographic classification is based on the address to which the enrollee's cash benefit check is mailed or the mailing address recorded in the health insurance master file.

Source: U.S., Department of Health and Human Services, Centers for Medicare and Medicaid Services, Office of Information Services, *Medicare County Enrollment as of July 1, 2004,* Internet site <http://cms.hhs.gov/> (accessed 17, May 2006).

Table 7.04. MEDICARE: ENROLLMENT IN THE UNITED STATES AND FLORIDA, SPECIFIED YEARS

Medicare enrollment	United States	Florida	Percentage of U.S.
All beneficiaries, hospital and/or medical insurance, 2005	41,003,057	3,008,193	7.3
Enrollment age (years), 2004			
0-64	6,394,913	396,102	6.2
65-69	9,462,761	682,479	7.2
70-74	8,130,271	613,234	7.5
75-79	7,091,343	550,712	7.8
80-84	5,266,951	408,074	7.7
85 and over	4,446,059	331,494	7.5
Disabled beneficiaries, 2005	6,483,556	398,585	6.1
Medicare home health agency utilization, 2004			
Reimbursement (dollars)	12,885,434,951	1,259,924,579	9.8
Patients	2,979,297	277,846	9.3
Visits	95,536,624	10,762,667	11.3
Average reimbursement per patient (dollars)	4,325	4,535	104.9
Average visits per patient	32	39	121.9
Medicare part B buy-ins, 2004	6,304,752	406,006	6.4
Medicare part B buy-ins, 2005	6,576,810	431,764	6.6

Note: Home Health Agency data is calendar year; all other data as of July 1.

Source: U.S., Department of Health and Human Services, Centers for Medicare and Medicaid Services, Research, Statistics, Data & Systems, Internet site <http://cms.hhs.gov/> (accessed 10, October 2007).

Table 7.05. MEDICARE: PERSONS AGED 65 AND OVER ENROLLED IN HOSPITAL INSURANCE IN THE STATE AND COUNTIES OF FLORIDA, JULY 1, 2004

County	Total HI and SMI enrollment	Percentage aged 65 and over	Disabled with SMI and HI	County	Total HI and SMI enrollment	Percentage aged 65 and over	Disabled with SMI and HI
Florida	2,980,077	87.1	346,648	Lake	62,228	89.7	5,783
				Lee	109,375	90.0	9,886
Alachua	26,009	81.9	4,255	Leon	23,755	85.6	2,935
Baker	2,913	70.4	768	Levy	7,958	79.4	1,495
Bay	25,440	81.7	4,348	Liberty	983	73.2	243
Bradford	3,636	80.0	655	Madison	3,242	78.3	663
Brevard	106,916	87.3	12,183	Manatee	62,825	90.1	5,569
Broward	242,923	88.3	25,863	Marion	76,383	87.7	8,581
Calhoun	2,184	77.5	460	Martin	36,471	92.9	2,344
Charlotte	46,884	90.4	4,123	Miami-Dade	323,990	89.2	32,911
Citrus	41,301	88.6	4,358	Monroe	11,264	87.3	1,309
Clay	19,752	83.8	2,779	Nassau	9,924	83.4	1,468
Collier	56,386	93.5	3,353	Okaloosa	26,155	86.2	3,277
Columbia	10,044	77.9	1,996	Okeechobee	6,532	82.3	1,078
DeSoto	5,253	83.4	801	Orange	108,374	81.6	17,640
Dixie	2,904	76.3	639	Osceola	26,504	78.6	5,014
Duval	98,728	82.0	15,803	Palm Beach	246,749	92.2	17,325
Escambia	48,411	82.3	7,842	Pasco	93,155	85.3	12,324
Flagler	18,728	88.8	1,895	Pinellas	193,434	86.9	22,503
Franklin	1,945	83.1	309	Polk	98,246	84.1	14,065
Gadsden	7,154	74.9	1,547	Putnam	15,035	79.6	2,857
Gilchrist	2,488	77.6	491	St. Johns	24,576	87.7	2,721
Glades	1,830	86.4	227	St. Lucie	46,767	85.7	6,093
Gulf	2,677	82.3	447	Santa Rosa	19,141	82.0	3,120
Hamilton	1,907	75.3	433	Sarasota	97,414	92.6	6,467
Hardee	3,428	79.8	652	Seminole	47,387	85.4	6,041
Hendry	4,075	82.5	669	Sumter	20,514	90.4	1,782
Hernando	43,552	87.1	5,126	Suwannee	7,894	81.1	1,380
Highlands	26,555	89.9	2,504	Taylor	3,438	79.0	659
Hillsborough	143,686	82.4	22,485	Union	1,345	72.0	311
Holmes	3,711	76.6	828	Volusia	105,377	86.4	12,989
Indian River	33,082	91.7	2,527	Wakulla	3,005	81.8	473
Jackson	8,741	76.1	1,968	Walton	8,010	81.7	1,365
Jefferson	2,343	81.2	399	Washington	4,254	75.2	994
Lafayette	864	81.6	144	Unknown	1,923	93.4	106

HI Hospital insurance.
SMI Supplemental medical insurance.
Note: Geographic classification is based on the address to which the enrollee's cash benefit check is mailed or the mailing address recorded in the health insurance master file. Beginning July 1, 2004, CMS Medicare enrollment data are from the Medicare Beneficiary Data System.

Source: U.S., Department of Health and Human Services, Centers for Medicare and Medicaid Services, Medicare Enrollment Reports, Internet site <http://cms.hhs.gov/> (accessed 10, October 2007).

Table 7.12. SOCIAL SECURITY: NUMBER OF BENEFICIARIES AND AMOUNT OF BENEFITS IN CURRENT-PAYMENT STATUS BY TYPE OF BENEFICIARY IN THE STATE AND COUNTIES OF FLORIDA, DECEMBER 2005

Residence of beneficiary	Total	Retired workers 1/	Disabled workers	Spouses	Children	Widows and widowers 2/
			Number of beneficiaries			
Florida	3,430,205	2,331,733	396,450	176,102	232,490	293,430
Alachua	31,420	19,620	4,315	1,485	3,215	2,785
Baker	3,835	1,935	845	175	500	380
Bay	30,680	18,390	4,750	1,795	2,580	3,165
Bradford	4,600	2,735	770	230	430	435
Brevard	123,475	84,340	14,110	6,790	7,350	10,885
Broward	269,990	184,765	29,300	11,855	18,955	25,115
Calhoun	2,660	1,440	475	160	265	320
Charlotte	50,785	38,100	4,455	2,565	2,025	3,640
Citrus	49,015	35,490	5,150	2,550	2,205	3,620
Clay	25,730	16,060	3,535	1,385	2,470	2,280
Collier	65,420	49,040	3,940	4,875	2,490	5,075
Columbia	12,525	7,435	2,225	535	1,210	1,120
DeSoto	5,990	3,905	835	290	495	465
Dixie	3,655	2,125	715	160	315	340
Duval	116,730	70,160	18,155	5,095	11,585	11,735
Escambia	57,155	34,175	8,420	3,625	4,970	5,965
Flagler	23,715	17,445	2,495	1,150	1,220	1,405
Franklin	2,260	1,495	330	115	120	200
Gadsden	8,780	5,085	1,625	240	1,125	705
Gilchrist	3,095	1,815	565	145	285	285
Glades	2,195	1,545	240	115	130	165
Gulf	3,160	1,820	475	235	240	390
Hamilton	2,570	1,350	515	125	290	290
Hardee	4,060	2,440	600	185	460	375
Hendry	5,110	3,060	755	285	570	440
Hernando	51,345	36,045	6,225	2,535	2,985	3,555
Highlands	30,510	22,505	2,760	1,645	1,415	2,185
Hillsborough	171,555	106,210	25,875	8,070	15,585	15,815
Holmes	4,590	2,595	855	245	385	510
Indian River	36,700	26,725	2,885	2,315	1,600	3,175
Jackson	10,695	5,960	1,890	455	1,290	1,100
Jefferson	2,750	1,715	435	115	220	265
Lafayette	1,000	585	155	55	80	125
Lake	77,260	56,960	7,335	3,745	3,550	5,670
Lee	128,230	93,620	11,520	6,760	6,590	9,740
Leon	28,775	18,935	3,405	1,215	2,585	2,635
Levy	9,920	6,130	1,635	480	770	905
Liberty	1,190	645	245	50	135	115
Madison	3,855	2,170	665	165	425	430
Manatee	72,040	52,440	6,580	3,580	3,475	5,965
Marion	91,590	64,990	10,140	4,495	5,175	6,790
Martin	40,095	30,140	2,630	2,425	1,515	3,385
Miami-Dade	338,210	229,765	35,295	21,055	25,705	26,390
Monroe	12,840	9,085	1,450	695	615	995
Nassau	12,580	7,895	1,720	830	980	1,155
Okaloosa	30,550	19,420	3,565	2,190	2,210	3,165
Okeechobee	7,775	4,885	1,175	380	600	735

See footnotes at end of table.

Continued . . .

Table 7.12. SOCIAL SECURITY: NUMBER OF BENEFICIARIES AND AMOUNT OF BENEFITS IN CURRENT-PAYMENT STATUS BY TYPE OF BENEFICIARY IN THE STATE AND COUNTIES OF FLORIDA, DECEMBER 2005 (Continued)

Residence of beneficiary	Total	Retired workers 1/	Disabled workers	Spouses	Children	Widows and widowers 2/
			Number of beneficiaries (Continued)			
Orange	131,385	79,230	20,775	6,320	13,695	11,365
Osceola	34,605	19,860	6,250	1,675	4,250	2,570
Palm Beach	273,180	201,945	19,965	14,380	13,385	23,505
Pasco	109,080	73,705	14,635	4,890	6,820	9,030
Pinellas	214,925	147,690	26,380	9,110	11,485	20,260
Polk	118,300	77,335	16,445	5,465	9,245	9,810
Putnam	18,170	10,735	3,050	945	1,680	1,760
St. Johns	29,955	20,430	3,130	1,765	2,015	2,615
St. Lucie	54,750	37,680	6,810	2,425	3,855	3,980
Santa Rosa	24,115	14,630	3,590	1,530	2,135	2,230
Sarasota	109,040	82,095	7,530	6,315	4,030	9,070
Seminole	57,300	36,790	7,220	2,875	5,095	5,320
Sumter	26,920	20,935	2,145	1,280	900	1,660
Suwannee	9,910	6,080	1,535	505	845	945
Taylor	4,290	2,460	750	205	405	470
Union	1,720	910	340	70	230	170
Volusia	121,245	82,795	14,785	5,725	7,405	10,535
Wakulla	3,910	2,495	590	155	365	305
Walton	9,515	5,920	1,455	525	725	890
Washington	5,220	2,820	1,035	275	535	555
			Amount of monthly cash benefits ($1,000)			
Florida	3,178,953	2,325,523	372,089	86,740	111,114	283,486
Alachua	28,708	19,789	3,888	781	1,632	2,611
Baker	3,242	1,852	763	80	235	308
Bay	26,462	17,356	4,233	832	1,213	2,821
Bradford	3,896	2,511	716	97	198	372
Brevard	116,655	85,186	13,821	3,420	3,669	10,556
Broward	256,367	187,714	28,242	5,657	9,594	25,158
Calhoun	2,094	1,246	415	60	115	256
Charlotte	49,199	38,642	4,648	1,276	991	3,636
Citrus	46,180	35,182	5,216	1,257	1,030	3,494
Clay	23,174	15,695	3,462	671	1,220	2,122
Collier	67,813	53,983	4,033	2,852	1,281	5,660
Columbia	10,564	6,890	1,982	239	508	940
DeSoto	5,173	3,668	739	132	211	418
Dixie	3,045	1,923	636	65	137	279
Duval	104,379	68,913	16,509	2,533	5,550	10,870
Escambia	48,721	32,017	7,517	1,722	2,222	5,241
Flagler	23,356	18,131	2,652	584	580	1,403
Franklin	1,944	1,370	286	54	63	166
Gadsden	6,915	4,474	1,327	101	455	553
Gilchrist	2,624	1,670	535	58	118	238
Glades	1,970	1,472	231	54	57	152
Gulf	2,856	1,819	449	115	108	362
Hamilton	2,097	1,231	461	51	118	232
Hardee	3,241	2,180	472	76	203	307

See footnotes at end of table.

Continued . . .

Table 7.12. SOCIAL SECURITY: NUMBER OF BENEFICIARIES AND AMOUNT OF BENEFITS IN CURRENT-PAYMENT STATUS BY TYPE OF BENEFICIARY IN THE STATE AND COUNTIES OF FLORIDA, DECEMBER 2005 (Continued)

Residence of beneficiary	Total	Retired workers 1/	Disabled workers	Spouses	Children	Widows and widowers 2/
	Amount of monthly cash benefits ($1,000) (Continued)					
Hendry	4,323	2,893	665	120	244	399
Hernando	48,116	35,771	6,295	1,219	1,403	3,424
Highlands	27,865	21,801	2,589	781	618	2,072
Hillsborough	154,314	104,626	23,612	3,935	7,286	14,852
Holmes	3,605	2,223	759	93	155	373
Indian River	36,263	27,978	2,830	1,287	808	3,353
Jackson	8,604	5,303	1,685	182	577	853
Jefferson	2,306	1,568	367	51	99	216
Lafayette	832	531	135	23	33	103
Lake	73,342	57,090	7,170	1,880	1,709	5,489
Lee	125,836	97,535	11,508	3,582	3,317	9,890
Leon	27,263	19,649	3,072	664	1,293	2,582
Levy	8,509	5,695	1,495	211	336	769
Liberty	975	581	215	19	61	95
Madison	3,080	1,931	565	73	186	322
Manatee	69,885	53,890	6,405	1,871	1,697	6,020
Marion	84,814	64,112	9,770	2,202	2,337	6,388
Martin	40,904	32,327	2,748	1,355	815	3,659
Miami-Dade	272,345	200,037	29,024	8,605	11,626	23,051
Monroe	12,305	9,234	1,420	350	328	969
Nassau	12,187	8,341	1,744	460	513	1,123
Okaloosa	26,375	18,242	3,166	1,044	1,066	2,855
Okeechobee	6,895	4,721	1,079	170	260	662
Orange	115,975	77,555	18,725	2,999	6,231	10,463
Osceola	29,307	18,772	5,778	700	1,806	2,249
Palm Beach	282,979	222,000	20,049	8,000	6,988	25,941
Pasco	100,380	72,152	14,143	2,295	3,201	8,587
Pinellas	202,408	147,499	24,659	4,611	5,757	19,876
Polk	107,366	76,191	15,109	2,701	4,151	9,208
Putnam	15,609	10,132	2,774	433	703	1,565
St. Johns	29,287	21,468	3,071	980	1,074	2,691
St. Lucie	51,601	38,210	6,620	1,201	1,714	3,852
Santa Rosa	21,501	14,226	3,462	737	1,070	2,002
Sarasota	108,756	86,124	7,547	3,411	2,082	9,587
Seminole	53,664	37,447	6,987	1,422	2,587	5,220
Sumter	26,478	21,676	2,138	660	394	1,604
Suwannee	8,374	5,537	1,417	224	388	801
Taylor	3,770	2,365	708	95	184	413
Union	1,413	828	303	29	104	145
Volusia	112,598	81,848	14,253	2,807	3,595	10,090
Wakulla	3,373	2,330	535	73	171	259
Walton	8,294	5,614	1,317	247	319	792
Washington	4,194	2,519	906	110	226	431

1/ Includes special age-72 beneficiaries.
2/ Includes nondisabled and disabled widows and widowers, widowed mothers and fathers, and parents.
Note: Detail may not add to totals because of rounding.

Source: U.S., Department of Health and Human Services, Social Security Administration, *OASDI Beneficiaries by State and County, 2005,* Internet site <http://www.ssa.gov/> (accessed 21, March 2007).

Table 7.14. SOCIAL SECURITY: AVERAGE MONTHLY BENEFITS OF BENEFICIARIES AGED 65 AND OVER AND RETIRED WORKERS IN THE STATE AND COUNTIES OF FLORIDA, DECEMBER 2005

(in dollars)

County	All beneficiaries aged 65 and over	Retired workers	County	All beneficiaries aged 65 and over	Retired workers
Florida	974.99	997.34	Lake	980.19	1,002.28
Alachua	986.05	1,008.61	Lee	1017.84	1,041.82
Baker	924.29	957.11	Leon	1016.21	1,037.71
Bay	912.46	943.77	Levy	905.38	929.04
Bradford	891.92	918.10	Liberty	860.56	900.78
Brevard	982.00	1,010.03	Madison	850.20	889.86
Broward	1000.64	1,015.96	Manatee	1006.48	1,027.65
Calhoun	833.83	865.28	Marion	964.73	986.49
Charlotte	989.42	1,014.23	Martin	1047.92	1,072.56
Citrus	968.11	991.32	Miami-Dade	851.48	870.62
Clay	951.00	977.27	Monroe	988.11	1,016.40
Collier	1071.31	1,100.80	Nassau	1023.65	1,056.49
Columbia	899.87	926.70	Okaloosa	902.15	939.34
DeSoto	925.21	939.31	Okeechobee	943.56	966.43
Dixie	884.33	904.94	Orange	954.64	978.86
Duval	961.47	982.23	Osceola	918.73	945.22
Escambia	902.92	936.85	Palm Beach	1080.54	1,099.31
Flagler	1016.29	1,039.32	Pasco	958.63	978.93
Franklin	884.79	916.39	Pinellas	980.26	998.71
Gadsden	858.29	879.84	Polk	965.23	985.21
Gilchrist	894.57	920.11	Putnam	921.00	943.83
Glades	936.08	952.75	St. Johns	1024.91	1,050.81
Gulf	954.73	999.45	St. Lucie	994.44	1,014.07
Hamilton	875.17	911.85	Santa Rosa	938.38	972.39
Hardee	877.15	893.44	Sarasota	1025.33	1,049.08
Hendry	925.53	945.42	Seminole	992.31	1,017.86
Hernando	970.54	992.40	Sumter	1011.67	1,035.40
Highlands	946.61	968.72	Suwannee	885.58	910.69
Hillsborough	961.49	985.09	Taylor	925.95	961.38
Holmes	816.75	856.65	Union	890.82	909.89
Indian River	1022.98	1,046.88	Volusia	967.78	988.56
Jackson	855.00	889.77	Wakulla	911.24	933.87
Jefferson	889.54	914.29	Walton	916.97	948.31
Lafayette	878.20	907.69	Washington	853.08	893.26

Source: U.S., Department of Health and Human Services, Social Security Administration, *OASDI Beneficiaries by State and County, 2005,* Internet site <http://www.ssa.gov/> (accessed 21, March 2007).

Table 7.15. PUBLIC ASSISTANCE: DIRECT ASSISTANCE PAYMENTS, CALENDAR YEARS 2002 THROUGH 2005, AND MEDICAL ASSISTANCE PAYMENTS, FISCAL YEARS 2002–03 THROUGH 2005–06, BY PROGRAM IN FLORIDA

(rounded to thousands of dollars)

Type of assistance	2002	2003	2004	2005
Direct assistance, total	2,000,291	2,104,100	2,139,111	2,217,060
Basic Supplemental Security Income (SSI)	1,814,408	1,907,671	1,953,493	2,031,442
Old-Age Assistance (OAA)	332,735	345,419	344,037	357,444
Aid to the Blind (AB)	14,353	14,553	14,030	13,646
Aid to the Disabled (AD)	1,467,319	1,547,699	1,595,426	1,660,352
SSI State Supplementation 1/	9,707	19,813	9,198	9,198
TANF 2/	176,176	176,616	176,420	176,420
	2002–03	2003–04	2004–05	2005–06
Medical assistance, total 3/	4,010,338	4,421,732	4,408,366	3,915,225
Aid to the Blind/Disabled	2,949,853	3,250,191	3,239,097	2,980,396
Aid to Families with Dependent Children (AFDC)	122,046	141,577	145,647	135,006
Aid to the Elderly	440,838	474,315	472,513	291,404
Other Title XIX recipients	497,601	555,649	551,108	508,419

1/ Payments to persons eligible for state benefits but not eligible under federal requirements.
2/ Temporary Assistance for Needy Families.
3/ Federal fiscal year ending September 30.
Source: U.S., Department of Health and Human Services, Social Security Administration, *Social Security Bulletin: Annual Statistical Supplement, 2006,* Internet site <http://www.ssa.gov/> (accessed 2, October 2007), and previous editions, and State of Florida, Agency for Health Care Administration, HFCA 2082, Federal Fiscal Year Ending September 30, 2006, unpublished data.

Table 7.16. MEDICAL ASSISTANCE: NUMBER OF RECIPIENTS BY AGE OF RECIPIENT AND BY TYPE OF SERVICE, IN FLORIDA, FEDERAL FISCAL YEAR 2005–06

Type of service	Total	Aged 5 and under	Aged 6 to 20	Aged 21 to 64	Aged 65 to 84	Aged 85 and over
Unduplicated total	2,129,978	517,828	671,135	660,870	215,703	64,442
Inpatient hospital	322,360	42,462	41,000	169,677	52,444	16,777
Mental hospital–aged	165	16	0	105	43	1
Intermediate care facilities	3,146	1	122	2,840	176	7
Skilled nursing facilities	81,138	158	194	12,848	37,326	30,612
Physician	1,603,446	450,775	518,689	491,904	117,441	24,637
Dental	336,384	76,189	214,890	33,783	9,543	1,979
Other practitioners	365,777	52,099	126,923	141,834	34,768	10,153
Outpatient hospital	837,789	195,133	194,882	333,807	94,678	19,289
Clinic	175,338	16,245	63,827	64,730	27,228	3,308
Home health	360,204	53,474	70,414	199,935	25,161	11,220
Family planning	136,099	1,293	47,155	87,325	289	37
Lab and X-ray	925,810	237,056	261,482	364,693	47,004	15,575
Prescribed drugs	1,216,491	286,743	302,133	403,635	173,296	50,684
Early and periodic screening	387,557	271,240	115,672	563	38	44
Rural health clinic	175,996	60,583	54,314	53,497	6,060	1,542
Other care	329,831	47,829	76,362	107,703	68,951	28,986

Note: Data are for fiscal year ending September 30.
Source: State of Florida, Agency for Health Care Administration, HCFA 2082, Federal Fiscal Year Ending September 30, 2006, unpublished data.

Table 7.18. PUBLIC ASSISTANCE: AVERAGE MONTHLY AID TO FAMILIES WITH DEPENDENT CHILDREN (AFDC) CASES BY TYPE OF RECIPIENT AND AVERAGE MONTHLY PAYMENTS FOR ALL CASES IN THE STATE, DEPARTMENT OF CHILDREN AND FAMILIES DISTRICTS, AND COUNTIES OF FLORIDA, FISCAL YEAR 2006–07

District or region and county	Average monthly cases				Average monthly expenditure (dollars)
	Assistance groups (families)	Adults	Children	Persons	
Florida	48,730	11,645	67,144	78,789	11,424,788
District 1	2,816	460	3,674	4,134	672,074
Escambia	1,821	311	2,472	2,783	435,836
Okaloosa	455	73	553	626	108,030
Santa Rosa	419	58	504	562	99,222
Walton	121	18	145	163	28,985
District 2	2,704	585	3,713	4,298	627,639
Bay	505	129	705	834	116,850
Calhoun	48	4	62	66	10,656
Franklin	35	6	43	49	7,743
Gadsden	293	58	407	465	66,458
Gulf	53	15	78	93	12,060
Holmes	135	25	166	191	32,417
Jackson	175	12	230	242	40,706
Jefferson	71	7	96	103	15,939
Leon	884	252	1,253	1,505	206,685
Liberty	27	2	31	33	6,309
Madison	152	20	187	207	34,651
Taylor	129	17	170	187	30,218
Wakulla	80	18	118	136	18,682
Washington	117	20	167	187	28,264
District 3	2,579	498	3,520	4,018	604,473
Alachua	886	197	1,242	1,439	206,924
Bradford	145	31	185	216	34,260
Columbia	378	70	512	582	89,171
Dixie	73	16	101	117	17,414
Gilchrist	88	9	107	116	20,152
Hamilton	90	13	137	150	21,076
Lafayette	21	3	25	28	5,014
Levy	204	37	274	311	49,500
Putnam	430	76	597	673	100,159
Suwannee	196	38	247	285	45,069
Union	69	8	93	101	15,735
District 4	4,492	591	5,859	6,450	1,066,232
Baker	124	28	181	209	30,164
Clay	437	48	533	581	101,448
Duval	3,394	466	4,483	4,949	808,650
Nassau	205	17	260	277	47,350
St. Johns	333	32	402	434	78,621
District 7	4,909	1,318	7,022	8,340	1,145,071
Brevard	1,088	201	1,450	1,651	251,813
Orange	2,491	711	3,651	4,362	582,210
Osceola	699	248	1,023	1,271	162,785
Seminole	631	158	898	1,056	148,264

See footnote at end of table. Continued. . .

Department of Children and Families Districts Effective July 1, 2001

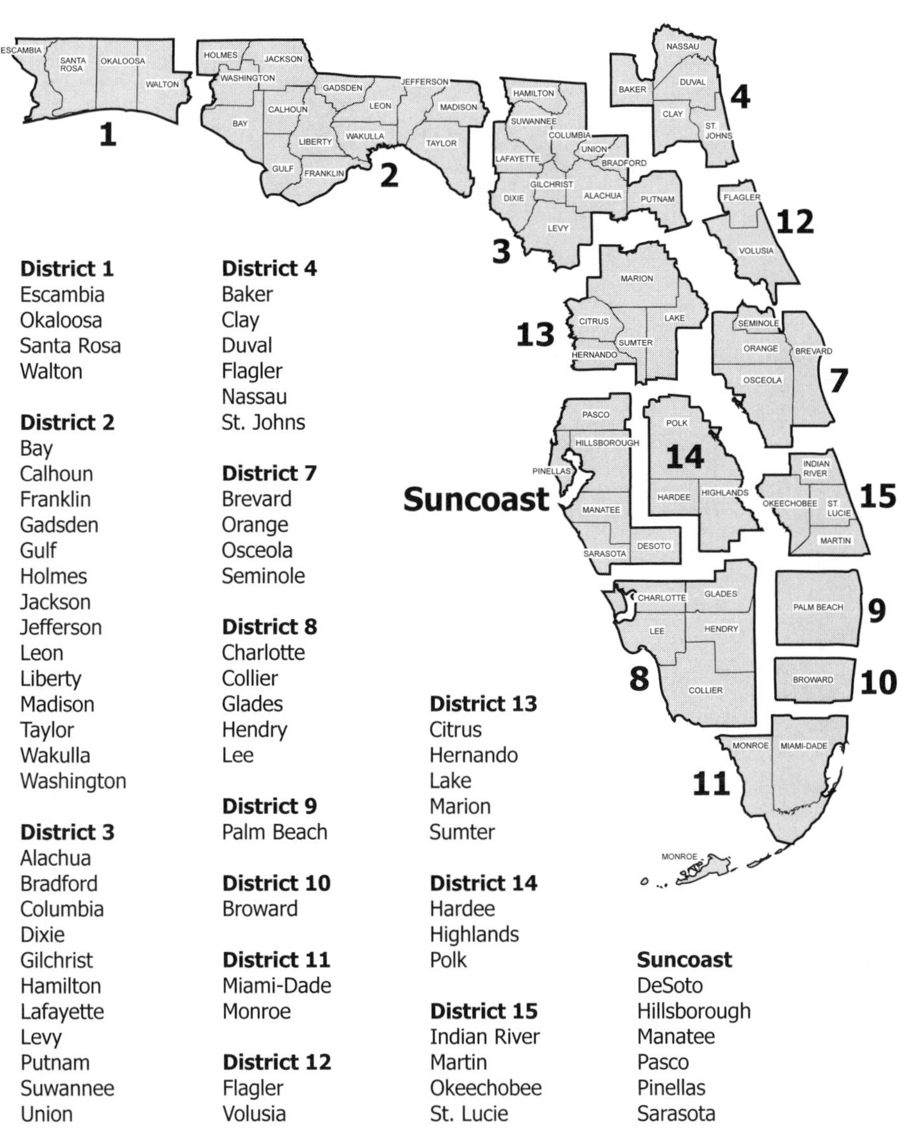

District 1
Escambia
Okaloosa
Santa Rosa
Walton

District 2
Bay
Calhoun
Franklin
Gadsden
Gulf
Holmes
Jackson
Jefferson
Leon
Liberty
Madison
Taylor
Wakulla
Washington

District 3
Alachua
Bradford
Columbia
Dixie
Gilchrist
Hamilton
Lafayette
Levy
Putnam
Suwannee
Union

District 4
Baker
Clay
Duval
Flagler
Nassau
St. Johns

District 7
Brevard
Orange
Osceola
Seminole

District 8
Charlotte
Collier
Glades
Hendry
Lee

District 9
Palm Beach

District 10
Broward

District 11
Miami-Dade
Monroe

District 12
Flagler
Volusia

District 13
Citrus
Hernando
Lake
Marion
Sumter

District 14
Hardee
Highlands
Polk

District 15
Indian River
Martin
Okeechobee
St. Lucie

Suncoast
DeSoto
Hillsborough
Manatee
Pasco
Pinellas
Sarasota

Table 7.18. PUBLIC ASSISTANCE: AVERAGE MONTHLY AID TO FAMILIES WITH DEPENDENT CHILDREN (AFDC) CASES BY TYPE OF RECIPIENT AND AVERAGE MONTHLY PAYMENTS FOR ALL CASES IN THE STATE, DEPARTMENT OF CHILDREN AND FAMILIES DISTRICTS, AND COUNTIES OF FLORIDA, FISCAL YEAR 2006–07 (Continued)

District or region and county	Average monthly cases: Assistance groups (families)	Adults	Children	Persons	Average monthly expenditure (dollars)
District 8	1,382	134	1,873	2,007	315,693
Charlotte	184	18	237	255	42,196
Collier	265	27	383	410	62,768
Glades	12	2	23	25	3,035
Hendry	158	23	233	256	36,239
Lee	763	64	997	1,061	171,455
District 9	2,057	482	2,936	3,418	482,199
Palm Beach	2,057	482	2,936	3,418	482,199
District 10	3,774	997	5,296	6,293	887,750
Broward	3,774	997	5,296	6,293	887,750
District 11	7,294	3,323	10,558	13,881	1,703,550
Miami-Dade	7,187	3,304	10,427	13,731	1,678,039
Monroe	108	19	131	150	25,511
District 12	1,508	433	2,100	2,533	354,386
Flagler	170	43	233	276	38,286
Volusia	1,339	390	1,867	2,257	316,100
District 13	2,588	458	3,382	3,840	604,244
Citrus	345	78	461	539	80,733
Hernando	383	70	484	554	88,956
Lake	666	146	889	1,035	155,924
Marion	1,013	140	1,323	1,463	236,672
Sumter	181	24	225	249	41,960
District 14	2,379	240	3,211	3,451	558,454
Hardee	163	5	209	214	39,062
Highlands	262	43	356	399	59,636
Polk	1,954	192	2,646	2,838	459,756
District 15	1,257	288	1,785	2,073	292,211
Indian River	249	66	352	418	58,176
Martin	169	46	245	291	39,789
Okeechobee	123	18	149	167	28,889
St. Lucie	716	158	1,039	1,197	165,357
Suncoast Region	8,990	1,838	12,215	14,053	2,110,813
DeSoto	128	13	159	172	29,686
Hillsborough	3,992	910	5,578	6,488	936,339
Manatee	614	57	833	890	147,685
Pasco	1,141	268	1,518	1,786	264,737
Pinellas	2,662	544	3,553	4,097	625,787
Sarasota	452	46	574	620	106,579

Note: Detail may not add to total because of rounding.

Source: State of Florida, Department of Children and Families, unpublished data.

Table 7.19. PUBLIC ASSISTANCE: RECIPIENTS OF SUPPLEMENTAL SECURITY INCOME AND AMOUNT OF PAYMENTS IN THE STATE AND COUNTIES OF FLORIDA, DECEMBER 2006

	Beneficiaries							
		Reason for eligibility		Age			SSI recipients	
County	Total	Aged	Blind and disabled	Under 18	18 to 64	65 and over	with OASDI	Payments ($1,000)
Florida	428,246	100,661	327,585	80,596	203,426	144,224	141,258	191,385
Alachua	4,708	421	4,287	1,002	2,895	811	1,469	2,127
Baker	557	42	515	111	362	84	197	238
Bay	3,653	308	3,345	689	2,318	646	1,355	1,574
Bradford	773	62	711	131	497	145	267	385
Brevard	8,597	929	7,668	2,033	5,029	1,535	2,824	3,919
Broward	32,609	8,976	23,633	5,902	14,703	12,004	10,330	14,202
Calhoun	520	49	471	63	319	138	223	223
Charlotte	1,745	246	1,499	320	1,044	381	690	719
Citrus	2,234	235	1,999	319	1,482	433	853	967
Clay	1,989	212	1,777	462	1,183	344	600	927
Collier	2,362	755	1,607	347	1,025	990	850	975
Columbia	2,286	197	2,089	484	1,410	392	822	1,017
DeSoto	771	83	688	167	445	159	309	330
Dixie	711	50	661	110	476	125	288	320
Duval	18,962	2,181	16,781	4,371	10,811	3,780	5,892	8,660
Escambia	8,394	649	7,745	1,814	5,220	1,360	2,672	3,757
Flagler	1,152	177	975	252	622	278	339	529
Franklin	351	56	295	28	206	117	174	146
Gadsden	2,477	251	2,226	644	1,300	533	961	1,098
Gilchrist	412	39	373	67	267	78	157	177
Glades	185	24	161	39	92	54	70	72
Gulf	368	37	331	45	233	90	155	163
Hamilton	575	68	507	120	314	141	247	250
Hardee	848	146	702	140	470	238	407	321
Hendry	1,047	206	841	246	496	305	370	465
Hernando	2,835	260	2,575	587	1,755	493	1,042	1,259
Highlands	2,126	284	1,842	476	1,172	478	853	923
Hillsborough	30,899	4,893	26,006	7,684	15,578	7,637	9,586	14,595
Holmes	794	97	697	81	511	202	345	319
Indian River	1,433	146	1,287	307	859	267	520	624
Jackson	1,945	235	1,710	376	1,063	506	763	818
Jefferson	671	78	593	147	373	151	246	344
Lafayette	128	14	114	33	69	26	42	53

Continued . . .

Table 7.19. PUBLIC ASSISTANCE: RECIPIENTS OF SUPPLEMENTAL SECURITY INCOME AND AMOUNT OF PAYMENTS IN THE STATE AND COUNTIES OF FLORIDA, DECEMBER 2006 (CONTINUED)

	Beneficiaries							
		Reason for eligibility		Age			SSI recipients	
County	Total	Aged	Blind and disabled	Under 18	18 to 64	65 and over	with OASDI	Payments ($1,000)
Lake	4,583	566	4,017	1,085	2,586	912	1,616	2,068
Lee	7,583	1,093	6,490	1,926	3,942	1,715	2,305	3,316
Leon	4,209	406	3,803	1,066	2,382	761	1,340	1,930
Levy	1,284	116	1,168	204	855	225	499	549
Liberty	284	27	257	59	171	54	96	140
Madison	1,040	109	931	222	590	228	370	481
Manatee	3,953	477	3,476	1,040	2,114	799	1,437	1,776
Marion	6,646	757	5,889	1,308	3,980	1,358	2,398	2,965
Martin	1,441	185	1,256	375	796	270	496	647
Miami-Dade	128,591	56,783	71,808	13,750	40,488	74,353	42,111	56,797
Monroe	1,101	249	852	110	595	396	409	450
Nassau	941	78	863	157	613	171	326	394
Okaloosa	2,242	182	2,060	417	1,471	354	785	993
Okeechobee	883	91	792	179	530	174	338	394
Orange	25,251	3,754	21,497	7,371	12,089	5,791	7,019	11,967
Osceola	6,313	942	5,371	1,717	3,050	1,546	1,865	2,806
Palm Beach	16,301	4,014	12,287	3,044	7,762	5,495	5,170	7,311
Pasco	8,002	756	7,246	1,612	5,106	1,284	2,877	3,568
Pinellas	16,999	2,107	14,892	3,405	10,063	3,531	6,008	7,574
Polk	15,083	1,368	13,715	4,250	8,319	2,514	4,987	6,953
Putnam	2,833	221	2,612	556	1,775	502	1,030	1,246
St. Johns	1,853	231	1,622	364	1,092	397	718	776
St. Lucie	5,334	617	4,717	1,425	2,887	1,022	1,737	2,413
Santa Rosa	2,003	168	1,835	301	1,354	348	708	843
Sarasota	3,552	534	3,018	769	1,978	805	1,216	1,519
Seminole	5,514	829	4,685	1,346	2,826	1,342	1,681	2,386
Sumter	1,378	121	1,257	301	823	254	545	574
Suwannee	1,333	149	1,184	248	796	289	523	588
Taylor	701	67	634	144	434	123	262	327
Union	332	28	304	66	204	62	124	156
Volusia	9,135	993	8,142	1,832	5,554	1,749	3,327	3,949
Wakulla	577	57	520	122	343	112	217	244
Walton	923	78	845	124	632	167	376	414
Washington	931	102	829	104	627	200	424	375

Source: U.S., Department of Health and Human Services, Social Security Administration, *SSI Recipients by State and County*, December 2006, Internet site <http:/www.ssa.gov/> (accessed 1, June 2007.)

Table 7.20. MEDICAID: RECIPIENTS AND EXPENDITURE IN THE STATE AND COUNTIES OF FLORIDA, FISCAL YEAR 2005–06

County	Recipients	Expenditure (dollars)	County	Recipients	Expenditure (dollars)
Florida	2,977,172	11,698,893,251	Lake	39,658	139,230,917
Alachua	37,123	174,295,959	Lee	69,729	285,334,554
Baker	5,410	20,445,747	Leon	38,172	130,730,036
Bay	31,940	126,605,067	Levy	9,111	30,458,313
Bradford	6,024	24,013,648	Liberty	1,684	7,109,304
Brevard	64,624	267,156,855	Madison	5,598	23,452,905
Broward	253,961	962,134,833	Manatee	39,420	147,379,385
Calhoun	3,517	14,368,544	Marion	54,503	188,892,323
Charlotte	16,260	62,507,231	Martin	12,983	52,454,427
Citrus	20,212	84,300,735	Miami-Dade	552,435	2,490,907,013
Clay	20,262	65,839,935	Monroe	7,794	35,963,337
Collier	38,966	104,804,156	Nassau	8,552	32,982,577
Columbia	16,349	64,704,577	Okaloosa	24,143	89,697,717
DeSoto	7,526	22,213,798	Okeechobee	8,740	28,223,138
Dixie	4,213	15,057,816	Orange	195,516	694,304,976
Duval	148,333	578,165,481	Osceola	62,399	163,372,120
Escambia	60,352	235,462,472	Palm Beach	153,605	616,421,291
Flagler	10,104	26,112,326	Pasco	65,019	240,347,694
Franklin	2,269	7,732,000	Pinellas	125,248	708,501,285
Gadsden	13,014	47,910,172	Polk	113,696	375,028,953
Gilchrist	3,682	12,037,545	Putnam	21,039	75,141,817
Glades	1,094	2,621,497	St. Johns	14,345	66,877,443
Gulf	2,910	11,240,218	St. Lucie	47,653	166,669,376
Hamilton	3,738	13,604,923	Santa Rosa	18,138	57,827,224
Hardee	8,432	23,181,019	Sarasota	35,232	159,554,541
Hendry	11,151	29,464,264	Seminole	44,897	146,592,369
Hernando	24,568	81,218,881	Sumter	10,609	33,548,875
Highlands	17,435	57,555,419	Suwannee	10,215	40,556,651
Hillsborough	208,166	758,193,510	Taylor	4,928	21,532,566
Holmes	7,323	26,243,400	Union	2,792	9,284,018
Indian River	16,075	54,435,569	Volusia	81,324	317,172,273
Jackson	11,067	63,432,955	Wakulla	4,480	14,731,979
Jefferson	2,885	14,662,755	Walton	7,611	27,105,002
Lafayette	1,432	5,118,533	Washington	5,487	24,665,016

Source: State of Florida, Agency for Health Care Administration, Medicaid Program Analysis, September 27, 2007, State Fiscal Year 2005–06.

Table 7.21. TEMPORARY ASSISTANCE FOR NEEDY FAMILIES: RECIPIENTS AND BENEFITS IN THE STATE AND COUNTIES OF FLORIDA, JULY 2006 THROUGH JUNE 2007

County	Families	Persons	Benefits ($1,000)	County	Families	Persons	Benefits ($1,000)
Florida	95,893	181,627	137,097	Lake	1,318	2,486	1,871
Alachua	1,867	3,541	2,483	Lee	1,358	2,217	2,057
Baker	231	431	362	Leon	1,740	3,459	2,480
Bay	1,074	2,047	1,402	Levy	373	649	594
Bradford	278	487	411	Liberty	47	62	76
Brevard	1,975	3,548	3,022	Madison	296	432	416
Broward	7,518	14,936	10,653	Manatee	1,107	1,742	1,772
Calhoun	78	131	128	Marion	1,866	3,204	2,840
Charlotte	370	576	506	Martin	345	701	477
Citrus	656	1,184	969	Miami-Dade	16,912	36,928	20,136
Clay	753	1,131	1,217	Monroe	234	390	306
Collier	536	945	753	Nassau	355	535	568
Columbia	740	1,338	1,070	Okaloosa	811	1,273	1,296
DeSoto	205	326	356	Okeechobee	249	406	347
Dixie	133	218	209	Orange	5,164	10,694	6,987
Duval	5,940	10,161	9,704	Osceola	1,677	3,644	1,953
Escambia	3,064	5,388	5,230	Palm Beach	4,160	8,179	5,786
Flagler	341	632	459	Pasco	2,304	4,255	3,177
Franklin	75	127	93	Pinellas	5,305	9,576	7,509
Gadsden	566	1,042	797	Polk	3,632	5,801	5,517
Gilchrist	147	243	242	Putnam	844	1,654	1,202
Glades	34	68	36	St. Johns	524	800	943
Gulf	115	236	145	St. Lucie	1,551	3,088	1,984
Hamilton	157	294	253	Santa Rosa	723	1,124	1,191
Hardee	270	378	469	Sarasota	795	1,264	1,279
Hendry	301	556	435	Seminole	1,272	2,531	1,779
Hernando	759	1,231	1,067	Sumter	367	594	504
Highlands	546	978	716	Suwannee	380	665	541
Hillsborough	8,379	15,807	11,236	Taylor	233	401	363
Holmes	237	398	389	Union	127	211	189
Indian River	592	1,186	698	Volusia	2,794	5,591	3,793
Jackson	291	413	488	Wakulla	142	278	224
Jefferson	113	176	191	Walton	213	326	348
Lafayette	42	67	60	Washington	205	361	339

Note: Recurring monthly payroll only. Does not include supplemental payrolls.

Source: State of Florida, Department of Children and Families, Office of Economic Self-Sufficiency, Economic Self-Sufficiency Datamart.

Table 7.22. FOOD STAMPS: RECIPIENTS AND BENEFITS IN THE STATE AND COUNTIES OF FLORIDA, JULY 2006 THROUGH JUNE 2007

County	Families	Persons	Benefits in food stamps	County	Families	Persons	Benefits in food stamps
Florida	980,448	1,953,596	1,345,596,367	Lake	11,571	26,399	15,802,196
Alachua	15,383	30,671	21,820,143	Lee	18,926	39,885	23,154,119
Baker	1,593	3,879	2,497,337	Leon	13,652	28,111	19,656,874
Bay	10,110	21,989	13,779,481	Levy	2,994	6,711	3,861,647
Bradford	2,035	4,459	2,776,722	Liberty	420	957	560,473
Brevard	21,717	45,199	28,789,164	Madison	1,965	4,191	2,583,628
Broward	81,367	155,786	106,379,030	Manatee	11,209	23,945	14,273,998
Calhoun	849	1,784	1,068,946	Marion	16,875	37,205	22,683,923
Charlotte	4,703	9,892	5,319,439	Martin	3,820	7,479	4,406,853
Citrus	6,410	13,978	8,421,805	Miami-Dade	248,622	419,881	321,107,522
Clay	5,888	14,062	8,086,724	Monroe	3,448	5,124	2,953,545
Collier	8,254	16,323	9,811,347	Nassau	2,675	5,907	3,671,155
Columbia	4,965	11,410	6,616,382	Okaloosa	6,173	13,654	7,518,246
DeSoto	2,098	4,587	2,783,754	Okeechobee	2,421	5,327	2,998,955
Dixie	1,438	3,185	1,929,657	Orange	51,665	116,813	71,688,231
Duval	51,520	113,884	79,859,926	Osceola	18,262	42,773	24,774,760
Escambia	18,681	42,227	26,690,464	Palm Beach	44,615	87,528	57,905,224
Flagler	3,418	8,101	4,787,520	Pasco	22,050	48,106	30,607,252
Franklin	666	1,425	843,053	Pinellas	49,427	91,130	61,110,367
Gadsden	4,503	9,771	6,383,636	Polk	35,010	77,528	48,228,040
Gilchrist	1,078	2,500	1,372,082	Putnam	7,995	18,273	11,852,760
Glades	374	785	456,488	St. Johns	4,414	8,921	5,287,783
Gulf	897	1,949	1,164,973	St. Lucie	14,967	31,342	20,372,326
Hamilton	1,193	2,832	1,830,316	Santa Rosa	5,085	12,083	7,376,640
Hardee	1,946	4,681	2,590,260	Sarasota	10,742	20,674	12,524,076
Hendry	3,034	7,237	4,679,098	Seminole	13,278	28,590	17,608,150
Hernando	7,030	16,280	9,853,505	Sumter	3,327	7,310	3,792,361
Highlands	5,033	10,992	6,468,922	Suwannee	3,261	7,313	4,591,417
Hillsborough	69,702	146,035	95,929,031	Taylor	1,807	3,867	2,584,036
Holmes	1,800	4,122	2,268,801	Union	927	2,168	1,405,361
Indian River	5,818	11,526	6,957,152	Volusia	27,152	54,282	34,491,246
Jackson	2,972	6,725	4,054,458	Wakulla	1,120	2,590	1,576,777
Jefferson	1,084	2,170	1,367,789	Walton	1,757	3,891	2,116,054
Lafayette	416	974	629,972	Washington	1,686	3,941	2,202,995

Note: Based on Florida system benefit authorizations for the regular Food Stamp Program. Does not include hurricane-related disaster benefits.

Source: State of Florida, Department of Children and Families, Office of Economic Self-Sufficiency, Economic Self-Sufficiency Datamart.

Table 7.23. ELDER ASSISTANCE: LIVING SITUATION, HURRICANE ASSISTANCE, AND FOOD STAMP RECIPIENTS IN THE STATE AND COUNTIES OF FLORIDA, 2003 OR 2006

PSA and County	Living situation 2006		Hurricane assistance 2003 A/		Food stamp recipients, March 2006		
	Living alone	Living in rural areas	DOEA customers	Percentage with special needs 1/	Possible eligible 2/	Partici- pants	Participa- tion rate
Florida	952,285	406,412	98,173	15.61	559,220	190,817	34.12
PSA 1	29,658	25,493	4,180	15.12	16,749	3,055	18.24
Escambia	14,247	5,831	1,336	17.44	8,349	1,712	20.51
Okaloosa	7,886	3,737	1,137	14.78	3,387	534	15.77
Santa Rosa	4,665	6,707	1,105	12.40	2,876	566	19.68
Walton	2,860	9,218	602	15.61	2,137	243	11.37
PSA 2	29,889	47,142	4,586	19.08	22,277	4,945	22.20
Bay	8,022	3,209	1,007	15.19	5,115	1,056	20.65
Calhoun	735	1,687	217	23.50	697	194	27.83
Franklin	720	2,011	116	15.52	729	84	11.52
Gadsden	2,120	5,008	357	32.49	1,991	566	28.43
Gulf	893	2,027	203	37.44	689	127	18.43
Holmes	1,078	3,060	299	44.82	976	324	33.20
Jackson	3,051	7,821	428	10.75	2,782	477	17.15
Jefferson	554	2,694	203	4.43	597	155	25.96
Leon	8,087	4,966	679	11.49	3,964	1,057	26.66
Liberty	335	1,042	135	16.30	379	75	19.79
Madison	1,051	2,826	229	9.61	1,232	243	19.72
Taylor	1,112	2,540	193	46.11	1,076	212	19.70
Wakulla	866	4,450	241	17.43	763	121	15.86
Washington	1,265	3,801	279	6.81	1,287	254	19.74
PSA 3	88,369	142,268	8,031	24.06	56,627	10,375	18.32
Alachua	7,964	10,406	701	23.54	5,070	1,167	23.02
Bradford	1,139	2,932	158	29.11	1,197	234	19.55
Citrus	10,659	17,973	1,294	4.17	6,509	859	13.20
Columbia	3,276	7,651	479	24.84	2,844	550	19.34
Dixie	994	3,221	164	78.66	1,107	195	17.62
Gilchrist	720	3,413	132	51.52	783	109	13.92
Hamilton	578	1,577	227	33.92	580	141	24.31
Hernando	10,452	8,430	728	13.32	5,161	751	14.55
Lafayette	376	1,298	109	0.92	309	46	14.89
Lake	17,671	18,901	968	17.87	9,109	1,521	16.70
Levy	2,421	9,387	290	75.52	2,123	412	19.41
Marion	19,796	30,248	1,334	21.59	12,438	2,387	19.19
Putnam	4,645	9,260	710	57.75	3,922	993	25.32
Sumter	5,058	9,083	320	6.56	3,201	420	13.12
Suwannee	2,265	7,393	310	11.61	1,872	469	25.05
Union	355	1,095	107	27.10	402	121	30.10
PSA 4	87,837	43,573	10,300	20.71	47,074	9,779	20.77
Baker	691	2,046	344	16.86	564	189	33.51
Clay	4,819	6,938	708	9.60	2,942	571	19.41
Duval	34,579	4,580	5,310	15.31	21,010	4,640	22.08
Flagler	4,715	6,657	599	23.37	1,900	363	19.11
Nassau	2,877	6,178	371	12.13	1,920	341	17.76
St. Johns	7,214	6,174	799	28.41	2,937	550	18.73
Volusia	32,942	11,000	2,169	36.05	15,801	3,125	19.78

See footnotes at end of table. Continued . . .

Table 7.23. ELDER ASSISTANCE: LIVING SITUATION, HURRICANE ASSISTANCE, AND FOOD STAMP RECIPIENTS IN THE STATE AND COUNTIES OF FLORIDA, 2003 OR 2006 (Continued)

PSA and County	Living situation 2006		Hurricane assistance 2003 A/		Food stamp recipients, March 2006		
	Living alone	Living in rural areas	DOEA customers	Percentage with special needs 1/	Possible eligible 2/	Partici-pants	Participa-tion rate
PSA 5	106,126	10,755	5,830	16.31	49,848	8,999	18.05
Pasco	29,078	10,504	1,860	22.26	15,565	2,514	16.15
Pinellas	77,048	251	3,970	13.53	34,283	6,485	18.92
PSA 6	105,448	51,995	8,756	14.62	60,341	15,627	25.90
Hardee	1,050	2,158	197	25.38	1,186	344	29.01
Highlands	7,748	11,812	604	12.25	4,652	777	16.70
Hillsborough	46,149	9,923	4,702	12.87	28,216	9,004	31.91
Manatee	22,115	4,360	1,284	15.42	9,059	1,257	13.88
Polk	28,386	23,742	1,969	17.93	17,228	4,245	24.64
PSA 7	83,254	20,695	8,557	17.97	46,489	13,729	29.53
Brevard	32,433	5,330	2,564	13.49	15,127	2,340	15.47
Orange	29,977	4,246	3,195	25.23	19,267	7,307	37.92
Osceola	6,926	8,799	1,345	10.48	5,103	2,440	47.82
Seminole	13,918	2,320	1,453	16.86	6,992	1,642	23.48
PSA 8	103,539	42,198	3,786	21.08	42,138	6,669	15.83
Charlotte	14,194	4,904	680	13.97	5,808	580	9.99
Collier	18,659	5,260	533	16.70	7,126	1,474	20.68
DeSoto	1,444	4,838	152	22.37	1,044	260	24.90
Glades	575	2,248	78	24.36	533	56	10.51
Hendry	1,259	1,759	135	12.59	1,087	361	33.21
Lee	34,715	17,959	1,049	27.84	15,989	2,514	15.72
Sarasota	32,693	5,230	1,159	21.74	10,551	1,424	13.50
PSA 9	125,230	17,643	6,646	11.74	52,365	10,466	19.99
Indian River	10,633	2,242	627	11.00	4,103	620	15.11
Martin	11,358	4,191	876	10.39	3,989	430	10.78
Okeechobee	1,789	2,736	287	16.38	1,378	243	17.63
Palm Beach	87,728	3,496	4,069	9.83	35,147	7,440	21.17
St. Lucie	13,722	4,978	787	21.98	7,748	1,733	22.37
PSA 10	99,374	380	16,671	7.81	52,308	15,107	28.88
Broward	99,374	380	16,671	7.81	52,308	15,107	28.88
PSA 11	93,561	4,270	20,830	14.90	113,004	92,066	81.47
Miami-Dade	89,501	2,294	20,458	14.78	110,286	91,421	82.89
Monroe	4,060	1,976	372	21.51	2,718	645	23.73

DOEA Department of Elder Affairs.
PSA Planning and Service Area.
A/ Estimates based on a 2003 Florida Department of Elder Affairs statewide survey applied to persons aged 60 and over measuring elder Floridian's needs.
1/ DOEA customers identified as needing special assistance in evacuating or who require a special needs shelter.
2/ Persons aged 60 and over with incomes below 125 percent of poverty.
Note: Data are for persons aged 60 and over.

Source: State of Florida, Department of Elder Affairs, *2006 Florida County Profiles* and *Assessing the Needs of Elder Floridians, 2004,* Internet site <http://elderaffairs.state.fl.us/> (accessed 13, August 2007).

Table 7.24. GRANDPARENTING: CHARACTERISTICS BY LIVING SITUATION IN THE STATE AND COUNTIES OF FLORIDA, 2006

PSA and County	Grand-parents not living with grand-children	Grand-parents living with grand-children 1/	Grand-parents responsible for grand-children 2/
Florida	3,949,339	182,733	56,664
PSA 1	127,172	5,510	2,016
Escambia	56,958	2,799	966
Okaloosa	34,245	1,536	609
SantaRosa	23,444	811	365
Walton	12,525	364	76
PSA 2	115,677	5,960	2,697
Bay	32,073	1,161	477
Calhoun	2,585	183	118
Franklin	2,994	93	80
Gadsden	7,768	744	390
Gulf	3,479	167	103
Holmes	4,026	199	82
Jackson	9,929	503	239
Jefferson	2,661	223	105
Leon	31,830	1,597	554
Liberty	1,111	35	12
Madison	3,743	272	109
Taylor	4,175	149	62
Wakulla	4,496	345	165
Washington	4,807	289	201
PSA 3	411,368	12,348	5,020
Alachua	31,925	1,578	654
Bradford	4,895	302	151
Citrus	53,240	1,140	463
Columbia	12,547	672	323
Dixie	3,890	178	89
Gilchrist	3,450	160	58
Hamilton	2,257	173	80
Hernando	54,214	1,243	430
Lafayette	1,292	96	48
Lake	85,801	2,293	808
Levy	9,704	382	123
Marion	93,069	2,401	948
Putnam	18,121	612	272
Sumter	25,937	630	322
Suwannee	9,269	416	208
Union	1,757	72	43
PSA 4	360,701	17,392	6,385
Baker	3,575	206	59
Clay	25,809	1,672	557
Duval	123,556	8,269	3,101
PSA 4 (Cont.)			
Flagler	26,842	871	311
Nassau	13,785	758	253
St.Johns	33,054	1,192	491
Volusia	134,080	4,424	1,613
PSA 5	379,039	8,529	2,760
Pasco	121,058	2,791	789
Pinellas	257,981	5,738	1,971
PSA 6	435,794	18,314	6,328
Hardee	4,988	253	92
Highlands	36,442	818	287
Hillsborough	180,221	10,726	3,520
Manatee	87,941	1,885	552
Polk	126,202	4,632	1,877
PSA 7	365,016	22,816	7,375
Brevard	139,273	4,643	1,729
Orange	130,914	10,978	3,287
Osceola	34,015	3,020	972
Seminole	60,814	4,175	1,387
PSA 8	494,743	9,429	3,234
Charlotte	67,363	1,213	408
Collier	99,511	2,231	558
DeSoto	8,488	226	113
Glades	2,811	52	10
Hendry	5,387	384	136
Lee	170,361	3,488	1,337
Sarasota	140,822	1,835	672
PSA 9	512,278	14,165	4,364
IndianRiver	44,771	1,012	393
Martin	49,161	845	190
Okeechobee	8,195	305	90
Palm Beach	345,087	9,523	2,907
St.Lucie	65,064	2,480	784
PSA 10	331,130	17,973	4,681
Broward	331,130	17,973	4,681
PSA 11	416,421	50,297	11,804
Miami-Dade	397,694	49,623	11,642
Monroe	18,727	674	162

PSA Planning and Service Area.
1/ Number of grandparents aged 60 and over living with grandchildren aged 18 and under.
2/ Number of grandparents aged 60 and over who are responsible for grandchildren aged 18 and under.

Source: State of Florida, Department of Elder Affairs, *2006 Florida County Profiles,* Internet site <http://elderaffairs.state.fl.us/> (accessed 13, August 2007).

Table 7.56. AVERAGE WEEKLY WAGES: AMOUNT RECEIVED BY PERSONS COVERED BY UNEMPLOYMENT COMPENSATION LAW IN FLORIDA, 1968 THROUGH 2006

(in dollars)

Year	Average weekly wages 1/	Year	Average weekly wages 1/	Year	Average weekly wages 1/
1968	111.71	1981	252.92	1994	453.38
1969	122.57	1982	271.25	1995	465.23
1970	129.33	1983	288.34	1996	479.30
1971	131.97	1984	306.55	1997	493.80
1972	138.02	1985	314.88	1998	522.28
1973	143.30	1986	329.60	1999	541.19
1974	155.82	1987	344.32	2000	581.74
1975	167.02	1988	362.41	2001	607.00
1976	175.27	1989	382.00	2002	624.00
1977	185.69	1990	392.18	2003	645.00
1978	195.01	1991	408.82	2004	677.00
1979	210.73	1992	424.66	2005	708.00
1980	227.97	1993	443.95	2006 A/	740.00

A/ Preliminary.
1/ Data prior to 1972 do not include state, local, or federal government figures. Beginning in 1972 state data were included, and beginning in 1974 local data were included. Does not include federal data after 1974. Data are for fiscal years from 1971 to date; data are for calendar years prior to 1971.
Note: In 1972 and 1978 changes were made extending coverage of workers.

Table 7.57. UNEMPLOYMENT INSURANCE: CONTRIBUTIONS AND DISBURSEMENTS FOR UNEMPLOYMENT INSURANCE IN FLORIDA, 1968 THROUGH 2006

(rounded to thousands of dollars)

Year	Contributions deposits 1/	Total disbursements 2/	Year	Contributions deposits 1/	Total disbursements 2/	Year	Contributions deposits 1/	Total disbursements 2/
1968	34,094	22,343	1981	305,028	206,012	1994	927,283	801,120
1969	42,145	20,875	1982	326,706	379,067	1995	694,134	632,215
1970	48,594	37,306	1983	451,459	406,075	1996	647,922	635,512
1971	57,425	49,704	1984	526,691	279,457	1997	607,804	610,951
1972	71,799	45,441	1985	514,281	277,463	1998	463,692	628,370
1973	85,861	44,962	1986	478,859	315,337	1999	549,539	633,496
1974	99,304	117,453	1987	469,296	285,736	2000	398,303	635,034
1975	263,243	496,688	1988	468,348	304,930	2001	525,447	918,288
1976	342,166	407,060	1989	480,211	355,749	2002	553,559	1,169,354
1977	360,650	271,917	1990	461,103	488,961	2003	721,918	1,146,980
1978	424,988	136,723	1991	560,898	897,263	2004	973,414	1,330,824
1979	389,370	135,457	1992	1,275,490	1,512,423	2005	976,566	1,170,113
1980	321,578	197,981	1993	1,259,207	1,199,657	2006	806,176	1,170,794

1/ Includes interest, reimbursable interstate and state and local government benefits.
2/ Includes payable interstate benefits.
Source for Tables 7.56 and 7.57: State of Florida, Department of Labor and Employment Security, Division of Employment Security, *Historical Series of Unemployment Insurance Statistical Data, 1937-1979,* and Bureau of Labor Statistics, Internet site <http://www.bls.gov> (accessed 14, August 2007) and State of Florida, Department of Financial Services, *Florida's Comprehensive Annual Financial Report, Fiscal year ending June 30, 2006,* Internet site <http://www.fldfs.com/> (accessed 20, April 2007).

PHYSICAL GEOGRAPHY AND ENVIRONMENT

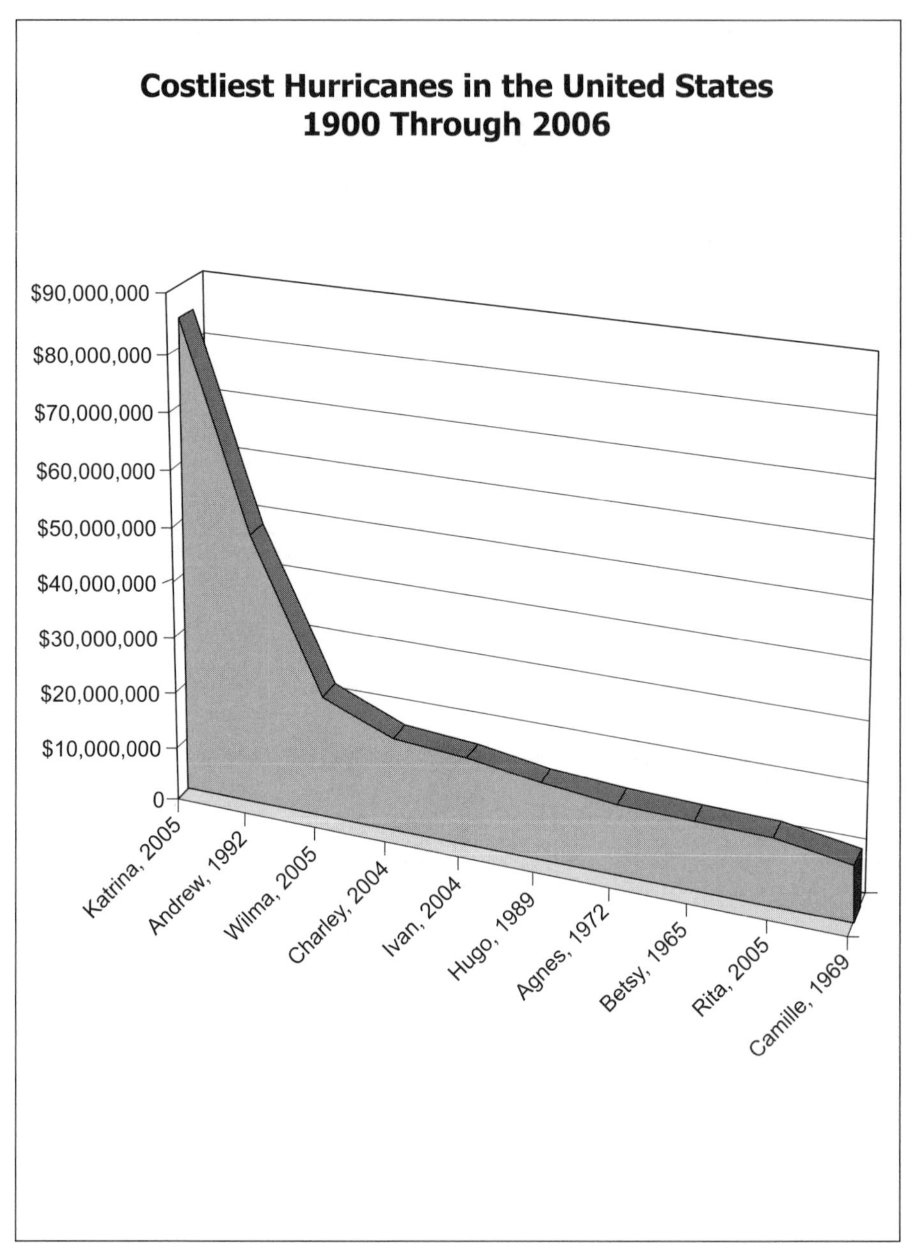

Source: Table 8.77

Section 8.00
Physical Geography and Environment

This section presents data on the physical geography and environment of the state of Florida. Geographically covered in this section are land and water area, coastlines, and elevations. Environmental subjects include solid waste, water usage, climate, hurricanes, and air pollution.

Sources. The Geography Division of the U.S Census Bureau provides data on the land and water area of the state and counties of Florida based on Topically Integrated Geographic Encoding and Reinforcement (TIGER) mapping files from the 2000 censuses of Population and Housing. Data for states can be found in the Census Bureau's *Statistical Abstract of the United States.* Florida county data from the 2000 census are presented on Table 8.03. Additional land area data are provided by the National Oceanic and Atmospheric Administration.

Solid waste statistics are published online by the Bureau of Solid and Hazardous Waste, Florida Department of Environmental Protection (DEP) in *Solid Waste Annual Report.* The DEP Division of Air Resources Management publishes particulate matter concentrations as a gauge to air pollution standards. "Air Quality Technical Reports" may be found on the DEP Web site.

Data on water use are reported by the U.S. Department of the Interior Geological Survey and published in *Estimated Use of Water in the United States in 2000.* Florida data are provided by the Tallahassee, Florida office of the Geological Survey and are published in a U.S. Geological Survey Scientific Investigations Report titled, "Water Withdrawals, Use, Discharge, and Trends in Florida, 2000." Copies of this report are available on the Internet. There are five water management districts in Florida. A map of these districts with the location of each district headquarter is on page 326.

Tables in this section containing information relating to temperature, precipitation, and other climatic phenomena data are provided by the U.S. Department of Commerce's National Oceanic and Atmospheric Administration (NOAA) in *Climatological Data: Florida* and *Comparative Climatic Data.* A map of the National Weather Station Offices located throughout the state is on page 332.

Hurricane landfall, force, cost, and death data are published by the National Hurricane Center in periodic NOAA technical memoranda available on the NOAA Web site.

Section 8.00
Physical Geography and Environment

Tables listed by major heading

Table 8.01. GEOGRAPHY: LAND AND WATER AREAS, COASTLINE, AND ELEVATIONS FOR FLORIDA, OTHER SUNBELT STATES, OTHER POPULOUS STATES AND THE UNITED STATES, 2000

State	Area (square miles)					Elevation (feet)		
			Water					Approx-imate
	Total	Land 1/	Total	Inland 2/	Coastal 3/	Highest	Lowest	mean
				Sunbelt states				
Florida	65,755	53,927	11,828	4,672	1,311	345	A/	100
Alabama	52,419	50,744	1,675	956	519	2,405	A/	500
Arizona	113,998	113,635	364	364	0	12,633	70	4,100
Arkansas	53,179	52,068	1,110	1,110	0	2,753	55	650
California	163,696	155,959	7,736	2,674	222	14,494	-282	2,900
Georgia	59,425	57,906	1,519	1,016	48	4,784	A/	600
Louisiana	51,840	43,562	8,278	4,154	1,935	535	-8	100
Mississippi	48,430	46,907	1,523	785	590	806	A/	300
New Mexico	121,590	121,356	234	234	0	13,161	2,842	5,700
North Carolina	53,819	48,711	5,108	3,960	0	6,684	A/	700
Oklahoma	69,898	68,667	1,231	1,231	0	4,973	289	1,300
South Carolina	32,020	30,110	1,911	1,008	72	3,560	A/	350
Tennessee	42,143	41,217	926	926	0	6,643	178	900
Texas	268,581	261,797	6,784	5,056	404	8,749	A/	1,700
Virginia	42,774	39,594	3,180	1,006	1,728	5,729	A/	950
				Other populous states				
Illinois	57,914	55,584	2,331	756	0	1,235	279	600
Indiana	36,418	35,867	551	316	0	1,257	320	700
Massachusetts	10,555	7,840	2,715	423	977	3,487	A/	500
Michigan	96,716	56,804	39,912	1,611	0	1,979	571	900
New Jersey	8,721	7,417	1,304	396	401	1,803	A/	250
New York	54,556	47,214	7,342	1,895	981	5,344	A/	1,000
Ohio	44,825	40,948	3,877	378	0	1,549	455	850
Pennsylvania	46,055	44,817	1,239	490	0	3,213	A/	1,100
United States	3,794,083	3,537,438	256,645	78,797	42,225	20,320	-282	2,500

A/ Sea level.
1/ Dry land and land temporarily or partially covered by water, as marshland and swamps.
2/ Inland water is defined as lakes, reservoirs, ponds and rivers, canals, estuaries, and bays from the point downstream at which they are narrower than one nautical mile to the point upstream where they appear as a single line feature on the Census Bureau's TIGER File.
3/ Coastal water is within embayments separated from territorial waters by 1 to 24 nautical miles. Excludes territorial waters (waters between the 3-mile limit and the shoreline).

Source: U.S., Department of Commerce, Census Bureau, *Statistical Abstract of the United States, 2007,* and U.S., Department of Commerce, Geography Division, unpublished data.

Table 8.03. LAND AND WATER AREA: AREA OF THE STATE AND COUNTIES OF FLORIDA, APRIL 1, 2000

(square miles)

County	Total	Land area	Water area 1/	County	Total	Land area	Water area 1/
Florida	65,754.6	53,926.8	11,827.8	Lake	1,156.4	953.2	203.3
				Lee	1,211.9	803.6	408.3
Alachua	969.1	874.3	94.9	Leon	701.8	666.7	35.0
Baker	588.9	585.2	3.7	Levy	1,412.3	1,118.4	293.9
Bay	1,033.3	763.7	269.6	Liberty	843.2	835.9	7.3
Bradford	300.0	293.1	6.9	Madison	715.8	691.8	24.0
Brevard	1,557.0	1,018.2	538.8	Manatee	892.8	741.0	151.7
Broward	1,319.6	1,205.4	114.2	Marion	1,663.0	1,578.9	84.2
Calhoun	574.3	567.3	7.0	Martin	752.8	555.6	197.2
Charlotte	859.1	693.6	165.5	Miami-Dade	2,431.3	1,946.1	485.2
Citrus	773.2	583.8	189.3	Monroe	3,737.2	996.9	2,740.2
Clay	643.7	601.1	42.6	Nassau	725.9	651.6	74.3
Collier	2,304.9	2,025.3	279.6	Okaloosa	1,082.0	935.6	146.4
Columbia	801.0	797.1	4.0	Okeechobee	891.6	773.9	117.6
DeSoto	639.5	637.3	2.2	Orange	1,004.2	907.5	96.7
Dixie	863.7	704.0	159.7	Osceola	1,506.4	1,321.9	184.5
Duval	918.2	773.7	144.6	Palm Beach	2,386.3	1,974.1	412.2
Escambia	875.6	662.4	213.2	Pasco	868.0	744.9	123.1
Flagler	570.8	485.0	85.8	Pinellas	607.7	279.9	327.8
Franklin	1,037.5	544.3	493.1	Polk	2,010.0	1,874.4	135.6
Gadsden	528.5	516.1	12.4	Putnam	827.2	721.9	105.3
Gilchrist	355.5	348.9	6.6	St. Johns	821.4	609.0	212.4
Glades	986.4	773.6	212.8	St. Lucie	688.1	572.5	115.6
Gulf	744.6	554.6	190.0	Santa Rosa	1,173.6	1,016.9	156.7
Hamilton	519.3	514.9	4.5	Sarasota	725.2	571.6	153.6
Hardee	638.3	637.3	1.0	Seminole	344.9	308.2	36.7
Hendry	1,189.8	1,152.5	37.3	Sumter	580.3	545.7	34.6
Hernando	589.1	478.3	110.8	Suwannee	691.9	687.6	4.3
Highlands	1,106.3	1,028.3	78.0	Taylor	1,232.0	1,041.9	190.1
Hillsborough	1,266.2	1,050.9	215.3	Union	249.7	240.3	9.4
Holmes	488.7	482.5	6.3	Volusia	1,432.4	1,103.3	329.2
Indian River	616.9	503.2	113.7	Wakulla	735.7	606.7	129.1
Jackson	954.6	915.6	38.9	Walton	1,238.0	1,057.6	180.5
Jefferson	636.7	597.7	38.9	Washington	615.8	579.9	35.9
Lafayette	547.9	542.8	5.1				

1/ Water area measurement figures in the 2000 census data reflect all water, including inland, coastal, territorial, new reservoirs, and other man-made lakes.

Source: U.S., Department of Commerce, Census Bureau, Geography Division, Internet site <http://www.census.gov/> (accessed 22, August 2006).

Table 8.15. SOLID WASTE: TONNAGE BY DISPOSAL PROCESS AND PER CAPITA AMOUNT IN THE STATE AND COUNTIES OF FLORIDA, 2002 AND 2003

County	Disposal process 1/ Recycled 2002	Recycled 2003	Landfilled 2002	Landfilled 2003	Combusted 2002	Combusted 2003	Per capita tons 2002	Per capita tons 2003
Florida	8,271.7	8,589.4	17,018.7	17,915.0	3,913.3	4,010.1	1.76	1.79
Alachua	79.8	75.1	168.4	177.1	0.0	0.0	1.09	1.09
Baker	2.3	2.9	17.0	16.7	0.0	0.0	0.84	0.84
Bay	44.5	34.7	93.5	172.3	72.8	77.5	1.39	1.84
Bradford	5.4	6.9	17.3	15.9	0.0	0.0	0.86	0.85
Brevard	326.9	419.5	708.3	704.5	0.0	0.0	2.10	2.21
Broward	671.3	624.9	1,426.9	1,523.4	765.3	811.9	1.72	1.74
Calhoun	0.7	0.9	3.6	3.7	2.0	2.1	0.48	0.50
Charlotte	34.4	43.3	120.2	130.3	0.0	0.0	1.04	1.14
Citrus	66.8	62.4	163.4	172.1	0.0	0.0	1.87	1.86
Clay	38.6	45.8	105.1	147.8	0.0	0.0	0.96	1.24
Collier	181.1	193.1	446.3	477.6	0.0	0.0	2.26	2.29
Columbia	13.8	12.0	59.6	56.8	0.0	0.0	1.26	1.17
DeSoto	4.4	2.9	27.9	24.7	0.0	0.0	0.99	0.82
Dixie	3.8	4.7	10.8	11.2	0.0	0.0	1.01	1.08
Duval	596.5	715.7	990.9	1,483.5	0.0	0.0	1.96	2.66
Escambia	85.3	75.4	337.1	473.9	0.0	0.0	1.41	1.81
Flagler	26.4	46.4	98.2	88.2	0.0	0.0	2.19	2.19
Franklin	1.5	2.3	15.0	16.6	0.0	0.0	1.62	1.80
Gadsden	4.5	5.3	30.3	30.1	0.0	0.0	0.76	0.76
Gilchrist	1.4	1.4	7.5	5.8	0.0	0.0	0.59	0.46
Glades	0.4	0.3	7.0	8.9	0.0	0.0	0.69	0.86
Gulf	7.4	1.7	12.7	15.4	3.7	4.7	1.57	1.40
Hamilton	1.0	0.9	3.9	1.9	0.0	0.0	0.36	0.20
Hardee	2.5	3.0	20.9	21.3	0.0	0.0	0.85	0.89
Hendry	5.6	9.1	29.1	37.8	11.7	2.4	1.28	1.35
Hernando	55.2	57.2	165.7	141.2	0.0	0.0	1.62	1.41
Highlands	17.6	20.1	91.3	78.5	0.0	0.0	1.22	1.09
Hillsborough	508.1	577.8	573.0	791.5	525.8	491.4	1.52	1.72
Holmes	0.9	0.6	5.6	5.0	0.0	0.0	0.35	0.30
Indian River	90.8	43.3	283.9	308.7	0.0	0.0	3.17	2.91
Jackson	3.8	3.6	31.9	39.8	0.0	0.0	0.75	0.89
Jefferson	1.4	3.0	8.9	10.6	0.0	0.0	0.78	1.00
Lafayette	0.6	0.4	3.2	3.1	0.0	0.0	0.53	0.47
Lake	44.1	54.5	61.6	32.0	80.0	98.7	0.80	0.77

See footnote at end of table.

Continued . . .

Table 8.15. SOLID WASTE: TONNAGE BY DISPOSAL PROCESS AND PER CAPITA AMOUNT IN THE STATE AND COUNTIES OF FLORIDA, 2002 AND 2003 (Continued)

County	Disposal process 1/						Per capita tons	
	Recycled		Landfilled		Combusted			
	2002	2003	2002	2003	2002	2003	2002	2003
Lee	329.4	464.2	410.1	432.1	262.4	326.8	2.11	2.47
Leon	152.1	171.5	398.9	251.9	0.0	0.0	2.22	1.66
Levy	2.2	2.3	40.5	24.1	0.0	0.0	1.18	0.72
Liberty	0.6	3.6	4.3	6.5	0.0	0.0	0.68	1.40
Madison	2.6	2.6	16.6	17.5	0.0	0.0	1.01	1.05
Manatee	234.3	286.3	332.9	343.1	0.0	0.0	2.04	2.19
Marion	92.9	93.9	219.5	236.8	0.0	0.0	1.15	1.17
Martin	60.6	113.3	134.9	256.1	0.0	0.0	1.49	2.75
Miami-Dade	718.0	747.0	2,364.3	2,402.7	865.5	843.5	1.71	1.70
Monroe	40.7	34.6	141.4	146.0	0.0	0.0	2.24	2.24
Nassau	10.6	2.3	91.9	97.6	0.0	0.0	1.68	1.58
Okaloosa	49.2	42.1	337.5	189.2	0.0	0.0	2.19	1.28
Okeechobee	10.9	9.5	37.5	32.9	0.0	0.0	1.33	1.14
Orange	661.1	853.8	1,471.0	1,820.6	0.0	0.0	2.23	2.72
Osceola	46.7	24.1	225.6	234.5	0.0	0.0	1.41	1.23
Palm Beach	659.4	639.8	732.6	814.5	447.3	438.9	1.55	1.56
Pasco	145.0	227.6	112.0	112.3	241.9	243.5	1.32	1.55
Pinellas	757.8	524.7	833.6	615.5	561.6	596.1	2.41	1.85
Polk	225.2	210.9	622.9	652.2	60.9	50.6	1.81	1.78
Putnam	19.4	18.7	64.4	67.1	0.0	0.0	1.17	1.19
St. Johns	44.8	38.0	207.1	225.6	0.0	0.0	1.88	1.89
St. Lucie	119.0	85.6	209.9	168.8	0.0	0.0	1.62	1.20
Santa Rosa	79.6	78.7	276.5	144.1	1.5	1.5	2.86	1.74
Sarasota	244.2	170.6	391.9	297.4	0.0	0.0	1.87	1.34
Seminole	102.9	121.5	369.5	303.0	0.0	0.0	1.22	1.07
Sumter	17.7	12.0	31.4	39.8	3.7	1.7	0.86	0.85
Suwannee	30.2	32.8	98.8	95.2	0.0	0.0	3.61	3.44
Taylor	3.1	4.0	18.2	17.4	0.0	0.0	1.08	1.04
Union	3.0	2.7	9.7	10.9	0.0	0.0	0.92	0.99
Volusia	469.6	379.2	558.4	499.2	0.0	0.0	2.24	1.87
Wakulla	2.8	4.2	0.0	10.9	7.1	4.7	0.41	0.79
Walton	6.5	34.8	97.3	107.4	0.0	0.0	2.28	3.02
Washington	1.1	0.9	11.4	14.1	0.0	14.1	0.58	0.58

1/ In thousand tons, rounded to hundreds.

Source: State of Florida, Department of Environmental Protection, Division of Waste Management, Bureau of Solid and Hazardous Waste, *2004 Solid Waste Annual Report Data*, and previous edition, Internet site <http://www.dep.state.fl.us/> (accessed 21, March 2007).

Table 8.16. SOLID WASTE: MUNICIPAL TONNAGE COLLECTED AND RECYCLED BY TYPE OF GENERATOR IN THE STATE AND COUNTIES OF FLORIDA, 2003

County	Total municipal solid waste: Amount collected: Tons	Per capita per year (pounds)	Per capita per day (pounds)	Percentage recycled	Residential: Amount collected (tons)	Residential: Percentage recycled	Commercial: Amount collected (tons)	Commercial: Percentage recycled
Florida	30,498,866	3,573	9.79	28.05	13,180,976	24.20	17,317,890	30.97
Alachua	252,245	2,181	5.98	29.79	78,197	30.67	174,048	29.39
Baker	19,533	1,671	4.58	14.61	8,790	9.74	10,743	18.60
Bay	284,522	3,675	10.07	12.19	89,460	6.09	195,062	14.99
Bradford	22,840	1,694	4.64	30.32	15,988	18.19	6,852	58.63
Brevard	1,124,020	4,427	12.13	37.33	584,490	21.93	539,530	54.00
Broward	2,960,335	3,486	9.55	21.11	976,911	14.55	1,983,424	24.34
Calhoun	6,704	998	2.73	13.98	5,154	5.18	1,550	43.23
Charlotte	173,646	2,285	6.26	24.94	104,188	12.56	69,458	43.52
Citrus	234,536	3,729	10.22	26.62	122,137	8.23	112,399	46.60
Clay	193,591	2,482	6.80	23.67	77,736	33.31	115,855	17.20
Collier	670,699	4,587	12.57	28.79	220,029	33.91	450,670	26.29
Columbia	68,711	2,334	6.39	17.41	24,229	16.22	44,482	18.05
DeSoto	27,552	1,635	4.48	10.46	26,300	10.11	1,252	17.73
Dixie	14,778	2,012	5.51	0.00	14,778	0.00	0	0.00
Duval	2,199,204	5,323	14.58	32.55	808,775	19.35	1,390,429	40.22
Escambia	549,289	3,622	9.92	13.73	252,673	3.28	296,616	22.63
Flagler	134,607	4,375	11.99	34.51	24,856	20.13	109,751	37.76
Franklin	18,880	3,603	9.87	12.25	13,593	12.24	5,287	12.28
Gadsden	35,363	1,521	4.17	14.88	20,510	6.62	14,853	26.29
Gilchrist	7,198	928	2.54	20.05	6,611	18.80	587	34.07
Glades	9,258	1,726	4.73	3.16	7,883	1.95	1,375	10.11
Gulf	21,799	2,792	7.65	7.70	13,297	7.29	8,502	8.34
Hamilton	2,864	408	1.12	32.40	1,924	36.49	940	24.04
Hardee	24,311	1,775	4.86	12.40	14,760	14.43	9,551	9.26
Hendry	49,301	2,701	7.40	18.51	42,399	18.51	6,902	18.52
Hernando	198,417	2,821	7.73	28.82	113,098	36.94	85,319	18.06
Highlands	98,634	2,182	5.98	20.43	56,456	21.08	42,178	19.55
Hillsborough	1,860,725	3,447	9.44	31.05	744,291	32.38	1,116,434	30.17
Holmes	5,625	594	1.63	11.20	3,515	12.20	2,110	9.53
Indian River	352,019	5,810	15.92	12.31	264,014	12.31	88,005	12.31
Jackson	43,465	1,774	4.86	8.34	13,040	5.07	30,425	9.75
Jefferson	13,567	2,002	5.49	22.00	10,854	22.00	2,713	22.01
Lafayette	3,488	949	2.60	12.18	2,791	11.14	697	16.36
Lake	185,133	1,538	4.21	29.45	148,923	29.55	36,210	29.02

Continued . . .

Table 8.16. SOLID WASTE: MUNICIPAL TONNAGE COLLECTED AND RECYCLED BY TYPE OF GENERATOR IN THE STATE AND COUNTIES OF FLORIDA, 2003 (Continued)

County	Total municipal solid waste: Amount collected: Tons	Per capita per year (pounds)	Per capita per day (pounds)	Percentage recycled	Residential: Amount collected (tons)	Percentage recycled	Commercial: Amount collected (tons)	Percentage recycled
Lee	1,223,069	4,941	13.54	37.95	406,174	32.39	816,895	40.71
Leon	423,374	3,314	9.08	40.50	142,488	39.37	280,886	41.07
Levy	26,379	1,439	3.94	8.65	14,916	10.89	11,463	5.75
Liberty	10,103	2,796	7.66	35.93	2,200	27.64	7,903	38.24
Madison	20,087	2,099	5.75	12.82	12,451	5.22	7,636	25.21
Manatee	629,378	4,388	12.02	45.49	252,048	65.95	377,330	31.82
Marion	330,730	2,346	6.43	28.39	219,433	21.00	111,297	42.97
Martin	369,363	5,493	15.05	30.67	277,123	30.72	92,240	30.51
Miami-Dade	3,993,203	3,404	9.33	18.71	1,762,289	13.01	2,230,914	23.21
Monroe	180,616	4,485	12.29	19.17	99,664	34.65	80,952	0.11
Nassau	99,891	3,168	8.68	2.29	50,678	1.15	49,213	3.45
Okaloosa	231,352	2,555	7.00	18.21	57,119	29.32	174,233	14.57
Okeechobee	42,409	2,278	6.24	22.47	31,383	22.47	11,026	22.47
Orange	2,674,440	5,440	14.91	31.92	750,437	42.77	1,924,003	27.69
Osceola	258,642	2,458	6.73	9.33	144,839	10.18	113,803	8.24
Palm Beach	1,893,175	3,125	8.56	33.79	916,601	33.46	976,574	34.11
Pasco	583,442	3,109	8.52	39.01	268,382	15.31	315,060	59.21
Pinellas	1,736,290	3,695	10.12	30.22	850,782	13.57	885,508	46.22
Polk	913,628	3,569	9.78	23.08	340,820	34.61	572,808	16.22
Putnam	85,841	2,385	6.54	21.79	56,650	14.03	29,191	36.86
St. Johns	263,673	3,771	10.33	14.42	112,576	28.72	151,097	3.78
St. Lucie	254,491	2,402	6.58	33.65	127,831	33.63	126,660	33.67
Santa Rosa	224,356	3,481	9.54	35.06	89,734	35.07	134,622	35.06
Sarasota	468,012	2,684	7.35	36.45	243,366	36.45	224,646	36.45
Seminole	426,470	2,160	5.92	28.95	277,206	26.45	149,264	33.58
Sumter	53,525	1,699	4.66	22.39	21,410	31.58	32,115	16.25
Suwannee	128,046	6,885	18.86	0.00	95,213	0.00	32,833	0.00
Taylor	21,425	2,075	5.69	18.67	9,760	18.97	11,665	18.43
Union	13,555	1,975	5.41	19.73	7,184	11.90	6,371	28.55
Volusia	878,446	3,732	10.22	43.17	512,385	36.26	366,061	52.83
Wakulla	19,817	1,589	4.35	21.00	17,899	17.23	1,918	56.20
Walton	142,168	6,041	16.55	24.49	88,491	30.07	53,677	15.29
Washington	12,611	1,151	3.15	7.48	8,794	2.59	3,817	18.73

Source: State of Florida, Department of Environmental Protection, Division of Waste Management, Bureau of Solid and Hazardous Waste, *2004 Solid Waste Annual Report Data,* Internet site <http://www.dep.state.fl.us/> (accessed 21, March 2007).

Table 8.35. WATER USE: WATER WITHDRAWALS BY WATER TYPE, SOURCE AND CATEGORY IN FLORIDA, OTHER SUNBELT STATES AND THE UNITED STATES, 2000

(in millions of gallons per day)

State	Total	Water type		Water source		Major category (freshwater only)			
		Fresh	Saline	Ground	Surface	Irrigation 1/	Public supply 2/	Industrial 3/	Power 4/
Florida	20,100	8,140	12,000	5,020	15,100	4,290	2,440	291	658
Alabama	9,990	9,990	0	440	9,550	43	834	833	8,190
Arizona	6,730	6,720	8	3,430	3,300	5,400	1,080	20	100
Arkansas	10,900	10,900	0	6,920	3,950	7,910	421	134	2,180
California	51,200	38,400	12,800	15,400	35,800	30,500	6,120	188	352
Georgia	6,500	6,410	92	1,450	5,060	1,140	1,250	622	3,250
Louisiana	10,400	10,400	0	1,630	8,730	1,020	753	2,680	5,610
Mississippi	2,960	2,810	148	2,180	781	1,410	359	242	362
New Mexico	3,260	3,260	0	1,540	1,710	2,860	296	11	56
North Carolina	11,400	9,730	1,620	580	10,800	287	945	293	7,850
Oklahoma	2,020	1,760	256	1,030	990	718	675	26	146
South Carolina	7,170	7,170	0	330	6,840	267	566	565	5,710
Tennessee	10,800	10,800	0	417	10,400	22	890	842	9,040
Texas	29,600	24,800	4,850	8,970	20,700	8,630	4,230	1,450	9,820
Virginia	8,830	5,200	3,640	314	8,520	26	720	470	3,850
United States	408,000	345,000	62,300	84,500	323,000	137,000	43,300	18,500	136,000

1/ Includes water withdrawn for crop irrigation, livestock, and fish farming purposes and recreational irrigation including turf grass for golf courses and landscape irrigation.
2/ Includes water withdrawn by water supply systems or domestic self-supplied users.
3/ Includes water withdrawn for commercial, industrial, and mining purposes.
4/ Includes water withdrawn for all uses at fossil fuel or nuclear power plants.

Source: U.S., Department of the Interior, Geological Survey, Reston, Virginia: *Estimated Use of Water in the United States in 2000,* by S.S. Hutson and other, 2004, U.S. Geological Survey Circular 1268. Copies of this report and other national water-use data are available at http://water.usgs.gov/watuse or by contacting the USGS at Box 25286, Denver Center, Denver, Colorado 80225.

Table 8.36. WATER USE: WITHDRAWALS BY CATEGORY OF USE AND BY SOURCE IN FLORIDA, 2000

(in millions of gallons per day)

Category	Freshwater			Saline		
	Total	Ground	Surface	Total	Ground	Surface
Total	8,192	5,079	3,113	11,956	4	11,952
Public supply	2,437	2,199	237	0	0	0
Domestic self-supplied	199	199	0	0	0	0
Commercial-industrial-mining	563	431	133	1	0	1
Agricultural irrigation	3,923	1,990	1,933	0	0	0
Recreational irrigation	412	230	181	0	0	0
Power generation	658	30	629	11,955	4	11,951

Note: Detail may not add to totals due to rounding.
Source: U.S., Department of the Interior, Geological Survey, Tallahassee, Florida: Water withdrawals, use, discharge, and trends in Florida, 2000, by R.L. Marella, 2004, U.S. Geological Survey Scientific Investigations Report 2004-5151. Copies of this report and other Florida water-use data are available at http://fl.water.usgs.gov or by contacting the USGS at 2010 Levy Avenue, Tallahassee, Florida 32310.

Table 8.39. WATER USE: FRESHWATER WITHDRAWALS BY CATEGORY OF USE AND BY WATER MANAGEMENT DISTRICT IN FLORIDA, 2000

(in millions of gallons per day)

Category	Northwest Florida	St. Johns River	South Florida	Southwest Florida	Suwannee River
Total	950.57	3,393.87	7,952.66	7,527.15	323.34
Public supply	192.07	572.59	1,119.52	536.82	15.79
Domestic self-supplied	21.75	51.70	52.43	52.74	20.06
Commercial-industrial-mining	78.16	123.62	124.01	151.92	86.77
Agricultural irrigation 1/	46.26	606.53	2,466.59	707.89	95.74
Recreational irrigation 2/	23.07	104.60	209.89	72.74	1.43
Power generation	589.26	1,934.83	3,980.22	6,005.04	103.55

1/ Withdrawals for crops, livestock, and fish farming.
2/ Withdrawals for turf grass and landscaping.
Note: Values may not be identical to the data reported by the water management districts due to differences in data collection or revisions. Detail may not add to totals because of rounding. Data are revised.

Table 8.40. WATER USE: FRESHWATER WITHDRAWALS BY CATEGORY OF USE IN FLORIDA SPECIFIED YEARS 1975 THROUGH 2000

(in millions of gallons per day)

Category	1975	1980	1985	1990	1995	2000
Total	6,773	6,701	6,313	7,583	7,230	8,192
Public supply	1,124	1,406	1,685	1,925	2,079	2,437
Domestic self-supplied	228	243	259	299	297	199
Commercial-industrial-mining	883	700	709	770	692	563
Agricultural irrigation 1/	2,930	3,026	2,798	3,495	3,244	3,923
Recreational irrigation 2/	(NA)	(NA)	182	310	281	411
Power generation	1,608	1,326	680	784	637	659

(NA) Not available.
1/ Withdrawals for crops, livestock, and fish farming.
2/ Withdrawals for turf grass and landscaping. Included under agricultural irrigation prior to 1985.
Note: Detail may not add to totals due to rounding.

Source for Tables 8:39 and 8:40: U.S., Department of Interior, Geological Survey, Tallahassee, Florida: Water withdrawals, use, discharge, and trends in Florida, 2000, by R.L. Marella, 2004, U.S. Geological Survey Scientific Investigations Report 2004-5151. Copies of this report and other Florida water-use data are available at <http://fl.water.usgs.gov> or by contacting the USGS at 2010 Levy Avenue, Tallahassee, Florida 32310.

Table 8.41. WATER USE: WATER WITHDRAWALS BY SOURCE IN THE STATE AND COUNTIES OF FLORIDA, 2000

(in millions of gallons per day)

County	Total	Ground Total	Ground Fresh	Ground Saline	Surface Total	Surface Fresh	Surface Saline
Florida	20,147.59	5,082.49	5,078.67	3.82	15,065.10	3,113.10	11,952.00
Alachua	60.15	59.58	59.58	0.00	0.57	0.57	0.00
Baker	7.88	6.15	6.15	0.00	1.73	1.73	0.00
Bay	322.95	12.22	12.22	0.00	310.73	45.68	265.05
Bradford	5.85	5.79	5.79	0.00	0.06	0.06	0.00
Brevard	1,262.01	143.53	143.53	0.00	1,118.48	39.20	1,079.28
Broward	1,814.20	273.46	273.46	0.00	1,540.74	28.35	1,512.39
Calhoun	6.13	4.34	4.34	0.00	1.79	1.79	0.00
Charlotte	63.99	35.95	35.95	0.00	28.04	28.04	0.00
Citrus	425.24	30.05	30.05	0.00	395.19	1.29	393.90
Clay	34.09	33.57	33.57	0.00	0.52	0.52	0.00
Collier	230.04	202.49	202.49	0.00	27.55	27.55	0.00
Columbia	14.09	13.88	13.88	0.00	0.21	0.21	0.00
DeSoto	133.38	123.87	123.87	0.00	9.51	9.51	0.00
Dixie	3.53	3.50	3.50	0.00	0.03	0.03	0.00
Duval	817.13	154.33	154.33	0.00	662.80	1.65	661.15
Escambia	317.25	91.94	91.94	0.00	225.31	225.31	0.00
Flagler	28.15	24.55	24.55	0.00	3.60	3.60	0.00
Franklin	2.25	2.25	2.25	0.00	0.00	0.00	0.00
Gadsden	16.33	8.93	8.93	0.00	7.40	7.40	0.00
Gilchrist	16.15	15.83	15.83	0.00	0.32	0.32	0.00
Glades	74.67	21.03	21.03	0.00	53.64	53.64	0.00
Gulf	4.75	3.10	3.10	0.00	1.65	1.65	0.00
Hamilton	41.72	41.61	41.61	0.00	0.11	0.11	0.00
Hardee	91.14	90.53	90.53	0.00	0.61	0.61	0.00
Hendry	512.11	197.12	197.12	0.00	314.99	314.99	0.00
Hernando	50.45	49.46	49.46	0.00	0.99	0.99	0.00
Highlands	174.55	157.29	157.29	0.00	17.26	17.26	0.00
Hillsborough	3,479.72	197.44	197.44	0.00	3,282.28	94.28	3,188.00
Holmes	4.09	3.77	3.77	0.00	0.32	0.32	0.00
Indian River	287.45	87.36	87.36	0.00	200.09	161.08	39.01
Jackson	113.10	21.87	21.87	0.00	91.23	91.23	0.00
Jefferson	8.56	8.39	8.39	0.00	0.17	0.17	0.00
Lafayette	6.94	6.78	6.78	0.00	0.16	0.16	0.00
Lake	100.61	90.84	90.84	0.00	9.77	9.77	0.00

See footnote at end of table.

Continued . . .

Water Management Districts

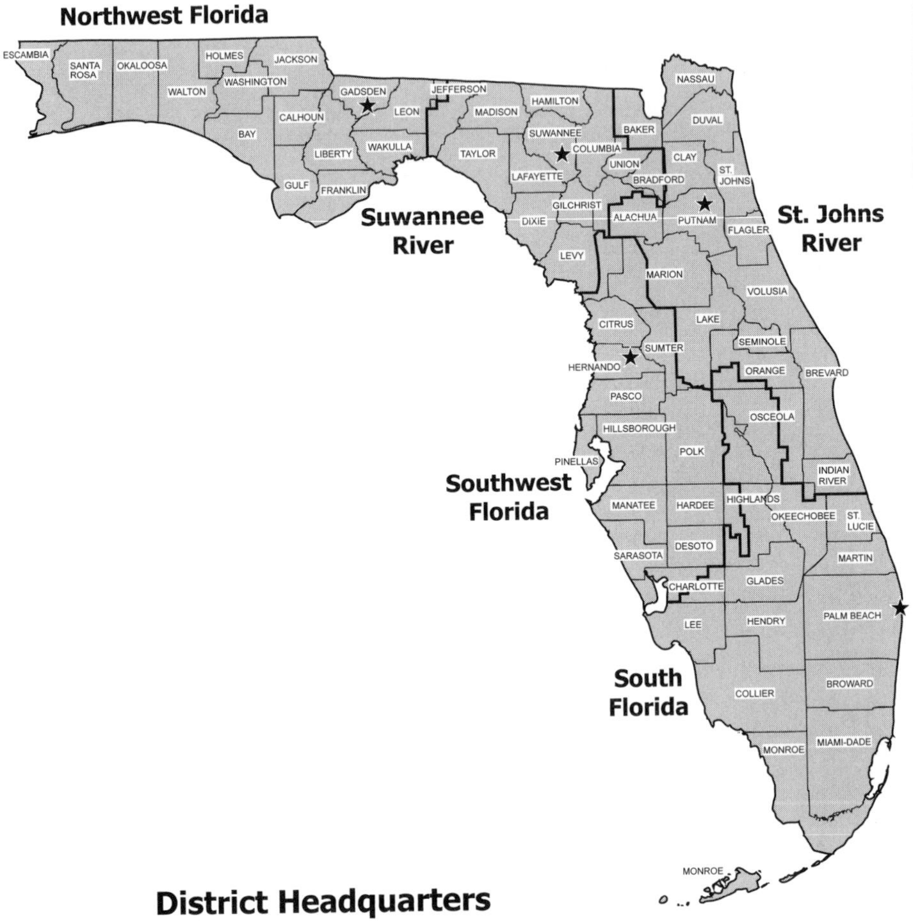

District Headquarters

District	City	County
Northwest Florida	Havana	Gadsden
Suwannee River	Live Oak	Suwannee
St. Johns River	Palatka	Putnam
Southwest Florida	Brooksville	Hernando
South Florida	West Palm Beach	Palm Beach

Table 8.41. WATER USE: WATER WITHDRAWALS BY SOURCE IN THE STATE AND COUNTIES OF FLORIDA, 2000 (Continued)

(in millions of gallons per day)

County	Total	Ground Total	Ground Fresh	Ground Saline	Surface Total	Surface Fresh	Surface Saline
Lee	652.84	120.80	120.80	0.00	532.04	39.77	492.27
Leon	45.66	45.36	45.36	0.00	0.30	0.30	0.00
Levy	31.07	28.44	28.44	0.00	2.63	2.63	0.00
Liberty	1.82	1.82	1.82	0.00	0.00	0.00	0.00
Madison	9.23	9.06	9.06	0.00	0.17	0.17	0.00
Manatee	186.95	122.30	122.30	0.00	64.65	64.65	0.00
Marion	69.78	67.68	67.68	0.00	2.10	2.10	0.00
Martin	198.87	43.60	43.60	0.00	155.27	155.27	0.00
Miami-Dade	603.46	541.59	537.91	3.68	61.87	28.68	33.19
Monroe	2.20	1.58	1.44	0.14	0.62	0.62	0.00
Nassau	48.19	46.53	46.53	0.00	1.66	0.48	1.18
Okaloosa	32.61	32.15	32.15	0.00	0.46	0.46	0.00
Okeechobee	71.83	59.80	59.80	0.00	12.03	12.03	0.00
Orange	298.08	281.36	281.36	0.00	16.72	16.72	0.00
Osceola	143.55	117.52	117.52	0.00	26.03	26.03	0.00
Palm Beach	1,712.20	273.70	273.70	0.00	1,438.50	1,005.48	433.02
Pasco	2,098.43	139.69	139.69	0.00	1,958.74	2.24	1,956.50
Pinellas	465.89	43.20	43.20	0.00	422.69	3.58	419.11
Polk	364.26	330.53	330.53	0.00	33.73	33.73	0.00
Putnam	89.27	40.35	40.35	0.00	48.92	48.92	0.00
St. Johns	55.71	52.55	52.55	0.00	3.16	3.16	0.00
St. Lucie	1,757.71	80.84	80.84	0.00	1,676.87	198.92	1,477.95
Santa Rosa	31.20	30.85	30.85	0.00	0.35	0.35	0.00
Sarasota	46.28	40.37	40.37	0.00	5.91	5.91	0.00
Seminole	90.25	88.47	88.47	0.00	1.78	1.78	0.00
Sumter	44.49	26.80	26.80	0.00	17.69	17.69	0.00
Suwannee	127.82	26.41	26.41	0.00	101.41	101.41	0.00
Taylor	49.81	46.79	46.79	0.00	3.02	3.02	0.00
Union	2.93	2.91	2.91	0.00	0.02	0.02	0.00
Volusia	234.74	97.02	97.02	0.00	137.72	137.72	0.00
Wakulla	33.17	4.79	4.79	0.00	28.38	28.38	0.00
Walton	12.32	10.51	10.51	0.00	1.81	1.81	0.00
Washington	4.32	4.32	4.32	0.00	0.00	0.00	0.00

Note: Values may not be identical to the data reported or published by the water management districts due to differences in data collection procedures and categories used or revisions in reported values.

Source: U.S., Department of Interior, Geological Survey, Tallahassee, Florida: Water withdrawals, use, discharge, and trends in Florida, 2000, by R.L. Marella, 2004, U.S. Geological Survey Scientific Investigations Report 2004-5151. Copies of this report and other Florida water-use data are available at <http://fl.water.usgs.gov> or by contacting the USGS at 2010 Levy Avenue, Tallahassee, Florida 32310.

Table 8.42. WATER USE: PUBLIC SUPPLIED POPULATION, WATER USE, AND WITHDRAWALS IN THE STATE AND COUNTIES OF FLORIDA, 2000

(in millions of gallons per day)

County	Population served	Water use Total	Water use Per capita	Withdrawals Total	Withdrawals Ground	Withdrawals Surface	Treated water
Florida	14,029,530	2,429.68	174	2,436.79	2,199.36	237.43	95.29
Alachua	179,118	28.26	158	28.26	28.26	0.00	0.00
Baker	4,326	0.88	203	0.88	0.88	0.00	0.00
Bay	129,300	51.17	396	51.17	6.28	44.89	0.00
Bradford	8,338	1.38	166	1.38	1.38	0.00	0.00
Brevard	458,282	53.35	116	27.74	13.66	14.08	0.00
Broward	1,603,081	258.06	161	258.06	258.06	0.00	0.09
Calhoun	4,224	0.75	178	0.75	0.75	0.00	0.00
Charlotte	115,564	14.21	123	7.28	3.29	3.99	3.29
Citrus	66,234	13.97	211	13.97	13.97	0.00	0.00
Clay	100,785	14.77	147	14.77	14.77	0.00	0.00
Collier	226,175	52.40	232	52.40	47.17	5.23	22.46
Columbia	21,235	3.67	173	3.67	3.67	0.00	0.00
DeSoto	11,233	1.90	169	10.59	4.49	6.10	0.00
Dixie	4,622	0.67	145	0.67	0.67	0.00	0.00
Duval	736,838	119.12	162	119.12	119.12	0.00	0.00
Escambia	279,294	43.56	156	44.63	44.63	0.00	0.00
Flagler	43,953	6.22	142	6.22	6.22	0.00	0.00
Franklin	9,258	1.92	207	1.92	1.92	0.00	0.00
Gadsden	27,632	4.34	157	4.34	3.06	1.28	0.00
Gilchrist	1,850	0.27	146	0.27	0.27	0.00	0.00
Glades	4,782	0.55	115	0.55	0.55	0.00	0.00
Gulf	10,338	1.47	142	1.47	1.47	0.00	0.00
Hamilton	6,366	0.95	149	0.95	0.95	0.00	0.00
Hardee	13,571	1.78	131	1.78	1.78	0.00	0.00
Hendry	20,457	4.72	231	4.72	0.95	3.77	0.00
Hernando	116,025	20.27	175	20.27	20.26	0.01	0.00
Highlands	69,820	9.14	131	9.14	9.14	0.00	0.00
Hillsborough	854,750	155.07	181	166.39	85.51	80.88	0.00
Holmes	5,860	1.38	235	1.38	1.38	0.00	0.00
Indian River	95,337	13.93	146	13.93	13.93	0.00	6.23
Jackson	16,348	2.46	150	2.46	2.46	0.00	0.00
Jefferson	5,010	0.72	144	0.72	0.72	0.00	0.00
Lafayette	1,264	0.20	158	0.20	0.20	0.00	0.00
Lake	171,137	39.92	233	39.92	39.92	0.00	0.00
Lee	357,289	52.37	147	52.37	49.09	3.28	24.37
Leon	198,937	35.70	179	35.70	35.70	0.00	0.00

See footnote at end of table.

Continued . . .

Table 8.42. WATER USE: PUBLIC SUPPLIED POPULATION, WATER USE, AND WITHDRAWALS IN THE STATE AND COUNTIES OF FLORIDA, 2000 (Continued)

(in millions of gallons per day)

County	Population served	Water use Total	Water use Per capita	Withdrawals Total	Withdrawals Ground	Withdrawals Surface	Treated water
Levy	11,066	2.16	195	2.16	2.16	0.00	0.00
Liberty	2,764	0.39	141	0.39	0.39	0.00	0.00
Madison	7,166	1.65	230	1.65	1.65	0.00	0.00
Manatee	250,270	39.81	159	49.92	13.87	36.05	0.00
Marion	136,842	27.99	205	27.99	27.99	0.00	0.00
Martin	87,100	18.45	212	18.45	18.45	0.00	2.82
Miami-Dade	2,207,800	377.27	171	394.29	394.29	0.00	0.00
Monroe	78,885	17.02	216	0.00	0.00	0.00	0.00
Nassau	24,875	6.81	274	6.81	6.81	0.00	0.00
Okaloosa	158,504	22.97	145	22.97	22.97	0.00	0.00
Okeechobee	21,600	2.23	103	2.23	0.54	1.69	0.00
Orange	813,152	186.15	229	211.76	211.76	0.00	0.00
Osceola	128,932	30.00	233	30.00	30.00	0.00	0.00
Palm Beach	1,035,732	229.84	222	229.84	194.57	35.27	18.27
Pasco	275,800	35.23	128	102.67	102.67	0.00	0.00
Pinellas	914,110	116.02	127	39.88	39.88	0.00	0.00
Polk	396,543	75.49	190	75.49	75.43	0.06	0.00
Putnam	23,311	3.20	137	3.20	3.20	0.00	0.00
St. Johns	105,104	16.49	157	16.49	16.49	0.00	0.00
St. Lucie	122,960	17.95	146	17.95	17.95	0.00	5.65
Santa Rosa	110,108	14.54	132	13.47	13.47	0.00	0.00
Sarasota	277,065	36.09	130	28.71	27.86	0.85	12.11
Seminole	339,403	66.90	197	66.90	66.90	0.00	0.00
Sumter	28,243	4.44	157	4.44	4.44	0.00	0.00
Suwannee	9,393	1.40	149	1.40	1.40	0.00	0.00
Taylor	10,289	1.73	168	1.73	1.73	0.00	0.00
Union	3,155	0.36	114	0.36	0.36	0.00	0.00
Volusia	414,851	54.90	132	54.90	54.90	0.00	0.00
Wakulla	9,285	2.19	236	2.19	2.19	0.00	0.00
Walton	39,024	7.35	188	7.35	7.35	0.00	0.00
Washington	7,565	1.16	153	1.16	1.16	0.00	0.00

Note: Public supply refers to municipal or other private water utilities which serve the public.

Source: U.S., Department of Interior, Geological Survey, Tallahassee, Florida: Water withdrawals, use, discharge, and trends in Florida, 2000, by R.L. Marella, 2004, U.S. Geological Survey Scientific Investigations Report 2004-5151. Copies of this report and other Florida water-use data are available at <http://fl.water.usgs.gov> or by contacting the USGS at 2010 Levy Avenue, Tallahassee, Florida 32310.

Table 8.43. WATER USE: WATER WITHDRAWALS BY CATEGORY IN THE STATE AND COUNTIES OF FLORIDA, 2000

(in millions of gallons per day)

County	All water: Total (fresh and saline)	All water: Percentage fresh	Public supply (fresh)	Domestic (fresh)	Industrial 1/ (fresh)	Water used for irrigation: Agricultural 2/ (fresh)	Water used for irrigation: Recreational 3/ (fresh)	Thermoelectric (fresh and saline)
Florida	20,146.41	40.66	2,436.79	198.68	563.30	3,923.01	411.73	12,614.08
Alachua	60.15	100.00	28.26	4.12	2.50	18.18	4.46	2.63
Baker	7.88	100.00	0.88	1.90	0.43	4.44	0.23	0.00
Bay	322.95	17.93	51.17	2.01	0.30	1.28	2.25	265.94
Bradford	5.85	100.00	1.38	1.89	1.25	1.02	0.31	0.00
Brevard	1,262.01	14.48	27.74	1.90	1.05	136.82	14.83	1,079.67
Broward	1,814.20	16.64	258.06	2.11	0.54	4.10	37.00	1,512.39
Calhoun	6.13	100.00	0.75	0.93	0.00	4.45	0.00	0.00
Charlotte	63.99	100.00	7.28	3.55	2.49	47.19	3.48	0.00
Citrus	425.24	7.37	13.97	7.20	1.09	3.35	4.18	395.45
Clay	34.09	100.00	14.77	4.24	6.87	5.96	2.25	0.00
Collier	230.04	100.00	52.40	2.67	5.81	142.99	26.17	0.00
Columbia	14.09	100.00	3.67	3.74	0.34	5.89	0.45	0.00
DeSoto	133.38	100.00	10.59	2.16	1.39	118.87	0.37	0.00
Dixie	3.53	100.00	0.67	0.98	0.26	1.62	0.00	0.00
Duval	817.13	19.09	119.12	4.46	12.51	4.07	7.49	669.48
Escambia	317.25	100.00	44.63	1.60	60.42	2.73	5.56	202.31
Flagler	28.15	100.00	6.22	0.62	0.27	15.70	5.34	0.00
Franklin	2.25	100.00	1.92	0.19	0.00	0.01	0.13	0.00
Gadsden	16.33	100.00	4.34	1.85	0.92	8.92	0.30	0.00
Gilchrist	16.15	100.00	0.27	1.33	0.26	14.29	0.00	0.00
Glades	74.67	100.00	0.55	0.61	4.07	69.02	0.42	0.00
Gulf	4.75	100.00	1.47	0.32	2.55	0.21	0.20	0.00
Hamilton	41.72	100.00	0.95	0.74	34.39	5.64	0.00	0.00
Hardee	91.14	100.00	1.78	0.64	5.93	81.73	0.25	0.81
Hendry	512.11	100.00	4.72	1.67	0.72	503.91	1.09	0.00
Hernando	50.45	100.00	20.27	1.41	19.77	4.29	4.71	0.00
Highlands	174.55	100.00	9.14	1.68	0.58	160.31	2.76	0.08
Hillsborough	3,479.72	8.38	166.39	4.71	19.67	87.15	13.80	3,188.00
Holmes	4.09	100.00	1.38	1.35	0.00	0.97	0.39	0.00
Indian River	287.45	86.43	13.93	1.87	0.12	222.49	10.03	39.01
Jackson	113.10	100.00	2.46	3.22	1.50	15.70	0.39	89.83
Jefferson	8.56	100.00	0.72	0.84	0.20	6.53	0.27	0.00
Lafayette	6.94	100.00	0.20	0.61	0.20	5.93	0.00	0.00
Lake	100.61	100.00	39.92	4.27	11.04	36.15	9.23	0.00
Lee	652.84	24.60	52.37	8.86	15.95	60.51	22.66	492.49
Levy	31.07	100.00	2.16	3.95	2.02	22.45	0.49	0.00

See footnotes at end of table.

Continued . . .

Table 8.43. WATER USE: WATER WITHDRAWALS BY CATEGORY IN THE STATE AND COUNTIES OF FLORIDA, 2000 (Continued)

(in millions of gallons per day)

County	All water: Total (fresh and saline)	All water: Percentage fresh	Public supply (fresh)	Domestic (fresh)	Industrial 1/ (fresh)	Water used for irrigation: Agricultural 2/ (fresh)	Water used for irrigation: Recreational 3/ (fresh)	Thermo-electric (fresh and saline)
Liberty	1.82	100.00	0.39	0.45	0.82	0.16	0.00	0.00
Madison	9.23	100.00	1.65	1.23	0.15	5.94	0.26	0.00
Manatee	186.95	100.00	49.92	0.17	1.00	105.72	5.04	25.10
Marion	69.78	100.00	27.99	16.42	2.08	17.21	6.08	0.00
Martin	198.87	100.00	18.45	4.20	3.15	140.02	7.88	25.17
Miami-Dade	603.46	93.89	394.29	4.83	41.65	110.35	13.39	38.95
Monroe	2.20	93.64	0.00	0.08	0.10	0.03	1.85	0.14
Nassau	47.01	100.00	6.81	3.48	32.46	0.70	3.56	1.18
Okaloosa	32.61	100.00	22.97	1.27	4.14	0.75	3.48	0.00
Okeechobee	71.83	100.00	2.23	1.52	0.36	67.04	0.68	0.00
Orange	298.08	100.00	211.76	8.82	24.21	26.99	25.54	0.76
Osceola	143.55	100.00	30.00	4.61	0.84	105.96	2.11	0.03
Palm Beach	1,712.20	74.71	229.84	10.12	18.97	946.16	74.09	433.02
Pasco	2,098.43	6.76	102.67	4.50	5.53	22.73	6.36	1,956.64
Pinellas	465.89	10.04	39.88	0.41	0.64	0.46	5.39	419.11
Polk	364.26	100.00	75.49	12.45	77.59	166.86	11.94	19.93
Putnam	89.27	100.00	3.20	4.99	50.26	15.19	1.04	14.59
St. Johns	55.71	100.00	16.49	1.91	0.01	28.59	8.71	0.00
St. Lucie	1,757.71	15.92	17.95	7.39	8.88	237.34	8.20	1,477.95
Santa Rosa	31.20	100.00	13.47	0.81	5.57	5.00	6.35	0.00
Sarasota	46.28	100.00	28.71	0.43	0.64	7.54	8.96	0.00
Seminole	90.25	100.00	66.90	2.73	0.08	11.08	9.46	0.00
Sumter	44.49	100.00	4.44	4.57	17.34	14.62	3.52	0.00
Suwannee	127.82	100.00	1.40	2.70	1.54	21.02	0.09	101.07
Taylor	49.81	100.00	1.73	0.95	45.11	1.93	0.09	0.00
Union	2.93	100.00	0.36	1.10	0.40	1.07	0.00	0.00
Volusia	234.74	100.00	54.90	3.02	0.49	32.91	12.25	131.17
Wakulla	33.17	100.00	2.19	1.44	0.62	0.28	0.20	28.44
Walton	12.32	100.00	7.35	0.17	0.92	2.09	1.79	0.00
Washington	4.32	100.00	1.16	1.42	0.22	1.13	0.39	0.00

1/ Includes selected commercial and mining withdrawals, including water withdrawn or diverted solely for dewatering purposes.
2/ Water withdrawn for crop irrigation, livestock, and fish farming purposes.
3/ Water withdrawn for turf grass (golf, commercial, and public) and landscape irrigation.

Source: U.S., Department of Interior, Geological Survey, Tallahassee, Florida: Water withdrawals, use, discharge, and trends in Florida, 2000, by R.L. Marella, 2004, U.S. Geological Survey Scientific Investigations Report 2004-5151. Copies of this report and other Florida water-use data are available at <http://fl.water.usgs.gov> or by contacting the USGS at 2010 Levy Avenue, Tallahassee, Florida 32310.

National Weather Station Offices

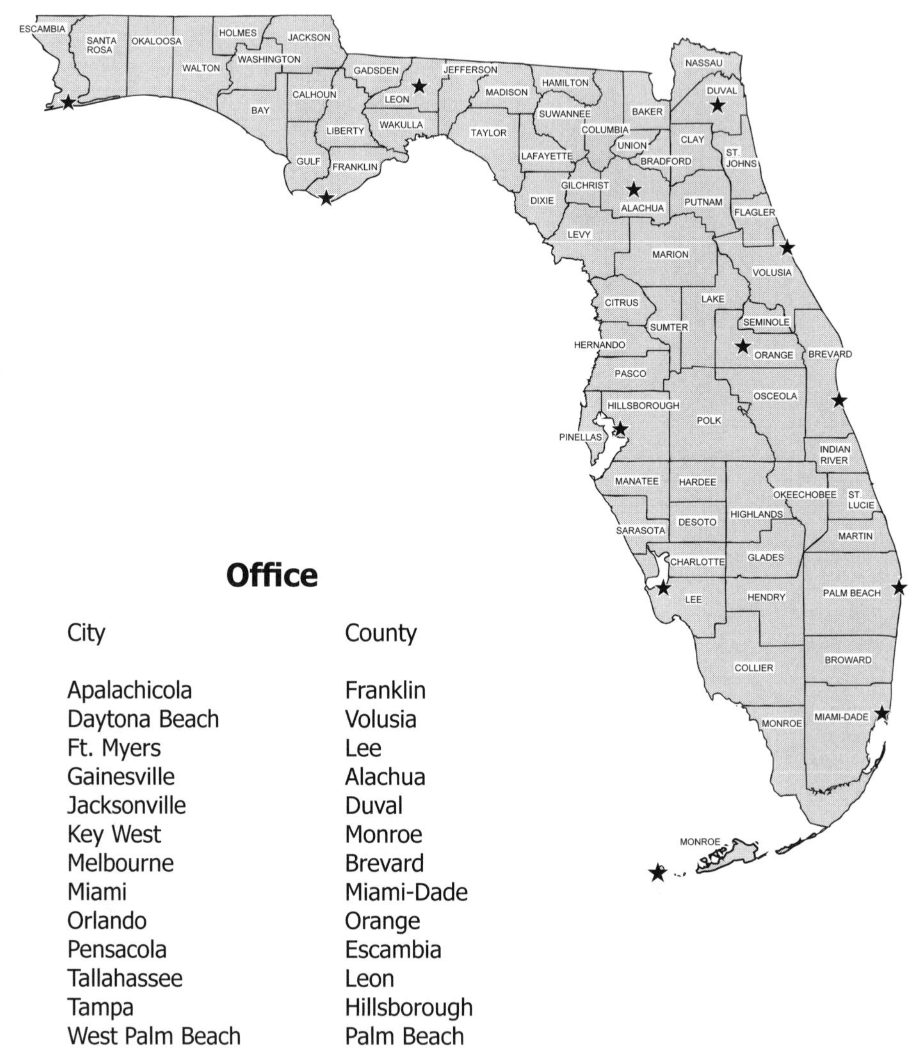

Office

City	County
Apalachicola	Franklin
Daytona Beach	Volusia
Ft. Myers	Lee
Gainesville	Alachua
Jacksonville	Duval
Key West	Monroe
Melbourne	Brevard
Miami	Miami-Dade
Orlando	Orange
Pensacola	Escambia
Tallahassee	Leon
Tampa	Hillsborough
West Palm Beach	Palm Beach

Table 8.70. CLIMATE: TEMPERATURE CHARACTERISTICS AND TOTAL PRECIPITATION AT NATIONAL WEATHER STATION OFFICES IN FLORIDA BY MONTH, 2006

(temperature in degrees Fahrenheit)

Station and month	Temperature						Precipitation (inches)
	Average maximum	Average minimum	Heating degree days	Cooling degree days	Days with maximum 90 degrees or more	Days with minimum 32 degrees or less	
Apalachicola							
January	68.8	43.6	273	9	0	2	1.82
February	66.6	42.4	292	6	0	4	4.90
March	73.3	49.2	141	32	0	0	0.40
April	81.1	60.7	3	188	0	0	1.75
May	84.6	61.0	0	246	7	0	3.95
June	88.3	70.2	0	432	11	0	4.93
July	92.4	73.3	0	559	25	0	2.89
August	92.1	74.3	0	573	27	0	5.43
September	87.8	68.3	0	399	14	0	8.19
October	80.7	A/ 57.4	B/ 47	B/ 182	0	0	2.15
November	70.8	46.1	205	17	0	0	2.35
December	A/ 69.7	A/ 48.7	B/ 191	B/ 19	0	1	7.19
Daytona Beach							
January	72.4	50.3	156	51	0	0	0.24
February	70.0	47.2	200	28	0	2	4.33
March	75.7	53.0	91	78	0	0	0.08
April	83.6	61.9	0	240	4	0	1.11
May	88.0	64.6	0	360	17	0	0.78
June	88.6	71.2	0	454	10	0	5.72
July	88.7	73.4	0	506	12	0	4.48
August	91.0	73.5	0	545	22	0	4.81
September	88.3	70.8	0	445	9	0	2.97
October	82.7	61.6	13	244	5	0	2.53
November	74.0	55.2	96	91	0	0	1.10
December	74.6	57.2	76	113	0	0	3.21
Gainesville							
January	70.2	45.3	247	33	0	3	3.43
February	67.9	41.6	289	12	0	5	5.08
March	75.4	46.8	157	42	0	1	0.32
April	82.9	57.6	7	172	1	0	3.50
May	87.8	61.4	5	311	13	0	0.63
June	89.8	68.0	0	426	21	0	4.79
July	91.5	70.1	0	499	24	0	5.51
August	92.1	72.3	0	543	27	0	2.77
September	88.3	67.0	0	387	12	0	3.11
October	A/ 83.1	A/ 55.7	B/ 51	B/ 194	5	0	2.58
November	A/ 72.1	A/ 47.1	B/ 192	B/ 34	0	0	0.94
December	A/ 72.5	A/ 49.3	B/ 162	B/ 42	0	2	2.77
Jacksonville							
January	69.3	45.0	253	19	0	3	2.30
February	66.9	41.7	297	5	0	4	3.91
March	74.3	47.1	176	50	0	0	0.68
April	82.2	57.5	16	171	1	0	1.22
May	87.5	61.7	2	307	14	0	2.01
June	89.6	69.0	0	435	16	0	7.25

See footnotes at end of table. Continued . . .

Table 8.70. CLIMATE: TEMPERATURE CHARACTERISTICS AND TOTAL PRECIPITATION AT NATIONAL WEATHER STATION OFFICES IN FLORIDA BY MONTH, 2006 (Continued)

(temperature in degrees Fahrenheit)

Station and month	Temperature: Average maximum	Average minimum	Heating degree days	Cooling degree days	Days with maximum 90 degrees or more	Days with minimum 32 degrees or less	Precipitation (inches)
Jacksonville (Continued)							
July	91.4	71.1	0	511	26	0	3.97
August	92.8	73.0	0	562	27	0	7.08
September	88.3	69.1	0	419	12	0	4.55
October	81.0	56.3	53	172	2	0	1.81
November	71.8	48.1	189	46	0	0	0.39
December	71.0	49.7	184	45	0	1	2.90
Key West							
January	74.7	64.8	24	179	0	0	0.23
February	74.5	64.3	24	152	0	0	0.71
March	A/ 78.1	A/ 67.8	B/ 0	B/ 253	0	0	0.05
April	81.7	71.5	0	357	0	0	0.01
May	83.8	73.8	0	438	0	0	4.30
June	87.1	76.7	0	514	2	0	6.04
July	88.5	79.3	0	591	7	0	6.46
August	89.3	79.9	0	612	14	0	4.04
September	A/ 88.4	A/ 78.4	B/ 0	B/ 559	10	0	6.86
October	85.0	76.5	0	496	0	0	2.92
November	A/ 77.6	A/ 68.3	B/ 7	B/ 252	0	0	3.21
December	77.9	70.7	0	296	0	0	4.82
Melbourne							
January	74.0	51.5	134	71	0	2	0.61
February	71.8	48.0	185	48	0	2	2.20
March	77.7	54.1	59	93	1	0	0.28
April	84.2	63.8	0	279	6	0	1.10
May	87.0	65.0	0	348	11	0	2.06
June	88.2	72.0	0	461	10	0	6.40
July	88.6	73.2	0	500	8	0	8.17
August	90.6	73.3	0	534	24	0	8.99
September	89.1	71.3	0	464	11	0	6.19
October	84.2	64.3	10	305	5	0	0.73
November	76.2	56.6	70	120	0	0	3.73
December	76.7	62.2	31	178	0	0	1.72
Miami							
January	76.3	62.2	33	174	0	0	0.32
February	76.2	58.9	45	125	0	0	3.47
March	79.8	64.3	7	234	1	0	1.10
April	84.9	69.6	0	378	3	0	0.23
May	87.5	71.4	0	457	9	0	8.62
June	88.9	76.5	0	541	14	0	7.05
July	89.0	76.9	0	567	12	0	7.32
August	90.4	77.2	0	591	23	0	12.95
September	89.3	76.2	0	540	14	0	16.73
October	87.0	73.3	0	477	6	0	1.64
November	79.7	66.3	22	269	0	0	1.63
December	79.7	69.2	3	302	0	0	3.11

See footnotes at end of table. Continued . . .

Table 8.70. CLIMATE: TEMPERATURE CHARACTERISTICS AND TOTAL PRECIPITATION AT NATIONAL WEATHER STATION OFFICES IN FLORIDA BY MONTH, 2006 (Continued)

(temperature in degrees Fahrenheit)

Station and month	Temperature: Average maximum	Average minimum	Heating degree days	Cooling degree days	Days with maximum 90 degrees or more	Days with minimum 32 degrees or less	Precipitation (inches)
Naples							
January	75.9	56.2	65	102	0	0	0.56
February	73.9	53.5	101	70	0	0	3.21
March	79.2	59.0	18	153	0	0	0.08
April	83.4	65.5	0	290	0	0	C/
May	85.8	68.8	0	387	4	0	2.74
June	88.5	74.0	0	496	13	0	10.33
July	89.1	74.1	0	523	13	0	12.16
August	90.4	75.3	0	562	24	0	11.60
September	89.1	74.7	0	517	13	0	7.50
October	86.3	68.3	1	390	5	0	1.15
November	78.0	61.1	41	184	0	0	0.41
December	A/ 79.9	A/ 62.7	B/ 16	B/ 219	0	0	0.45
Orlando							
January	74.7	51.6	115	66	0	0	0.43
February	72.7	49.1	153	45	0	0	2.36
March	79.8	55.0	36	118	0	0	0.02
April	87.0	61.9	0	291	9	0	1.05
May	89.3	64.7	0	381	19	0	3.36
June	90.7	71.6	0	490	24	0	6.61
July	91.4	73.9	0	554	24	0	7.01
August	92.5	73.8	0	568	27	0	4.33
September	90.4	71.7	0	488	22	0	4.09
October	85.0	63.4	9	301	11	0	1.95
November	75.8	56.1	72	107	0	0	1.54
December	76.8	58.4	48	136	0	0	3.60
Pensacola							
January	67.2	48.8	224	17	0	1	2.99
February	64.4	44.4	292	4	0	2	3.76
March	73.6	53.0	108	62	0	0	0.24
April	81.0	63.1	1	221	0	0	3.31
May	A/ 85.0	A/ 66.8	B/ 0	B/ 344	5	0	3.50
June	92.7	72.7	0	540	28	0	0.58
July	91.5	75.8	0	581	25	0	4.27
August	90.7	75.0	0	560	20	0	4.83
September	A/ 86.4	A/ 69.3	B/ 0	B/ 391	5	0	9.83
October	79.0	59.1	47	179	1	0	2.82
November	69.3	47.6	208	19	0	0	4.02
December	65.2	45.8	290	5	0	4	5.11
Tallahassee							
January	69.4	44.4	256	14	0	5	2.36
February	67.1	40.5	316	11	0	10	7.35
March	75.9	46.7	162	56	1	3	0.29
April	A/ 84.6	A/ 57.0	B/ 10	B/ 192	6	0	1.08
May	87.5	61.2	0	296	13	0	4.04
June	91.4	67.9	0	447	22	0	8.34

See footnotes at end of table. Continued . . .

Table 8.70. CLIMATE: TEMPERATURE CHARACTERISTICS AND TOTAL PRECIPITATION AT NATIONAL WEATHER STATION OFFICES IN FLORIDA BY MONTH, 2006 (Continued)

(temperature in degrees Fahrenheit)

Station and month	Temperature						Precipitation (inches)
	Average maximum	Average minimum	Heating degree days	Cooling degree days	Days with maximum 90 degrees or more	Days with minimum 32 degrees or less	
Tallahassee (Continued)							
July	93.4	71.6	0	551	29	0	3.93
August	93.7	73.6	0	582	29	0	5.37
September	86.9	66.1	0	354	10	0	2.09
October	80.7	54.4	67	154	4	0	3.76
November	70.8	46.0	216	25	0	0	2.38
December	69.3	45.2	247	14	0	6	8.35
Tampa							
January	71.8	53.4	130	63	0	0	0.70
February	70.0	51.2	145	30	0	0	9.08
March	77.0	57.6	41	120	0	0	C/
April	83.3	65.0	0	280	0	0	1.03
May	86.0	68.5	0	388	5	0	1.43
June	88.9	74.4	0	507	14	0	8.93
July	90.2	75.2	0	556	19	0	9.46
August	90.4	76.1	0	575	20	0	6.78
September	89.3	74.8	0	519	17	0	12.40
October	85.1	67.1	4	357	4	0	0.87
November	77.1	58.7	55	150	1	0	2.76
December	77.5	61.4	40	188	0	0	3.17
West Palm Beach							
January	75.6	58.4	66	134	0	0	1.62
February	74.6	54.7	89	86	0	0	2.79
March	79.2	61.5	18	193	1	0	1.78
April	84.0	67.6	0	330	2	0	4.69
May	86.2	68.9	0	398	4	0	3.13
June	88.9	75.3	0	521	17	0	4.27
July	88.6	76.3	0	550	8	0	4.91
August	90.7	76.6	0	585	23	0	7.14
September	88.9	74.9	0	515	11	0	6.07
October	85.9	70.1	0	412	3	0	1.95
November	78.7	62.7	38	215	0	0	4.75
December	78.4	67.9	7	267	0	0	11.05

A/ Monthly means or totals based on incomplete time series.
B/ Adjusted total. Monthly value totals based on proportional available data across the entire month.
C/ Trace of precipitation.
Note: Degree day totals are the sums of the negative (heating) or positive (cooling) departures of average daily temperatures from 65 degrees Fahrenheit.

Source: U.S., Department of Commerce, National Oceanic and Atmospheric Administration, National Environmental Satellite, Data and Information Services, *Climatological Data: Florida,* 2006 monthly reports, Internet site <http://nndc.noaa.gov/> (accessed 13, June 2007).

Table 8.74. CLIMATE: CHARACTERISTICS FOR JACKSONVILLE, MIAMI, LOS ANGELES, ATLANTA CHICAGO, AND NEW YORK, SPECIFIED DATES THROUGH 2006

Characteristic	Jacksonville Florida	Miami Florida	Los Angeles California	Atlanta Georgia	Chicago Illinois	New York New York 1/
Normal temperature 2/						
January average	53.1	68.1	58.3	42.7	22.0	32.1
July average	81.6	83.7	74.2	80.0	73.3	76.5
Annual average	68.0	76.7	66.2	62.1	49.1	54.6
January normal high	64.2	76.5	68.1	51.9	29.6	38.0
July normal high	90.8	90.9	83.8	89.4	83.5	84.2
Annual average high	78.4	84.2	75.6	72.0	58.3	61.7
January normal low	41.9	59.6	48.5	33.5	14.3	26.2
July normal low	72.4	76.5	64.6	70.6	63.2	68.8
Annual average low	57.6	69.1	56.6	52.3	39.8	47.5
Extreme temperatures 3/						
Highest temperature of record	105	98	112	105	104	106
Lowest temperature of record	7	30	5	-8	-27	-15
Length of record (years)	65	64	66	58	48	138
Normal annual precipitation 2/ (inches)	52.34	58.53	15.14	50.20	36.27	49.69
Average number of days precipitation 0.01 or more 3/	116	131	35	115	124	121
Length of record (years)	65	64	66	72	48	137
Average total snow and ice pellets 3/ (inches)	0.0	0.0	0.0	2.1	38.2	28.8
Length of record (years)	60	59	44	67	47	138
Average annual percentage of possible sunshine 3/ 4/	63	70	73	60	54	58
Length of record (years)	50	20	32	65	16	109
Average annual wind speed 3/ (MPH)	7.8	9.2	5.4	9.1	10.3	9.3
Length of record (years)	57	57	32	68	48	69
Heating and cooling degree days 2/ 5/						
Heating degree days	1,354	149	928	2,827	6,498	4,754
Cooling degree days	2,627	4,361	1,506	1,810	830	1,151
Average relative humidity 3/						
Length of record	70	42	47	46	48	72
Annual (percentage)						
Morning	89	83	73	82	80	72
Afternoon	56	61	52	56	64	56

T Trace.
MPH Miles per hour.
1/ Central Park data.
2/ Based on 1971-2000 period of record.
3/ Record through 2006.
4/ Percentage of days that are either clear or partly cloudy.
5/ Degree day normals are used to determine relative estimates of heating requirements for buildings. Each day that the average temperature for a day is below 65 degrees F. produces one heating degree day and each day it is above 65 degrees F. produces one cooling degree day.
Note: All temperatures are in degrees Fahrenheit.

Source: U.S., Department of Commerce, National Oceanic and Atmospheric Administraton, National Climatic Data Center, *Comparative Climatic Data,* Internet site <http://www.ncdc.noaa.gov/> (accessed 25, June 2007).

Table 8.76. HURRICANES: AREA OF LANDFALL, NAME, YEAR, FORCE CATEGORY, AND RANK OF THE FIFTEEN DEADLIEST HURRICANES IN THE UNITED STATES, 1851 THROUGH 2006

Area of landfall/name	Year	Force category 1/	Deaths Number	Deaths Rank
Galveston, Texas/(NA)	1900	4	A/ 8,000	1
Lake Okeechobee, S.E. Florida/(NA)	1928	4	B/ 2,500	2
S.E. Louisiana; Mississippi/Katrina	2005	3	1,500	3
Cheniere Caminanada, Louisiana/(NA)	1893	4	C/ 1,100-1,400	4
Sea Islands, South Carolina; Georgia/(NA)	1893	3	1,000-2,000	5
Georgia; South Carolina/(NA)	1881	2	700	6
S.W. Louisiana; N. Texas/Audrey	1957	4	D/ 416	7
Florida Keys/(NA)	1935	5	408	8
Last Island, Louisiana/(NA)	1856	4	E/ 400	9
Miami, Florida; Mississippi; Alabama; Pensacola, FL/(NA	1926	4	372	10
Grand Isle, Louisiana/(NA)	1909	3	350	11
Florida Keys; S. Texas/(NA)	1919	4	F/ 287	12
New Orleans, Louisiana/(NA)	1915	4	E/ 275	13
Galveston, Texas/(NA)	1915	4	275	13
New England/(NA)	1938	3	256	15

(NA) Not available.
A/ Could be as high as 12,000. B/ Could be as high as 3,000.
C/ Total including offshore losses near 2,000. D/ At least.
E/ Total including offshore losses is 600. F/ Could include some offshore losses.
1/ Assigned based on the Saffir/Simpson scale. Ratings are 1-5 and a "5" indicates central pressure less than 920 millibars or winds greater than 155 mph or storm surge higher than 18 feet and damage classified as catastrophic.

Table 8.77. HURRICANES: AREA OF LANDFALL, NAME, YEAR, FORCE CATEGORY, AND RANK OF THE TEN COSTLIEST HURRICANES IN THE UNITED STATES, 1900 THROUGH 2006

Area of landfall/name	Year	Force category 1/	Value of damage 2/ Amount ($1,000)	Value of damage 2/ Rank
S.E. Louisiana, Mississippi, Florida/Katrina	2005	3	84,645,000	1
S.E. Florida; S.E. Louisiana/Andrew	1992	5	48,058,000	2
S.W. and S.E. Florida/Wilma	2005	3	21,527,000	3
S.W. Florida/Charley	2004	4	16,322,000	4
Alabama; N.W. Florida/Ivan	2004	3	15,451,000	5
South Carolina/Hugo	1989	4	13,480,000	6
Florida; N.E. United States/Agnes	1972	1	12,424,000	7
S.E. Florida and S.E. Louisiana/Betsy	1965	3	11,883,000	8
Louisiana; Texas; Florida/Rita	2005	3	11,808,000	9
Miississippi; S.E. Louisiana; Virginia/Camille	1969	5	9,781,000	10

1/ Assigned based on the Saffir/Simpson scale. Ratings are 1-5 and a "5" indicates central pressure less than 920 millibars or winds greater than 155 mph or storm surge higher than 18 feet and damage classified as catastrophic.
2/ Adjusted to 2006 dollars on basis of U.S. Department of Commerce Implicit Price Deflator for construction.

Source for Tables 8.76 and 8.77: U.S., Department of Commerce, National Oceanic and Atmospheric Administration, National Hurricane Center, *The Deadliest, Costliest, and Most Intense United States Tropical Cyclones from 1851 to 2006,* NOAA Technical Memorandum NWS TPC-5, updated April 2007, Internet site <http://www.nhc.noaa.gov/> (accessed 11, June 2007).

Table 8.80. AIR POLLUTION: PARTICULATE MATTER (PM) CONCENTRATIONS IN SPECIFIED CITIES OF FLORIDA, 2006

			PM10 concentration (UG/M^3)	
County 1/	Area	Site Address	2nd highest 24-hour value 2/	Annual arith-metic mean 3/
Alachua	Gainesville	N.W. 53rd Ave. & N.W. 43rd Street	39	17.9
Bay	Panama City	Cherry Street & Henderson Ave. S.T.P	59	22.2
Brevard	Cocoa	6315 Depot Avenue	26	A/ 14.1
Broward	Ft. Lauderdale	Lincoln Park Elementary	35	18.3
	Davie	3205 S.W. 70th Avenue	30	14.7
	Pompano Beach	851 S.W. 3rd Avenue	83	21.1
	Hollywood	2701 Plunkett Street	82	22.3
	County	4010 Winston Park Boulevard	34	14.8
Duval	Jacksonville	Rosselle and Copeland	48	25.1
Escambia	Pensacola	Ellyson Industrial Field	42	20.1
Hamilton	County	County Road 137	52	19.8
Hillsborough	Ruskin	Highway 41, Gibsonton	67	32.9
	Tampa	4702 Central Avenue	117	32.3
	Brandon	2929 S. Kingsway Avenue	40	23.0
Lee	Ft. Myers Beach	Princeton Street	81	A/ 20.3
Manatee	County	Holland House 100 yards east of US 41	49	24.3
Miami-Dade	Miami	N.W. 20 Street and 12 Avenue	43	26.3
Nassau	Fernandina Beach	5th Street North of Lime Avenue	30	A/ 18.4
Orange	Orlando	E. Washington Street	36	19.0
	Winter Park	Morris Boulevard	35	19.2
Palm Beach	Belle Glade	38745 SR 80	42	20.1
	Delray Beach	225 S. Congress Avenue	49	25.9
Pinellas	St. Petersburg	N.E. Corner of 13th Avenue	43	24.4
	Largo	1301 Ulmerton Road	36	22.3
	Tarpon Springs	County Road 77 Booker	35	18.3
Polk	Mulberry	N.W. 4th Circle	56	20.5
Putnam	Palatka	Comfort and Port Road	70	25.7
Sarasota	Sarasota	1642 12th Street	50	24.4
	Venice	200 Warfield Avenue	32	18.1
Seminole	County	County Homes Road	61	20.9
Volusia	Daytona Beach	1185-A Dunn Avenue	65	21.6

UG/M^3 Micrograms per cubic meter.

A/ The mean does not satisfy summary criteria.

1/ Source includes more sites than could be reported here. Major cities in each county are reported. If more than one site was available, the one with the highest annual arithmetic mean is reported.

2/ Florida standard is 150 UG/M^3, not to be exceeded more than once per year.

3/ Florida standard is 50 UG/M^3.

Note: Particulate describes airborne solid or liquid particles of about 0.1 to 50 microns in diameter (1 micron = 0.0001 centimeter). PM consists of sulfate, nitrate, and acidic particles formed by oxidation of the pollutant gases sulfur dioxide and nitrogen dioxide; of soot and organic particles released in forest fires and other low-temperature combustion processes; of lead-containing particles emitted from motor vehicles; of products of industrial processes and high temperature fuel combustion; of local soil; and of airborne sea salt. PM10 is a subset of particulate matter and refers to airborne particles that are 10 microns or less in size.

Source: State of Florida, Department of Environmental Protection, Division of Air Resources Management, Air Quality Technical Reports, Internet site <http://www.dep.state.fl.us/air/> (accessed 9, April 2007).

AGRICULTURE

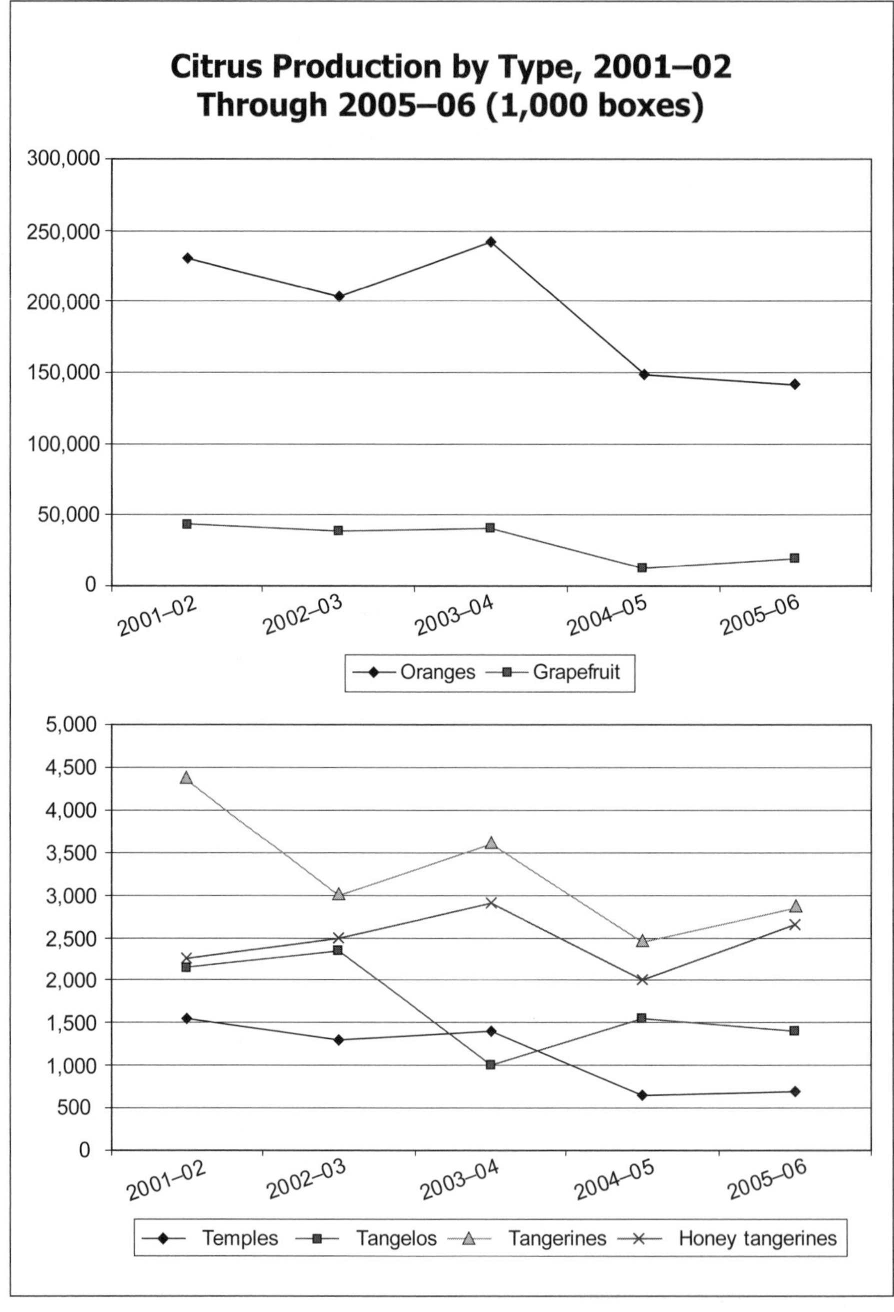

Source: Table 9.51

Section 9.00
Agriculture

Section 9.00 presents statistics on Florida's agriculture and farming and includes data on veterinarians; agricultural employment; farms (land, real estate, operators, and income); and crops and livestock.

Explanatory notes. Since 1840, the U.S. Department of Agriculture (USDA) has conducted a Census of Agriculture every five years. Congress authorized agricultural censuses in 1978 and 1982 to coincide with the economic censuses. After 1982, the agricultural census again reverted to a five-year cycle conducted in years ending in "2" and "7." The USDA released state and county data from the 2002 census in June 2004. These data are presented in several tables throughout this section.

NAICS. Agriculture census tables are based on the North American Industry Classification System (NAICS). This system of classifying establishments by economic activity replaced the Standard Industrial Classification (SIC) system in 1997. See the Glossary for a definition and for a listing of industry categories.

Farms. As defined since the 1978 census, a farm is "any place from which $1,000 or more of agricultural products were sold or normally would have been sold during the census year." Because data for selected items are collected from a sample of operators, the results are subject to sampling variability. Dollar values have not been adjusted for changes in price levels between census years.

State criteria. When comparisons are made between Florida and other states, the other states selected either have a similar climate (the southern tier of Sunbelt states) or produce similar crops (citrus in Arizona and California, sugarcane in Hawaii and Louisiana, etc.).

Sources. Data on the number of active licensed veterinarians and veterinarian establishments are available in license information downloadable data files from the Florida Department of Business and Professional Regulation on their Web site.

Agricultural-related establishment, employment, and payroll data based on the NAICS system for 2006 from the Labor Market Statistics office of the Florida Agency for Workforce Innovation appear on Tables 9.15 and 9.27. (See discussion in the Section 6.00 introduction.)

The USDA provides timely and detailed data on farm income and farm real estate debt in various reports from the Department's Economic Research Service (ERS) and in the annual publication *Agricultural Statistics*. Economic census data, primarily covering characteristics of farms and farm operators using the NAICS format, are from the *2002 Census of Agriculture*, published by the USDA's Natural Agricultural Statistics Service (NASS).

The U.S. Department of Commerce's Bureau of Economic Analysis (BEA) provides additional farm income and employment data, some of which also appears in Section 5.00.

Water-use data for agricultural irrigation are from the Tallahassee, FL office of the U.S. Geological Survey report "Water withdrawals, use, discharge, and trends in Florida, 2000" (See discussion in the Section 8.00 introduction.)

The Florida Department of Citrus' Economic and Market Research office provided orange juice sales data in the publication *Citrus Reference Book,* available on their Web site.

Information about citrus production, cash receipts, other crop cultivation, and livestock is found in several reports from the Florida Agricultural Statistics Service, on the state's Department of Agriculture and Consumer Services Web site. A map of counties by crop-reporting district appears on page 378. A complete series of crop estimates for the state dating back to 1919 is available from the reporting service upon request.

Section 9.00
Agriculture

Tables listed by major heading

Heading | Page

Tables listed by major heading

Table 9.04. VETERINARIANS: ACTIVE VETERINARY MEDICINE LICENSES ISSUED IN THE STATE AND COUNTIES OF FLORIDA, JUNE 23, 2007

County	Veterin-arians	Veterinary establish-ments 1/	County	Veterin-arians	Veterinary establish-ments 1/
Total	6,045	1,806	Jefferson	5	1
			Lafayette	3	1
Foreign	13	0	Lake	41	27
Out-of-state	922	2	Lee	94	61
Unknown	1,533	73	Leon	73	34
Alachua	212	34	Levy	20	2
Baker	1	1	Liberty	0	0
Bay	32	17	Madison	3	1
Bradford	4	2	Manatee	50	28
Brevard	96	59	Marion	155	41
Broward	334	149	Martin	48	27
Calhoun	1	1	Miami-Dade	261	157
Charlotte	28	10	Monroe	35	20
Citrus	25	16	Nassau	19	7
Clay	40	25	Okaloosa	42	30
Collier	47	30	Okeechobee	8	3
Columbia	8	3	Orange	171	82
DeSoto	9	4	Osceola	27	12
Dixie	2	1	Palm Beach	296	151
Duval	152	85	Pasco	68	33
Escambia	65	30	Pinellas	211	107
Flagler	14	4	Polk	86	42
Franklin	3	1	Putnam	14	10
Gadsden	8	5	St. Johns	37	15
Gilchrist	4	1	St. Lucie	32	15
Glades	0	0	Santa Rosa	26	13
Gulf	1	1	Sarasota	104	43
Hamilton	2	2	Seminole	107	49
Hardee	5	4	Sumter	7	5
Hendry	2	4	Suwannee	10	5
Hernando	26	13	Taylor	2	2
Highlands	13	8	Union	0	0
Hillsborough	242	113	Volusia	93	52
Holmes	1	0	Wakulla	1	2
Indian River	36	19	Walton	7	7
Jackson	4	2	Washington	4	2

1/ Includes limited service veterinary practices.

Caution: Data were collected from unaudited, raw data files as reported by the Department of Business and Professional Regulation and may contain reporting errors.

Source: State of Florida, Department of Business and Professional Regulation, Licensee Information Download files: Veterinary Medicine, Internet site <http://www.myflorida.com/dbpr/> (accessed 23, June 2007).

Table 9.10. EMPLOYMENT: ESTIMATES OF AVERAGE MONTHLY EMPLOYMENT OF FARM PROPRIETORS AND WAGE AND SALARY WORKERS IN THE UNITED STATES AND IN THE STATE AND COUNTIES OF FLORIDA, 2004 AND 2005

County	Farm proprietors	Farm wage and salary employees: Number	Farm wage and salary employees: As a percentage of all wage and salary employees	County	Farm proprietors	Farm wage and salary employees: Number	Farm wage and salary employees: As a percentage of all wage and salary employees
			2004 A/				
United States	2,124,000	825,000	0.59	Lafayette	256	183	10.11
				Lake	1,514	1,272	1.51
Florida	39,245	52,218	0.65	Lee	575	1,187	0.54
Alachua	1,316	450	0.34	Leon	292	98	0.06
Baker	194	106	1.52	Levy	664	291	3.05
Bay	80	18	0.02	Liberty	55	2	0.09
Bradford	329	15	0.20	Madison	599	111	2.00
Brevard	551	208	0.10	Manatee	753	3,964	3.07
Broward	256	657	0.08	Marion	1,901	1,077	1.06
Calhoun	156	119	3.77	Martin	286	496	0.80
Charlotte	241	313	0.72	Miami-Dade	1,415	5,641	0.51
Citrus	344	73	0.22	Monroe	0	0	0.00
Clay	249	61	0.14	Nassau	284	285	1.50
Collier	244	4,395	3.10	Okaloosa	427	11	0.01
Columbia	728	36	0.17	Okeechobee	507	800	7.24
DeSoto	890	536	4.67	Orange	812	2,644	0.38
Dixie	192	19	0.70	Osceola	551	294	0.44
Duval	356	430	0.08	Palm Beach	660	4,940	0.84
Escambia	564	64	0.04	Pasco	1,080	621	0.65
Flagler	108	108	0.60	Pinellas	145	105	0.02
Franklin	0	0	0.00	Polk	2,815	1,566	0.74
Gadsden	340	1,547	9.56	Putnam	449	386	1.91
Gilchrist	450	157	5.09	St. Johns	174	408	0.79
Glades	220	116	7.10	St. Lucie	536	331	0.46
Gulf	0	0	0.00	Santa Rosa	526	96	0.28
Hamilton	312	38	0.99	Sarasota	348	272	0.16
Hardee	1,241	674	7.15	Seminole	342	250	0.15
Hendry	459	1,606	10.04	Sumter	855	237	1.80
Hernando	490	131	0.33	Suwannee	1,019	257	2.43
Highlands	828	967	3.07	Taylor	156	8	0.11
Hillsborough	3,012	8,532	1.27	Union	265	9	0.21
Holmes	705	10	0.27	Volusia	1,059	1,806	1.06
Indian River	467	833	1.60	Wakulla	106	4	0.08
Jackson	1,056	91	0.59	Walton	581	25	0.15
Jefferson	444	203	5.84	Washington	416	28	0.43

See footnote at end of table. Continued . . .

Table 9.10. EMPLOYMENT: ESTIMATES OF AVERAGE MONTHLY EMPLOYMENT OF FARM PROPRIETORS AND WAGE AND SALARY WORKERS IN THE UNITED STATES AND IN THE STATE AND COUNTIES OF FLORIDA, 2004 AND 2005 (Continued)

County	Farm proprietors	Farm wage and salary employees		County	Farm proprietors	Farm wage and salary employees	
		Number	As a percentage of all wage and salary employees			Number	As a percentage of all wage and salary employees
				2005			
United States	2,135,000	779,000	0.55	Lafayette	255	165	9.16
				Lake	1,505	1,115	1.28
Florida	39,029	44,994	0.54	Lee	572	978	0.42
Alachua	1,308	371	0.28	Leon	291	89	0.06
Baker	193	85	1.15	Levy	661	194	1.89
Bay	80	21	0.03	Liberty	55	0	0.00
Bradford	327	19	0.25	Madison	596	102	1.80
Brevard	548	171	0.08	Manatee	749	3,413	2.46
Broward	255	533	0.07	Marion	1,890	990	0.92
Calhoun	155	105	3.42	Martin	285	453	0.68
Charlotte	240	371	0.83	Miami-Dade	1,406	4,941	0.45
Citrus	342	61	0.18	Monroe	0	0	0.00
Clay	248	51	0.11	Nassau	283	57	0.29
Collier	243	3,613	2.54	Okaloosa	425	15	0.01
Columbia	724	41	0.18	Okeechobee	505	757	6.52
DeSoto	885	440	3.51	Orange	807	2,316	0.32
Dixie	191	17	0.58	Osceola	548	282	0.39
Duval	354	204	0.04	Palm Beach	657	4,204	0.68
Escambia	561	62	0.04	Pasco	1,073	510	0.50
Flagler	107	199	0.96	Pinellas	144	54	0.01
Franklin	0	0	0.00	Polk	2,798	1,272	0.57
Gadsden	338	1,371	8.50	Putnam	447	345	1.70
Gilchrist	448	141	4.44	St. Johns	173	383	0.69
Glades	219	107	6.56	St. Lucie	533	439	0.58
Gulf	0	0	0.00	Santa Rosa	523	75	0.21
Hamilton	310	38	0.98	Sarasota	346	189	0.11
Hardee	1,233	636	6.24	Seminole	340	228	0.12
Hendry	457	1,294	7.67	Sumter	850	226	1.40
Hernando	488	126	0.30	Suwannee	1,013	193	1.81
Highlands	823	995	3.11	Taylor	155	9	0.12
Hillsborough	2,995	7,592	1.09	Union	264	8	0.18
Holmes	702	9	0.24	Volusia	1,052	1,539	0.87
Indian River	465	490	0.91	Wakulla	105	5	0.09
Jackson	1,050	75	0.47	Walton	578	25	0.14
Jefferson	442	162	4.66	Washington	414	23	0.35

A/ Revised.

Source: U.S., Department of Commerce, Bureau of Economic Analysis, Regional Economic Information System (REIS), 1969–2005, Internet site <http://www.bea.gov/> (accessed 30, May 2006).

Table 9.15. PRODUCTION AND SERVICES: AVERAGE MONTHLY PRIVATE REPORTING UNITS EMPLOYMENT, AND PAYROLL COVERED BY UNEMPLOYMENT COMPENSATION LAW IN THE STATE AND COUNTIES OF FLORIDA, 2006

County	Number of reporting units	Number of employees	Payroll ($1,000)	County	Number of reporting units	Number of employees	Payroll ($1,000)
		Agriculture production–crops (NAICS code 111)					
Florida	2,413	55,913	103,742	Levy	13	122	357
Alachua	18	397	733	Madison	6	45	53
Brevard	24	144	291	Manatee	66	4,878	7,289
Broward	76	688	1,258	Marion	31	330	538
Charlotte	15	503	865	Martin	39	549	1,055
Clay	6	50	174	Miami-Dade	342	7,198	13,996
Collier	54	4,345	7,268	Okaloosa	3	20	43
Columbia	7	51	83	Okeechobee	19	200	538
DeSoto	45	538	1,149	Orange	175	3,053	6,490
Duval	14	266	861	Osceola	20	266	645
Flagler	10	284	581	Palm Beach	205	5,817	13,945
Gadsden	25	1,879	3,176	Pasco	38	487	888
Gilchrist	5	22	47	Pinellas	15	76	140
Glades	8	95	218	Polk	137	1,704	3,393
Hamilton	8	53	58	Putnam	29	404	574
Hardee	56	552	820	St. Johns	35	455	914
Hendry	39	1,506	3,807	St. Lucie	34	552	1,293
Hernando	10	89	260	Santa Rosa	16	103	162
Highlands	94	1,119	2,511	Sarasota	27	243	425
Hillsborough	220	9,408	13,083	Seminole	25	263	548
Indian River	32	731	1,693	Sumter	17	285	518
Jackson	11	100	95	Suwannee	18	122	221
Jefferson	10	172	303	Volusia	102	1,968	2,773
Lake	116	1,605	3,145	Walton	3	26	80
Lee	37	1,337	2,491	Washington	5	15	34
Leon	7	90	174	Unknown 1/	12	29	150
		Agriculture production–livestock (NAICS code 112)					
Florida	713	5,890	13,458	Hillsborough	34	647	1,529
				Indian River	7	37	86
Alachua	15	135	316	Jackson	8	36	75
Bradford	5	25	63	Jefferson	8	107	222
Broward	19	51	121	Lafayette	20	181	269
Clay	6	21	43	Lake	9	89	217
Collier	7	17	48	Lee	5	11	25
Columbia	3	18	38	Leon	5	21	38
DeSoto	10	77	202	Levy	17	180	421
Gilchrist	9	147	310	Madison	4	9	10
Hardee	16	177	404	Manatee	11	87	159
Hernando	12	80	171	Marion	114	1,119	2,369
Highlands	23	294	691	Martin	9	28	53

See footnotes at end of table. Continued . . .

Table 9.15. PRODUCTION AND SERVICES: AVERAGE MONTHLY PRIVATE REPORTING UNITS EMPLOYMENT, AND PAYROLL COVERED BY UNEMPLOYMENT COMPENSATION LAW IN THE STATE AND COUNTIES OF FLORIDA, 2006 (Continued)

County	Number of reporting units	Number of employees	Payroll ($1,000)	County	Number of reporting units	Number of employees	Payroll ($1,000)
			Agriculture production–livestock (NAICS code 112) (Continued)				
Miami-Dade	28	112	314	St. Lucie	8	54	188
Nassau	3	27	49	Sarasota	17	31	84
Okeechobee	48	682	1,542	Seminole	9	22	38
Orange	7	11	28	Sumter	14	76	189
Osceola	19	147	324	Suwannee	15	144	254
Palm Beach	44	78	217	Volusia	15	41	82
Pasco	14	261	543	Washington	3	21	49
Polk	30	124	227	Unknown 1/	5	7	50
			Agriculture and forestry support activities (NAICS code 115)				
Florida	1,262	27,431	48,862	Levy	12	75	187
				Marion	89	1,126	2,370
Alachua	4	39	126	Martin	11	111	219
Brevard	7	12	17	Miami-Dade	84	1,920	3,277
Broward	39	160	324	Nassau	5	106	509
Citrus	8	23	38	Okeechobee	13	223	249
Collier	29	1,161	1,782	Orange	40	1,103	2,074
Columbia	6	11	21	Osceola	6	44	89
DeSoto	52	1,154	1,732	Palm Beach	124	2,164	4,276
Gadsden	7	133	287	Pasco	20	179	244
Glades	3	23	70	Pinellas	12	32	45
Hardee	57	1,055	1,572	Polk	142	3,366	5,615
Hendry	45	1,737	3,178	St. Johns	10	83	109
Highlands	92	2,323	3,863	St. Lucie	46	1,479	3,212
Hillsborough	40	1,965	2,243	Santa Rosa	8	35	140
Indian River	62	1,885	3,404	Sarasota	13	62	222
Jackson	6	28	88	Seminole	11	45	80
Jefferson	4	16	70	Taylor	4	49	222
Lake	14	258	476	Volusia	12	42	68
Lee	13	96	209	Statewide 1/	5	2,417	4,741
Leon	7	33	63	Unknown 1/	29	161	323

NAICS North American Industry Classification System. See Glossary for details.
1/ Reporting units without a fixed location within the state or of unknown county location.
Note: Private employment. Data are preliminary. For a list of four-digit code industries included see Table 9.27. Only counties for which data are disclosed are shown. Detail may not add to totals due to disclosure editing and/or rounding. See Tables in 23.70, 23.72, 23.73, and 23.74 for public employment data.

Source: State of Florida, Agency for Workforce Innovation, Labor Market Statistics, "Quarterly Census of Employment and Wages" (ES-202), Annual NAICS files, Internet site <http://www.labormarketinfo.com/index.htm> (accessed 17, July 2007).

Table 9.21. LABOR AND PROPRIETORS' INCOME: FARM LABOR AND EXPENSE IN FLORIDA 2002 THROUGH 2005

(in thousands of dollars)

Item	2002	2003	2004	2005
Cash receipts from marketing	6,446,099	6,673,397	7,211,413	7,869,455
Livestock and products	1,353,220	1,364,351	1,648,820	1,629,275
Crops	5,092,879	5,309,046	5,562,593	6,240,180
Other income	289,031	340,278	417,376	612,783
Government payments	83,377	133,750	209,850	433,697
Imputed income and miscellaneous income received 1/	205,654	206,528	207,526	179,086
Production expenses	4,924,252	5,292,221	5,370,213	5,829,341
Feed purchased	395,136	400,446	390,446	390,446
Livestock purchased	164,909	176,423	225,690	248,199
Seed purchased	336,995	367,924	337,924	407,924
Fertilizer and lime purchased	536,572	626,061	626,061	616,061
Petroleum products purchased	142,444	145,645	144,136	194,648
Hired farm labor expenses 2/	1,577,162	1,611,933	1,647,563	1,608,759
All other production expenses 3/	1,771,034	1,963,789	1,998,393	2,363,304
Value of inventory change	-17,763	-7,317	-32,736	-18,262
Livestock	-20,770	-6,764	-24,235	-15,927
Crops	-7,067	1,530	-6,944	(L)
Materials and supplies	10,074	-2,083	-1,557	-2,380
Derivation of farm labor and proprietors' income:				
Total cash receipts and other income	6,735,130	7,013,675	7,628,789	8,482,238
Less: Total production expenses	4,924,252	5,292,221	5,370,213	5,829,341
Realized net income	1,810,878	1,721,454	2,258,576	2,652,897
Plus: Value of inventory change	-17,763	-7,317	-32,736	-18,262
Total net income including corporate farms	1,793,115	1,714,137	2,225,840	2,634,635
Less: Net income of corporate farms	1,031,270	1,001,179	1,817,017	2,305,400
Total net farm proprietors' income	761,838	712,959	408,822	329,243
Plus: Farm wages and perquisites	1,039,636	883,742	1,097,727	1,121,080
Plus: Farm supplements to wages and salaries	168,550	170,287	176,747	154,199
Total farm labor and proprietors' income	1,970,024	1,766,988	1,683,296	1,604,522

(L) Less than $50,000.

1/ Includes the value of home consumption and other farm related income components, such as machine hire and custom work income and income from forest products.

2/ Consists of hired workers' cash wages, social security and medicare, perquisites, and contract labor, machine hire and custom work expenses.

3/ Includes repair and operation of machinery; depreciation, interest, rent and taxes; and other miscellaneous expenses, including agricultural chemicals.

Note: Data for 2003 and 2004 have been revised.

Source: U.S., Department of Commerce, Bureau of Economic Analysis, Regional Economic Information System (REIS), 1969–2005, Internet site <http://www.bea.gov/> (accessed 30, May 2007).

Table 9.22. FARM INCOME AND EXPENSE: FARM LABOR AND PROPRIETORS' INCOME IN THE UNITED STATES AND IN THE STATE AND COUNTIES OF FLORIDA 2004 AND 2005

(in thousands of dollars)

County	Cash receipts and other income 1/	Less production expenses	Total net farm income 2/	Total net farm proprietors' income	Total farm labor and proprietors' income
			2004 A/		
United States	275,122,404	224,662,948	58,857,085	35,402,000	57,936,000
Florida	7,628,789	5,370,213	2,225,840	408,822	1,683,296
Alachua	65,926	52,333	13,014	6,922	16,924
Baker	29,577	23,753	5,741	3,455	5,569
Bay	3,201	1,652	1,535	1,492	2,037
Bradford	22,739	18,531	4,075	3,257	3,633
Brevard	48,802	36,371	12,103	224	6,104
Broward	60,034	42,025	17,825	1,691	18,446
Calhoun	18,531	15,234	2,475	1,342	4,568
Charlotte	61,667	46,978	14,420	2,647	10,272
Citrus	8,281	7,388	799	565	2,125
Clay	35,657	29,746	5,795	306	2,994
Collier	341,798	214,970	126,703	15,342	106,415
Columbia	29,429	28,334	809	609	1,295
DeSoto	229,589	159,436	69,141	10,529	26,376
Dixie	6,238	4,947	1,237	850	1,363
Duval	32,239	28,191	3,947	3,213	17,611
Escambia	23,011	19,951	1,900	1,735	3,763
Flagler	34,030	26,279	7,721	6,185	8,883
Franklin	0	0	0	0	0
Gadsden	110,570	84,990	25,498	14,264	49,132
Gilchrist	64,699	54,330	9,957	592	5,029
Glades	81,366	60,506	19,938	955	4,809
Gulf	0	0	0	0	0
Hamilton	15,666	14,028	1,409	1,053	1,490
Hardee	223,840	135,978	86,714	14,932	30,216
Hendry	365,243	254,949	109,099	7,087	55,917
Hernando	29,660	23,621	5,810	3,469	6,903
Highlands	264,089	173,662	89,053	12,453	40,021
Hillsborough	407,328	290,514	115,911	35,552	185,981
Holmes	43,965	31,790	11,661	11,081	11,295
Indian River	122,195	90,578	31,391	1,616	26,493
Jackson	70,979	54,655	12,262	9,410	11,163
Jefferson	24,234	18,418	5,601	4,727	9,370
Lafayette	66,273	50,459	15,517	6,894	10,701

See footnotes at end of table. Continued . . .

Table 9.22. FARM INCOME AND EXPENSE: FARM LABOR AND PROPRIETORS' INCOME IN THE UNITED STATES AND IN THE STATE AND COUNTIES OF FLORIDA 2004 AND 2005 (Continued)

(in thousands of dollars)

County	Cash receipts and other income 1/	Less production expenses	Total net farm income 2/	Total net farm proprietors' income	Total farm labor and proprietors' income
			2004 A/ (Continued)		
Lake	203,728	157,070	46,284	15,961	49,482
Lee	140,636	122,669	17,788	4,853	37,700
Leon	7,733	7,220	446	(L)	2,529
Levy	74,369	46,976	26,864	15,618	25,694
Liberty	920	771	136	76	100
Madison	40,526	32,718	7,505	6,854	8,972
Manatee	286,599	189,467	96,453	16,123	90,060
Marion	150,953	125,482	24,953	6,054	35,790
Martin	182,211	128,138	53,715	1,246	13,387
Miami-Dade	525,346	387,032	138,279	1,461	142,028
Monroe	0	0	0	0	0
Nassau	32,631	26,905	5,583	5,415	15,010
Okaloosa	10,982	9,738	720	528	817
Okeechobee	188,949	140,416	46,463	6,276	32,906
Orange	323,742	257,258	66,260	9,266	84,003
Osceola	148,318	82,594	64,216	3,207	15,564
Palm Beach	1,076,065	645,401	430,383	12,493	172,162
Pasco	112,968	90,669	21,530	5,385	21,871
Pinellas	13,788	11,542	2,244	1,499	4,381
Polk	328,621	214,116	113,094	31,650	71,348
Putnam	49,124	31,724	17,330	5,922	13,632
St. Johns	53,801	43,230	10,802	3,630	12,561
St. Lucie	231,370	147,063	83,902	1,463	12,553
Santa Rosa	37,466	28,898	6,104	5,184	7,298
Sarasota	30,709	22,538	7,892	1,897	9,179
Seminole	25,804	18,187	7,488	2,616	8,961
Sumter	47,825	37,482	9,778	5,874	11,976
Suwannee	149,119	115,183	33,421	23,091	28,879
Taylor	6,160	4,597	1,493	1,390	1,577
Union	13,986	12,493	1,391	1,107	1,385
Volusia	148,412	102,060	46,186	21,377	55,997
Wakulla	4,485	3,657	808	716	765
Walton	26,701	20,075	5,887	4,958	5,882
Washington	13,886	12,247	1,381	1,161	1,949

See footnotes at end of table.

Continued . . .

Table 9.22. FARM INCOME AND EXPENSE: FARM LABOR AND PROPRIETORS' INCOME IN THE UNITED STATES AND IN THE STATE AND COUNTIES OF FLORIDA 2004 AND 2005 (Continued)

(in thousands of dollars)

County	Cash receipts and other income 1/	Less production expenses	Total net farm income 2/	Total net farm proprietors' income	Total farm labor and proprietors' income
			2005		
United States	287,418,068	240,675,255	47,076,768	26,609,000	50,903,000
Florida	8,482,238	5,829,341	2,634,635	329,243	1,604,522
Alachua	73,916	57,702	15,233	8,079	18,668
Baker	28,390	24,987	3,404	1,933	3,980
Bay	3,565	1,792	1,763	1,714	2,376
Bradford	20,832	19,634	1,183	882	1,495
Brevard	57,618	40,057	17,304	520	6,270
Broward	67,168	45,006	22,033	2,356	16,924
Calhoun	20,930	16,451	4,717	2,854	6,176
Charlotte	72,592	52,109	20,288	3,660	13,658
Citrus	9,367	8,120	1,198	880	2,303
Clay	34,823	32,998	1,743	313	2,816
Collier	409,384	233,623	175,642	8,706	97,089
Columbia	28,049	31,076	-3,327	-3,310	-2,352
DeSoto	271,639	174,804	96,109	8,627	23,292
Dixie	6,604	5,379	1,193	799	1,374
Duval	32,599	30,133	2,406	1,912	11,234
Escambia	23,844	21,963	2,028	1,852	4,007
Flagler	39,246	29,117	10,112	6,219	12,695
Franklin	0	0	0	0	0
Gadsden	128,487	89,002	39,391	13,045	48,602
Gilchrist	66,811	58,288	8,127	268	5,163
Glades	83,573	70,493	12,380	847	4,967
Gulf	0	0	0	0	0
Hamilton	14,318	15,374	-2,516	-2,493	-1,876
Hardee	257,785	147,840	109,075	11,468	27,551
Hendry	409,477	280,128	128,395	2,380	45,609
Hernando	30,169	25,250	4,819	2,753	6,978
Highlands	291,952	190,448	100,471	9,799	42,940
Hillsborough	460,407	310,520	149,403	32,355	196,884
Holmes	40,875	33,991	6,784	6,405	6,622
Indian River	160,314	98,515	61,610	1,256	19,336
Jackson	76,690	59,882	17,397	8,527	10,180
Jefferson	26,621	19,990	6,296	5,315	9,754
Lafayette	62,625	53,050	9,075	6,727	10,578
Lake	227,934	166,427	61,264	17,384	51,209

See footnotes at end of table. Continued . . .

Table 9.22. FARM INCOME AND EXPENSE: FARM LABOR AND PROPRIETORS' INCOME IN THE UNITED STATES AND IN THE STATE AND COUNTIES OF FLORIDA 2004 AND 2005 (Continued)

(in thousands of dollars)

County	Cash receipts and other income 1/	Less production expenses	Total net farm income 2/	Total net farm proprietors' income	Total farm labor and proprietors' income
			2005 (Continued)		
Lee	172,298	128,287	43,868	4,062	36,449
Leon	7,643	8,168	-560	-546	2,359
Levy	80,911	50,802	29,790	16,740	24,294
Liberty	905	863	(L)	(L)	(L)
Madison	38,781	35,030	2,372	2,109	4,344
Manatee	350,722	203,253	146,963	16,290	92,123
Marion	153,544	136,904	16,351	2,510	33,743
Martin	202,142	134,395	67,458	1,658	15,524
Miami-Dade	585,049	415,656	169,327	4,024	149,710
Monroe	0	0	0	0	0
Nassau	27,789	28,008	-158	-166	1,465
Okaloosa	11,153	10,680	557	398	813
Okeechobee	203,864	150,511	51,857	4,647	32,396
Orange	357,819	264,125	93,506	980	75,769
Osceola	164,394	84,685	78,596	1,742	12,210
Palm Beach	1,145,320	753,186	391,754	8,236	160,183
Pasco	113,379	96,556	16,566	3,156	19,740
Pinellas	15,602	12,254	3,346	2,356	4,949
Polk	390,003	230,968	158,078	28,962	66,794
Putnam	50,629	33,866	16,744	5,417	13,062
St. Johns	55,483	49,361	6,339	2,764	13,715
St. Lucie	285,994	155,916	129,751	478	16,642
Santa Rosa	40,626	31,667	9,597	3,262	5,100
Sarasota	35,763	24,392	11,173	2,783	8,285
Seminole	30,298	19,489	10,718	3,881	10,649
Sumter	51,882	40,888	10,670	6,249	12,678
Suwannee	140,480	121,292	18,146	14,889	20,228
Taylor	5,425	4,973	281	254	472
Union	13,707	13,310	205	120	425
Volusia	169,316	106,500	62,713	25,012	58,893
Wakulla	4,473	4,091	380	327	463
Walton	23,848	21,552	2,397	1,939	3,051
Washington	14,392	13,564	816	661	1,475

(L) Less than $50,000.
A/ Revised.
1/ Includes government payments, imputed income, and rent received.
2/ Includes corporate farms.
Note: See also tables in Section 5.00.

Source: U.S., Department of Commerce, Bureau of Economic Analysis, Regional Economic Information System (REIS), 1969–2005, Internet site <http://www.bea.gov/> (accessed 30, May 2007).

Table 9.25. INCOME: ESTIMATED CASH RECEIPTS FROM FARM MARKETINGS BY SPECIFIED COMMODITY IN THE UNITED STATES AND LEADING STATES IN RANK ORDER, 2005

(in millions of dollars)

Commodity and state	Cash receipts	Commodity and state	Cash receipts	Commodity and state	Cash receipts
All commodities		All livestock 1/		All crops	
United States	238,941	United States	124,980	United States	113,962
California	31,707	Texas	10,662	California	23,253
Texas	16,355	California	8,454	Illinois	6,859
Iowa	14,621	Iowa	7,947	Iowa	6,674
Nebraska	11,470	Nebraska	7,545	**Florida**	6,306
Kansas	9,975	Kansas	6,868	Texas	5,694
Minnesota	9,301	North Carolina	5,602	Minnesota	4,338
Illinois	8,847	Wisconsin	5,014	Washington	3,987
North Carolina	8,264	Minnesota	4,963	Nebraska	3,925
Florida	7,760	Arizona	4,215	Indiana	3,537
Wisconsin	6,759	Oklahoma	4,215	Ohio	3,138
Greenhouses 2/ (6)		Potatoes (14)		Tomatoes (16)	
United States	16,202	United States	2,377	United States	2,277
California	3,448	Idaho	523	California	942
Florida	1,879	Washington	431	**Florida**	805
Texas	1,323	California	198	Ohio	89
Oregon	980	Wisconsin	162	Virginia	88
North Carolina	975	North Dakota	133	Georgia	75
Michigan	648	**Florida**	114	Tennessee	42
Ohio	584	Colorado	106	Indiana	37
Pennsylvania	415	Oregon	93	Michigan	33
New York	382	Minnesota	93	New Jersey	28
Georgia	379	Maine	91	Pennsylvania	26
Oranges (18)		Strawberries (21)		Tobacco (24)	
United States	1,605	United States	1,383	United States	1,096
Florida	1,015	California	1,110	North Carolina	408
California	581	**Florida**	197	Kentucky	343
Texas	8	North Carolina	19	Tennessee	109
Arizona	1	Oregon	14	Virginia	70
		Pennsylvania	13	South Carolina	62
		New York	8	Georgia	40
		Washington	7	Connecticut	12
		Ohio	6	Ohio	11
		Wisconsin	5	Pennsylvania	11
		Michigan	5	**Florida**	8

1/ Includes poultry and products.
2/ Includes nurseries.
Note: Commodities listed are among 25 leading commodities ranked by value of farm marketings. The number after the commodity name indicates rank order in cash receipts in the United States. Receipts include commodity credit corporation loans.

Source: U.S., Department of Agriculture, Economic Research Service, "Receipts of 10 Leading States in Cash Receipts for Top 25 Commodities, 2005," Internet site <http://www.ers.usda.gov/> (accessed 21, March 2007).

Table 9.26. INCOME: CASH RECEIPTS BY COMMODITY AND COMMODITY GROUP IN FLORIDA, 2004 THROUGH 2006

Commodity	2004 A/ Cash receipts ($1,000)	2004 A/ Percentage of total	2005 A/ Cash receipts ($1,000)	2005 A/ Percentage of total	2006 B/ Cash receipts ($1,000)	2006 B/ Percentage of total
Cash receipts 1/	7,078,818	100.00	7,702,314	100.00	6,974,161	100.00
Crops	5,621,904	79.42	6,295,677	81.74	5,669,269	81.29
Citrus	1,470,960	20.78	1,670,132	21.68	1,444,978	20.72
Grapefruit	245,244	3.46	518,106	6.73	172,149	2.47
Oranges	1,138,435	16.08	1,054,745	13.69	1,200,915	17.22
Tangelos	8,626	0.12	8,219	0.11	9,378	0.13
Tangerines	73,740	1.04	85,748	1.11	58,502	0.84
Temples	4,915	0.07	3,314	0.04	4,034	0.06
Other fruits and nuts	270,245	3.82	283,813	3.68	337,318	4.84
Avocados	14,253	0.20	12,148	0.16	12,360	0.18
Pecans	695	0.01	1,015	0.01	810	0.01
Blueberries	25,200	0.36	32,760	0.43	32,900	0.47
Strawberries	177,997	2.51	196,790	2.55	239,148	3.43
Other	52,100	0.74	41,100	0.53	52,100	0.75
Vegetables and melons	1,448,222	20.46	1,844,132	23.94	1,568,869	22.50
Cabbage	30,932	0.44	31,294	0.41	30,690	0.44
Cucumbers	83,426	1.18	94,130	1.22	98,077	1.41
Green peppers	218,411	3.09	213,428	2.77	187,330	2.69
Potatoes	97,234	1.37	113,087	1.47	145,138	2.08
Snap beans	133,198	1.88	142,324	1.85	141,804	2.03
Squash	45,392	0.64	47,970	0.62	38,760	0.56
Sweet corn	110,382	1.56	108,058	1.40	117,271	1.68
Tomatoes	500,472	7.07	804,972	10.45	551,128	7.90
Watermelons	67,200	0.95	126,945	1.65	111,042	1.59
Other	161,575	2.28	161,924	2.10	147,629	2.12
Field crops	677,061	9.56	572,141	7.43	499,082	7.16
Corn	6,056	0.09	4,256	0.06	5,607	0.08
Cotton	24,458	0.35	31,704	0.41	39,579	0.57
Hay	11,440	0.16	17,954	0.23	18,451	0.26
Peanuts	65,884	0.93	68,537	0.89	51,900	0.74
Soybeans	3,153	0.04	1,970	0.03	950	0.01
Sugarcane	526,278	7.43	417,549	5.42	356,888	5.12
Tobacco	17,226	0.24	8,305	0.11	4,319	0.06
Wheat	2,096	0.03	1,296	0.02	818	0.01
Other	20,470	0.29	20,570	0.27	20,570	0.29
Foliage and floriculture	884,126	12.49	956,580	12.42	800,399	11.48
Other crops and products 1/	871,290	12.31	968,879	12.58	1,018,623	14.61
Livestock and products	1,456,914	20.58	1,406,637	18.26	1,304,892	18.71
Milk	431,616	6.10	421,662	5.47	343,599	4.93
Cattle and calves	451,857	6.38	502,268	6.52	484,288	6.94
Poultry and eggs	369,324	5.22	303,206	3.94	297,159	4.26
Broilers	208,440	2.94	201,564	2.62	181,425	2.60
Eggs	159,878	2.26	100,723	1.31	115,002	1.65
Other poultry	1,006	0.01	919	0.01	732	0.01
Aquaculture	68,539	0.97	57,340	0.74	57,231	0.82
Catfish	1,139	0.02	1,434	0.02	1,761	0.03
Other aquaculture 2/	67,400	0.95	55,906	0.73	55,470	0.80

See footnotes at end of table. Continued . . .

Table 9.26. INCOME: CASH RECEIPTS BY COMMODITY AND COMMODITY GROUP IN FLORIDA 2004 THROUGH 2006 (Continued)

Commodity	2004 A/ Cash receipts ($1,000)	2004 A/ Percentage of total	2005 A/ Cash receipts ($1,000)	2005 A/ Percentage of total	2006 B/ Cash receipts ($1,000)	2006 B/ Percentage of total
Livestock and products (Cont.)						
Hogs	6,406	0.09	4,674	0.06	3,766	0.05
Honey	20,090	0.28	11,834	0.15	13,908	0.20
Other livestock and products	109,082	1.54	105,653	1.37	104,941	1.50

A/ Revised.
B/ Preliminary.
1/ Include mushrooms, sod, ornamental shrubs and trees and aquatic plants. Excludes forestry products.
2/ Other aquaculture includes tropical fish, farmed alligators, and farmed clams and oysters.
Note: Percents for individual commodities do not add to totals for some groups due to rounding.

Source: State of Florida, Department of Agriculture and Consumer Services, Florida Agricultural Statistics Service, *Florida Agriculture: Farm Cash Receipts and Expenditures, 2006,* released August 2007, Internet site <http://www.nass.usda.gov/> (accessed 19, September 2007).

Table 9.27. PRODUCTION AND SERVICES: AVERAGE MONTHLY PRIVATE REPORTING UNITS EMPLOYMENT, AND PAYROLL COVERED BY UNEMPLOYMENT COMPENSATION LAW BY INDUSTRY IN FLORIDA, 2006

NAICS code	Industry	Number of reporting units	Number of employees	Payroll ($1,000)
11	Agriculture, forestry, fishing, and hunting 1/	4,933	92,634	175,476
111	Crop production	2,413	55,913	103,742
1111	Oilseed and grain farming	11	87	197
1112	Vegetable and melon farming	296	17,729	26,899
1113	Fruit and tree nut farming	513	9,573	18,330
1114	Greenhouse and nursery production	1,318	24,269	48,969
1119	Other crop farming	275	4,256	9,347
112	Animal production	713	5,890	13,458
1121	Cattle ranching and farming	372	3,277	7,619
1123	Poultry and egg production	17	775	1,687
1124	Sheep and goat farming	8	27	62
1125	Animal aquaculture	62	319	996
1129	Other animal production	252	1,489	3,065
115	Agriculture and forestry support activities	1,262	27,431	48,862
1151	Support activities for crop production	900	25,374	43,604
1152	Support activities for animal production	293	1,599	3,478
1153	Support activities for forestry	69	457	1,780

NAICS North American Industrial Classification System. See Glossary for definition.
1/ Includes industries not shown separately. See Table 10.34.
Note: Private employment. Data are preliminary. Detail may not add to totals due to disclosure editing and/or rounding. See Tables 23.70, 23.72, 23.73, and 23.74 for public employment data.

Source: State of Florida, Agency for Workforce Innovation, Labor Market Statistics, "Quarterly Census of Employment and Wages" (ES-202), Annual NAICS files, Internet site <http://www.labormarketinfo.com/index.htm> (accessed 17, July 2007).

Table 9.34. FARMS: SPECIFIED CHARACTERISTICS OF FARMS IN FLORIDA
1997 AND 2002

Item	All farms		
	1997	2002	Percentage change
Number of farms	45,808	44,081	-3.8
Land in farms (acres)	10,659,777	10,414,877	-2.3
Average size of farm (acres)	233	236	1.3
Estimated market value of land and buildings (dollars) 1/			
Average per farm	540,572	665,376	23.1
Average per acre	2,344	2,836	21.0
Estimated market value of all machinery and equipment ($1,000) 1/	1,613,796	1,723,447	6.8
Average per farm (dollars)	35,239	39,884	13.2
Farms by size			
1 to 9 acres	10,622	10,267	-3.3
10 to 49 acres	18,680	18,360	-1.7
50 to 179 acres	9,804	8,776	-10.5
180 to 499 acres	3,785	3,684	-2.7
500 to 999 acres	1,324	1,330	0.5
1,000 to 1,999 acres	749	822	9.7
2,000 acres or more	844	842	-0.2
Total cropland	30,792	27,348	-11.2
Acres	3,610,304	3,715,257	2.9
Harvested cropland	23,520	20,495	-12.9
Acres	2,434,379	2,313,537	-5.0
Irrigated land	14,573	13,456	-7.7
Acres	1,873,823	1,815,174	-3.1
Market value of agricultural products sold ($1,000)	6,137,802	6,242,272	1.7
Average per farm (dollars)	133,990	141,609	5.7
Crops, including nursery and greenhouse crops	4,853,417	5,041,433	3.9
Livestock, poultry, and their products	1,284,385	1,200,839	-6.5
Farms by value of sales			
Less than $2,500	19,006	19,114	0.6
$2,500 to $4,999	5,607	4,544	-19.0
$5,000 to $9,999	5,131	4,285	-16.5
$10,000 to $24,999	5,286	5,240	-0.9
$25,000 to $49,999	3,049	3,305	8.4
$50,000 to $99,999	2,349	2,486	5.8
$100,000 to $499,999	3,395	3,239	-4.6
$500,000 or more	1,985	1,868	-5.9
Farms by type of organization			
Family or individual	37,138	37,119	-0.1
Partnership	3,212	2,429	-24.4
Corporation	4,989	4,076	-18.3
Other—cooperative, estate or trust, institutional, etc	469	457	-2.6
Livestock/poultry inventory			
Cattle and calves			
Farms	23,007	19,182	-16.6
Number	1,858,255	1,738,874	-6.4
Beef cows	0	0	
Farms	18,945	15,717	-17.0
Number	1,012,614	982,404	-3.0
Milk cows	0	0	
Farms	952	923	-3.0
Number	160,818	144,843	-9.9

See footnotes at end of table.

Continued . . .

Table 9.34. FARMS: SPECIFIED CHARACTERISTICS OF FARMS IN FLORIDA 1997 AND 2002 (Continued)

Item	All farms 1997	All farms 2002	All farms Percentage change
Livestock/poultry inventory (Continued)			
Hogs and pigs			
Farms	2,352	1,471	-37.5
Number	62,967	33,479	-46.8
Broilers and other meat-type chickens sold			
Farms	468	446	-4.7
Number	139,309,122	109,236,689	-21.6
Crops harvested			
Corn for grain			
Farms	1,324	519	-60.8
Acres	67,439	26,790	-60.3
Bushels	5,247,737	2,456,508	-53.2
Soybeans for beans			
Farms	391	77	-80.3
Acres	39,680	7,478	-81.2
Bushels	988,263	242,878	-75.4
Tobacco			
Farms	196	115	-41.3
Acres	6,951	3,851	-44.6
Pounds	16,350,368	9,609,134	-41.2
Potatoes			
Farms	156	106	-32.1
Acres	41,258	35,386	-14.2
Hundred weight	8,813,440	8,663,744	-1.7
Sugarcane for sugar			
Farms	162	120	-25.9
Acres	421,727	440,768	4.5
Tons	15,728,855	16,174,145	2.8
Vegetables harvested for sale 2/			
Farms	1,792	1,507	-15.9
Acres	253,321	219,412	-13.4
All land in orchards			
Farms	11,080	10,115	-8.7
Acres	996,717	894,955	-10.2
Total production on farms by NAICS code	34,799	44,081	26.7
Oilseed and grain (1111)	1,118	348	-68.9
Vegetable and melon (1112)	1,250	1,139	-8.9
Fruit and tree nut (1113)	8,245	9,335	13.2
Greenhouse, nursery, and floriculture (1114)	4,902	4,530	-7.6
Other crop farming (1119)	2,137	2,679	25.4
Beef cattle ranching and farming (112111)	12,040	15,304	27.1
Dairy cattle and milk production (11212)	296	517	74.7
Hog and pig farming (1122)	468	601	28.4
Poultry and egg production (1123)	560	739	32.0
Sheep and goat farming (1124)	272	608	123.5
Animal aquaculture and other animal (1125, 1129)	3,202	8,281	158.6

NAICS North American Industry Classification System. See Glossary for definition.

1/ Data are based on a sample of farms.

2/ Vegetable acreage is counted only once even when it is replanted.

Note: Livestock and poultry inventories are as of December 31. Crop and livestock production, sales, and expense data are for the calendar year, except for a few crops for which the production and calendar years overlap. The agriculture census is on a 5-year cycle collecting data for years ending in 2 or 7.

Source: U.S., Department of Agriculture, Natural Agricultural Statistics Service, *2002 Census of Agriculture: Florida State Level Data,* Volume 1, Chapter 1, released June 2004, Internet site <http://www.nass.usda.gov/> (accessed 11, May 2007).

Table 9.35. FARMS: NUMBER, LAND IN FARMS, AND VALUE OF LAND AND BUILDINGS IN THE STATE AND COUNTIES OF FLORIDA, 1997 AND 2002

County	Number of farms 1997	Number of farms 2002	Land in farms (acres) Total 1997	Land in farms (acres) Total 2002	Average size of farm 1997	Average size of farm 2002	Average market value 1/ (dollars) 1997	Average market value 1/ (dollars) 2002
Florida	34,799	44,081	10,454,217	10,414,877	300	236	662,538	665,376
Alachua	1,086	1,493	198,193	222,728	182	149	360,956	486,109
Baker	157	204	13,035	18,061	83	89	247,169	309,168
Bay	70	116	6,732	10,863	96	94	178,733	243,482
Bradford	274	378	43,579	44,819	159	119	262,500	267,420
Brevard	470	555	276,573	187,570	588	338	909,187	783,045
Broward	347	494	30,897	23,741	89	48	414,044	450,331
Calhoun	130	151	43,799	49,107	337	325	395,452	485,551
Charlotte	209	284	290,340	191,529	1,389	674	1,877,627	1,171,466
Citrus	294	432	49,192	47,209	167	109	339,900	309,677
Clay	211	340	70,834	78,542	336	231	623,247	558,561
Collier	235	273	277,279	180,852	1,180	662	2,152,046	1,652,022
Columbia	600	688	97,100	90,227	162	131	348,563	285,920
DeSoto	715	1,153	322,402	388,177	451	337	1,133,735	786,445
Dixie	155	215	33,508	31,249	216	145	211,203	275,161
Duval	320	382	35,531	31,241	111	82	390,172	496,454
Escambia	466	674	54,617	64,581	117	96	248,484	337,473
Flagler	91	100	87,737	68,364	964	684	1,235,927	1,085,977
Franklin	19	20	5,125	(D)	270	(D)	358,268	356,396
Gadsden	290	343	57,933	68,140	200	199	545,860	550,780
Gilchrist	365	408	78,090	81,489	214	200	428,540	374,556
Glades	188	231	380,377	407,950	2,023	1,766	1,663,359	3,158,103
Gulf	33	30	3,823	4,521	116	151	131,637	301,835
Hamilton	256	239	66,379	52,027	259	218	302,842	431,687
Hardee	1,045	1,142	345,643	346,191	331	303	859,608	718,746
Hendry	403	456	604,677	552,352	1,500	1,211	4,288,707	4,518,569
Hernando	432	617	52,999	65,315	123	106	415,946	429,492
Highlands	779	1,035	489,579	576,900	628	557	1,190,743	1,206,393
Hillsborough	2,639	2,969	247,502	284,910	94	96	391,045	454,871
Holmes	578	672	87,582	90,875	152	135	217,569	223,042
Indian River	437	480	168,399	191,333	385	399	1,243,117	1,146,115
Jackson	844	920	244,552	226,890	290	247	300,497	400,313
Jefferson	342	418	126,590	132,727	370	318	498,805	584,211
Lafayette	221	195	93,434	91,988	423	472	547,086	619,141
Lake	1,389	1,798	185,311	180,245	133	100	406,637	447,801

See footnotes at end of table.

Continued . . .

Table 9.35. FARMS: NUMBER, LAND IN FARMS, AND VALUE OF LAND AND BUILDINGS IN THE STATE AND COUNTIES OF FLORIDA, 1997 AND 2002 (Continued)

County	Number of farms 1997	Number of farms 2002	Land in farms (acres) Total 1997	Land in farms (acres) Total 2002	Average size of farm 1997	Average size of farm 2002	Average market value 1/ (dollars) 1997	Average market value 1/ (dollars) 2002
Lee	509	643	129,001	126,484	253	197	723,893	726,318
Leon	243	281	67,539	74,004	278	263	456,258	530,636
Levy	549	897	157,376	180,314	287	201	364,963	367,195
Liberty	47	67	7,238	9,900	154	148	227,102	199,919
Madison	486	529	131,577	156,995	271	297	380,680	408,912
Manatee	697	852	267,993	301,231	384	354	921,872	1,086,878
Marion	1,669	2,930	265,572	270,562	159	92	491,266	443,694
Martin	305	418	183,724	206,198	602	493	1,617,780	1,179,554
Miami-Dade	1,576	2,244	85,093	90,373	54	40	408,330	545,496
Monroe	13	18	1,241	102	95	6	296,297	104,627
Nassau	238	315	35,165	(D)	148	(D)	275,889	412,099
Okaloosa	342	465	50,822	55,119	149	119	249,245	292,073
Okeechobee	459	638	391,871	392,495	854	615	1,227,122	1,263,840
Orange	862	901	175,017	146,637	203	163	603,726	634,638
Osceola	485	519	610,825	652,673	1,259	1,258	1,646,904	2,067,337
Palm Beach	855	1,110	604,703	535,965	707	483	2,397,652	1,623,283
Pasco	951	1,222	161,939	168,716	170	138	500,412	570,545
Pinellas	129	111	1,895	1,589	15	14	283,991	362,615
Polk	2,464	3,114	621,489	626,634	252	201	531,715	588,641
Putnam	391	466	85,794	92,619	219	199	467,078	471,370
St. Johns	149	204	49,631	37,653	333	185	748,864	808,080
St. Lucie	500	477	227,414	221,537	455	464	1,182,701	1,564,070
Santa Rosa	438	505	87,971	83,790	201	166	297,052	401,815
Sarasota	315	371	128,655	121,310	408	327	899,896	841,623
Seminole	344	376	37,222	27,987	108	74	331,507	424,814
Sumter	718	902	183,374	187,373	255	208	467,695	502,601
Suwannee	840	1,054	158,406	170,149	189	161	289,572	363,639
Taylor	126	101	56,784	53,720	451	532	396,058	732,184
Union	213	275	62,503	59,635	293	217	408,651	308,858
Volusia	910	1,114	111,502	93,842	123	84	447,093	329,264
Wakulla	88	126	11,426	10,900	130	87	223,264	210,229
Walton	476	540	78,844	79,910	166	148	202,967	325,288
Washington	322	391	55,268	53,251	172	136	229,495	329,229

(D) Data withheld to avoid disclosure of information about individual farms.
1/ Average estimated market value of land and buildings per farm. Data are based on a sample of farms.
Note: The agriculture census is on a 5-year cycle collecting data for years ending in 2 and 7.

Source: U.S., Department of Agriculture, Natural Agricultural Statistics Service, *2002 Census of Agriculture: Florida County Level Data,* Volume 1, Chapter 1, released June 2004, Internet site <http://www.nass.usda.gov/> (accessed 11, May 2007).

Table 9.36. FARMS: LAND IN FARMS BY USE IN THE STATE AND COUNTIES OF FLORIDA, 2002

(acres)

County	Total land in farms	Land according to use: Cropland Total	Cropland Harvested	Woodland 1/	Pasture-land 2/	Other 3/	Irrigated land
Florida	10,414,877	3,715,257	2,313,537	2,485,733	3,400,193	813,694	1,815,174
Alachua	222,728	80,269	39,281	44,207	86,289	11,963	13,488
Baker	18,061	3,668	1,844	7,532	5,113	1,748	920
Bay	10,863	2,976	1,256	5,394	1,309	1,184	421
Bradford	44,819	18,097	5,410	11,294	13,148	2,280	295
Brevard	187,570	23,106	15,651	57,518	90,039	16,907	24,792
Broward	23,741	6,984	4,385	3,600	9,477	3,680	4,883
Calhoun	49,107	24,142	19,186	19,412	3,642	1,911	1,765
Charlotte	191,529	41,928	(D)	96,158	35,374	18,069	24,516
Citrus	47,209	12,331	4,051	13,772	15,266	5,840	867
Clay	78,542	8,199	2,904	47,922	18,436	3,985	1,286
Collier	180,852	91,398	(D)	31,918	(D)	(D)	55,181
Columbia	90,227	26,712	9,636	39,378	17,629	6,508	1,929
DeSoto	388,177	115,356	87,005	36,676	201,221	34,924	79,147
Dixie	31,249	8,488	2,874	12,417	8,804	1,540	1,751
Duval	31,241	10,666	4,368	11,089	6,675	2,811	2,005
Escambia	64,581	39,246	28,456	14,565	6,254	4,516	2,329
Flagler	68,364	8,355	5,292	46,149	10,948	2,912	4,443
Franklin	(D)	(D)	(D)	668	(D)	162	(NA)
Gadsden	68,140	15,253	7,616	43,511	5,117	4,259	3,834
Gilchrist	81,489	26,686	14,651	30,158	21,226	3,419	3,832
Glades	407,950	73,043	52,786	(D)	(D)	(D)	49,147
Gulf	4,521	1,027	114	2,757	595	142	(NA)
Hamilton	52,027	17,443	8,465	23,699	6,806	4,079	4,503
Hardee	346,191	115,676	70,728	70,046	142,963	17,506	56,882
Hendry	552,352	296,006	203,203	50,803	167,269	38,274	206,043
Hernando	65,315	24,260	12,139	12,823	23,725	4,507	1,393
Highlands	576,900	168,996	99,362	149,947	211,057	46,900	99,269
Hillsborough	284,910	126,158	59,342	33,131	92,497	33,124	42,969
Holmes	90,875	36,695	17,694	29,034	15,682	9,464	584
Indian River	191,333	102,916	65,311	34,139	45,828	8,450	95,174
Jackson	226,890	114,428	73,936	61,904	38,481	12,077	13,374
Jefferson	132,727	29,884	16,347	78,797	10,462	13,584	4,081
Lafayette	91,988	17,114	7,044	24,456	48,378	2,040	4,147
Lake	180,245	73,958	35,899	29,434	59,966	16,887	20,153
Lee	126,484	36,422	25,762	30,061	44,560	15,441	23,935
Leon	74,004	11,425	3,705	51,455	5,788	5,336	2,523

See footnotes at end of table. Continued . . .

Table 9.36. FARMS: LAND IN FARMS BY USE IN THE STATE AND COUNTIES OF FLORIDA, 2002 (Continued)

(acres)

County	Total land in farms	Land according to use: Cropland Total	Cropland Harvested	Woodland 1/	Pasture-land 2/	Other 3/	Irrigated land
Levy	180,314	69,859	39,122	59,242	42,164	9,049	19,501
Liberty	9,900	1,232	223	7,042	(D)	(D)	(D)
Madison	156,995	42,483	21,744	67,437	32,144	14,931	3,646
Manatee	301,231	117,173	60,900	38,266	104,172	41,620	54,710
Marion	270,562	86,712	30,601	63,934	98,998	20,918	5,605
Martin	206,198	97,840	55,470	33,915	63,551	10,892	55,805
Miami-Dade	90,373	66,564	55,142	3,740	7,370	12,699	43,615
Monroe	102	29	(D)	(D)	6	(D)	(D)
Nassau	(D)	5,181	2,699	18,905	10,596	(D)	111
Okaloosa	55,119	19,684	10,739	25,349	5,333	4,753	435
Okeechobee	392,495	115,292	38,984	23,206	238,584	15,413	22,085
Orange	146,637	25,489	16,904	25,744	87,296	8,108	15,103
Osceola	652,673	76,148	27,448	186,679	359,041	30,805	18,651
Palm Beach	535,965	480,973	428,683	13,659	11,619	29,714	418,455
Pasco	168,716	52,943	21,332	42,185	64,300	9,288	11,751
Pinellas	1,589	(D)	319	131	(D)	(D)	319
Polk	626,634	189,970	134,101	78,191	303,046	55,427	116,094
Putnam	92,619	16,743	9,177	47,771	21,114	6,991	5,738
St. Johns	37,653	24,960	22,236	2,511	7,749	2,433	21,759
St. Lucie	221,537	118,847	97,929	(D)	(D)	(D)	102,629
Santa Rosa	83,790	51,976	45,057	22,676	4,634	4,504	6,064
Sarasota	121,310	33,362	6,418	33,732	50,831	3,385	5,002
Seminole	27,987	3,763	2,564	7,850	15,165	1,209	1,698
Sumter	187,373	44,950	18,131	68,472	62,463	11,488	3,975
Suwannee	170,149	68,545	40,012	57,981	27,702	15,921	17,910
Taylor	53,720	3,052	870	41,327	4,291	5,050	196
Union	59,635	18,791	6,395	29,508	9,269	2,067	1,012
Volusia	93,842	18,906	12,522	32,903	30,261	11,772	8,792
Wakulla	10,900	3,055	1,018	5,935	1,268	642	145
Walton	79,910	32,143	12,570	25,387	16,861	5,519	1,533
Washington	53,251	18,404	8,512	24,164	7,480	3,203	958

(D) Data withheld to avoid disclosure of information about individual farms.
(NA) Not available.
1/ Includes woodland pasture.
2/ Pastureland and rangeland other than cropland and woodland pasture.
3/ Land in house lots, ponds, roads, wasteland, etc.
Note: Because data for selected items are collected from a sample of operators, the results are subject to sampling variability. The agriculture census is on a 5-year cycle collecting data for years ending in 2 or 7.

Source: U.S., Department of Agriculture, Natural Agricultural Statistics Service, *2002 Census of Agriculture: Florida County Level Data,* Volume 1, Chapter 1, released June 2004, Internet site <http://www.nass.usda.gov/> (accessed 11, May 2007).

Table 9.37. INCOME: CASH RECEIPTS BY COMMODITY GROUP AND SPECIFIED COMMODITY IN FLORIDA, 2002 THROUGH 2006

(in thousands of dollars)

Commodity 1/	2002	2003	2004	2005	2006
All commodities	6,396,056	6,614,451	7,078,818	7,702,314	6,974,160
Livestock and products	1,239,055	1,240,273	1,456,914	1,406,637	1,304,892
Meat animals	338,336	352,758	458,263	506,942	488,054
Cattle and calves	333,413	348,411	451,857	502,268	484,288
Hogs	4,923	4,347	6,406	4,674	3,766
Dairy products, wholesale milk	352,237	329,868	431,616	421,662	343,599
Poultry and eggs	331,103	357,346	369,324	303,206	297,159
Broilers	195,579	178,955	208,440	201,564	181,425
Farm chickens	510	364	700	635	502
Chicken eggs	109,014	145,027	159,878	100,723	115,002
Crops	5,157,001	5,374,178	5,621,903	6,295,677	5,669,268
Food grains, wheat	639	1,235	2,096	1,296	818
Feed crops	18,230	17,334	17,496	22,211	24,058
Corn	5,653	6,226	6,056	4,256	5,607
Hay	12,577	11,109	11,440	17,954	18,451
Cotton	20,940	39,649	24,458	31,704	39,579
Tobacco	18,244	19,577	17,226	8,305	4,319
Oil crops	36,636	65,870	69,037	70,507	52,850
Peanuts	35,208	63,825	65,884	68,537	51,900
Soybeans	1,428	2,045	3,153	1,970	950
Vegetables	1,461,742	1,478,035	1,448,222	1,844,132	1,568,869
Potatoes	129,471	129,261	97,234	113,087	145,138
Cabbage, fresh	28,928	23,089	30,932	31,294	30,690
Corn, sweet, fresh	100,531	90,016	110,382	108,058	117,271
Cucumbers	92,649	93,151	83,426	94,130	98,077
Peppers, green, fresh	180,600	177,920	218,411	213,428	187,330
Tomatoes, fresh	528,255	550,572	500,472	804,972	551,128
Squash	40,050	47,580	45,392	47,970	38,760
Miscellaneous vegetables	155,063	152,300	160,300	159,650	144,650
Watermelons	62,238	61,920	67,200	126,945	111,042
Fruits and nuts	1,443,324	1,499,415	1,741,205	1,953,945	1,782,296
Grapefruit	223,857	182,976	245,244	518,106	172,149
Oranges	891,973	1,014,492	1,143,350	1,058,059	1,204,949
Tangelos	11,488	14,832	8,626	8,219	9,378
Tangerines	70,703	58,483	73,740	85,748	58,502
Avocados	17,287	14,695	14,253	12,148	12,360
Strawberries	153,472	129,177	177,997	196,790	239,148
Blueberries	18,560	18,200	25,200	32,760	32,900
Other berries	100	100	100	100	100
Pecans	885	1,460	695	1,015	810
Miscellaneous fruits and nuts	55,000	65,000	52,000	41,000	52,000
All other crops	2,157,247	2,253,063	2,302,164	2,363,577	2,196,480
Cane for sugar	485,733	557,614	526,278	417,549	356,888
Greenhouse/nursery	1,586,371	1,608,824	1,687,126	1,859,580	1,753,399
Floriculture	833,371	830,824	884,126	956,580	800,399
Other greenhouse	750,000	125,286	800,000	900,000	950,000
Mushrooms, agaricus	44,431	45,868	48,200	48,318	47,623

1/ Totals include data for "other" categories not shown.

Note: Data are estimates. Value of sales for some individual commodities may be understated; balance is included in totals. Data are revised.

Source: U.S., Department of Agriculture, Economic Research Service, "Cash Receipts by Commodity Groups and Selected Commodities, United States and States, 2000-2006," Internet site <http://www.ers.usda.gov/> (accessed 20, September 2007).

Table 9.38. INCOME: MARKET VALUE OF AGRICULTURAL PRODUCTS SOLD IN THE STATE AND COUNTIES OF FLORIDA, 2002

(in thousands of dollars, except where indicated)

County	All products Total	All products Average per farm (dollars)	Crops 1/	Livestock poultry and their products
Florida	6,242,272	141,609	5,041,433	1,200,839
Alachua	58,665	39,293	37,620	21,044
Baker	25,425	124,634	9,515	15,911
Bay	2,157	18,592	1,881	275
Bradford	17,913	47,388	1,673	16,240
Brevard	42,159	75,961	35,306	6,853
Broward	49,625	100,455	44,596	5,028
Calhoun	14,390	95,300	13,152	1,238
Charlotte	48,302	170,079	42,632	5,671
Citrus	6,606	15,293	4,705	1,901
Clay	37,052	108,975	3,792	33,259
Collier	267,636	980,353	263,794	3,842
Columbia	46,767	67,976	7,947	38,820
DeSoto	180,096	156,198	150,446	29,650
Dixie	6,542	30,427	(D)	(D)
Duval	22,452	58,775	7,008	15,444
Escambia	15,676	23,258	10,370	5,306
Flagler	23,789	237,894	22,326	1,464
Franklin	385	19,257	0	385
Gadsden	91,377	266,404	90,268	1,108
Gilchrist	44,558	109,210	6,194	38,364
Glades	72,064	311,966	52,489	19,575
Gulf	489	16,308	(D)	(D)
Hamilton	12,169	50,914	6,440	5,728
Hardee	166,203	145,537	129,599	36,604
Hendry	375,812	824,149	357,076	18,736
Hernando	21,708	35,183	8,176	13,532
Highlands	236,005	228,024	204,808	31,197
Hillsborough	392,432	132,176	333,745	58,687
Holmes	30,223	44,975	2,920	27,303
Indian River	116,913	243,569	110,225	6,688
Jackson	36,470	39,641	24,845	11,624
Jefferson	21,154	50,608	9,317	11,837
Lafayette	48,116	246,751	3,355	44,762
Lake	178,076	99,041	166,274	11,801

See footnotes at end of table. Continued . . .

Table 9.38. INCOME: MARKET VALUE OF AGRICULTURAL PRODUCTS SOLD IN THE STATE AND COUNTIES OF FLORIDA, 2002 (Continued)

(in thousands of dollars, except where indicated)

County	All products		Crops 1/	Livestock poultry and their products
	Total	Average per farm (dollars)		
Lee	113,406	176,370	109,147	4,260
Leon	6,659	23,699	4,432	2,228
Levy	83,226	92,782	25,949	57,277
Liberty	1,497	22,339	(D)	(D)
Madison	24,645	46,587	10,068	14,577
Manatee	268,480	315,118	247,023	21,457
Marion	87,530	29,874	18,314	69,217
Martin	127,655	305,395	99,523	28,132
Miami-Dade	578,000	257,576	573,350	4,650
Monroe	2,533	140,738	672	1,861
Nassau	27,497	87,291	2,139	25,358
Okaloosa	6,540	14,065	3,575	2,965
Okeechobee	144,376	226,295	36,677	107,699
Orange	242,688	269,354	239,492	3,195
Osceola	64,941	125,128	43,953	20,988
Palm Beach	759,867	684,565	752,826	7,040
Pasco	84,200	68,904	34,616	49,584
Pinellas	7,960	71,710	7,622	338
Polk	284,787	91,454	249,232	35,554
Putnam	46,670	100,150	40,961	5,709
St. Johns	59,681	292,552	56,944	2,737
St. Lucie	127,907	268,149	112,346	15,561
Santa Rosa	20,997	41,579	19,149	1,848
Sarasota	17,801	47,982	13,343	4,458
Seminole	19,211	51,094	17,949	1,262
Sumter	30,644	33,974	14,022	16,622
Suwannee	135,960	128,995	32,497	103,464
Taylor	13,354	132,221	727	12,627
Union	10,711	38,948	4,275	6,436
Volusia	106,297	95,419	98,465	7,832
Wakulla	1,584	12,571	642	942
Walton	20,055	37,139	4,538	15,517
Washington	5,506	14,081	2,288	3,217

(D) Data withheld to avoid disclosure of information about individual farms.
1/ Includes nursery and greenhouse products.
Note: The agriculture census is on a 5-year cycle collecting data for years ending in 2 and 7.

Source: U.S., Department of Agriculture, Natural Agricultural Statistics Service, *2002 Census of Agriculture: Florida County Level Data,* Volume 1, Chapter 2, released June 2004, Internet site <http://www.nass.usda.gov/> (accessed 11, May 2007).

Table 9.39. FARM OPERATORS: NUMBER OF OPERATORS BY PRINCIPAL OCCUPATION AGE, RACE, AND HISPANIC ORIGIN AND NUMBER OF FARMS AND ACRES OPERATED BY FEMALES IN THE STATE AND COUNTIES OF FLORIDA, 2002

County	Total	Principal occupation: Farming	Principal occupation: Other	Average age (years)	Black	Non-white 1/	Hispanic origin 2/	Female operators: Number of farms	Female operators: Land in farms (acres)
Florida	44,081	22,998	21,083	57.0	1,363	1,427	3,696	8,116	816,437
Alachua	1,493	728	765	57.0	174	43	70	359	26,358
Baker	204	106	98	57.1	15	0	1	14	549
Bay	116	69	47	56.3	3	8	1	24	343
Bradford	378	169	209	57.5	9	7	7	52	3,066
Brevard	555	296	259	58.2	9	11	12	116	16,443
Broward	494	252	242	54.3	16	34	118	103	(D)
Calhoun	151	75	76	58.3	5	6	4	20	2,673
Charlotte	284	128	156	60.9	0	16	8	50	6,500
Citrus	432	205	227	55.4	0	16	10	97	3,128
Clay	340	174	166	55.4	0	17	13	84	3,077
Collier	273	148	125	53.7	0	11	49	34	2,811
Columbia	688	329	359	57.8	69	12	44	115	12,541
DeSoto	1,153	606	547	57.5	7	54	25	150	40,829
Dixie	215	77	138	58.1	0	3	4	35	3,526
Duval	382	178	204	58.9	6	8	5	74	3,210
Escambia	674	364	310	57.2	47	38	12	100	4,505
Flagler	100	42	58	54.8	0	2	0	8	(D)
Franklin	20	17	3	46.6	0	0	0	0	0
Gadsden	343	194	149	59.1	54	2	6	37	5,308
Gilchrist	408	218	190	54.8	4	1	18	105	13,593
Glades	231	124	107	58.1	0	22	3	45	27,519
Gulf	30	10	20	56.1	0	0	0	1	(D)
Hamilton	239	133	106	57.5	19	4	2	18	3,853
Hardee	1,142	602	540	59.4	0	5	68	163	27,891
Hendry	456	242	214	57.3	9	9	51	55	16,620
Hernando	617	335	282	56.9	5	21	50	132	7,848
Highlands	1,035	590	445	56.5	29	15	60	156	44,575
Hillsborough	2,969	1,608	1,361	56.8	60	113	290	589	25,110
Holmes	672	344	328	58.9	14	15	8	68	7,138
Indian River	480	264	216	58.0	14	3	17	84	7,326
Jackson	920	473	447	57.5	104	14	11	121	17,510
Jefferson	418	147	271	57.3	40	6	21	89	21,308
Lafayette	195	119	76	56.0	0	4	7	35	6,915
Lake	1,798	816	982	56.3	39	69	141	327	16,030
Lee	643	329	314	55.1	8	13	31	130	8,133
Leon	281	137	144	58.7	61	8	8	67	13,769

See footnotes at end of table. Continued . . .

Table 9.39. FARM OPERATORS: NUMBER OF OPERATORS BY PRINCIPAL OCCUPATION AGE, RACE, AND HISPANIC ORIGIN AND NUMBER OF FARMS AND ACRES OPERATED BY FEMALES IN THE STATE AND COUNTIES OF FLORIDA, 2002 (Continued)

County	Total	Principal occupation		Average age (years)	Black	Non-white 1/	Hispanic origin 2/	Female operators	
		Farming	Other					Number of farms	Land in farms (acres)
Levy	897	543	354	55.1	23	25	49	173	12,054
Liberty	67	30	37	57.0	0	0	0	10	1,656
Madison	529	262	267	58.6	43	9	15	98	28,554
Manatee	852	448	404	57.0	5	46	52	145	22,597
Marion	2,930	1,787	1,143	56.7	173	38	190	850	42,190
Martin	418	239	179	55.4	4	16	25	75	11,946
Miami-Dade	2,244	1,152	1,092	55.2	28	163	1,357	360	4,752
Monroe	18	8	10	54.2	0	2	2	2	(D)
Nassau	315	165	150	57.1	6	2	3	37	(D)
Okaloosa	465	216	249	59.0	0	15	13	67	7,159
Okeechobee	638	354	284	56.7	0	8	46	78	13,177
Orange	901	459	442	56.7	7	83	38	188	9,059
Osceola	519	275	244	57.6	1	20	18	102	29,333
Palm Beach	1,110	595	515	53.8	43	71	156	328	12,122
Pasco	1,222	620	602	56.9	12	22	119	235	12,021
Pinellas	111	46	65	57.2	0	5	9	35	359
Polk	3,114	1,623	1,491	60.3	22	27	119	436	66,576
Putnam	466	227	239	57.0	18	16	11	63	5,380
St. Johns	204	106	98	53.4	4	11	7	40	4,356
St. Lucie	477	265	212	57.6	3	24	33	68	12,629
Santa Rosa	505	265	240	55.9	9	39	7	68	3,442
Sarasota	371	194	177	55.2	3	15	22	92	20,122
Seminole	376	166	210	56.8	16	11	3	80	3,103
Sumter	902	478	424	57.6	36	28	53	151	20,239
Suwannee	1,054	615	439	58.1	36	33	50	174	19,260
Taylor	101	42	59	60.2	0	0	0	10	457
Union	275	121	154	55.9	9	5	4	34	2,578
Volusia	1,114	541	573	55.2	15	25	85	270	14,503
Wakulla	126	61	65	55.7	19	0	12	23	929
Walton	540	260	280	56.0	3	26	20	96	7,468
Washington	391	187	204	59.1	5	32	3	71	5,764

(D) Data withheld to avoid disclosure of information about individual farms.

1/ Includes operators reporting as American Indian or Alaska Native, Hawaiian or other Pacific Islander, Asian, and more than one race.

2/ Persons of Hispanic origin may be of any race. Includes persons of Latino or Spanish origin.

Note: Data were collected for a maximum or three operators per farm. The agriculture census is on a 5-year cycle collecting data for years ending in 2 and 7.

Source: U.S., Department of Agriculture, National Agricultural Statistics Service, *2002 Census of Agriculture Florida County Level Data,* Volume 1, Chapter 2, released June 2004, Internet site <http://www.nass.usda.gov/> (accessed 11, May 2007).

Table 9.42. INCOME: CASH RECEIPTS FROM FARMING IN FLORIDA, OTHER AGRICULTURAL STATES, AND THE UNITED STATES, 2006

(amounts in thousands of dollars)

State	Total	Rank among states	Percentage change from previous year	Crops	Livestock and products	Government payments
Florida	6,974,161	9	-9.5	5,669,269	1,304,892	140,767
California	31,402,706	1	-4.2	23,787,727	7,614,979	530,193
Texas	16,026,756	2	-3.4	5,703,021	10,323,735	1,507,639
Iowa	15,108,261	3	4.0	7,229,148	7,879,113	1,252,368
Nebraska	12,042,344	4	4.9	4,358,958	7,683,386	812,068
Kansas	10,335,795	5	2.3	3,365,144	6,970,651	648,182
Minnesota	9,769,512	6	5.0	5,127,587	4,641,925	767,576
Illinois	8,635,700	7	-2.4	6,840,840	1,794,860	1,045,199
North Carolina	8,199,349	8	-0.8	2,925,338	5,274,011	738,423
Wisconsin	6,791,282	10	-0.3	2,135,279	4,656,003	414,088
Arkansas	6,164,069	11	-4.8	2,396,712	3,767,357	515,613
Washington	6,138,973	12	3.8	4,524,433	1,614,540	196,466
Georgia	6,005,101	13	-3.3	2,240,211	3,764,890	483,093
Indiana	5,973,217	14	10.0	3,918,946	2,054,271	541,283
Missouri	5,621,258	15	-0.6	2,627,578	2,993,680	510,223
Colorado	5,614,394	16	4.1	1,552,540	4,061,854	244,612
Ohio	5,479,712	17	6.3	3,448,407	2,031,305	441,641
Oklahoma	5,093,622	18	-5.5	974,121	4,119,501	243,297
South Dakota	4,716,173	19	-2.5	2,064,550	2,651,623	411,846
Pennsylvania	4,691,681	20	-0.8	1,723,338	2,968,343	134,499
United States	239,271,907	(X)	-0.6	119,951,478	119,320,429	15,789,146

(X) Not applicable.
Source: U.S., Department of Agriculture, *Cash Receipts and Four Leading Commodities for the 50 States, 2006,* Internet site <http://www.usda.gov/> (accessed 20, September 2007).

Table 9.43. FARM REAL ESTATE DEBT: AMOUNT OUTSTANDING BY LENDER IN FLORIDA AND THE UNITED STATES, 2002 AND 2003

(in thousands of dollars)

Lender	Florida 2002	Florida 2003	Florida As a percentage of U.S. total	United States 2002	United States 2003
Total	4,084,119	4,272,143	3.4	118,566,346	124,734,230
Federal Credit System 1/	965,113	1,030,382	2.2	43,416,173	46,352,321
Farm Service Agency 2/	49,878	44,971	1.4	3,655,172	3,295,558
Life insurance companies 3/	1,502,753	1,536,454	11.6	13,000,000	13,291,455
All operating banks	1,163,375	1,244,639	3.1	37,995,001	40,649,006
Individuals and others 4/	403,000	415,697	2.0	20,243,000	20,573,890

1/ Includes mortgages in process of foreclosure.
2/ Includes farm ownership loans, soil and water loans to individuals, rural and labor housing loans on farms and association loans for grazing, Indian tribe land acquisition loans, and one-half of economic emergency loans.
3/ Includes U.S. legal reserve companies only. Includes regular mortgages and purchase-money mortgages.
4/ Estimate.
Note: Includes operator households.
Source: U.S., Department of Agriculture, *Agricultural Statistics, 2006,* Internet site <http://www.usda.gov/> (accessed 12, June 2007).

Table 9.50. IRRIGATION: ESTIMATED AGRICULTURAL ACREAGE IRRIGATED AND WATER USE BY CROP AND TYPE IN FLORIDA, 2000

Product	Acreage irrigated	Irrigated water use (millions of gallons per day) Total	Ground	Surface	Reclaimed
Total	2,058,396	4,610.67	2,181.61	2,112.85	316.21
Agricultural irrigation	1,866,451	3,972.61	1,951.18	1,931.52	89.91
Vegetable crops 1/	209,925	404.34	282.35	118.69	3.30
Fruit crops	844,003	1,883.83	1,091.67	773.14	19.02
Blueberries	913	1.23	1.20	0.03	0.00
Citrus 2/	824,602	1,844.18	1,056.16	769.00	19.02
Grapes	514	0.37	0.32	0.05	0.00
Peaches	5	0.01	0.01	0.00	0.00
Pecans	569	0.93	0.83	0.10	0.00
Strawberries	6,588	13.60	13.10	0.50	0.00
Other	9,523	21.84	18.50	3.34	0.00
Fruit crops nonspecified	1,289	1.67	1.55	0.12	0.00
Field crops	533,683	1,022.92	132.93	871.91	18.08
Cotton	14,018	9.05	8.26	0.79	0.00
Field corn	28,967	36.37	33.87	1.87	0.63
Peanuts	25,036	21.36	20.10	1.26	0.00
Potatoes	33,196	32.17	25.58	6.59	0.00
Rice	12,335	33.24	0.00	33.24	0.00
Sorghum	1,480	1.04	0.91	0.13	0.00
Soybeans	2,246	1.07	0.99	0.08	0.00
Sugarcane	404,123	856.86	31.05	825.81	0.00
Tobacco	5,049	5.41	5.31	0.10	0.00
Wheat	244	0.32	0.29	0.03	0.00
Other	6,989	26.03	6.57	2.01	17.45
Ornamentals/grasses	278,840	661.52	444.23	167.78	49.51
Field grown	24,190	68.89	54.49	11.41	2.99
Greenhouse grown	564	2.19	1.40	0.79	0.00
Container grown	36,387	132.13	104.28	26.37	1.48
Pasture hay (alfalfa/tame)	130,028	204.41	161.11	41.83	1.47
Sod	76,221	210.13	122.95	87.18	0.00
Other crops/grasses that utilize reclaimed water	11,450	43.77	0.00	0.20	43.57
Livestock/Aquaculture	(X)	40.49	38.77	1.72	0.00
Livestock	(X)	32.47	30.96	1.51	0.00
Fish farming	(X)	8.02	7.81	0.21	0.00
Other	(X)	0.00	0.00	0.00	0.00
Nonagricultural irrigation	192,085	638.06	230.43	181.33	226.30
Turf grass recreation (golf)	116,581	398.97	162.77	131.89	104.31
Other grass and landscape	57,530	205.24	67.66	49.44	88.14
Public access areas and	0	0.00	0.00	0.00	0.00
landscape	17,974	33.85	0.00	0.00	33.85

(X) Not applicable.
1/ Includes crops not shown separately.
2/ Includes oranges, grapefruit, limes, lemons, and all other citrus.

Source: U.S., Department of Interior, Geological Survey, Tallahassee, Florida: Water withdrawals, use, discharge, and trends in Florida, 2000, by R.L. Marella, 2004, U.S. Geological Survey Scientific Investigations Report 2004-5151. Copies of this report and other Florida water-use data are available at <http://fl.water.usgs.gov/> or by contacting the USGS at 2010 Levy Avenue, Tallahassee, Florida 32310.

Table 9.51. CITRUS: ESTIMATED PRODUCTION AND VALUE OF CITRUS BY TYPE IN FLORIDA CROP YEARS 2001–02 THROUGH 2005–06

Type of citrus	2001–02	2002–03	2003–04	2004–05	2005–06 A/
			Production (1,000 boxes)		
All citrus	287,265	251,005	291,800	169,250	174,800
Oranges	230,000	203,000	242,000	149,800	147,900
Early and midseason	122,500	106,600	121,700	76,600	71,200
Late (Valencia)	102,000	91,000	116,000	70,700	72,900
Navel	5,500	5,400	4,300	2,500	3,800
Grapefruit	46,700	38,700	40,900	12,800	19,300
White	18,900	16,200	15,900	3,400	6,500
Colored	27,800	22,500	25,000	9,400	12,800
Other citrus	10,565	9,305	8,900	6,650	7,600
Temples	1,550	1,300	1,400	650	700
Tangelos	2,150	2,350	1,000	1,550	1,400
Tangerines 1/	4,350	3,000	3,600	2,450	2,850
Honey tangerines	2,250	2,500	2,900	2,000	2,650
K-early citrus	30	(X)	(X)	(X)	(X)
Limes	150	(X)	(X)	(X)	(X)
Lemons 2/	85	155	(X)	(X)	(X)
			Value of production ($1,000)		
All citrus	966,803	787,378	891,500	754,169	1,043,293
Oranges	797,602	643,804	699,927	522,892	807,576
Early and midseason	346,037	266,997	259,413	199,002	318,038
Late (Valencia)	428,533	350,210	422,212	299,699	468,062
Navel	23,032	26,597	18,302	24,191	21,476
Grapefruit	107,653	94,518	136,295	172,365	174,084
White	37,073	28,702	30,862	40,560	59,945
Colored	70,580	65,816	105,433	131,805	114,139
Other citrus	61,520	57,007	57,450	58,912	61,633
Temples	3,395	2,615	1,502	1,615	2,214
Tangelos	5,307	6,114	7,484	3,794	7,512
Tangerines 1/	29,942	25,320	21,889	24,776	29,516
Honey tangerines	21,612	20,897	26,575	28,727	22,391
K-early citrus	36	(X)	(X)	(X)	(X)
Limes	929	(X)	(X)	(X)	(X)
Lemons 2/	299	2,061	(X)	(X)	(X)

(X) Not applicable.
A/ Preliminary.
1/ Excludes honey tangerines and, after 2001–02, Dancy and Robinson.
2/ Florida lemons bloom and harvest during the calendar year; data are for the years 2001 and 2002.
Note: Some data may be revised.

Source: State of Florida, Department of Agriculture and Consumer Services, Florida Agricultural Statistics Service, *Florida Agricultural Statistics: Citrus Summary, 2005–06,* Internet site <http://www.nass.usda.gov/> (accessed 9 April, 2007).

Table 9.52. ORANGES AND GRAPEFRUIT: BEARING ACREAGE, PRODUCTION, AND YIELD PER ACRE IN FLORIDA, OTHER CITRUS STATES, AND THE UNITED STATES, CROP YEARS 1999–2000 THROUGH 2005–06

State and year	Oranges			Grapefruit		
	Bearing acreage (1,000 acres)	Production (1,000 tons)	Yield per acre (tons)	Bearing acreage (1,000 acres)	Production (1,000 tons)	Yield per acre (tons)
Florida						
1999–2000	602.1	10,485	17.4	114.1	2,270	19.9
2000–01 A/	605.0	10,049	16.6	107.8	1,955	18.1
2001–02	586.9	10,350	17.6	101.3	1,985	19.6
2002–03	587.6	9,135	15.5	95.5	1,645	17.2
2003–04	564.8	10,890	19.3	82.3	1,738	21.1
2004–05	541.8	6,741	12.4	71.0	544	7.7
2005–06 B/	491.0	6,657	13.6	59.8	820	13.7
Arizona						
1999–2000	6.2	41	6.6	2.8	15	5.4
2000–01	6.4	34	5.3	2.0	8	4.0
2001–02	6.4	19	3.0	2.0	5	2.5
2002–03	5.8	18	3.1	1.5	4	2.7
2003–04	5.5	18	3.3	1.5	5	3.3
2004–05	5.0	16	3.2	1.5	5	3.3
2005–06 B/	4.3	17	4.0	1.2	3	2.5
California						
1999–2000	195.5	2,400	12.3	16.6	241	14.5
2000–01	194.5	2,043	10.5	15.4	211	13.7
2001–02	195.0	1,931	9.9	14.0	198	14.1
2002–03	189.5	2,326	12.3	13.0	188	14.5
2003–04	184.0	1,894	10.3	12.5	194	15.5
2004–05	182.0	2,419	13.3	12.0	205	17.1
2005–06 B/	181.0	2,156	11.9	11.5	201	17.5
Texas						
1999–2000	9.1	71	7.8	20.0	237	11.9
2000–01	9.1	95	10.4	20.0	288	14.4
2001–02	9.3	74	8.0	19.0	236	12.4
2002–03	8.8	66	7.5	18.5	226	12.2
2003–04	8.8	70	8.0	18.5	228	12.3
2004–05	8.8	76	8.6	18.5	264	14.3
2005–06 B/	8.8	68	7.7	18.5	208	11.2
United States						
1999–2000	812.9	12,997	16.0	153.5	2,763	18.0
2000–01	815.0	12,221	15.0	145.2	2,462	17.0
2001–02	797.6	12,374	15.5	136.3	2,424	17.8
2002–03	791.7	11,545	14.6	128.5	2,063	16.1
2003–04	763.1	12,872	16.9	114.8	2,165	18.9
2004–05	737.6	9,252	12.5	103.0	1,018	9.9
2005–06 B/	685.1	8,898	13.0	91.0	1,232	13.5

A/ Excludes economic abandonment of 85,000 tons of colored seedless grapefruit.
B/ Preliminary.
Note: Some data may be revised.

Source: State of Florida, Department of Agriculture and Consumer Services, Florida Agricultural Statistics Service, *Florida Agricultural Statistics: Citrus Summary, 2005–06,* Internet site <http://www.nass.usda.gov/> (accessed 9 April, 2007).

Table 9.53. ORANGES AND GRAPEFRUIT: SEASON AVERAGE ON-TREE PRICES PER BOX AND VALUE OF PRODUCTION IN FLORIDA AND THE UNITED STATES, CROP YEARS 1998–99 THROUGH 2005–06

Crop year	Season average price (in dollars per box)			Value of production (in thousands of dollars)		
	Total	Fresh use	Processing	Total	Fresh use	Processing
			Oranges 1/			
Florida						
1998–99	4.84	8.78	4.59	900,044	95,303	804,741
1999–2000	3.67	5.37	3.60	856,052	50,399	805,653
2000–01	3.21	4.29	3.16	716,055	41,590	674,465
2001–02	3.47	4.84	3.41	797,602	45,396	752,206
2002–03	3.17	5.61	3.05	643,804	54,527	589,277
2003–04	2.89	3.87	2.85	699,927	38,302	661,625
2004–05	3.49	6.87	3.31	522,892	50,828	472,064
2005–06 A/	5.46	5.80	5.44	807,576	42,605	764,971
United States						
1998–99	5.47	13.78	4.20	1,250,484	457,953	792,531
1999–2000	3.58	5.61	3.17	1,066,942	309,879	757,063
2000–01	3.85	7.71	2.98	1,109,894	452,788	657,106
2001–02	4.25	8.97	3.26	1,243,537	506,482	737,055
2002–03	3.56	6.52	2.79	965,171	400,187	564,984
2003–04	3.74	8.63	2.74	1,143,268	493,089	650,179
2004–05	4.41	9.24	2.86	981,893	541,149	440,744
2005–06 A/	5.96	9.87	4.87	1,251,062	501,359	749,703
			Grapefruit			
Florida						
1998–99	2.30	5.04	0.30	108,411	100,401	8,010
1999–2000	3.53	6.52	1.98	188,332	118,752	69,580
2000–01 B/	2.19	4.81	0.59	100,869	84,056	16,813
2001–02	2.31	5.25	0.56	107,653	91,297	16,356
2002–03	2.44	5.63	0.29	94,518	87,711	6,807
2003–04	3.33	7.32	0.60	136,295	121,850	14,445
2004–05	13.47	19.51	5.13	172,365	144,765	27,600
2005–06 A/	9.02	13.96	6.26	174,084	96,502	77,582
United States						
1998–99	3.17	6.12	0.24	202,909	196,085	6,824
1999–2000	3.87	6.84	1.77	262,371	195,724	66,647
2000–01	2.50	5.10	0.42	154,388	141,435	12,953
2001–02	2.64	5.43	0.44	159,115	145,752	13,363
2002–03	3.03	6.33	0.18	160,153	155,872	4,281
2003–04	3.66	7.23	0.46	196,143	184,193	11,950
2004–05	12.65	18.79	2.83	324,456	298,803	25,653
2005–06 A/	9.53	13.87	5.39	293,011	213,334	79,677

A/ Preliminary.
B/ Excludes economic abandonment of 2 million boxes of colored seedless.
1/ Includes early, midseason, and late type (Valencia) oranges.
Note: Charges for picking, hauling, and packing are deducted from the weighted average of prices obtained from all segments of the citrus industry to arrive at the final on-tree price received by producers. United States data include Arizona, California, Florida, and Texas. Some data may be revised.

Source: State of Florida, Department of Agriculture and Consumer Services, Florida Agricultural Statistics Service, *Florida Agricultural Statistics: Citrus Summary, 2005–06,* Internet site <http://www.nass.usda.gov/> (accessed 9 April, 2007).

Table 9.54. CITRUS: ESTIMATED PRODUCTION OF PRINCIPAL TYPES OF CITRUS IN THE STATE AND COUNTIES OF FLORIDA, CROP YEAR 2005–06

(in 1,000 boxes)

District and county	Total 1/	Oranges: All oranges	Oranges: Early and mid-season	Oranges: Valencias	All grapefruit	Specialty fruit 2/
Florida	174,800	147,900	75,000	72,900	19,300	7,600
District						
Indian River	18,484	6,300	2,400	3,900	11,600	584
Northern	13,122	10,648	8,685	1,963	973	1,501
Central	60,761	53,052	26,615	26,437	4,527	3,182
Western	48,232	46,500	25,300	21,200	600	1,132
Southern	34,201	31,400	12,000	19,400	1,600	1,201
County						
Brevard	626	485	295	190	101	40
Charlotte	2,246	1,863	579	1,284	224	159
Collier	6,134	5,698	2,317	3,381	238	198
DeSoto	20,429	20,033	8,132	11,901	106	290
Glades	1,740	1,645	843	802	39	56
Hardee	14,900	14,347	9,396	4,951	168	385
Hendry	15,752	14,661	5,309	9,352	667	424
Hernando	337	312	308	4	7	18
Highlands	23,819	21,817	8,620	13,197	1,149	853
Hillsborough	5,277	4,960	3,734	1,226	57	260
Indian River	7,511	2,072	1,134	938	5,279	160
Lake	6,417	4,608	3,773	835	732	1,077
Lee	1,806	1,585	554	1,031	154	67
Manatee	7,139	6,832	3,933	2,899	168	139
Marion	425	341	310	31	27	57
Martin	5,511	5,004	1,539	3,465	404	103
Okeechobee	1,388	1,174	647	527	163	51
Orange	1,791	1,547	1,090	457	93	151
Osceola	4,694	3,807	2,594	1,213	717	170
Palm Beach	321	36	29	7	131	154
Pasco	3,633	3,429	2,833	596	69	135
Polk	32,542	27,690	15,592	12,098	2,673	2,179
St. Lucie	9,264	3,166	925	2,241	5,749	349
Sarasota	477	322	99	223	99	56
Seminole	190	135	114	21	19	36
Volusia	285	232	209	23	41	12
Other 3/	146	99	92	7	26	21

1/ Does not include lemon and lime production.
2/ Includes tangelos, temples, and tangerines.
3/ Includes Alachua, Citrus, Pinellas, and Putnam counties.
Note: Citrus districts are based on citrus marketings/production areas. Several counties are in more than one district.

Source: State of Florida, Department of Agriculture and Consumer Services, Florida Agricultural Statistics Service, *Florida Agricultural Statistics: Citrus Summary, 2005–06,* Internet site <http://www.nass.usda.gov/> (accessed 9 April, 2007).

Table 9.55. CITRUS: ACREAGE BY TYPE OF FRUIT IN THE STATE AND SPECIFIED COUNTIES OF FLORIDA, JANUARY 1, 2006

County	Total	Oranges: All oranges 1/	Oranges: Early and mid-season	Oranges: Valencias	All grape-fruit 1/	Specialty fruit 2/
Florida	621,373	529,241	237,771	285,769	63,419	28,713
Brevard	5,080	4,289	2,212	2,035	404	387
Charlotte	11,883	10,180	3,264	6,916	1,013	690
Citrus	145	113	104	9	20	12
Collier	33,394	31,189	12,530	18,659	1,061	1,144
DeSoto	61,083	59,869	23,783	35,456	438	776
Glades	8,555	8,127	4,507	3,594	175	253
Hardee	45,084	43,487	27,898	14,557	477	1,120
Hendry	79,726	73,583	27,165	46,322	3,324	2,819
Hernando	921	827	793	13	11	83
Highlands	62,671	59,116	19,409	39,270	1,311	2,244
Hillsborough	14,783	13,848	10,251	3,460	180	755
Indian River	40,191	18,144	9,000	8,966	20,877	1,170
Lake	15,198	11,191	8,230	2,807	899	3,108
Lee	10,658	9,569	3,626	5,941	695	394
Manatee	18,548	17,749	9,766	7,707	433	366
Marion	1,185	967	795	168	41	177
Martin	35,038	32,138	10,598	21,492	2,113	787
Okeechobee	9,222	7,832	4,246	3,584	1,022	368
Orange	4,548	3,998	2,318	1,662	98	452
Osceola	12,170	10,532	6,660	3,860	1,067	571
Palm Beach	1,668	154	109	45	426	1,088
Pasco	8,190	7,645	5,966	1,555	97	448
Polk	86,398	76,430	35,783	38,535	3,564	6,404
Putnam	182	106	89	17	4	72
St. Lucie	51,387	25,672	7,257	18,084	23,073	2,642
Sarasota	1,652	1,070	337	732	417	165
Seminole	529	382	295	85	19	128
Volusia	1,231	993	743	237	156	82
Other 3/	53	41	37	1	4	8

1/ Includes unidentified variety acreage.
2/ Includes temples, tangelos, tangerines, lemons, and other.
3/ Alachua and Pinellas counties.

Source: State of Florida, Department of Agriculture and Consumer Services, Florida Agricultural Statistics Service, *Florida Agricultural Statistics: Citrus Summary, 2005–06,* Internet site <http://www.nass.usda.gov/> (accessed 9 April, 2007).

Table 9.56. ORANGE JUICE SALES: GALLONS SOLD AND CONSUMER RETAIL DOLLARS SPENT IN UNITED STATES FOOD AND OUTLET STORES, SEASONS 1990–91 THROUGH 2005–06

Season 1/	Total: Volume (million gallons)	Total: Value (million dollars)	Total: Price (dollars/ gallon)	Frozen: Volume (million gallons)	Frozen: Value (million dollars)	Frozen: Price (dollars/ gallon)
1990–91	754.2	2,848.0	3.78	305.4	944.6	3.09
1991–92	749.9	2,874.4	3.83	290.1	897.9	3.10
1992–93	807.9	2,742.1	3.39	287.3	777.7	2.71
1993–94	803.8	2,732.6	3.40	263.6	720.3	2.73
1994–95	806.7	2,768.6	3.43	243.3	660.8	2.72
1995–96	807.4	2,945.6	3.65	222.0	645.6	2.91
1996–97	832.3	3,169.3	3.81	204.2	615.0	3.01
1997–98	864.7	3,254.9	3.76	187.6	541.1	2.88
1998–99	852.6	3,576.4	4.19	165.0	517.2	3.13
1999–00	872.5	3,780.3	4.33	149.3	479.8	3.21
2000–01	888.7	3,886.6	4.37	135.5	429.6	3.17
2001–02	861.2	3,777.7	4.39	112.9	363.7	3.22
2002–03	836.4	3,677.2	4.40	95.3	317.3	3.33
2003–04	807.3	3,511.4	4.35	79.2	262.7	3.32
2004–05	795.3	3,512.8	4.42	70.1	230.6	3.29
2005–06	746.3	3,501.5	4.69	62.3	215.8	3.46

Season 1/	Refrigerated 2/: Not from concentrate: Volume (million gallons)	Not from concentrate: Value (million dollars)	Not from concentrate: Price (dollars/ gallon)	Reconstituted: Volume (million gallons)	Reconstituted: Value (million dollars)	Reconstituted: Price (dollars/ gallon)
1990–91	125.7	652.9	5.20	309.7	1,177.8	3.80
1991–92	140.6	735.5	5.23	305.7	1,170.1	3.83
1992–93	175.4	833.7	4.75	332.6	1,067.4	3.21
1993–94	191.6	882.3	4.60	336.2	1,071.3	3.19
1994–95	207.5	965.5	4.65	345.0	1,090.3	3.16
1995–96	198.4	960.9	4.84	376.5	1,288.1	3.42
1996–97	220.0	1,088.4	4.95	398.2	1,415.8	3.56
1997–98	260.3	1,249.3	4.80	407.4	1,416.5	3.48
1998–99	287.0	1,508.5	5.26	391.2	1,500.6	3.84
1999–00	311.4	1,671.9	5.37	403.4	1,582.9	3.92
2000–01	346.4	1,835.4	5.30	398.8	1,578.8	3.96
2001–02	363.3	1,906.7	5.25	375.9	1,458.2	3.88
2002–03	379.8	1,960.2	5.16	352.8	1,355.0	3.84
2003–04	389.3	1,970.7	5.06	331.4	1,238.9	3.74
2004–05	374.7	1,967.5	5.25	343.8	1,278.6	3.72
2005–06	373.4	2,030.4	5.44	304.2	1,219.4	4.01

1/ October of the previous year through September of the present year. Data for 1990–91 through 1994–95 includes food stores only; data for 1995–96 through November 2001 includes grocery and supercenter outlet stores and Wal-Mart sales estimates thereafter.

2/ Includes glass and plastic containers and cartons.

Note: Data are Nielsen retail orange juice sales from scanner supermarkets doing over $2 million in annual retail sales. Canned and aseptic shelf-stable orange juice included in totals only.

Source: State of Florida, Department of Citrus, Economic and Market Research, *Citrus Reference Book 2007,* Internet site <http://www.floridajuice.com/> (accessed 29, May 2007).

Table 9.61. FIELD CROPS: ACREAGE HARVESTED, PRODUCTION, YIELD, AND VALUE OF PRODUCTION IN FLORIDA, CROP YEARS 2005 AND 2006

Crop	Harvested acres (1,000) 2005	Harvested acres (1,000) 2006	Unit	Production Total (1,000) 2005	Production Total (1,000) 2006	Yield per acre 2005	Yield per acre 2006	Value ($1,000) 2005	Value ($1,000) 2006
Corn 1/	28	30	Bu.	2,632	2,460	94	82	5,264	6,888
Cotton	85	101	2/	135	150	762	713	31,104	33,048
Cottonseed	(X)	(X)	Tons	41	47	(X)	(X)	3,083	4,348
Hay, all	290	260	Tons	711	598	2	2	70,034	60,398
Peanuts 3/	152	120	Lbs.	410,400	300,000	2,700	2,500	68,537	51,900
Soybeans 4/	8	5	Bu.	256	135	32	27	1,382	797
Sugarcane 5/	401	405	Tons	12,746	14,178	32	36	356,888	(NA)
Tobacco, flue-cured, Type 14	3	1	Tons	5,500	2,860	2,200	2,600	8,300	4,319
Wheat	8	5	Bu.	360	210	45	42	1,116	662

(X) Not applicable.
(NA) Not available.
1/ Harvested for grain.
2/ Production in 1,000 (480 pound net weight) bales. Yield in pounds.
3/ Harvested for dry nuts.
4/ Harvested for beans.
5/ For sugar and seed.
Note: Data for 2005 may be revised. All 2006 estimates are preliminary.

Table 9.62. CORN: ACREAGE HARVESTED FOR GRAIN AND BUSHELS PRODUCED IN THE STATE, CROP-REPORTING DISTRICTS, AND SPECIFIED COUNTIES OF FLORIDA, 2006

District and county	Acres harvested	Production (bushels)
Florida	30,000	2,460,000
District 10–Northwest	15,000	1,322,000
Escambia	1,700	107,100
Gadsden	1,300	110,500
Holmes	1,400	98,000
Jackson	4,700	514,170
Jefferson	3,200	284,800
Okaloosa	400	25,200
Santa Rosa	300	18,000
Walton	500	31,000
District 10 (Continued)		
Washington	900	92,430
Other counties 1/	600	40,800
District 30–Northeast	12,100	1,016,400
Columbia	500	15,850
Hamilton	3,500	455,000
Madison	3,600	174,600
Suwannee	2,000	156,400
Other counties	2,500	214,550
Other counties 2/	2,900	121,600

1/ Includes Calhoun county.
2/ Includes Alachua, Gilchrist, Levy, and Putnam counties.
Note: See accompanying map for counties in crop-reporting districts. Data are preliminary.

Source for Tables 9.61 and 9.62: State of Florida, Department of Agriculture and Consumer Services, Florida Agricultural Statistics Service, *Florida Agricultural Facts (NASS), 2007,* Internet site <http://www.nass.usda.gov/> (accessed 14, May 2007).

Crop-reporting Districts

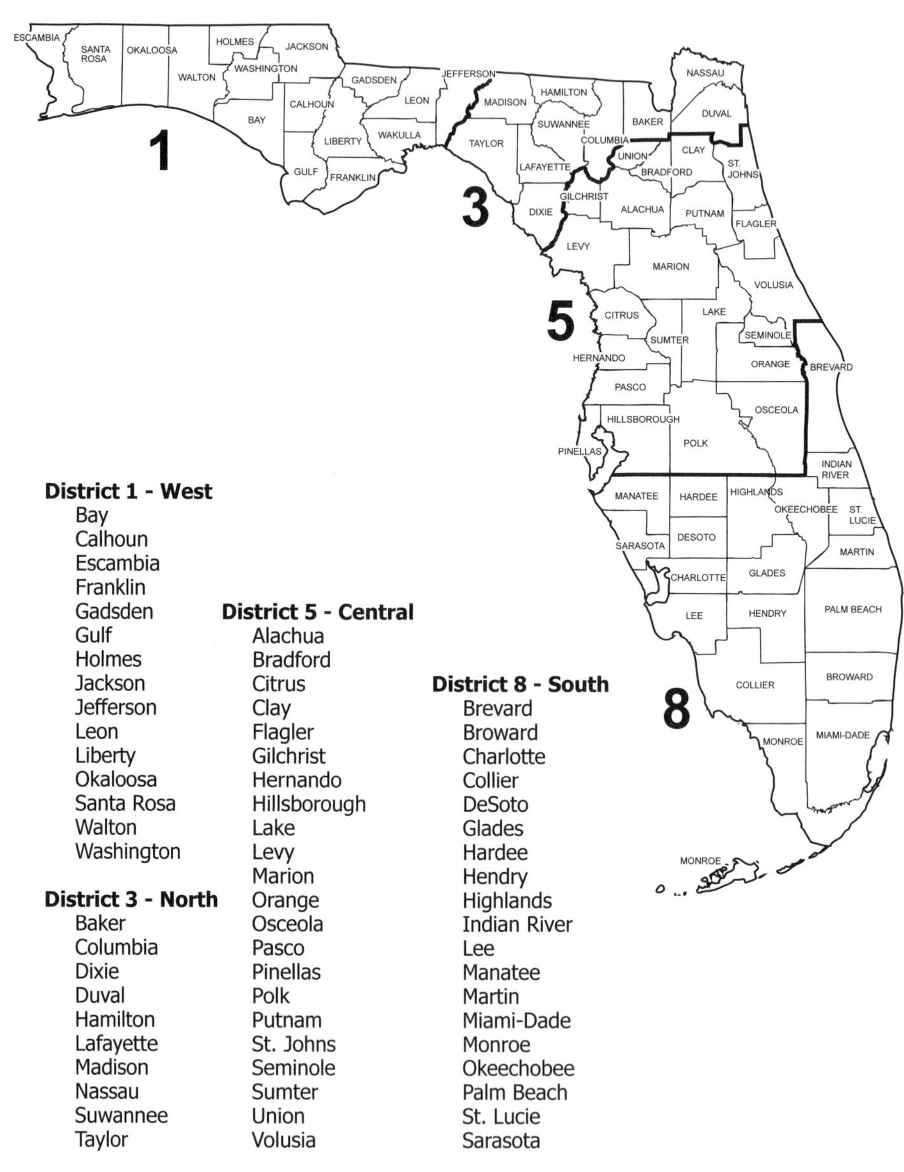

District 1 - West
- Bay
- Calhoun
- Escambia
- Franklin
- Gadsden
- Gulf
- Holmes
- Jackson
- Jefferson
- Leon
- Liberty
- Okaloosa
- Santa Rosa
- Walton
- Washington

District 3 - North
- Baker
- Columbia
- Dixie
- Duval
- Hamilton
- Lafayette
- Madison
- Nassau
- Suwannee
- Taylor

District 5 - Central
- Alachua
- Bradford
- Citrus
- Clay
- Flagler
- Gilchrist
- Hernando
- Hillsborough
- Lake
- Levy
- Marion
- Orange
- Osceola
- Pasco
- Pinellas
- Polk
- Putnam
- St. Johns
- Seminole
- Sumter
- Union
- Volusia

District 8 - South
- Brevard
- Broward
- Charlotte
- Collier
- DeSoto
- Glades
- Hardee
- Hendry
- Highlands
- Indian River
- Lee
- Manatee
- Martin
- Miami-Dade
- Monroe
- Okeechobee
- Palm Beach
- St. Lucie
- Sarasota

Table 9.63. WHEAT: ACREAGE PLANTED AND HARVESTED, PRODUCTION, AND YIELD IN THE STATE OF FLORIDA, 2005 AND 2006

District	Planted acres 2005	Planted acres 2006	Harvested acres 2005	Harvested acres 2006	Production: Total (bushels) 2005	Production: Total (bushels) 2006	Production: Yield per acre (bushels) 2005	Production: Yield per acre (bushels) 2006
Florida	18,000	8,000	8,000	5,000	360,000	210,000	45.0	42.0
District 10–West	16,500	6,200	7,300	3,900	338,100	164,800	46.3	42.3
District 30–North	800	1,300	700	1,000	21,900	41,000	31.3	41.0
District 50–Central 1/	700	500	(NA)	100	(NA)	4,200	(NA)	42.0

(NA) Not available.
1/ Wheat harvested and produced in 2005 for cover crop and/or forage.

Table 9.64. PEANUTS: ACREAGE HARVESTED AND PRODUCTION IN THE STATE CROP-REPORTING DISTRICTS, AND SPECIFIED COUNTIES OF FLORIDA, 2005

District and county	Acres harvested	Production (1,000 pounds)	District and county	Acres harvested	Production (1,000 pounds)
Florida	152,000	410,400	District 30–North	25,000	72,000
			Columbia	4,400	10,956
District 10–West	84,800	220,056	Hamilton	3,400	9,146
Calhoun	2,800	6,888	Lafayette	1400	3661
Escambia	8,600	23,392	Madison	7,400	18,796
Gadsden	1,300	2,509	Suwannee	8,400	29,441
Holmes	4,900	11,515	District 50–Central	37,700	107,068
Jackson	35,400	87,084	Alachua	6,300	15,372
Jefferson	2,100	5,586	Gilchrist	3,400	11,271
Okaloosa	3,100	8,060	Levy	18,400	53,444
Santa Rosa	19,800	58,014	Marion	8,500	24,055
Walton	4,900	10,339	Sumter	1,100	2,926
Washington	1,900	6,669	Other counties	4,500	11,276

Table 9.65. SOYBEANS: ACREAGE HARVESTED FOR GRAIN AND BUSHELS PRODUCED IN THE STATE AND SPECIFIED COUNTIES OF FLORIDA, 2006

District and county	Acres harvested	Production (bushels)	District and county	Acres harvested	Production (bushels)
Florida	5,000	135,000	District 10 (Continued)		
			Other counties 1/	1,500	45,400
District 10–West	3,800	106,100	District 30–North	1,200	28,900
Escambia	700	19,800	Madison	800	19,900
Jackson	1600	40,900	Other counties 2/	400	9,000

1/ Includes Calhoun, Gadsden, Holmes, Jefferson, and Washington counties.
2/ Includes Suwannee county.
Note: All 2006 data for tables 9.63 and 9.65 are preliminary; 2005 data may be revised. See accompanying map for counties in crop-reporting districts.

Source for Tables 9.63, 9.64, and 9.65: State of Florida, Department of Agriculture and Consumer Services, Florida Agricultural Statistics Service, *Florida Agricultural Facts (NASS), 2007,* Internet site <http://www.nass.usda.gov/> (accessed 14, May 2007).

Table 9.66. COTTON: ACREAGE HARVESTED AND PRODUCTION IN THE STATE, CROP-REPORTING DISTRICTS, AND SPECIFIED COUNTIES OF FLORIDA, 2005

District and county	Acres harvested	Production (bales)
Florida	85,000	135,000
District 10–North	83,800	133,200
Calhoun	8,400	13,000
Escambia	11,000	17,200
Holmes	2,100	3,300
Jackson	34,300	55,600
Jefferson	500	800
District 10–North (Continued)		
Okaloosa	2,700	4,300
Santa Rosa	19,200	30,000
Walton	3,200	5,200
Washington	2,400	3,800
Other counties, all districts	1,200	1,800

Note: See accompanying map for counties in crop-reporting districts.

Table 9.67. SUGARCANE FOR SUGAR: ACREAGE HARVESTED AND PRODUCTION IN THE STATE AND SPECIFIED COUNTIES OF FLORIDA, 2005

County	Acres harvested	Production (tons)
Florida	376,000	11,806,000
Glades	34,000	1,190,000
Hendry	30,000	1,050,000
Palm Beach	312,000	9,566,000

Table 9.68. TOBACCO: ACREAGE HARVESTED AND PRODUCTION OF FLUE-CURED TOBACCO IN THE STATE, CROP-REPORTING DISTRICTS, AND SPECIFIED COUNTIES OF FLORIDA, 2005

District and county	Acres harvested	Production (pounds)
Florida	2,500	5,500,000
District 30	1,860	4,426,800
Columbia	120	286,800
Suwannee	460	1,094,800
District 30 (Continued)		
Other counties	1,280	3,045,200
Other, state	640	1,073,200

Note: County estimates are greatly reduced due to limited number of growers. See accompanying map for counties in crop-reporting district.

Source for Tables 9.66, 9.67, and 9.68: State of Florida, Department of Agriculture and Consumer Services, Florida Agricultural Statistics Service, *Florida Agricultural Facts (NASS), 2007,* Internet site <http://www.nass.usda.gov/> (accessed 14, May 2007).

Table 9.69. VEGETABLES, MELONS, AND BERRIES: ACREAGE PLANTED AND HARVESTED PRODUCTION, AND VALUE OF CROPS IN FLORIDA, CROP YEAR 2005–06

Crop	Acreage planted	Acreage harvested	Production (1,000 cwt)	Total value ($1,000)
All crops, total	217,800	199,200	48,834	1,670,398
Vegetables, total	155,700	135,900	30,555	1,140,846
Snap beans	33,400	28,700	2,727	141,804
Cabbage	7,800	6,200	2,046	30,690
Sweet corn	33,000	26,300	4,866	117,271
Cucumbers	10,000	9,500	2,375	73,863
Bell peppers	19,800	16,500	4,046	187,330
Squash	10,500	10,200	1,020	38,760
Tomatoes	41,200	38,500	13,475	551,128
Watermelons	25,900	25,300	8,349	111,042
Potatoes	28,800	28,100	7,816	146,462
Strawberries	7,400	7,300	2,044	239,148
Blueberries	(X)	2,600	70	32,900

cwt Hundred weight.
(X) Not applicable.

Source: State of Florida, Department of Agriculture and Consumer Services, Florida Agricultural Statistics Service, *Florida Agricultural Facts (NASS), 2007,* Internet site <http://www.nass.usda.gov/> (accessed 14, May 2007).

Table 9.70. LIVESTOCK: CASH RECEIPTS FROM MARKETINGS IN FLORIDA 1997 THROUGH 2006

(in thousands of dollars)

Year	Total livestock and products: Amount	Total livestock and products: Percentage of total farm cash receipts	Cattle and calves	Hogs	Milk	Chickens and eggs	Honey
1997	1,385,551	21	320,424	12,335	407,715	353,128	11,738
1998	1,390,311	19	291,182	5,772	424,424	367,166	14,426
1999	1,347,573	20	309,852	5,743	412,112	354,186	12,326
2000	1,315,908	19	367,857	7,144	383,604	335,487	13,154
2001	1,389,601	21	361,915	7,267	428,446	376,238	14,080
2002	1,239,055	19	333,413	4,923	352,237	305,101	23,324
2003	1,240,273	19	348,411	4,347	329,868	324,443	19,681
2004	1,456,914	21	451,857	6,406	431,616	369,018	20,090
2005	1,406,637	18	502,268	4,674	421,662	302,922	11,834
2006	1,304,892	18	484,288	3,766	343,599	296,929	13,908

Note: Data are for calendar year, except for hogs, chickens and eggs, and honey, which report for a marketing year of December through November. Value of eggs is for total production including consumption on farms where produced. Data do not include government payments. Some data are revised.

Source: State of Florida, Department of Agriculture and Consumer Services, Florida Agricultural Statistics Service, *Livestock, Dairy, and Poultry Summary, 2006,* Internet site <http://www.nass.usda.gov/> (accessed 25, July 2007).

Table 9.71. CATTLE AND CALVES: NUMBER AND RANK OF CATTLE AND CALVES AND BEEF COWS IN THE STATE AND COUNTIES OF FLORIDA, JANUARY 1, 2007

(number in thousands, rounded to hundreds)

County	Cattle and calves 1/		Beef cows 2/		County	Cattle and calves 1/		Beef cows 2/	
	Number	Rank	Number	Rank		Number	Rank	Number	Rank
Florida	17,300	(X)	9,500	(X)	Lee	140	31	80	27
					Leon	50	50	20	54
Alachua	480	11	260	13	Levy	400	16	210	15
Baker	40	54	20	54	Liberty	10	61	5	61
Bradford	110	35	70	32	Madison	190	26	110	24
Brevard	240	22	140	19	Manatee	540	10	300	10
Broward	120	32	50	37	Marion	410	15	270	12
Calhoun	40	54	20	54	Martin	250	21	130	21
Charlotte	200	24	130	21	Miami-Dade	30	60	20	54
Citrus	80	43	50	37	Nassau	70	48	20	54
Clay	90	39	40	42	Okaloosa	40	54	20	54
Collier	120	32	80	27	Okeechobee	1,560	1	690	2
Columbia	180	27	100	25	Orange	120	32	80	27
DeSoto	770	7	480	7	Osceola	1,140	2	760	1
Dixie	40	54	20	54	Palm Beach	40	54	30	48
Duval	80	43	30	48	Pasco	480	11	260	13
Escambia	90	39	35	45	Polk	1,020	3	650	3
Flagler	60	49	40	42	Putnam	100	36	60	34
Gadsden	50	50	25	52	St. Johns	40	54	25	52
Gilchrist	350	18	80	27	St. Lucie	260	20	210	15
Glades	710	8	350	8	Santa Rosa	50	50	35	45
Hamilton	80	43	50	37	Sarasota	200	24	130	21
Hardee	880	5	520	5	Seminole	90	39	60	34
Hendry	850	6	490	6	Sumter	470	13	310	9
Hernando	170	28	70	32	Suwannee	440	14	160	18
Highlands	1,010	4	610	4	Taylor	50	50	30	48
Hillsborough	610	9	300	10	Union	80	43	45	41
Holmes	170	28	80	27	Volusia	100	36	50	37
Indian River	160	30	100	25	Wakulla	10	61	5	61
Jackson	360	17	170	17	Walton	90	39	60	34
Jefferson	100	36	40	42	Washington	80	43	35	45
Lafayette	210	23	30	48	Other 3/	20	(X)	10	(X)
Lake	280	19	140	19					

(X) Not applicable.
1/ All classes, beef and dairy.
2/ Beef production brood cows only, which have calved at least once.
3/ Includes Bay, Franklin, Gulf, Monroe, and Pinellas counties.

Source: State of Florida, Department of Agriculture and Consumer Services, Florida Agricultural Statistics Service, *Florida Agricultural Facts (NASS), 2007,* Internet site <http://www.nass.usda.gov/> (accessed 14, May 2007).

Table 9.72. CATTLE AND CALVES: MARKETINGS, PRICE, AND CASH RECEIPTS IN FLORIDA AND THE UNITED STATES, 2002 THROUGH 2006

Year	Florida: Marketings 1/ (1,000 lbs.)	Florida: Price per 100 lbs. (dollars): Cattle	Florida: Price per 100 lbs. (dollars): Calves	Florida: Cash receipts 2/ ($1,000)	United States: Marketings 1/ (1,000 lbs.)	United States: Price per 100 lbs. (dollars): Cattle	United States: Price per 100 lbs. (dollars): Calves	United States: Cash receipts 2/ ($1,000)
2002	497,000	47.90	88.20	333,413	56,072,764	66.50	96.40	38,048,819
2003	478,730	50.50	96.60	348,411	56,758,262	79.70	102.00	45,092,283
2004	491,080	63.20	121.00	451,857	53,764,917	85.80	119.00	47,295,574
2005	481,360	80.00	130.00	502,268	53,161,063	89.70	135.00	49,295,310
2006	477,110	78.20	120.00	484,288	54,739,022	87.20	133.00	49,148,364

1/ Excludes custom slaughter for use on farms where produced and interfarm sales within states.
2/ Receipts from marketings and sales of farm slaughter.

Table 9.73. LIVESTOCK INVENTORY: NUMBER ON FARMS IN FLORIDA, LEADING STATE AND THE UNITED STATES, 2006 OR 2007

Type of livestock	Florida: Rank among states	Florida: Number (1,000 head)	Leading state: Name	Leading state: Number	United States
Cattle and calves 1/	18	1,730	Texas	14,000	97,003
Beef cows 1/	11	950	Texas	5,303	32,894
Hogs 2/	36	20	Iowa	17,200	62,149

1/ January 1, 2007.
2/ December 1, 2006.

Source for Tables 9.72, and 9.73: State of Florida, Department of Agriculture and Consumer Services, Florida Agricultural Statistics Service, *Livestock, Dairy, and Poultry Summary, 2006,* Internet site <http://www.nass.usda.gov/> (accessed 25, July 2007).

Table 9.74. HONEY: PRODUCTION AND VALUE IN FLORIDA AND THE UNITED STATES 2000 THROUGH 2006

Year	Florida: Number of colonies (1,000)	Florida: Production (1,000 pounds)	Florida: Value ($1,000)	United States: Number of colonies (1,000)	United States: Production (1,000 pounds)	United States: Value ($1,000)
2000	232	24,360	13,154	2,620	220,339	132,742
2001	220	22,000	14,080	2,506	185,461	132,225
2002	220	20,460	23,324	2,574	171,718	228,338
2003	210	14,910	19,681	2,599	181,727	253,106
2004	205	20,090	20,090	2,556	183,582	201,790
2005	160	13,760	11,834	2,413	174,818	160,428
2006	170	13,770	13,908	2,392	154,846	161,314

Source: U.S., Deparment of Agriculture, Economics, Statistics, and Market Information System, National Agricultural Statistics Service (NASS), Internet site <http://www.nass.usda.gov/> (accessed 25, July 2007).

Table 9.86. DAIRY PRODUCTION: NUMBER OF MILK COWS AND ANNUAL MILK PRODUCTION IN FLORIDA, OTHER LEADING PRODUCTION STATES, AND THE UNITED STATES, 2006

State	Milk cows 2/ (1,000)	Production 1/ Total milk (1,000,000 pounds)	Rank among states	Per milk cow (pounds)	Milkfat in milk (percentage)
Florida	132	2,167	20	16,417	3.66
California	1,780	38,830	1	21,815	3.68
Wisconsin	1,243	23,398	2	18,824	3.72
New York	638	12,045	3	18,879	3.71
Idaho	488	10,895	4	22,326	3.64
Pennsylvania	554	10,742	5	19,390	3.72
Minnesota	450	8,364	6	18,587	3.73
New Mexico	355	7,638	7	21,515	3.61
Texas	355	7,145	8	21,328	3.74
Michigan	320	7,100	9	22,188	3.63
Washington	237	5,464	10	23,055	3.70
Ohio	274	4,860	11	17,737	3.75
Iowa	205	4,130	12	20,146	3.71
Arizona	173	3,954	13	22,855	3.59
Indiana	165	3,299	14	19,994	3.68
Vermont	141	2,592	15	18,383	3.74
Colorado	110	2,547	16	23,155	3.55
United States	9,112	181,798	(X)	19,951	3.69

(X) Not applicable
1/ Average number on farms during year, excluding heifers not yet fresh.
2/ Excludes milk fed to calves.

Table 9.87. CHICKEN AND EGGS: CASH RECEIPTS IN FLORIDA, MARKETING YEARS 1997 THROUGH 2006

(in thousands of dollars)

Year	Total	Broilers	Eggs 1/	Other chickens 2/
1997	353,128	229,383	123,701	44
1998	367,166	252,840	113,197	1,029
1999	354,186	246,126	107,570	490
2000	335,487	226,625	108,187	675
2001	376,238	253,680	122,253	305
2002	305,101	195,579	109,012	510
2003	324,443	178,955	145,107	381
2004	369,018	208,440	159,878	700
2005	302,922	201,564	100,723	635
2006	296,929	181,425	115,002	502

1/ Total production, including consumption on farms where produced.
2/ Value of sales.
Note: Data are for marketing years beginning December 1 and ending November 30. Some data may be revised.

Source for Tables 9.86 and 9.87: State of Florida, Department of Agriculture and Consumer Services, Florida Agricultural Statistics Service, *Livestock, Dairy, and Poultry Summary, 2006,* Internet site <http://www.nass.usda.gov/> (accessed 25, July 2007).

FORESTRY, FISHERIES, AND MINERALS

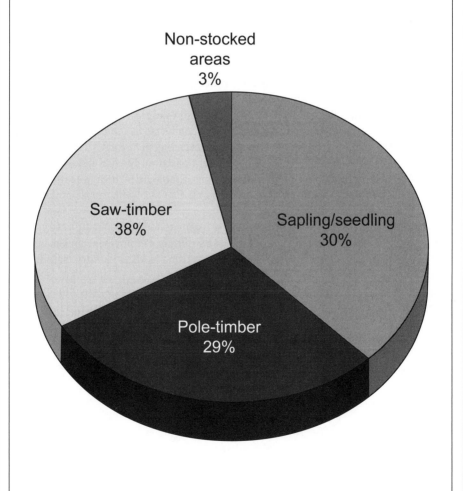

Timberland Area by Stand-size Class in Florida, 2005 (%)

Non-stocked areas 3%

Saw-timber 38%

Sapling/seedling 30%

Pole-timber 29%

Source: Table 10.02

Section 10.00
Forestry, Fisheries, and Minerals

This section depicts statistical data on Florida's abundant forestry, fishing, and mining resources and industries.

Sources. The U.S. Department of Agriculture's (USDA) Forest Service conducts a national inventory of forest and timberland. Data on Florida's forest land and timberland come from the South Regional Forest Inventory and Analysis division of the USDA's Forest Service. Information about the harvest of forest products is published in *Florida's Timber Industry: An Assessment of Timber Product Output and Use* and is available on the Forest Service's Southern Research Station Web site. The Forest Service also publishes data on national forests in an Internet report, *Land Areas of the National Forest System.*

The Fisheries Statistics and Economics Division of the National Oceanic and Atmospheric Administration (NOAA) within the U.S. Department of Commerce publishes fishery products, plants, and cooperatives statistics online in the annual report, *Fisheries of the United States.* New from this source and to this year's *Abstract* are "catch and release" recreational finfishing data and statistics on anglers and angler trips by state found on Tables 10.34 and 10.35.

The Marine Fisheries Information System in the office of the Fish and Wildlife Research Institute within the Florida Fish and Wildlife Conservation Commission provides unpublished data on fish and shellfish landings and trips. Table 19.45 in Section 19.00 gives information on the number of commercial boats registered in Florida by county.

Basic data about mineral production are from *The Minerals Yearbook*, published by the U.S. Geological Survey, Department of the Interior.

Industry employment. The *Economic Census*, conducted by the U.S. Census Bureau in years ending in "2" and "7," reports employment based on NAICS industry classifications. Employment data from the *2002 Economic Census: Mining* appear in Table 10.61.

Current statewide private forestry, fishing, and mining employment and payroll data (also using NAICS industry classifications) are provided by the Labor Market Statistics office of the Florida Agency for Workforce Innovation. (See the introduction to Sections 6.00 and 9.00 and the Glossary.)

Section 10.00
Forestry, Fisheries, and Minerals

Tables listed by major heading

Table 10.01. FOREST LAND: LAND AREA BY LAND CLASS IN THE STATE AND COUNTIES OF FLORIDA, 2005

(in acres)

County	All land	Forest land				Non-forest land
		Total	Timber-land	Other forest land	Reserved timber-land	
Florida	35,026,317	16,146,905	15,551,947	97,517	497,441	18,139,798
Alachua	638,522	326,047	326,047	0	0	300,987
Baker	293,124	254,959	245,618	0	9,341	38,165
Bay	514,314	355,481	355,481	0	0	158,832
Bradford	206,904	154,725	154,725	0	0	52,179
Brevard	618,896	164,808	164,808	0	0	443,595
Broward	745,138	8,110	0	8,110	0	725,460
Calhoun	395,483	326,522	316,560	9,963	0	68,960
Charlotte	466,173	152,998	152,998	0	0	313,174
Citrus	404,961	227,004	227,004	0	0	177,957
Clay	337,684	297,608	297,608	0	0	40,076
Collier	857,368	535,343	268,372	0	266,971	281,813
Columbia	525,151	379,921	379,921	0	0	145,230
DeSoto	405,009	58,451	58,451	0	0	346,558
Dixie	454,075	373,741	373,741	0	0	80,334
Duval	522,886	238,320	219,637	9,341	9,341	284,567
Escambia	426,957	249,464	249,464	0	0	177,493
Flagler	287,887	223,561	223,561	0	0	64,326
Franklin	400,826	347,944	337,981	0	9,963	51,884
Gadsden	341,479	244,416	244,416	0	0	97,064
Gilchrist	209,051	132,802	132,802	0	0	76,249
Glades	624,805	98,297	98,297	0	0	526,507
Gulf	345,668	279,030	279,030	0	0	66,638
Hamilton	333,839	227,748	227,748	0	0	94,603
Hardee	401,495	111,661	111,661	0	0	289,835
Hendry	772,664	87,359	87,359	0	0	673,736
Hernando	302,140	180,859	180,859	0	0	110,788
Highlands	684,664	146,675	139,332	0	7,343	537,989
Hillsborough	703,343	104,608	94,818	0	9,790	587,813
Holmes	297,008	236,034	228,562	7,472	0	60,974
Indian River	351,139	41,106	41,106	0	0	310,033
Jackson	614,373	399,929	389,966	9,963	0	214,444
Jefferson	408,059	307,272	297,706	0	9,565	91,676
Lafayette	367,101	284,136	284,136	0	0	82,965
Lake	663,069	288,463	278,673	0	9,790	374,605

See footnote at end of table.

Continued . . .

Table 10.01. FOREST LAND: LAND AREA BY LAND CLASS IN THE STATE AND COUNTIES OF FLORIDA, 2005 (Continued)

(in acres)

County	All land	Forest land: Total	Forest land: Timber-land	Forest land: Other forest land	Forest land: Reserved timber-land	Non-forest land
Lee	514,392	175,549	158,713	16,836	0	338,843
Leon	384,796	246,709	246,709	0	0	135,307
Levy	755,355	489,619	489,619	0	0	254,561
Liberty	521,504	512,828	490,619	12,246	9,963	8,676
Madison	429,589	309,950	309,950	0	0	119,639
Manatee	444,873	81,979	81,979	0	0	360,446
Marion	1,090,021	554,273	554,273	0	0	504,468
Martin	394,510	71,186	71,186	0	0	323,324
Miami-Dade	1,395,266	37,355	8,110	8,110	21,134	1,048,196
Monroe	615,517	36,870	15,736	0	21,134	458,012
Nassau	424,541	286,092	286,092	0	0	138,449
Okaloosa	633,868	489,563	469,637	0	19,926	144,069
Okeechobee	550,364	59,008	59,008	0	0	491,356
Orange	615,523	164,693	145,112	0	19,580	450,830
Osceola	920,381	210,580	210,580	0	0	709,800
Palm Beach	1,388,163	58,093	58,093	0	0	1,296,697
Pasco	490,872	188,414	188,414	0	0	302,459
Pinellas	197,961	20,040	9,547	0	10,493	177,920
Polk	1,138,062	300,054	279,069	10,493	10,493	824,214
Putnam	536,639	424,306	414,964	0	9,341	112,011
St. Johns	387,741	249,612	249,612	0	0	115,690
St. Lucie	365,145	35,915	35,915	0	0	329,230
Santa Rosa	644,986	465,377	465,377	0	0	168,492
Sarasota	348,858	88,764	71,804	0	16,961	249,601
Seminole	176,272	54,492	54,492	0	0	121,780
Sumter	338,538	136,063	136,063	0	0	202,474
Suwannee	409,084	226,607	210,260	0	16,348	171,302
Taylor	631,563	571,358	571,358	0	0	60,205
Union	151,610	136,430	136,430	0	0	15,180
Volusia	734,169	445,249	445,249	0	0	274,561
Wakulla	401,257	327,208	312,264	4,981	9,963	74,048
Walton	694,801	554,426	554,426	0	0	136,898
Washington	378,840	292,839	292,839	0	0	73,551

Note: Data are preliminary.

Source: U.S., Department of Agriculture, Forest Service, South Regional Forest Inventory and Analysis, Internet site <http://www.srs.fs.usda.gov/> (accessed 26, April 2007).

Table 10.02. TIMBERLAND: LAND AREA BY STAND-SIZE CLASS IN THE STATE AND COUNTIES OF FLORIDA, 2005

(in acres)

County	All classes	Stand-size class: Saw-timber	Stand-size class: Pole-timber	Stand-size class: Sapling/ seedling	Non-stocked areas
Florida	15,551,947	5,872,539	4,499,326	4,670,846	509,236
Alachua	326,047	122,798	46,129	157,120	0
Baker	245,618	50,194	53,215	109,513	32,695
Bay	355,481	37,867	124,816	190,307	2,491
Bradford	154,725	67,243	52,451	35,030	0
Brevard	164,808	57,528	28,595	68,192	10,493
Broward	0	0	0	0	0
Calhoun	316,560	101,095	102,647	102,855	9,963
Charlotte	152,998	82,789	23,136	27,394	19,679
Citrus	227,004	62,517	79,744	71,802	12,941
Clay	297,608	119,508	89,063	68,208	20,830
Collier	268,372	185,699	37,331	41,287	4,055
Columbia	379,921	155,674	101,645	122,602	0
DeSoto	58,451	48,660	9,790	0	0
Dixie	373,741	129,518	104,397	121,143	18,683
Duval	219,637	100,306	63,254	56,077	0
Escambia	249,464	131,782	49,430	68,253	0
Flagler	223,561	64,785	94,391	55,043	9,341
Franklin	337,981	126,846	113,412	87,760	9,963
Gadsden	244,416	128,390	37,677	78,349	0
Gilchrist	132,802	32,610	78,199	19,657	2,335
Glades	98,297	14,193	42,122	41,982	0
Gulf	279,030	83,884	112,541	72,355	10,252
Hamilton	227,748	56,585	73,890	82,188	15,086
Hardee	111,661	106,414	5,246	0	0
Hendry	87,359	57,589	9,967	19,803	0
Hernando	180,859	105,670	40,572	34,617	0
Highlands	139,332	71,419	6,834	53,210	7,870
Hillsborough	94,818	44,386	14,721	27,841	7,870
Holmes	228,562	74,047	83,473	71,042	0
Indian River	41,106	24,399	6,917	9,790	0
Jackson	389,966	131,927	154,376	91,210	12,454
Jefferson	297,706	131,297	86,417	64,759	15,233
Lafayette	284,136	62,400	110,911	71,123	39,701
Lake	278,673	138,827	57,013	80,385	2,448

See footnote at end of table.

Continued . . .

Table 10.02. TIMBERLAND: LAND AREA BY STAND-SIZE CLASS IN THE STATE AND COUNTIES OF FLORIDA, 2005 (Continued)

(in acres)

County	All classes	Stand-size class			Non-stocked areas
		Saw-timber	Pole-timber	Sapling/ seedling	
Lee	158,713	39,244	76,334	28,675	14,460
Leon	246,709	118,911	60,610	67,189	0
Levy	489,619	216,696	140,567	120,679	11,677
Liberty	490,619	180,088	154,387	141,971	14,172
Madison	309,950	77,979	149,555	79,544	2,872
Manatee	81,979	47,206	14,490	20,283	0
Marion	554,273	197,795	115,893	234,881	5,703
Martin	71,186	44,234	0	26,952	0
Miami-Dade	8,110	0	0	8,110	0
Monroe	15,736	0	7,625	8,110	0
Nassau	286,092	110,436	75,449	88,116	12,092
Okaloosa	469,637	216,933	101,456	141,284	9,963
Okeechobee	59,008	51,956	7,052	0	0
Orange	145,112	88,077	39,727	17,309	0
Osceola	210,580	88,281	22,906	65,457	33,936
Palm Beach	58,093	25,761	21,329	4,920	6,083
Pasco	188,414	71,300	81,442	30,776	4,895
Pinellas	9,547	9,547	0	0	0
Polk	279,069	97,993	98,015	49,452	33,608
Putnam	414,964	148,322	123,258	127,038	16,348
St.Johns	249,612	61,748	89,430	98,433	0
St. Lucie	35,915	30,668	0	2,623	2,623
Santa Rosa	465,377	211,752	137,813	95,886	19,926
Sarasota	71,804	37,011	25,003	0	9,790
Seminole	54,492	42,078	12,413	0	0
Sumter	136,063	84,959	29,371	21,733	0
Suwannee	210,260	58,312	68,592	81,020	2,335
Taylor	571,358	63,301	208,170	287,387	12,501
Union	136,430	25,464	63,561	38,063	9,341
Volusia	445,249	175,058	98,791	159,008	12,392
Wakulla	312,264	105,837	124,595	79,341	2,491
Walton	554,426	169,059	141,971	238,415	4,981
Washington	292,839	67,688	115,197	107,289	2,665

Note: Data are preliminary.

Source: U.S., Department of Agriculture, Forest Service, South Regional Forest Inventory and Analysis, Internet site <http://www.srs.fs.usda.gov/> (accessed 26, April 2007).

Table 10.03. TIMBERLAND: AREA BY OWNERSHIP CLASS IN THE STATE AND COUNTIES OF FLORIDA, 1995 AND 2005

(in hundreds of acres)

	1995				2005			
		Ownership class				Ownership class		
		Government-owned				Government-owned		
County	All owner-ships	State county and municipal	Federal 1/	Private indivi-duals 2/	All owner-ships	State county and municipal	Federal 1/	Private indivi-duals 2/
Florida	146,506.6	12,157.8	16,159.9	118,188.9	155,519.5	24,529.7	17,116.4	113,873.5
Alachua	2,774.6	49.7	0.2	2,724.7	3,260.5	93.4	0.0	3,167.1
Baker	3,265.2	2.3	905.1	2,357.9	2,456.2	280.2	899.0	1,277.0
Bay	3,963.7	72.7	214.7	3,676.3	3,554.8	348.6	99.6	3,106.6
Bradford	1,352.0	164.3	0.0	1,187.7	1,547.3	122.1	0.0	1,425.1
Brevard	930.9	56.0	124.6	750.4	1,648.1	484.4	202.8	960.8
Broward	0.0	0.0	0.0	0.0	0.0	0.0	0.0	0.0
Calhoun	3,025.9	1.2	0.1	3,024.6	3,165.6	0.0	63.6	3,102.0
Charlotte	302.9	73.1	0.0	229.8	1,530.0	551.0	0.0	979.0
Citrus	1,859.3	492.4	0.0	1,367.0	2,270.0	737.9	0.0	1,532.1
Clay	2,882.5	708.4	6.4	2,167.7	2,976.1	675.1	0.0	2,301.0
Collier	1,904.6	90.5	0.0	1,814.1	2,683.7	1,235.4	81.1	1,367.3
Columbia	3,574.8	55.1	800.9	2,718.9	3,799.2	361.2	560.5	2,877.5
DeSoto	477.6	31.3	0.0	446.3	584.5	0.0	0.0	584.5
Dixie	3,857.1	50.3	171.3	3,635.5	3,737.4	280.2	0.0	3,457.2
Duval	2,296.1	120.8	167.7	2,007.7	2,196.4	428.0	0.0	1,768.4
Escambia	2,507.9	54.0	29.5	2,424.4	2,494.6	0.0	54.2	2,440.5
Flagler	2,375.9	16.5	0.0	2,359.4	2,235.6	0.0	0.0	2,235.6
Franklin	3,014.9	460.7	270.0	2,284.3	3,379.8	1,895.4	174.4	1,310.1
Gadsden	2,534.0	103.3	0.0	2,430.7	2,444.2	210.8	0.0	2,233.4
Gilchrist	1,346.7	2.8	0.0	1,343.9	1,328.0	93.4	0.0	1,234.6
Glades	916.5	0.6	0.0	915.9	983.0	81.1	0.0	901.9
Gulf	3,102.3	351.8	7.6	2,743.0	2,790.3	398.5	92.9	2,298.9
Hamilton	2,400.9	130.9	0.0	2,270.0	2,277.5	163.5	0.0	2,114.0
Hardee	795.3	8.1	0.0	787.2	1,116.6	0.0	0.0	1,116.6
Hendry	628.3	4.6	0.0	623.7	873.6	0.0	0.0	873.6
Hernando	1,558.5	569.7	7.1	981.7	1,808.6	783.2	0.0	1,025.4
Highlands	787.6	5.5	225.0	557.1	1,393.3	97.9	454.8	840.6
Hillsborough	964.7	178.5	0.0	786.2	948.2	570.7	0.0	377.5
Holmes	2,107.4	38.4	4.6	2,064.5	2,285.6	99.6	27.8	2,158.2
Indian River	228.4	8.5	0.0	219.9	411.1	140.2	0.0	270.8
Jackson	3,254.3	93.8	54.4	3,106.1	3,899.7	298.9	0.0	3,600.8
Jefferson	2,844.0	140.6	0.0	2,703.4	2,977.1	310.4	0.0	2,666.6
Lafayette	2,973.2	27.7	0.0	2,945.5	2,841.4	93.4	0.0	2,747.9
Lake	2,484.9	208.3	696.9	1,579.7	2,786.7	711.6	685.3	1,389.9

See footnotes at end of table. Continued . . .

Table 10.03. TIMBERLAND: AREA BY OWNERSHIP CLASS IN THE STATE AND COUNTIES OF FLORIDA, 1995 AND 2005 (Continued)

(in hundreds of acres)

	1995				2005			
	Ownership class				Ownership class			
		Government-owned				Government-owned		
County	All owner-ships	State county and municipal	Federal 1/	Private indivi-duals 2/	All owner-ships	State county and municipal	Federal 1/	Private indivi-duals 2/
Lee	608.7	89.0	0.0	519.7	1,587.1	677.4	0.0	909.7
Leon	3,053.9	100.5	1,037.6	1,915.8	2,467.1	254.9	786.2	1,426.0
Levy	4,627.9	472.8	159.4	3,995.7	4,896.2	509.0	93.4	4,293.8
Liberty	5,032.3	222.7	2,581.7	2,227.9	4,906.2	285.8	2,646.0	1,974.5
Madison	3,263.7	68.8	7.3	3,187.6	3,099.5	186.8	0.0	2,912.7
Manatee	400.0	91.9	0.0	308.1	819.8	97.9	0.0	721.9
Marion	5,682.8	373.2	2,456.1	2,853.5	5,542.7	186.8	2,937.2	2,418.7
Martin	406.5	121.5	0.0	284.9	711.9	382.5	0.0	329.3
Miami-Dade	0.0	0.0	0.0	0.0	81.1	81.1	0.0	0.0
Monroe	0.0	0.0	0.0	0.0	157.4	76.3	81.1	0.0
Nassau	3,233.7	64.4	0.1	3,169.3	2,860.9	373.7	0.0	2,487.3
Okaloosa	4,482.8	605.1	2,113.1	1,764.5	4,696.4	597.8	2,567.9	1,530.7
Okeechobee	433.3	7.9	0.0	425.4	590.1	0.0	0.0	590.1
Orange	1,493.0	302.9	2.7	1,187.4	1,451.1	562.6	0.0	888.5
Osceola	1,815.1	322.9	3.8	1,488.4	2,105.8	467.8	0.0	1,638.0
Palm Beach	0.0	0.0	0.0	0.0	580.9	500.9	0.0	80.0
Pasco	1,591.3	652.0	0.2	939.0	1,884.1	697.3	0.0	1,186.8
Pinellas	64.6	25.8	0.0	38.8	95.5	0.0	0.0	95.5
Polk	2,431.6	198.0	152.0	2,081.6	2,790.7	303.0	310.5	2,177.3
Putnam	3,477.8	238.5	250.1	2,989.2	4,149.6	908.2	256.9	2,984.5
St.Johns	2,453.3	47.5	0.0	2,405.7	2,496.1	93.4	0.0	2,402.7
St. Lucie	205.9	4.3	0.0	201.6	359.2	74.0	0.0	285.2
Santa Rosa	4,780.5	1,311.8	563.0	2,905.7	4,653.8	1,332.1	609.3	2,712.3
Sarasota	488.0	30.3	0.0	457.8	718.0	415.2	0.0	302.9
Seminole	725.5	67.7	1.5	656.2	544.9	104.9	0.0	440.0
Sumter	1,498.9	782.3	0.0	716.7	1,360.6	692.3	0.0	668.3
Suwannee	2,315.1	56.7	0.0	2,258.4	2,102.6	0.0	0.0	2,102.6
Taylor	5,794.4	548.0	0.0	5,246.4	5,713.6	560.5	0.0	5,153.1
Union	1,213.9	39.4	0.0	1,174.5	1,364.3	0.0	0.0	1,364.3
Volusia	4,409.4	385.9	28.4	3,995.0	4,452.5	1,554.2	86.2	2,812.1
Wakulla	3,142.7	13.6	1,744.7	1,384.4	3,122.6	0.0	2,090.3	1,032.3
Walton	5,167.8	363.1	1,372.3	3,432.4	5,544.3	563.0	1,255.6	3,725.6
Washington	2,919.4	177.1	0.0	2,742.3	2,928.4	443.9	0.0	2,484.5

1/ Includes national forests, Bureau of Land Management, Tribal Trust, and other federal lands.
2/ Includes individuals, corporations, farmers, and ranchers.
Note: 1995 data are revised; 2005 data are preliminary.
Source: U.S., Department of Agriculture, Forest Service, South Regional Forest Inventory and Analysis, Internet site <http://www.srs.fs.usda.gov/> (accessed 26, April 2007).

Table 10.07. FOREST PRODUCTS: HARVEST BY PRODUCT AND BY SPECIES GROUP IN THE STATE AND COUNTIES OF FLORIDA, 2003

(in thousands of cubic feet)

County	Softwood				Hardwood			
	All products 1/	Saw logs	Veneer logs	Pulpwood	All products 1/	Saw logs	Veneer logs	Pulpwood
Florida	468,577	166,217	30,492	243,796	40,109	4,454	1,437	26,939
Alachua	13,683	4,344	1,740	6,422	3,172	0	0	3,120
Baker	14,974	5,389	652	8,734	474	0	0	474
Bay	15,041	5,787	0	8,992	653	191	0	462
Bradford	7,683	4,208	217	3,167	110	0	0	110
Brevard	546	216	217	81	28	0	0	28
Broward	0	0	0	0	15	0	0	15
Calhoun	12,811	2,794	0	9,711	1,320	748	0	572
Charlotte	132	0	0	0	0	0	0	0
Citrus	1,238	345	217	587	59	0	0	59
Clay	12,906	4,392	652	7,757	198	0	0	198
Collier	70	70	0	0	0	0	0	0
Columbia	14,044	4,712	217	8,973	282	0	125	157
DeSoto	127	127	0	0	0	0	0	0
Dixie	18,008	9,325	217	7,251	2,667	173	125	1,985
Duval	13,698	7,106	870	5,184	584	5	87	492
Escambia	12,589	3,747	861	7,290	1,157	0	0	1,157
Flagler	9,788	3,185	1,958	3,553	945	0	0	945
Franklin	3,770	2,305	0	1,262	576	0	0	0
Gadsden	9,941	3,123	1,681	4,954	1,345	268	64	998
Gilchrist	3,721	1,056	217	2,418	511	0	83	395
Glades	841	393	435	13	0	0	0	0
Gulf	10,563	1,614	0	8,823	842	412	0	430
Hamilton	14,809	4,569	217	9,523	653	0	0	205
Hardee	428	0	217	211	6	0	0	6
Hendry	652	0	0	652	0	0	0	0
Hernando	1,453	742	217	324	326	3	0	323
Highlands	864	152	217	11	0	0	0	0
Hillsborough	149	124	0	0	17	0	0	17
Holmes	7,828	3,524	360	3,774	751	29	0	722
Indian River	244	212	0	0	0	0	0	0
Jackson	17,533	4,528	1,441	9,126	2,345	265	181	1,899
Jefferson	7,881	1,877	1,899	3,624	2,695	89	64	878
Lafayette	8,708	4,308	0	4,101	920	0	41	879
Lake	2,668	940	217	296	185	0	0	25

See footnote at end of table.

Continued . . .

Table 10.07. FOREST PRODUCTS: HARVEST BY PRODUCT AND BY SPECIES GROUP IN THE STATE AND COUNTIES OF FLORIDA, 2003 (Continued)

(in thousands of cubic feet)

County	Softwood All products 1/	Softwood Saw logs	Softwood Veneer logs	Softwood Pulpwood	Hardwood All products 1/	Hardwood Saw logs	Hardwood Veneer logs	Hardwood Pulpwood
Lee	132	0	0	0	0	0	0	0
Leon	6,146	875	720	4,469	887	63	64	710
Levy	19,545	6,668	2,611	8,041	1,606	473	166	945
Liberty	9,533	1,719	0	7,572	971	583	0	388
Madison	16,523	4,495	675	10,469	2,228	0	83	481
Manatee	16	16	0	0	0	0	0	0
Marion	10,655	3,078	1,523	5,025	604	181	81	342
Martin	218	0	217	1	2	0	0	2
Miami-Dade	0	0	0	0	0	0	0	0
Monroe	38	38	0	0	0	0	0	0
Nassau	24,638	13,732	435	9,960	293	244	0	49
Okaloosa	5,975	1,341	893	3,477	243	26	0	217
Okeechobee	42	28	0	0	0	0	0	0
Orange	839	303	217	141	18	0	0	18
Osceola	2,655	383	217	364	49	0	0	49
Palm Beach	0	0	0	0	10	0	0	10
Pasco	1,608	930	0	52	19	0	0	19
Pinellas	0	0	0	0	0	0	0	0
Polk	2,462	1,398	217	254	217	0	0	57
Putnam	14,440	4,498	1,740	7,973	1,708	0	0	1,708
St. Johns	15,364	7,486	870	6,287	631	0	0	631
St. Lucie	1	0	0	1	63	0	0	63
Santa Rosa	12,173	4,164	861	6,900	935	31	0	904
Sarasota	314	76	217	21	44	0	0	44
Seminole	1,127	131	435	387	216	0	0	158
Sumter	2,151	1,016	217	147	77	13	0	64
Suwannee	8,541	2,538	240	5,618	465	0	83	382
Taylor	30,779	11,068	217	18,364	3,004	437	190	713
Union	11,677	5,518	652	5,389	84	0	0	84
Volusia	5,595	2,054	870	1,684	641	0	0	312
Wakulla	4,913	2,658	0	2,171	885	0	0	885
Walton	9,615	2,526	574	6,241	366	26	0	340
Washington	11,471	2,266	938	5,974	1,007	194	0	813

1/ Includes composite products, fuelwood, post-poles-pilings, and other products.

Source: U.S., Department of Agriculture, Forest Service, Southern Research Station, Forest Inventory and Analysis, *Florida's Timber Industry: An Assessment of Timber Product Output and Use, 2003,* Internet site <http://www.srs.fs.usda.gov/> (accessed 6, February 2007).

Table 10.25. NATIONAL FOREST LAND: GROSS AND NET AREA OF NATIONAL FOREST AND OTHER LAND ADMINISTERED BY THE NATIONAL FOREST SYSTEM IN FLORIDA AND THE UNITED STATES AS OF SEPTEMBER 30, 2006

(in acres)

Unit name and area	Gross area within unit boundaries	National forest system lands	Other lands within unit boundaries
Florida	1,255,421	1,113,052	142,369
Apalachicola National Forest	632,890	565,688	67,202
National wilderness areas			
Bradwell Bay 1/	24,602	24,602	0
Mud Swamp/New River	8,090	8,090	0
Choctawhatchee National Forest	1,152	1,152	0
Ocala National Forest	430,447	383,584	46,863
National wilderness areas			
Alexander Springs	7,941	7,941	0
Billies Bay	3,092	3,092	0
Juniper Prairie	14,281	14,277	4
Little Lake George	2,833	2,833	0
National game refuge, Ocala	79,735	79,735	0
Osceola National Forest	190,932	162,628	28,304
National wilderness area, Big Gum Swamp	13,660	13,660	0
United States	232,393,777	192,797,480	39,596,297

1/ Protected under the Clean Air Act, without visibility protection.

Table 10.26. NATIONAL FOREST LAND: NET AREA OF LAND ADMINISTERED BY THE NATIONAL FOREST SYSTEM IN THE STATE AND COUNTIES OF FLORIDA AND THE UNITED STATES AS OF SEPTEMBER 30, 2006

County	National forest area	Acres
Florida	(X)	1,157,390
Baker	Nekoosa Purchase Units	32
	Osceola National Forest	79,438
	Pinhook Purchase Units	23,232
Columbia	Nekoosa Purchase Units	191
	Osceola National Forest	83,190
	Pinhook Purchase Units	16,830
Franklin	Apalachicola National Forest	21,816
	Tates Hell-New River Purchase Units	976
Lake	Ocala National Forest	84,372
Leon	Apalachicola National Forest	104,568
Liberty	Apalachicola National Forest	267,298
	Tates Hell-New River Purchase Units	3,077
Marion	Ocala National Forest	275,590
Okaloosa	Choctawhatchee National Forest	523
Putnam	Ocala National Forest	23,622
Santa Rosa	Choctawhatchee National Forest	108
Wakulla	Apalachicola National Forest	172,006
Walton	Choctawhatchee National Forest	521
United States	(X)	188,067,642

(X) Not applicable.

Source for Tables 10.25 and 10.26: U.S., Department of Agriculture, Forest Service, *Land Areas of the National Forest System as of September 30, 2006,* Internet site <http://www.fs.fed.us/land/> (accessed 9, April 2007).

Table 10.30. FORESTRY AND LOGGING: AVERAGE MONTHLY PRIVATE REPORTING UNITS EMPLOYMENT AND PAYROLL COVERED BY UNEMPLOYMENT COMPENSATION LAW IN THE STATE AND COUNTIES OF FLORIDA, 2006

Forestry and logging (NAICS code 113)

County	Number of reporting units	Number of employees	Payroll ($1,000)	County	Number of reporting units	Number of employees	Payroll ($1,000)
Florida	363	2,889	8,130	Levy	17	178	396
				Liberty	11	112	248
Bay	15	78	237	Madison	12	104	275
Bradford	5	43	124	Marion	7	70	262
Calhoun	12	113	294	Nassau	26	257	1,117
Clay	14	64	179	Okaloosa	7	22	61
Columbia	8	41	122	Palm Beach	5	9	21
DeSoto	4	24	60	Pasco	6	30	72
Dixie	12	97	286	Polk	5	34	74
Duval	9	31	72	Putnam	21	130	360
Escambia	9	49	138	Santa Rosa	6	34	92
Flagler	4	22	71	Suwannee	12	156	395
Gadsden	5	12	21	Taylor	18	208	625
Hamilton	6	21	52	Union	6	45	96
Holmes	11	27	47	Volusia	7	24	59
Jefferson	3	33	117	Walton	3	7	14
Lake	5	23	40	Washington	7	34	73
Leon	4	29	80	Unknown 1/	5	13	40

NAICS North American Industrial Classification System. See Glossary for definition.
1/ Reporting units without a fixed location within the state or of unknown county location.
Note: Private employment. Data are preliminary. For a list of four-digit code industries included see Table 10.31. Only counties for which data are disclosed are shown. Detail may not add to totals due to disclosure editing and/or rounding. See Tables 23.70, 23.72, 23.73, and 23.74 for public employment data.

Table 10.31. FORESTRY AND FISHING INDUSTRIES: AVERAGE MONTHLY PRIVATE REPORTING UNITS, EMPLOYMENT, AND PAYROLL COVERED BY UNEMPLOYMENT COMPENSATION LAW BY INDUSTRY IN FLORIDA, 2006

NAICS code	Industry	Number of reporting units	Number of employees	Payroll ($1,000)
113	Forestry	363	2,889	8,130
1131	Timber tract operations	52	523	1,999
1132	Forest products	42	412	832
1133	Logging	269	1,954	5,300
114	Fishing, hunting, and trapping	182	512	1,283
1141	Commercial fishing	160	420	1,001
1142	Hunting and trapping	22	91	282

NAICS North American Industrial Classification System. See Glossary for definition.
Note: Private employment. Data are preliminary. Detail may not add to totals due to disclosure editing and/or rounding. See Tables 23.70, 23.72, 23.73, and 23.74 for public employment data.
Source for Tables 10.30 and 10.31: State of Florida, Agency for Workforce Innovation, Labor Market Statistics, "Quarterly Census of Employment and Wages" (ES-202), Annual NAICS files, Internet site <http://www.labormarketinfo.com/index.htm> (accessed 17, July 2007).

Table 10.34. FISHERIES: MARINE RECREATIONAL FINFISH HARVESTED AND RELEASED IN FLORIDA, SPECIFIED STATES, AND THE UNITED STATES, 2005

(in thousands)

State	Harvested		Number	State	Harvested		Number
	Number	Pounds	released		Number	Pounds	released
Florida	74,382	54,451	79,517	Mississippi	1,120	1,615	2,266
				New Hampshire	622	1,898	921
Alabama	3,472	7,079	5,253	New Jersey	7,905	19,452	26,498
California	10,764	10,152	9,430	New York	5,600	13,852	18,410
Connecticut	1,679	5,036	4,850	North Carolina	13,381	24,148	16,443
Delaware	1,702	2,474	4,058	Oregon 1/	559	2,182	44
Georgia	1,384	1,670	3,676	Rhode Island	1,556	4,247	2,793
Hawaii	4,154	20,696	483	South Carolina	3,564	3,151	5,523
Louisiana	13,462	25,301	18,747	Texas 1/	1,745	(NA)	(NA)
Maine	1,042	1,456	3,515	Virginia	13,031	15,799	18,675
Maryland	6,605	9,021	16,643	Washington 1/	478	2,786	96
Massachusetts	5,176	17,002	10,994	United States 2/	174,282	245,416	249,069

(NA) Not available.
1/ Numbers include only private and for-hire fisheries. Texas only estimates harvest (no weight or release data).
2/ Includes Puerto Rico.
Note: Fishing within U.S. coastal waters for pleasure, amusement, relaxation, or home consumption.

Table 10.35. FISHING: ANGLERS AND ANGLER TRIPS IN FLORIDA, COASTAL STATES AND THE UNITED STATES, 2005

State	Anglers		Trips	State	Anglers		Trips
	Out-of-state	In-state			Out-of-state	In-state	
Florida	2,950	3,632	27,697	Mississippi	38	137	895
				New Hampshire	85	118	519
Alabama	162	325	1,588	New Jersey	474	865	6,718
California	(NA)	(NA)	4,341	New York	113	924	6,159
Connecticut	80	333	1,644	North Carolina	1,291	970	6,823
Delaware	187	118	1,056	Oregon	(NA)	(NA)	172
Georgia	43	204	859	Rhode Island	238	143	1,593
Hawaii	160	241	2,505	South Carolina	472	359	2,188
Louisiana	136	770	3,936	Texas	(NA)	(NA)	987
Maine	175	216	1,114	Virginia	502	687	3,791
Maryland	432	683	3,254	Washington	(NA)	(NA)	135
Massachusetts	398	738	4,543	United States 1/	7,970	11,570	83,365

(NA) Not available.
1/ Includes Puerto Rico.
Note: Fishing within U.S. coastal waters for pleasure, amusement, relaxation, or home consumption.

Source for Tables 10.34 and 10.35: U.S., Department of Commerce, National Oceanic and Atmospheric Administration, Fisheries Statistics and Economics Division, *Fisheries of the United States, 2005,* Internet site <http://www.st.nmfs.gov/> (accessed 6, February 2007).

Table 10.36. FISHERIES: NUMBER OF PROCESSING AND WHOLESALING PLANTS AND AVERAGE ANNUAL EMPLOYMENT IN FLORIDA, GEOGRAPHIC AREAS, OTHER MAJOR PRODUCTION STATES AND THE UNITED STATES, 2004

Area	Number of plants			Average annual employment		
	Total	Processing	Wholesale	Total	Processing	Wholesale
Area						
New England	539	97	442	7,356	3,780	3,576
Mid-Atlantic	551	63	488	8,506	3,993	4,513
South Atlantic 1/	511	110	418	6,950	3,381	3,703
Gulf	462	196	266	9,672	7,546	2,126
Pacific	907	321	586	23,908	18,124	5,784
Inland States	200	8	192	3,515	1,015	2,500
State						
Florida	377	80	297	4,265	1,842	2,423
Maine	223	32	191	1,755	813	942
Massachusetts	228	48	180	4,400	2,302	2,098
North Carolina	100	25	75	1,481	742	739
Louisiana	198	75	123	3,236	2,475	761
Alaska	292	152	140	8,719	8,535	184
Washington	204	61	143	5,343	4,252	1,091
California	367	82	285	8,580	4,418	4,162
United States 2/	3,242	814	2,428	65,690	43,092	22,598

1/ Detail may not add to total; some data are reported as Inland States.
2/ Includes American Samoa, Hawaii, and Puerto Rico.
Source: U.S., Department of Commerce, National Oceanic and Atmospheric Administration, Fisheries Statistics and Economics Division, *Fisheries of the United States, 2005,* Internet site <http://www.st.nmfs.gov/> (accessed 6, February 2007).

Table 10.37. FISHING, HUNTING, AND TRAPPING: AVERAGE MONTHLY PRIVATE REPORTING UNITS, EMPLOYMENT, AND PAYROLL COVERED BY UNEMPLOYMENT COMPENSATION LAW IN THE STATE AND COUNTIES OF FLORIDA, 2006

County	Number of reporting units	Number of employees	Payroll ($1,000)	County	Number of reporting units	Number of employees	Payroll ($1,000)
			Fishing, hunting, and trapping (NAICS code 114)				
Florida	182	512	1,283	Indian River	4	7	15
				Lee	35	81	201
Bay	3	3	8	Miami-Dade	10	16	49
Broward	4	3	10	Monroe	22	124	337
Citrus	3	8	12	Okaloosa	7	15	35
Duval	17	35	103	Pasco	7	14	14
Hillsborough	6	14	24	Pinellas	13	23	36

NAICS North American Industrial Classification System. See Glossary for definition.
Note: Private employment. For a list of four-digit code industries included see Table 10.34. Data are preliminary. Only counties for which data are disclosed are shown. Detail may not add to totals due to disclosure editing and/or rounding. See Tables 23.70, 23.72, 23.73, and 23.74 for public employment data.

Source: State of Florida, Agency for Workforce Innovation, Labor Market Statistics, "Quarterly Census of Employment and Wages" (ES-202), Annual NAICS files, Internet site <http://www.labormarketinfo.com/index.htm/> (accessed 17, July 2007).

Table 10.40. FISH AND SHELLFISH: QUANTITY OF LANDINGS BY TYPE OF SPECIES AND TRIPS IN THE STATE AND SPECIFIED COUNTIES OF FLORIDA, 2006

Area and county	Landings 1/ (pounds)			
	Total	Fish	Shellfish 2/	Trips 3/
Florida	94,133,863	49,238,805	44,895,058	206,826
East coast	26,796,095	13,681,829	12,972,686	65,203
West coast	67,329,275	35,440,105	31,875,010	141,591
Inland/out-of-state 4/	8,492	116,872	47,362	32
Bay	2,995,010	2,381,818	613,193	3,296
Brevard	4,740,645	1,954,548	2,786,098	11,042
Broward	996,221	413,533	582,688	2,377
Charlotte	1,460,685	993,015	467,670	4,545
Citrus	2,233,296	643,577	1,589,719	8,189
Clay	145,968	0	145,968	351
Collier	1,843,247	1,258,672	584,574	4,858
Dixie	496,880	140,589	356,291	2,072
Duval	6,517,592	1,276,092	5,241,500	6,560
Escambia	1,035,859	723,501	312,358	1,916
Flagler	66,374	46,145	20,229	139
Franklin	5,730,938	1,802,755	3,928,182	24,665
Gulf	6,779,454	5,342,323	1,437,131	2,069
Hernando	1,345,665	557,350	788,316	5,165
Hillsborough	2,363,070	755,188	1,607,882	3,072
Indian River	1,035,726	1,026,067	9,659	3,640
Lee	9,878,287	2,089,319	7,788,968	14,480
Levy	869,984	108,422	761,562	4,040
Manatee	3,117,951	2,875,807	242,144	3,502
Martin	2,444,744	2,391,396	53,347	5,473
Miami-Dade	2,349,672	775,774	1,573,898	7,949
Monroe	12,415,278	5,653,845	6,761,433	33,907
Nassau	943,898	68,671	875,228	819
Okaloosa	1,380,704	1,303,417	77,287	1,779
Palm Beach	1,979,045	1,906,852	72,193	8,937
Pasco	339,049	118,189	220,860	2,024
Pinellas	9,455,351	7,648,903	1,806,448	14,164
Putnam	445,068	48,622	396,446	1,484
St. Johns	936,074	367,522	568,551	2,920
St. Lucie	2,613,726	2,494,996	118,729	7,314
Santa Rosa	298,434	264,645	33,789	874
Sarasota	154,639	80,188	74,451	641
Taylor	286,017	34,450	251,567	1,342
Volusia	1,439,763	911,610	528,153	6,054
Wakulla	2,764,350	647,515	2,116,835	4,507
Walton	70,968	16,618	54,350	480
Out-of-state	164,234	116,872	47,362	180

1/ Based on whole weight of species with some exceptions, e.g. stone crab claws.
2/ Includes, hard clams, conchs, whelks, crabs, lobsters, octopus, oysters, scallops, sponges, squid, shrimp for food, and shrimp for bait.
3/ Only commercial fishing trips where seafood products were sold to wholesale and retail dealers.
4/ Seafood dealers residing in inland counties or out-of-state who reported commercial landings in Florida.
Note: Data are preliminary. Landings are usually recorded in county where products first crossed the shore.

Source: State of Florida, Fish and Wildlife Conservation Commission, Fish and Wildlife Research Institute, Marine Fisheries Information System, 2006 Annual Landings Summary, Internet site <http://myfwc.com/> (accessed 16, May 2007).

Table 10.60. MINERAL INDUSTRIES: ESTABLISHMENTS, EMPLOYMENT, PAYROLL, VALUE ADDED BY MINING, AND CAPITAL EXPENDITURE BY INDUSTRY IN FLORIDA, 2002

NAICS Code	Industry	Number of establishments: Total	Number of establishments: With 20 employees or more	All employees: Number	All employees: Payroll 1/ ($1,000)	Value added by mining ($1,000)	Capital expenditure ($1,000)
21	Mining	283	56	5,951	252,814	1,024,483	137,821
211	Oil and gas extraction	36	2	192	10,664	86,394	22,294
212	Mining (except oil and gas)	170	52	5,428	231,931	913,380	111,473
21231	Stone mining and quarrying	60	32	1,963	79,431	321,961	31,443
213	Support activities for mining	77	2	331	10,219	24,709	4,054

1/ For pay period including March 12. Industries with 100 employees or more are shown.
Note: The mining industries census is on a 5-year cycle collecting data for years ending in 2 and 7. Data are for the North American Industry Classification System (NAICS). See Glossary for definitions.

Table 10.61. MINERAL INDUSTRIES: CHARACTERISTICS OF MINERAL INDUSTRIES IN FLORIDA, 2002

(in thousands of dollars, except where indicated)

Item	2002
Companies 1/	236
Establishments during year (number)	283
0-19 employees	227
20-99 employees	44
100 employees or more	12
Employees for pay periods including March 12 (number)	5,951
Total compensation	329,386
Annual payroll	252,814
Annual fringe benefits not included in payroll	76,572
Production, development, and exploration workers (number)	4,924
Annual wages	204,382
Cost of supplies	676,287
Quantity of electricity purchased (1,000 kWh)	3,139,712
Cost of purchased communication services	2,161
Value of shipments and receipts	1,562,949
Value added by mining	1,024,483
Inventories, end of 2001	187,131
Inventories, end of 2002	209,152
Capital expenditure (except land and mineral rights)	137,821
For land and mineral rights 2/	41,891
Rental payments during year	43,554

kWh Kilowatt hour.
1/ A business organization consisting of one or more establishments under common ownership or control.
2/ Excludes mining service industries and natural gas liquids industries where data were not collected.
Note: The mining industries census is on a 5-year cycle collecting data for years ending in 2 and 7. Data are for the North American Industry Classification System (NAICS). See Glossary for definitions.

Source for Tables 10.60 and 10.61: U.S., Department of Commerce, Census Bureau, *2002 Economic Census: Mining,* Geographic Area Series EC02-21A-FL, issued May 2005, Internet site <http://www.census.gov/> (accessed 11, May 2007).

Table 10.71. NONFUEL MINERAL PRODUCTION: QUANTITY AND VALUE IN FLORIDA 2002 THROUGH 2004

(quantity in thousand metric tons; value in thousands of dollars)

Mineral	2002 Quantity	2002 Value	2003 Quantity	2003 Value	2004 A/ Quantity	2004 A/ Value
Total	(X)	2,030,000	(X)	2,070,000	(X)	2,320,000
Cement:						
Masonry	591	64,000	674	82,900	763	97,600
Portland	3,950	297,000	4,190	323,000	5,230	432,000
Clays, kaolin	32	3,370	31	3,250	31	3,280
Gemstones	(NA)	1	(NA)	1	(NA)	1
Peat	559	11,500	373	7,440	478	9,710
Sand and gravel:						
Construction	26,400	114,000	30,900	141,000	29,300	146,000
Industrial	645	8,640	624	7,270	679	8,520
Stone (crushed) 1/	97,700	573,000	97,100	587,000	105,000	675,000
Combined value 2/	(X)	963,000	(X)	918,000	(X)	945,000

(X) Not applicable.
(NA) Not available.
A/ Preliminary.
1/ Excludes certain stones; included with "Combined value."
2/ Includes minerals not listed separately.
Note: Production as measured by mine shipments, sales, or marketable production (including consumption by producers). Some data are estimated while other may be revised.

Source: U.S., Department of the Interior, U.S. Geological Survey, *The Minerals Yearbook, Volume II, Area Reports: Domestic,2004,* Internet site <http://minerals.usgs.gov/> (accessed 19, September 2007).

Table 10.72. MINING: AVERAGE MONTHLY PRIVATE REPORTING UNITS, EMPLOYMENT AND PAYROLL COVERED BY UNEMPLOYMENT COMPENSATION LAW BY INDUSTRY IN FLORIDA, 2006

Industry	Number of reporting units	Number of employees	Payroll ($1,000)
Mining	312	4,532	20,350
Oil and gas extraction	19	111	675
Mining, except oil and gas	175	3,961	17,473
Metal ore mining	3	203	1,371
Nonmetallic mineral mining and quarrying	172	3,758	16,102
Support activities for mining	118	460	2,202

NAICS North American Industry Classification System. See Glossary for definition.
Note: Private employment. Data are preliminary. Detail may not add to totals due to disclosure editing and/or rounding. See Tables 23.70, 23.72, 23.73, and 23.74 for public employment data.

Source: State of Florida, Agency for Workforce Innovation, Labor Market Statistics, "Quarterly Census of Employment and Wages" (ES-202), Annual NAICS files, Internet site <http://www.labormarketinfo.com/index.htm> (accessed 17, July 2007).

CONSTRUCTION

Private Construction Employment, 2006

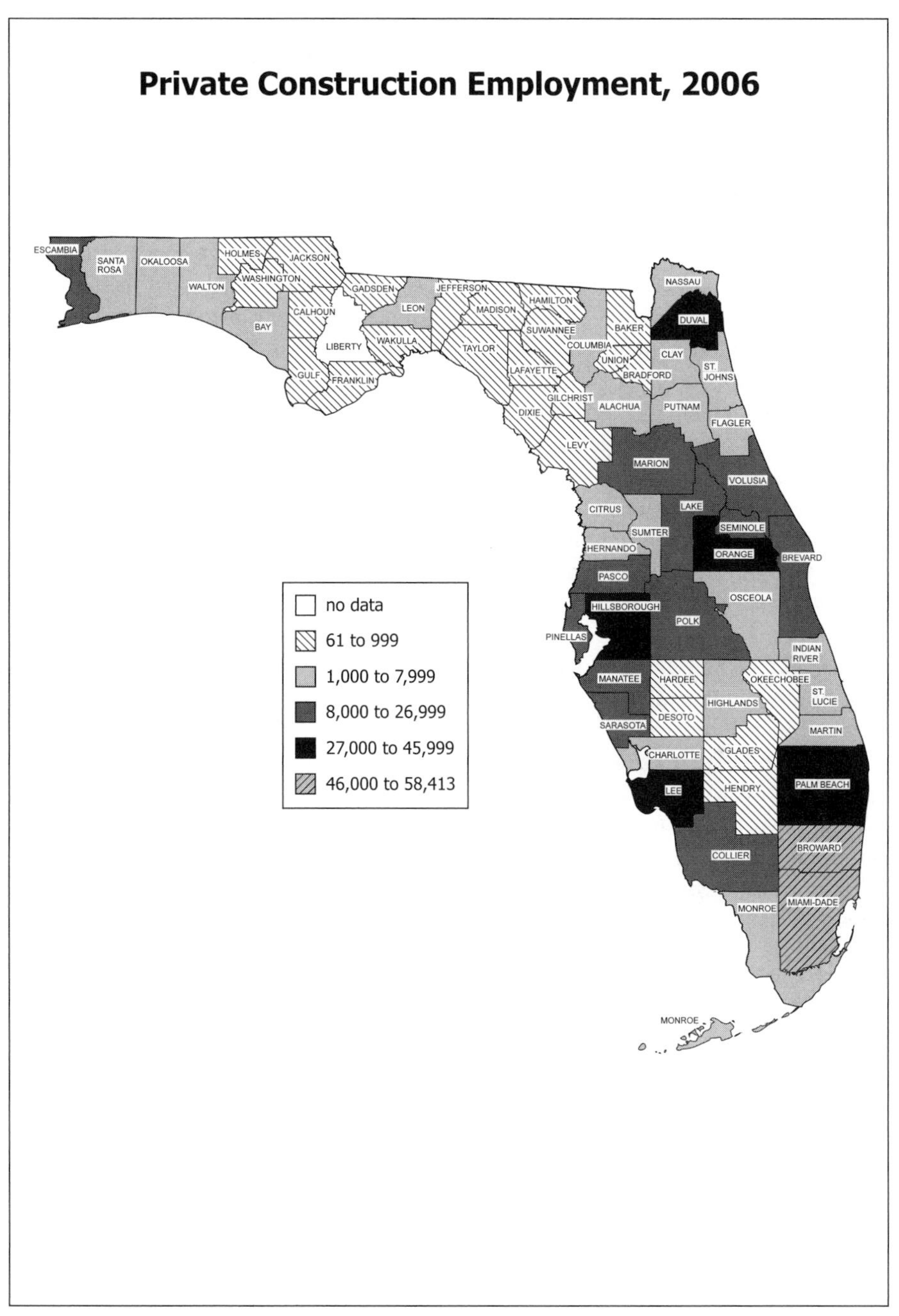

Source: Table 11.20

Section 11.00
Construction

This section focuses on Florida's various construction industry activity indicators: establishments, employment, and payroll; building permits and housing starts; and manufactured housing.

Explanatory notes. The U.S. Census Bureau conducts an economic census in years ending in "2" and "7." This section includes construction data from the 2002 economic census.

Establishment, employment, and payroll statistics for the building construction industry, and characteristics of that industry based on the North American Industry Classification System (NAICS), are in this section. Several tables present economic census and current construction industry data based on the NAICS system. (See introduction to Section 6.00 and the Glossary.)

Sources. The U.S. Census Bureau publishes employment and payroll data for construction-related establishments in the *2002 Economic Census: Construction* on their Web site. Current employment and payroll data for Florida and its counties by specified industry are from the Labor Market Statistics office of the Florida Agency for Workforce Innovation.

The principal sources of building permit data for Florida are the Bureau of Economic and Business Research (BEBR) at the University of Florida, which compiles and publishes data reported to the U.S. Census Bureau, and the U.S. Census Bureau. Florida and U.S. housing start data from the Census Bureau for new, privately owned units are published in the *Statistical Abstract of the United States*. The Census Bureau annually publishes private residential building permit data for states in *New Privately Owned Housing Units Authorized Unadjusted Units for Regions, Divisions, and States* on the Internet.

The Bureau of Economic and Business Research (BEBR) compiles and makes available Census Bureau annual county single- and multifamily construction start and building permit data. BEBR also publishes monthly and annual summaries of data provided by the Census Bureau on the type and value of building permits for construction issued by local administrative offices throughout Florida in *Building Permit Activity in Florida*.

Data on manufactured home placements and average sales prices for Florida, other states, and the United States featured in Table 11.26 are available on the Census Bureau's Web site.

Section 11.00
Construction

Tables listed by major heading

Table 11.01. CONSTRUCTION: ESTABLISHMENTS, EMPLOYMENT, AND PAYROLL IN FLORIDA, 2002

NAICS code	Industry	Number of establishments	Number of employees 1/ Total	Number of employees 1/ Construction workers (percentage)	Payroll ($1,000) Amount	Payroll ($1,000) Construction workers (percentage)
23	Construction	40,830	424,868	70.9	13,252,374	62.4
236	Construction of buildings	10,775	95,083	54.3	3,626,554	42.7
2361	Residential building construction	8,816	60,553	51.5	2,228,326	40.6
2362	Nonresidential building construction	1,959	34,530	59.1	1,398,228	46.1
237	Heavy and civil engineering construction	2,776	61,530	73.0	2,028,854	62.4
2371	Utility system construction	965	23,576	73.8	840,405	64.3
2372	Land subdivision	822	5,664	35.9	242,892	27.8
2373	Highway, street, and bridge construction	444	24,767	80.1	700,745	70.6
2379	Other heavy and civil engineering construction	545	7,523	75.3	244,812	67.0
238	Specialty trade contractors	27,279	268,255	76.3	7,596,965	71.7
2381	Foundation, structure, and building exterior contractors	6,131	72,763	80.7	1,838,487	72.1
2382	Building equipment contractors	8,920	110,381	75.4	3,548,900	72.4
2383	Building finishing contractors	8,200	52,909	74.0	1,347,258	71.3
2389	Other specialty trade contractors	4,028	32,202	72.8	862,320	68.7

1/ Paid employment for the pay period including March 12.

Note: The economic censuses are conducted on a 5-year cycle collecting data for years ending in 2 and 7. Data are for North American Industry Classification System (NAICS) code 23 and may not be comparable to earlier years. See Glossary for definition.

Table 11.02. CONSTRUCTION: VALUE OF CONSTRUCTION WORK FOR SPECIFIED ESTABLISHMENTS BY TYPE OF CONSTRUCTION IN FLORIDA, 2002

(in thousands of dollars)

Type of construction	Total	New construction	Additions, alterations, or reconstruction	Maintenance and repair
Total	78,720,223	59,304,061	12,725,345	6,690,817
Building construction, total	59,719,745	44,547,420	10,045,487	5,126,839
Single-family houses, detached and attached	29,187,830	24,210,999	2,899,670	2,077,161
Apartment buildings 1/ (2 or more units)	6,146,849	5,171,909	505,830	469,110
Office buildings	5,064,215	2,780,406	1,776,191	507,618
Commercial buildings 2/	5,084,915	3,179,910	1,177,869	727,136
Nonbuilding construction, total	16,065,853	11,822,016	2,679,858	1,563,979
Highways, streets, and related work	3,491,266	2,166,899	991,219	333,149
Sewers, water mains, and related facilities	2,310,009	1,710,105	338,730	261,173

1/ Includes rentals, apartment type condominiums, and cooperatives.

2/ Includes stores, restaurants, automobile service stations, and other commercial buildings except warehouses and mini-storage.

Note: Totals includes establishments not listed separately.

Source for Tables 11.01 and 11.02: U.S., Department of Commerce, Census Bureau, *2002 Economic Census: Construction,* Geographic Area Series EC02-23A-FL, issued September 2005, Internet site <http://www.census.gov/> (accessed 11, May 2007).

Table 11.03. HOUSING STARTS: NEW PRIVATELY OWNED HOUSING UNITS STARTED IN FLORIDA AND THE UNITED STATES, 1995 THROUGH 2006

(in thousands)

Year	Florida	United States	Year	Florida	United States
1995	123.4	1,354.1	2002	177.0	1,704.9
1996	129.1	1,476.8	2003	197.3	1,847.7
1997	135.2	1,474.0	2004	185.7	1,955.8
1998	143.9	1,616.9	2005	173.6	2,068.3
1999	152.8	1,640.9	2006		
2000	147.9	1,568.7	Total units	165.4	1,801.6
2001	161.2	1,602.7	Single-family units	123.7	1,465.6

Note: Data from 1997-2006 have been revised.
Source: U.S., Department of Commerce, Census Bureau, *Statistical Abstract of the United States, 2007,* and previous editions.

Table 11.04. BUILDING PERMIT ACTIVITY: PRIVATE RESIDENTIAL HOUSING UNITS AUTHORIZED BY BUILDING PERMITS IN FLORIDA, OTHER SUNBELT STATES, OTHER POPULOUS STATES, AND THE UNITED STATES, 2002 THROUGH 2006

State	2002	2003	2004	2005	2006
Florida	185,431	213,567	255,893	287,250	203,238
Other sunbelt states					
Alabama 1/	18,403	22,256	27,411	30,612	32,034
Arizona	66,031	74,996	90,644	90,851	65,363
Arkansas 1/	12,436	14,839	15,855	17,932	13,885
California	159,573	191,948	207,390	205,020	160,502
Georgia	97,523	96,704	108,356	109,336	104,200
Louisiana	18,425	22,220	22,989	22,811	28,671
Mississippi 1/	11,276	12,010	14,532	13,396	16,618
New Mexico	12,066	13,759	12,555	14,180	13,573
North Carolina	79,824	79,226	93,077	97,910	99,979
Oklahoma 1/	12,979	14,968	17,068	18,362	15,840
South Carolina	34,104	38,191	43,230	54,157	50,776
Tennessee 1/	34,273	37,530	44,791	46,615	46,003
Texas 1/	165,027	177,194	188,842	210,611	216,642
Virginia	59,445	55,936	63,220	61,518	47,704
Other populous states					
Illinois	60,971	62,211	59,753	66,942	58,802
Indiana	39,596	39,421	39,233	38,476	29,069
Massachusetts	17,465	20,257	22,477	24,549	19,580
Michigan	49,968	53,913	54,721	45,328	29,191
New Jersey	30,441	32,984	35,936	38,588	34,323
New York	49,149	49,708	53,497	61,949	54,382
Ohio	51,246	53,041	51,695	47,727	34,422
Pennsylvania	45,114	47,356	49,665	44,525	39,128
United States	1,747,678	1,889,214	2,070,077	2,155,316	1,838,903

1/ Percentage of population in permit-issuing places is less than 90.
Note: Data for 2003 and earlier are based on a national sample of 8,500 permit-issuing places selected from a universe of 19,000 such places. Starting in 2004, the data are derived from a sample of 9,000 permit-issuing places selected from a universe of 20,000 such places. See also Table 24.20.
Source: U.S., Department of Commerce, Census Bureau, *New Privately Owned Housing Units Authorized Unadjusted Units for Regions, Divisions, and States, Annual 2006,* Internet site <http://www.census.gov/> (accessed 14, May 2007).

Table 11.05. CONSTRUCTION ACTIVITY: SINGLE- AND MULTIFAMILY HOUSING UNITS PERMITTED AND CONSTRUCTION STARTS IN THE STATE AND COUNTIES OF FLORIDA 2005 AND 2006

	Single-family housing units				Multifamily housing units			
	Permitted		Construction starts		Permitted		Construction starts	
County	2005	2006	2005	2006	2005	2006	2005	2006
Florida	200,832	144,455	195,246	145,282	72,046	55,403	67,219	45,584
Alachua	1,345	1,037	1,320	1,019	637	780	625	553
Baker	279	227	264	226	0	0	3	0
Bay	1,324	902	1,388	864	3,322	2,962	2,931	2,615
Bradford	0	0	10	0	0	0	0	0
Brevard	6,420	4,311	6,165	4,347	1,556	1,190	1,452	1,037
Broward	3,451	3,119	3,340	3,087	2,919	3,573	3,540	2,428
Calhoun	47	45	44	40	0	0	0	0
Charlotte	2,852	2,462	2,747	2,459	1,164	1,175	1,063	937
Citrus	2,620	2,979	2,488	2,774	2	0	1	0
Clay	3,830	1,338	3,887	1,448	281	1,075	309	732
Collier	4,040	2,828	3,871	2,927	2,301	1,959	2,071	1,478
Columbia	484	464	466	443	66	6	61	16
DeSoto	0	0	11	0	0	0	0	0
Dixie	0	0	4	0	0	0	0	0
Duval	8,433	6,448	8,091	6,458	5,510	3,633	4,985	3,130
Escambia	1,969	1,215	1,926	1,205	484	567	554	372
Flagler	3,334	1,499	3,439	1,641	650	352	601	296
Franklin	27	10	52	9	2	0	1	0
Gadsden	250	382	224	361	0	0	0	0
Gilchrist	101	92	100	90	0	0	0	0
Glades	69	73	67	70	0	0	0	0
Gulf	0	0	22	0	0	0	0	0
Hamilton	42	38	43	33	0	0	0	0
Hardee	91	229	88	210	41	5	58	3
Hendry	66	66	76	65	0	2	0	0
Hernando	3,877	2,862	3,716	2,898	226	275	185	195
Highlands	1,200	1,369	1,105	1,239	23	63	38	46
Hillsborough	12,440	8,639	12,481	8,534	2,872	2,681	2,945	1,889
Holmes	0	0	4	0	0	0	0	0
Indian River	3,590	2,841	3,243	2,998	340	304	455	213
Jackson	195	179	188	167	0	2	0	0
Jefferson	116	100	110	94	8	0	7	0
Lafayette	28	25	27	24	0	0	0	0
Lake	5,678	5,567	5,521	5,305	316	480	346	331
Lee	22,200	14,501	21,910	14,648	6,610	3,622	5,576	3,547

See footnote at end of table. Continued . . .

Table 11.05. CONSTRUCTION ACTIVITY: SINGLE- AND MULTIFAMILY HOUSING UNITS PERMITTED AND CONSTRUCTION STARTS IN THE STATE AND COUNTIES OF FLORIDA 2005 AND 2006 (Continued)

	Single-family housing units				Multifamily housing units			
	Permitted		Construction starts		Permitted		Construction starts	
County	2005	2006	2005	2006	2005	2006	2005	2006
Leon	1,528	1,504	1,448	1,423	1,335	1,354	1,110	1,084
Levy	40	25	68	23	0	27	0	16
Liberty	21	14	19	15	0	0	0	0
Madison	13	13	18	12	0	0	0	0
Manatee	4,740	3,284	4,604	3,280	1,368	915	1,325	895
Marion	6,542	6,770	6,380	6,503	841	320	691	400
Martin	1,121	941	1,113	887	886	38	698	173
Miami-Dade	8,961	6,798	8,701	6,851	12,911	10,180	12,882	8,043
Monroe	428	299	405	314	30	25	23	17
Nassau	1,404	971	1,379	994	51	252	50	145
Okaloosa	1,257	1,056	1,338	1,028	1,297	649	1,080	627
Okeechobee	0	0	17	0	0	0	0	0
Orange	10,694	9,511	10,357	9,396	6,533	4,241	5,120	3,539
Osceola	5,820	5,629	5,866	5,200	2,169	2,238	2,195	1,631
Palm Beach	9,535	4,439	9,507	4,732	4,653	3,911	3,978	3,355
Pasco	8,046	5,029	7,451	5,400	1,794	873	1,992	617
Pinellas	2,787	1,812	2,734	1,839	1,161	390	1,000	513
Polk	10,061	7,760	9,255	7,992	1,208	1,758	1,307	1,273
Putnam	20	28	43	27	40	59	58	30
St. Johns	4,754	2,511	4,637	2,689	974	513	1,064	459
St. Lucie	7,879	4,636	7,832	4,716	886	730	883	581
Santa Rosa	1,332	923	1,229	974	22	4	24	2
Sarasota	7,004	3,417	6,740	3,761	1,264	779	1,348	726
Seminole	3,712	2,690	3,649	2,690	358	13	291	83
Sumter	5,033	3,577	4,422	3,858	0	10	4	12
Suwannee	14	8	31	6	4	0	1	2
Taylor	89	77	85	73	16	0	13	1
Union	46	68	41	66	0	0	0	0
Volusia	5,197	3,132	5,183	3,140	1,786	1,032	1,344	1,134
Wakulla	675	571	621	586	0	0	1	0
Walton	1,681	1,115	1,619	1,124	1,129	386	930	408
Washington	0	0	16	0	0	0	0	0

Note: Permits are issued by local reporting agencies and may be pulled and not used, or renewed after expiration. Construction starts can be for permits issued any time within a 12-month period. These data are compiled using monthly reports. Some counties do not report monthly and only report annually as shown in Table 11.15. Construction starts are calculated using a monthly ratio of starts-to-permits. Because of a difference in methodology between the annual survey depicted in Table 11.15 and the aggregation of the monthly surveys presented here, and the absence of annual start-to-permit ratios, these data are not comparable to those presented in Table 11.15.

Source: University of Florida, Bureau of Economic and Business Research (BEBR), unpublished data.

Table 11.15. BUILDING PERMIT ACTIVITY: VALUE REPORTED ON BUILDING PERMITS AND NEW HOUSING UNITS AUTHORIZED BY BUILDING PERMITS IN THE STATE, COUNTIES MUNICIPALITIES, AND UNINCORPORATED AREAS OF FLORIDA, 2006

Area 1/	Number of months reported	Total residential value ($1,000)	Number of housekeeping units 2/ Single-family	Multifamily
Florida	(X)	35,716,293	146,236	57,002
Alachua	(X)	211,058	1,009	940
Alachua	12	13,018	116	2
Gainesville	7	52,222	147	576
Newberry	0	2,472	12	0
Waldo	12	0	0	0
Unincorporated area	12	143,347	734	362
Baker	(X)	30,991	226	0
Macclenny	12	11,907	119	0
Unincorporated area	12	19,085	107	0
Bay	(X)	379,634	920	2,156
Callaway	0	8,681	67	2
Lynn Haven	12	13,709	84	0
Mexico Beach	12	1,486	7	0
Panama City Beach	12	183,731	51	1,346
Unincorporated area	12	172,027	711	808
Bradford	(X)	9,607	124	0
County office	12	9,607	124	0
Brevard	(X)	988,009	3,967	1,077
Cape Canaveral	12	9,629	14	28
Cocoa	11	9,132	57	0
Cocoa Beach	12	11,618	19	15
Indialantic	12	649	2	0
Indian Harbour Beach	10	3,704	6	13
Malabar	12	10,417	28	0
Melbourne	12	76,091	315	197
Melbourne Beach	12	690	2	0
Melbourne Village	12	1,071	3	0
Palm Bay	12	347,803	1,764	7
Palm Shores	12	150	1	0
Rockledge	11	42,102	97	244
Satellite Beach	12	12,997	40	0
Titusville	12	42,566	288	72
West Melbourne	12	35,102	142	0
Unincorporated area	12	384,289	1,189	501
Broward	(X)	988,266	3,550	3,166
Coconut Creek	12	27,907	132	0
Cooper City	12	232	1	0
Coral Springs	12	14,695	76	22
Dania Beach	12	20,029	103	24
Davie	0	73,058	510	71
Deerfield Beach	12	19,820	138	0
Ft. Lauderdale	12	139,727	289	1,021
Hallandale Beach	11	28,142	12	181
Hillsboro Beach	12	0	0	0
Hollywood	12	17,969	69	106
Lauderdale Lakes	0	0	0	0
Lauderhill	12	12,880	163	0
Lighthouse Point	12	20,565	110	0
Margate	10	853	10	0
Miramar	12	167,962	397	566

See footnotes at end of table. Continued . . .

Table 11.15. BUILDING PERMIT ACTIVITY: VALUE REPORTED ON BUILDING PERMITS AND NEW HOUSING UNITS AUTHORIZED BY BUILDING PERMITS IN THE STATE, COUNTIES MUNICIPALITIES, AND UNINCORPORATED AREAS OF FLORIDA, 2006 (Continued)

Area 1/	Number of months reported	Total residential value ($1,000)	Number of housekeeping units 2/ Single-family	Multifamily
Broward (Continued)				
North Lauderdale	12	15,176	243	0
Oakland Park	12	25,397	166	0
Parkland	12	129,365	326	56
Pembroke Park	12	0	0	0
Pembroke Pines	12	13,550	5	103
Plantation	12	57,016	38	201
Pompano Beach	12	56,988	334	178
Sea Ranch Lakes	12	0	0	0
Sunrise	12	77,706	18	500
Tamarac	11	37,314	254	26
Weston	12	1,663	11	0
Wilton Manors	12	9,308	19	50
Unincorporated area	0	20,947	126	61
Calhoun	(X)	5,131	40	0
Blountstown	12	0	0	0
Unincorporated area	12	5,131	40	0
Charlotte	(X)	840,057	3,052	1,283
Punta Gorda	12	52,653	67	174
Unincorporated area	12	787,405	2,985	1,109
Citrus	(X)	391,293	2,056	41
Crystal River	12	2,013	10	3
Inverness	12	6,307	54	4
Unincorporated area	12	382,973	1,992	34
Clay	(X)	354,867	1,336	1,076
Green Cove Springs	12	9,650	55	0
Orange Park	12	1,191	6	4
Penney Farms	12	678	6	0
Unincorporated area	12	343,348	1,269	1,072
Collier	(X)	1,228,774	2,829	1,959
Everglades	12	3,474	15	0
Marco Island	12	44,680	73	0
Naples	12	172,266	96	48
Unincorporated area	12	1,008,355	2,645	1,911
Columbia	(X)	46,108	467	6
Lake City	12	9,354	91	6
Unincorporated area	5	36,754	376	0
DeSoto	(X)	30,552	167	20
County office	12	30,552	167	20
Dixie	(X)	10,597	71	12
Horseshoe Beach	0	3,746	14	12
Unincorporated area	12	6,850	57	0
Duval	(X)	1,280,636	6,450	3,633
Atlantic Beach	12	18,480	58	0
Baldwin	12	669	8	0
Jacksonville	12	1,215,167	6,291	3,521
Jacksonville Beach	12	39,947	74	112
Neptune Beach	12	6,374	19	0
Escambia	(X)	276,424	1,218	666
Pensacola	12	20,429	104	0
Unincorporated area	12	255,994	1,114	666

See footnotes at end of table. Continued . . .

Table 11.15. BUILDING PERMIT ACTIVITY: VALUE REPORTED ON BUILDING PERMITS AND NEW HOUSING UNITS AUTHORIZED BY BUILDING PERMITS IN THE STATE, COUNTIES MUNICIPALITIES, AND UNINCORPORATED AREAS OF FLORIDA, 2006 (Continued)

Area 1/	Number of months reported	Total residential value ($1,000)	Number of housekeeping units 2/ Single-family	Multifamily
Flagler	(X)	491,109	1,499	340
Beverly Beach	0	220	1	0
Bunnell	12	494	5	0
Flagler Beach	0	0	0	0
Marineland	0	50	1	0
Palm Coast	12	381,124	1,283	298
Unincorporated area	11	109,222	209	42
Franklin	(X)	47,275	225	0
Apalachicola	12	867	6	0
Unincorporated area	0	46,408	219	0
Gadsden	(X)	70,254	458	0
Gretna	12	0	0	0
Midway	12	38,892	289	0
Quincy	0	0	0	0
Unincorporated area	12	31,363	169	0
Gilchrist	(X)	11,777	92	0
Trenton	0	11,777	92	0
Unincorporated area	0	0	0	0
Glades	(X)	10,992	73	0
Moore Haven	0	0	0	0
Unincorporated area	0	0	0	0
Gulf	(X)	44,370	235	0
County office	12	44,370	235	0
Hamilton	(X)	4,858	40	0
County office	12	4,858	40	0
Hardee	(X)	19,145	216	0
County office	12	19,145	216	0
Hendry	(X)	38,257	282	2
Clewiston	12	5,343	66	2
LaBelle	12	2,196	12	0
Unincorporated area	12	30,717	204	0
Hernando	(X)	616,500	2,862	275
Brooksville	10	31,300	68	176
Weeki Wachee	12	2,144	8	0
Unincorporated area	12	583,057	2,786	99
Highlands	(X)	257,722	1,415	125
Avon Park	1	2,201	7	25
Sebring	12	19,865	60	69
Unincorporated area	12	235,656	1,348	31
Hillsborough	(X)	1,723,725	8,639	2,815
Plant City	12	46,087	328	15
Tampa	12	383,997	1,940	985
Temple Terrace	12	18,504	97	0
Unincorporated area	12	1,275,137	6,274	1,815
Holmes	(X)	13,181	97	0
Holmes	12	13,181	97	0
Indian River	(X)	723,207	2,839	304
Fellsmere	12	5,384	23	0
Indian River Shores	12	31,366	28	0
Orchid	12	4,058	3	0
Sebastian	12	62,848	317	6
Unincorporated area	12	619,550	2,468	298

See footnotes at end of table.

Continued . . .

Table 11.15. BUILDING PERMIT ACTIVITY: VALUE REPORTED ON BUILDING PERMITS AND NEW HOUSING UNITS AUTHORIZED BY BUILDING PERMITS IN THE STATE, COUNTIES MUNICIPALITIES, AND UNINCORPORATED AREAS OF FLORIDA, 2006 (Continued)

Area 1/	Number of months reported	Total residential value ($1,000)	Number of housekeeping units 2/ Single-family	Multifamily
Jackson	(X)	26,185	179	2
County office	12	26,185	179	2
Jefferson	(X)	15,144	100	0
County office	12	15,144	100	0
Lafayette	(X)	4,430	26	0
County office	12	4,430	26	0
Lake	(X)	949,786	5,637	472
Eustis	12	52,569	210	102
Fruitland Park	12	22,438	83	4
Groveland	12	102,431	479	0
Howey-in-the-Hills	12	1,646	6	0
Lady Lake	12	8,028	54	0
Leesburg	12	131,278	471	194
Mascotte	5	24,061	100	0
Minneola	12	8,578	35	0
Mount Dora	12	51,273	199	0
Tavares	12	48,382	264	24
Umatilla	0	0	0	0
Unincorporated area	0	499,100	3,736	148
Lee	(X)	3,732,955	14,700	4,046
Bonita Springs	12	277,607	747	329
Cape Coral	12	465,099	3,727	770
Ft. Myers	12	513,424	1,435	1,188
Ft. Myers Beach	12	32,953	18	64
Sanibel	12	11,949	16	0
Unincorporated area	12	2,431,922	8,757	1,695
Leon	(X)	269,158	1,301	588
Tallahassee	12	174,723	804	588
Unincorporated area	12	94,435	497	0
Levy	(X)	45,161	275	3
Cedar Key	12	1,733	6	0
Chiefland	12	411	3	0
Otter Creek	0	0	0	0
Williston	12	2,568	13	0
Unincorporated area	12	40,449	253	3
Liberty	(X)	2,801	22	0
Bristol	11	85	1	0
Unincorporated area	12	2,716	21	0
Madison	(X)	11,522	89	0
Lee	12	85	1	0
Madison	0	417	12	0
Unincorporated area	12	11,020	76	0
Manatee	(X)	801,138	2,565	1,001
Anna Maria	12	2,420	5	0
Bradenton	12	51,778	221	38
Bradenton Beach	0	5,253	1	25
Holmes Beach	12	8,762	25	0
Palmetto	12	76,123	51	197
Unincorporated area	12	656,803	2,262	741
Marion	(X)	1,060,228	6,753	310
Belleview	12	12,165	56	46
Dunnellon	12	3,606	20	0

See footnotes at end of table.

Continued . . .

Table 11.15. BUILDING PERMIT ACTIVITY: VALUE REPORTED ON BUILDING PERMITS AND NEW HOUSING UNITS AUTHORIZED BY BUILDING PERMITS IN THE STATE, COUNTIES MUNICIPALITIES, AND UNINCORPORATED AREAS OF FLORIDA, 2006 (Continued)

Area 1/	Number of months reported	Total residential value ($1,000)	Number of housekeeping units 2/ Single-family	Multifamily
Marion (Continued)				
Ocala	12	112,019	612	192
Unincorporated area	12	932,438	6,065	72
Martin	(X)	278,219	936	28
Jupiter Island	12	22,796	15	0
Ocean Breeze Park	12	0	0	0
Sewall's Point	12	5,014	5	0
Stuart	12	2,578	8	8
Unincorporated area	12	247,831	908	20
Miami-Dade	(X)	3,323,113	6,548	13,469
Aventura	11	25,544	4	179
Bal Harbour	12	4,975	3	0
Bay Harbor Islands	12	13,625	3	60
Biscayne Park	12	0	0	0
Coral Gables	12	65,165	63	153
Doral	12	163,622	475	602
El Portal	8	560	2	0
Florida City	11	19,187	143	0
Golden Beach	0	383	1	0
Hialeah	12	23,756	12	231
Hialeah Gardens	12	15,090	101	64
Homestead	12	212,160	991	662
Indian Creek	12	0	0	0
Islandia	0	0	0	0
Key Biscayne	0	2,142	16	0
Medley	12	900	6	0
Miami	12	1,278,778	133	7,348
Miami Beach	0	71,494	23	285
Miami Lakes	0	13,007	65	0
Miami Shores	12	0	0	0
Miami Springs	12	1,225	5	0
North Bay Village	12	15,260	1	52
North Miami	12	1,018	3	3
North Miami Beach	0	11,831	84	0
Opa-locka	12	6,028	38	37
Palmetto Bay	12	8,710	27	0
South Miami	4	7,456	19	0
Sunny Isles Beach	12	547,558	1	1,349
Surfside	0	0	0	0
Sweetwater	12	750	4	0
Village of Pinecrest	12	47,022	61	0
Virginia Gardens	0	0	0	0
West Miami	12	0	0	0
Unincorporated area	12	765,870	4,264	2,444
Monroe	(X)	93,785	430	27
Islamorada Village of Islands	12	26,367	99	0
Key Colony Beach	12	7,865	8	5
Key West	0	6,447	30	0
Layton	12	200	1	0
Marathon	12	24,705	96	8
Unincorporated area	0	28,202	196	14

See footnotes at end of table.

Continued . . .

Table 11.15. BUILDING PERMIT ACTIVITY: VALUE REPORTED ON BUILDING PERMITS AND NEW HOUSING UNITS AUTHORIZED BY BUILDING PERMITS IN THE STATE, COUNTIES MUNICIPALITIES, AND UNINCORPORATED AREAS OF FLORIDA, 2006 (Continued)

Area 1/	Number of months reported	Total residential value ($1,000)	Number of housekeeping units 2/ Single-family	Multifamily
Nassau	(X)	258,619	986	250
Callahan	9	2,461	21	0
Fernandina Beach	12	28,474	158	0
Hilliard	12	651	6	0
Unincorporated area	12	227,033	801	250
Okaloosa	(X)	283,616	1,699	91
Crestview	12	83,032	692	0
Destin	12	35,783	166	3
Ft. Walton Beach	12	7,446	34	17
Niceville	12	20,623	83	26
Valparaiso	12	1,770	11	0
Unincorporated area	12	134,962	713	45
Okeechobee	(X)	20,472	202	0
Okeechobee	12	5,788	33	0
Unincorporated area	0	14,685	169	0
Orange	(X)	2,341,794	9,527	4,619
Apopka	12	177,636	754	130
Bay Lake	12	0	0	0
Eatonville	12	779	8	0
Edgewood	3	0	0	0
Lake Buena Vista	12	0	0	0
Maitland	12	47,648	48	219
Ocoee	12	136,145	556	0
Orlando	12	568,563	1,563	2,790
Winter Garden	12	153,110	865	0
Winter Park	12	64,174	112	6
Unincorporated area	12	1,193,740	5,621	1,474
Osceola	(X)	1,498,452	5,772	2,234
Kissimmee	12	61,553	397	2
St. Cloud	12	235,020	1,310	0
Unincorporated area	12	1,201,879	4,065	2,232
Palm Beach	(X)	2,017,000	4,652	3,725
Atlantis	12	770	2	0
Belle Glade	12	2,669	22	2
Boca Raton	12	82,427	55	247
Boynton Beach	12	75,211	453	7
Briny Breezes	12	0	0	0
Cloud Lake	5	0	0	0
Delray Beach	12	67,958	116	264
Glen Ridge	0	0	0	0
Golf	12	6,348	30	0
Greenacres	12	43,003	276	0
Haverhill	12	196	1	0
Highland Beach	12	1,199	1	0
Hypoluxo	12	0	0	0
Juno Beach	1	0	0	0
Jupiter Inlet Colony	11	2,011	3	0
Jupiter	12	133,326	313	159
Lake Clarke Shores	12	1,619	3	0
Lake Park	12	0	0	0
Lake Worth	12	17,039	40	94
Lantana	12	291	2	0

See footnotes at end of table. Continued . . .

Table 11.15. BUILDING PERMIT ACTIVITY: VALUE REPORTED ON BUILDING PERMITS AND NEW HOUSING UNITS AUTHORIZED BY BUILDING PERMITS IN THE STATE, COUNTIES MUNICIPALITIES, AND UNINCORPORATED AREAS OF FLORIDA, 2006 (Continued)

Area 1/	Number of months reported	Total residential value ($1,000)	Number of housekeeping units 2/ Single-family	Multifamily
Palm Beach (Continued)				
Manalapan	12	10,416	4	0
Mangonia Park	12	0	0	0
North Palm Beach	12	146	1	0
Ocean Ridge	12	3,410	4	0
Pahokee	0	2,015	36	0
Palm Beach Gardens	2	138,493	224	274
Palm Beach Shores	12	29,071	0	77
Palm Beach	0	39,435	26	7
Palm Springs	12	7,493	69	2
Riviera Beach	12	252,238	275	432
Royal Palm Beach	12	6,184	51	0
South Bay	7	0	0	0
South Palm Beach	12	0	0	0
Tequesta	11	6,488	27	0
Wellington	12	95,089	224	0
West Palm Beach	12	270,406	131	1,177
Unincorporated area	12	722,046	2,263	983
Pasco	(X)	966,491	5,007	862
Dade City	12	4,064	37	6
New Port Richey	12	5,571	47	0
Port Richey	12	4,996	11	0
St. Leo	12	483	2	0
San Antonio	12	5,873	12	0
Zephyrhills	12	10,858	107	4
Unincorporated area	12	934,646	4,791	852
Pinellas	(X)	471,088	1,786	394
Belleair	10	3,995	6	0
Clearwater	12	19,672	108	2
Dunedin	12	15,145	36	6
Gulfport	12	8,914	30	0
Indian Rocks Beach	0	0	0	0
Indian Shores	12	15,069	1	27
Kenneth City	12	417	12	0
Largo	12	30,008	36	134
Oldsmar	12	4,048	25	0
Pinellas Park	12	31,902	213	5
Redington Shores	12	10,351	21	0
Safety Harbor	12	3,130	22	0
Seminole	12	13,308	49	0
South Pasadena	12	900	3	3
St. Pete Beach	12	6,840	15	0
St. Petersburg	12	108,414	496	164
Tarpon Springs	12	71,353	337	0
Treasure Island	12	6,465	5	16
Unincorporated area	12	121,157	371	37
Polk	(X)	1,116,655	7,609	1,714
Auburndale	12	55,769	292	40
Bartow	12	26,841	173	0
Davenport	12	15,242	86	0
Dundee	0	5,326	44	0
Eagle Lake	12	3,628	26	0

See footnotes at end of table.

Continued . . .

Table 11.15. BUILDING PERMIT ACTIVITY: VALUE REPORTED ON BUILDING PERMITS AND NEW HOUSING UNITS AUTHORIZED BY BUILDING PERMITS IN THE STATE, COUNTIES MUNICIPALITIES, AND UNINCORPORATED AREAS OF FLORIDA, 2006 (Continued)

Area 1/	Number of months reported	Total residential value ($1,000)	Number of housekeeping units 2/	
			Single-family	Multifamily
Polk (Continued)				
Ft. Meade	10	2,705	22	0
Frostproof	7	140	2	0
Haines City	12	70,145	441	0
Lake Alfred	12	14,210	64	0
Lake Hamilton	12	353	3	0
Lake Wales	12	14,733	103	0
Lakeland	12	201,299	844	851
Mulberry	12	296	3	0
Polk City	10	2,184	10	6
Winter Haven	12	134,400	684	350
Unincorporated area	12	569,385	4,812	467
Putnam	(X)	42,869	282	57
Palatka	12	2,043	16	0
Welaka	12	7,499	16	57
Unincorporated area	0	33,326	250	0
St. Johns	(X)	756,657	2,502	508
St. Augustine	12	10,623	34	44
St. Augustine Beach	12	18,548	76	0
Unincorporated area	12	727,486	2,392	464
St. Lucie	(X)	670,852	4,636	728
Ft. Pierce	7	77,539	216	325
Port St. Lucie	12	512,569	4,067	116
Unincorporated area	12	80,745	353	287
Santa Rosa	(X)	142,483	923	4
County office	12	142,483	923	4
Sarasota	(X)	746,309	3,418	687
Longboat Key	12	28,188	10	17
North Port	12	281,455	2,094	122
Sarasota	12	51,001	111	14
Venice	12	53,594	140	142
Unincorporated area	12	332,070	1,063	392
Seminole	(X)	547,708	2,710	13
Altamonte Springs	9	2,123	9	7
Casselberry	12	35,979	183	0
Lake Mary	12	33,349	214	0
Longwood	12	14,406	69	0
Oviedo	12	49,572	169	0
Sanford	12	95,619	825	6
Winter Springs	12	47,357	274	0
Unincorporated area	12	269,303	967	0
Sumter	(X)	563,367	3,558	18
Wildwood	12	9,772	60	18
Unincorporated area	12	553,595	3,498	0
Suwannee	(X)	31,005	172	102
Live Oak	11	5,090	7	102
Unincorporated area	12	25,915	165	0
Taylor	(X)	12,278	75	0
Perry	8	2,437	17	0
Unincorporated area	12	9,841	58	0

See footnotes at end of table.

Continued . . .

Table 11.15. BUILDING PERMIT ACTIVITY: VALUE REPORTED ON BUILDING PERMITS AND NEW HOUSING UNITS AUTHORIZED BY BUILDING PERMITS IN THE STATE, COUNTIES MUNICIPALITIES, AND UNINCORPORATED AREAS OF FLORIDA, 2006 (Continued)

Area 1/	Number of months reported	Total residential value ($1,000)	Number of housekeeping units 2/ Single-family	Multifamily
Union	(X)	7,783	71	0
County office	12	7,783	71	0
Volusia	(X)	808,785	2,906	909
Daytona Beach	12	85,321	363	10
Daytona Beach Shores	12	59,215	1	161
De Land	12	85,238	458	32
Deltona	12	108,058	512	0
Edgewater	12	12,412	103	0
Holly Hill	12	2,964	20	6
Lake Helen	12	4,039	15	0
New Smyrna Beach	0	45,673	118	283
Oak Hill	12	1,159	10	0
Orange City	12	34,568	60	96
Ormond Beach	12	37,657	115	0
Pierson	0	212	2	0
Ponce Inlet	12	10,364	24	0
Port Orange	12	63,826	246	8
South Daytona	12	55,863	4	186
Unincorporated area	12	202,216	855	127
Wakulla	(X)	76,432	571	0
County office	12	76,432	571	0
Walton	(X)	569,746	1,032	245
De Funiak Springs	12	2,463	15	0
Unincorporated area	12	567,283	1,017	245
Washington	(X)	7,834	125	0
County office	12	7,834	125	0

(X) Not applicable.
(NA) Not available.
1/ Permitting for unincorporated areas may include incorporated areas in the same county not shown separately. The definition is more service-based than geographical.
2/ Excludes mobile homes.
Special Area Coverage: Clay County excludes the portion of Keystone Heights that is in Bradford County. Marineland in Flagler County also covers the portion that is in St. Johns County. Gilchrist County covers the Levy County portion of Fanning Springs. Santa Rosa County covers Navarre Beach, located entirely in Escambia County. Sarasota County covers the Manatee County portion of Longboat Key.
Note: Data are based on voluntary reports from local building officials processed by the Bureau of the Census by the 12th working day of the month. Data may also include estimates for nonreports. Value figures are estimated on a cost-per-foot basis by each jurisdiction and may not be comparable to other locations.

Source: University of Florida, Bureau of Economic and Business Research, *Building Permit Activity in Florida: 2006 Annual Report,* May 7, 2007.

Table 11.19. EMPLOYMENT AND PAYROLL: AVERAGE MONTHLY PRIVATE REPORTING UNITS EMPLOYMENT, AND PAYROLL COVERED BY UNEMPLOYMENT COMPENSATION LAW BY CONSTRUCTION INDUSTRY IN FLORIDA, 2005 AND 2006

NAICS code	Industry	Number of reporting units	Number of employees	Payroll ($1,000)
			2005 A/	
23	Construction	70,558	580,075	1,850,633
236	Construction of buildings	17,869	125,364	528,598
2361	Residential building construction	15,450	87,155	363,613
2362	Nonresidential building construction	2,419	38,209	164,984
237	Heavy and civil engineering construction	4,698	70,262	265,227
2371	Utility system construction	1,456	21,909	74,869
2372	Land subdivision	1,954	16,933	78,870
2373	Highway, street, and bridge construction	591	20,923	71,462
2379	Other heavy construction	697	10,498	40,026
238	Specialty trade contractors	47,991	384,449	1,056,809
2381	Building foundation and exterior contractors	10,941	106,614	269,037
2382	Building equipment contractors	13,847	147,635	444,671
2383	Building finishing contractors	16,925	78,621	194,044
2389	Other specialty trade contractors	6,278	51,580	149,057
			2006 B/	
23	Construction	74,873	634,897	2,155,672
236	Construction of buildings	19,026	136,393	609,749
2361	Residential building construction	16,494	94,032	416,710
2362	Nonresidential building construction	2,532	42,361	193,040
237	Heavy and civil engineering construction	4,929	76,747	311,039
2371	Utility system construction	1,526	24,537	88,323
2372	Land subdivision	2,078	19,730	97,456
2373	Highway, street, and bridge construction	581	22,140	83,555
2379	Other heavy construction	744	10,341	41,704
238	Specialty trade contractors	50,918	421,757	1,234,884
2381	Building foundation and exterior contractors	11,479	116,187	316,992
2382	Building equipment contractors	14,540	162,083	514,510
2383	Building finishing contractors	18,061	86,551	228,177
2389	Other specialty trade contractors	6,838	56,936	175,205

NAICS North American Classification Industry System. See Glossary for definition.
A/ Revised.
B/ Preliminary.
Note: Private employment. Detail may not add to totals due to disclosure editing and/or rounding. See Tables 23.70, 23.72, 23.73, and 23.74 for public employment data.

Source: State of Florida, Agency for Workforce Innovation, Labor Market Statistics, "Quarterly Census of Employment and Wages" (ES-202), Annual NAICS files, Internet site <http://www.labormarketinfo.com/index.htm> (accessed 17, July 2007).

Table 11.20. EMPLOYMENT AND PAYROLL: AVERAGE MONTHLY PRIVATE REPORTING UNITS EMPLOYMENT, AND PAYROLL COVERED BY UNEMPLOYMENT COMPENSATION LAW IN THE STATE AND COUNTIES OF FLORIDA, 2006

County	Number of reporting units	Number of employees	Payroll ($1,000)	County	Number of reporting units	Number of employees	Payroll ($1,000)
			Construction (NAICS code 23)				
Florida	74,873	634,897	2,155,672	Lee	3,450	35,917	122,157
Alachua	786	5,916	16,688	Leon	915	7,778	22,623
Baker	112	643	1,418	Levy	169	972	2,426
Bay	939	7,253	20,370	Madison	36	92	154
Bradford	77	354	766	Manatee	1,386	10,703	36,094
Brevard	2,298	17,375	62,525	Marion	1,438	10,927	30,760
Broward	5,767	58,413	216,197	Martin	858	7,100	21,658
Calhoun	46	221	466	Miami-Dade	5,919	51,986	192,143
Charlotte	905	5,936	17,621	Monroe	474	2,457	7,220
Citrus	639	4,329	10,361	Nassau	341	1,247	3,082
Clay	817	5,120	15,232	Okaloosa	970	6,310	17,835
Collier	2,089	23,334	84,031	Okeechobee	164	900	2,294
Columbia	256	1,347	3,050	Orange	4,395	44,547	175,001
DeSoto	107	474	1,119	Osceola	982	6,194	18,053
Dixie	39	136	251	Palm Beach	5,302	45,786	165,641
Duval	3,554	36,747	132,831	Pasco	1,738	11,939	33,456
Escambia	1,128	10,151	29,955	Pinellas	3,393	26,622	83,967
Flagler	467	2,137	5,360	Polk	1,994	15,447	47,053
Franklin	68	254	629	Putnam	303	1,606	3,418
Gadsden	129	876	2,770	St. Johns	716	4,316	13,101
Gilchrist	80	212	407	St. Lucie	1,079	7,267	21,888
Glades	31	155	408	Santa Rosa	728	4,484	18,180
Gulf	97	460	1,115	Sarasota	2,558	17,925	58,185
Hamilton	25	122	161	Seminole	2,117	22,090	80,293
Hardee	54	287	651	Sumter	161	3,409	8,201
Hendry	100	633	1,516	Suwannee	128	514	1,085
Hernando	770	4,603	10,955	Taylor	47	494	1,330
Highlands	384	2,140	4,909	Union	37	197	395
Hillsborough	4,292	43,427	155,066	Volusia	2,541	14,339	40,931
Holmes	66	265	507	Wakulla	146	533	1,194
Indian River	768	5,778	17,432	Walton	417	2,998	8,513
Jackson	109	836	1,875	Washington	88	560	1,391
Jefferson	50	293	769	Statewide 1/	448	10,181	43,143
Lafayette	17	61	87	Out-of-state 2/	25	171	813
Lake	1,207	11,292	34,785	Unknown 1/	1,122	4,818	18,019

NAICS North American Industry Classification System. See Glossary for definition.

1/ Reporting units without a fixed location within the state or of unknown county location.

2/ Employment based in Florida, but working out of the state or country.

Note: Construction includes construction of buildings (NAICS code 236), heavy and civil engineering construction (NAICS code 237), and specialty trade contractors (NAICS code 238). Private employment. Data are preliminary. Only counties for which data are disclosed are shown. Detail may not add to totals due to disclosure editing and/or rounding. See Tables 23.70, 23.72, 23.73, and 23.74 for public employment data.

Source: State of Florida, Agency for Workforce Innovation, Labor Market Statistics, "Quarterly Census of Employment and Wages" (ES-202), Annual NAICS files, Internet site <http://www.labormarketinfo.com/index.htm> (accessed 17, July 2007).

Table 11.21. CONSTRUCTION OF BUILDINGS: AVERAGE MONTHLY PRIVATE REPORTING UNITS, EMPLOYMENT, AND PAYROLL COVERED BY UNEMPLOYMENT COMPENSATION LAW IN THE STATE AND COUNTIES OF FLORIDA, 2006

County	Number of reporting units	Number of employees	Payroll ($1,000)	County	Number of reporting units	Number of employees	Payroll ($1,000)
		Construction of buildings (NAICS code 236)					
Florida	19,026	136,393	609,749	Lake	321	1,648	6,838
				Lee	830	6,379	27,960
Alachua	219	1,281	4,942	Leon	260	1,502	5,554
Baker	28	70	144	Levy	27	64	151
Bay	274	1,502	4,504	Liberty	6	12	28
Bradford	25	84	173	Madison	11	21	38
Brevard	554	4,181	25,509	Manatee	331	1,562	7,496
Broward	1,440	11,367	54,921	Marion	330	2,169	6,651
Calhoun	11	21	38	Martin	228	1,067	3,978
Charlotte	205	1,066	3,572	Miami-Dade	1,675	14,444	72,645
Citrus	136	473	1,403	Monroe	143	957	2,747
Clay	221	1,169	4,776	Nassau	100	386	994
Collier	526	4,923	22,415	Okaloosa	294	2,044	6,764
Columbia	54	329	712	Okeechobee	32	200	569
DeSoto	19	72	155	Orange	1,180	11,443	62,728
Dixie	8	13	26	Osceola	208	1,103	3,853
Duval	885	9,290	42,926	Palm Beach	1,413	12,266	56,007
Escambia	319	2,107	6,962	Pasco	321	1,326	4,117
Flagler	122	474	1,443	Pinellas	850	4,983	19,439
Franklin	22	61	151	Polk	449	2,856	10,696
Gadsden	36	312	1,371	Putnam	48	119	290
Gilchrist	19	34	80	St. Johns	201	916	3,363
Glades	7	25	61	St. Lucie	225	950	3,294
Gulf	24	55	135	Santa Rosa	210	1,357	10,445
Hamilton	9	74	84	Sarasota	667	3,743	15,664
Hardee	16	131	297	Seminole	542	5,149	23,904
Hendry	18	118	339	Sumter	27	81	262
Hernando	138	671	1,616	Suwannee	31	91	164
Highlands	94	292	630	Union	6	12	23
Hillsborough	1,033	8,104	39,434	Volusia	583	2,432	8,256
Holmes	20	51	85	Wakulla	51	141	328
Indian River	200	1,313	4,950	Walton	150	540	1,764
Jackson	29	90	183	Washington	22	108	205
Jefferson	11	70	183	Statewide 1/	117	2,379	10,574
Lafayette	6	25	41	Unknown 1/	387	1,665	6,179

NAICS North American Industry Classification System. See Glossary for definition.

1/ Reporting units without a fixed location within the state or of unknown county location.

Note: Private employment. Data are preliminary. For a list of four-digit code industries included see Table 11.19. Only counties for which data are disclosed are shown. Detail may not add to totals due to disclosure editing and/or rounding. See Tables 23.70, 23.72, 23.73, and 23.74 for public employment data.

Source: State of Florida, Agency for Workforce Innovation, Labor Market Statistics, "Quarterly Census of Employment and Wages" (ES-202), Annual NAICS files, Internet site <http://www.labormarketinfo.com/index.htm> (accessed 17, July 2007).

Table 11.22. SPECIALTY TRADE CONTRACTORS: AVERAGE MONTHLY PRIVATE REPORTING UNITS, EMPLOYMENT, AND PAYROLL COVERED BY UNEMPLOYMENT COMPENSATION LAW IN THE STATE AND COUNTIES OF FLORIDA, 2006

County	Number of reporting units	Number of employees	Payroll ($1,000)	County	Number of reporting units	Number of employees	Payroll ($1,000)
		Specialty trade contractors (NAICS code 238)					
Florida	50,918	421,757	1,234,884	Lee	2,406	26,233	81,554
Alachua	523	4,304	10,540	Leon	581	5,335	13,506
Baker	79	560	1,250	Levy	133	439	869
Bay	605	4,495	11,176	Madison	23	61	92
Bradford	46	196	402	Manatee	969	7,519	22,053
Brevard	1,625	11,683	31,388	Marion	1,018	7,415	19,141
Broward	3,948	39,846	130,787	Martin	558	5,145	14,379
Calhoun	29	135	271	Miami-Dade	3,746	30,880	89,560
Charlotte	652	4,356	12,324	Monroe	304	1,314	3,775
Citrus	467	3,290	7,508	Nassau	213	737	1,688
Clay	555	3,489	8,672	Okaloosa	617	3,820	9,443
Collier	1,416	15,947	49,701	Okeechobee	114	635	1,604
Columbia	187	909	2,029	Orange	2,963	28,399	88,533
DeSoto	75	315	814	Osceola	719	4,600	12,302
Dixie	27	99	183	Palm Beach	3,517	28,555	88,984
Duval	2,423	23,122	70,051	Pasco	1,330	8,927	22,050
Escambia	744	7,199	20,301	Pinellas	2,321	19,147	55,651
Flagler	324	1,517	3,510	Polk	1,423	10,606	28,680
Franklin	40	155	315	Putnam	236	1,246	2,273
Gadsden	87	400	879	St. Johns	460	2,851	7,572
Gilchrist	56	167	304	St. Lucie	802	5,762	15,009
Glades	20	55	99	Santa Rosa	478	2,806	6,866
Gulf	61	346	650	Sarasota	1,768	12,705	36,825
Hamilton	15	45	73	Seminole	1,453	14,240	45,519
Hardee	33	126	266	Sumter	119	2,352	6,506
Hendry	71	418	982	Suwannee	85	294	565
Hernando	595	3,676	8,780	Taylor	26	134	253
Highlands	268	1,634	3,580	Union	24	108	214
Hillsborough	2,975	29,688	92,749	Volusia	1,841	10,291	26,774
Holmes	44	208	407	Wakulla	88	367	799
Indian River	523	3,837	10,295	Walton	222	2,107	5,548
Jackson	70	527	1,143	Washington	54	279	558
Jefferson	34	126	287	Statewide 1/	242	4,338	16,474
Lafayette	11	36	45	Out-of-state 2/	13	29	130
Lake	820	6,551	17,552	Unknown 1/	596	2,616	9,808

NAICS North American Industry Classification System. See Glossary for definition.
1/ Reporting units without a fixed location within the state or of unknown county location.
2/ Employment based in Florida, but working out of the state or country.
Note: Private employment. Data are preliminary. For a list of four-digit code industries included see Table 11.19. Only counties for which data are disclosed are shown. Detail may not add to totals due to disclosure editing and/or rounding. See Tables 23.70, 23.72, 23.73, and 23.74 for public employment data.
Source: State of Florida, Agency for Workforce Innovation, Labor Market Statistics, "Quarterly Census of Employment and Wages" (ES-202), Annual NAICS files, Internet site <http://www.labormarketinfo.com/ index.htm> (accessed 17, July 2007).

Table 11.23. BUILDING MATERIAL AND GARDEN SUPPLY STORES: AVERAGE MONTHLY PRIVATE REPORTING UNITS, EMPLOYMENT, AND PAYROLL COVERED BY UNEMPLOYMENT COMPENSATION LAW IN THE STATE AND COUNTIES OF FLORIDA, 2006

County	Number of reporting units	Number of employees	Payroll ($1,000)	County	Number of reporting units	Number of employees	Payroll ($1,000)
	Building material and garden supply stores (NAICS code 444)						
Florida	5,354	90,409	236,583	Lee	213	4,419	13,396
				Leon	75	1,389	3,448
Alachua	61	1,079	2,535	Levy	12	73	126
Baker	9	44	73	Madison	9	91	218
Bay	60	863	2,067	Manatee	77	1,340	2,880
Bradford	6	37	82	Marion	102	1,685	4,002
Brevard	167	2,929	6,697	Martin	55	1,109	2,850
Broward	459	7,698	19,976	Miami-Dade	658	8,919	23,011
Calhoun	5	26	63	Monroe	32	487	1,145
Charlotte	54	943	2,271	Nassau	28	438	945
Citrus	44	584	1,201	Okaloosa	55	1,060	2,356
Clay	48	966	1,943	Okeechobee	12	95	194
Collier	133	2,597	8,270	Orange	271	4,868	14,629
Columbia	15	284	579	Osceola	45	915	2,238
DeSoto	8	79	187	Palm Beach	388	5,770	15,158
Dixie	6	103	258	Pasco	97	1,427	3,119
Duval	241	4,547	12,631	Pinellas	237	3,900	10,219
Escambia	100	1,834	5,172	Polk	133	3,412	7,984
Flagler	36	521	1,325	Putnam	23	370	659
Franklin	5	75	169	St. Johns	55	766	2,150
Gadsden	7	71	145	St. Lucie	75	1,137	3,434
Gilchrist	4	47	113	Santa Rosa	46	816	1,770
Gulf	6	42	107	Sarasota	146	2,140	6,152
Hamilton	4	31	48	Seminole	124	3,589	9,690
Hardee	10	44	111	Sumter	18	397	796
Hendry	12	121	206	Suwannee	23	275	564
Hernando	50	762	1,695	Taylor	10	79	141
Highlands	33	607	1,245	Union	5	15	34
Hillsborough	282	5,833	15,778	Volusia	155	2,396	6,058
Holmes	7	35	46	Wakulla	5	67	113
Indian River	46	828	2,015	Walton	32	324	834
Jackson	18	216	417	Washington	4	30	71
Jefferson	6	48	89	Statewide 1/	4	30	71
Lafayette	4	71	163	Out-of-state 2/	17	586	3,018
Lake	84	1,830	4,510	Unknown 1/	74	171	753

NAICS North American Industry Classification System. See Glossary for definition.
1/ Reporting units without a fixed location within the state or of unknown county location.
2/ Employment based in Florida, but working out of the state or country.
Note: Private employment. Data are preliminary. Only counties for which data are disclosed are shown. Detail may not add to totals due to disclosure editing and/or rounding. See Tables in 23.70, 23.72, 23.73, and 23.74 for public employment data.
Source: State of Florida, Agency for Workforce Innovation, Labor Market Statistics, "Quarterly Census of Employment and Wages" (ES-202), Annual NAICS files, Internet site <http://www.labormarketinfo.com/index.htm> (accessed 17, July 2007).

Table 11.24. LUMBER AND CONSTRUCTION SUPPLY AND HARDWARE AND PLUMBING MERCHANT WHOLESALERS: AVERAGE MONTHLY PRIVATE REPORTING UNITS, EMPLOYMENT, AND PAYROLL COVERED BY UNEMPLOYMENT COMPENSATION LAW IN THE STATE AND COUNTIES OF FLORIDA, 2006

County	Number of reporting units	Number of employees	Payroll ($1,000)	County	Number of reporting units	Number of employees	Payroll ($1,000)
Lumber and construction supply merchant wholesalers (NAICS code 4233)							
Florida	1,682	18,819	74,579	Manatee	18	128	504
				Marion	18	174	570
Alachua	13	122	416	Martin	24	219	1,040
Bay	12	116	419	Miami-Dade	294	2,922	10,275
Brevard	32	256	996	Okaloosa	11	126	409
Broward	171	1,801	7,493	Orange	110	1,864	8,661
Charlotte	12	96	338	Palm Beach	121	1,283	5,092
Citrus	6	43	119	Pasco	22	157	502
Clay	9	54	215	Pinellas	62	445	1,614
Collier	39	369	1,383	Polk	40	784	2,934
Columbia	7	57	172	Putnam	3	15	45
Duval	102	1,762	7,189	St. Johns	13	56	213
Escambia	25	481	1,732	St. Lucie	23	217	650
Flagler	5	18	64	Santa Rosa	5	17	47
Hernando	7	57	181	Sarasota	35	332	1,354
Highlands	12	26	39	Seminole	53	559	2,231
Hillsborough	108	1,913	7,858	Sumter	3	105	351
Indian River	19	104	376	Volusia	27	228	860
Lake	17	201	707	Walton	6	51	163
Lee	50	583	2,298	Statewide 1/	33	238	1,956
Leon	18	309	1,360	Unknown 1/	60	126	703
Hardware and plumbing merchant wholesalers (NAICS code 4237)							
Florida	1,331	16,119	71,921	Martin	17	60	217
Alachua	10	61	228	Miami-Dade	199	2,863	12,559
Brevard	22	225	799	Monroe	6	8	23
Broward	134	1,258	6,247	Okaloosa	12	71	249
Charlotte	5	37	113	Orange	81	1,596	7,703
Citrus	7	42	192	Osceola	12	69	260
Clay	6	22	80	Palm Beach	73	609	2,677
Collier	16	93	350	Pasco	17	99	375
Columbia	5	12	28	Pinellas	64	616	2,606
Duval	86	2,457	11,163	Polk	34	390	1,733
Escambia	30	336	1,498	St. Johns	7	39	195
Highlands	4	38	149	St. Lucie	13	100	375
Hillsborough	101	1,630	7,506	Santa Rosa	4	6	29
Indian River	12	58	176	Sarasota	31	358	1,339
Lake	19	102	370	Seminole	50	573	2,870
Lee	40	318	1,314	Sumter	3	42	185
Leon	15	153	597	Volusia	23	104	344
Manatee	14	204	1,039	Statewide 1/	38	236	1,516
Marion	24	226	953	Unknown 1/	62	153	1,016

NAICS North American Industry Classification System. See Glossary for definition.
1/ Reporting units without a fixed location within the state or of unknown county location.
Note: See Note on Table 11.23.

Source: State of Florida, Agency for Workforce Innovation, Labor Market Statistics, "Quarterly Census of Employment and Wages" (ES-202), Annual NAICS files, Internet site <http://www.labormarketinfo.com/index.htm> (accessed 17, July 2007).

Table 11.25. COMMERCIAL EQUIPMENT MERCHANT WHOLESALERS: AVERAGE MONTHLY PRIVATE REPORTING UNITS, EMPLOYMENT, AND PAYROLL COVERED BY UNEMPLOYMENT COMPENSATION LAW IN THE STATE AND COUNTIES OF FLORIDA, 2006

County	Number of reporting units	Number of employees	Payroll ($1,000)	County	Number of reporting units	Number of employees	Payroll ($1,000)
		Commercial equipment merchant wholesalers (NAICS code 4234)					
Florida	4,494	46,437	283,976	Marion	35	170	641
				Martin	26	68	430
Alachua	37	265	1,020	Miami-Dade	1,002	8,209	51,802
Bay	21	122	524	Monroe	8	50	176
Brevard	74	708	4,010	Okaloosa	12	66	317
Broward	496	5,772	32,657	Orange	244	3,192	20,188
Charlotte	12	18	81	Osceola	15	49	197
Citrus	13	26	73	Palm Beach	298	3,375	24,847
Clay	13	61	230	Pasco	41	118	451
Collier	42	353	3,123	Pinellas	216	3,709	19,203
Duval	156	3,614	18,919	Polk	51	600	2,460
Escambia	44	260	1,211	St. Johns	22	71	475
Flagler	5	4	8	Santa Rosa	13	81	286
Hernando	12	33	105	Sarasota	84	346	1,415
Highlands	8	13	23	Seminole	134	1,903	14,179
Hillsborough	317	4,340	23,955	Sumter	6	18	59
Indian River	17	44	188	Volusia	66	567	1,814
Lake	36	154	522	Walton	8	10	31
Lee	74	514	2,460	Statewide 1/	287	3,998	38,326
Leon	44	402	2,559	Out-of-state 2/	5	26	180
Manatee	40	222	1,505	Unknown 1/	400	770	7,208

NAICS North American Industry Classification System. See Glossary for definition.
1/ Reporting units without a fixed location within the state or of unknown county location.
2/ Employment based in Florida, but working out of the state or country.
Note: Private employment. Data are preliminary. Only counties for which data are disclosed are shown. Detail may not add to totals due to disclosure editing and/or rounding. See Tables 23.70, 23.72, 23.73, and 23.74 for public employment data.

Source: State of Florida, Agency for Workforce Innovation, Labor Market Statistics, "Quarterly Census of Employment and Wages" (ES-202), Annual NAICS files, Internet site <http://www.labormarketinfo.com/index.htm> (accessed 17, July 2007).

Table 11.26. MANUFACTURED HOMES: PLACEMENTS OF NEW MOBILE HOMES AND AVERAGE SALES PRICES IN FLORIDA, SELECTED STATES, AND THE UNITED STATES, 2006

State 1/	Placements (1,000) Total 2/	Placements (1,000) Single-wide	Placements (1,000) Double-wide	Average sale price (dollars) Total 2/	Average sale price (dollars) Single-wide	Average sale price (dollars) Double-wide
Florida	11.7	1.8	9.4	66,900	35,800	69,200
Alabama	4.0	1.4	2.5	55,200	33,600	66,100
Arizona	5.3	0.3	4.5	78,000	37,800	76,300
Arkansas	2.2	0.7	1.5	57,500	32,800	67,400
California	8.6	0.7	6.7	92,900	44,600	88,400
Georgia	3.7	1.1	2.6	56,400	28,800	65,500
Illinois	1.9	0.7	1.2	59,400	34,800	76,600
Indiana	1.5	0.4	1.1	61,900	34,200	69,000
Kentucky	3.5	1.1	2.4	55,300	33,700	64,300
Louisiana	6.9	3.6	3.3	51,700	36,600	68,500
Michigan	2.1	0.3	1.8	59,500	33,500	65,000
Minnesota	1.1	0.2	0.9	64,900	41,800	66,900
Mississippi	4.1	2.3	1.8	47,700	34,300	63,400
Missouri	2.4	0.7	1.7	55,600	32,500	65,200
Nevada	1.3	(D)	1.2	86,800	(D)	82,600
New Mexico	1.3	0.3	0.9	66,700	35,400	71,600
New York	1.9	0.4	1.5	63,800	37,900	68,800
North Carolina	4.3	1.0	3.3	63,700	36,100	72,200
Ohio	2.3	0.6	1.7	59,500	36,500	66,500
Oklahoma	2.8	1.1	1.7	55,700	32,900	70,700
Oregon	1.7	(D)	1.2	86,100	(D)	76,300
Pennsylvania	3.4	0.6	2.9	63,700	43,000	68,300
South Carolina	2.7	0.6	2.0	65,400	32,900	72,600
Tennessee	3.8	1.2	2.5	55,700	34,400	65,200
Texas	9.3	3.7	5.5	58,500	36,300	70,900
Virginia	2.2	0.7	1.5	57,500	38,300	66,200
Washington	2.7	(D)	2.1	84,200	(D)	73,700
West Virginia	2.5	0.6	1.8	59,000	33,700	68,100
Wisconsin	1.2	0.3	0.9	58,800	35,600	65,000
United States	111.3	28.8	78.2	64,200	35,900	71,400

(D) Data withheld to avoid disclosure of information about individual companies.
1/ States with 2006 placements of 1,100 or more are listed.
2/ Includes manufactured homes with more than two sections.

Source: U.S., Department of Commerce, Census Bureau, Internet site <http://www.census.gov/> (accessed 5, July 2007).

MANUFACTURING

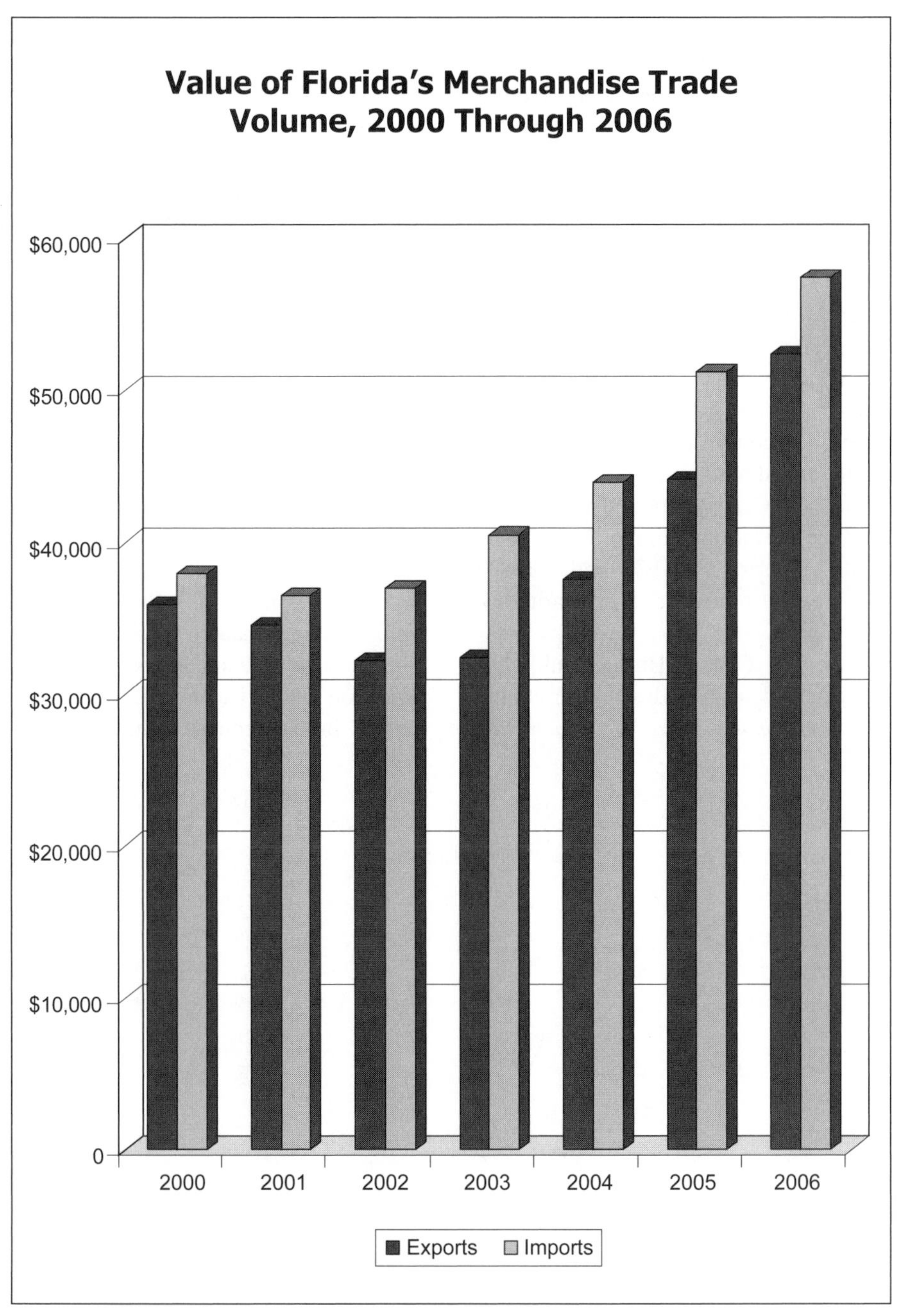

Source: Table 12.85

Section 12.00
Manufacturing

This section presents summary and detailed statistics on Florida's manufacturing industry. It includes data on private establishments, employment, and payroll by industry classification and by county and highlights specific manufacturing industries within the state. Also included are data about merchandise trade and export commodities.

Explanatory notes. The U.S. Census Bureau conducts a complete count of manufactures every five years, in years ending in "2" and "7," as part of its comprehensive economic census. Industries are categorized based on the North American Industry Classification System (NAICS). (See the introduction to Section 6.00 and the Glossary.) NAICS codes 31-33 represent the manufacturing industry.

Sources. The Census Bureau publishes employment data by industry and county in *2002 Economic Census: Manufacturing*. Table 12.05 depicts manufacturing industry data by kind of business and Table 12.06 presents data for counties. In addition to the 5-year censuses, the Census Bureau also conducts a sample survey called the *Annual Survey of Manufactures* in intervening years. Geographic Area Statistics from the *Survey* for specified metropolitan areas appear at the beginning of this section in Table 12.01.

The Florida Agency for Workforce Innovation's Labor Market Statistics office provides current data on the number of units, employees, and payroll for manufacturing establishments based on the NAICS system. This section details employment for a number of private manufacturing industries and most include county breakdowns.

The U.S. Census Bureau's Foreign Trade Division provides data on Florida's merchandise trade volume and exports. These data appear on Enterprise Florida, Inc.'s Marketing and Information Department Web site.

Section 12.00
Manufacturing

Tables listed by major heading

Tables listed by major heading

Table 12.01. MANUFACTURING: CHARACTERISTICS IN THE STATE AND SELECTED METROPOLITAN AREAS OF FLORIDA, SPECIFIED YEARS 1992 THROUGH 2005

Year and source 2/	Number of establishments 1/ Total	Number of establishments 1/ With 20 employees or more	All employees Number (1,000)	All employees Payroll (million dollars)	All employees Percentage of U.S. total	Value added by manufacture (million dollars)	New capital expenditure (million dollars)
Florida							
1992–census	16,382	3,758	472.4	12,991.0	2.79	32,641.4	2,111.5
1993–ASM	(NA)	(NA)	479.9	13,257.9	2.83	33,615.2	1,772.3
1994–ASM	(NA)	(NA)	472.0	13,257.5	2.77	35,100.6	2,040.9
1995–ASM	(NA)	(NA)	480.5	13,941.0	2.76	37,460.0	2,345.9
1996–ASM	(NA)	(NA)	486.1	14,852.5	2.81	38,621.3	2,643.9
1997–census	15,992	3,628	433.1	13,185.1	2.58	40,213.4	A/ 2,979.5
1998–ASM	(NA)	(NA)	426.8	13,334.3	2.52	41,094.4	2,956.8
1999–ASM	(NA)	(NA)	424.0	13,803.0	2.54	41,807.4	2,735.4
2000–ASM	(NA)	(NA)	422.4	14,096.0	2.54	41,406.2	2,845.0
2001–ASM	(NA)	(NA)	401.3	13,590.6	2.53	39,974.4	2,506.5
2002–census	15,202	3,192	377.1	14,082.4	2.57	41,912.6	2,465.1
2003–ASM	(NA)	(NA)	358.3	13,972.0	2.58	42,391.3	2,447.8
2004–ASM	(NA)	(NA)	353.9	13,961.5	2.64	45,367.0	2,524.1
2005–ASM	(NA)	(NA)	347.5	14,209.0	2.64	47,289.8	2,761.3
Miami-Ft. Lauderdale MSA 3/							
1992–census	5,215	1,185	122.1	3,047.6	0.67	7,132.2	337.2
1997–census	4,998	1,034	103.5	2,779.2	0.62	8,144.9	391.1
2002–census	5,522	948	100.7	3,417.6	0.69	10,491.0	482.9
Orlando MSA							
1992–census	1,574	390	53.3	1,661.5	0.29	3,754.2	195.2
1997–census	1,564	390	47.1	1,627.7	0.28	4,679.8	527.3
2002–census	1,506	370	46.4	2,114.5	0.32	5,846.3	330.3
Tampa-St. Petersburg-Clearwater MSA							
1992–census	2,583	639	83.6	2,330.5	0.46	5,164.9	315.5
1997–census	2,580	642	77.1	2,246.2	0.46	6,317.4	516.7
2002–census	2,453	590	72.4	2,722.1	0.49	7,429.1	427.9

(NA) Not available.

A/ Beginning in 1997 data are for total capital expenditure (including new and used) and are not comparable to earlier years.

1/ Includes establishments with payroll at any time during the year.

2/ Data for 1992 are from the Census of Manufactures and are based on SIC classifications for industries. Data for 1997 and 2002 are from the Economic Census based on the NAICS industry classification system and may not be comparable to earlier years. See Glossary for definitions. Data for Annual Survey of Manufactures (ASM) years are estimates based on a representative sample of establishments canvassed annually and may differ from results of a complete canvas of all establishments.

3/ Consists of Broward, Miami-Dade, and Palm Beach counties.

Note: Data are reported for metropolitan areas with 40,000 manufacturing employees or more in 1992. The manufactures census is on a 5-year cycle collecting data for years ending in 2 and 7. See Glossary for definitions of metropolitan areas and maps at the front of the book for area boundaries.

Source: U.S., Department of Commerce, Census Bureau, *2002 Economic Census: Manufacturing,* Geographic Area Series EC02-31A-FL (RV), Issued September 2005, previous manufacturing censuses, and *Annual Survey of Manufactures: Geographic Area Statistics, 2005,* M05(AS)-3, issued November 2006, and previous editions, Internet site <http://www.census.gov/> (accessed 19, February 2007).

Table 12.05. MANUFACTURING: ESTABLISHMENTS, EMPLOYMENT, AND PAYROLL IN FLORIDA, 2002

NAICS code	Industry	Number of establishments	Number of employees 1/	Annual payroll ($1,000)
31-33	Manufacturing	15,202	377,137	14,082,395
311	Food	1,009	33,656	1,101,798
3111	Animal food	40	967	33,993
3112	Grain and oilseed milling	7	156	6,111
3113	Sugar and confectionery	69	3,267	124,184
3114	Fruit and vegetable preserving	68	6,987	289,963
3115	Dairy product	41	1,973	75,856
3116	Meat product	78	6,387	156,387
3117	Seafood product	34	2,422	67,361
3118	Bakeries and tortilla	527	8,389	237,953
3119	Other food	145	3,108	109,990
312	Beverage and tobacco product	99	7,375	259,890
3121	Beverage	80	5,701	195,661
3122	Tobacco	19	1,674	64,229
313	Textile mills	135	1,405	42,067
3131	Fiber, yarn, and thread mills	10	299	6,900
3132	Fabric mills	59	707	23,856
3133	Textile and fabric finishing and fabric coating mills	66	399	11,311
314	Textile product mills	511	5,118	121,763
3141	Textile furnishing mills	190	2,052	45,929
3149	Other textile product mills	321	3,066	75,834
315	Apparel	457	9,163	200,455
3151	Apparel knitting mills	18	612	11,247
3152	Cut and sew apparel	374	7,931	175,617
3159	Apparel accessories and other apparel	65	620	13,591
316	Leather and allied product	70	1,059	26,105
3161	Leather and hide tanning and finishing	6	111	3,332
3162	Footwear	19	447	9,502
3169	Other leather and allied product	45	501	13,271
321	Wood product	528	15,891	458,953
3211	Sawmills and wood preservation	65	2,108	66,481
3212	Veneer, plywood, and engineered wood product	110	6,572	196,491
3219	Other wood product	353	7,211	195,981
322	Paper	163	10,352	480,148
3221	Pulp, paper, and paperboard mills	16	4,715	268,268
3222	Converted paper product	147	5,637	211,880
323	Printing and related support activities	2,021	22,228	729,031
324	Petroleum and coal products	51	1,129	46,695
325	Chemical	548	19,136	901,604
3251	Basic chemical	56	1,559	78,521
3252	Resin, synthetic rubber, and artificial and synthetic fibers and filaments	28	2,293	104,964

See footnotes at end of table. Continued . . .

Table 12.05. MANUFACTURING: ESTABLISHMENTS, EMPLOYMENT, AND PAYROLL IN FLORIDA, 2002 (Continued)

NAICS code	Industry	Number of estab-lishments	Number of employees 1/	Annual payroll ($1,000)
325	Chemical (Continued)			
3253	Pesticide, fertilizer, and other agriculture chemical	66	4,313	215,533
3254	Pharmaceutical and medicine	66	5,339	255,719
3255	Paint, coating, and adhesive	84	1,627	70,596
3256	Soap, cleaning compound, and toilet preparation	133	2,499	109,691
3259	Other chemical product	115	1,506	66,580
326	Plastics and rubber products	630	17,047	527,253
3261	Plastics product	547	15,061	464,476
3262	Rubber product	83	1,986	62,777
327	Nonmetallic mineral product	964	21,263	746,990
3271	Clay product and refractory	58	393	12,476
3272	Glass and glass product	132	1,996	70,613
3273	Cement and concrete product	595	15,785	540,696
3274	Lime and gypsum product	27	1,007	43,390
3279	Other nonmetallic mineral product	152	2,082	79,815
331	Primary metal	120	3,556	142,471
3311	Iron and steel mills and ferroalloy	6	A/	(D)
3312	Steel product from purchased steel	19	1,040	40,892
3313	Alumina and aluminum production and processing	24	917	35,024
3314	Nonferrous metal (except aluminum) production and processing	30	B/	(D)
3315	Foundries	41	749	25,681
332	Fabricated metal product	1,990	37,690	1,230,250
3321	Forging and stamping	61	1,781	66,369
3322	Cutlery and handtool	44	925	31,815
3323	Architectural and structural metals	702	18,297	568,686
3324	Boiler, tank, and shipping container	48	1,888	75,254
3325	Hardware	35	1,124	29,704
3326	Spring and wire product	66	1,659	50,505
3327	Machine shops, turned product; and screw, nut, and bolt	670	5,009	169,404
3328	Coating, engraving, heat treating, and allied activities	170	1,732	55,883
3329	Other fabricated metal product	194	5,275	182,630
333	Machinery	872	21,262	906,145
3331	Agriculture, construction, and mining machinery	73	1,206	43,726
3332	Industrial machinery	103	2,250	107,383
3333	Commercial and service industry machinery	125	5,220	278,449
3334	Ventilation, heating, air conditioning, and commercial refrigeration equipment	86	2,600	81,983
3335	Metalworking machinery	202	2,644	102,347
3336	Engine, turbine, and power transmission equipment	37	766	31,801
3339	Other general-purpose machinery	246	6,576	260,456
334	Computer and electronic product	700	55,250	2,923,711
3341	Computer and peripheral equipment	68	2,003	113,768
3342	Communications equipment	122	14,947	977,079
3343	Audio and video equipment	31	693	27,664

See footnotes at end of table.

Continued . . .

Table 12.05. MANUFACTURING: ESTABLISHMENTS, EMPLOYMENT, AND PAYROLL IN FLORIDA, 2002 (Continued)

NAICS code	Industry	Number of estab-lishments	Number of employees 1/	Annual payroll ($1,000)
334	Computer and electronic product (Continued)			
3344	Semiconductor and other electronic component	200	15,171	611,859
3345	Navigational, measuring, electromedical, and control instruments	237	21,555	1,163,684
3346	Magnetic and optical media	42	881	29,657
335	Electrical equipment, appliance, and component	257	9,375	314,492
3351	Electric lighting equipment	55	C/	(D)
3353	Electrical equipment	84	2,968	111,485
3359	Other electrical equipment and component	110	4,855	162,406
336	Transportation equipment	716	31,633	1,119,536
3361	Motor vehicle manufacturing	12	D/	(D)
3362	Motor vehicle body and trailer	88	3,667	112,163
3363	Motor vehicle parts	180	6,163	171,791
3364	Aerospace product and parts	96	7,900	401,221
3366	Ship and boat building	306	13,096	409,343
3369	Other transportation equipment	32	515	15,903
337	Furniture and related product	1,486	17,975	499,237
3371	Household and institutional furniture and kitchen cabinet	1,181	10,831	294,226
3372	Office furniture (including fixtures)	181	3,686	104,952
3379	Other furniture related product	124	3,458	100,059
339	Miscellaneous	1,875	35,574	1,303,801
3391	Medical equipment and supplies	811	22,884	919,481
3399	Other miscellaneous	1,064	12,690	384,320

(D) Data withheld to avoid disclosure of information about individual firms.
Employment range: A/ 250-499. B/ 50-999. C/ 1,000-2,499. D/ 100-249.
1/ Industries with 100 employees or more are shown.
Note: The economic censuses are conducted on a 5-year cycle collecting data for years ending in 2 and 7. Data are for North American Industry Classification System (NAICS) codes 31-33 and may not be comparable to earlier years. See Glossary for definition.

Source: U.S., Department of Commerce, Census Bureau, *2002 Economic Census: Manufacturing,* Geographic Area Series EC02-31A-FL (RV), issued September 2005, Internet site <http://www.census.gov/> (accessed 11, May 2007).

Table 12.06. MANUFACTURING: ESTABLISHMENTS, EMPLOYMENT, VALUE ADDED BY MANUFACTURE, VALUE OF SHIPMENTS, AND NEW CAPITAL EXPENDITURE IN THE STATE AND COUNTIES OF FLORIDA, 2002

(in thousands of dollars, except where indicated)

County	Establish-ments (number)	All employees Number 1/	All employees Payroll	Value added by manu-facture	Value of shipments	Capital expen-diture
Florida	15,202	377,137	14,082,395	41,912,600	78,474,770	2,465,056
Alachua	154	3,873	133,440	393,735	834,956	24,600
Baker	0	0	0	0	0	0
Bay	133	3,671	140,689	404,555	844,800	30,348
Bradford	0	0	0	0	0	0
Brevard	459	18,347	864,589	2,580,956	3,961,072	131,769
Broward	1,836	32,179	1,146,172	3,751,169	6,775,856	153,167
Calhoun	0	0	0	0	0	0
Charlotte	86	638	21,602	64,113	106,507	1,906
Citrus	62	546	15,559	26,709	73,721	1,537
Clay 2/	71	(NA)	(D)	(D)	(D)	11,765
Collier	252	2,733	100,840	235,764	437,510	10,058
Columbia	39	836	23,172	60,758	182,781	2,451
DeSoto	0	0	0	0	0	0
Dixie	0	0	0	0	0	0
Duval	690	27,340	1,091,920	3,975,300	7,011,260	221,828
Escambia	223	5,927	244,507	812,864	1,873,203	49,417
Flagler	50	1,628	53,715	165,543	378,529	7,469
Franklin	0	0	0	0	0	0
Gadsden	33	1,352	38,618	77,692	188,356	(D)
Gilchrist	0	0	0	0	0	0
Glades	0	0	0	0	0	0
Gulf	0	0	0	0	0	0
Hamilton 3/	3	(NA)	(D)	(D)	(D)	(D)
Hardee	0	0	0	0	0	0
Hendry 3/	15	(NA)	(D)	(D)	(D)	(D)
Hernando	75	885	31,841	118,485	210,057	9,325
Highlands	49	996	29,580	96,027	227,144	3,011
Hillsborough	930	29,054	1,032,341	3,157,296	6,740,022	200,814
Holmes	0	0	0	0	0	0
Indian River	100	2,408	78,267	184,361	331,121	7,107
Jackson	18	620	17,408	70,419	155,450	2,303
Jefferson	0	0	0	0	0	0
Lafayette	0	0	0	0	0	0
Lake	165	3,847	119,775	333,511	609,340	19,592
Lee	403	6,726	198,273	582,985	986,100	29,088
Leon	103	1,833	67,833	149,246	366,017	10,153
Levy	0	0	0	0	0	0

See footnotes at end of table.

Continued . . .

Table 12.06. MANUFACTURING: ESTABLISHMENTS, EMPLOYMENT, VALUE ADDED BY MANUFACTURE, VALUE OF SHIPMENTS, AND NEW CAPITAL EXPENDITURE IN THE STATE AND COUNTIES OF FLORIDA, 2002 (Continued)

(in thousands of dollars, except where indicated)

County	Establish-ments (number)	All employees Number 1/	All employees Payroll	Value added by manu-facture	Value of shipments	Capital expen-diture
Liberty	0	0	0	0	0	0
Madison 3/	10	(NA)	(D)	(D)	(D)	(D)
Manatee	268	9,640	340,163	1,009,947	2,421,772	129,526
Marion	245	9,065	279,539	724,731	1,381,488	31,763
Martin	152	2,586	94,697	214,640	538,099	10,804
Miami-Dade	2,608	50,316	1,596,870	5,021,323	8,442,440	225,097
Monroe	0	0	0	0	0	0
Nassau	36	1,314	73,283	300,417	552,743	11,548
Okaloosa	125	2,338	86,251	203,117	313,588	8,951
Okeechobee	0	0	0	0	0	0
Orange	827	29,196	1,249,946	4,072,426	7,145,403	245,387
Osceola	83	1,565	51,091	124,227	328,890	15,441
Palm Beach	1,078	18,234	674,541	1,718,538	3,204,558	104,618
Pasco	208	3,047	98,617	229,564	451,828	29,106
Pinellas	1,240	39,396	1,559,302	3,923,790	7,087,910	188,674
Polk	452	16,088	599,415	2,229,138	4,938,430	207,531
Putnam	38	2,309	94,319	363,832	714,730	34,813
St. Johns	92	1,841	59,518	172,392	341,322	(D)
St. Lucie	146	2,384	80,936	322,990	595,720	42,186
Santa Rosa	62	987	28,332	108,545	264,490	12,251
Sarasota	386	7,803	271,420	631,906	1,074,299	36,485
Seminole	431	11,768	693,673	1,316,175	2,031,831	49,880
Sumter	25	821	24,000	62,949	241,253	3,310
Suwannee	21	1,616	39,452	32,970	191,925	(D)
Taylor	24	1,604	60,482	227,781	435,430	13,588
Union	0	0	0	0	0	0
Volusia	383	8,609	289,091	687,362	1,294,455	63,634
Wakulla	0	0	0	0	0	0
Walton	31	700	19,377	71,348	89,794	1,744
Washington 3/	9	(NA)	(D)	(D)	(D)	(D)

(NA) Not available.
(D) Data withheld to avoid disclosure of information about individual companies.
1/ Industries with 100 employees or more are shown for the state and those with 500 employees or more are shown for counties.
Employment ranges: 2/ 1,000-2,499. 3/ 500-999.
Note: The economic censuses are conducted on a 5-year cycle collecting data for years ending in 2 and 7. Data are for North American Industry Classification System (NAICS) codes 31-33 and may not be comparable to earlier years. See Glossary for definition.

Source: U.S., Department of Commerce, Census Bureau, *2002 Economic Census: Manufacturing,* Geographic Area Series EC02-31A-FL (RV), Issued September 2005, Internet site <http://www.census.gov/> (accessed 11, May 2007).

Table 12.50. EMPLOYMENT AND PAYROLL: AVERAGE MONTHLY PRIVATE REPORTING UNITS EMPLOYMENT, AND PAYROLL COVERED BY UNEMPLOYMENT COMPENSATION LAW BY MANUFACTURING INDUSTRY IN FLORIDA, 2005 AND 2006

NAICS code	Industry	Number of reporting units	Number of employees	Payroll ($1,000)
			2005 A/	
31-33	Manufacturing	16,579	399,135	1,443,851
311	Food manufacturing	1,127	31,698	96,016
3111	Animal food manufacturing	42	511	1,535
3112	Grain and oilseed milling	9	135	786
3113	Sugar and confectionery product manufacturing	83	3,075	11,767
3114	Fruit and vegetable preserving and specialty	72	6,283	25,230
3115	Dairy product manufacturing	47	2,401	8,334
3116	Animal slaughtering and processing	74	4,346	9,737
3117	Seafood product preparation and packaging	41	2,309	5,980
3118	Bakeries and tortilla manufacturing	613	8,891	20,053
3119	Other food manufacturing	146	3,747	12,594
312	Beverage and tobacco product manufacturing	172	10,656	40,565
3121	Beverage manufacturing	137	8,363	31,421
3122	Tobacco manufacturing	35	2,294	9,144
313	Textile mills	168	1,906	5,019
3131	Fiber, yarn, and thread mills	12	56	68
3132	Fabric mills	50	660	1,975
3133	Textile and fabric finishing mills	106	1,190	2,976
314	Textile product mills	521	5,670	13,135
3141	Textile furnishings mills	165	1,940	4,093
3149	Other textile product mills	356	3,730	9,042
315	Apparel manufacturing	398	5,789	12,897
3151	Apparel knitting mills	16	337	647
3152	Cut and sew apparel manufacturing	344	4,884	10,710
3159	Accessories and other apparel manufacturing	38	568	1,540
316	Leather and allied product manufacturing	89	1,264	3,450
3161	Leather and hide tanning and finishing	7	12	26
3162	Footwear manufacturing	23	208	567
3169	Other leather product manufacturing	59	1,044	2,858
321	Wood product manufacturing	631	22,418	66,189
3211	Sawmills and wood preservation	79	2,966	9,003
3212	Plywood and engineered wood product manufacturing	140	8,766	24,799
3219	Other wood product manufacturing	412	10,687	32,387
322	Paper manufacturing	215	10,495	44,723
3221	Pulp, paper, and paperboard mills	32	2,807	15,525
3222	Converted paper product manufacturing	183	7,688	29,198
323	Printing and related support activities	2,225	23,611	68,582
324	Petroleum and coal products manufacturing	72	2,879	11,257

See footnotes at end of table. Continued . . .

Table 12.50. EMPLOYMENT AND PAYROLL: AVERAGE MONTHLY PRIVATE REPORTING UNITS EMPLOYMENT, AND PAYROLL COVERED BY UNEMPLOYMENT COMPENSATION LAW BY MANUFACTURING INDUSTRY IN FLORIDA, 2005 AND 2006 (Continued)

NAICS code	Industry	Number of reporting units	Number of employees	Payroll ($1,000)
		2005 A/ (Continued)		
325	Chemical manufacturing	646	20,440	89,529
3251	Basic chemical manufacturing	66	1,184	6,127
3252	Resin, rubber, and artificial fibers manufacturing	62	2,565	10,589
3253	Agricultural chemical manufacturing	79	6,050	28,468
3254	Pharmaceutical and medicine manufacturing	94	4,141	19,123
3255	Paint, coating, and adhesive manufacturing	93	1,696	5,959
3256	Soap, cleaning compound, and toiletry manufacturing	145	2,914	11,513
3259	Other chemical product and preparation manufacturing	107	1,891	7,751
326	Plastics and rubber products manufacturing	618	15,368	43,935
3261	Plastics product manufacturing	527	12,636	35,162
3262	Rubber product manufacturing	91	2,732	8,773
327	Nonmetallic mineral product manufacturing	910	25,674	87,744
3271	Clay product and refractory manufacturing	114	859	2,666
3272	Glass and glass product manufacturing	128	2,303	6,609
3273	Cement and concrete product manufacturing	502	18,861	65,242
3274	Lime and gypsum product manufacturing	26	1,450	6,607
3279	Other nonmetallic mineral products	140	2,200	6,620
331	Primary metal manufacturing	158	5,378	17,749
3311	Iron and steel mills and ferroalloy manufacturing	19	639	3,197
3312	Steel product manufacturing from purchased steel	26	607	2,271
3313	Alumina and aluminum production	42	2,417	6,940
3314	Other nonferrous metal production	22	471	1,461
3315	Foundries	49	1,245	3,880
332	Fabricated metal product manufacturing	2,050	39,723	119,905
3321	Forging and stamping	60	1,398	4,359
3322	Cutlery and handtool manufacturing	57	819	2,748
3323	Architectural and structural metals manufacturing	720	18,993	54,918
3324	Boiler, tank, and shipping container manufacturing	74	2,620	9,158
3325	Hardware manufacturing	29	589	1,718
3326	Spring and wire product manufacturing	38	1,879	5,408
3327	Machine shops and threaded product manufacturing	651	5,416	16,308
3328	Coating, engraving, and heat treating metals	180	1,504	4,373
3329	Other fabricated metal product manufacturing	241	6,504	20,914
333	Machinery manufacturing	924	26,027	100,196
3331	Agricultural, construction, and mining machinery manufacturing	59	1,625	5,519
3332	Industrial machinery manufacturing	104	2,165	8,108
3333	Commercial and service industry machinery	156	7,874	37,804
3334	HVAC and commercial refrigeration equipment	97	3,471	9,571
3335	Metalworking machinery manufacturing	207	2,821	8,110
3336	Turbine and power transmission equipment manufacturing	50	1,392	6,663
3339	Other general purpose machinery manufacturing	251	6,680	24,420
334	Computer and electronic product manufacturing	875	51,066	273,243
3341	Computer and peripheral equipment manufacturing	88	3,360	15,843
3342	Communications equipment manufacturing	156	10,861	73,685

See footnotes at end of table.

Continued . . .

Table 12.50. EMPLOYMENT AND PAYROLL: AVERAGE MONTHLY PRIVATE REPORTING UNITS EMPLOYMENT, AND PAYROLL COVERED BY UNEMPLOYMENT COMPENSATION LAW BY MANUFACTURING INDUSTRY IN FLORIDA, 2005 AND 2006 (Continued)

NAICS code	Industry	Number of reporting units	Number of employees	Payroll ($1,000)
		2005 A/ (Continued)		
334	Computer and electronic product manufacturing (Continued)			
3343	Audio and video equipment manufacturing	34	548	2,106
3344	Semiconductor and electronic component manufacturing	234	17,798	95,424
3345	Electronic instrument manufacturing	308	17,017	81,551
3346	Magnetic media manufacturing and reproducing	55	1,483	4,633
335	Electrical equipment and appliance manufacturing	326	8,290	26,476
3351	Electric lighting equipment manufacturing	69	1,791	5,014
3352	Household appliance manufacturing	35	165	481
3353	Electrical equipment manufacturing	94	2,868	9,853
3359	Other electrical equipment and component manufacturing	128	3,467	11,127
336	Transportation equipment manufacturing	888	42,117	170,993
3362	Motor vehicle body and trailer manufacturing	107	3,127	8,956
3363	Motor vehicle parts manufacturing	184	6,076	19,049
3364	Aerospace product and parts manufacturing	195	17,709	95,774
3366	Ship and boat building	359	13,555	41,431
3369	Other transportation equipment manufacturing	28	177	787
337	Furniture and related product manufacturing	1,730	19,164	49,530
3371	Household and institutional furniture manufacturing	1,452	12,977	33,298
3372	Office furniture and fixtures manufacturing	164	2,593	7,365
3379	Other furniture related product manufacturing	114	3,594	8,866
339	Miscellaneous manufacturing	1,836	29,502	102,719
3391	Medical equipment and supplies manufacturing	995	20,054	76,722
3399	Other miscellaneous manufacturing	841	9,449	25,997

See footnotes at end of table.

Continued . . .

Table 12.50. EMPLOYMENT AND PAYROLL: AVERAGE MONTHLY PRIVATE REPORTING UNITS EMPLOYMENT, AND PAYROLL COVERED BY UNEMPLOYMENT COMPENSATION LAW BY MANUFACTURING INDUSTRY IN FLORIDA, 2005 AND 2006 (Continued)

NAICS code	Industry	Number of reporting units	Number of employees	Payroll ($1,000)
			2006 B/	
31-33	Manufacturing	16,729	402,301	1,533,177
311	Food manufacturing	1,112	30,556	96,406
3111	Animal food manufacturing	37	516	1,504
3112	Grain and oilseed milling	9	174	1,181
3113	Sugar and confectionery product manufacturing	87	2,944	11,580
3114	Fruit and vegetable preserving and specialty	69	5,996	25,295
3115	Dairy product manufacturing	48	2,472	8,712
3116	Animal slaughtering and processing	78	4,207	10,314
3117	Seafood product preparation and packaging	31	1,881	5,544
3118	Bakeries and tortilla manufacturing	620	8,583	20,302
3119	Other food manufacturing	133	3,784	11,972
312	Beverage and tobacco product manufacturing	173	10,769	43,423
3121	Beverage manufacturing	146	8,491	33,793
3122	Tobacco manufacturing	27	2,277	9,630
313	Textile mills	143	1,378	3,933
3131	Fiber, yarn, and thread mills	9	90	239
3132	Fabric mills	46	474	1,499
3133	Textile and fabric finishing mills	88	814	2,195
314	Textile product mills	518	5,694	13,602
3141	Textile furnishings mills	169	1,923	3,795
3149	Other textile product mills	349	3,771	9,807
315	Apparel manufacturing	373	5,126	11,633
3151	Apparel knitting mills	13	90	213
3152	Cut and sew apparel manufacturing	325	4,554	10,261
3159	Accessories and other apparel manufacturing	35	482	1,158
316	Leather and allied product manufacturing	90	1,390	3,694
3162	Footwear manufacturing	22	162	394
3169	Other leather product manufacturing	61	1,152	2,950
321	Wood product manufacturing	638	21,589	64,964
3211	Sawmills and wood preservation	77	2,674	8,432
3212	Plywood and engineered wood product manufacturing	152	8,458	24,045
3219	Other wood product manufacturing	409	10,456	32,487
322	Paper manufacturing	210	10,376	45,152
3221	Pulp, paper, and paperboard mills	28	2,804	15,495
3222	Converted paper product manufacturing	182	7,572	29,656
323	Printing and related support activities	2,144	23,296	69,978
324	Petroleum and coal products manufacturing	69	2,973	12,343

See footnotes at end of table.

Continued . . .

Table 12.50. EMPLOYMENT AND PAYROLL: AVERAGE MONTHLY PRIVATE REPORTING UNITS EMPLOYMENT, AND PAYROLL COVERED BY UNEMPLOYMENT COMPENSATION LAW BY MANUFACTURING INDUSTRY IN FLORIDA, 2005 AND 2006 (Continued)

NAICS code	Industry	Number of reporting units	Number of employees	Payroll ($1,000)
		2006 B/ (Continued)		
325	Chemical manufacturing	633	19,662	87,320
3251	Basic chemical manufacturing	70	1,541	8,125
3252	Resin, rubber, and artificial fibers manufacturing	59	2,396	10,477
3253	Agricultural chemical manufacturing	73	5,234	25,558
3254	Pharmaceutical and medicine manufacturing	93	4,028	18,882
3255	Paint, coating, and adhesive manufacturing	92	1,778	6,365
3256	Soap, cleaning compound, and toiletry manufacturing	140	2,870	10,905
3259	Other chemical product and preparation manufacturing	106	1,815	7,010
326	Plastics and rubber products manufacturing	622	15,997	48,462
3261	Plastics product manufacturing	538	13,287	39,327
3262	Rubber product manufacturing	84	2,709	9,135
327	Nonmetallic mineral product manufacturing	1,180	29,533	113,373
3271	Clay product and refractory manufacturing	107	861	2,885
3272	Glass and glass product manufacturing	120	2,377	7,551
3273	Cement and concrete product manufacturing	785	22,765	87,269
3274	Lime and gypsum product manufacturing	27	1,021	5,115
3279	Other nonmetallic mineral products	141	2,509	10,553
331	Primary metal manufacturing	168	5,755	19,982
3311	Iron and steel mills and ferroalloy manufacturing	24	667	3,695
3312	Steel product manufacturing from purchased steel	20	624	2,714
3313	Alumina and aluminum production	48	2,598	7,450
3314	Other nonferrous metal production	23	534	1,776
3315	Foundries	53	1,332	4,347
332	Fabricated metal product manufacturing	2,099	40,945	134,390
3321	Forging and stamping	57	1,327	4,383
3322	Cutlery and handtool manufacturing	57	722	2,764
3323	Architectural and structural metals manufacturing	758	19,785	64,138
3324	Boiler, tank, and shipping container manufacturing	71	2,684	9,747
3325	Hardware manufacturing	26	503	1,685
3326	Spring and wire product manufacturing	35	1,933	5,723
3327	Machine shops and threaded product manufacturing	662	6,062	19,388
3328	Coating, engraving, and heat treating metals	185	1,667	5,076
3329	Other fabricated metal product manufacturing	248	6,261	21,486
333	Machinery manufacturing	919	26,213	107,641
3331	Agricultural, construction, and mining machinery manufacturing	58	1,441	4,888
3332	Industrial machinery manufacturing	109	1,894	8,098
3333	Commercial and service industry machinery	159	8,070	42,705
3334	HVAC and commercial refrigeration equipment	99	4,309	12,587
3335	Metalworking machinery manufacturing	201	2,835	8,686
3336	Turbine and power transmission equipment manufacturing	42	1,185	5,214
3339	Other general purpose machinery manufacturing	251	6,480	25,462
334	Computer and electronic product manufacturing	827	49,824	281,888
3341	Computer and peripheral equipment manufacturing	79	3,429	16,870
3342	Communications equipment manufacturing	143	10,396	74,948

See footnotes at end of table.

Continued . . .

Table 12.50. EMPLOYMENT AND PAYROLL: AVERAGE MONTHLY PRIVATE REPORTING UNITS EMPLOYMENT, AND PAYROLL COVERED BY UNEMPLOYMENT COMPENSATION LAW BY MANUFACTURING INDUSTRY IN FLORIDA, 2005 AND 2006 (Continued)

NAICS code	Industry	Number of reporting units	Number of employees	Payroll ($1,000)
		2006 B/ (Continued)		
334	Computer and electronic product manufacturing (Continued)			
3343	Audio and video equipment manufacturing	28	603	2,008
3344	Semiconductor and electronic component manufacturing	228	17,462	99,140
3345	Electronic instrument manufacturing	296	17,137	85,921
3346	Magnetic media manufacturing and reproducing	53	798	3,001
335	Electrical equipment and appliance manufacturing	332	9,027	31,588
3351	Electric lighting equipment manufacturing	67	1,774	4,951
3352	Household appliance manufacturing	26	209	495
3353	Electrical equipment manufacturing	101	3,237	13,135
3359	Other electrical equipment and component manufacturing	138	3,808	13,008
336	Transportation equipment manufacturing	892	43,466	183,653
3362	Motor vehicle body and trailer manufacturing	113	3,339	9,914
3363	Motor vehicle parts manufacturing	170	5,560	17,449
3364	Aerospace product and parts manufacturing	214	18,275	103,676
3366	Ship and boat building	345	14,512	46,589
3369	Other transportation equipment manufacturing	33	222	663
337	Furniture and related product manufacturing	1,709	18,816	51,554
3371	Household and institutional furniture manufacturing	1,418	12,961	34,413
3372	Office furniture and fixtures manufacturing	183	2,685	8,645
3379	Other furniture related product manufacturing	108	3,170	8,496
339	Miscellaneous manufacturing	1,878	29,916	108,200
3391	Medical equipment and supplies manufacturing	983	20,365	80,607
3399	Other miscellaneous manufacturing	895	9,551	27,593

NAICS North American Industry Classification System. See Glossary for definition.
A/ Revised.
B/ Preliminary.
Note: Private employment. Detail may not add to totals due to disclosure editing and/or rounding. See Tables 23.70, 23.72, 23.73, and 23.74 for public employment data.

Source: State of Florida, Agency for Workforce Innovation, Labor Market Statistics, "Quarterly Census of Employment and Wages" (ES-202), Annual NAICS files, Internet site <http://www.labormarketinfo.com/index.htm> (accessed 17, July 2007).

Table 12.51. MANUFACTURING: AVERAGE MONTHLY PRIVATE REPORTING UNITS, EMPLOYMENT AND PAYROLL COVERED BY UNEMPLOYMENT COMPENSATION LAW IN THE STATE AND COUNTIES OF FLORIDA, 2005 AND 2006

County	Number of reporting units	Number of employees	Payroll ($1,000)	County	Number of reporting units	Number of employees	Payroll ($1,000)
		Manufacturing, 2005 A/ (NAICS code 31-33)					
Florida	16,579	399,135	1,443,851	Lee	480	6,783	21,145
				Leon	130	2,178	7,133
Alachua	158	3,943	13,219	Levy	31	761	1,788
Baker	6	249	835	Liberty	7	290	909
Bay	136	3,315	11,337	Madison	13	794	1,800
Bradford	19	463	1,290	Manatee	302	10,084	35,365
Brevard	513	23,399	114,698	Marion	241	9,922	30,196
Broward	1,845	31,370	122,849	Martin	197	3,153	10,781
Calhoun	4	53	99	Miami-Dade	2,668	48,672	148,732
Charlotte	89	887	2,603	Monroe	72	286	761
Citrus	76	662	1,576	Nassau	34	1,194	6,484
Clay	93	1,748	5,393	Okaloosa	151	4,588	16,442
Collier	253	3,226	11,133	Okeechobee	24	235	631
Columbia	38	2,455	7,777	Orange	944	30,264	128,507
DeSoto	13	363	1,114	Osceola	80	1,670	6,126
Dixie	8	466	1,355	Palm Beach	1,121	19,431	82,446
Duval	727	27,114	102,328	Pasco	231	3,659	11,287
Escambia	229	6,379	23,082	Pinellas	1,253	37,989	139,070
Flagler	47	1,195	3,272	Polk	473	18,157	62,850
Gadsden	33	1,472	3,903	Putnam	40	2,578	10,533
Gilchrist	6	114	320	St. Johns	105	3,152	11,603
Gulf	7	219	526	St. Lucie	158	2,932	8,527
Hardee	10	220	565	Santa Rosa	63	1,041	3,283
Hendry	18	1,175	4,983	Sarasota	442	8,745	27,442
Hernando	87	1,134	3,547	Seminole	422	8,231	26,122
Highlands	54	1,065	3,358	Sumter	39	1,052	2,847
Hillsborough	1,040	31,743	110,058	Taylor	26	1,626	5,684
Holmes	12	144	332	Union	8	207	500
Indian River	108	2,143	6,062	Volusia	433	10,136	31,241
Jackson	23	718	1,979	Walton	27	594	1,578
Jefferson	9	73	156	Statewide 1/	144	1,378	11,051
Lafayette	8	134	214	Out-of-state 2/	16	134	1,080
Lake	186	4,603	12,867	Unknown 1/	298	610	3,966

See footnotes at end of table.

Continued . . .

Table 12.51. MANUFACTURING: AVERAGE MONTHLY PRIVATE REPORTING UNITS, EMPLOYMENT AND PAYROLL COVERED BY UNEMPLOYMENT COMPENSATION LAW IN THE STATE AND COUNTIES OF FLORIDA, 2005 AND 2006 (Continued)

County	Number of reporting units	Number of employees	Payroll ($1,000)	County	Number of reporting units	Number of employees	Payroll ($1,000)
			Manufacturing, 2006 B/ (NAICS code 31-33)				
Florida	16,729	402,301	1,533,177	Lee	498	7,535	24,516
				Leon	124	2,216	7,712
Alachua	168	4,517	15,979	Levy	32	744	1,897
Baker	5	276	973	Liberty	8	308	1,045
Bay	143	3,706	13,818	Madison	12	706	1,770
Bradford	21	447	1,291	Manatee	321	10,027	36,908
Brevard	544	24,197	123,924	Marion	239	9,873	31,710
Broward	1,853	31,809	132,118	Martin	195	3,038	10,807
Calhoun	5	57	113	Miami-Dade	2,564	47,724	154,340
Charlotte	91	952	2,813	Monroe	71	293	836
Citrus	76	928	2,420	Nassau	35	1,164	6,456
Clay	100	1,899	6,477	Okaloosa	134	4,650	16,999
Collier	261	3,260	11,236	Okeechobee	26	278	728
Columbia	40	2,423	7,915	Orange	919	28,462	128,781
DeSoto	15	387	1,226	Osceola	83	1,602	6,011
Dixie	9	481	1,345	Palm Beach	1,164	20,147	92,424
Duval	744	26,542	106,209	Pasco	264	4,127	13,282
Escambia	248	6,280	23,530	Pinellas	1,189	37,665	143,792
Flagler	57	1,224	3,488	Polk	491	17,814	62,978
Gadsden	36	1,527	4,215	Putnam	45	2,484	9,951
Gilchrist	8	130	378	St. Johns	111	3,192	12,819
Glades	4	34	121	St. Lucie	163	3,397	10,135
Gulf	9	261	851	Santa Rosa	77	1,031	3,278
Hardee	10	222	506	Sarasota	433	8,799	33,449
Hendry	22	1,053	4,641	Seminole	438	8,585	29,141
Hernando	92	1,424	4,638	Sumter	45	1,442	4,192
Highlands	59	1,101	3,546	Taylor	25	1,589	5,563
Hillsborough	1,053	32,180	114,465	Union	8	186	481
Holmes	12	148	365	Volusia	439	10,567	33,632
Indian River	102	2,323	7,440	Wakulla	12	576	2,600
Jackson	21	609	1,874	Walton	35	663	1,817
Jefferson	11	62	139	Statewide 1/	134	1,757	15,309
Lafayette	6	122	196	Out-of-state 2/	16	139	1,034
Lake	200	4,481	13,199	Unknown 1/	308	599	4,054

NAICS North American Industrial Classification System. See Glossary for definition.
A/ Revised. B/ Preliminary.
1/ Reporting units without a fixed location within the state or of unknown county location.
2/ Employment based in Florida, but working out of the state or country.
Note: Private employment. For a list of three- and four-digit code industries included see Table 12.50. Only counties for which data are disclosed are shown. Detail may not add to totals due to disclosure editing and/or rounding. See Tables 23.70, 23.72, 23.73, and 23.74 for public employment data.

Source: State of Florida, Agency for Workforce Innovation, Labor Market Statistics, "Quarterly Census of Employment and Wages" (ES-202), Annual NAICS files, Internet site <http://www.labormarketinfo.com/index.htm> (accessed 17, July 2007).

Table 12.52. FOOD MANUFACTURING: AVERAGE MONTHLY PRIVATE REPORTING UNITS EMPLOYMENT, AND PAYROLL COVERED BY UNEMPLOYMENT COMPENSATION LAW IN THE STATE AND COUNTIES OF FLORIDA, 2006

County	Number of reporting units	Number of employees	Payroll ($1,000)	County	Number of reporting units	Number of employees	Payroll ($1,000)
			Food manufacturing (NAICS code 311)				
Florida	1,112	30,556	96,406	Manatee	10	1,605	9,373
Alachua	8	73	74	Marion	11	397	1,192
Bay	4	18	20	Martin	8	316	785
Bradford	3	66	221	Miami-Dade	321	4,410	11,940
Brevard	12	95	224	Okeechobee	8	121	349
Broward	114	1,839	3,994	Orange	62	2,373	7,849
Charlotte	5	25	36	Osceola	8	98	428
Collier	12	32	49	Palm Beach	75	2,103	7,974
Duval	47	1,881	6,396	Pasco	15	82	217
Escambia	11	108	132	Pinellas	47	1,116	3,199
Hendry	5	905	4,285	Polk	35	4,508	15,352
Highlands	6	132	556	St. Lucie	14	439	1,747
Hillsborough	69	2,859	7,898	Sarasota	18	138	245
Indian River	3	30	116	Seminole	35	437	955
Lake	9	474	1,473	Volusia	24	399	942
Lee	29	414	912	Statewide 1/	10	40	467
Leon	4	38	36	Unknown 1/	17	74	214
			Fruit and vegetable preserving and specialty (NAICS code 3114)				
Florida	69	5,996	25,295	Lake	3	427	1,420
Broward	4	98	286	Miami-Dade	11	218	466
Hendry	2	310	1,154	Orange	4	332	1,560
Hillsborough	4	107	563	Polk	10	1,826	6,822
			Bakeries and tortilla manufacturing (NAICS code 3118)				
Florida	620	8,583	20,302	Martin	4	58	59
				Miami-Dade	222	2,015	4,313
Alachua	7	67	67	Orange	37	958	2,566
Brevard	7	54	130	Palm Beach	39	506	1,247
Broward	81	871	1,463	Pinellas	20	108	146
Collier	9	25	38	Polk	6	1,074	3,466
Duval	24	674	2,174	St. Johns	4	3	2
Escambia	6	60	58	St. Lucie	5	9	13
Hillsborough	28	525	858	Seminole	20	331	728
Lee	19	311	672	Volusia	15	175	278
Manatee	7	293	1,066	Unknown 1/	8	62	151

NAICS North American Industry Classification System. See Glossary for definition.
1/ Reporting units without a fixed location within the state or of unknown county location.
Note: Private employment. Data are preliminary. For a list of other four-digit code industries included see Table 12.50. Only counties for which data are disclosed are shown. Detail may not add to totals due to disclosure editing and/or rounding. See Tables 23.70, 23.72, 23.73, and 23.74 for public employment data.

Source: State of Florida, Agency for Workforce Innovation, Labor Market Statistics, "Quarterly Census of Employment and Wages" (ES-202), Annual NAICS files, Internet site <http://www.labormarketinfo.com/index.htm> (accessed 17, July 2007).

Table 12.53. BEVERAGE AND TOBACCO PRODUCTS, TEXTILE MILLS, APPAREL, AND LEATHER AND ALLIED PRODUCTS: AVERAGE MONTHLY PRIVATE REPORTING UNITS, EMPLOYMENT AND PAYROLL COVERED BY UNEMPLOYMENT COMPENSATION LAW IN THE STATE AND COUNTIES OF FLORIDA, 2006

County	Number of reporting units	Number of employees	Payroll ($1,000)	County	Number of reporting units	Number of employees	Payroll ($1,000)
			Beverage and tobacco product manufacturing (NAICS code 312)				
Florida	173	10,769	43,423	Lee	3	34	90
Broward	15	865	4,213	Marion	3	178	517
Duval	9	2,836	12,985	Miami-Dade	33	711	2,474
Escambia	4	30	83	Pinellas	12	58	129
Hillsborough	26	3,405	12,084	Unknown 1/	4	9	39
			Textile mills (NAICS code 313)				
Florida	143	1,378	3,933	Orange	9	60	133
				Palm Beach	14	372	1,046
Broward	20	190	602	Pinellas	9	53	114
Miami-Dade	47	339	900	Volusia	9	114	284
			Apparel manufacturing (NAICS code 315)				
Florida	373	5,126	11,633	Miami-Dade	138	2,179	4,794
				Orange	11	25	44
Brevard	6	29	33	Palm Beach	33	108	276
Broward	49	375	841	Pasco	4	5	5
Duval	13	160	262	Pinellas	19	319	478
Hillsborough	28	1,504	3,952	Polk	5	9	17
Lee	5	25	47	Seminole	7	24	66
Leon	5	20	26	Volusia	5	11	12
			Leather and allied products (NAICS code 316)				
Florida	90	1,390	3,694	Miami-Dade	17	199	444
Broward	10	210	620	Palm Beach	10	72	346
Hillsborough	4	27	53	Unknown 1/	3	5	21

NAICS North American Industry Classification System. See Glossary for definition.

1/ Reporting units without a fixed location within the state or of unknown county location.

Note: Private employment. Data are preliminary. For a list of four-digit code industries included see Table 12.50. Only counties for which data are disclosed are shown. Detail may not add to totals due to disclosure editing and/or rounding. See Tables 23.70, 23.72, 23.73, and 23.74 for public employment data.

Source: State of Florida, Agency for Workforce Innovation, Labor Market Statistics, "Quarterly Census of Employment and Wages" (ES-202), Annual NAICS files, Internet site <http://www.labormarketinfo.com/index.htm> (accessed 17, July 2007).

Table 12.57. WOOD PRODUCTS AND PLYWOOD AND ENGINEERED WOOD PRODUCTS: AVERAGE MONTHLY PRIVATE REPORTING UNITS, EMPLOYMENT, AND PAYROLL COVERED BY UNEMPLOYMENT COMPENSATION LAW IN THE STATE AND COUNTIES OF FLORIDA, 2006

County	Number of reporting units	Number of employees	Payroll ($1,000)	County	Number of reporting units	Number of employees	Payroll ($1,000)
			Wood products (NAICS code 321)				
Florida	638	21,589	64,964	Levy	7	73	228
Alachua	10	393	1,092	Liberty	4	173	490
Bay	9	211	593	Manatee	8	157	516
Bradford	6	85	255	Marion	25	1,199	3,535
Brevard	13	791	2,014	Martin	5	116	412
Broward	41	726	2,544	Miami-Dade	58	1,108	3,191
Calhoun	3	55	110	Orange	26	669	2,025
Columbia	10	843	2,076	Osceola	4	150	327
Dixie	3	444	1,208	Palm Beach	42	1,309	3,774
Duval	28	1,109	3,855	Pasco	9	253	711
Escambia	10	170	529	Pinellas	33	600	2,035
Flagler	3	124	294	Polk	32	1,892	5,466
Gadsden	4	438	1,491	St. Lucie	11	390	848
Hernando	3	142	289	Sarasota	12	552	2,071
Hillsborough	51	2,518	9,046	Seminole	11	471	1,517
Indian River	5	144	414	Sumter	5	118	408
Jackson	4	257	775	Volusia	14	194	576
Lake	18	624	1,669	Walton	5	137	375
Lee	19	683	2,053	Washington	3	21	30
			Plywood and engineered wood products (NAICS code 3212)				
Florida	152	8,458	24,045	Lee	6	415	1,202
Brevard	5	724	1,874	Marion	6	314	876
Columbia	4	174	487	Miami-Dade	8	349	1,074
Duval	8	616	2,441	Orange	5	292	773
Escambia	3	96	272	Palm Beach	11	823	2,257
Gadsden	3	407	1,385	Polk	12	629	1,862
Hernando	3	142	289	St. Lucie	6	370	806
Hillsborough	10	441	1,264	Seminole	3	191	538
Lake	9	361	893	Volusia	3	37	92

NAICS North American Industry Classification System. See Glossary for definition.

Note: Private employment. Data are preliminary. For a list of other three- and four-digit code industries included see Table 12.50. Only counties for which data are disclosed are shown. Detail may not add to totals due to disclosure editing and/or rounding. See Tables 23.70, 23.72, 23.73, and 23.74 for public employment data.

Source: State of Florida, Agency for Workforce Innovation, Labor Market Statistics, "Quarterly Census of Employment and Wages" (ES-202), Annual NAICS files, Internet site <http://www.labormarketinfo.com/index.htm> (accessed 17, July 2007).

Table 12.62. FURNITURE AND RELATED PRODUCTS AND HOUSEHOLD AND INSTITUTIONAL FURNITURE: AVERAGE MONTHLY PRIVATE REPORTING UNITS, EMPLOYMENT, AND PAYROLL COVERED BY UNEMPLOYMENT COMPENSATION LAW IN THE STATE AND COUNTIES OF FLORIDA, 2006

County	Number of reporting units	Number of employees	Payroll ($1,000)	County	Number of reporting units	Number of employees	Payroll ($1,000)
Furniture and related products (NAICS code 337)							
Florida	1,709	18,816	51,554	Marion	21	1,010	2,240
Alachua	17	204	742	Martin	28	118	328
Bay	13	133	331	Miami-Dade	315	3,065	7,520
Brevard	43	354	907	Monroe	8	18	54
Broward	189	1,951	6,334	Nassau	5	24	57
Charlotte	19	199	604	Okaloosa	10	58	163
Clay	5	29	68	Orange	72	1,034	3,081
Collier	59	492	1,745	Osceola	6	30	79
Columbia	3	14	27	Palm Beach	137	1,057	3,418
Duval	67	750	2,070	Pasco	25	164	345
Escambia	13	132	366	Pinellas	111	1,505	4,153
Flagler	5	33	75	Polk	36	242	552
Gadsden	5	258	435	Putnam	4	58	118
Hernando	11	83	180	St. Johns	6	40	90
Highlands	9	76	151	St. Lucie	13	127	334
Hillsborough	83	1,247	3,441	Santa Rosa	14	83	226
Indian River	17	73	182	Sarasota	58	568	1,718
Lake	19	161	312	Seminole	45	537	1,460
Lee	75	759	2,348	Volusia	44	385	959
Leon	11	253	601	Washington	4	20	42
Levy	4	18	30	Statewide 1/	8	20	70
Manatee	29	792	2,068	Unknown 1/	5	4	25
Household and institutional furniture manufacturing (NAICS code 3371)							
Florida	1,418	12,961	34,413	Manatee	24	577	1,497
Alachua	15	147	521	Marion	19	962	2,147
Bay	10	119	310	Martin	26	107	297
Brevard	33	206	538	Miami-Dade	249	1,986	4,696
Broward	148	944	2,925	Monroe	8	18	54
Charlotte	19	199	604	Nassau	5	24	57
Clay	5	29	68	Okaloosa	10	58	163
Collier	57	348	1,387	Orange	59	551	1,500
Columbia	3	14	27	Osceola	3	18	39
Duval	54	526	1,357	Palm Beach	113	765	2,352
Escambia	12	122	362	Pasco	23	162	342
Flagler	4	28	61	Pinellas	88	780	2,143
Gadsden	5	258	435	Polk	29	175	408
Hernando	10	79	172	Putnam	4	58	118
Highlands	9	76	151	St. Johns	5	22	57
Hillsborough	67	544	1,220	St. Lucie	12	127	334
Indian River	16	72	180	Santa Rosa	12	71	192
Lake	17	150	300	Sarasota	51	451	1,421
Lee	69	724	2,241	Seminole	34	456	1,272
Leon	8	63	186	Volusia	36	284	728
Levy	4	18	30	Washington	4	20	42

1/ Reporting units without a fixed location within the state or of unknown county location.
Note: See Note on Table 12.57.
Source: State of Florida, Agency for Workforce Innovation, Labor Market Statistics, "Quarterly Census of Employment and Wages" (ES-202), Annual NAICS files, Internet site <http://www.labormarketinfo.com/index.htm> (accessed 17, July 2007).

Table 12.63. PAPER AND MISCELLANEOUS PRODUCTS: AVERAGE MONTHLY PRIVATE REPORTING UNITS, EMPLOYMENT, AND PAYROLL COVERED BY UNEMPLOYMENT COMPENSATION LAW IN THE STATE AND COUNTIES OF FLORIDA, 2006

County	Number of reporting units	Number of employees	Payroll ($1,000)	County	Number of reporting units	Number of employees	Payroll ($1,000)
			Paper manufacturing (NAICS code 322)				
Florida	210	10,376	45,152	Miami-Dade	33	1,142	3,715
				Orange	9	313	1,103
Brevard	3	12	25	Palm Beach	2	4	10
Broward	19	159	384	Pinellas	15	376	1,165
Duval	31	1,801	7,205	Polk	8	713	2,616
Escambia	9	995	5,291	Sarasota	5	33	134
Hillsborough	29	954	3,925	Seminole	4	222	854
Marion	3	126	387	Volusia	3	42	91
			Miscellaneous manufacturing (NAICS code 339)				
Florida	1,878	29,916	108,200	Martin	23	105	377
Alachua	30	595	2,136	Miami-Dade	252	4,478	18,546
Bay	14	107	343	Monroe	6	15	34
Brevard	69	503	1,407	Okaloosa	17	172	397
Broward	208	3,068	8,521	Orange	123	1,119	3,771
Charlotte	12	40	91	Osceola	8	24	93
Citrus	9	30	65	Palm Beach	149	1,547	5,645
Clay	10	44	109	Pasco	35	304	832
Collier	35	357	1,071	Pinellas	149	5,485	19,749
Duval	73	3,843	19,142	Polk	40	322	815
Escambia	38	393	1,263	St. Johns	14	29	74
Flagler	9	24	62	St. Lucie	18	108	259
Highlands	3	13	30	Santa Rosa	12	57	118
Hillsborough	101	1,929	7,208	Sarasota	56	541	1,774
Lake	21	113	317	Seminole	62	752	2,006
Lee	56	455	1,530	Sumter	4	7	17
Leon	21	102	316	Volusia	56	1,459	5,032
Manatee	40	848	2,360	Statewide 1/	15	66	329
Marion	25	228	656	Unknown 1/	25	55	397

NAICS North American Industry Classification System. See Glossary for definition.

1/ Reporting units without a fixed location within the state or of unknown county location.

Note: Private employment. Data are preliminary. For a list of four-digit code industries included see Table 12.50. Only counties for which data are disclosed are shown. Detail may not add to totals due to disclosure editing and/or rounding. See Tables 23.70, 23.72, 23.73, and 23.74 for public employment data.

Source: State of Florida, Agency for Workforce Innovation, Labor Market Statistics, "Quarterly Census of Employment and Wages" (ES-202), Annual NAICS files, Internet site <http://www.labormarketinfo.com/index.htm> (accessed 17, July 2007).

Table 12.64. PRINTING AND RELATED SUPPORT ACTIVITIES AND PLASTICS AND RUBBER PRODUCTS AVERAGE MONTHLY PRIVATE REPORTING UNITS, EMPLOYMENT AND PAYROLL COVERED BY UNEMPLOYMENT COMPENSATION LAW IN THE STATE AND COUNTIES OF FLORIDA, 2006

County	Number of reporting units	Number of employees	Payroll ($1,000)	County	Number of reporting units	Number of employees	Payroll ($1,000)
Printing and related support activities (NAICS code 323)							
Florida	2,144	23,296	69,978	Marion	17	102	234
Alachua	19	217	605	Martin	17	308	1,086
Bay	17	223	646	Miami-Dade	360	4,370	11,857
Brevard	41	290	698	Monroe	9	21	32
Broward	303	2,969	9,782	Okaloosa	19	114	229
Charlotte	12	72	157	Orange	138	1,874	6,295
Citrus	9	35	51	Palm Beach	150	944	3,299
Clay	11	53	130	Pasco	29	103	235
Collier	29	219	639	Pinellas	136	3,689	10,815
Duval	114	1,275	4,022	Polk	46	475	1,184
Escambia	34	284	681	Putnam	3	52	149
Flagler	4	16	25	St. Johns	11	105	278
Hernando	11	41	79	St. Lucie	19	95	178
Hillsborough	158	1,852	5,785	Santa Rosa	4	21	47
Indian River	10	50	113	Sarasota	67	491	1,519
Lake	17	173	503	Seminole	59	455	1,316
Lee	69	484	1,829	Volusia	53	444	1,094
Leon	33	464	1,249	Statewide 1/	7	9	51
Manatee	31	181	553	Unknown 1/	40	45	463
Plastics and rubber products (NAICS code 326)							
Florida	622	15,997	48,462	Martin	3	35	85
Brevard	31	421	1,032	Miami-Dade	85	2,587	6,989
Broward	56	1,416	4,595	Orange	36	1,682	5,208
Collier	8	131	534	Osceola	5	150	422
Duval	30	618	2,437	Palm Beach	31	350	865
Hernando	6	68	179	Pasco	10	189	604
Highlands	7	181	486	Pinellas	51	1,585	4,969
Hillsborough	35	1,041	3,326	Polk	35	1,045	3,273
Indian River	7	171	431	St. Lucie	7	410	1,086
Lake	7	92	222	Sarasota	17	579	1,835
Lee	13	140	406	Seminole	16	208	491
Manatee	13	216	782	Volusia	17	303	981
Marion	16	810	2,615	Unknown 1/	16	29	196

NAICS North American Industry Classification System. See Glossary for definition.
1/ Reporting units without a fixed location within the state or of unknown county location.
Note: Private employment. Data are preliminary. For a list of other three- and four-digit code industries see Table 12.50. Only counties for which data are disclosed are shown. Detail may not add to totals due to disclosure editing and/or rounding. See Tables 23.70, 23.72, 23.73, and 23.74 for public employment data.

Source: State of Florida, Agency for Workforce Innovation, Labor Market Statistics, "Quarterly Census of Employment and Wages" (ES-202), Annual NAICS files, Internet site <http://www.labormarketinfo.com/index.htm> (accessed 17, July 2007).

Table 12.67. CHEMICALS AND ALLIED PRODUCTS: AVERAGE MONTHLY PRIVATE REPORTING UNITS, EMPLOYMENT, AND PAYROLL COVERED BY UNEMPLOYMENT COMPENSATION LAW IN THE STATE AND COUNTIES OF FLORIDA, 2006

County	Number of reporting units	Number of employees	Payroll ($1,000)	County	Number of reporting units	Number of employees	Payroll ($1,000)
			Chemicals (NAICS code 325)				
Florida	633	19,662	87,320	Marion	8	149	545
				Martin	4	22	78
Alachua	8	75	303	Miami-Dade	99	2,165	9,455
Brevard	16	282	964	Nassau	3	336	2,179
Broward	57	890	6,079	Orange	29	1,260	4,518
Duval	34	1,332	6,076	Palm Beach	39	958	3,511
Escambia	12	1,351	6,701	Pasco	8	93	237
Flagler	5	26	83	Pinellas	45	1,560	5,760
Gadsden	3	24	68	Polk	46	2,963	14,012
Highlands	3	232	880	Santa Rosa	5	169	1,122
Hillsborough	54	1,549	7,901	Sarasota	18	324	1,149
Lake	8	233	716	Seminole	13	109	381
Lee	12	119	438	Volusia	15	768	2,227
Manatee	8	96	429	Unknown 1/	22	86	557
			Agricultural chemicals (NAICS code 3253)				
Florida	73	5,234	25,558	Orange	5	331	1,585
Hillsborough	9	997	5,506	Polk	19	2,268	10,988
			Pharmaceutical and medicine (NAICS code 3254)				
Florida	93	4,028	18,882	Palm Beach	9	682	2,555
Alachua	3	24	74	Pinellas	8	915	3,794
Broward	8	453	4,609	Polk	3	16	74
Miami-Dade	22	965	4,792	Sarasota	5	36	139
			Soap, cleaning compound, and toiletry preparations (NAICS code 3256)				
Florida	140	2,870	10,905	Orange	4	34	140
Broward	22	234	748	Palm Beach	8	57	172
Duval	9	669	2,896	Pinellas	9	166	486
Hillsborough	13	253	1,106	Seminole	4	7	25
Miami-Dade	40	631	2,624	Statewide 1/	3	4	52

NAICS North American Industry Classification System. See Glossary for definition.

1/ Reporting units without a fixed location within the state or of unknown county location.

Note: Private employment. Data are preliminary. For a list of other four-digit code industries included see Table 12.50. Only counties for which data are disclosed are shown. Detail may not add to totals due to disclosure editing and/or rounding. See Tables 23.70, 23.72, 23.73, and 23.74 for public employment data.

Source: State of Florida, Agency for Workforce Innovation, Labor Market Statistics, "Quarterly Census of Employment and Wages" (ES-202), Annual NAICS files, Internet site <http://www.labormarketinfo.com/index.htm> (accessed 17, July 2007).

Table 12.71. NONMETALLIC MINERAL PRODUCT AND CEMENT AND CONCRETE PRODUCTS: AVERAGE MONTHLY PRIVATE REPORTING UNITS, EMPLOYMENT, AND PAYROLL COVERED BY UNEMPLOYMENT COMPENSATION LAW IN THE STATE AND COUNTIES OF FLORIDA, 2006

County	Number of reporting units	Number of employees	Payroll ($1,000)	County	Number of reporting units	Number of employees	Payroll ($1,000)
		Nonmetallic mineral product manufacturing (NAICS code 327)					
Florida	1,180	29,533	113,373	Leon	7	144	463
Alachua	16	834	3,060	Manatee	17	294	1,143
Bay	12	363	1,237	Marion	17	494	1,826
Bradford	3	23	68	Martin	13	290	1,082
Brevard	40	736	2,597	Miami-Dade	127	3,437	13,382
Broward	81	2,147	7,480	Okaloosa	15	185	528
Charlotte	13	269	956	Orange	79	2,257	8,069
Citrus	13	154	495	Osceola	9	349	1,086
Clay	13	249	1,051	Palm Beach	92	2,166	11,151
Collier	25	656	2,525	Pasco	32	771	3,019
Columbia	4	53	292	Pinellas	45	667	2,049
Duval	50	1,816	7,353	Polk	45	875	3,433
Escambia	17	638	2,658	Putnam	8	110	377
Flagler	11	159	514	St. Johns	10	76	258
Gadsden	8	197	514	St. Lucie	18	483	1,674
Hendry	4	52	200	Santa Rosa	5	103	292
Hernando	18	497	2,357	Sarasota	30	717	2,163
Highlands	5	155	560	Seminole	24	416	2,808
Hillsborough	71	2,547	9,951	Sumter	11	214	787
Indian River	7	120	441	Volusia	34	594	1,920
Lake	28	1,112	3,494	Walton	7	122	411
Lee	58	1,610	5,770	Unknown 1/	4	6	20
		Cement and concrete products (NAICS code 3273)					
Florida	785	22,765	87,269	Leon	6	85	303
				Manatee	13	276	1,070
Alachua	13	806	2,990	Marion	13	345	1,372
Bay	10	330	1,198	Martin	7	167	663
Brevard	27	466	1,788	Miami-Dade	77	2,704	10,893
Broward	39	1,218	4,254	Okaloosa	9	144	410
Charlotte	10	253	928	Orange	56	1,773	6,778
Citrus	9	140	461	Osceola	8	343	1,072
Clay	13	249	1,051	Palm Beach	56	1,593	8,305
Collier	15	518	2,126	Pasco	28	754	2,992
Columbia	3	50	286	Pinellas	22	454	1,579
Duval	35	971	3,377	Polk	32	717	2,869
Escambia	12	273	816	Putnam	7	101	357
Flagler	8	147	472	St. Johns	8	74	256
Gadsden	6	191	509	St. Lucie	12	347	1,314
Hendry	4	52	200	Santa Rosa	5	103	292
Hernando	13	473	2,294	Sarasota	20	523	1,737
Hillsborough	46	1,931	7,404	Seminole	10	225	826
Indian River	4	105	389	Sumter	11	214	787
Lake	24	1,094	3,446	Volusia	22	524	1,726
Lee	39	1,503	5,499	Walton	6	98	337

NAICS North American Industry Classification System. See Glossary for definition.

1/ Reporting units without a fixed location within the state or of unknown county location.

Note: See Note on Table 12.67.

Source: State of Florida, Agency for Workforce Innovation, Labor Market Statistics, "Quarterly Census of Employment and Wages" (ES-202), Annual NAICS files, Internet site <http://www.labormarketinfo.com/index.htm> (accessed 17, July 2007).

Table 12.72. FABRICATED METAL PRODUCTS AND ARCHITECTURAL AND STRUCTURAL METALS AVERAGE MONTHLY PRIVATE REPORTING UNITS, EMPLOYMENT, AND PAYROLL COVERED BY UNEMPLOYMENT COMPENSATION LAW IN THE STATE AND COUNTIES OF FLORIDA, 2006

County	Number of reporting units	Number of employees	Payroll ($1,000)	County	Number of reporting units	Number of employees	Payroll ($1,000)
Fabricated metal products (NAICS code 332)							
Florida	2,099	40,945	134,390	Martin	25	227	846
				Miami-Dade	229	5,253	14,999
Alachua	14	416	1,630	Monroe	9	38	217
Bay	24	272	946	Nassau	5	23	79
Brevard	82	1,448	4,189	Okaloosa	11	138	471
Broward	246	3,342	11,492	Okeechobee	7	70	158
Citrus	14	156	324	Orange	127	1,937	6,745
Clay	22	428	1,519	Osceola	9	35	82
Collier	22	304	958	Palm Beach	127	1,748	6,181
DeSoto	3	7	14	Pasco	33	381	965
Dixie	4	34	129	Pinellas	200	2,907	9,283
Duval	89	2,822	9,133	Polk	77	1,648	5,644
Flagler	46	1,051	2,741	Putnam	7	64	139
Flagler	5	37	132	St. Johns	17	390	1,368
Hernando	7	92	193	St. Lucie	18	156	501
Highlands	6	30	80	Santa Rosa	8	93	283
Hillsborough	143	3,733	12,759	Sarasota	51	2,937	13,308
Holmes	3	76	204	Seminole	57	795	2,214
Indian River	12	174	474	Sumter	4	351	835
Lake	21	404	1,177	Suwannee	5	33	86
Lee	52	1,020	3,296	Taylor	7	354	747
Leon	20	537	1,916	Volusia	52	869	2,929
Manatee	60	1,389	4,417	Walton	4	13	30
Marion	31	1,580	4,272	Unknown 1/	38	54	590
Architectural and structural metals (NAICS code 3323)							
Florida	758	19,785	64,138	Martin	7	83	251
Alachua	4	22	47	Miami-Dade	96	2,744	7,375
Bay	9	72	168	Monroe	3	18	121
Brevard	27	601	1,895	Okaloosa	3	13	34
Broward	80	1,228	4,596	Okeechobee	4	59	133
Citrus	7	131	275	Orange	44	768	2,615
Clay	8	232	815	Palm Beach	54	1,091	3,655
Duval	41	1,749	5,114	Pasco	11	264	607
Escambia	22	647	1,710	Pinellas	46	813	2,590
Hillsborough	57	1,420	4,349	Polk	23	697	2,357
Indian River	8	142	389	Putnam	5	58	132
Lake	6	303	960	St. Lucie	4	25	48
Lee	32	819	2,613	Seminole	18	447	1,181
Leon	10	237	832	Sumter	3	349	831
Levy	4	18	41	Volusia	19	362	1,123
Manatee	22	397	1,157	Walton	4	13	30
Marion	12	494	1,396	Unknown 1/	8	15	59

NAICS North American Industry Classification System. See Glossary for definition.

1/ Reporting units without a fixed location within the state or of unknown county location.

Note: Private employment. Data are preliminary. For a list of other four-digit code industries included see Table 12.50. Only counties for which data are disclosed are shown. Detail may not add to totals due to disclosure editing and/or rounding. See Tables 23.70, 23.72, 23.73, and 23.74 for public employment data.

Source: State of Florida, Agency for Workforce Innovation, Labor Market Statistics, "Quarterly Census of Employment and Wages" (ES-202), Annual NAICS files, Internet site <http://www.labormarketinfo.com/index.htm> (accessed 17, July 2007).

Table 12.74. MACHINERY INDUSTRY: AVERAGE MONTHLY PRIVATE REPORTING UNITS EMPLOYMENT, AND PAYROLL COVERED BY UNEMPLOYMENT COMPENSATION LAW IN THE STATE AND COUNTIES OF FLORIDA, 2006

County	Number of reporting units	Number of employees	Payroll ($1,000)	County	Number of reporting units	Number of employees	Payroll ($1,000)
			Machinery (NAICS code 333)				
Florida	919	26,213	107,641	Manatee	30	592	1,856
Alachua	8	446	1,590	Marion	18	603	2,338
Bay	4	237	872	Martin	6	35	117
Brevard	27	1,635	7,370	Miami-Dade	96	1,719	4,968
Broward	102	2,405	8,921	Okaloosa	4	47	180
Charlotte	7	92	323	Orange	45	4,194	27,409
Citrus	3	23	93	Palm Beach	46	559	1,945
Collier	11	107	373	Pasco	20	1,002	3,758
Duval	43	1,381	5,288	Pinellas	92	2,919	9,933
Escambia	5	52	160	Polk	37	1,203	3,930
Flagler	4	21	92	St. Lucie	10	184	755
Hernando	10	155	491	Sarasota	29	495	1,692
Highlands	3	6	31	Seminole	17	689	2,424
Hillsborough	54	1,065	4,864	Suwannee	5	20	40
Indian River	6	134	412	Volusia	35	1,531	5,287
Lake	13	487	1,742	Statewide 1/	11	55	447
Lee	32	778	2,585	Unknown 1/	36	56	370
			Commercial and service industry (NAICS code 3333)				
Florida	159	8,070	42,705	Miami-Dade	14	404	1,383
				Orange	15	3,279	21,981
Brevard	6	1,348	6,422	Palm Beach	8	145	501
Broward	21	346	1,330	Pasco	7	278	1,117
Duval	5	168	987	Pinellas	11	240	944
Hernando	4	22	110	Polk	4	198	610
Hillsborough	12	552	2,932	St. Lucie	4	82	400
Indian River	3	57	179	Sarasota	3	30	147
Manatee	3	63	214	Seminole	4	21	37
			HVAC and commercial refrigeration equipment (NAICS code 3334)				
Florida	99	4,309	12,587	Miami-Dade	17	538	1,316
Broward	14	489	1,689	Orange	4	18	45
Duval	7	396	1,066	Pinellas	8	782	1,992
Lee	6	131	604	Sarasota	4	179	484

NAICS North American Industry Classification System. See Glossary for definition.
HVAC Heating, ventilation, air conditioning.
1/ Reporting units without a fixed location within the state or of unknown county location.
Note: Private employment. Data are preliminary. For a list of other four-digit code industries included see Table 12.50. Only counties for which data are disclosed are shown. Detail may not add to totals due to disclosure editing and/or rounding. See Tables 23.70, 23.72, 23.73, and 23.74 for public employment data.

Source: State of Florida, Agency for Workforce Innovation, Labor Market Statistics, "Quarterly Census of Employment and Wages" (ES-202), Annual NAICS files, Internet site <http://www.labormarketinfo.com/index.htm> (accessed 17, July 2007).

Table 12.77. COMPUTER, ELECTRONIC PRODUCTS, COMMUNICATIONS EQUIPMENT, AND SEMICONDUCTOR AND ELECTRONIC COMPONENTS: AVERAGE MONTHLY PRIVATE REPORTING UNITS, EMPLOYMENT, AND PAYROLL COVERED BY UNEMPLOYMENT COMPENSATION LAW IN THE STATE AND COUNTIES OF FLORIDA, 2006

County	Number of reporting units	Number of employees	Payroll ($1,000)	County	Number of reporting units	Number of employees	Payroll ($1,000)
Computer and electronic products (NAICS code 334)							
Florida	827	49,824	281,888	Manatee	17	733	3,596
				Marion	11	1,163	5,264
Alachua	13	290	1,441	Martin	15	474	1,744
Bay	4	25	92	Miami-Dade	87	3,277	15,123
Brevard	78	12,985	77,759	Okaloosa	13	600	2,260
Broward	93	4,962	39,210	Orange	59	2,467	12,225
Citrus	5	13	32	Palm Beach	64	3,289	23,695
Duval	17	474	1,829	Pasco	9	203	657
Escambia	6	63	297	Pinellas	77	9,855	54,930
Flagler	3	69	186	Polk	9	273	899
Hillsborough	43	1,813	7,019	Sarasota	19	692	3,244
Indian River	3	34	225	Seminole	39	1,303	5,757
Lake	8	208	555	Volusia	22	1,023	3,771
Lee	17	316	1,020	Statewide 1/	22	793	6,780
Leon	7	527	2,704	Unknown 1/	31	40	409
Communications equipment (NAICS code 3342)							
Florida	143	10,396	74,948	Marion	4	96	702
				Miami-Dade	15	177	567
Alachua	3	11	24	Orange	8	281	1,446
Brevard	15	556	3,027	Palm Beach	13	1,714	14,490
Hillsborough	9	780	3,244	Polk	3	131	429
Lee	4	41	119	Seminole	6	67	396
Manatee	7	525	2,478	Unknown 1/	4	7	69
Semiconductor and electronic components (NAICS code 3344)							
Florida	228	17,462	99,140	Orange	19	1,337	6,407
Alachua	3	26	131	Palm Beach	23	827	5,362
Broward	18	356	1,459	Pasco	3	85	293
Hillsborough	11	888	3,033	Pinellas	29	3,197	18,495
Lee	6	171	510	Seminole	14	669	3,128
Manatee	5	56	195	Volusia	9	333	1,491
Miami-Dade	9	326	1,180	Unknown 1/	7	7	59

NAICS North American Industry Classification System. See Glossary for definition.

1/ Reporting units without a fixed location within the state or of unknown county location.

Note: Private employment. Data are preliminary. For a list of other four-digit industries included see Table 12.50. Only counties for which data are disclosed are shown. Detail may not add to totals due to disclosure editing and/or rounding. See Tables 23.70, 23.72, 23.73, and 23.74 for public employment data.

Source: State of Florida, Agency for Workforce Innovation, Labor Market Statistics, "Quarterly Census of Employment and Wages" (ES-202), Annual NAICS files, Internet site <http://www.labormarketinfo.com/index.htm> (accessed 17, July 2007).

Table 12.83. SHIP AND BOAT BUILDING: AVERAGE MONTHLY PRIVATE REPORTING UNITS EMPLOYMENT, AND PAYROLL COVERED BY UNEMPLOYMENT COMPENSATION LAW IN THE STATE AND COUNTIES OF FLORIDA, 2006

County	Number of reporting units	Number of employees	Payroll ($1,000)	County	Number of reporting units	Number of employees	Payroll ($1,000)
			Ship and boat building (NAICS code 3366)				
Florida	345	14,512	46,589	Marion	3	29	56
Bay	13	922	2,968	Martin	19	213	771
Broward	55	963	3,387	Miami-Dade	28	1,273	3,911
Clay	5	37	113	Monroe	8	39	71
Duval	14	1,076	4,032	Orange	5	947	2,901
Escambia	8	114	304	Palm Beach	28	625	2,814
Highlands	3	9	18	Pinellas	25	920	2,429
Hillsborough	8	819	2,921	St. Lucie	14	701	2,050
Indian River	6	98	311	Sarasota	6	338	1,265
Lee	16	297	939	Volusia	10	906	2,921
Manatee	13	942	2,971	Walton	3	49	138

NAICS North American Industry Classification System. See Glossary for definition.
Note: See Note on Table 12.84.

Table 12.84. MEDICAL EQUIPMENT AND SUPPLIES: AVERAGE MONTHLY PRIVATE REPORTING UNITS, EMPLOYMENT, AND PAYROLL COVERED BY UNEMPLOYMENT COMPENSATION LAW IN THE STATE AND COUNTIES OF FLORIDA, 2006

County	Number of reporting units	Number of employees	Payroll ($1,000)	County	Number of reporting units	Number of employees	Payroll ($1,000)
			Medical equipment and supplies (NAICS code 3391)				
Florida	983	20,365	80,607	Marion	13	132	418
Bay	5	10	42	Martin	9	17	65
Brevard	27	179	529	Miami-Dade	125	3,818	16,884
Broward	117	2,017	5,426	Okaloosa	10	42	129
Charlotte	9	32	82	Orange	62	523	2,194
Citrus	6	23	53	Palm Beach	82	995	3,885
Clay	7	17	45	Pasco	18	83	212
Collier	22	276	875	Pinellas	89	3,545	13,427
Duval	37	3,311	17,496	Polk	16	120	331
Escambia	21	297	1,064	St. Johns	8	13	30
Flagler	5	10	24	St. Lucie	10	61	151
Hernando	5	22	64	Santa Rosa	5	25	49
Hillsborough	64	1,354	5,496	Sarasota	26	297	990
Lake	9	29	100	Seminole	31	479	1,318
Lee	27	150	529	Volusia	24	1,073	4,002
Leon	13	68	242	Statewide 1/	8	50	281
Manatee	21	646	1,813	Unknown 1/	14	27	215

NAICS North American Industry Classification System. See Glossary for definition.
1/ Reporting units without a fixed location within the state or of unknown county location.
Note: Private employment. Data are preliminary. For a list of other four-digit code industries see Table 12.50. Only counties for which data are disclosed are shown. Detail may not add to totals due to disclosure editing and/or rounding. See Tables 23.70, 23.72, 23.73, and 23.74 for public employment data.
Source for tables 12.83 and 12.84: State of Florida, Agency for Workforce Innovation, Labor Market Statistics, "Quarterly Census of Employment and Wages" (ES-202), Annual NAICS files, Internet site <http://www.labormarketinfo.com/index.htm> (accessed 17, July 2007).

Table 12.85. TRADE: VALUE OF FLORIDA'S MERCHANDISE TRADE VOLUME, 2000 THROUGH 2006

Year	Value ($1,000,000) Total trade	Exports	Imports	Percentage change from previous year Total trade	Exports	Imports
2000	73,751.5	35,851.0	37,900.5	6.0	5.0	7.0
2001	70,959.5	34,529.9	36,429.6	-3.8	-3.7	-3.9
2002	69,118.9	32,163.5	36,955.4	-2.6	-6.9	1.4
2003	72,865.3	32,403.8	40,461.6	5.4	0.7	9.5
2004	81,400.8	37,501.3	43,899.5	11.7	15.7	8.5
2005	95,284.0	44,114.9	51,169.1	17.1	17.6	16.6
2006	109,745.1	52,345.4	57,399.8	15.2	18.7	12.2

Note: Data are from the Foreign Trade Division of the U.S. Census Bureau.

Table 12.86. TRADE: VALUE OF FLORIDA PRODUCTS EXPORTED BY INDUSTRY IN FLORIDA 2004, 2005, AND 2006

Industry	Value ($1,000,000) 2004	2005	2006	Percentage of total 2006	Percentage change 2005 to 2006
Exports of all commodities, total	37,501.3	44,114.9	52,345.4	100.00	18.7
Industrial machinery	8,760.6	10,695.2	12,641.1	24.15	18.2
Electrical machinery	6,198.1	6,929.3	8,188.9	15.64	18.2
Vehicles, not railway	4,037.9	6,011.9	8,155.4	15.58	35.7
Optical and medical instruments	1,868.7	2,406.0	3,055.7	5.84	27.0
Aircraft, spacecraft	1,399.2	1,745.8	2,275.0	4.35	30.3
Fertilizers	1,563.9	1,739.7	1,619.2	3.09	-6.9
Plastics and plastic products	804.7	913.5	1,093.8	2.09	19.7
Pharmaceutical products	967.4	1,022.9	950.7	1.82	-7.1
Cotton and yarn, fabric	869.2	801.0	912.9	1.74	14.0
Knit, crocheted apparel	913.6	839.7	788.0	1.51	-6.2
Precious stones, metals	550.1	465.7	786.6	1.50	68.9
Paper, paperboard	484.9	506.7	584.9	1.12	15.4
Ships and boats	377.0	445.3	581.7	1.11	30.6
Knit, crocheted fabrics	514.1	617.6	575.8	1.10	-6.8
Special other	434.7	520.5	548.6	1.05	5.4
Perfumery, cosmetic, etc.	414.3	464.9	533.1	1.02	14.7
Organic chemicals	545.4	462.6	489.4	0.93	5.8
Miscellaneous chemical products	364.6	378.3	419.3	0.80	10.8
Iron/steel products	229.8	317.0	418.9	0.80	32.2
Toys and sport equipment	217.7	279.2	374.2	0.71	34.0
Furniture and bedding	223.2	332.1	356.1	0.68	7.2
Tanning, dye, paint, putty	258.0	269.7	325.2	0.62	20.5
Iron and steel	158.1	187.6	284.7	0.54	51.7
Meat	248.0	368.3	262.0	0.50	-28.9
Aluminum and aluminum products	145.8	195.7	248.0	0.47	26.7
Rubber and rubber products	205.8	200.9	240.1	0.46	19.5
Manmade staple fibers	273.5	254.8	239.1	0.46	-6.2
Woven apparel	425.7	357.2	234.1	0.45	-34.5
Tools, cutlery, and parts of base metal	160.9	203.8	230.0	0.44	12.9
Wood and wood products	161.3	198.2	223.1	0.43	12.5
All other commodities	2,305.4	2,496.4	2,927.7	5.59	17.3

Note: Data are from the Foreign Trade Division of the U.S. Census Bureau.

Source for Tables 12.85 and 12.86: Enterprise Florida, Inc., Marketing and Information Department, Internet site <http://www.eflorida.com/> (accessed 16, April 2007).

Table 12.87. TRADE: VALUE OF FLORIDA PRODUCTS EXPORTED BY SELECTED DESTINATIONS, 2004, 2005, AND 2006

Location 1/	Value ($1,000,000)			Percentage change	
	2004	2005	2006	2004 to 2005	2005 to 2006
Total	37,501.3	44,114.9	52,345.4	17.6	18.7
Brazil	6,024.3	6,671.0	7,718.2	10.7	15.7
Venezuela	2,635.7	3,419.6	4,410.2	29.7	29.0
Germany	1,500.5	1,618.9	3,467.7	7.9	114.2
Colombia	1,958.7	2,343.7	2,804.0	19.7	19.6
Costa Rica	2,179.2	2,290.5	2,643.9	5.1	15.4
Dominican Republic	2,128.2	2,266.7	2,510.1	6.5	10.7
Argentina	1,351.1	1,678.3	1,957.2	24.2	16.6
Chile	1,147.2	1,450.6	1,715.0	26.5	18.2
Honduras	1,586.9	1,628.2	1,695.8	2.6	4.2
Mexico	1,045.5	1,091.4	1,591.3	4.4	45.8
Guatemala	1,058.0	1,172.2	1,267.7	10.8	8.1
Peru	734.2	879.9	1,239.8	19.8	40.9
Bahamas	703.1	1,015.1	1,201.2	44.4	18.3
El Salvador	934.6	944.8	1,011.2	1.1	7.0
United Arab Emirates	340.8	818.5	981.5	140.1	19.9
Saudi Arabia	534.2	1,193.6	974.1	123.4	-18.4
Ecuador	763.5	918.4	962.2	20.3	4.8
Panama	639.6	767.4	892.9	20.0	16.4
United Kingdom	1,003.7	942.3	872.3	-6.1	-7.4
Paraguay	561.6	788.4	835.7	40.4	6.0
Trinidad and Tobago	493.8	599.5	763.5	21.4	27.3
Jamaica	580.0	610.9	720.5	5.3	17.9
India	133.0	374.6	558.1	181.7	49.0
Haiti	403.1	407.5	501.5	1.1	23.1
China	329.6	426.5	487.7	29.4	14.3
Republic of South Africa	141.8	239.0	424.5	68.5	77.6
Netherlands	368.9	315.3	406.9	-14.5	29.1
Japan	469.5	278.6	392.7	-40.7	40.9
Netherlands Antilles	265.8	290.3	391.7	9.2	35.0
France	228.1	298.7	370.0	30.9	23.9
Cayman Islands	255.5	387.5	359.6	51.7	-7.2
Nicaragua	274.9	308.5	354.2	12.2	14.8
Spain	490.6	282.5	348.0	-42.4	23.2
Italy	189.0	220.3	292.7	16.6	32.9
Barbados	208.3	239.2	278.8	14.8	16.5
Kuwait	255.2	385.5	264.3	51.1	-31.4
Uruguay	152.5	174.1	230.6	14.2	32.4
Australia	279.4	305.3	209.1	9.3	-31.5
Switzerland	145.0	87.9	208.4	-39.3	137.0
Turks and Caicos Islands	70.3	132.6	206.4	88.6	55.6
Qatar	49.3	124.1	201.7	151.8	62.5
Ireland	103.8	226.2	194.0	117.9	-14.3
Aruba	148.6	177.1	173.0	19.2	-2.3
Hong Kong	139.9	184.4	169.8	31.8	-7.9
Belgium	324.4	149.8	135.0	-53.8	-9.8
Bolivia	115.3	123.5	129.5	7.1	4.8
Oman	32.6	127.8	94.1	292.2	-26.4
Antigua	50.4	67.2	93.6	33.3	39.4
Guyana	60.0	78.1	93.3	30.2	19.4
Bermuda	84.1	80.0	92.8	-4.8	16.0

1/ Florida's top 50 merchandise export destinations.
Note: Data are from the Foreign Trade Division of the U.S. Census Bureau.
Source: Enterprise Florida, Inc., Marketing and Information Department, Internet site <http://www.eflorida.com/> (accessed 16, April 2007).

TRANSPORTATION

Top Ten Specialty Tags Sold in Florida, 2005–06

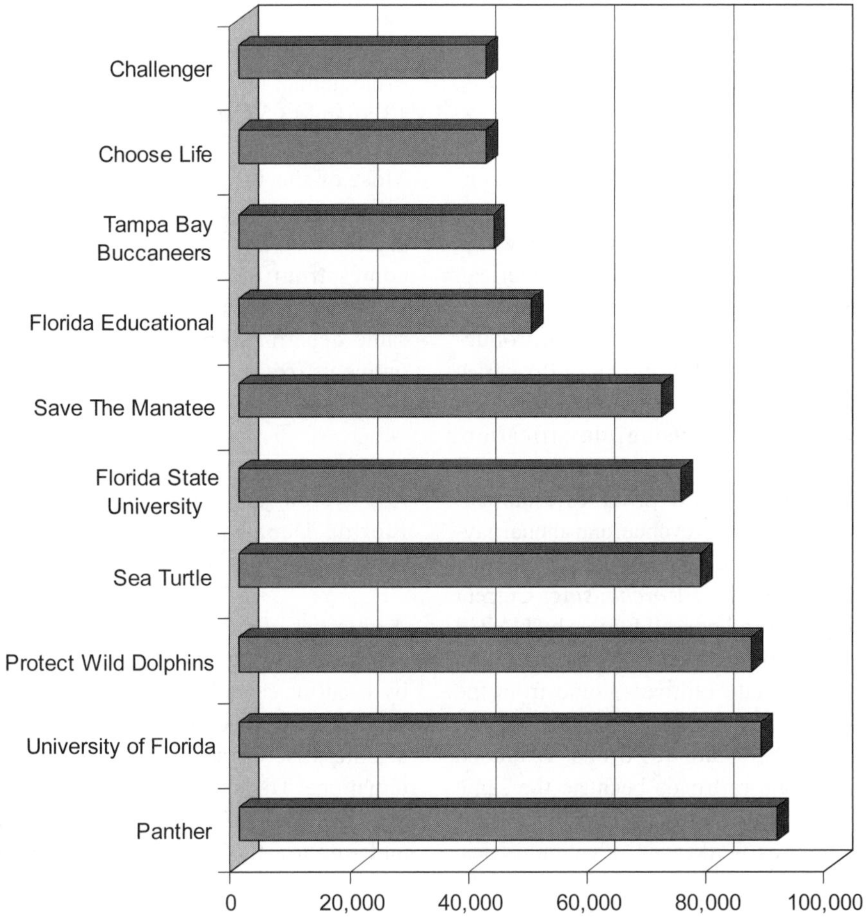

Source: Table 13.32

Section 13.00
Transportation

This section presents data on Florida's transportation industry. Included are statistics on establishments, employment, and payroll; commodity flow; trucks and motorcycles; roads and highways; motor vehicle registrations, tags, and crashes; driver licenses; traffic citations; transportation and warehousing; air, water, and railroad transportation; port activity; exports and imports traveling through customs; airport activity; and aircraft pilots.

Explanatory notes. Every five years, in years ending in "2" and "7," the U.S. Census Bureau conducts an economic census that includes transportation and warehousing based upon the North American Industry Classification (NAICS) industry classification system (see the introduction to Section 6.00 and the Glossary). NAICS codes 48-49 denote the transportation and warehousing classification.

Sources. Table 13.01 provides establishment, employment, revenue, and annual payroll data from the *2002 Economic Census: Transportation and Warehousing.* Current employment and payroll figures by NAICS categories for all modes of transportation except interstate railroads come from the Florida Agency for Workforce Innovation, Labor Market Statistics office. Excluded are interstate railroads because the same unemployment law does not cover their employees as workers in other industries.

The Census Bureau reports commodity flow data and data about trucks traveiling the state's highways from the economic census in the publication, *2002 Economic Census: Transportation, 2002 Commodity Flow Survey.*

The U.S. Department of Transportation (DOT) provides data on roads and highways; tax receipts; bridges; fatalities and annual vehicle miles of travel by functional system; and vehicle registration by type in *Highway Statistics*, a publication of the Federal Highway Administration available on the Internet. The DOT National Highway Traffic and Safety Administration published an evaluation report on the repeal of Florida's motorcycle helmet law on their Web site. Tables 13.51 and 13.52 depict data from this report.

Most of the information about licenses, drivers of motor vehicles, motor vehicle registrations and tags, and traffic citations comes from the Florida Department of Highway Safety and Motor Vehicles. The same department publishes accident data online in *Traffic Crash Facts,* and automobile tag and revenue data in *Revenue Report.*

Data on miles of track in the state's rail system are from the Rail Office, Florida Department of Transportation publication, *Florida Rail System Plan.*

Authorities of the various ports in the state have provided data on their activities, either by fiscal or calendar year, in Table 13.61. The Marketing and Information Department at Enterprise Florida furnished Annual International Trade Statistics from the Census Bureau's Foreign Trade Division on exports and imports through Florida's customs.

Online itinerant and local airport operations data are available from the Federal Aviation Administration (FAA) of the U.S. DOT on their Web site. The FAA also provides unpublished aircraft pilot data.

Section 13.00
Transportation

Tables listed by major heading

Tables listed by major heading

Table 13.01. TRANSPORTATION AND WAREHOUSING: ESTABLISHMENTS, EMPLOYMENT REVENUE, AND ANNUAL PAYROLL BY KIND OF BUSINESS IN FLORIDA, 2002

NAICS code	Industry	Number of establishments	Number of employees 1/	Revenue ($1,000)	Annual payroll ($1,000)
48-49	Transportation and warehousing 2/	11,193	176,357	25,805,912	5,674,523
481	Air transportation 2/	378	6,595	1,614,282	251,620
4811	Scheduled air transportation 2/	160	3,896	956,180	135,440
4812	Nonscheduled air transportation	218	2,699	658,102	116,180
483	Water transportation	235	12,212	8,807,749	530,007
4831	Deep sea, coastal, and Great Lakes water transportation	178	11,839	8,783,298	520,825
4832	Inland water transportation	57	373	24,451	9,182
484	Truck transportation	4,619	48,607	5,652,207	1,585,087
4841	General freight trucking	2,346	A/	(D)	(D)
4842	Specialized freight trucking	2,273	B/	(D)	(D)
485	Transit and ground passenger transportation	860	9,862	691,036	205,137
4851	Urban transit systems	53	1,191	67,546	29,651
4852	Interurban and rural bus transportation	29	490	52,847	8,388
4853	Taxi and limousine service	367	2,203	219,496	42,624
4854	School and employee bus transportation	138	1,753	62,832	34,246
4855	Charter bus industry	65	2,105	168,064	44,331
4859	Other transit and ground passenger transportation	208	2,120	120,251	45,897
486	Pipeline transportation	6	42	19,998	2,441
487	Scenic and sightseeing transportation	394	2,184	145,899	40,998
4871	Scenic and sightseeing transportation, land	26	575	33,053	11,246
4872	Scenic and sightseeing transportation, water	359	1,593	109,897	29,349
4879	Scenic and sightseeing transportation, other	9	16	2,949	403
488	Support activities for transportation	3,223	47,053	5,226,944	1,549,555
4881	Support activities for air transportation	563	16,588	1,295,508	427,036
4882	Support activities for rail transportation	35	C/	(D)	(D)
4883	Support activities for water transportation	392	D/	(D)	(D)
4884	Support activities for road transportation	511	2,869	176,353	58,793
4885	Freight transportation arrangement	1,605	11,885	1,943,881	428,648
4889	Other support activities for transportation	117	D/	(D)	(D)
492	Couriers and messengers	932	29,189	3,108,305	885,931
4921	Couriers	515	27,285	2,890,138	842,518
4922	Local messengers and local delivery	417	1,904	218,167	43,413
493	Warehousing and storage	546	20,613	539,492	623,747

(D) Data withheld to avoid disclosure of information about individual firms.
Employment ranges: A/ 25,000-49,999. B/ 10,000-24,999. C/ 500-999. D/ 5,000-9,999.
1/ Paid employment for the pay period including March 12.
2/ Excludes large, certificated passenger carriers that report to the Office of Airline Statistics, U.S. Department of Transportation.
Note: The economic censuses are conducted on a 5-year cycle collecting data for years ending in 2 and 7. Data are for North American Industry Classification System (NAICS) codes 48-49 and may not be comparable to earlier years. See Glossary for definition.

Source: U.S., Department of Commerce, Census Bureau, *2002 Economic Census: Transportation and Warehousing*, Geographic Area Series EC02-48A-FL, issued August 2005, Internet site <http://www.census.gov/> (accessed 11, May 2007).

Table 13.05. COMMODITY FLOW: SHIPMENT CHARACTERISTIC BY MODE OF TRANSPORTATION IN FLORIDA, 2002

Mode of transportation	Value (million dollars)	Percentage of total	Tons (1,000)	Percentage of total	Ton-miles 1/	Percentage of total	Average miles per shipment
Total	296,989	100.0	455,084	100.0	61,074	100.0	484
Single modes	245,096	82.5	444,398	97.7	58,629	96.0	154
Truck 2/	226,639	76.3	361,197	79.4	40,866	66.9	125
For-hire	97,189	32.7	210,389	46.2	30,286	49.6	565
Private	128,728	43.3	149,286	32.8	9,967	16.3	43
Rail	6,701	2.3	A/	A/	17,082	28.0	1,152
Water	320	0.1	A/	A/	A/	A/	A/
Air (includes truck and air)	10,922	3.7	238	A/	337	0.6	1,645
Pipeline 3/	513	0.2	A/	A/	A/	A/	A/
Multiple modes 4/	39,863	13.4	1,724	0.4	1,252	2.0	1,060
Parcel, U.S. Postal Service or courier	39,094	13.2	884	0.2	833	1.4	1,060
Truck and rail	191	A/	308	A/	316	0.5	1,146
Other and unknown modes	12,030	4.1	8,963	2.0	1,193	2.0	62

A/ Less than one unit of measure or estimate does not meet sampling standards.
1/ Ton-miles estimates are based on estimated distances traveled along a modeled transportation network.
2/ "Truck" as a single mode includes shipments that were made by only private truck, only for-hire truck, or a combination of private truck and for-hire truck.
3/ Estimates for pipeline exclude shipments of crude petroleum.
4/ Includes multiple modes not shown separately.
Note: Data are from a survey. See source for methodology discussion.

Table 13.06. COMMODITY FLOW: TRUCK SHIPMENT CHARACTERISTIC BY DISTANCE SHIPPED IN FLORIDA, 2002

Distance shipped	Value (million dollars)	Percentage of total	Tons (1,000)	Percentage of total	Ton-miles 1/	Percentage of total
Total, all transportation modes	296,989	100.0	455,084	100.0	61,074	100.0
Less than 99 miles	143,110	48.2	370,501	81.4	11,148	18.3
100 to 249 miles	45,999	15.5	42,721	9.4	7,980	13.1
250 to 499 miles	27,758	9.3	12,974	2.9	5,545	9.1
500 to 749 miles	12,687	4.3	7,640	1.7	5,639	9.2
750 to 999 miles	24,386	8.2	9,199	2.0	10,146	16.6
1,000 to 1,499 miles	27,011	9.1	9,092	2.0	12,951	21.2
1,500 miles or more	16,037	5.4	2,957	0.6	7,664	12.5
Truck 2/	226,639	100.0	361,197	100.0	40,866	100.0
Less than 99 miles	126,524	55.8	294,531	81.5	8,663	21.2
100 to 249 miles	36,501	16.1	39,982	11.1	7,380	18.1
250 to 499 miles	22,865	10.1	9,808	2.7	4,058	9.9
500 to 749 miles	8,529	3.8	4,793	1.3	3,461	8.5
750 to 999 miles	11,988	5.3	5,574	1.5	5,907	14.5
1,000 to 1,499 miles	12,350	5.4	4,394	1.2	5,845	14.3
1,500 miles or more	7,881	3.5	2,113	0.6	5,553	13.6

1/ Ton-miles estimates are based on estimated distances traveled along a modeled transportation network.
2/ "Truck" as a single mode includes shipments that were made by only private truck, only for-hire truck, or a combination of private truck and for-hire truck.
Note: Data are from a survey. See source for methodology discussion.
Source for Tables 13.16 and 13.17: U.S., Department of Commerce, Census Bureau, *2002 Economic Census: Transportation, 2002 Commodity Flow Survey, Florida,* EC02TCF-FL, issued December 2004, Internet site <http://www.census.gov/> (accessed 11, May 2007).

Table 13.07. TRUCKS: NUMBER, MILES, AND AVERAGE ANNUAL MILES IN FLORIDA, 2002

Business and range	Number (1,000)	Truck miles (1,000,000)	Average miles per truck (1,000)
Total 1/	4,329.3	56,606.3	13.1
Business			
For-hire transportation or warehousing	36.5	A/	A/
Vehicle leasing or rental	89.3	1,918.3	21.5
Agriculture, forestry, fishing, or hunting	56.5	795.2	14.1
Utilities	53.3	657.6	12.3
Construction	255.1	5,248.5	20.6
Manufacturing	54.0	1,107.4	20.5
Wholesale trade	61.1	1,013.6	16.6
Retail trade	71.0	1,389.4	19.6
Waste management, landscaping, or administrative/support services	61.2	854.0	14.0
Arts, entertainment, or recreation services	1.3	9.2	7.0
Accomodation or food services	33.6	527.8	15.7
Other services	127.5	1,982.5	15.6
Personal transportation	3,136.6	36,353.4	11.6
Range of operation			
Off-the-road	71.1	1,161.8	16.3
50 miles or less	2,950.8	36,930.9	12.5
51 to 100 miles	298.9	5,462.6	18.3
101 to 200 miles	91.7	1,326.9	14.5
201 to 500 miles	50.3	A/	A/
501 miles or more	68.0	1,201.1	17.7
Primary jurisdiction			
Operated within the home base state	3,531.4	48,100.7	13.6
Operated in states other than the home base state	77.5	1,292.5	16.7
Months operated			
12	3,431.4	47,979.7	14.0
7 to 11	341.8	5,143.5	15.1
2 to 6	368.5	3,335.8	9.1
1 or less	98.8	142.8	1.4
Vehicle not used	88.8	4.5	0.1
Vehicle size			
Light	4,147.5	52,340.1	12.6
Medium	67.5	1,109.1	16.4
Light-heavy	37.8	679.8	18.0
Heavy-heavy	76.5	2,477.3	32.4
Average weight (pounds)			
Less than 6,001	3,446.7	41,218.5	12.0
6,001 to 8,500	560.9	8,353.6	14.9
8,501 to 10,000	139.8	2,768.1	19.8
10,001 to 14,000	35.2	568.3	16.1
14,001 to 16,000	22.3	357.3	16.0
16,001 to 19,500	10.0	183.5	18.3
19,501 to 26,000	37.8	679.8	18.0
26,001 to 33,000	17.3	345.8	20.0
33,001 to 40,000	6.2	115.8	18.8
40,001 to 50,000	7.8	200.4	25.6
50,001 to 60,000	8.7	191.9	22.1
60,001 to 80,000	35.6	1,598.0	44.9
80,001 to 100,000	1.0	25.4	26.1

A/ Estimate does not meet sampling standards. 1/ Includes trucks not shown separately.
Note: Data are from a survey. See source for methodology discussion.
Source: U.S., Department of Commerce, Census Bureau, *2002 Economic Census: Transportation, 2002 Commodity Flow Survey, Florida,* EC02TCF-FL, issued December 2004, Internet site <http://www.census.gov/> (accessed 11, May 2007).

Table 13.16. ROADS AND HIGHWAYS: EXISTING MILEAGE OF PUBLIC ROADS AND HIGHWAYS BY JURISDICTION IN FLORIDA, DECEMBER 2002 THROUGH 2005

Jurisdiction	2002	2003	2004	2005
Total	119,785	120,376	119,525	120,557
Rural mileage	50,933	51,897	41,256	39,468
State highway agency	7,060	7,058	5,988	5,969
County roads	39,520	40,553	30,647	29,278
Town, township, municipal	2,409	2,342	2,690	2,392
Other jurisdictions 1/	0	0	0	0
Federal agency 2/	1,944	1,944	1,931	1,829
Urban mileage	68,852	68,479	78,269	81,089
State highway agency	4,999	4,994	6,059	6,071
County roads	30,906	30,537	39,655	41,917
Town, township, municipal	32,806	32,807	32,414	32,953
Federal agency 2/	141	141	141	148

1/ Includes state park, state toll, other state agency, other local agency and other roadways not identified by ownership.
2/ Includes mileage in federal parks, forests, and reservations that are not part of the state and local highway system.

Table 13.17. ROADS AND HIGHWAYS: EXISTING MILEAGE OF PUBLIC ROADS AND HIGHWAYS BY FUNCTIONAL SYSTEM OF HIGHWAY AND BY PAVEMENT CONDITION IN FLORIDA, DECEMBER 31, 2005

Function	Total existing mileage	Total miles measured	Pavement conditions 1/ Poor	Mediocre	Fair	Good	Very good
Total	120,557	(X)	(NA)	(NA)	(NA)	(NA)	(NA)
Rural	39,467	(X)	(NA)	(NA)	(NA)	(NA)	(NA)
Interstate	749	744	0	0	4	278	462
Other principal arterial	2,854	2,848	0	23	273	1,735	817
Minor arterial	2,401	2,395	5	0	234	1,740	416
Major collector	4,119	844	0	0	95	478	271
Minor collector	3,353	(X)	(NA)	(NA)	(NA)	(NA)	(NA)
Local	25,991	(X)	(NA)	(NA)	(NA)	(NA)	(NA)
Urban	81,090	(X)	(NA)	(NA)	(NA)	(NA)	(NA)
Interstate	722	717	0	1	41	350	325
Other freeways and expressways	550	547	0	2	38	405	102
Other principal arterial	3,560	3,540	20	75	1,151	1,804	490
Minor arterial	4,030	1,740	23	75	760	796	86
Collector	6,796	363	16	16	123	200	8
Local	65,432	(X)	(NA)	(NA)	(NA)	(NA)	(NA)

(X) Not applicable.
(NA) Not available.
1/ Based on the International Roughness Index (IRI) or a combination of IRI and the Present Serviceability Rating (PSR) values. See source for rating explanation.

Source for Tables 13.16 and 13.17: U.S., Department of Transportation, Federal Highway Administration, *Highway Statistics, 2005,* Internet site <http://www.fhwa.dot.gov/> (accessed 20, March 2007), and previous editions.

Table 13.21. ROADS AND HIGHWAYS: FEDERAL HIGHWAY TRUST FUNDS RECEIPTS BY HIGHWAY USER IN FLORIDA, 2003, 2004 AND 2005

(in thousands of dollars)

Item	2003	2004	2005
Federal highway trust fund receipts, total	1,801,837	1,820,745	2,091,712
Highway account	1,551,004	1,567,749	1,811,267
Motor fuel	1,432,139	1,436,842	1,618,257
Gasoline, total	1,161,562	1,142,198	1,285,994
Gasoline	1,161,168	1,142,198	1,285,977
Gasohol	394	0	17
Special fuels	270,577	294,644	332,263
Other	118,865	130,907	193,010
Federal use tax	36,613	38,199	46,236
Trucks and trailers	66,561	74,678	126,959
Tires	15,691	18,030	19,815
Mass transit account	250,833	252,996	280,445
Gasoline, total	215,281	212,919	235,925
Gasoline	215,141	212,919	235,920
Gasohol	140	0	5
Special fuels	35,552	40,077	44,520

Note: Total Federal Highway Trust Fund receipts are reported by the U.S. Department of the Treasury. Payments into the Highway Trust Fund attributable to highway users in the state are estimated by the Federal Highway Administration.

Table 13.22. ROADS AND HIGHWAYS: PERSONS FATALLY INJURED IN MOTOR VEHICLE CRASHES BY FUNCTIONAL SYSTEM IN FLORIDA, 2001 THROUGH 2005

Functional system	2001	2002	2003	2004	2005
Total	3,011	3,132	3,169	3,244	3,543
Rural	623	1,418	1,586	1,624	1,310
Interstate	135	239	251	259	164
Other principal arterial	190	429	437	451	303
Minor arterial	57	200	354	650	112
Major collector	6	23	21	11	11
Minor collector	4	5	3	2	0
Local	231	522	520	251	720
Urban	597	1,695	1,577	1,607	1,978
Interstate	121	200	159	189	301
Other freeways and expressways	32	67	66	99	100
Other principal arterial	246	750	670	697	828
Minor arterial	76	273	375	449	301
Collector	13	22	44	38	44
Local	109	383	263	135	404
Unknown	1,791	19	6	13	255

Note: Data obtained from the Fatality Analysis Reporting System, National Highway Traffic Safety Administration.

Source for Tables 13.21 and 13.22: U.S., Department of Transportation, Federal Highway Administration, *Highway Statistics, 2005,* Internet site <http://www.fhwa.dot.gov/> (accessed 20, March 2007), and previous editions.

Table 13.29. ROADS AND HIGHWAYS: ESTIMATED ANNUAL VEHICLE MILES OF TRAVEL BY FUNCTIONAL SYSTEM OF HIGHWAY IN FLORIDA, 2004 AND 2005

(in millions of miles)

Functional system of highway	Total		Rural		Urban	
	2004	2005	2004	2005	2004	2005
Total	196,444	201,531	36,297	36,887	160,147	164,644
Interstate	33,409	34,416	9,530	9,814	23,879	24,602
Other freeways and expressways	11,283	11,875	0	0	11,283	11,875
Other principal arterial	50,283	51,468	10,423	10,861	39,860	40,607
Minor arterial	33,189	33,841	4,390	4,601	28,799	29,240
Collector	24,580	24,726	5,051	5,145	19,529	19,581
Local	43,700	45,205	6,903	6,466	36,797	38,739

Note: Data are estimated highway travel based on traffic counts taken at selected highway locations.

Table 13.30. MOTOR VEHICLE REGISTRATIONS: NUMBER BY TYPE OF VEHICLE IN FLORIDA 1986 THROUGH 2005

(in thousands, rounded to hundreds, except where indicated)

Year	All motor vehicles 1/	Percentage change from previous year	Automobiles 2/	Buses	Trucks 2/	Motorcycles
1986	10,591.2	4.9	8,263.3	34.2	2,064.0	229.7
1987	10,903.1	2.9	8,521.6	34.8	2,127.1	219.5
1988	11,183.1	2.6	8,713.2	35.5	2,234.9	199.5
1989	11,410.8	2.0	8,972.7	36.2	2,197.9	203.9
1990	11,155.6	-2.2	8,694.9	36.8	2,218.1	205.8
1991	10,176.1	-8.8	7,910.3	37.5	2,032.3	196.0
1992	10,426.1	2.5	8,131.4	38.1	2,062.8	193.7
1993	10,358.4	-0.6	8,072.5	38.8	2,058.3	188.8
1994	10,429.2	0.7	7,519.2	39.6	2,693.0	177.4
1995	10,559.5	1.2	7,594.9	40.3	2,734.3	190.1
1996	11,091.9	5.0	7,285.6	41.2	3,561.9	203.3
1997	11,083.5	-0.1	7,374.8	42.1	3,457.1	209.5
1998	11,498.4	3.7	7,437.6	43.1	3,795.7	222.0
1999	11,625.4	1.1	7,304.6	44.0	4,041.1	235.7
2000	11,781.0	1.3	7,352.7	45.0	4,383.3	255.2
2001	14,645.6	24.3	8,937.6	45.6	5,356.9	305.5
2002	14,309.1	-2.3	8,471.5	46.1	5,446.0	345.5
2003	14,918.5	4.3	8,564.2	46.7	5,915.2	392.4
2004	15,519.4	4.0	8,440.8	47.3	6,569.3	461.9
2005	16,207.6	4.4	8,311.7	48.2	7,331.6	516.1

1/ Includes motorcycles.
2/ Beginning in 1994, personal passenger vans, passenger minivans, and utility-type vehicles were classified by the source as trucks rather than automobiles. Therefore, caution should be used when making comparisons to earlier years.
Note: Includes federal, state, county, and municipal vehicles. Excludes vehicles owned by the military service.

Source for Tables 13.29 and 13.30: U.S., Department of Transportation, Federal Highway Administration, *Highway Statistics, 2005,* Internet site <http://www.fhwa.dot.gov/> (accessed 20, March 2007), and previous editions.

Table 13.31. MOTOR VEHICLE TAGS: TOTAL, PASSENGER CAR, AND LEASE VEHICLE TAGS SOLD AND REVENUE COLLECTED IN THE STATE AND COUNTIES OF FLORIDA FISCAL YEAR 2005-06

County	Total tags		Passenger car tags		Lease vehicle tags		
	Number	Percentage change from 2004-05	Number	Percentage change from 2004-05	Number	Percentage change from 2004-05	Total revenue ($1,000)
Florida 1/	19,495,041	3.6	10,978,272	2.5	1,357,182	3.3	636,081.9
Alachua	231,082	2.9	138,779	2.8	3,506	-2.3	6,076.9
Baker	30,699	5.8	12,201	5.0	85	-6.6	830.4
Bay	211,760	3.4	105,121	2.3	1,811	-2.8	5,448.7
Bradford	31,390	3.7	13,235	1.5	82	17.1	867.6
Brevard	611,834	2.1	349,716	0.6	11,296	-7.5	16,179.5
Broward	1,637,132	3.6	1,017,665	1.8	252,723	12.6	49,419.7
Calhoun	13,917	5.7	5,512	0.8	15	15.4	386.1
Charlotte	209,066	3.0	110,263	0.6	3,807	1.9	5,694.9
Citrus	184,115	6.1	84,768	3.5	1,810	5.5	4,623.5
Clay	199,454	6.7	106,284	6.5	2,585	6.8	5,385.4
Collier	345,049	4.0	208,624	3.0	16,969	7.3	10,592.7
Columbia	73,147	6.2	32,670	4.5	517	-27.5	2,244.0
DeSoto	37,161	3.5	13,674	-1.6	218	2.3	1,221.0
Dixie	19,354	5.7	6,127	3.1	23	43.8	523.7
Duval	813,478	0.7	499,304	0.3	29,588	3.4	24,409.0
Escambia	317,621	0.7	176,265	-0.8	9,076	2.1	8,650.6
Flagler	85,544	6.8	50,836	6.1	1,735	11.4	2,441.5
Franklin	16,081	0.9	5,754	1.0	33	-5.7	400.1
Gadsden	39,488	2.0	20,524	1.7	144	-9.4	1,162.1
Gilchrist	19,140	5.9	6,672	3.6	21	5.0	584.2
Glades	9,332	7.0	2,663	7.2	19	26.7	286.9
Gulf	19,514	1.0	7,242	1.0	42	7.7	497.4
Hamilton	12,081	4.8	5,134	2.0	33	-17.5	344.7
Hardee	28,206	1.5	10,928	-0.4	287	29.9	941.4
Hendry	48,224	-2.4	19,390	-1.3	357	-87.6	1,934.0
Hernando	173,370	6.5	94,969	5.5	2,247	11.4	4,728.7
Highlands	129,320	3.8	55,888	2.0	1,213	6.4	3,713.3
Hillsborough	1,189,885	5.6	713,231	4.2	43,217	7.9	36,510.3
Holmes	20,817	4.6	8,171	2.0	41	-16.3	565.7
Indian River	168,655	3.9	89,734	1.8	4,560	7.4	4,648.3
Jackson	56,395	5.8	25,933	3.6	260	-34.3	1,530.9
Jefferson	20,372	0.3	8,533	-2.9	1,142	-32.6	686.3
Lafayette	8,422	4.7	2,648	2.4	77	37.5	258.8
Lake	347,531	6.1	169,710	5.5	6,681	8.9	9,708.6

See footnotes at end of table.

Continued . . .

Table 13.31. MOTOR VEHICLE TAGS: TOTAL, PASSENGER CAR, AND LEASE VEHICLE TAGS SOLD AND REVENUE COLLECTED IN THE STATE AND COUNTIES OF FLORIDA FISCAL YEAR 2005–06 (Continued)

County	Total tags Number	Total tags Percentage change from 2004–05	Passenger car tags Number	Passenger car tags Percentage change from 2004–05	Lease vehicle tags Number	Lease vehicle tags Percentage change from 2004–05	Total revenue ($1,000)
Lee	655,958	5.1	361,073	4.1	22,031	2.7	20,343.0
Leon	251,371	2.6	148,925	2.6	6,821	-7.2	6,773.4
Levy	51,338	7.9	19,696	5.7	221	-26.3	1,543.6
Liberty	8,128	4.2	2,680	1.0	9	-25.0	270.8
Madison	19,401	1.2	8,494	2.0	100	49.3	567.5
Manatee	320,047	2.8	178,572	2.5	8,882	2.3	9,097.7
Marion	379,635	5.7	192,790	4.5	4,223	7.8	10,727.3
Martin	187,846	2.4	103,315	1.8	7,755	6.8	5,258.5
Miami-Dade	2,183,782	4.3	1,450,420	2.7	208,097	10.1	75,785.6
Monroe	128,073	-5.2	47,618	-9.4	2,105	9.5	2,951.9
Nassau	80,576	6.1	39,534	5.4	718	4.4	2,142.6
Okaloosa	243,227	2.1	128,415	0.8	3,019	2.1	6,185.0
Okeechobee	54,816	2.1	18,215	0.7	266	3.9	1,629.1
Orange	1,043,571	3.8	657,202	3.7	68,465	0.1	32,883.1
Osceola	246,864	4.1	152,661	4.2	4,809	-6.9	7,186.3
Palm Beach	1,138,484	1.8	743,582	1.0	83,786	1.7	37,109.2
Pasco	482,142	4.6	259,390	3.8	9,422	7.5	13,731.9
Pinellas	1,461,505	1.1	598,588	0.6	459,276	-2.0	47,931.9
Polk	622,547	4.8	309,278	4.0	10,466	-2.3	20,455.7
Putnam	88,582	2.8	37,440	2.1	432	4.3	2,282.2
St. Johns	202,755	7.6	108,046	4.1	4,929	4.3	6,602.9
St. Lucie	261,016	4.4	146,617	3.3	7,070	-7.4	7,771.3
Santa Rosa	161,617	4.0	78,262	1.2	1,072	16.6	4,123.8
Sarasota	437,563	2.3	263,606	1.0	18,007	4.2	12,321.6
Seminole	438,322	2.6	271,056	1.8	14,779	-8.5	12,539.4
Sumter	75,917	11.6	37,040	14.0	903	40.4	2,569.3
Suwannee	46,877	3.0	19,092	1.7	167	-39.7	1,404.5
Taylor	36,082	4.2	10,941	1.5	122	-26.9	2,721.5
Union	12,672	5.1	4,895	1.0	38	5.6	448.5
Volusia	591,252	4.3	312,961	2.5	10,303	6.1	16,064.0
Wakulla	31,008	5.5	10,970	4.5	65	18.2	755.6
Walton	57,792	8.7	26,429	7.0	528	12.3	1,662.7
Washington	24,302	6.1	9,660	3.0	65	-4.4	643.1

1/ Details may not add to totals due to reporting practices involving tags outside the computer system and refunds.

Note: Totals include pleasure, commercial, and dealer boats. Florida and Pinellas County totals also include IRP. See Table 2.36 for mobile home and recreational vehicle tag sales.

Source: State of Florida, Department of Highway Safety and Motor Vehicles, *Revenue Report, July 1, 2005 through June 30, 2006,* Internet site <http://www.hsmv.state.fl.us/> (accessed 16, March 2007).

Table 13.32. MOTOR VEHICLE TAGS: SPECIALTY TAGS SOLD AND REVENUE COLLECTED IN FLORIDA, FISCAL YEAR 2005–06

Specialty license plates	Number	Revenue (dollars)	Percentage of total
Total	1,477,967	31,777,561	100.00
Agriculture in the Classroom	17,446	348,920	1.10
Air Force	11,596	173,940	0.55
American Red Cross	1,168	29,200	0.09
Animal Friend	10,338	258,450	0.81
Aquaculture	7,874	196,860	0.62
Army	13,034	195,510	0.62
Barry University	1,267	31,675	0.10
Bethune-Cookman College	6,670	166,750	0.52
Boy Scouts of America	3,402	68,040	0.21
Challenger/Columbia	41,645	1,041,125	3.28
Choose Life	41,776	835,521	2.63
Clearwater Christian College	69	1,725	0.01
Coast Guard	4,507	67,605	0.21
Conserve Wildlife	30,631	459,465	1.45
Discover Florida Oceans	11,056	276,400	0.87
Eckerd College	409	10,225	0.03
Edward Waters College	873	21,825	0.07
Embry-Riddle Aeronautical University	1,545	38,625	0.12
End Breast Cancer	17,879	446,975	1.41
Everglades River of Grass	14,232	284,640	0.90
Family First	4,139	103,475	0.33
Family Values	1,584	39,600	0.12
Fish Florida	16,680	366,960	1.15
Flagler College	1,333	33,325	0.10
Florida A & M University	20,581	514,525	1.62
Florida Atlantic University	2,332	58,300	0.18
Florida College	274	6,850	0.02
Florida Educational	49,382	740,735	2.33
Florida Fine Arts	31,327	626,532	1.97
Florida Gulf Coast University	1,364	34,100	0.11
Florida Hospital College of Health Sciences	119	2,975	0.01
Florida Institute of Technology	1,081	27,025	0.09
Florida International University	2,554	63,850	0.20
Florida Marlins	3,131	78,275	0.25
Florida Memorial College	1,342	33,550	0.11
Florida Panthers	3,274	81,850	0.26
Florida Salute to Veterans	28,377	425,655	1.34
Florida Sheriff's Youth Ranch	6,940	138,800	0.44
Florida Southern College	476	11,900	0.04
Florida State University	74,500	1,862,500	5.86
Florida Wildflower	18,939	284,085	0.89
Girl Scouts of America	106	2,120	0.01
Golf Capital of the World	22,898	572,450	1.80
Hospice: Everyday is a Gift	8,891	222,275	0.70
Imagine—Florida Food Banks	6,066	151,650	0.48
Indian River Lagoon	24,479	367,185	1.16
Invest in Children	23,501	470,020	1.48
Jacksonville Jaguars	12,073	301,825	0.95
Jacksonville University	996	24,900	0.08
Keep Kids Drug Free	11,072	276,800	0.87
Kids Deserve Justice	1,152	28,800	0.09
Large Mouth Bass	20,095	502,375	1.58
Live the Dream	4,219	105,475	0.33

Continued . . .

Table 13.32. MOTOR VEHICLE TAGS: SPECIALTY TAGS SOLD AND REVENUE COLLECTED IN FLORIDA, FISCAL YEAR 2005–06 (Continued)

Specialty license plates	Number	Revenue (dollars)	Percentage of total
Lynn University	246	6,150	0.02
Miami Dolphins	24,375	609,375	1.92
Miami Heat	14,599	364,975	1.15
Motorcycle Specialty	15,483	232,245	0.73
Navy	11,119	166,785	0.52
New College	497	12,425	0.04
Nova Southeastern University	1,585	39,625	0.12
Orlando Magic	3,949	98,725	0.31
Orlando Predators	36	900	0.00
Palm Beach Atlantic University	352	8,800	0.03
Protect the Panther	90,648	2,266,200	7.13
Parents Make a Difference	1,472	36,800	0.12
Police Athletic League	17,678	353,560	1.11
Protect Florida Whales	19,493	487,325	1.53
Protect Our Reefs	38,180	954,500	3.00
Protect Wild Dolphins	86,197	1,723,940	5.43
Ringling School of Art and Design	473	11,825	0.04
Rollins University	1,227	30,675	0.10
St. Leo University	495	12,375	0.04
St. Thomas University	193	4,825	0.02
Salutes Firefighters	16,762	335,230	1.05
Save Our Seas	15,194	379,845	1.20
Save the Manatee	71,227	1,424,540	4.48
Sea Turtle	77,853	1,362,428	4.29
Share the Road— Bike Florida	10,663	159,945	0.50
Southeastern College	101	2,525	0.01
Special Olympics	5,821	87,315	0.27
Sportsmen's National Land Trust	5,726	143,150	0.45
Stetson University	1,187	29,675	0.09
Stop Child Abuse	7,764	194,100	0.61
Stop Heart Disease	8,133	203,325	0.64
Support Law Enforcement	8,710	174,200	0.55
Support Soccer	3,628	90,700	0.29
Tampa Bay Buccaneers	42,893	1,072,325	3.37
Tampa Bay Devil Rays	1,357	33,925	0.11
Tampa Bay Estuary	10,634	159,510	0.50
Tampa Bay Lightning	4,946	123,650	0.39
Tampa Bay Storm	23	575	0.00
U.S. Paratrooper	3,906	78,120	0.25
U.S. Marine Corps	36,724	550,860	1.73
U.S. Olympic	10,773	161,595	0.51
United We Stand	19,431	485,775	1.53
University of Central Florida	12,283	307,075	0.97
University of Florida	87,979	2,199,475	6.92
University of Miami	29,706	742,650	2.34
University of North Florida	1,672	41,800	0.13
University of South Florida	9,227	230,675	0.73
University of Tampa	1,144	28,600	0.09
University of West Florida	1,327	33,175	0.10
Warner Southern College	182	4,550	0.01

Source: State of Florida, Department of Highway Safety and Motor Vehicles, *Revenue Report, July 1, 2005 through June 30, 2006,* Internet site <http://www.hsmv.state.fl.us/> (accessed 16, March 2007).

Table 13.33. MOTOR VEHICLE REGISTRATIONS: OUT-OF-STATE VEHICLES REGISTERED IN FLORIDA BY STATE OF PREVIOUS REGISTRATION
2002 THROUGH 2006

State in 2006 rank order	2002	2003	2004	2005	2006 Number	2006 Percentage of total
Total	529,260	539,183	580,146	584,146	534,221	100.00
Georgia	49,240	52,679	55,353	58,737	52,759	9.88
New York	56,814	57,050	61,097	61,978	50,041	9.37
New Jersey	24,610	29,755	33,406	35,234	29,087	5.44
Ohio	26,475	26,311	28,239	30,979	27,184	5.09
North Carolina	24,257	24,000	25,946	28,411	26,011	4.87
Pennsylvania	25,267	24,203	28,211	29,213	25,831	4.84
Michigan	22,968	23,843	25,635	26,954	24,941	4.67
Alabama	24,699	23,784	24,420	26,885	23,847	4.46
Virginia	21,016	21,052	23,071	24,668	21,961	4.11
Texas	22,052	22,894	23,418	25,216	20,931	3.92
Massachusetts	20,185	19,895	22,998	24,087	20,796	3.89
Illinois	17,246	19,118	20,905	21,586	18,071	3.38
California	17,140	17,334	18,946	19,372	16,530	3.09
Tennessee	16,184	16,027	16,933	18,661	16,453	3.08
Indiana	13,780	13,901	14,910	15,237	13,718	2.57
Maryland	15,242	14,363	15,034	15,692	13,685	2.56
South Carolina	12,401	13,310	13,484	14,344	12,547	2.35
Connecticut	10,165	10,678	12,387	12,777	10,641	1.99
Louisiana	7,448	7,295	7,558	7,916	8,060	1.51
Kentucky	7,183	7,435	7,621	8,270	7,307	1.37
Missouri	6,848	7,000	7,391	7,856	6,961	1.30
Wisconsin	6,492	6,707	7,217	7,782	6,810	1.27
New Hampshire	6,111	6,152	6,875	6,954	6,388	1.20
Mississippi	5,777	5,576	5,911	6,296	6,194	1.16
Arizona	4,711	5,057	5,658	6,208	5,695	1.07
Maine	5,238	6,035	6,482	6,581	5,594	1.05
Colorado	6,094	5,981	6,373	6,365	5,212	0.98
Minnesota	4,685	5,012	4,949	5,243	4,600	0.86
Oklahoma	3,533	3,349	4,132	4,182	3,796	0.71
Rhode Island	4,464	4,857	4,697	4,499	3,731	0.70
Washington	2,907	3,285	4,032	3,574	3,124	0.58
West Virginia	3,197	3,108	3,192	3,155	2,808	0.53
Iowa	3,028	3,048	3,187	3,092	2,803	0.52
Arkansas	2,723	2,649	2,991	3,062	2,688	0.50
Nevada	(NA)	2,599	2,767	3,022	2,566	0.48
Other states	18,128	18,864	19,383	20,273	18,056	3.38
Other areas 1/	5,877	5,151	5,112	6,085	6,794	1.27

(NA) Not available.
1/ Includes Washington D.C., Canada, Puerto Rico, other Caribbean islands, Armed Forces, and other foreign countries.

Source: State of Florida, Department of Highway Safety and Motor Vehicles, Division of Motor Vehicles, unpublished data.

Table 13.34. MOTOR VEHICLE REGISTRATIONS: OUT-OF-STATE VEHICLES REGISTERED BY COUNTY OF REGISTRATION IN THE STATE AND COUNTIES OF FLORIDA, 2005 AND 2006

County	2005	2006 Number	2006 Percentage of total	County	2005	2006 Number	2006 Percentage of total
Florida	610,504	534,221	100.00	Lake	11,596	10,103	1.89
				Lee	25,470	21,133	3.96
Alachua	6,095	5,523	1.03	Leon	6,991	6,585	1.23
Baker	578	587	0.11	Levy	1,013	908	0.17
Bay	11,599	10,110	1.89	Liberty	95	78	0.01
Bradford	549	627	0.12	Madison	691	713	0.13
Brevard	18,364	15,499	2.90	Manatee	8,436	6,812	1.28
Broward	36,462	32,817	6.14	Marion	13,520	11,509	2.15
Calhoun	349	280	0.05	Martin	6,105	5,073	0.95
Charlotte	8,827	7,514	1.41	Miami-Dade	56,757	54,232	10.15
Citrus	6,074	5,307	0.99	Monroe	4,488	3,954	0.74
Clay	6,601	6,120	1.15	Nassau	3,292	3,474	0.65
Collier	15,009	12,402	2.32	Okaloosa	14,056	11,818	2.21
Columbia	1,763	1,600	0.30	Okeechobee	1,067	950	0.18
DeSoto	912	819	0.15	Orange	37,769	31,833	5.96
Dixie	290	241	0.05	Osceola	12,506	10,170	1.90
Duval	27,656	25,747	4.82	Palm Beach	34,032	29,002	5.43
Escambia	17,452	14,735	2.76	Pasco	16,223	13,696	2.56
Flagler	5,111	4,597	0.86	Pinellas	33,397	29,916	5.60
Franklin	603	448	0.08	Polk	15,027	13,292	2.49
Gadsden	1,152	853	0.16	Putnam	2,110	1,995	0.37
Gilchrist	368	450	0.08	St. Johns	7,268	6,998	1.31
Glades	228	215	0.04	St. Lucie	8,751	7,380	1.38
Gulf	610	489	0.09	Santa Rosa	8,120	6,719	1.26
Hamilton	474	511	0.10	Sarasota	14,422	11,518	2.16
Hardee	542	417	0.08	Seminole	14,613	12,962	2.43
Hendry	1,445	1,171	0.22	Sumter	4,143	3,931	0.74
Hernando	6,172	4,908	0.92	Suwannee	1,094	939	0.18
Highlands	3,777	3,208	0.60	Taylor	537	365	0.07
Hillsborough	31,963	27,731	5.19	Union	209	226	0.04
Holmes	1,174	1,094	0.20	Volusia	20,738	17,769	3.33
Indian River	5,986	5,160	0.97	Wakulla	767	695	0.13
Jackson	2,313	2,071	0.39	Walton	2,999	2,592	0.49
Jefferson	725	678	0.13	Washington	857	854	0.16
Lafayette	122	98	0.02				

Source: State of Florida, Department of Highway Safety and Motor Vehicles, Division of Motor Vehicles, unpublished data.

Table 13.35. TRANSPORTATION AND WAREHOUSING: AVERAGE MONTHLY PRIVATE REPORTING UNITS, EMPLOYMENT, AND PAYROLL COVERED BY UNEMPLOYMENT COMPENSATION LAW BY TRANSPORTATION AND WAREHOUSING INDUSTRY IN FLORIDA, 2005 AND 2006

NAICS code	Industry	Number of reporting units	Number of employees	Payroll ($1,000)
			2005 A/	
48-49	Transportation and warehousing	13,634	209,620	664,389
481	Air transportation	583	31,208	124,739
4811	Scheduled air transportation	278	27,909	110,744
4812	Nonscheduled air transportation	305	3,299	13,995
482	Rail transportation	37	56	108
483	Water transportation	181	12,462	54,690
4831	Sea, coastal, and Great Lakes transportation	136	11,582	51,251
4832	Inland water transportation	45	880	3,439
484	Truck transportation	5,777	49,038	148,889
4841	General freight trucking	3,413	32,033	100,318
4842	Specialized freight trucking	2,364	17,005	48,571
485	Transit and ground passenger transportation	865	12,782	27,382
4851	Urban transit systems	62	1,960	5,594
4852	Interurban and rural bus transportation	20	737	1,481
4853	Taxi and limousine service	424	2,504	5,932
4854	School and employee bus transportation	39	1,899	2,741
4855	Charter bus industry	83	1,838	3,537
4859	Other ground passenger transportation	237	3,844	8,097
486	Pipeline transportation	24	229	1,035
4869	Other pipeline transportation	10	151	620
487	Scenic and sightseeing transportation	611	2,386	4,985
4871	Scenic and sightseeing transportation, land	56	370	701
4872	Scenic and sightseeing transportation, water	535	1,969	4,149
4879	Scenic and sightseeing transportation, other	20	48	136
488	Support activities for transportation	3,691	44,744	130,170
4881	Support activities for air transportation	648	14,862	43,261
4882	Support activities for rail transportation	32	532	1,408
4883	Support activities for water transportation	457	8,537	27,266
4884	Support activities for road transportation	662	6,625	11,282
4885	Freight transportation arrangement	1,718	12,464	42,776
4889	Other support activities for transportation	174	1,724	4,176
491	Postal service	72	252	952
492	Couriers and messengers	1,149	30,595	90,911
4921	Couriers	703	28,864	86,781
4922	Local messengers and local delivery	446	1,731	4,131
493	Warehousing and storage	644	25,869	80,528

See footnotes at end of table. Continued . . .

Table 13.35. TRANSPORTATION AND WAREHOUSING: AVERAGE MONTHLY PRIVATE REPORTING UNITS, EMPLOYMENT, AND PAYROLL COVERED BY UNEMPLOYMENT COMPENSATION LAW BY TRANSPORTATION AND WAREHOUSING INDUSTRY IN FLORIDA, 2005 AND 2006 (Continued)

NAICS code	Industry	Number of reporting units	Number of employees	Payroll ($1,000)
			2006 B/	
48-49	Transportation and warehousing	13,992	214,140	708,333
481	Air transportation	589	29,810	124,286
4811	Scheduled air transportation	270	26,835	110,477
4812	Nonscheduled air transportation	319	2,975	13,809
482	Rail transportation	22	32	64
483	Water transportation	181	12,356	60,748
4831	Sea, coastal, and Great Lakes transportation	135	11,458	56,818
4832	Inland water transportation	46	897	3,930
484	Truck transportation	6,031	49,610	156,423
4841	General freight trucking	3,532	32,659	105,889
4842	Specialized freight trucking	2,499	16,951	50,534
485	Transit and ground passenger transportation	873	13,134	29,428
4851	Urban transit systems	70	1,966	5,741
4852	Interurban and rural bus transportation	19	611	1,293
4853	Taxi and limousine service	439	2,871	6,709
4854	School and employee bus transportation	38	1,834	2,670
4855	Charter bus industry	81	1,810	3,673
4859	Other ground passenger transportation	226	4,042	9,343
486	Pipeline transportation	21	242	1,179
4869	Other pipeline transportation	8	152	679
487	Scenic and sightseeing transportation	630	2,362	5,308
4871	Scenic and sightseeing transportation, land	49	350	669
4872	Scenic and sightseeing transportation, water	554	1,931	4,396
4879	Scenic and sightseeing transportation, other	27	81	243
488	Support activities for transportation	3,738	47,320	144,378
4881	Support activities for air transportation	666	16,547	49,666
4882	Support activities for rail transportation	34	592	1,490
4883	Support activities for water transportation	450	9,007	30,247
4884	Support activities for road transportation	670	6,524	11,561
4885	Freight transportation arrangement	1,741	12,838	46,650
4889	Other support activities for transportation	177	1,813	4,764
491	Postal service	80	206	288
492	Couriers and messengers	1,171	31,289	98,727
4921	Couriers	722	29,514	94,235
4922	Local messengers and local delivery	449	1,775	4,493
493	Warehousing and storage	656	27,779	87,504

NAICS North American Industry Classification System. See Glossary for definition.
A/ Revised. B/ Preliminary.
Note: Private employment. Public employment data are in Section 23.00. Detail may not add to totals.
Source: State of Florida, Agency for Workforce Innovation, Labor Market Statistics, "Quarterly Census of Employment and Wages" (ES-202), Annual NAICS files, Internet site <http://www.labormarketinfo.com/index.htm> (accessed 17, July 2007).

Table 13.36. TRANSPORTATION AND WAREHOUSING: AVERAGE MONTHLY PRIVATE REPORTING UNITS, EMPLOYMENT, AND PAYROLL COVERED BY UNEMPLOYMENT COMPENSATION LAW IN THE STATE AND COUNTIES OF FLORIDA, 2005 AND 2006

County	Number of reporting units	Number of employees	Payroll ($1,000)	County	Number of reporting units	Number of employees	Payroll ($1,000)
		Transportation and warehousing, 2005 A/ (NAICS codes 48-49)					
Florida	13,634	209,620	664,389	Levy	29	97	201
				Liberty	7	22	55
Alachua	87	1,274	3,113	Madison	13	103	316
Bay	116	1,085	3,033	Manatee	153	1,174	3,038
Bradford	30	206	690	Marion	189	1,756	5,385
Brevard	309	3,143	8,252	Martin	104	801	2,576
Broward	1,416	21,432	64,295	Miami-Dade	3,062	55,168	196,104
Charlotte	73	390	941	Monroe	140	775	1,928
Citrus	55	126	252	Nassau	61	485	1,299
Clay	97	476	1,438	Okaloosa	122	955	2,377
Collier	223	1,447	4,464	Okeechobee	32	360	962
Columbia	39	346	881	Orange	832	19,832	57,030
DeSoto	19	50	104	Osceola	101	374	1,019
Dixie	13	51	133	Palm Beach	778	7,722	23,404
Duval	832	22,631	70,377	Pasco	211	1,131	3,421
Escambia	203	2,794	8,359	Pinellas	461	4,668	12,560
Flagler	36	71	128	Polk	424	11,083	32,386
Franklin	6	32	34	Putnam	36	205	473
Gadsden	23	407	804	St. Johns	85	430	1,193
Gilchrist	5	9	17	St. Lucie	139	1,654	4,745
Gulf	7	18	36	Santa Rosa	68	438	1,465
Hamilton	14	100	350	Sarasota	185	1,782	4,537
Hardee	11	116	161	Seminole	212	1,882	5,729
Hernando	100	2,120	6,099	Sumter	30	277	693
Highlands	55	291	642	Suwannee	31	132	234
Hillsborough	813	16,635	53,266	Taylor	6	55	143
Holmes	19	93	253	Union	13	380	974
Indian River	75	451	1,211	Volusia	256	1,657	4,125
Jackson	18	538	1,031	Wakulla	14	71	138
Jefferson	9	84	274	Walton	27	95	192
Lafayette	3	56	159	Washington	12	132	290
Lake	128	2,199	6,412	Statewide 1/	159	8,663	36,524
Lee	368	3,194	12,608	Out-of-state 2/	11	25	89
Leon	108	1,463	3,510	Unknown 1/	267	677	2,502

See footnotes at end of table.

Continued . . .

Table 13.36. TRANSPORTATION AND WAREHOUSING: AVERAGE MONTHLY PRIVATE REPORTING UNITS, EMPLOYMENT, AND PAYROLL COVERED BY UNEMPLOYMENT COMPENSATION LAW IN THE STATE AND COUNTIES OF FLORIDA, 2005 AND 2006 (Continued)

County	Number of reporting units	Number of employees	Payroll ($1,000)	County	Number of reporting units	Number of employees	Payroll ($1,000)
	Transportation and warehousing, 2006 B/ (NAICS codes 48-49)						
Florida	13,992	214,140	708,333	Leon	107	1,361	3,683
				Levy	37	117	259
Alachua	90	1,402	3,420	Liberty	7	16	45
Bay	120	1,099	3,147	Madison	16	116	365
Bradford	28	237	849	Manatee	165	1,342	3,422
Brevard	306	2,918	7,428	Marion	193	2,303	6,986
Broward	1,490	21,771	69,160	Martin	110	765	2,533
Charlotte	77	367	980	Miami-Dade	2,900	55,210	210,121
Citrus	62	174	350	Monroe	147	775	2,098
Clay	99	716	2,279	Nassau	64	457	1,375
Collier	242	1,453	4,459	Okaloosa	121	1,002	2,574
Columbia	48	377	947	Okeechobee	32	335	1,031
DeSoto	23	71	161	Orange	891	21,522	63,221
Dixie	12	60	164	Osceola	115	349	1,082
Duval	888	23,530	76,531	Palm Beach	799	7,979	24,675
Escambia	194	3,007	9,066	Pasco	242	1,223	3,360
Flagler	41	66	134	Pinellas	463	4,855	13,788
Franklin	9	36	40	Polk	433	11,407	34,565
Gadsden	23	483	963	Putnam	43	221	516
Gilchrist	8	13	29	St. Johns	89	580	1,705
Glades	4	20	39	St. Lucie	150	1,823	4,851
Gulf	7	17	35	Santa Rosa	70	342	1,176
Hamilton	14	95	329	Sarasota	185	1,566	4,430
Hardee	13	138	189	Seminole	229	2,436	7,242
Hendry	21	57	139	Sumter	27	231	606
Hernando	99	2,066	5,752	Suwannee	39	199	462
Highlands	73	352	737	Taylor	10	62	155
Hillsborough	813	15,963	55,221	Union	14	380	993
Holmes	21	99	283	Volusia	251	1,596	3,954
Indian River	82	595	1,592	Wakulla	11	65	136
Jackson	23	584	1,219	Walton	24	103	199
Jefferson	7	83	265	Washington	10	111	294
Lafayette	3	53	153	Statewide 1/	149	7,467	34,366
Lake	146	2,289	6,465	Out-of-state 2/	8	18	77
Lee	388	3,569	13,147	Unknown 1/	330	976	3,651

NAICS North American Industry Classification System. See Glossary for definition.
A/ Revised. B/ Preliminary.
1/ Reporting units without a fixed location within the state or of unknown county location.
2/ Employment based in Florida, but working out of the state or country.
Note: Private employment. For a list of industries included see Table 13.35. Only counties for which data are disclosed are shown. Detail may not add to totals due to disclosure editing and/or rounding. See Tables 23.70, 23.72, 23.73, and 23.74 for public employment data.
Source: State of Florida, Agency for Workforce Innovation, Labor Market Statistics, "Quarterly Census of Employment and Wages" (ES-202), Annual NAICS files, Internet site <http://www.labormarketinfo.com/index.htm> (accessed 17, July 2007).

Table 13.37. TRANSPORTATION AND WAREHOUSING: AVERAGE MONTHLY PRIVATE REPORTING UNITS, EMPLOYMENT, AND PAYROLL COVERED BY UNEMPLOYMENT COMPENSATION LAW IN THE STATE AND COUNTIES OF FLORIDA, 2006

County	Number of reporting units	Number of employees	Payroll ($1,000)	County	Number of reporting units	Number of employees	Payroll ($1,000)
			Truck transportation (NAICS code 484)				
Florida	6,031	49,610	156,423	Liberty	7	16	45
Alachua	41	215	508	Madison	12	42	121
Baker	24	77	261	Manatee	89	490	1,472
Bay	45	413	1,070	Marion	135	1,267	4,069
Brevard	150	810	2,226	Martin	37	362	1,302
Broward	505	2,775	8,431	Miami-Dade	688	4,595	15,297
Charlotte	42	127	278	Monroe	10	61	165
Citrus	46	130	291	Nassau	46	111	342
Clay	64	505	1,489	Okaloosa	28	223	486
Collier	102	288	845	Okeechobee	17	298	961
Columbia	37	276	642	Orange	420	4,600	15,074
DeSoto	17	51	115	Osceola	59	82	187
Dixie	11	59	163	Palm Beach	258	1,583	5,358
Duval	465	7,080	25,328	Pasco	177	830	2,239
Escambia	116	1,104	2,745	Pinellas	199	1,109	2,866
Flagler	29	42	77	Polk	298	4,882	15,492
Gadsden	16	272	446	Putnam	34	170	404
Gilchrist	7	13	25	St. Johns	30	105	359
Gulf	4	11	23	St. Lucie	82	268	802
Hardee	10	129	178	Santa Rosa	46	143	384
Hendry	15	50	126	Sarasota	89	360	1,166
Hernando	70	514	1,936	Seminole	101	549	1,668
Highlands	53	195	443	Sumter	24	207	555
Hillsborough	376	4,304	14,582	Suwannee	31	174	417
Holmes	17	82	244	Taylor	6	33	61
Indian River	30	136	261	Union	12	367	979
Jackson	14	113	276	Volusia	124	443	1,178
Jefferson	4	50	180	Wakulla	9	63	135
Jefferson	3	53	153	Walton	16	83	165
Lake	90	1,383	3,616	Washington	7	22	41
Lee	200	1,028	3,226	Statewide 1/	80	2,582	8,797
Leon	51	446	1,215	Out-of-state 2/	7	17	71
Levy	29	99	225	Unknown 1/	129	263	985
			Transit and ground passenger transportation (NAICS code 485)				
Florida	873	13,134	29,428	Escambia	8	262	570
				Franklin	3	25	25
Bay	5	8	16	Highlands	4	115	218
Brevard	27	270	537	Hillsborough	26	316	602
Broward	129	1,287	2,595	Indian River	5	27	41
Charlotte	8	10	58	Lake	4	222	831
Collier	23	184	393	Lee	26	86	190
Duval	34	2,138	4,432	Leon	8	118	228

See footnotes at end of table.

Continued . . .

Table 13.37. TRANSPORTATION AND WAREHOUSING: AVERAGE MONTHLY PRIVATE REPORTING UNITS, EMPLOYMENT, AND PAYROLL COVERED BY UNEMPLOYMENT COMPENSATION LAW IN THE STATE AND COUNTIES OF FLORIDA, 2006 (Continued)

County	Number of reporting units	Number of employees	Payroll ($1,000)	County	Number of reporting units	Number of employees	Payroll ($1,000)
Transit and ground passenger transportation (NAICS code 485) (Continued)							
Manatee	9	33	76	Pinellas	40	495	1,065
Marion	8	49	80	Polk	9	43	74
Miami-Dade	152	2,271	5,842	St. Johns	4	6	6
Monroe	9	73	209	St. Lucie	13	56	97
Orange	79	2,564	5,295	Sarasota	18	109	156
Osceola	11	31	70	Seminole	18	59	130
Palm Beach	88	1,477	3,944	Suwannee	5	20	33
Pasco	9	30	57	Statewide 1/	4	35	127
Scenic and sightseeing transportation (NAICS code 487)							
Florida	630	2,362	5,308	Miami-Dade	63	201	617
Bay	23	104	151	Monroe	85	383	888
Brevard	8	23	162	Okaloosa	44	131	246
Broward	81	340	830	Orange	18	24	55
Charlotte	6	19	34	Osceola	3	7	17
Collier	30	173	378	Palm Beach	62	107	351
Duval	15	93	162	Pinellas	32	189	302
Indian River	8	13	19	St. Johns	9	68	94
Lee	29	68	160	Sarasota	8	35	47
Manatee	6	9	18	Volusia	17	37	78
Martin	13	26	64	Unknown 1/	17	33	157
Warehousing and storage (NAICS code 493)							
Florida	656	27,779	87,504	Miami-Dade	102	2,773	9,138
Bay	4	44	73	Okaloosa	6	34	106
Brevard	15	201	522	Orange	67	3,507	11,744
Broward	77	2,194	7,577	Osceola	5	21	43
Collier	10	43	127	Polk	33	5,206	15,129
Duval	67	3,254	10,223	St. Johns	4	9	118
Hillsborough	59	1,879	6,140	Sarasota	11	347	1,046
Lake	10	283	925	Seminole	14	70	274
Leon	8	52	148	Volusia	9	23	43
Manatee	4	20	46	Statewide 1/	6	77	793
Martin	4	6	7	Unknown 1/	10	16	91

NAICS North American Industry Classification System. See Glossary for definition.
1/ Reporting units without a fixed location within the state or of unknown county location.
2/ Employment based in Florida, but working out of the state or country.
Note: Private employment. Data are preliminary. For a list of four-digit industries included see Table 13.35. Only counties for which data are disclosed are shown. Detail may not add to totals due to disclosure editing and/or rounding. See Tables 23.70, 23.72, 23.73, and 23.74 for public employment data.

Source: State of Florida, Agency for Workforce Innovation, Labor Market Statistics, "Quarterly Census of Employment and Wages" (ES-202), Annual NAICS files, Internet site <http://www.labormarketinfo.com/index.htm> (accessed 17, July 2007).

Table 13.38. AIR AND WATER TRANSPORTATION AND SUPPORT ACTIVITIES FOR TRANSPORTATION AVERAGE MONTHLY PRIVATE REPORTING UNITS, EMPLOYMENT, AND PAYROLL COVERED BY UNEMPLOYMENT COMPENSATION LAW IN THE STATE AND COUNTIES OF FLORIDA, 2006

County	Number of reporting units	Number of employees	Payroll ($1,000)	County	Number of reporting units	Number of employees	Payroll ($1,000)
			Air transportation (NAICS code 481)				
Florida	589	29,810	124,286	Monroe	4	37	72
Brevard	8	129	617	Okaloosa	7	134	584
Broward	92	4,183	14,317	Orange	37	3,705	12,996
Collier	11	230	1,152	Palm Beach	46	520	1,953
Duval	22	367	1,108	Pinellas	8	90	360
Escambia	7	215	455	Polk	4	5	12
Hillsborough	15	3,009	8,443	Sarasota	7	72	171
Lake	4	5	21	Seminole	14	166	556
Lee	13	306	775	Volusia	10	114	235
Miami-Dade	175	13,310	61,109	Unknown 1/	42	196	798
			Water transportation (NAICS code 483)				
Florida	181	12,356	60,748	Hillsborough	14	1,592	10,893
Bay	3	32	117	Miami-Dade	53	8,826	40,492
Brevard	5	27	89	Palm Beach	13	108	763
Broward	35	679	2,948	Pinellas	5	27	57
Duval	15	800	4,584	Seminole	5	12	22
			Support activities for transportation (NAICS code 488)				
Florida	3,738	47,320	144,378	Levy	6	11	15
Alachua	16	124	412	Manatee	34	475	945
Bay	30	300	1,124	Marion	22	122	449
Brevard	66	950	1,834	Martin	41	178	602
Broward	415	6,485	18,900	Miami-Dade	1,355	17,036	51,345
Charlotte	8	27	102	Monroe	26	99	387
Citrus	8	24	38	Nassau	11	180	681
Clay	20	95	420	Okaloosa	21	141	335
Collier	48	125	409	Okeechobee	12	34	62
Columbia	4	30	74	Orange	162	2,947	6,946
Duval	207	4,901	17,496	Osceola	19	99	291
Escambia	39	880	3,711	Palm Beach	230	1,892	5,934
Flagler	7	19	44	Pasco	32	133	422
Hamilton	4	42	165	Pinellas	96	1,205	3,939
Hendry	4	6	12	Polk	62	739	2,336
Hernando	12	26	61	Putnam	4	18	49
Highlands	10	27	53	St. Johns	36	256	783
Hillsborough	208	2,598	8,381	St. Lucie	33	179	508
Holmes	3	16	39	Santa Rosa	8	105	614
Indian River	22	125	367	Sarasota	38	181	501
Lake	27	194	449	Seminole	47	703	2,117
Lee	64	629	1,688	Volusia	55	335	683
Leon	20	243	627	Unknown 1/	83	270	846

NAICS North American Industry Classification System. See Glossary for definition.
1/ Reporting units without a fixed location within the state or of unknown county location.
Note: See Note on Table 13.37.
Source: State of Florida, Agency for Workforce Innovation, Labor Maket Statistics, "Quarterly Census of Employment and Wages" (ES-202), Annual NAICS files, Internet site <http://www.labormarketinfo.com/index.htm> (accessed 17, July 2007).

Table 13.40. DRIVER LICENSES: NUMBER ISSUED BY TYPE AND BY AGE OF DRIVER IN FLORIDA, JANUARY 1, 2007

Age	Restricted and learner	Operator	Chauffeur	Commercial	Age	Restricted and learner	Operator	Chauffeur	Commercial
Total	482,200	14,332,172	76	677,430	45	2,909	283,969	4	22,272
					46	2,965	280,406	4	22,026
15	76,236	2	0	0	47	2,759	272,463	1	21,004
16	83,271	58,811	0	0	48	2,719	267,907	4	20,361
17	60,929	112,772	0	0	49	2,574	266,148	1	20,072
18	33,725	168,577	0	62	50	2,517	258,018	0	19,752
19	22,503	197,604	0	309	51	2,425	249,715	1	18,445
20	17,812	213,420	0	557	52	2,290	246,121	0	17,851
21	15,730	230,113	1	1,222	53	2,268	237,379	0	16,461
22	14,260	240,807	1	1,992	54	2,093	232,857	2	15,977
23	11,122	246,831	3	2,885	55	1,962	226,299	1	15,071
24	9,236	259,103	3	3,849	56	1,855	219,565	2	14,077
25	7,644	265,097	4	4,709	57	1,737	219,305	0	13,584
26	7,017	269,182	0	5,973	58	1,658	222,116	2	12,977
27	6,241	263,466	0	7,244	59	1,520	233,664	1	13,291
28	5,809	257,786	4	8,185	60	1,390	215,671	1	11,934
29	5,419	256,296	1	9,479	61	1,239	181,668	1	10,079
30	5,038	247,657	1	10,261	62	1,061	183,578	1	9,885
31	4,737	245,401	0	11,264	63	994	192,758	0	9,904
32	4,584	248,222	1	12,721	64	994	189,558	3	8,738
33	4,488	246,560	2	13,769	65	799	167,481	1	7,808
34	4,322	257,407	1	15,662	66	801	160,738	1	6,888
35	4,086	272,622	3	17,584	67	707	153,274	0	6,079
36	3,897	277,738	2	18,351	68	663	152,660	0	5,625
37	3,769	266,736	1	18,117	69	559	144,095	2	4,875
38	3,594	258,544	1	18,636	70	463	138,871	1	4,245
39	3,472	257,137	3	18,905	71	427	133,499	0	3,612
40	3,415	262,696	1	20,284	72	350	127,939	2	2,961
41	3,403	272,402	2	21,049	73	295	119,436	0	2,290
42	3,369	285,908	0	22,452	74	270	122,010	0	1,992
43	3,288	287,855	3	22,718	75	255	115,876	0	1,683
44	3,152	286,703	0	22,372	76+	1,114	1,103,673	2	5,000

Note: Data are essentially an inventory of current licenses as of January 1, 2007, according to the records of the Florida Department of Highway Safety and Motor Vehicles. Figures do not include temporary permits.

Source: State of Florida, Department of Highway Safety and Motor Vehicles, Division of Driver Licenses, unpublished data.

Table 13.41. DRIVER LICENSES: NUMBER ISSUED BY COUNTY OF DRIVER'S MAILING ADDRESS AND BY SEX OF LICENSE HOLDER IN THE STATE AND COUNTIES OF FLORIDA, JANUARY 1, 2007

County of driver's mailing address	Male	Female	County of driver's mailing address	Male	Female
Florida	7,407,264	7,608,024	Lee	229,987	235,454
Alachua	82,498	88,966	Leon	88,537	97,898
Baker	8,058	8,893	Levy	15,001	16,451
Bay	69,331	71,543	Liberty	1,998	2,222
Bradford	8,092	8,936	Madison	5,728	6,497
Brevard	220,605	230,533	Manatee	119,609	126,611
Broward	700,742	701,331	Marion	126,199	138,391
Calhoun	4,128	4,572	Martin	61,831	63,475
Charlotte	65,057	69,351	Miami-Dade	907,003	870,301
Citrus	57,445	61,893	Monroe	43,988	35,390
Clay	69,835	74,942	Nassau	27,865	29,597
Collier	130,184	127,430	Okaloosa	78,472	80,062
Columbia	21,741	23,964	Okeechobee	13,717	13,661
DeSoto	10,143	10,128	Orange	418,986	418,302
Dixie	5,260	5,498	Osceola	101,238	100,609
Duval	305,254	331,538	Palm Beach	499,912	520,220
Escambia	114,761	122,898	Pasco	172,360	184,573
Flagler	35,512	37,641	Pinellas	366,865	389,979
Franklin	4,116	4,262	Polk	206,614	220,171
Gadsden	14,590	16,361	Putnam	26,018	27,865
Gilchrist	5,173	5,716	St. Johns	68,796	73,314
Glades	3,461	3,294	St. Lucie	96,853	101,244
Gulf	5,193	5,555	Santa Rosa	57,933	60,692
Hamilton	4,054	4,549	Sarasota	152,826	164,098
Hardee	8,032	7,854	Seminole	162,693	172,331
Hendry	12,177	11,599	Sumter	28,976	31,682
Hernando	64,684	70,898	Suwannee	14,328	15,734
Highlands	35,659	38,755	Taylor	7,178	7,708
Hillsborough	437,283	453,502	Union	3,513	3,913
Holmes	6,862	7,618	Volusia	199,371	208,775
Indian River	54,676	58,386	Wakulla	9,556	10,268
Jackson	15,504	17,657	Walton	20,447	20,945
Jefferson	5,076	5,411	Washington	7,917	8,671
Lafayette	1,659	1,801	Unknown county 1/	9,673	8,631
Lake	110,250	119,528	Out-of-state 2/	358,181	329,486

1/ Licenses mailed to addresses which do not permit specification of county. Also includes licenses with incorrect or unknown zip codes.

2/ Licenses mailed to out-of-state addresses.

Note: Data are essentially an inventory of current licenses as of January 1, 2007, according to the records of the Florida Department of Highway Safety and Motor Vehicles. Figures include restricted, operator, chauffeur, and commercial licenses. Figures do not include temporary permits.

Source: State of Florida, Department of Highway Safety and Motor Vehicles, Division of Driver Licenses, unpublished data.

Table 13.42. TRAFFIC CITATIONS: NUMBER BY TYPE OF VIOLATION IN THE STATE OF FLORIDA, 2002 THROUGH 2006

Type of violation	2002	2003	2004	2005	2006	Percentage change 2002 to 2006
Total	4,368,083	4,361,619	4,418,401	4,766,625	5,097,673	16.7
Criminal, total	515,033	531,230	557,201	594,545	636,578	23.6
DUI	69,551	65,113	68,625	67,450	63,591	-8.6
Reckless driving	13,589	13,002	11,787	12,348	12,211	-10.1
Leave scene/accident	20,998	19,154	20,246	19,515	19,753	-5.9
Fleeing	7,317	7,005	6,674	4,925	5,166	-29.4
No/improper/expired driver license	98,678	111,332	124,668	145,587	170,006	72.3
Driving w/license suspended/revoked	169,238	186,493	195,767	209,411	227,245	34.3
Violation of driver license restriction	18,061	15,865	15,519	11,166	11,132	-38.4
Unlawful use of driver license	10,828	11,540	10,889	6,748	6,616	-38.9
No/improper/expired tag	87,675	82,895	80,726	84,360	85,084	-3.0
Other criminal	19,098	18,831	22,300	33,035	35,774	87.3
Non-moving, total	1,427,691	1,432,897	1,443,530	1,501,695	1,643,694	15.1
Load/leak/drop	3,635	95	84	4,074	3,895	7.2
Over weight/length/height 1/	382	444	464	(X)	(X)	(X)
Improper parking	11,492	10,887	12,678	12,622	13,626	18.6
No helmet	5,930	5,891	7,129	7,185	7,568	27.6
Defect/unsafe equipment	243,306	241,729	227,650	224,236	236,663	-2.7
Seat belt violation	406,897	361,155	300,213	326,978	348,542	-14.3
Expired or failure to display license	107,749	110,871	111,452	117,436	125,909	16.9
Expired or failure to display tag	256,921	286,958	312,718	340,266	370,023	44.0
No proof insurance	229,002	248,430	265,334	286,095	322,520	40.8
Bicycle or pedestrian	20,179	20,133	20,302	18,258	16,469	-18.4
Other	142,198	146,304	185,506	164,545	198,479	39.6
Non-criminal moving, total	2,425,359	2,397,492	2,417,670	2,670,385	2,817,401	16.2
Exceed 55 mph 2/	70,927	8,430	(X)	(X)	(X)	(X)
Exceed 65 mph 2/	22,722	1,038	(X)	(X)	(X)	(X)
Speed posted zone	1,085,657	1,155,218	1,125,429	1,212,486	1,351,074	24.4
Speed too fast for conditions	22,320	22,570	17,133	11,860	10,778	-51.7
Careless driving	216,880	214,633	228,107	233,184	226,886	4.6
Failed to yield right of way	142,305	148,762	161,459	158,447	112,084	-21.2
Ran stop sign	114,670	102,988	101,365	105,525	113,919	-0.7
Ran red light	315,293	314,503	332,994	365,727	391,204	24.1
Traffic control device	6,395	5,607	7,695	19,894	17,790	178.2
Improper turn	37,601	37,796	39,714	41,362	45,023	19.7
Improper passing	38,044	35,143	36,457	38,735	41,305	8.6
Following too close	23,556	23,445	25,691	28,483	26,813	13.8
Wrong side of road	12,574	12,333	12,675	13,385	14,344	14.1
Improper lane change	85,620	88,067	88,687	64,897	73,833	-13.8
Improper backing	26,112	25,508	26,253	26,896	26,795	2.6
Drive without lights	15,441	15,592	15,511	17,005	17,661	14.4
Fail to dim lights	2,635	2,674	2,843	3,040	3,080	16.9
Exceed bumper height	19,556	18,871	17,183	19,508	21,090	7.8
Child restraint	427	641	691	743	757	77.3
Other	166,624	163,673	177,783	309,208	322,965	93.8

(X) Not applicable.
1/ Merged into non-moving other in 2005.
2/ Merged into speed posted zone in 2004.

Source: State of Florida, Department of Highway Safety and Motor Vehicles, Division of Driver Licenses, *2006 Annual Report, Uniform Traffic Citation Statistics,* Internet site <http://www.hsmv.state.fl.us/> (accessed 29, May 2007).

Table 13.43. TRAFFIC CITATIONS: NUMBER ISSUED IN THE STATE AND COUNTIES OF FLORIDA, 2002 THROUGH 2006

County	2002	2003	2004	2005	2006	Percentage change 2002 to 2006
Florida	4,368,083	4,361,619	4,418,401	4,766,325	5,097,673	16.7
Alachua	66,086	78,052	80,190	86,596	93,080	40.8
Baker	5,247	6,681	6,236	6,528	7,546	43.8
Bay	40,919	41,041	41,015	41,466	44,585	9.0
Bradford	14,151	15,205	14,510	13,024	16,191	14.4
Brevard	123,822	126,861	142,764	153,493	147,473	19.1
Broward	517,543	587,378	556,653	528,038	530,052	2.4
Calhoun	5,189	5,699	3,267	3,174	4,150	-20.0
Charlotte	25,324	24,819	22,023	20,871	27,643	9.2
Citrus	16,027	17,300	15,986	19,895	24,717	54.2
Clay	25,581	23,694	28,869	36,625	43,336	69.4
Collier	58,775	67,182	71,030	88,795	91,856	56.3
Columbia	17,410	15,892	13,715	15,742	16,544	-5.0
DeSoto	5,084	6,518	6,044	6,166	7,682	51.1
Dixie	3,920	2,567	2,627	3,415	3,700	-5.6
Duval	317,113	307,947	278,430	284,903	312,191	-1.6
Escambia	49,883	51,562	48,208	51,731	62,605	25.5
Flagler	12,643	10,679	11,637	13,209	17,603	39.2
Franklin	3,634	3,926	3,296	3,174	2,888	-20.5
Gadsden	17,902	15,587	12,451	13,769	17,381	-2.9
Gilchrist	2,553	2,879	2,384	2,777	3,584	40.4
Glades	7,118	6,180	5,022	4,063	8,480	19.1
Gulf	3,102	2,228	2,655	2,516	2,040	-34.2
Hamilton	5,491	4,852	5,568	4,427	4,206	-23.4
Hardee	8,801	9,215	6,315	7,734	10,024	13.9
Hendry	8,947	8,877	7,141	7,951	8,324	-7.0
Hernando	25,826	32,058	32,606	36,172	45,776	77.2
Highlands	17,313	18,267	14,809	21,139	22,344	29.1
Hillsborough	213,483	229,982	271,627	317,064	320,622	50.2
Holmes	2,986	4,130	3,511	4,662	6,121	105.0
Indian River	25,538	22,566	20,450	23,011	27,080	6.0
Jackson	9,655	10,600	10,020	12,945	13,283	37.6
Jefferson	8,798	4,217	5,158	6,036	4,536	-48.4
Lafayette	1,769	1,626	1,356	1,362	1,153	-34.8
Lake	38,868	38,302	42,560	57,012	57,832	48.8

Continued . . .

Table 13.43. TRAFFIC CITATIONS: NUMBER ISSUED IN THE STATE AND COUNTIES OF FLORIDA, 2002 THROUGH 2006 (Continued)

County	2002	2003	2004	2005	2006	Percentage change 2002 to 2006
Lee	95,777	104,789	89,151	109,582	129,836	35.6
Leon	76,523	52,033	58,907	65,863	74,657	-2.4
Levy	9,502	7,835	6,738	8,822	8,963	-5.7
Liberty	6,635	5,808	2,807	3,041	2,489	-62.5
Madison	12,335	15,527	10,479	11,371	10,995	-10.9
Manatee	39,925	49,524	45,526	47,845	51,897	30.0
Marion	39,384	41,490	48,921	48,748	56,390	43.2
Martin	33,016	29,445	32,250	37,103	36,310	10.0
Miami-Dade	731,164	673,264	740,641	788,803	865,266	18.3
Monroe	40,275	29,801	20,322	18,688	20,036	-50.3
Nassau	12,453	12,557	10,912	12,766	14,267	14.6
Okaloosa	33,018	38,735	41,081	44,611	47,489	43.8
Okeechobee	8,220	10,284	9,711	9,420	10,409	26.6
Orange	214,070	185,967	244,446	291,082	347,656	62.4
Osceola	61,352	64,083	65,885	67,432	82,972	35.2
Palm Beach	376,252	371,944	360,952	374,190	393,278	4.5
Pasco	64,685	63,884	55,526	69,116	70,009	8.2
Pinellas	184,122	180,695	193,672	198,687	193,789	5.3
Polk	118,776	118,576	106,522	119,489	137,269	15.6
Putnam	18,344	17,395	12,960	17,104	17,548	-4.3
St. Johns	34,344	40,875	38,573	43,375	44,508	29.6
St. Lucie	71,398	61,998	61,338	69,666	66,878	-6.3
Santa Rosa	23,745	24,820	23,861	28,038	32,144	35.4
Sarasota	59,526	62,707	64,366	83,810	85,365	43.4
Seminole	95,122	85,301	92,983	104,148	95,983	0.9
Sumter	17,280	16,410	18,991	21,602	22,433	29.8
Suwannee	6,674	4,389	5,319	6,474	6,903	3.4
Taylor	4,467	5,871	5,046	4,962	5,140	15.1
Union	1,502	1,719	1,744	1,888	1,587	5.7
Volusia	151,385	151,773	131,517	134,194	127,938	-15.5
Wakulla	5,530	7,678	7,011	5,422	6,829	23.5
Walton	6,982	10,991	11,669	10,913	13,301	90.5
Washington	7,799	8,882	8,441	8,585	10,511	34.8

Source: State of Florida, Department of Highway Safety and Motor Vehicles, Division of Driver Licenses, *2006 Annual Report, Uniform Traffic Citation Statistics,* Internet site <http://www.hsmv.state.fl.us/> (accessed 29, May 2007).

Table 13.44. TRAFFIC CITATIONS: SEAT BELT AND CHILD RESTRAINT CONVICTIONS IN THE STATE AND COUNTIES OF FLORIDA, 2006

County	Total	Percentage of state	Driver	Passenger Under age 18	Passenger Aged 18 and over	Child restraint
Florida	298,108	100.00	245,892	13,920	21,933	16,363
Alachua	6,079	2.04	5,064	251	558	206
Baker	653	0.22	509	23	74	47
Bay	3,059	1.03	2,392	124	372	171
Bradford	1,209	0.41	903	69	143	94
Brevard	10,494	3.52	8,525	287	1,212	470
Broward	17,987	6.03	15,970	707	733	577
Calhoun	249	0.08	196	16	28	9
Charlotte	3,148	1.06	2,539	69	277	263
Citrus	2,106	0.71	1,664	44	251	147
Clay	3,109	1.04	2,487	64	391	167
Collier	7,660	2.57	5,833	535	620	672
Columbia	1,503	0.50	1,190	133	111	69
DeSoto	441	0.15	322	44	41	34
Dixie	373	0.13	311	10	36	16
Duval	27,502	9.23	22,487	1,168	2,727	1,120
Escambia	4,125	1.38	3,307	247	405	166
Flagler	1,485	0.50	1,238	38	100	109
Franklin	128	0.04	93	11	18	6
Gadsden	642	0.22	45	145	0	452
Gilchrist	412	0.14	287	27	54	44
Glades	298	0.10	171	29	37	61
Gulf	305	0.10	255	10	28	12
Hamilton	88	0.03	52	16	2	18
Hardee	597	0.20	419	86	31	61
Hendry	582	0.20	379	85	45	73
Hernando	3,811	1.28	3,103	100	415	193
Highlands	1,699	0.57	1,322	105	144	128
Hillsborough	15,582	5.23	12,319	1,021	1,181	1,061
Holmes	294	0.10	250	18	16	10
Indian River	2,010	0.67	1,694	71	143	102
Jackson	600	0.20	455	44	48	53
Jefferson	136	0.05	111	10	11	4
Lafayette	90	0.03	71	8	8	3
Lake	3,217	1.08	2,559	197	293	168

Continued . . .

Table 13.44. TRAFFIC CITATIONS: SEAT BELT AND CHILD RESTRAINT CONVICTIONS IN THE STATE AND COUNTIES OF FLORIDA, 2006 (Continued)

County	Total	Percentage of state	Driver	Passenger Under age 18	Passenger Aged 18 and over	Child restraint
Lee	3,877	1.30	2,824	504	312	237
Leon	6,715	2.25	5,623	263	569	260
Levy	636	0.21	527	32	52	25
Liberty	217	0.07	181	19	4	13
Madison	367	0.12	292	38	25	12
Manatee	4,295	1.44	3,297	310	346	342
Marion	6,034	2.02	5,351	284	264	135
Martin	1,860	0.62	1,513	82	126	139
Miami-Dade	24,380	8.18	21,811	701	884	984
Monroe	1,897	0.64	1,695	51	77	74
Nassau	1,020	0.34	802	25	164	29
Okaloosa	1,989	0.67	1,611	89	226	63
Okeechobee	1,084	0.36	937	61	36	50
Orange	16,165	5.42	13,797	479	971	918
Osceola	5,501	1.85	4,200	276	490	535
Palm Beach	18,435	6.18	15,153	863	1,064	1,355
Pasco	5,807	1.95	4,959	149	443	256
Pinellas	10,426	3.50	8,540	512	923	451
Polk	10,144	3.40	8,051	887	628	578
Putnam	2,127	0.71	1,607	109	173	238
St. Johns	1,400	0.47	1,143	63	115	79
St. Lucie	3,612	1.21	2,776	183	381	272
Santa Rosa	7,781	2.61	6,523	278	483	497
Sarasota	2,608	0.87	2,143	67	252	146
Seminole	6,097	2.05	4,777	335	450	535
Sumter	1,139	0.38	822	134	129	54
Suwannee	458	0.15	379	37	12	30
Taylor	532	0.18	3	27	50	452
Union	194	0.07	160	11	11	12
Volusia	11,620	3.90	9,415	309	1,333	563
Wakulla	601	0.20	513	24	42	22
Walton	426	0.14	349	17	46	14
Washington	338	0.11	283	20	22	13
Unknown	16,653	5.59	15,313	869	277	194

Source: State of Florida, Department of Highway Safety and Motor Vehicles, Division of Driver Licenses, *2006 Annual Report, Uniform Traffic Citation Statistics,* Internet site <http://www.hsmv.state.fl.us/> (accessed 29, May 2007).

Table 13.45. TRAFFIC STATISTICS: DRIVERS, VEHICLES, MILEAGE, CRASHES, INJURIES AND DEATHS IN FLORIDA, 1991 THROUGH 2006

Year	Licensed drivers	Registered vehicles 1/	Vehicle miles (millions)	Crashes	Nonfatal injuries	Deaths	Mileage death rate 2/
1991	12,170,821	11,184,146	113,484	195,312	195,122	2,523	2.22
1992	11,550,126	11,205,298	114,000	196,176	205,432	2,480	2.18
1993	11,767,409	11,159,938	119,768	199,039	212,497	2,719	2.27
1994	11,992,578	11,393,982	120,929	206,183	223,458	2,722	2.25
1995	12,019,156	11,557,811	127,800	228,589	233,900	2,847	2.23
1996	12,343,598	12,003,930	129,637	241,377	243,320	2,806	2.16
1997	12,691,835	12,170,375	133,276	240,639	240,001	2,811	2.11
1998	13,012,132	11,277,808	136,680	245,440	241,863	2,889	2.11
1999	13,398,895	11,611,993	140,868	243,409	232,225	2,920	2.07
2000	14,041,846	11,948,485	149,857	246,541	231,588	2,999	2.00
2001	14,346,373	13,448,202	171,029	256,169	234,600	3,013	1.76
2002	14,604,720	12,989,278	178,680	250,470	229,611	3,143	1.76
2003	14,847,416	14,080,886	185,642	243,294	221,639	3,179	1.71
2004	15,007,005	14,512,264	196,722	252,902	227,192	3,257	1.66
2005	15,272,680	15,062,993	200,974	268,605	233,930	3,533	1.76
2006	15,491,878	15,612,161	203,783	256,200	214,914	3,365	1.65

1/ Data from 1998 to present excludes count of trailers with tags.
2/ The number of deaths per 100 million vehicle miles traveled.
Note: Some data may be revised. See Note on Table 13.47.

Table 13.46. MOTOR VEHICLE CRASHES: NUMBER OF DRIVERS ASSIGNED A CONTRIBUTING CAUSE BY TYPE OF CIRCUMSTANCE IN FLORIDA, 2006

Cause of crash	All crashes		Fatal crashes		Injury crashes	
	Number	Percentage of total	Number	Percentage of total	Number	Percentage of total
Total	195,907	100.00	4,185	100.00	141,275	100.00
Careless driving	71,886	36.69	1,102	26.33	52,439	37.12
Failed to yield right of way	33,705	17.20	444	10.61	26,439	18.71
Improper backing	2,804	1.43	3	0.07	1,577	1.12
Improper lane change	6,026	3.08	86	2.05	4,155	2.94
Improper turn	6,290	3.21	67	1.60	4,674	3.31
Alcohol, under influence	7,629	3.89	517	12.35	3,644	2.58
Drugs, under influence	770	0.39	156	3.73	316	0.22
Followed too closely	7,736	3.95	8	0.19	5,795	4.10
Disregarded traffic signal	7,386	3.77	123	2.94	5,844	4.14
Exceeded safe speed limit	5,252	2.68	291	6.95	3,894	2.76
Exceeded stated speed limit	3,252	1.66	68	1.62	2,553	1.81
Disregarded stop sign	1,977	1.01	43	1.03	1,306	0.92
Improper passing	1,670	0.85	137	3.27	1,186	0.84
Drove left of center	1,561	0.80	280	6.69	1,046	0.74
Driver distraction	1,851	0.94	26	0.62	1,364	0.97
Other	30,783	15.71	540	12.90	21,623	15.31

Note: Contributing causes are reported by the investigating officer for drivers in traffic crashes. There may be up to three contributing causes per driver. See Note on Table 13.47.

Source for Tables 13.45 and 13.46: State of Florida, Department of Highway Safety and Motor Vehicles, Office of Management Research and Development, *Traffic Crash Facts, 2006,* Internet site <http://www.hsmv.state.fl.us/> (accessed 20, September 2007).

Table 13.47. MOTOR VEHICLE CRASHES: COMPARATIVE SAFETY EQUIPMENT USAGE BY TYPE OF INJURY IN FLORIDA, 2006

Safety equipment usage	Total 1/	Type of injury (percentage) No injury	Possible	Nonincapacitating	Incapacitating	Fatal
Drivers	354,111	62.10	21.07	11.90	4.29	0.41
Safety belt	138,051	69.12	19.16	8.97	2.62	0.13
Safety belt and air bag (deployed)	43,675	36.89	27.13	25.59	9.76	0.63
Safety belt and air bag (not deployed)	140,439	66.66	21.22	9.09	2.93	0.09
Air bag only (deployed)	2,218	26.60	26.51	28.63	14.25	3.97
Air bag only (not deployed)	4,699	42.56	20.47	21.30	11.94	3.66
Not using safety equipment	23,197	51.79	18.39	17.39	9.73	2.66
Other vehicle occupants	174,430	65.04	20.14	10.59	3.87	0.36
Safety belt	76,032	67.57	20.50	9.25	2.55	0.13
Safety belt and air bag (deployed)	10,539	36.25	27.82	24.96	10.31	0.65
Safety belt and air bag (not deployed)	40,718	63.49	23.02	10.20	3.19	0.10
Air bag only (deployed)	643	31.10	22.86	28.62	14.77	2.64
Air bag only (not deployed)	2,728	48.79	20.12	18.44	10.37	2.27
Not using safety equipment	31,391	68.48	13.74	10.74	5.96	1.10
Motorcyclist	10,250	9.02	16.42	41.27	27.86	5.37
With safety helmet	5,980	8.38	15.52	42.32	28.09	5.59
Driver	5,444	8.14	15.39	42.14	28.31	5.91
Passenger	536	10.82	16.79	44.22	25.93	2.24
Without safety helmet	4,250	9.98	17.34	39.93	27.67	5.08
Driver	3,782	9.04	17.53	39.74	28.42	5.26
Passenger	468	17.52	15.81	41.45	21.58	3.63
Bicyclist	4,733	7.20	28.19	45.47	16.48	2.66
With safety helmet	548	5.47	23.36	52.19	16.24	2.74
Driver	545	5.50	23.49	52.11	16.33	2.57
Passenger	3	0.00	0.00	66.67	0.00	33.33
Without safety helmet	4,157	7.48	28.55	44.72	16.57	2.67
Driver	4,085	6.78	28.67	45.12	16.74	2.69
Passenger	72	47.22	22.22	22.22	6.94	1.39
Children 2/	64,761	70.99	28.84	(NA)	(NA)	0.17
With restraint	51,846	70.33	29.61	(NA)	(NA)	0.06
Less than 4 years	11,047	76.27	23.66	(NA)	(NA)	0.06
4 to 5 years	5,175	73.95	26.01	(NA)	(NA)	0.04
6 to 17 years	35,624	67.96	31.98	(NA)	(NA)	0.06
Without restraint	12,902	73.64	25.75	(NA)	(NA)	0.61
Less than 4 years	727	60.80	38.24	(NA)	(NA)	0.96
4 to 5 years	678	69.91	29.06	(NA)	(NA)	1.03
6 to 17 years	11,497	74.67	24.76	(NA)	(NA)	0.57

(NA) Not available.
1/ Includes "use not stated" data not shown elsewhere.
2/ Injury breakdowns are unavailable for children and are listed together under "possible" injury.
Note: Legally reportable accidents are those involving death, bodily injury, or one or more of the following circumstances (1) driver leaves the accident scene where death, injury, or property damage has occurred; (2) driver is under the influence of alcohol or drugs; and, (3) a wrecker is required to remove an inoperative vehicle.

Source: State of Florida, Department of Highway Safety and Motor Vehicles, Office of Management Research and Development, *Traffic Crash Facts, 2006,* Internet site <http://www.hsmv.state.fl.us/> (accessed 20, September 2007).

Table 13.48. MOTOR VEHICLE CRASHES: DRIVERS INVOLVED IN ALL CRASHES AND ALCOHOL-RELATED CRASHES BY AGE IN FLORIDA, 2006

Age category	Drivers in all crashes		Drivers in fatal crashes		Drinking drivers in all crashes		Drinking drivers in fatal crashes	
	Number	Rate per 10,000 licensed drivers	Number	Rate per 10,000 licensed drivers	Number	Rate per 10,000 licensed drivers	Number	Rate per 10,000 licensed drivers
Total	343,353	221.63	4,328	2.79	15,712	10.14	739	0.48
Under 15	557	(NA)	5	(NA)	15	(NA)	0	(NA)
15-24	86,563	415.42	1,081	5.19	4,317	20.72	231	1.11
25-34	70,838	261.24	875	3.23	3,921	14.46	180	0.66
35-44	66,817	225.41	792	2.67	3,275	11.05	152	0.51
45-54	53,944	191.65	648	2.30	2,532	9.00	91	0.32
55-64	32,505	146.54	417	1.88	1,000	4.51	54	0.24
65-74	16,193	110.03	236	1.60	320	2.17	16	0.11
75-84	9,726	101.86	179	1.87	109	1.14	7	0.07
85 and over	2,460	90.18	75	2.75	20	0.73	3	0.11
Not stated	3,750	(NA)	20	(NA)	203	(NA)	5	(NA)

(NA) Not available.
Note: Excludes bicycles, mopeds, all terrain vehicles (ATVs), or trains. See Note on Table 13.49.

Table 13.49. MOTOR VEHICLE CRASHES: VEHICLES INVOLVED IN CRASHES BY TYPE OF VEHICLE IN FLORIDA, 2006

Vehicle type	All crashes	Fatal crashes		Injury crashes		Property damage only crashes	
		Number	Percentage of total	Number	Percentage of total	Number	Percentage of total
Total	370,035	4,830	1.31	251,225	67.89	113,980	30.80
Automobile	235,067	2,369	1.01	157,915	67.18	74,783	31.81
Passenger van	26,692	301	1.13	18,572	69.58	7,819	29.29
Light truck (2 rear tires)	69,729	956	1.37	47,160	67.63	21,613	31.00
Medium truck (4 rear tires)	5,150	80	1.55	3,224	62.60	1,846	35.84
Heavy truck	5,189	118	2.27	3,034	58.47	2,037	39.26
Truck-tractor (cab)	4,978	170	3.42	2,658	53.39	2,150	43.19
Motor home (RV)	225	7	3.11	117	52.00	101	44.89
Bus	2,514	32	1.27	1,357	53.98	1,125	44.75
Bicycle	4,665	130	2.79	4,271	91.55	264	5.66
Motorcycle	9,259	578	6.24	8,182	88.37	499	5.39
Moped	721	9	1.25	665	92.23	47	6.52
All terrain vehicle	771	23	2.98	684	88.72	64	8.30
Train	39	0	0.00	17	43.59	22	56.41
Low speed vehicle	184	8	4.35	151	82.07	25	13.59
Other	4,702	46	0.98	3,071	65.31	1,585	33.71
Unknown vehicle type	150	3	2.00	147	98.00	0	0.00

Note: Legally reportable accidents are those involving death, bodily injury, or one or more of the following circumstances (1) driver leaves the accident scene where death, injury, or property damage has occurred; (2) driver is under the influence of alcohol or drugs; and, (3) a wrecker is required to remove an inoperative vehicle.

Source for Tables 13.48 and 13.49: State of Florida, Department of Highway Safety and Motor Vehicles, Office of Management Research and Development, *Traffic Crash Facts, 2006,* Internet site <http://www.hsmv.state.fl.us/> (accessed 20, September 2007).

Table 13.50. MOTOR VEHICLE CRASHES: PERSONS KILLED OR INJURED IN CRASHES AND ALCOHOL-RELATED CRASHES IN THE STATE AND COUNTIES OF FLORIDA, 2006

	Total crashes			Fatalities			Injuries		
		Alcohol-related			Alcohol-related			Alcohol-related	
County	Number	Total	Per-centage	Number	Total	Per-centage	Number	Total	Per-centage
Florida 1/	256,200	22,858	8.9	3,365	1,099	32.7	214,914	16,319	7.6
Alachua	4,221	304	7.2	43	17	39.5	3,128	171	5.5
Baker	272	45	16.5	17	4	23.5	318	47	14.8
Bay	2,596	405	15.6	46	24	52.2	2,117	259	12.2
Bradford	360	40	11.1	8	3	37.5	330	40	12.1
Brevard	4,544	676	14.9	98	43	43.9	4,284	481	11.2
Broward	26,441	1,684	6.4	256	59	23.0	20,376	1,282	6.3
Calhoun	76	14	18.4	4	1	25.0	89	18	20.2
Charlotte	2,064	211	10.2	32	11	34.4	1,724	175	10.2
Citrus	981	157	16.0	32	11	34.4	1,026	112	10.9
Clay	1,454	188	12.9	27	11	40.7	1,297	120	9.3
Collier	2,705	372	13.8	56	16	28.6	2,276	235	10.3
Columbia	808	122	15.1	29	8	27.6	867	106	12.2
DeSoto	382	52	13.6	18	0	0.0	461	45	9.8
Dixie	132	31	23.5	11	9	81.8	125	30	24.0
Duval	15,440	1,287	8.3	144	55	38.2	10,946	787	7.2
Escambia	4,722	683	14.5	37	15	40.5	4,329	495	11.4
Flagler	822	109	13.3	30	12	40.0	890	78	8.8
Franklin	77	17	22.1	3	1	33.3	69	10	14.5
Gadsden	575	87	15.1	22	11	50.0	608	91	15.0
Gilchrist	131	20	15.3	3	0	0.0	164	22	13.4
Glades	167	17	10.2	8	4	50.0	145	10	6.9
Gulf	92	22	23.9	1	0	0.0	83	19	22.9
Hamilton	208	25	12.0	4	2	50.0	221	16	7.2
Hardee	352	44	12.5	6	2	33.3	347	41	11.8
Hendry	390	59	15.1	23	11	47.8	388	52	13.4
Hernando	1,758	199	11.3	33	9	27.3	2,149	156	7.3
Highlands	859	91	10.6	21	9	42.9	746	70	9.4
Hillsborough	23,971	1,937	8.1	191	60	31.4	20,174	1,273	6.3
Holmes	152	23	15.1	9	1	11.1	197	23	11.7
Indian River	1,532	189	12.3	27	5	18.5	1,511	151	10.0
Jackson	546	62	11.4	19	4	21.1	567	52	9.2
Jefferson	163	29	17.8	12	5	41.7	181	29	16.0
Lafayette	81	15	18.5	1	0	0.0	65	6	9.2
Lake	2,700	303	11.2	57	15	26.3	2,523	202	8.0
Lee	5,625	654	11.6	121	40	33.1	4,698	468	10.0
Leon	5,287	0	0.0	28	9	32.1	3,577	254	7.1

See footnotes at end of table.

Continued . . .

Table 13.50. MOTOR VEHICLE CRASHES: PERSONS KILLED OR INJURED IN CRASHES AND ALCOHOL-RELATED CRASHES IN THE STATE AND COUNTIES OF FLORIDA, 2006 (Continued)

	Total crashes			Fatalities			Injuries		
		Alcohol-related			Alcohol-related			Alcohol-related	
County	Number	Total	Percentage	Number	Total	Percentage	Number	Total	Percentage
Levy	456	59	12.9	13	6	46.2	439	58	13.2
Liberty	62	5	8.1	4	0	0.0	93	5	5.4
Madison	277	30	10.8	11	2	18.2	278	27	9.7
Manatee	3,993	554	13.9	56	19	33.9	3,095	356	11.5
Marion	4,193	294	7.0	67	25	37.3	4,205	241	5.7
Martin	1,570	232	14.8	32	12	37.5	1,245	126	10.1
Miami-Dade	42,582	1,792	4.2	347	75	21.6	31,030	1,286	4.1
Monroe	1,337	223	16.7	23	12	52.2	1,152	143	12.4
Nassau	571	84	14.7	20	7	35.0	601	63	10.5
Okaloosa	2,050	333	16.2	25	14	56.0	1,650	212	12.8
Okeechobee	425	70	16.5	19	8	42.1	446	60	13.5
Orange	17,506	1,322	7.6	184	64	34.8	15,148	952	6.3
Osceola	3,002	243	8.1	65	20	30.8	2,978	189	6.3
Palm Beach	14,948	1,265	8.5	212	62	29.2	13,278	945	7.1
Pasco	6,202	593	9.6	96	38	39.6	7,397	539	7.3
Pinellas	13,939	1,533	11.0	120	48	40.0	11,681	987	8.4
Polk	7,623	687	9.0	159	41	25.8	7,018	477	6.8
Putnam	1,014	124	12.2	24	9	37.5	877	134	15.3
St. Johns	1,908	271	14.2	20	5	25.0	1,781	232	13.0
St. Lucie	2,535	283	11.2	51	17	33.3	2,015	153	7.6
Santa Rosa	1,541	219	14.2	25	11	44.0	1,827	196	10.7
Sarasota	3,593	457	12.7	55	17	30.9	2,977	310	10.4
Seminole	2,906	430	14.8	39	13	33.3	2,383	283	11.9
Sumter	766	74	9.7	25	6	24.0	863	81	9.4
Suwannee	463	80	17.3	22	10	45.5	474	61	12.9
Taylor	246	42	17.1	4	3	75.0	202	37	18.3
Union	103	13	12.6	10	2	20.0	125	12	9.6
Volusia	6,552	771	11.8	122	50	41.0	5,579	605	10.8
Wakulla	212	45	21.2	4	2	50.0	188	21	11.2
Walton	654	88	13.5	23	11	47.8	589	56	9.5
Washington	263	45	17.1	11	3	27.3	283	43	15.2

1/ Includes data not distributed by county.

Note: Legally reportable accidents are those involving death, bodily injury, or one or more of the following circumstances (1) driver leaves the accident scene where death, injury, or property damage has occurred; (2) driver is under the influence of alcohol or drugs; and, (3) a wrecker is required to remove an inoperable vehicle.

Source: State of Florida, Department of Highway Safety and Motor Vehicles, Office of Management Research and Development, *Traffic Crash Facts, 2006,* Internet site <http://www.hsmv.state.fl.us/> (accessed 20, September 2007).

Table 13.51. MOTORCYCLES: NUMBER REGISTERED, CRASHES, AND INJURY CHARACTERISTICS AMONG CRASH-INVOLVED MOTORCYCLISTS IN FLORIDA, 1998 TO 2002

Characteristic	1998	1999	2000	2001	2002	Percentage change 1998 to 2002
Motorcycle registrations	207,371	220,923	240,844	289,760	323,301	55.9
Crashes	4,536	4,662	5,334	6,069	(NA)	(NA)
Injuries, total 1/	1,264	1,460	1,643	2,055	2,132	68.7
Extremity	637	752	795	961	1,027	61.2
Head, brain, skull	188	263	329	445	474	152.1
Neck, spine	36	29	35	42	40	11.1
Internal organs	138	140	162	218	217	57.2
Torso area	197	211	237	295	286	45.2
Other	68	65	85	94	88	29.4
Hospital-admitted	1,264	1,460	1,643	2,055	2,132	68.7
Male	1,085	1,264	1,420	1,811	1,872	72.5
Female	178	196	223	244	260	46.1
Under 21 years	181	194	189	248	244	34.8
21 to 24 years	131	124	158	236	199	51.9
25 to 34 years	319	391	431	481	487	52.7
35 to 44 years	296	340	399	501	533	80.1
45 to 54 years	212	254	296	373	395	86.3
55 to 64 years	82	106	123	150	190	131.7
65 and over years	43	51	47	66	84	95.3
Fatalities, total	173	164	241	274	301	74.0
Per 10,000 registered motorcycles	8.3	7.4	10.0	9.5	9.3	12.0
Died at scene	84	87	123	142	159	89.3
Helmeted	77	80	93	65	59	-23.4
Unhelmeted 2/	7	7	30	77	100	1,328.6
Transported to hospital	89	77	118	132	142	59.6
Helmeted	80	71	83	56	44	-45.0
Unhelmeted 2/	9	6	35	76	98	988.9

(NA) Not available.
1/ Principal diagnosis. 2/ Includes unknown.
Note: See Note on Table 13.52.

Table 13.52. MOTORCYCLES: COMPARATIVE HELMET USE AMONG CRASH-INVOLVED MOTORCYCLISTS IN FLORIDA, 1997–1999 TO 2001–2003

Item	1997–1999	2001–2003	Percentage change
Crash-involved motorcyclists, total	5,251	7,710	46.8
Percentage not helmeted	26.8	51.4	(X)
Under age 21	610	781	28.0
Percentage not helmeted	39.8	49.3	(X)
Incapacitating injuries	1,428	1,890	32.4
Percentage not helmeted	20.8	50.3	(X)
Under age 21	145	199	37.2
Percentage not helmeted	35.4	49.5	(X)
Number killed	515	933	81.2
Percentage not helmeted	9.4	60.8	(X)
Under age 21	35	101	188.6
Percentage not helmeted	25.7	45.0	(X)

(X) Not applicable.

Note: Florida amended the 1967 all-rider motorcycle helmet law effective July 1, 2000. The law now only requires helmet use by riders under the age of 21.

Source for Tables 13.51 and 13.52: U.S., Department of Transportation, National Highway Traffic Safety Administration, *Evaluation of the Repeal of the All-Rider Motorcycle Helmet Law in Florida,* Internet site <http://www.nhtsa.dot.gov/> (accessed 22, August 2006).

Table 13.60. RAILROADS: MILES OF RAILROAD TRACK OPERATED AND PERCENTAGE OF STATE SYSTEM BY RAILROAD COMPANY IN FLORIDA, 2006

Company	Tracks (in miles)	Percentage of state system	Company	Tracks (in miles)	Percentage of state system
Total	2,796	100.0	Florida Midland	33	1.2
			Florida Northern	103	3.7
Alabama and Gulf Coast	45	1.6	Georgia and Florida	50	1.8
Apalachicola Northern	96	3.4	Norfolk Southern	149	5.3
Bay Line	63	2.3	Seminole Gulf	115	4.1
CSX Transportation 1/	1,638	58.6	South Central Florida Express	171	6.1
First Coast 2/	32	1.1	South Florida Rail Corridor 3/	81	2.9
Florida Central	76	2.7	Talleyrand Terminal	10	0.4
Florida East Coast	371	13.3			

(X) Not applicable.

1/ Amtrak operates in Florida but owns no trackage in the state other than yard and terminal tracks. It operates mainly over CSXT main tracks. It also operates over trackage owned by the State of Florida between West Palm Beach and Miami (81 miles).

2/ First Coast Railroad leases 32 miles from CSXT, but the mileage is included with the First Coast and subtracted from CSXT.

3/ Not an operating carrier, trackage included in CSX data.

Source: State of Florida, Department of Transportation, Rail Office, *2006 Florida Rail System Plan,* Internet site <http://www.dot.state.fl.us/> (accessed 10, May 2007).

Table 13.61. PORT ACTIVITY: TONNAGE HANDLED IN SPECIFIED PORTS IN FLORIDA SPECIFIED FISCAL OR CALENDAR YEAR

Port and type of cargo	Short tons	Port and type of cargo	Short tons
Canaveral (fiscal year 2006), total	4,541,499	Manatee (Continued)	
Bulk cargo	3,800,000	General cargo	1,223,223
Breakbulk	723,000	Liquid bulk cargo	5,354,185
Roll on/roll off	18,499		
		Miami (fiscal year 2006), total	8,600,000
Everglades (fiscal year 2006), total	26,706,223	Trailer cargo	3,700,000
Containerized cargo	5,688,442	Containerized cargo	4,700,000
Bulk cargo	2,954,310	Other cargo	197,000
Breakbulk	344,528		
Petroleum	17,566,394	Palm Beach (fiscal year 2006), total	3,313,742
Roll on/roll off	152,549	General cargo	1,303,053
		Dry bulk cargo	2,010,689
Jacksonville 1/ (fiscal year 2006), total JPA terminals	8,696,543	Panama City (fiscal year 2005-06), total	1,788,875
Containerized cargo	4,075,907	General cargo	1,255,455
Breakbulk	1,212,917	Bulk cargo	533,420
Bulk cargo	2,203,249		
Auto/tractors	1,204,470		
		Tampa (fiscal year 2006), total	48,188,580
Manatee (fiscal year 2006), total	9,184,009	General cargo	1,279,623
Containerized cargo	54,898	Dry bulk cargo	21,222,946
Dry bulk cargo	2,551,703	Liquid bulk cargo	25,686,011

1/ Tonnage passing through facilities owned by the Jacksonville Port Authority only; therefore they differ from movements into and out of the Port of Jacksonville.

Source: Data are reported in annual or cumulative monthly reports of each port authority.

Table 13.73. EXPORTS AND IMPORTS: VALUE OF SHIPMENTS HANDLED BY CUSTOMS DISTRICTS IN FLORIDA, 2006

Top merchandise commodities	Exports: Value (million dollars)	Exports: Percentage change from prior year	Top merchandise commodities	Imports: Value (million dollars)	Imports: Percentage change from prior year
Florida	52,345.4	18.7	**Florida**	57,399.8	12.2
Industrial machinery	12,641.1	18.2	Vehicles, not railway	9,249.8	14.4
Electrical machinery	8,188.9	18.2	Mineral fuel, oil, etc.	7,052.2	11.7
Vehicles, not railway	8,155.4	35.7	Knit, crocheted apparel	4,553.3	4.8
Optical and medical instruments	3,055.7	27.0	Electrical machinery	3,452.1	11.4
Aircraft, spacecraft	2,275.0	30.3	Industrial machinery	3,262.8	5.4
Fertilizers	1,619.2	-6.9	Copper and copper products	3,223.7	144.8
Plastics and plastic products	1,093.8	19.7	Special woven fabrics	2,650.2	-3.8
Pharmaceutical products	950.7	-7.1	Aircraft, spacecraft	2,110.7	2.1
Cotton and yarn, fabric	912.9	14.0	Fish and seafood	1,661.5	11.0
Knit, crocheted apparel	788.0	-6.2	Precious stones, metals	1,583.3	15.3
Precious stones, metals	786.6	68.9	Special other	1,438.6	-0.3
Paper, paperboard	584.9	15.4	Beverages, spirits, vinegar	1,209.5	26.0
Ships and boats	581.7	30.6	Optical and medical instruments	1,138.7	3.5
Knit, crocheted fabrics	575.8	-6.8	Furniture and bedding	935.9	-1.5
Special other	548.6	5.4	Wood and wood products	871.2	-7.5
Perfumery, cosmetics, etc.	533.1	14.7	Live trees and plants	723.9	7.4
Organic chemicals	489.4	5.8	Aluminum and products	649.4	42.5
Miscellaneous chemical products	419.3	10.8	Paper, paperboard	587.4	39.9
Iron/steel products	418.9	32.2	Plastics and plastic products	583.0	0.7
Toys and sport equipment	374.2	34.0	Iron and steel	541.0	71.7
Furniture and bedding	356.1	7.2	Inorganic chemicals	537.1	-13.5
Tanning, dye, paint, putty	325.2	20.5	Perfumery, cosmetics, etc.	532.5	-0.4
Iron and steel	284.7	51.7	Leather art; saddlery, bags	527.1	20.7
Meat	262.0	-28.9	Edible fruits and nuts	470.5	20.3
Aluminum and products	248.0	26.7	Stone, plaster, and cement art	468.6	29.4
Rubber and rubber products	240.1	19.5	Art and antiques	455.0	-0.3
Manmade staple fibers	239.1	-6.2	Ships and boats	451.6	-1.2
Woven apparel	234.1	-34.5	Iron/steel products	437.1	13.5
Tools, cutlery of base metal	230.0	12.9	Ceramic products	405.3	7.5
Wood and wood products	223.1	12.5	Footwear	405.2	4.8
Manmade filament, fabric	197.1	37.2	Salt, sulfur, earth, and stone	384.1	5.6
Copper and copper products	196.3	113.3	Spices, coffee and tea	376.4	18.9
Mineral fuel, oil, etc.	196.1	62.2	Prepared vegetables, fruits	349.1	18.9
Miscellaneous food	185.4	5.1	Prepared meat, fish, etc.	334.7	15.4
Beverages, spirits, vinegar	170.5	23.6	Tobacco and substitutes	306.1	17.1
Prepared vegetables, fruits	169.6	18.3	Edible vegetables and roots	266.1	11.2
Woodpulp, etc.	160.6	9.9	Toys and sport equipment	234.2	-20.9
Books, newspapers	157.7	-23.8	Rubber and rubber products	231.6	-4.4
Photographic/cinematographic	156.3	19.9	Organic chemicals	201.4	-38.9
Inorganic chemicals	150.4	49.4	Clocks and watches	187.3	1.7
Railway or tramway stock	136.5	35.6	Miscellaneous manufactured	183.4	10.9
Stone, plaster, and cement art	132.0	16.8	Pharmaceutical products	163.7	-28.5
Special woven fabrics	128.9	1.1	Miscellaneous textile articles	138.3	4.2
Miscellaneous base metals	128.1	24.1	Glass and glassware	122.4	15.5
Miscellaneous manufactured	117.4	16.7	Meat	106.2	-12.1
Food industry waste	113.2	-6.7	Miscellaneous base metals	102.0	13.7

Note: Data from the Foreign Trade Division of the U.S. Census Bureau.
Source: Enterprise Florida, Marketing and Information Department, Annual International Trade Statistics, Internet site <http://www.eflorida.com/> (accessed 16, April 2007).

Table 13.90. AIRPORT ACTIVITY: OPERATIONS AT AIRPORTS WITH FEDERAL AVIATION ADMINISTRATION (FAA)-OPERATED AND CONTRACTED TRAFFIC CONTROL TOWERS IN FLORIDA, CALENDAR YEAR 2006

Location and type of operation	Total operations 1/	Air carrier 2/	Air taxi 3/	General aviation 4/	Military
Florida	6,085,104	1,161,016	560,991	4,190,028	173,069
Itinerant	4,300,426	1,161,016	560,991	2,481,411	97,008
Local	1,784,678	0	0	1,708,617	76,061
Boca Raton	91,026	0	7,832	82,901	293
Itinerant	54,494	0	7,832	46,609	53
Local	36,532	0	0	36,292	240
Daytona Beach International	282,368	3,930	4,954	272,516	968
Itinerant	220,121	3,930	4,954	210,325	912
Local	62,247	0	0	62,191	56
Ft. Lauderdale	297,237	179,848	60,379	56,572	438
Itinerant	297,075	179,848	60,379	56,410	438
Local	162	0	0	162	0
Ft. Lauderdale Executive	202,264	0	16,200	185,422	642
Itinerant	164,059	0	16,200	147,766	93
Local	38,205	0	0	37,656	549
Ft. Myers Page Field	77,897	2	4,940	72,748	207
Itinerant	53,812	2	4,940	48,701	169
Local	24,085	0	0	24,047	38
Ft. Myers/S.W. International	90,954	67,556	11,242	11,295	861
Itinerant	90,553	67,556	11,242	11,008	747
Local	401	0	0	287	114
Ft. Pierce	107,460	0	669	106,597	194
Itinerant	69,813	0	669	68,962	182
Local	37,647	0	0	37,635	12
Gainesville Regional	93,426	1,517	11,302	71,201	9,406
Itinerant	64,481	1,517	11,302	46,158	5,504
Local	28,945	0	0	25,043	3,902
Hollywood/North Perry	164,378	0	4	164,129	245
Itinerant	57,608	0	4	57,580	24
Local	106,770	0	0	106,549	221
Jacksonville Cecil Field	75,897	497	612	35,645	39,143
Itinerant	33,686	497	612	19,806	12,771
Local	42,211	0	0	15,839	26,372
Jacksonville/Craig Municipal	162,966	0	7,481	142,882	12,603
Itinerant	95,788	0	7,481	75,940	12,367
Local	67,178	0	0	66,942	236
Jacksonville International	118,844	60,610	33,962	17,309	6,963
Itinerant	115,989	60,610	33,962	16,756	4,661
Local	2,855	0	0	553	2,302

See footnotes at end of table.

Continued . . .

Table 13.90. AIRPORT ACTIVITY: OPERATIONS AT AIRPORTS WITH FEDERAL AVIATION ADMINISTRATION (FAA)-OPERATED AND CONTRACTED TRAFFIC CONTROL TOWERS IN FLORIDA, CALENDAR YEAR 2006 (Continued)

Location and type of operation	Total operations 1/	Air carrier 2/	Air taxi 3/	General aviation 4/	Military
Key West International	87,049	7,526	21,880	47,045	10,598
Itinerant	64,761	7,526	21,880	34,321	1,034
Local	22,288	0	0	12,724	9,564
Kendall-Tamiami Executive	208,090	23	2,818	204,864	385
Itinerant	105,975	23	2,818	103,005	129
Local	102,115	0	0	101,859	256
Lakeland/Linder Regional	118,713	0	1,099	114,521	3,093
Itinerant	78,187	0	1,099	75,820	1,268
Local	40,526	0	0	38,701	1,825
Leesburg	13,637	0	25	13,610	2
Itinerant	7,602	0	25	7,575	2
Local	6,035	0	0	6,035	0
Melbourne International	158,867	2,481	2,328	153,518	540
Itinerant	88,731	2,481	2,328	83,403	519
Local	70,136	0	0	70,115	21
Miami International	386,959	297,032	64,080	24,403	1,444
Itinerant	386,444	297,032	64,080	23,984	1,348
Local	515	0	0	419	96
Miami/Opa-Locka	121,061	203	6,598	103,348	10,912
Itinerant	81,441	203	6,598	68,681	5,959
Local	39,620	0	0	34,667	4,953
Naples	134,947	55	11,940	122,674	278
Itinerant	102,035	55	11,940	89,956	84
Local	32,912	0	0	32,718	194
New Smyrna	134,822	228	800	133,587	207
Itinerant	45,138	228	800	43,917	193
Local	89,684	0	0	89,670	14
Orlando Executive	163,811	0	13,470	149,820	521
Itinerant	108,620	0	13,470	94,688	462
Local	55,191	0	0	55,132	59
Orlando International	356,012	265,134	68,242	21,924	712
Itinerant	356,012	265,134	68,242	21,924	712
Local	0	0	0	0	0
Orlando/Kissimmee Municipal	153,297	10	2,543	150,447	297
Itinerant	82,932	10	2,543	80,323	56
Local	70,365	0	0	70,124	241
Orlando/Sanford	318,860	9,677	1,176	307,794	213
Itinerant	140,737	9,677	1,176	129,714	170
Local	178,123	0	0	178,080	43

See footnotes at end of table.

Continued . . .

Table 13.90. AIRPORT ACTIVITY: OPERATIONS AT AIRPORTS WITH FEDERAL AVIATION ADMINISTRATION (FAA)-OPERATED AND CONTRACTED TRAFFIC CONTROL TOWERS IN FLORIDA, CALENDAR YEAR 2006 (Continued)

Location and type of operation	Total operations 1/	Air carrier 2/	Air taxi 3/	General aviation 4/	Military
Ormond Beach	147,889	1,017	17	146,446	409
Itinerant	81,957	1,017	17	80,612	311
Local	65,932	0	0	65,834	98
Palm Beach International	192,755	60,294	40,138	91,296	1,027
Itinerant	189,757	60,294	40,138	88,421	904
Local	2,998	0	0	2,875	123
Panama City International	86,453	4,085	11,441	62,425	8,502
Itinerant	50,442	4,085	11,441	32,060	2,856
Local	36,011	0	0	30,365	5,646
Pensacola Regional	111,601	10,277	28,366	57,813	15,145
Itinerant	79,368	10,277	28,366	29,099	11,626
Local	32,233	0	0	28,714	3,519
Pompano Beach	101,686	0	167	101,504	15
Itinerant	37,984	0	167	37,808	9
Local	63,702	0	0	63,696	6
St. Augustine	111,832	9	7,268	98,748	5,807
Itinerant	66,835	9	7,268	56,843	2,715
Local	44,997	0	0	41,905	3,092
St. Petersburg/A. Whitted	79,219	0	2,994	73,550	2,675
Itinerant	40,567	0	2,994	36,176	1,397
Local	38,652	0	0	37,374	1,278
St. Petersburg-Clearwater	203,961	6,627	7,009	173,484	16,841
Itinerant	121,304	6,627	7,009	96,731	10,937
Local	82,657	0	0	76,753	5,904
Sarasota/Bradenton	162,883	15,837	11,078	133,274	2,694
Itinerant	120,898	15,837	11,078	92,104	1,879
Local	41,985	0	0	41,170	815
Stuart/Witham Field	83,821	0	6,381	76,622	818
Itinerant	60,599	0	6,381	53,696	522
Local	23,222	0	0	22,926	296
Tallahassee Regional	102,261	4,849	29,620	51,688	16,104
Itinerant	85,289	4,849	29,620	38,077	12,743
Local	16,972	0	0	13,611	3,361
Tampa International	257,193	161,690	55,082	39,831	590
Itinerant	256,937	161,690	55,082	39,575	590
Local	256	0	0	256	0
Titusville/Space Coast Regional	185,870	2	769	183,967	1,132
Itinerant	64,882	2	769	63,557	554
Local	120,988	0	0	120,410	578

See footnotes at end of table. Continued . . .

Table 13.90. AIRPORT ACTIVITY: OPERATIONS AT AIRPORTS WITH FEDERAL AVIATION ADMINISTRATION (FAA)-OPERATED AND CONTRACTED TRAFFIC CONTROL TOWERS IN FLORIDA, CALENDAR YEAR 2006 (Continued)

Location and type of operation	Total operations 1/	Air carrier 2/	Air taxi 3/	General aviation 4/	Military
Vero Beach	136,838	0	4,085	132,608	145
Itinerant	77,513	0	4,085	73,320	108
Local	59,325	0	0	59,288	37

1/ An aircraft arrival at or departure from an airport with FAA traffic control.
2/ Air carrier authorized by the Department of Transportation to provide scheduled service over specified routes with limited nonscheduled operations.
3/ Performs at least five round trips per week between two or more points and publishes flight schedules or transports mail.
4/ All operations not classified as an air carrier, air taxi, or military.
Note: Itinerant includes all aircraft arrivals and departures other than local. Local includes aircraft operatior which operate in the local traffic pattern or within sight of the tower.

Source: U.S., Department of Transportation, Federal Aviation Administration, Internet site <http://www.apo.data.faa.gov/> (accessed 16, April 2007).

Table 13.91. AIRPORT ACTIVITY: INSTRUMENT OPERATIONS AT AIRPORTS WITH FEDERAL AVIATION ADMINISTRATION (FAA)-OPERATED AND CONTRACTED TRAFFIC CONTROL TOWERS IN FLORIDA, CALENDAR YEAR 2006

Location and type of operation	Total operations 1/	Air carrier 2/	Air taxi 3/	General aviation 4/	Military
Florida	3,993,322	1,177,309	591,007	1,959,282	265,724
Daytona Beach International	403,885	12,729	14,019	372,179	4,958
Jacksonville International	419,148	67,523	69,597	236,578	45,450
Miami International	913,515	477,132	160,387	267,464	8,532
Orlando International	704,273	283,174	95,763	318,637	6,699
Palm Beach International	356,055	65,484	68,120	221,016	1,435
Southwest Florida International	229,350	71,249	30,309	125,719	2,073
Tallahassee Regional	123,766	4,713	33,288	70,785	14,980
Tampa International	550,355	182,917	83,325	266,895	17,218

1/ An aircraft arrival at or departure from an airport with FAA traffic control.
2/ Air carrier authorized by the Department of Transportation to provide scheduled service over specified routes with limited nonscheduled operations.
3/ Performs at least five round trips per week between two or more points and publishes flight schedules or transports mail.
4/ All operations not classified as an air carrier, air taxi, or military.
Note: All VFR tower and federal contract tower Instrument Operations have been removed. Instrument operations include primary and secondary airport arrivals and departures, and overflight operations in which an aircraft transits the area without intent to land.

Source: U.S., Department of Transportation, Federal Aviation Administration, Internet site <http://www.apo.data.faa.gov/> (accessed 18, June 2007).

Table 13.93. AIRCRAFT PILOTS: ACTIVE AIRCRAFT PILOTS BY TYPE OF CERTIFICATE AND FLIGHT INSTRUCTORS IN THE STATE AND COUNTIES OF FLORIDA DECEMBER 31, 2006

	Pilots						
			Airplane pilots 1/				
County	Total 2/	Student 3/	Private	Commercial	Airline transport 4/	Miscel-laneous 5/	Flight instructors
Florida	48,512	7,364	15,943	10,649	14,493	7,002	8,135
Alachua	496	105	216	103	70	77	57
Baker	25	3	16	3	3	3	0
Bay	566	104	180	144	138	76	89
Bradford	24	4	10	7	3	3	2
Brevard	2,498	338	799	599	758	473	507
Broward	5,061	603	1,208	1,055	2,193	535	932
Calhoun	13	0	9	3	1	2	1
Charlotte	444	56	162	90	133	66	65
Citrus	308	48	150	58	51	57	45
Clay	689	73	184	141	291	118	91
Collier	1,145	107	478	220	339	156	187
Columbia	126	13	65	30	17	13	16
DeSoto	39	6	15	13	4	9	8
Dixie	19	2	9	5	3	4	2
Duval	1,607	268	529	424	386	252	241
Escambia	1,562	668	277	242	373	245	107
Flagler	269	36	85	76	72	35	64
Franklin	34	5	13	5	11	5	4
Gadsden	45	5	22	12	6	11	8
Gilchrist	22	0	17	4	1	3	2
Glades	12	2	5	3	2	2	0
Gulf	34	7	15	6	6	3	2
Hamilton	6	0	3	1	2	0	1
Hardee	18	1	11	5	1	2	2
Hendry	59	6	24	14	15	13	13
Hernando	233	37	104	47	45	35	40
Highlands	177	24	75	50	28	39	37
Hillsborough	2,180	319	884	417	559	347	285
Holmes	23	4	9	5	5	4	5
Indian River	745	62	257	211	215	71	208
Jackson	55	12	16	17	10	7	9
Jefferson	31	4	18	4	5	4	2
Lafayette	1	0	0	1	0	1	0
Lake	673	88	270	150	161	133	127
Lee	1,473	194	583	298	397	200	211
Leon	418	58	188	103	68	75	62

See footnotes at end of table. Continued . . .

Table 13.93. AIRCRAFT PILOTS: ACTIVE AIRCRAFT PILOTS BY TYPE OF CERTIFICATE AND FLIGHT INSTRUCTORS IN THE STATE AND COUNTIES OF FLORIDA DECEMBER 31, 2006 (Continued)

	Pilots						
			Airplane pilots 1/				
County	Total 2/	Student 3/	Private	Commercial	Airline transport 4/	Miscel- laneous 5/	Flight instructors
Levy	70	12	32	18	8	9	11
Liberty	2	0	0	1	1	0	0
Madison	10	0	8	0	2	1	0
Manatee	700	77	261	137	222	96	108
Marion	778	109	333	195	141	102	105
Martin	778	75	244	143	313	137	142
Miami-Dade	3,925	657	1,191	774	1,298	579	549
Monroe	663	78	242	109	233	108	84
Nassau	304	32	98	60	112	39	58
Okaloosa	1,099	220	302	256	321	156	126
Okeechobee	89	7	47	24	11	17	13
Orange	2,488	301	743	593	850	366	505
Osceola	461	81	121	107	152	68	107
Palm Beach	3,484	428	1,172	682	1,201	530	602
Pasco	825	116	347	164	196	119	130
Pinellas	2,341	285	886	475	692	321	359
Polk	1,056	154	450	229	215	171	196
Putnam	134	15	63	28	28	30	17
St. Johns	710	104	231	136	239	120	111
St. Lucie	642	129	191	152	168	85	122
Santa Rosa	924	268	166	206	283	204	75
Sarasota	1,026	122	424	251	228	134	170
Seminole	1,537	255	487	426	369	140	331
Sumter	108	14	46	21	26	22	14
Suwannee	100	8	40	26	24	16	21
Taylor	16	0	5	10	1	4	6
Union	11	4	4	1	2	0	0
Volusia	2,859	505	832	805	715	306	709
Wakulla	49	5	13	11	19	9	11
Walton	173	36	52	36	49	31	20
Washington	20	5	6	7	2	3	1

1/ Includes pilots with airplane only certificates and with airplane and helicopter and/or glider certificates.
2/ Includes recreational pilots not shown separately.
3/ Category of certificate unknown.
4/ Includes airline transport airplane only and airline transport airplane and helicopter certificates.
5/ Includes helicopter, gyroplane, glider and recreational certificates.

Source: U.S., Department of Transportation, Federal Aviation Administration, Office of Aviation Policy and Plans, unpublished data.

COMMUNICATIONS

Telecommunications Industry Employment, 2006 (%)

Wired telecommunications carriers 50%

Wireless telecommunications carriers 26%

Telecommunications resellers 2%

Satellite telecommunications 1%

Cable and other program distribution 21%

Other telecommunications 1%

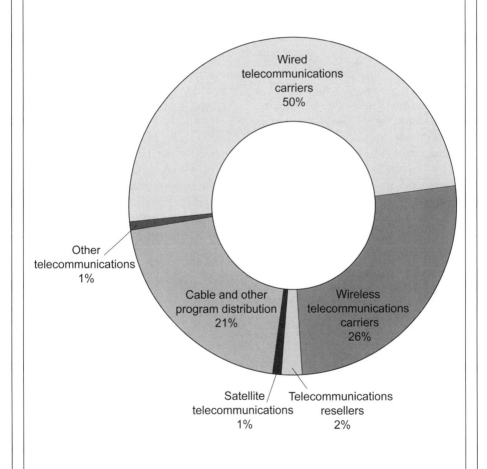

Source: Table 14.04

Section 14.00
Communications

This section depicts data about communications throughout the state. The communications services industry has increased immensely in recent years, due to the rise in electronic communications. Section 14.00 reports industry data on establishments, employment, and payroll; broadcasting; telecommunications and carriers; post offices; publishing and motion pictures; computer-related communication; and telephone companies.

Explanatory notes. The U.S. Census Bureau conducts an economic census in years ending in "2" and "7." Recent changes in industry classification through implementation of the North American Industry Classification System (NAICS) have resulted in more service-related classifications than those previously designated by the old Standard Industrial Classification (SIC) system. (See the introduction to Section 6.00 and the Glossary.)

Information (NAICS code 51) represents one of these redefined categories. Information includes publishing industries (511), motion picture and sound recording industries (512), broadcasting and telecommunications (513), and information services and data processing services (514). Tables 14.01 through 14.06 present data about these categories from the U.S. Census Bureau's *2002 Economic Census: Information*.

Sources. The Florida Agency for Workforce Innovation, Labor Market Statistics office provides the current employment and payroll data depicted in several tables throughout this section, beginning with Table 14.35. (See the introduction to Section 6.00 and the Glossary.)

The U.S. Postal Service and the Florida Public Service Commission provide additional communication-related data presented in this section. The U.S. Postal Service furnishes unpublished postal revenue data, by zip code, for first class post offices throughout the state on Table 14.33. The Florida Public Service Commission reports exchanges and access line data for telephone companies servicing Florida in the Internet publication, *Comparative Rate Statistics: Electric, Natural Gas, Telephone, Water and Wastewater*.

Section 14.00
Communications

Tables listed by major heading

Table 14.01. INFORMATION: ESTABLISHMENTS, EMPLOYMENT, REVENUE, AND ANNUAL PAYROLL BY KIND OF BUSINESS IN FLORIDA, 2002

NAICS code	Industry	Establish-ments	Employ-ment 1/	Revenue ($1,000)	Annual payroll ($1,000)
51	Information	7,758	184,701	A/	8,088,549
511	Publishing industries (except Internet)	1,658	45,237	7,429,219	1,983,242
512	Motion picture and sound recording industries	1,174	13,058	A/	263,446
515	Broadcasting (except Internet)	525	15,278	3,382,339	791,737
516	Internet publishing and broadcasting	154	1,196	188,613	56,682
517	Telecommunications	2,982	90,142	A/	4,099,504
518	Internet service providers, web search portals, and data processing services	1,170	18,264	2,661,998	856,175
519	Other information services	95	1,526	119,959	37,763

A/ Not available or not comparable.
1/ Paid employment for the pay period including March 12.
Note: The economic censuses are conducted on a 5-year cycle collecting data for years ending in 2 and 7. Data are for North American Industry Classification System (NAICS) code 51 and may not be comparable to earlier years. See Glossary for definition.

Table 14.02. PUBLISHING AND BROADCASTING: ESTABLISHMENTS, EMPLOYMENT, REVENUE AND ANNUAL PAYROLL BY KIND OF BUSINESS IN FLORIDA, 2002

NAICS code	Industry	Establish-ments	Employ-ment 1/	Revenue ($1,000)	Annual payroll ($1,000)
511	Publishing industries (except Internet)	1,658	45,237	7,429,219	1,983,242
5111	Newspaper, periodical, book, and directory publishers	1,187	36,552	5,629,833	1,287,713
51111	Newspaper publishers	320	23,665	2,802,001	781,338
51112	Periodical publishers	498	7,627	1,772,439	308,421
51113	Book publishers	181	1,981	316,938	76,309
51114	Directory and mailing list publishers	129	2,738	651,324	98,384
51119	Other publishers	59	541	87,131	23,261
5112	Software publishers	471	8,685	1,799,386	695,529
515	Broadcasting (except Internet)	525	15,278	3,382,339	791,737
5151	Radio and television broadcasting	489	13,914	2,933,037	706,808
51511	Radio broadcasting	364	6,291	798,645	228,846
51512	Television broadcasting	125	7,623	2,134,392	477,962
5152	Cable and other subscription programming	36	1,364	449,302	84,929
516	Internet publishing and broadcasting	154	1,196	188,613	56,682

1/ Paid employment for the pay period including March 12.
Note: The economic censuses are conducted on a 5-year cycle collecting data for years ending in 2 and 7. Data are for North American Industry Classification System (NAICS) codes and may not be comparable to earlier years. See Glossary for definition.

Source for Tables 14.01 and 14.02: U.S., Department of Commerce, Census Bureau, *2002 Economic Census: Information,* Geographic Area Series EC02-51A-FL, issued June 2005, Internet site <http://www.census.gov/> (accessed 11, May 2007).

Table 14.03. MOTION PICTURE AND SOUND RECORDING: ESTABLISHMENTS, EMPLOYMENT REVENUE, AND ANNUAL PAYROLL BY KIND OF BUSINESS IN FLORIDA, 2002

NAICS code	Industry	Establish-ments	Employ-ment 1/	Revenue ($1,000)	Annual payroll ($1,000)
512	Motion picture and sound recording industries	1,174	13,058	A/	263,446
5121	Motion picture and video industries	984	11,775	A/	206,911
51211	Motion picture and video production	614	3,987	B/	116,312
51212	Motion picture and video distribution	26	90	B/	4,148
51213	Motion picture and video exhibition	235	7,150	642,760	68,660
51219	Postproduction and other motion picture and video industries	109	548	45,824	17,791
5122	Sound recording industries	190	1,283	A/	56,535
51221	Record production	15	38	8,310	2,226
51222	Integrated record production/distribution	21	364	B/	24,145
51223	Music publishers	35	311	87,102	13,201
51224	Sound recording studios	88	260	25,515	7,914
51229	Other sound recording industries	31	310	31,146	9,049

A/ Not available or not comparable.
B/ Receipts not collected at this level of detail for multi-establishment firms.
1/ Paid employment for the pay period including March 12.
Note: See Note for Table 14.04.

Table 14.04. TELECOMMUNICATIONS, INTERNET SERVICES, AND OTHER INFORMATION SERVICES: ESTABLISHMENTS, EMPLOYMENT, REVENUE, AND ANNUAL PAYROLL BY KIND OF BUSINESS IN FLORIDA, 2002

NAICS code	Industry	Establish-ments	Employ-ment 1/	Revenue ($1,000)	Annual payroll ($1,000)
517	Telecommunications	2,982	90,142	A/	4,099,504
5171	Wired telecommunications carriers	1,464	44,624	B/	2,550,905
5172	Wireless telecommunications carriers (except satellite)	785	23,597	B/	870,935
5173	Telecommunications resellers	252	1,634	372,348	53,434
5174	Satellite telecommunications	49	636	247,025	31,442
5175	Cable and other program distribution	383	18,967	B/	567,658
5179	Other telecommunications	49	684	84,622	25,130
518	Internet service providers, web search portals, and data processing services	1,170	18,264	2,661,998	856,175
5181	Internet service providers and web search portals	344	3,089	535,377	145,021
5182	Data processing, hosting, and related services	826	15,175	2,126,621	711,154
519	Other information services	95	1,526	119,959	37,763
51911	News syndicates	35	374	56,723	14,475
51912	Libraries and archives	47	390	23,424	8,686
51919	All other information services	13	762	39,812	14,602

A/ Not available or not comparable.
B/ Receipts not collected at this level of detail for multi-establishment firms.
1/ Paid employment for the pay period including March 12.
Note: The economic censuses are conducted on a 5-year cycle collecting data for years ending in 2 and 7. Data are for North American Industry Classification System (NAICS) codes and may not be comparable to earlier years. See Glossary for definition.
Source for Tables 14.03 and 14.04: U.S., Department of Commerce, Census Bureau, *2002 Economic Census: Information,* Geographic Area Series EC02-51A-FL, issued June 2005, Internet site <http://www.census.gov/> (accessed 11, May 2007).

Table 14.05. BROADCASTING: ESTABLISHMENTS, EMPLOYMENT, AND ANNUAL PAYROLL IN THE STATE AND SPECIFIED COUNTIES OF FLORIDA, 2002

County	Establish-ments	Employ-ment 1/	Payroll ($1,000)	County	Establish-ments	Employ-ment 1/	Payroll ($1,000)
Florida	525	15,278	791,737	Lee	23	796	29,165
				Leon 3/	13	(NA)	(D)
Alachua	8	186	5,607	Miami-Dade	87	4,212	306,419
Bay	15	248	7,285	Orange 4/	41	(NA)	(D)
Brevard	12	106	2,809	Palm Beach	44	1,295	67,506
Broward	43	1,512	73,036	Pinellas	18	618	33,423
Duval	37	1,115	41,508	Sarasota 2/	17	(NA)	(D)
Escambia 2/	9	(NA)	(D)	Seminole 2/	8	(NA)	(D)
Hillsborough	32	1,248	64,262	Volusia	10	65	2,080

(NA) Not available.
(D) Data withheld to avoid disclosure of information about individual firms.
1/ Paid employment for the pay period including March 12.
Employment ranges: 2/ 500-999. 3/ 100-249. 4/ 20-99.
Note: Data are for NAICS code 515. See also note on Table 14.06.

Table 14.06. TELECOMMUNICATIONS: ESTABLISHMENTS, EMPLOYMENT, AND ANNUAL PAYROLL IN THE STATE AND SPECIFIED COUNTIES OF FLORIDA, 2002

County	Establish-ments	Employ-ment 1/	Payroll ($1,000)	County	Establish-ments	Employ-ment 1/	Payroll ($1,000)
Florida	2,982	90,142	4,099,504	Marion	41	484	19,454
Alachua 2/	33	(NA)	(D)	Martin	23	504	17,546
Bay	30	648	20,534	Miami-Dade	536	11,790	474,123
Brevard	69	1,239	43,383	Monroe	21	296	8,928
Broward	338	10,109	409,106	Nassau 4/	8	(NA)	(D)
Charlotte	15	208	11,990	Okaloosa	31	507	19,698
Citrus	9	155	5,618	Okeechobee	6	58	2,483
Clay 2/	21	(NA)	(D)	Orange	210	8,583	381,510
Collier	34	737	26,188	Osceola	18	207	8,505
Columbia	7	97	3,852	Palm Beach	179	5,154	193,476
Duval	185	8,068	298,932	Pasco	33	233	8,165
Escambia	61	1,043	42,404	Pinellas	135	3,534	159,244
Flagler	7	94	2,421	Polk	62	1,439	47,085
Gulf 3/	5	(NA)	(D)	Putnam	7	94	3,274
Hernando	15	98	4,167	St. Johns	18	225	7,411
Highlands	12	151	5,980	St. Lucie	18	863	19,688
Hillsborough	344	16,871	1,202,630	Santa Rosa	16	268	10,707
Indian River	19	275	8,742	Sarasota	43	940	35,031
Jackson	5	83	2,620	Seminole	70	4,780	207,017
Lake	23	915	40,038	Suwannee 4/	3	(NA)	(D)
Lee	83	4,265	152,753	Taylor 4/	2	(NA)	(D)
Leon	63	51,239	1,312	Volusia	44	847	29,274
Madison 4/	4	(NA)	(D)	Walton 4/	6	(NA)	(D)
Manatee	26	599	24,452	Washington 4/	4	(NA)	(D)

(NA) Not available.
(D) Data withheld to avoid disclosure of information about individual firms.
1/ Paid employment for the pay period including March 12.
Employment ranges: 2/ 500-999. 3/ 100-249. 4/ 20-99.
Note: The economic censuses are conducted on a 5-year cycle collecting data for years ending in 2 and 7. Data are for North American Industry Classification System (NAICS) code 517 and may not be comparable to earlier years. See Glossary for definition.
Source for Tables 14.05 and 14.06: U.S., Department of Commerce, Census Bureau, *2002 Economic Census: Information,* Geographic Area Series EC02-51A-FL, issued June 2005, Internet site <http://www.census.gov/> (accessed 11, May 2007).

Table 14.33. POST OFFICES: ZIP CODES AND NET POSTAL REVENUE IN THE STATE AND SPECIFIED CITIES OF FLORIDA, FISCAL YEAR 2005-06

First class post office	ZIP code	Net revenue (dollars)	Change 1/
Florida	(X)	3,459,251,467	4.5
Alachua	32615	1,309,151	5.6
Altamonte Springs	32714	9,004,908	10.6
Alva	33920	321,455	22.7
Anna Maria	34216	330,639	-6.1
Anthony	32617	341,082	7.3
Apalachicola	32320	435,322	-12.4
Apopka	32712	6,447,001	-69.9
Arcadia	34266	1,400,811	0.9
Auburndale	33823	1,800,644	6.5
Avon Park	33825	1,631,878	8.5
Bartow	33830	2,928,963	3.9
Bay Pines	33744	666,158	-3.6
Belle Glade	33430	921,363	-1.6
Belleview	34420	1,791,883	0.3
Blountstown	32424	1,318,150	16.0
Boca Grande	33921	468,120	-2.5
Boca Raton	33431	78,280,584	18.9
Bonifay	32425	796,954	5.0
Bonita Springs	34135	5,877,585	1.4
Boynton Beach	33436	11,203,487	0.2
Bradenton	34206	17,822,666	2.8
Bradenton Beach	34217	971,941	-7.4
Brandon	33511	7,545,415	0.6
Bronson	32621	449,128	6.1
Brooksville	34601	12,478,441	3.0
Bunnell	32110	1,167,006	-0.5
Bushnell	33513	942,185	1.7
Callahan	32011	1,119,726	29.4
Cantonment	32533	869,618	3.3
Cape Canaveral	32920	1,558,075	2.1
Casselberry	32707	6,245,877	0.8
Chattahoochee	32324	365,249	-3.9
Chiefland	32626	1,107,641	8.7
Chipley	32428	957,485	4.6
Christmas	32709	451,194	3.6
Clarcona	32710	600,237	2.8
Clearwater	33758	74,307,220	-2.4
Clermont	34711	5,763,515	11.0
Clewiston	33440	983,519	-0.9
Cocoa	32926	4,417,176	-4.2
Cocoa Beach	32931	1,484,134	-3.6
Coleman	33521	554,533	13.1
Crawfordville	32327	1,044,062	7.7
Crescent City	32112	399,463	2.8
Crestview	32539	2,275,050	8.7
Cross City	32628	350,604	4.5
Crystal River	34429	2,257,268	-6.6
Dade City	33525	2,429,560	5.1
Dania	33004	2,336,921	3.9
Davenport	33837	1,282,527	9.9
Daytona Beach	32114	56,040,007	5.7
De Bary	32713	1,854,022	27.2
Deerfield Beach	33441	12,645,448	1.1
Defuniak Springs	32433	1,373,286	1.7
Deland	32720	5,436,365	-3.1
Deleon Springs	32130	580,814	5.7
Delray Beach	33484	11,721,812	-5.4
Deltona	32738	4,068,484	-0.5
Destin	32541	4,508,689	-1.7
Dover	33527	411,151	0.9
Dundee	33838	701,678	13.1
Dunedin	34698	4,190,197	6.1
Dunnellon	34430	1,741,492	6.9
Eagle Lake	33839	793,007	7.2
Eastpoint	32328	327,780	-4.3
Eaton Park	33840	953,198	-1.3
Edgewater	32132	1,650,153	3.9
Eglin Air Force Base	32542	661,523	-9.3
Elfers	34680	1,888,608	1.4
Ellenton	34222	1,892,495	-1.3
Englewood	34223	3,415,913	-2.4
Estero	33928	2,254,985	19.0
Eustis	32726	1,818,206	4.3
Fernandina Beach	32034	3,191,185	1.1
Flagler Beach	32136	42,378,668	-0.3
Floral City	34436	452,136	-0.8
Ft. Lauderdale	33310	319,697,046	0.6
Ft. McCoy	32134	352,680	5.6
Ft. Meade	33841	348,783	1.0
Ft. Myers	33906	61,173,832	2.3
Ft. Myers Beach	33931	1,665,578	-5.4
Ft. Pierce	34981	26,160,041	10.8
Ft. Walton Beach	32548	7,566,215	3.9
Freeport	32439	482,293	37.2
Frostproof	33843	538,118	3.8
Fruitland Park	34731	968,792	3.3
Gainesville	32608	29,205,969	3.1
Gibsonton	33534	368,703	14.9
Goldenrod	32733	1,811,473	25.7
Gonzalez	32560	617,708	1.8
Gotha	34734	789,924	1.4
Graceville	32440	528,496	4.7
Grand Island	32735	327,581	2.7
Green Cove Springs	32043	1,359,402	3.1
Groveland	34736	693,903	9.3
Gulf Breeze	32561	4,328,751	2.3

See footnotes at end of table.

Continued . . .

Table 14.33. POST OFFICES: ZIP CODES AND NET POSTAL REVENUE IN THE STATE AND SPECIFIED CITIES OF FLORIDA, FISCAL YEAR 2005–06 (Continued)

First class post office	ZIP code	Net revenue (dollars)	Change 1/	First class post office	ZIP code	Net revenue (dollars)	Change 1/
Haines City	33844	1,486,183	3.3	Live Oak	32060	1,739,034	3.8
Hallandale	33009	6,277,564	-0.5	Longboat Key	34228	1,219,402	-0.1
Havana	32333	469,877	1.9	Longwood	32779	7,407,658	4.5
Hawthorne	32640	338,719	1.3	Loxahatchee	33470	1,442,716	7.8
Hernando	34442	1,132,339	-2.1	Lutz	33549	3,640,100	12.2
Hialeah	33010	24,018,745	9.3	Lynn Haven	32444	2,199,647	-0.5
High Springs	32643	692,271	4.5	Macclenny	32063	774,128	2.4
Highland City	33846	411,560	6.6	Madison	32340	782,501	-2.2
Hilliard	32046	330,062	2.5	Maitland	32751	8,001,809	-5.1
Hobe Sound	33455	1,890,695	-0.5	Malabar	32950	466,880	6.3
Hollywood	33022	193,151,723	63.9	Mango	33550	986,348	3.1
Homestead	33030	4,591,152	3.8	Marathon	33050	1,594,944	-7.7
Homosassa	34487	655,604	30.4	Marco	34145	2,855,800	-6.2
Homosassa Springs	34447	1,350,649	-0.9	Marianna	32446	1,872,587	5.9
Howey-in-the-Hills	34737	395,090	40.2	Mary Esther	32569	2,349,960	8.3
Immokalee	34142	864,270	0.4	Mayo	32066	366,188	9.2
Indian Rocks Beach	33785	1,214,912	0.3	Melbourne	32901	33,344,192	5.5
Indiantown	34956	429,654	-5.3	Melrose	32666	328,820	0.0
Interlachen	32148	452,529	2.4	Merritt Island	32953	3,563,790	3.8
Inverness	34450	3,463,140	4.6	Miami	33152	286,348,491	2.0
Islamorada	33036	626,474	-4.5	Miami Beach	33139	11,310,839	3.5
Jacksonville	32203	286,320,717	-2.8	Middleburg	32068	1,212,864	3.1
Jasper	32052	359,375	6.7	Midway	32343	2,128,475	595.5
Jensen Beach	34957	2,636,182	-2.2	Milton	32570	3,828,187	1.0
Jupiter	33458	10,210,380	3.2	Mims	32754	774,920	4.1
Kathleen	33849	531,027	1.2	Minneola	34755	895,498	-0.1
Key Largo	33037	1,737,577	0.8	Monticello	32344	674,695	3.6
Key West	33040	4,840,859	-10.2	Mount Dora	32757	2,508,403	0.8
Keystone Heights	32656	1,454,797	3.4	Mulberry	33860	1,782,035	-18.9
Kissimmee	34744	12,804,640	2.9	Naples	34102	33,005,400	-1.9
La Belle	33935	1,167,263	4.3	New Port Richey	34653	7,161,458	9.6
Lady Lake	32159	5,279,606	5.5	New Smyrna Beach	32168	3,560,498	5.5
Lake Alfred	33850	772,081	1.1	Newberry	32669	697,177	5.4
Lake Butler	32054	474,629	9.7	Niceville	32578	2,385,891	2.4
Lake City	32055	4,451,250	6.8	Nokomis	34275	2,478,574	1.7
Lake Helen	32744	384,061	2.2	Oakland	34760	471,483	31.7
Lake Mary	32746	13,536,808	6.7	Ocala	34478	21,779,236	13.1
Lake Monroe	32747	1,170,901	-0.4	Ocoee	34761	2,490,943	7.5
Lake Placid	33852	1,529,273	0.1	Odessa	33556	1,287,628	14.6
Lake Wales	33853	2,243,517	-0.1	Okahumpka	34762	543,856	15.2
Lake Worth	33461	14,452,363	-1.0	Okeechobee	34972	2,313,859	-0.5
Lakeland	33805	36,529,857	8.6	Old Town	32680	342,182	4.0
Land O'Lakes	34639	2,505,996	15.3	Oldsmar	34677	13,190,991	53.1
Largo	33770	15,435,639	2.1	Oneco	34264	1,092,826	4.4
Laurel	34272	341,722	-3.4	Opa Locka	33054	3,390,716	4.7
Lecanto	34461	2,551,608	4.0	Orange City	32763	2,491,331	-3.4
Leesburg	34748	4,962,510	3.3	Orange Park	32073	9,212,815	9.4
Lehigh Acres	33936	2,695,566	-1.7	Orlando	32862	231,227,647	4.2
Lithia	33547	796,282	16.8	Ormond Beach	32174	7,429,113	4.7

See footnotes at end of table.

Continued . . .

Table 14.33. POST OFFICES: ZIP CODES AND NET POSTAL REVENUE IN THE STATE AND SPECIFIED CITIES OF FLORIDA, FISCAL YEAR 2005–06 (Continued)

First class post office	ZIP code	Net revenue (dollars)	Change 1/	First class post office	ZIP code	Net revenue (dollars)	Change 1/
Osprey	34229	1,983,401	-0.4	Sebastian	32958	2,210,876	5.2
Oviedo	32765	4,646,091	12.7	Sebring	33870	3,925,552	0.6
Oxford	34484	935,464	29.0	Seffner	33584	1,511,345	7.4
Palatka	32177	2,228,551	1.6	Shalimar	32579	1,409,344	-3.2
Palm Beach	33480	3,073,813	-2.3	Sharpes	32959	701,667	3.0
Palm City	34990	2,885,174	0.7	Silver Springs	34489	1,461,429	-3.8
Palm Harbor	34683	10,282,721	-12.6	Sorrento	32776	574,615	12.7
Palmetto	34221	1,839,164	3.7	Starke	32091	867,386	2.1
Panama City	32401	15,353,808	10.0	Stuart	34994	10,517,269	5.3
Parrish	34219	430,089	1.9	Summerfield	34491	1,185,992	0.5
Pensacola	32522	32,626,524	2.9	Summerland Key	33042	1,222,977	-4.4
Perry	32347	1,078,763	-0.3	Tallahassee	32301	133,455,031	2.2
Pinellas Park	33781	4,925,976	-0.3	Tallevast	34270	3,164,521	7.6
Placida	33946	1,009,440	2.2	Tampa	33630	409,624,103	5.0
Plant City	33566	3,640,497	5.6	Tarpon Springs	34689	6,287,167	5.8
Plymouth	32768	490,042	2.7	Tavares	32778	6,144,005	79.2
Polk City	33868	524,838	2.6	Tavernier	33070	900,596	-3.2
Pompano Beach	33069	53,132,320	-6.9	Thonotosassa	33592	463,190	2.0
Ponte Vedra Beach	32082	3,813,587	-1.2	Titusville	32780	4,913,718	3.0
Port Orange	32127	4,936,571	5.0	Trenton	32693	530,806	2.5
Port Richey	34668	6,743,940	2.3	Umatilla	32784	700,518	6.4
Port St. Joe	32456	941,521	1.0	Valparaiso	32580	675,415	-1.6
Port Salerno	34992	929,731	4.9	Valrico	33594	2,640,495	8.5
Punta Gorda	33950	13,098,544	7.2	Venice	34285	9,392,834	4.4
Quincy	32351	3,629,472	-4.4	Vero Beach	32960	12,167,334	1.3
Riverview	33569	3,289,840	19.9	Wabasso	32970	979,916	-11.8
Rockledge	32955	3,082,716	7.9	Wauchula	33873	825,250	1.3
Roseland	32957	452,801	-1.8	Weirsdale	32195	889,847	-10.1
Ruskin	33570	3,643,151	2.6	West Palm Beach	33406	86,986,806	10.4
Safety Harbor	34695	1,618,767	6.4	Wildwood	34785	799,864	10.3
St. Augustine	32084	9,815,984	7.8	Williston	32696	782,146	7.5
St. Cloud	34769	3,151,629	11.9	Wimauma	33598	329,132	18.7
St. James City	33956	363,480	-10.6	Windermere	34786	2,754,678	6.2
St. Leo	33574	323,240	-2.9	Winter Garden	34787	2,748,537	8.7
St. Petersburg	33730	133,979,062	-2.7	Winter Haven	33880	6,125,138	4.1
San Antonio	33576	463,089	19.8	Winter Park	32789	11,185,578	-4.2
Sanford	32771	4,273,653	5.1	Yulee	32097	793,629	11.6
Sanibel	33957	1,669,429	-1.3	Zellwood	32798	334,510	11.8
Santa Rosa Beach	32459	1,293,277	-1.8	Zephyrhills	33540	4,925,672	-2.9
Sarasota	34230	38,762,664	1.4				

(X) Not applicable.
1/ Percentage change from previous year.
Note: Data are for first class post offices. Florida total includes revenue from all post offices.

Source: U.S., Postal Service Headquarters, unpublished data.

Table 14.35. EMPLOYMENT: AVERAGE MONTHLY PRIVATE EMPLOYMENT COVERED BY UNEMPLOYMENT COMPENSATION LAW BY INDUSTRY IN FLORIDA, 2005 AND 2006

NAICS code	Industry	2005 A/	2006 B/
51	Information	168,573	167,394
511	Publishing industries, except Internet	41,988	42,965
5111	Newspaper, book, and directory publishers	34,129	34,600
5112	Software publishers	7,859	8,365
512	Motion picture and sound recording industries	14,442	14,141
5121	Motion picture and video industries	13,393	13,109
5122	Sound recording industries	1,049	1,032
515	Broadcasting, except Internet	18,866	18,960
5151	Radio and television broadcasting	13,951	13,960
5152	Cable and other subscription programming	4,915	5,000
516	Internet publishing and broadcasting	1,308	1,484
517	Telecommunications	64,864	63,367
5171	Wired telecommunications carriers	37,288	33,234
5172	Wireless telecommunications carriers	12,376	14,086
5173	Telecommunications resellers	5,014	4,655
5174	Satellite telecommunications	663	717
5175	Cable and other program distribution	9,318	10,350
5179	Other telecommunications	205	326
518	ISPs, search portals, and data processing	25,736	25,124
5181	ISPs and web search portals	6,913	5,892
5182	Data processing and related services	18,824	19,232
519	Other information services	1,368	1,353

NAICS North American Industry Classification System. See Glossary for definition.
A/ Revised.
B/ Preliminary.
Note: Private employment. Detail may not add to totals due to disclosure editing and/or rounding. See Tables 23.70, 23.72, 23.73, and 23.74 for public employment data.

Source: State of Florida, Agency for Workforce Innovation, Labor Market Statistics, "Quarterly Census of Employment and Wages" (ES-202), Annual NAICS files, Internet site <http://www.labormarketinfo.com/index.htm> (accessed 17, July 2007).

Table 14.36. PUBLISHING AND MOTION PICTURE INDUSTRIES: AVERAGE MONTHLY PRIVATE REPORTING UNITS, EMPLOYMENT, AND PAYROLL COVERED BY UNEMPLOYMENT COMPENSATION LAW IN THE STATE AND COUNTIES OF FLORIDA, 2006

Industry	Number of reporting units	Number of employees	Payroll ($1,000)	Industry	Number of reporting units	Number of employees	Payroll ($1,000)
			Publishing industries, except Internet (NAICS code 511)				
Florida	1,941	42,965	199,731	Marion	21	475	1,309
				Martin	19	520	1,995
Alachua	41	841	2,978	Miami-Dade	221	4,256	20,197
Brevard	48	839	3,382	Monroe	7	174	605
Broward	229	4,903	32,979	Okaloosa	22	1,029	5,157
Clay	8	46	136	Orange	101	3,866	18,484
Collier	32	930	4,534	Osceola	12	76	217
Duval	69	1,768	6,437	Palm Beach	180	3,205	14,115
Escambia	20	673	2,053	Pasco	17	136	374
Flagler	6	52	189	Pinellas	99	2,746	11,216
Hernando	9	55	146	Polk	34	840	3,237
Highlands	4	77	199	Santa Rosa	7	81	174
Hillsborough	136	5,405	29,120	Sarasota	66	1,283	5,198
Indian River	10	376	1,503	Seminole	68	2,017	11,862
Jackson	3	10	23	Taylor	3	32	68
Lake	19	341	853	Volusia	39	1,223	4,336
Lee	39	1,306	4,380	Statewide 1/	53	266	1,930
Leon	35	723	2,477	Out-of-state 2/	8	8	53
Manatee	35	553	2,110	Unknown 1/	129	245	1,597
			Motion picture and sound recording (NAICS code 512)				
Florida	1,720	14,141	38,915	Monroe	11	49	136
Alachua	14	157	142	Okaloosa	7	150	135
Bay	6	81	65	Orange	174	1,741	6,316
Brevard	26	289	307	Osceola	20	137	219
Broward	234	1,992	5,269	Palm Beach	154	1,367	3,209
Collier	19	132	188	Pasco	10	182	197
Columbia	3	41	82	Pinellas	76	483	740
Duval	58	437	751	Polk	26	304	309
Escambia	13	162	130	Putnam	3	12	9
Hillsborough	86	888	2,281	St. Johns	9	41	65
Lake	13	74	62	Sarasota	28	158	213
Lee	37	271	503	Seminole	53	346	458
Leon	18	339	346	Volusia	20	179	240
Manatee	21	216	171	Walton	3	5	5
Martin	10	154	198	Statewide 1/	15	57	321
Miami-Dade	416	2,775	11,348	Unknown 1/	76	286	3,810

NAICS North American Industry Classification System. See Glossary for definition.

1/ Reporting units without a fixed location within the state or of unknown county location.

2/ Employment based in Florida, but working out of the state or country.

Note: Private employment. Data are preliminary. For a list of four-digit industries included see Table 14.35. Only counties for which data are disclosed are shown. Detail may not add to totals due to disclosure editing and/or rounding. See Tables 23.70, 23.72, 23.73, and 23.74 for public employment data.

Source: State of Florida, Agency for Workforce Innovation, Labor Market Statistics, "Quarterly Census of Employment and Wages" (ES-202), Annual NAICS files, Internet site <http://www.labormarketinfo.com/index.htm> (accessed 17, July 2007).

Table 14.37. TELECOMMUNICATIONS AND COMPUTER-RELATED COMMUNICATION: AVERAGE MONTHLY PRIVATE REPORTING UNITS, EMPLOYMENT, AND PAYROLL COVERED BY UNEMPLOYMENT COMPENSATION LAW IN THE STATE AND COUNTIES OF FLORIDA, 2006

County	Number of reporting units	Number of employees	Payroll ($1,000)	County	Number of reporting units	Number of employees	Payroll ($1,000)
			Telecommunications (NAICS code 517)				
Florida	3,010	63,367	294,358	Manatee	25	541	2,305
Alachua	36	537	2,311	Marion	35	1,326	3,625
Bay	23	860	4,063	Martin	20	202	890
Brevard	36	1,012	4,121	Miami-Dade	486	7,379	36,055
Broward	348	7,374	36,845	Monroe	14	144	708
Charlotte	19	104	465	Nassau	5	47	194
Citrus	11	186	691	Okaloosa	31	548	2,279
Collier	34	566	2,259	Orange	207	7,923	33,044
Columbia	9	80	331	Osceola	31	198	847
Duval	154	3,127	15,441	Palm Beach	194	2,687	13,978
Escambia	58	1,806	7,897	Pasco	38	466	1,810
Flagler	3	66	268	Pinellas	142	3,469	13,752
Gadsden	7	45	211	Polk	69	1,074	4,310
Hernando	11	104	485	Putnam	8	58	241
Hillsborough	253	10,450	53,107	St. Johns	15	218	1,087
Indian River	8	105	557	Sarasota	41	1,113	8,086
Jackson	4	77	299	Seminole	78	2,494	12,237
Jefferson	3	12	41	Sumter	4	24	109
Lake	26	879	3,325	Volusia	37	1,074	3,729
Levy	75	1,184	4,723	Statewide 1/	75	627	3,354
Leon	62	845	3,913	Out-of-state 2/	7	15	315
Levy	4	31	135	Unknown 1/	152	513	2,797
			ISPs, search portals, and data processing (NAICS code 518)				
Florida	1,998	25,124	125,043	Marion	13	102	357
				Miami-Dade	291	1,896	9,451
Alachua	18	134	881	Monroe	8	14	99
Bay	5	23	77	Nassau	4	4	27
Brevard	40	672	3,236	Okaloosa	28	304	1,535
Broward	275	3,226	16,817	Orange	125	2,956	12,939
Charlotte	8	7	47	Palm Beach	164	1,678	9,805
Clay	9	8	44	Pasco	22	53	219
Collier	17	168	935	Pinellas	124	1,520	6,054
Duval	91	2,331	12,666	Polk	9	57	172
Escambia	33	117	554	St. Johns	10	17	92
Hernando	10	35	112	St. Lucie	15	16	61
Hillsborough	4	38	86	Santa Rosa	8	15	38
Hillsborough	145	3,373	22,744	Sarasota	30	144	622
Indian River	12	20	92	Seminole	65	1,077	4,768
Lake	11	37	139	Volusia	36	289	979
Lee	40	250	1,579	Statewide 1/	59	1,760	8,415
Leon	26	1,202	3,337	Out-of-state 2/	7	18	151
Manatee	11	42	198	Unknown 1/	165	363	2,562

NAICS North American Industry Classification System. See Glossary for definition.
1/ Reporting units without a fixed location within the state or of unknown county location.
2/ Employment based in Florida, but working out of the state or country.
Note: See Note on Table 14.36.
Source: State of Florida, Agency for Workforce Innovation, Labor Market Statistics, "Quarterly Census of Employment and Wages" (ES-202), Annual NAICS files, Internet site <http://www.labormarketinfo.com/index.htm> (accessed 17, July 2007).

Table 14.38. INFORMATION INDUSTRY: AVERAGE MONTHLY PRIVATE REPORTING UNITS EMPLOYMENT, AND PAYROLL COVERED BY UNEMPLOYMENT COMPENSATION LAW IN THE STATE AND COUNTIES OF FLORIDA, 2006

County	Number of reporting units	Number of employees	Payroll ($1,000)	County	Number of reporting units	Number of employees	Payroll ($1,000)
			Newspaper, book, and directory publishers (NAICS code 5111)				
Florida	1,577	34,600	133,460	Marion	20	472	1,297
Alachua	32	628	1,575	Martin	19	520	1,995
Brevard	31	746	2,711	Miami-Dade	191	3,939	17,194
Broward	178	3,249	14,695	Monroe	6	173	605
Clay	8	46	136	Okaloosa	17	353	897
Collier	26	663	2,810	Orange	73	2,623	11,084
Duval	60	1,679	5,670	Osceola	10	73	212
Escambia	17	658	1,967	Palm Beach	156	2,943	13,035
Flagler	6	52	189	Pasco	15	133	366
Hernando	8	54	141	Pinellas	81	2,563	10,103
Highlands	4	77	199	Polk	32	800	3,021
Hillsborough	106	3,881	14,926	Santa Rosa	7	81	174
Indian River	8	330	1,207	Sarasota	55	1,194	4,501
Jackson	3	10	23	Seminole	48	644	2,861
Lake	15	330	812	Volusia	34	1,195	4,197
Lee	35	1,292	4,314	Statewide 1/	28	191	1,277
Leon	33	708	2,360	Out-of-state 2/	7	3	21
Manatee	31	525	1,902	Unknown 1/	88	175	971
			Radio and television broadcasting (NAICS code 5151)				
Florida	476	13,960	71,183	Marion	2	60	250
				Miami-Dade	97	3,673	23,209
Alachua	9	195	654	Monroe	8	79	225
Bay	10	187	578	Okaloosa	6	101	280
Brevard	8	100	257	Pasco	32	1,806	9,994
Broward	38	997	5,942	Palm Beach	35	900	4,848
Charlotte	5	45	153	Pinellas	22	561	2,728
Columbia	3	24	59	Polk	9	100	322
Duval	19	1,063	4,324	St. Lucie	4	73	180
Escambia	8	327	1,609	Sarasota	10	193	750
Hillsborough	27	1,139	5,788	Seminole	6	61	269
Jackson	3	26	71	Volusia	9	34	78
Lee	18	760	3,297	Walton	3	15	36
Leon	16	421	1,341	Statewide 1/	10	631	2,799
Martin	3	8	16	Unknown 1/	15	49	209
			Internet publishing and broadcasting (NAICS code 5161)				
Florida	356	1,484	9,424	Palm Beach	45	232	1,309
Brevard	4	5	12	Pinellas	23	102	432
Broward	44	333	1,703	Sarasota	14	36	133
Hillsborough	22	71	1,564	Seminole	9	13	50
Leon	3	14	54	Volusia	6	15	36
Miami-Dade	42	188	949	Statewide 1/	11	110	877
Orange	30	111	800	Unknown 1/	42	42	340

NAICS North American Industry Classification System. See Glossary for definition.
1/ Reporting units without a fixed location within the state or of unknown county location.
2/ Employment based in Florida, but working out of the state or country.
Note: See Note on Table 14.39.
Source: State of Florida, Agency for Workforce Innovation, Labor Market Statistics, "Quarterly Census of Employment and Wages" (ES-202), Annual NAICS files, Internet site <http://www.labormarketinfo.com/index.htm> (accessed 17, July 2007).

Table 14.39. TELECOMMUNICATIONS CARRIERS: AVERAGE MONTHLY PRIVATE REPORTING UNITS, EMPLOYMENT, AND PAYROLL COVERED BY UNEMPLOYMENT COMPENSATION LAW IN THE STATE AND COUNTIES OF FLORIDA, 2006

County	Number of reporting units	Number of employees	Payroll ($1,000)	County	Number of reporting units	Number of employees	Payroll ($1,000)
			Wired telecommunications carriers (NAICS code 5171)				
Florida	1,214	33,234	171,547	Miami-Dade	133	4,319	22,919
				Orange	90	3,500	16,779
Alachua	10	211	995	Osceola	15	165	741
Broward	110	3,709	21,429	Palm Beach	45	1,199	6,780
Duval	85	2,530	12,712	Pinellas	69	1,644	6,327
Escambia	22	922	4,432	St. Johns	6	151	849
Gadsden	5	36	180	Seminole	37	2,003	9,637
Hillsborough	123	5,820	33,984	Volusia	15	371	1,801
Leon	34	387	2,083	Statewide 1/	31	219	1,468
Martin	8	142	686	Unknown 1/	61	101	711
			Wireless telecommunications carriers (NAICS code 5172)				
Florida	964	14,086	53,861	Miami-Dade	177	1,660	5,685
				Okaloosa	14	84	284
Alachua	13	85	335	Orange	68	2,000	6,867
Broward	107	1,650	6,519	Osceola	11	22	69
Charlotte	10	27	94	Palm Beach	93	843	4,526
Clay	3	17	54	Pasco	12	40	141
Collier	7	51	167	Pinellas	41	440	937
Columbia	3	23	68	Polk	17	96	390
Duval	47	403	1,611	Putnam	3	15	40
Escambia	26	456	1,749	St. Johns	3	22	61
Hernando	6	20	73	Santa Rosa	7	20	69
Hillsborough	69	2,852	11,826	Sarasota	13	98	605
Lee	18	139	568	Seminole	21	350	1,853
Leon	20	138	702	Volusia	11	124	351
Manatee	7	34	109	Statewide 1/	20	163	399
Martin	9	48	162	Unknown 1/	46	352	1,588
			Cable and other program distribution (NAICS code 5175)				
Florida	169	10,350	36,127	Marion	4	94	303
				Miami-Dade	27	116	729
Broward	19	1,114	4,098	Statewide 1/	6	22	68
Collier	4	243	852	Unknown 1/	7	4	31

NAICS North American Industry Classification System. See Glossary for definition.
1/ Reporting units without a fixed location within the state or of unknown county location.
Note: Private employment. Data are preliminary. Only counties for which data are disclosed are shown. Detail may not add to totals due to disclosure editing and/or rounding. See Tables 23.70, 23.72, 23.73, and 23.74 for public employment data.

Source: State of Florida, Agency for Workforce Innovation, Labor Market Statistics, "Quarterly Census of Employment and Wages" (ES-202), Annual NAICS files, Internet site <http://www.labormarketinfo.com/index.htm> (accessed 17, July 2007).

Table 14.60. TELEPHONE COMPANIES: SPECIFIED CHARACTERISTICS OF COMPANIES IN FLORIDA, DECEMBER 2006

Companies and headquarters	Number of exchanges	Florida access lines 1/ Beginning 2005	Beginning 2006	Percentage of state total	Annual growth rate (percentage)
Florida	284	9,727,883	9,030,289	100.00	-7.17
BellSouth Telecommunications Miami	102	5,499,237	5,137,730	56.89	-6.57
Embarq Florida, Inc. Tallahassee	104	2,038,675	1,897,680	21.01	-6.92
Frontier Communications of the South Atmore, Alabama	2	4,376	4,110	0.05	-6.08
GTC, Inc. 2/ Florala, Alabama	2	2,478	2,402	0.03	-3.07
GTC, Inc. 3/ Perry	2	10,974	10,747	0.12	-2.07
GTC, Inc. 4/ Port St. Joe	13	35,875	33,646	0.37	-6.21
ITS Telecommunications Indiantown	1	3,915	3,776	0.04	-3.55
Northeast Florida Telephone Company Macclenny	2	10,195	10,112	0.11	-0.81
Quincy Telephone Company Quincy	3	15,087	14,032	0.16	-6.99
Smart City Telecommunications Lake Buena Vista	2	16,151	16,406	0.18	1.58
Verizon Florida, Inc. Tampa	24	1,998,995	1,809,910	20.04	-9.46
Windstream Florida, Inc. Live Oak	27	91,925	89,738	0.99	-2.38

1/ An access line is the line going to a home or building for the main telephone located there.
2/ Formerly Florala Telephone Company.
3/ Formerly Gulf Telephone Company.
4/ Formerly St. Joseph Telephone.
Note: Telephone companies listed above have headquarters in Florida, except as specified. Detail may not add to totals due to rounding.

Source: State of Florida, Public Service Commission, *Comparative Rate Statistics: Electric, Natural Gas, Telephone, Water and Wastewater, December 31, 2006,* Internet site <http://www.psc.state.fl.us/> (accessed 16, April 2007).

POWER AND ENERGY

Per Capita Energy Consumption in Florida by Type of Fuel, 1992 Through 2004 (million BTU)

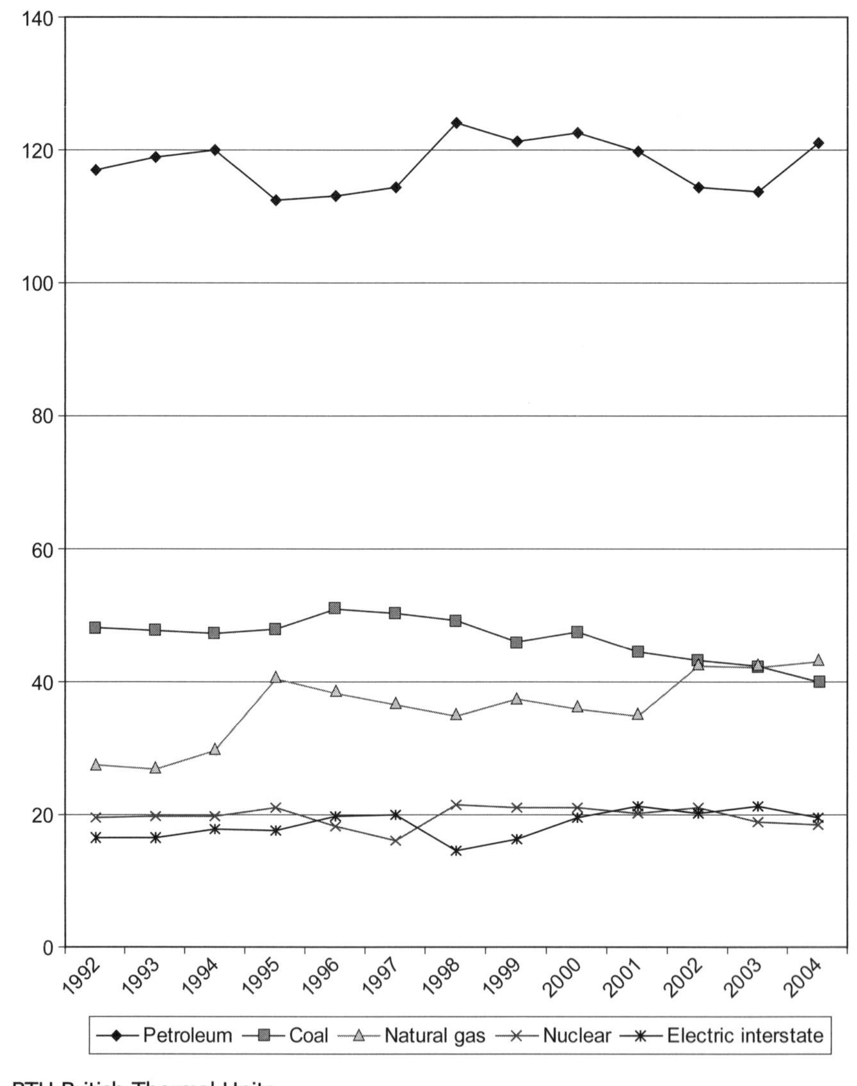

BTU British Thermal Units

Source: Table 15.07

Section 15.00
Power and Energy

Data in this section describe the status of the Florida utilities industries, and the consumption and production of electricity, natural gas, gasoline, fuel oil, and nuclear power.

Sources. The U.S. Census Bureau conducts an economic census in years ending in "2" and "7." Economic census data about the utilities industry by kind of business and by metropolitan area are from the *2002 Economic Census: Utilities,* based on North American Industry Classification System (NAICS) categories (see the introduction to Section 6.00 and the Glossary) and are shown in Tables 15.01 and 15.02. Census data for Metropolitan Statistical Areas presented on Table 15.02 are those defined as of December 2006.

The U.S. Department of Energy's Energy Information Administration (EIA) provides various types of energy information in publications on the EIA Web site. Energy consumption comes from the Internet publication, *State Energy Consumption, Price, and Expenditure Estimates (SEDS).* Nuclear power plant data appears in the EIA publication, *Electric Power Annual.* Natural gas data appear in *Natural Gas Annual.*

The Oil and Gas Section of the Florida Department of Environmental Protection publishes crude oil and natural gas data in the *Florida Oil and Gas Annual Production Report.*

The Florida Public Service Commission (PSC) publishes major sources of data on electric energy and rates in Florida. Electric utility sales, customers, and counties served by private and public utilities and rural cooperatives; residential, commercial, and industrial electric rates; and capacity, generation, and consumption come from the PSC's *Statistics of the Florida Electric Utility Industry.* Typical electric and natural gas bill data and growth and use comparisons appear in *Comparative Rate Statistics: Electric, Natural Gas, Telephone, Water, and Wastewater.* A map indicating the location of municipal electric utility companies statewide is on page 523.

Public power and sector rate comparisons appear in the *Annual Directory and Statistical Report* (copyrighted) published by the Electric Power Statistics office of the American Public Power Association.

The state's Labor Market Statistics office of the Agency for Workforce Innovation provides current employment and payroll information about the utilities industry throughout the state. (See the introduction to Section 6.00.)

Annual gasoline pump prices appear on the AAA Web site in the *Daily Fuel Gauge Report.* The Florida Department of Community Affairs (DCA) publishes an online annual *Florida Motor Gasoline and Diesel Fuel Report.* Another source of state motor fuel data is *Highway Statistics*, published by the U.S. Department of Transportation's Federal Highway Administration.

Information on consumer prices of energy as measured by the Florida County Retail Price Index (FCRPI) appears in Section 24.00.

Section 15.00
Power and Energy

Tables listed by major heading

Heading | Page

Table 15.01. UTILITIES: ESTABLISHMENTS, EMPLOYMENT, AND ANNUAL PAYROLL BY KIND OF BUSINESS IN FLORIDA, 2002

NAICS code	Industry	Number of establishments	Number of employees 1/	Payroll ($1,000)
22	Utilities	563	28,476	1,644,351
2211	Electric power generation, transmission, and distribution	307	24,981	1,514,749
22111	Electric power generation	141	7,976	508,867
22112	Electric power transmission, control, and distribution	166	17,005	1,005,882
2212	Natural gas distribution	35	1,517	66,212
2213	Water, sewage, and other systems	221	1,978	63,390
22131	Water supply and irrigation systems	164	1,465	49,039
22132	Sewage treatment facilities	57	513	14,351

1/ Paid employment for the pay period including March 12.
Note: The economic censuses are conducted on a 5-year cycle collecting data for years ending in 2 and 7. Data are for North American Classification System (NAICS) code 22 and may not be comparable to earlier years. See Glossary for definition.

Source: U.S., Department of Commerce, Census Bureau, *2002 Economic Census: Utilities,* Geographic Area Series EC02-22A-FL, issued August 2005, Internet site <http://www.census.gov/> (accessed 11, May 2007).

Table 15.02. UTILITIES: ANNUAL PAYROLL IN THE STATE, METROPOLITAN STATISTICAL AREAS (MSAS) OF FLORIDA, 2002

(in thousands of dollars)

Area	Amount	Area	Amount
Florida	1,644,351	Metropolitan Statistical Area (Continued)	
Metropolitan Statistical Area		Ocala	12,123
Cape Coral-Ft. Myers	42,832	Orlando-Kissimmee	97,037
Deltona-Daytona Beach-Ormond Beach	24,579	Palm Bay-Melbourne-Titusville	(D)
Ft. Walton Beach-Crestview-Destin	10,519	Palm Coast	(X)
Gainesville	8,421	Panama City-Lynn Haven	18,467
Jacksonville	42,760	Pensacola-Ferry Pass-Brent	72,995
Lakeland	35,210	Port St. Lucie	(D)
Miami-Ft. Lauderdale-Miami Beach	(D)	Punta Gorda	(D)
Naples-Marco Island	11,294	Sarasota-Bradenton-Venice	(D)
		Sebastian-Vero Beach	(D)
		Tallahassee	12,569
		Tampa-St. Petersburg-Clearwater	303,287

(X) Not applicable.
(D) Data withheld to avoid disclosure of information about individual firms.
Note: The economic censuses are conducted on a 5-year cycle collecting data for years ending in 2 and 7. Data are for North American Classification System (NAICS) code 22 and may not be comparable to earlier years. See Glossary for definition. MSAs as defined December 2006. See map at front of book.

Source: U.S., Department of Commerce, Census Bureau, *2002 Economic Census: Utilities,* Geographic Area Series EC02-22A-FL, issued August 2005, Internet site <http://www.census.gov/> (accessed 11, May 2007).

Table 15.06. ENERGY CONSUMPTION ESTIMATES: AMOUNT CONSUMED BY TYPE OF FUEL IN FLORIDA, 1992 THROUGH 2004

(in trillions of British thermal units)

Year	Total	Petro-leum 1/	Coal	Natural gas	Nuclear	Electric interstate 2/	Hydro-electric
1992	3,319.2	1,580.1	649.4	371.1	263.0	223.3	2.4
1993	3,375.1	1,634.1	654.5	368.0	271.9	228.7	2.2
1994	3,511.8	1,683.9	663.4	417.7	278.9	251.5	2.8
1995	3,653.9	1,611.8	686.9	579.3	302.0	252.7	2.4
1996	3,757.8	1,654.1	745.8	561.1	267.5	287.8	2.2
1997	3,778.5	1,707.8	751.3	547.2	241.0	298.5	2.5
1998	3,923.7	1,889.8	749.5	529.6	326.4	221.4	2.0
1999	3,978.6	1,889.8	716.3	583.4	329.4	253.6	1.4
2000	4,142.8	1,960.5	760.4	574.5	336.8	313.6	0.9
2001	4,113.9	1,958.0	725.9	569.8	330.0	346.4	1.5
2002	4,228.0	1,908.3	719.7	705.9	351.8	336.9	1.9
2003	4,287.3	1,940.3	723.8	720.3	322.8	361.8	2.7
2004	4,452.5	2,119.9	699.1	755.2	325.5	342.4	2.7

1/ Includes asphalt and road oil, aviation gasoline, jet fuel, distillates, kerosene, lubricants, motor gasoline, residual fuel, liquefied petroleum gas, and other.
2/ Combines electric sales and energy losses associated with interstate sales.
Note: Some data may be revised.

Table 15.07. ENERGY CONSUMPTION ESTIMATES: PER CAPITA ENERGY CONSUMPTION BY TYPE OF FUEL IN FLORIDA, 1992 THROUGH 2004

(in millions of British thermal units)

Year	Total	Petro-leum 1/	Coal	Natural gas	Nuclear	Electric interstate 2/	Hydro-electric
1992	245.9	117.1	48.1	27.5	19.5	16.5	0.2
1993	245.8	119.0	47.7	26.8	19.8	16.7	0.2
1994	250.1	119.9	47.2	29.7	19.9	17.9	0.2
1995	254.9	112.4	47.9	40.4	21.1	17.6	0.2
1996	257.0	113.1	51.0	38.4	18.3	19.7	0.2
1997	252.9	114.3	50.3	36.6	16.1	20.0	0.2
1998	257.6	124.1	49.2	34.8	21.4	14.5	0.1
1999	255.4	121.3	46.0	37.4	21.1	16.3	0.1
2000	259.2	122.7	47.6	35.9	21.1	19.6	0.1
2001	251.9	119.9	44.4	34.9	20.2	21.2	0.1
2002	253.6	114.4	43.2	42.3	21.1	20.2	0.1
2003	251.1	113.7	42.4	42.2	18.9	21.2	0.2
2004	254.2	121.0	39.9	43.1	18.6	19.5	0.2

1/ Includes asphalt and road oil, aviation gasoline, jet fuel, distillates, kerosene, lubricants, motor gasoline, residual fuel, liquefied petroleum gas, and other.
2/ Combines electric sales and energy losses associated with interstate sales.
Note: Per capita is computed using Census Bureau data for 2000 and *Florida Estimates of Population* for all other years. Some data may be revised.

Source: U.S., Department of Energy, Energy Information Administration, *State Energy Consumption, Price, and Expenditure Estimates (SEDS), 2004,* Internet site <http://www.eia.doe.gov/> (accessed 5, June 2007).

Municipal Electric Utilities

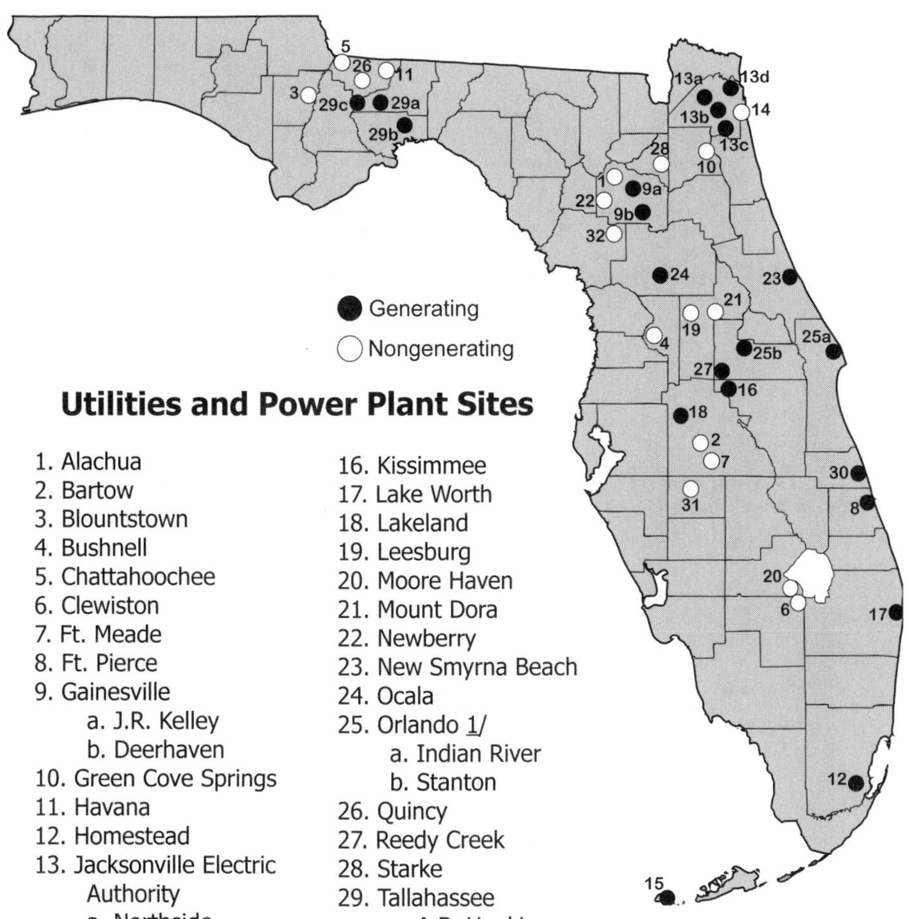

Utilities and Power Plant Sites

1. Alachua
2. Bartow
3. Blountstown
4. Bushnell
5. Chattahoochee
6. Clewiston
7. Ft. Meade
8. Ft. Pierce
9. Gainesville
   a. J.R. Kelley
   b. Deerhaven
10. Green Cove Springs
11. Havana
12. Homestead
13. Jacksonville Electric Authority
    a. Northside
    b. Kennedy
    c. Southside
    d. St. Johns
14. Jacksonville Beach
15. Key West
16. Kissimmee
17. Lake Worth
18. Lakeland
19. Leesburg
20. Moore Haven
21. Mount Dora
22. Newberry
23. New Smyrna Beach
24. Ocala
25. Orlando 1/
    a. Indian River
    b. Stanton
26. Quincy
27. Reedy Creek
28. Starke
29. Tallahassee
    a. A.B. Hopkins
    b. S.O. Purdom
    c. C.H. Corn
30. Vero Beach
31. Wauchula
32. Williston

1/ Includes St. Cloud

Table 15.08. ENERGY CONSUMPTION: AMOUNT CONSUMED BY SECTOR IN FLORIDA OTHER LEADING CONSUMPTION STATES, AND THE UNITED STATES, 2004

State	Total consumption Amount (trillion BTU)	Total consumption Rank	Residential Percentage	Residential Rank	Commercial Percentage	Commercial Rank	Industrial Percentage	Industrial Rank	Transportation Percentage	Transportation Rank
Florida	4,452.5	3	29.3	3	23.4	4	12.4	19	34.8	3
Texas	11,971.4	1	13.0	1	11.0	3	53.5	1	22.6	2
California	8,364.6	2	18.6	2	18.6	1	24.5	3	38.3	1
NewYork	4,254.0	4	28.6	4	32.9	2	12.6	21	26.0	4
Pennsylvannia	4,049.4	5	24.6	5	17.5	6	32.8	6	25.2	5
Ohio	4,022.8	6	23.4	7	17.5	7	33.8	5	25.3	6
Illinois	3,960.5	7	24.2	6	18.8	5	31.6	7	25.3	7
Louisiana	3,816.3	8	9.7	22	7.5	21	63.0	2	19.9	12
Georgia	3,141.1	9	22.9	9	17.0	12	30.5	9	29.5	8
Michigan	3,119.4	10	25.6	8	20.2	8	28.4	10	25.9	10
Indiana	2,945.7	11	18.0	13	12.7	16	47.5	4	21.8	14
United States	100,278.6	(X)	21.2	(X)	17.7	(X)	33.3	(X)	27.8	(X)

BTU British thermal units.
(X) Not applicable.

Source: U.S., Department of Energy, Energy Information Administration, *State Energy Consumption, Price, and Expenditure Estimates (SEDS), 2004,* Internet site <http://www.eia.doe.gov/> (accessed 5, June 2007).

Table 15.09. CRUDE OIL AND NATURAL GAS: AMOUNT PRODUCED BY FIELD IN FLORIDA 2004 THROUGH 2006

Field	Crude oil (barrels) 2004	2005	2006	Natural gas (1,000 cubic feet) 2004	2005	2006
Total	2,875,385	2,584,713	2,359,853	3,544,522	2,969,669	2,949,590
South Florida	881,479	865,837	853,284	93,704	105,818	89,249
Bear Island	104,087	135,402	121,678	9,851	25,960	12,519
Corkscrew	29,684	30,092	29,429	0	0	0
Lake Trafford	376	430	458	0	0	0
Lehigh Park	31,669	20,579	32,917	3,862	2,510	4,016
Raccoon Point	444,796	427,622	396,055	56,512	54,830	50,721
Sunniland	9,155	11,758	11,977	842	1,082	1,102
West Felda	261,712	239,954	260,770	22,637	21,436	20,891
Northwest Florida	1,993,906	1,718,876	1,506,569	3,450,818	2,863,851	2,860,341
Blackjack Creek	46,314	86,587	103,839	201,494	244,547	286,176
Jay	1,947,583	1,632,289	1,402,653	3,249,324	2,619,304	2,574,165
McLellan	9	0	77	0	0	0

Source: State of Florida, Department of Environmental Protection, Florida Geological Survey, Oil and Gas Section, *Florida Oil and Gas Annual Production Report, 2006,* Internet site <http:www.dep.state.fl.us/> (accessed 21, March 2007).

Table 15.14. ELECTRIC UTILITY INDUSTRY: SALES, CUSTOMERS, AND COUNTIES SERVED BY PRIVATELY AND PUBLICLY OWNED UTILITIES AND BY RURAL ELECTRIC COOPERATIVES IN FLORIDA, 2005

Utility	Electricity sales to ultimate customers (MWH)	Number of ultimate customers December 1/	Counties served
Investor-owned systems			
Florida Power and Light	102,413,604	4,321,767	Alachua, Baker, Bradford, Brevard, Broward, Charlotte, Clay, Collier, Columbia, DeSoto, Duval, Flagler, Glades, Hardee, Hendry, Highlands, Indian River, Lee, Manatee, Martin, Miami-Dade, Monroe, Nassau, Okeechobee, Palm Beach, Putnam, St. Johns, St. Lucie, Sarasota, Seminole, Suwannee, Union, Volusia
Progress Energy Florida, Inc.	39,176,585	1,583,391	Alachua, Bay, Brevard, Citrus, Columbia, Dixie, Flagler, Franklin, Gadsden, Gilchrist, Gulf, Hamilton, Hardee, Hernando, Highlands, Jefferson, Lafayette, Lake, Leon, Levy, Liberty, Madison, Marion, Orange, Osceola, Pasco, Pinellas, Polk, Seminole, Sumter, Suwannee, Taylor, Volusia, Wakulla
Florida Public Utilities	824,643	27,546	Calhoun, Jackson, Liberty, Nassau
Gulf Power	11,641,664	404,087	Bay, Escambia, Holmes, Jackson, Okaloosa, Santa Rosa, Walton, Washington
Tampa Electric	18,911,837	635,747	Hillsborough, Pasco, Pinellas, Polk
Generating municipal systems			
Ft. Pierce	599,720	25,841	St. Lucie
Gainesville	1,854	90,660	Alachua
Homestead	375,636	18,094	Miami-Dade
Jacksonville	13,236,849	402,438	Clay, Duval, St. Johns
Key West	717,588	29,223	Monroe
Kissimmee	1,322,340	56,028	Osceola
Lake Worth	512,602	26,823	Palm Beach
Lakeland	2,808,851	118,262	Polk
New Smyrna Beach	31,299	22,935	Volusia
Ocala	1,330,623	49,884	Marion
Orlando 2/	3,173,477	201,461	Orange
Reedy Creek	1,194,607	1,231	Orange
Tallahassee	2,723,848	107,780	Leon
Vero Beach	737,381	32,688	Indian River
Florida Keys 3/	675,828	30,968	Monroe

See footnotes at end of table.

Continued . . .

Table 15.14. ELECTRIC UTILITY INDUSTRY: SALES, CUSTOMERS, AND COUNTIES SERVED BY PRIVATELY AND PUBLICLY OWNED UTILITIES AND BY RURAL ELECTRIC COOPERATIVES IN FLORIDA, 2005 (Continued)

Utility	Electricity sales to ultimate customers (MWH)	Number of ultimate customers December 1/	Counties served
Nongenerating municipal systems			
Alachua	97,801	3,525	Alachua
Bartow	275,035	11,563	Polk
Blountstown	37,811	1,314	Calhoun
Bushnell	25,660	1,044	Sumter
Chattahoochee	43,771	1,284	Gadsden
Clewiston	116	4,164	Hendry
Ft. Meade	41,665	2,696	Polk
Green Cove Springs	116,547	3,545	Clay
Havana	22,855	1,349	Gadsden
Jacksonville Beach	761,697	31,942	Duval, St. Johns
Leesburg	514,179	20,659	Lake
Moore Haven	18,620	977	Glades
Mount Dora	96,291	5,855	Lake
Newberry	26,418	1,286	Alachua
Quincy	157,039	4,761	Gadsden
Starke	69,477	2,725	Bradford
Wauchula	64,247	2,625	Hardee
Williston	31,887	1,410	Levy
Winter Park	257,994	13,750	Orange
Nongenerating rural electric cooperatives			
Central Florida	490,826	31,702	Alachua, Dixie, Gilchrist, Levy, Marion
Choctawhatchee	686,166	38,894	Holmes, Okaloosa, Santa Rosa, Walton
Clay	3,079,308	155,591	Alachua, Baker, Bradford, Clay, Columbia, Duval, Flagler, Lake, Levy, Marion, Putnam, Suwannee Union, Volusia
Escambia River	165,253	9,581	Escambia, Santa Rosa
Glades	340,932	15,715	Glades, Hendry, Highlands, Okeechobee
Gulf Coast	321,089	19,530	Bay, Calhoun, Gulf, Jackson, Walton, Washington
Lee County	3,334,418	177,634	Charlotte, Collier, Hendry, Lee
Okefenokee 4/	164,677	9,318	Baker, Nassau
Peace River	535,469	29,973	Brevard, DeSoto, Hardee, Highlands, Hillsborough, Indian River, Manatee, Osceola, Polk, Sarasota
Sumter	2,425,467	142,357	Citrus, Hernando, Lake, Levy, Marion, Pasco, Sumter
Suwannee Valley	481,042	23,047	Columbia, Hamilton, Lafayette, Suwannee
Talquin	1,018,333	52,178	Franklin, Gadsden, Leon, Liberty, Wakulla
Tri-county	265,599	17,018	Dixie, Jefferson, Madison, Taylor

See footnotes at end of table.

Continued . . .

Table 15.14. ELECTRIC UTILITY INDUSTRY: SALES, CUSTOMERS, AND COUNTIES SERVED BY PRIVATELY AND PUBLICLY OWNED UTILITIES AND BY RURAL ELECTRIC COOPERATIVES IN FLORIDA, 2005 (Continued)

Utility	Electricity sales to ultimate customers (MWH)	Number of ultimate customers December 1/	Counties served
Nongenerating rural electric cooperatives (Continued)			
West Florida	380,502	26,967	Calhoun, Holmes, Jackson, Washington
Withlacoochee	3,452,789	186,112	Citrus, Hernando, Pasco, Polk, Sumter

MWH Megawatt-hours (1,000 kilowatt-hours).
1/ Year-end monthly average.
2/ Includes St. Cloud.
3/ Generating rural system.
4/ Florida customers only.

Source: State of Florida, Public Service Commission, Division of Research and Regulatory Review, *Statistics of the Florida Electric Utility Industry, 2005,* Internet site <http://www.psc.state.fl.us/> (accessed 19, February 2007).

Table 15.15. UTILITIES: AVERAGE MONTHLY PRIVATE REPORTING UNITS, EMPLOYMENT AND PAYROLL COVERED BY UNEMPLOYMENT COMPENSATION LAW BY INDUSTRY IN FLORIDA, 2006

NAICS code	Industry	Number of reporting units	Number of em- ployees	Payroll ($1,000)
22	Utilities	722	24,421	131,976
2211	Power generation and supply	315	19,342	114,184
2212	Natural gas distribution	60	1,555	6,607
2213	Water, sewage and other systems	347	3,524	11,186

NAICS North American Industry Classification System. See Glossary for definition.
Note: Private employment. Data are preliminary. Detail may not add to totals due to disclosure editing and/or rounding. See Tables 23.70, 23.72, 23.73, and 23.74 for public employment data.

Source: State of Florida, Agency for Workforce Innovation, Labor Market Statistics, "Quarterly Census of Employment and Wages" (ES-202), Annual NAICS files, Internet site <http://www.labormarketinfo.com/index.htm> (accessed 17, July 2007).

Table 15.16. POWER GENERATION, NATURAL GAS DISTRIBUTION, AND WATER, SEWAGE, AND OTHER SYSTEMS: AVERAGE MONTHLY PRIVATE REPORTING UNITS, EMPLOYMENT, AND PAYROLL COVERED BY UNEMPLOYMENT COMPENSATION LAW IN THE STATE AND COUNTIES OF FLORIDA, 2006

County	Number of reporting units	Number of employees	Payroll ($1,000)	County	Number of reporting units	Number of employees	Payroll ($1,000)
		Power generation and supply (NAICS code 2211)					
Florida	315	19,342	114,184	Nassau	3	74	306
				Okaloosa	8	91	406
Collier	6	176	1,042	Pasco	6	546	2,576
Duval	7	228	1,366	Pinellas	2	1,335	8,216
Gulf	3	117	513	Polk	6	382	2,386
Jackson	4	143	638	Putnam	5	393	2,332
Lee	14	607	3,199	Santa Rosa	4	96	360
Marion	3	180	982	Volusia	12	337	1,941
		Natural gas distribution (NAICS code 2212)					
Florida	60	1,555	6,607	Miami-Dade	8	122	499
		Water, sewage, and other systems (NAICS code 2213)					
Florida	347	3,524	11,186	Marion	15	118	381
Brevard	8	55	107	Miami-Dade	10	39	123
Broward	22	181	644	Monroe	4	75	281
Charlotte	4	21	63	Okaloosa	8	108	296
Citrus	5	44	107	Orange	8	31	257
Collier	5	59	176	Palm Beach	19	56	320
Duval	11	185	766	Pasco	11	159	439
Escambia	8	68	152	Polk	7	31	98
Flagler	4	9	15	Putnam	3	13	27
Hernando	5	10	16	St. Johns	6	29	82
Highlands	9	42	116	St. Lucie	8	39	114
Hillsborough	15	76	229	Santa Rosa	10	151	409
Indian River	5	31	63	Seminole	10	196	587
Lake	13	112	306	Volusia	7	17	18
Lee	13	244	873	Wakulla	3	48	110
Manatee	5	20	47	Walton	8	142	471

NAICS North American Industry Classification System. See Glossary for definition.

Note: Private employment. Data are preliminary. For a list of other utility industries see Table 15.01. Only counties for which data are disclosed are shown. Detail may not add to totals due to disclosure editing and/or rounding. See Tables 23.70, 23.72, 23.73, and 23.74 for public employment data.

Source: State of Florida, Agency for Workforce Innovation, Labor Market Statistics, "Quarterly Census of Employment and Wages" (ES-202), Annual NAICS files, Internet site <http://www.labormarketinfo.com/index.htm> (accessed 17, July 2007).

Table 15.25. ELECTRIC RATES: RESIDENTIAL ELECTRIC RATES CHARGED BY MUNICIPAL COOPERATIVE, AND INVESTOR-OWNED UTILITIES IN FLORIDA
DECEMBER 31, 2005

(in dollars)

Utility	Minimum bill or customer charge	500 kWh	750 kWh	1,000 kWh	1,500 kWh
Municipal					
Alachua	8.00	59.40	85.10	110.80	162.20
Bartow	6.63	55.86	80.47	105.08	154.31
Blountstown	3.50	39.39	57.34	75.28	111.17
Bushnell	7.40	63.23	91.14	119.05	174.88
Chattahoochee	4.50	48.68	70.78	92.87	137.05
Clewiston	6.50	58.75	84.88	111.00	163.25
Ft. Meade	12.96	66.41	93.14	119.86	173.31
Ft. Pierce	5.35	59.99	87.31	114.62	169.26
Gainesville	4.89	51.96	75.49	102.41	156.24
Green Cove Springs	6.00	65.73	95.60	125.46	185.19
Havana	6.00	68.41	99.62	130.82	193.23
Homestead	5.50	59.83	86.99	114.15	168.48
Jacksonville	5.50	47.33	68.24	89.15	130.98
Jacksonville Beach	4.50	59.80	87.45	115.09	170.39
Key West	6.00	68.95	100.43	131.90	194.85
Kissimmee	10.17	65.81	93.63	121.44	183.41
Lakeland	6.35	63.88	92.64	121.40	148.80
Lake Worth	7.42	64.68	93.31	121.94	179.20
Leesburg	8.72	56.74	80.75	104.76	152.78
Moore Haven	8.50	53.95	76.68	99.40	144.85
Mount Dora	5.05	52.09	75.62	99.14	146.18
New Smyrna Beach	5.65	57.12	82.85	108.58	160.05
Newberry	7.50	59.56	85.60	111.62	163.68
Ocala	7.00	31.30	88.44	115.58	169.88
Orlando	7.00	48.31	68.96	89.61	135.92
Quincy	6.00	57.26	82.89	108.52	159.78
Reedy Creek	2.85	47.85	70.35	92.84	137.84
St. Cloud	7.28	50.25	71.72	93.20	141.37
Starke	6.45	72.25	105.16	138.05	214.85
Tallahassee	4.94	61.86	90.20	118.77	175.69
Vero Beach	7.21	69.36	100.44	131.51	193.66
Wauchula	8.62	60.66	86.67	112.69	164.73
Williston	8.00	62.17	89.26	116.34	170.51
Winter Park	8.03	51.69	73.52	95.34	144.00

See footnotes at end of table.

Continued . . .

Table 15.25. ELECTRIC RATES: RESIDENTIAL ELECTRIC RATES CHARGED BY MUNICIPAL COOPERATIVE, AND INVESTOR-OWNED UTILITIES IN FLORIDA DECEMBER 31, 2005 (Continued)

(in dollars)

Utility	Minimum bill or customer charge	500 kWh	750 kWh	1,000 kWh	1,500 kWh
Cooperative					
Central Florida	8.50	62.75	89.88	117.00	171.25
Choctawhatchee	18.00	59.14	79.71	100.28	141.41
Clay	9.00	54.35	77.03	99.70	150.05
Escambia River	9.00	55.00	78.00	101.00	147.00
Florida Keys	10.00	71.94	102.90	133.87	195.81
Glades	10.50	70.25	100.13	130.00	189.75
Gulf Coast	10.00	55.50	78.25	101.00	146.50
Lee County	5.00	51.70	75.05	98.40	145.10
Okefenokee	10.00	52.10	73.15	94.20	136.30
Peace River	11.25	65.10	92.03	118.95	172.80
Sumter	8.25	59.10	84.53	109.95	160.80
Suwannee Valley	8.73	61.20	87.43	113.66	166.13
Talquin	8.00	54.00	77.00	100.00	146.00
Tri-county	10.00	64.00	91.00	118.00	172.00
West Florida	13.90	61.34	85.05	108.77	156.21
Withlacoochee River	9.75	56.55	79.94	103.34	150.14
Investor-owned					
Florida Power and Light 1/	5.25	46.82	67.59	90.69	136.91
Florida Public Utilities					
Marianna Division	10.00	38.92	53.37	67.82	96.74
Fernandina Beach Division 1/	10.00	35.34	48.00	60.66	86.00
Gulf Power	10.00	47.87	66.79	85.71	123.58
Progress Energy Florida	(NA)	51.71	73.51	95.34	144.02
Tampa Electric	8.50	52.07	73.85	95.62	139.19

kWh Kilowatt-hour.
1/ Includes 1.5 percent embedded gross receipts taxes.
Note: Cost excludes local taxes, franchise fees, and gross receipts taxes not embedded in rates. Full year fuel costs are included for all utilities and purchased power costs are included for municipal utilities.

Source: State of Florida, Public Service Commission, Division of Research and Regulatory Review, *Statistics of the Florida Electric Utility Industry, 2005,* Internet site <http://www.psc.state.fl.us/> (accessed 19, February 2007).

Table 15.26. ELECTRIC RATES: COMMERCIAL AND INDUSTRIAL ELECTRIC RATES CHARGED BY MUNICIPAL, COOPERATIVE, AND INVESTOR-OWNED UTILITIES IN FLORIDA, DECEMBER 31, 2005

(in dollars)

Utility	15,000 kWh	45,000 kWh	150,000 kWh	400,000 kWh	800,000 kWh
Municipal					
Alachua	1,678	4,542	15,088	38,213	76,403
Bartow	1,825	4,783	15,900	39,455	78,891
Blountstown	1,322	3,953	13,159	35,079	70,151
Bushnell	2,000	5,395	17,930	45,293	90,563
Chattahoochee	1,444	4,419	14,730	37,607	75,214
Clewiston	1,798	5,053	16,760	43,435	86,835
Ft. Meade	1,717	5,220	17,190	42,550	85,010
Ft. Pierce	1,742	4,707	16,776	40,793	81,551
Gainesville	1,571	4,206	13,982	34,514	68,964
Green Cove Springs	2,027	5,506	18,294	40,509	80,893
Havana	1,848	5,533	18,429	49,134	98,262
Homestead	1,913	5,200	17,253	43,865	87,695
Jacksonville	1,331	3,496	11,535	28,850	57,500
Jacksonville Beach	2,098	5,624	18,710	47,032	94,048
Key West	2,100	5,779	19,219	49,069	98,119
Kissimmee	2,067	5,422	18,326	44,720	89,383
Lakeland	1,760	4,850	16,807	41,774	83,172
Lake Worth	2,245	5,959	19,748	49,578	99,106
Leesburg	1,582	4,136	13,743	34,073	68,127
Moore Haven	1,678	4,289	14,219	34,844	69,654
Mount Dora	1,331	3,584	11,912	30,057	60,099
Newberry	1,844	4,751	15,803	36,893	73,741
New Smyrna Beach	1,746	4,758	15,783	40,198	80,362
Ocala	1,674	4,535	18,067	38,159	76,297
Orlando	1,324	3,455	11,481	28,287	56,719
Quincy	1,401	3,805	12,541	32,108	63,108
Reedy Creek	1,599	4,102	13,626	33,396	66,772
St. Cloud	1,372	3,577	11,887	29,560	59,104
Starke	2,291	6,854	22,824	60,849	121,689
Tallahassee	1,806	4,793	15,824	39,714	79,388
Vero Beach	1,952	5,496	18,216	47,221	94,371
Wauchula	1,603	5,083	16,791	42,823	85,581
Williston	1,787	4,936	16,175	41,050	82,050
Winter Park	1,353	3,506	11,663	29,933	59,855

See footnotes at end of table.

Continued . . .

Table 15.26. ELECTRIC RATES: COMMERCIAL AND INDUSTRIAL ELECTRIC RATES CHARGED BY MUNICIPAL, COOPERATIVE, AND INVESTOR-OWNED UTILITIES IN FLORIDA, DECEMBER 31, 2005 (Continued)

(in dollars)

Utility	15,000 kWh	45,000 kWh	150,000 kWh	400,000 kWh	800,000 kWh
Cooperative					
Central Florida	1,843	4,880	16,150	40,150	80,250
Choctawhatchee	1,310	3,410	10,655	26,726	53,423
Clay	1,464	3,994	13,185	33,785	65,910
Escambia River	1,645	4,405	14,590	36,840	73,640
Florida Keys	2,211	6,514	21,829	57,327	114,703
Glades	2,134	6,060	19,600	37,495	74,815
Gulf Coast	1,385	3,830	12,737	32,612	65,212
Lee County	1,401	3,798	13,200	32,575	65,135
Okefenokee	1,401	3,529	11,530	28,480	56,860
Peace River	1,628	4,297	14,205	35,630	71,210
Sumter	1,492	3,962	13,090	32,990	65,930
Suwannee Valley	1,830	4,947	13,546	33,253	66,465
Talquin	1,396	3,823	12,930	29,880	59,460
Tri-county	1,690	4,315	14,150	35,100	70,100
West Florida	1,477	4,032	13,323	23,106	46,112
Withlacoochee River	1,422	3,806	12,628	31,801	63,577
Investor-owned					
Florida Power and Light 1/	1,422	3,744	12,247	29,814	59,698
Florida Public Utilities					
Fernandina Beach Division 1/	784	2,077	6,728	16,853	33,631
Marianna Division	890	2,395	7,570	19,097	38,119
Gulf Power	1,185	3,078	10,772	25,549	50,943
Progress Energy Florida	1,262	3,506	11,663	29,933	59,855
Tampa Electric	1,427	3,653	12,078	29,813	59,371

kWh Kilowatt-hour.
1/ Includes 1.5 percent embedded gross receipts taxes.
Note: Cost excludes local taxes, franchise fees, and gross receipts taxes not embedded in rates. Full year fuel costs are included for all utilities and purchased power costs are included for municipal utilities.

Source: State of Florida, Public Service Commission, Division of Research and Regulatory Review, *Statistics of the Florida Electric Utility Industry, 2005,* Internet site <http://www.psc.state.fl.us/> (accessed 19, February 2007).

Table 15.27. ELECTRIC UTILITY INDUSTRY: CAPACITY, NET GENERATION, FUEL CONSUMPTION, SALES, PER CAPITA CONSUMPTION, AND REVENUE IN FLORIDA, 2001 THROUGH 2005

Item	2001	2002	2003	2004	2005
Nameplate capacity, total (mW)	40,515	43,351	45,097	45,875	48,437
Conventional steam	23,537	23,360	22,336	22,128	22,099
Internal combustion and gas turbine	6,988	7,140	7,152	7,514	9,864
Combined cycle	6,028	8,889	11,642	12,273	12,399
Hydroelectric	58	58	59	58	63
Steam-nuclear	3,898	3,898	3,902	3,902	3,903
Other	6	6	6	0	110
Net generation, total (gWh)	178,485	187,863	196,563	198,372	204,476
By prime mover					
Conventional steam	118,191	107,753	111,213	103,200	102,056
Internal combustion and combustion turbine	5,616	6,211	4,191	3,444	3,452
Combined cycle 1/	23,088	40,356	50,052	60,478	70,303
Hydroelectric	22	19	38	30	33
Steam-nuclear	31,568	33,524	31,069	31,220	28,632
By fuel type					
Coal	73,005	71,092	76,294	68,708	69,683
Oil	34,858	27,494	29,030	28,513	28,096
Natural gas	39,032	55,734	60,132	69,901	78,032
Nuclear	31,568	33,524	31,069	31,220	28,632
Hydroelectric	22	19	38	30	33
Sales to ultimate consumers, total (gWh)	197,113	207,590	214,493	204,588	222,308
Residential	99,811	106,445	110,821	105,168	114,156
Commercial	70,552	73,812	75,647	73,382	78,809
Industrial	21,620	22,040	22,453	20,372	23,431
Other public utilities	5,130	5,293	5,572	5,666	5,912
Per capita consumption 1/ (kWh)					
Sales per capita, total	12,021	12,421	12,603	11,760	12,696
Residential sales per capita	6,087	6,369	6,512	6,045	6,519
Net generation per capita (kWh)	12,867	13,321	13,569	13,437	13,716
Revenues per gWh by class of service ($1,000)					
Total	77.7	73.9	77.8	87.4	88.7
Residential	87.0	82.4	86.3	96.2	97.7
Commercial	66.2	62.1	66.3	74.2	76.0
Industrial	69.2	68.5	70.4	85.1	82.3
Other	92.0	89.4	92.9	103.2	110.9

mW Megawatt (1,000 kilowatts).
gWh Gigawatt-hours (million kilowatt-hours).
kWh Kilowatt-hours.
1/ Total sales divided by population.
Note: Detail may not add to totals because of rounding. Some data may be revised.

Source: State of Florida, Public Service Commission, Division of Research and Regulatory Review, *Statistics of the Florida Electric Utility Industry, 2005,* and previous editions, Internet site <http://www.psc.state.fl.us/ (accessed 19, February 2007).

Table 15.28. ELECTRIC UTILITY INDUSTRY: ACTUAL AND PROJECTED FUEL REQUIREMENTS IN FLORIDA, 2005 THROUGH 2015

Year	Coal (1,000 short tons)	Oil 1/ (1,000 barrels)	Natural gas (billion cubic feet)	Nuclear (U-235) (trillion BTU)	Year	Coal (1,000 short tons)	Oil 1/ (1,000 barrels)	Natural gas (billion cubic feet)	Nuclear (U-235) (trillion BTU)
2005	30,356	45,314	576	309	2011	32,950	12,857	1,076	344
2006	30,433	34,127	556	344	2012	35,241	11,385	1,071	347
2007	31,960	34,178	697	331	2013	40,306	10,140	1,030	341
2008	32,299	30,069	767	351	2014	44,365	9,712	993	349
2009	32,096	18,652	910	332	2015	45,938	9,178	1,033	342
2010	32,242	12,345	1,014	346					

BTU British Thermal Units.
1/ Light oil combined with heavy oil.
Source: State of Florida, Public Service Commission, Division of Research and Regulatory Review, *Statistics of the Florida Electric Utility Industry, 2005,* Internet site <http://www.psc.state.fl.us/> (accessed 19, February 2007).

Table 15.29. ELECTRIC UTILITY INDUSTRY: TYPICAL BILL AND GROWTH AND USE COMPARISONS OF INVESTOR-OWNED ELECTRIC UTILITY COMPANIES IN FLORIDA, 2006

(amounts in dollars)

Item	Florida Power and Light Company	Progress Energy Florida Inc.	Tampa Electric Company	Gulf Power Company	Florida Public Utilities Company: Northwest	Florida Public Utilities Company: Northeast
Typical electric bill comparisons 1/						
Minimum bill or customer charge	5.17	8.03	8.50	10.00	10.00	10.00
100 kWh	15.25	17.91	18.35	18.00	15.95	14.71
250 kWh	30.36	32.73	33.10	30.01	24.87	21.77
500 kWh	55.55	57.45	57.69	50.02	39.75	33.54
750 kWh	80.72	82.13	82.28	70.03	54.62	45.30
1,000 kWh	105.89	106.82	106.87	90.03	69.48	57.06
1,500 kWh	166.27	166.24	156.06	130.05	99.23	80.60
Growth and use						
Average residential consumption (kWh)	13,970	13,983	15,164	15,032	14,649	15,121
Percentage increase	-1.60	-1.80	-1.00	-0.98	0.36	-3.18
Number of residential customers	3,906,270	1,487,586	581,955	364,647	10,330	13,218
Percentage increase	2.00	5.37	2.60	2.87	0.85	2.62
Annual residential revenue ($1,000,000)	6,493	2,361	957	492	11	12
Percentage increase	24.30	18.00	14.20	8.17	4.04	-7.01
Average revenue per kWh sold (cents)	11.90	11.79	10.97	9.02	7.31	5.79
Annual retail operating revenue ($1,000,000)	11,629	4,159	2,014	912	24	25
Percentage increase	27.40	19.67	3.00	8.22	5.46	0.66

kWh Kilowatt-hour.
1/ Residential service. Excludes local taxes and franchise fees. December 2005 fuel and other adjustment clause factors are included. See source for base rate explanation.

Source: State of Florida, Public Service Commission, *Comparative Rate Statistics: Electric, Natural Gas, Telephone, Water and Wastewater, December 31, 2006,* Internet site <http://www.psc.state.fl.us/> (accessed 16, April 2007).

Table 15.30. UTILITIES: PUBLIC POWER COMPARISONS IN FLORIDA, OTHER POPULOUS STATES, AND THE UNITED STATES, 2005

State	Ultimate customers Total	Sales Megawatt-hours	Sales Revenue ($1,000)	Generation (MWh)	Residential customers 1/	Public power customers as a percentage of total residential customers
			Sunbelt states			
Florida	1,255,875	35,060,910	2,903,136	35,712,973	1,065,343	13.2
Alabama	490,893	16,480,247	1,048,336	8,772	410,357	20.1
Arizona	966,789	26,972,877	2,026,507	26,393,983	870,369	35.4
Arkansas	168,990	5,897,471	340,554	2,450,683	144,797	11.5
California	3,104,831	59,569,930	5,747,860	57,230,528	2,674,941	21.4
Georgia	334,407	11,994,137	808,304	13,572,001	276,934	7.2
Louisiana	159,477	4,449,623	360,892	2,939,124	133,868	7.0
Mississippi	132,871	4,297,852	295,978	54,443	104,469	8.7
New Mexico	80,190	2,233,201	162,604	1,227,925	65,108	8.2
North Carolina	564,167	15,524,092	1,284,032	12,596,017	472,612	12.0
Oklahoma	192,671	4,663,088	323,757	7,744,029	163,945	10.3
South Carolina	319,321	15,508,275	942,304	26,331,035	265,604	13.7
Tennessee	2,082,162	69,864,784	4,627,440	0	1,779,408	69.2
Texas	1,559,421	43,500,004	3,479,346	51,484,609	1,366,222	15.5
Virginia	161,280	4,949,522	317,501	79,922	131,392	4.3
			Other populous states			
Illinois	257,672	6,820,711	460,775	2,741,150	222,440	4.4
Indiana	257,654	7,878,630	470,819	2,577,186	218,735	8.1
Massachusetts	386,514	8,009,339	840,328	2,090,534	338,979	13.1
Michigan	304,039	8,020,026	565,058	6,684,178	258,267	6.0
New Jersey	62,914	1,187,317	133,066	87,514	54,428	1.6
New York	1,257,408	24,943,562	3,476,518	26,627,808	1,120,826	16.5
Ohio	375,461	10,013,854	758,458	2,578,568	333,704	6.9
Pennsylvania	83,203	1,490,511	132,095	42,268	72,804	1.4
United States	20,048,423	542,511,906	40,988,345	403,119,699	17,239,729	14.3

1/ Full-service and delivery-only customers.

Source: American Public Power Association, Electric Power Statistics, *2007-08 Annual Directory and Statistical Report* (copyrighted), Internet site <http://www.appanet.org/> (accessed 21, March 2007).

Table 15.31. UTILITIES: SECTOR RATE COMPARISONS IN FLORIDA, OTHER SUNBELT STATES, AND OTHER POPULOUS STATES, 2005

(cents per kilowatt-hour)

State	Residential			Commercial			Industrial		
	Public	Private	Co-op	Public	Private	Co-op	Public	Private	Co-op
				Sunbelt states					
Florida	9.3	9.7	9.6	8.0	8.2	8.8	6.1	6.5	7.2
Alabama	6.8	8.2	8.7	6.9	7.6	8.3	5.1	4.6	5.5
Arizona	8.6	8.9	10.0	7.2	7.9	8.6	4.7	6.4	5.6
Arkansas	6.7	7.9	8.5	5.9	6.0	7.8	4.9	4.9	4.5
California	10.5	13.1	10.6	9.8	13.0	11.4	8.5	10.2	7.1
Georgia	8.0	8.7	8.6	7.3	7.6	8.3	4.6	5.4	4.9
Louisiana	8.2	9.4	7.2	8.1	8.7	7.2	7.4	6.7	5.9
Mississippi	7.4	9.5	8.3	7.5	8.7	8.5	5.5	5.9	6.1
New Mexico	8.9	8.8	10.4	8.0	7.7	8.9	5.9	5.5	5.6
North Carolina	9.7	8.1	9.7	8.0	6.5	8.1	5.9	4.9	5.1
Oklahoma	8.1	7.7	8.6	7.5	6.7	8.5	4.7	5.1	5.0
South Carolina	8.2	8.6	9.0	7.7	7.2	8.4	4.7	4.4	5.3
Tennessee	7.0	5.1	7.1	7.1	5.5	7.6	5.5	3.5	5.2
Texas	8.9	9.2	10.1	7.7	8.2	9.7	6.4	5.7	7.3
Virginia	7.2	7.8	10.6	6.6	5.9	10.5	5.3	4.2	6.1
				Other populous states					
Illinois	7.5	8.2	10.2	7.0	8.5	8.2	5.1	4.5	6.0
Indiana	6.8	7.5	7.9	6.4	6.6	6.8	5.2	4.3	5.2
Massachusetts	10.9	13.7	(X)	11.1	13.4	(X)	9.7	8.5	(X)
Michigan	7.9	8.3	10.1	7.4	7.9	8.7	6.0	5.3	5.9
New Jersey	11.5	11.7	11.3	11.5	10.5	11.4	10.1	8.2	8.2
New York	15.5	16.0	9.4	14.7	15.7	8.6	3.5	11.7	6.3
Ohio	8.6	8.1	8.3	8.6	7.5	7.7	6.2	4.8	4.9
Pennsylvania	9.6	9.8	10.8	9.2	8.5	9.7	7.5	6.3	7.5

(X) Not applicable.

Source: American Public Power Association, Electric Power Statistics, *2007-08 Annual Directory and Statistical Report* (copyrighted), Internet site <http://www.appanet.org/> (accessed 21, March 2007).

Table 15.40. NATURAL GAS: TYPICAL NATURAL GAS BILLS FOR INDUSTRIAL, COMMERCIAL AND RESIDENTIAL SERVICE OF INVESTOR-OWNED NATURAL GAS COMPANIES IN FLORIDA, DECEMBER 31, 2006

(amounts in dollars)

Company	Industrial						
	Minimum bill	500 therms	600 therms	700 therms	800 therms	900 therms	1000 therms
Chesapeake Utilities Corporation 1/ 2/	15.00-27.50	307.61	259.72	298.42	337.12	375.83	414.53
Florida City Gas 1/ 3/	11.00-12.00	1,107.30	1,276.53	1,487.29	1,698.04	1,908.80	2,119.55
Florida Public Utilities Company 1/ 3/	15.00-45.00	954.64	1,136.56	1,318.49	1,500.42	1,682.34	1,864.27
Indiantown Gas Company 2/	9.00	198.18	236.01	273.85	311.68	349.52	387.35
Peoples Gas System 1/ 3/	20.00-30.00	938.46	1,122.15	1,305.84	1,489.54	1,673.23	1,786.79
St. Joe Natural Gas Company 1/ 3/	9.00	728.62	872.54	1,016.46	1,160.38	1,304.31	1,448.23
Sebring Gas System, Inc. 2/	12.00	258.64	307.96	357.29	406.62	455.94	505.27

Company	Commercial						
	Minimum bill	50 therms	70 therms	90 therms	150 therms	200 therms	300 therms
Chesapeake Utilities Corporation 1/ 2/	15.00	44.26	55.97	67.67	102.78	132.04	190.57
Florida City Gas 1/ 3/	8.00-11.00	120.97	166.16	211.35	342.46	453.45	668.78
Florida Public Utilities Company 1/ 3/	15.00	110.74	149.03	187.32	302.21	397.94	589.41
Indiantown Gas Company 2/	9.00	27.92	35.48	43.05	65.75	84.67	122.51
Peoples Gas System 1/ 3/	20.00	111.85	148.58	185.32	295.54	387.38	571.08
St. Joe Natural Gas Company 1/ 3/	9.00	80.96	109.75	138.53	224.88	296.85	440.77
Sebring Gas System, Inc. 2/	9.00-12.00	37.57	49.00	60.43	94.71	123.28	159.98

Company	Residential						
	Minimum bill	20 therms	30 therms	40 therms	50 therms	75 therms	100 therms
Chesapeake Utilities Corporation 1/ 2/	15.00	26.70	32.56	38.41	44.26	58.89	73.52
Florida City Gas 1/ 3/	8.00	53.19	75.78	98.38	120.97	177.46	231.48
Florida Public Utilities Company 1/ 3/	8.00	50.55	71.82	93.09	114.37	167.55	220.74
Indiantown Gas Company 2/	9.00	16.57	20.35	24.13	27.92	37.38	46.84
Peoples Gas System 1/ 3/	10.00	49.01	68.52	88.03	107.53	156.30	205.06
St. Joe Natural Gas Company 1/ 3/	9.00	37.82	52.23	66.64	81.04	117.07	153.09
Sebring Gas System, Inc. 2/	9.00	20.43	26.14	31.86	37.57	51.86	66.14

1 Therm = 100,000 British Thermal Units.

1/ Includes conservation costs for those companies participating in conservation.

2/ These companies no longer purchase gas for their customers. These companies deliver gas that the end use customers purchase, therefore no gas costs are included.

3/ Includes costs gas costs for those companies participating in purchased gas adjustment clause.

Source: State of Florida, Public Service Commission, *Comparative Rate Statistics: Electric, Natural Gas, Telephone, Water and Wastewater, December 31, 2006,* Internet site <http://www.psc.state.fl.us/> (accessed 16, April 2007).

Table 15.42. NATURAL GAS: PRODUCTION, MOVEMENT, AND CONSUMPTION IN FLORIDA AND THE UNITED STATES, 2004 AND 2005

(quantity in millions of cubic feet)

Item	Florida		United States	
	2004	2005	2004	2005
Marketed production 1/	3,123	2,616	19,517,491	18,950,734
Net interstate movements	734,265	774,283	0	0
Net movements across U.S. borders	0	0	3,495,034	3,720,962
Net storage changes 2/	0	0	114,228	-51,072
Extraction loss	618	495	926,600	876,497
Supplemental gas supplies	0	0	60,365	63,691
Balancing item 3/	-2,591	2,323	356,956	331,241
Consumption, total	734,178	778,727	22,388,975	22,241,202
Delivered to consumers	722,326	768,084	20,724,883	20,544,907
Lease fuel	1,178	987	731,563	756,324
Plant fuel	102	286	366,341	355,193
Pipeline and distribution use	10,572	9,370	566,187	584,779

1/ Gross withdrawals from gas and oil wells less gas used for repressuring, nonhydrocarbon gases removed, and quantities vented and flared.
2/ Positive numbers indicate an increase in storage, thus a decrease in supply.
3/ Represents an imbalance between available supplies and consumption.
Note: Some data may be revised.

Table 15.43. NATURAL GAS: VOLUME CONSUMED, CONSUMERS, AND PRICE OF NATURAL GAS DELIVERED TO CONSUMERS IN FLORIDA AND THE UNITED STATES, 2005

Item	Residential	Commercial	Industrial	Vehicle fuel	Electric utilities
Florida					
Volume consumed (MCF)	16,124	57,690	63,133	727	630,410
Consumers	656,069	55,479	432	(NA)	(NA)
Average price (dollars per thousand cubic feet)	20.15	13.28	9.48	12.94	8.75
United States					
Volume consumed (MCF)	4,806,136	3,101,526	6,745,835	22,265	5,869,145
Consumers	63,573,466	5,196,428	205,217	(NA)	(NA)
Average price (dollars per thousand cubic feet)	12.84	11.59	8.56	9.09	8.48

MCF Million cubic feet.
(NA) Not available.

Source for Tables 15.42 and 15.43: U.S., Department of Energy, Energy Information Administration, *Natural Gas Annual, 2005,* Internet site <http://www.eia.doe.gov/> (accessed 21, March 2007).

Table 15.50. NUCLEAR POWER PLANTS: NUMBER OF UNITS, NET GENERATION, AND NET SUMMER CAPABILITY IN FLORIDA, OTHER LEADING GENERATING STATES, AND THE UNITED STATES, 2005

Leading state	Number of units	Net generation: Total (megawatt-hours)	Net generation: Percentage of total	Net summer capability: Total (megawatts)	Net summer capability: Percentage of total
Florida	5	28,758,826	13.1	3,902	7.3
Illinois	11	93,263,001	48.0	11,388	26.8
Pennsylvania	9	76,289,432	35.0	9,195	20.5
South Carolina	7	53,137,554	51.8	6,472	28.7
New York	6	42,443,152	28.9	5,150	13.2
North Carolina	5	39,981,739	30.8	4,938	18.2
Texas	4	38,232,493	9.6	4,860	4.8
California	4	36,154,898	18.1	4,324	7.0
Michigan	4	32,871,574	27.0	3,982	13.1
Alabama	5	31,694,223	23.0	5,008	16.3
Georgia	4	31,534,259	23.1	4,060	11.1
United States	104	781,986,365	19.3	99,988	10.2

Source: U.S., Department of Energy, Energy Information Administration, *Electric Power Annual 2005,* Internet site <http://www.eia.doe.gov/> (accessed 20, February 2007).

Table 15.51. ENERGY CONSUMPTION ESTIMATES: AMOUNT CONSUMED BY SECTOR IN FLORIDA SPECIFIED YEARS, 1975 THROUGH 2004

(in trillions of British thermal units)

Year	Total	Residential	Commercial 1/	Industrial 2/	Transportation 3/
1975	1,945.1	459.4	332.3	405.7	747.7
1980	2,525.8	610.6	383.3	581.3	950.6
1985	2,713.8	714.7	557.3	484.0	957.8
1990	3,298.5	891.2	721.9	547.9	1,137.4
1995	3,653.9	1,031.9	794.6	614.3	1,213.2
1996	3,757.8	1,065.2	805.7	664.7	1,222.2
1997	3,778.5	1,048.6	823.6	640.2	1,266.2
1998	3,923.7	1,139.0	869.5	629.2	1,285.9
1999	3,978.6	1,123.2	894.1	634.1	1,327.2
2000	4,142.8	1,178.2	945.8	612.9	1,405.8
2001	4,113.9	1,191.0	958.0	579.3	1,385.6
2002	4,228.0	1,262.0	999.9	549.0	1,417.2
2003	4,287.3	1,306.3	1,017.2	569.4	1,394.4
2004	4,452.5	1,306.7	1,041.6	554.1	1,550.0

1/ Consists of service-providing facilities and equipment of businesses; federal, state, and local governments (including institutional living quarters and sewage treatment facilities); and other private and public organizations.

2/ Consists of all facilities and equipment used for producing, processing, or assembling goods.

3/ Consists of all vehicles whose primary purpose is transporting people and/or goods.

Note: Data prior to 2000 were based on the Standard Industrial Code system (SIC) and are not comparable to data from 2000 forward, which is based on the North American Industry Classification System (NAICS).

Source: U.S., Department of Energy, Energy Information Administration, *State Energy Consumption, Price, and Expenditure Estimates (SEDS), 2004,* Internet site <http://www.eia.doe.gov/> (accessed 5, June 2007).

Table 15.60. MOTOR FUELS: CONSUMPTION BY USE IN FLORIDA, 1966 THROUGH 2005

(in thousands of gallons)

Year	Total quantity consumed 1/	Nonhighway use 2/	Highway use
1966	2,562,586	120,505	2,428,962
1967	2,711,163	135,851	2,561,698
1968	2,959,259	138,496	2,803,754
1969	3,215,457	129,949	3,069,173
1970	3,484,439	153,969	3,312,830
1971	3,771,337	146,210	3,585,727
1972	4,215,995	124,098	4,045,322
1973	4,695,983	126,054	4,494,951
1974	4,510,456	123,058	4,342,185
1975	4,639,217	135,547	4,456,610
1976	4,827,840	136,774	4,650,302
1977	5,023,007	131,635	4,846,201
1978	5,337,604	139,114	5,152,263
1979	5,374,535	142,358	5,171,693
1980	5,293,548	164,430	5,116,312
1981	5,390,545	137,165	5,240,229
1982	5,469,775	139,779	5,317,892
1983	5,723,316	163,810	5,548,590
1984	5,934,391	181,767	5,740,587
1985	6,110,435	254,402	5,843,396
1986	6,394,295	263,337	6,116,961
1987	6,700,629	275,337	6,387,472
1988	6,863,376	281,739	6,530,151
1989	7,034,489	292,036	6,680,708
1990	7,043,054	306,520	6,674,542
1991	6,930,325	319,863	6,549,254
1992	7,163,374	264,516	6,827,210
1993	7,431,207	169,860	7,187,669
1994	7,487,188	178,304	7,308,884
1995	7,680,638	206,176	7,474,462
1996	7,800,062	201,216	7,598,846
1997	8,019,637	206,247	7,813,390
1998	8,371,333	241,386	8,129,947
1999	8,675,760	218,669	8,457,091
2000	7,593,619	225,147	7,368,472
2001	8,999,570	238,595	8,760,975
2002	9,354,667	278,781	9,075,886
2003	9,324,909	285,653	9,610,562
2004	10,122,346	290,875	9,831,471
2005	10,418,160	322,803	10,095,357

1/ Includes losses allowed for evaporation and handling.
2/ Gasoline. Includes gasohol.
Note: Includes gasoline and all other fuels (except under nonhighway use) under state motor fuel laws. Data for earlier years may not be comparable due to revised estimation procedures.

Source: U.S., Department of Transportation, Federal Highway Administration, *Highway Statistics, 2005,* Internet site <http://www.fhwa.dot.gov/> (accessed 20, March 2007), and previous editions.

Table 15.66. GASOLINE: AVERAGE PUMP PRICES IN SPECIFIED METROPOLITAN AREAS IN FLORIDA, OTHER SUNBELT STATES, AND THE UNITED STATES, 2006 AND 2007

(prices in dollars per gallon)

Area	Regular		Mid-grade		Premium		Diesel	
	2006	2007	2006	2007	2006	2007	2006	2007
Florida	2.790	3.010	3.022	3.261	3.078	3.321	3.009	2.914
Metropolitan area								
Bradenton-Sarasota-Venice	2.852	2.997	3.090	3.246	3.147	3.306	2.963	2.907
Daytona Beach	2.884	3.006	3.124	3.257	3.182	3.317	3.013	2.942
Ft. Lauderdale	2.904	3.081	3.146	3.338	3.204	3.399	2.959	2.992
Ft. Myers-Cape Coral	2.888	3.017	3.128	3.268	3.186	3.328	2.972	2.917
Gainesville	2.876	3.061	3.116	3.317	3.173	3.378	2.990	2.987
Jacksonville	2.811	2.974	3.045	3.221	3.101	3.281	2.949	2.916
Miami	2.896	3.090	3.137	3.348	3.195	3.409	3.025	2.979
Orlando	2.812	2.950	3.047	3.196	3.103	3.255	2.953	2.896
Pensacola	2.825	2.948	3.060	3.193	3.117	3.252	2.937	2.853
Tallahassee	2.841	2.978	3.078	3.226	3.134	3.286	2.948	2.871
Tampa-St. Petersburg-Clearwater	2.783	2.957	3.015	3.203	3.071	3.262	2.935	2.855
West Palm Beach-Boca Raton	2.955	3.113	3.201	3.373	3.260	3.435	3.027	3.001
Other sunbelt states								
Alabama	2.610	2.927	2.790	3.129	2.873	3.222	2.886	2.791
Arkansas	2.620	2.930	2.764	3.092	2.940	3.288	2.919	2.772
Arizona	2.715	3.051	2.831	3.182	2.994	3.365	3.039	2.999
California	3.029	3.275	3.224	3.486	3.277	3.544	3.290	3.142
Georgia	2.587	2.949	2.781	3.170	2.904	3.310	2.902	2.814
Louisiana	2.699	2.945	2.877	3.139	3.011	3.286	2.914	2.804
Mississippi	2.655	2.884	2.800	3.042	2.926	3.179	2.852	2.717
New Mexico	2.888	3.271	3.076	3.484	3.208	3.635	3.088	2.999
North Carolina	2.679	2.975	2.843	3.157	2.968	3.296	2.954	2.873
Oklahoma	2.504	2.902	2.590	3.001	2.734	3.168	2.945	2.715
South Carolina	2.529	2.851	2.689	3.031	2.819	3.178	2.828	2.737
Tennessee	2.587	2.911	2.738	3.081	2.870	3.229	2.881	2.772
Texas	2.584	2.948	2.734	3.119	2.833	3.231	2.906	2.818
Virginia	2.591	2.912	2.718	3.055	2.823	3.173	2.873	2.815
United States	2.897	3.043	3.075	3.230	3.186	3.348	2.975	2.892

Note: Data are from the Oil Price Information Service for June 14, 2007.

Source: AAA, *Daily Fuel Gauge Report,* Internet site <http://www.fuelgaugereport.com/> (accessed 14, June 2007).

Table 15.67. GASOLINE: TOTAL AND PER CAPITA GALLONS SOLD IN THE STATE AND COUNTIES OF FLORIDA, 2004, 2005, AND 2006

County	Total sales (1,000 gallons) 2004	2005	2006	Percentage change 2004 to 2006	Per capita sales (gallons) 2004	2005	2006	Percentage change 2004 to 2006
Florida	8,605,523	8,605,920	8,605,274	0.0	491.3	480.3	469.7	-4.4
Alachua	117,411	117,785	117,557	0.1	497.1	489.2	479.6	-3.5
Baker	15,161	15,215	15,384	1.5	632.7	635.2	637.7	0.8
Bay	91,997	85,473	87,007	-5.4	580.7	528.5	528.0	-9.1
Bradford	15,075	14,612	15,357	1.9	543.4	519.7	539.2	-0.8
Brevard	251,995	254,634	247,105	-1.9	483.3	478.7	455.5	-5.8
Broward	818,891	810,356	816,044	-0.3	475.2	465.5	462.1	-2.8
Calhoun	5,089	4,424	4,723	-7.2	373.9	317.3	332.3	-11.1
Charlotte	85,957	80,805	80,415	-6.4	547.5	524.6	521.9	-4.7
Citrus	60,290	58,809	53,197	-11.8	467.0	443.4	391.4	-16.2
Clay	76,940	75,877	75,045	-2.5	470.7	447.3	427.4	-9.2
Collier	146,293	144,907	141,704	-3.1	477.8	456.0	428.8	-10.3
Columbia	45,089	43,702	46,554	3.2	745.8	711.0	742.6	-0.4
DeSoto	11,817	12,080	12,249	3.7	346.5	370.5	381.7	10.2
Dixie	6,573	6,068	5,771	-12.2	440.3	394.6	365.8	-16.9
Duval	440,745	444,809	453,254	2.8	524.4	516.5	515.3	-1.7
Escambia	143,876	137,091	144,991	0.8	468.3	451.5	478.1	2.1
Flagler	36,820	37,172	38,022	3.3	528.4	472.8	443.0	-16.2
Franklin	4,923	8,514	6,300	28.0	462.3	785.1	564.2	22.0
Gadsden	26,016	25,571	31,029	19.3	555.2	535.9	641.0	15.5
Gilchrist	5,982	6,014	6,374	6.6	376.2	370.7	383.5	1.9
Glades	4,427	3,825	3,276	-26.0	412.5	356.5	302.9	-26.6
Gulf	5,703	5,443	5,454	-4.4	352.7	330.3	326.0	-7.6
Hamilton	10,533	10,596	10,090	-4.2	736.4	740.2	701.6	-4.7
Hardee	14,416	15,688	14,134	-2.0	518.8	573.9	518.8	0.0
Hendry	18,998	18,924	19,345	1.8	508.1	493.1	491.9	-3.2
Hernando	68,916	70,355	76,149	10.5	474.6	466.6	489.4	3.1
Highlands	39,871	38,541	37,967	-4.8	433.1	412.4	399.9	-7.7
Hillsborough	566,848	569,845	575,605	1.5	511.4	503.6	497.8	-2.7
Holmes	8,997	8,414	8,501	-5.5	473.2	439.2	440.3	-7.0
Indian River	70,417	69,610	67,112	-4.7	555.2	535.3	503.2	-9.4
Jackson	33,124	34,350	35,975	8.6	677.8	691.3	712.5	5.1
Jefferson	10,223	9,704	8,382	-18.0	726.9	681.8	582.2	-19.9
Lafayette	2,165	2,701	2,236	3.3	287.3	338.9	270.7	-5.8
Lake	126,870	126,249	127,619	0.6	503.7	480.0	466.3	-7.4
Lee	282,354	294,120	301,173	6.7	541.7	535.3	524.8	-3.1

See footnote at end of table.

Continued . . .

Table 15.67. GASOLINE: TOTAL AND PER CAPITA GALLONS SOLD IN THE STATE AND COUNTIES OF FLORIDA, 2004, 2005, AND 2006 (Continued)

	Total sales (1,000 gallons)				Per capita sales (gallons)			
County	2004	2005	2006	Percentage change 2004 to 2006	2004	2005	2006	Percentage change 2004 to 2006
Leon	118,795	119,851	118,632	-0.1	450.2	442.1	427.7	-5.0
Levy	20,719	18,152	17,519	-15.4	552.7	477.9	453.1	-18.0
Liberty	2,594	2,672	3,496	34.8	352.7	352.4	451.5	28.0
Madison	12,649	11,568	8,765	-30.7	648.7	587.3	440.7	-32.1
Manatee	149,965	144,492	139,577	-6.9	507.9	474.7	446.0	-12.2
Marion	173,005	174,654	189,036	9.3	589.8	572.8	599.2	1.6
Martin	79,936	81,048	79,626	-0.4	580.8	574.6	551.7	-5.0
Miami-Dade	1,020,342	1,021,292	1,017,660	-0.3	428.7	421.7	413.3	-3.6
Monroe	60,908	57,027	56,477	-7.3	749.8	692.0	678.7	-9.5
Nassau	30,268	28,969	28,331	-6.4	465.6	440.5	422.8	-9.2
Okaloosa	106,482	103,058	104,787	-1.6	573.2	545.5	544.7	-5.0
Okeechobee	29,981	31,448	29,984	0.0	788.9	832.7	793.1	0.5
Orange	585,184	583,392	571,932	-2.3	577.1	559.1	532.7	-7.7
Osceola	145,606	164,664	166,649	14.5	644.8	700.2	678.7	5.3
Palm Beach	546,483	550,155	540,474	-1.1	439.9	434.6	418.1	-5.0
Pasco	189,975	192,766	189,753	-0.1	487.4	473.7	450.3	-7.6
Pinellas	395,202	385,146	373,637	-5.5	418.8	406.4	392.1	-6.4
Polk	241,649	236,906	244,324	1.1	457.3	437.2	440.7	-3.6
Putnam	32,949	32,834	32,628	-1.0	450.0	445.1	438.8	-2.5
St. Johns	95,816	98,076	95,914	0.1	641.6	623.6	582.4	-9.2
St. Lucie	116,396	122,049	121,853	4.7	514.5	508.5	484.9	-5.8
Santa Rosa	63,608	65,162	66,274	4.2	475.7	477.6	473.4	-0.5
Sarasota	162,665	162,820	163,921	0.8	454.0	442.6	435.2	-4.1
Seminole	199,769	202,204	200,177	0.2	495.3	491.1	475.7	-4.0
Sumter	40,080	42,689	44,338	10.6	603.5	576.5	555.1	-8.0
Suwannee	23,784	23,608	22,869	-3.8	630.6	618.4	589.3	-6.5
Taylor	12,359	12,046	12,153	-1.7	590.2	565.3	561.2	-4.9
Union	3,595	3,837	3,888	8.2	245.9	255.0	252.3	2.6
Volusia	216,431	215,577	211,250	-2.4	446.9	435.8	418.3	-6.4
Wakulla	10,413	9,545	10,855	4.2	408.3	355.3	384.4	-5.9
Walton	34,197	34,985	36,863	7.8	676.6	653.6	655.3	-3.1
Washington	12,916	10,947	10,536	-18.4	575.7	474.0	442.6	-23.1

Note: Includes gasohol. Per capita is computed using Bureau of Economic and Business Research *Florida Estimates of Population.* Consumption for 2006 is estimated based on trend and historical data. County gasoline data derived from local option gas tax receipts.

Source: State of Florida, Department of Community Affairs, *2006 Florida Motor Gasoline and Diesel Fuel Report,* and previous editions, February 2007, Internet site <http://www.dep.state.fl.us/> (accessed 2, August 2007).

WHOLESALE AND RETAIL TRADE

Gross and Taxable Sales Reported by the Lumber, Builders, and Contractors Group in Florida, 2006

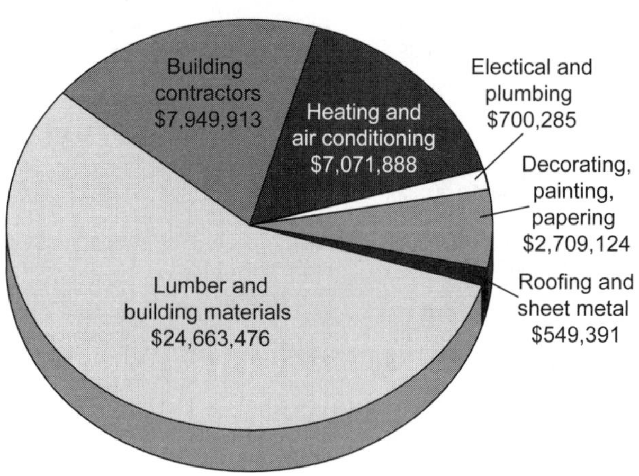

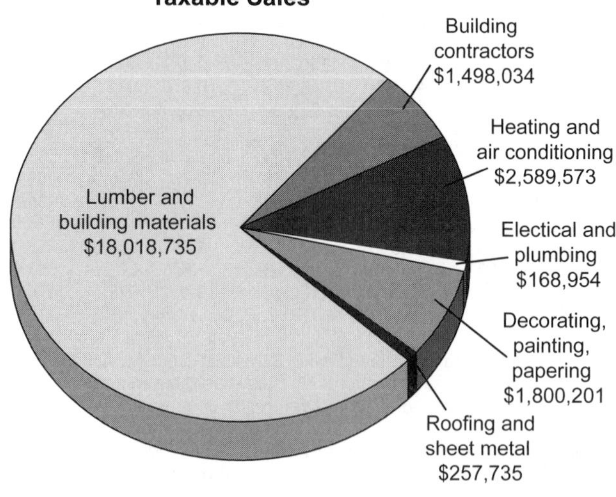

Source: Table 16.81

Section 16.00
Wholesale and Retail Trade

This section presents data on Florida's wholesale and retail trade industries. Included are statistics on establishments, employment, sales, and payroll.

Explanatory notes. The U.S. Census Bureau conducts an economic census every five years in years ending in "2" and "7." Wholesale and retail trade industries are grouped by North American Industry Classification System (NAICS) categories as explained in the introduction to Section 6.00 and in the Glossary. NAICS code 42 represents the wholesale trade industry. This code is broken down into two subsets; Durable goods (NAICS 421) and Nondurable goods (NAICS 422). NAICS codes 44-45 represent retail trade establishments.

Sources. Data from the *2002 Economic Census: Wholesale Trade* and *2002 Economic Census: Retail Trade* are featured in several tables of this section. The number of establishments, employment, payroll, sales, and expenses appear where possible by kind of business and by county in which the establishments are located. Current covered employment and payroll information by kind of business and county by NAICS classification is from the office of Labor Market Statistics (LMS), Florida Agency for Workforce Innovation. (See the introduction to Section 6.00.) Data from several different types of wholesale and retail establishments are presented in various tables throughout this section.

The Florida Department of Revenue is the source for information on sales reported by firms in connection with the sales and use tax laws. In addition to the data presented in this section, monthly and annual county gross and taxable sales by business category are available from the Bureau of Economic and Business Research (BEBR), University of Florida on a subscription basis. These business categories vary in coverage and classification from the Census Bureau figures. Data on retail sales tax collections appear in Table 23.43. Table 24.30 in Section 24.00 features a time series of gross and taxable sales.

The Florida Department of Health reports health professionals operating at the retail level who are required to have a license (e.g., dispensing opticians or pharmacists). These data appear in Section 20.00.

Section 16.00
Wholesale and Retail Trade

Tables listed by major heading

Heading | Page

Table 16.01. WHOLESALE TRADE: ESTABLISHMENTS, EMPLOYMENT, SALES AND ANNUAL PAYROLL BY KIND OF BUSINESS IN FLORIDA, 2002

NAICS code	Kind of business	Number of establishments	Number of emplyees 1/	Sales ($1,000)	Annual payroll ($1,000)
42	Wholesale trade	31,332	299,340	219,490,896	11,884,840
423	Durable goods merchants	19,158	165,370	104,892,869	6,995,462
4231	Motor vehicle and motor vehicle parts and supplies 2/	2,032	(NA)	(D)	(D)
4232	Furniture and home furnishings	1,135	8,173	3,622,597	270,738
4233	Lumber and other construction materials	1,246	1,204	5,684,304	468,962
4234	Professional and commercial equipment and supplies	3,179	36,337	27,898,882	1,826,598
4235	Metal and mineral 3/ (except petroleum)	577	(NA)	(D)	(D)
4236	Electrical goods	2,762	26,734	14,558,131	1,354,151
4237	Hardware, plumbing, heating equipment and supplies	1,280	10,729	3,918,873	421,244
4238	Machinery, equipment, and supplies 4/	3,887	(NA)	(D)	(D)
4239	Miscellaneous durable goods	3,060	19,101	7,865,688	629,942
424	Wholesale trade, nondurable goods	10,024	118,181	83,916,044	4,340,840
4241	Paper and paper product	802	8,195	3,441,787	316,893
4242	Drugs, and druggists' sundries	734	11,297	16,052,006	551,509
4243	Apparel, piece goods, and notions	1,277	9,066	4,394,676	309,326
4244	Grocery and related products	2,704	44,134	25,536,547	1,480,321
4245	Farm product raw material	116	583	1,264,887	22,540
4246	Chemical and allied products	932	6,103	2,845,991	257,760
4247	Petroleum and petroleum products	358	3,973	12,466,330	160,435
4248	Beer, wine, and distilled alcoholic beverage	196	11,472	6,345,404	550,117
4249	Miscellaneous nondurable goods	2,905	23,358	11,568,416	691,939
425	Electronic markets and agents and brokers	2,150	15,789	30,681,983	548,538

(NA) Not available.
(D) Data withheld to avoid disclosure of information about individual firms.
1/ Paid employment for pay period including March 12.
Employment ranges: 2/ 10,000 to 24,999. 3/ 5,000 to 9,999. 4/ 25,000 to 24,999.
Note: The economic censuses are conducted on a 5-year cycle collecting data for years ending in 2 and 7. Data are for North American Industry Classification System (NAICS) code 42 and may not be comparable to earlier years. See Glossary for definition.

Source: U.S., Department of Commerce, Census Bureau, *2002 Economic Census: Wholesale Trade,* Geographic Area Series EC02-42A-FL, issued September 2005, Internet site <http://www.census.gov/> (accessed 11, May 2007).

Table 16.06. WHOLESALE AND RETAIL TRADE: SALES IN THE STATE AND COUNTIES OF FLORIDA, 2002

(in thousands of dollars)

County	Wholesale trade	Retail trade	County	Wholesale trade	Retail trade
Florida	219,490,896	191,805,685	Lake	(D)	2,028,795
Alachua	(D)	2,367,427	Lee	2,009,534	6,365,752
Baker	(D)	129,758	Leon	893,786	2,685,149
Bay	478,815	1,864,639	Levy	43,257	269,567
Bradford	29,818	144,818	Liberty	(D)	15,331
Brevard	2,412,569	5,233,118	Madison	23,425	76,607
Broward	35,028,568	22,012,210	Manatee	1,290,926	2,703,995
Calhoun	(D)	81,863	Marion	1,392,032	2,860,280
Charlotte	(D)	1,434,629	Martin	584,752	1,921,445
Citrus	138,239	1,176,143	Miami-Dade	39,021,392	24,568,286
Clay	237,703	1,535,243	Monroe	185,125	1,183,949
Collier	1,040,455	4,196,902	Nassau	(D)	422,949
Columbia	(D)	578,398	Okaloosa	397,090	2,476,204
DeSoto	(D)	243,399	Okeechobee	111,989	335,976
Dixie	(D)	42,537	Orange	29,640,652	12,403,154
Duval	18,867,449	10,185,744	Osceola	(D)	1,751,198
Escambia	2,013,186	3,340,536	Palm Beach	14,804,170	16,480,821
Flagler	63,288	342,357	Pasco	(D)	3,074,472
Franklin	(D)	80,841	Pinellas	17,745,138	12,038,819
Gadsden	244,379	254,369	Polk	6,542,016	4,522,310
Gilchrist	(D)	38,483	Putnam	69,106	498,261
Glades	(D)	7,812	St. Johns	893,844	1,340,944
Gulf	(D)	58,149	St. Lucie	747,068	1,886,487
Hamilton	(D)	53,286	Santa Rosa	171,246	805,701
Hardee	158,529	150,747	Sarasota	1,432,109	4,434,320
Hendry	(D)	297,216	Seminole	4,761,803	5,082,697
Hernando	(D)	1,066,482	Sumter	(D)	247,536
Highlands	(D)	737,104	Suwannee	121,621	270,491
Hillsborough	24,551,768	13,909,770	Taylor	(D)	170,746
Holmes	(D)	50,619	Union	(D)	28,928
Indian River	(D)	1,524,526	Volusia	2,036,909	4,714,294
Jackson	(D)	397,784	Wakulla	(D)	81,316
Jefferson	(D)	65,437	Walton	139,978	305,302
Lafayette	(D)	30,563	Washington	(D)	120,694

(D) Data withheld to avoid disclosure of information about individual industries.
Note: The economic censuses are conducted on a 5-year cycle collecting data for years ending in 2 and 7. Data are for North American Industry Classification System (NAICS) codes 42 and 44-45 and may not be comparable to earlier years. See Glossary for definition.

Source: U.S., Department of Commerce, Census Bureau, *2002 Economic Census: Wholesale Trade,* Geographic Area Series EC02-42A-FL, issued September 2005, and *2002 Economic Census: Retail Trade,* Geographic Area Series EC-02-44A-FL, issued August 2005, Internet site <http://www.census.gov/> (both accessed 11, May 2007).

Table 16.11. RETAIL TRADE: ESTABLISHMENTS, EMPLOYMENT, SALES, AND ANNUAL PAYROLL BY KIND OF BUSINESS IN FLORIDA, 2002

NAICS code	Kind of business	Number of establishments	Number of employees 1/	Sales ($1,000)	Annual payroll ($1,000)
44-45	Retail trade	69,543	902,760	191,805,685	18,371,874
441	Motor vehicle and parts dealers	7,913	114,851	54,890,631	4,120,935
4411	Automobile dealers	3,010	78,041	46,631,965	3,141,340
4412	Other motor vehicle dealers	1,571	11,990	4,920,839	370,807
4413	Automotive parts, accessories, and tire stores	3,332	24,820	3,337,827	608,788
442	Furniture and home furnishings stores	4,738	34,034	6,736,064	843,886
4421	Furniture stores	2,085	15,857	3,868,747	479,118
4422	Home furnishings stores	2,653	18,177	2,867,317	364,768
443	Electronics and appliance stores	2,915	22,074	5,120,963	534,952
444	Building material, garden equipment and supplies dealers	4,663	63,583	13,409,608	1,565,672
4441	Building material and supplies dealers	3,798	58,265	12,614,849	1,458,476
4442	Lawn and garden equipment and supplies	865	5,318	794,759	107,196
445	Food and beverage stores	8,276	197,036	27,645,118	3,050,448
4451	Grocery stores	5,687	185,216	25,849,406	2,858,814
4452	Specialty food stores	1,508	7,157	768,832	118,235
4453	Beer, wine, and liquor stores	1,081	4,663	1,026,880	73,399
446	Health and personal care stores	5,820	74,842	12,147,910	1,434,884
447	Gasoline stations	6,544	44,764	13,491,646	691,464
448	Clothing and clothing accessories stores	11,360	94,631	11,737,460	1,435,631
4481	Clothing stores	6,849	69,801	8,302,612	1,003,010
4482	Shoe stores	1,970	13,892	1,638,431	182,470
4483	Jewelry, luggage, and leather goods stores	2,541	10,938	1,796,417	250,151
451	Sporting goods, hobby, book, and music stores	3,424	29,970	3,827,333	440,194
4511	Sporting goods, hobby, and musical instrument stores	2,473	20,198	2,646,690	312,205
4512	Book, periodical, and music stores	951	9,772	1,180,643	127,989
452	General merchandise stores	2,197	148,201	26,741,845	2,595,616
4521	Department stores	520	83,094	12,797,307	1,428,879
4529	Other general merchandise stores	1,677	65,107	13,944,538	1,166,737
453	Miscellaneous store retailers	8,141	46,839	5,611,286	767,079
4531	Florists	1,164	5,738	352,565	77,140
4532	Office supplies, stationery, and gift stores	2,706	19,803	2,598,371	301,992
4533	Used merchandise stores	1,277	6,325	486,753	92,557
4539	Other miscellaneous store retailers	2,994	14,973	2,173,597	295,390
454	Nonstore retailers	3,552	31,935	10,445,821	891,113
4541	Electronic shopping and mail-order houses	1,256	18,791	8,566,364	567,385
4542	Vending machine operators	383	1,943	234,452	43,683
4543	Direct selling establishments	1,913	11,201	1,645,005	280,045

1/ Paid employment for pay period including March 12.

Note: The economic censuses are conducted on a 5-year cycle collecting data for years ending in 2 and 7. Data are for North American Industry Classification System (NAICS) codes 44-45 and may not be comparable to earlier years. See Glossary for definition.

Source: U.S., Department of Commerce, Census Bureau, *2002 Economic Census: Retail Trade,* Geographic Area Series EC02-44A-FL, issued August 2005, Internet site <http://www.census.gov/> (accessed 11, May 2007).

Table 16.43. EMPLOYMENT AND PAYROLL: AVERAGE MONTHLY PRIVATE REPORTING UNITS EMPLOYMENT, AND PAYROLL COVERED BY UNEMPLOYMENT COMPENSATION LAW BY WHOLESALE AND RETAIL TRADE INDUSTRY IN FLORIDA, 2005 AND 2006

NAICS code	Industry	Number of reporting units	Number of employees	Payroll ($1,000)
			2005 A/	
42	Wholesale trade	41,772	338,058	1,485,652
423	Merchant wholesalers, durable goods	21,322	181,067	809,745
4231	Motor vehicle and parts merchant wholesalers	1,774	19,555	70,816
4232	Furniture and furnishing merchant wholesalers	892	5,556	20,762
4233	Lumber and construction supply merchant wholesalers	1,663	16,974	63,027
4234	Commercial equipment merchant wholesalers	4,744	44,843	254,736
4235	Metal and mineral merchant wholesalers	578	4,494	19,350
4236	Electric goods merchant wholesalers	2,932	23,573	118,915
4237	Hardware and plumbing merchant wholesalers	1,350	14,913	62,075
4238	Machinery and supply merchant wholesalers	4,097	33,503	136,185
4239	Miscellaneous durable goods merchant wholesalers	3,292	17,656	63,878
424	Merchant wholesalers, nondurable goods	10,786	121,307	512,057
4241	Paper and paper product merchant wholesalers	794	7,672	30,154
4242	Druggists' goods merchant wholesalers	1,040	18,305	123,196
4243	Apparel and piece goods merchant wholesalers	1,180	6,787	22,740
4244	Grocery and related product wholesalers	2,803	43,479	159,916
4245	Farm product raw material merchant wholesalers	108	939	3,405
4246	Chemical merchant wholesalers	1,003	7,188	34,286
4247	Petroleum merchant wholesalers	453	4,275	22,113
4248	Alcoholic beverage merchant wholesalers	336	11,358	49,320
4249	Miscellaneous nondurable goods merchant wholesalers	3,069	21,305	66,927
425	Electronic markets and agents and brokers	9,664	35,684	163,850
44-45	Retail trade	72,601	985,094	2,119,922
441	Motor vehicle and parts dealers	8,970	132,232	474,365
4411	Automobile dealers	3,436	86,647	350,344
4412	Other motor vehicle dealers	1,804	16,116	52,893
4413	Auto parts, accessories, and tire stores	3,730	29,468	71,128
442	Furniture and home furnishings stores	4,668	42,987	112,999
4421	Furniture stores	2,152	24,274	68,683
4422	Home furnishings stores	2,516	18,713	44,316
443	Electronics and appliance stores	4,237	35,592	107,149
444	Building material and garden supply stores	5,163	86,105	216,509
4441	Building material and supplies dealers	4,162	79,423	201,596
4442	Lawn and garden equipment and supplies stores	1,001	6,682	14,913
445	Food and beverage stores	8,841	194,737	311,208
4451	Grocery stores	5,878	175,869	276,716
4452	Specialty food stores	1,858	13,663	26,300
4453	Beer, wine, and liquor stores	1,105	5,205	8,191
446	Health and personal care stores	6,726	65,521	167,366

See footnotes at end of table.

Continued . . .

Table 16.43. EMPLOYMENT AND PAYROLL: AVERAGE MONTHLY PRIVATE REPORTING UNITS EMPLOYMENT, AND PAYROLL COVERED BY UNEMPLOYMENT COMPENSATION LAW BY WHOLESALE AND RETAIL TRADE INDUSTRY IN FLORIDA, 2005 AND 2006 (Continued)

NAICS code	Industry	Number of reporting units	Number of employees	Payroll ($1,000)
		2005 A/ (Continued)		
44-45	Retail trade (Continued)			
447	Gasoline stations	5,511	39,302	61,334
448	Clothing and clothing accessories stores	10,563	98,757	151,225
4481	Clothing stores	6,253	74,032	103,089
4482	Shoe stores	1,849	13,260	19,829
4483	Jewelry, luggage, and leather goods stores	2,461	11,465	28,307
451	Sporting goods, hobby, book and music stores	3,871	30,857	50,139
4511	Sporting goods and musical instrument stores	2,807	20,587	35,989
4512	Book, periodical, and music stores	1,064	10,270	14,149
452	General merchandise stores	2,541	176,923	284,869
4521	Department stores	670	95,681	153,653
4529	Other general merchandise stores	1,871	81,243	131,216
453	Miscellaneous store retailers	9,303	59,356	110,412
4531	Florists	1,176	5,411	8,502
4532	Office supplies, stationery, and gift stores	2,918	26,679	50,284
4533	Used merchandise stores	1,234	5,224	8,027
4539	Other miscellaneous store retailers	3,975	22,042	43,599
454	Nonstore retailers	2,207	22,725	72,347
4541	Electronic shopping and mail-order houses	1,048	14,617	49,165
4542	Vending machine operators	415	2,402	5,638
4543	Direct selling establishments	744	5,706	17,544

See footnotes at end of table. Continued . . .

Table 16.43. EMPLOYMENT AND PAYROLL: AVERAGE MONTHLY PRIVATE REPORTING UNITS EMPLOYMENT, AND PAYROLL COVERED BY UNEMPLOYMENT COMPENSATION LAW BY WHOLESALE AND RETAIL TRADE INDUSTRY IN FLORIDA, 2005 AND 2006 (Continued)

NAICS code	Industry	Number of reporting units	Number of employees	Payroll ($1,000)
			2006 B/	
42	Wholesale trade	42,106	347,754	1,620,592
423	Merchant wholesalers, durable goods	20,492	186,618	886,527
4231	Motor vehicle and parts merchant wholesalers	1,691	19,664	74,454
4232	Furniture and furnishing merchant wholesalers	849	5,643	20,642
4233	Lumber and construction supply merchant wholesalers	1,682	18,819	74,579
4234	Commercial equipment merchant wholesalers	4,494	46,437	283,976
4235	Metal and mineral merchant wholesalers	568	4,619	20,978
4236	Electric goods merchant wholesalers	2,821	22,715	123,026
4237	Hardware and plumbing merchant wholesalers	1,331	16,119	71,921
4238	Machinery and supply merchant wholesalers	3,960	34,342	149,149
4239	Miscellaneous durable goods merchant wholesalers	3,096	18,260	67,803
424	Merchant wholesalers, nondurable goods	10,296	121,526	531,655
4241	Paper and paper product merchant wholesalers	754	7,432	31,041
4242	Druggists' goods merchant wholesalers	1,028	18,083	125,980
4243	Apparel and piece goods merchant wholesalers	1,108	6,652	24,130
4244	Grocery and related product wholesalers	2,728	43,778	166,243
4245	Farm product raw material merchant wholesalers	96	905	3,310
4246	Chemical merchant wholesalers	988	7,026	35,029
4247	Petroleum merchant wholesalers	473	4,323	23,509
4248	Alcoholic beverage merchant wholesalers	344	11,699	51,852
4249	Miscellaneous nondurable goods merchant wholesalers	2,777	21,627	70,562
425	Electronic markets and agents and brokers	11,318	39,609	202,410
44-45	Retail trade	73,398	1,006,239	2,224,578
441	Motor vehicle and parts dealers	9,070	135,300	496,301
4411	Automobile dealers	3,461	88,553	366,096
4412	Other motor vehicle dealers	1,845	16,903	56,259
4413	Auto parts, accessories, and tire stores	3,764	29,845	73,945
442	Furniture and home furnishings stores	4,722	45,296	118,530
4421	Furniture stores	2,063	24,278	68,826
4422	Home furnishings stores	2,659	21,018	49,704
443	Electronics and appliance stores	4,302	36,896	108,499
444	Building material and garden supply stores	5,354	90,409	236,583
4441	Building material and supplies dealers	4,347	83,778	221,191
4442	Lawn and garden equipment and supplies stores	1,007	6,631	15,392
445	Food and beverage stores	8,785	194,018	319,161
4451	Grocery stores	5,787	174,374	282,376
4452	Specialty food stores	1,785	14,117	27,788
4453	Beer, wine, and liquor stores	1,213	5,527	8,997
446	Health and personal care stores	6,854	68,192	177,498

See footnotes at end of table.

Continued . . .

Table 16.43. EMPLOYMENT AND PAYROLL: AVERAGE MONTHLY PRIVATE REPORTING UNITS EMPLOYMENT, AND PAYROLL COVERED BY UNEMPLOYMENT COMPENSATION LAW BY WHOLESALE AND RETAIL TRADE INDUSTRY IN FLORIDA, 2005 AND 2006 (Continued)

NAICS code	Industry	Number of reporting units	Number of employees	Payroll ($1,000)
		2006 B/ (Continued)		
44-45	Retail trade (Continued)			
447	Gasoline stations	5,761	40,068	64,067
448	Clothing and clothing accessories stores	10,502	103,286	163,508
4481	Clothing stores	6,332	77,354	111,183
4482	Shoe stores	1,759	13,912	21,371
4483	Jewelry, luggage, and leather goods stores	2,411	12,019	30,954
451	Sporting goods, hobby, book and music stores	3,946	32,939	55,123
4511	Sporting goods and musical instrument stores	2,909	22,966	41,191
4512	Book, periodical, and music stores	1,037	9,973	13,931
452	General merchandise stores	2,511	179,031	298,974
4521	Department stores	646	80,204	131,872
4529	Other general merchandise stores	1,865	98,827	167,102
453	Miscellaneous store retailers	9,227	58,226	110,234
4531	Florists	1,120	5,060	7,987
4532	Office supplies, stationery, and gift stores	2,805	25,324	48,227
4533	Used merchandise stores	1,148	4,716	7,290
4539	Other miscellaneous store retailers	4,154	23,127	46,729
454	Nonstore retailers	2,364	22,578	76,102
4541	Electronic shopping and mail-order houses	1,183	14,741	52,996
4542	Vending machine operators	435	2,347	5,061
4543	Direct selling establishments	746	5,490	18,045

NAICS North American Industry Classification System. See Glossary for definition.
A/ Revised.
B/ Preliminary.
Note: Private employment. Detail may not add to totals due to disclosure editing and/or rounding. See Tables 23.70, 23.72, 23.73, and 23.74 for public employment data.

Source: State of Florida, Agency for Workforce Innovation, Labor Market Statistics, "Quarterly Census of Employment and Wages" (ES-202), Annual NAICS files, Internet site <http://www.labormarketinfo.com/index.htm> (accessed 17, July 2007).

Table 16.44. WHOLESALE TRADE: AVERAGE MONTHLY PRIVATE REPORTING UNITS, EMPLOYMENT AND PAYROLL COVERED BY UNEMPLOYMENT COMPENSATION LAW IN THE STATE AND COUNTIES OF FLORIDA, 2005 AND 2006

County	Number of reporting units	Number of employees	Payroll ($1,000)	County	Number of reporting units	Number of employees	Payroll ($1,000)
		Wholesale trade, 2005 A/ (NAICS code 42)					
Florida	41,772	338,058	1,485,652	Leon	289	2,859	11,102
Alachua	273	2,493	9,142	Levy	40	252	531
Baker	19	144	323	Liberty	6	36	85
Bay	218	2,572	7,798	Madison	15	74	209
Bradford	18	99	231	Manatee	420	3,182	13,370
Brevard	694	4,869	18,444	Marion	417	3,687	11,570
Broward	5,107	41,356	184,353	Martin	305	1,459	5,928
Calhoun	13	124	185	Miami-Dade	9,488	67,222	279,443
Charlotte	162	641	2,313	Monroe	152	520	1,956
Citrus	126	603	1,770	Nassau	70	326	1,387
Clay	173	701	2,420	Okaloosa	201	1,381	4,024
Collier	507	3,221	14,554	Okeechobee	43	219	547
Columbia	90	859	2,557	Orange	2,253	28,421	117,785
DeSoto	21	239	540	Osceola	202	2,153	6,724
Dixie	8	18	76	Palm Beach	3,041	20,564	96,502
Duval	1,486	22,818	100,820	Pasco	380	1,857	5,506
Escambia	423	5,269	17,359	Pinellas	1,909	14,988	63,324
Flagler	75	178	648	Polk	788	9,415	31,462
Franklin	22	151	526	Putnam	56	335	1,031
Gadsden	31	410	1,456	St. Johns	262	1,447	6,781
Gilchrist	13	54	127	St. Lucie	321	3,863	11,000
Glades	10	64	158	Santa Rosa	149	563	1,849
Gulf	13	155	693	Sarasota	746	4,523	17,481
Hamilton	6	6	10	Seminole	1,041	8,651	45,651
Hardee	26	200	608	Sumter	47	362	981
Hendry	47	200	606	Suwannee	50	303	719
Hernando	150	892	2,658	Taylor	20	62	128
Highlands	114	592	1,574	Union	5	18	29
Hillsborough	2,534	29,798	127,569	Volusia	595	4,419	14,082
Holmes	17	79	143	Wakulla	18	166	558
Indian River	207	771	2,903	Walton	54	273	787
Jackson	35	331	871	Washington	11	119	207
Jefferson	13	38	135	Statewide 1/	1,742	21,100	159,286
Lake	361	2,069	7,037	Out-of-state 2/	68	178	1,168
Lee	833	6,312	24,856	Unknown 1/	2,719	4,725	36,920

See footnotes at end of table.

Continued . . .

Table 16.44. WHOLESALE TRADE: AVERAGE MONTHLY PRIVATE REPORTING UNITS, EMPLOYMENT AND PAYROLL COVERED BY UNEMPLOYMENT COMPENSATION LAW IN THE STATE AND COUNTIES OF FLORIDA, 2005 AND 2006 (Continued)

County	Number of reporting units	Number of employees	Payroll ($1,000)	County	Number of reporting units	Number of employees	Payroll ($1,000)
			Wholesale trade, 2006 B/ (NAICS code 42)				
Florida	42,106	347,754	1,620,592	Lee	840	6,632	27,131
				Leon	288	2,714	10,580
Alachua	264	2,433	8,571	Levy	40	242	471
Baker	23	133	308	Liberty	6	31	88
Bay	205	2,384	7,309	Madison	15	67	199
Bradford	24	203	844	Manatee	476	3,702	17,213
Brevard	712	5,084	20,590	Marion	433	3,849	12,789
Broward	5,084	42,188	204,748	Martin	366	1,676	6,803
Calhoun	15	140	233	Miami-Dade	8,982	67,218	295,738
Charlotte	163	662	2,311	Monroe	134	522	2,103
Citrus	134	603	1,879	Nassau	78	363	1,527
Clay	191	784	2,777	Okaloosa	174	1,333	4,249
Collier	470	2,998	14,823	Okeechobee	51	230	479
Columbia	96	809	2,377	Orange	2,246	28,779	129,616
DeSoto	22	238	574	Osceola	224	2,379	7,680
Dixie	8	22	82	Palm Beach	2,982	21,110	104,834
Duval	1,474	23,429	111,503	Pasco	425	2,142	6,961
Escambia	413	5,185	17,690	Pinellas	1,842	14,827	64,325
Flagler	78	223	772	Polk	789	9,739	34,183
Franklin	20	124	398	Putnam	61	381	1,139
Gadsden	30	518	1,735	St. Johns	266	2,109	10,966
Gilchrist	16	61	140	St. Lucie	366	4,422	13,167
Glades	15	76	188	Santa Rosa	138	550	1,870
Gulf	12	59	314	Sarasota	706	4,324	17,081
Hamilton	6	10	26	Seminole	1,055	8,966	44,968
Hardee	28	244	778	Sumter	53	412	1,272
Hendry	50	259	692	Suwannee	51	320	828
Hernando	162	848	2,753	Taylor	15	51	118
Highlands	125	596	1,639	Union	4	12	17
Hillsborough	2,507	30,396	135,986	Volusia	622	4,545	14,470
Holmes	18	94	210	Wakulla	17	74	234
Indian River	205	914	4,058	Walton	68	457	1,405
Jackson	33	316	956	Washington	10	96	185
Jefferson	16	64	219	Statewide 1/	1,893	23,049	184,333
Lafayette	5	33	80	Out-of-state 2/	63	229	1,584
Lake	372	2,091	7,114	Unknown 1/	3,330	5,988	45,310

NAICS North American Industry Classification System. See Glossary for details.
A/ Revised. B/ Preliminary.
1/ Reporting units without a fixed location within the state or of unknown county location.
2/ Employment based in Florida, but working out of the state or country.
Note: Private employment. For a list of three- and four-digit industries included see Table 16.43. Only counties for which data are disclosed are shown. Detail may not add to totals due to disclosure editing and/or rounding. See Tables 23.70, 23.72, 23.73, and 23.74 for public employment data.
Source: State of Florida, Agency for Workforce Innovation, Labor Market Statistics, "Quarterly Census of Employment and Wages" (ES-202), Annual NAICS files, Internet site <http://www.labormarketinfo.com/index.htm> (accessed 17, July 2007).

Table 16.45. RETAIL TRADE: AVERAGE MONTHLY PRIVATE REPORTING UNITS, EMPLOYMENT AND PAYROLL COVERED BY UNEMPLOYMENT COMPENSATION LAW IN THE STATE AND COUNTIES OF FLORIDA, 2005 AND 2006

County	Number of reporting units	Number of employees	Payroll ($1,000)	County	Number of reporting units	Number of employees	Payroll ($1,000)
			Retail trade, 2005 A/ (NAICS codes 44-45)				
Florida	72,601	985,094	2,119,922	Lee	2,341	34,330	79,484
				Leon	988	16,552	28,986
Alachua	880	13,194	23,658	Levy	137	1,406	2,355
Baker	71	800	1,135	Liberty	13	96	153
Bay	737	9,800	18,307	Madison	59	608	858
Bradford	82	815	1,376	Manatee	1,043	16,932	33,192
Brevard	1,966	27,478	55,191	Marion	1,103	16,087	31,998
Broward	7,383	97,033	228,639	Martin	758	10,446	22,773
Calhoun	46	399	621	Miami-Dade	11,123	119,707	263,044
Charlotte	521	7,707	15,268	Monroe	689	5,461	12,423
Citrus	486	5,517	10,678	Nassau	242	2,801	4,725
Clay	577	8,111	14,547	Okaloosa	902	12,611	23,820
Collier	1,496	18,551	43,971	Okeechobee	152	1,634	2,870
Columbia	267	3,099	6,138	Orange	4,380	66,798	142,999
DeSoto	61	1,605	3,275	Osceola	711	11,149	20,847
Dixie	44	337	601	Palm Beach	5,296	69,768	159,173
Duval	3,294	53,402	119,371	Pasco	1,163	16,566	31,021
Escambia	1,165	16,803	33,373	Pinellas	3,863	53,713	118,976
Flagler	192	2,711	4,998	Polk	1,769	24,728	49,910
Franklin	69	567	1,001	Putnam	242	2,924	4,960
Gadsden	145	1,386	2,209	St. Johns	686	8,055	14,844
Gilchrist	32	277	536	St. Lucie	705	9,514	20,067
Glades	11	99	165	Santa Rosa	350	4,689	8,159
Gulf	48	398	608	Sarasota	1,725	22,335	51,609
Hamilton	42	281	376	Seminole	1,759	27,690	62,876
Hardee	78	696	1,288	Sumter	139	2,138	3,662
Hendry	112	1,605	2,820	Suwannee	149	1,565	2,729
Hernando	443	6,466	11,446	Taylor	81	987	1,541
Highlands	325	4,068	7,528	Union	33	225	328
Hillsborough	4,302	68,181	160,195	Volusia	1,867	25,463	49,165
Holmes	64	400	483	Wakulla	56	504	681
Indian River	640	8,240	16,724	Walton	255	2,418	4,292
Jackson	186	2,189	3,754	Washington	63	708	1,118
Jefferson	63	382	563	Statewide 1/	322	16,778	37,363
Lafayette	19	144	243	Out-of-state 2/	49	243	1,214
Lake	893	12,633	24,958	Unknown 1/	648	2,090	9,661

See footnotes at end of table.

Continued . . .

Table 16.45. RETAIL TRADE: AVERAGE MONTHLY PRIVATE REPORTING UNITS, EMPLOYMENT AND PAYROLL COVERED BY UNEMPLOYMENT COMPENSATION LAW IN THE STATE AND COUNTIES OF FLORIDA, 2005 AND 2006 (Continued)

County	Number of reporting units	Number of employees	Payroll ($1,000)	County	Number of reporting units	Number of employees	Payroll ($1,000)
			Retail trade, 2006 B/ (NAICS codes 44-45)				
Florida	73,398	1,006,239	2,224,578	Lee	2,399	36,262	85,452
				Leon	1,019	16,966	30,916
Alachua	905	13,645	25,447	Levy	132	1,418	2,464
Baker	72	768	1,105	Liberty	12	88	115
Bay	774	9,828	19,031	Madison	61	553	847
Bradford	83	991	1,675	Manatee	1,076	15,916	32,365
Brevard	1,988	27,978	56,274	Marion	1,138	16,206	33,166
Broward	7,503	100,710	243,512	Martin	773	10,438	23,058
Calhoun	45	354	572	Miami-Dade	10,845	124,551	285,259
Charlotte	546	8,634	17,155	Monroe	656	5,411	11,561
Citrus	488	5,530	10,734	Nassau	236	2,982	5,153
Clay	563	8,868	16,436	Okaloosa	881	12,117	23,492
Collier	1,497	19,325	47,227	Okeechobee	150	1,557	2,909
Columbia	267	3,108	6,365	Orange	4,475	67,276	148,954
DeSoto	59	1,760	3,882	Osceola	769	11,506	21,452
Dixie	45	394	662	Palm Beach	5,441	72,368	167,730
Duval	3,337	52,878	125,334	Pasco	1,194	17,237	33,213
Escambia	1,174	16,854	34,013	Pinellas	3,763	52,983	119,852
Flagler	211	2,844	5,379	Polk	1,795	25,818	53,169
Franklin	63	540	973	Putnam	242	2,868	5,031
Gadsden	142	1,349	2,240	St. Johns	703	8,236	16,173
Gilchrist	29	263	511	St. Lucie	712	9,455	20,408
Glades	11	94	160	Santa Rosa	361	4,729	8,560
Gulf	54	422	668	Sarasota	1,715	22,120	51,295
Hamilton	45	285	383	Seminole	1,800	28,387	60,171
Hardee	74	721	1,314	Sumter	144	2,271	4,019
Hendry	122	1,665	2,764	Suwannee	153	1,632	2,985
Hernando	450	6,670	12,298	Taylor	80	940	1,550
Highlands	313	4,229	8,009	Union	35	217	330
Hillsborough	4,382	71,087	171,000	Volusia	1,892	25,349	50,664
Holmes	61	366	507	Wakulla	60	736	1,106
Indian River	641	8,270	16,971	Walton	328	3,101	5,749
Jackson	189	2,161	3,788	Washington	65	730	1,190
Jefferson	61	368	542	Statewide 1/	328	14,696	39,416
Lafayette	19	151	271	Out-of-state 2/	106	266	1,402
Lake	927	13,470	26,790	Unknown 1/	719	2,280	9,409

NAICS North American Industry Classification System. See Glossary for definition.
A/ Revised. B/ Preliminary.
1/ Reporting units without a fixed location within the state or of unknown county location.
2/ Employment based in Florida, but working out of the state or country.
Note: See Note on Table 16.44.
Source: State of Florida, Agency for Workforce Innovation, Labor Market Statistics, "Quarterly Census of Employment and Wages" (ES-202), Annual NAICS files, Internet site <http://www.labormarketinfo.com/index.htm> (accessed 17, July 2007).

Table 16.46. AUTOMOTIVE DEALERS AND GASOLINE SERVICE STATIONS: AVERAGE MONTHLY PRIVATE REPORTING UNITS, EMPLOYMENT, AND PAYROLL COVERED BY UNEMPLOYMENT COMPENSATION LAW IN THE STATE AND COUNTIES OF FLORIDA, 2006

County	Number of reporting units	Number of employees	Payroll ($1,000)	County	Number of reporting units	Number of employees	Payroll ($1,000)
	Automotive dealers and gasoline service stations (NAICS code 441)						
Florida	9,070	135,300	496,301	Lee	306	4,899	19,518
				Leon	135	1,967	6,120
Alachua	93	1,767	6,039	Levy	16	172	448
Baker	12	67	141	Madison	8	30	48
Bay	108	1,367	4,226	Manatee	137	2,078	7,204
Bradford	9	116	262	Marion	176	2,408	8,208
Brevard	279	3,910	12,956	Martin	119	1,419	5,553
Broward	934	15,500	65,090	Miami-Dade	1,275	15,324	59,869
Calhoun	12	57	123	Monroe	62	472	1,575
Charlotte	75	1,116	3,599	Nassau	25	232	748
Citrus	74	926	3,074	Okaloosa	119	1,602	5,230
Clay	77	939	2,756	Okeechobee	22	223	614
Collier	137	2,267	9,200	Orange	561	9,108	32,697
Columbia	47	598	1,724	Osceola	96	970	3,125
DeSoto	12	221	680	Palm Beach	495	8,278	32,740
Dixie	8	36	83	Pasco	186	2,308	7,358
Duval	470	8,952	36,804	Pinellas	440	7,658	27,069
Escambia	165	2,534	7,854	Polk	282	4,035	13,732
Flagler	24	238	671	Putnam	45	492	1,222
Franklin	4	22	69	St. Johns	58	824	2,763
Gadsden	21	186	545	St. Lucie	102	1,633	5,349
Gilchrist	3	8	12	Santa Rosa	52	445	1,089
Gulf	5	20	38	Sarasota	166	3,420	12,829
Hamilton	5	14	34	Seminole	213	3,513	12,351
Hardee	15	108	248	Sumter	18	168	388
Hendry	12	174	611	Suwannee	23	189	501
Hernando	50	632	1,936	Taylor	15	130	334
Highlands	54	737	2,174	Union	5	16	32
Hillsborough	540	11,171	41,165	Volusia	293	3,651	11,697
Holmes	7	43	90	Wakulla	10	58	114
Indian River	60	765	2,539	Walton	21	116	293
Jackson	27	328	1,005	Washington	11	58	106
Jefferson	6	27	49	Statewide 1/	16	188	931
Lake	137	1,886	6,334	Unknown 1/	69	350	1,823

NAICS North American Industry Classification System. See Glossary for definition.
1/ Reporting units without a fixed location within the state or of unknown county location.
Note: Private employment. Data are preliminary. For a list of four-digit code industries included see Table 16.43. Only counties for which data are disclosed are shown. Detail may not add to totals due to disclosure editing and/or rounding. See Tables 23.70, 23.72, 23.73, and 23.74 for public employment data.

Source: State of Florida, Agency for Workforce Innovation, Labor Market Statistics, "Quarterly Census of Employment and Wages" (ES-202), Annual NAICS files, Internet site <http://www.labormarketinfo.com/index.htm> (accessed 17, July 2007).

Table 16.47. AUTOMOBILE DEALERS: AVERAGE MONTHLY PRIVATE REPORTING UNITS EMPLOYMENT, AND PAYROLL COVERED BY UNEMPLOYMENT COMPENSATION LAW IN THE STATE AND COUNTIES OF FLORIDA, 2006

County	Number of reporting units	Number of employees	Payroll ($1,000)	County	Number of reporting units	Number of employees	Payroll ($1,000)
		Automobile dealers (NAICS code 4411)					
Florida	3,461	88,553	366,096	Madison	4	13	21
				Manatee	52	1,131	4,520
Alachua	34	1,180	4,340	Marion	73	1,328	5,397
Bay	37	819	3,000	Martin	31	725	3,226
Bradford	3	77	200	Miami-Dade	454	10,352	46,866
Brevard	109	2,564	9,581	Monroe	7	148	595
Broward	322	11,229	50,997	Nassau	7	142	520
Charlotte	25	632	2,434	Okaloosa	36	981	3,752
Citrus	27	551	2,198	Okeechobee	4	71	227
Clay	25	483	1,772	Orange	275	6,285	24,668
Collier	55	1,577	7,207	Osceola	46	558	2,126
Columbia	18	332	1,134	Palm Beach	184	5,863	25,616
Duval	175	6,190	28,503	Pasco	82	1,544	5,569
Escambia	74	1,695	5,974	Pinellas	183	5,120	19,586
Flagler	6	67	274	Polk	115	2,665	10,076
Gadsden	10	97	314	Putnam	15	300	850
Hardee	10	72	185	St. Johns	18	489	1,906
Hendry	5	132	536	St. Lucie	44	1,024	3,746
Hernando	12	355	1,350	Santa Rosa	16	221	657
Highlands	25	473	1,499	Sarasota	63	2,501	10,373
Hillsborough	218	6,755	28,250	Seminole	106	2,704	10,072
Indian River	26	498	1,884	Suwannee	13	133	391
Jackson	10	227	750	Taylor	4	53	160
Lake	52	1,196	4,702	Volusia	116	2,164	7,682
Lee	110	3,016	13,861	Washington	3	14	35
Leon	54	1,337	4,721	Statewide 1/	4	3	18
Levy	4	99	327	Unknown 1/	27	46	458

NAICS North American Industry Classification System. See Glossary for definition.
1/ Reporting units without a fixed location within the state or of unknown county location.
Note: Private employment. Data are preliminary. For a list of other four-digit code industries see Table 16.43. Only counties for which data are disclosed are shown. Detail may not add to totals due to disclosure editing and/or rounding. See Tables 23.70, 23.72, 23.73, and 23.74 for public employment data.

Source: State of Florida, Agency for Workforce Innovation, Labor Market Statistics, "Quarterly Census of Employment and Wages" (ES-202), Annual NAICS files, Internet site <http://www.labormarketinfo.com/index.htm> (accessed 17, July 2007).

Table 16.48. AUTO PARTS, ACCESSORIES, AND TIRE STORES: AVERAGE MONTHLY PRIVATE REPORTING UNITS, EMPLOYMENT, AND PAYROLL COVERED BY UNEMPLOYMENT COMPENSATION LAW IN THE STATE AND COUNTIES OF FLORIDA, 2006

County	Number of reporting units	Number of employees	Payroll ($1,000)	County	Number of reporting units	Number of employees	Payroll ($1,000)
	Auto parts, accessories, and tire stores (NAICS code 4413)						
Florida	3,764	29,845	73,945	Lee	119	867	2,180
				Leon	65	508	1,129
Alachua	51	455	1,282	Levy	9	60	95
Baker	4	29	47	Madison	4	17	28
Bay	48	336	723	Manatee	49	661	1,880
Bradford	6	39	62	Marion	66	621	1,432
Brevard	99	861	2,146	Martin	34	242	639
Broward	307	1,973	5,264	Miami-Dade	653	3,838	9,181
Calhoun	8	33	63	Monroe	9	74	169
Charlotte	28	222	513	Nassau	14	60	143
Citrus	21	171	303	Okaloosa	59	365	758
Clay	37	364	753	Okeechobee	8	62	132
Collier	57	410	1,169	Orange	242	2,025	5,290
Columbia	21	187	362	Osceola	36	286	625
DeSoto	8	60	124	Palm Beach	193	1,830	5,124
Dixie	4	13	26	Pasco	70	505	1,003
Duval	223	1,806	4,857	Pinellas	152	1,361	3,392
Escambia	69	629	1,321	Polk	126	941	2,260
Flagler	10	115	221	Putnam	24	154	285
Gadsden	8	48	89	St. Johns	21	164	410
Gilchrist	3	8	12	St. Lucie	35	405	1,078
Gulf	5	20	38	Santa Rosa	27	193	376
Hamilton	4	10	19	Sarasota	56	463	1,103
Hardee	5	36	63	Seminole	79	624	1,667
Hendry	7	42	73	Sumter	10	108	229
Hernando	30	201	379	Suwannee	8	52	96
Highlands	16	179	482	Taylor	6	45	100
Hillsborough	245	2,933	6,665	Union	3	12	28
Holmes	4	28	60	Volusia	110	843	2,232
Indian River	20	163	366	Walton	14	78	169
Jackson	15	94	199	Washington	8	44	71
Jefferson	4	23	32	Statewide 1/	7	148	758
Lake	51	366	776	Unknown 1/	21	196	908

NAICS North American Industry Classification System. See Glossary for definition.
1/ Reporting units without a fixed location within the state or of unknown county location.
Note: Private employment. Data are preliminary. For a list of other four-digit code industries see Table 16.43. Only counties for which data are disclosed are shown. Detail may not add to totals due to disclosure editing and/or rounding. See Tables 23.70, 23.72, 23.73, and 23.74 for public employment data.

Source: State of Florida, Agency for Workforce Innovation, Labor Market Statistics, "Quarterly Census of Employment and Wages" (ES-202), Annual NAICS files, Internet site <http://www.labormarketinfo.com/index.htm> (accessed 17, July 2007).

Table 16.49. FURNITURE AND HOME FURNISHINGS STORES: AVERAGE MONTHLY PRIVATE REPORTING UNITS, EMPLOYMENT, AND PAYROLL COVERED BY UNEMPLOYMENT COMPENSATION LAW IN THE STATE AND COUNTIES OF FLORIDA, 2006

County	Number of reporting units	Number of employees	Payroll ($1,000)	County	Number of reporting units	Number of employees	Payroll ($1,000)
		Furniture and home furnishings stores (NAICS code 442)					
Florida	4,722	45,296	118,530	Madison	3	15	29
				Manatee	72	505	1,152
Alachua	54	539	1,168	Marion	65	556	1,290
Bay	55	434	922	Martin	68	644	1,707
Bradford	4	52	144	Miami-Dade	614	5,014	12,777
Brevard	130	1,050	2,672	Monroe	22	106	224
Broward	535	4,948	14,089	Nassau	11	44	81
Charlotte	55	363	835	Okaloosa	66	477	997
Citrus	32	177	268	Okeechobee	7	30	52
Clay	35	483	884	Orange	246	2,682	7,228
Collier	155	1,179	3,255	Osceola	35	230	529
Columbia	16	130	323	Palm Beach	429	3,396	8,116
Duval	193	2,049	5,170	Pasco	71	422	854
Escambia	66	721	1,755	Pinellas	210	1,644	3,728
Flagler	19	39	100	Polk	121	1,110	2,694
Franklin	5	76	220	Putnam	12	68	143
Gadsden	9	50	80	St. Johns	49	285	534
Hardee	3	12	43	St. Lucie	45	218	561
Hendry	7	31	62	Santa Rosa	19	96	280
Hernando	24	216	513	Sarasota	137	1,185	3,102
Highlands	27	176	379	Seminole	138	1,658	4,131
Hillsborough	244	2,938	7,811	Sumter	7	99	244
Indian River	53	393	930	Suwannee	6	29	46
Jackson	9	51	76	Taylor	5	34	64
Lake	61	371	897	Volusia	114	1,077	2,830
Lee	196	2,906	9,406	Walton	31	256	681
Leon	59	568	1,425	Washington	3	10	13
Levy	7	26	51	Unknown 1/	33	136	533

NAICS North American Industry Classification System. See Glossary for definition.
1/ Reporting units without a fixed location within the state or of unknown county location.
Note: Private employment. Data are preliminary. For a list of four-digit code industries included see Table 16.43. Only counties for which data are disclosed are shown. Detail may not add to totals due to disclosure editing and/or rounding. See Tables 23.70, 23.72, 23.73, and 23.74 for public employment data.

Source: State of Florida, Agency for Workforce Innovation, Labor Market Statistics, "Quarterly Census of Employment and Wages" (ES-202), Annual NAICS files, Internet site <http://www.labormarketinfo.com/index.htm> (accessed 17, July 2007).

Table 16.50. FOOD AND BEVERAGE STORES: AVERAGE MONTHLY PRIVATE REPORTING UNITS EMPLOYMENT, AND PAYROLL COVERED BY UNEMPLOYMENT COMPENSATION LAW IN THE STATE AND COUNTIES OF FLORIDA, 2006

County	Number of reporting units	Number of employees	Payroll ($1,000)	County	Number of reporting units	Number of employees	Payroll ($1,000)
		Food and beverage stores (NAICS code 445)					
Florida	8,785	194,018	319,161	Leon	92	3,320	4,872
Alachua	106	3,452	4,934	Levy	28	381	534
Baker	12	196	267	Liberty	4	29	29
Bay	86	1,798	2,885	Madison	6	161	223
Bradford	15	201	346	Manatee	150	3,451	5,520
Brevard	224	5,052	7,969	Marion	130	2,914	4,534
Broward	833	19,872	33,366	Martin	69	2,023	3,563
Calhoun	6	161	185	Miami-Dade	1,333	25,690	42,482
Charlotte	53	1,660	2,766	Monroe	65	1,391	2,760
Citrus	53	1,306	1,930	Nassau	30	625	1,011
Clay	58	1,572	2,395	Okaloosa	79	1,639	2,683
Collier	140	4,089	7,612	Okeechobee	32	381	552
Columbia	29	357	576	Orange	540	11,257	19,085
DeSoto	11	179	284	Osceola	109	2,133	3,416
Dixie	12	147	165	Palm Beach	622	15,003	26,284
Duval	453	9,166	16,455	Pasco	161	4,114	6,320
Escambia	143	2,245	3,430	Pinellas	494	11,188	17,574
Flagler	23	778	1,119	Polk	257	4,545	7,016
Franklin	16	200	251	Putnam	35	573	848
Gadsden	34	319	387	St. Johns	69	2,221	3,510
Gilchrist	6	84	98	St. Lucie	118	2,130	3,459
Glades	4	52	63	Santa Rosa	28	766	1,065
Gulf	9	177	229	Sarasota	186	4,763	8,077
Hamilton	12	86	102	Seminole	177	4,729	7,815
Hardee	18	173	252	Sumter	26	544	802
Hendry	34	692	754	Suwannee	17	228	341
Hernando	59	1,585	2,404	Taylor	8	133	213
Highlands	38	928	1,322	Volusia	232	5,308	8,460
Hillsborough	585	12,637	20,401	Wakulla	8	176	259
Holmes	18	148	157	Walton	37	651	1,110
Indian River	75	1,530	2,839	Washington	8	74	103
Jackson	26	451	537	Statewide 1/	24	290	1,214
Lake	110	2,643	4,237	Out-of-state 2/	3	14	118
Lee	239	6,807	11,698	Unknown 1/	54	212	626

NAICS North American Industry Classification System. See Glossary for definition.
1/ Reporting units without a fixed location within the state or of unknown county location.
2/ Employment based in Florida, but working out of the state or country.
Note: Private employment. Data are preliminary. For a list of four-digit code industries included see Table 16.43. Only counties for which data are disclosed are shown. Detail may not add to totals due to disclosure editing and/or rounding. See Tables 23.70, 23.72, 23.73, and 23.74 for public employment data.

Source: State of Florida, Agency for Workforce Innovation, Labor Market Statistics, "Quarterly Census of Employment and Wages" (ES-202), Annual NAICS files, Internet site <http://www.labormarketinfo.com/index.htm> (accessed 17, July 2007).

Table 16.52. CLOTHING AND CLOTHING ACCESSORIES STORES: AVERAGE MONTHLY PRIVATE REPORTING UNITS, EMPLOYMENT, AND PAYROLL COVERED BY UNEMPLOYMENT COMPENSATION LAW IN THE STATE AND COUNTIES OF FLORIDA, 2006

County	Number of reporting units	Number of employees	Payroll ($1,000)	County	Number of reporting units	Number of employees	Payroll ($1,000)
	Clothing and clothing accessories stores (NAICS code 448)						
Florida	10,502	103,286	163,508	Manatee	171	1,853	2,548
				Marion	88	822	1,093
Alachua	126	1,306	1,316	Martin	93	826	1,141
Baker	3	15	20	Miami-Dade	2,146	18,668	32,764
Bay	93	736	981	Monroe	143	693	1,236
Bradford	6	26	29	Nassau	28	154	218
Brevard	213	1,957	2,606	Okaloosa	156	2,020	2,797
Broward	1,142	9,874	15,877	Okeechobee	10	64	116
Charlotte	52	569	702	Orange	729	9,596	15,333
Citrus	37	301	385	Osceola	84	1,002	1,312
Clay	63	511	643	Palm Beach	908	9,719	17,180
Collier	279	2,291	4,430	Pasco	94	980	1,225
Columbia	21	142	174	Pinellas	461	3,973	5,791
DeSoto	4	33	26	Polk	170	1,375	1,676
Duval	470	5,863	9,899	Putnam	18	86	113
Escambia	145	1,462	1,818	St. Johns	125	1,123	1,545
Gadsden	8	38	41	St. Lucie	42	314	371
Hardee	5	34	36	Santa Rosa	24	202	271
Hendry	6	31	46	Sarasota	257	2,092	3,186
Hernando	33	240	307	Seminole	239	2,619	3,439
Highlands	29	190	231	Sumter	8	71	76
Hillsborough	574	6,014	9,406	Suwannee	8	28	38
Holmes	3	5	9	Taylor	4	18	25
Indian River	119	988	1,862	Volusia	192	2,015	2,422
Jackson	19	131	169	Wakulla	5	13	14
Jefferson	4	6	7	Walton	58	624	968
Lake	72	636	795	Washington	5	14	15
Lee	366	3,655	5,521	Statewide 1/	59	2,410	5,217
Leon	155	2,296	2,288	Out-of-state 2/	16	38	144
Madison	4	31	28	Unknown 1/	91	354	1,411

NAICS North American Industry Classification System. See Glossary for definition.
1/ Reporting units without a fixed location within the state or of unknown county location.
2/ Employment based in Florida, but working out of the state or country.
Note: Private employment. Data are preliminary. For a list of four-digit code industries included see Table 16.43. Only counties for which data are disclosed are shown. Detail may not add to totals due to disclosure editing and/or rounding. See Tables 23.70, 23.72, 23.73, and 23.74 for public employment data.
Source: State of Florida, Agency for Workforce Innovation, Labor Market Statistics, "Quarterly Census of Employment and Wages" (ES-202), Annual NAICS files, Internet site <http://www.labormarketinfo.com/index.htm> (accessed 17, July 2007).

Table 16.53. GENERAL MERCHANDISE STORES: AVERAGE MONTHLY PRIVATE REPORTING UNITS, EMPLOYMENT, AND PAYROLL COVERED BY UNEMPLOYMENT COMPENSATION LAW IN THE STATE AND COUNTIES OF FLORIDA, 2006

County	Number of reporting units	Number of employees	Payroll ($1,000)	County	Number of reporting units	Number of employees	Payroll ($1,000)
		General merchandise stores (NAICS code 452)					
Florida	2,511	179,031	298,974	Leon	36	3,096	4,455
Alachua	35	2,026	3,092	Manatee	41	3,211	5,443
Bay	38	2,356	3,922	Marion	54	3,748	5,911
Brevard	71	6,145	9,421	Martin	21	1,668	2,544
Broward	194	13,742	22,866	Miami-Dade	355	17,226	31,393
Calhoun	4	22	26	Monroe	11	386	619
Charlotte	18	2,238	3,661	Nassau	13	852	1,154
Citrus	18	1,123	1,684	Okaloosa	33	2,760	4,586
Clay	25	2,277	3,452	Orange	138	11,532	19,773
Collier	31	2,988	5,673	Osceola	38	3,722	5,940
Columbia	10	737	1,230	Palm Beach	147	12,560	23,696
Dixie	4	25	29	Pasco	64	4,305	6,643
Duval	132	9,579	15,898	Pinellas	114	7,926	13,419
Escambia	54	3,998	6,698	Polk	96	6,047	9,416
Gulf	5	29	31	Putnam	13	671	1,013
Hernando	26	2,050	3,136	St. Johns	18	862	1,408
Highlands	15	864	1,336	Sarasota	44	3,142	5,308
Hillsborough	136	11,294	19,029	Seminole	59	5,388	8,638
Indian River	18	1,786	2,763	Union	3	17	17
Lake	40	3,336	5,008	Volusia	60	5,237	8,346
Lee	76	5,954	10,159	Unknown 1/	14	29	83

NAICS North American Industry Classification System. See Glossary for definition.
1/ Reporting units without a fixed location within the state or of unknown county location.
Note: Private employment. Data are preliminary. For a list of four-digit code industries included see Table 16.43. Only counties for which data are disclosed are shown. Detail may not add to totals due to disclosure editing and/or rounding. See Tables 23.70, 23.72, 23.73, and 23.74 for public employment data.

Source: State of Florida, Agency for Workforce Innovation, Labor Market Statistics, "Quarterly Census of Employment and Wages" (ES-202), Annual NAICS files, Internet site <http://www.labormarketinfo.com/index.htm> (accessed 17, July 2007).

Table 16.81. GROSS AND TAXABLE SALES: SALES REPORTED TO THE DEPARTMENT OF REVENUE BY KIND OF BUSINESS IN FLORIDA, 2006

(amounts rounded to thousands of dollars)

Code	Kind of business Description	Gross sales	Change 1/	Taxable sales	Change 1/
	Total	895,361,248	11.52	334,828,571	6.82
	Food and beverage group	86,470,465	9.22	46,427,008	6.00
01	Grocery stores	49,109,413	11.41	14,601,261	4.87
02	Meat markets	195,255	-11.68	17,097	7.89
03	Seafood dealers	270,548	30.49	29,576	13.16
04	Vegetable and fruit markets	277,261	3.50	48,023	18.36
05	Bakeries	668,926	-3.46	268,499	7.57
06	Delicatessens	779,181	4.78	486,796	11.12
07	Candy and confectionery	1,286,598	-9.52	494,852	-0.47
08	Restaurants and lunchrooms	30,951,140	7.86	27,841,049	6.95
09	Taverns and night clubs	2,932,143	3.27	2,639,855	2.44
	Apparel group	13,044,821	9.96	11,217,605	7.71
10	Clothing stores, alterations	11,316,569	10.36	9,651,708	7.67
11	Shoe stores	1,728,251	7.43	1,565,897	7.97
	General merchandise group	111,914,237	9.70	52,707,762	7.76
17	Feed, seed, and fertilizer stores	1,759,883	-5.00	488,207	38.85
18	Hardware, paints, machinery	6,134,086	-2.82	3,456,695	10.75
19	Farm implements and supplies	6,537,895	17.55	3,950,361	-3.55
20	General merchandise stores	95,256,968	9.77	43,748,920	8.20
21	Second-hand stores	1,801,347	64.57	775,201	24.83
22	Dry goods stores	424,058	0.62	288,379	-0.51
	Automotive group	132,155,051	8.29	62,519,836	1.55
23	Motor vehicle dealers	87,155,265	4.18	49,182,480	0.47
24	Auto accessories, tires, parts	9,397,046	9.41	4,254,178	8.03
25	Filling and service stations	13,657,777	6.79	1,340,283	4.91
26	Garages, auto paint, and body shops	6,605,892	7.38	4,455,095	7.45
27	Aircraft dealers	5,099,232	11.60	334,994	7.49
28	Motorboat and yacht dealers	10,239,839	62.98	2,952,805	0.51
	Furniture and appliances group	67,429,844	7.84	25,032,550	3.79
29	Furniture stores, new and used	11,729,182	6.38	8,049,498	2.94
30	Household appliances	6,222,671	5.09	3,800,334	6.24
31	Store and office equipment	6,739,350	0.48	3,394,806	2.09
32	Music stores, radios, televisions	42,738,641	9.94	9,787,913	4.18
	Lumber, builders, contractors group	43,644,077	13.77	24,333,233	8.08
33	Building contractors	7,949,913	27.85	1,498,034	12.07
34	Heating and air conditioning	7,071,888	18.22	2,589,573	15.48
35	Electrical and plumbing	700,285	78.91	168,954	98.85
36	Decorating, painting, papering	2,709,124	47.03	1,800,201	70.45
37	Roofing and sheet metal	549,391	8.36	257,735	15.09
38	Lumber and building materials	24,663,476	5.30	18,018,735	2.55
	General classification group	433,216,847	11.97	111,005,482	8.68
39	Hotels, apartment houses, etc. 2/	16,154,790	5.87	14,905,908	5.36
41	Barber and beauty shops	2,206,692	6.80	803,725	-1.13
42	Book stores	1,835,183	9.45	1,145,151	4.90
43	Cigar stands and tobacco shops	302,168	3.18	134,704	5.51
44	Florists	869,876	9.05	378,313	7.61
45	Fuel and L.P. gas dealers	11,638,422	13.65	781,698	12.68
46	Funeral directors and monuments	263,417	-0.69	25,385	-0.01
47	Scrap metal, junk yards	1,128,377	90.52	56,542	12.20
48	Itinerant vendors	1,545,438	5.92	510,351	4.09
49	Laundry and cleaning services	779,742	18.84	318,543	17.91
50	Machine shops and foundries	4,768,929	53.22	592,440	39.91

See footnotes at end of table.

Continued . . .

Table 16.81. GROSS AND TAXABLE SALES: SALES REPORTED TO THE DEPARTMENT OF REVENUE BY KIND OF BUSINESS IN FLORIDA, 2006 (Continued)

(amounts rounded to thousands of dollars)

Code	Description	Gross sales	Change 1/	Taxable sales	Change 1/
	General classification group (Continued)				
51	Horse, cattle, pet dealers	2,185,903	-18.11	545,300	-16.52
52	Photographers, photo and art supplies	1,426,560	3.08	747,687	-0.20
53	Shoe repair shops	35,757	25.16	12,415	3.90
54	Storage and warehousing	605,446	15.21	415,280	12.01
55	Gift, card, novelty shops	3,164,799	-3.52	2,116,001	0.22
56	Newsstands	283,769	91.60	55,996	8.55
57	Social clubs and associations	695,996	19.33	575,654	15.27
58	Industrial machinery equipment	11,344,025	1.08	2,838,586	2.51
59	Admissions	9,523,073	13.52	7,290,127	8.14
60	Holiday season vendors	66,990	41.45	45,680	41.15
61	Rental of tangible property	14,930,387	13.43	7,629,656	8.23
62	Fabrication and sales of cabinets	4,692,894	18.93	1,771,364	22.11
63	Manufacturing and mining	72,530,985	18.83	10,968,314	13.80
64	Bottlers, soft drinks, etc.	1,278,155	-26.92	121,409	-12.94
65	Pawn shops	357,347	17.41	221,367	6.18
66	Communications	3,664,819	1.13	1,499,120	-0.09
67	Transportation	1,281,222	34.10	195,923	28.15
68	Graphic arts and printing	7,709,302	5.80	1,802,125	9.10
69	Insurance, banking, etc.	1,174,122	-31.75	442,247	-8.14
70	Sanitary and industrial supplies	3,698,768	1.94	1,264,217	5.39
71	Packaging materials and paper boxes	1,743,384	5.48	245,486	15.02
72	Repair of tangible personal property	6,124,801	9.31	1,929,538	8.87
73	Advertising	2,870,299	-10.54	338,786	14.37
74	Top soil, clay, sand, fill dirt	3,147,256	23.53	845,178	25.79
75	Trading stamp redemption centers	10,629	1,004.10	4,432	871.94
76	Nurseries and landscaping	3,140,836	23.31	887,094	19.62
77	Vending machines	937,331	5.08	477,382	7.98
78	Importing and exporting	22,587,968	23.10	970,572	17.79
79	Medical, dental, surgical, optical	11,981,598	3.87	625,036	-7.31
80	Wholesale dealers	131,997,911	15.66	12,585,916	17.73
81	Schools and colleges	567,440	38.73	134,966	9.18
82	Office space and commercial rentals	25,969,492	9.51	20,862,475	10.21
83	Parking lots, boat docking, storage	710,584	5.79	552,506	7.80
84	Utilities, electricity or gas	27,065,141	18.71	6,753,377	23.14
87	Motion picture industry	726,355	45.00	513,120	37.74
90	Flea markets	172,727	5.81	82,424	-4.94
92	Other professional services	3,776,175	52.54	393,979	45.44
93	Other personal services	6,649,240	16.54	2,508,259	8.53
94	Other industrial services	894,325	37.43	83,728	16.60
95	Governmental, public sector	411,931	39.79	121,514	29.08
96	Social services, public interest organizations	8	74.33	8	74.33
98	Commercial fisherman	20,902	25.14	3,111	106.79
99	Miscellaneous	7,053,065	1.75	1,460,463	-9.13

1/ Percentage change from 2005.
2/ Includes sales reported under categories 85 and 89; hotels, apartment houses, etc.
Note: Audited sales reported to the Florida Department of Revenue for the 6% regular sales tax, 6% use tax, and 3% vehicle and farm equipment sales tax. Sales occurred, for the most part, from December 1, 2005, through November 30, 2006. Data are not comparable with U.S. census data.

Source: State of Florida, Department of Revenue, unpublished data prepared by the University of Florida, Bureau of Economic and Business Research.

Table 16.82. GROSS AND TAXABLE SALES: SALES REPORTED TO THE DEPARTMENT OF REVENUE IN THE STATE AND COUNTIES OF FLORIDA, 2005 AND 2006

(amounts rounded to thousands of dollars)

County	Gross sales 2005	Gross sales 2006	Gross sales Percentage change	Taxable sales 2005	Taxable sales 2006	Taxable sales Percentage change
Florida	802,889,236	895,361,248	11.5	313,461,537	334,828,571	6.8
Alachua	6,561,037	7,317,222	11.5	3,355,806	3,796,217	13.1
Baker	1,571,914	1,521,017	-3.2	131,328	133,905	2.0
Bay	5,130,196	5,729,097	11.7	2,947,951	3,115,204	5.7
Bradford	385,363	476,879	23.7	184,627	224,220	21.4
Brevard	15,819,248	16,826,384	6.4	7,368,728	7,393,751	0.3
Broward	78,837,794	92,957,940	17.9	29,697,000	32,779,429	10.4
Calhoun	138,543	199,946	44.3	55,741	57,685	3.5
Charlotte	3,926,186	4,051,291	3.2	2,491,569	2,489,977	-0.1
Citrus	2,441,682	2,616,698	7.2	1,374,322	1,435,030	4.4
Clay	3,419,706	3,728,982	9.0	1,797,546	1,880,520	4.6
Collier	11,380,614	12,295,944	8.0	6,829,235	7,025,880	2.9
Columbia	1,791,374	2,700,469	50.7	837,957	916,890	9.4
DeSoto	831,758	1,429,234	71.8	271,047	273,741	1.0
Dixie	211,616	503,418	137.9	75,232	76,858	2.2
Duval	38,136,809	42,332,115	11.0	14,888,482	15,921,737	6.9
Escambia	9,393,486	9,722,037	3.5	4,687,993	4,574,171	-2.4
Flagler	1,423,814	1,661,189	16.7	736,996	770,842	4.6
Franklin	232,350	244,183	5.1	141,536	140,694	-0.6
Gadsden	1,002,862	1,099,463	9.6	280,132	289,427	3.3
Gilchrist	138,064	147,024	6.5	56,093	60,008	7.0
Glades	110,041	114,920	4.4	29,549	31,351	6.1
Gulf	213,646	231,272	8.3	101,085	109,157	8.0
Hamilton	135,827	169,180	24.6	45,332	48,491	7.0
Hardee	448,526	510,327	13.8	166,205	167,906	1.0
Hendry	1,237,096	1,388,912	12.3	339,630	363,963	7.2
Hernando	5,810,859	5,883,798	1.3	1,443,119	1,584,588	9.8
Highlands	2,039,543	2,137,464	4.8	1,107,077	1,124,746	1.6
Hillsborough	55,391,975	58,484,186	5.6	21,806,276	22,904,109	5.0
Holmes	221,391	231,947	4.8	73,554	76,729	4.3
Indian River	3,752,256	3,950,315	5.3	2,214,844	2,146,524	-3.1
Jackson	1,052,693	1,112,084	5.6	417,359	435,175	4.3
Jefferson	152,281	170,248	11.8	49,016	51,950	6.0
Lafayette	93,260	103,896	11.4	23,984	24,271	1.2
Lake	6,258,837	6,861,261	9.6	3,405,532	3,693,022	8.4
Lee	19,206,735	21,059,157	9.6	11,590,866	12,661,797	9.2
Leon	6,952,732	7,156,299	2.9	3,738,369	3,870,122	3.5
Levy	773,572	803,261	3.8	314,313	334,440	6.4

See footnotes at end of table. Continued . . .

Table 16.82. GROSS AND TAXABLE SALES: SALES REPORTED TO THE DEPARTMENT OF REVENUE IN THE STATE AND COUNTIES OF FLORIDA, 2005 AND 2006 (Continued)

(amounts rounded to thousands of dollars)

County	Gross sales 2005	Gross sales 2006	Gross sales Percentage change	Taxable sales 2005	Taxable sales 2006	Taxable sales Percentage change
Liberty	97,715	91,739	-6.1	22,275	19,564	-12.2
Madison	195,391	222,759	14.0	75,110	76,687	2.1
Manatee	9,246,345	9,938,298	7.5	4,280,945	4,476,411	4.6
Marion	9,548,942	10,446,580	9.4	4,319,768	4,704,899	8.9
Martin	5,911,541	6,154,611	4.1	3,019,612	3,170,236	5.0
Miami-Dade	103,274,017	122,584,979	18.7	35,154,113	39,247,887	11.6
Monroe	3,654,661	3,833,720	4.9	2,434,133	2,561,819	5.2
Nassau	1,643,380	1,781,476	8.4	700,835	753,904	7.6
Okaloosa	6,963,577	7,043,866	1.2	3,526,006	3,507,887	-0.5
Okeechobee	988,428	1,067,524	8.0	460,930	471,029	2.2
Orange	61,976,433	70,920,585	14.4	30,751,002	32,392,761	5.3
Osceola	9,002,575	9,667,939	7.4	3,727,309	3,935,907	5.6
Palm Beach	43,480,376	47,593,662	9.5	22,079,073	23,481,737	6.4
Pasco	8,205,958	9,153,737	11.5	4,262,637	4,593,838	7.8
Pinellas	32,750,332	34,447,795	5.2	13,597,265	13,951,253	2.6
Polk	25,737,879	28,538,097	10.9	7,106,103	7,497,227	5.5
Putnam	1,668,647	1,531,417	-8.2	587,693	603,065	2.6
St. Johns	3,792,340	4,283,245	12.9	2,290,940	2,466,309	7.7
St. Lucie	7,381,730	8,164,925	10.6	2,877,208	2,900,527	0.8
Santa Rosa	2,218,560	2,191,138	-1.2	1,103,397	1,079,006	-2.2
Sarasota	12,418,014	13,633,622	9.8	6,907,242	7,205,198	4.3
Seminole	15,324,710	16,883,581	10.2	7,186,047	7,595,579	5.7
Sumter	2,719,538	1,915,896	-29.6	568,314	734,793	29.3
Suwannee	704,690	866,094	22.9	303,028	401,892	32.6
Taylor	498,711	482,894	-3.2	186,483	191,050	2.4
Union	210,556	223,185	6.0	46,144	49,489	7.2
Volusia	13,399,970	14,447,680	7.8	6,773,063	6,972,083	2.9
Wakulla	232,329	280,699	20.8	119,694	139,381	16.4
Walton	1,798,217	2,005,141	11.5	1,164,968	1,268,620	8.9
Washington	297,632	279,348	-6.1	146,699	132,219	-9.9
Out-of-state	129,025,450	144,311,337	11.8	22,557,354	25,188,870	11.7
In/out state 1/	1,894,903	2,444,621	29.0	50,716	72,924	43.8

1/ Reports that have not yet been allocated to counties.

Note: Taxable sales are audited by the Department of Revenue; gross sales are unaudited and may contain significant inaccuracies and different reporting conventions by taxpayers. Taxable sales are sales subject to the 6 percent regular sales tax and 3 percent vehicle and farm equipment sales tax. Sales occurred, for the most part, December 1, 2004 through November 30, 2006. Kind of business data for counties are available from the Bureau of Economic and Business Research, University of Florida. Data are not comparable with retail sales reported by the U.S. Bureau of the Census.

Source: State of Florida, Department of Revenue, unpublished data prepared by the University of Florida, Bureau of Economic and Business Research.

FINANCE, INSURANCE, AND REAL ESTATE

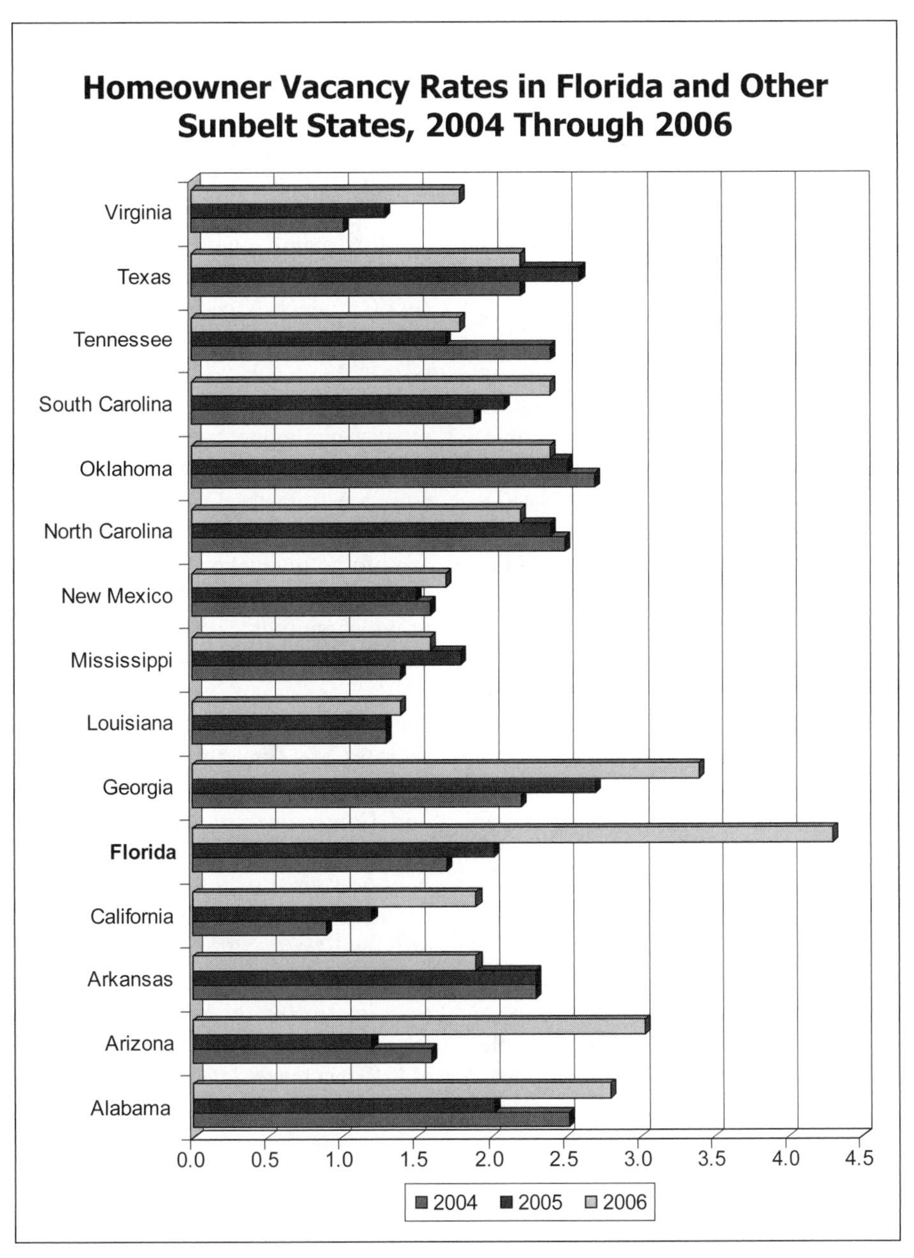

Source: Table 17.47

Section 17.00
Finance, Insurance, and Real Estate

This section provides statistics on the finance, insurance, and real estate industries in Florida. Tables include information on establishments, employment, revenue, and payroll; the banking industry; insurance carriers; real estate, including rental and leasing; homeowner and vacancy rates; life insurance companies, including policies, purchases, benefit payments, premium receipts, mortgages, and agency owned real estate; and other Florida, accident and health, and property and casualty insurance.

Explanatory notes. Changes in the industry classification system resulted in a separation of the finance and insurance industries from those that are real estate. Under the North American Industry Classification System (NAICS), the NAICS code 52 represents the finance and insurance industries and code 53 represents the real estate and rental and leasing industry. Finance and insurance industries covered in this section are primarily credit intermediation and related activities (522); securities, commodity contracts, investments (523); insurance carriers and related activities (524); and funds, trusts, and other financial vehicles (525). Real estate rental and leasing encompasses real estate (531), rental and leasing services (532), and lessors of nonfinancial intangible assets (533).

Sources. Table 17.01 at the front of section 17.00 depicts the finance and insurance industry by kind of business based on the NAICS classification system (See Glossary) as reported in the *2002 Economic Census: Finance and Insurance* published by the U.S. Census Bureau. Table 17.46 depicts county-level census real estate data from the *2002 Economic Census: Real Estate and Rental and Leasing.*

Historical and recent summaries of banking data for Florida are published by the state Office of Financial Regulation in *Annual Report of the Division of Banking.* Another major source of banking data is the Federal Deposit Insurance Corporation (FDIC), which issues *Statistics on Banking* and *FDIC/OTS Summary of Deposits.*

Current figures on the number of establishments, employment, and payroll for the finance and insurance industry by NAICS code are from the Office of Labor Market Statistics in the Florida Agency for Workforce Innovation, (See the introduction to Section 6.00.) The same agency provides similar data for the real estate and rental and leasing industry in the state.

Data on homeowner and rental vacancy rates are from the U.S. Census Bureau, published in *Housing Vacancies and Homeownership Annual Statistics.*

A basic source of information on activities of insurance companies in Florida is provided by the Florida Department of Insurance in the *Florida Office of Insurance Regulation Annual Report.* Data on life insurance are from the American Council of Life Insurance, *Life Insurers Fact Book.*

Section 17.00
Finance, Insurance, and Real Estate

Tables listed by major heading

Section 17.00
Finance, Insurance, and Real Estate—Continued

Tables listed by major heading

Table 17.01. FINANCE AND INSURANCE: ESTABLISHMENTS, EMPLOYMENT, REVENUE AND PAYROLL BY KIND OF BUSINESS IN FLORIDA, 2002

NAICS code	Industry	Number of establishments	Number of employees 1/	Revenue ($1,000)	Annual payroll ($1,000)
52	Finance and insurance	28,053	341,471	(NA)	15,993,236
521	Monetary authorities—central bank	2	538	435,844	25,760
522	Credit intermediation and related activities	12,230	177,192	(NA)	7,401,276
5221	Depository credit intermediation	6,191	106,245	(NA)	4,142,134
52211	Commercial banking 2/	4,677	83,267	(NA)	3,279,320
52212	Savings institutions 2/	820	11,870	(NA)	497,925
52213	Credit unions 3/	685	(NA)	(D)	(D)
5222	Nondepository credit intermediation	3,518	44,586	17,367,788	2,270,530
52221	Credit card issuing	32	5,669	1,587,533	262,707
52222	Sales financing	478	7,876	5,590,628	400,249
52229	Other nondepository credit intermediation	3,008	31,041	10,189,627	1,607,574
5223	Activities related to credit intermediation	2,521	26,361	4,984,502	988,612
52231	Mortgage and nonmortgage loan brokers	1,398	6,796	963,978	254,153
52232	Financial transactions processing, reserve, and clearinghouse activities	251	14,928	3,505,088	593,125
52239	Other activities related to credit intermediation	872	4,637	515,436	141,334
523	Securities intermediation and related activities	4,548	38,604	10,109,635	3,034,300
5231	Securities and commodity contracts intermediation and brokerage	2,100	28,274	7,239,852	2,349,193
52311	Investment banking and securities dealing	257	3,981	1,215,858	405,698
52312	Securities brokerage	1,710	23,536	5,895,082	1,907,284
52313	Commodity contracts dealing	41	158	38,841	8,792
52314	Commodity contracts brokerage	92	599	90,071	27,419
5239	Other financial investment activities 3/	2,446	(NA)	(D)	(D)
52391	Miscellaneous intermediation	416	1,402	537,683	73,817
52392	Portfolio management	715	5,285	1,649,149	409,210
52393	Investment advice	1,150	2,771	556,115	161,441
52399	All other financial investment activities 4/	165	(NA)	(D)	(D)
524	Insurance carriers and related activities	11,050	124,384	(NA)	5,496,438
5241	Insurance carriers 2/	2,133	72,222	(NA)	3,381,064
52411	Direct life, health, and medical insurance carriers 2/	824	35,939	(NA)	1,714,313
52412	Other direct insurance carriers 2/	1,251	35,747	(NA)	1,629,128
52413	Reinsurance carriers 2/	58	536	(NA)	37,623
5242	Agencies, brokerages, and other insurance related activities	8,917	52,162	7,061,722	2,115,374
52421	Insurance agencies and brokerages	8,043	38,734	5,408,698	1,571,859
52429	Other insurance related activities	874	13,428	1,653,024	543,515
525	Funds, trusts, and other financial vehicles (part)	223	753	570,186	35,462

(NA) Not available.
(D) Data withheld to avoid disclosure of information about individual industries.
1/ Paid employment for the pay period including March 12.
2/ Revenue not collected at this level of detail for multiestablishment firms.
Employment ranges: 3/ 10,000-24,999. 4/ 500-999.
Note: The economic censuses are conducted on a 5-year cycle collecting data for years ending in 2 and 7. Data are for North American Classification System (NAICS) code 52 and may not be comparable to earlier years. See Glossary for definition.

Source: U.S., Department of Commerce, Census Bureau, *2002 Economic Census: Finance and Insurance*, Geographic Area Series EC02-52A-FL, issued August 2005, Internet site <http://www.census.gov/> (accessed 11, May 2007).

Table 17.07. BANKING OFFICES: NUMBER OF FDIC-INSURED COMMERCIAL BANKS BY CHARTER CLASS AND OFFICE TYPE IN FLORIDA DECEMBER 31, 2004 AND 2005

Charter class	All offices	Commercial banks Total	Unit banks	Banks operating branches	Branches
Total by charter class	4,410	262	56	206	4,148
National	2,208	61	10	51	2,147
State	2,202	201	46	155	2,001
Member of Federal Reserve System	1,254	28	6	22	1,226
Nonmember of Federal Reserve System	948	173	40	133	775
Total in operation					
December 31, 2004	4,996	295	62	233	4,771
December 31, 2005	5,113	300	66	234	4,813
Net change	117	5	4	1	42
Beginning operation	(NA)	19	(NA)	(NA)	(NA)
Ceasing operation	(NA)	14	(NA)	(NA)	(NA)
Failed banks	(NA)	0	(NA)	(NA)	(NA)
Mergers, absorptions, and consolidations	(NA)	14	(NA)	(NA)	(NA)

(NA) Not available.

Table 17.08. BANKING ACTIVITY: NUMBER OF FDIC-INSURED COMMERCIAL BANKS AND AMOUNT OF ASSETS, LIABILITIES, AND DEPOSITS BY ASSET SIZE IN FLORIDA, DECEMBER 31, 2006

(in thousands of dollars)

Item	All commercial banks	Assets: Less than 100 million	100 million to one billion	More than one billion
Institutions reporting (number)	269	71	179	19
Employment (number)	24,930	1,650	13,582	9,698
Assets, total	113,033,887	4,393,954	54,888,057	53,751,876
Cash and due from depository institutions	4,012,236	227,818	2,111,038	1,673,380
Securities	18,787,232	761,003	8,820,694	9,205,535
Net loans and leases	80,560,676	2,680,090	39,249,655	38,630,931
Other real estate owned	30,491	113	24,065	6,313
Goodwill and other intangibles	1,486,291	13,947	367,784	1,104,560
Liabilities and capital, total	113,033,883	4,393,953	54,888,054	53,751,876
Liabilities	100,978,807	3,506,869	49,437,235	48,034,703
Equity capital	12,055,076	887,084	5,450,819	5,717,173
Deposits, total	85,929,544	3,307,564	44,366,349	38,255,631
Held in domestic offices	85,256,513	3,292,114	44,068,192	37,896,207
Transaction accounts	12,739,132	913,557	7,787,932	4,037,643
Nontransaction accounts	72,517,382	2,378,557	36,280,261	33,858,564
Time deposits, total	36,173,580	1,470,112	20,643,488	14,059,980
Less than $100,000	15,180,586	662,025	9,563,183	4,955,378
$100,000 or more	20,992,994	808,087	11,080,305	9,104,602
Held in foreign offices	673,031	15,450	298,157	359,424
Noninterest-bearing	5,346	5,346	0	0
Interest-bearing	667,685	10,104	298,157	359,424

Note: Asset size of bank determined from domestic and foreign consolidated assets.

Source for Tables 17.07 and 17.08: Federal Deposit Insurance Corporation, Division of Research and Statistics, *Statistics on Banking, 2006,* Internet site <http://www.fdic.gov/> (accessed 19, September 2007).

Table 17.09. BANKING ACTIVITY: NUMBER OF FDIC-INSURED COMMERCIAL AND SAVINGS BANKS AND BANKING OFFICES AND AMOUNT OF DEPOSITS IN THE STATE AND COUNTIES OF FLORIDA, JUNE 30, 2006

County	Number of banks 1/	Number of banking offices 2/	Deposits ($1,000,000)	County	Number of banks 1/	Number of banking offices 2/	Deposits ($1,000,000)
Florida	365	5,310	363,415	Lake	22	101	4,545
Alachua	14	64	2,843	Lee	37	203	10,861
Baker	2	3	176	Leon	14	81	3,989
Bay	17	56	2,423	Levy	3	13	326
Bradford	3	3	172	Liberty	1	1	7
Brevard	21	133	7,238	Madison	6	6	196
Broward	60	452	35,363	Manatee	28	115	5,265
Calhoun	4	6	160	Marion	21	89	4,776
Charlotte	17	60	3,418	Martin	18	62	3,791
Citrus	16	47	2,154	Miami-Dade	79	612	73,205
Clay	12	28	1,139	Monroe	10	54	2,387
Collier	36	131	10,665	Nassau	10	17	814
Columbia	6	16	876	Okaloosa	23	85	3,486
DeSoto	5	7	350	Okeechobee	7	10	543
Dixie	3	4	91	Orange	34	240	18,783
Duval	26	176	23,200	Osceola	16	57	2,383
Escambia	17	80	4,108	Palm Beach	64	489	37,193
Flagler	10	20	1,425	Pasco	24	109	5,412
Franklin	3	10	256	Pinellas	36	329	19,206
Gadsden	4	6	221	Polk	15	136	5,716
Gilchrist	3	5	115	Putnam	6	16	618
Glades	3	3	44	St. Johns	19	60	2,490
Gulf	6	8	249	St. Lucie	14	61	3,855
Hamilton	2	2	68	Santa Rosa	14	34	1,363
Hardee	3	5	352	Sarasota	41	183	11,284
Hendry	4	10	460	Seminole	32	135	6,027
Hernando	14	40	2,617	Sumter	7	18	642
Highlands	8	31	1,531	Suwannee	5	8	294
Hillsborough	45	296	18,125	Taylor	3	4	142
Holmes	3	3	169	Union	2	2	61
Indian River	17	58	3,686	Volusia	27	151	8,151
Jackson	9	17	479	Wakulla	4	9	222
Jefferson	2	2	121	Walton	14	32	890
Lafayette	2	2	55	Washington	4	4	143

1/ Number of banks in each county includes each bank operating at least one office within the county, regardless of the location of its main office; therefore, a bank operating a branch in a second county would be counted as a bank in each county, but only once in the state total.
2/ Includes each location at which deposit business is transacted.

Source: Federal Deposit Insurance Corporation, Division of Supervision, *FDIC/OTS Summary of Deposits,* June 30, 2006, Internet site <http://www3.fdic.gov/> (accessed 20, March 2007).

Table 17.20. STATE-CHARTERED BANKS AND TRUST COMPANIES: NUMBER, ASSETS CAPITAL ACCOUNTS, LOANS, AND DEPOSITS IN FLORIDA SPECIFIED YEARS 1895 THROUGH 2006

(amounts in thousands of dollars)

Year	Number	Assets	Capital accounts	Loans	Deposits
1895	21	1,692	666	943	974
1900	22	4,510	1,006	2,637	3,408
1905	41	14,338	3,222	9,332	10,291
1910	113	27,599	5,607	17,711	20,884
1915	192	42,656	9,811	26,280	30,527
1920	212	114,374	13,272	71,347	95,349
1925	271	539,101	33,427	309,492	501,553
1930	151	92,928	16,422	38,534	70,235
1935	102	64,276	9,768	13,662	53,552
1940	114	116,169	14,233	31,285	101,545
1945	112	450,838	20,135	36,851	430,256
1950	130	619,824	37,603	128,517	580,607
1955	146	1,138,114	67,726	329,340	1,064,763
1960	181	1,781,837	139,368	711,387	1,620,185
1965	243	2,571,685	216,444	1,139,398	2,541,195
1970	282	5,603,445	425,945	2,668,971	4,996,082
1975	449	11,757,147	989,185	5,860,781	10,346,695
1980	358	22,416,088	1,679,111	10,380,658	17,942,643
1985	251	24,160,155	1,627,920	13,372,532	21,321,726
1990	261	37,247,099	2,587,920	23,793,358	33,324,544
1991	260	39,051,128	2,852,114	24,076,458	35,021,312
1992	256	41,551,323	3,196,327	25,095,945	37,137,219
1993	248	51,271,342	4,265,301	32,194,235	44,490,477
1994	238	58,803,093	4,783,598	38,780,991	50,081,893
1995	224	58,344,123	5,143,296	38,320,163	49,393,436
1996	194	40,904,042	3,693,747	26,214,925	33,128,637
1997	180	35,464,125	3,266,522	23,194,221	28,937,982
1998	166	37,565,723	3,194,845	24,301,914	30,948,982
1999	182	41,547,418	3,527,556	27,790,873	33,141,500
2000	183	32,747,606	2,898,730	21,587,117	27,017,949
2001	185	34,522,545	3,054,353	22,710,763	28,848,026
2002	188	41,053,816	3,706,098	27,108,241	33,993,565
2003	194	45,857,980	4,215,925	31,037,365	37,629,271
2004	191	52,379,026	5,291,263	34,413,986	42,334,789
2005	205	63,349,176	6,464,610	46,095,000	50,549,292
2006	211	72,137,907	7,950,044	53,034,000	56,789,420

(NA) Not available.

Note: Data for 1990 through 2006 excludes nondeposit trust companies and industrial savings banks.

Source: State of Florida, Office of Financial Regulation, *Annual Report of the Division of Banking, 1995,* and unpublished data.

Table 17.21. STATE-CHARTERED BANKS AND TRUST COMPANIES: NUMBER ASSETS, AND DEPOSITS IN THE STATE AND COUNTIES OF FLORIDA, DECEMBER 31, 2006

(amounts in thousands of dollars)

County	Number	Assets	Deposits	County	Number	Assets	Deposits
Florida	210	72,137,907	56,885,944	Lafayette	1	61,519	54,056
				Lake	6	2,014,501	1,683,166
Alachua	3	735,742	598,699	Lee	7	1,718,481	1,328,798
Bay	1	257,491	221,575	Leon	5	3,576,174	2,868,655
Bradford	1	57,086	47,979	Levy	2	325,950	244,993
Brevard	5	507,817	507,817	Madison	1	50,581	43,808
Broward	11	2,585,780	2,029,336	Manatee	6	1,702,752	1,447,874
Charlotte	3	1,087,724	965,230	Marion	4	680,115	585,374
Citrus	4	375,385	314,862	Martin	2	555,904	457,167
Clay	1	170,100	152,448	Miami-Dade	24	16,289,774	12,819,002
Collier	8	4,969,815	3,637,866	Monroe	3	2,332,495	1,866,163
Columbia	2	265,238	226,167	Nassau	1	222,898	195,356
DeSoto	1	136,430	111,498	Okaloosa	6	1,689,268	1,411,300
Duval	8	1,651,229	1,374,303	Orange	8	8,620,411	6,148,698
Escambia	5	1,468,025	1,191,378	Osceola	1	424,008	320,081
Flagler	1	310,266	234,988	Palm Beach	12	2,250,706	1,797,491
Franklin	2	443,747	391,006	Pasco	1	61,251	44,385
Gilchrist	0	0	0	Pinellas	9	2,751,553	2,047,514
Gulf	1	276,503	238,689	Polk	4	1,235,358	1,024,048
Hardee	1	533,194	483,750	Putnam	1	154,027	127,860
Hendry	1	218,177	192,853	St. Johns	3	1,234,135	938,745
Hernando	2	114,323	90,244	St. Lucie	1	153,245	139,926
Highlands	1	295,880	264,139	Sarasota	7	1,527,923	1,257,722
Hillsborough	14	2,947,882	2,367,479	Seminole	2	562,264	312,610
Holmes	1	200,870	172,790	Taylor	1	71,351	54,755
Indian River	1	110,920	101,544	Volusia	8	849,629	717,020
Jackson	3	112,676	90,421	Wakulla	1	442,964	360,720
Jefferson	1	394,211	320,676	Walton	1	352,159	260,920

Source: State of Florida, Office of the Financial Regulation, unpublished data.

Table 17.23. STATE-CHARTERED BANKS AND TRUST COMPANIES: ASSETS, DEPOSITS CAPITAL, NET INCOME, AND NUMBER OF BANKS BY ASSET SIZE IN FLORIDA, DECEMBER 31, 2006

(in thousands of dollars, except where indicated)

Item	All banks	Less than 50 million	50-500 million	Over 500 million
Assets	72,137,907	568,558	31,703,504	39,865,845
Deposits	56,789,420	343,814	25,660,896	30,784,710
Capital	7,950,044	218,852	3,488,485	4,242,707
Net income 1/	790,909	-10,596	310,340	491,041
Number of institutions	210	18	161	31

1/ After taxes and extraordinary items.
Note: Nondeposit trust companies and industrial savings banks are excluded.

Table 17.24. INTERNATIONAL BANKS: NUMBER AND ASSETS OF AGENCIES BY NATION OF ORIGIN IN FLORIDA, DECEMBER 31, 2004, 2005 AND 2006

Nation of origin	2004 Number 1/	2004 Assets ($1,000)	2005 Number 1/	2005 Assets ($1,000)	2006 Number 1/	2006 Assets ($1,000)
Total	35	17,022,626	31	19,560,951	31	21,084,647
Argentina	1	65,199	1	69,019	1	92,716
Brazil	1	363,165	1	374,947	1	468,166
Chile	2	650,110	2	904,434	2	853,794
Colombia	3	261,097	3	346,417	3	528,973
Ecuador	1	98,499	1	100,593	1	109,715
England	0	0	0	0	2	9,908,715
France	3	1,485,105	2	1,369,318	2	1,485,727
Israel	2	282,337	2	511,665	2	666,685
Italy	1	31,187	1	35,085	1	36,876
Netherlands	1	822,408	1	861,764	1	1,021,160
Panama	1	280,908	1	198,436	1	228,246
Peru	1	351,791	1	368,245	1	333,132
Portugal	1	0	0	0	0	0
Puerto Rico	1	13,537	1	679,506	1	917,463
Spain	8	3,126,243	7	3,239,739	9	3,965,136
United Kingdom	3	9,091,675	2	10,297,613	1	0
Venezuela	2	99,365	2	204,170	2	468,143

1/ Total includes agencies reporting $0 assets.

Source for Tables 17.23 and 17.24: State of Florida, Office of Financial Regulation, unpublished data.

Table 17.30. CREDIT UNIONS: FINANCIAL CONDITION OF STATE-CHARTERED CREDIT UNIONS IN FLORIDA, DECEMBER 31, 2006

(in thousands of dollars, except where indicated)

Item	Amount	Item	Amount
Number of institutions 1/	94	Gross income, total	1,291,228
Net loans	12,543,060	Operating expense, total	1,133,446
Assets, total	18,181,946	Net income	157,781
Shares and deposits, total	15,239,885	Ratio of expense to $100 gross income (dollars)	87.8
Liabilities and equity, total	17,249,471		

1/ Does not include credit unions in liquidation.

Table 17.31. CREDIT UNIONS: ASSETS AND DEPOSITS OF STATE-CHARTERED CREDIT UNIONS IN THE STATE AND COUNTIES OF FLORIDA, DECEMBER 31, 2006

(amounts in thousands of dollars)

County	Number of institutions	Assets	Deposits	County	Number of institutions	Assets	Deposits
Florida	94	18,181,946	15,239,885	Lee	2	4,600	3,547
				Leon	8	789,247	668,842
Alachua	4	1,220,791	1,057,570	Madison	1	3,415	2,798
Bay	1	56,959	50,087	Marion	1	17,621	14,745
Brevard	2	1,710,893	1,456,012	Martin	1	12,898	11,004
Broward	7	3,040,915	2,333,285	Miami-Dade	11	1,540,137	1,247,451
Calhoun	1	23,764	20,066	Nassau	1	9,692	7,116
Clay	1	7,029	5,598	Orange	5	1,473,001	1,285,942
Duval	12	5,469,661	4,714,518	Palm Beach	4	235,931	177,238
Escambia	4	252,271	215,586	Pinellas	5	635,902	542,193
Gadsden	1	109,141	98,983	Polk	3	131,544	113,377
Hillsborough	6	543,798	428,181	Putnam	2	72,883	61,379
Holmes	1	10,904	8,284	Santa Rosa	1	16,285	13,705
Jackson	2	22,213	16,620	Sarasota	3	290,557	262,786
Jefferson	1	6,376	5,519	Taylor	1	16,349	13,335
Lake	1	414,154	366,717	Washington	1	43,015	37,402

Source for Tables 17.30 and 17.31: State of Florida, Office of Financial Regulation unpublished data.

Table 17.38. EMPLOYMENT AND PAYROLL: AVERAGE MONTHLY PRIVATE REPORTING UNITS EMPLOYMENT, AND PAYROLL COVERED BY UNEMPLOYMENT COMPENSATION LAW BY FINANCE AND INSURANCE INDUSTRY IN FLORIDA, 2005 AND 2006

NAICS code	Industry	Number of reporting units	Number of employees	Payroll ($1,000)
			2005 A/	
52	Finance and insurance	33,516	354,344	1,749,741
521	Monetary authorities - central bank	10	643	2,332
522	Credit intermediation and related activities	13,578	182,177	821,214
5221	Depository credit intermediation	4,999	99,443	408,566
5222	Nondepository credit intermediation	5,393	60,363	307,316
5223	Activities related to credit intermediation	3,186	22,371	105,331
523	Securities, commodity contracts, investments	7,289	37,481	320,022
5231	Securities and commodity contracts brokerage	2,823	25,124	233,970
5232	Securities and commodity exchanges	22	157	1,062
5239	Other financial investment activities	4,444	12,201	84,990
524	Insurance carriers and related activities	12,143	130,836	591,174
5241	Insurance carriers	2,900	71,144	335,338
5242	Insurance agencies, brokerages, and related	9,243	59,692	255,836
525	Funds, trusts, and other financial vehicles	496	3,206	15,000
5251	Insurance and employee benefit funds	112	1,366	6,038
5259	Other investment pools and funds	384	1,840	8,962
53	Real estate and rental and leasing	34,052	171,925	559,656
531	Real estate	29,224	123,933	420,216
5311	Lessors of real estate	6,238	34,095	98,475
5312	Offices of real estate agents and brokers	16,162	42,766	166,733
5313	Activities related to real estate	6,824	47,073	155,008
532	Rental and leasing services	4,642	46,715	129,514
5321	Automotive equipment rental and leasing	1,184	17,444	50,102
5322	Consumer goods rental	2,337	18,946	39,132
5323	General rental centers	362	3,058	9,974
5324	Machinery and equipment rental and leasing	759	7,267	30,307
533	Lessors of nonfinancial intangible assets	186	1,277	9,925

See footnotes at end of table.

Continued . . .

Table 17.38. EMPLOYMENT AND PAYROLL: AVERAGE MONTHLY PRIVATE REPORTING UNITS EMPLOYMENT, AND PAYROLL COVERED BY UNEMPLOYMENT COMPENSATION LAW BY FINANCE AND INSURANCE INDUSTRY IN FLORIDA, 2005 AND 2006 (Continued)

NAICS code	Industry	Number of reporting units	Number of employees	Payroll ($1,000)
			2006 B/	
52	Finance and insurance	35,894	365,645	1,880,013
521	Monetary authorities - central bank	27	611	2,635
522	Credit intermediation and related activities	14,681	190,586	888,802
5221	Depository credit intermediation	5,205	103,251	442,376
5222	Nondepository credit intermediation	5,752	61,303	317,693
5223	Activities related to credit intermediation	3,724	26,032	128,733
523	Securities, commodity contracts, investments	8,008	38,581	348,900
5231	Securities and commodity contracts brokerage	2,937	24,890	250,417
5232	Securities and commodity exchanges	19	57	412
5239	Other financial investment activities	5,052	13,633	98,072
524	Insurance carriers and related activities	12,694	132,939	623,957
5241	Insurance carriers	3,099	72,245	354,764
5242	Insurance agencies, brokerages, and related	9,595	60,695	269,193
525	Funds, trusts, and other financial vehicles	484	2,928	15,719
5251	Insurance and employee benefit funds	116	1,433	6,651
5259	Other investment pools and funds	368	1,495	9,067
53	Real estate and rental and leasing	36,443	178,294	589,818
531	Real estate	31,600	130,261	445,400
5311	Lessors of real estate	6,487	35,120	106,634
5312	Offices of real estate agents and brokers	18,018	45,603	172,904
5313	Activities related to real estate	7,095	49,537	165,862
532	Rental and leasing services	4,648	46,769	134,641
5321	Automotive equipment rental and leasing	1,208	17,129	48,942
5322	Consumer goods rental	2,302	18,265	39,936
5323	General rental centers	344	2,981	10,415
5324	Machinery and equipment rental and leasing	794	8,395	35,349
533	Lessors of nonfinancial intangible assets	195	1,264	9,776

NAICS North American Industry Classification System. See Glossary for definition.
A/ Revised.
B/ Preliminary.
Note: Private employment. Detail may not add to totals due to disclosure editing and/or rounding. See Tables 23.70, 23.72, 23.73, and 23.74 for public employment data.

Source: State of Florida, Agency for Workforce Innovation, Labor Market Statistics, "Quarterly Census of Employment and Wages" (ES-202), Annual NAICS files, Internet site <http://www.labormarketinfo.com/index.htm> (accessed 17, July 2007).

Table 17.39. EMPLOYMENT AND PAYROLL: AVERAGE MONTHLY PRIVATE REPORTING UNITS EMPLOYMENT, AND PAYROLL COVERED BY UNEMPLOYMENT COMPENSATION LAW IN THE STATE AND COUNTIES OF FLORIDA, 2005 AND 2006

County	Number of reporting units	Number of employees	Payroll ($1,000)	County	Number of reporting units	Number of employees	Payroll ($1,000)
		Finance and insurance, 2005 A/ (NAICS code 52)					
Florida	33,516	354,344	1,749,741	Lee	1,031	6,647	29,736
				Leon	452	4,979	21,356
Alachua	273	4,122	15,088	Levy	26	264	722
Baker	17	134	318	Madison	17	78	198
Bay	222	3,761	12,772	Manatee	457	2,586	10,211
Bradford	15	101	253	Marion	388	3,602	13,245
Brevard	718	5,178	20,191	Martin	313	1,817	10,599
Broward	3,991	42,611	207,516	Miami-Dade	4,893	45,998	260,024
Calhoun	15	66	132	Monroe	136	1,220	5,088
Charlotte	203	1,260	5,112	Nassau	73	451	1,549
Citrus	135	754	2,574	Okaloosa	341	3,036	11,120
Clay	186	895	3,113	Okeechobee	29	230	675
Collier	634	4,171	31,682	Orange	1,936	23,487	123,399
Columbia	54	342	1,586	Osceola	221	1,061	3,427
DeSoto	20	177	553	Palm Beach	3,254	24,460	157,669
Dixie	8	27	52	Pasco	454	2,386	7,837
Duval	1,677	44,633	208,635	Pinellas	2,020	23,194	109,480
Escambia	423	4,140	15,762	Polk	611	8,130	30,297
Flagler	109	584	2,361	Putnam	66	452	1,164
Franklin	17	101	361	St. Johns	294	1,395	7,477
Gadsden	24	184	531	St. Lucie	252	2,778	9,442
Gilchrist	11	54	158	Santa Rosa	136	572	1,968
Glades	3	11	23	Sarasota	876	7,273	41,652
Gulf	13	154	538	Seminole	949	10,187	44,864
Hamilton	4	21	39	Sumter	29	118	370
Hardee	18	220	597	Suwannee	29	327	1,000
Hendry	20	204	566	Taylor	17	132	426
Hernando	159	1,014	3,432	Union	5	16	35
Highlands	103	518	1,716	Volusia	676	4,029	14,197
Hillsborough	2,434	46,385	222,510	Wakulla	10	208	550
Holmes	12	171	545	Walton	55	296	958
Indian River	246	1,549	7,277	Washington	21	83	281
Jackson	54	312	880	Statewide 1/	407	5,233	36,436
Jefferson	12	126	452	Out-of-state 2/	47	136	1,747
Lake	301	1,862	6,828	Unknown 1/	860	1,601	16,266

See footnotes at end of table.

Continued . . .

Table 17.39. EMPLOYMENT AND PAYROLL: AVERAGE MONTHLY PRIVATE REPORTING UNITS EMPLOYMENT, AND PAYROLL COVERED BY UNEMPLOYMENT COMPENSATION LAW IN THE STATE AND COUNTIES OF FLORIDA, 2005 AND 2006 (Continued)

County	Number of reporting units	Number of employees	Payroll ($1,000)	County	Number of reporting units	Number of employees	Payroll ($1,000)
			Finance and insurance, 2006 B/ (NAICS code 52)				
Florida	35,894	365,645	1,880,013	Lee	1,116	6,794	30,423
				Leon	476	5,151	22,895
Alachua	288	4,288	16,479	Levy	29	277	832
Baker	19	147	325	Madison	16	83	218
Bay	226	3,683	12,960	Manatee	498	2,909	12,368
Bradford	18	118	276	Marion	425	3,899	15,204
Brevard	745	5,330	21,869	Martin	327	1,937	9,704
Broward	4,276	43,995	225,087	Miami-Dade	5,146	47,461	289,307
Calhoun	16	63	160	Monroe	129	1,227	5,469
Charlotte	235	1,551	5,968	Nassau	74	361	1,403
Citrus	144	786	2,776	Okaloosa	339	3,131	12,878
Clay	221	1,055	3,873	Okeechobee	34	260	873
Collier	661	4,250	29,779	Orange	2,040	23,013	119,511
Columbia	57	351	1,556	Osceola	259	1,197	3,874
DeSoto	22	177	580	Palm Beach	3,442	24,845	166,287
Dixie	8	31	68	Pasco	528	2,670	9,413
Duval	1,705	44,612	217,324	Pinellas	2,056	25,235	125,974
Escambia	436	5,064	19,470	Polk	689	8,291	32,675
Flagler	119	594	2,417	Putnam	72	488	1,398
Franklin	17	98	377	St. Johns	340	1,545	9,031
Gadsden	26	181	523	St. Lucie	265	2,909	10,456
Gilchrist	11	49	124	Santa Rosa	148	603	2,160
Gulf	18	167	578	Sarasota	934	7,117	43,355
Hamilton	6	32	54	Seminole	1,045	10,854	49,086
Hardee	17	243	725	Sumter	38	377	1,124
Hendry	21	218	655	Suwannee	30	320	996
Hernando	176	1,015	3,671	Taylor	16	136	482
Highlands	112	587	1,860	Union	6	13	32
Hillsborough	2,628	47,249	237,456	Volusia	714	4,146	15,171
Holmes	13	150	435	Walton	78	392	1,602
Indian River	249	1,604	7,910	Washington	21	88	274
Jackson	56	302	886	Statewide 1/	415	5,108	39,123
Jefferson	12	127	481	Out-of-state 2/	65	143	2,185
Lake	342	1,862	7,176	Unknown 1/	1,164	2,392	19,422

NAICS North American Industry Classification System. See Glossary for definition.
A/ Revised. B/ Preliminary.
1/ Reporting units without a fixed location within the state or of unknown county location.
2/ Employment based in Florida, but working out of the state or country.

Note: Private employment. For a list of three- and four-digit industries included see Table 17.38. Only counties for which data are disclosed are shown. Detail may not add to totals due to disclosure editing and/or rounding. See Tables 23.70, 23.72, 23.73, and 23.74 for public employment data.

Source: State of Florida, Agency for Workforce Innovation, Labor Market Statistics, "Quarterly Census of Employment and Wages" (ES-202), Annual NAICS files, Internet site <http://www.labormarketinfo.com/index.htm> (accessed 17, July 2007).

Table 17.40. CREDIT INTERMEDIATION AND RELATED ACTIVITIES: AVERAGE MONTHLY PRIVATE REPORTING UNITS, EMPLOYMENT, AND PAYROLL COVERED BY UNEMPLOYMENT COMPENSATION LAW IN THE STATE AND COUNTIES OF FLORIDA, 2006

County	Number of reporting units	Number of employees	Payroll ($1,000)	County	Number of reporting units	Number of employees	Payroll ($1,000)
	Credit intermediation and related activities (NAICS code 522)						
Florida	14,681	190,586	888,802	Leon	173	2,348	9,074
Alachua	110	1,314	4,227	Levy	14	211	628
Baker	11	95	242	Madison	6	54	143
Bay	82	3,007	10,122	Manatee	206	1,566	6,236
Bradford	10	84	213	Marion	162	2,740	10,544
Brevard	304	2,914	10,953	Martin	117	1,024	4,371
Broward	1,763	24,527	118,287	Miami-Dade	2,085	26,263	140,874
Calhoun	9	51	133	Monroe	58	942	3,637
Charlotte	97	1,033	3,666	Nassau	32	231	829
Citrus	58	469	1,588	Okaloosa	153	1,875	8,363
Clay	92	583	2,250	Okeechobee	17	162	596
Collier	266	2,398	15,725	Orange	878	11,892	53,357
Columbia	25	232	687	Osceola	131	810	2,574
DeSoto	12	134	451	Palm Beach	1,270	11,306	59,935
Duval	740	23,558	110,624	Pasco	226	1,460	5,141
Escambia	179	3,031	10,827	Pinellas	852	12,121	55,719
Flagler	53	389	1,545	Polk	269	2,206	7,822
Franklin	10	67	262	Putnam	32	297	838
Gadsden	12	145	351	St. Johns	131	875	3,558
Gilchrist	5	41	111	St. Lucie	112	2,406	8,598
Gulf	11	116	409	Santa Rosa	64	399	1,484
Hamilton	3	10	26	Sarasota	343	3,071	14,604
Hardee	6	217	677	Seminole	398	4,784	19,749
Hendry	8	146	491	Sumter	16	291	787
Hernando	72	562	2,071	Suwannee	11	233	805
Highlands	42	338	960	Taylor	8	105	378
Hillsborough	1,136	23,416	113,453	Volusia	293	2,363	7,564
Holmes	6	101	340	Walton	41	314	1,293
Indian River	89	741	3,642	Washington	7	53	128
Jackson	28	210	676	Statewide 1/	159	1,784	14,741
Lake	132	1,134	4,114	Out-of-state 2/	23	89	782
Lee	524	3,651	15,018	Unknown 1/	475	1,187	8,126

NAICS North American Industry Classification System. See Glossary for definition.
1/ Reporting units without a fixed location within the state or of unknown county location.
2/ Employment based in Florida, but working out of the state or country.
Note: Private employment. Data are preliminary. For a list of four-digit code industries included see Table 17.38. Only counties for which data are disclosed are shown. Detail may not add to totals due to disclosure editing and/or rounding. See Tables 23.70, 23.72, 23.73, and 23.74 for public employment data.

Source: State of Florida, Agency for Workforce Innovation, Labor Market Statistics, "Quarterly Census of Employment and Wages" (ES-202), Annual NAICS files, Internet site <http://www.labormarketinfo.com/index.htm> (accessed 17, July 2007).

Table 17.41. CREDIT INTERMEDIATION AND SECURITIES AND COMMODITY CONTRACTS BROKERAGE: AVERAGE MONTHLY PRIVATE REPORTING UNITS, EMPLOYMENT AND PAYROLL COVERED BY UNEMPLOYMENT COMPENSATION LAW IN THE STATE AND COUNTIES OF FLORIDA, 2006

County	Number of reporting units	Number of employees	Payroll ($1,000)	County	Number of reporting units	Number of employees	Payroll ($1,000)
			Depository credit intermediation (NAICS code 5221)				
Florida	5,205	103,251	442,376	Levy	11	207	622
				Madison	5	51	136
Alachua	50	1,060	3,329	Manatee	103	1,264	4,958
Baker	7	84	214	Marion	65	1,557	5,951
Bay	37	1,629	5,237	Martin	61	809	3,729
Bradford	5	67	175	Miami-Dade	584	16,449	84,907
Brevard	129	2,077	7,130	Monroe	29	896	3,482
Broward	452	8,752	39,341	Nassau	17	156	474
Calhoun	5	40	113	Okaloosa	75	1,446	5,152
Charlotte	56	848	2,885	Okeechobee	11	145	537
Citrus	41	420	1,473	Orange	297	5,998	24,643
Clay	34	308	890	Osceola	50	544	1,702
Collier	112	1,859	12,879	Palm Beach	502	7,676	37,722
Columbia	13	177	559	Pasco	106	1,065	3,304
DeSoto	6	97	262	Pinellas	298	4,457	17,369
Duval	264	11,722	53,394	Polk	138	1,716	5,643
Escambia	88	2,357	8,184	Putnam	17	258	719
Flagler	18	149	443	St. Johns	50	592	2,289
Gadsden	7	97	246	St. Lucie	49	2,221	7,851
Gulf	8	111	403	Santa Rosa	25	307	963
Hardee	4	204	619	Sarasota	147	2,076	9,009
Hendry	6	143	482	Seminole	99	1,871	6,457
Hernando	36	393	1,186	Sumter	13	285	774
Highlands	26	304	865	Suwannee	4	45	98
Hillsborough	344	9,753	39,248	Taylor	7	103	367
Holmes	5	88	278	Volusia	126	1,288	4,440
Indian River	46	645	2,881	Walton	24	274	907
Jackson	18	167	474	Washington	4	44	113
Lake	77	971	3,557	Statewide 1/	22	191	2,300
Lee	193	2,433	9,605	Out-of-state 2/	13	70	705
Leon	88	1,651	6,138	Unknown 1/	48	114	1,024
			Nondepository credit intermediation (NAICS code 5222)				
Florida	5,752	61,303	317,693	Calhoun	3	9	16
Alachua	48	234	842	Charlotte	23	101	491
Baker	4	11	28	Citrus	11	39	96
Bradford	5	17	38	Clay	41	218	1,165
Brevard	117	586	2,866	Collier	79	362	2,012
Broward	763	12,388	62,792	Columbia	9	47	109

See footnotes at end of table.

Continued . . .

Table 17.41. CREDIT INTERMEDIATION AND SECURITIES AND COMMODITY CONTRACTS BROKERAGE: AVERAGE MONTHLY PRIVATE REPORTING UNITS, EMPLOYMENT AND PAYROLL COVERED BY UNEMPLOYMENT COMPENSATION LAW IN THE STATE AND COUNTIES OF FLORIDA, 2006 (Continued)

County	Number of reporting units	Number of employees	Payroll ($1,000)	County	Number of reporting units	Number of employees	Payroll ($1,000)
			Nondepository credit intermediation (NAICS code 5222) (Continued)				
Duval	307	9,877	46,656	Okeechobee	6	17	59
Escambia	64	415	1,643	Orange	336	3,541	18,380
Flagler	21	195	983	Osceola	39	160	505
Hernando	25	135	793	Palm Beach	455	2,516	16,757
Highlands	10	18	57	Pasco	71	206	833
Hillsborough	487	9,209	48,926	Pinellas	319	3,799	16,439
Indian River	34	64	282	Polk	94	411	1,939
Jackson	9	42	201	Putnam	14	37	117
Lake	44	127	454	St. Johns	50	175	821
Lee	172	750	3,612	St. Lucie	41	118	522
Leon	53	546	2,270	Santa Rosa	26	63	398
Manatee	63	220	1,005	Sarasota	120	688	4,251
Marion	63	369	1,253	Seminole	201	2,108	10,343
Martin	32	151	418	Volusia	106	873	2,524
Miami-Dade	892	6,539	40,777	Walton	9	25	335
Monroe	11	20	50	Statewide 1/	85	1,280	10,429
Nassau	10	60	283	Out-of-state 2/	5	6	25
Okaloosa	57	300	2,635	Unknown 1/	251	601	4,461
			Activities related to credit intermediation (NAICS code 5223)				
Florida	3,724	26,032	128,733	Lake	11	36	103
Alachua	12	21	56	Lee	159	468	1,801
Bay	10	40	200	Leon	32	152	666
Brevard	58	250	957	Manatee	40	82	273
Broward	548	3,387	16,155	Martin	24	63	224
Charlotte	18	84	290	Miami-Dade	609	3,276	15,190
Citrus	6	10	20	Monroe	18	26	105
Clay	17	58	195	Okaloosa	21	129	576
Collier	75	177	834	Orange	245	2,354	10,333
Duval	169	1,958	10,574	Osceola	42	106	367
Escambia	27	259	1,000	Palm Beach	313	1,114	5,457
Flagler	14	44	120	Pasco	49	189	1,004
Hernando	11	35	93	Pinellas	235	3,864	21,911
Highlands	6	16	38	Polk	37	79	240
Hillsborough	305	4,454	25,278	St. Johns	31	108	448
Indian River	9	32	479	St. Lucie	22	68	225

See footnotes at end of table.

Continued . . .

Table 17.41. CREDIT INTERMEDIATION AND SECURITIES AND COMMODITY CONTRACTS BROKERAGE: AVERAGE MONTHLY PRIVATE REPORTING UNITS, EMPLOYMENT AND PAYROLL COVERED BY UNEMPLOYMENT COMPENSATION LAW IN THE STATE AND COUNTIES OF FLORIDA, 2006 (Continued)

County	Number of reporting units	Number of employees	Payroll ($1,000)	County	Number of reporting units	Number of employees	Payroll ($1,000)
Activities related to credit intermediation (NAICS code 5223) (Continued)							
Santa Rosa	13	30	123	Walton	8	14	51
Sarasota	76	308	1,344	Statewide 1/	52	313	2,012
Seminole	98	806	2,949	Out-of-state 2/	5	13	52
Volusia	61	202	599	Unknown 1/	176	472	2,642
Securities and commodity contracts brokerage (NAICS code 5231)							
Florida	2,937	24,890	250,417	Manatee	31	176	1,522
				Marion	32	170	1,389
Alachua	23	99	896	Martin	28	227	2,282
Bay	21	122	870	Miami-Dade	522	4,331	53,721
Brevard	77	463	3,689	Monroe	12	28	311
Broward	320	2,435	22,167	Nassau	6	8	47
Charlotte	26	157	1,120	Okaloosa	24	127	1,197
Citrus	14	52	412	Orange	143	1,546	13,601
Clay	15	49	375	Osceola	12	21	78
Collier	60	556	6,422	Palm Beach	377	3,644	45,000
Duval	101	2,089	15,234	Pasco	24	110	730
Escambia	29	211	1,859	Pinellas	156	2,495	20,751
Flagler	14	26	266	Polk	53	247	2,067
Hernando	16	58	363	St. Johns	35	214	2,895
Highlands	13	37	349	St. Lucie	15	29	140
Hillsborough	163	2,310	19,452	Santa Rosa	15	22	105
Indian River	26	148	1,443	Sarasota	102	819	10,324
Jackson	6	6	17	Seminole	60	432	3,798
Lake	32	75	530	Volusia	65	243	1,939
Lee	79	413	3,821	Statewide 1/	46	308	3,905
Leon	33	212	1,822	Unknown 1/	83	109	3,108

NAICS North American Industry Classification System. See Glossary for definition.
1/ Reporting units without a fixed location within the state or of unknown county location.
2/ Employment based in Florida, but working out of the state or country.
Note: Private employment. Data are preliminary. For a list of other finance and insurance industries see Table 17.38. Only counties for which data are disclosed are shown. Detail may not add to totals due to disclosure editing and/or rounding. See Tables 23.70, 23.72, 23.73, and 23.74 for public employment data.

Source: State of Florida, Agency for Workforce Innovation, Labor Market Statistics, "Quarterly Census of Employment and Wages" (ES-202), Annual NAICS files, Internet site <http://www.labormarketinfo.com/index.htm> (accessed 17, July 2007).

Table 17.43. INSURANCE CARRIERS AND RELATED ACTIVITIES: AVERAGE MONTHLY PRIVATE REPORTING UNITS, EMPLOYMENT, AND PAYROLL COVERED BY UNEMPLOYMENT COMPENSATION LAW IN THE STATE AND COUNTIES OF FLORIDA, 2006

County	Number of reporting units	Number of employees	Payroll ($1,000)	County	Number of reporting units	Number of employees	Payroll ($1,000)
		Insurance carriers and related activities (NAICS code 524)					
Florida	12,694	132,939	623,957	Leon	213	2,012	9,348
				Levy	15	66	204
Alachua	131	2,827	11,168	Madison	6	21	51
Baker	6	47	68	Manatee	177	984	4,038
Bay	106	523	1,841	Marion	175	863	2,908
Bradford	7	33	60	Martin	134	583	2,432
Brevard	277	1,760	6,561	Miami-Dade	1,639	14,039	69,942
Broward	1,555	15,489	73,980	Monroe	42	223	1,439
Calhoun	6	10	23	Nassau	28	116	455
Charlotte	91	328	1,090	Okaloosa	135	1,096	3,195
Citrus	54	243	694	Okeechobee	11	89	255
Clay	96	348	1,092	Orange	692	8,565	45,127
Collier	204	1,049	5,312	Osceola	72	270	1,020
Columbia	21	99	251	Palm Beach	1,041	7,037	38,495
DeSoto	8	41	127	Pasco	218	980	3,087
Dixie	5	17	38	Pinellas	746	9,610	43,020
Duval	686	17,731	83,377	Polk	287	4,933	19,420
Escambia	189	1,734	6,427	Putnam	32	173	520
Flagler	39	153	565	St. Johns	121	374	1,657
Franklin	6	31	112	St. Lucie	106	438	1,615
Gadsden	11	33	120	Santa Rosa	53	162	504
Gilchrist	3	6	9	Sarasota	311	2,782	15,166
Gulf	6	50	168	Seminole	444	5,285	24,010
Hardee	10	24	45	Sumter	13	47	120
Hendry	12	71	160	Suwannee	14	83	180
Hernando	68	357	1,082	Taylor	6	29	90
Highlands	46	171	467	Union	4	2	3
Hillsborough	960	20,461	98,373	Volusia	261	1,332	5,175
Holmes	6	48	93	Wakulla	3	12	39
Indian River	82	370	1,519	Walton	20	46	168
Jackson	21	84	192	Washington	12	34	140
Jefferson	6	17	30	Statewide 1/	144	2,769	18,018
Lake	134	572	2,256	Out-of-state 2/	32	43	620
Lee	379	2,523	10,633	Unknown 1/	251	572	3,531

NAICS North American Industry Classification System. See Glossary for definition.
1/ Reporting units without a fixed location within the state or of unknown county location.
2/ Employment based in Florida, but working out of the state or country.
Note: Private employment. Data are preliminary. For a list of four-digit code industries included see Table 17.38. Only counties for which data are disclosed are shown. Detail may not add to totals due to disclosure editing and/or rounding. See Tables 23.70, 23.72, 23.73, and 23.74 for public employment data.

Source: State of Florida, Agency for Workforce Innovation, Labor Market Statistics, "Quarterly Census of Employment and Wages" (ES-202), Annual NAICS files, Internet site <http://www.labormarketinfo.com/index.htm> (accessed 17, July 2007).

Table 17.44. INSURANCE CARRIERS, AGENCIES, BROKERAGES, AND RELATED INDUSTRIES AVERAGE MONTHLY PRIVATE REPORTING UNITS, EMPLOYMENT, AND PAYROLL COVERED BY UNEMPLOYMENT COMPENSATION LAW IN THE STATE AND COUNTIES OF FLORIDA, 2006

County	Number of reporting units	Number of employees	Payroll ($1,000)	County	Number of reporting units	Number of employees	Payroll ($1,000)
			Insurance carriers (NAICS code 5241)				
Florida	3,099	72,245	354,764	Marion	47	325	1,423
				Martin	19	72	391
Alachua	40	2,010	7,697	Miami-Dade	311	6,444	35,927
Bay	28	195	721	Monroe	11	27	147
Brevard	59	559	2,487	Nassau	6	23	67
Broward	332	8,521	41,811	Okaloosa	29	574	1,461
Charlotte	18	61	263	Orange	186	4,914	26,859
Citrus	12	76	240	Osceola	21	77	495
Clay	28	143	514	Palm Beach	214	2,143	11,775
Collier	53	295	1,515	Pasco	47	407	1,407
Columbia	5	31	79	Pinellas	193	4,567	19,776
Duval	240	13,237	64,335	Polk	81	3,725	15,026
Escambia	53	618	2,823	Putnam	8	64	255
Flagler	10	47	221	St. Johns	36	80	292
Hernando	13	76	215	St. Lucie	30	173	792
Highlands	6	17	57	Santa Rosa	16	40	160
Hillsborough	309	15,233	74,369	Sarasota	63	1,210	6,729
Indian River	21	98	490	Seminole	96	2,235	10,488
Jackson	6	29	80	Volusia	65	346	1,526
Lake	22	68	261	Walton	6	19	46
Lee	102	724	3,266	Statewide 1/	65	1,506	11,432
Leon	58	743	4,411	Out-of-state 2/	8	19	317
Manatee	33	169	841	Unknown 1/	62	147	905
			Insurance agencies, brokerages, and related (NAICS code 5242)				
Florida	9,595	60,695	269,193	Charlotte	73	267	826
				Citrus	42	167	454
Alachua	91	816	3,471	Clay	68	206	578
Baker	4	15	30	Collier	151	754	3,797
Bay	78	328	1,120	Columbia	16	68	172
Bradford	6	31	57	DeSoto	6	32	96
Brevard	218	1,201	4,074	Dixie	4	16	34
Broward	1,223	6,967	32,169	Duval	446	4,494	19,042
Calhoun	6	10	23	Escambia	136	1,116	3,604

See footnotes at end of table.

Continued. . .

Table 17.44. INSURANCE CARRIERS, AGENCIES, BROKERAGES, AND RELATED INDUSTRIES AVERAGE MONTHLY PRIVATE REPORTING UNITS, EMPLOYMENT, AND PAYROLL COVERED BY UNEMPLOYMENT COMPENSATION LAW IN THE STATE AND COUNTIES OF FLORIDA, 2006 (Continued)

County	Number of reporting units	Number of employees	Payroll ($1,000)	County	Number of reporting units	Number of employees	Payroll ($1,000)
Insurance agencies, brokerages, and related (NAICS code 5242) (Continued)							
Flagler	29	106	344	Nassau	22	93	387
Franklin	4	21	90	Okaloosa	106	522	1,734
Gadsden	9	30	111	Okeechobee	10	84	241
Gilchrist	3	6	9	Orange	506	3,652	18,269
Gulf	5	50	168	Osceola	51	193	525
Hardee	9	23	43	Palm Beach	827	4,894	26,720
Hendry	11	64	140	Pasco	171	574	1,680
Hernando	55	281	867	Pinellas	553	5,042	23,245
Highlands	40	154	409	Polk	206	1,208	4,394
Hillsborough	651	5,229	24,004	Putnam	24	109	265
Holmes	6	48	93	St. Johns	85	295	1,366
Indian River	61	272	1,029	St. Lucie	76	265	822
Jackson	15	55	113	Santa Rosa	37	122	343
Jefferson	5	16	28	Sarasota	248	1,572	8,437
Lake	112	504	1,995	Seminole	348	3,050	13,523
Lee	277	1,799	7,367	Sumter	9	33	85
Leon	155	1,269	4,936	Suwannee	11	50	89
Levy	12	42	149	Taylor	5	29	90
Madison	6	21	50	Walton	196	986	3,649
Manatee	144	815	3,197	Walton	14	28	123
Marion	128	538	1,485	Washington	11	30	130
Martin	115	511	2,041	Statewide 1/	79	1,263	6,586
Miami-Dade	1,328	7,595	34,015	Out-of-state 2/	24	24	303
Monroe	31	196	1,292	Unknown 1/	189	425	2,626

NAICS North American Industry Classification System. See Glossary for definition.
1/ Reporting units without a fixed location within the state or of unknown county location.
2/ Employment based in Florida, but working out of the state or country.
Note: Private employment. Data are preliminary. For a list of other finance and insurance industries see Table 17.38. Only counties for which data are disclosed are shown. Detail may not add to totals due to disclosure editing and/or rounding. See Tables 23.70, 23.72, 23.73, and 23.74 for public employment data.

Source: State of Florida, Agency for Workforce Innovation, Labor Market Statistics, "Quarterly Census of Employment and Wages" (ES-202), Annual NAICS files, Internet site <http://www.labormarketinfo.com/index.htm> (accessed 17, July 2007).

Table 17.45. REAL ESTATE AND RENTAL AND LEASING: AVERAGE MONTHLY PRIVATE REPORTING UNITS, EMPLOYMENT, AND PAYROLL COVERED BY UNEMPLOYMENT COMPENSATION LAW IN THE STATE AND COUNTIES OF FLORIDA, 2006

County	Number of reporting units	Number of employees	Payroll ($1,000)	County	Number of reporting units	Number of employees	Payroll ($1,000)
Real estate and rental and leasing (NAICS code 53)							
Florida	36,443	178,294	589,818	Leon	422	2,210	4,994
				Levy	54	148	234
Alachua	350	1,913	4,670	Madison	15	38	58
Baker	15	38	37	Manatee	639	2,299	6,096
Bay	312	1,606	3,797	Marion	500	1,728	3,956
Bradford	23	58	127	Martin	350	1,279	4,682
Brevard	818	3,025	7,153	Miami-Dade	5,141	23,990	87,090
Broward	4,041	22,395	74,882	Monroe	357	1,067	2,873
Charlotte	330	1,061	2,535	Nassau	86	252	748
Citrus	204	558	1,098	Okaloosa	420	3,384	8,192
Clay	214	807	2,045	Okeechobee	53	126	313
Collier	1,143	3,605	12,749	Orange	2,284	18,930	71,822
Columbia	62	244	620	Osceola	479	2,538	7,804
DeSoto	38	145	220	Palm Beach	3,064	14,802	52,088
Dixie	6	9	21	Pasco	578	1,869	3,904
Duval	1,364	8,609	33,529	Pinellas	1,899	9,141	27,342
Escambia	431	2,225	5,637	Polk	705	2,933	7,523
Flagler	217	533	2,255	Putnam	66	170	322
Franklin	32	239	597	St. Johns	373	1,168	3,360
Gadsden	25	93	188	St. Lucie	361	1,318	3,702
Glades	6	15	25	Santa Rosa	201	611	1,269
Gulf	27	156	274	Sarasota	1,058	3,541	10,240
Hamilton	5	10	22	Seminole	890	3,978	15,469
Hardee	21	47	81	Sumter	57	202	332
Hendry	37	142	295	Suwannee	28	70	132
Hernando	201	515	936	Taylor	16	106	133
Highlands	142	445	962	Union	5	16	33
Hillsborough	2,070	12,178	47,457	Volusia	843	3,445	8,618
Holmes	8	31	51	Wakulla	21	51	84
Indian River	285	1,103	2,917	Walton	210	1,069	4,191
Jackson	45	164	247	Washington	18	45	53
Jefferson	8	16	17	Statewide 1/	168	3,691	14,380
Lake	461	1,748	4,528	Out-of-state 2/	21	122	636
Lee	1,625	6,630	20,388	Unknown 1/	481	1,500	6,540

NAICS North American Industry Classification System. See Glossary for definition.
1/ Reporting units without a fixed location within the state or of unknown county location.
2/ Employment based in Florida, but working out of the state or country.
Note: Private employment. Data are preliminary. For a list of three- and four-digit code industries included see Table 17.38. Only counties for which data are disclosed are shown. Detail may not add to totals due to disclosure editing and/or rounding. See Tables 23.70, 23.72, 23.73, and 23.74 for public employment data.

Source: State of Florida, Agency for Workforce Innovation, Labor Market Statistics, "Quarterly Census of Employment and Wages" (ES-202), Annual NAICS files, Internet site <http://www.labormarketinfo.com/index.htm> (accessed 17, July 2007).

Table 17.46. REAL ESTATE: ESTABLISHMENTS, EMPLOYMENT, AND PAYROLL IN THE STATE AND COUNTIES OF FLORIDA, 2002

County	Number of estab- lishments	Number of em- ployees 1/	Annual payroll ($1,000)	County	Number of estab- lishments	Number of em- ployees 1/	Annual payroll ($1,000)
Florida	25,009	136,409	3,905,597	Lake	296	1,045	25,416
Alachua	284	2,022	44,773	Lee	939	4,992	147,904
Baker	10	38	222	Leon	352	2,050	45,544
Bay	230	926	19,655	Levy	30	97	1,857
Bradford	14	67	1,219	Liberty 2/	1	(NA)	(D)
Brevard	609	2,597	60,005	Madison	6	28	320
Broward	2,797	16,288	519,879	Manatee	360	1,592	42,162
Calhoun	4	13	116	Marion	302	1,406	28,699
Charlotte	221	740	16,610	Martin	246	1,690	49,290
Citrus	139	456	9,683	Miami-Dade	3,921	20,060	580,181
Clay	135	544	11,848	Monroe	293	987	20,559
Collier	731	2,804	100,254	Nassau	59	236	5,522
Columbia	45	152	3,647	Okaloosa	337	2,255	42,622
DeSoto	31	105	1,833	Okeechobee	36	82	1,712
Dixie	6	16	190	Orange	1,526	15,770	448,805
Duval	1,039	7,421	273,606	Osceola	354	3,628	101,152
Escambia	353	1,432	32,796	Palm Beach	2,078	11,739	372,206
Flagler	88	225	7,426	Pasco	349	1,131	22,257
Franklin	28	147	5,094	Pinellas	1,467	6,109	158,459
Gadsden	23	50	1,009	Polk	544	2,794	62,492
Gilchrist	8	36	785	Putnam	55	249	6,577
Glades 2/	1	(NA)	(D)	St. Johns	244	906	19,709
Gulf	12	28	464	St. Lucie	210	772	17,645
Hamilton	4	12	109	Santa Rosa	108	330	5,619
Hardee	22	59	1,154	Sarasota	705	2,370	64,207
Hendry	27	90	1,392	Seminole	593	2,721	74,763
Hernando	125	359	6,582	Sumter	54	121	1,344
Highlands	82	281	6,284	Suwannee	22	79	1,318
Hillsborough	1,449	10,131	335,370	Taylor	11	40	386
Holmes	3	12	120	Union 2/	2	(NA)	(D)
Indian River	219	658	14,897	Volusia	620	2,594	57,673
Jackson	33	102	1,897	Wakulla	19	33	742
Jefferson	3	17	155	Walton	79	619	18,640
Lafayette 2/	2	(NA)	(D)	Washington	14	37	417

(NA) Not available.
(D) Data withheld to avoid disclosure of confidential information.
1/ Employment for the pay period including March 12th.
Employment range: 2/ 0-19.
Note: The economic censuses are conducted on a 5-year cycle collecting data for years ending in 2 and 7. Data are for North American Industry Classification System (NAICS) code 53 and may not be comparable to earlier years. See Glossary for definition.

Source: U.S., Department of Commerce, Census Bureau, *2002 Economic Census: Real Estate and Rental and Leasing*, Geographic Area Series EC02-53A-FL, Issued August 2005, Internet site <http://www.census.gov/> (accessed 11, May 2007).

Table 17.47. REAL ESTATE: HOMEOWNER AND RENTAL VACANCY RATES IN FLORIDA OTHER SUNBELT STATES, OTHER POPULOUS STATES, AND THE UNITED STATES, SPECIFIED YEARS 1990 THROUGH 2006

State	Homeowner vacancy rates					Rental vacancy rates				
	1990	2000	2004	2005	2006	1990	2000	2004	2005	2006
						Sunbelt states				
Florida	2.7	2.6	1.7	2.0	4.3	9.0	10.8	11.7	10.1	10.7
Alabama	1.5	2.3	2.5	2.0	2.8	8.1	14.4	14.8	13.2	13.4
Arizona	2.5	1.6	1.6	1.2	3.0	10.7	10.7	11.3	11.6	9.3
Arkansas	2.5	2.4	2.3	2.3	1.9	7.9	11.4	13.5	13.7	13.5
California	1.8	1.2	0.9	1.2	1.9	6.0	4.5	5.4	6.0	5.8
Georgia	1.8	1.9	2.2	2.7	3.4	9.4	9.7	16.3	14.6	13.0
Louisiana	1.7	1.7	1.3	1.3	1.4	13.1	11.2	7.3	8.8	7.9
Mississippi	1.6	2.0	1.4	1.8	1.6	8.7	11.6	12.5	13.2	12.9
New Mexico	2.4	2.4	1.6	1.5	1.7	13.7	13.2	8.1	7.7	8.1
North Carolina	1.6	1.9	2.5	2.4	2.2	7.2	11.2	13.3	13.8	11.7
Oklahoma	3.1	2.2	2.7	2.5	2.4	14.6	15.2	13.9	12.6	11.2
South Carolina	1.0	1.4	1.9	2.1	2.4	8.4	15.5	14.7	10.0	10.6
Tennessee	2.4	1.9	2.4	1.7	1.8	9.5	7.1	10.0	10.3	10.5
Texas	2.5	1.6	2.2	2.6	2.2	9.7	10.8	13.9	13.6	13.5
Virginia	1.7	2.2	1.0	1.3	1.8	5.8	7.7	11.4	7.8	8.3
						Other populous states				
Illinois	1.3	1.1	1.7	1.9	2.3	6.1	7.8	14.8	13.4	12.6
Indiana	1.5	1.1	2.5	2.4	3.2	5.3	10.6	12.9	14.2	14.0
Massachusetts	1.4	0.6	0.7	1.1	1.8	6.9	3.5	6.5	5.7	6.2
Michigan	1.1	1.3	2.2	2.7	3.4	7.3	9.6	13.0	13.1	18.1
New Jersey	1.8	1.0	0.7	1.2	1.6	5.9	4.3	6.2	6.2	7.3
New York	1.8	1.5	1.3	2.0	1.8	4.9	5.5	6.1	5.1	5.8
Ohio	1.2	1.3	2.1	2.6	2.7	5.5	9.0	13.0	13.4	12.3
Pennsylvania	1.1	1.4	1.4	1.6	1.6	7.2	8.3	11.7	10.0	10.6
United States	1.7	1.6	1.7	1.9	2.4	7.2	8.0	10.2	9.8	9.7

Note: Data are based on a monthly sample survey conducted by the Census Bureau. See Glossary for definitions.

Source: U.S., Department of Commerce, Census Bureau, *Housing Vacancies and Homeownership Annual Statistics: 2006,* Internet site <http://www.census.gov/> (accessed 20, March 2007).

Table 17.60. LIFE INSURANCE: COMPANIES, POLICIES, PURCHASES, BENEFIT PAYMENTS PREMIUM RECEIPTS, MORTGAGES, AND REAL ESTATE OWNED BY U.S. LIFE INSURANCE COMPANIES IN FLORIDA AND THE UNITED STATES, 2005

Item	Florida	United States
Purchases of individual life	109,218	1,734,093
Insurance in force		
Amount ($1,000,000)	1,142,814	22,213,142
Individual policies (1,000)	7,985	156,635
Amount ($1,000,000)	785,502	13,782,163
Group ($1,000,000)	349,717	8,276,672
Credit policies 1/ (1,000)	1,066	24,466
Amount ($1,000,000)	7,596	154,307
Insurance and annuity benefit payments ($1,000)	22,015,883	380,430,614
Policy and contract dividends	1,003,939	20,051,120
Death payments	3,539,123	58,144,589
Annuity payments	3,963,120	76,708,471
Surrender values	13,180,104	214,255,013
Other payments 2/	329,596	11,271,422
Payments to beneficiaries, total ($1,000)	3,539,123	58,144,589
Individual	2,392,871	37,973,267
Group	1,105,377	19,499,671
Credit	40,876	671,651
Premium receipts of companies ($1,000,000)	34,772	589,422
Life	6,981	123,414
Annuity	19,146	280,987
Health	6,900	108,739
Deposit-type funds	1,745	76,282
Mortgages owned by companies, total ($1,000)	17,971,566	287,464,259
Farm	1,143,677	13,926,062
Nonfarm	16,827,889	273,538,198
Real estate owned by companies	2,394,635	32,354,502

1/ Includes group credit certificates.
2/ Includes matured endowments, disability payments, and payments on guaranteed interest contracts.

Source: American Council of Life Insurers, *Life Insurers Fact Book, 2006,* Internet site <http://www.acli.org/> (accessed 26, March 2007).

Table 17.61. FLORIDA INSURANCE: EXPERIENCE BY TYPE OF INSURANCE IN FLORIDA, 2005

(amounts in thousands of dollars)

	Direct premiumns written	Direct losses paid	Direct premiumns earned	Direct losses incurred	Losses incurred/ premiums earned ratio (percentage)
Fire	325,675	205,455	298,222	367,071	123.10
Homeowners	4,960,334	6,050,601	4,429,998	6,728,392	151.90
Commercial multiple peril	1,659,797	1,799,460	1,578,676	2,265,112	143.50
Medical malpractice	660,598	238,262	716,143	271,411	37.90
Workers' compensation	3,225,696	1,260,963	3,108,528	1,792,140	57.70
Other liability	1,386,229	563,507	1,298,662	816,472	62.90
Private passenger auto liability	7,694,510	4,655,217	7,592,531	4,853,382	63.90
Commercial auto liability	1,305,519	725,280	1,243,220	815,522	65.60
Private passenger physical damage	3,038,214	2,444,285	2,994,381	2,534,495	84.60
Commercial auto physical damage	351,338	214,975	338,031	227,020	67.20
Product liability	126,006	36,898	118,979	63,400	53.30
Directors and officers liability	487,943	145,329	326,957	301,586	92.20

Table 17.62. ACCIDENT AND HEALTH INSURANCE: COVERAGES OF INTEREST BY COVERAGE TYPE IN FLORIDA, 2005

Coverage type	Direct premiums earned	Direct losses incurred	Covered lives	Average premium earned per life
Prepaid health services	9,124,298	0	35,728	255
Prepaid health clinic	8,719,816	5,628,393	13,020	670
Administrative services only (ASO)	2,431,857,746	2,229,743,231	1,405,933	1,730
Accident only	234,995,148	110,095,481	6,707,087	35
Accidental death and dismemberment	74,224,431	33,040,367	6,384,092	12
Blanket accident/sickness	6,292,335	3,919,454	462,604	14
Dental	821,762,138	580,083,619	5,472,854	150
Disability income	943,675,157	1,015,786,498	2,941,442	321
Excess/stop loss	229,649,345	164,836,425	1,131,051	203
Hospital indemnity	89,661,949	43,181,223	444,079	202
Limited benefits	227,177,718	124,808,206	1,202,489	189
Long term care	614,094,459	420,196,915	408,074	1,505
Short term care	11,164,002	10,057,464	7,966	1,401
Medicare supplement	1,339,746,906	1,131,958,403	768,095	1,744
Champus/Tricare supplement	2,111,681	1,528,038	5,272	401
Prescription drug	7,824,706	7,978,149	10,582	739
Sickness	923,358	467,102	4,498	205
Student	9,478,955	8,783,439	23,710	400
Travel	4,593,455	2,634,898	551,553	8
Vision	61,333,490	52,928,069	2,370,317	26

Source for Tables 17.61 and 17.62: State of Florida, Office of Insurance Regulation, *Florida Office of Insurance Regulation 2006 Annual Report,* Internet site <http://www.floir.com/> (accessed 16, August 2007).

Table 17.63. ACCIDENT AND HEALTH INSURANCE: PREMIUMS EARNED AND LOSSES INCURRED BY MAJOR MEDICAL PLANS IN FLORIDA, 2005

Market segment	Total direct premiums earned	Direct losses incurred	Loss ratio	Covered lives	Average earned premium per life
Fully regulated major medical plans, total (instate)	13,383,211,376	10,667,846,393	79.7	3,774,078	3,546
Guarantee issue	81,286,431	68,629,082	84.4	29,202	2,784
Individually underwritten	962,816,696	643,463,407	66.8	424,774	2,267
Sole proprietor	163,826,093	133,572,176	81.5	31,613	5,182
2-5 member groups	817,502,232	613,531,296	75.0	242,439	3,372
6-50 member groups	2,745,026,118	1,943,100,064	70.8	786,510	3,490
51 or more member groups	8,482,142,528	7,089,064,370	83.6	2,233,435	3,798
Short-term major medical	1,568	0	0.0	1	1,568
Conversion	130,609,710	176,485,998	135.1	26,104	5,003
Other major medical plans, total (out-of-state)	1,287,714,860	894,298,465	69.4	471,712	2,730
Group guarantee issue	12,295,544	13,046,342	106.1	1,482	8,297
Individually underwritten	481,718,925	270,691,466	56.2	223,236	2,158
Sole proprietor	5,820,464	5,209,311	89.5	1,155	5,039
2-5 member groups	25,626,557	19,995,660	78.0	3,839	6,675
6-50 member groups	24,196,681	16,662,645	68.9	7,127	3,395
51 or more member groups	737,092,634	567,219,518	77.0	234,621	3,142
Short-term major medical	349,555	210,131	60.1	154	2,270
Conversion	614,500	1,263,392	205.6	98	6,270

Table 17.64. AUTOMOBILE INSURANCE: EXPERIENCE OF VOLUNTARY PRIVATE PASSENGER AUTOMOBILE INSURANCE IN FLORIDA, 2002 THROUGH 2004

(amounts in dollars)

Item	Accident year		
	2002	2003	2004
Calendar year earned premium	8,904,866,369	10,194,342,996	11,067,974,548
Accident year paid losses	5,866,663,343	5,658,502,652	5,283,539,192
Accident year reserves outstanding	392,391,074	855,416,756	2,000,856,384
Allocated loss adjustment expense incurred	251,060,093	246,519,536	261,585,845
Unallocated loss adjustment expense incurred	864,928,804	910,838,292	1,038,267,350
Accident year incurred loss and loss adjustment expense	7,375,043,314	7,671,277,236	8,584,248,771
Developed loss and loss adjustment expense incurred	7,498,922,063	8,061,228,415	9,722,874,702
Policyholders dividends	22,634,961	15,279,139	11,384,765
All other expenses	1,907,215,073	2,107,396,064	2,300,828,730
Underwriting gain (or loss)	-523,905,728	10,439,378	-967,113,649

Note: Valuation as of March 31, 2005. Accident year refers to the year in which the accident occurred.

Source for Tables 17.63 and 17.64: State of Florida, Office of Insurance Regulation, *Florida Office of Insurance Regulation 2006 Annual Report*, Internet site <http://www.floir.com/> (accessed 16, August 2007).

Table 17.72. PROPERTY AND CASUALTY INSURANCE: PREMIUM AND LOSS SUMMARY BY LINE OF BUSINESS IN FLORIDA, 2005

Line of business	Direct premiumns written ($1,000)	Direct losses paid ($1,000)	Premiums written/ losses ratio (percentage)	Premiums earned/losses incurred ratio (percentage)
Total	32,010,135	23,682,271	0.74	0.83
Fire	339,936	201,550	0.59	1.12
Allied lines	412,661	878,479	2.13	3.04
Multiple peril crop	127,792	142,961	1.12	1.34
Federal flood	649,856	816,868	1.26	1.21
Farmowners multiple peril	22,008	34,155	1.55	1.00
Homeowners multiple peril	4,985,092	6,408,489	1.29	1.42
Commercial multiple peril (non-liability portion)	1,092,885	1,771,001	1.62	1.81
Commercial multiple peril (liability portion)	768,696	317,617	0.41	0.55
Mortgage guaranty	446,371	21,100	0.05	0.10
Ocean marine	261,902	173,731	0.66	1.00
Inland marine	740,179	351,445	0.47	0.52
Financial guaranty	115,050	294	0.00	0.01
Medical malpractice	618,763	388,034	0.63	0.42
Earthquake	8,660	14,055	1.62	1.77
Accident and health, total	272,752	162,756	0.39	0.69
Group accident and health	145,565	105,244	0.72	0.67
Credit A&H (group and individual)	20,437	2,452	0.12	0.07
Collectively renewable A&H	360	339	0.94	2.82
Non-cancelable A&H	15	82	5.53	5.53
Guaranteed renewable A&H	65,731	31,537	0.48	1.56
Non-renewable for stated reasons only	24,944	15,635	0.63	0.60
Other accident only	6,487	3,789	0.58	0.62
All other A&H	9,211	3,679	0.40	0.49
Workers' compensation	3,662,187	1,468,674	0.40	0.55
Other liability	1,876,020	849,359	0.45	0.55
Products liability	136,620	46,170	0.34	0.43
Automobile, total	14,300,941	9,322,857	0.11	0.71
Private passenger auto no-fault (PIP)	2,550,373	1,633,570	0.64	0.65
Other private passenger auto liability	6,176,114	3,747,424	0.61	0.65
Commercial auto no-fault (PIP)	70,171	39,733	0.57	0.64
Other commercial auto liability	1,549,682	879,158	0.57	0.65
Private passenger auto physical damage	3,519,879	2,763,652	0.79	0.82
Commercial auto physical damage	434,724	259,320	0.60	0.56
Aircraft (all perils)	142,476	73,600	0.52	0.81
Fidelity	54,581	20,579	0.38	0.41
Surety	345,380	-33,309	-0.10	-0.17
Burglary and theft	6,268	1,787	0.29	0.61
Boiler and machinery	46,436	32,784	0.71	0.39
Credit	52,989	21,587	0.41	0.74
Aggregate write-ins for other lines of business	523,632	195,646	0.37	0.56

PIP Personal injury protection.
Note: Excludes surplus lines carriers, Citizen Property Insurance Corporation, and risk retention groups.

Source: State of Florida, Office of Insurance Regulation, *Florida Office of Insurance Regulation 2006 Annual Report,* Internet site <http://www.floir.com/> (accessed 16, August 2007).

PERSONAL AND BUSINESS SERVICES

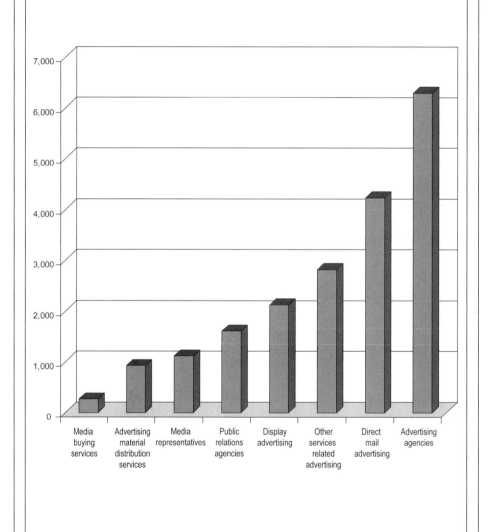

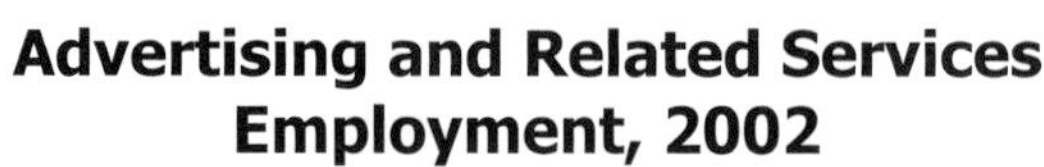

Source: Table 18.02

Section 18.00
Personal and Business Services

This section highlights Florida's personal and business services industries. Included are private establishments, employment, and payroll for a large list of services offered by businesses throughout the state.

Explanatory notes. Due to the development of the North American Industry Classification System (NAICS), an expansion of the services industry categories is the most significant change in the way industry data are reported. (See the introduction to Section 6.00 and the Glossary.) Services industries are presented in various sections throughout this volume, depending upon the nature of the service provided.

Industries reported in this chapter focus primarily on personal and business-related services and include administrative and support and waste management (56); professional, scientific, and technical services (54); and other services, except public administration (81). Information about establishments with other NAICS service-related codes are available in Sections 14.00, 19.00, 20.00, and 22.00.

Sources. Economic census data from several volumes of the *2002 Economic Census* published by the U.S. Census Bureau are represented in various tables at the beginning of this section. Volume titles include: *Administrative and Support and Waste Management and Remediation Services*; *Other Services;* and *Professional, Scientific, and Technical Services.* Each volume is available on the Census Bureau's Web site.

Current preliminary 2006 and revised 2005 establishment, employment, and payroll data by NAICS categories are from the Labor Market Statistics office of the Florida Agency for Workforce Innovation. (See the introduction to Section 6.00.)

Professional individuals licensed by the state operate many service establishments. Table 18.56 features licensed architects, interior designers, and accountants from the Florida Department of Business and Professional Regulation database on the Internet.

Section 18.00
Personal and Business Services

Tables listed by major heading

Tables listed by major heading

Table 18.01. ADMINISTRATIVE AND SUPPORT AND WASTE MANAGEMENT AND REMEDIATION SERVICES AND OTHER SERVICES: ESTABLISHMENTS, EMPLOYMENT, AND PAYROLL IN FLORIDA, 2002

NAICS code	Industry	Number of establishments	Number of employees 1/	Annual Payroll ($1,000)
56	Administrative and support and waste management and remediation services	27,437	991,958	23,087,482
561	Administrative and support services	26,631	976,071	22,520,309
5611	Office administrative services	1,871	22,013	906,141
5612	Facilities support services	194	11,067	428,828
5613	Employment services	2,661	683,383	15,725,340
5614	Business support services	2,880	63,266	1,345,338
5615	Travel arrangement and reservation services	2,354	27,314	824,637
5616	Investigation and security services	1,931	49,500	1,029,093
5617	Services to buildings and dwellings	13,292	99,292	1,830,634
5619	Other support services	1,448	20,236	430,298
562	Waste management and remediation services	806	15,887	567,173
5621	Waste collection	319	9,332	349,271
5622	Waste treatment and disposal	101	1,496	58,960
5629	Remediation and other waste management services	386	5,059	158,942
81	Other services (except public administration)	34,370	191,822	4,150,341
811	Repair and maintenance	14,439	66,457	1,649,793
8111	Automotive repair and maintenance	9,384	42,204	952,049
8112	Electronic and precision equipment repair and maintenance	1,149	7,244	250,315
8113	Commercial and industrial machinery and equipment (except auto and electronic) repair and maintenance	1,431	7,028	208,093
8114	Personal and household goods repair and maintenance	2,475	9,981	239,336
812	Personal and laundry services	13,043	75,363	1,250,802
8121	Personal care services	6,873	34,513	530,657
8122	Death care services	884	8,046	174,788
8123	Drycleaning and laundry services	2,521	19,469	330,287
8129	Other personal services	2,765	13,335	215,070
813	Religious, grantmaking, civic, professional, and similar organizations	6,888	50,002	1,249,746
8132	Grantmaking and giving services	708	6,133	212,821
8133	Social advocacy organizations	477	2,821	70,804
8134	Civic and social organizations	1,276	11,305	155,258
8139	Business, professional, labor, political, and similar organizations	4,427	29,743	810,863

1/ Paid employment for the pay period including March 12.

Note: The economic censuses are conducted on a 5-year cycle collecting data for years ending in 2 and 7. Data are for North American Industry Classification System (NAICS) codes 56 and 81 and may not be comparable to earlier years. See Glossary for definition.

Source: U.S., Department of Commerce, Census Bureau, *2002 Economic Census: Administrative and Support and Waste Management and Remediation Services,* Geographic Area Series EC02-56A-FL, issued August 2005, and *2002 Economic Census: Other Services (Except Public Administration),* Geographic Area Series EC02-81A-FL, issued August 2005, Internet site <http://www.census.gov/> (both accessed 11, May 2007).

Table 18.02. PROFESSIONAL, SCIENTIFIC, AND TECHNICAL SERVICES: ESTABLISHMENTS EMPLOYMENT, AND PAYROLL IN FLORIDA, 2002

NAICS code	Industry	Number of estab- lishments	Number of em- ployees 1/	Annual Payroll ($1,000)
54	Professional, scientific, and technical services	56,822	378,593	17,197,105
5411	Legal services	14,745	81,742	4,865,147
54111	Offices of lawyers	13,825	76,333	4,680,642
54119	Other legal services	920	5,409	184,505
5412	Accounting, tax return preparations, bookkeeping, and payroll services	8,242	66,281	1,886,417
5413	Architectural, engineering, and related services	7,649	72,942	3,521,571
54131	Architectural services	1,691	9,801	457,618
54133	Engineering services 2/	3,738	(NA)	(D)
54134	Drafting services	285	653	19,102
54135	Building inspection services	397	999	27,710
54136	Geophysical surveying and mapping services 3/	34	(NA)	(D)
54137	Surveying and mapping (except geophysical) services	759	6,779	222,537
54138	Testing laboratories	281	3,359	125,914
5414	Specialized design services	2,657	7,176	224,456
54141	Interior design services	1,407	4,115	135,046
54142	Industrial design services	92	181	6,141
54143	Graphic design services	1,028	2,571	73,878
54149	Other specialized design services	130	309	9,391
5415	Computer systems design and related services	5,917	49,094	2,854,747
5416	Management, scientific, and technical consulting services	9,500	41,423	1,864,386
54161	Management consulting services	7,980	36,246	1,649,715
54162	Environmental consulting services	549	2,741	113,027
54169	Other scientific and technical consulting services	971	2,436	101,644
5417	Scientific research and development services	629	8,797	471,773
54171	Research and development in the physical, engineering, and life sciences	549	7,850	429,756
54172	Research and development in the social sciences and humanities	80	947	42,017
5418	Advertising and related services	2,806	19,274	746,224
54181	Advertising agencies	905	6,296	294,102
54182	Public relations agencies	445	1,608	73,929
54183	Media buying services	77	268	11,479
54184	Media representatives	207	1,054	37,414
54185	Display advertising	213	2,064	58,886
54186	Direct mail advertising	266	4,235	151,674
54187	Advertising material distribution services	52	930	48,493
54189	Other services related to advertising	641	2,819	70,247
5419	Other professional, scientific, and technical services	4,677	31,864	762,384
54191	Marketing research and public opinion polling	373	8,079	160,584
54192	Photographic services	1,038	3,833	70,354
54193	Translation and interpretation services	168	432	11,365
54194	Veterinary services	1,665	14,363	337,264
54199	All other professional, scientific, and technical services	1,433	5,157	182,817

(NA) Not available.
(D) Data withheld to avoid disclosure of information about individual firms.
1/ Paid employment for pay period including March 12.
Employment range: 2/ 25,000-49,999. 3/ 100-249.

Note: The economic censuses are conducted on a 5-year cycle collecting data for years ending in 2 and 7. Data are for North American Industry Classification System (NAICS) code 54 and may not be comparable to earlier years. See Glossary for definition.

Source: U.S., Department of Commerce, Census Bureau, *2002 Economic Census: Professional, Scientific, and Technical Services,* Geographic Area Series EC02-54A-FL, issued August 2005, Internet site <http://www.census.gov/> (accessed 11, May 2007).

Table 18.05. ADMINISTRATIVE AND SUPPORT AND WASTE MANAGEMENT AND REMEDIATION SERVICES: ESTABLISHMENTS, EMPLOYMENT, AND PAYROLL IN THE STATE AND COUNTIES OF FLORIDA, 2002

County	Number of establishments	Number of employees 1/	Annual payroll ($1,000)	County	Number of establishments	Number of employees 1/	Annual payroll ($1,000)
Florida	27,437	991,958	23,087,482	Lake	290	3,591	83,368
Alachua	245	3,213	65,600	Lee	913	28,071	618,739
Baker	17	62	884	Leon	371	14,342	194,951
Bay	195	4,514	88,371	Levy	25	123	1,146
Bradford 2/	21	(NA)	(D)	Liberty	0	0	0
Brevard	707	11,411	310,502	Madison 2/	11	(NA)	(D)
Broward	3,502	80,827	1,913,289	Manatee	416	40,535	793,896
Calhoun 3/	1	(NA)	(D)	Marion	322	4,062	62,318
Charlotte	222	7,157	148,880	Martin	313	4,225	87,616
Citrus	147	1,348	21,513	Miami-Dade	3,387	127,865	2,887,328
Clay	168	6,257	87,455	Monroe	197	933	19,692
Collier	682	10,089	233,042	Nassau	68	310	6,885
Columbia	40	1,199	25,017	Okaloosa	234	7,683	171,626
DeSoto	23	93	1,783	Okeechobee	29	619	17,564
Dixie 3/	5	(NA)	(D)	Orange	1,884	71,442	1,523,482
Duval	1,444	55,038	1,061,518	Osceola	286	3,427	65,956
Escambia	313	15,749	350,769	Palm Beach	2,692	85,599	2,686,798
Flagler 4/	84	(NA)	(D)	Pasco	435	3,987	71,166
Franklin 3/	8	(NA)	(D)	Pinellas	1,595	132,003	3,826,787
Gadsden	23	527	12,593	Polk	556	23,137	321,793
Gilchrist	11	25	397	Putnam	61	251	4,985
Glades 5/	6	(NA)	(D)	St. Johns	219	5,464	92,974
Gulf 2/	14	(NA)	(D)	St. Lucie	295	3,860	65,405
Hamilton 3/	2	(NA)	(D)	Santa Rosa	131	1,856	30,761
Hardee	21	321	8,283	Sarasota	825	45,491	1,236,320
Hendry 2/	13	(NA)	(D)	Seminole	742	16,109	351,413
Hernando	156	1,302	22,305	Sumter	25	120	1,355
Highlands 6/	100	(NA)	(D)	Suwannee	27	164	3,294
Hillsborough	1,861	109,954	2,684,682	Taylor	12	56	1,343
Holmes 3/	5	(NA)	(D)	Union	8	61	1,691
Indian River	235	3,215	63,513	Volusia	684	9,831	205,327
Jackson	30	494	9,079	Wakulla	15	51	827
Jefferson	6	20	365	Walton	53	776	15,225
Lafayette	0	0	0	Washington 2/	9	(NA)	(D)

(NA) Not available.
(D) Data withheld to avoid disclosure of information about individual firms.
1/ Paid employment for the pay period including March 12.
Employment ranges: 2/ 20-99. 3/ 0-19. 4/ 1,000-2,499. 5/ 100-249. 6/ 25,000-49,999.
Note: The economic censuses are conducted on a 5-year cycle collecting data for years ending in 2 and 7. Data are for North American Industry Classification System (NAICS) code 56 and may not be comparable to earlier years. See Glossary for definition.

Source: U.S., Department of Commerce, Census Bureau, *2002 Economic Census: Administrative and Support and Waste Management and Remediation Services,* Geographic Area Series EC02-56A-FL, issued August 2005, Internet site <http://www.census.gov/> (accessed 11, May 2007).

Table 18.06. PROFESSIONAL, SCIENTIFIC, AND TECHNICAL SERVICES: ESTABLISHMENTS EMPLOYMENT, AND PAYROLL IN THE STATE AND COUNTIES OF FLORIDA, 2002

County	Number of establishments	Number of employees 1/	Annual payroll ($1,000)	County	Number of establishments	Number of employees 1/	Annual payroll ($1,000)
Florida	56,822	378,593	17,197,105	Lake	457	1,840	66,904
Alachua	701	5,184	199,236	Lee	1,460	8,785	330,652
Baker 2/	15	(NA)	(D)	Leon	1,160	9,339	513,992
Bay	368	2,465	88,719	Levy	36	165	3,778
Bradford	31	102	2,369	Liberty 7/	1	(NA)	(D)
Brevard	1,438	17,427	835,137	Madison	18	78	2,134
Broward	7,878	40,124	1,716,878	Manatee	688	3,726	116,300
Calhoun	13	65	756	Marion	520	2,804	90,022
Charlotte	291	1,598	62,397	Martin 8/	586	(NA)	(D)
Citrus	196	614	16,916	Miami-Dade	9,660	55,525	2,905,134
Clay 3/	301	(NA)	(D)	Monroe	316	1,524	47,736
Collier	1,082	4,702	204,027	Nassau	120	490	18,594
Columbia	83	492	12,451	Okaloosa	542	5,125	243,019
DeSoto	24	90	2,568	Okeechobee	31	138	2,663
Dixie	9	44	723	Orange	3,783	35,073	1,799,734
Duval	2,574	20,417	1,013,806	Osceola	269	921	28,640
Escambia 4/	705	(NA)	(D)	Palm Beach	5,857	31,097	1,523,771
Flagler	118	354	15,711	Pasco 8/	624	(NA)	(D)
Franklin	28	65	2,599	Pinellas	3,479	28,272	1,089,908
Gadsden 5/	45	(NA)	(D)	Polk	864	5,390	201,524
Gilchrist	17	41	983	Putnam 9/	96	(NA)	(D)
Glades	0	0	0	St. Johns	481	3,107	77,335
Gulf	20	112	4,464	St. Lucie 3/	339	(NA)	(D)
Hamilton	9	15	181	Santa Rosa 6/	191	(NA)	(D)
Hardee 2/	19	(NA)	(D)	Sarasota	1,464	10,452	435,747
Hendry	33	127	3,005	Seminole	1,512	9,816	454,722
Hernando 6/	195	(NA)	(D)	Sumter	45	183	4,286
Highlands	121	841	20,252	Suwannee	42	177	3,933
Hillsborough	4,085	43,940	2,175,364	Taylor	25	98	2,594
Holmes	17	73	1,298	Union 2/	5	(NA)	(D)
Indian River	373	1,879	68,601	Volusia	1,126	5,983	194,686
Jackson	39	311	8,377	Wakulla	38	165	3,790
Jefferson 2/	22	(NA)	(D)	Walton	99	225	6,110
Lafayette 7/	5	(NA)	(D)	Washington	33	139	3,424

(NA) Not available.
(D) Data withheld to avoid disclosure of information about individual firms.
1/ Paid employment for pay period including March 12.
Employment ranges: 2/ 20-99. 3/ 1,000-2,499. 4/ 5,000-9,999. 5/ 100-249. 6/ 500-999. 7/ 0-19. 8/ 2,500-4,999. 9/ 250-499.
Note: The economic censuses are conducted on a 5-year cycle collecting data for years ending in 2 and 7. Data are for North American Industry Classification System (NAICS) code 54 and may not be comparable to earlier years. See Glossary for definition.

Source: U.S., Department of Commerce, Census Bureau, *2002 Economic Census: Professional, Scientific, and Technical Services,* Geographic Area Series EC02-54A-FL, issued August 2005, Internet site <http://www.census.gov/> (accessed 11, May 2007).

Table 18.20. OTHER SERVICES, EXCEPT PUBLIC ADMINISTRATION: AVERAGE MONTHLY PRIVATE REPORTING UNITS, EMPLOYMENT, AND PAYROLL COVERED BY UNEMPLOYMENT COMPENSATION LAW BY INDUSTRY IN FLORIDA, 2005 AND 2006

NAICS code	Industry	Number of reporting units	Number of employees	Payroll ($1,000)
			2005 A/	
81	Other services (except public administration)	48,266	243,559	523,004
811	Repair and maintenance	15,770	75,984	194,155
8111	Automotive repair and maintenance	10,783	52,727	123,455
8112	Electronic equipment repair and maintenance	1,151	7,263	25,562
8113	Commercial machinery repair and maintenance	1,518	7,802	25,019
8114	Household goods repair and maintenance	2,318	8,193	20,118
812	Personal and laundry services	13,203	77,451	133,415
8121	Personal care services	7,683	35,781	58,482
8122	Death care services	801	7,102	17,400
8123	Dry-cleaning and laundry services	2,477	20,042	34,600
8129	Other personal services	2,242	14,526	22,933
813	Membership associations and organizations	8,378	76,301	170,714
8131	Religious organizations	961	9,511	17,979
8132	Grant making and giving services	505	6,021	19,002
8133	Social advocacy organizations	749	8,330	19,230
8134	Civic and social organizations	1,151	17,988	22,867
8139	Professional and similar organizations	5,012	34,450	91,635
814	Private households 1/	10,915	13,823	24,721
			2006 B/	
81	Other services (except public administration)	48,408	248,161	558,007
811	Repair and maintenance	15,771	76,895	203,894
8111	Automotive repair and maintenance	10,757	53,358	129,011
8112	Electronic equipment repair and maintenance	1,141	7,368	27,554
8113	Commercial machinery repair and maintenance	1,539	7,949	26,656
8114	Household goods repair and maintenance	2,334	8,220	20,673
812	Personal and laundry services	13,508	78,959	142,595
8121	Personal care services	7,976	36,114	61,788
8122	Death care services	801	7,031	17,707
8123	Dry-cleaning and laundry services	2,446	20,170	36,596
8129	Other personal services	2,285	15,644	26,504
813	Membership associations and organizations	8,424	78,502	185,723
8131	Religious organizations	988	9,890	19,180
8132	Grant making and giving services	507	5,927	18,965
8133	Social advocacy organizations	818	7,953	19,307
8134	Civic and social organizations	1,147	17,642	23,519
8139	Professional and similar organizations	4,964	37,090	104,751
814	Private households 1/	10,705	13,805	25,796

NAICS North American Industry Classification System. See Glossary for definition.
A/ Revised.
B/ Preliminary.
1/ Private households which employ workers in domestic services such as cooks, maids, sitters, butlers personal secretaries, gardeners and caretakers, and managers of personal affairs.
Note: Private employment. Detail may not add to totals due to disclosure editing and/or rounding. See Tables 23.70, 23.72, 23.73, and 23.74 for public employment data.

Source: State of Florida, Agency for Workforce Innovation, Labor Market Statistics, "Quarterly Census of Employment and Wages" (ES-202), Annual NAICS files, Internet site <http://www.labormarketinfo.com/index.htm> (accessed 17, July 2007).

Table 18.22. PROFESSIONAL, SCIENTIFIC, AND TECHNICAL SERVICES: AVERAGE MONTHLY PRIVATE REPORTING UNITS, EMPLOYMENT, AND PAYROLL COVERED BY UNEMPLOYMENT COMPENSATION LAW BY INDUSTRY IN FLORIDA, 2005 AND 2006

NAICS code	Industry	Number of reporting units	Number of employees	Payroll ($1,000)
			2005 A/	
54	Professional, scientific, and technical services	77,834	429,568	1,992,982
5411	Legal services	18,021	90,948	519,476
5412	Accounting and bookkeeping services	9,670	52,211	199,727
5413	Architectural and engineering services	9,273	86,579	393,784
5414	Specialized design services	4,173	10,967	34,511
5415	Computer systems design and related services	9,689	54,503	301,272
5416	Management and technical consulting services	17,283	59,843	290,975
5417	Scientific research and development services	975	12,378	69,513
5418	Advertising and related services	3,916	24,075	89,229
5419	Other professional and technical services	4,834	38,065	94,495

2006 B/

NAICS code	Industry	Number of reporting units	Number of employees	Payroll ($1,000)
54	Professional, scientific, and technical services	81,280	451,078	2,209,828
5411	Legal services	18,367	92,299	552,297
5412	Accounting and bookkeeping services	9,809	53,888	222,799
5413	Architectural and engineering services	9,633	93,002	451,634
5414	Specialized design services	4,306	11,538	40,379
5415	Computer systems design and related services	10,345	56,780	330,852
5416	Management and technical consulting services	18,468	65,296	329,626
5417	Scientific research and development services	995	12,403	73,213
5418	Advertising and related services	3,970	24,928	97,610
5419	Other professional and technical services	5,387	40,944	111,418

NAICS North American Industry Classification System. See Glossary for definition.
A/ Revised.
B/ Preliminary.
Note: Private employment. Detail may not add to totals due to disclosure editing and/or rounding. See Tables 23.70, 23.72, 23.73, and 23.74 for public employment data.

Source: State of Florida, Agency for Workforce Innovation, Labor Market Statistics, "Quarterly Census of Employment and Wages" (ES-202), Annual NAICS files, Internet site <http://www.labormarketinfo.com/index.htm> (accessed 17, July 2007).

Table 18.23. ADMINISTRATIVE AND SUPPORT AND WASTE MANAGEMENT AND REMEDIATION SERVICES: AVERAGE MONTHLY PRIVATE REPORTING UNITS, EMPLOYMENT, AND PAYROLL COVERED BY UNEMPLOYMENT COMPENSATION LAW BY INDUSTRY IN FLORIDA, 2005 AND 2006

NAICS code	Industry	Number of reporting units	Number of employees	Payroll ($1,000)
			2005 A/	
56	Adminstrative and support and waste management and remediation services	38,206	819,171	1,859,613
561	Administrative and support services	37,078	801,294	1,797,378
5611	Office administrative services	3,784	27,689	136,105
5612	Facilities support services	205	20,910	91,731
5613	Employment services	3,890	464,772	949,197
5614	Business support services	3,792	58,270	145,739
5615	Travel arrangement and reservation services	2,577	28,648	80,993
5616	Investigation and security services	2,536	57,435	119,200
5617	Services to buildings and dwellings	18,081	129,725	233,580
5619	Other support services	2,213	13,845	40,833
562	Waste management and remediation services	1,128	17,877	62,234
5621	Waste collection	493	8,696	28,724
5622	Waste treatment and disposal	155	3,099	12,404
5629	Remediation and other waste services	480	6,082	21,106
			2006 B/	
56	Adminstrative and support and waste management and remediation services	39,359	822,284	1,954,502
561	Administrative and support services	38,184	802,996	1,886,056
5611	Office administrative services	3,991	30,307	154,379
5612	Facilities support services	225	21,526	99,426
5613	Employment services	3,802	451,904	949,520
5614	Business support services	3,799	59,567	155,636
5615	Travel arrangement and reservation services	2,570	29,972	89,525
5616	Investigation and security services	2,601	58,728	130,737
5617	Services to buildings and dwellings	19,022	136,148	261,457
5619	Other support services	2,174	14,845	45,376
562	Waste management and remediation services	1,175	19,288	68,445
5621	Waste collection	500	9,484	31,895
5622	Waste treatment and disposal	154	3,530	14,620
5629	Remediation and other waste services	521	6,274	21,931

NAICS North American Industry Classification System. See Glossary for definition.
A/ Revised.
B/ Preliminary.
Note: Private employment. Detail may not add to totals due to disclosure editing and/or rounding. See Tables 23.70, 23.72, 23.73, and 23.74 for public employment data.

Source: State of Florida, Agency for Workforce Innovation, Labor Market Statistics, "Quarterly Census of Employment and Wages" (ES-202), Annual NAICS files, Internet site <http://www.labormarketinfo.com/index.htm> (accessed 17, July 2007).

Table 18.24. OTHER SERVICES, EXCEPT PUBLIC ADMINISTRATION: AVERAGE MONTHLY PRIVATE REPORTING UNITS, EMPLOYMENT AND PAYROLL COVERED BY UNEMPLOYMENT COMPENSATION LAW IN THE STATE AND COUNTIES OF FLORIDA 2005 AND 2006

County	Number of reporting units	Number of employees	Payroll ($1,000)	County	Number of reporting units	Number of employees	Payroll ($1,000)
Other services, except public administration, 2005 A/ (NAICS code 81)							
Florida	48,266	243,559	523,004	Lee	1,425	6,915	16,905
				Leon	876	5,920	16,883
Alachua	665	3,407	6,003	Levy	66	164	236
Baker	31	89	142	Liberty	4	22	41
Bay	389	2,466	5,420	Madison	25	80	138
Bradford	37	293	1,002	Manatee	679	3,058	5,785
Brevard	1,173	6,164	11,654	Marion	557	2,585	4,959
Broward	5,286	26,587	59,183	Martin	602	3,061	6,767
Calhoun	14	38	58	Miami-Dade	7,699	34,958	70,877
Charlotte	300	1,259	2,286	Monroe	355	1,472	3,369
Citrus	256	1,343	2,192	Nassau	132	664	1,153
Clay	324	1,720	2,923	Okaloosa	498	2,780	5,680
Collier	1,093	4,890	10,795	Okeechobee	64	284	692
Columbia	109	595	817	Orange	2,616	18,651	40,073
DeSoto	45	138	218	Osceola	331	1,477	3,253
Dixie	14	62	106	Palm Beach	4,975	21,383	49,950
Duval	2,198	12,841	28,455	Pasco	728	3,301	5,904
Escambia	700	4,499	8,434	Pinellas	2,563	13,519	26,803
Flagler	128	520	1,021	Polk	962	5,155	10,938
Franklin	22	56	127	Putnam	125	651	869
Gadsden	73	306	422	St. Johns	382	2,578	9,640
Gilchrist	20	117	203	St. Lucie	414	1,751	3,494
Glades	7	26	40	Santa Rosa	246	1,091	2,054
Gulf	17	43	84	Sarasota	1,261	6,554	13,015
Hamilton	20	58	78	Seminole	980	4,392	9,603
Hardee	45	125	173	Sumter	64	216	382
Hendry	49	178	331	Suwannee	50	192	331
Hernando	265	1,151	1,702	Taylor	28	91	159
Highlands	174	676	1,219	Union	8	23	30
Hillsborough	2,636	16,510	37,782	Volusia	1,202	5,952	9,990
Holmes	21	106	204	Wakulla	31	102	193
Indian River	472	1,701	3,226	Walton	91	575	1,169
Jackson	63	326	553	Washington	33	136	241
Jefferson	24	66	99	Statewide 1/	185	1,636	5,557
Lafayette	8	16	19	Out-of-state 2/	7	9	44
Lake	516	2,374	4,397	Unknown 1/	808	1,419	4,460

See footnotes at end of table.

Continued . . .

Table 18.24. OTHER SERVICES, EXCEPT PUBLIC ADMINISTRATION: AVERAGE MONTHLY PRIVATE REPORTING UNITS, EMPLOYMENT AND PAYROLL COVERED BY UNEMPLOYMENT COMPENSATION LAW IN THE STATE AND COUNTIES OF FLORIDA 2005 AND 2006 (Continued)

County	Number of reporting units	Number Number of employees	Payroll ($1,000)	County	Number of reporting units	Number Number of employees	Payroll ($1,000)
		Other services, except public administration, 2006 B/ (NAICS code 81)					
Florida	48,408	248,161	558,007	Lee	1,425	7,470	18,873
				Leon	861	6,222	17,623
Alachua	673	3,659	6,931	Levy	69	191	278
Baker	34	106	164	Liberty	3	12	28
Bay	386	2,545	5,830	Madison	28	78	137
Bradford	37	159	270	Manatee	701	3,358	6,836
Brevard	1,184	5,600	11,172	Marion	579	2,639	5,313
Broward	5,244	26,417	61,850	Martin	609	2,805	6,236
Calhoun	14	34	54	Miami-Dade	7,525	34,773	74,742
Charlotte	322	1,246	2,518	Monroe	352	1,422	3,432
Citrus	261	1,393	2,180	Nassau	140	753	1,352
Clay	327	1,739	2,817	Okaloosa	483	2,750	5,858
Collier	1,075	4,851	11,407	Okeechobee	69	280	610
Columbia	106	367	628	Orange	2,662	19,435	44,270
DeSoto	40	128	211	Osceola	371	1,552	3,086
Dixie	13	50	88	Palm Beach	4,975	21,528	52,622
Duval	2,206	12,788	28,954	Pasco	750	3,364	6,658
Escambia	710	4,378	8,515	Pinellas	2,514	13,306	27,705
Flagler	134	561	947	Polk	984	5,067	10,948
Franklin	23	75	180	Putnam	114	679	968
Gadsden	71	251	383	St. Johns	410	2,718	10,492
Gilchrist	19	50	70	St. Lucie	420	1,950	4,299
Glades	6	28	41	Santa Rosa	237	1,043	1,916
Gulf	17	39	101	Sarasota	1,263	6,886	14,045
Hamilton	19	72	102	Seminole	1,016	4,990	11,486
Hardee	51	148	209	Sumter	61	229	406
Hendry	51	174	304	Suwannee	52	209	386
Hernando	260	1,247	1,967	Taylor	28	96	186
Highlands	182	710	1,268	Union	8	28	37
Hillsborough	2,657	17,301	39,446	Volusia	1,202	6,357	14,185
Holmes	20	84	201	Wakulla	38	98	193
Indian River	462	1,731	3,464	Walton	103	688	1,351
Jackson	62	297	695	Washington	39	154	317
Jefferson	26	70	95	Statewide 1/	191	2,347	7,765
Lafayette	9	20	20	Out-of-state 2/	8	11	88
Lake	532	2,437	4,780	Unknown 1/	885	1,925	5,417

NAICS North American Industry Classification System. See Glossary for definition.
A/ Revised. B/ Preliminary.
1/ Reporting units without a fixed location within the state or of unknown county location.
2/ Employment based in Florida, but working out of the state or country.
Note: Private employment. For a list of three- and four-digit industries included see Table 18.20. Only counties for which data are disclosed are shown. Detail may not add to totals due to disclosure editing and/or rounding. See Tables 23.70, 23.72, 23.73, and 23.74 for public employment data.
Source: State of Florida, Agency for Workforce Innovation, Labor Market Statistics, "Quarterly Census of Employment and Wages" (ES-202), Annual NAICS files, Internet site <http://www.labormarketinfo.com/index.htm> (accessed 17, July 2007).

Table 18.28. REPAIR AND MAINTENANCE: AVERAGE MONTHLY PRIVATE REPORTING UNITS EMPLOYMENT, AND PAYROLL COVERED BY UNEMPLOYMENT COMPENSATION LAW IN THE STATE AND COUNTIES OF FLORIDA, 2006

County	Number of reporting units	Number of employees	Payroll ($1,000)	County	Number of reporting units	Number of employees	Payroll ($1,000)
		Repair and maintenance (NAICS code 811)					
Florida	15,771	76,895	203,894	Lee	557	2,872	9,241
				Leon	217	1,460	3,579
Alachua	166	839	1,886	Levy	32	106	174
Baker	15	57	94	Madison	14	44	85
Bay	138	1,163	3,460	Manatee	231	1,148	2,747
Bradford	20	51	97	Marion	251	1,157	2,691
Brevard	428	1,709	4,445	Martin	176	854	2,122
Broward	1,846	8,696	25,339	Miami-Dade	2,156	8,521	19,758
Calhoun	3	8	22	Monroe	85	323	856
Charlotte	118	469	1,186	Nassau	46	259	570
Citrus	98	415	910	Okaloosa	188	1,074	3,038
Clay	122	569	1,185	Okeechobee	38	170	446
Collier	258	1,019	2,768	Orange	893	5,890	15,349
Columbia	50	156	343	Osceola	154	625	1,291
DeSoto	8	22	59	Palm Beach	1,205	5,121	13,988
Dixie	7	37	62	Pasco	325	1,343	3,575
Duval	753	5,184	14,734	Pinellas	914	4,106	10,747
Escambia	289	1,629	4,130	Polk	392	2,056	5,407
Flagler	51	156	341	Putnam	51	210	511
Franklin	6	9	18	St. Johns	90	398	1,046
Gadsden	19	68	160	St. Lucie	188	806	2,258
Gilchrist	7	24	38	Santa Rosa	95	480	1,141
Gulf	10	28	85	Sarasota	372	1,390	3,330
Hamilton	7	31	63	Seminole	362	2,226	5,650
Hardee	18	45	95	Sumter	23	83	170
Hendry	24	73	150	Suwannee	25	113	248
Hernando	106	455	891	Taylor	13	56	141
Highlands	76	386	855	Union	3	8	14
Hillsborough	942	5,908	16,756	Volusia	438	1,709	3,758
Holmes	11	37	85	Wakulla	17	61	135
Indian River	112	475	1,166	Walton	27	85	169
Jackson	20	81	161	Washington	16	42	113
Lafayette	4	7	5	Statewide 1/	79	1,146	4,787
Lake	211	821	2,106	Unknown 1/	146	304	1,019

NAICS North American Industry Classification System. See Glossary for definition.
1/ Reporting units without a fixed location within the state or of unknown county location.
Note: Private employment. Data are preliminary. For a list of four-digit code industries included see Table 18.20. Only counties for which data are disclosed are shown. Detail may not add to totals due to disclosure editing and/or rounding. See Tables 23.70, 23.72, 23.73, and 23.74 for public employment data.

Source: State of Florida, Agency for Workforce Innovation, Labor Market Statistics, "Quarterly Census of Employment and Wages" (ES-202), Annual NAICS files, Internet site <http://www.labormarketinfo.com/index.htm> (accessed 17, July 2007).

Table 18.29. PERSONAL AND LAUNDRY SERVICES: AVERAGE MONTHLY PRIVATE REPORTING UNITS EMPLOYMENT, AND PAYROLL COVERED BY UNEMPLOYMENT COMPENSATION LAW IN THE STATE AND COUNTIES OF FLORIDA, 2006

County	Number of reporting units	Number of employees	Payroll ($1,000)	County	Number of reporting units	Number of employees	Payroll ($1,000)
			Personal and laundry services (NAICS code 812)				
Florida	13,508	78,959	142,595	Leon	163	1,158	1,922
				Levy	16	49	67
Alachua	165	933	1,616	Madison	3	22	39
Baker	10	24	31	Manatee	198	909	1,501
Bay	94	640	1,006	Marion	177	995	1,634
Bradford	8	82	133	Martin	130	610	1,090
Brevard	376	2,053	3,447	Miami-Dade	1,946	11,890	21,017
Broward	1,607	9,717	17,128	Monroe	74	198	377
Calhoun	5	18	21	Nassau	49	166	277
Charlotte	104	437	771	Okaloosa	124	786	1,281
Citrus	88	411	624	Okeechobee	13	49	90
Clay	129	599	875	Orange	875	6,285	12,146
Collier	302	1,281	2,637	Osceola	142	569	1,023
Columbia	29	129	180	Palm Beach	1,226	7,021	14,184
DeSoto	11	45	52	Pasco	246	1,071	1,737
Duval	683	3,860	6,662	Pinellas	765	4,173	7,557
Escambia	166	1,289	2,139	Polk	214	1,409	2,918
Flagler	42	157	231	Putnam	30	141	182
Franklin	4	6	14	St. Johns	124	776	1,451
Gadsden	16	35	47	St. Lucie	118	436	765
Gilchrist	6	14	22	Santa Rosa	58	201	303
Gulf	3	7	9	Sarasota	355	2,063	4,176
Hamilton	4	24	23	Seminole	362	1,731	2,933
Hardee	9	28	32	Sumter	16	87	157
Hendry	8	33	58	Suwannee	13	66	100
Hernando	94	427	554	Taylor	7	22	27
Highlands	46	152	193	Volusia	355	2,108	3,447
Hillsborough	778	5,949	10,694	Wakulla	9	16	20
Holmes	3	10	29	Walton	28	97	141
Indian River	100	408	722	Washington	11	49	70
Jackson	17	136	401	Statewide 1/	24	582	830
Lake	165	1,063	1,616	Out-of-state 2/	3	6	63
Lee	416	2,634	5,441	Unknown 1/	136	574	1,594

NAICS North American Industry Classification System. See Glossary for definition.
1/ Reporting units without a fixed location within the state or of unknown county location.
2/ Employment based in Florida, but working out of the state or country.
Note: Private employment. Data are preliminary. For a list of four-digit industries included see Table 18.20. Only counties for which data are disclosed are shown. Detail may not add to totals due to disclosure editing and/or rounding. See Tables 23.70, 23.72, 23.73, and 23.74 for public employment data.

Source: State of Florida, Agency for Workforce Innovation, Labor Market Statistics, "Quarterly Census of Employment and Wages" (ES-202), Annual NAICS files, Internet site <http://www.labormarketinfo.com/index.htm> (accessed 17, July 2007).

Table 18.30. PRIVATE HOUSEHOLDS: AVERAGE MONTHLY PRIVATE REPORTING UNITS EMPLOYMENT, AND PAYROLL COVERED BY UNEMPLOYMENT COMPENSATION LAW IN THE STATE AND COUNTIES OF FLORIDA, 2006

County	Number of reporting units	Number of employees	Payroll ($1,000)	County	Number of reporting units	Number of employees	Payroll ($1,000)
			Private households 1/ (NAICS code 814)				
Florida	10,705	13,805	25,796	Leon	241	286	355
				Levy	10	18	20
Alachua	244	309	346	Madison	9	7	6
Baker	4	4	8	Manatee	136	165	311
Bay	60	74	100	Marion	85	125	203
Bradford	4	5	5	Martin	203	313	776
Brevard	126	148	239	Miami-Dade	2,188	2,508	4,155
Broward	836	1,136	2,181	Monroe	88	120	398
Calhoun	3	3	5	Nassau	14	22	37
Charlotte	35	44	76	Okaloosa	72	103	151
Citrus	34	60	84	Okeechobee	5	9	18
Clay	42	59	83	Orange	480	576	989
Collier	262	376	992	Osceola	26	26	29
Columbia	17	31	53	Palm Beach	1,718	2,386	6,182
DeSoto	8	11	13	Pasco	61	90	97
Dixie	3	3	2	Pinellas	416	553	910
Duval	466	601	1,100	Polk	225	324	474
Escambia	121	167	180	Putnam	15	22	24
Flagler	10	8	10	St. Johns	122	131	222
Gadsden	26	40	45	St. Lucie	40	46	71
Glades	4	9	12	Santa Rosa	56	60	85
Hamilton	5	10	12	Sarasota	260	366	716
Hardee	13	13	16	Seminole	166	185	306
Hendry	7	11	25	Sumter	10	19	37
Hernando	24	35	43	Suwannee	6	8	6
Highlands	30	39	46	Taylor	3	3	6
Hillsborough	556	696	1,050	Volusia	141	183	306
Indian River	184	241	469	Wakulla	6	7	9
Jackson	13	14	12	Walton	13	22	31
Jefferson	11	22	34	Washington	5	7	7
Lake	91	100	130	Statewide 2/	36	45	79
Lee	189	238	512	Unknown 2/	405	546	860

NAICS North American Industry Classification System. See Glossary for definition.

1/ Private households which employ workers in domestic services such as cooks, maids, sitters, butlers personal secretaries, gardeners and caretakers, and managers of personal affairs.

2/ Reporting units without a fixed location within the state or of unknown county location.

Note: Private employment. Data are preliminary. Only counties for which data are disclosed are shown. Detail may not add to totals due to disclosure editing and/or rounding. See Tables 23.70, 23.72, 23.73, and 23.74 for public employment data.

Source: State of Florida, Agency for Workforce Innovation, Labor Market Statistics, "Quarterly Census of Employment and Wages" (ES-202), Annual NAICS files, Internet site <http://www.labormarketinfo.com/index.htm> (accessed 17, July 2007).

Table 18.31. MEMBERSHIP ASSOCIATIONS AND ORGANIZATIONS: AVERAGE MONTHLY PRIVATE REPORTING UNITS, EMPLOYMENT, AND PAYROLL COVERED BY UNEMPLOYMENT COMPENSATION LAW IN THE STATE AND COUNTIES OF FLORIDA, 2006

County	Number of reporting units	Number of employees	Payroll ($1,000)	County	Number of reporting units	Number of employees	Payroll ($1,000)
	Membership associations and organizations (NAICS code 813)						
Florida	8,424	78,502	185,723	Leon	240	3,318	11,767
				Levy	11	17	17
Alachua	98	1,578	3,082	Manatee	136	1,136	2,278
Baker	5	21	30	Marion	66	362	786
Bay	94	668	1,265	Martin	100	1,028	2,248
Bradford	5	20	35	Miami-Dade	1,235	11,854	29,811
Brevard	254	1,691	3,041	Monroe	105	782	1,800
Broward	955	6,868	17,201	Nassau	31	307	469
Calhoun	3	5	6	Okaloosa	99	787	1,388
Charlotte	65	296	485	Okeechobee	13	51	56
Citrus	41	506	562	Orange	414	6,684	15,785
Clay	34	511	674	Osceola	49	333	743
Collier	253	2,176	5,010	Palm Beach	826	7,000	18,268
Columbia	10	51	52	Pasco	118	860	1,249
DeSoto	13	51	88	Pinellas	419	4,474	8,491
Duval	304	3,143	6,458	Polk	153	1,279	2,149
Escambia	134	1,293	2,066	Putnam	18	305	250
Flagler	31	240	365	St. Johns	74	1,413	7,774
Franklin	10	58	141	St. Lucie	74	662	1,205
Gadsden	10	108	132	Santa Rosa	28	302	387
Gilchrist	3	10	8	Sarasota	276	3,068	5,824
Hardee	11	62	66	Seminole	126	848	2,597
Hendry	12	57	72	Sumter	12	40	42
Hernando	36	330	479	Suwannee	8	22	31
Highlands	30	134	174	Taylor	5	15	11
Hillsborough	381	4,748	10,947	Volusia	268	2,357	6,673
Indian River	66	606	1,106	Wakulla	6	15	30
Jackson	12	67	120	Walton	35	484	1,011
Jefferson	7	33	41	Washington	7	57	127
Lake	65	453	928	Statewide 1/	52	575	2,069
Lee	263	1,726	3,679	Unknown 1/	198	501	1,944

NAICS North American Industry Classification System. See Glossary for definition.
1/ Reporting units without a fixed location within the state or of unknown county location.
Note: Private employment. Data are preliminary. For a list of four-digit industries included see Table 18.20. Only counties for which data are disclosed are shown. Detail may not add to totals due to disclosure editing and/or rounding. See Tables 23.70, 23.72, 23.73, and 23.74 for public employment data.

Source: State of Florida, Agency for Workforce Innovation, Labor Market Statistics, "Quarterly Census of Employment and Wages" (ES-202), Annual NAICS files, Internet site <http://www.labormarketinfo.com/index.htm> (accessed 17, July 2007).

Table 18.32. CIVIL AND SOCIAL ORGANIZATIONS: AVERAGE MONTHLY PRIVATE REPORTING UNITS, EMPLOYMENT, AND PAYROLL COVERED BY UNEMPLOYMENT COMPENSATION LAW IN THE STATE AND COUNTIES OF FLORIDA, 2006

County	Number of reporting units	Number of employees	Payroll ($1,000)	County	Number of reporting units	Number of employees	Payroll ($1,000)
		Civic and social organizations (NAICS code 8134)					
Florida	1,147	17,642	23,519	Lee	46	349	466
				Leon	23	521	735
Alachua	19	346	409	Manatee	21	242	248
Bay	14	54	61	Marion	16	80	173
Brevard	33	148	158	Martin	16	248	311
Broward	95	1,217	1,958	Miami-Dade	109	696	1,593
Charlotte	9	57	58	Monroe	18	263	604
Citrus	10	51	32	Okaloosa	23	202	160
Clay	8	282	244	Okeechobee	4	24	17
Collier	26	712	1,261	Orange	57	2,503	3,745
Columbia	4	24	23	Osceola	6	35	61
DeSoto	4	12	7	Palm Beach	81	740	1,536
Duval	67	762	1,115	Pasco	31	251	195
Escambia	20	346	364	Pinellas	65	1,948	2,198
Flagler	4	63	40	Polk	25	545	580
Hardee	4	38	29	St. Johns	12	298	319
Hendry	4	24	12	Santa Rosa	3	14	22
Hernando	10	62	41	Sarasota	42	1,189	1,267
Highlands	10	53	34	Seminole	18	66	114
Hillsborough	74	1,677	1,841	Volusia	34	767	565
Indian River	9	144	174	Walton	3	13	14
Lake	13	71	85	Unknown 1/	18	21	89

NAICS North American Industry Classification System. See Glossary for definition.
1/ Reporting units without a fixed location within the state or of unknown county location.
Note: Private employment. Data are preliminary. For a list of other four-digit industries see Table 18.20. Only counties for which data are disclosed are shown. Detail may not add to totals due to disclosure editing and/or rounding. See Tables 23.70, 23.72, 23.73, and 23.74 for public employment data.

Source: State of Florida, Agency for Workforce Innovation, Labor Market Statistics, "Quarterly Census of Employment and Wages" (ES-202), Annual NAICS files, Internet site <http://www.labormarketinfo.com/index.htm> (accessed 17, July 2007).

Table 18.35. PROFESSIONAL AND SIMILAR ORGANIZATIONS: AVERAGE MONTHLY PRIVATE REPORTING UNITS, EMPLOYMENT, AND PAYROLL COVERED BY UNEMPLOYMENT COMPENSATION LAW IN THE STATE AND COUNTIES OF FLORIDA, 2006

County	Number of reporting units	Number of employees	Payroll ($1,000)	County	Number of reporting units	Number of employees	Payroll ($1,000)
		Professional and similar organizations (NAICS code 8139)					
Florida	4,964	37,090	104,751	Manatee	75	388	671
				Marion	31	104	287
Alachua	37	231	627	Martin	69	648	1,580
Baker	3	9	15	Miami-Dade	750	8,017	20,074
Bay	61	435	861	Monroe	70	442	1,014
Brevard	161	769	1,482	Nassau	22	196	361
Broward	600	3,921	10,814	Okaloosa	58	457	964
Charlotte	44	174	287	Okeechobee	7	24	35
Citrus	19	84	109	Orange	208	1,710	5,584
Clay	11	115	246	Osceola	21	198	421
Collier	195	1,084	2,754	Palm Beach	543	4,472	11,834
Columbia	3	9	11	Pasco	46	226	406
DeSoto	4	5	5	Pinellas	240	1,194	3,006
Duval	142	805	1,833	Polk	84	388	876
Escambia	65	303	617	Putnam	10	45	41
Flagler	20	64	114	St. Johns	34	927	7,101
Franklin	6	41	122	St. Lucie	40	298	621
Gadsden	4	10	14	Santa Rosa	16	71	109
Hendry	6	22	49	Sarasota	170	1,521	3,521
Hernando	19	147	207	Seminole	55	345	1,271
Highlands	13	49	89	Sumter	5	12	17
Hillsborough	202	1,510	4,802	Suwannee	4	12	20
Indian River	37	243	492	Taylor	4	11	8
Jackson	7	17	50	Volusia	192	1,311	5,575
Jefferson	3	12	11	Wakulla	3	5	7
Lake	36	178	406	Walton	25	355	815
Lee	166	1,004	2,247	Washington	5	13	69
Leon	148	2,000	8,460	Statewide 1/	29	92	437
Levy	5	7	7	Unknown 1/	108	310	1,216

NAICS North American Industry Classification System. See Glossary for definition.
1/ Reporting units without a fixed location within the state or of unknown county location.
Note: Private employment. Data are preliminary. For a list of four-digit industries included see Table 18.23. Only counties for which data are disclosed are shown. Detail may not add to totals due to disclosure editing and/or rounding. See Tables 23.70, 23.72, 23.73, and 23.74 for public employment data.

Source: State of Florida, Agency for Workforce Innovation, Labor Market Statistics, "Quarterly Census of Employment and Wages" (ES-202), Annual NAICS files, Internet site <http://www.labormarketinfo.com/index.htm> (accessed 17, July 2007).

Table 18.51. PROFESSIONAL, SCIENTIFIC AND TECHNICAL SERVICES: AVERAGE MONTHLY PRIVATE REPORTING UNITS, EMPLOYMENT, AND PAYROLL COVERED BY UNEMPLOYMENT COMPENSATION LAW IN THE STATE AND COUNTIES OF FLORIDA, 2006

County	Number of reporting units	Number of employees	Payroll ($1,000)	County	Number of reporting units	Number of employees	Payroll ($1,000)
	Professional, scientific and technical services (NAICS code 54)						
Florida	81,280	451,078	2,209,828	Lee	1,986	10,098	43,525
Alachua	853	5,860	22,110	Leon	1,405	10,562	54,150
Baker	19	102	287	Levy	53	243	603
Bay	452	3,608	16,977	Madison	17	115	300
Bradford	55	318	681	Manatee	1,039	3,919	15,201
Brevard	1,811	11,764	54,124	Marion	732	3,162	11,341
Broward	10,520	48,990	236,477	Martin	730	2,984	13,525
Calhoun	8	20	44	Miami-Dade	12,586	62,938	352,768
Charlotte	413	1,702	6,820	Monroe	375	1,074	5,195
Citrus	296	1,087	6,224	Nassau	188	521	1,976
Clay	434	1,792	6,086	Okaloosa	695	6,276	30,232
Collier	1,504	5,173	26,829	Okeechobee	53	227	499
Columbia	104	519	1,542	Orange	5,193	45,829	244,760
DeSoto	30	126	353	Osceola	505	1,752	5,832
Dixie	10	91	178	Palm Beach	7,739	35,369	192,950
Duval	3,243	27,184	146,353	Pasco	940	3,559	12,128
Escambia	854	6,079	24,771	Pinellas	4,499	28,430	118,461
Flagler	219	696	2,422	Polk	1,142	6,380	24,780
Franklin	30	57	208	Putnam	120	395	1,042
Gadsden	55	157	355	St. Johns	723	2,443	10,534
Gilchrist	18	75	158	St. Lucie	515	2,715	9,140
Glades	7	17	49	Santa Rosa	281	1,385	5,348
Gulf	27	80	236	Sarasota	1,957	10,020	43,516
Hamilton	12	19	31	Seminole	2,171	10,404	46,087
Hardee	29	111	262	Sumter	93	298	856
Hendry	41	135	361	Suwannee	44	215	539
Hernando	296	1,055	3,083	Taylor	29	126	416
Highlands	143	937	2,021	Union	9	24	45
Hillsborough	5,466	43,826	230,316	Volusia	1,436	7,106	24,079
Holmes	28	107	217	Wakulla	38	328	941
Indian River	525	2,215	10,218	Walton	212	567	1,761
Jackson	53	276	728	Washington	24	84	173
Jefferson	21	98	244	Statewide 1/	1,205	15,472	70,614
Lafayette	10	40	71	Out-of-state 2/	76	248	1,805
Lake	637	3,097	13,837	Unknown 1/	4,245	8,399	50,028

NAICS North American Industry Classification System. See Glossary for definition.
1/ Reporting units without a fixed location within the state or of unknown county location.
2/ Employment based in Florida, but working out of the state or country.
Note: Private employment. Data are preliminary. For a list of three- and four-digit industries included see Table 18.22. Only counties for which data are disclosed are shown. Detail may not add to totals due to disclosure editing and/or rounding. See Tables 23.70, 23.72, 23.73, and 23.74 for public employment data.

Source: State of Florida, Agency for Workforce Innovation, Labor Market Statistics, "Quarterly Census of Employment and Wages" (ES-202), Annual NAICS files, Internet site <http://www.labormarketinfo.com/index.htm> (accessed 17, July 2007).

Table 18.52. MANAGEMENT OF COMPANIES AND ENTERPRISES: AVERAGE MONTHLY PRIVATE REPORTING UNITS, EMPLOYMENT, AND PAYROLL COVERED BY UNEMPLOYMENT COMPENSATION LAW IN THE STATE AND COUNTIES OF FLORIDA, 2006

County	Number of reporting units	Number of employees	Payroll ($1,000)	County	Number of reporting units	Number of employees	Payroll ($1,000)
	Management of companies and enterprises (NAICS code 55)						
Florida	2,872	73,935	514,812	Manatee	70	2,611	9,744
				Marion	20	325	1,149
Alachua	20	152	815	Martin	25	180	1,652
Bay	17	189	990	Miami-Dade	332	7,482	74,706
Brevard	37	1,244	5,804	Monroe	25	177	1,529
Broward	295	6,116	40,894	Nassau	14	36	94
Charlotte	17	83	612	Okaloosa	28	363	1,717
Citrus	4	36	140	Orange	194	9,929	72,257
Clay	20	265	969	Palm Beach	316	7,535	76,443
Collier	79	866	8,832	Pasco	22	297	1,218
DeSoto	5	17	66	Pinellas	143	9,326	49,634
Duval	134	6,560	41,979	Polk	41	5,367	23,841
Escambia	34	997	6,076	St. Johns	19	47	567
Flagler	6	6	86	St. Lucie	16	76	899
Hardee	4	10	64	Santa Rosa	5	252	977
Hernando	6	23	71	Sarasota	70	711	3,805
Highlands	12	46	281	Seminole	57	563	3,161
Hillsborough	168	5,215	32,956	Volusia	48	887	4,327
Indian River	25	121	1,066	Walton	5	11	135
Lake	18	138	683	Statewide 1/	133	1,976	18,873
Lee	67	1,528	13,744	Out-of-state 2/	18	266	986
Leon	31	426	2,341	Unknown 1/	225	604	6,508

NAICS North American Industry Classification System. See Glossary for definition.
1/ Reporting units without a fixed location within the state or of unknown county location.
2/ Employment based in Florida, but working out of the state or country.
Note: Private employment. Data are preliminary. Only counties for which data are disclosed are shown. Detail may not add to totals due to disclosure editing and/or rounding. See Tables 23.70, 23.72, 23.73, and 23.74 for public employment data.

Source: State of Florida, Agency for Workforce Innovation, Labor Market Statistics, "Quarterly Census of Employment and Wages" (ES-202), Annual NAICS files, Internet site <http://www.labormarketinfo.com/index.htm> (accessed 17, July 2007).

Table 18.53. ADMINISTRATIVE AND SUPPORT AND WASTE MANAGEMENT AND REMEDIATION SERVICES: AVERAGE MONTHLY PRIVATE REPORTING UNITS, EMPLOYMENT AND PAYROLL COVERED BY UNEMPLOYMENT COMPENSATION LAW IN THE STATE AND COUNTIES OF FLORIDA, 2006

County	Number of reporting units	Number of employees	Payroll ($1,000)	County	Number of reporting units	Number of employees	Payroll ($1,000)
	Administrative and support and waste management and remediation services (NAICS code 56)						
Florida	39,359	822,284	1,954,502	Leon	483	6,318	11,980
Alachua	374	4,721	8,205	Levy	35	80	166
Baker	19	157	269	Madison	7	39	81
Bay	306	3,932	8,957	Manatee	617	26,468	66,014
Bradford	30	87	219	Marion	457	5,048	9,147
Brevard	975	22,359	81,637	Martin	430	3,579	7,461
Broward	4,412	55,680	145,047	Miami-Dade	4,274	68,475	168,640
Calhoun	6	20	36	Monroe	255	1,372	4,027
Charlotte	282	1,496	3,421	Nassau	113	655	1,570
Citrus	215	2,103	5,582	Okaloosa	385	5,107	12,197
Clay	244	1,626	3,879	Okeechobee	55	426	1,156
Collier	951	8,956	22,184	Orange	2,389	69,645	169,868
Columbia	65	646	1,745	Osceola	477	3,720	6,986
DeSoto	35	235	447	Palm Beach	3,617	59,223	157,839
Duval	1,747	39,560	94,059	Pasco	686	5,917	12,956
Escambia	439	9,153	16,454	Pinellas	2,155	58,248	114,595
Flagler	178	1,139	2,540	Polk	823	20,749	42,055
Franklin	15	69	106	Putnam	78	544	933
Gadsden	35	685	1,560	St. Johns	312	2,146	5,438
Gilchrist	20	68	107	St. Lucie	428	4,009	8,077
Glades	13	59	161	Santa Rosa	202	2,299	6,924
Gulf	15	56	96	Sarasota	1,123	13,366	29,385
Hamilton	5	15	185	Seminole	1,023	16,874	39,688
Hendry	46	297	525	Sumter	91	504	970
Hernando	252	1,726	3,335	Suwannee	32	149	260
Highlands	166	1,989	3,623	Taylor	12	49	72
Hillsborough	2,463	86,131	182,447	Volusia	924	10,145	19,199
Holmes	15	60	94	Wakulla	16	83	180
Indian River	368	2,276	4,614	Walton	116	749	1,746
Jackson	36	232	477	Washington	10	39	61
Jefferson	17	125	299	Statewide 1/	698	164,377	390,238
Lake	471	4,111	9,855	Out-of-state 2/	42	1,457	6,535
Lee	1,380	13,628	32,822	Unknown 1/	1,357	6,387	22,231

NAICS North American Industry Classification System. See Glossary for definition.
1/ Reporting units without a fixed location within the state or of unknown county location.
2/ Employment based in Florida, but working out of the state or country.
Note: Private employment. Data are preliminary. For a list of three- and four-digit industries included see Table 18.23. Only counties for which data are disclosed are shown. Detail may not add to totals due to disclosure editing and/or rounding. See Tables 23.70, 23.72, 23.73, and 23.74 for public employment data.

Source: State of Florida, Agency for Workforce Innovation, Labor Market Statistics, "Quarterly Census of Employment and Wages" (ES-202), Annual NAICS files, Internet site <http://www.labormarketinfo.com/index.htm> (accessed 17, July 2007).

Table 18.54. ADMINISTRATIVE AND SUPPORT SERVICES: AVERAGE MONTHLY PRIVATE REPORTING UNITS, EMPLOYMENT, AND PAYROLL COVERED BY UNEMPLOYMENT COMPENSATION LAW IN THE STATE AND COUNTIES OF FLORIDA, 2006

County	Number of reporting units	Number of employees	Payroll ($1,000)	County	Number of reporting units	Number of employees	Payroll ($1,000)
			Administrative and support services (NAICS code 561)				
Florida	38,184	802,996	1,886,056	Leon	469	6,129	11,356
Alachua	362	4,390	7,116	Levy	31	73	154
Baker	17	155	267	Madison	4	26	49
Bay	286	3,537	7,528	Manatee	603	26,196	65,065
Bradford	28	84	213	Marion	440	4,961	8,862
Brevard	943	21,876	79,943	Martin	419	3,407	6,818
Broward	4,308	53,080	136,232	Miami-Dade	4,185	66,609	161,870
Calhoun	6	19	35	Monroe	239	1,200	3,447
Charlotte	268	1,303	2,773	Nassau	107	533	1,177
Citrus	205	2,078	5,473	Okaloosa	363	4,852	11,361
Clay	233	1,527	3,559	Okeechobee	48	356	888
Collier	933	8,676	21,157	Orange	2,329	68,266	165,166
Columbia	57	571	1,385	Osceola	464	3,659	6,799
DeSoto	32	203	338	Palm Beach	3,543	58,114	153,718
Duval	1,686	38,211	88,466	Pasco	645	5,126	10,590
Escambia	416	8,953	15,816	Pinellas	2,103	57,564	112,178
Flagler	176	1,136	2,536	Polk	782	20,047	39,631
Franklin	13	62	90	Putnam	70	520	866
Gadsden	33	677	1,527	St. Johns	304	2,054	5,264
Gilchrist	18	58	93	St. Lucie	412	3,908	7,727
Glades	11	58	158	Santa Rosa	194	2,217	6,674
Gulf	15	56	96	Sarasota	1,099	12,882	27,421
Hamilton	5	15	185	Seminole	998	16,172	37,728
Hendry	43	270	434	Sumter	87	496	949
Hernando	248	1,709	3,300	Suwannee	28	143	248
Highlands	155	1,927	3,449	Taylor	10	46	59
Hillsborough	2,402	84,736	176,267	Volusia	895	9,689	17,830
Holmes	12	52	78	Wakulla	15	83	178
Indian River	362	2,193	4,323	Walton	99	621	1,385
Jackson	28	157	209	Washington	9	36	56
Jefferson	17	125	299	Statewide 1/	687	164,325	389,859
Lake	448	3,558	7,786	Out-of-state 2/	40	1,457	6,534
Lee	1,339	12,865	30,351	Unknown 1/	1,321	6,296	21,881

NAICS North American Industry Classification System. See Glossary for definition.
1/ Reporting units without a fixed location within the state or of unknown county location.
2/ Employment based in Florida, but working out of the state or country.
Note: Private employment. Data are preliminary. For a list of four-digit industries included see Table 18.23. Only counties for which data are disclosed are shown. Detail may not add to totals due to disclosure editing and/or rounding. See Tables 23.70, 23.72, 23.73, and 23.74 for public employment data.

Source: State of Florida, Agency for Workforce Innovation, Labor Market Statistics, "Quarterly Census of Employment and Wages" (ES-202), Annual NAICS files, Internet site <http://www.labormarketinfo.com/index.htm> (accessed 17, July 2007).

Table 18.56. ARCHITECTS, INTERIOR DESIGNERS, AND ACCOUNTANTS: NUMBER LICENSED IN THE STATE AND COUNTIES OF FLORIDA, JUNE 23, 2007

Location of licensee	Architects	Interior designers	Account- ants	Location of licensee	Architects	Interior designers	Account- ants
Total	9,415	2,837	27,850	Jefferson	3	2	9
				Lafayette	1	0	5
Foreign	6	0	37	Lake	30	14	177
Out-of-state	2,730	115	2,378	Lee	105	91	410
Unknown	2,539	484	4,759	Leon	112	58	750
Alachua	86	15	293	Levy	2	0	19
Baker	1	0	11	Liberty	0	0	5
Bay	19	4	110	Madison	2	0	9
Bradford	1	0	9	Manatee	45	24	285
Brevard	67	47	415	Marion	25	15	166
Broward	372	249	2,743	Martin	29	32	166
Calhoun	1	0	8	Miami-Dade	944	345	2,978
Charlotte	12	3	68	Monroe	32	8	76
Citrus	5	0	53	Nassau	14	11	43
Clay	15	11	149	Okaloosa	39	14	132
Collier	86	121	295	Okeechobee	0	0	18
Columbia	2	1	35	Orange	350	173	1,413
DeSoto	1	0	6	Osceola	20	8	65
Dixie	0	0	1	Palm Beach	351	300	1,974
Duval	194	121	1,180	Pasco	13	8	215
Escambia	89	22	268	Pinellas	194	114	1,361
Flagler	10	5	26	Polk	48	14	385
Franklin	3	1	7	Putnam	7	0	25
Gadsden	4	2	32	St. Johns	37	25	234
Gilchrist	0	0	1	St. Lucie	20	16	111
Glades	0	0	1	Santa Rosa	16	7	92
Gulf	0	0	6	Sarasota	124	88	455
Hamilton	2	0	3	Seminole	142	70	629
Hardee	0	0	8	Sumter	0	0	12
Hendry	2	0	16	Suwannee	0	1	17
Hernando	7	3	55	Taylor	1	0	8
Highlands	3	2	40	Union	0	0	3
Hillsborough	330	127	1,976	Volusia	48	21	387
Holmes	1	0	5	Wakulla	8	0	31
Indian River	38	35	142	Walton	22	10	19
Jackson	3	0	21	Washington	2	0	9

Caution: Data were collected from unaudited, raw data files as reported by the Department of Business and Professional Regulation and may contain reporting errors.
Note: Total includes all active and inactive licenses and excludes business licenses.

Source: State of Florida, Department of Business and Professional Regulation, Licensee Information Download files: Architecture and Interior Design and Accountancy, Internet site <http://www.myflorida.com/dbpr/> (accessed 23, June 2007).

TOURISM AND RECREATION

Boating and Personal Watercraft Accidents by Age of Operator, 2006 (%)

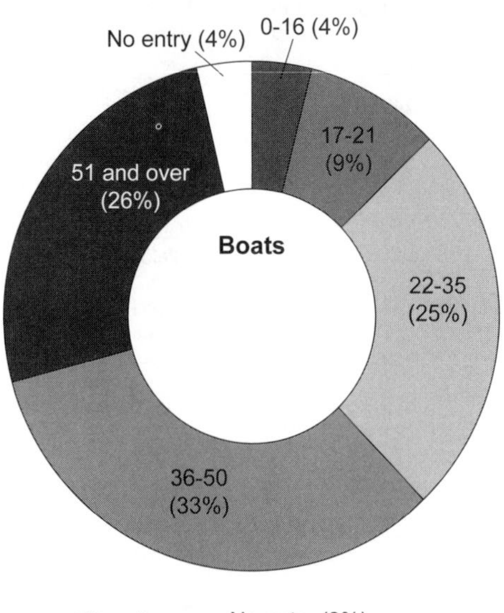

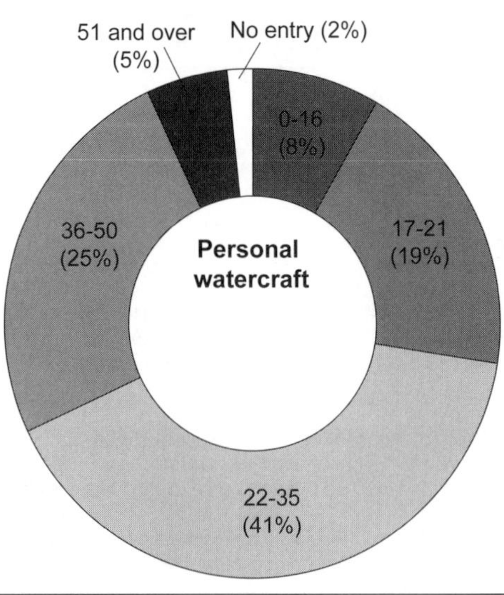

Source: Table 19.46

Section 19.00
Tourism and Recreation

Florida's beaches and attractions combined with tropical-like weather draw visitors from around the world year-round. As a large tourist state, much of Florida's economy relies on its visitors. This section presents data on Florida's tourism and recreation industries and includes establishments, employment, and payroll; characteristics of Floridians taking vacations within the state as well as domestic and international visitors; air and auto visitors; traffic counts of vehicles entering and leaving the state; recreational and commercial boating statistics; state and national parks and areas visitors; tourist development tases; and tourist facilities, such as hotels, motels, and food service establishments.

Explanatory notes. Estimates of the number of tourists entering Florida by automobile are made using traffic counts and information from welcome stations. Tourist arrivals by air are based on arrivals at major airports. Individual visitors are interviewed on a randomly selected basis about expenditures and length of stay. Sample results are expanded to the total visitor population.

Sources. Tables from the *2002 Economic Census* publications, *Arts, Entertainment, and Recreation* and *Accommodation and Foodservices* published by the U.S. Census Bureau, appear in the front of this chapter. These tables are based on the NAICS industry classification system (See the introduction to Section 6.00 and the Glossary). Current data on employment in tourist- and recreation-related industries come from the Florida Agency for Workforce Innovation, Labor Market Statistics. (See the introduction to Section 6.00.)

VISIT FLORIDA issues reports of tourist characteristics of domestic and international visitors as well as Floridian's traveling within the state in their annual *Florida Visitor Study.*

The Transportation Statistics Office of the Florida Department of Transportation records traffic counts at strategic highway locations around the state. Data on tourist facilities (hotels, motels, and food service establishments) regulated by the Division of Hotels and Restaurants are available from the Florida Department of Business and Professional Regulation.

The Florida Department of Highway Safety and Motor Vehicles provides county-level pleasure and commercial boat registrations in *Revenue Report.* Data on recreational boating and personal watercraft accidents are published by the Florida Fish and Wildlife Conservation Commission and are available online in the *Boating Accident Statistical Report.*

The Florida Department of Revenue (DOR) provides information on the gross and taxable sales of businesses. Some businesses have been classified for purposes of presenting data in this section as "tourist- and recreation-related" businesses. DOR also provides information on the tourist-development or local option taxes collected in several counties on its Web site.

The state's Recreation and Parks Management Information System in the Department of Environmental Protection provides unpublished information on attendance at state parks and areas, and the U.S. Department of the Interior's National Park Service publishes national park data online in their *National Park Service Statistical Abstract.*

Section 19.00
Tourism and Recreation

Tables listed by major heading

(Continued)

Tables listed by major heading

Table 19.01. ARTS, ENTERTAINMENT, AND RECREATION: ESTABLISHMENTS, EMPLOYMENT RECEIPTS, AND ANNUAL PAYROLL BY KIND OF BUSINESS IN FLORIDA, 2002

NAICS code	Industry	Number of establishments	Number of employees 1/	Receipts ($1,000)	Annual payroll ($1,000)
71	Arts, entertainment, and recreation	6,308	146,735	11,319,842	3,131,214
711	Performing arts, spectator sports, and related industries	2,313	28,353	3,281,444	1,117,465
7111	Performing arts companies	546	6,123	481,832	125,605
7112	Spectator sports	388	11,635	1,758,039	759,847
7113	Promoters	366	7,798	675,764	127,414
7114	Agents/managers	237	591	102,503	19,504
7115	Independent artists, writers, and performers	776	2,206	263,306	85,095
712	Museums, historical sites, similar institutions	315	5,989	378,885	117,504
713	Amusement, gambling, and recreation	3,680	112,393	7,659,513	1,896,245
7131	Amusement parks and arcades	168	36,918	3,612,913	620,068
7132	Gambling industries	79	4,869	530,009	99,945
7139	Other amusement and recreation services	3,433	70,606	3,516,591	1,176,232

1/ Paid employment for the pay period including March 12.

Note: The economic censuses are conducted on a 5-year cycle collecting data for years ending in 2 and 7. Data are for North American Industry Classification System (NAICS) code 71 and may not be comparable to earlier years. See Glossary for definition.

Table 19.02. ACCOMMODATION AND FOOD SERVICES: ESTABLISHMENTS, EMPLOYMENT SALES, AND ANNUAL PAYROLL BY KIND OF BUSINESS IN FLORIDA, 2002

NAICS code	Industry	Number of establishments	Number of employees 1/	Sales ($1,000)	Annual payroll ($1,000)
72	Accommodation and foodservices	30,215	621,207	29,266,940	7,940,944
721	Accommodation	3,838	145,617	10,078,151	2,627,504
7211	Traveler accommodation	3,334	141,946	9,805,356	2,569,872
72111	Hotels (except casino hotels) and motels	3,183	141,176	9,745,796	2,557,991
72119	Other traveler accommodation	151	770	59,560	11,881
7212	Recreational vehicle parks and recreational camps	404	3,161	244,706	51,360
7213	Rooming and boarding houses	100	510	28,089	6,272
722	Foodservices and drinking places	26,377	475,590	19,288,789	5,313,440
7221	Full-service restaurants	11,799	253,841	10,312,688	3,053,498
7222	Limited-service eating places	11,335	179,862	6,924,145	1,746,484
7223	Special foodservices	1,378	27,049	1,289,438	352,694
72231	Foodservice contractors	797	22,116	1,058,829	301,701
72232	Caterers	416	4,199	165,874	41,915
72233	Mobile foodservices	165	734	64,735	9,078
7224	Drinking places (alcoholic beverages)	1,865	14,838	762,518	160,764

1/ Paid employment for the pay period including March 12.

Note: The economic censuses are conducted on a 5-year cycle collecting data for years ending in 2 and 7. Data are for North American Industry Classification System (NAICS) code 72 and may not be comparable to earlier years. See Glossary for definition.

Source for Tables 19.01 and 19.02: U.S., Department of Commerce, Census Bureau, *2002 Economic Census: Arts, Entertainment, and Recreation,* Geographic Area Series EC02-71A-FL, issued August 2005, and *2002 Economic Census: Accommodation and Foodservices,* Geographic Area Series EC02-72A-FL, issued July 2005, Internet site <http://www.census.gov/> (accessed 11, May 2007).

Table 19.05. ARTS, ENTERTAINMENT, AND RECREATION AND ACCOMMODATION AND FOOD SERVICES: RECEIPTS OR SALES IN THE STATE AND COUNTIES OF FLORIDA, 2002

(in thousands of dollars)

County	Arts, entertainment and recreation receipts	Accommodation and food-services sales	County	Arts, entertainment and recreation receipts	Accommodation and food-services sales
Florida	11,319,842	29,266,940	Lake	(D)	240,784
Alachua	(D)	326,772	Lee	215,964	839,873
Baker	(D)	14,066	Leon	66,552	393,582
Bay	(D)	373,164	Levy	3,927	25,561
Bradford	(D)	22,727	Liberty	(D)	(D)
Brevard	225,638	604,443	Madison	1,044	10,946
Broward	1,238,342	2,799,987	Manatee	61,250	297,414
Calhoun	(D)	(D)	Marion	54,576	240,967
Charlotte	27,371	138,202	Martin	105,835	220,032
Citrus	21,277	80,485	Miami-Dade	988,233	4,162,169
Clay	30,109	149,730	Monroe	88,106	638,620
Collier	353,264	697,888	Nassau	(D)	180,124
Columbia	2,235	66,455	Okaloosa	50,950	357,413
DeSoto	(D)	13,552	Okeechobee	(D)	34,759
Dixie	2,073	5,231	Orange	3,561,741	4,688,186
Duval	377,495	1,173,952	Osceola	436,757	654,999
Escambia	55,391	392,107	Palm Beach	879,007	2,266,130
Flagler	(D)	62,587	Pasco	45,749	275,807
Franklin	(D)	21,903	Pinellas	366,662	1,567,142
Gadsden	(D)	13,882	Polk	81,933	452,479
Gilchrist	(D)	4,680	Putnam	3,510	37,432
Glades	(D)	2,816	St. Johns	100,940	330,651
Gulf	2,155	9,165	St. Lucie	36,465	170,144
Hamilton	0	4,303	Santa Rosa	12,115	85,173
Hardee	(D)	9,334	Sarasota	192,609	579,129
Hendry	5,137	21,138	Seminole	100,966	476,453
Hernando	11,970	100,504	Sumter	(D)	29,352
Highlands	29,440	63,160	Suwannee	(D)	20,362
Hillsborough	848,189	1,643,887	Taylor	(D)	14,647
Holmes	(D)	4,516	Union	0	2,291
Indian River	85,073	139,857	Volusia	(D)	734,596
Jackson	2,629	30,504	Wakulla	(D)	10,978
Jefferson	(D)	3,649	Walton	5,309	308,779
Lafayette	0	(D)	Washington	(D)	12,754

(D) Data withheld to avoid disclosure of information about individual firms.

Note: The economic censuses are conducted on a 5-year cycle collecting data for years ending in 2 and 7. Data are for North American Industry Classification System (NAICS) codes 71 and 72 and may not be comparable to earlier years. See Glossary for definition.

Source: U.S., Department of Commerce, Census Bureau, *2002 Economic Census: Arts, Entertainment, and Recreation,* Geographic Area Series EC02-71A-FL, issued August 2005, and *2002 Economic Census: Accommodation and Foodservices,* Geographic Area Series EC02-72A-FL, issued July 2005, Internet site <http://www.census.gov/> (accessed 11, May 2007).

Table 19.20. TOURISTS: CHARACTERISTICS OF DOMESTIC VISITORS TO FLORIDA
2004 AND 2005

Characteristic	2004 Total	2004 Air	2004 Non-air	2005 Total	2005 Air	2005 Non-air
Visitors (1,000)	73,379	34,276	39,104	73,379	34,276	39,104
Percentage	100.0	46.7	53.3	100.0	46.7	53.3
Purpose of trip (percentage)						
Leisure	84.1	77.1	90.5	82.6	77.1	91.0
General vacation	37.4	33.2	41.2	37.3	34.2	39.0
Visit friends/relatives	29.8	28.9	30.6	24.9	25.6	27.7
Special Event	6.2	6.3	6.1	6.4	6.9	6.2
Getaway weekend	5.8	4.7	6.7	7.3	4.7	10.7
Other personal	5.0	4.1	5.8	6.7	5.8	7.4
Business	15.9	22.9	9.5	17.4	22.9	9.0
Convention	3.8	5.8	2.0	4.0	6.7	1.7
Seminar/training	3.4	4.8	2.1	2.5	3.7	1.4
Other group meetings	1.3	2.3	0.4	1.5	2.3	0.7
Sales/consulting	2.0	2.6	1.3	3.0	4.3	1.4
Other	5.4	7.4	3.7	6.4	5.9	3.8
Average expenditure per person per day (dollars)	136.0	163.1	107.3	138.9	157.0	115.9
Transportation	39.5	59.7	19.7	41.1	57.5	20.8
Food	29.0	30.5	27.4	29.4	30.6	28.4
Accommodations	21.4	23.8	18.2	22.4	24.1	19.7
Shopping	19.6	21.1	17.0	19.8	19.6	19.9
Entertainment	19.5	19.8	19.4	19.6	18.2	21.7
Miscellaneous	7.0	8.1	5.5	6.5	7.0	5.5
Length of stay (average nights)	5.1	5.2	5.0	5.2	5.5	5.1
1-3 nights	42.0	37.2	46.3	42.8	32.9	48.9
4-7 nights	42.1	46.3	38.3	40.4	50.0	34.5
8 nights or over	15.9	16.5	15.4	16.8	17.0	16.6
Travel party size (average persons)	2.3	2.0	2.7	2.3	2.0	2.7
One adult	31	45	15	34	44	19
Couples	33	26	39	32	26	41
Families	23	16	32	22	17	29
Three or more adults	6	6	7	7	6	7
Two males or two females	7	7	7	5	6	3
Accommodations (percentage)						
Hotel/motel	50.1	53.4	50.1	47.5	49.3	47.2
Private home	30.6	30.0	34.2	30.7	31.4	34.1
Condominium/timeshare	5.6	5.8	6.3	7.3	7.7	8.6
Ship	4.0	3.5	1.2	3.5	2.7	1.5
Other	6.6	4.0	5.5	8.2	6.1	6.2
Reservation type for accommodations						
Made reservation	76	81	70	77	83	72
On-line	18	18	18	19	23	17
Direct to location	14	13	14	13	13	16
800 phone number	14	12	16	12	8	17
Travel agent	8	11	4	10	12	4
Corporate travel department	6	11	2	7	11	1
Other	15	15	15	16	16	17
No reservation	24	19	30	23	17	28

See footnotes at end of table. Continued . . .

Table 19.20. TOURISTS: CHARACTERISTICS OF DOMESTIC VISITORS TO FLORIDA 2004 AND 2005 (Continued)

Characteristic	2004 Total	2004 Air	2004 Non-air	2005 Total	2005 Air	2005 Non-air
Primary activities 1/ (percentage)						
Shopping	30.0	35.1	29.1	32.2	36.6	33.0
Touring, sightseeing	33.2	29.4	35.4	27.3	24.8	29.1
Beach/saterfront	32.5	29.6	35.7	24.8	21.8	29.8
Theme/amusement park	25.3	26.4	25.3	23.3	26.2	23.6
Nightlife	8.6	11.3	6.3	8.9	11.1	6.9
Play golf	4.3	4.5	4.4	6.2	5.5	7.6
National/state park	6.1	6.1	6.0	5.9	6.1	5.6
Look at real estate	6.0	6.9	5.9	5.9	6.8	5.1
Sports event	4.4	4.8	4.4	4.5	4.7	5.4
Group tour	5.0	4.1	4.3	4.1	3.5	4.2
Museum/art exhibit	2.9	2.9	2.9	4.1	4.1	4.3
Historical sites	4.9	3.1	5.8	3.9	3.8	4.5
Boat/sail	5.3	5.7	4.9	3.6	3.7	3.4
Nature/culture-eco-travel	3.9	3.0	4.7	3.3	1.9	3.6
Festival/craft fair	3.5	3.2	3.8	3.0	2.2	3.2
Gambling	2.9	2.6	3.2	2.9	3.4	2.5
Performing arts (concerts, plays, stage shows)	3.0	3.4	2.3	2.7	3.2	2.1
Hunt/fish	4.4	2.0	6.1	2.3	1.8	2.9
Camping	2.5	0.4	1.4	2.2	0.4	0.9
Other adventure sports	2.2	2.4	1.4	1.8	1.9	1.6
Hike/bike	1.3	1.0	1.6	1.3	1.2	1.5
Boat/car/home show	1.0	1.0	0.6	1.3	1.5	0.7
No activity mentioned	15.4	15.7	14.4	20.1	17.6	19.8
Rental car use (percentage)	27	50	9	26	49	6
Rented car and flew	22	50	0	23	49	0
Rented car, did not fly	5	0	9	3	0	6
Seasonality (percentage)						
Winter (December, January, February)	31	31	29	28	30	26
Spring (March, April, May)	26	27	25	28	29	26
Summer (June, July, August)	24	22	28	25	21	30
Fall (September, October, November)	19	20	17	19	20	19
Household income of visitors (percentage)						
Under $20,000	4.9	2.2	6.2	5.6	3.7	7.4
$20,000 to $29,999	5.7	5.0	6.0	6.1	3.8	8.5
$30,000 to $49,999	17.6	12.4	22.2	14.0	10.9	16.7
$50,000 to $74,999	21.9	20.4	24.4	21.5	18.8	25.0
$75,000 to $99,999	23.7	24.5	22.3	24.7	27.9	20.5
$100,000 to $124,999	12.6	16.0	10.1	13.1	14.3	13.1
$125,000 and over	13.5	19.6	8.9	15.0	20.5	8.8
Average (dollars)	77,500	87,800	69,700	79,900	88,900	70,800
Age of adult traveler (percentage)						
18 to 34 years	28.2	27.2	29.1	27.4	26.9	29.3
35 to 54 years	45.9	49.7	42.6	43.2	48.9	39.2
Over 55 years	25.9	23.1	28.3	29.5	24.2	31.5
Average age (years)	45.4	45.0	45.7	46.3	45.3	46.4

1/ Multiple responses were allowed.
Note: Data are for domestic visitors only and exclude Canadian and other international visitors.

Source: State of Florida, VISIT FLORIDA, *2005 Florida Visitor Study*.

Table 19.21. TOURISTS: KEY DEMOGRAPHICS OF FLORIDA RESIDENTS TAKING TRIPS FOR PLEASURE WITHIN FLORIDA, 2005

Characteristic	Percent-age	Characteristic	Percent-age	Characteristic	Percent-age
Sex		Hispanic origin	9.6	Household income	
Male	47.5	Not of Hispanic origin	90.4	Less than $20,000	7.1
Female	52.5	Race		$20,000 - $49,000	27.2
Age		White	83.6	$50,000 - $79,999	29.3
18-34	26.5	Black	8.3	$80,000 - $99,999	11.4
35-49	39.3	Asian or Pacific Islander	0.5	Over $100,000	25.0
50-64	25.4	American Indian or		Marital status	
Over 65	8.7	Alaskan Native	1.9	Married	64.3
Mean (years)	44.2	Multi-racial or mixed race	1.3	Widowed	5.7
Median (years)	43.0	Other	4.3	Never married	15.7
				Divorced/separated	14.3

Table 19.22. TOURISTS: FLORIDA RESIDENTS TAKING TRIPS FOR PLEASURE WITHIN FLORIDA, 2001 TO 2005

Destination and average nights spent	Percentage 2001	2002	2003	2004	2005	Percentage points change 2004 to 2005
MSA						
Orlando	37.7	28.7	32.2	35.8	37.3	1.5
Non-MSA	15.1	18.4	17.1	17.3	20.7	3.4
Tampa	6.4	10.1	11.6	9.1	7.4	-1.7
Miami	4.9	6.4	8.4	5.7	4.9	-0.8
Daytona	6.8	5.3	3.4	4.9	(NA)	(NA)
Average nights spent on trip						
Trip in Florida	3.9	3.8	3.8	3.8	3.2	-0.6
Trip out of Florida	9.0	9.2	9.0	8.5	9.4	0.9

MSA Metropolitan Statistical Area.
(NA) Not available.

Table 19.23. TOURISTS: FLORIDA RESIDENTS TAKING TRIPS FOR PLEASURE BY TIME OF YEAR, 2004 AND 2005

Trip characteristic	Persons 2004	Persons 2005	Percentage 2004	Percentage 2005	Percentage change 2004 to 2005
Out-of-state trips, total	34,106,212	36,951,570	16.7	17.7	8.3
January through March	6,331,093	7,150,233	12.4	13.7	12.9
April through June	8,526,553	9,185,701	16.7	17.6	7.7
July through September	11,436,814	11,951,850	22.4	22.9	4.5
October through December	8,118,095	8,402,829	15.9	16.1	3.5
In-state trips, total	13,471,954	13,302,565	39.5	36.0	-1.3
January through March	2,500,782	2,874,394	39.5	40.2	14.9
April through June	3,990,427	3,444,638	46.8	37.5	-13.7
July through September	4,357,426	4,326,570	38.1	36.2	-0.7
October through December	2,763,607	2,478,834	34.0	29.5	-10.3

Note: Quarterly figures are weighted; therefore, they do not add up to annual totals.

Source for Tables 19.21, 19.22 and 19.23: State of Florida, VISIT FLORIDA, *2005 Florida Visitor Study.*

Table 19.24. TOURISTS: PERCENTAGE DISTRIBUTION OF DOMESTIC VISITORS TRAVELING BY AIR AND AUTOMOBILE TO FLORIDA BY ORIGIN AND COUNTY DESTINATION, 2005

Origin	Total	Air	Auto	County of destination	Total	Air	Auto
New York	11.5	15.8	7.6	Orange	28.9	35.1	25.6
Georgia	10.1	1.7	18.6	Hillsborough	7.7	9.1	3.4
New Jersey	5.6	7.6	4.1	Broward	6.2	9.4	2.4
Illinois	5.1	6.6	3.9	Miami-Dade	6.0	7.9	3.1
North Carolina	5.0	1.7	5.8	Volusia	4.7	2.9	5.7
California	5.0	9.2	0.7	Duval	4.3	2.3	5.9
Pennsylvania	4.7	5.8	3.4	Palm Beach	4.2	5.8	3.0
Ohio	4.2	4.5	3.8	Okaloosa	3.8	0.8	7.0
Alabama	4.0	0.9	7.7	Pinellas	3.1	2.8	3.8
Texas	3.9	3.5	4.1	Lee	3.0	3.1	2.8
Michigan	3.9	4.1	3.6	Monroe	2.8	2.3	2.3
South Carolina	3.5	0.7	5.5	Escambia	2.6	1.1	4.6
				Brevard	2.5	2.1	2.7
				Bay	2.3	0.3	5.1
				Sarasota	2.1	2.7	1.8

Source: State of Florida, VISIT FLORIDA, *2005 Florida Visitor Study.*

Table 19.25. TOURISTS: INTERNATIONAL TRAVELERS TO FLORIDA BY SPECIFIED COUNTRY OF ORIGIN, 2000 THROUGH 2005

(in thousands of person-trips)

Country or region	2000	2001	2002	2003	2004	2005 Number	2005 Percentage change 2000 to 2005
Total	8,068	7,149	6,019	5,869	6,341	6,412	-20.5
Canada (air and auto)	2,042	1,887	1,603	1,669	1,911	2,033	-0.4
Overseas	6,026	5,262	4,416	4,200	4,430	4,379	-27.3
Argentina	338	227	75	86	74	A/ 95	-71.9
Brazil	365	218	134	145	167	181	-50.4
France	160	139	134	110	122	121	-24.4
Germany	325	303	202	225	265	282	-13.2
Italy	151	117	96	75	113	79	-47.7
Japan	147	110	65	60	82	66	-55.1
Netherlands	97	98	55	67	53	36	-62.9
Spain	101	77	66	91	77	A/ 95	-5.9
United Kingdom	1,651	1,516	1,294	1,378	1,480	1,490	-9.8
Venezuela	451	393	301	239	224	A/ 221	-51.0
Other overseas	2,337	2,162	1,644	1,361	1,531	1,436	-38.6

A/ Due to an extremely small sample size, estimates for these countries were developed. Caution is urged when interpreting the data.
Source: State of Florida, VISIT FLORIDA, *2005 Florida Visitor Study.*

Table 19.26. TRAFFIC COUNTS: AVERAGE DAILY TRAFFIC ENTERING AND LEAVING FLORIDA AND PASSING OTHER SPECIFIC POINTS, MONTHS OF 2006

Location and direction		January	February	March	April	May	June
I-95 Georgia	N	25,366	28,976	33,008	36,465	30,408	30,225
	S	27,919	29,688	30,197	31,425	27,076	29,415
Florida Turpike Wildwood	N	18,227	17,951	21,479	18,879	19,190	20,393
	S	17,720	18,842	21,916	18,665	19,240	20,188
I-75 Georgia	N	16,899	18,367	22,545	23,866	19,769	21,823
	S	18,168	18,321	21,817	18,821	18,670	21,161
I-10 Alabama	E	15,297	16,140	17,740	16,995	17,510	18,862
	W	15,141	15,901	18,083	17,167	17,247	18,660
U.S. 231 Alabama	N	5,449	5,754	7,138	7,627	7,459	8,083
	S	5,719	5,942	7,166	7,006	7,696	8,324
I-4 Orlando	E	78,713	81,705	87,068	85,731	80,618	83,940
	W	80,748	84,525	89,693	88,919	83,196	86,593

Location and direction		July	August	September	October	November	December
I-95 Georgia	N	31,153	27,184	24,709	26,355	29,092	29,301
	S	31,155	27,213	25,447	29,459	31,255	31,925
Florida Turpike Wildwood	N	20,459	18,109	17,004	18,270	15,503	24,230
	S	20,686	17,642	17,489	19,440	17,102	26,656
I-75 Georgia	N	22,000	17,579	16,507	20,000	20,006	19,753
	S	22,323	17,100	18,728	19,879	21,434	22,052
I-10 Alabama	E	19,336	16,448	15,731	16,009	16,658	16,433
	W	19,423	16,653	15,509	15,621	16,362	16,192
U.S. 231 Alabama	N	8,731	6,794	6,611	6,360	6,286	5,874
	S	8,649	6,752	6,739	6,600	6,566	6,409
I-4 Orlando	E	87,774	83,960	(NA)	(NA)	(NA)	(NA)
	W	90,543	86,788	(NA)	(NA)	(NA)	(NA)

(NA) Not available.

Source: State of Florida, Department of Transportation, Transportation Statistics Office, unpublished data.

Table 19.45. BOATS: NUMBER REGISTERED BY TYPE IN THE STATE AND COUNTIES OF FLORIDA, FISCAL YEAR 2005–06

County	Total 1/	Pleasure boats	Commercial boats	County	Total 1/	Pleasure boats	Commercial boats
Florida 2/	964,326	938,144	21,582	Lake	22,772	22,560	154
				Lee	48,254	47,048	1,015
Alachua	10,811	10,667	115	Leon	13,143	12,966	162
Baker	2,150	2,141	9	Levy	4,310	3,964	311
Bay	19,611	18,831	685	Liberty	1,044	1,027	16
Bradford	2,107	2,088	18	Madison	1,119	1,114	5
Brevard	38,372	37,219	824	Manatee	19,791	19,088	516
Broward	47,533	46,190	892	Marion	20,046	19,754	244
Calhoun	1,444	1,426	16	Martin	16,495	15,840	496
Charlotte	21,353	20,798	476	Miami-Dade	56,731	54,772	1,522
Citrus	17,556	16,945	555	Monroe	27,387	24,686	2,587
Clay	12,311	12,139	140	Nassau	5,808	5,632	163
Collier	23,676	22,862	725	Okaloosa	18,757	18,272	383
Columbia	4,544	4,506	31	Okeechobee	5,656	5,472	175
DeSoto	2,359	2,304	54	Orange	33,869	33,496	166
Dixie	2,652	2,402	247	Osceola	9,065	8,951	87
Duval	31,748	31,081	535	Palm Beach	42,516	41,525	764
Escambia	16,708	16,388	240	Pasco	25,253	24,716	473
Flagler	4,743	4,667	67	Pinellas	52,987	51,423	1,164
Franklin	3,115	2,363	743	Polk	31,535	31,114	361
Gadsden	2,446	2,415	29	Putnam	8,101	7,870	210
Gilchrist	1,647	1,616	31	St. Johns	12,362	12,022	290
Glades	1,411	1,340	56	St. Lucie	13,240	12,778	411
Gulf	2,962	2,737	224	Santa Rosa	13,482	13,295	155
Hamilton	874	874	0	Sarasota	24,303	23,781	362
Hardee	1,568	1,560	8	Seminole	18,997	18,772	134
Hendry	2,892	2,779	103	Sumter	4,118	4,066	45
Hernando	9,722	9,575	131	Suwannee	2,903	2,875	24
Highlands	10,158	10,035	82	Taylor	3,727	3,575	137
Hillsborough	45,494	44,787	589	Union	775	772	3
Holmes	1,879	1,861	16	Volusia	30,013	29,308	555
Indian River	11,190	10,794	353	Wakulla	4,406	4,127	276
Jackson	4,470	4,448	22	Walton	5,292	5,181	109
Jefferson	1,211	1,189	19	Washington	2,273	2,253	20
Lafayette	862	852	9				

1/ Includes vessels registered to dealers, canoes, and Class 5 vessels not shown separately.
2/ Includes data not distributed by county.

Source: State of Florida, Department of Highway Safety and Motor Vehicles, *Revenue Report, July 1, 2005 through June 30, 2006,* Internet site <http://www.hsmv.state.fl.us/> (accessed 16, March 2007).

Table 19.46. RECREATIONAL BOATING ACCIDENTS: BOATING AND PERSONAL WATERCRAFT ACCIDENTS BY LOCATION, TYPE, OPERATION, AND OPERATOR IN FLORIDA, 2006

Item	Boats 1/		Personal water-craft 2/
	Number	Fatal	
Location			
River/creek	148	17	26
Ocean/gulf	133	9	34
Bay/sound	133	10	32
Lake/pond	106	19	53
Canal/cut	56	2	10
Inlet/pass	53	1	17
Port/harbor	31	0	2
Marsh/swamp	8	2	0
Other	3	1	0
Accidents, total	671	69	174
Type 3/			
Capsizing	25	11	3
Collision			
Fixed object	116	7	25
Floating object/person	16	0	9
Skier hit object	9	1	2
Struck by boat	11	1	6
Struck by skeg/prop	9	0	0
Struck underwater object	22	1	1
Vessel	195	7	92
Skier mishap/fall	11	0	1
Fall on PWC	22	6	22
Fall in boat	21	0	0
Fall overboard	45	15	3
Fire or explosion, fuel	18	0	3
Fire or explosion, non-fuel	13	0	0
Flooding/swamping	60	6	2
Grounding	35	3	2
Sinking	10	1	0
Starting engine	2	0	0
Vessel wake damage	16	0	1
Other	15	2	2
Vessels in accidents	946	61	248
Operation at time of accident 4/			
At anchor	52	5	0
Being towed	15	2	2
Operation at time of accident (Continued)			
Cruising	407	36	90
Changing direction	160	8	91
Changing speed	42	1	19
Docked	84	4	2
Docking/undocking	33	3	1
Drifting	64	8	20
Launching/loading	2	0	1
Rowing/paddling	5	2	0
Sailing	9	0	0
Towing	17	1	0
Wake/surf jumping	18	2	18
Other	23	3	4
No information	30	0	0
Operators, total	853	69	241
Age (years)			
0-16	34	3	20
17-21	76	2	46
22-35	213	16	98
36-50	281	26	60
51 and over	219	22	13
No entry	30	0	4
Experience (hours)			
Less than 10	76	7	58
10–100	156	9	70
100+	426	13	38
No entry	195	40	75
No boater education by age (years)			
All ages	616	59	203
1-16	23	1	15
17-21	54	2	38
22-35	171	13	83
36-50	209	26	52
51 and over	131	17	11
No entry	28	0	4

1/ Registered recreational vessels.
2/ Accidents involving a small vessel designed to be operated by a person sitting, standing, or kneeling on, or being towed behind the vessel, rather than in the conventional manner of sitting or standing inside the vessel.
3/ Based on first harmful event.
4/ Each accident may contain multiple entries.
Note: A reportable boat accident is any boating accident that results in death, disappearance of any person, injury requiring medical treatment beyond first aid, and/or property damage totaling more than $500.
Source: State of Florida, Fish and Wildlife Conservation Commission, *2006 Boating Accident Statistical Report,* Internet site <http://myfwc.com/> (accessed 16, May 2007).

Table 19.48. RECREATIONAL BOATING ACCIDENTS: VESSELS, ACCIDENTS, AND PROPERTY DAMAGES RESULTING FROM RECREATIONAL BOATING AND PERSONAL WATERCRAFT ACCIDENTS IN THE STATE AND COUNTIES OF FLORIDA, 2006

	Registered vessels		Reported accidents 1/					Damages (dollars)	
			Boating			Personal watercraft			
County	Boats	Personal water-craft	Num-ber	Fatal-ities	Injuries	Num-ber	Injuries	Boating	Personal water-craft
Florida	988,652	117,438	671	69	420	174	146	8,639,845	469,965
Alachua	11,162	864	1	0	0	0	0	5,000	0
Baker	2,265	151	1	0	0	1	0	2,500	2,500
Bay	19,860	2,498	16	1	8	5	4	138,500	7,500
Bradford	2,194	207	0	0	0	0	0	0	0
Brevard	38,985	4,208	25	5	14	5	5	59,600	5,400
Broward	49,287	7,761	29	3	11	7	6	310,102	8,500
Calhoun	1,497	32	0	0	0	0	0	0	0
Charlotte	21,961	1,598	9	0	10	2	2	108,750	1,250
Citrus	17,370	1,103	6	1	10	1	1	12,950	0
Clay	12,744	1,843	6	2	3	3	2	35,462	2,462
Collier	23,751	3,187	27	0	17	5	2	343,600	11,000
Columbia	4,778	322	0	0	0	0	0	0	0
DeSoto	2,382	184	0	0	0	0	0	0	0
Dixie	2,656	99	5	1	4	0	0	17,125	0
Duval	33,518	4,125	19	5	7	3	0	88,050	4,000
Escambia	17,672	1,755	21	1	12	4	4	113,335	6,800
Flagler	4,915	440	4	0	4	0	0	13,000	0
Franklin	2,673	214	11	1	3	2	1	47,750	750
Gadsden	2,587	99	0	0	0	0	0	0	0
Gilchrist	1,760	94	2	0	2	1	1	1,000	0
Glades	1,370	30	6	0	5	0	0	547,000	0
Gulf	2,942	193	2	0	2	1	1	2,600	2,600
Hamilton	935	26	0	0	0	0	0	0	0
Hardee	1,625	146	0	0	0	0	0	0	0
Hendry	3,057	151	0	0	0	0	0	0	0
Hernando	9,855	1,069	2	0	1	0	0	3,000	0
Highlands	10,478	1,313	4	1	5	0	0	3,000	0
Hillsborough	47,469	6,397	13	3	4	3	2	62,920	9,500
Holmes	2,069	52	0	0	0	0	0	0	0
Indian River	11,146	751	13	1	5	6	2	62,200	16,200
Jackson	4,753	230	2	0	1	0	0	5,000	0
Jefferson	1,330	44	0	0	0	0	0	0	0
Lafayette	923	55	1	0	1	1	1	2,000	2,000

See footnote at end of table. Continued . . .

Table 19.48. RECREATIONAL BOATING ACCIDENTS: VESSELS, ACCIDENTS, AND PROPERTY DAMAGES RESULTING FROM RECREATIONAL BOATING AND PERSONAL WATERCRAFT ACCIDENTS IN THE STATE AND COUNTIES OF FLORIDA, 2006 (Continued)

County	Registered vessels: Boats	Registered vessels: Personal watercraft	Reported accidents 1/ Boating: Number	Boating: Fatalities	Boating: Injuries	Personal watercraft: Number	Personal watercraft: Injuries	Damages (dollars): Boating	Damages (dollars): Personal watercraft
Lake	23,183	2,646	15	6	18	7	13	56,450	18,950
Lee	49,423	5,353	32	5	13	7	2	231,300	65,000
Leon	13,587	996	1	1	0	0	0	0	0
Levy	4,088	157	2	1	2	0	0	2,700	0
Liberty	1,124	31	0	0	0	0	0	0	0
Madison	1,207	48	0	0	0	0	0	0	0
Manatee	19,695	2,214	4	0	2	0	0	55,000	0
Marion	20,624	1,745	8	1	7	2	2	3,000	3,000
Martin	16,456	1,259	14	0	5	0	0	279,850	0
Miami-Dade	58,133	9,990	42	5	38	11	11	604,705	30,300
Monroe	26,406	1,913	75	3	35	12	12	2,625,250	54,950
Nassau	6,000	437	8	0	1	0	0	47,505	0
Okaloosa	19,486	2,893	19	1	16	8	8	78,900	23,300
Okeechobee	5,852	260	0	0	0	0	0	0	0
Orange	35,002	7,336	15	6	14	10	6	127,866	25,366
Osceola	9,408	1,585	11	0	7	3	4	21,300	0
Palm Beach	43,504	6,591	65	1	41	20	21	1,713,843	26,500
Pasco	26,210	3,478	5	0	6	1	1	53,500	1,500
Pinellas	54,350	8,060	41	2	19	18	11	287,247	44,712
Polk	32,607	3,237	8	2	6	2	3	30,697	1,500
Putnam	8,744	574	5	0	6	3	4	3,600	3,600
St. Johns	12,579	1,493	19	0	8	8	5	88,656	27,775
St. Lucie	13,563	1,252	5	0	2	0	0	44,750	0
Santa Rosa	14,250	1,659	6	2	9	1	3	8,950	3,000
Sarasota	24,525	2,813	10	1	8	1	0	69,500	2,000
Seminole	19,457	3,479	9	2	12	2	0	58,450	35,000
Sumter	4,227	192	1	0	1	0	0	200	0
Suwannee	3,007	187	1	0	1	1	1	1,000	1,000
Taylor	3,823	124	3	2	1	0	0	10,000	0
Union	849	38	0	0	0	0	0	0	0
Volusia	30,571	3,029	17	3	10	5	3	128,050	18,050
Wakulla	4,446	179	3	0	1	1	1	23,132	4,000
Walton	5,507	555	2	0	2	1	1	0	0
Washington	2,381	106	0	0	0	0	0	0	0

1/ A reportable boat accident is any boating accident that results in death, disappearance of any person, injury requiring medical treatment beyond first aid, and/or property damage totaling more than $500.

Source: State of Florida, Fish and Wildlife Conservation Commission, *2006 Boating Accident Statistical Report,* Internet site <http://myfwc.com/> (accessed 16, May 2007).

Table 19.52. STATE PARKS AND AREAS: ATTENDANCE AT PARKS BY DEPARTMENT OF ENVIRONMENTAL PROTECTION DISTRICTS IN THE STATE AND SPECIFIED COUNTIES OF FLORIDA, FISCAL YEARS 2005–06 AND 2006–07

Property designation	County	2005–06	2006–07	Percentage change
Total	(X)	18,128,702	19,519,202	7.7
District 1	(X)	2,606,335	2,991,474	14.8
Alfred B. Maclay Gardens	Leon	147,278	168,241	14.2
Bald Point	Franklin	39,572	52,373	32.3
Big Lagoon	Escambia	108,705	123,372	13.5
Blackwater River	Santa Rosa	64,074	73,787	15.2
Camp Helen	Bay	20,120	23,811	18.3
Constitution Convention	Gulf	2,728	3,170	16.2
Deer Lake	Walton	6,325	6,495	2.7
DeSoto Site	Leon	1,243	1,179	-5.1
Econfina River	Taylor	9,883	10,808	9.4
Eden	Walton	52,645	48,146	-8.5
Falling Waters	Washington	34,313	33,863	-1.3
Florida Caverns	Jackson	94,307	99,519	5.5
Grayton Beach	Walton	105,871	105,486	-0.4
Henderson Beach	Okaloosa	220,418	239,120	8.5
John Gorrie	Franklin	2,294	3,074	34.0
Lake Jackson Mounds	Leon	51,799	35,305	-31.8
Lake Talquin	Gadsden, Leon, Liberty	13,496	14,420	6.8
Letchworth Mounds	Jefferson	14,664	7,454	-49.2
Natural Bridge Battlefield	Leon	11,826	9,503	-19.6
Navarre Beach	Santa Rosa	3,012	0	-100.0
Ochlockonee River	Wakulla	31,095	31,176	0.3
Orman House	Franklin	948	1,227	29.4
Perdido Key	Escambia	22,242	38,346	72.4
Ponce De Leon Springs	Holmes, Walton	40,065	39,681	-1.0
Rocky Bayou	Okaloosa	77,780	79,016	1.6
St. Andrews	Bay	747,150	890,590	19.2
St. George Island	Franklin	80,324	157,837	96.5
St. Joseph Peninsula	Gulf	138,929	166,744	20.0
San Marcos de Apalache	Wakulla	9,359	11,466	22.5
Shell Island	Bay	83,354	98,423	18.1
Tarkiln Bayou	Escambia	7,874	4,845	-38.5
Three Rivers	Jackson	18,093	18,370	1.5
Topsail Hill	Walton	148,897	181,439	21.9
Torreya	Liberty	20,442	23,781	16.3
Wakulla Springs	Wakulla	175,210	189,407	8.1
District 2	(X)	2,775,461	3,013,956	8.6
Amelia Island	Nassau	217,440	206,355	-5.1
Big Shoals	Columbia	23,361	21,853	-6.5
Big Talbot Island	Duval	153,445	174,464	13.7
Cedar Key	Levy	19,582	20,511	4.7

See footnotes at end of table. Continued . . .

Table 19.52. STATE PARKS AND AREAS: ATTENDANCE AT PARKS BY DEPARTMENT OF ENVIRONMENTAL PROTECTION DISTRICTS IN THE STATE AND SPECIFIED COUNTIES OF FLORIDA, FISCAL YEARS 2005–06 AND 2006–07 (Continued)

Property designation	County	2005–06	2006–07	Percentage change
District 2 (Continued)				
Cedar Key Scrub	Levy	16,505	16,631	0.8
Crystal River	Citrus	17,891	19,044	6.4
Crystal River Preserve	Citrus	202,359	272,841	34.8
Devil's Millhopper	Alachua	39,126	44,680	14.2
Dudley Farm	Alachua	11,549	10,838	-6.2
Fanning Springs	Levy	218,450	281,346	28.8
Forest Capital	Taylor	28,755	28,193	-2.0
Ft. Clinch	Nassau	196,176	214,631	9.4
Ft. Cooper	Citrus	19,058	24,912	30.7
Ft. George Island	Duval	60,499	35,532	-41.3
Gold Head Branch	Clay	66,158	65,220	-1.4
Homosassa Springs	Citrus	297,134	326,623	9.9
Ichetucknee Springs	Columbia, Suwannee	167,629	181,387	8.2
Lafayette Blue Springs	Lafayette	10,648	23,111	117.0
Little Talbot Island	Leon	113,088	104,922	-7.2
Madison Blue Springs	Madison	14,933	51,880	247.4
Manatee Springs	Dixie	127,338	134,110	5.3
Marjorie Kinnan Rawlings	Alachua	18,824	20,094	6.7
Nature and Heritage Tourism Center	Columbia	26,668	27,798	4.2
O'Leno	Alachua, Columbia	57,624	61,589	6.9
Olustee Battlefield	Baker	34,181	34,702	1.5
Paynes Prairie	Alachua	155,454	194,662	25.2
Peacock Springs	Suwannee	6,534	5,352	-18.1
Pumpkin Hill Creek	Duval	871	842	-3.3
Rainbow Springs	Marion	222,081	197,588	-11.0
River Rise	Columbia	4,013	3,893	-3.0
San Felasco Hammock	Alachua	48,973	57,382	17.2
Stephen Foster	Hamilton	78,825	47,335	-39.9
Suwannee River	Hamilton, Madison, Suwannee	35,025	28,417	-18.9
Troy Springs	Suwannee	8,901	17,151	92.7
Waccasassa Bay	Levy	25,253	26,315	4.2
Yulee Sugar Mill Ruins	Citrus	31,110	31,752	2.1
District 3	(X)	3,092,953	3,386,904	9.5
Addison Blockhouse	Volusia	0	144	0.0
Anastasia	St. Johns	413,037	488,804	18.3
Blue Spring	Volusia	374,226	455,925	21.8
Bulow Creek	Flagler, Volusia	64,110	60,961	-4.9
Bulow Plantation Ruins	Flagler	24,255	22,910	-5.5
Catfish Creek	Polk	2,671	3,827	43.3
Colt Creek	Polk	0	7,033	0.0
De Leon Springs	Volusia	235,626	232,243	-1.4

See footnotes at end of table.

Continued . . .

Table 19.52. STATE PARKS AND AREAS: ATTENDANCE AT PARKS BY DEPARTMENT OF ENVIRONMENTAL PROTECTION DISTRICTS IN THE STATE AND SPECIFIED COUNTIES OF FLORIDA, FISCAL YEARS 2005–06 AND 2006–07 (Continued)

Property designation	County	2005–06	2006–07	Percentage change
District 3 (Continued)				
Dunn's Creek	Putnam	1,988	3,134	57.6
Faver-Dykes	St. Johns	35,085	35,736	1.9
Ft. Mose	St. Johns	19,449	6,214	-68.0
Gamble Rogers	Flagler	125,729	134,607	7.1
Haw Creek	Flagler, Volusia	16,111	14,196	-11.9
Hontoon Island	Volusia, Lake	33,968	42,710	25.7
Kissimmee Prairie	Okeechobee	8,807	9,923	12.7
Lake Griffin	Lake	29,577	35,329	19.4
Lake Kissimmee	Polk	51,623	53,669	4.0
Lake Louisa	Lake	87,651	103,427	18.0
Lower Wekiva River	Lake, Seminole	8,241	9,896	20.1
North Peninsula	Volusia	81,774	88,912	8.7
Ravine	Putnam	139,504	152,236	9.1
Rock Springs Run	Orange	14,712	14,864	1.0
St. Sebastian River	Brevard	63,317	40,391	-36.2
Sebastian Inlet	Brevard, Indian River	631,838	712,256	12.7
Silver River	Marion	209,842	229,453	9.3
Tomoka	Volusia	92,908	113,768	22.5
Tosohatchee	Orange	17,404	8,904	-48.8
Washington Oaks	Flagler	67,059	65,020	-3.0
Wekiwa Springs	Orange, Seminole	242,441	240,412	-0.8
District 4	(X)	5,585,452	5,741,595	2.8
Alafia River	Hillsborough	45,652	57,803	26.6
Anclote Key	Pasco, Pinellas	151,377	169,436	11.9
Caladesi Island	Pinellas	250,549	294,547	17.6
Cayo Costa	Lee	46,892	46,535	-0.8
Charlotte Harbor	Charlotte	313	2,438	678.9
Collier-Seminole	Collier	72,178	79,600	10.3
Dade Battlefield	Sumter	15,027	18,838	25.4
Delnor-Wiggins Pass	Collier	546,781	461,819	-15.5
Don Pedro Island	Charlotte	48,050	47,700	-0.7
Egmont Key	Hillsborough	168,528	170,907	1.4
Estero Bay	Lee	7,670	11,708	52.6
Fakahatchee Strand	Collier	137,238	118,337	-13.8
Gamble Plantation	Manatee	66,933	67,264	0.5
Gasparilla Island	Lee	516,326	581,735	12.7
Highlands Hammock	Hardee	208,201	214,607	3.1
Hillsborough River	Hillsborough	157,648	182,296	15.6
Honeymoon Island	Pinellas	906,176	976,553	7.8
Koreshan	Lee	60,324	64,585	7.1
Lake June	Highlands	1,637	1,320	-19.4
Lake Manatee	Manatee	45,983	54,958	19.5

See footnotes at end of table. Continued . . .

Table 19.52. STATE PARKS AND AREAS: ATTENDANCE AT PARKS BY DEPARTMENT OF ENVIRONMENTAL PROTECTION DISTRICTS IN THE STATE AND SPECIFIED COUNTIES OF FLORIDA, FISCAL YEARS 2005–06 AND 2006–07 (Continued)

Property designation	County	2005–06	2006–07	Percentage change
District 4 (Continued)				
Little Manatee River	Manatee	24,170	30,798	27.4
Lovers Key	Lee	968,854	851,944	-12.1
Madira Bickel Mound	Manatee	2,989	2,765	-7.5
Mound Key	Lee	3,615	3,283	-9.2
Myakka River	Manatee, Sarasota	307,067	310,084	1.0
Oscar Scherer	Sarasota	105,850	112,186	6.0
Paynes Creek	Hardee	32,312	29,658	-8.2
Skyway State Fishing Piers	Hillsborough, Pinellas	235,623	330,787	40.4
Stump Pass Beach	Charlotte	390,680	378,075	-3.2
Terra Ceia	Manatee	4,421	6,553	48.2
Werner-Boyce Salt Springs	Pasco	33,801	35,874	6.1
Ybor City Museum	Hillsborough	22,587	26,602	17.8
District 5	(X)	4,068,501	4,385,273	7.8
Atlantic Ridge	Martin	422	338	-19.9
Avalon	St. Lucie	165,015	171,335	3.8
Bahia Honda	Monroe	462,268	495,818	7.3
Barnacle, The	Miami-Dade	28,890	39,955	38.3
Cape Florida	Miami-Dade	687,851	782,132	13.7
Coral Reef	Monroe	881,790	861,045	-2.4
Curry Hammock	Monroe	46,992	50,643	7.8
Ft. Pierce Inlet	St. Lucie	192,402	187,354	-2.6
Ft. Zachary Taylor	Monroe	252,798	280,755	11.1
Hugh Taylor Birch	Broward	179,621	236,127	31.5
Indian Key	Monroe	9,375	24,821	164.8
Jack Island	Martin, Palm Beach	36,595	38,098	4.1
Jonathan Dickinson	Martin	144,519	154,426	6.9
Key Largo Hammock	Monroe	13,165	11,699	-11.1
Lignumvitae Key	Monroe	16,731	23,030	37.6
Lloyd Beach	Broward	477,373	467,124	-2.1
Long Key	Monroe	62,160	72,860	17.2
MacArthur Beach	Palm Beach	90,685	113,713	25.4
Oleta River	Miami-Dade	269,712	319,048	18.3
St. Lucie Inlet	St. Lucie	14,046	13,886	-1.1
San Pedro	Monroe	74	608	721.6
Savannas	St. Lucie	17,193	19,421	13.0
Seabranch	Martin	7,651	10,570	38.2
Windley Key Fossil Reef	Monroe	11,173	10,467	-6.3

(X) Not applicable.

Note: Data include areas reporting actual visitor counts from full-time entrance stations and areas reporting estimates of attendance from sample counts. Some parks may have been closed for repairs. Totals may include data from parks that are closed or no longer under the state system.

Source: State of Florida, Department of Environmental Protection, Recreation and Parks Management Information System, unpublished data.

Table 19.53. STATE PARKS AND AREAS: ACREAGE ACQUIRED AND ATTENDANCE AT STATE PARKS AND AREAS IN FLORIDA, FISCAL YEARS 2000-01 THROUGH 2005-06

State park or area	2000-01	2001-02	2002-03	2003-04	2004-05	2005-06
State parks (number)	155	156	157	158	158	159
Acres, total	571,211	593,457	603,953	730,573	723,852	724,629
Added acres	22,234	22,246	10,496	126,620	-6,721	777
Greenways and trails 1/						
Acres, total	74,435.65	74,445.82	76,984.82	78,897.03	83,084.97	83,716.78
Acquired acres	1,829.68	7.35	1,184.71	118.19	35.06	4.79
Attendance, total	18,148,400	18,115,379	19,011,528	20,956,953	18,909,154	21,313,680
State parks	18,075,329	17,722,275	18,240,624	19,106,966	17,296,273	18,174,879
Aquatic preserves	73,071	76,516	109,577	122,783	224,401	439,804
Greenways and trails 1/	(X)	316,588	661,327	1,727,204	1,388,480	2,698,997

(X) Not applicable.
1/ Data are for acreage and attendance managed by the Office of Greenways and Trails.

Source: State of Florida, Department of Environmental Protection, *Statistical Abstract*, Internet site <http://www.dep.state.fl.us/> (accessed 23, July 2007).

Table 19.54. NATIONAL PARK SYSTEMS: RECREATIONAL VISITS TO NATIONAL PARK SERVICE AREAS IN FLORIDA, 2005 AND 2006

Park, monument, or memorial	County	2005	2006	Percentage change
Florida	(X)	7,794.3	7,983.2	2.4
Big Cypress Preserve	Broward, Hendry	768.7	825.9	7.4
Biscayne Park	Miami-Dade	563.7	608.8	8.0
Canaveral Seashore	Brevard, Volusia	1,007.4	1,005.4	-0.2
Castillo de San Marcos Monument	St. Johns	600.3	630.9	5.1
DeSoto Memorial	Miami-Dade	240.2	245.5	2.2
Dry Tortugas	Monroe	61.8	64.1	3.8
Everglades Park	Miami-Dade	1,233.8	954.0	-22.7
Ft. Caroline Memorial	Duval	145.7	224.1	53.8
Ft. Matanzas Monument	St. Johns	1,002.4	922.3	-8.0
Gulf Islands Seashore 1/	Escambia, Okaloosa, Santa Rosa	1,267.1	1,986.8	56.8
Timucuan Preserve	Duval	903.2	1,012.0	12.0

(X) Not applicable. 1/ Part located in Mississippi; excluded from total. Due to major damage from Hurricanes Katrina and Ivan, use caution when comparing data to previous years.
Note: Data are in thousands, rounded to hundreds.

Source: U.S., Department of the Interior, National Park Service, *National Park Service Statistical Abstract, 2006,* and previous edition.

Table 19.55. TOURIST DEVELOPMENT TAXES: LOCAL OPTION TAX COLLECTIONS IN THE STATE AND COUNTIES OF FLORIDA, FISCAL YEARS 2005–06 AND 2006–07

County	2005–06 ($1,000)	2006–07 Amount ($1,000)	2006–07 Percentage change	County	2005–06 ($1,000)	2006–07 Amount ($1,000)	2006–07 Percentage change
Florida	436,326	397,529	-8.9	Leon	3,368	2,848	-15.4
				Levy	162	137	-15.2
Alachua	2,016	2,058	2.1	Madison	87	79	-8.8
Baker	32	27	-16.1	Manatee	4,760	4,264	-10.4
Bay	5,520	4,364	-20.9	Marion	1,129	950	-15.9
Bradford	53	52	-2.4	Martin	677	221	-67.3
Brevard	8,524	7,188	-15.7	Miami-Dade	25,026	22,772	-9.0
Broward	38,855	33,165	-14.6	Monroe	14,179	8,036	-43.3
Charlotte	1,626	1,413	-13.1	Nassau	1,563	1,071	-31.5
Citrus	554	488	-12.0	Okaloosa	7,365	5,694	-22.7
Clay	379	351	-7.4	Okeechobee	228	186	-18.1
Collier	13,056	13,247	1.5	Orange	126,085	127,898	1.4
Columbia	421	338	-19.8	Osceola	33,007	19,812	-40.0
Duval	9,676	7,802	-19.4	Palm Beach	23,540	23,951	1.7
Escambia	4,524	4,239	-6.3	Pasco	812	638	-21.5
Flagler	782	712	-8.9	Pinellas	21,651	20,474	-5.4
Franklin	670	532	-20.6	Polk	6,866	6,788	-1.1
Gadsden	39	53	35.1	Putnam	112	65	-41.5
Gilchrist	0	3	(X)	St. Johns	5,288	4,345	-17.8
Gulf	304	372	22.1	St. Lucie	2,818	1,959	-30.5
Hamilton	47	42	-11.8	Santa Rosa	432	572	32.3
Hendry	132	117	-11.4	Sarasota	7,433	6,644	-10.6
Hernando	378	358	-5.4	Seminole	2,638	2,064	-21.8
Highlands	355	302	-14.8	Sumter	278	247	-11.2
Hillsborough	20,423	20,355	-0.3	Suwannee	103	61	-41.1
Holmes	11	7	-35.9	Taylor	126	121	-4.2
Indian River	1,583	1,260	-20.4	Volusia	8,134	6,583	-19.1
Jackson	349	288	-17.7	Wakulla	34	32	-5.9
Jefferson	0	5	(X)	Walton	8,744	6,918	-20.9
Lake	2,286	1,956	-14.4	Washington	57	75	32.2
Lee	17,030	20,928	22.9				

Note: Data reflect both state- and locally-administered tourist development tax collections.
Source: State of Florida, Department of Revenue, Internet site <http://dor.myflorida.com/> (accessed 20, July 2007).

Table 19.60. TOURIST FACILITIES: HOTELS AND MOTELS BY NUMBER OF UNITS AND FOOD SERVICE ESTABLISHMENTS BY SEATING CAPACITY IN THE STATE AND COUNTIES OF FLORIDA, JULY 2, 2007

County	Licensed hotels		Licensed motels 1/		Food service establishments	
	Number	Units	Number	Units	Number of licenses	Seating capacity
Florida	1,336	210,089	3,249	172,660	40,723	3,574,210
Alachua	13	1,742	51	2,781	487	39,703
Baker	0	0	3	147	34	1,870
Bay	14	1,442	111	5,744	503	47,463
Bradford	1	29	11	328	42	3,018
Brevard	24	2,886	91	5,885	1,165	97,935
Broward	133	20,284	298	8,631	3,912	323,703
Calhoun	0	0	2	24	23	1,243
Charlotte	3	332	19	682	315	28,336
Citrus	1	111	25	1,010	264	19,685
Clay	6	552	10	753	304	26,001
Collier	29	4,451	46	2,308	901	90,408
Columbia	3	272	30	1,575	121	8,359
DeSoto	1	63	5	137	46	2,986
Dixie	0	0	8	127	21	1,469
Duval	64	9,099	82	6,775	2,081	173,951
Escambia	19	1,873	61	4,387	579	53,343
Flagler	4	268	14	365	150	12,358
Franklin	3	51	12	297	47	3,829
Gadsden	3	171	12	238	56	3,021
Gilchrist	0	0	5	69	15	1,071
Glades	0	0	9	165	13	602
Gulf	3	101	8	68	32	1,644
Hamilton	0	0	14	413	25	1,726
Hardee	1	48	4	64	33	1,936
Hendry	3	170	13	276	60	4,413
Hernando	2	139	14	534	282	20,924
Highlands	5	555	21	646	167	15,271
Hillsborough	78	13,783	111	6,597	2,531	210,451
Holmes	0	0	4	181	20	1,354
Indian River	5	542	29	1,100	327	27,241
Jackson	1	64	17	838	83	5,589
Jefferson	0	0	9	199	26	1,292
Lafayette	0	0	3	39	7	387
Lake	14	1,114	56	1,772	497	41,972
Lee	49	5,610	126	4,466	1,434	137,698

See footnotes at end of table.

Continued . . .

Table 19.60. TOURIST FACILITIES: HOTELS AND MOTELS BY NUMBER OF UNITS AND FOOD SERVICE ESTABLISHMENTS BY SEATING CAPACITY IN THE STATE AND COUNTIES OF FLORIDA, JULY 2, 2007 (Continued)

County	Licensed hotels		Licensed motels 1/		Food service establishments	
	Number	Units	Number	Units	Number of licenses	Seating capacity
Leon	26	2,935	38	2,812	585	51,354
Levy	1	10	22	386	73	4,564
Liberty	0	0	1	13	6	471
Madison	1	60	5	147	23	1,350
Manatee	6	609	63	2,677	632	54,683
Marion	15	1,575	67	2,676	539	42,076
Martin	7	559	20	486	408	33,610
Miami-Dade	272	33,870	151	8,531	5,190	367,370
Monroe	31	2,607	198	5,520	479	43,500
Nassau	7	1,067	21	554	176	15,058
Okaloosa	11	832	48	3,549	511	48,717
Okeechobee	0	0	10	425	77	5,758
Orange	162	52,932	108	26,644	3,151	408,539
Osceola	31	12,434	99	14,161	696	85,994
Palm Beach	76	11,457	122	4,648	3,002	278,285
Pasco	8	629	35	1,487	684	57,990
Pinellas	60	7,375	278	11,371	2,299	204,362
Polk	19	1,513	96	4,973	919	72,987
Putnam	1	73	27	480	105	7,304
St. Johns	23	2,573	92	3,042	537	41,424
St. Lucie	13	1,572	30	1,416	428	30,449
Santa Rosa	3	142	9	518	210	14,245
Sarasota	21	2,361	64	2,622	890	80,463
Seminole	16	2,178	28	2,482	848	69,753
Sumter	2	151	12	515	122	11,533
Suwannee	1	68	9	241	50	3,918
Taylor	1	60	19	434	39	3,082
Union	0	0	0	0	6	372
Volusia	30	3,347	217	9,320	1,134	97,070
Wakulla	3	155	3	69	38	2,650
Walton	7	1,193	15	572	224	20,072
Washington	0	0	8	268	39	2,955

1/ Includes bed and breakfasts.

Caution: Data were collected from unaudited, raw data files as reported by the Department of Business and Professional Regulation and may contain reporting errors.

Note: Total public lodgings are shown in Table 2.30 and apartment buildings, rooming houses, resort condominiums, resort dwellings, and transient apartments appear in Table 2.31.

Source: State of Florida, Department of Business and Professional Regulation, Licensee Information Download files: Lodging, Internet site <http://www.myflorida.com/dbpr/> (accessed 2, July 2007).

Table 19.70. TOURIST- AND RECREATION-RELATED BUSINESSES: GROSS AND TAXABLE SALES AND SALES AND USE TAX COLLECTIONS BY KIND OF BUSINESS IN FLORIDA, 2005 AND 2006

(rounded to thousands of dollars)

Kind of business	Gross sales	Taxable sales	Sales and use tax collections
2005			
Candy, nut, confectionery, and dairy product stores	1,421,993	497,207	19,156
Restaurants, lunchrooms, catering services	28,696,108	26,030,715	1,279,307
Taverns and night clubs	2,839,298	2,577,053	113,227
Motorboats, yachts, and marine parts	6,282,930	2,937,801	178,408
Music, electronics, and radio and television stores	38,874,423	9,395,211	524,782
Hotels, apartments, and house lessors	15,259,073	14,147,450	884,646
Bookstores	1,676,686	1,091,645	60,440
Tobacco shops	292,869	127,665	4,375
Photo and art supplies, photographers, and art galleries	1,383,880	749,206	28,426
Gift, novelty, hobby, and toy stores	3,280,239	2,111,329	91,274
Newsstands	148,104	51,585	2,644
Social clubs and associations	583,258	499,410	25,722
Admissions	8,388,722	6,741,174	408,224
Holiday season vendors	47,359	32,362	1,225
Rental of tangible property	13,163,118	7,049,773	387,654
2006			
Candy, nut, confectionery, and dairy product stores	1,286,598	494,852	18,359
Restaurants, lunchrooms, catering services	30,951,140	27,841,049	1,302,062
Taverns and night clubs	2,932,143	2,639,855	107,386
Motorboats, yachts, and marine parts	10,239,839	2,952,805	178,608
Music, electronics, and radio and television stores	42,738,641	9,787,913	533,894
Hotels, apartments, and house lessors	16,154,790	14,905,908	908,964
Bookstores	1,835,183	1,145,151	61,957
Tobacco shops	302,168	134,704	4,124
Photo and art supplies, photographers, and art galleries	1,426,560	747,687	28,232
Gift, novelty, hobby, and toy stores	3,164,799	2,116,001	87,566
Newsstands	283,769	55,996	2,839
Social clubs and associations	695,996	575,654	28,925
Admissions	9,523,073	7,290,127	429,367
Holiday season vendors	66,990	45,680	1,076
Rental of tangible property	14,930,387	7,629,656	412,425

Note: Audited sales reported for the 6 percent regular sales tax, 6 percent use tax, and 3 percent vehicle and farm equipment sales tax. Sales occurred, for the most part, from December 1, 2004, through November 30, 2006. Kind of business data for counties are available from the Bureau of Economic and Business Research, University of Florida. Data includes all sales in the category. See Table 16.81 for taxable sales for all businesses; see Table 23.43 for tax collections.

Source: State of Florida, Department of Revenue, unpublished data prepared by the University of Florida, Bureau of Economic and Business Research.

Table 19.72. TOURIST- AND RECREATION-RELATED BUSINESSES: AVERAGE MONTHLY PRIVATE REPORTING UNITS, EMPLOYMENT, AND PAYROLL COVERED BY UNEMPLOYMENT COMPENSATION LAW BY INDUSTRY IN FLORIDA, 2005 AND 2006

NAICS code	Industry	Number of reporting units	Number of employees	Payroll ($1,000)
			2005 A/	
4452	Specialty food stores	1,858	13,663	26,300
4453	Beer, wine, and liquor stores	1,105	5,205	8,191
4483	Jewelry, luggage, and leather goods stores	2,461	11,465	28,307
451	Sporting goods, hobby, book and music stores	3,871	30,857	50,139
481	Air transportation	583	31,208	124,739
4811	Scheduled air transportation	278	27,909	110,744
4812	Nonscheduled air transportation	305	3,299	13,995
482	Rail transportation	37	56	108
483	Water transportation	181	12,462	54,690
485	Transit and ground passenger transportation	865	12,782	27,382
4851	Urban transit systems	62	1,960	5,594
4853	Taxi and limousine service	424	2,504	5,932
4855	Charter bus industry	83	1,838	3,537
4859	Other ground passenger transportation	237	3,844	8,097
487	Scenic and sightseeing transportation	611	2,386	4,985
4871	Scenic and sightseeing transportation, land	56	370	701
4872	Scenic and sightseeing transportation, water	535	1,969	4,149
512	Motion picture and sound recording industries	1,738	14,442	40,036
5121	Motion picture and video industries	1,480	13,393	35,243
532	Rental and leasing services	4,642	46,715	129,514
5321	Automotive equipment rental and leasing	1,184	17,444	50,102
5615	Travel arrangement and reservation services	2,577	28,648	80,993
71	Arts, entertainment, and recreation	8,732	169,516	417,206
711	Performing arts and spectator sports	3,719	28,827	132,707
7111	Performing arts companies	740	7,249	17,328
7112	Spectator sports	697	13,552	88,014
7115	Independent artists, writers, and performers	1,567	2,515	10,001
712	Museums, historical sites, zoos, and parks	335	5,796	11,326
713	Amusements, gambling, and recreation	4,678	134,893	273,174
7131	Amusement parks and arcades	244	54,295	127,992
7132	Gambling industries	71	2,823	6,034
7139	Other amusement and recreation industries	4,363	77,776	139,149
72	Accommodation and food services	34,182	715,564	1,006,490
721	Accommodation	4,134	156,147	318,567
7211	Traveler accommodation	3,619	152,575	313,151
7212	RV parks and recreational camps	431	3,090	4,700
722	Food services and drinking places	30,048	559,417	687,923
7221	Full-service restaurants	13,789	306,429	412,268
7222	Limited-service eating places	12,656	207,862	212,189
7224	Drinking places, alcoholic beverages	2,193	18,246	22,768

See footnotes at end of table.

Continued . . .

Table 19.72. TOURIST- AND RECREATION-RELATED BUSINESSES: AVERAGE MONTHLY PRIVATE REPORTING UNITS, EMPLOYMENT, AND PAYROLL COVERED BY UNEMPLOYMENT COMPENSATION LAW BY INDUSTRY IN FLORIDA, 2005 AND 2006 (Continued)

NAICS code	Industry	Number of reporting units	Number of employees	Payroll ($1,000)
			2006 B/	
4452	Specialty food stores	1,785	14,117	27,788
4453	Beer, wine, and liquor stores	1,213	5,527	8,997
4483	Jewelry, luggage, and leather goods stores	2,411	12,019	30,954
451	Sporting goods, hobby, book and music stores	3,946	32,939	55,123
481	Air transportation	589	29,810	124,286
4811	Scheduled air transportation	270	26,835	110,477
4812	Nonscheduled air transportation	319	2,975	13,809
482	Rail transportation	22	32	64
483	Water transportation	181	12,356	60,748
485	Transit and ground passenger transportation	873	13,134	29,428
4851	Urban transit systems	70	1,966	5,741
4853	Taxi and limousine service	439	2,871	6,709
4855	Charter bus industry	81	1,810	3,673
4859	Other ground passenger transportation	226	4,042	9,343
487	Scenic and sightseeing transportation	630	2,362	5,308
4871	Scenic and sightseeing transportation, land	49	350	669
4872	Scenic and sightseeing transportation, water	554	1,931	4,396
512	Motion picture and sound recording industries	1,720	14,141	38,915
5121	Motion picture and video industries	1,447	13,109	34,340
532	Rental and leasing services	4,648	46,769	134,641
5321	Automotive equipment rental and leasing	1,208	17,129	48,942
5615	Travel arrangement and reservation services	2,570	29,972	89,525
71	Arts, entertainment, and recreation	8,982	174,005	441,697
711	Performing arts and spectator sports	3,899	29,959	144,481
7111	Performing arts companies	720	7,526	19,364
7112	Spectator sports	689	13,707	96,810
7115	Independent artists, writers, and performers	1,739	2,958	11,063
712	Museums, historical sites, zoos, and parks	326	5,873	12,067
713	Amusements, gambling, and recreation	4,757	138,173	285,149
7131	Amusement parks and arcades	254	53,567	127,641
7132	Gambling industries	69	2,432	6,560
7139	Other amusement and recreation industries	4,434	82,175	150,948
72	Accommodation and food services	35,221	730,386	1,068,436
721	Accommodation	4,115	154,956	324,917
7211	Traveler accommodation	3,612	151,405	319,351
7212	RV parks and recreational camps	423	3,054	4,775
722	Food services and drinking places	31,106	575,429	743,519
7221	Full-service restaurants	14,225	315,812	446,525
7222	Limited-service eating places	13,157	213,817	227,654
7224	Drinking places, alcoholic beverages	2,159	19,120	26,033

NAICS North American Industry Classification System. See Glossary for definition.
A/ Revised. B/ Preliminary.
Note: Private employment. See Tables 23.70, 23.72, 23.73, and 23.74 for public employment data.
Source: State of Florida, Agency for Workforce Innovation, Labor Market Statistics, "Quarterly Census of Employment and Wages" (ES-202), Annual NAICS files, Internet site <http://www.labormarketinfo.com/index.htm> (accessed 17, July 2007).

Table 19.73. ACCOMMODATION AND FOOD SERVICES: AVERAGE MONTHLY PRIVATE REPORTING UNITS, EMPLOYMENT, AND PAYROLL COVERED BY UNEMPLOYMENT COMPENSATION LAW IN THE STATE AND COUNTIES OF FLORIDA, 2005 AND 2006

County	Number of reporting units	Number of employees	Payroll ($1,000)	County	Number of reporting units	Number of employees	Payroll ($1,000)
		Accommodation and food services, 2005 A/ (NAICS code 72)					
Florida	34,182	715,564	1,006,490	Lee	1,101	20,605	28,649
				Leon	549	12,978	12,618
Alachua	497	11,624	11,382	Levy	74	928	737
Baker	29	489	417	Liberty	3	57	54
Bay	443	8,777	11,414	Madison	18	295	238
Bradford	36	500	469	Manatee	522	9,392	11,240
Brevard	910	17,165	19,233	Marion	427	7,699	8,638
Broward	3,597	65,405	103,463	Martin	306	5,600	6,923
Calhoun	14	140	119	Miami-Dade	4,535	86,075	136,529
Charlotte	196	3,324	4,013	Monroe	534	10,041	19,527
Citrus	196	2,643	2,651	Nassau	136	3,847	6,280
Clay	240	4,808	5,190	Okaloosa	493	11,090	13,650
Collier	701	15,400	27,203	Okeechobee	64	963	1,092
Columbia	115	2,181	2,079	Orange	2,207	90,490	146,922
DeSoto	30	436	454	Osceola	515	13,770	22,888
Dixie	24	200	148	Palm Beach	2,520	52,839	80,230
Duval	1,652	34,663	41,392	Pasco	533	9,165	10,245
Escambia	528	11,599	13,083	Pinellas	2,125	37,462	49,658
Flagler	113	1,882	2,250	Polk	725	13,361	13,714
Franklin	42	581	646	Putnam	91	1,221	1,126
Gadsden	39	501	435	St. Johns	394	8,581	11,935
Gilchrist	25	213	209	St. Lucie	316	5,229	6,043
Glades	18	105	105	Santa Rosa	183	3,545	3,800
Gulf	25	232	208	Sarasota	786	15,556	22,418
Hamilton	15	145	142	Seminole	703	14,060	17,054
Hardee	28	275	272	Sumter	74	1,067	1,162
Hendry	64	747	773	Suwannee	45	622	508
Hernando	216	4,199	4,123	Taylor	40	502	431
Highlands	142	2,110	2,170	Union	10	196	320
Hillsborough	2,102	45,637	60,470	Volusia	953	17,981	20,747
Holmes	15	179	147	Wakulla	41	558	459
Indian River	238	3,690	4,856	Walton	136	3,395	6,178
Jackson	63	1,031	920	Washington	31	398	307
Jefferson	15	113	102	Statewide 1/	69	6,653	10,842
Lafayette	8	62	44	Out-of-state 2/	20	569	3,006
Lake	389	6,991	7,833	Unknown 1/	138	729	1,905

See footnotes at end of table.

Continued . . .

Table 19.73. ACCOMMODATION AND FOOD SERVICES: AVERAGE MONTHLY PRIVATE REPORTING UNITS, EMPLOYMENT, AND PAYROLL COVERED BY UNEMPLOYMENT COMPENSATION LAW IN THE STATE AND COUNTIES OF FLORIDA, 2005 AND 2006 (Continued)

County	Number of reporting units	Number of employees	Payroll ($1,000)	County	Number of reporting units	Number of employees	Payroll ($1,000)
	Accommodation and food services, 2006 B/ (NAICS code 72)						
Florida	35,221	730,386	1,068,436	Lee	1,126	22,001	32,870
				Leon	574	13,397	13,569
Alachua	511	11,442	11,942	Levy	73	786	657
Baker	28	444	379	Liberty	4	60	60
Bay	454	9,472	12,657	Madison	18	328	279
Bradford	38	618	570	Manatee	524	9,571	11,761
Brevard	949	17,970	20,971	Marion	455	7,733	8,828
Broward	3,630	64,723	94,880	Martin	319	5,890	7,731
Calhoun	12	135	127	Miami-Dade	4,457	87,226	154,233
Charlotte	217	4,027	4,744	Monroe	498	9,225	19,597
Citrus	204	2,791	2,879	Nassau	134	3,694	6,298
Clay	248	5,036	5,497	Okaloosa	475	11,229	15,183
Collier	741	15,064	27,958	Okeechobee	63	971	1,155
Columbia	123	2,299	2,361	Orange	2,371	92,530	157,573
DeSoto	35	422	463	Osceola	555	13,548	22,511
Dixie	25	212	177	Palm Beach	2,618	54,579	86,724
Duval	1,749	36,001	44,452	Pasco	564	9,403	10,821
Escambia	561	12,170	13,942	Pinellas	2,146	36,800	49,648
Flagler	110	2,015	2,531	Polk	739	13,580	14,924
Franklin	42	554	697	Putnam	100	1,166	1,160
Gadsden	42	497	466	St. Johns	426	9,277	13,394
Gilchrist	18	170	173	St. Lucie	326	5,341	6,368
Glades	16	76	92	Santa Rosa	203	3,537	3,644
Gulf	31	306	329	Sarasota	790	15,201	23,306
Hamilton	12	69	50	Seminole	789	14,917	19,294
Hardee	28	321	308	Sumter	86	1,395	1,582
Hendry	65	849	1,047	Suwannee	46	708	598
Hernando	230	4,546	4,585	Taylor	34	448	392
Highlands	141	2,082	2,249	Union	9	201	296
Hillsborough	2,139	47,068	64,345	Volusia	984	18,054	21,666
Holmes	18	209	179	Wakulla	42	594	541
Indian River	250	3,719	5,025	Walton	169	4,193	7,637
Jackson	64	1,010	968	Washington	37	414	354
Jefferson	17	111	97	Statewide 1/	92	7,046	14,055
Lafayette	7	51	48	Out-of-state 2/	34	384	1,114
Lake	409	7,245	8,452	Unknown 1/	177	1,238	2,976

NAICS North American Industry Classification System. See Glossary for definition.
A/ Revised. B/ Preliminary.
1/ Reporting units without a fixed location within the state or of unknown county location.
2/ Employment based in Florida, but working out of the state or country.
Note: Private employment. For a list of three- and four-digit code industries included see Table 19.72. Only counties for which data are disclosed are shown. Detail may not add to totals due to disclosure editing and/or rounding. See Tables 23.70, 23.72, 23.73, and 23.74 for public employment data.

Source: State of Florida, Agency for Workforce Innovation, Labor Market Statistics, "Quarterly Census of Employment and Wages" (ES-202), Annual NAICS files, Internet site <http://www.labormarketinfo.com/index.htm> (accessed 17, July 2007).

Table 19.75. FOOD SERVICES AND DRINKING PLACES: AVERAGE MONTHLY PRIVATE REPORTING UNITS, EMPLOYMENT, AND PAYROLL COVERED BY UNEMPLOYMENT COMPENSATION LAW IN THE STATE AND COUNTIES OF FLORIDA, 2006

County	Number of reporting units	Number of employees	Payroll ($1,000)	County	Number of reporting units	Number of employees	Payroll ($1,000)
		Food services and drinking places (NAICS code 722)					
Florida	31,106	575,429	743,519	Lee	984	17,733	23,826
				Leon	507	11,948	11,842
Alachua	428	10,240	10,412	Levy	59	696	568
Baker	25	412	345	Liberty	4	60	60
Bay	375	7,333	8,855	Madison	15	236	189
Bradford	31	555	524	Manatee	466	8,873	10,810
Brevard	860	15,888	17,597	Marion	389	6,883	7,742
Broward	3,254	53,449	71,223	Martin	302	5,269	6,488
Calhoun	11	133	126	Miami-Dade	4,014	63,487	94,670
Charlotte	190	3,686	4,303	Monroe	329	4,911	9,125
Citrus	173	2,462	2,446	Nassau	113	1,870	2,207
Clay	235	4,764	5,161	Okaloosa	427	10,300	13,840
Collier	675	10,564	16,604	Okeechobee	53	912	1,058
Columbia	90	1,926	1,978	Orange	2,095	52,130	73,649
DeSoto	29	359	394	Osceola	427	8,372	10,941
Dixie	20	179	138	Palm Beach	2,442	43,985	62,025
Duval	1,613	31,626	36,889	Pasco	506	8,214	8,873
Escambia	492	10,995	12,482	Pinellas	1,890	29,974	37,243
Flagler	92	1,658	1,754	Polk	638	12,333	13,276
Franklin	29	403	512	Putnam	84	1,072	1,035
Gadsden	28	441	404	St. Johns	339	6,850	8,300
Gilchrist	15	166	164	St. Lucie	293	4,703	5,469
Glades	8	48	47	Santa Rosa	177	3,118	3,029
Gulf	26	247	247	Sarasota	700	12,590	17,159
Hamilton	7	56	39	Seminole	744	13,852	17,588
Hardee	21	280	262	Sumter	67	1,284	1,462
Hendry	49	667	719	Suwannee	36	604	505
Hernando	213	4,362	4,378	Taylor	28	399	333
Highlands	117	1,823	1,923	Union	9	200	295
Hillsborough	1,968	40,760	52,679	Volusia	800	15,081	17,137
Holmes	16	192	170	Wakulla	37	565	497
Indian River	218	3,279	4,314	Walton	137	2,213	3,241
Jackson	50	892	841	Washington	29	368	313
Jefferson	13	95	81	Statewide 1/	73	6,798	10,974
Lafayette	6	47	45	Out-of-state 2/	30	349	806
Lake	349	6,262	7,015	Unknown 1/	137	947	1,871

NAICS North American Industry Classification System. See Glossary for definition.
1/ Reporting units without a fixed location within the state or of unknown county location.
2/ Employment in Florida, but working out of the state or country.
Note: Private employment. Data are preliminary. For a list of four-digit industries included see Table 19.72. Only counties for which data are disclosed are shown. Detail may not add to totals due to disclosure editing and/or rounding. See Tables 23.70, 23.72, 23.73, and 23.74 for public employment data.
Source: State of Florida, Agency for Workforce Innovation, Labor Market Statistics, "Quarterly Census of Employment and Wages" (ES-202), Annual NAICS files, Internet site <http://www.labormarketinfo.com/index.htm> (accessed 17, July 2007).

Table 19.76. ACCOMMODATION: AVERAGE MONTHLY PRIVATE REPORTING UNITS EMPLOYMENT, AND PAYROLL COVERED BY UNEMPLOYMENT COMPENSATION LAW IN THE STATE AND COUNTIES OF FLORIDA, 2006

County	Number of reporting units	Number of employees	Payroll ($1,000)	County	Number of reporting units	Number of employees	Payroll ($1,000)
			Accommodation (NAICS code 721)				
Florida	4,115	154,956	324,917	Levy	14	90	89
				Madison	3	92	90
Alachua	83	1,203	1,530	Manatee	58	697	951
Baker	3	32	33	Marion	66	850	1,086
Bay	79	2,139	3,802	Martin	17	620	1,242
Bradford	7	63	46	Miami-Dade	443	23,738	59,563
Brevard	89	2,083	3,375	Monroe	169	4,314	10,471
Broward	376	11,275	23,657	Nassau	21	1,824	4,091
Charlotte	27	341	441	Okaloosa	48	928	1,343
Citrus	31	329	433	Okeechobee	10	60	97
Clay	13	272	335	Orange	276	40,400	83,923
Collier	66	4,501	11,355	Osceola	128	5,176	11,570
Columbia	33	372	383	Palm Beach	176	10,594	24,699
DeSoto	6	62	69	Pasco	58	1,188	1,948
Dixie	5	33	39	Pinellas	256	6,826	12,405
Duval	136	4,375	7,563	Polk	101	1,247	1,648
Escambia	69	1,175	1,460	Putnam	16	94	125
Flagler	18	357	777	St. Johns	87	2,427	5,094
Franklin	13	150	184	St. Lucie	33	638	898
Gadsden	14	56	62	Santa Rosa	26	419	615
Glades	8	28	45	Sarasota	90	2,611	6,148
Hamilton	5	12	11	Seminole	45	1,065	1,706
Hardee	7	41	46	Sumter	19	111	119
Hendry	16	182	328	Suwannee	10	104	93
Hernando	17	184	207	Taylor	6	49	59
Highlands	24	259	325	Volusia	184	2,973	4,529
Hillsborough	171	6,309	11,666	Wakulla	5	29	43
Indian River	32	440	711	Walton	32	1,980	4,396
Jackson	14	118	127	Washington	8	46	41
Lake	60	983	1,437	Statewide 1/	19	248	3,081
Lee	142	4,268	9,044	Out-of-state 2/	4	34	309
Leon	67	1,450	1,726	Unknown 1/	40	291	1,105

NAICS North American Industry Classification System. See Glossary for definition.
1/ Reporting units without a fixed location within the state or of unknown county location.
2/ Employment in Florida, but working out of the state or country.
Note: Private employment. Data are preliminary. For a list of four-digit code industries included see Table 19.72. Only counties for which data are disclosed are shown. Detail may not add to totals due to disclosure editing and/or rounding. See Tables 23.70, 23.72, 23.73, and 23.74 for public employment data.
Source: State of Florida, Agency for Workforce Innovation, Labor Market Statistics, "Quarterly Census of Employment and Wages" (ES-202), Annual NAICS files, Internet site <http://www.labormarketinfo.com/index.htm> (accessed 17, July 2007).

Table 19.78. AMUSEMENTS, GAMBLING, AND RECREATION: AVERAGE MONTHLY PRIVATE REPORTING UNITS, EMPLOYMENT, AND PAYROLL COVERED BY UNEMPLOYMENT COMPENSATION LAW IN THE STATE AND COUNTIES OF FLORIDA, 2006

County	Number of reporting units	Number of employees	Payroll ($1,000)	County	Number of reporting units	Number of employees	Payroll ($1,000)
	Amusements, gambling, and recreation (NAICS code 713)						
Florida	4,757	138,173	285,149	Manatee	85	2,128	5,262
Alachua	45	875	912	Marion	54	1,141	1,338
Bay	61	980	1,352	Martin	103	1,732	3,581
Bradford	3	25	22	Miami-Dade	440	5,733	10,564
Brevard	123	2,554	4,572	Monroe	92	716	1,716
Broward	568	9,557	14,952	Nassau	19	190	514
Charlotte	48	899	1,303	Okaloosa	69	958	1,284
Citrus	33	471	555	Okeechobee	10	177	391
Clay	28	404	500	Orange	217	50,938	125,715
Collier	161	6,138	16,955	Osceola	45	596	737
Columbia	8	105	112	Palm Beach	483	13,012	28,612
Dixie	6	12	11	Pasco	88	1,547	2,045
Duval	163	2,876	4,295	Pinellas	259	4,150	6,591
Escambia	65	861	1,177	Polk	95	2,436	3,454
Flagler	21	270	517	Putnam	10	44	48
Franklin	11	57	97	St. Johns	54	1,227	2,066
Gadsden	3	59	59	St. Lucie	53	728	1,286
Hendry	8	39	55	Santa Rosa	31	407	380
Hernando	38	594	768	Sarasota	129	2,374	4,492
Highlands	28	425	595	Seminole	100	1,460	2,197
Hillsborough	239	7,602	12,033	Sumter	6	141	147
Holmes	5	27	32	Suwannee	6	28	27
Indian River	48	2,053	4,260	Taylor	7	33	46
Jackson	9	121	160	Volusia	126	1,986	2,722
Lake	58	778	1,038	Wakulla	5	73	104
Lee	215	5,005	11,473	Walton	9	142	248
Leon	39	869	919	Washington	5	38	60
Levy	9	44	54	Statewide 1/	17	61	136
Madison	3	9	12	Unknown 1/	73	151	373

NAICS North American Industry Classification System. See Glossary for definition.
1/ Reporting units without a fixed location within the state or of unknown county location.
Note: Private employment. Data are preliminary. For a list of four-digit code industries included see Table 19.72. Only counties for which data are disclosed are shown. Detail may not add to totals due to disclosure editing and/or rounding. See Tables 23.70, 23.72, 23.73, and 23.74 for public employment data.

Source: State of Florida, Agency for Workforce Innovation, Labor Market Statistics, "Quarterly Census of Employment and Wages" (ES-202), Annual NAICS files, Internet site <http://www.labormarketinfo.com/index.htm> (accessed 17, July 2007).

Table 19.80. SPORTS-RELATED BUSINESSES: AVERAGE MONTHLY PRIVATE REPORTING UNITS EMPLOYMENT, AND PAYROLL COVERED BY UNEMPLOYMENT COMPENSATION LAW BY INDUSTRY IN FLORIDA, 2005 AND 2006

NAICS code	Industry	Number of reporting units	Number of employees	Payroll ($1,000)
			2005	
611620	Sports and recreation instruction	825	3,275	5,499
7112	Spectator sports	697	13,552	88,014
711211	Sports teams and clubs	122	5,799	66,690
711212	Racetracks	73	5,611	11,244
711219	Other spectator sports	502	2,143	10,080
7113	Promoters of performing arts and sports	434	4,818	11,902
711310	Promoters with facilities	170	3,826	8,538
711320	Promoters without facilities	264	991	3,364
713910	Golf courses and country clubs	686	34,306	68,748
713930	Marinas	649	5,063	12,329
713940	Fitness and recreational sports centers	1,840	26,966	40,887
713950	Bowling centers	151	3,373	3,831
			2006 A/	
611620	Sports and recreation instruction	845	3,488	6,153
7112	Spectator sports	689	13,707	96,810
711211	Sports teams and clubs	114	6,040	77,992
711212	Racetracks	71	5,786	12,159
711219	Other spectator sports	504	1,881	6,659
7113	Promoters of performing arts and sports	450	5,046	12,471
711310	Promoters with facilities	169	3,968	9,227
711320	Promoters without facilities	281	1,078	3,244
713910	Golf courses and country clubs	720	36,097	75,365
713930	Marinas	620	5,041	13,072
713940	Fitness and recreational sports centers	1,917	28,936	43,870
713950	Bowling centers	153	3,504	4,050

NAICS North American Industry Classification System. See Glossary for definition.
A/ Preliminary.

Source: State of Florida, Agency for Workforce Innovation, Labor Market Statistics, "Quarterly Census of Employment and Wages" (ES-202), Annual NAICS files, Internet site <http://www.labormarketinfo.com/ index.htm> (accessed 17, July 2007).

HEALTH, EDUCATION, AND CULTURAL SERVICES

Licensed Massage Therapists, July 2, 2007

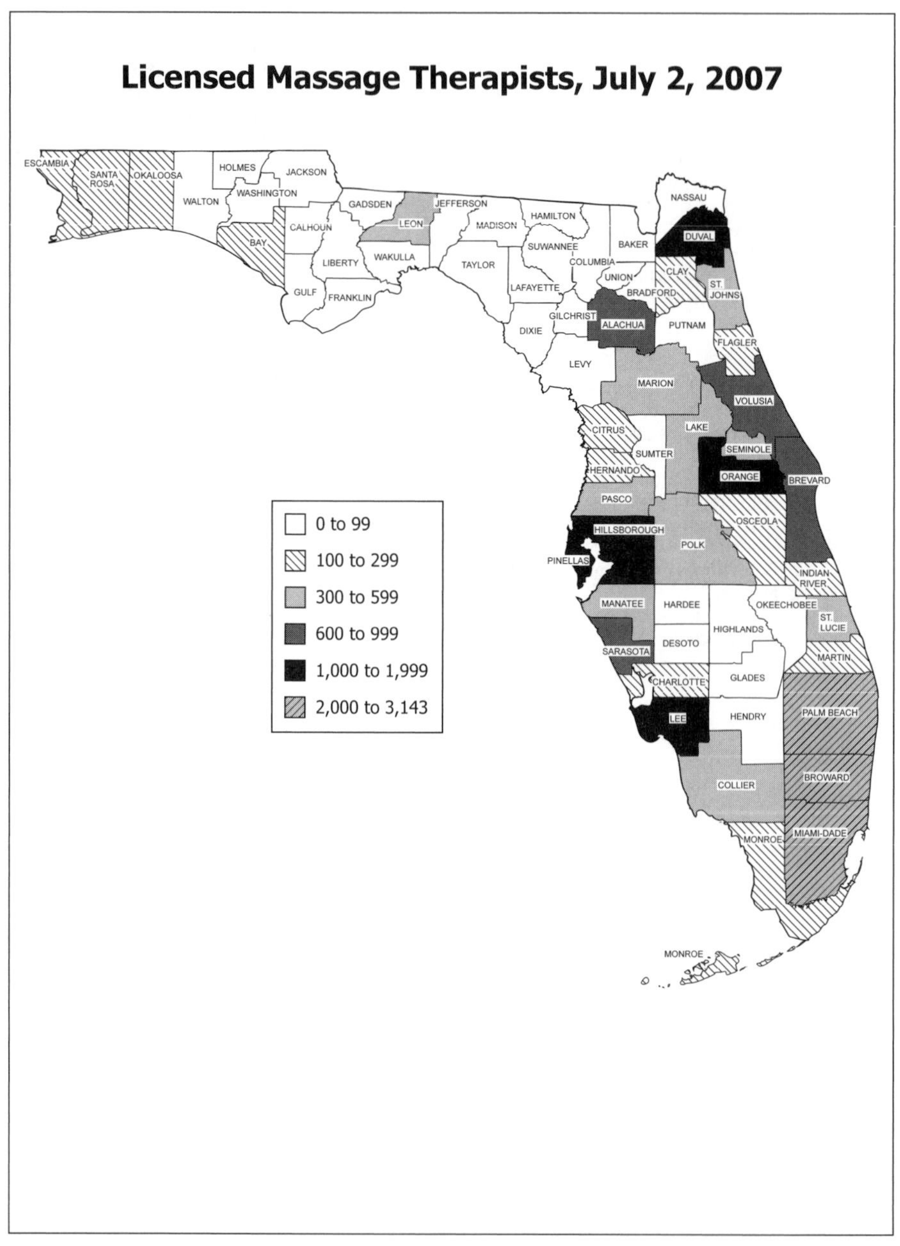

Source: Table 20.36

Section 20.00
Health, Education, and Cultural Services

This section presents data on the health industry, educational financing and staffing, and cultural affairs of the state. Health-related tables include statistics on industry establishments, employment, and payroll; physicians, nurses, dentists, and health practitioners, and health-related retailers and hospitals. Education tables include educational services, classroom teacher new hire estimates and projections, instructional and administrative school staff and salaries, student-teacher ratios; and funding. Cultural tables include data on public libraries and state funding for culture and the arts.

Sources. The U.S. Census Bureau conducts an economic census every five years in years ending in "2" and "7." Data from the 2002 census pertaining to health, social assistance, and educational services are published in two *2002 Economic Census* publications; *Health Care and Social Assistance* and *Educational Services*. The 2002 census uses the North American Industry Classification System (NAICS), explained in the Glossary, to report data about the various health- and education-related industries. Major services categories appearing in this section are educational services (NAICS code 61); health care and social assistance (62); and arts, entertainment, and recreation (71).

Current covered employment and payroll data by NAICS classification are from the Labor Market Statistics office of the Florida Agency for Workforce Innovation. (See introduction to Section 6.00.)

Information on physicians, dentists, nurses, opticians, pharmacists, and other licensed health service practitioners and professionals comes from the Florida Department of Health. Data on veterans' hospitals are published on the U.S. Department of Veterans Affairs Web site. The U.S. Census Bureau provides health and education program expenditure data in *Federal Aid to States* on the Census Bureau Web site.

Education-related financial and staff data come from the Florida Department of Education (FLDOE) in various published and unpublished data reports produced primarily by the Education Information and Accountability Services (EIAS) office in EIAS series reports. Much of the EIAS data are on the FLDOE Web site. New hire data are from the Division of Accountability, Research, and Measurement's Office of Policy Research and Improvement and can be found in *New Hires in Florida Public Schools* on the FLDOE Web site.

Public library expenditure and collection statistics are published by the Florida Department of States' Division of Library and Information Services in *Florida Library Directory with Statistics* on the Internet. Another State Department office, the Division of Cultural Affairs, provides county-level information on state arts grant funding to Florida groups and individuals.

Section 20.00
Health, Education, and Cultural Services

Tables listed by major heading

Tables listed by major heading

Table 20.01. HEALTH CARE AND SOCIAL ASSISTANCE: ESTABLISHMENTS, EMPLOYMENT, RECEIPTS AND PAYROLL BY KIND OF BUSINESS IN FLORIDA, 2002

NAICS code	Industry	Number of establishments	Number of employees 1/	Revenue ($1,000)	Annual payroll ($1,000)
62	Health care and social assistance	44,372	807,392	70,972,374	27,074,198
621	Ambulatory health care services	34,533	299,682	32,293,521	12,569,507
6211	Offices of physicians	15,975	129,959	17,211,245	7,321,907
6212	Offices of dentists	6,414	39,853	3,752,926	1,409,182
6213	Offices of other health practitioners	7,583	31,738	2,482,389	893,958
6214	Outpatient care centers	1,704	32,139	3,313,767	1,033,838
6215	Medical and diagnostic laboratories	1,036	13,583	2,141,422	607,220
6216	Home health care services	1,298	43,229	2,466,100	1,015,576
6219	Other ambulatory health care services	523	9,181	925,672	287,826
622	Hospitals	259	266,512	27,479,967	9,769,961
6221	General medical and surgical hospitals	208	249,370	26,176,551	9,229,327
6222	Psychiatric and substance abuse hospitals	25	8,583	424,541	227,172
6223	Specialty (except psychiatric and substance abuse) hospitals	26	8,559	878,875	313,462
623	Nursing and residential care facilities	3,001	149,056	7,190,691	3,180,682
6231	Nursing care facilities	819	82,896	4,111,954	1,927,905
6232	Residential mental retardation/health and substance abuse facility	787	18,465	752,381	367,222
6233	Community care facilities for the elderly	1,151	41,400	2,029,580	746,986
6239	Other residential care facilities	244	6,295	296,776	138,569
624	Social assistance	6,579	92,142	4,008,195	1,554,048
6241	Individual and family services	2,290	34,851	1,858,051	712,969
6242	Community food and housing/emergency and other relief services	457	6,215	475,134	140,101
6243	Vocational rehabilitation services	310	10,751	432,321	164,372
6244	Child day care services	3,522	40,325	1,242,689	536,606

1/ Paid employment for the pay period including March 12.

Note: The economic censuses are conducted on a 5-year cycle collecting data for years ending in 2 and 7. Data are for North American Industry Classification System (NAICS) code 62 and may not be comparable to earlier years. See Glossary for definition.

Table 20.02. HEALTH CARE AND SOCIAL ASSISTANCE: REVENUE AND EXPENDITURE FOR FIRMS EXEMPT FROM FEDERAL INCOME TAX BY KIND OF BUSINESS IN FLORIDA, 2002

NAICS code	Industry	Revenue ($1,000)	Expenditure ($1,000)
62	Health care and social assistance	27,081,329	25,427,543
621	Ambulatory health care services	2,485,261	2,283,965
622	Hospitals	19,420,140	18,252,099
623	Nursing and residential care facilities	2,266,446	2,180,189
624	Social assistance	2,909,482	2,711,290

Note: The economic censuses are conducted on a 5-year cycle collecting data for years ending in 2 and 7. Data are for North American Industry Classification System (NAICS) code 62 and may not be comparable to earlier years. See Glossary for definition.

Source Tables 20.01 and 20.02: U.S., Department of Commerce, Census Bureau, *2002 Economic Census: Health Care and Social Assistance,* Geographic Area Series EC02-62A-FL, issued August 2005, Internet site <http://www.census.gov/> (accessed 11, May 2007).

Table 20.03. HEALTH CARE AND SOCIAL ASSISTANCE: ESTABLISHMENTS, EMPLOYMENT AND PAYROLL IN THE STATE AND COUNTIES OF FLORIDA, 2002

County	Number of estab-lishments	Number of em-ployees 1/	Annual payroll ($1,000)	County	Number of estab-lishments	Number of em-ployees 1/	Annual payroll ($1,000)
Florida	44,372	807,392	27,074,198	Lake	523	10,705	352,104
				Lee	1,165	22,609	810,490
Alachua 2/	649	(NA)	(D)	Leon	621	15,443	488,843
Baker	29	1,718	54,325	Levy	54	536	9,695
Bay	447	8,163	255,200	Liberty	11	118	2,007
Bradford	41	670	17,535	Madison	36	829	18,200
Brevard	1,191	24,861	827,328	Manatee	615	10,898	337,268
Broward	5,073	77,929	2,676,556	Marion	621	12,332	395,259
Calhoun	20	530	9,497	Martin	412	6,724	234,090
Charlotte	440	7,736	255,113	Miami-Dade	6,986	110,539	3,741,672
Citrus	285	5,429	170,616	Monroe	229	2,669	88,158
Clay	322	5,327	154,962	Nassau	97	1,506	40,278
Collier	706	12,336	442,915	Okaloosa	467	7,747	241,167
Columbia	136	3,188	113,027	Okeechobee	89	1,406	41,106
DeSoto	51	2,003	33,457	Orange	2,251	49,698	1,825,857
Dixie	16	189	3,107	Osceola	329	5,949	195,378
Duval	2,045	47,068	1,581,843	Palm Beach	4,075	62,693	2,241,499
Escambia	691	18,076	584,167	Pasco	797	12,752	422,114
Flagler	106	1,119	34,086	Pinellas	2,962	63,305	2,039,580
Franklin 3/	28	(NA)	(D)	Polk	862	20,080	646,197
Gadsden	58	3,204	81,441	Putnam	144	2,199	58,869
Gilchrist 3/	18	(NA)	(D)	St. Johns	327	4,894	151,284
Glades 4/	4	(NA)	(D)	St. Lucie	486	7,782	249,259
Gulf	25	403	8,303	Santa Rosa	175	2,564	75,653
Hamilton	22	355	7,526	Sarasota	1,291	21,659	709,317
Hardee	57	1,078	21,998	Seminole	902	12,260	425,690
Hendry	49	680	15,986	Sumter	66	814	24,489
Hernando	359	5,132	165,093	Suwannee	47	1,194	27,894
Highlands	259	4,240	120,257	Taylor	43	687	19,611
Hillsborough	2,793	53,635	1,928,644	Union	17	395	14,437
Holmes	32	524	11,392	Volusia	1,105	20,412	670,080
Indian River	378	6,641	217,057	Wakulla 3/	23	(NA)	(D)
Jackson	82	1,728	42,386	Walton	57	804	17,894
Jefferson 5/	22	(NA)	(D)	Washington	40	659	13,977
Lafayette	13	160	2,352				

(NA) Not available.
(D) Data withheld to avoid disclosure of information about individual firms.
1/ Paid employment for the pay period including March 12.
Employment ranges: 2/ 10,000-24,999. 3/ 100-249. 4/ 20-99. 5/ 250-499.
Note: The economic censuses are conducted on a 5-year cycle collecting data for years ending in 2 and 7. Data are for North American Industry Classification System (NAICS) code 62 and may not be comparable to earlier years. See Glossary for definition.

Source: U.S., Department of Commerce, Census Bureau, *2002 Economic Census: Health Care and Social Assistance,* Geographic Area Series EC02-62A-FL, issued August 2005, Internet site <http://www.census.gov/> (accessed 11, May 2007).

Table 20.05. EMPLOYMENT AND PAYROLL: AVERAGE MONTHLY PRIVATE REPORTING UNITS EMPLOYMENT, AND PAYROLL COVERED BY UNEMPLOYMENT COMPENSATION LAW BY SPECIFIED SERVICES INDUSTRY IN FLORIDA, 2005 AND 2006

NAICS code	Industry	Number of reporting units	Number of employees	Payroll ($1,000)
			2005 A/	
61	Educational services	5,168	95,299	254,955
6111	Elementary and secondary schools	963	32,042	75,786
6112	Junior colleges	37	1,943	5,012
6113	Colleges and universities	210	31,096	95,757
6114	Business, computer and management training	655	6,484	23,845
6115	Technical and trade schools	572	8,469	23,531
6116	Other schools and instruction	2,288	12,388	23,642
6117	Educational support services	443	2,876	7,382
62	Health care and social assistance	45,434	809,945	2,635,945
621	Ambulatory health care services	36,181	333,605	1,383,172
6211	Offices of physicians	17,357	151,731	820,337
6212	Offices of dentists	6,418	42,216	151,335
6213	Offices of other health practitioners	7,866	35,679	103,841
6214	Outpatient care centers	1,332	29,469	92,604
6215	Medical and diagnostic laboratories	1,331	16,647	63,344
6216	Home health care services	1,416	49,164	124,877
622	Hospitals	530	235,825	794,349
6221	General medical and surgical hospitals	261	220,352	749,669
6222	Psychiatric and substance abuse hospitals	84	7,878	19,717
6223	Other hospitals	185	7,596	24,963
623	Nursing and residential care facilities	2,627	148,533	302,742
6231	Nursing care facilities	809	81,798	179,361
6232	Residential mental health facilities	357	18,089	35,226
6233	Community care facilities for the elderly	1,183	39,587	69,900
6239	Other residential care facilities	278	9,059	18,255
624	Social assistance	6,096	91,981	155,683
6241	Individual and family services	1,901	28,415	57,144
6242	Emergency and other relief services	326	6,518	13,868
6243	Vocational rehabilitation services	403	13,900	25,601
6244	Child day care services	3,466	43,149	59,070
71	Arts, entertainment, and recreation	8,732	169,516	417,206
711	Performing arts and spectator sports	3,719	28,827	132,707
7111	Performing arts companies	740	7,249	17,328
7112	Spectator sports	697	13,552	88,014
7113	Promoters of performing arts and sports	434	4,818	11,902
7114	Agents and managers for public figures	281	693	5,461
712	Museums, historical sites, zoos, and parks	335	5,796	11,326
713	Amusements, gambling, and recreation	4,678	134,893	273,174
7131	Amusement parks and arcades	244	54,295	127,992
7132	Gambling industries	71	2,823	6,034
7139	Other amusement and recreation industries	4,363	77,776	139,149

See footnotes at end of table. Continued . . .

Table 20.05. EMPLOYMENT AND PAYROLL: AVERAGE MONTHLY PRIVATE REPORTING UNITS EMPLOYMENT, AND PAYROLL COVERED BY UNEMPLOYMENT COMPENSATION LAW BY SPECIFIED SERVICES INDUSTRY IN FLORIDA, 2005 AND 2006 (Continued)

NAICS code	Industry	Number of reporting units	Number of employees	Payroll ($1,000)
			2006 B/	
61	Educational services	5,449	99,920	280,506
6111	Elementary and secondary schools	1,054	34,431	84,818
6112	Junior colleges	34	1,572	4,176
6113	Colleges and universities	257	32,962	108,110
6114	Business, computer and management training	655	5,642	21,804
6115	Technical and trade schools	575	8,526	25,530
6116	Other schools and instruction	2,380	13,265	26,828
6117	Educational support services	494	3,521	9,240
62	Health care and social assistance	47,045	840,134	2,837,619
621	Ambulatory health care services	37,504	348,577	1,490,653
6211	Offices of physicians	17,725	157,886	875,038
6212	Offices of dentists	6,557	43,134	160,951
6213	Offices of other health practitioners	8,377	36,161	108,035
6214	Outpatient care centers	1,465	32,028	104,060
6215	Medical and diagnostic laboratories	1,372	18,258	72,990
6216	Home health care services	1,572	51,656	139,919
622	Hospitals	562	238,930	840,469
6221	General medical and surgical hospitals	265	222,346	789,346
6222	Psychiatric and substance abuse hospitals	97	7,979	20,838
6223	Other hospitals	200	8,605	30,285
623	Nursing and residential care facilities	2,633	154,152	330,670
6231	Nursing care facilities	791	84,759	196,217
6232	Residential mental health facilities	374	19,579	40,088
6233	Community care facilities for the elderly	1,219	40,680	75,072
6239	Other residential care facilities	249	9,133	19,293
624	Social assistance	6,346	98,476	175,826
6241	Individual and family services	2,056	31,695	68,325
6242	Emergency and other relief services	323	6,378	14,686
6243	Vocational rehabilitation services	429	14,520	27,601
6244	Child day care services	3,538	45,883	65,214
71	Arts, entertainment, and recreation	8,982	174,005	441,697
711	Performing arts and spectator sports	3,899	29,959	144,481
7111	Performing arts companies	720	7,526	19,364
7112	Spectator sports	689	13,707	96,810
7113	Promoters of performing arts and sports	450	5,046	12,471
7114	Agents and managers for public figures	301	722	4,773
712	Museums, historical sites, zoos, and parks	326	5,873	12,067
713	Amusements, gambling, and recreation	4,757	138,173	285,149
7131	Amusement parks and arcades	254	53,567	127,641
7132	Gambling industries	69	2,432	6,560
7139	Other amusement and recreation industries	4,434	82,175	150,948

NAICS North American Industry Classification System. See Glossary for definition.
A/ Revised. B/ Preliminary.
Note: Private employment. Totals may include industries not shown separately.
Source: State of Florida, Agency for Workforce Innovation, Labor Market Statistics, "Quarterly Census of Employment and Wages" (ES-202), Annual NAICS files, Internet site <http://www.labormarketinfo.com/index.htm> (accessed 17, July 2007).

Table 20.06. OFFICES OF PHYSICIANS: AVERAGE MONTHLY PRIVATE REPORTING UNITS EMPLOYMENT, AND PAYROLL COVERED BY UNEMPLOYMENT COMPENSATION LAW IN THE STATE AND COUNTIES OF FLORIDA, 2006

County	Number of reporting units	Number of employees	Payroll ($1,000)	County	Number of reporting units	Number of employees	Payroll ($1,000)
Offices of physicians (NAICS code 6211)							
Florida	17,725	157,886	875,038	Levy	10	76	178
				Madison	7	29	91
Alachua	209	2,406	13,245	Manatee	283	3,227	15,173
Baker	6	15	111	Marion	306	3,086	15,794
Bay	184	1,574	9,096	Martin	133	1,410	7,855
Bradford	4	22	62	Miami-Dade	3,279	19,123	95,786
Brevard	414	5,027	30,595	Monroe	87	403	1,642
Broward	1,910	14,750	87,174	Nassau	33	125	563
Calhoun	3	16	31	Okaloosa	187	1,416	6,038
Charlotte	203	1,483	7,845	Okeechobee	22	187	779
Citrus	118	1,270	6,388	Orange	872	10,188	64,913
Clay	104	934	4,210	Osceola	155	1,464	6,916
Collier	294	2,496	16,121	Palm Beach	1,745	13,168	78,685
Columbia	54	464	1,799	Pasco	390	3,145	16,442
DeSoto	15	69	256	Pinellas	1,100	10,440	58,829
Duval	658	12,299	71,777	Polk	264	4,932	22,582
Escambia	223	3,245	19,998	Putnam	63	476	1,603
Flagler	40	219	1,088	St. Johns	160	1,074	5,403
Franklin	5	36	88	St. Lucie	157	1,287	6,632
Gadsden	7	34	109	Santa Rosa	82	542	2,206
Gulf	6	36	108	Sarasota	513	3,936	21,987
Hamilton	3	20	53	Seminole	342	2,675	14,636
Hardee	9	58	172	Sumter	19	272	1,037
Hernando	153	1,185	6,768	Suwannee	9	45	131
Highlands	91	660	2,711	Taylor	12	104	351
Hillsborough	1,155	9,674	58,040	Union	4	16	73
Holmes	9	33	90	Volusia	370	3,183	16,490
Indian River	179	1,664	9,075	Wakulla	3	18	90
Jackson	25	156	589	Walton	29	127	516
Lake	238	2,069	10,880	Washington	7	52	160
Lee	418	5,554	32,368	Statewide 1/	28	880	3,793
Leon	171	2,744	14,232	Unknown 1/	132	295	1,843

NAICS North American Industry Classification System. See Glossary for definition.
1/ Reporting units without a fixed location within the state or of unknown county location.
Note: Private employment. Data are preliminary. For a list of other four-digit code industries see Table 20.05. Only counties for which data are disclosed are shown. Detail may not add to totals due to disclosure editing and/or rounding. See Tables 23.70, 23.72, 23.73, and 23.74 for public employment data.

Source: State of Florida, Agency for Workforce Innovation, Labor Market Statistics, "Quarterly Census of Employment and Wages" (ES-202), Annual NAICS files, Internet site <http://www.labormarketinfo.com/index.htm> (accessed 17, July 2007).

Table 20.07. OFFICES OF DENTISTS: AVERAGE MONTHLY PRIVATE REPORTING UNITS EMPLOYMENT, AND PAYROLL COVERED BY UNEMPLOYMENT COMPENSATION LAW IN THE STATE AND COUNTIES OF FLORIDA, 2006

County	Number of reporting units	Number of employees	Payroll ($1,000)	County	Number of reporting units	Number of employees	Payroll ($1,000)
			Offices of dentists (NAICS code 6212)				
Florida	6,557	43,134	160,951	Manatee	109	702	2,710
Alachua	96	702	2,670	Marion	77	619	2,153
Baker	3	29	89	Martin	74	448	1,821
Bay	57	400	1,674	Miami-Dade	1,051	5,842	18,678
Bradford	3	24	73	Monroe	31	157	464
Brevard	181	1,398	5,371	Nassau	10	83	283
Broward	838	4,732	15,949	Okaloosa	62	486	1,591
Calhoun	3	18	66	Okeechobee	8	65	183
Charlotte	44	336	1,521	Orange	318	2,211	9,048
Citrus	25	203	757	Osceola	47	425	1,652
Clay	66	492	1,739	Palm Beach	692	3,840	14,653
Collier	131	738	3,349	Pasco	103	643	2,445
Columbia	11	76	283	Pinellas	380	2,641	10,235
DeSoto	3	15	55	Polk	118	858	3,267
Duval	277	2,091	7,946	Putnam	14	121	338
Escambia	111	824	3,312	St. Johns	51	342	1,281
Flagler	10	107	548	St. Lucie	51	394	1,634
Gadsden	6	35	74	Santa Rosa	23	195	727
Hendry	7	51	125	Sarasota	217	1,216	5,023
Hernando	39	297	1,168	Seminole	175	1,514	5,379
Highlands	25	171	547	Sumter	5	32	115
Hillsborough	389	3,316	13,678	Suwannee	7	52	137
Indian River	53	400	1,462	Volusia	151	966	3,398
Jackson	10	59	154	Wakulla	4	18	41
Lake	80	596	2,113	Walton	12	60	184
Lee	168	1,185	5,270	Washington	5	19	28
Leon	71	592	2,503	Statewide 1/	7	80	247
Levy	7	40	102	Unknown 1/	20	42	207

NAICS North American Industry Classification System. See Glossary for definition.
1/ Reporting units without a fixed location within the state or of unknown county location.
Note: Private employment. Data are preliminary. For a list of other four-digit code industries see Table 20.05. Only counties for which data are disclosed are shown. Detail may not add to totals due to disclosure editing and/or rounding. See Tables 23.70, 23.72, 23.73, and 23.74 for public employment data.

Source: State of Florida, Agency for Workforce Innovation, Labor Market Statistics, "Quarterly Census of Employment and Wages" (ES-202), Annual NAICS files, Internet site <http://www.labormarketinfo.com/index.htm> (accessed 17, July 2007).

Table 20.11. HOSPITALS AND NURSING AND RESIDENTIAL CARE FACILITIES: AVERAGE MONTHLY PRIVATE REPORTING UNITS, EMPLOYMENT, AND PAYROLL COVERED BY UNEMPLOYMENT COMPENSATION LAW IN THE STATE AND COUNTIES OF FLORIDA, 2006

County	Number of reporting units	Number of employees	Payroll ($1,000)	County	Number of reporting units	Number of employees	Payroll ($1,000)
			Hospitals (NAICS code 622)				
Florida	562	238,930	840,469	Manatee	7	2,821	9,048
Alachua	11	10,065	35,570	Miami-Dade	127	37,905	149,307
Brevard	15	7,339	23,528	Monroe	4	784	2,842
Broward	45	10,871	39,417	Okaloosa	5	2,121	6,472
Charlotte	6	2,418	7,807	Orange	32	20,773	72,205
Citrus	4	1,561	4,548	Osceola	8	2,859	10,303
Columbia	6	1,078	3,220	Palm Beach	42	16,531	59,594
Duval	23	18,189	61,739	Pasco	10	3,637	12,968
Escambia	6	6,737	23,054	Pinellas	32	14,695	49,120
Hernando	6	2,125	6,273	Polk	9	7,902	25,054
Highlands	3	1,585	5,276	St. Lucie	7	1,804	7,016
Hillsborough	30	18,903	68,317	Santa Rosa	5	1,272	3,469
Indian River	5	2,115	7,287	Sarasota	10	6,403	22,385
Lake	9	3,739	12,192	Seminole	11	3,380	11,814
Leon	5	4,294	14,546	Volusia	10	7,408	26,218
			Nursing and residential care facilities (NAICS code 623)				
Florida	2,633	154,152	330,670	Madison	5	514	908
Alachua	37	1,813	3,434	Manatee	34	2,605	5,117
Bay	47	1,682	3,695	Marion	40	2,545	4,975
Bradford	5	331	582	Martin	23	1,743	3,581
Brevard	64	5,061	11,477	Miami-Dade	351	15,467	34,144
Broward	238	10,526	22,460	Monroe	4	238	515
Charlotte	33	1,817	3,704	Nassau	7	331	711
Citrus	23	1,778	3,735	Okaloosa	24	1,395	2,827
Clay	17	1,717	3,548	Okeechobee	8	523	1,181
Collier	31	2,995	6,508	Orange	126	7,847	18,693
Columbia	10	489	908	Osceola	20	1,425	2,937
DeSoto	4	40	84	Palm Beach	187	12,310	27,894
Duval	92	6,724	14,347	Pasco	50	2,764	5,684
Escambia	47	3,879	8,226	Pinellas	236	13,970	29,661
Flagler	8	188	385	Polk	68	4,162	8,477
Gadsden	7	206	371	Putnam	9	640	1,226
Gilchrist	3	244	479	St. Johns	18	1,518	2,999
Hardee	18	312	618	St. Lucie	36	2,006	4,339
Hendry	5	226	494	Santa Rosa	12	703	1,526
Hernando	21	1,260	2,339	Sarasota	77	5,451	11,577
Highlands	24	1,006	2,038	Seminole	61	3,607	8,009
Hillsborough	142	8,292	18,434	Sumter	5	154	267
Indian River	20	1,450	2,976	Suwannee	6	772	1,488
Jackson	16	572	1,026	Volusia	97	5,961	11,992
Jefferson	4	218	398	Walton	7	441	793
Lake	34	2,787	6,181	Washington	6	282	547
Lee	59	4,556	10,357	Statewide 1/	11	232	889
Leon	44	2,204	4,192	Unknown 1/	19	261	678

NAICS North American Industry Classification System. See Glossary for definition.
1/ Employment based in Florida, but working out of the state or country.
Note: See Note on Table 20.07.
Source: State of Florida, Agency for Workforce Innovation, Labor Market Statistics, "Quarterly Census of Employment and Wages" (ES-202), Annual NAICS files, Internet site <http://www.labormarketinfo.com/index.htm> (accessed 17, July 2007).

Table 20.20. EDUCATIONAL SERVICES: ESTABLISHMENTS, EMPLOYMENT, RECEIPTS, AND PAYROLL BY KIND OF BUSINESS IN FLORIDA, 2002

NAICS code	Industry	Number of establishments	Number of employees 1/	Receipts ($1,000)	Annual payroll ($1,000)
61	Educational services	3,070	23,223	1,883,151	593,497
6114	Business schools and computer and management training	514	4,631	477,905	172,993
61141	Business and secretarial schools	20	235	14,581	5,462
61142	Computer training	216	2,187	204,774	87,929
61143	Professional and management development training	278	2,209	258,550	79,602
6115	Technical and trade schools	496	6,904	716,145	208,318
611511	Cosmetology and barber schools	69	428	25,630	7,791
611512	Flight training	123	2,416	285,091	82,187
611513	Apprenticeship training	62	428	21,580	9,072
611519	Other trade and technical schools	242	3,632	383,844	109,268
6116	Other schools and instruction	1,788	10,404	547,303	174,243
61161	Fine arts schools	501	2,417	115,779	33,426
61162	Sports and recreation instruction	666	2,783	193,078	56,078
61163	Language schools	59	436	20,732	8,503
61169	All other schools and instruction	562	4,768	217,714	76,236
611691	Exam preparation and tutoring	297	2,637	97,019	37,337
611692	Automobile driving schools	103	826	37,875	12,141
611699	All other miscellaneous schools and instruction	162	1,305	82,820	26,758
6117	Educational support services	272	1,284	141,798	37,943

1/ Paid employment for the pay period including March 12.

Note: The economic censuses are conducted on a 5-year cycle collecting data for years ending in 2 and 7. Data are for North American Industry Classification System (NAICS) code 61 and may not be comparable to earlier years. See Glossary for definition.

Table 20.21. EDUCATIONAL SERVICES: REVENUE AND EXPENDITURE FOR FIRMS EXEMPT FROM FEDERAL INCOME TAX BY KIND OF BUSINESS IN FLORIDA, 2002

(in thousands of dollars)

NAICS code	Industry	Revenue	Expenditure
61	Educational services	232,400	213,045
6114	Business schools and computer and management training	47,232	45,430
6115	Technical and trade schools	56,245	52,983
6116	Other schools and instruction	89,778	80,473
6117	Educational support services	39,145	34,159

Note: The economic censuses are conducted on a 5-year cycle collecting data for years ending in 2 and 7. Data are for North American Industry Classification System (NAICS) code 61 and may not be comparable to earlier years. See Glossary for definition.

Source for Tables 20.20 and 20.21: U.S., Department of Commerce, Census Bureau, *2002 Economic Census: Educational Services,* Geographic Area Series EC02-61A-FL, issued June 2005, Internet site <http://www.census.gov/> (accessed 11, May 2007).

Table 20.22. EDUCATIONAL SERVICES: ESTABLISHMENTS, EMPLOYMENT, AND PAYROLL IN THE STATE AND COUNTIES OF FLORIDA, 2002

County	Number of establishments	Number of employees 1/	Annual payroll ($1,000)	County	Number of establishments	Number of employees 1/	Annual payroll ($1,000)
Florida	3,070	23,223	593,497	Lake 5/	28	(NA)	(D)
Alachua 2/	52	(NA)	(D)	Lee 2/	65	(NA)	(D)
Baker	0	0	0	Leon 6/	74	(NA)	(D)
Bay 3/	19	(NA)	(D)	Levy	6	7	115
Bradford 4/	3	(NA)	(D)	Liberty	0	0	0
Brevard	106	605	10,436	Madison 4/	1	(NA)	(D)
Broward	377	2,994	61,603	Manatee	47	438	13,411
Calhoun	0	0	0	Marion	19	65	889
Charlotte	15	68	1,103	Martin	22	80	1,936
Citrus 3/	14	(NA)	(D)	Miami-Dade	469	4,291	117,306
Clay 5/	18	(NA)	(D)	Monroe	29	126	3,062
Collier	48	152	3,698	Nassau 5/	18	(NA)	(D)
Columbia 4/	4	(NA)	(D)	Okaloosa	33	168	3,031
DeSoto 3/	1	(NA)	(D)	Okeechobee	0	0	0
Dixie	0	0	0	Orange	221	2,131	59,582
Duval	143	1,284	49,066	Osceola 5/	32	(NA)	(D)
Escambia 2/	50	(NA)	(D)	Palm Beach	270	1,448	34,317
Flagler 3/	3	(NA)	(D)	Pasco 5/	27	(NA)	(D)
Franklin 4/	2	(NA)	(D)	Pinellas 7/	192	(NA)	(D)
Gadsden 3/	6	(NA)	(D)	Polk	43	247	5,490
Gilchrist 4/	1	(NA)	(D)	Putnam	5	12	86
Glades	0	0	0	St. Johns	30	181	3,345
Gulf	0	0	0	St. Lucie	16	63	1,282
Hamilton	0	0	0	Santa Rosa 5/	16	(NA)	(D)
Hardee	0	0	0	Sarasota	87	389	9,177
Hendry 4/	2	(NA)	(D)	Seminole 7/	98	(NA)	(D)
Hernando 4/	10	(NA)	(D)	Sumter 4/	4	(NA)	(D)
Highlands 4/	7	(NA)	(D)	Suwannee 4/	2	(NA)	(D)
Hillsborough	224	2,081	57,284	Taylor 4/	1	(NA)	(D)
Holmes	0	0	0	Union	0	0	0
Indian River 2/	24	(NA)	(D)	Volusia 3/	77	(NA)	(D)
Jackson 4/	3	(NA)	(D)	Wakulla 4/	2	(NA)	(D)
Jefferson 4/	2	(NA)	(D)	Walton 4/	1	(NA)	(D)
Lafayette 4/	1	(NA)	(D)	Washington	0	0	0

(NA) Not available.
(D) Data withheld to avoid disclosure of information about individual firms.
1/ Paid employment for pay period including March 12.
Employment ranges: 2/ 250-499. 3/ 20-99. 4/ 0-19. 5/ 100-249. 6/ 500-999. 7/ 1,000-2,499.
Note: The economic censuses are conducted on a 5-year cycle collecting data for years ending in 2 and 7. Data are for North American Industry Classification System (NAICS) code 61 and may not be comparable to earlier years. See Glossary for definition.

Source: U.S., Department of Commerce, Census Bureau, *2002 Economic Census: Educational Services,* Geographic Area Series EC-02-61A-FL, issued June 2005, Internet site <http://www.census.gov/> (accessed 11, May 2007).

Table 20.26. EDUCATIONAL SERVICES: AVERAGE MONTHLY PRIVATE REPORTING UNITS EMPLOYMENT, AND PAYROLL COVERED BY UNEMPLOYMENT COMPENSATION LAW IN THE STATE AND COUNTIES OF FLORIDA, 2005 AND 2006

County	Number of reporting units	Number of employees	Payroll ($1,000)	County	Number of reporting units	Number of employees	Payroll ($1,000)
			Educational services, 2005 A/ (NAICS code 61)				
Florida	5,168	95,299	254,955	Madison	4	90	109
				Manatee	70	652	1,457
Alachua	80	1,553	2,707	Marion	39	608	986
Bay	29	285	438	Martin	39	426	832
Brevard	152	2,671	6,431	Miami-Dade	739	18,346	55,540
Broward	599	13,665	40,664	Monroe	32	282	654
Charlotte	21	136	270	Nassau	14	87	154
Citrus	20	125	229	Okaloosa	37	406	1,667
Clay	43	524	1,066	Orange	378	8,978	25,911
Collier	72	993	2,892	Osceola	44	246	473
Columbia	11	92	144	Palm Beach	469	7,152	18,812
Duval	254	4,649	11,343	Pasco	68	1,021	2,480
Escambia	69	2,159	4,325	Pinellas	323	4,583	11,808
Flagler	9	14	12	Polk	89	2,842	5,742
Gadsden	11	85	173	Putnam	11	43	64
Hernando	21	183	282	St. Johns	44	996	2,010
Highlands	17	104	149	St. Lucie	35	397	808
Hillsborough	377	7,017	17,362	Santa Rosa	23	204	904
Indian River	28	582	1,453	Sarasota	113	1,314	3,660
Lake	56	876	2,233	Seminole	142	2,114	5,194
Lee	101	1,801	4,946	Volusia	106	4,249	11,454
Leon	104	935	1,960	Statewide 1/	70	742	2,435
Levy	11	53	87	Unknown 1/	148	387	1,517
			Educational services, 2006 B/ (NAICS code 61)				
Florida	5,449	99,920	280,506	Manatee	77	676	1,718
				Marion	46	709	1,187
Alachua	77	1,506	2,706	Martin	40	446	920
Bay	31	316	523	Miami-Dade	773	19,230	61,122
Bradford	6	18	28	Monroe	27	322	809
Brevard	163	2,785	7,177	Nassau	17	93	159
Broward	616	14,077	45,495	Okaloosa	41	463	1,545
Charlotte	19	158	278	Orange	401	8,895	26,364
Citrus	18	122	297	Osceola	45	324	618
Clay	43	596	1,161	Palm Beach	483	7,104	20,392
Collier	68	1,027	3,190	Pasco	74	1,165	2,924
Columbia	13	113	183	Pinellas	313	4,528	12,215
Duval	273	4,685	11,314	Polk	99	3,028	6,393
Escambia	71	2,155	4,468	Putnam	11	48	67
Flagler	13	19	31	St. Johns	52	1,080	2,328
Gadsden	12	120	269	St. Lucie	33	360	739
Hernando	24	191	296	Santa Rosa	24	235	1,078
Highlands	17	104	161	Sarasota	123	1,417	3,993
Hillsborough	394	7,867	20,241	Seminole	157	2,626	6,484
Indian River	29	629	1,648	Volusia	109	4,208	11,873
Lake	62	904	2,711	Wakulla	3	38	52
Lee	120	1,951	5,684	Walton	8	44	101
Leon	105	955	1,962	Statewide 1/	73	1,222	3,737
Levy	11	48	78	Unknown 1/	189	620	2,481

A/ Revised. B/ Preliminary.

1/ Reporting units without a fixed location within the state or of unknown county location.

Note: See Note on Table 20.07. For a list of other educational services included see Table 20.05.

Source: State of Florida, Agency for Workforce Innovation, Labor Market Statistics, "Quarterly Census of Employment and Wages" (ES-202), Annual NAICS files, Internet site <http://www.labormarketinfo.com/index.htm> (accessed 17, July 2007).

Table 20.27. SCHOOLS: AVERAGE MONTHLY PRIVATE REPORTING UNITS, EMPLOYMENT, AND PAYROLL COVERED BY UNEMPLOYMENT COMPENSATION LAW IN THE STATE AND COUNTIES OF FLORIDA, 2006

County	Number of reporting units	Number of employees	Payroll ($1,000)	County	Number of reporting units	Number of employees	Payroll ($1,000)
		Elementary and secondary schools (NAICS code 6111)					
Florida	1,054	34,431	84,818	Manatee	19	364	810
Alachua	30	745	1,321	Marion	9	230	444
Bay	6	182	377	Martin	13	314	681
Brevard	29	934	2,175	Miami-Dade	206	6,895	18,553
Broward	94	4,361	11,821	Monroe	4	37	77
Charlotte	3	55	133	Okaloosa	6	217	453
Clay	7	219	507	Orange	54	2,125	5,714
Collier	12	517	1,635	Osceola	8	155	339
Columbia	5	54	82	Palm Beach	93	3,488	9,116
Duval	54	1,765	4,036	Pasco	16	358	762
Escambia	24	866	1,414	Pinellas	57	1,758	4,064
Hernando	5	170	273	Polk	22	1,008	2,206
Hillsborough	79	2,091	5,129	St. Johns	8	265	520
Indian River	8	356	884	St. Lucie	10	201	363
Lake	15	727	2,124	Sarasota	20	587	1,549
Lee	23	860	2,093	Seminole	27	854	1,964
Leon	14	465	916	Volusia	17	357	724
Levy	5	39	66	Unknown 1/	14	35	105
		Junior colleges (NAICS code 6112)					
Florida	34	1,572	4,176	Orange	3	227	706
Miami-Dade	8	240	632	Unknown 1/	4	5	44
		Colleges and universities (NAICS code 6113)					
Florida	257	32,962	108,110	Palm Beach	16	1,688	5,256
Broward	34	6,471	25,093	Pinellas	15	1,211	3,797
Clay	3	85	174	Polk	7	1,584	3,392
Collier	3	349	1,078	St. Johns	3	527	1,306
Duval	19	1,479	3,825	Sarasota	7	432	1,559
Hillsborough	22	2,775	7,290	Seminole	5	352	1,105
Lee	5	174	480	Volusia	7	3,298	9,986
Miami-Dade	23	7,533	29,126	Statewide 1/	7	98	281
Orange	24	1,901	6,004	Unknown 1/	18	138	381

See footnotes at end of table. Continued . . .

Table 20.27. SCHOOLS: AVERAGE MONTHLY PRIVATE REPORTING UNITS, EMPLOYMENT, AND PAYROLL COVERED BY UNEMPLOYMENT COMPENSATION LAW IN THE STATE AND COUNTIES OF FLORIDA, 2006 (Continued)

County	Number of reporting units	Number of employees	Payroll ($1,000)	County	Number of reporting units	Number of employees	Payroll ($1,000)
	Business, computer and management training (NAICS code 6114)						
Florida	655	5,642	21,804	Nassau	4	6	26
Alachua	5	138	275	Okaloosa	5	10	461
Brevard	21	84	453	Orange	56	929	2,954
Broward	75	437	1,606	Osceola	4	9	20
Collier	10	22	86	Palm Beach	51	268	1,038
Duval	24	142	482	Pinellas	46	429	1,803
Escambia	7	90	354	Polk	8	30	66
Hernando	6	3	3	St. Johns	8	8	70
Hillsborough	57	845	2,965	Santa Rosa	4	40	222
Lake	8	13	35	Sarasota	15	42	135
Leon	20	83	223	Seminole	28	311	1,063
Manatee	9	26	91	Volusia	12	16	53
Martin	3	5	6	Statewide 1/	17	73	487
Miami-Dade	71	1,141	4,291	Unknown 1/	50	80	528
	Technical and trade schools (NAICS code 6115)						
Florida	575	8,526	25,530	Martin	3	34	82
				Miami-Dade	80	1,159	3,768
Alachua	7	102	281	Okaloosa	10	116	389
Brevard	17	173	519	Orange	29	1,885	6,125
Broward	75	1,124	3,729	Osceola	5	39	47
Clay	5	21	42	Palm Beach	48	487	1,451
Collier	8	33	135	Pasco	7	45	87
Duval	24	353	962	Pinellas	34	425	1,159
Escambia	15	132	249	Polk	8	82	262
Hillsborough	40	538	1,587	St. Lucie	4	40	100
Lake	7	13	95	Sarasota	14	130	315
Lee	20	149	298	Seminole	20	586	1,216
Leon	6	42	94	Volusia	21	303	748
Manatee	7	19	34	Statewide 1/	13	53	313
Marion	6	14	18	Unknown 1/	13	19	154

NAICS North American Industry Classification System. See Glossary for definition.
1/ Reporting units without a fixed location within the state or of unknown county location.
Note: Private employment. Data are preliminary. For a list of other educational services included see Table 20.05. Only counties for which data are disclosed are shown. Detail may not add to totals due to disclosure editing and/or rounding. See Tables 23.70, 23.72, 23.73, and 23.74 for public employment data.

Source: State of Florida, Agency for Workforce Innovation, Labor Market Statistics, "Quarterly Census of Employment and Wages" (ES-202), Annual NAICS files, Internet site <http://www.labormarketinfo.com/index.htm> (accessed 17, July 2007).

Table 20.28. HEALTH CARE AND SOCIAL ASSISTANCE: AVERAGE MONTHLY PRIVATE EMPLOYMENT COVERED BY UNEMPLOYMENT COMPENSATION LAW IN THE STATE AND COUNTIES OF FLORIDA, 2006

		Social assistance 1/				
County	Health care and social assistance (NAICS 62)	Total (NAICS 624)	Individual and family services (NAICS 6241)	Emergency and other relief services (NAICS 6242)	Vocational rehabilitation services (NAICS 6243)	Child day care services (NAICS 6244)
Florida	840,134	98,476	31,695	6,378	14,520	45,883
Alachua	18,789	1,722	510	95	(NA)	1,090
Baker	516	85	(NA)	(NA)	(NA)	52
Bay	7,304	1,199	497	96	(NA)	564
Bradford	763	128	(NA)	(NA)	(NA)	56
Brevard	24,560	2,801	545	251	879	1,127
Broward	70,820	10,999	3,336	782	947	5,934
Calhoun	471	67	(NA)	(NA)	(NA)	64
Charlotte	7,427	369	132	41	64	131
Citrus	6,321	372	(NA)	21	52	278
Clay	5,886	743	231	(NA)	(NA)	442
Collier	13,449	980	246	47	(NA)	610
Columbia	2,863	486	(NA)	(NA)	(NA)	401
DeSoto	621	113	13	(NA)	(NA)	96
Dixie	128	(NA)	(NA)	(NA)	(NA)	(NA)
Duval	52,315	6,264	2,313	567	779	2,605
Escambia	19,016	2,039	744	249	276	771
Flagler	1,396	104	14	(NA)	(NA)	68
Franklin	80	14	(NA)	(NA)	(NA)	(NA)
Gadsden	511	127	(NA)	(NA)	(NA)	80
Gilchrist	389	54	(NA)	(NA)	(NA)	51
Glades	48	(NA)	(NA)	(NA)	(NA)	(NA)
Gulf	369	146	(NA)	(NA)	(NA)	(NA)
Hamilton	291	(NA)	(NA)	(NA)	(NA)	(NA)
Hardee	1,162	269	(NA)	(NA)	(NA)	143
Hendry	840	231	(NA)	(NA)	(NA)	191
Hernando	6,173	635	(NA)	30	(NA)	248
Highlands	4,599	431	54	(NA)	(NA)	248
Hillsborough	58,544	6,821	1,834	567	1,054	3,366
Holmes	407	94	(NA)	(NA)	(NA)	84
Indian River	7,333	864	355	27	(NA)	353
Jackson	1,467	440	166	(NA)	(NA)	109
Jefferson	292	43	(NA)	(NA)	(NA)	(NA)
Lafayette	126	(NA)	(NA)	(NA)	(NA)	(NA)
Lake	11,589	899	208	(NA)	(NA)	485
Lee	18,574	2,456	748	163	526	1,019
Leon	14,599	1,962	886	104	81	891
Levy	811	329	(NA)	(NA)	(NA)	99
Liberty	(NA)	26	(NA)	(NA)	(NA)	(NA)
Madison	916	171	(NA)	(NA)	(NA)	47

See footnotes at end of table.

Continued . . .

Table 20.28. HEALTH CARE AND SOCIAL ASSISTANCE: AVERAGE MONTHLY PRIVATE EMPLOYMENT COVERED BY UNEMPLOYMENT COMPENSATION LAW IN THE STATE AND COUNTIES OF FLORIDA, 2006 (Continued)

County	Health care and social assistance (NAICS 62)	Social assistance 1/ Total (NAICS 624)	Individual and family services (NAICS 6241)	Emergency and other relief services (NAICS 6242)	Vocational rehabilitation services (NAICS 6243)	Child day care services (NAICS 6244)
Manatee	12,748	1,778	700	101	(NA)	557
Marion	11,538	1,517	466	97	376	577
Martin	8,415	785	240	30	264	252
Miami-Dade	112,959	15,524	5,031	1,173	2,517	6,803
Monroe	2,236	363	166	(NA)	(NA)	106
Nassau	977	186	88	(NA)	(NA)	98
Okaloosa	7,312	1,007	198	28	(NA)	601
Okeechobee	1,766	397	(NA)	(NA)	(NA)	158
Orange	55,241	5,491	982	579	925	3,005
Osceola	7,304	731	(NA)	(NA)	40	456
Palm Beach	67,030	7,395	2,777	137	1,388	3,092
Pasco	14,675	1,760	460	63	140	1,097
Pinellas	58,748	5,671	1,832	176	1,375	2,287
Polk	22,379	1,861	700	46	307	808
Putnam	2,190	283	14	(NA)	(NA)	250
St. Johns	5,703	649	288	95	(NA)	253
St. Lucie	8,200	1,669	840	(NA)	(NA)	715
Santa Rosa	3,462	409	52	(NA)	(NA)	230
Sarasota	22,936	1,533	729	252	75	477
Seminole	14,931	1,770	407	122	186	1,055
Sumter	1,227	142	(NA)	(NA)	(NA)	35
Suwannee	1,220	155	(NA)	(NA)	(NA)	61
Taylor	727	64	(NA)	(NA)	(NA)	20
Union	264	(NA)	(NA)	(NA)	(NA)	(NA)
Volusia	24,432	1,923	804	186	84	848
Wakulla	278	34	(NA)	(NA)	(NA)	30
Walton	1,604	369	316	(NA)	(NA)	50
Washington	797	184	(NA)	(NA)	(NA)	75
Statewide 2/	4,768	73	62	(NA)	(NA)	(NA)
Out-of-state 3/	81	(NA)	(NA)	(NA)	(NA)	(NA)
Unknown 2/	1,660	91	27	18	(NA)	43

NAICS North American Industry Classification System. See Glossary for definition.
(NA) Not available.

1/ Industries in the social assistance subsector provide a wide variety of social assistance services directly to their clients. These services do not include residential or accommodation services, except on a short stay basis.

2/ Reporting units without a fixed location within the state or of unknown county location.

3/ Employment based in Florida, but working out of the state or country.

Note: Private employment. Data are preliminary. For a list of other educational services included see Table 20.05. Only counties for which data are disclosed are shown. Detail may not add to totals due to disclosure editing and/or rounding. See Tables 23.70, 23.72, 23.73, and 23.74 for public employment data.

Source: State of Florida, Agency for Workforce Innovation, Labor Market Statistics, "Quarterly Census of Employment and Wages" (ES-202), Annual NAICS files, Internet site <http://www.labormarketinfo.com/index.htm> (accessed 17, July 2007).

Table 20.29. PERFORMING ARTS AND SPECTATOR SPORTS: AVERAGE MONTHLY PRIVATE REPORTING UNITS, EMPLOYMENT, AND PAYROLL COVERED BY UNEMPLOYMENT COMPENSATION LAW IN THE STATE AND COUNTIES OF FLORIDA, 2006

County	Reporting units	Employ- ment	Payroll ($1,000)	County	Reporting units	Employ- ment	Payroll ($1,000)
			Performing arts and spectator sports (NAICS code 711)				
Florida	3,899	29,959	144,481	Miami-Dade	664	6,002	36,208
				Monroe	26	44	128
Alachua	45	788	2,472	Nassau	7	12	56
Bay	13	60	107	Okaloosa	19	53	174
Brevard	68	296	545	Orange	357	2,249	12,782
Broward	545	2,779	9,629	Osceola	44	647	1,085
Charlotte	9	6	19	Palm Beach	443	2,417	7,153
Clay	12	76	199	Pasco	55	180	311
Collier	43	394	2,660	Pinellas	168	2,098	9,847
Duval	104	1,294	12,354	Polk	62	649	2,011
Escambia	32	243	402	Putnam	4	6	7
Flagler	10	23	47	St. Johns	30	98	853
Hernando	19	41	178	St. Lucie	21	130	1,000
Hillsborough	173	2,621	19,807	Santa Rosa	14	39	97
Indian River	17	86	328	Sarasota	94	1,892	4,560
Lake	37	80	182	Seminole	99	324	1,756
Lee	74	949	1,940	Sumter	9	29	72
Leon	32	77	192	Volusia	80	1,321	4,008
Manatee	36	149	1,287	Walton	9	29	96
Marion	68	472	1,063	Statewide 1/	48	299	5,415
Martin	36	98	310	Unknown 1/	219	392	2,302

1/ Reporting units without a fixed location within the state or of unknown county location.
Note: See Note on Table 20.30.

Table 20.30. MUSEUMS, HISTORICAL SITES, ZOOS, AND PARKS: AVERAGE MONTHLY PRIVATE REPORTING UNITS, EMPLOYMENT, AND PAYROLL COVERED BY UNEMPLOYMENT COMPENSATION LAW IN THE STATE AND COUNTIES OF FLORIDA, 2006

County	Reporting units	Employ- ment	Payroll ($1,000)	County	Reporting units	Employ- ment	Payroll ($1,000)
			Museums, historical sites, zoos, and parks (NAICS code 712)				
Florida	326	5,873	12,067	Monroe	16	197	440
Brevard	6	139	261	Okaloosa	4	88	123
Broward	27	430	935	Orange	19	493	921
Collier	11	98	273	Osceola	5	20	31
Duval	9	358	720	Palm Beach	46	658	1,684
Hillsborough	9	640	1,272	Pinellas	20	235	435
Lake	4	12	14	Polk	3	109	222
Lee	8	31	61	St. Johns	12	253	693
Leon	5	104	146	Santa Rosa	2	105	179
Martin	5	37	88	Sarasota	11	198	374
Miami-Dade	44	960	2,132	Volusia	7	53	102

NAICS North American Industry Classification System. See Glossary for definition.

Note: Private employment. Data are preliminary. Only counties for which data are disclosed are shown. Detail may not add to totals due to disclosure editing and/or rounding. See Tables 23.70, 23.72, 23.73, and 23.74 for public employment data.

Source for Tables 20.29 and 20.30: State of Florida, Agency for Workforce Innovation, Labor Market Statistics, "Quarterly Census of Employment and Wages" (ES-202), Annual NAICS files, Internet site <http://www.labormarketinfo.com/index.htm> (accessed 17, July 2007).

Table 20.33. PHYSICIANS: LICENSED DOCTORS OF MEDICINE AND OSTEOPATHY IN THE STATE AND COUNTIES OF FLORIDA, JULY 2, 2007

Location of licensee	Doctors of— Medicine	Osteopathy	Location of licensee	Doctors of— Medicine	Osteopathy
Total	53,164	5,003	Jefferson	6	0
			Lafayette	1	0
Foreign	35	0	Lake	456	45
Out-of-state	2,309	346	Lee	1,093	171
Unknown	10,795	1,035	Leon	628	24
Alachua	1,527	39	Levy	18	3
Baker	9	2	Liberty	0	0
Bay	318	26	Madison	5	3
Bradford	8	2	Manatee	571	58
Brevard	1,142	78	Marion	506	45
Broward	4,122	567	Martin	334	48
Calhoun	7	0	Miami-Dade	6,451	318
Charlotte	307	45	Monroe	163	24
Citrus	205	33	Nassau	69	9
Clay	258	35	Okaloosa	370	31
Collier	695	57	Okeechobee	41	1
Columbia	94	10	Orange	2,454	201
DeSoto	18	1	Osceola	274	26
Dixie	2	1	Palm Beach	3,298	374
Duval	2,419	132	Pasco	568	62
Escambia	699	31	Pinellas	2,365	396
Flagler	76	13	Polk	809	40
Franklin	7	0	Putnam	72	7
Gadsden	27	3	St. Johns	418	26
Gilchrist	4	1	St. Lucie	299	38
Glades	1	1	Santa Rosa	232	29
Gulf	10	0	Sarasota	1,005	82
Hamilton	3	2	Seminole	687	70
Hardee	9	0	Sumter	18	4
Hendry	14	1	Suwannee	13	1
Hernando	220	26	Taylor	14	4
Highlands	156	10	Union	10	0
Hillsborough	3,137	236	Volusia	840	86
Holmes	11	0	Wakulla	9	5
Indian River	325	29	Walton	46	7
Jackson	42	2	Washington	10	1

Caution: Data were collected from unaudited, raw data files as reported by the Department of Health and may contain reporting errors.

Note: Active licenses only. Excludes delinquent active, involuntary inactive, and voluntary inactive licenses.

Source: State of Florida, Department of Health, Internet site <http://ww2.doh.state.fl.us/> (accessed 2, July 2007).

Table 20.35. DENTISTS, DENTAL HYGIENISTS, AND DENTAL RADIOGRAPHERS: NUMBER LICENSED IN THE STATE AND COUNTIES OF FLORIDA, JULY 2, 2007

Location of licensee	Dentists	Dental hygienists	Dental radio-graphers	Location of licensee	Dentists	Dental hygienists	Dental radio-graphers
Total	11,659	11,777	21,900	Jefferson	2	9	15
				Lafayette	0	2	7
Foreign	11	3	1	Lake	105	156	256
Out-of-state	253	308	50	Lee	259	334	544
Unknown	1,831	1,517	253	Leon	116	160	283
Alachua	258	195	288	Levy	9	14	32
Baker	4	25	21	Liberty	1	3	9
Bay	70	111	120	Madison	3	6	17
Bradford	4	18	39	Manatee	145	204	213
Brevard	267	371	566	Marion	106	177	250
Broward	1,205	1,042	2,645	Martin	115	132	140
Calhoun	4	6	12	Miami-Dade	1,443	1,022	4,217
Charlotte	67	89	110	Monroe	31	36	140
Citrus	37	62	91	Nassau	18	53	66
Clay	87	163	236	Okaloosa	105	100	213
Collier	206	172	287	Okeechobee	10	26	40
Columbia	20	37	48	Orange	549	501	906
DeSoto	6	8	22	Osceola	56	71	129
Dixie	3	6	15	Palm Beach	972	859	1,501
Duval	415	415	1,105	Pasco	123	195	502
Escambia	155	165	203	Pinellas	584	630	1,512
Flagler	30	36	36	Polk	140	215	531
Franklin	1	1	7	Putnam	13	25	66
Gadsden	11	21	49	St. Johns	110	137	110
Gilchrist	1	4	12	St. Lucie	67	127	261
Glades	0	1	2	Santa Rosa	45	131	82
Gulf	4	9	8	Sarasota	265	253	416
Hamilton	2	1	18	Seminole	235	247	411
Hardee	4	2	19	Sumter	6	15	34
Hendry	5	14	51	Suwannee	7	18	16
Hernando	54	85	168	Taylor	3	5	19
Highlands	34	40	129	Union	0	6	27
Hillsborough	638	525	1,626	Volusia	210	279	464
Holmes	3	7	12	Wakulla	3	12	14
Indian River	79	99	127	Walton	14	19	29
Jackson	14	29	42	Washington	6	11	10

Caution: Data were collected from unaudited, raw data files as reported by the Department of Health and may contain reporting errors.

Note: Active licenses only. Excludes delinquent active, involuntary inactive, and voluntary inactive licenses.

Source: State of Florida, Department of Health, Internet site <http://ww2.doh.state.fl.us/> (accessed 2, July 2007).

Table 20.36. HEALTH PRACTITIONERS: NUMBER LICENSED IN THE STATE AND COUNTIES OF FLORIDA, JULY 2, 2007

Location of licensee	Chiro- practors	Optome- trists	Podia- trists	Therapists: Occupa- tional	Therapists: Physical	Therapists: Massage	Nursing home adminis- trators	Psychol- ogists
Total	5,354	2,775	1,720	6,002	12,016	28,788	1,543	4,015
Foreign	3	1	1	8	10	10	0	0
Out-of-state	345	200	70	88	242	295	22	85
Unknown	706	421	377	533	1,770	1,995	175	353
Alachua	68	30	13	203	273	604	10	177
Baker	1	2	1	3	1	15	1	3
Bay	24	19	9	45	86	189	12	17
Bradford	2	1	0	3	0	15	1	2
Brevard	124	66	35	167	314	824	38	91
Broward	636	326	204	614	1,125	2,884	119	576
Calhoun	2	1	0	1	5	5	2	0
Charlotte	34	11	12	46	97	216	12	9
Citrus	23	10	6	36	80	148	19	7
Clay	30	22	6	62	104	190	15	19
Collier	88	29	24	82	199	563	19	48
Columbia	6	10	0	13	24	38	5	3
DeSoto	5	0	0	2	6	21	1	4
Dixie	1	0	0	3	2	3	0	0
Duval	127	100	49	234	504	1,146	55	129
Escambia	47	27	13	71	130	258	24	60
Flagler	23	4	4	26	32	116	6	4
Franklin	1	0	1	1	3	4	1	0
Gadsden	2	0	1	5	3	17	2	13
Gilchrist	2	0	1	2	2	15	1	0
Glades	0	0	0	0	1	1	0	0
Gulf	1	0	0	1	5	7	1	0
Hamilton	0	0	0	0	1	3	2	0
Hardee	2	1	0	1	5	16	0	0
Hendry	5	2	0	5	9	19	1	3
Hernando	44	11	11	31	66	173	8	6
Highlands	22	10	6	30	61	77	7	5
Hillsborough	230	137	71	380	634	1,552	72	301
Holmes	1	2	0	0	4	8	1	0
Indian River	41	17	11	60	94	230	16	27
Jackson	6	4	0	8	11	28	4	7
Jefferson	1	0	0	7	0	8	0	1
Lafayette	0	0	0	1	1	0	1	0

See footnotes at end of table. Continued . . .

Table 20.36. HEALTH PRACTITIONERS: NUMBER LICENSED IN THE STATE AND COUNTIES OF FLORIDA, JULY 2, 2007 (Continued)

Location of licensee	Chiro-practors	Optome-trists	Podia-trists	Therapists: Occupa-tional	Therapists: Physical	Therapists: Massage	Nursing home adminis-trators	Psychol-ogists
Lake	55	21	17	67	124	330	29	13
Lee	149	92	42	160	366	1,022	42	63
Leon	41	40	10	81	157	342	19	162
Levy	6	2	1	3	5	32	1	2
Liberty	0	0	0	2	0	3	0	2
Madison	1	1	0	4	3	7	1	0
Manatee	72	37	25	160	226	547	40	47
Marion	66	23	14	88	147	304	20	39
Martin	70	29	14	62	114	276	12	29
Miami-Dade	353	221	190	601	924	3,143	84	689
Monroe	16	13	3	14	41	195	0	16
Nassau	8	10	5	7	25	93	6	7
Okaloosa	37	29	8	39	87	208	11	16
Okeechobee	4	2	1	4	9	44	3	0
Orange	213	131	46	320	600	1,539	86	130
Osceola	39	15	3	42	67	234	6	5
Palm Beach	498	189	167	416	876	2,467	139	333
Pasco	93	29	20	100	192	558	36	37
Pinellas	344	116	72	339	647	1,845	127	146
Polk	92	48	29	102	208	537	31	37
Putnam	2	3	2	13	26	61	1	5
St. Johns	39	29	17	111	231	326	19	41
St. Lucie	54	16	10	53	104	333	11	17
Santa Rosa	23	19	1	31	78	133	15	16
Sarasota	147	53	38	149	310	980	55	88
Seminole	95	82	26	124	265	577	33	64
Sumter	10	2	2	5	17	41	1	4
Suwannee	5	1	1	3	3	27	5	2
Taylor	2	2	0	2	6	12	1	1
Union	0	0	0	0	2	6	0	1
Volusia	153	50	27	113	218	759	47	43
Wakulla	4	0	0	3	5	21	4	4
Walton	9	6	3	10	20	82	3	5
Washington	1	0	0	2	9	11	2	1

Caution: Data were collected from unaudited, raw data files as reported by the Department of Health and may contain reporting errors.

Note: Active licenses only. Excludes delinquent active, involuntary inactive, and voluntary inactive licenses.

Source: State of Florida, Department of Health, Internet site <http://ww2.doh.state.fl.us/> (accessed 2, July 2007).

Table 20.37. NURSES: LICENSED REGISTERED AND PRACTICAL NURSES IN THE STATE AND COUNTIES OF FLORIDA, JULY 2, 2007

Location of licensee	Total registered and practical nurses	Regis- tered nurses	Practical nurses	Location of licensee	Total registered and practical nurses	Regis- tered nurses	Practical nurses
Total	277,986	212,890	65,096	Jefferson	159	104	55
				Lafayette	54	28	26
Foreign	301	288	13	Lake	4,315	3,154	1,161
Out-of-state	6,067	5,260	807	Lee	7,755	5,993	1,762
Unknown	30,105	25,635	4,470	Leon	3,407	2,620	787
Alachua	5,224	4,492	732	Levy	420	276	144
Baker	383	274	109	Liberty	65	28	37
Bay	2,628	1,831	797	Madison	245	108	137
Bradford	278	162	116	Manatee	4,878	3,574	1,304
Brevard	7,736	6,115	1,621	Marion	4,360	3,255	1,105
Broward	25,578	19,817	5,761	Martin	2,051	1,694	357
Calhoun	199	103	96	Miami-Dade	20,717	15,969	4,748
Charlotte	2,662	1,859	803	Monroe	882	794	88
Citrus	2,168	1,451	717	Nassau	855	713	142
Clay	3,041	2,489	552	Okaloosa	2,427	1,674	753
Collier	3,381	2,559	822	Okeechobee	419	235	184
Columbia	1,112	763	349	Orange	12,363	9,747	2,616
DeSoto	316	156	160	Osceola	2,382	1,674	708
Dixie	130	71	59	Palm Beach	15,784	12,322	3,462
Duval	10,862	8,833	2,029	Pasco	6,950	4,900	2,050
Escambia	4,377	3,186	1,191	Pinellas	16,406	11,909	4,497
Flagler	1,411	1,050	361	Polk	7,303	4,908	2,395
Franklin	128	68	60	Putnam	826	470	356
Gadsden	494	273	221	St. Johns	2,631	2,188	443
Gilchrist	223	146	77	St. Lucie	3,642	2,645	997
Glades	42	25	17	Santa Rosa	2,472	1,922	550
Gulf	194	110	84	Sarasota	6,184	4,493	1,691
Hamilton	125	77	48	Seminole	5,574	4,428	1,146
Hardee	195	88	107	Sumter	717	539	178
Hendry	250	141	109	Suwannee	631	381	250
Hernando	2,743	1,857	886	Taylor	201	93	108
Highlands	1,366	939	427	Union	177	113	64
Hillsborough	15,039	11,317	3,722	Volusia	7,743	5,711	2,032
Holmes	232	100	132	Wakulla	306	192	114
Indian River	1,852	1,423	429	Walton	528	330	198
Jackson	980	582	398	Washington	335	166	169

Caution: Data were collected from unaudited, raw data files as reported by the Department of Health and may contain reporting errors.

Note: Active licenses only. Excludes delinquent active, involuntary inactive, and voluntary inactive licenses.

Source: State of Florida, Department of Health, Internet site <http://ww2.doh.state.fl.us/> (accessed 2, July 2007).

Table 20.38. HEALTH-RELATED RETAILERS: LICENSED DISPENSING OPTICIANS, PHARMACISTS AND PHARMACIST INTERNS IN THE STATE AND COUNTIES OF FLORIDA, JULY 2, 2007

Location of licensee	Dispensing opticians	Pharmacists	Pharmacist interns	Location of licensee	Dispensing opticians	Pharmacists	Pharmacist interns
Total	3,561	24,206	7,129	Jefferson	1	14	2
				Lafayette	0	1	0
Foreign	2	10	70	Lake	48	198	38
Out-of-state	49	638	1,413	Lee	141	512	74
Unknown	180	6,423	913	Leon	41	327	531
Alachua	44	462	381	Levy	9	15	2
Baker	1	5	1	Liberty	0	8	1
Bay	27	151	19	Madison	0	22	7
Bradford	5	17	3	Manatee	66	280	42
Brevard	109	419	86	Marion	81	216	35
Broward	390	2,059	729	Martin	38	144	9
Calhoun	0	17	2	Miami-Dade	465	1,754	550
Charlotte	29	96	12	Monroe	11	63	2
Citrus	24	85	12	Nassau	7	33	6
Clay	38	149	38	Okaloosa	19	122	12
Collier	45	236	29	Okeechobee	4	15	4
Columbia	6	46	10	Orange	142	1,206	269
DeSoto	3	13	2	Osceola	18	103	20
Dixie	1	5	1	Palm Beach	250	1,366	547
Duval	91	805	256	Pasco	95	381	43
Escambia	37	226	43	Pinellas	186	1,198	231
Flagler	14	39	5	Polk	82	350	75
Franklin	0	7	0	Putnam	11	39	4
Gadsden	4	30	7	St. Johns	39	207	30
Gilchrist	3	7	3	St. Lucie	49	169	28
Glades	0	0	0	Santa Rosa	20	154	15
Gulf	1	5	0	Sarasota	96	358	52
Hamilton	0	6	0	Seminole	67	457	86
Hardee	0	3	2	Sumter	7	18	0
Hendry	6	11	0	Suwannee	4	20	5
Hernando	41	107	13	Taylor	5	9	2
Highlands	15	59	15	Union	0	5	0
Hillsborough	256	1,645	245	Volusia	95	425	60
Holmes	0	15	3	Wakulla	3	17	3
Indian River	26	118	18	Walton	8	36	2
Jackson	4	35	10	Washington	2	15	1

Caution: Data were collected from unaudited, raw data files as reported by the Department of Health and may contain reporting errors.

Note: Active licenses only. Excludes delinquent active, involuntary inactive, and voluntary inactive licenses.

Source: State of Florida, Department of Health, Internet site <http://ww2.doh.state.fl.us/> (accessed 2, July 2007).

Table 20.40. PUBLIC LIBRARIES: OPERATING EXPENDITURE AND NUMBER OF VOLUMES IN REGIONS AND COUNTIES OF FLORIDA, FISCAL YEAR 2004–05

Area and library	Total operating expenditure (dollars)	Collection volumes 1/
Total	475,354,804	33,387,319
Miami-Dade System	52,913,596	4,558,560
Broward County Division of Libraries	59,841,971	2,536,130
Hillsborough County Library Cooperative	30,185,007	1,960,505
Tampa-Hillsborough County	28,593,113	1,763,763
Temple Terrace	672,332	85,888
Bruton Memorial	919,562	110,854
Orange County Library District	29,620,012	1,567,378
Pinellas Public Library Cooperative	25,952,861	2,070,855
Clearwater	5,658,179	508,013
Dunedin	2,136,539	110,113
East Lake Community	464,481	34,143
Gulf Beaches	477,790	62,459
Gulfport	557,072	74,479
Largo	2,823,917	207,091
Oldsmar	605,924	34,994
Palm Harbor	1,050,383	139,307
Pinellas Park	1,877,816	111,603
Safety Harbor	971,463	71,037
St. Pete Beach	584,701	49,521
St. Petersburg	5,580,722	498,199
Seminole Community	818,249	69,963
Tarpon Springs	963,710	98,867
Jacksonville	31,353,636	2,955,642
Palm Beach County System	30,988,225	1,185,325
Lee County System	26,939,756	1,117,943
Polk County Library Cooperative	7,805,222	725,499
Auburndale	484,440	62,712
Bartow	698,506	46,076
Dr. C. C. Pearce Municipal	111,581	16,215
Dundee	82,602	15,773
Eagle Lake	30,710	6,924
Ft. Meade	170,350	23,605
Haines City	385,036	46,951
Lakeland	2,667,764	233,131
Lake Alfred	63,137	22,500
Lake Wales	598,358	68,375
Latt Maxcy Memorial	157,796	32,719
Polk City Community	38,784	4,815
Polk County Historical and Genealogical	193,726	35,562
Stephen H. Grimes Law	253,931	26,000
Winter Haven	1,294,464	75,422
Polk County Cooperative Office	574,037	8,719
Brevard County System	14,751,322	1,231,798
Volusia County	12,649,712	786,758
West Florida Regional	4,684,554	456,057
Seminole County System	5,372,493	526,569
Pasco County Cooperative	6,751,714	584,025
Pasco County System	6,400,631	554,915
Zephyrhills	351,083	29,110
Sarasota County	10,192,300	810,609
Collier County	7,667,090	655,761
Marion County System	5,688,899	448,438
Manatee County System	6,050,435	356,745
Leon County System	6,354,966	609,661
Lake County System	6,553,727	468,356
Fruitland Park	142,082	25,236
Helen Lehmann Memorial	44,314	16,965
Lady Lake	336,549	34,558
Leesburg	1,164,837	121,323
Tavares	451,344	37,490
Umatilla	324,290	27,952
W.T. Bland	676,866	51,878
Lake County System Office	3,413,445	152,954
Alachua County District	11,409,681	769,436
St. Lucie County System	4,142,684	304,780
Osceola County System	5,981,878	325,289
Hialeah	2,127,871	151,913
Heartland Cooperative	2,665,825	312,961
DeSoto County	243,490	49,933
Hardee County	245,038	48,142
Highlands County System	1,251,891	157,100
Okeechobee County	433,878	57,786
Okaloosa County Cooperative	3,237,562	241,590
Destin	416,762	36,795
Ft. Walton Beach	529,553	61,302
Mary Esther	197,374	19,320
Niceville	720,053	48,663
Robert L. F. Sikes	331,489	40,264
Valparaiso	262,644	29,676
Okaloosa Cooperative Office	779,687	5,570
Northwest Regional System	2,541,810	213,913
Bay County	1,894,216	165,928
Gulf County	193,234	32,289
Liberty County	111,342	15,696
Clay County System	2,108,045	234,564
Charlotte-Glades System	2,986,739	195,327
Charlotte County	2,896,657	179,421
Glades County	50,280	15,906

See footnotes at end of table.

Continued . . .

Table 20.40. PUBLIC LIBRARIES: OPERATING EXPENDITURE AND NUMBER OF VOLUMES IN REGIONS AND COUNTIES OF FLORIDA, FISCAL YEAR 2004–05 (Continued)

Area and library	Total operating expenditure (dollars)	Collection volumes 1/
St. Johns County System	4,108,621	319,301
Hernando County System	2,382,406	201,157
Martin County	3,940,413	289,544
Citrus County System	2,702,758	176,384
Indian River County	4,111,051	417,229
Panhandle Cooperative System	1,606,492	184,802
Calhoun County	292,528	39,528
Holmes County	84,437	21,053
Jackson County	609,468	81,731
Washington County	206,747	42,490
West Palm Beach	2,811,673	115,041
Boca Raton	2,539,300	145,806
Monroe County System	2,480,452	190,501
Flagler County	958,608	113,029
Sumter County System	746,411	64,426
Bushnell	129,536	11,212
Coleman	40,067	5,891
E. C. Rowell	38,124	11,005
Wildwood	71,865	14,038
The Villages	54,256	6,484
Panasoffkee Community	95,361	12,746
Putnam County System	635,780	123,028
Suwannee River Regional Library System	1,707,046	173,562
New River Cooperative	1,167,672	117,688
Emily Taber (Baker County)	192,555	41,492
Bradford County	447,752	42,286
Union County	161,055	28,609
Nassau County System	994,848	164,081
Boynton Beach City	1,614,110	136,186
Delray Beach	1,428,953	123,941
Columbia County	1,218,287	126,904
North Miami	936,739	102,833
Walton County	681,594	75,691
Wilderness Coast Public Libraries	959,841	112,873
Franklin County	178,730	31,732
Jefferson County	198,365	38,297
Wilderness Coast Public Libraries (Continued)		
Wakulla County	246,203	39,955
Wilderness Coast Cooperative Office	336,543	2,889
Gadsden County	616,936	116,230
Altamonte Springs	405,011	34,582
North Miami Beach	955,760	51,651
Three Rivers Regional System	685,819	82,893
Dixie County	138,022	31,829
Gilchrist County	121,030	25,534
Lafayette County	133,453	23,470
Three Rivers Regional Office	293,314	2,060
Hendry County System	678,707	105,629
Levy County System	353,700	67,537
Lake Worth	533,412	57,044
Riviera Beach	448,186	80,810
Oakland Park	710,047	39,378
Winter Park	2,663,393	111,891
Taylor County	304,469	52,687
Parkland	540,000	26,200
Eustis Memorial	716,719	109,283
Ft. Myers Beach	574,777	61,217
New Port Richey	760,289	86,801
Maitland	668,347	85,104
Lynn Haven	175,941	24,508
Palm Springs	503,608	41,761
North Palm Beach	542,393	47,462
Wilton Manors	454,306	24,575
Lighthouse Point	390,700	42,485
Brockway Memorial	420,294	54,839
Lantana	176,430	19,376
Lake Park	338,238	29,582
Sanibel	1,209,664	54,362
Highland Beach	258,545	31,000
Apalachicola Municipal	16,465	12,038

1/ Includes volumes of books and bound periodicals.

Note: Libraries are omitted if they failed to report to the Division of Library Services or if they failed to meet or are not part of a system which met all of the following criteria: at least 10 hours of public service per week, a book collection of at least 2,000 volumes, at least 200 volumes purchased a year, and expenditure of at least $15,000 per year.

Source: State of Florida, Department of State, Division of Library and Information Services, *2006 Florida Library Directory with Statistics,* Internet site <http://dlis.dos.state.fl.us/bld/> (accessed 1, June 2007).

Table 20.50. ELEMENTARY AND SECONDARY SCHOOLS: NEW HIRES IN FLORIDA PUBLIC SCHOOLS, FALL 2006

Subject field	New hires	New hires who were not certified in the appropriate field	
		Number	Percentage
Basic, total	17,471	1,766	10.1
Elementary education 1/	7,675	464	6.0
Reading	827	503	60.8
English/Language arts	1,716	207	12.1
Math	1,508	138	9.2
Science	1,366	139	10.2
Social studies	1,110	62	5.6
Foreign language	429	26	6.1
Physical education	476	32	6.7
Art	292	6	2.1
Music	434	18	4.1
English for speakers of other languages	348	111	31.9
Drop out prevention	241	23	9.5
Permanent substitutes	691	6	0.9
Other	358	31	8.7
Exceptional student education, total	2,201	360	16.4
Mentally handicapped	146	27	18.5
Specific learning disabled	124	19	15.3
Emotionally handicapped	147	24	16.3
Varying exceptionalities	1,712	278	16.2
Physically impaired	7	5	71.4
Hospital/homebound	55	7	12.7
Exceptional, total	3,082	515	16.7
Speech impaired	246	5	2.0
Hearing impaired	26	3	11.5
Visually impaired	17	0	0.0
Autistic	108	16	14.8
Severely emotionally handicapped	125	36	28.8
Profoundly mentally handicapped	46	3	6.5
Occupational/physical therapy	26	0	0.0
PreK handicapped	96	2	2.1
Gifted	189	90	47.6
Other exceptional	2	0	0.0
Vocational, total	590	64	10.8
Agribusiness	40	3	7.5
Business	144	14	9.7
Marketing	31	6	19.4
Health professional	44	4	9.1
Public service	13	1	7.7
Home economics/family consumer sciences	114	13	11.4
Trades/industrial	85	9	10.6
Industrial arts/technology education	57	9	15.8
Other vocational	62	5	8.1
Instructional, total	22,256	2,377	10.7
Classroom, total	21,143	2,345	11.1
Nonclassroom, total	1,113	32	2.9
Guidance counselor	435	15	3.4
Media specialist	123	7	5.7
Social worker	51	1	2.0
School psychologist	103	1	1.0
Other nonclassroom	401	8	2.0

1/ Includes elementary language arts, math, science, and social studies.

Source: State of Florida, Department of Education, Division of Accountability, Research, and Measurement, Office of Policy Research and Improvement, *New Hires in Florida Public Schools: Fall 1997 Through Fall 2006,* Internet site <http://www.firn.edu/> (accessed 30, April 2007).

Table 20.51. ELEMENTARY AND SECONDARY SCHOOLS: CLASSROOM TEACHER NEW HIRES IN THE STATE AND COUNTIES OF FLORIDA, FALL 2006

County	Total new hires	Percentage 1/	Filled out of field Number	Filled out of field Percentage	County	Total new hires	Percentage 1/	Filled out of field Number	Filled out of field Percentage
Florida	21,143	12.6	2,345	11.1	Lake	366	15.2	48	13.1
					Lee	637	13.5	40	6.3
Alachua	270	15.6	32	11.9	Leon	265	12.8	4	1.5
Baker	36	12.2	16	44.4	Levy	52	13.1	5	9.6
Bay	189	10.4	0	0.0	Liberty	11	9.9	6	54.5
Bradford	29	11.1	6	20.7	Madison	26	15.1	4	15.4
Brevard	464	9.5	33	7.1	Manatee	397	15.1	21	5.3
Broward	948	6.0	70	7.4	Marion	431	16.4	66	15.3
Calhoun	26	15.2	5	19.2	Martin	112	10.0	0	0.0
Charlotte	147	13.9	11	7.5	Miami-Dade	2,562	11.9	207	8.1
Citrus	121	11.4	7	5.8	Monroe	98	15.9	11	11.2
Clay	487	20.1	56	11.5	Nassau	118	17.0	1	0.8
Collier	409	14.6	20	4.9	Okaloosa	265	13.8	13	4.9
Columbia	77	11.4	16	20.8	Okeechobee	67	15.5	17	25.4
DeSoto	54	17.9	3	5.6	Orange	1,440	12.7	195	13.5
Dixie	15	11.3	3	20.0	Osceola	598	20.2	18	3.0
Duval	1,145	14.5	209	18.3	Palm Beach	1,093	9.7	0	0.0
Escambia	411	14.1	35	8.5	Pasco	576	13.6	23	4.0
Flagler	189	20.9	11	5.8	Pinellas	840	11.5	68	8.1
Franklin	14	14.1	0	0.0	Polk	1,084	16.4	49	4.5
Gadsden	111	26.2	22	19.8	Putnam	65	8.8	14	21.5
Gilchrist	30	16.8	2	6.7	St. Johns	160	10.3	6	3.8
Glades	24	27.6	7	29.2	St. Lucie	438	20.6	112	25.6
Gulf	18	12.2	1	5.6	Santa Rosa	208	12.9	26	12.5
Hamilton	21	17.8	9	42.9	Sarasota	213	7.6	30	14.1
Hardee	58	17.3	25	43.1	Seminole	458	10.7	92	20.1
Hendry	74	17.5	18	24.3	Sumter	54	12.0	8	14.8
Hernando	286	18.3	25	8.7	Suwannee	44	12.1	1	2.3
Highlands	116	13.7	24	20.7	Taylor	27	11.8	0	0.0
Hillsborough	1,682	15.6	480	28.5	Union	16	8.6	4	25.0
Holmes	28	12.0	2	7.1	Volusia	540	11.7	72	13.3
Indian River	153	14.0	15	9.8	Wakulla	43	14.1	15	34.9
Jackson	72	14.3	0	0.0	Walton	70	14.8	0	0.0
Jefferson	36	39.1	4	11.1	Washington	19	7.1	0	0.0
Lafayette	10	14.5	2	20.0					

1/ New hires as a percentage of all teachers.

Source: State of Florida, Department of Education, Division of Accountability, Research, and Measurement, Office of Policy Research and Improvement, *New Hires in Florida Public Schools: Fall 1997 Through Fall 2006,* Internet site <http://www.firn.edu/> (accessed 30, April 2007).

Table 20.56. ELEMENTARY AND SECONDARY SCHOOLS: TOTAL ADMINISTRATIVE AND INSTRUCTIONAL STAFF AND DISTRIBUTION OF ADMINISTRATIVE STAFF IN THE STATE AND COUNTIES OF FLORIDA, FALL 2006

County	Total staff 1/	Administrative staff: Total	Officials administrators managers	Consultants/ supervisors of instruction	Principals	Assistant principals	Community education coordinators	Deans/ curriculum coordinators
Florida	190,617	11,248	2,640	574	3,101	4,525	17	391
Alachua	2,007	139	43	13	47	35	1	0
Baker	340	27	10	2	6	9	0	0
Bay	2,074	120	19	5	37	28	0	31
Bradford	307	30	10	2	8	10	0	0
Brevard	5,515	305	43	1	101	115	0	45
Broward	17,721	762	78	3	233	448	0	0
Calhoun	196	12	7	0	5	0	0	0
Charlotte	1,209	76	27	1	19	28	0	1
Citrus	1,227	91	26	3	21	35	0	6
Clay	2,710	137	41	4	35	57	0	0
Collier	3,197	201	45	29	49	44	2	32
Columbia	765	45	18	1	14	12	0	0
DeSoto	348	28	14	0	5	9	0	0
Dixie	154	15	7	1	5	2	0	0
Duval	9,035	652	221	12	161	257	0	1
Escambia	3,266	171	47	15	64	42	1	2
Flagler	1,027	81	36	0	12	21	0	12
Franklin	116	10	5	0	3	0	0	2
Gadsden	516	57	23	8	13	12	1	0
Gilchrist	219	26	14	1	4	5	0	2
Glades	104	11	6	0	3	2	0	0
Gulf	175	14	5	2	6	1	0	0
Hamilton	146	21	12	3	5	1	0	0
Hardee	390	34	17	0	7	9	0	1
Hendry	485	38	11	5	10	12	0	0
Hernando	1,753	86	24	5	20	36	1	0
Highlands	955	56	16	5	17	17	0	1
Hillsborough	12,211	661	50	6	214	365	0	26
Holmes	275	27	15	0	7	5	0	0
Indian River	1,253	88	22	2	25	38	1	0
Jackson	582	38	9	0	16	13	0	0
Jefferson	112	13	10	0	2	1	0	0
Lafayette	83	9	4	2	2	1	0	0
Lake	2,746	165	31	3	40	52	0	39
Lee	5,346	365	84	44	104	118	1	14
Leon	2,372	161	38	14	43	66	0	0
Levy	468	41	18	1	13	9	0	0
Liberty	128	12	6	1	3	2	0	0
Madison	212	31	10	7	7	4	0	3

See footnotes at end of table.

Continued . . .

Table 20.56. ELEMENTARY AND SECONDARY SCHOOLS: TOTAL ADMINISTRATIVE AND INSTRUCTIONAL STAFF AND DISTRIBUTION OF ADMINISTRATIVE STAFF IN THE STATE AND COUNTIES OF FLORIDA, FALL 2006 (Continued)

		Administrative staff						
County	Total staff 1/	Total	Officials administrators managers	Consultants/ supervisors of instruction	Principals	Assistant principals	Community education coordinators	Deans/ curriculum coordinators
Manatee	3,104	281	69	22	54	75	0	61
Marion	3,002	193	38	14	52	69	2	18
Martin	1,256	67	15	2	21	29	0	0
Miami-Dade	24,632	1,323	237	34	353	698	1	0
Monroe	715	65	19	13	14	18	1	0
Nassau	796	49	18	3	16	7	0	5
Okaloosa	2,144	117	36	2	38	35	0	6
Okeechobee	503	41	15	1	12	10	0	3
Orange	12,614	615	93	54	190	273	1	4
Osceola	3,306	165	43	7	45	66	0	4
Palm Beach	12,672	790	216	41	194	339	0	0
Pasco	4,834	277	65	26	71	100	0	15
Pinellas	8,347	527	114	41	147	209	3	13
Polk	7,394	399	91	19	130	158	0	1
Putnam	877	85	34	8	20	22	1	0
St. Johns	1,802	137	53	11	29	36	0	8
St. Lucie	2,424	136	37	1	40	55	0	3
Santa Rosa	1,794	93	14	7	32	39	0	1
Sarasota	3,118	163	42	6	44	71	0	0
Seminole	4,730	230	28	3	63	111	0	25
Sumter	517	34	12	3	13	5	0	1
Suwannee	417	33	15	0	8	10	0	0
Taylor	266	24	9	4	6	4	0	1
Union	210	16	8	1	4	3	0	0
Volusia	5,225	294	64	15	79	135	0	1
Wakulla	350	30	13	2	7	8	0	0
Walton	539	38	10	4	15	9	0	0
Washington	321	33	13	7	7	6	0	0
Deaf/Blind	253	70	46	18	2	1	0	3
Dozier	36	2	0	0	2	0	0	0
Florida Virtual	338	36	36	0	0	0	0	0
FAU Developmental	44	4	2	0	1	1	0	0
FSU Developmental	169	12	6	1	4	1	0	0
FAMU Developmental	47	7	4	1	2	0	0	0
UF P.K. Yonge Developmental	76	6	3	2	0	1	0	0

1/ Administrative and instructional staff only as of December 5, 2006. Excludes noninstructional, nonadministrative professional staff, aides, technicians, clerical/secretarial, service workers, skilled crafts workers, and unskilled laborers.

Note: Data are for public schools only.

Source: State of Florida, Department of Education, Education Information and Accountability Services, *Statistical Brief: Staff in Florida's Public Schools, Fall 2006,* January 2007, Series 2007-05B, Internet site <http://www.firn.edu/doe/> (accessed 20, February 2007).

Table 20.57. ELEMENTARY AND SECONDARY SCHOOLS: DISTRIBUTION OF INSTRUCTIONAL STAFF IN THE STATE AND COUNTIES OF FLORIDA, FALL 2006

County	Total	Teachers: Elementary 1/	Teachers: Secondary 2/	Teachers: Exceptional student education	Guidance counselors	Visiting teachers/ school social workers	School psychologists	Librarians/ audio-visual workers	Other 3/
Florida	188,277	70,923	63,641	25,888	6,032	984	1,376	2,796	16,637
Alachua	2,042	722	683	318	69	3	14	49	184
Baker	325	139	126	31	10	0	2	5	12
Bay	2,050	722	630	382	77	9	13	37	180
Bradford	280	112	106	38	10	0	0	6	8
Brevard	5,545	2,253	1,734	865	179	9	30	92	383
Broward	17,215	6,486	6,181	1,755	576	140	154	238	1,685
Calhoun	195	68	65	35	6	0	1	6	14
Charlotte	1,219	399	438	193	39	8	11	20	111
Citrus	1,210	443	390	162	39	4	9	22	141
Clay	2,658	1,128	896	388	89	12	14	40	91
Collier	3,097	1,371	1,006	398	105	7	23	54	133
Columbia	746	310	265	98	27	1	3	13	29
DeSoto	345	134	112	34	9	2	1	6	47
Dixie	147	61	52	19	5	0	0	1	9
Duval	8,795	3,692	2,825	1,177	239	33	59	142	628
Escambia	3,322	1,206	1,200	483	94	9	14	61	255
Flagler	986	329	332	120	27	1	4	9	164
Franklin	110	43	37	14	3	0	0	4	9
Gadsden	504	190	153	66	18	2	4	12	59
Gilchrist	203	72	80	26	10	0	0	4	11
Glades	97	51	30	6	3	0	0	3	4
Gulf	168	52	73	19	7	1	2	4	10
Hamilton	140	55	45	18	4	0	0	3	15
Hardee	376	158	124	44	11	0	2	8	29
Hendry	473	194	156	55	15	0	0	10	43
Hernando	1,722	673	615	193	65	9	9	23	135
Highlands	946	342	359	120	28	5	5	15	72
Hillsborough	11,930	5,149	3,448	1,614	339	138	143	166	933
Holmes	261	92	108	28	8	0	0	7	18
Indian River	1,270	487	433	151	30	10	11	20	128
Jackson	591	211	186	76	26	0	1	12	79
Jefferson	105	38	33	9	3	1	0	3	18
Lafayette	78	35	26	7	3	0	0	2	5
Lake	2,729	1,022	935	297	96	11	17	47	304
Lee	5,255	1,933	1,813	666	132	29	29	61	592
Leon	2,360	871	766	381	75	15	15	43	194
Levy	447	168	164	62	16	2	0	11	24
Liberty	119	40	42	20	2	0	1	2	12
Madison	198	69	72	28	6	0	0	3	20

See footnotes at end of table. Continued . . .

Table 20.57. ELEMENTARY AND SECONDARY SCHOOLS: DISTRIBUTION OF INSTRUCTIONAL STAFF IN THE STATE AND COUNTIES OF FLORIDA, FALL 2006 (Continued)

County	Total	Teachers			Guidance coun- selors	Visiting teachers/ school social workers	School psycholo- gists	Librar- ians/ audio- visual workers	Other 3/
		Elemen- tary 1/	Second- ary 2/	Exceptional student education					
Manatee	2,933	1,151	1,058	384	99	20	22	48	151
Marion	2,954	1,134	1,074	408	92	18	15	49	164
Martin	1,272	406	462	214	39	1	7	24	119
Miami-Dade	24,044	9,533	7,039	3,677	989	147	240	366	2,053
Monroe	705	237	253	104	19	2	8	4	78
Nassau	762	271	289	127	27	3	6	17	22
Okaloosa	2,091	841	815	228	57	7	10	32	101
Okeechobee	492	194	147	72	17	1	3	8	50
Orange	13,416	4,258	4,367	1,590	351	64	90	182	2,514
Osceola	3,475	1,242	1,210	424	93	13	34	39	420
Palm Beach	12,247	4,399	4,752	1,691	383	21	74	117	810
Pasco	4,771	1,744	1,623	815	164	28	36	86	275
Pinellas	8,361	2,720	2,853	1,384	246	89	56	140	873
Polk	7,226	2,800	2,482	942	211	17	47	120	607
Putnam	864	305	235	136	31	0	8	15	134
St. Johns	1,803	652	676	225	61	4	10	30	145
St. Lucie	2,455	891	844	319	99	8	14	38	242
Santa Rosa	1,766	673	706	218	53	3	9	29	75
Sarasota	3,140	1,170	1,040	523	93	15	21	22	256
Seminole	4,654	1,820	1,775	600	117	22	31	46	243
Sumter	519	203	200	47	16	3	2	11	37
Suwannee	401	171	157	29	11	2	1	7	23
Taylor	265	103	83	40	6	3	0	4	26
Union	203	68	65	26	5	0	0	3	36
Volusia	5,152	1,872	1,779	941	194	28	32	65	241
Wakulla	332	122	124	57	9	0	0	7	13
Walton	537	195	216	53	16	0	1	12	44
Washington	303	93	130	31	12	0	2	6	29
Deaf/Blind	214	0	5	162	5	4	6	0	32
Dozier	34	0	21	11	1	0	0	0	1
Florida Virtual	311	0	281	0	8	0	0	0	22
FAU Developmental	43	21	15	2	1	0	0	1	3
FSU Developmental	161	76	67	8	4	0	0	2	4
FAMU Developmental	40	18	21	0	0	0	0	1	0
UF P.K. Yonge Developmental	72	20	38	4	3	0	0	1	6

1/ Prekindergarten and Kindergarten through grade 5 or 6.
2/ Grades 6 through 12.
3/ Includes other teachers and nonadministrative/instructional professional staff.
Note: Data are for public schools only as of December 5, 2006.

Source: State of Florida, Department of Education, Education Information and Accountability Services, *Statistical Brief: Staff in Florida's Public Schools, Fall 2006,* January 2007, Series 2007-05B, Internet site <http://www.firn.edu/doe/> (accessed 20, February 2007).

Table 20.59. ELEMENTARY AND SECONDARY SCHOOLS: NUMBER AND AVERAGE SALARY OF SPECIFIED DISTRICT STAFF PERSONNEL IN THE STATE AND COUNTIES OF FLORIDA, 2005–06

(salaries in dollars)

County	Superin-tendent salary	Principals: High school Num-ber	Principals: High school Average Salary	Principals: Middle/junior high school Num-ber	Principals: Middle/junior high school Average Salary	Principals: Elementary Num-ber	Principals: Elementary Average Salary	Board members Num-ber	Board members Average Salary
Florida	127,617	432	86,039	547	80,087	1,727	79,182	349	29,928
Alachua	141,520	8	68,656	7	74,310	24	70,211	5	33,500
Baker	107,896	1	54,916	1	54,916	4	64,041	5	24,201
Bay	114,939	5	72,499	8	68,755	19	69,842	5	30,194
Bradford	92,613	1	70,856	1	72,313	5	66,627	5	24,512
Brevard	181,553	15	90,061	12	80,371	63	75,363	5	35,573
Broward	233,950	31	102,538	29	99,753	138	95,593	9	39,688
Calhoun	88,215	1	73,197	1	69,684	1	67,739	5	23,349
Charlotte	135,000	3	94,660	4	79,341	10	76,846	5	31,499
Citrus	111,897	3	76,615	4	74,390	10	72,875	5	30,598
Clay	115,460	6	81,789	5	83,463	22	81,758	5	31,450
Collier	169,600	7	102,833	10	86,191	25	80,350	5	34,092
Columbia	102,021	3	78,266	2	76,182	8	71,270	5	27,033
DeSoto	94,593	1	73,564	1	76,917	4	71,368	5	25,740
Dixie	88,625	1	74,520	1	70,380	2	68,310	5	23,458
Duval	275,011	26	81,138	32	78,216	102	74,552	7	38,643
Escambia	125,925	10	68,293	11	68,828	37	68,091	5	33,255
Flagler	125,000	2	77,371	2	77,585	4	73,725	5	27,035
Franklin	92,968	0	0	0	0	2	57,261	5	23,105
Gadsden	98,562	3	63,904	2	62,223	7	59,939	5	26,086
Gilchrist	92,262	2	66,026	0	0	2	65,762	5	23,022
Glades	89,320	0	0	1	68,800	2	64,750	5	23,112
Gulf	91,012	2	69,443	2	66,940	2	65,706	5	23,560
Hamilton	90,014	1	67,410	0	0	3	63,263	5	23,406
Hardee	94,627	1	78,276	1	74,478	4	70,184	5	24,516
Hendry	96,670	2	71,570	2	62,240	6	68,720	5	25,307
Hernando	116,740	5	78,427	4	75,614	10	74,534	5	30,200
Highlands	106,899	3	74,240	4	78,332	9	68,279	5	29,116
Hillsborough	215,010	20	87,583	48	78,265	122	74,420	7	39,529
Holmes	89,896	2	60,735	1	58,822	2	60,297	5	22,511
Indian River	0	3	86,741	4	77,372	16	70,527	5	30,523
Jackson	99,971	3	67,501	1	61,397	5	61,950	5	26,286
Jefferson	88,356	1	65,061	1	65,212	1	65,436	5	23,386
Lafayette	88,324	1	65,059	0	0	1	62,207	5	22,293
Lake	122,480	8	81,630	9	85,367	23	82,162	5	33,786
Lee	152,000	13	90,923	17	88,284	49	86,888	5	36,883

See footnotes at end of table. Continued . . .

Table 20.59. ELEMENTARY AND SECONDARY SCHOOLS: NUMBER AND AVERAGE SALARY OF SPECIFIED DISTRICT STAFF PERSONNEL IN THE STATE AND COUNTIES OF FLORIDA, 2005–06 (Continued)

(salaries in dollars)

County	Superin-tendent salary	Principals: High school Num-ber	Principals: High school Average Salary	Principals: Middle/junior high school Num-ber	Principals: Middle/junior high school Average Salary	Principals: Elementary Num-ber	Principals: Elementary Average Salary	Board members Num-ber	Board members Average Salary
Leon	125,228	5	82,491	9	75,725	23	78,312	5	33,983
Levy	95,646	2	74,067	2	66,814	4	66,680	5	25,212
Liberty	86,268	1	62,559	0	0	1	59,626	3	22,181
Madison	90,047	1	67,503	1	67,437	3	62,822	5	23,834
Manatee	195,825	6	101,413	11	80,009	32	85,870	5	34,499
Marion	124,579	7	86,774	9	79,902	29	78,033	5	34,336
Martin	112,781	3	90,483	4	85,456	11	83,446	5	30,879
Miami-Dade	305,001	51	89,767	65	80,890	210	86,571	8	37,950
Monroe	123,608	3	94,023	2	85,008	7	83,993	5	28,403
Nassau	126,207	4	73,013	3	71,440	9	67,301	5	24,310
Okaloosa	108,168	4	94,841	8	87,355	21	80,036	5	32,464
Okeechobee	94,700	2	81,557	3	69,120	5	66,539	5	25,357
Orange	210,662	18	90,551	31	78,158	114	78,349	8	41,104
Osceola	130,805	10	86,996	10	78,053	20	83,100	5	31,600
Palm Beach	180,000	24	85,216	31	81,607	104	80,081	7	36,480
Pasco	124,987	8	86,691	12	75,500	39	74,648	1	19,600
Pinellas	185,850	17	85,714	25	80,268	85	76,994	7	38,533
Polk	150,760	16	81,688	19	77,007	73	72,437	7	36,929
Putnam	118,565	3	83,025	4	71,173	12	67,674	5	26,687
St. Johns	129,320	5	92,109	6	84,482	16	80,502	5	31,264
St. Lucie	158,990	6	80,882	10	78,280	19	78,280	5	33,363
Santa Rosa	114,260	6	85,407	7	78,043	16	74,260	5	30,741
Sarasota	159,650	9	93,664	8	92,361	23	89,623	5	33,973
Seminole	166,220	7	97,071	14	81,592	37	78,072	5	36,091
Sumter	116,730	3	83,585	3	74,477	6	73,941	5	27,426
Suwannee	95,716	1	77,915	1	73,819	3	72,016	5	25,319
Taylor	90,497	1	68,759	1	70,843	2	70,145	5	22,977
Union	83,600	1	72,360	1	65,632	1	60,869	5	22,430
Volusia	161,200	9	92,294	12	80,577	48	77,561	5	35,157
Wakulla	112,942	1	83,500	2	73,800	3	67,700	5	24,328
Walton	98,563	2	82,837	3	81,521	5	79,286	5	26,380
Washington	93,260	2	76,003	2	67,837	2	67,209	5	24,075

(NA) Not available.

Note: Data are for public schools only. The number of months worked varies from district to district. Salaries have not been adjusted for a full 12-month calendar year. Does not include special schools such as university developmental schools.

Source: State of Florida, Department of Education, Education Information and Accountability Services (EIAS), *Statistical Brief: Florida District Staff Salaries of Selected Positions, 2005–06,* July 2006, Series 2007-02B, Internet site <http://www.firn.edu/doe/> (accessed 20, February 2007).

Table 20.60. ELEMENTARY AND SECONDARY SCHOOLS: NUMBER AND AVERAGE SALARY OF TEACHERS BY DEGREE ATTAINMENT IN THE STATE AND COUNTIES OF FLORIDA, 2006–07

(salaries in dollars)

County	Total 1/ Number	Total 1/ Average salary	Bachelor's Number	Bachelor's Percentage of total	Bachelor's Average salary	Master's Number	Master's Percentage of total	Master's Average salary
Florida	183,181	45,307	111,639	60.9	41,997	64,785	35.4	49,793
Alachua	1,952	40,181	865	44.3	36,953	923	47.3	42,101
Baker	324	40,518	254	78.4	38,136	68	21.0	48,907
Bay	1,956	41,679	1,242	63.5	39,327	642	32.8	45,457
Bradford	266	39,389	194	72.9	37,820	64	24.1	43,001
Brevard	5,120	43,963	3,148	61.5	41,506	1,880	36.7	47,674
Broward	16,756	47,962	9,582	57.2	45,348	6,493	38.8	51,126
Calhoun	194	40,251	119	61.3	37,625	68	35.1	44,573
Charlotte	1,185	46,319	629	53.1	42,352	518	43.7	50,407
Citrus	1,198	42,700	689	57.5	39,610	484	40.4	46,692
Clay	2,667	42,398	1,895	71.1	40,767	749	28.1	46,174
Collier	3,035	50,804	1,558	51.3	45,689	1,367	45.0	55,846
Columbia	727	42,000	462	63.5	39,075	252	34.7	46,973
DeSoto	354	42,053	264	74.6	40,218	84	23.7	47,586
Dixie	145	41,345	106	73.1	39,363	38	26.2	46,619
Duval	8,611	45,014	5,876	68.2	42,398	2,616	30.4	50,461
Escambia	3,221	39,075	1,891	58.7	36,151	1,251	38.8	43,057
Flagler	833	46,871	521	62.5	43,972	296	35.5	51,572
Franklin	100	37,981	53	53.0	34,580	43	43.0	41,257
Gadsden	488	35,842	336	68.9	34,504	143	29.3	38,757
Gilchrist	204	39,892	137	67.2	38,256	62	30.4	43,224
Glades	96	41,447	72	75.0	39,036	22	22.9	48,661
Gulf	163	41,204	95	58.3	38,785	67	41.1	44,453
Hamilton	142	42,349	107	75.4	40,887	33	23.2	46,509
Hardee	381	40,261	305	80.1	38,794	73	19.2	45,793
Hendry	451	41,667	324	71.8	39,363	117	25.9	47,095
Hernando	1,688	39,089	1,114	66.0	36,322	543	32.2	44,291
Highlands	911	41,876	645	70.8	39,672	251	27.6	47,124
Hillsborough	13,246	43,412	8,243	62.2	40,496	4,816	36.4	48,058
Holmes	255	39,622	158	62.0	36,756	96	37.6	44,309
Indian River	1,105	43,162	724	65.5	40,833	317	28.7	46,924
Jackson	584	39,306	338	57.9	35,682	214	36.6	43,361
Jefferson	99	41,770	66	66.7	39,774	29	29.3	45,401
Lafayette	76	37,461	60	78.9	36,380	15	19.7	41,888
Lake	2,703	41,397	1,791	66.3	39,279	888	32.9	45,477
Lee	4,804	44,706	3,073	64.0	41,828	1,595	33.2	49,593
Leon	2,341	43,412	1,283	54.8	40,173	958	40.9	46,810

See footnotes at end of table. Continued . . .

Table 20.60. ELEMENTARY AND SECONDARY SCHOOLS: NUMBER AND AVERAGE SALARY OF TEACHERS BY DEGREE ATTAINMENT IN THE STATE AND COUNTIES OF FLORIDA, 2006–07 (Continued)

(salaries in dollars)

County	Total 1/		Bachelor's			Master's		
	Number	Average salary	Number	Percentage of total	Average salary	Number	Percentage of total	Average salary
Levy	432	41,780	281	65.0	40,223	138	31.9	44,613
Liberty	109	39,191	71	65.1	36,799	38	34.9	43,660
Madison	185	40,823	121	65.4	37,967	58	31.4	46,322
Manatee	2,738	47,480	1,506	55.0	43,614	1,137	41.5	51,630
Marion	2,886	42,068	1,942	67.3	39,852	853	29.6	46,122
Martin	1,224	45,646	749	61.2	43,057	435	35.5	49,130
Miami-Dade	23,629	49,191	12,462	52.7	44,004	8,552	36.2	52,908
Monroe	690	50,775	405	58.7	47,687	272	39.4	55,339
Nassau	742	43,787	459	61.9	40,567	277	37.3	48,937
Okaloosa	2,090	47,538	1,220	58.4	43,709	790	37.8	51,998
Okeechobee	471	41,809	376	79.8	39,579	84	17.8	50,263
Orange	13,110	44,288	8,275	63.1	41,754	4,537	34.6	48,423
Osceola	3,193	42,851	2,067	64.7	40,184	1,036	32.4	47,537
Palm Beach	11,805	48,529	7,574	64.2	45,052	4,009	34.0	54,409
Pasco	4,665	43,472	2,971	63.7	41,109	1,601	34.3	47,469
Pinellas	8,284	45,679	5,118	61.8	43,510	2,987	36.1	48,904
Polk	6,992	41,505	5,239	74.9	39,491	1,637	23.4	47,263
Putnam	823	43,981	574	69.7	41,190	233	28.3	50,337
St. Johns	1,732	45,032	1,057	61.0	42,483	653	37.7	48,884
St. Lucie	2,474	43,399	1,605	64.9	40,334	803	32.5	48,509
Santa Rosa	1,754	43,196	1,145	65.3	40,608	577	32.9	48,072
Sarasota	3,039	52,348	1,265	41.6	45,180	1,652	54.4	56,731
Seminole	4,459	46,475	2,439	54.7	41,837	1,815	40.7	51,206
Sumter	373	45,508	261	70.0	43,050	110	29.5	51,107
Suwannee	408	43,721	291	71.3	42,179	111	27.2	47,544
Taylor	238	42,111	147	61.8	37,317	75	31.5	49,119
Union	161	35,489	110	68.3	33,732	48	29.8	39,362
Volusia	4,972	43,485	2,981	60.0	39,778	1,819	36.6	48,468
Wakulla	329	40,857	199	60.5	38,519	118	35.9	44,392
Walton	509	45,121	331	65.0	42,264	156	30.6	50,293
Washington	284	42,324	179	63.0	38,747	99	34.9	48,173

1/ Includes teachers with specialist and doctorate degrees not shown separately.

Note: Average salary paid to a professional on the instructional salary schedule negotiated by a Florida school district. Data were obtained from the Florida DOE Staff Database, Survey 3, February 5-9, 2007, as of June 8, 2007. Data are for public schools only and exclude special and developmental research schools.

Source: State of Florida, Department of Education, Education Information and Accountability Services, *Statistical Brief: Teacher Salary, Experience, and Degree Level, 2006–07,* July 2007, Series 2007-18B, Internet site <http://www.fldoe.org/eias/> (accessed 8, August 2007).

Table 20.62. ELEMENTARY AND SECONDARY SCHOOLS: STUDENT-TEACHER RATIOS AND SPECIFIED PERSONNEL PERCENTAGES AND RATIOS IN THE STATE AND COUNTIES OF FLORIDA, 2005–06

County	FTE students per FTE teacher		Percentage of full-time staff who are—		Ratio of—	
	Elementary 1/	Secondary	Teachers 2/	Administrators	Teacher aides to teachers 2/	Administrators to teachers 2/
Florida	20.28	19.82	51.07	3.31	5.15	15.42
Alachua	20.42	20.49	41.70	3.48	3.20	12.00
Baker	19.98	16.93	49.05	4.84	5.56	10.14
Bay	20.04	19.72	50.35	3.48	3.93	14.48
Bradford	18.61	16.25	48.47	5.73	3.68	8.46
Brevard	17.51	21.55	53.81	3.28	6.88	16.39
Broward	21.78	19.89	55.17	2.57	7.29	21.49
Calhoun	18.06	14.30	54.66	3.86	7.72	14.16
Charlotte	22.08	21.01	43.69	3.13	2.85	13.94
Citrus	18.65	20.83	46.16	3.82	3.96	12.09
Clay	17.52	19.61	53.20	3.10	5.48	17.13
Collier	18.69	20.15	48.80	3.66	4.25	13.34
Columbia	18.61	17.54	47.26	3.36	3.44	14.06
DeSoto	19.24	19.83	43.90	3.87	3.00	11.33
Dixie	19.89	18.52	42.52	5.32	2.78	8.00
Duval	20.22	20.01	59.31	4.78	5.99	12.39
Escambia	19.53	17.13	49.93	2.68	6.21	18.61
Flagler	22.88	18.78	48.78	4.11	5.75	11.87
Franklin	18.03	16.69	48.09	4.37	4.00	11.00
Gadsden	17.60	15.75	41.91	5.74	3.25	7.30
Gilchrist	18.48	16.34	47.87	5.59	3.33	8.57
Glades	15.77	16.68	45.50	5.82	3.73	7.81
Gulf	20.38	15.70	46.84	4.65	4.86	10.07
Hamilton	18.37	18.91	40.94	5.70	3.05	7.17
Hardee	19.87	14.94	45.99	3.87	3.46	11.89
Hendry	21.04	21.68	43.71	3.61	3.50	12.11
Hernando	18.00	18.24	48.50	2.86	3.74	16.93
Highlands	20.02	15.73	48.86	3.30	4.87	14.80
Hillsborough	18.16	27.36	51.71	2.30	7.10	22.49
Holmes	19.25	15.61	48.07	5.15	4.48	9.33
Indian River	18.84	19.30	50.19	3.57	4.51	14.04
Jackson	20.16	17.73	45.40	3.60	2.73	12.60
Jefferson	18.91	15.77	41.15	7.52	5.16	5.47
Lafayette	16.54	18.23	45.10	4.58	3.13	9.85
Lake	20.83	18.58	47.27	3.17	4.38	14.90
Lee	21.76	18.36	50.94	3.70	5.91	13.76
Leon	20.77	18.27	46.51	3.70	3.40	12.58

See footnotes at end of table. Continued . . .

Table 20.62. ELEMENTARY AND SECONDARY SCHOOLS: STUDENT-TEACHER RATIOS AND SPECIFIED PERSONNEL PERCENTAGES AND RATIOS IN THE STATE AND COUNTIES OF FLORIDA, 2005–06 (Continued)

County	FTE students per FTE teacher		Percentage of full-time staff who are—		Ratio of—	
	Elementary 1/	Secondary	Teachers 2/	Administrators	Teacher aides to teachers 2/	Administrators to teachers 2/
Levy	19.03	17.89	43.27	4.53	3.35	9.56
Liberty	19.18	16.08	50.72	6.28	3.50	8.07
Madison	23.10	18.35	42.72	6.91	3.93	6.17
Manatee	21.14	17.46	48.38	4.93	3.93	9.81
Marion	20.99	19.09	42.40	3.39	2.69	12.49
Martin	22.91	18.93	51.73	3.14	4.16	16.49
Miami-Dade	19.93	23.57	54.20	3.27	8.16	16.58
Monroe	18.10	16.37	45.45	4.58	3.92	9.91
Nassau	21.38	18.65	47.07	3.33	4.24	14.13
Okaloosa	18.94	18.68	51.77	3.18	3.95	16.29
Okeechobee	20.54	21.63	47.54	4.59	4.08	10.36
Orange	23.15	18.63	49.52	2.71	4.86	18.30
Osceola	22.27	20.38	44.32	2.54	3.44	17.42
Palm Beach	21.33	18.57	54.73	3.71	6.24	14.76
Pasco	19.04	18.67	49.85	3.10	4.52	16.05
Pinellas	21.48	19.67	49.18	3.45	3.97	14.25
Polk	18.60	16.63	50.24	3.17	3.85	15.83
Putnam	22.16	22.77	39.45	3.98	2.40	9.91
St. Johns	22.45	18.87	49.78	4.42	5.44	11.27
St. Lucie	24.17	21.86	46.59	2.93	4.75	15.90
Santa Rosa	20.18	17.53	60.53	3.37	4.90	17.95
Sarasota	18.28	17.53	49.48	2.83	4.73	17.49
Seminole	19.86	18.64	55.48	2.99	5.75	18.56
Sumter	20.05	17.97	46.16	3.47	3.30	13.30
Suwannee	18.78	16.98	51.47	4.63	5.47	11.12
Taylor	17.55	16.28	41.20	4.49	2.29	9.16
Union	16.74	14.71	50.40	3.98	5.58	12.66
Volusia	20.38	18.63	47.36	3.10	4.51	15.25
Wakulla	21.31	17.56	46.91	4.75	3.65	9.86
Walton	20.18	15.46	46.24	4.12	4.44	11.22
Washington	20.61	12.61	44.22	5.78	4.26	7.64

FTE Full-time equivalent.
1/ Kindergarten through grade 6.
2/ Teachers in grades prekindergarten through grade 12 and exceptional education, primary education specialists, and others including postsecondary vocational instructors and adult education instructors.
Note: Data are for public schools only. Florida includes special schools.

Source: State of Florida, Department of Education, Education Information and Accountability Services, (EIAS), *Profiles of Florida School Districts, 2005-2006, Student and Staff Data,* Internet site <http://www.fldoe.org/eias/> (accessed 19, June 2007).

Table 20.63. ELEMENTARY AND SECONDARY SCHOOLS: ALL FUNDS REVENUE BY MAJOR SOURCE IN THE STATE AND COUNTIES OF FLORIDA, 2003–04

(in thousands of dollars, except where indicated)

County	Total all revenue receipts	Revenue per FTE student 1/ (dollars)	Revenue receipts from– Federal sources Amount	Federal sources Percentage of total	State sources Amount	State sources Percentage of total	Local sources Amount	Local sources Percentage of total
Florida 2/	21,308,681	8,167	2,220,113	10.42	9,591,215	45.01	9,497,353	44.57
Alachua	230,106	8,055	32,471	14.11	113,147	49.17	84,489	36.72
Baker	30,756	6,714	3,590	11.67	22,106	71.88	5,059	16.45
Bay	208,812	7,811	23,887	11.44	94,715	45.36	90,210	43.20
Bradford	29,160	7,508	4,079	13.99	19,264	66.06	5,817	19.95
Brevard	532,506	7,284	51,555	9.68	282,175	52.99	198,776	37.33
Broward	2,209,787	7,967	206,770	9.36	1,077,893	48.78	925,124	41.86
Calhoun	15,636	7,019	2,256	14.43	11,387	72.82	1,993	12.75
Charlotte	147,200	8,041	13,733	9.33	37,007	25.14	96,459	65.53
Citrus	119,261	7,519	12,028	10.09	49,107	41.18	58,126	48.74
Clay	213,447	6,869	16,210	7.59	138,293	64.79	58,944	27.62
Collier	412,261	10,131	36,695	8.90	57,573	13.97	317,993	77.13
Columbia	70,097	7,173	9,880	14.09	45,046	64.26	15,172	21.64
DeSoto	39,723	7,500	7,019	17.67	23,082	58.11	9,621	24.22
Dixie	17,005	7,952	2,712	15.95	10,561	62.10	3,732	21.95
Duval	921,832	7,225	102,463	11.12	451,760	49.01	367,610	39.88
Escambia	333,589	7,585	45,109	13.52	177,022	53.07	111,457	33.41
Flagler	89,473	10,163	5,611	6.27	37,105	41.47	46,757	52.26
Franklin	14,524	10,985	2,054	14.14	2,384	16.42	10,086	69.44
Gadsden	59,940	9,265	13,504	22.53	36,490	60.88	9,945	16.59
Gilchrist	20,243	7,492	3,064	15.14	13,471	66.55	3,707	18.31
Glades	14,313	13,771	2,200	15.37	8,200	57.29	3,913	27.34
Gulf	18,836	8,771	2,639	14.01	5,849	31.05	10,348	54.94
Hamilton	26,555	13,267	3,344	12.59	18,529	69.77	4,683	17.64
Hardee	38,864	7,539	6,829	17.57	19,700	50.69	12,334	31.74
Hendry	57,169	7,443	8,992	15.73	32,693	57.19	15,485	27.09
Hernando	154,807	7,977	13,298	8.59	75,466	48.75	66,043	42.66
Highlands	89,022	7,669	14,072	15.81	44,316	49.78	30,634	34.41
Hillsborough	1,553,970	8,506	209,240	13.46	842,093	54.19	502,637	32.35
Holmes	31,386	9,367	4,416	14.07	23,669	75.41	3,300	10.51
Indian River	143,615	8,745	12,093	8.42	35,749	24.89	95,773	66.69
Jackson	54,530	7,522	9,309	17.07	35,169	64.50	10,052	18.43
Jefferson	23,217	16,161	3,490	15.03	16,451	70.85	3,276	14.11
Lafayette	7,762	7,362	1,320	17.00	5,063	65.22	1,380	17.77
Lake	262,229	7,656	22,069	8.42	125,129	47.72	115,031	43.87
Lee	643,141	9,587	54,259	8.44	155,621	24.20	433,261	67.37

See footnotes at end of table. Continued . . .

Table 20.63. ELEMENTARY AND SECONDARY SCHOOLS: ALL FUNDS REVENUE BY MAJOR SOURCE IN THE STATE AND COUNTIES OF FLORIDA, 2003–04 (Continued)

(in thousands of dollars, except where indicated)

County	Total all revenue receipts	Revenue per FTE student 1/ (dollars)	Revenue receipts from– Federal sources Amount	Federal sources Percentage of total	State sources Amount	State sources Percentage of total	Local sources Amount	Local sources Percentage of total
Leon	283,782	8,721	29,379	10.35	135,343	47.69	119,061	41.95
Levy	45,741	7,533	5,852	12.79	29,144	63.72	10,745	23.49
Liberty	11,196	8,288	1,909	17.05	7,929	70.82	1,358	12.13
Madison	24,631	7,641	4,311	17.50	16,259	66.01	4,061	16.49
Manatee	340,359	8,408	32,771	9.63	120,291	35.34	187,297	55.03
Marion	301,047	7,476	38,082	12.65	164,277	54.57	98,687	32.78
Martin	164,973	9,251	14,531	8.81	34,573	20.96	115,868	70.23
Miami-Dade	3,178,325	8,396	383,661	12.07	1,513,259	47.61	1,281,405	40.32
Monroe	102,187	11,340	8,947	8.76	14,522	14.21	78,717	77.03
Nassau	74,313	7,083	5,632	7.58	29,189	39.28	39,493	53.14
Okaloosa	223,824	7,199	25,071	11.20	111,728	49.92	87,025	38.88
Okeechobee	52,587	7,357	7,097	13.50	32,340	61.50	13,149	25.00
Orange	1,393,925	8,245	122,384	8.78	570,676	40.94	700,866	50.28
Osceola	346,692	7,811	29,886	8.62	178,249	51.41	138,558	39.97
Palm Beach	1,522,792	8,945	123,523	8.11	478,565	31.43	920,704	60.46
Pasco	450,976	7,924	40,439	8.97	262,509	58.21	148,028	32.82
Pinellas	924,309	7,901	94,762	10.25	392,053	42.42	437,494	47.33
Polk	616,819	7,245	74,474	12.07	340,113	55.14	202,232	32.79
Putnam	89,071	7,245	12,491	14.02	51,085	57.35	25,494	28.62
St. Johns	185,940	7,827	11,321	6.09	58,308	31.36	116,311	62.55
St. Lucie	269,564	8,307	28,752	10.67	123,848	45.94	116,963	43.39
Santa Rosa	172,364	7,129	17,165	9.96	100,542	58.33	54,657	31.71
Sarasota	413,145	10,163	25,758	6.23	68,762	16.64	318,626	77.12
Seminole	492,293	7,653	35,485	7.21	245,373	49.84	211,436	42.95
Sumter	50,170	7,468	6,586	13.13	25,463	50.75	18,121	36.12
Suwannee	41,110	7,064	5,791	14.09	26,828	65.26	8,491	20.65
Taylor	28,307	8,201	5,271	18.62	14,931	52.75	8,105	28.63
Union	15,665	7,168	2,006	12.81	11,236	71.72	2,423	15.47
Volusia	527,034	8,277	49,529	9.40	229,670	43.58	247,835	47.02
Wakulla	33,544	7,194	2,930	8.73	23,410	69.79	7,205	21.48
Walton	57,993	9,099	6,287	10.84	10,563	18.21	41,144	70.95
Washington	39,229	8,752	5,769	14.71	26,890	68.55	6,569	16.75

FTE Full-time equivalent.
1/ All adult revenues excluded.
2/ Includes special schools.
Note: Data are for public schools only, and include capital outlay, debt service, pre-K, and adult revenues.

Source: State of Florida, Department of Education, Bureau of School Business Services, Office of Funding and Financial Reporting, *Profiles of Florida School Districts, 2003–04, Financial Data Statistical Report,* EIAS Series 2006-07, July 2006, Internet site <http://www.firn.edu/doe/> (accessed 20, February 2007).

Table 20.65. ELEMENTARY AND SECONDARY SCHOOLS: ALL FUNDS EXPENDITURE BY MAJOR TYPE IN THE STATE AND COUNTIES OF FLORIDA, 2003–04

(in thousands of dollars, except where indicated)

County	Total expenditure all funds	Total current expenditure	Current expenditure per FTE 1/ (dollars)	Capital outlay	Debt service
Florida	22,187,434	17,603,134	6,715	3,352,732	1,231,569
Alachua	237,072	200,024	6,978	18,955	18,093
Baker	30,043	28,395	6,250	650	999
Bay	205,050	173,343	6,386	18,382	13,326
Bradford	29,360	27,191	7,066	2,059	111
Brevard	538,438	449,760	6,174	71,444	17,235
Broward	2,322,341	1,868,638	6,674	340,988	112,715
Calhoun	15,617	14,712	6,603	905	0
Charlotte	135,941	120,219	6,487	11,560	4,162
Citrus	128,875	108,994	6,831	19,327	554
Clay	210,535	176,221	5,661	28,909	5,406
Collier	495,525	320,478	7,812	150,270	24,777
Columbia	70,916	62,493	6,397	7,620	803
DeSoto	40,097	37,305	7,053	2,075	717
Dixie	17,454	15,596	7,251	1,742	116
Duval	946,298	791,614	6,210	126,808	27,876
Escambia	326,841	282,202	6,400	33,366	11,273
Flagler	89,266	60,201	6,834	24,538	4,527
Franklin	12,413	10,761	8,190	1,300	352
Gadsden	64,478	53,293	8,310	8,858	2,327
Gilchrist	21,225	19,422	7,202	1,392	412
Glades	16,622	8,751	8,436	7,437	434
Gulf	18,646	15,753	7,299	1,812	1,081
Hamilton	26,199	15,112	7,436	11,030	57
Hardee	39,139	35,546	6,864	3,149	444
Hendry	56,968	52,163	6,851	3,316	1,489
Hernando	148,233	116,311	5,985	19,833	12,089
Highlands	90,212	79,757	6,878	7,870	2,585
Hillsborough	1,621,807	1,254,477	6,851	286,065	81,265
Holmes	33,678	23,061	6,891	10,531	86
Indian River	138,399	111,022	6,749	21,305	6,072
Jackson	63,146	49,235	7,067	11,206	2,705
Jefferson	28,623	12,699	8,603	15,607	317
Lafayette	8,073	7,631	7,197	379	63
Lake	328,594	210,976	6,075	102,183	15,435
Lee	663,861	468,870	6,923	158,342	36,649

See footnotes at end of table.

Continued . . .

Table 20.65. ELEMENTARY AND SECONDARY SCHOOLS: ALL FUNDS EXPENDITURE BY MAJOR TYPE IN THE STATE AND COUNTIES OF FLORIDA, 2003–04 (Continued)

(in thousands of dollars, except where indicated)

County	Total expenditure all funds	Total current expenditure	Current expenditure per FTE 1/ (dollars)	Capital outlay	Debt service
Leon	276,047	224,778	6,775	38,543	12,726
Levy	45,907	41,233	6,799	3,875	799
Liberty	10,643	10,158	7,467	386	99
Madison	24,257	22,180	6,891	1,149	928
Manatee	387,515	270,734	6,553	93,747	23,034
Marion	324,695	264,753	6,550	41,600	18,341
Martin	179,572	122,713	6,879	55,971	887
Miami-Dade	3,320,457	2,728,912	7,102	232,803	358,742
Monroe	111,229	71,123	7,877	36,742	3,364
Nassau	68,722	62,629	5,991	5,487	607
Okaloosa	217,895	198,554	6,479	13,324	6,016
Okeechobee	53,235	47,085	6,597	5,868	282
Orange	1,356,480	1,096,871	6,495	180,551	79,057
Osceola	347,394	272,084	6,100	52,531	22,780
Palm Beach	1,804,097	1,223,445	7,184	464,834	115,818
Pasco	423,816	373,365	6,524	34,646	15,805
Pinellas	955,678	791,637	6,765	159,114	4,926
Polk	617,591	553,444	6,472	36,477	27,671
Putnam	91,829	81,470	6,871	7,390	2,969
St. Johns	191,867	157,531	6,862	22,208	12,128
St. Lucie	254,029	206,206	6,361	25,874	21,949
Santa Rosa	164,885	147,432	6,118	14,764	2,689
Sarasota	414,260	318,176	7,792	84,791	11,292
Seminole	486,210	389,292	6,052	63,022	33,896
Sumter	56,732	45,122	6,705	9,812	1,799
Suwannee	41,640	39,498	6,904	1,600	543
Taylor	29,491	26,118	7,745	1,937	1,435
Union	15,468	14,775	6,815	532	162
Volusia	571,788	411,469	6,465	120,872	39,447
Wakulla	34,231	29,408	6,290	2,586	2,237
Walton	54,929	45,875	7,160	6,565	2,489
Washington	34,857	32,841	6,864	1,914	102

FTE Full-time equivalent.
1/ Does not include capital outlay or debt service.
Note: Data are for public schools only.

Source: State of Florida, Department of Education, Bureau of School Business Services, Office of Funding and Financial Reporting, *Profiles of Florida School Districts, 2003–04, Financial Data Statistical Report,* EIAS Series 2006-07, July 2006, Internet site <http://www.firn.edu/doe/> (accessed 20, February 2007).

Table 20.66. ELEMENTARY AND SECONDARY SCHOOLS: GENERAL FUND EXPENDITURE FOR INSTRUCTION, PUPIL PERSONNEL SERVICES, AND INSTRUCTIONAL SUPPORT SERVICES IN THE STATE AND COUNTIES OF FLORIDA, 2003–04

(in thousands of dollars)

County	Instruction	Pupil personnel services	Instructional support services	County	Instruction	Pupil personnel services	Instructional support services
Florida	10,234,231	868,662	1,941,915	Lake	122,341	11,276	22,751
				Lee	258,251	22,151	46,204
Alachua	106,044	13,501	30,489	Leon	124,183	11,498	32,778
Baker	15,060	1,779	3,440	Levy	23,728	1,789	4,045
Bay	103,080	7,386	17,395	Liberty	6,158	294	956
Bradford	15,322	1,024	2,234	Madison	11,828	662	2,222
Brevard	278,293	16,332	44,083	Manatee	160,481	13,653	31,085
Broward	1,086,627	101,160	217,166	Marion	151,272	17,513	32,275
Calhoun	8,293	500	1,713	Martin	71,057	6,732	12,423
Charlotte	67,252	7,475	16,071	Miami-Dade	1,605,345	144,641	284,524
Citrus	61,115	5,051	12,315	Monroe	39,835	3,801	7,826
Clay	105,547	9,957	20,788	Nassau	35,777	2,450	5,515
Collier	183,193	14,040	32,637	Okaloosa	122,863	7,126	16,939
Columbia	35,526	4,481	7,735	Okeechobee	26,537	2,611	5,006
DeSoto	21,994	1,539	3,793	Orange	641,021	38,441	135,531
Dixie	8,179	741	1,448	Osceola	154,306	15,381	37,237
Duval	468,847	48,714	101,131	Palm Beach	720,037	47,355	138,765
Escambia	156,391	15,306	35,349	Pasco	217,195	19,478	44,843
Flagler	33,078	4,405	6,197	Pinellas	462,069	37,080	82,979
Franklin	6,210	434	708	Polk	329,193	22,053	51,970
Gadsden	26,490	3,246	7,358	Putnam	45,551	4,097	9,404
Gilchrist	10,744	977	1,960	St. Johns	92,523	8,979	15,551
Glades	4,442	517	1,128	St. Lucie	116,372	11,650	24,612
Gulf	8,535	778	1,659	Santa Rosa	82,731	6,506	14,272
Hamilton	7,925	1,007	2,170	Sarasota	191,945	20,598	33,416
Hardee	20,170	2,118	3,831	Seminole	238,775	17,294	33,206
Hendry	29,749	3,100	5,790	Sumter	27,008	1,762	4,690
Hernando	64,054	6,631	14,400	Suwannee	23,016	1,903	3,832
Highlands	43,254	4,581	9,318	Taylor	14,831	1,303	2,459
Hillsborough	718,576	57,532	124,228	Union	8,193	675	1,245
Holmes	12,957	593	1,695	Volusia	241,406	20,313	43,372
Indian River	62,700	3,744	11,583	Wakulla	16,477	1,723	3,084
Jackson	27,056	2,640	6,021	Walton	25,584	1,881	5,334
Jefferson	6,577	574	1,877	Washington	19,130	1,696	2,714
Lafayette	3,935	436	1,138				

Note: Data are for all government fund types and expendable trust funds and exclude special revenue expenditure. Data are for public schools only.

Source: State of Florida, Department of Education, Bureau of School Business Services, Office of Funding and Financial Reporting, *Profiles of Florida School Districts, 2003–04, Financial Data Statistical Report,* EIAS Series 2006-07, July 2006, Internet site <http://www.firn.edu/doe/> (accessed 20, February 2007).

Table 20.67. ELEMENTARY AND SECONDARY SCHOOLS: OPERATING TAX MILLAGE, OPERATING TAX YIELD, ASSESSED VALUE OF NONEXEMPT PROPERTY, AND ASSESSED VALUATION PER FTE STUDENT IN THE STATE AND COUNTIES OF FLORIDA, 2003-04

			Assessed value of nonexempt property	
County	Operating tax millage	Operating tax yield ($1,000)	Tax roll amount 2003 ($1,000)	Valuation per FTE student (dollars)
Florida	(X)	5,835,476	989,504,170	352,088
Alachua	6.4940	48,223	7,816,644	249,327
Baker	6.3730	2,766	456,784	96,712
Bay	6.5690	51,655	8,277,376	287,761
Bradford	6.6940	3,604	566,721	141,412
Brevard	6.4050	133,103	21,874,824	275,438
Broward	6.1240	604,916	103,976,830	351,858
Calhoun	6.6140	1,579	251,304	106,665
Charlotte	6.1080	63,625	10,964,886	569,724
Citrus	6.2960	38,146	6,377,731	386,045
Clay	6.6310	35,706	5,668,140	170,512
Collier	4.5240	198,300	46,139,966	1,029,099
Columbia	6.3890	9,423	1,552,515	149,059
DeSoto	6.2420	5,967	1,006,249	183,834
Dixie	6.7330	2,389	373,521	160,499
Duval	6.5400	232,208	37,374,610	270,372
Escambia	6.7880	62,916	9,756,466	208,517
Flagler	6.3710	27,508	4,544,976	505,594
Franklin	4.1530	6,416	1,626,152	1,158,864
Gadsden	6.6490	5,990	948,376	139,207
Gilchrist	6.5010	2,242	362,984	121,896
Glades	6.1970	2,585	439,065	400,169
Gulf	5.8830	7,406	1,325,114	584,077
Hamilton	6.4660	3,137	510,643	235,412
Hardee	6.5780	8,633	1,381,409	254,389
Hendry	6.5270	9,660	1,557,911	191,467
Hernando	6.3300	33,679	5,600,585	270,971
Highlands	6.7370	20,440	3,193,682	251,458
Hillsborough	6.2700	302,470	50,779,806	258,483
Holmes	6.3380	1,847	306,722	87,059
Indian River	6.1790	63,040	10,739,236	604,514
Jackson	6.4900	6,198	1,005,281	130,358
Jefferson	6.7040	2,218	348,298	233,833
Lafayette	6.2550	887	149,349	137,265
Lake	6.4400	63,939	10,450,920	288,799
Lee	6.3460	260,078	43,139,910	591,843
Leon	6.4170	60,630	9,945,660	285,110

See footnotes at end of table. Continued . . .

Table 20.67. ELEMENTARY AND SECONDARY SCHOOLS: OPERATING TAX MILLAGE, OPERATING TAX YIELD, ASSESSED VALUE OF NONEXEMPT PROPERTY, AND ASSESSED VALUATION PER FTE STUDENT IN THE STATE AND COUNTIES OF FLORIDA, 2003–04 (Continued)

County	Operating tax millage	Operating tax yield ($1,000)	Assessed value of nonexempt property: Tax roll amount 2003 ($1,000)	Assessed value of nonexempt property: Valuation per FTE student (dollars)
Levy	6.4900	7,115	1,154,036	174,440
Liberty	6.7560	866	134,904	83,799
Madison	6.6190	2,482	394,640	116,690
Manatee	6.2960	111,096	18,574,280	424,678
Marion	6.4350	59,647	9,757,028	223,467
Martin	6.2630	79,421	13,348,450	683,305
Miami-Dade	6.4180	799,452	131,120,086	324,326
Monroe	3.4220	48,101	14,796,250	1,526,510
Nassau	6.5380	27,700	4,459,829	402,603
Okaloosa	6.5930	60,440	9,649,714	286,839
Okeechobee	6.4120	7,500	1,231,305	158,405
Orange	6.3880	377,091	62,138,122	336,215
Osceola	6.4790	74,663	12,130,330	249,334
Palm Beach	6.2510	586,278	98,725,684	530,754
Pasco	6.3820	84,175	13,883,582	224,324
Pinellas	6.2430	294,979	49,736,379	399,840
Polk	6.3170	113,191	18,861,514	211,234
Putnam	6.4660	16,128	2,625,629	202,426
St. Johns	6.2740	74,743	12,540,138	502,008
St. Lucie	6.3550	65,318	10,819,143	307,548
Santa Rosa	6.5400	34,284	5,518,134	215,807
Sarasota	6.7930	220,315	34,139,702	781,623
Seminole	6.2410	117,455	19,810,401	281,901
Sumter	6.7060	12,745	2,000,620	279,681
Suwannee	6.5780	5,314	850,345	142,077
Taylor	6.0380	4,903	854,723	251,980
Union	6.3990	1,028	169,024	73,671
Volusia	6.2270	127,966	21,631,743	306,504
Wakulla	6.3660	4,066	672,276	134,451
Walton	4.8960	30,021	6,454,559	968,391
Washington	6.8640	3,462	530,953	147,789

FTE Full-time equivalent.
(X) Not applicable.
Note: Data are for public schools only.

Source: State of Florida, Department of Education, Bureau of School Business Services, Office of Funding and Financial Reporting, *Profiles of Florida School Districts, 2003–04, Financial Data Statistical Report,* EIAS Series 2006-07, July 2006, Internet site <http://www.firn.edu/doe/> (accessed 20, February 2007).

Table 20.69. ELEMENTARY AND SECONDARY SCHOOLS: EXPENDITURE FOR FOOD SERVICES AND PUPIL TRANSPORTATION SERVICES IN THE STATE AND COUNTIES OF FLORIDA 2003–04

(in dollars)

County	Food services	Transportation services	County	Food services	Transportation services
Florida	861,421,269	720,115,965	Lake	11,737,685	11,088,794
			Lee	22,174,637	30,790,446
Alachua	10,632,531	8,610,961	Leon	8,467,574	7,450,822
Baker	1,575,768	1,493,234	Levy	2,310,886	2,942,338
Bay	9,766,545	6,277,034	Liberty	463,799	456,943
Bradford	1,349,092	1,213,126	Madison	1,288,085	1,274,355
Brevard	22,406,642	15,210,286	Manatee	12,050,072	9,775,600
Broward	77,581,275	66,712,227	Marion	14,732,289	16,855,060
Calhoun	779,983	744,062	Martin	5,568,908	4,944,019
Charlotte	6,573,036	5,403,280	Miami-Dade	130,871,610	78,557,556
Citrus	4,217,595	6,034,412	Monroe	2,506,912	3,201,455
Clay	7,349,252	8,471,384	Nassau	3,352,400	3,249,354
Collier	14,967,408	15,263,175	Okaloosa	9,351,283	7,691,192
Columbia	3,344,399	3,408,023	Okeechobee	2,816,680	2,110,321
DeSoto	2,057,476	1,689,542	Orange	46,449,933	49,929,949
Dixie	1,016,525	933,750	Osceola	13,366,460	11,541,466
Duval	41,854,782	34,611,295	Palm Beach	53,021,604	36,072,160
Escambia	16,599,856	14,030,519	Pasco	21,457,408	16,674,101
Flagler	2,740,924	3,444,011	Pinellas	33,071,250	36,366,058
Franklin	493,671	454,455	Polk	34,959,200	22,603,755
Gadsden	3,738,340	2,952,066	Putnam	5,109,438	4,034,565
Gilchrist	1,239,473	840,271	St. Johns	6,713,344	6,394,025
Glades	445,245	341,178	St. Lucie	12,085,053	13,386,879
Gulf	691,556	764,313	Santa Rosa	7,749,979	10,531,587
Hamilton	971,056	765,468	Sarasota	12,896,708	13,413,245
Hardee	2,174,263	1,630,914	Seminole	19,383,021	17,986,766
Hendry	3,492,437	2,256,329	Sumter	2,738,323	1,883,255
Hernando	5,738,829	7,068,084	Suwannee	2,113,229	2,129,380
Highlands	5,103,334	4,245,999	Taylor	1,395,659	1,596,908
Hillsborough	74,872,681	52,343,871	Union	756,645	633,572
Holmes	1,340,841	978,265	Volusia	19,228,389	13,293,666
Indian River	6,679,011	3,425,765	Wakulla	1,447,824	1,927,581
Jackson	3,184,038	2,444,156	Walton	2,406,756	2,166,424
Jefferson	586,030	823,560	Washington	1,422,766	1,803,782
Lafayette	391,566	473,571			

Note: Data are for public schools only. Detail may not add to total due to rounding.

Source: State of Florida, Department of Education, Bureau of School Business Services, Office of Funding and Financial Reporting, *Profiles of Florida School Districts, 2003–04, Financial Data Statistical Report,* EIAS Series 2006-07, July 2006, Internet site <http://www.firn.edu/doe/> (accessed 20, February 2007).

Table 20.70. NONPUBLIC SCHOOLS: TOTAL ADMINISTRATIVE AND INSTRUCTIONAL STAFF IN THE STATE AND COUNTIES OF FLORIDA, 2005–06

County	Total	Adminis-tration	Instructional staff				
			Pre-K	Kinder-garten	Elementary	Secondary	Other 1/
Florida	36,971	4,346	4,857	2,393	11,226	12,052	2,097
Alachua	586	85	86	41	178	156	40
Baker	3	1	0	0	1	1	0
Bay	175	18	35	13	46	52	11
Bradford	43	6	2	4	18	11	2
Brevard	1,228	149	127	80	375	428	69
Broward	3,715	375	415	186	1,108	1,416	215
Calhoun	0	0	0	0	0	0	0
Charlotte	130	22	12	10	45	37	4
Citrus	121	15	15	10	40	33	8
Clay	374	53	38	24	127	113	19
Collier	461	49	80	25	126	156	25
Columbia	66	8	3	6	23	17	9
DeSoto	28	4	5	2	9	7	1
Dixie	4	1	0	0	1	1	1
Duval	2,783	401	327	175	798	899	183
Escambia	707	74	108	43	210	224	48
Flagler	47	7	12	4	16	5	3
Franklin	12	1	2	1	6	2	0
Gadsden	66	9	6	4	18	24	5
Gilchrist	24	3	2	1	2	13	3
Glades	0	0	0	0	0	0	0
Gulf	18	2	3	1	6	5	1
Hamilton	18	2	0	2	8	6	0
Hardee	6	2	0	0	2	2	0
Hendry	30	2	17	2	6	2	1
Hernando	178	18	28	11	61	53	7
Highlands	99	15	14	9	33	22	6
Hillsborough	2,411	298	342	174	692	760	145
Holmes	8	2	0	0	1	5	0
Indian River	270	38	13	18	97	89	15
Jackson	33	4	6	4	11	7	1
Jefferson	37	3	2	3	10	17	2
Lafayette	10	1	3	1	3	1	1
Lake	583	70	52	42	185	212	22

See footnotes at end of table. Continued . . .

Table 20.70. NONPUBLIC SCHOOLS: TOTAL ADMINISTRATIVE AND INSTRUCTIONAL STAFF IN THE STATE AND COUNTIES OF FLORIDA, 2005–06 (Continued)

County	Total	Adminis-tration	Instructional staff				
			Pre-K	Kinder-garten	Elementary	Secondary	Other 1/
Lee	957	119	129	74	282	300	53
Leon	698	93	131	41	187	202	44
Levy	44	6	1	7	16	11	3
Liberty	0	0	0	0	0	0	0
Madison	34	4	2	3	11	11	3
Manatee	464	43	45	30	163	166	17
Marion	683	51	91	41	224	246	30
Martin	236	24	34	21	80	62	15
Miami-Dade	6,100	789	1,061	433	1,608	1,827	382
Monroe	68	7	12	6	22	18	3
Nassau	72	10	12	5	27	16	2
Okaloosa	219	21	29	14	84	54	17
Okeechobee	22	2	3	2	9	4	2
Orange	3,218	312	350	197	1,120	1,103	136
Osceola	405	45	103	31	111	99	16
Palm Beach	2,799	313	276	154	835	1,056	165
Pasco	356	47	49	28	95	117	20
Pinellas	2,026	247	208	117	698	639	117
Polk	818	91	151	57	231	247	41
Putnam	155	15	10	13	51	57	9
St. Johns	235	28	50	15	70	57	15
St. Lucie	473	37	32	38	177	164	25
Santa Rosa	70	7	16	6	14	15	12
Sarasota	737	74	64	43	245	279	32
Seminole	1,004	128	121	71	344	284	56
Sumter	12	1	1	1	4	5	0
Suwannee	52	6	7	5	22	11	1
Taylor	63	4	0	1	33	25	0
Union	5	1	0	0	2	2	0
Volusia	629	74	98	39	190	195	33
Wakulla	11	4	2	1	2	1	1
Walton	18	3	9	2	3	1	0
Washington	14	2	5	1	4	2	0

1/ Librarians and guidance.
Note: See Glossary under Private school for definition of nonpublic schools.

Source: State of Florida, Department of Education, Office of Independent Education and Parental Choice, *Florida's Nonpublic Schools: Annual Report, 2005-2006,* August 2006, Internet site <http://www.floridaschoolchoice.org/> (accessed 2, February 2007).

Table 20.74. FEDERAL AID: SPECIFIED FEDERAL HEALTH AND EDUCATION PROGRAM EXPENDITURES IN FLORIDA, OTHER SUNBELT STATES, AND THE UNITED STATES, 2004

(in millions of dollars, except where indicated)

State	Total 1/	Per capita (dollars)	Compensatory education for the disadvantaged	Temporary Assistance to Needy Families (TANF)	ETA employment/ training
Florida	18,174.5	1,045.38	104.2	642.3	268.7
Alabama	6,057.1	1,338.48	32.9	105.9	131.9
Arizona	7,815.2	1,361.55	31.0	243.8	131.8
Arkansas	4,123.7	1,499.52	19.7	41.0	68.7
California	47,282.9	1,319.20	322.3	3,765.2	1,134.5
Georgia	9,539.6	1,069.69	0.7	380.3	166.7
Louisiana	7,035.4	1,561.09	0.0	264.7	120.7
Mississippi	5,297.4	1,826.19	16.1	99.2	84.2
New Mexico	4,248.9	2,232.73	14.2	130.5	55.0
North Carolina	11,354.0	1,329.43	38.2	332.2	257.0
Oklahoma	4,936.6	1,401.03	18.1	171.4	74.0
South Carolina	5,543.9	1,320.64	2.0	101.5	102.7
Tennessee	9,128.7	1,548.99	16.2	214.1	153.0
Texas	25,674.4	1,142.53	164.6	523.4	527.4
Virginia	6,598.1	881.94	21.5	176.1	236.8
United States	408,143.4	1,389.87	1,401.9	17,467.9	8,318.6

ETA Employment and Training Administration.
1/ Includes other amounts not shown separately.
Source: U.S., Department of Commerce, Census Bureau, *Federal Aid to States for Fiscal Year 2004,* issued January 2006, Internet site <http://www.census.gov/> (accessed 19, September 2007).

Table 20.75. CULTURE AND THE ARTS: STATE GRANTS TO GROUPS AND INDIVIDUALS IN THE STATE AND SPECIFIED COUNTIES OF FLORIDA, 2007-08

(in dollars)

County	Amount	County	Amount	County	Amount	County	Amount
Florida	13,335,059	Franklin	717	Leon	429,072	Pasco	17,320
		Glades	10,000	Levy	18,938	Pinellas	1,042,322
Alachua	544,563	Gulf	10,000	Liberty	9,400	Polk	252,363
Baker	4,667	Hamilton	7,739	Madison	7,333	Putnam	39,401
Bay	48,615	Hardee	5,245	Manatee	13,270	St. Johns	118,929
Brevard	261,579	Hendry	2,664	Marion	20,136	St. Lucie	18,681
Broward	744,199	Hernando	9,568	Martin	35,315	Sarasota	1,085,562
Calhoun	1,907	Highlands	24,039	Miami-Dade	2,455,106	Seminole	79,982
Charlotte	35,343	Hillsborough	1,233,025	Monroe	330,866	Sumter	10,400
Citrus	21,818	Holmes	626	Nassau	38,840	Suwannee	16,032
Collier	188,053	Indian River	251,597	Okaloosa	87,374	Volusia	422,556
DeSoto	20,663	Jackson	6,334	Okeechobee	20,128	Wakulla	1,450
Duval	790,278	Jefferson	900	Orange	869,867	Walton	6,928
Escambia	113,790	Lake	14,904	Osceola	18,336	Washington	750
Flagler	78,374	Lee	129,292	Palm Beach	1,307,903		

Source: State of Florida, Department of State, Division of Cultural Affairs, *2008 Grant Awards by County,* Internet site<http://www.florida-arts.org> (accessed 16, August 2007).

GOVERNMENT AND ELECTIONS

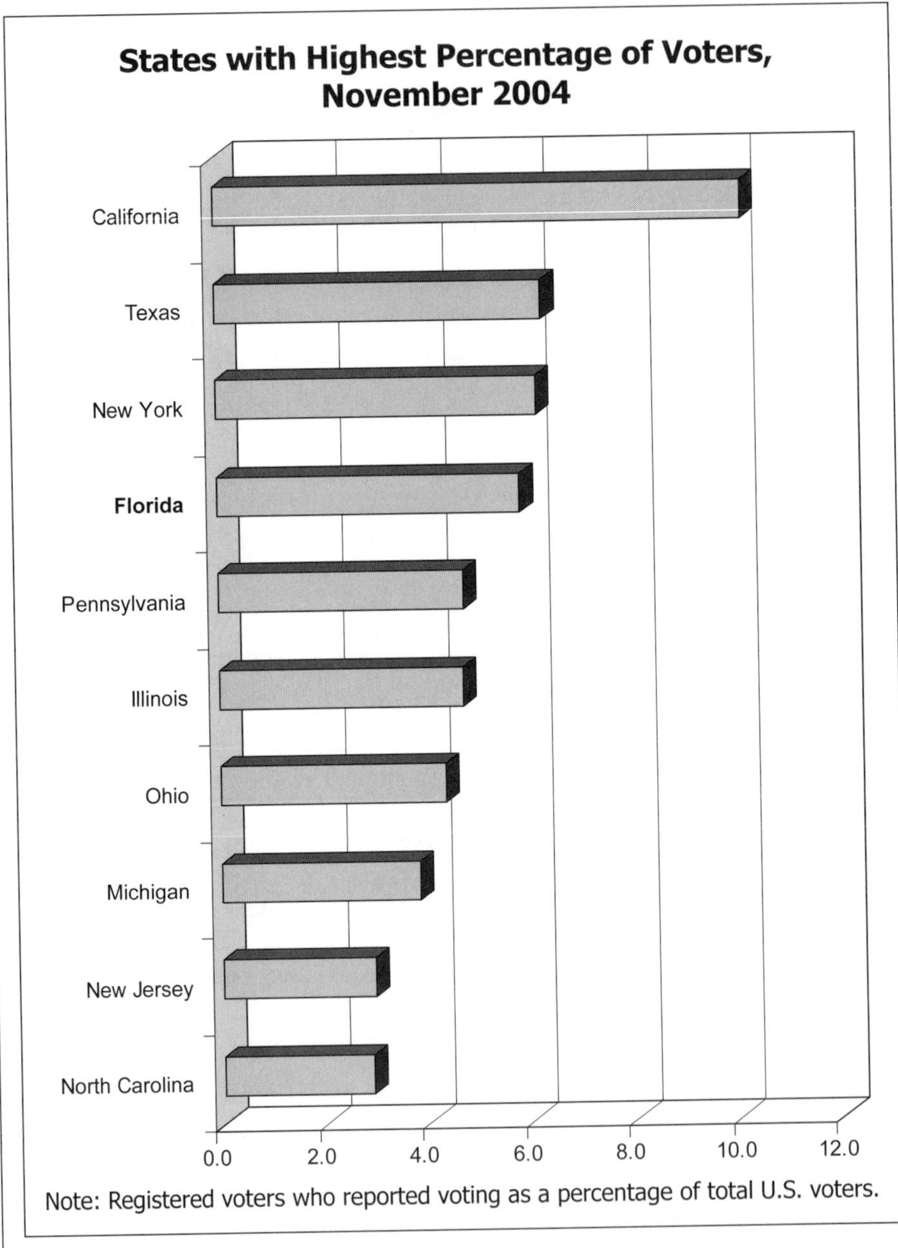

Source: Table 21.22

Section 21.00
Government and Elections

This section presents statistics on the government structure and voting in the state. It includes the number and type of government units within Florida; voting-age population estimates and projections; registered voters by race and Hispanic origin and by party affiliation; registered voters who reported voting in various elections; voter turnout and election results; female, black, and Hispanic elected officials; and Congress composition and apportionment.

Sources. The Census Bureau conducts a government census in years ending in "2" and "7" to coincide with the economic censuses. Results from the 2002 census on governmental unit characteristics within the state are published in *2002 Census of Governments, Volume1, No. 1: Governmental Organization* and appear on Table 21.01. The Census Bureau tracked voting patterns during the 2004 election cycle in *Current Population Survey: Voting and Registration in the Election of November 2004.* Tables 21.22 and 21.23 show results for Florida.

The U.S. Census Bureau also provides historical apportionment decennial census data for states. Apportionment figures from the 1840 to 2000 censuses are presented on Table 21.43.

Selected benchmark voting-age population census counts and estimates from the Census Bureau are shown on Table 21.20 as published in *Annual Estimates of the Resident Population by Selected Age Groups for the United States and State* on the Internet. County-level estimates and characteristics of the state's voting-age population are published by the Population Program of the Bureau of Economic and Business Research (BEBR) in *Florida Population Studies* and appear in Tables 21.25 and 21.26.

The Division of Elections in the Florida Department of State provides information on registered voters by party, voter turnout, and election results on their Web site.

Data on women in state legislatures are published in copyrighted information releases from the Center for the American Woman and Politics, Eagleton Institute of Politics, Rutgers University. Copyrighted Black elected officials data are published annually online in *Black Elected Officials: A Statistical Summary* by the Joint Center for Political and Economic Studies, Washington, DC. Information on Hispanic elected officials and on the composition of Congress and state legislatures is available in the *Statistical Abstract of the United States.*

Section 21.00
Government and Elections

Tables listed by major heading

Table 21.01. GOVERNMENTAL UNITS: NUMBER BY TYPE IN FLORIDA AND THE UNITED STATES, 2002

Type of unit	Florida	United States
All units	1,192	87,576
Percentage change from 1997	10.2	0.1
Local government, total	1,191	87,525
Local government general purpose	470	38,967
County 1/	66	3,034
Municipal	404	19,429
Local government special purpose	721	48,558
School districts	95	13,506
Special districts	626	35,052
Single-function districts, total	431	31,877
Education services	13	2,098
Education 2/	8	518
Libraries	5	1,580
Social services	51	1,521
Hospitals	28	711
Health	15	753
Welfare	8	57
Transportation	22	1,458
Highways	7	743
Airports	8	510
Other 3/	7	205
Fire protection	57	5,725
Environment and housing	250	14,124
Natural resources 4/	124	6,979
Drainage and flood control	57	3,247
Soil and water conservation	60	2,506
Other	7	1,226
Parks and recreation	16	1,287
Housing and community development	105	3,399
Sewerage	3	2,004
Solid waste management	2	455
Utilities	26	3,890
Water supply	14	3,405
Other 5/	12	485
Industrial development and mortgage credit	6	234
Other	6	1,161
Multiple-function districts, total	195	3,175
Natural resources and water supply	5	102
Sewerage and water supply	7	1,446
Other	183	1,627

1/ In 1968, Duval County and the City of Jacksonville consolidated to form one government, designated the City of Jacksonville. Jacksonville is counted as a municipal government, rather than as a county government, in census reporting.
2/ Primarily school building authorities.
3/ Includes parking facilities and water transport and terminals.
4/ Functions within the "natural resources" category may overlap.
5/ Includes electric power, gas supply, and transit.
Note: The government census is on a 5-year cycle collecting data for years ending in 2 and 7. Totals may include other categories not shown separately. Therefore, detail may not add to totals.
Source: U.S., Department of Commerce, Census Bureau, *2002 Census of Governments, Volume I, No. 1: Government Organization,* issued December 2002, Internet site <http://www.census.gov/> (accessed 11, May 2007).

Table 21.20. VOTING-AGE POPULATION: ESTIMATES BY SEX AND AGE IN FLORIDA, OTHER SUNBELT STATES, OTHER POPULOUS STATES, AND THE UNITED STATES 2000 AND 2006

State	April 1, 2000					July 1, 2006				
		Persons aged 18 and over					Persons aged 18 and over			
			Percentage—					Percentage—		
	Total population (1,000)	Number (1,000)	Aged 18 to 24	Aged 65 and over	Aged 85 and over	Total population (1,000)	Number (1,000)	Aged 18 to 24	Aged 65 and over	Aged 85 and over
	Sunbelt states									
Florida	15,982	12,336	10.8	22.8	2.7	18,090	14,068	11.3	21.6	3.3
Alabama	4,447	3,324	13.2	17.4	2.0	4,599	3,485	12.8	17.7	2.3
Arizona	5,131	3,764	13.7	17.7	1.8	6,166	4,538	13.0	17.4	2.3
Arkansas	2,673	1,993	13.1	18.8	2.3	2,811	2,120	12.6	18.4	2.6
California	33,872	24,622	13.7	14.6	1.7	36,458	26,925	14.1	14.6	2.1
Georgia	8,186	6,017	13.9	13.1	1.5	9,364	6,909	13.2	13.2	1.6
Louisiana	4,469	3,249	14.6	15.9	1.8	4,288	3,198	14.2	16.4	2.1
Mississippi	2,845	2,069	15.0	16.6	2.1	2,911	2,151	14.1	16.8	2.3
New Mexico	1,819	1,310	13.6	16.2	1.8	1,955	1,446	14.2	16.8	2.2
North Carolina	8,049	6,085	13.3	15.9	1.7	8,857	6,701	12.5	16.1	2.0
Oklahoma	3,451	2,558	14.0	17.8	2.2	3,579	2,685	13.7	17.6	2.4
South Carolina	4,012	3,002	13.6	16.2	1.7	4,321	3,282	12.9	16.9	2.1
Tennessee	5,689	4,291	12.8	16.4	1.9	6,039	4,596	11.9	16.7	2.1
Texas	20,852	14,965	14.7	13.8	1.6	23,508	17,014	14.4	13.7	1.8
Virginia	7,079	5,340	12.7	14.8	1.6	7,643	5,836	12.8	15.2	1.9
	Other populous states									
Illinois	12,419	9,174	13.2	16.4	2.1	12,832	9,617	13.3	16.0	2.4
Indiana	6,080	4,506	13.6	16.7	2.0	6,314	4,736	13.0	16.6	2.3
Massachusetts	6,349	4,849	11.9	17.7	2.4	6,437	4,988	12.7	17.2	2.7
Michigan	9,938	7,343	12.7	16.6	1.9	10,096	7,617	12.9	16.6	2.3
New Jersey	8,414	6,327	10.7	17.6	2.1	8,725	6,635	11.5	17.0	2.5
New York	18,976	14,286	12.4	17.1	2.2	19,306	14,792	13.1	17.1	2.5
Ohio	11,353	8,465	12.5	17.8	2.1	11,478	8,708	12.6	17.6	2.5
Pennsylvania	12,281	9,359	11.7	20.5	2.5	12,441	9,636	12.4	19.6	3.1
United States	281,422	209,128	13.0	16.7	2.0	299,398	225,663	13.1	16.5	2.3

Note: Includes Armed Forces residing in each state.

Source: U.S., Department of Commerce, Census Bureau, Population Division, *Annual Estimates of the Resident Population by Selected Age Groups for the United States and State: July 1, 2006 and April 1, 2000,* Internet site <http://www.census.gov/> (accessed 3, July 2007).

Table 21.22. VOTERS: VOTING-AGE POPULATION AND REGISTERED VOTERS BY RACE AND VOTING STATUS IN FLORIDA, OTHER STATES, AND THE UNITED STATES, NOVEMBER 2004

State	Voting-age population (1,000)	White (1,000)	Black (1,000)	Hispanic origin (1,000)	Registered voters Number (1,000)	Registered voters Percent-age	Reported voted Number (1,000)	Reported voted Percent-age
Florida	13,133	10,871	1,832	2,422	8,219	62.6	7,372	56.1
Alabama	3,332	2,450	799	39	2,418	72.6	2,060	61.8
Alaska	451	359	13	22	334	74.0	293	65.0
Arizona	4,122	3,747	142	1,160	2,485	60.3	2,239	54.3
Arkansas	2,010	1,649	295	73	1,328	66.1	1,140	56.7
California	26,085	20,083	1,678	8,127	14,193	54.4	12,807	49.1
Colorado	3,398	3,098	123	574	2,307	67.9	2,097	61.7
Connecticut	2,606	2,278	233	170	1,695	65.0	1,524	58.5
Delaware	612	485	108	44	415	67.7	385	62.8
Georgia	6,338	4,390	1,688	376	3,948	62.3	3,332	52.6
Hawaii	938	208	17	55	497	53.0	433	46.2
Idaho	996	942	5	89	663	66.5	585	58.7
Illinois	9,303	7,648	1,277	1,031	6,437	69.2	5,672	61.0
Indiana	4,536	4,088	368	182	3,031	66.8	2,598	57.3
Iowa	2,212	2,120	37	69	1,674	75.7	1,522	68.8
Kansas	1,990	1,768	99	132	1,338	67.2	1,188	59.7
Kentucky	3,042	2,775	204	44	2,231	73.3	1,930	63.4
Louisiana	3,277	2,260	976	68	2,413	73.6	2,067	63.1
Maine	1,022	990	8	9	824	80.6	736	72.0
Maryland	4,043	2,737	1,070	282	2,676	66.2	2,413	59.7
Massachusetts	4,840	4,297	292	323	3,483	72.0	3,085	63.7
Michigan	7,452	6,163	957	201	5,364	72.0	4,818	64.7
Minnesota	3,766	3,435	128	108	3,080	81.8	2,887	76.7
Mississippi	2,081	1,335	698	46	1,510	72.5	1,263	60.7
Missouri	4,243	3,636	433	115	3,336	78.6	2,815	66.3
Montana	690	647	0	12	519	75.1	482	69.9
Nebraska	1,294	1,181	51	119	918	70.9	793	61.3
Nevada	1,699	1,445	113	301	965	56.8	871	51.3
New Hampshire	982	943	6	11	716	72.9	677	68.9
New Jersey	6,413	5,174	845	906	4,085	63.7	3,693	57.6
New Mexico	1,375	1,151	34	544	936	68.1	837	60.9
New York	14,492	11,055	2,354	1,976	8,624	59.5	7,698	53.1
North Carolina	6,250	4,709	1,241	327	4,292	68.7	3,639	58.2
North Dakota	466	443	3	6	412	88.5	330	70.8
Ohio	8,469	7,381	895	209	6,003	70.9	5,485	64.8
Oklahoma	2,602	2,031	190	135	1,781	68.4	1,541	59.2
Oregon	2,727	2,498	48	165	2,049	75.2	1,924	70.6
Pennsylvania	9,356	8,218	853	255	6,481	69.3	5,845	62.5
Rhode Island	813	732	46	58	522	64.2	467	57.4
South Carolina	3,061	2,188	837	52	2,238	73.1	1,899	62.0
South Dakota	564	530	2	10	425	75.5	378	67.1
Tennessee	4,402	3,655	651	128	2,739	62.2	2,319	52.7
Texas	15,813	13,246	1,669	5,232	9,681	61.2	7,950	50.3
Utah	1,629	1,561	10	104	1,141	70.1	1,022	62.8
Vermont	482	463	2	3	354	73.5	316	65.4
Virginia	5,364	4,101	961	301	3,441	64.1	3,134	58.4
Washington	4,596	3,792	141	248	3,133	68.2	2,851	62.0
West Virginia	1,395	1,331	42	5	935	67.0	798	57.2
Wisconsin	4,126	3,793	195	203	3,225	78.2	3,010	73.0
Wyoming	373	358	3	20	265	71.0	247	66.3
United States 1/	215,694	176,618	24,910	27,129	142,070	65.9	125,736	58.3

1/ Includes District of Columbia.

Source: U.S., Department of Commerce, Census Bureau, Population Division, *Current Population Survey: Voting and Registration in the Election of November 2004,* Internet release date May 25, 2005, Internet site <http://www.census.gov/> (accessed 14, May 2007).

Table 21.23. VOTERS: REGISTERED VOTERS WHO REPORTED VOTING BY SEX, RACE, AND HISPANIC ORIGIN IN FLORIDA, OTHER SUNBELT STATES, OTHER POPULOUS STATES AND THE UNITED STATES, NOVEMBER 2004

State	Registered voters 1/ (1,000)	Reported voted (percentage)					
		Total	Male	Female	White	Black	Hispanic origin 2/
		Sunbelt states					
Florida	8,219	56.1	53.9	58.2	58.4	44.5	34.0
Alabama	2,418	61.8	59.6	63.8	62.2	63.9	A/
Arizona	2,485	54.3	51.5	57.0	55.9	46.6	25.5
Arkansas	1,328	56.7	54.4	58.9	58.6	49.4	A/
California	14,193	49.1	47.1	51.0	51.2	61.7	25.6
Georgia	3,948	52.6	49.0	56.0	53.6	54.4	7.0
Louisiana	2,413	63.1	63.0	63.1	64.0	62.1	A/
Mississippi	1,510	60.7	55.4	65.4	58.9	66.8	A/
New Mexico	936	60.9	59.6	62.0	62.1	A/	50.6
North Carolina	4,292	58.2	54.6	61.5	58.1	63.1	8.2
Oklahoma	1,781	59.2	58.0	60.3	62.6	54.7	18.9
South Carolina	2,238	62.0	59.8	64.0	63.4	59.5	A/
Tennessee	2,739	52.7	50.8	54.5	53.5	51.3	7.2
Texas	9,681	50.3	48.1	52.4	50.6	55.8	29.3
Virginia	3,441	58.4	56.9	59.8	63.0	49.6	23.1
		Other populous states					
Illinois	6,437	61.0	59.1	62.7	61.6	66.9	28.5
Indiana	3,031	57.3	57.1	57.4	57.8	53.8	22.6
Massachusetts	3,483	63.7	62.2	65.2	67.0	43.5	32.9
Michigan	5,364	64.7	62.7	66.5	66.3	62.6	35.5
New Jersey	4,085	57.6	54.9	60.0	59.7	54.7	30.6
New York	8,624	53.1	51.9	54.2	57.6	44.3	31.0
Ohio	6,003	64.8	63.9	65.5	65.1	65.5	43.1
Pennsylvania	6,481	62.5	61.3	63.5	64.4	55.6	34.5
United States	142,070	58.3	56.3	60.1	60.3	56.3	28.0

A/ The base is too small to show the derived measure.
1/ Includes races not shown separately.
2/ Persons of Hispanic origin may be of any race.

Source: U.S., Department of Commerce, Census Bureau, Population Division, *Current Population Survey: Voting and Registration in the Election of November 2004,* Internet release date May 25, 2005, Internet site <http://www.census.gov/> (accessed 14, May 2007).

Table 21.25. VOTING-AGE POPULATION: ESTIMATES BY SPECIFIED SEX, RACE, AND AGE OF PERSONS AGED 18 AND OVER IN THE STATE AND COUNTIES OF FLORIDA
APRIL 1, 2006

		Percentage—								
		Sex		Non-Hispanic			Age			
County	Voting-age population	Male	Female	White	Black	Hispanic	18-34	35-54	55-64	65 and over
Florida	14,235,367	48.3	51.7	65.3	13.9	18.6	27.2	36.1	14.6	22.1
Alachua	197,502	48.4	51.6	69.8	18.7	7.5	47.7	29.7	10.8	11.8
Baker	18,462	54.2	45.8	82.9	13.6	2.6	31.8	40.2	14.1	13.9
Bay	128,161	48.8	51.2	83.7	10.2	3.4	26.6	38.9	15.9	18.5
Bradford	22,712	58.0	42.0	74.2	21.7	2.8	32.3	37.3	13.6	16.8
Brevard	431,958	48.4	51.6	84.0	8.2	5.6	22.1	36.3	15.9	25.7
Broward	1,339,069	47.8	52.2	55.6	21.7	19.6	27.5	40.0	13.4	19.1
Calhoun	10,952	54.3	45.7	76.9	16.6	4.4	32.8	34.9	13.2	19.0
Charlotte	135,956	47.2	52.8	90.0	4.9	3.7	14.6	27.3	17.9	40.2
Citrus	114,841	47.4	52.6	92.9	2.5	3.3	14.9	27.5	19.1	38.5
Clay	129,907	48.8	51.2	84.1	7.6	5.2	28.4	41.5	15.2	14.8
Collier	260,250	49.6	50.4	73.8	4.9	20.4	22.2	31.4	16.9	29.6
Columbia	48,517	51.2	48.8	79.4	15.9	3.3	28.7	35.8	15.8	19.8
DeSoto	26,098	56.7	43.3	62.2	11.6	25.5	32.2	28.6	14.3	25.0
Dixie	12,385	54.3	45.7	88.2	9.2	1.8	26.2	33.2	16.9	23.8
Duval	657,065	47.8	52.2	63.0	27.7	5.7	32.7	39.8	13.4	14.1
Escambia	238,924	48.9	51.1	73.6	20.0	3.0	33.8	34.1	13.7	18.5
Flagler	73,009	47.5	52.5	83.0	9.6	5.7	16.8	31.2	18.8	33.1
Franklin	9,657	53.3	46.7	84.3	13.1	1.9	23.7	34.7	18.4	23.3
Gadsden	36,389	47.1	52.9	37.7	54.1	7.4	31.9	37.0	14.3	16.8
Gilchrist	12,932	52.0	48.0	90.0	6.4	3.1	29.7	35.0	15.6	19.7
Glades	8,571	56.0	44.0	69.6	9.7	16.2	27.1	33.3	16.1	23.5
Gulf	13,503	59.9	40.1	74.1	20.4	4.0	27.8	38.4	14.8	19.0
Hamilton	11,359	60.9	39.1	54.9	35.4	8.9	34.5	37.4	13.3	14.8
Hardee	20,054	55.3	44.7	57.6	9.4	32.2	36.6	32.8	11.7	18.8
Hendry	27,400	54.8	45.2	44.7	12.7	41.5	41.3	32.5	11.3	14.9
Hernando	127,353	47.1	52.9	88.4	4.2	6.3	17.7	29.3	17.4	35.7
Highlands	78,455	48.0	52.0	77.6	7.7	13.5	18.7	26.0	15.6	39.6
Hillsborough	870,642	48.3	51.7	61.6	15.0	20.4	32.1	38.8	13.3	15.8
Holmes	15,084	53.3	46.7	87.9	8.1	2.1	30.5	34.2	14.9	20.4
Indian River	109,945	47.9	52.1	84.0	7.5	7.6	19.1	30.7	16.6	33.6
Jackson	39,992	55.3	44.7	68.7	26.5	3.5	30.3	36.6	14.2	18.9
Jefferson	11,500	52.8	47.2	61.1	33.5	4.7	26.8	38.4	16.4	18.4
Lafayette	6,501	63.2	36.8	73.0	16.1	10.1	38.5	33.3	11.8	16.4

Continued . . .

Table 21.25. VOTING-AGE POPULATION: ESTIMATES BY SPECIFIED SEX, RACE, AND AGE OF PERSONS AGED 18 AND OVER IN THE STATE AND COUNTIES OF FLORIDA APRIL 1, 2006 (Continued)

		Percentage—								
		Sex		Non-Hispanic			Age			
County	Voting-age population	Male	Female	White	Black	Hispanic	18-34	35-54	55-64	65 and over
Lake	221,481	48.1	51.9	84.3	7.2	7.4	19.6	31.6	16.8	32.0
Lee	467,565	48.5	51.5	80.6	5.9	12.5	21.3	31.6	17.3	29.8
Leon	217,307	46.9	53.1	62.5	30.5	4.3	46.5	31.8	11.2	10.5
Levy	30,168	47.7	52.3	84.9	9.4	4.8	23.3	34.2	18.0	24.5
Liberty	6,133	63.5	36.5	69.8	22.0	5.8	36.7	38.1	11.7	13.5
Madison	15,323	53.0	47.0	58.0	36.5	4.6	33.4	33.7	13.6	19.3
Manatee	244,723	48.1	51.9	80.6	7.3	11.0	22.8	32.6	15.8	28.9
Marion	250,431	47.6	52.4	81.6	9.8	7.5	21.0	32.3	16.4	30.3
Martin	116,955	48.5	51.5	87.0	4.5	7.7	16.9	32.2	17.2	33.7
Miami-Dade	1,841,729	47.4	52.6	16.6	18.2	63.5	30.3	38.4	13.4	17.9
Monroe	66,599	52.9	47.1	77.3	4.6	16.8	21.2	40.5	18.9	19.5
Nassau	52,460	48.9	51.1	90.6	6.6	1.9	24.0	39.0	18.1	18.9
Okaloosa	147,256	49.7	50.3	81.6	9.5	5.3	30.5	38.0	14.6	16.9
Okeechobee	28,885	53.6	46.4	71.9	8.3	18.5	29.3	34.6	13.4	22.7
Orange	801,252	49.2	50.8	53.5	19.2	22.9	36.9	38.9	11.7	12.4
Osceola	186,434	49.1	50.9	51.2	7.8	37.7	32.7	39.7	13.4	14.2
Palm Beach	1,012,014	47.6	52.4	70.8	13.5	13.8	23.3	34.6	14.5	27.6
Pasco	335,645	47.7	52.3	88.9	2.4	7.1	20.8	32.8	16.0	30.4
Pinellas	767,719	47.4	52.6	83.0	8.9	5.5	22.2	35.8	15.8	26.2
Polk	429,154	48.5	51.5	73.9	12.7	12.0	26.7	34.4	15.2	23.7
Putnam	56,696	48.5	51.5	77.7	14.8	6.6	24.5	33.9	16.9	24.7
St. Johns	129,697	48.3	51.7	90.3	5.4	3.1	24.3	39.4	16.7	19.6
St. Lucie	202,141	48.3	51.7	74.5	13.7	10.6	22.8	33.7	15.7	27.9
Santa Rosa	106,423	49.7	50.3	89.2	4.5	3.5	27.6	41.1	15.3	16.0
Sarasota	318,018	47.0	53.0	90.2	3.5	5.3	15.8	29.5	17.8	36.9
Seminole	320,039	48.6	51.4	73.2	10.0	13.5	30.0	41.6	14.2	14.2
Sumter	69,920	53.4	46.6	81.0	9.6	8.7	20.1	28.3	15.1	36.5
Suwannee	30,251	49.0	51.0	82.4	10.0	6.7	26.3	34.0	16.0	23.7
Taylor	16,630	52.8	47.2	76.9	19.6	1.9	28.6	37.2	16.0	18.3
Union	11,994	69.4	30.6	69.4	24.5	4.8	34.0	44.7	11.5	9.8
Volusia	404,644	48.2	51.8	81.8	8.7	8.1	24.0	33.8	15.9	26.3
Wakulla	22,065	53.4	46.6	84.9	11.4	2.8	27.5	41.5	16.2	14.8
Walton	44,468	50.5	49.5	87.7	6.7	3.6	24.2	37.5	16.0	22.2
Washington	18,043	53.4	46.6	81.2	13.6	3.0	28.2	36.3	15.4	20.1

Source: University of Florida, Bureau of Economic and Business Research, Population Program, *Florida Population Studies,* June 2007, Volume 40, Bulletin No. 148.

Table 21.26. VOTING-AGE POPULATION: PROJECTIONS, APRIL 1, 2030, OF PERSONS AGED 18 AND OVER BY SEX, RACE, AND AGE IN THE STATE AND COUNTIES OF FLORIDA

County	Voting-age population	Percentage— Sex Male	Female	Non-Hispanic White	Black	Hispanic	Age 18-34	35-54	55-64	65 and over
Florida	21,219,318	48.3	51.7	56.1	15.3	25.5	23.8	28.9	14.8	32.5
Alachua	259,600	48.5	51.5	61.6	21.0	12.1	41.7	26.3	10.8	21.2
Baker	26,331	52.6	47.4	84.2	10.4	4.4	27.2	32.0	13.9	26.9
Bay	182,745	48.5	51.5	78.0	10.9	7.8	20.6	29.1	16.0	34.3
Bradford	28,208	56.7	43.3	73.7	20.4	4.1	28.8	32.2	12.4	26.6
Brevard	626,270	48.3	51.7	77.6	9.5	10.0	18.7	26.3	15.4	39.6
Broward	1,838,340	47.8	52.2	36.4	27.3	31.7	25.6	33.6	14.7	26.1
Calhoun	14,012	53.3	46.7	75.0	16.4	6.1	29.1	32.8	12.2	25.9
Charlotte	204,236	47.6	52.4	84.6	6.9	6.2	12.9	20.8	15.9	50.4
Citrus	171,071	47.9	52.1	88.6	3.3	6.4	13.2	21.1	16.0	49.7
Clay	230,755	48.7	51.3	77.5	9.7	8.9	24.5	32.1	15.0	28.4
Collier	488,736	48.9	51.1	66.6	5.8	26.4	19.2	24.2	15.3	41.3
Columbia	69,907	51.3	48.7	77.8	14.6	6.0	25.0	27.6	14.0	33.4
DeSoto	38,007	54.6	45.4	52.1	9.3	37.7	29.0	25.9	12.8	32.3
Dixie	17,737	52.2	47.8	89.5	7.5	2.2	23.5	24.4	13.5	38.5
Duval	936,800	47.6	52.4	51.4	31.8	11.7	27.3	31.9	14.7	26.1
Escambia	300,604	48.5	51.5	67.8	22.0	5.8	30.2	27.8	12.8	29.1
Flagler	180,763	47.3	52.7	79.3	10.0	8.4	15.0	21.7	15.4	47.8
Franklin	12,501	53.4	46.6	82.5	13.1	3.4	21.6	28.4	14.2	35.8
Gadsden	44,581	47.7	52.3	30.8	52.3	14.8	29.3	30.0	12.8	27.9
Gilchrist	21,590	50.6	49.4	89.0	6.2	4.2	21.6	27.5	15.1	35.7
Glades	11,025	56.5	43.5	59.3	8.2	28.6	23.9	29.9	16.7	29.5
Gulf	17,156	57.6	42.4	77.3	16.8	4.3	24.0	29.6	12.7	33.7
Hamilton	13,724	58.8	41.2	53.8	31.8	13.0	29.7	31.9	12.6	25.9
Hardee	24,881	53.5	46.5	42.0	9.2	47.7	36.3	31.5	11.0	21.2
Hendry	38,026	51.8	48.2	30.3	9.6	59.0	40.1	32.2	10.2	17.6
Hernando	204,681	47.9	52.1	82.4	5.2	10.8	15.2	22.2	15.6	47.0
Highlands	110,479	48.4	51.6	67.6	8.2	22.5	16.7	20.9	14.5	47.8
Hillsborough	1,310,265	48.2	51.8	48.4	17.8	29.6	28.4	31.9	14.1	25.5
Holmes	18,436	52.7	47.3	85.3	9.4	2.8	28.7	31.5	12.2	27.6
Indian River	175,419	48.2	51.8	78.5	8.1	12.0	16.1	22.5	15.2	46.2
Jackson	50,650	55.5	44.5	66.4	27.0	4.5	25.9	29.1	12.7	32.2
Jefferson	14,206	52.4	47.6	65.3	25.7	7.7	22.0	30.8	14.6	32.6
Lafayette	8,201	61.1	38.9	69.0	14.4	15.4	34.5	32.6	10.7	22.2

Continued . . .

Table 21.26. VOTING-AGE POPULATION: PROJECTIONS, APRIL 1, 2030, OF PERSONS AGED 18 AND OVER BY SEX, RACE, AND AGE IN THE STATE AND COUNTIES OF FLORIDA (Continued)

		Percentage—								
		Sex		Non-Hispanic			Age			
County	Voting-age population	Male	Female	White	Black	Hispanic	18-34	35-54	55-64	65 and over
Lake	410,079	48.4	51.6	78.0	8.2	12.3	16.6	24.1	15.6	43.7
Lee	862,684	48.5	51.5	70.5	7.0	21.0	19.0	24.5	15.3	41.2
Leon	291,798	47.0	53.0	53.2	36.4	6.1	42.4	27.1	11.0	19.5
Levy	45,904	48.3	51.7	80.2	8.4	10.3	21.0	27.4	15.5	36.1
Liberty	7,791	60.6	39.4	65.7	24.3	6.5	33.3	32.6	11.6	22.5
Madison	18,645	53.2	46.8	54.2	33.9	10.3	28.8	33.0	11.9	26.4
Manatee	369,986	48.7	51.3	70.2	8.3	19.9	20.7	27.1	15.3	36.9
Marion	418,758	48.2	51.8	76.0	9.7	12.9	18.0	25.1	15.4	41.5
Martin	169,629	48.5	51.5	81.8	4.7	12.5	14.7	22.9	15.3	47.2
Miami-Dade	2,434,298	47.1	52.9	6.9	18.0	72.8	27.0	31.9	15.7	25.4
Monroe	67,975	50.5	49.5	75.1	4.8	18.5	20.6	24.8	14.7	39.9
Nassau	86,990	48.6	51.4	90.5	5.0	3.7	18.8	28.3	16.5	36.4
Okaloosa	211,448	48.9	51.1	75.2	10.3	10.4	24.8	29.9	14.7	30.6
Okeechobee	36,606	51.8	48.2	65.3	8.3	24.8	26.9	29.2	13.6	30.3
Orange	1,307,357	49.1	50.9	36.1	22.8	35.0	31.9	33.6	13.9	20.6
Osceola	406,417	49.2	50.8	34.2	9.8	52.0	27.3	32.6	16.2	24.0
Palm Beach	1,522,322	47.7	52.3	60.7	16.4	20.2	21.2	27.2	14.3	37.2
Pasco	555,739	48.5	51.5	81.4	3.7	12.4	18.9	25.8	15.4	39.9
Pinellas	872,209	48.4	51.6	73.3	12.3	10.3	20.5	28.2	14.9	36.3
Polk	649,199	48.7	51.3	61.1	14.1	22.9	23.4	28.6	15.0	33.1
Putnam	69,131	48.6	51.4	70.2	15.2	13.3	22.8	27.4	15.3	34.4
St. Johns	251,449	48.5	51.5	88.7	4.6	5.5	21.0	29.2	15.5	34.3
St. Lucie	375,608	48.3	51.7	66.5	14.2	17.6	19.9	25.0	15.0	40.1
Santa Rosa	179,627	49.7	50.3	85.0	4.9	7.0	23.8	32.2	15.5	28.5
Sarasota	471,295	47.8	52.2	84.8	3.7	10.3	13.3	21.0	15.5	50.2
Seminole	477,431	48.9	51.1	62.5	12.2	20.7	25.4	35.3	14.8	24.4
Sumter	145,194	50.3	49.7	83.8	5.6	10.0	17.7	21.8	13.8	46.7
Suwannee	45,570	50.1	49.9	77.1	7.9	14.1	21.2	29.4	14.8	34.6
Taylor	21,106	52.4	47.6	76.6	18.2	3.2	23.7	31.8	14.5	30.0
Union	15,388	65.9	34.1	70.7	21.1	6.6	31.8	36.4	11.2	20.5
Volusia	577,534	48.5	51.5	75.0	8.9	14.4	20.7	26.1	15.2	37.9
Wakulla	40,870	53.2	46.8	86.4	9.5	3.0	22.3	31.1	15.1	31.5
Walton	87,769	49.5	50.5	84.7	5.9	7.4	19.6	29.0	15.4	36.0
Washington	25,569	54.9	45.1	80.0	12.2	5.3	27.0	31.0	12.9	29.1

Source: University of Florida, Bureau of Economic and Business Research, Population Program, *Florida Population Studies,* June 2007, Volume 40, Bulletin No. 148.

Table 21.30. VOTERS: REGISTERED VOTERS BY PARTY IN THE STATE AND COUNTIES OF FLORIDA, MAY 2007

County	Total	Republican		Democrat		Minor		No party affiliation	
		Number	Percentage	Number	Percentage	Number	Percentage	Number	Percentage
Florida	10,251,312	3,852,823	37.6	4,150,002	40.5	321,301	3.1	1,927,186	18.8
Alachua	124,350	35,281	28.4	64,470	51.8	3,500	2.8	21,099	17.0
Baker	13,249	3,819	28.8	8,470	63.9	169	1.3	791	6.0
Bay	105,525	48,236	45.7	38,260	36.3	3,249	3.1	15,780	15.0
Bradford	14,599	4,695	32.2	8,340	57.1	303	2.1	1,261	8.6
Brevard	305,970	138,819	45.4	110,873	36.2	10,751	3.5	45,527	14.9
Broward	947,128	245,513	25.9	478,104	50.5	12,994	1.4	210,517	22.2
Calhoun	8,547	1,262	14.8	6,744	78.9	125	1.5	416	4.9
Charlotte	118,277	51,418	43.5	36,614	31.0	5,082	4.3	25,163	21.3
Citrus	96,763	40,298	41.6	36,087	37.3	2,850	2.9	17,528	18.1
Clay	112,285	63,338	56.4	28,340	25.2	3,441	3.1	17,166	15.3
Collier	191,993	98,608	51.4	46,528	24.2	7,978	4.2	38,879	20.3
Columbia	36,998	12,660	34.2	19,441	52.5	1,352	3.7	3,545	9.6
DeSoto	15,935	4,289	26.9	8,940	56.1	362	2.3	2,344	14.7
Dixie	10,776	1,961	18.2	7,761	72.0	250	2.3	804	7.5
Duval	547,847	201,775	36.8	245,615	44.8	20,203	3.7	80,254	14.6
Escambia	179,538	78,794	43.9	72,042	40.1	5,315	3.0	23,387	13.0
Flagler	51,105	19,824	38.8	18,923	37.0	1,484	2.9	10,874	21.3
Franklin	7,508	1,476	19.7	5,475	72.9	106	1.4	451	6.0
Gadsden	28,443	3,433	12.1	23,113	81.3	372	1.3	1,525	5.4
Gilchrist	9,768	3,280	33.6	5,284	54.1	223	2.3	981	10.0
Glades	6,241	1,690	27.1	3,794	60.8	78	1.2	679	10.9
Gulf	9,049	2,702	29.9	5,723	63.2	117	1.3	507	5.6
Hamilton	7,649	1,344	17.6	5,689	74.4	193	2.5	423	5.5
Hardee	11,136	3,319	29.8	6,587	59.2	118	1.1	1,112	10.0
Hendry	15,822	5,065	32.0	8,473	53.6	501	3.2	1,783	11.3
Hernando	123,105	49,788	40.4	46,886	38.1	4,884	4.0	21,547	17.5
Highlands	62,205	27,582	44.3	24,290	39.0	1,923	3.1	8,410	13.5
Hillsborough	632,901	220,104	34.8	257,793	40.7	21,509	3.4	133,495	21.1
Holmes	10,957	2,595	23.7	7,606	69.4	101	0.9	655	6.0
Indian River	81,540	41,046	50.3	24,136	29.6	2,961	3.6	13,397	16.4
Jackson	27,276	6,575	24.1	18,786	68.9	342	1.3	1,573	5.8
Jefferson	9,733	2,054	21.1	6,918	71.1	227	2.3	534	5.5
Lafayette	4,335	766	17.7	3,347	77.2	67	1.5	155	3.6
Lake	168,130	78,274	46.6	56,573	33.6	7,100	4.2	26,183	15.6

See footnote at end of table.

Continued . . .

Table 21.30. VOTERS: REGISTERED VOTERS BY PARTY IN THE STATE AND COUNTIES OF FLORIDA, MAY 2007 (Continued)

County	Total	Republican Number	Republican Percentage	Democrat Number	Democrat Percentage	Minor Number	Minor Percentage	No party affiliation Number	No party affiliation Percentage
Lee	246,521	119,359	48.4	69,585	28.2	8,226	3.3	49,351	20.0
Leon	149,572	42,113	28.2	85,230	57.0	3,810	2.5	18,419	12.3
Levy	23,320	6,872	29.5	13,103	56.2	1,113	4.8	2,232	9.6
Liberty	3,842	356	9.3	3,323	86.5	33	0.9	130	3.4
Madison	11,595	1,922	16.6	8,856	76.4	192	1.7	625	5.4
Manatee	190,602	83,934	44.0	61,635	32.3	6,282	3.3	38,751	20.3
Marion	201,389	85,924	42.7	78,277	38.9	12,156	6.0	25,032	12.4
Martin	92,568	47,344	51.1	25,521	27.6	5,424	5.9	14,279	15.4
Miami-Dade	1,052,601	357,568	34.0	442,672	42.1	12,050	1.1	240,311	22.8
Monroe	49,383	18,737	37.9	17,193	34.8	1,848	3.7	11,605	23.5
Nassau	45,476	23,097	50.8	15,388	33.8	1,749	3.8	5,242	11.5
Okaloosa	122,583	71,978	58.7	28,696	23.4	1,578	1.3	20,331	16.6
Okeechobee	17,358	5,318	30.6	9,836	56.7	469	2.7	1,735	10.0
Orange	508,864	176,558	34.7	203,286	39.9	15,268	3.0	113,752	22.4
Osceola	133,711	41,828	31.3	53,553	40.1	5,086	3.8	33,244	24.9
Palm Beach	779,588	240,934	30.9	346,544	44.5	29,617	3.8	162,493	20.8
Pasco	272,991	109,112	40.0	99,797	36.6	15,785	5.8	48,297	17.7
Pinellas	592,930	227,404	38.4	222,442	37.5	26,481	4.5	116,603	19.7
Polk	286,044	111,366	38.9	118,455	41.4	9,291	3.2	46,932	16.4
Putnam	43,444	12,915	29.7	24,111	55.5	970	2.2	5,448	12.5
St. Johns	123,528	65,591	53.1	33,601	27.2	4,815	3.9	19,521	15.8
St. Lucie	149,329	52,888	35.4	61,781	41.4	6,082	4.1	28,578	19.1
Santa Rosa	101,186	56,817	56.2	27,134	26.8	3,058	3.0	14,177	14.0
Sarasota	256,145	118,873	46.4	80,001	31.2	7,263	2.8	50,008	19.5
Seminole	242,111	105,559	43.6	78,162	32.3	7,974	3.3	50,416	20.8
Sumter	52,059	24,188	46.5	19,093	36.7	1,995	3.8	6,783	13.0
Suwannee	23,924	7,036	29.4	14,272	59.7	1,245	5.2	1,371	5.7
Taylor	12,193	2,640	21.7	8,765	71.9	246	2.0	542	4.4
Union	6,543	1,467	22.4	4,674	71.4	70	1.1	332	5.1
Volusia	299,108	105,935	35.4	118,068	39.5	9,418	3.1	65,687	22.0
Wakulla	16,752	4,471	26.7	10,531	62.9	455	2.7	1,295	7.7
Walton	32,001	16,640	52.0	10,821	33.8	742	2.3	3,798	11.9
Washington	15,368	4,396	28.6	9,571	62.3	280	1.8	1,121	7.3

Note: See Table 21.25 for voting-age population.

Source: State of Florida, Department of State, Division of Elections, "Voter Registration by Party Affiliation and County, May 2007," Internet site <http://election.dos.state.fl.us/> (accessed 3, July 2007).

Table 21.31. VOTER TURNOUT: NUMBER REPORTED REGISTERED AND VOTED IN THE STATE AND COUNTIES OF FLORIDA, NOVEMBER 7, 2006

County	Registered voters	Voter turnout Number	Voter turnout Percent-age
Florida	10,433,148	4,884,544	46.8
Alachua	147,411	71,150	48.3
Baker	12,997	6,380	49.1
Bay	107,996	48,570	45.0
Bradford	14,275	7,231	50.7
Brevard	315,877	188,153	59.6
Broward	923,647	411,489	44.6
Calhoun	8,517	3,457	40.6
Charlotte	117,250	55,774	47.6
Citrus	98,226	51,970	52.9
Clay	113,010	51,969	46.0
Collier	186,236	87,673	47.1
Columbia	36,260	15,769	43.5
DeSoto	15,676	6,672	42.6
Dixie	10,566	5,164	48.9
Duval	537,453	227,365	42.3
Escambia	187,489	87,864	46.9
Flagler	49,688	29,860	60.1
Franklin	7,452	4,012	53.8
Gadsden	28,098	14,147	50.3
Gilchrist	9,591	5,405	56.4
Glades	6,162	2,849	46.2
Gulf	9,086	4,935	54.3
Hamilton	7,974	3,635	45.6
Hardee	11,001	4,555	41.4
Hendry	15,670	5,508	35.1
Hernando	119,604	57,305	47.9
Highlands	60,709	30,606	50.4
Hillsborough	634,037	291,909	46.0
Holmes	10,751	5,581	51.9
Indian River	87,085	43,898	50.4
Jackson	26,607	13,271	49.9
Jefferson	9,749	6,078	62.3
Lafayette	4,322	2,205	51.0
Lake	178,144	87,074	48.9
Lee	326,923	155,846	47.7
Leon	143,482	91,272	63.6
Levy	24,141	11,449	47.4
Liberty	4,042	1,840	45.5
Madison	11,504	6,011	52.3
Manatee	198,974	100,637	50.6
Marion	200,190	101,727	50.8
Martin	99,349	53,313	53.7
Miami-Dade	1,090,048	410,985	37.7
Monroe	47,175	24,235	51.4
Nassau	44,032	22,651	51.4
Okaloosa	124,257	56,518	45.5
Okeechobee	18,929	8,375	44.2
Orange	568,546	221,594	39.0
Osceola	127,261	45,249	35.6
Palm Beach	764,463	371,368	48.6
Pasco	263,167	130,170	49.5
Pinellas	617,939	294,632	47.7
Polk	293,480	142,958	48.7
Putnam	42,303	19,930	47.1
St. Johns	125,071	61,437	49.1
St. Lucie	145,616	70,797	48.6
Santa Rosa	98,543	42,733	43.4
Sarasota	250,497	142,532	56.9
Seminole	244,642	119,569	48.9
Sumter	49,471	30,584	61.8
Suwannee	23,613	11,096	47.0
Taylor	12,529	5,665	45.2
Union	6,464	2,934	45.4
Volusia	291,683	153,526	52.6
Wakulla	16,731	9,674	57.8
Walton	34,318	16,377	47.7
Washington	15,149	7,377	48.7

Source: State of Florida, Department of State, Division of Elections, Internet site <http://election.dos.state.fl.us/> (accessed 21, February 2007).

Table 21.32. ELECTION RESULTS: VOTES CAST FOR PRESIDENT AND VICE PRESIDENT IN THE GENERAL ELECTION BY PARTY IN THE STATE AND COUNTIES OF FLORIDA, NOVEMBER 2, 2004

County	Bush and Cheney (REP)	Kerry and Edwards (DEM)	Nader and Camejo (REF)	Badnarik and Campagna (LIB)	Peroutka and Baldwin (CPF)	Cobb and LaMarche (GRE)	Brown and Herbert (SPF)	Harris and Trowe (SWP)
Florida	3,964,522	3,583,544	32,971	11,996	6,626	3,917	3,502	2,732
Alachua	47,762	62,504	559	363	61	52	13	14
Baker	7,738	2,180	22	7	2	3	1	2
Bay	53,404	21,068	359	89	32	48	12	12
Bradford	7,557	3,244	28	14	7	3	2	0
Brevard	153,068	110,309	1,197	511	208	117	27	25
Broward	244,674	453,873	3,813	1,123	941	646	1,100	702
Calhoun	3,782	2,116	38	8	4	6	3	6
Charlotte	44,428	34,256	556	179	70	63	115	119
Citrus	39,500	29,277	452	107	68	35	11	17
Clay	62,078	18,971	258	114	40	22	6	6
Collier	83,631	43,892	598	181	104	83	129	65
Columbia	16,758	8,031	109	47	13	17	6	10
DeSoto	5,524	3,913	48	12	9	2	2	0
Dixie	4,434	1,960	29	5	8	1	3	2
Duval	220,190	158,610	1,221	631	179	141	55	34
Escambia	93,566	48,329	548	218	527	48	27	15
Flagler	19,633	18,578	181	54	17	10	3	4
Franklin	3,472	2,401	37	3	8	7	0	3
Gadsden	6,253	14,629	54	18	9	8	3	10
Gilchrist	4,936	2,017	32	17	5	4	2	2
Glades	2,443	1,718	16	4	3	1	1	2
Gulf	4,805	2,407	41	8	6	5	2	3
Hamilton	2,792	2,260	16	2	3	4	2	0
Hardee	5,049	2,149	39	6	1	1	3	1
Hendry	5,757	3,960	24	7	15	10	0	2
Hernando	42,635	37,187	521	94	59	19	18	14
Highlands	25,878	15,347	188	28	27	12	12	4
Hillsborough	245,576	214,132	1,954	769	364	227	93	107
Holmes	6,412	1,810	42	14	12	1	6	3
Indian River	36,938	23,956	292	93	60	37	13	25
Jackson	12,122	7,555	74	24	16	9	7	0
Jefferson	3,298	4,135	27	6	4	5	1	2
Lafayette	2,460	845	11	1	6	1	1	0

See footnotes at end of table.   Continued . . .

Table 21.32. ELECTION RESULTS: VOTES CAST FOR PRESIDENT AND VICE PRESIDENT IN THE GENERAL ELECTION BY PARTY IN THE STATE AND COUNTIES OF FLORIDA, NOVEMBER 2, 2004 (Continued)

County	Bush and Cheney (REP)	Kerry and Edwards (DEM)	Nader and Camejo (REF)	Badnarik and Campagna (LIB)	Peroutka and Baldwin (CPF)	Cobb and LaMarche (GRE)	Brown and Herbert (SPF)	Harris and Trowe (SWP)
Lake	74,389	48,221	659	230	129	97	143	82
Lee	144,176	93,860	1,379	453	208	188	243	160
Leon	51,615	83,873	476	255	87	47	14	12
Levy	10,410	6,074	97	27	22	12	6	4
Liberty	1,927	1,070	14	2	6	0	1	1
Madison	4,191	4,050	41	10	5	4	1	2
Manatee	81,318	61,262	683	206	72	48	18	14
Marion	81,283	57,271	650	225	145	51	21	31
Martin	41,362	30,208	418	124	82	75	106	78
Miami-Dade	361,095	409,732	2,041	638	494	323	178	225
Monroe	19,467	19,654	283	87	14	19	5	6
Nassau	23,783	8,573	183	58	29	22	59	36
Okaloosa	69,693	19,368	372	171	95	41	11	5
Okeechobee	6,978	5,153	32	11	5	5	4	2
Orange	192,539	193,354	1,144	590	238	120	37	22
Osceola	43,117	38,633	281	91	32	34	7	9
Palm Beach	212,688	328,687	1,568	617	575	226	106	155
Pasco	103,230	84,749	1,440	577	205	217	292	206
Pinellas	225,686	225,460	2,402	864	410	255	140	140
Polk	123,559	86,009	799	225	121	63	34	20
Putnam	18,311	12,412	136	60	25	19	5	5
St. Johns	59,196	26,399	403	218	28	34	8	4
St. Lucie	47,592	51,835	436	99	45	32	14	10
Santa Rosa	52,059	14,659	296	97	154	25	15	2
Sarasota	104,692	88,442	1,259	507	176	126	243	207
Seminole	108,172	76,971	570	329	82	48	12	11
Sumter	19,800	11,584	248	41	38	34	57	40
Suwannee	11,153	4,522	85	25	8	5	3	1
Taylor	5,467	3,049	45	7	7	1	3	2
Union	3,396	1,251	16	2	4	5	1	0
Volusia	111,924	115,519	912	333	131	69	31	20
Wakulla	6,777	4,896	47	20	9	9	1	4
Walton	17,555	6,213	119	26	43	12	4	4
Washington	7,369	2,912	53	14	14	3	0	1

REP Republican Party, DEM Democratic Party, REF Reform Party, LIB Libertarian Party of Florida, CPF Constitution Party of Florida, GRE Green Party of Florida, SPF Socialist Party of Florida, SWP Florida Socialist Workers.

Source: State of Florida, Department of State, Division of Elections, Internet site <http://election.dos.state.fl.us/> (accessed 21, February 2007).

Table 21.33. ELECTION RESULTS: VOTES CAST FOR UNITED STATES SENATOR, NOVEMBER 2, 2004 AND NOVEMBER 7, 2006, AND FOR GOVERNOR AND LIEUTENANT GOVERNOR, NOVEMBER 7, 2006 IN THE STATE AND COUNTIES OF FLORIDA

	United States Senator 1/				Governor/Lieutenant Governor–2006	
	2004		2006			
County	Mel Martinez (R)	Betty Castor (D)	Bill Nelson (D)	Katherine Harris (R)	Charlie Crist/Jeff Kottkamp (R)	Jim Davis/ Daryl L. Jones (D)
Florida	3,672,864	3,590,201	2,890,548	1,826,127	2,519,845	2,178,289
Alachua	43,074	63,809	48,125	20,887	30,139	38,741
Baker	6,815	2,853	2,771	3,420	4,335	1,738
Bay	49,639	22,190	23,526	23,821	31,382	14,802
Bradford	6,534	3,938	3,539	3,486	4,458	2,438
Brevard	142,394	111,477	111,031	72,787	100,148	79,854
Broward	231,266	442,728	293,758	102,847	143,043	256,072
Calhoun	3,133	2,526	2,207	1,146	1,737	1,563
Charlotte	43,079	32,837	31,192	22,836	32,377	21,621
Citrus	33,998	31,699	29,741	20,332	29,038	19,905
Clay	58,131	20,831	19,871	30,697	37,632	12,610
Collier	81,948	40,332	39,741	44,988	59,821	25,303
Columbia	14,014	9,780	7,965	7,393	9,313	5,763
DeSoto	4,994	4,031	3,656	2,869	3,785	2,603
Dixie	3,322	2,735	2,802	2,030	2,651	2,109
Duval	205,001	163,748	120,044	101,107	132,607	87,718
Escambia	88,787	48,274	42,964	42,573	51,195	33,777
Flagler	18,294	18,812	17,957	11,278	15,376	13,589
Franklin	2,706	2,886	2,529	1,349	1,981	1,854
Gadsden	5,230	15,246	11,320	2,527	4,557	9,303
Gilchrist	4,060	2,578	2,843	2,338	3,160	1,906
Glades	2,147	1,821	1,826	1,081	1,572	1,292
Gulf	4,086	2,858	2,916	1,898	2,702	1,985
Hamilton	2,206	2,597	2,187	1,241	1,766	1,637
Hardee	4,024	2,806	2,328	2,157	2,580	1,720
Hendry	5,350	4,027	3,096	2,230	3,056	2,273
Hernando	36,557	39,634	34,316	20,975	29,907	24,412
Highlands	22,326	17,196	16,710	13,053	17,426	11,128
Hillsborough	207,331	230,298	176,114	105,813	153,134	128,946
Holmes	5,114	2,608	2,641	2,700	3,417	1,897
Indian River	34,338	23,511	23,704	18,696	26,812	15,529
Jackson	10,449	8,605	7,994	4,866	6,835	5,900
Jefferson	2,722	4,504	4,438	1,485	2,602	3,275
Lafayette	1,768	1,390	1,247	894	1,346	771
Lake	68,425	49,635	47,749	36,773	53,055	30,419
Lee	139,810	89,048	80,749	69,955	97,221	53,426

See footnotes at end of table. Continued . . .

Table 21.33. ELECTION RESULTS: VOTES CAST FOR UNITED STATES SENATOR, NOVEMBER 2, 2004 AND NOVEMBER 7, 2006, AND FOR GOVERNOR AND LIEUTENANT GOVERNOR, NOVEMBER 7, 2006 IN THE STATE AND COUNTIES OF FLORIDA (Continued)

County	United States Senator 1/				Governor/Lieutenant Governor–2006	
	2004		2006			
	Mel Martinez (R)	Betty Castor (D)	Bill Nelson (D)	Katherine Harris (R)	Charlie Crist/Jeff Kottkamp (R)	Jim Davis/ Daryl L. Jones (D)
Leon	45,453	86,180	66,776	21,959	38,296	50,540
Levy	8,735	7,129	6,298	4,848	6,317	4,558
Liberty	1,448	1,459	1,243	549	907	850
Madison	3,318	4,640	4,040	1,769	2,854	2,915
Manatee	72,829	64,795	55,168	42,713	58,035	38,547
Marion	73,530	60,814	55,933	42,965	57,111	39,744
Martin	39,076	29,868	29,448	22,465	31,071	20,570
Miami-Dade	367,867	366,482	243,075	143,162	183,457	215,930
Monroe	18,075	18,961	14,534	8,893	11,882	11,390
Nassau	21,893	9,519	9,985	11,955	15,454	6,378
Okaloosa	65,146	19,645	20,882	33,895	42,686	12,117
Okeechobee	5,959	5,464	5,243	2,917	4,227	3,853
Orange	188,121	187,549	136,547	78,409	116,412	96,795
Osceola	42,103	36,569	27,050	17,223	23,945	19,864
Palm Beach	200,442	318,042	264,962	96,176	140,531	219,199
Pasco	89,420	90,761	76,957	48,124	68,530	54,479
Pinellas	197,640	234,451	182,572	99,572	148,257	131,046
Polk	108,774	93,231	80,403	58,584	79,071	57,018
Putnam	15,941	13,701	11,117	8,303	10,960	8,140
St. Johns	56,251	27,319	27,329	32,311	40,979	18,554
St. Lucie	44,436	50,660	45,911	23,310	34,787	33,860
Santa Rosa	49,149	15,165	17,268	24,298	29,041	12,361
Sarasota	95,425	91,651	80,177	58,339	76,198	60,214
Seminole	102,898	76,579	62,454	47,119	68,149	40,724
Sumter	17,929	12,844	15,167	14,485	19,771	9,668
Suwannee	9,095	6,069	5,646	5,146	6,995	3,716
Taylor	4,241	3,972	3,375	2,139	3,172	2,327
Union	2,874	1,632	1,510	1,351	1,723	1,086
Volusia	104,032	114,932	96,406	53,817	76,618	72,216
Wakulla	5,240	6,048	6,517	2,802	4,837	4,421
Walton	16,038	6,770	7,145	8,685	10,971	4,835
Washington	6,414	3,452	3,813	3,316	4,435	2,495

(D) Democrat.
(R) Republican.
1/ Excludes other candidates.

Source: State of Florida, Department of State, Division of Elections, Internet site <http://election.dos.state.fl.us/> (accessed 21, February 2007).

Table 21.35. FEMALE OFFICIALS: WOMEN IN U.S. CONGRESS AND STATE LEGISLATURES IN FLORIDA AND THE UNITED STATES, 2007

Area	Total Congress	109th Congress Percent-age of total	Senate	House	Total legis-lators	Women legislators Number	Percent-age of total	Senate	House
Florida	27	18.5	0	5	160	38	23.8	11	27
United States	535	16.3	16	71	7,382	1,734	23.5	422	1,312

Source: Center for the American Woman and Politics (CAWP), Eagleton Institute of Politics, Rutgers University, (copyright), Internet site http://www.cawp.rutgers.edu/> (accessed 21, February 2007).

Table 21.36. BLACK OFFICIALS: BLACK ELECTED OFFICIALS BY OFFICE IN FLORIDA, THE SOUTH AND THE UNITED STATES, JANUARY 2000 AND 2001

Office	Florida 2000	Florida 2001	South 1/ 2000	South 1/ 2001	United States 2000	United States 2001
Total	226	243	6,170	6,179	9,040	9,101
U.S. and state legislatures 2/	23	25	374	379	637	648
City and county offices 3/	155	163	4,058	4,056	5,435	5,471
Law enforcement 4/	33	39	595	606	1,037	1,044
Education 5/	15	16	1,143	1,138	1,930	1,937

1/ Includes Alabama, Arkansas, Delaware, District of Columbia, Florida, Georgia, Kentucky, Louisiana, Maryland, Mississippi, North Carolina, Oklahoma, South Carolina, Tennessee, Texas, Virginia, and West Virginia.
2/ Includes elected state administrators.
3/ County commissioners, councilmen, mayors, vice mayors, aldermen, regional officers, and others.
4/ Judges, magistrates, constables, marshals, sheriffs, justices of the peace, and others.
5/ Members of state education agencies, college boards, school boards, and others.

Source: Joint Center for Political and Economic Studies, Washington, DC, *Black Elected Officials: A Statistical Summary, 2001* (copyright), Internet site <http://www.jointcenter.org/> (accessed 2, August 2006).

Table 21.37. HISPANIC OFFICIALS: HISPANIC ELECTED OFFICIALS BY OFFICE IN FLORIDA THE SOUTH, AND THE UNITED STATES, 2004 AND 2005

Office	Florida 2004	Florida 2005	South 1/ 2004	South 1/ 2005	United States 2004	United States 2005
Total	109	119	2,148	2,231	4,651	4,853
State executives and legislators, including U.S. representatives	16	21	66	77	231	266
County and municipal officials	59	66	908	943	2,059	2,149
Judicial and law enforcement	28	26	407	431	638	678
Education and school boards	6	6	766	780	1,723	1,760

1/ Includes Alabama, Arkansas, Delaware, District of Columbia, Florida, Georgia, Kentucky, Louisiana, Maryland, Mississippi, North Carolina, Oklahoma, South Carolina, Tennessee, Texas, Virginia, and West Virginia.

Source: U.S., Department of Commerce, Census Bureau, *Statistical Abstract of the United States 2007,* Internet site <http://www.census.gov/> (accessed 21, February 2007).

Table 21.42. COMPOSITION OF CONGRESS AND STATE LEGISLATURES: NUMBER OF UNITED STATES REPRESENTATIVES AND SENATORS AND STATE LEGISLATORS BY PARTY AFFILIATION, SPECIFIED YEARS 1997 THROUGH 2006

Year 1/	Florida				United States			
	Demo-crats	Repub-licans	Demo-crats	Repub-licans	Demo-crats	Repub-licans	Demo-crats	Repub-licans
	U.S. representatives		U.S. senators		U.S. representatives		U.S. senators	
1997	8	15	1	1	207	226	45	55
1999	8	15	1	1	212	222	45	55
2001	8	15	2	0	211	221	50	50
2003	7	18	2	0	205	228	48	51
2004	7	18	1	1	205	228	48	51
2005	7	18	1	1	202	231	44	55
2006	7	18	1	1	201	231	44	55
	State representatives		State senators		State representatives		State senators	
1997	59	61	17	23	2,886	2,539	998	931
1998	57	63	17	23	2,903	2,580	1,041	963
2000	43	77	15	25	2,818	2,600	955	931
2001	43	77	15	25	2,809	2,604	990	932
2002	39	81	14	25	2,694	2,687	939	974
2003	39	81	14	26	2,700	2,693	941	977
2005	36	84	14	26	2,704	2,683	951	963
2006	36	84	14	26	2,702	2,675	952	964

1/ U.S. representative and senator data refer to the beginning of the first session. State legislative data refer to election years.

Note: Excludes vacancies and persons classified as Independents.

Source: U.S., House of Representatives, Office of the Clerk, Internet site <http://clerk.house.gov/> (accessed 16, June 2006), and U.S., Department of Commerce, Census Bureau, *Statistical Abstract of the United States, 2007,* and previous editions, Internet site <http://www.census.gov/> (accessed 21, February 2007).

Table 21.43. APPORTIONMENT: MEMBERSHIP IN THE UNITED STATES HOUSE OF REPRESENTATIVES FOR FLORIDA AND THE UNITED STATES, 1840 THROUGH 2000

Census of–	Florida	United States	Census of–	Florida	United States
1840	A/ 1	232	1930	5	435
1850	1	237	1940	6	435
1860	1	243	1950	8	437
1870	2	293	1960	12	435
1880	2	332	1970	15	435
1890	2	357	1980	19	435
1900	3	391	1990	23	435
1910	4	435	2000	25	435

A/ Assigned after apportionment.

Note: Total membership includes representatives assigned to newly admitted states after the apportionment acts. Population figures used for apportionment purposes are those determined for states by each decennial census.

Source: U.S., Department of Commerce, Census Bureau, "Apportionment Population and Number of Representatives, by State: Census 2000," released December 28, 2000, Internet site <http://www.census.gov/> (accessed 19, June 2006), and previous reports.

COURTS AND LAW ENFORCEMENT

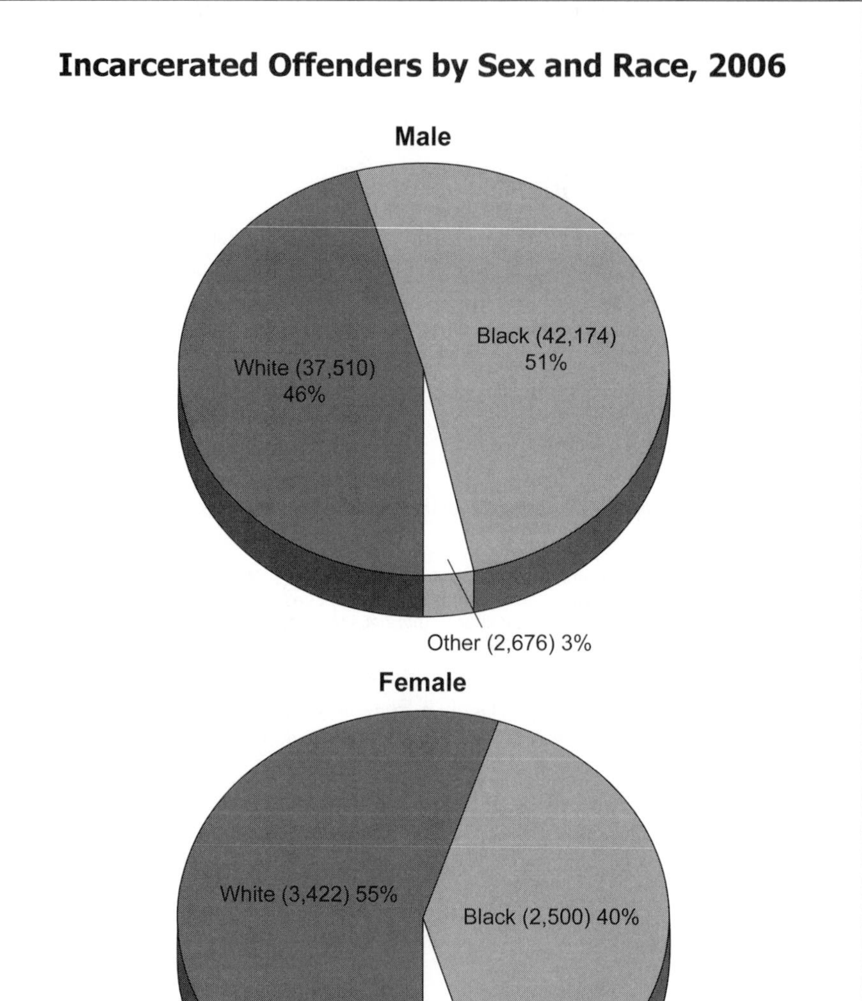

Source: Table 22.11

Section 22.00
Courts and Law Enforcement

This section presents data on criminal offenses and crime rates; firearms usage in crimes; domestic violence, hate crimes, and juvenile delinquency; prisoners and capital punishment; county detention facilities population; and victim services and legal assistance.

Explanatory notes. Data on criminal offenses are subject to certain limitations. Many crimes are not reported to law enforcement agencies and hence, are not counted in preparing crime statistics. Victims may report crimes to prosecuting authorities rather than to law enforcement agencies or, for various reasons, may not report at all.

An additional factor to consider when studying crime rates in Florida is the presence of large numbers of tourists. The crime rates in this section are based on resident population. Crime rates in Florida drop when adjustments are made for the tourist presence.

Sources. The principal source of data on crimes in Florida is the *Florida Uniform Crime Report,* the annual report of the Florida Statistical Analysis Center of the Florida Department of Law Enforcement (FDLE), published on the Internet. Other FDLE statistics, including the use of firearms in violent crimes and the number of domestic violence offenses, are also available on the FDLE Web site.

National sources for criminal justice system data include Internet publications from two divisions of the U.S. Department of Justice: the Federal Bureau of Investigation publishes the annual *Crime in the United States* and the Bureau of Justice Statistics publishes various reports in their *Bureau of Justice Statistics Bulletin.*

The Florida Department of Corrections (FDOC) publishes population under criminal sentence data for both incarerated and community supervision offenders in its *Annual Report* on the Internet. The FDOC Bureau of Planning, Research, and Statistics issues data on county jails in *Florida County Detention Facilities Annual Report,* also available on the Internet.

Online juvenile delinquency data are from the Office of Research and Planning in the Florida Department of Juvenile Justice and appear in the publication, *Profile of Delinquency Cases and Youths Referred at Each Stage of the Juvenile Justice System.*

The Florida Office of the Attorney General publishes victim compensation data in the *Annual Report* of the state Division of Victim Services. Hate crime statistics appear in *Hate Crimes in Florida.* Both reports are on the Internet.

The Florida Bar provides state and county data on its members and the office of Labor Market Statistics in the Florida Agency for Workforce Innovation, furnishes current legal services employment and payroll data.

Section 22.00
Courts and Law Enforcement

Tables listed by major heading

Tables listed by major heading

Table 22.01. CRIMINAL OFFENSES AND RATES: CRIME INDEX OFFENSES BY TYPE OF OFFENSE IN FLORIDA, 1999 THROUGH 2006

Item	Total index offenses 1/	Violent crime: Murder	Violent crime: Forcible sex	Violent crime: Robbery	Violent crime: Aggravated assault	Nonviolent crime: Burglary	Nonviolent crime: Larceny	Nonviolent crime: Motor vehicle theft
Number of index offenses 2/								
1999	934,349	856	12,583	31,996	83,424	180,785	532,462	92,243
2000	895,708	890	12,388	31,392	83,371	170,131	509,616	87,920
2001	911,292	867	12,756	32,808	83,892	175,671	515,501	89,797
2002	900,155	906	12,810	32,413	81,776	176,058	508,213	87,979
2003	881,615	924	12,756	31,512	79,044	170,577	505,266	81,536
2004	850,490	946	12,427	29,984	80,340	166,255	482,243	78,295
2005	838,063	881	12,230	30,092	82,622	164,777	472,257	75,204
2006	849,926	1,129	11,567	34,123	82,682	170,733	473,281	76,411
Percentage change from previous year								
1999	-8.9	-11.4	-0.9	-11.4	-7.2	-10.7	-8.0	-11.4
2000	-4.1	4.0	-1.5	-1.9	-0.1	-5.9	-4.3	-4.7
2001	1.7	-2.6	3.0	4.5	0.6	3.3	1.2	2.1
2002	-1.2	4.5	0.4	-1.2	-2.5	0.2	-1.4	-2.0
2003	-2.1	2.0	-0.4	-2.8	-3.3	-3.1	-0.6	-7.3
2004	-3.5	2.4	-2.6	-4.8	1.6	-2.5	-4.6	-4.0
2005	-1.5	-6.9	-1.6	0.4	2.8	-0.9	-2.1	-3.9
2006	1.4	28.1	-5.4	13.4	0.1	3.6	0.2	1.6
Rate per 100,000 population								
1999	6,098.1	5.6	82.1	208.8	544.5	1,179.9	3,475.1	602.0
2000	5,604.3	5.6	77.5	196.4	521.6	1,064.5	3,188.6	550.1
2001	5,579.9	5.3	78.1	200.9	513.7	1,075.6	3,156.4	549.8
2002	5,398.4	5.4	76.8	194.4	490.4	1,055.8	3,047.8	527.6
2003	5,164.2	5.4	74.7	184.6	463.0	999.2	2,959.7	477.6
2004	4,855.3	5.4	70.9	171.2	458.6	949.1	2,753.0	447.0
2005	4,677.2	4.9	68.3	167.9	461.1	919.6	2,635.6	419.7
2006	4,632.0	6.2	63.0	186.0	450.6	930.5	2,579.3	416.4
Percentage change from previous year								
1999	-10.8	-13.2	-3.0	-13.3	-9.1	-12.6	-9.9	-13.2
2000	-8.1	-0.3	-5.6	-5.9	-4.2	-9.8	-8.2	-8.6
2001	-0.4	-4.7	0.8	2.3	-1.5	1.0	-1.0	0.0
2002	-3.3	2.3	-1.6	-3.2	-4.5	-1.8	-3.4	-4.0
2003	-4.3	-0.4	-2.7	-5.0	-5.6	-5.4	-2.9	-9.5
2004	-6.0	-0.2	-5.1	-7.3	-0.9	-5.0	-7.0	-6.4
2005	-3.7	-9.0	-3.8	-1.9	0.5	-3.1	-4.3	-6.1
2006	-1.0	25.1	-7.6	10.7	-2.3	1.2	-2.1	-0.8

1/ The crimes selected for use in the index are chosen based on their serious nature, their frequency of occurrence, and the reliability of reporting from citizens to law enforcement agencies. The Crime Index is used as a basic measure of crime.

2/ Actual offenses known to law enforcement officers, not the number of persons who committed them or number of injuries they caused.

Note: Rates may not add to totals due to rounding. Percentage changes and rates per 100,000 by offense calculated by the Bureau of Economic and Business Research.

Source: State of Florida, Department of Law Enforcement, Florida Statistical Analysis Center, *Florida Uniform Crime Report, 2006,* and previous reports, Internet site <http://www.fdle.state.fl.us/> (accessed 6, August 2007).

Table 22.02. CRIMINAL OFFENSES AND RATES: CRIME INDEX OFFENSES, CRIME RATES, AND OFFENSES CLEARED IN THE STATE AND COUNTIES OF FLORIDA, 2006

County	Crime index offenses			Crime rate per 100,000 population		Offenses cleared 4/ (percentage)
	Total 1/	Violent 2/	Nonviolent 3/	2006	Percentage change 2005 to 2006	
Florida	849,926	129,501	720,425	4,632.0	-1.0	22.0
Alachua	13,363	2,260	11,103	5,481.6	12.5	19.9
Baker	496	93	403	1,983.7	-25.3	58.1
Bay	7,785	1,300	6,485	4,703.5	-2.8	54.2
Bradford	622	120	502	2,178.6	7.8	50.5
Brevard	21,904	3,622	18,282	4,033.5	5.5	23.1
Broward	75,314	10,764	64,550	4,295.9	-1.7	19.4
Calhoun	128	20	108	907.0	-15.7	51.6
Charlotte	6,193	739	5,454	3,863.0	4.7	20.9
Citrus	3,267	425	2,842	2,389.0	11.2	28.1
Clay	5,416	828	4,588	3,061.6	5.3	41.8
Collier	7,576	1,377	6,199	2,319.2	-4.9	25.3
Columbia	2,398	423	1,975	3,774.1	-6.5	21.1
DeSoto	1,147	237	910	3,458.6	-17.5	35.8
Dixie	540	77	463	3,444.5	2.6	20.9
Duval	53,472	7,078	46,394	6,081.7	-1.9	16.7
Escambia	15,365	2,442	12,923	4,962.1	5.6	27.7
Flagler	2,296	233	2,063	2,575.4	2.2	21.2
Franklin	303	28	275	2,542.8	-9.3	66.3
Gadsden	1,870	423	1,447	3,880.1	-5.8	22.5
Gilchrist	278	22	256	1,664.4	-33.7	17.3
Glades	349	61	288	3,232.7	11.2	26.1
Gulf	351	99	252	2,126.1	2.4	59.5
Hamilton	329	67	262	2,266.3	12.3	28.3
Hardee	886	144	742	3,259.0	-4.7	33.9
Hendry	1,531	299	1,232	3,958.3	-16.5	24.8
Hernando	6,218	687	5,531	3,960.4	7.0	30.9
Highlands	3,362	407	2,955	3,477.7	1.1	20.9
Hillsborough	62,143	9,259	52,884	5,336.8	-2.1	24.5
Holmes	263	50	213	1,348.6	-11.5	45.6
Indian River	4,422	479	3,943	3,269.2	-10.3	22.5
Jackson	1,182	268	914	2,352.4	-6.3	16.9
Jefferson	313	125	188	2,180.7	8.1	42.5
Lafayette	70	18	52	868.5	30.6	42.9
Lake	9,237	1,666	7,571	3,337.3	-1.5	25.5
Lee	23,200	3,157	20,043	3,961.7	0.9	19.4
Leon	12,586	2,116	10,470	4,618.8	-6.3	30.5
Levy	1,510	227	1,283	3,873.7	-4.8	30.0

See footnotes at end of table.   Continued . . .

Table 22.02. CRIMINAL OFFENSES AND RATES: CRIME INDEX OFFENSES, CRIME RATES, AND OFFENSES CLEARED IN THE STATE AND COUNTIES OF FLORIDA, 2006 (Continued)

County	Crime index offenses: Total 1/	Crime index offenses: Violent 2/	Crime index offenses: Non-violent 3/	Crime rate per 100,000 population: 2006	Crime rate per 100,000 population: Percentage change 2005 to 2006	Offenses cleared 4/ (percent-age)
Liberty	48	6	42	617.6	-16.4	41.7
Madison	736	136	600	3,714.5	-2.2	23.9
Manatee	18,276	3,113	15,163	5,831.7	4.9	20.9
Marion	10,390	2,326	8,064	3,297.6	-6.0	46.8
Martin	4,497	625	3,872	3,152.6	10.4	27.7
Miami-Dade	145,346	23,520	121,826	5,964.1	-4.3	15.9
Monroe	4,103	458	3,645	5,096.3	10.7	18.2
Nassau	2,856	990	1,866	4,188.4	23.0	31.7
Okaloosa	6,045	706	5,339	3,137.5	-0.7	36.5
Okeechobee	1,530	302	1,228	3,957.0	0.0	29.5
Orange	68,520	12,709	55,811	6,347.2	3.0	19.9
Osceola	10,832	1,439	9,393	4,232.9	-7.0	24.1
Palm Beach	63,798	9,301	54,497	4,953.3	-0.6	18.7
Pasco	17,086	1,817	15,269	4,026.3	10.6	25.6
Pinellas	47,401	7,333	40,068	4,999.6	-1.1	23.3
Polk	23,943	3,064	20,879	4,237.3	-5.8	23.2
Putnam	4,083	823	3,260	5,486.7	-7.1	41.3
St. Johns	4,823	678	4,145	2,917.9	0.4	17.0
St. Lucie	9,912	1,473	8,439	3,822.4	2.1	26.6
Santa Rosa	2,890	366	2,524	2,043.4	6.9	32.5
Sarasota	14,545	1,511	13,034	3,885.7	0.4	25.2
Seminole	13,581	1,461	12,120	3,228.4	-3.8	25.0
Sumter	1,342	269	1,073	1,624.7	-9.2	29.0
Suwannee	973	197	776	2,507.8	-10.6	28.3
Taylor	494	186	308	2,300.8	-30.8	18.0
Union	267	56	211	1,776.7	-13.8	69.7
Volusia	21,851	2,716	19,135	4,337.5	7.5	23.0
Wakulla	684	114	570	2,409.0	4.9	42.4
Walton	1,038	119	919	1,860.7	-29.2	25.0
Washington	351	47	304	1,521.3	-19.8	51.3

1/ Actual offenses known to law enforcement officers, not the number of persons who committed them or number of injuries they caused.

2/ Includes murder, forcible sex, robbery, and aggravated assault.

3/ Includes breaking and entering (burglary), larceny, and auto theft.

4/ Clearance of an offense occurs when an offender is identified, charged, and taken into custody, or occasionally when some element beyond law enforcement control precludes formal charges against the offender.

Note: Data are aggregates of offenses reported to municipal, county, and state law enforcement agencies and campus police departments.

Source: State of Florida, Department of Law Enforcement, Florida Statistical Analysis Center, *Florida Uniform Crime Report, 2006,* Internet site <http://www.fdle.state.fl.us/> (accessed 6, August 2007).

Table 22.03. CRIMINAL OFFENSES AND RATES: CRIME INDEX OFFENSES AND CRIME RATES IN THE STATE, COUNTIES, CITIES, AND SPECIFIED AREAS OF FLORIDA, 2006

Area	Number of index offenses 1/	Crime rate per 100,000 population
Florida	849,926	4,632.0
Alachua	13,363	5,481.6
Sheriff's office	4,916	4,477.0
Alachua	488	6,373.3
Gainesville	6,853	5,667.4
High Springs	209	4,567.3
Waldo	10	1,218.0
Santa Fe Community College	99	(X)
University of Florida	783	(X)
State agencies	5	(X)
Baker	496	1,983.7
Sheriff's office	495	1,979.7
State agencies	1	(X)
Bay	7,785	4,703.5
Sheriff's office	2,896	3,604.7
Lynn Haven	628	3,820.9
Mexico Beach	48	4,123.7
Panama City	2,531	6,742.1
Panama City Beach	915	9,145.4
Parker	140	2,986.3
Springfield	497	5,511.8
Florida State University Panama City	12	(X)
State agencies	1	(X)
Bradford	622	2,178.6
Sheriff's office	384	1,793.9
Hampton 2/	(NA)	(X)
Lawtey	13	1,949.0
Starke	225	3,717.2
Brevard	21,904	4,033.5
Sheriff's office	6,855	3,009.2
Cocoa	1,557	8,950.8
Cocoa Beach	1,180	9,229.6
Indialantic	100	3,377.2
Indian Harbour Beach	101	1,161.5
Melbourne	4,894	6,377.2
Melbourne Beach	43	1,299.9
Melbourne Village	8	1,118.9
Palm Bay	3,742	3,870.4
Rockledge	782	3,100.1
Satellite Beach	283	2,587.3
Titusville	1,978	4,493.4
West Melbourne	376	2,383.2
Melbourne Airport	1	(X)
State agencies	4	(X)
Broward	75,314	4,295.9
Sheriff's office	1,820	6,543.5
Coconut Creek	1,199	2,483.3
Cooper City	660	2,210.4
Coral Springs	3,241	2,500.5
Dania	1,696	5,939.4
Davie	3,160	3,759.4
Deerfield	3,152	4,169.1
Ft. Lauderdale	11,620	6,608.4
Hallandale	1,971	5,498.8
Hillsboro Beach	21	940.0
Hollywood	6,992	4,879.7
Lauderdale by the Sea	202	3,464.2
Lauderdale Lakes	1,829	5,687.0
Lauderhill	2,977	4,715.4
Lighthouse Point	248	2,275.4
Margate	1,162	2,100.1
Miramar	3,774	3,420.9
North Lauderdale	1,258	3,025.2
Oakland Park	2,955	6,964.9
Parkland	301	1,373.6
Pembroke Park	511	8,902.4
Pembroke Pines	5,249	3,458.2
Plantation	3,937	4,637.7
Pompano Beach	6,352	6,282.7
Sea Ranch Lakes	16	2,191.8
Southwest Ranches	186	2,508.4
Sunrise	3,769	4,203.2
Tamarac	1,388	2,342.3
West Park	659	4,774.0
Weston	1,063	1,724.8
Wilton Manors	737	5,874.4
Ft. Lauderdale International	317	(X)
Port Everglades	39	(X)
Seminole Indian Reservation	641	(X)
State agencies	212	(X)
Calhoun	128	907.0
Sheriff's office	63	568.8
Altha	9	1,601.4
Blountstown	56	2,261.7
Charlotte	6,193	3,863.0
Sheriff's office	5,697	3,973.8
Punta Gorda	490	2,890.5
State agencies	6	(X)
Citrus	3,267	2,389.0
Sheriff's office	2,908	2,186.3
Crystal River	359	9,606.6

See footnotes at end of table.

Continued . . .

Table 22.03. CRIMINAL OFFENSES AND RATES: CRIME INDEX OFFENSES AND CRIME RATES IN THE STATE, COUNTIES, CITIES, AND SPECIFIED AREAS OF FLORIDA, 2006 (Continued)

Area	Number of index offenses 1/	Crime rate per 100,000 population
Clay	5,416	3,061.6
Sheriff's office	4,724	2,925.3
Green Cove Springs	333	5,218.6
Orange Park	359	3,973.9
Collier	7,576	2,319.2
Sheriff's office	6,440	2,236.4
Naples	912	3,970.4
Marco Island	222	1,412.3
State agencies	2	(X)
Columbia	2,398	3,774.1
Sheriff's office	1,350	2,565.6
Lake City	1,048	9,597.9
DeSoto	1,147	3,458.6
Sheriff's office	830	3,142.9
Arcadia	317	4,692.8
Dixie	540	3,444.5
Sheriff's office	410	2,947.7
Cross City	130	7,352.9
Duval	53,472	6,081.7
Atlantic Beach	543	3,874.4
Baldwin 3/	0	(X)
Jacksonville	49,766	5,961.5
Jacksonville Beach	1,661	7,709.8
Neptune Beach	305	4,187.8
Jacksonville Port Authority	98	(X)
University of North Florida	166	(X)
Duval County School Board	924	(X)
State agencies	9	(X)
Escambia	15,365	4,962.1
Sheriff's office	11,731	4,607.4
Pensacola	3,419	6,212.6
Pensacola Junior College	104	(X)
University of West Florida	105	(X)
State agencies	6	(X)
Flagler	2,296	2,575.4
Sheriff's office	1,892	2,332.8
Bunnell	227	9,033.0
Flagler Beach	176	3,180.9
State agencies	1	(X)
Franklin	303	2,542.8
Sheriff's office	162	1,993.4
Apalachicola	91	3,629.8
Carrabelle	50	3,900.2
Gadsden	1,870	3,880.1
Sheriff's office	1,048	3,184.9
Chattahoochee	139	3,626.4
Greensboro	54	8,282.2
Gretna 2/	(NA)	(X)
Havana	89	5,045.4
Quincy	540	7,397.3
Gilchrist	278	1,664.4
Sheriff's office	207	1,378.4
Trenton	70	4,151.8
State agencies	1	(X)
Glades	349	3,232.7
Sheriff's office	349	3,232.7
Gulf	351	2,126.1
Sheriff's office	253	1,989.3
Port St. Joe	98	2,585.1
Hamilton	329	2,266.3
Sheriff's office	277	2,465.9
Jasper 2/	(NA)	(X)
Jennings	19	2,360.2
White Springs	32	4,134.4
State agencies	1	(X)
Hardee	886	3,259.0
Sheriff's office	547	3,022.6
Bowling Green	84	2,723.7
Wauchula	239	5,366.0
Zolfo Springs	16	1,031.6
Hendry	1,531	3,958.3
Sheriff's office	1,206	3,756.4
Clewiston	325	4,944.5
Hernando	6,218	3,960.4
Sheriff's office	5,729	3,827.4
Brooksville	489	6,678.5
Highlands	3,362	3,477.7
Sheriff's office	2,096	2,761.5
Avon Park	476	5,414.0
Lake Placid	140	7,945.5
Sebring	650	6,361.3
Hillsborough	62,143	5,336.8
Sheriff's office	35,496	4,564.4
Plant City	2,135	6,502.4
Tampa	22,629	6,838.9

See footnotes at end of table. Continued . . .

Table 22.03. CRIMINAL OFFENSES AND RATES: CRIME INDEX OFFENSES AND CRIME RATES IN THE STATE, COUNTIES, CITIES, AND SPECIFIED AREAS OF FLORIDA, 2006 (Continued)

Area	Number of index offenses 1/	Crime rate per 100,000 population
Hillsborough (Continued)		
Temple Terrace	1,099	4,771.0
Tampa International Airport	254	(X)
University of South Florida	502	(X)
State agencies	28	(X)
Holmes	263	1,348.6
Sheriff's office	212	1,264.2
Bonifay	50	1,830.2
State agencies	1	(X)
Indian River	4,422	3,269.2
Sheriff's office	3,024	3,472.4
Fellsmere	74	1,599.0
Indian River Shores	35	940.4
Sebastian	563	2,598.5
Vero Beach	718	3,953.7
State agencies	8	(X)
Jackson	1,182	2,352.4
Sheriff's office	780	2,038.2
Cottondale 2/	(NA)	(X)
Graceville	76	3,040.0
Marianna	296	4,510.8
Sneads	30	1,503.0
Jefferson	313	2,180.7
Sheriff's office	215	1,817.0
Monticello	98	3,888.9
Lafayette	70	868.5
Sheriff's office	70	868.5
Lake	9,237	3,337.3
Sheriff's office	4,675	2,879.5
Astatula	23	1,445.6
Clermont	787	3,561.6
Eustis	439	2,471.0
Fruitland Park	110	3,032.0
Groveland	172	2,903.9
Howey-in-the-Hills	5	432.5
Lady Lake	364	2,842.6
Leesburg	1,567	8,317.0
Mascotte	86	2,014.1
Mount Dora	565	5,078.7
Tavares	312	2,485.7
Umatilla	131	4,902.7
State agencies	1	(X)
Lee	23,200	3,961.7
Sheriff's office	13,643	3,799.7
Cape Coral	5,314	3,439.5
Fort Myers	3,847	5,852.8
Sanibel	101	1,597.8
Florida Gulf Coast University	63	(X)
Lee County Airport	224	(X)
State agencies	8	(X)
Leon	12,586	4,618.8
Sheriff's office	2,256	2,346.1
Tallahassee	9,324	5,287.6
Florida A & M University	298	(X)
Florida State University	540	(X)
Florida Capitol Police	27	(X)
Tallahassee Community College	89	(X)
State agencies	52	(X)
Levy	1,510	3,873.7
Sheriff's office	987	3,107.6
Cedar Key	16	1,731.6
Chiefland	232	10,841.1
Inglis	49	2,830.7
Williston	225	9,278.4
State agencies	1	(X)
Liberty	48	617.6
Sheriff's office	48	617.6
Madison	736	3,714.5
Sheriff's office	517	3,094.3
Madison	219	7,050.9
Manatee	18,276	5,831.7
Sheriff's office	13,741	5,962.2
Bradenton	3,050	5,554.4
Bradenton Beach	87	5,602.1
Holmes Beach	176	3,493.4
Longboat Key	96	1,252.4
Palmetto	1,125	8,178.2
State agencies	1	(X)
Marion	10,390	3,297.6
Sheriff's office	6,022	2,340.0
Belleview	298	7,722.2
Dunnellon	67	3,326.7
Ocala	4,001	7,716.0
State agencies	2	(X)

See footnotes at end of table. Continued . . .

Table 22.03. CRIMINAL OFFENSES AND RATES: CRIME INDEX OFFENSES AND CRIME RATES IN THE STATE, COUNTIES, CITIES, AND SPECIFIED AREAS OF FLORIDA, 2006 (Continued)

Area	Number of index offenses 1/	Crime rate per 100,000 population
Martin	4,497	3,152.6
Sheriff's office	3,530	2,861.5
Jupiter Island	19	3,025.5
Sewalls Point	24	1,203.0
Stuart	923	5,539.9
State agencies	1	(X)
Miami-Dade	145,346	5,964.1
Miami-Dade	58,841	5,179.5
Aventura	1,797	6,101.7
Bal Harbour Village	81	2,724.5
Bay Harbor Islands	92	1,766.5
Biscayne Park	87	2,620.5
Coral Gables	2,251	5,069.4
Doral	2,780	8,543.1
El Portal	111	4,349.5
Florida City	1,465	15,932.6
Golden Beach	18	1,910.8
Hialeah	9,937	4,351.8
Hialeah Gardens	851	4,156.1
Homestead	4,154	9,623.1
Key Biscayne	291	2,538.4
Medley	396	30,745.3
Miami	26,219	6,699.5
Miami Beach	8,697	9,438.4
Miami Gardens	8,149	7,574.9
Miami Lakes	999	3,660.4
Miami Shores	700	6,694.7
Miami Springs	488	3,556.1
North Bay Village	209	3,607.2
North Miami	4,305	7,207.0
North Miami Beach	2,635	6,476.1
Opa Locka	2,019	13,036.7
Palmetto Bay	1,002	3,985.4
Village of Pinecrest	654	3,348.7
South Miami	867	8,235.2
Sunny Isles Beach	556	3,068.3
Surfside	164	2,910.4
Sweetwater	258	1,806.6
Virginia Gardens	33	1,391.8
West Miami	172	2,994.4
Florida International University	550	(X)
Miami Dade Public Schools	3,289	(X)
Miccosukee Public Safety	120	(X)
State agencies	109	(X)
Monroe	4,103	5,096.3
Sheriff's office	2,245	4,131.9
Key Colony Beach	17	1,983.7
Key West	1,834	7,243.6
State agencies	7	(X)
Nassau	2,856	4,188.4
Sheriff's office	2,294	4,069.3
Fernandina Beach	559	4,731.3
State agencies	3	(X)
Okaloosa	6,045	3,137.5
Sheriff's office	3,949	2,996.0
Crestview	812	4,165.4
Fort Walton	982	4,702.6
Niceville	193	1,459.8
Shalimar	6	821.9
Valparaiso	101	1,545.1
State agencies	2	(X)
Okeechobee	1,530	3,957.0
Sheriff's office	1,174	3,558.3
Okeechobee	355	6,257.7
State agencies	1	(X)
Orange	68,520	6,347.2
Sheriff's office	38,329	5,447.5
Apopka	2,155	5,784.8
Eatonville	144	5,653.7
Edgewood	137	6,342.6
Maitland	430	2,678.3
Oakland	42	2,172.8
Ocoee	1,661	5,162.4
Orlando	22,618	10,094.8
Windermere	27	1,006.7
Winter Garden	1,399	4,919.1
Winter Park	1,066	3,724.7
University of Central Florida	487	(X)
State agencies	25	(X)
Osceola	10,832	4,232.9
Sheriff's office	6,680	4,033.2
Kissimmee	2,825	4,689.5
St. Cloud	1,320	4,394.9
State agencies	7	(X)
Palm Beach	63,798	4,953.3
Sheriff's office	21,635	3,839.1
Atlantis	51	2,385.4
Belle Glade	998	5,907.4
Boca Raton	3,189	3,730.3
Boynton Beach	4,072	6,071.2
Delray Beach	4,010	6,256.3
Greenacres City	1,564	4,928.5
Gulfstream	9	1,222.8
Highland Beach	44	1,058.5
Hypoluxo	39	1,583.4
Juno Beach	107	2,942.0

See footnotes at end of table.

Continued . . .

Table 22.03. CRIMINAL OFFENSES AND RATES: CRIME INDEX OFFENSES AND CRIME RATES IN THE STATE, COUNTIES, CITIES, AND SPECIFIED AREAS OF FLORIDA, 2006 (Continued)

Area	Number of index offenses 1/	Crime rate per 100,000 population
Palm Beach (Continued)		
Jupiter	1,516	3,030.3
Jupiter Inlet Colony	10	2,695.4
Lake Clarke Shores	49	1,412.5
Lake Park	737	8,087.3
Lake Worth	3,520	9,667.1
Lantana	626	6,185.2
Manalapan	15	4,166.7
Mangonia Park	464	18,274.9
North Palm Beach	397	3,160.3
Ocean Ridge	54	2,623.9
Pahokee	488	7,602.4
Palm Beach	218	2,246.0
Palm Beach Gardens	1,956	4,060.1
Palm Beach Shores	87	6,369.0
Palm Springs	1,067	7,352.5
Riviera Beach	4,052	12,128.8
Royal Palm Beach	935	3,082.3
South Bay	212	4,543.5
South Palm Beach	13	851.9
Tequesta	120	2,104.5
Wellington	1,882	3,387.1
West Palm Beach	8,506	7,904.0
Florida Atlantic University	279	(X)
Palm Beach County School	751	(X)
State agencies	126	(X)
Pasco	17,086	4,026.3
Sheriff's office	14,186	3,684.0
Dade City	444	6,476.1
New Port Richey	1,218	7,317.5
Port Richey	880	6,995.8
Zephyrhills	349	10,889.2
State agencies	9	(X)
Pinellas	47,401	4,999.6
Sheriff's office	8,804	3,138.0
Belleair	57	1,375.5
Belleair Beach	17	1,050.0
Belleair Bluffs	65	2,912.2
Clearwater	5,699	5,152.7
Dunedin	1,038	2,762.5
Gulfport	683	5,280.2
Indian Rocks Beach	155	2,899.9
Indian Shores	81	1,942.9
Kenneth City	217	4,768.2
Largo	3,172	4,181.9
Madeira Beach	364	8,063.8
North Redington Beach	30	1,988.1
Oldsmar	584	4,223.0
Pinellas Park	2,918	5,975.2
Pinellas (Continued)		
Redington Beaches	30	1,895.1
Safety Harbor	325	1,822.0
Seminole	749	4,001.9
South Pasadena	275	4,776.0
St. Pete Beach	603	6,000.0
St. Petersburg	20,162	7,930.8
Tarpon Springs	993	4,109.9
Treasure Island	297	3,957.4
St. Pete/Clearwater Airport	5	(X)
University of South Florida	68	(X)
State agencies	10	(X)
Polk	23,943	4,237.3
Sheriff's office	10,774	3,022.3
Auburndale	852	6,809.5
Bartow	1,264	7,811.6
Davenport	79	3,370.3
Dundee	234	7,485.6
Eagle Lake	37	1,391.5
Fort Meade	251	4,270.9
Frostproof	107	3,577.4
Haines City	1,031	5,736.4
Lake Alfred	142	3,349.8
Lake Hamilton	97	6,884.3
Lake Wales	760	5,958.4
Lakeland	5,751	6,276.8
Mulberry	290	8,383.9
Winter Haven	2,266	7,212.2
State agencies	8	(X)
Putnam	4,083	5,486.7
Sheriff's office	2,821	4,772.2
Crescent City	146	8,170.1
Interlachen 2/	(NA)	(X)
Palatka	1,105	9,678.5
Welaka	11	1,762.8
St. Johns	4,823	2,917.9
Sheriff's office	3,693	2,535.0
St. Augustine	945	6,896.8
St. Augustine Beach	179	3,029.8
Florida School Deaf and Blind	2	(X)
State agencies	4	(X)
St. Lucie	9,912	3,822.4
Sheriff's office	2,267	3,061.3
Ft. Pierce	3,726	9,065.3
Port St. Lucie	3,903	2,707.4
State agencies	16	(X)

See footnotes at end of table. Continued . . .

Table 22.03. CRIMINAL OFFENSES AND RATES: CRIME INDEX OFFENSES AND CRIME RATES IN THE STATE, COUNTIES, CITIES, AND SPECIFIED AREAS OF FLORIDA, 2006 (Continued)

Area	Number of index offenses 1/	Crime rate per 100,000 population
Santa Rosa	2,890	2,043.4
Sheriff's office	2,201	1,720.0
Gulf Breeze	184	3,186.7
Milton	502	6,528.8
State agencies	3	(X)
Sarasota	14,545	3,885.7
Sheriff's office	8,308	3,328.5
North Port	1,343	2,811.4
Sarasota	4,148	7,492.2
Venice	652	3,020.8
New College of Florida	83	(X)
Sarasota/Bradenton Airport	2	(X)
State agencies	9	(X)
Seminole	13,581	3,228.4
Sheriff's office	4,529	2,181.7
Altamonte Springs	1,890	4,389.8
Casselberry	1,094	4,388.3
Lake Mary	328	2,339.5
Longwood	772	5,544.0
Oviedo	527	1,649.7
Sanford	3,708	7,238.4
Winter Springs	728	2,143.0
State agencies	5	(X)
Sumter	1,342	1,624.7
Sheriff's office	860	1,171.8
Bushnell	139	5,973.4
Center Hill	22	2,463.6
Coleman	6	916.0
Webster	42	5,475.9
Wildwood	270	5,915.9
State agencies	3	(X)
Suwannee	973	2,507.8
Sheriff's office	603	1,874.7
Live Oak	369	5,562.3
State agencies	1	(X)
Taylor	494	2,300.8
Sheriff's office	205	1,401.0
Perry	289	4,225.8
Union	267	1,776.7
Sheriff's office	267	1,776.7
Volusia	21,851	4,337.5
Sheriff's office	6,001	2,697.5
Daytona Beach	6,028	9,277.1
Daytona Beach Shores	312	6,265.1
Deland	2,302	8,675.0
Edgewater	704	3,263.5
Holly Hill	984	7,800.9
Lake Helen	73	2,523.3
New Smyrna Beach	932	4,076.3
Oak Hill	70	3,428.0
Orange City	971	10,312.2
Ormond Beach	1,283	3,184.1
Ponce Inlet	49	1,498.0
Port Orange	1,313	2,341.8
South Daytona	608	4,414.4
Volusia County Beach Patrol	202	(X)
State agencies	19	(X)
Wakulla	684	2,409.0
Sheriff's office	683	2,405.5
State agencies	1	(X)
Walton	1,038	1,860.7
Sheriff's office	1,037	2,057.6
DeFuniak Springs 2/	(NA)	(X)
State agencies	1	(X)
Washington	351	1,521.3
Sheriff's office	199	1,024.7
Chipley	151	4,133.6
State agencies	1	(X)

(X) Not applicable.
(NA) Not available.
1/ Actual offenses known to enforcement officers. Index offenses include murder, forcible sex, robbery, aggravated assault, burglary, larceny, and auto theft.
2/ Agency unable to submit and were not included in county totals.
3/ Baldwin offenses are being reported by the Jacksonville Police Department.
Note: The data reflected in this table are by geographic jurisdiction and are not intended to depict an individual law enforcement agency's activity. Sheriff's office totals include the activity occurring within those incorporated jurisdictions who do not report directly to the Uniform Crime Reporting (UCR) program. County totals reflect all UCR activity occurring within that county. State agencies are listed only for counties with state agency activity.

Source: State of Florida, Department of Law Enforcement, Florida Statistical Analysis Center, *Florida Uniform Crime Report, 2006,* Internet site <http://www.fdle.state.fl.us/> (accessed 6, August 2007).

Table 22.04. CRIMINAL OFFENSES: ADULT AND JUVENILE ARRESTS BY OFFENSE AND BY SEX IN FLORIDA, 2006

Offense	Total all ages	Adult arrests			Juvenile arrests		
		Total	Male	Female	Total	Male	Female
Total	1,110,676	989,495	780,731	208,764	121,181	91,590	29,591
Index offenses, total	170,593	129,512	96,783	32,729	41,081	30,246	10,835
Murder	756	696	644	52	60	50	10
Forcible sex offenses	3,530	2,864	2,804	60	666	645	21
Forcible rape	1,960	1,696	1,680	16	264	258	6
Forcible sodomy	376	262	250	12	114	111	3
Forcible fondling	1,194	906	874	32	288	276	12
Robbery	9,703	7,027	6,265	762	2,676	2,473	203
Aggravated assault	35,917	30,471	23,596	6,875	5,446	4,064	1,382
Burglary	27,188	18,169	16,138	2,031	9,019	8,331	688
Larceny	81,597	61,828	40,311	21,517	19,769	11,728	8,041
Motor vehicle theft	11,902	8,457	7,025	1,432	3,445	2,955	490
Nonindex offenses, total	940,083	859,983	683,948	176,035	80,100	61,344	18,756
Manslaughter	140	132	106	26	8	8	0
Kidnap/abduction	864	827	753	74	37	25	12
Arson	473	262	210	52	211	187	24
Simple assault	89,707	71,907	55,183	16,724	17,800	11,409	6,391
Drug arrests	168,119	153,667	123,722	29,945	14,452	12,389	2,063
Bribery	60	51	40	11	9	9	0
Embezzlement	1,569	1,421	727	694	148	78	70
Fraud	16,240	15,565	9,954	5,611	675	437	238
Counterfeit/forgery	4,804	4,658	3,057	1,601	146	105	41
Extortion/blackmail	129	111	100	11	18	16	2
Intimidation	5,109	4,336	3,656	680	773	634	139
Prostitution/commercialized sex	5,443	5,377	2,192	3,185	66	33	33
Nonforcible sex offenses	3,861	3,491	3,257	234	370	340	30
Stolen property buy/receive/ possess	2,737	2,406	1,998	408	331	297	34
Driving under influence	55,278	54,890	43,477	11,413	388	295	93
Destruction/damage/vandalism	9,880	6,367	5,109	1,258	3,513	3,069	444
Gambling	352	319	288	31	33	31	2
Weapons violations	8,611	6,194	5,782	412	2,417	2,074	343
Liquor law violations	32,137	30,719	25,951	4,768	1,418	1,030	388
Miscellaneous	534,570	497,283	398,386	98,897	37,287	28,878	8,409

Note: A person is counted each time he/she is arrested or summoned; therefore, arrest counts do not reflect the specific number of persons arrested since one individual may be arrested several times for the same or different crimes.

Source: State of Florida, Department of Law Enforcement, Florida Statistical Analysis Center, *Florida Uniform Crime Report, 2006,* Internet site <http://www.fdle.state.fl.us/> (accessed 6, August 2007).

Table 22.05. FIREARMS: FIREARM USE IN VIOLENT CRIMES AND MANSLAUGHTER IN THE STATE AND COUNTIES OF FLORIDA, 2006

			Violent index crimes									
	Total		Murder		Forcible sex		Robbery		Aggravated assault		Man-slaughter	
County	Num-ber	Fire-arm	Num-ber	Fire-arm	Num-ber	Fire-arm	Num-ber	Fire-arm	Num-ber	Fire-arm	Num-ber	Fire-arm
Florida	129,666	31,180	1,129	740	11,567	162	34,123	14,362	82,682	15,905	165	11
Alachua	2,262	404	13	6	307	2	382	159	1,558	237	2	0
Baker	94	1	2	1	14	0	7	0	70	0	1	0
Bay	1,301	201	5	3	112	1	184	69	999	128	1	0
Bradford	120	24	0	0	9	0	13	3	98	21	0	0
Brevard	3,626	749	22	19	380	7	635	241	2,585	482	4	0
Broward	10,769	2,646	87	58	840	16	3,685	1,448	6,152	1,123	5	1
Calhoun	20	7	0	0	0	0	1	1	19	6	0	0
Charlotte	739	120	2	1	25	0	95	37	617	82	0	0
Citrus	425	63	1	0	72	0	36	8	316	55	0	0
Clay	828	192	7	5	158	1	101	46	562	140	0	0
Collier	1,379	151	7	2	203	2	291	60	876	87	2	0
Columbia	423	70	2	1	38	0	43	20	340	49	0	0
DeSoto	238	31	1	0	12	0	38	5	186	26	1	0
Dixie	79	16	1	1	5	0	12	6	59	9	2	0
Duval	7,083	3,105	115	71	474	18	2,419	1,305	4,070	1,710	5	1
Escambia	2,444	470	11	3	341	7	561	240	1,529	220	2	0
Flagler	233	42	4	1	42	0	37	14	150	27	0	0
Franklin	28	3	1	0	1	0	3	1	23	2	0	0
Gadsden	423	45	1	1	34	0	35	12	353	32	0	0
Gilchrist	22	3	1	0	2	0	0	0	19	3	0	0
Glades	61	7	1	1	7	0	8	5	45	1	0	0
Gulf	99	5	0	0	3	0	2	0	94	5	0	0
Hamilton	67	12	0	0	10	0	11	4	46	8	0	0
Hardee	144	24	0	0	8	0	17	8	119	16	0	0
Hendry	299	58	4	4	26	0	58	13	211	41	0	0
Hernando	687	89	5	3	81	0	60	18	541	68	0	0
Highlands	408	91	2	2	30	1	77	34	298	53	1	1
Hillsborough	9,279	2,077	61	32	632	11	2,464	984	6,102	1,050	20	0
Holmes	50	7	0	0	22	0	1	0	27	7	0	0
Indian River	479	89	7	2	51	0	121	44	300	43	0	0
Jackson	268	48	1	0	8	0	18	8	241	40	0	0
Jefferson	125	15	0	0	8	1	11	4	106	10	0	0
Lafayette	19	4	0	0	0	0	0	0	18	4	1	0

Continued . . .

Table 22.05. FIREARMS: FIREARM USE IN VIOLENT CRIMES AND MANSLAUGHTER IN THE STATE AND COUNTIES OF FLORIDA, 2006 (Continued)

County	Total		Violent index crimes								Man-slaughter	
			Murder		Forcible sex		Robbery		Aggravated assault			
	Number	Firearm	Number	Firearm	Number	Firearm	Number	Firearm	Number	Firearm	Number	Firearm
Lake	1,669	297	9	9	218	1	209	95	1,230	192	3	0
Lee	3,162	922	48	30	374	1	866	394	1,869	497	5	0
Leon	2,117	531	10	6	277	2	529	262	1,300	261	1	0
Levy	227	22	0	0	22	0	17	7	188	15	0	0
Liberty	6	0	0	0	2	0	0	0	4	0	0	0
Madison	136	20	3	2	13	0	11	2	109	16	0	0
Manatee	3,115	696	20	14	161	2	642	224	2,290	456	2	0
Marion	2,329	393	15	8	328	2	277	127	1,706	256	3	0
Martin	626	65	7	0	30	2	161	23	427	40	1	0
Miami-Dade	23,530	6,266	240	184	1,582	24	7,538	3,196	14,160	2,857	10	5
Monroe	459	41	1	1	62	0	103	6	292	34	1	0
Nassau	990	57	4	3	25	0	25	6	936	48	0	0
Okaloosa	706	137	5	1	88	2	106	39	507	95	0	0
Okeechobee	302	42	6	5	19	0	38	6	239	31	0	0
Orange	12,718	4,181	121	91	950	17	4,280	2,309	7,358	1,763	9	1
Osceola	1,439	264	13	9	135	2	324	126	967	127	0	0
Palm Beach	9,353	2,201	92	61	664	8	2,909	1,115	5,636	1,016	52	1
Pasco	1,818	379	28	17	184	0	335	113	1,270	249	1	0
Pinellas	7,343	1,297	40	21	871	16	1,652	545	4,770	714	10	1
Polk	3,070	737	21	14	444	7	731	275	1,868	441	6	0
Putnam	824	144	6	4	36	0	76	25	705	115	1	0
St. Johns	678	66	6	3	56	1	72	15	544	47	0	0
St. Lucie	1,473	331	12	12	181	3	301	127	979	189	0	0
Santa Rosa	367	67	3	0	93	1	52	15	218	51	1	0
Sarasota	1,511	230	10	3	123	0	355	85	1,023	142	0	0
Seminole	1,465	292	17	11	275	2	363	158	806	121	4	0
Sumter	272	50	2	1	37	0	39	25	191	24	3	0
Suwannee	197	28	0	0	23	0	20	10	154	18	0	0
Taylor	186	21	1	1	16	0	9	5	160	15	0	0
Union	56	14	1	1	10	0	9	3	36	10	0	0
Volusia	2,719	475	21	11	259	2	636	224	1,800	238	3	0
Wakulla	114	10	0	0	32	0	5	0	77	10	0	0
Walton	121	27	2	0	16	0	2	1	99	26	2	0
Washington	47	8	1	0	6	0	5	2	35	6	0	0

Source: State of Florida, Department of Law Enforcement, Florida Statistical Analysis Center, *Florida Uniform Crime Report, 2006,* Internet site <http://www.fdle.state.fl.us/> (accessed 6, August 2007).

Table 22.06. DOMESTIC VIOLENCE OFFENSES: NUMBER AND RELATIONSHIP OF THE VICTIM TO THE OFFENDER IN FLORIDA, 2006

Primary offense	Total	Percentage change from 2005	Arrests	Relationship of victim to offender: Spouse	Parent
Total	115,170	-4.3	62,787	28,129	11,672
Criminal homicide	164	-6.8	82	49	12
Manslaughter	19	11.8	13	2	3
Forcible sex offenses	2,405	-14.4	844	173	91
Forcible rape	1,089	-12.2	428	148	44
Forcible sodomy	369	-15.0	147	14	4
Forcible fondling	947	-16.7	269	11	43
Aggravated assault	20,193	-6.8	13,021	3,978	1,864
Aggravated stalking	259	2.0	134	92	8
Simple assault	88,110	-2.6	47,889	22,587	9,311
Threat/intimidation	3,690	-11.2	680	1,116	373
Simple stalking	330	-60.7	124	132	10

Primary offense	Relationship of victim to offender (Continued): Child	Sibling	Other family	Cohabitant	Other
Total	8,175	8,994	7,339	35,401	15,460
Criminal homicide	31	5	17	34	16
Manslaughter	9	1	1	2	1
Forcible sex offenses	634	280	709	229	289
Forcible rape	220	98	250	155	174
Forcible sodomy	99	69	114	27	42
Forcible fondling	315	113	345	47	73
Aggravated assault	1,796	1,903	1,594	5,795	3,263
Aggravated stalking	4	4	18	56	77
Simple assault	5,533	6,624	4,682	28,559	10,814
Threat/intimidation	161	171	309	645	915
Simple stalking	7	6	9	81	85

Source: State of Florida, Department of Law Enforcement, Florida Statistical Analysis Center, *Florida Uniform Crime Report, 2006,* and previous reports, Internet site <http://www.fdle.state.fl.us/> (accessed 6, August 2007).

Table 22.07. DOMESTIC VIOLENCE OFFENSES: NUMBER BY TYPE OF CRIME IN THE STATE AND COUNTIES OF FLORIDA, 2006

County	Total	Percentage change from 2005 A/	Rate per 100,000 population	Homicide and manslaughter	Forcible sex offenses	Assault: Aggravalted	Assault: Simple	Stalking	Threat/ intimidation
Florida	115,170	-4.3	627.7	183	2,405	20,193	88,110	589	3,690
Alachua	1,766	2.9	724.4	4	48	427	1,236	29	22
Baker	73	-34.2	292.0	0	0	13	60	0	0
Bay	1,384	4.1	836.2	1	20	216	1,102	16	29
Bradford	208	0.0	728.5	0	2	24	181	1	0
Brevard	3,950	4.2	727.4	1	102	732	3,020	25	70
Broward	7,669	-7.0	437.4	15	154	1,474	5,618	74	334
Calhoun	39	-4.9	276.3	0	0	7	32	0	0
Charlotte	660	-18.6	411.7	0	3	141	511	1	4
Citrus	1,018	10.9	744.4	0	29	94	847	1	47
Clay	1,156	-3.4	653.5	3	37	172	925	2	17
Collier	1,911	1.3	585.0	3	83	334	1,386	4	101
Columbia	529	-3.6	832.6	1	0	99	426	0	3
DeSoto	224	130.9	675.4	0	2	60	161	0	1
Dixie	58	-15.9	370.0	1	0	12	44	0	1
Duval	6,832	-1.9	777.0	16	124	794	5,875	12	11
Escambia	2,643	-1.4	853.6	4	57	448	2,036	1	97
Flagler	621	-2.2	696.6	3	6	58	491	4	59
Franklin	46	17.9	386.0	0	0	1	45	0	0
Gadsden	646	-32.9	1,340.4	0	16	233	397	0	0
Gilchrist	73	87.2	437.0	0	0	0	73	0	0
Glades	83	16.9	768.8	1	1	24	54	1	2
Gulf	28	16.7	169.6	0	0	18	10	0	0
Hamilton	73	21.7	502.9	0	1	11	56	0	5
Hardee	189	-1.0	695.2	0	2	28	159	0	0
Hendry	201	-23.3	519.7	0	1	43	139	2	16
Hernando	1,127	-12.1	717.8	1	18	146	929	0	33
Highlands	494	-12.7	511.0	1	6	112	364	0	11
Hillsborough	9,867	-1.8	847.4	9	185	1,614	7,909	6	144
Holmes	93	-24.4	476.9	0	8	11	73	1	0
Indian River	585	0.2	432.5	2	4	83	492	0	4
Jackson	200	23.5	398.0	1	1	60	138	0	0
Jefferson	13	-55.2	90.6	0	0	7	6	0	0
Lafayette	22	57.1	273.0	1	0	7	14	0	0
Lake	1,898	-8.3	685.7	1	39	334	1,490	12	22

See footnote at end of table. Continued . . .

Table 22.07. DOMESTIC VIOLENCE OFFENSES: NUMBER BY TYPE OF CRIME IN THE STATE AND COUNTIES OF FLORIDA, 2006 (Continued)

County	Total	Percentage change from 2005 A/	Rate per 100,000 population	Homicide and manslaughter	Forcible sex offenses	Assault		Stalking	Threat/ intimidation
						Aggravalted	Simple		
Lee	2,710	-6.3	462.8	8	81	436	2,153	8	24
Leon	1,201	44.9	440.7	0	21	241	925	3	11
Levy	256	7.1	656.7	0	4	65	186	1	0
Liberty	30	-37.5	386.0	0	2	2	22	2	2
Madison	106	15.2	535.0	0	0	29	77	0	0
Manatee	2,503	-1.2	798.7	1	19	519	1,914	3	47
Marion	2,369	6.2	751.9	3	5	483	1,875	3	0
Martin	773	8.9	541.9	1	11	110	609	4	38
Miami-Dade	13,267	-8.3	544.4	35	518	2,979	7,892	139	1,704
Monroe	345	-9.2	428.5	0	4	38	303	0	0
Nassau	223	-42.5	327.0	2	0	193	27	0	1
Okaloosa	941	6.8	488.4	1	11	121	794	0	14
Okeechobee	287	1.8	742.3	0	0	36	250	0	1
Orange	8,451	2.1	782.8	15	201	1,760	6,194	21	260
Osceola	1,913	6.6	747.5	0	34	272	1,573	20	14
Palm Beach	5,589	-12.9	433.9	12	97	1,157	4,207	25	91
Pasco	3,504	3.9	825.7	4	67	353	3,056	20	4
Pinellas	8,201	-3.4	865.0	10	126	1,171	6,636	44	214
Polk	4,708	3.5	833.2	4	120	535	3,984	3	62
Putnam	941	-0.7	1,264.5	3	7	194	727	4	6
St. Johns	772	-23.1	467.1	1	19	162	561	16	13
St. Lucie	1,013	-56.9	390.6	1	18	197	789	6	2
Santa Rosa	672	-1.6	475.2	1	12	85	563	0	11
Sarasota	1,415	-10.4	378.0	1	18	256	1,118	4	18
Seminole	2,038	-6.6	484.5	5	11	220	1,736	20	46
Sumter	218	-25.6	263.9	0	5	49	159	1	4
Suwannee	216	21.3	556.7	0	5	40	171	0	0
Taylor	149	-4.5	694.0	0	0	72	76	0	1
Union	26	-42.2	173.0	1	0	3	20	0	2
Volusia	3,300	-6.9	655.1	4	33	516	2,641	50	56
Wakulla	84	7.7	295.8	0	0	13	69	0	2
Walton	426	-24.3	763.6	1	1	33	382	0	9
Washington	144	9.9	624.1	0	6	16	122	0	0

A/ Percentage changes in rate should be interpreted with caution. In small counties with low numbers of crime, a small increase in crime can produce a large percentage change.

Source: State of Florida, Department of Law Enforcement, Florida Statistical Analysis Center, *Florida Uniform Crime Report, 2006,* Internet site <http://www.fdle.state.fl.us/> (accessed 6, August 2007).

Table 22.08. CRIME RATES: PROPERTY AND VIOLENT CRIME RATES IN FLORIDA AND THE UNITED STATES, 1994 THROUGH 2005

(rates per 100,000 population)

Year	Florida All crime	Florida Property crime 1/	Florida Violent crime 2/	United States All crime	United States Property crime 1/	United States Violent crime 2/
1994	8,250.0	7,103.2	1,146.8	5,373.6	4,660.0	713.6
1995	7,701.6	6,630.6	1,071.0	5,275.9	4,591.3	684.6
1996	7,497.3	6,446.3	1,051.0	5,086.6	4,450.1	636.5
1997	7,271.8	6,248.2	1,023.6	4,930.0	4,318.7	611.3
1998	6,886.1	5,947.4	938.7	4,619.3	4,051.8	567.5
1999	6,205.5	5,351.5	854.0	4,266.6	3,743.6	523.0
2000	5,694.7	4,882.7	812.0	4,124.8	3,618.3	506.5
2001	5,577.5	4,779.2	798.3	4,162.6	3,658.1	504.5
2002	5,427.6	4,656.4	771.2	4,125.0	3,630.6	494.4
2003	5,188.4	4,457.3	731.1	4,067.0	3,591.2	475.8
2004	4,894.3	4,182.5	711.8	3,977.3	3,514.1	463.2
2005	4,715.9	4,007.9	708.0	3,899.0	3,429.8	469.2

1/ Includes burglary, larceny-theft, and motor vehicle theft.
2/ Includes murder, forcible rape, robbery, and aggravated assault.
Note: Some data may be revised.

Source: U.S., Department of Justice, Federal Bureau of Investigation, *Crime in the United States, 2005,* Internet site <http://www.fbi.gov/> (accessed 22, February 2007), and previous editions.

Table 22.09. CAPITAL PUNISHMENT: PRISONERS UNDER SENTENCE OF DEATH BY RACE, SEX AND HISPANIC ORIGIN IN FLORIDA, THE SOUTH, AND THE UNITED STATES, DECEMBER 31, 2004 AND 2005

Item	Florida Number	Florida Percentage of United States	South 1/ Number	South 1/ Percentage of United States	United States
Prisoners under sentence of death on 12-31-04 A/	367	11.1	1,840	55.4	3,320
Changes during 2004					
Received under death sentence	15	11.7	70	54.7	128
Removed from death row 2/	9	6.7	87	64.9	134
Executed	1	1.7	43	71.7	60
Prisoners under sentence of death on 12-31-05	372	11.4	1,780	54.7	3,254
White	240	13.3	961	53.2	1,805
Black	132	9.6	794	57.9	1,372
Women	1	1.9	25	48.1	52
Hispanic origin 3/	31	8.6	157	43.4	362

A/ Revised.
1/ Includes Alabama, Arkansas, Delaware, Florida, Georgia, Kentucky, Louisiana, Maryland, Mississippi, North Carolina, Oklahoma, South Carolina, Tennessee, Texas, and Virginia.
2/ Excludes executions. Includes suicide, murder, and death by natural causes.
3/ Persons of Hispanic origin may be of any race.

Source: U.S., Department of Justice, Bureau of Justice Statistics, *Bureau of Justice Statistics Bulletin: Capital Punishment, 2005,* Internet site <http://www.ojp.usdoj.gov/> (accessed 22, February 2007).

Table 22.10. PRISONERS: NUMBER UNDER JURISDICTION OF THE STATE OR FEDERAL CORRECTIONAL AUTHORITIES IN FLORIDA AND THE UNITED STATES JUNE 30, 2003 THROUGH 2006

Item	2003	2004	2005 A/	2006 B/
Florida				
Total prisoners	80,352	84,733	87,544	89,082
Percentage change from previous year	9.2	5.5	3.3	1.8
Incarceration rate 1/	472	489	492	492
United States				
Total prisoners	1,464,197	1,491,834	1,447,812	1,487,940
Percentage change from previous year	3.1	1.9	-3.0	2.8
Incarceration rate 1/	480	486	488	497

A/ Revised.
B/ Preliminary.
1/ The number of prisoners with a sentence of more than one year per 100,000 residents.
Note: Population figures from 2003 forward are jurisdiction counts, not custody counts as in previous years.

Source: U.S., Department of Justice, Office of Justice Programs, *Bureau of Justice Statistics Bulletin: Prison and Jail Inmates at Midyear 2006*, June 2007, NCJ 217675, and previous editions, Internet site <http://www.ojp.usdoj.gov/> (accessed 29, June 2007).

Table 22.11. POPULATION UNDER CRIMINAL SENTENCE: INCARCERATED INMATES AND OFFENDERS UNDER COMMUNITY SUPERVISION OF THE FLORIDA DEPARTMENT OF CORRECTIONS, JUNE 30, 2002 THROUGH 2006

Type of supervision	2002	2003	2004	2005	2006
Under supervision, total	227,030	230,301	233,124	229,130	234,758
Incarcerated offenders	73,553	77,316	81,974	84,901	88,576
Male	69,164	72,520	76,675	79,221	82,360
White	30,383	32,244	34,202	35,793	37,510
Black	37,121	38,412	40,259	40,984	42,174
Other	1,660	1,864	2,214	2,444	2,676
Female	4,389	4,796	5,299	5,680	6,216
White	2,001	2,344	2,733	3,081	3,422
Black	2,118	2,171	2,313	2,322	2,500
Other	270	281	253	277	294
Community supervision	153,477	152,985	151,150	144,229	146,182
Probation	110,506	110,486	108,428	102,487	104,753
Felony	104,543	103,532	101,274	94,647	96,512
Misdemeanor	2,296	2,596	2,643	2,455	2,419
Administrative	1,694	1,725	1,508	1,998	2,274
Sex offender	1,973	2,633	3,003	3,387	3,548
Drug offender probation	15,258	16,633	17,425	17,732	17,860
Community control	13,314	12,327	11,624	10,524	9,526
Pretrial intervention	8,444	7,991	8,218	8,248	8,599
Post-prison release	5,955	5,548	5,455	5,238	5,444
Parole	2,155	2,197	2,175	2,161	2,167
Other 1/	3,800	3,351	3,280	3,077	3,277

1/ Includes conditional, control, conditional medical, and other post-prison releases.

Source: State of Florida, Department of Corrections, *2005–2006 Annual Report,* and previous editions, Internet site <http://www.dc.state.fl.us/> (accessed 22, February 2007).

Table 22.12. POPULATION UNDER CRIMINAL SENTENCE: INCARCERATED OFFENDERS AND OFFENDERS UNDER COMMUNITY SUPERVISION OF THE FLORIDA DEPARTMENT OF CORRECTIONS BY PRIMARY OFFENSE, JUNE 30, 2006

Primary offense	Incarcerated offenders		Community supervision				
	Total	Admitted 2005-06	Total 1/	Probation 2/	Community control	Conditional release	Parole
Total	88,576	35,098	146,182	122,613	9,526	2,827	2,167
Murder, manslaughter	11,370	929	2,248	1,475	100	214	451
First degree murder	5,662	296	461	245	21	49	145
Second degree murder	3,831	356	787	419	24	112	229
Third degree murder	101	9	33	25	0	4	4
Other homicide	78	10	56	41	2	2	11
Manslaughter	923	140	525	402	27	34	59
DUI manslaughter	775	118	386	343	26	13	3
Sexual offenses	9,765	1,735	6,981	6,182	456	255	85
Capital sexual battery	2,679	253	1,113	1,020	30	52	11
Life sexual battery	1,269	106	247	191	13	25	17
First degree sexual battery	1,090	159	766	691	33	26	16
Second degree sexual battery	830	183	642	535	62	41	4
Other sexual battery	188	6	65	50	1	0	13
Lewd, lascivious behavior	3,709	1,028	4,148	3,695	317	111	24
Robbery	10,614	2,022	4,177	2,895	321	550	388
With weapon	6,964	1,015	2,129	1,365	163	299	293
Without weapon	3,198	888	1,923	1,420	150	246	93
Home invasion	452	119	125	110	8	5	2
Violent personal offenses	10,843	4,788	21,771	19,001	1,432	502	160
Home invasion, other	4	2	3	2	0	0	1
Carjacking	742	158	190	150	27	10	3
Aggravated assault	934	621	3,173	2,791	212	46	43
Aggravated battery	2,796	980	3,333	2,841	269	170	20
Assault and battery on law enforcement officers	1,230	592	2,197	1,884	116	91	7
Other assault and battery	207	166	668	586	44	12	1
Aggravated stalking	158	103	501	445	47	3	2
Resisting arrest with violence	491	319	1,363	1,184	77	37	2
Kidnapping	1,580	269	950	787	63	51	26
Arson	395	129	550	475	42	11	14
Abuse of children	690	402	3,050	2,589	202	4	6
Leaving accident, injury/death	216	139	900	830	54	0	2
DUI, injury	227	97	536	484	46	0	5
Other violent offenses	1,173	811	4,357	3,953	233	67	28
Burglary	12,864	4,530	13,118	10,887	1,025	535	191
Burglary of structure	2,782	1,655	6,197	5,192	467	159	87
Burglary of dwelling	6,139	2,085	3,899	3,192	345	242	74
Armed burglary	1,911	347	699	532	85	64	11
Burglary with assault	1,817	315	808	658	70	64	14
Other burglary/trespass	215	128	1,515	1,313	58	6	5

See footnotes at end of table.

Continued . . .

Table 22.12. POPULATION UNDER CRIMINAL SENTENCE: INCARCERATED OFFENDERS AND OFFENDERS UNDER COMMUNITY SUPERVISION OF THE FLORIDA DEPARTMENT OF CORRECTIONS BY PRIMARY OFFENSE, JUNE 30, 2006 (Continued)

Primary offense	Incarcerated offenders		Community supervision				
	Total	Admitted 2005-06	Total 1/	Probation 2/	Community control	Conditional release	Parole
Theft, forgery, fraud	7,375	5,283	35,927	30,939	1,737	180	182
Grand theft, other	1,880	1,466	15,786	13,526	684	44	76
Grand theft, automobile	1,059	812	2,343	2,069	137	32	18
Stolen property	2,237	1,207	3,107	2,699	273	68	27
Forgery, uttering and counterfeiting	920	797	4,920	4,204	284	22	34
Worthless checks	76	67	1,445	1,261	51	0	4
Fraudulent practices	621	474	6,554	5,578	232	9	14
Other theft, property damage	582	460	1,772	1,602	76	5	9
Drugs	17,886	10,318	41,090	32,624	2,974	406	597
Sale/purchase/manufacturing	9,366	5,021	12,232	10,126	1,125	319	294
Trafficking	4,371	1,490	2,626	2,185	278	33	127
Other possession	4,149	3,807	26,232	20,313	1,571	54	176
Weapons	2,365	1,004	2,860	2,414	204	91	37
Discharging	329	158	573	498	53	7	6
Possession	2,032	845	2,254	1,887	149	84	30
Other weapons offenses	4	1	33	29	2	0	1
Other offenses	5,456	4,149	17,731	15,943	1,274	94	63
Escape	2,115	1,289	2,819	2,370	246	68	18
DUI, no injury	479	436	2,329	2,117	155	1	20
Other traffic	1,484	1,399	8,720	7,948	689	10	4
Racketeering	243	55	411	385	17	4	3
Pollution/hazardous materials	6	6	146	124	3	0	0
Criminal Justice system	1,022	866	2,037	1,811	141	8	6
Other offenses	107	98	1,269	1,188	23	3	12
Data unavailable	38	340	279	253	3	0	13

DUI Driving under the influence.
1/ Includes pretrial intervention, control releases, and other post-prison releases not shown separately.
2/ Includes drug offender probation.

Source: State of Florida, Department of Corrections, *2005–2006 Annual Report,* Internet site <http://www.dc.state.fl.us/> (accessed 22, February 2007).

Table 22.13. PRISONERS: CHARACTERISTICS BY RACE AND SEX OF OFFENDER IN FLORIDA, JUNE 30, 2006

Item	Total	White Male	White Female	Black Male	Black Female	Other Male	Other Female
Length of sentence (years)							
Total	88,576	37,510	3,422	42,174	2,500	2,676	294
Average 1/	14.6	14.4	7.0	15.8	7.1	14.9	9.2
Six months or less	37	18	0	14	0	5	0
Over six months, one year or less	4	2	1	1	0	0	0
Over one year, two or less	14,003	5,738	1,258	5,811	784	334	78
Over two years, three or less	10,452	4,448	584	4,597	454	330	39
Over three years, five or less	14,303	6,148	612	6,592	521	384	46
Over five years, ten or less	15,749	6,961	436	7,366	366	564	56
Over ten years, twenty or less	13,622	5,834	267	6,852	179	444	46
Twenty or more	20,403	8,361	262	10,941	195	615	29
Data unavailable	3	0	2	0	1	0	0
Class of felony 2/	88,576	37,510	3,422	42,174	2,500	2,676	294
Capital	5,030	2,664	101	2,014	49	194	8
Life felony	5,126	1,938	44	2,861	56	205	22
First degree, life	6,498	2,517	121	3,543	115	192	10
First degree	19,259	8,018	583	9,366	445	755	92
Second degree	31,409	13,064	1,070	15,448	839	902	86
Third degree	20,164	8,911	1,497	8,274	988	418	76
Misdemeanor	3	0	0	2	1	0	0
Data unavailable	1,087	398	6	666	7	10	0
Current age (years)							
Average age	36.6	37.9	36.9	35.6	35.5	35.1	35.3
Median age	36.0	37.0	37.0	34.0	35.0	33.0	34.0
16 and under	49	12	1	34	2	0	0
17	172	40	1	121	5	3	2
18	382	124	9	225	9	12	3
19	902	319	15	523	13	31	1
20 to 24	11,590	4,293	329	6,185	318	427	38
25 to 29	14,806	5,679	540	7,597	436	499	55
30 to 34	13,158	5,272	512	6,448	393	479	54
35 to 39	13,199	5,742	646	5,995	408	366	42
40 to 44	13,084	5,725	628	5,926	456	308	41
45 to 49	10,053	4,525	424	4,527	295	250	32
50 to 54	5,780	2,649	188	2,680	100	148	15
55 to 59	2,947	1,532	84	1,186	46	91	8
60 to 64	1,325	832	30	420	10	30	3
65 to 69	653	443	5	184	5	16	0
70 and over	473	323	8	123	3	16	0
Data unavailable	3	0	2	0	1	0	0
Years in prison	88,576	37,510	3,422	42,174	2,500	2,676	294
Six months or less	15,080	6,395	1,019	6,473	652	469	72
Six months to one year	12,413	5,387	782	5,338	522	341	43
1 to 2 years	15,574	6,766	719	7,049	513	476	51
2 to 3 years	9,772	4,257	324	4,534	284	343	30
3 to 5 years	10,892	4,729	243	5,300	235	346	39
5 to 10 years	12,728	5,270	213	6,645	179	368	53
10 to 20 years	8,857	3,312	87	5,096	94	265	3
20 years or more	3,257	1,394	33	1,739	20	68	3
Data unavailable	3	0	2	0	1	0	0

See footnotes at end of table. Continued . . .

Table 22.13. PRISONERS: CHARACTERISTICS BY RACE AND SEX OF OFFENDER IN FLORIDA, JUNE 30, 2006 (Continued)

Item	Total	White		Black		Other	
		Male	Female	Male	Female	Male	Female
Tested literacy skill levels 3/							
Median skill level	7.3	9.1	9.5	6.1	6.1	6.3	7.9
Beginning/basic literacy (1.0 - 4.9)	30,599	8,471	576	19,367	1,152	941	92
Functional literacy (5.0 - 8.9)	21,147	8,231	805	10,831	704	508	68
GED prep (9.0 - 12.9)	30,799	17,630	1,952	9,915	596	598	108
Data unavailable	6,031	3,178	89	2,061	48	629	26
Prior DC commitments							
None	47,020	23,022	2,609	17,768	1,448	1,934	239
One	18,062	7,328	459	9,354	460	422	39
Two	9,865	3,354	209	5,854	248	190	10
Three	5,849	1,815	78	3,716	161	75	4
Four or more	7,770	1,990	65	5,476	182	55	2
Data unavailable	10	1	2	6	1	0	0

DC Department of Corrections.
1/ Sentence lengths of 50 years or longer, life, and death were calculated as 50 years.
2/ Primary offense.
3/ Most recent Tests of Adult Basic Education (TABE) scores.

Table 22.14. PRISONERS: GENERAL CHARACTERISTICS OF PRISON RELEASES IN FLORIDA, FISCAL YEARS 2004–05 AND 2005–06

Item	2004–05		2005–06	
	Total	Percentage	Total	Percentage
Total	31,537	100.0	105,248	100.0
Male	28,301	89.7	80,529	76.5
Female	3,236	10.3	24,719	23.5
Race				
White	14,683	46.6	64,801	61.6
Black	16,059	50.9	36,077	34.3
Other	795	2.5	4,353	4.1
Age				
17 and under	33	0.1	174	0.2
18-24	5,703	18.1	26,629	25.3
25-34	10,331	32.8	32,337	30.7
35-49	12,863	40.8	35,805	34.0
50-59	2,154	6.8	7,962	7.6
60 and over	453	1.4	2,341	2.2
Prior DC commitments				
0	16,846	53.4	54,321	51.6
1	6,388	20.3	24,874	23.6
2	3,426	10.9	11,952	11.4
3	2,127	6.7	6,307	6.0
4 or more	2,745	8.7	7,794	7.4
Data unavailable 1/	5	(NA)	17	(NA)

(NA) Not available.
1/ Percentages are less than 0.05 percent.

Source for tables 22.13 and 22.14: State of Florida, Department of Corrections, *2005–2006 Annual Report*, and previous edition, Internet site <http://www.dc.state.fl.us/> (accessed 22, February 2007).

Table 22.15. POPULATION UNDER CRIMINAL SENTENCE: OFFENDERS BY TYPE OF SUPERVISION, BY RACE, AND BY COUNTY OF COMMITMENT OR SUPERVISION IN THE STATE AND COUNTIES OF FLORIDA, JUNE 30, 2007

County	Incarcerated offenders				Community supervision 1/			
	Total	White	Black	Other races	Total 2/	White	Black	Other races
Florida	92,838	42,924	46,610	3,304	153,692	95,896	49,813	7,963
Alachua	1,531	455	1,063	13	2,080	971	1,095	14
Baker	203	137	64	2	240	187	52	1
Bay	2,027	1,323	679	25	3,171	2,414	709	48
Bradford	238	120	116	2	250	193	55	2
Brevard	2,599	1,478	1,049	72	5,001	3,590	1,306	105
Broward	8,657	3,098	5,290	269	16,379	8,244	7,124	1,008
Calhoun	161	81	78	2	248	185	62	1
Charlotte	652	480	157	15	1,128	963	140	25
Citrus	624	517	90	17	1,144	1,044	81	19
Clay	559	344	202	13	792	645	125	22
Collier	832	593	216	23	1,769	1,508	206	55
Columbia	666	353	307	6	1,145	768	366	11
DeSoto	193	73	98	22	540	400	128	12
Dixie	109	71	38	0	259	209	48	2
Duval	5,693	1,773	3,861	59	4,431	2,262	2,073	96
Escambia	2,991	1,349	1,599	43	3,892	2,277	1,539	76
Flagler	179	103	73	3	559	406	137	16
Franklin	117	71	46	0	124	90	34	0
Gadsden	690	73	604	13	1,123	289	784	48
Gilchrist	25	20	5	0	113	97	16	0
Glades	51	24	21	6	58	41	13	4
Gulf	112	63	48	1	154	118	34	2
Hamilton	125	47	78	0	268	113	150	5
Hardee	124	67	37	20	337	253	58	26
Hendry	182	89	70	23	364	194	91	79
Hernando	522	368	129	25	1,346	1,133	168	45
Highlands	701	362	309	30	985	671	259	55
Hillsborough	8,561	3,577	4,448	536	13,608	7,809	4,777	1,020
Holmes	119	94	21	4	226	211	15	0
Indian River	781	419	348	14	804	591	181	32
Jackson	460	206	247	7	602	389	206	7
Jefferson	134	32	102	0	238	82	156	0
Lafayette	58	36	18	4	123	96	23	4
Lake	1,278	625	591	62	2,455	1,708	564	182
Lee	1,891	1,034	791	66	3,174	2,269	696	208

See footnotes at end of table. Continued . . .

Table 22.15. POPULATION UNDER CRIMINAL SENTENCE: OFFENDERS BY TYPE OF SUPERVISION, BY RACE, AND BY COUNTY OF COMMITMENT OR SUPERVISION IN THE STATE AND COUNTIES OF FLORIDA, JUNE 30, 2007 (Continued)

County	Incarcerated offenders				Community supervision 1/			
	Total	White	Black	Other races	Total 2/	White	Black	Other races
Leon	2,317	555	1,741	21	3,725	1,524	2,159	42
Levy	229	132	93	4	449	359	88	2
Liberty	73	42	28	3	52	39	11	2
Madison	196	50	145	1	227	73	150	4
Manatee	1,293	677	539	77	2,120	1,433	588	97
Marion	2,343	1,323	945	75	3,586	2,493	955	138
Martin	986	523	417	46	933	759	154	20
Miami-Dade	8,262	2,912	4,895	455	14,006	6,750	6,194	1,060
Monroe	522	316	178	28	1,620	1,364	223	33
Nassau	322	176	145	1	367	306	56	5
Okaloosa	955	599	341	15	2,171	1,668	456	47
Okeechobee	313	192	95	26	545	448	52	45
Orange	4,794	1,837	2,586	371	9,075	4,242	3,665	1,165
Osceola	861	494	256	111	1,920	1,204	360	356
Palm Beach	3,520	1,403	2,026	91	6,175	3,695	2,115	365
Pasco	1,567	1,306	215	46	3,483	3,049	271	163
Pinellas	5,669	2,801	2,764	104	10,222	7,253	2,665	301
Polk	4,313	2,488	1,685	140	6,189	4,147	1,776	266
Putnam	511	252	248	11	906	556	334	16
St. Johns	801	424	361	16	1,100	824	265	11
St. Lucie	1,666	642	981	43	2,500	1,529	841	130
Santa Rosa	409	342	62	5	983	888	90	5
Sarasota	1,089	621	428	40	2,458	1,996	393	69
Seminole	1,208	602	544	62	2,615	1,618	760	236
Sumter	327	162	157	8	437	294	130	13
Suwannee	403	225	172	6	590	410	157	23
Taylor	230	107	120	3	343	207	136	0
Union	86	45	40	1	90	71	18	1
Volusia	2,811	1,480	1,260	71	4,157	3,007	1,051	99
Wakulla	131	92	39	0	446	350	89	7
Walton	306	253	50	3	731	654	69	8
Washington	312	200	107	5	327	259	66	2
Interstate	163	93	52	18	3	2	1	0
Out-of-state	5	3	2	0	2	2	0	0

1/ Felony and misdemeanor probation, community control, pretrial intervention, control release, parole, and other supervision.
2/ Includes unknown race and data not distributed by county.

Source: State of Florida, Department of Corrections, unpublished data.

Table 22.16. COUNTY DETENTION FACILITIES: AVERAGE DAILY INMATE POPULATION AND INCARCERATION RATES IN THE STATE AND COUNTIES OF FLORIDA
2003 THROUGH 2005

County	Average daily population 1/					Incarceration rate 2/		
				Percentage change				
	2003	2004	2005	2003 to 2004	2004 to 2005	2003	2004	2005
Florida	55,042	55,448	55,946	0.7	0.9	3.3	3.3	3.4
Alachua	988	1,065	1,085	7.8	1.9	4.3	4.7	4.7
Baker	131	140	129	6.9	-7.9	5.7	6.1	5.6
Bay	938	1,023	874	9.1	-14.6	6.2	6.7	5.7
Bradford	154	195	221	26.6	13.3	5.8	7.4	8.3
Brevard	1,371	1,346	1,444	-1.8	7.3	2.8	2.7	2.9
Broward	4,732	5,102	5,408	7.8	6.0	2.8	3.1	3.2
Calhoun	37	55	46	48.6	-16.4	2.8	4.1	3.4
Charlotte	420	423	469	0.7	10.9	2.8	2.8	3.2
Citrus	390	407	410	4.4	0.7	3.2	3.3	3.3
Clay	455	461	406	1.3	-11.9	3.0	3.1	2.7
Collier	961	845	1,160	-12.1	37.3	3.5	3.0	4.2
Columbia	270	285	303	5.6	6.3	4.6	4.9	5.2
DeSoto	144	152	191	5.6	25.7	4.4	4.6	5.8
Dixie	88	96	103	9.1	7.3	6.1	6.6	7.1
Duval	2,971	3,391	3,421	14.1	0.9	3.7	4.2	4.2
Escambia	1,739	1,716	1,854	-1.3	8.0	5.8	5.7	6.2
Flagler	110	128	156	16.4	21.9	1.9	2.2	2.7
Franklin	87	90	92	3.4	2.2	8.5	8.8	9.1
Gadsden	215	229	202	6.5	-11.8	4.7	5.0	4.4
Gilchrist	34	26	29	-23.5	11.5	2.2	1.7	1.9
Glades	35	48	42	37.1	-12.5	3.3	4.5	3.9
Gulf	64	41	34	-35.9	-17.1	4.2	2.7	2.3
Hamilton	72	82	95	13.9	15.9	5.2	5.9	6.8
Hardee	130	112	115	-13.8	2.7	4.7	4.1	4.2
Hendry	163	150	183	-8.0	22.0	4.5	4.1	5.1
Hernando	357	394	478	10.4	21.3	2.6	2.9	3.5
Highlands	365	381	406	4.4	6.6	4.1	4.3	4.6
Hillsborough	3,821	3,670	4,483	-4.0	22.2	3.6	3.5	4.2
Holmes	94	89	72	-5.3	-19.1	5.0	4.8	3.9
Indian River	477	522	545	9.4	4.4	4.0	4.4	4.6
Jackson	260	232	273	-10.8	17.7	5.4	4.9	5.7
Jefferson	50	58	59	16.0	1.7	3.8	4.4	4.4
Lafayette	23	31	27	34.8	-12.9	3.2	4.3	3.8
Lake	854	902	973	5.6	7.9	3.7	3.9	4.2
Lee	1,337	1,445	1,677	8.1	16.1	2.8	3.0	3.5
Leon	1,035	1,063	1,072	2.7	0.8	4.2	4.3	4.3
Levy	114	131	168	14.9	28.2	3.2	3.6	4.7

See footnotes at end of table.

Continued . . .

Table 22.16. COUNTY DETENTION FACILITIES: AVERAGE DAILY INMATE POPULATION AND INCARCERATION RATES IN THE STATE AND COUNTIES OF FLORIDA 2003 THROUGH 2005 (Continued)

	Average daily population 1/					Incarceration rate 2/		
				Percentage change				
				2003 to	2004 to			
County	2003	2004	2005	2004	2005	2003	2004	2005
Liberty	24	26	30	8.3	15.4	3.4	3.7	4.2
Madison	83	84	93	1.2	10.7	4.4	4.4	4.9
Manatee	941	1,027	1,088	9.1	5.9	3.4	3.7	3.9
Marion	1,562	1,676	1,866	7.3	11.3	5.8	6.2	6.9
Martin	533	582	589	9.2	1.2	4.1	4.4	4.5
Miami-Dade	6,710	6,671	6,761	-0.6	1.3	2.9	2.9	2.9
Monroe	562	524	583	-6.8	11.3	6.9	6.5	7.2
Nassau	234	262	295	12.0	12.6	3.8	4.3	4.8
Okaloosa	544	619	694	13.8	12.1	3.1	3.5	3.9
Okeechobee	216	242	264	12.0	9.1	5.9	6.6	7.2
Orange	3,582	3,343	3,592	-6.7	7.4	3.7	3.5	3.8
Osceola	980	977	922	-0.3	-5.6	5.1	5.1	4.8
Palm Beach	2,565	2,784	2,767	8.5	-0.6	2.2	2.4	2.3
Pasco	1,140	1,067	1,120	-6.4	5.0	3.2	3.0	3.1
Pinellas	2,804	3,150	3,296	12.3	4.6	3.1	3.4	3.5
Polk	2,426	2,501	2,607	3.1	4.2	4.8	5.0	5.2
Putnam	214	277	224	29.4	-19.1	3.0	3.9	3.1
St. Johns	389	441	451	13.4	2.3	2.9	3.3	3.4
St. Lucie	1,069	1,160	1,238	8.5	6.7	5.3	5.7	6.1
Santa Rosa	362	393	340	8.6	-13.5	2.9	3.1	2.7
Sarasota	776	750	727	-3.4	-3.1	2.3	2.2	2.1
Seminole	887	980	931	10.5	-5.0	2.3	2.5	2.4
Sumter	151	155	0	2.6	-100.0	2.5	2.5	0.0
Suwannee	145	152	162	4.8	6.6	4.0	4.3	4.5
Taylor	91	104	90	14.3	-13.5	4.6	5.3	4.6
Union	24	25	25	4.2	0.0	1.8	1.8	1.8
Volusia	1,417	1,530	1,548	8.0	1.2	3.1	3.3	3.4
Wakulla	167	250	287	49.7	14.8	6.9	10.3	11.8
Walton	189	193	226	2.1	17.1	4.2	4.2	5.0
Washington	93	126	120	35.5	-4.8	4.3	5.8	5.6

1/ Average annual figures based on monthly data.

2/ Per 1,000 population based upon self-reports of county total population as well as county inmate population.

Note: Data are collected monthly from the 67 county jail systems state-wide. Due to major hurricanes and the resulting loss of data, several months have a relatively large number of facilities not reporting. The exclusion of these facilities in the statewide totals has a significant impact. Therefore, for these months, the statewide totals are not true representations of the jail activity in Florida.

Source: State of Florida, Department of Corrections, Bureau of Planning, Research, and Statistics, *Florida County Detention Facilities: 2005 Annual Report,* and previous reports, Internet site <http://www.dc.state.fl.us/> (accessed 1, October 2007).

Table 22.20. JUVENILE DELINQUENCY: CASES AND YOUTHS REFERRED FOR DELINQUENCY BY MOST SERIOUS OFFENSE IN FLORIDA, 2004–05 AND 2005–06

Offense	Cases received			Youths referred		
	2004–05	2005–06	Change	2004–05	2005–06	Change
Felony	46,385	47,947	3.4	36,621	37,644	2.8
Murder/manslaughter	93	96	3.2	92	95	3.3
Attempted murder	47	81	72.3	45	80	77.8
Sexual battery	795	748	-5.9	778	728	-6.4
Other sex offenses	1,155	1,091	-5.5	1,099	1,039	-5.5
Armed robbery	723	1,036	43.3	675	923	36.7
Other robbery	1,318	1,510	14.6	1,212	1,371	13.1
Arson	364	357	-1.9	334	323	-3.3
Burglary	12,728	12,668	-0.5	9,335	9,406	0.8
Auto theft	3,047	3,109	2.0	1,868	1,931	3.4
Grand larceny	3,034	3,386	11.6	2,329	2,639	13.3
Receiving stolen property	255	341	33.7	156	233	49.4
Concealed firearm	264	386	46.2	195	276	41.5
Aggravated assault/battery	10,306	10,330	0.2	8,990	8,833	-1.7
Forgery	426	398	-6.6	351	322	-8.3
Nonmarijuana drug	4,014	4,349	8.3	2,910	3,019	3.7
Marijuana	1,372	1,505	9.7	1,081	1,158	7.1
Escape	239	186	-22.2	114	94	-17.5
Resisting arrest with violence	395	388	-1.8	335	327	-2.4
Shooting/throwing missile	877	946	7.9	760	832	9.5
Traffic offenses	171	160	-6.4	123	120	-2.4
Other	4,762	4,876	2.4	3,839	3,895	1.5
Misdemeanor	73,215	72,171	-1.4	51,056	49,476	-3.1
Assault/battery	21,301	21,218	-0.4	15,623	15,281	-2.2
Prostitution	82	64	-22.0	62	43	-30.6
Other sex offenses	192	198	3.1	142	152	7.0
Misdemeanor theft	18,809	16,995	-9.6	15,003	13,392	-10.7
Receiving stolen property	1	4	300.0	0	3	(X)
Concealed weapon	562	619	10.1	353	409	15.9
Disorderly conduct	7,570	7,442	-1.7	4,820	4,849	0.6
Vandalism	3,038	3,232	6.4	1,877	1,940	3.4
Trespassing	4,873	4,911	0.8	2,689	2,667	-0.8
Loitering and prowling	1,334	1,491	11.8	722	741	2.6
Marijuana	8,326	8,812	5.8	5,478	5,793	5.8
Possess drug paraphernalia	887	805	-9.2	556	499	-10.3
Other misdemeanor drug	86	56	-34.9	56	33	-41.1
Possession of alcohol	1,736	1,842	6.1	1,410	1,475	4.6
Other alcohol offenses	74	79	6.8	57	68	19.3
Violation of game laws	106	98	-7.5	82	69	-15.9
Resisting arrest without violence	2,688	2,768	3.0	1,270	1,195	-5.9
Other misdemeanor	1,550	1,537	-0.8	856	867	1.3
Other delinquency	31,444	29,986	-4.6	7,577	7,108	-6.2
Contempt	2,098	2,014	-4.0	622	506	-18.6
Violation of ordinance	215	201	-6.5	124	118	-4.8
Traffic	50	64	28.0	25	39	56.0
Interstate compact	706	745	5.5	586	617	5.3
Nonlaw violation of community control or furlough	17,576	15,971	-9.1	3,836	3,477	-9.4
Prosecution previously deferred	7,214	7,302	1.2	1,654	1,565	-5.4
Transfer from other county	3,585	3,689	2.9	730	786	7.7

(X) Not applicable.

Note: Data for 2004–05 are revised. Percentage change is from fiscal year 2004–05 to 2005–06.

Source: State of Florida, Department of Juvenile Justice, Office of Research and Planning, *2005–06 Profile of Delinquency Cases and Youths Referred,* Internet site <http:/www.djj.state.fl.us/> (accessed 22, February 2007).

Table 22.21. JUVENILE DELINQUENCY: REFERRED CASES AT VARIOUS STAGES OF THE JUVENILE JUSTICE SYSTEM BY AGE, RACE, AND SEX IN FLORIDA, 2005–06

Item	Received	Disposition		
		Disposed 1/	Nonjudicial	Judicial
Total	150,104	151,027	53,202	100,564
Age				
0-9	947	954	398	514
10	1,052	1,112	523	548
11	2,220	2,360	1,083	1,257
12	5,946	6,149	2,580	3,540
13	12,936	13,115	5,210	8,010
14	21,522	21,884	8,139	14,205
15	30,316	30,372	10,575	20,458
16	34,873	34,920	11,686	24,174
17	36,494	36,316	12,015	25,082
18 and over	3,798	3,845	993	2,776
Male, total	110,864	111,222	37,574	77,206
White	45,193	45,328	16,002	30,187
Black	47,553	47,578	14,925	34,925
Other	3,249	3,181	1,154	2,140
Hispanic origin 2/	14,869	15,135	5,493	9,954
Female, total	39,240	39,805	15,628	23,358
White	18,111	18,260	7,617	9,975
Black	16,207	16,535	5,961	10,612
Other	936	953	399	537
Hispanic origin 2/	3,986	4,057	1,651	2,234

Item	Disposition (Continued)			
	Diverted from court	Placed on DJJ probation	Commit-ments 3/	Transferred to adult court
Total	32,518	37,469	10,445	3,628
Age				
0-9	340	42	0	0
10	432	122	5	0
11	831	416	61	0
12	1,933	1,364	238	0
13	3,592	3,231	778	4
14	5,191	5,776	1,661	69
15	6,356	8,039	2,486	252
16	6,687	9,052	2,759	1,024
17	6,763	8,572	2,255	2,079
18 and over	393	855	202	200
Male, total	21,336	28,850	8,610	3,378
White	10,131	12,540	3,098	914
Black	7,508	11,639	4,503	1,951
Other	588	822	202	115
Hispanic origin 2/	3,109	3,849	807	398
Female, total	11,182	8,619	1,835	250
White	5,615	3,824	812	101
Black	4,047	3,828	834	127
Other	290	222	52	1
Hispanic origin 2/	1,230	745	137	21

1/ May include more than one disposition per case. Therefore, detail may not add.
2/ Persons of Hispanic origin may be of any race.
3/ Placement in commitment programs ranging from day-treatment programs for less serious offenders to secure training schools and boot camps for more serious offenders.
Note: Since not all charges are always disposed in the same way, some duplication may exist.
Source: State of Florida, Department of Juvenile Justice, Office of Research and Planning, *2005–06 Profile of Delinquency Cases and Youths Referred,* Internet site <http:/www.djj.state.fl.us/> (accessed 22, February 2007).

Table 22.22. JUVENILE DELINQUENCY: YOUTHS REFERRED FOR DELINQUENCY TO THE JUVENILE JUSTICE SYSTEM BY AGE IN THE STATE AND COUNTIES OF FLORIDA, 2005–06

County	Total	0-9	10	11	12	13	14	15	16	17	18 and over
Florida	94,228	800	823	1,667	4,164	8,337	12,867	17,946	21,343	23,828	2,453
Alachua	1,535	17	17	24	83	174	219	288	343	322	48
Baker	149	1	2	2	7	8	15	25	38	47	4
Bay	991	10	11	24	54	68	150	174	224	261	15
Bradford	173	2	1	3	14	24	22	35	29	42	1
Brevard	2,973	23	35	63	126	265	366	527	665	789	114
Broward	7,795	65	69	139	347	703	1,052	1,454	1,768	2,005	193
Calhoun	62	2	1	0	2	5	10	16	10	14	2
Charlotte	667	6	5	10	31	67	95	126	159	153	15
Citrus	468	1	1	7	27	36	61	86	126	116	7
Clay	1,021	1	3	9	45	76	160	199	244	254	30
Collier	1,265	9	7	13	47	110	197	232	288	326	36
Columbia	377	1	1	3	13	41	55	91	71	91	10
DeSoto	190	5	0	1	9	21	28	39	42	43	2
Dixie	44	0	0	1	1	3	10	4	13	11	1
Duval	4,605	7	18	71	229	404	627	912	1,044	1,234	59
Escambia	2,167	10	17	49	114	213	341	423	455	479	66
Flagler	466	2	6	7	22	46	71	95	104	102	11
Franklin	62	0	1	1	1	5	7	9	14	20	4
Gadsden	336	3	1	4	10	22	53	88	78	67	10
Gilchrist	116	2	1	3	6	13	22	18	23	28	0
Glades	52	3	1	1	2	9	3	10	14	9	0
Gulf	72	0	2	2	4	6	8	11	14	18	7
Hamilton	65	2	0	0	2	8	10	12	13	17	1
Hardee	167	2	0	4	9	12	30	29	37	38	6
Hendry	317	2	3	3	8	25	45	68	69	85	9
Hernando	648	5	4	19	26	55	83	125	155	162	14
Highlands	600	13	10	11	28	46	82	120	133	148	9
Hillsborough	8,093	71	98	180	472	755	1,165	1,551	1,759	1,893	149
Holmes	72	1	0	3	4	9	4	8	19	23	1
Indian River	550	2	3	13	19	52	63	114	123	146	15
Jackson	206	2	1	1	17	22	40	35	43	37	8
Jefferson	49	0	1	0	3	4	4	11	12	13	1
Lafayette	3	0	0	0	0	0	0	2	0	1	0
Lake	1,494	15	11	39	77	139	179	280	347	362	45
Lee	2,578	24	13	34	92	206	305	508	655	686	55

See footnote at end of table. Continued . . .

Table 22.22. JUVENILE DELINQUENCY: YOUTHS REFERRED FOR DELINQUENCY TO THE JUVENILE JUSTICE SYSTEM BY AGE IN THE STATE AND COUNTIES OF FLORIDA, 2005–06 (Continued)

County	Total	0-9	10	11	12	13	14	15	16	17	18 and over
Leon	1,226	6	11	28	66	122	182	227	263	290	31
Levy	201	3	1	5	4	25	34	34	51	41	3
Liberty	20	0	0	0	4	2	3	2	5	4	0
Madison	98	2	2	3	5	5	10	19	19	31	2
Manatee	1,872	43	30	47	95	194	258	328	402	443	32
Marion	1,892	28	26	31	90	206	296	341	409	411	54
Martin	711	9	9	17	28	71	88	142	157	169	21
Miami-Dade	7,408	12	29	81	239	566	1,061	1,418	1,775	2,090	137
Monroe	262	0	1	1	10	23	40	48	60	72	7
Nassau	292	2	4	6	9	20	33	48	68	88	14
Okaloosa	840	8	4	12	24	60	95	164	194	253	26
Okeechobee	268	4	6	3	8	17	32	57	64	67	10
Orange	6,717	77	58	147	284	565	917	1,290	1,526	1,618	235
Osceola	1,713	41	28	40	75	180	237	288	341	397	86
Palm Beach	5,299	21	42	82	193	422	670	1,020	1,237	1,417	195
Pasco	1,639	8	4	25	54	133	222	316	387	429	61
Pinellas	5,395	53	56	76	256	498	733	1,098	1,197	1,316	112
Polk	4,223	68	71	107	247	442	628	805	882	883	90
Putnam	770	7	5	11	55	72	142	131	156	171	20
St. Johns	736	15	10	13	22	67	99	98	181	204	27
St. Lucie	1,583	10	12	29	84	152	232	334	324	358	48
Santa Rosa	609	2	5	7	23	48	75	112	154	166	17
Sarasota	1,334	14	6	17	43	99	167	261	308	383	36
Seminole	2,263	12	12	41	73	178	269	435	528	656	59
Sumter	247	0	2	5	8	21	34	60	56	55	6
Suwannee	255	3	5	4	12	33	30	43	57	61	7
Taylor	125	1	2	4	4	12	13	24	30	30	5
Union	46	0	2	0	3	5	6	9	10	10	1
Volusia	3,582	30	28	60	141	322	464	684	824	940	89
Wakulla	156	3	0	1	8	11	19	28	37	44	5
Walton	178	2	0	2	1	6	19	36	51	52	9
Washington	105	0	0	3	2	8	16	20	25	28	3

Note: The number of youths referred is determined by counting only the most serious offense for which a youth is charged during the fiscal year. This differs from the number of cases received in that the most serious offense on any given date is counted as one case. Therefore, the same youth may be referred for additional offenses on different dates throughout the year, resulting in more than one case received.

Source: State of Florida, Department of Juvenile Justice, Office of Research and Planning, *2005–06 Profile of Delinquency Cases and Youths Referred,* Internet site <http:/www.djj.state.fl.us/> (accessed 22, February 2007).

Table 22.23. JUVENILE DELINQUENCY: YOUTHS REFERRED FOR DELINQUENCY TO THE JUVENILE JUSTICE SYSTEM BY SEX AND RACE IN THE STATE AND COUNTIES OF FLORIDA, 2005–06

County	Total 1/	Percentage change from 2004-05	Male				Female			
			White	Black	Hispanic	Other	White	Black	Hispanic	Other
Florida	94,228	-1.1	29,194	25,763	9,509	1,877	13,331	10,868	3,010	676
Alachua	1,535	14.5	342	662	15	5	158	347	4	2
Baker	149	-15.3	77	21	1	0	28	22	0	0
Bay	991	1.6	479	196	18	13	178	97	6	4
Bradford	173	8.1	62	56	0	2	27	24	2	0
Brevard	2,973	9.2	1,352	539	92	36	664	251	23	16
Broward	7,795	-5.4	1,772	3,041	674	422	634	936	194	122
Calhoun	62	10.7	34	9	1	2	12	4	0	0
Charlotte	667	6.0	352	48	19	5	202	29	10	2
Citrus	468	-10.0	284	22	20	7	115	7	8	5
Clay	1,021	9.7	539	144	25	12	232	54	13	2
Collier	1,265	7.4	409	86	341	59	204	39	97	30
Columbia	377	-5.3	154	91	10	2	59	60	1	0
DeSoto	190	3.3	63	43	28	0	23	18	14	1
Dixie	44	-10.2	24	4	0	0	10	4	2	0
Duval	4,605	-10.8	1,014	2,039	93	46	544	798	40	31
Escambia	2,167	-1.1	559	862	28	19	293	380	16	10
Flagler	466	10.2	180	90	28	7	105	41	12	3
Franklin	62	6.9	42	9	1	0	7	3	0	0
Gadsden	336	-1.2	19	210	6	2	8	86	3	2
Gilchrist	173	8.1	62	56	0	2	27	24	2	0
Glades	52	8.3	18	15	9	0	4	3	1	2
Gulf	62	10.7	34	9	1	2	12	4	0	0
Hamilton	65	-21.7	10	24	3	0	6	21	1	0
Hardee	167	-2.9	64	25	29	1	28	10	9	1
Hendry	317	-1.6	63	61	93	9	25	26	35	5
Hernando	648	-10.1	343	74	36	3	153	27	10	2
Highlands	600	6.4	242	105	61	3	107	72	9	1
Hillsborough	8,093	1.1	2,001	2,461	1,027	49	1,024	1,157	340	34
Holmes	72	2.9	47	6	1	0	17	1	0	0
Indian River	550	3.6	252	108	39	2	92	47	10	0
Jackson	206	12.0	59	73	8	1	36	25	4	0
Jefferson	49	-3.9	11	22	0	0	7	9	0	0
Lafayette	3	-66.7	2	0	0	0	1	0	0	0
Lake	1,494	0.5	564	334	123	12	242	179	38	2
Lee	2,578	2.6	973	435	359	31	487	164	110	19
Leon	1,226	-8.5	272	544	14	12	140	231	7	6

See footnotes at end of table. Continued . . .

Table 22.23. JUVENILE DELINQUENCY: YOUTHS REFERRED FOR DELINQUENCY TO THE JUVENILE JUSTICE SYSTEM BY SEX AND RACE IN THE STATE AND COUNTIES OF FLORIDA, 2005–06 (Continued)

County	Total 1/	Percentage change from 2004-05	Male				Female			
			White	Black	Hispanic	Other	White	Black	Hispanic	Other
Levy	201	4.1	97	40	2	0	48	14	0	0
Liberty	20	0.0	12	3	0	0	4	1	0	0
Madison	98	-30.5	15	50	1	0	7	25	0	0
Manatee	1,872	-1.9	645	364	229	18	319	202	84	11
Marion	1,892	1.9	717	480	102	5	332	213	35	8
Martin	711	15.4	277	141	91	4	110	63	21	4
Miami-Dade	7,408	-6.2	321	2,536	2,270	466	121	992	577	125
Monroe	262	-10.6	119	41	37	1	30	15	16	3
Nassau	292	-3.6	168	31	4	1	78	6	3	1
Okaloosa	840	0.1	412	127	19	9	217	45	4	7
Okeechobee	268	-0.4	116	19	55	5	49	6	16	2
Orange	6,717	3.4	1,386	2,231	972	155	664	926	341	42
Osceola	1,713	2.1	510	237	513	20	190	78	159	6
Palm Beach	5,299	-0.6	1,388	1,667	474	215	631	700	150	74
Pasco	1,639	-8.2	931	123	102	7	393	45	35	3
Pinellas	5,395	-3.6	2,017	1,425	185	81	956	618	87	26
Polk	4,223	-0.8	1,525	974	429	15	656	462	150	12
Putnam	770	7.2	245	232	27	3	124	130	8	1
St. Johns	736	4.8	385	108	10	2	157	62	9	3
St. Lucie	1,583	9.1	415	536	120	26	215	220	44	7
Santa Rosa	609	-6.3	358	49	16	5	158	16	3	4
Sarasota	1,334	-5.8	656	198	69	15	274	86	31	5
Seminole	2,263	6.8	851	500	236	15	377	208	70	6
Sumter	247	6.5	112	58	6	2	38	27	4	0
Suwannee	255	-7.3	123	54	11	2	35	28	2	0
Taylor	125	-32.1	58	33	0	0	18	15	1	0
Union	46	-16.4	18	9	0	0	13	6	0	0
Volusia	3,582	2.1	1,492	709	207	22	723	336	84	9
Wakulla	156	2.6	94	24	0	1	29	7	0	1
Walton	178	-13.6	104	20	0	0	47	4	2	1
Washington	105	1.0	59	14	0	0	26	6	0	0

1/ Includes unknown race or out-of-state not shown separately.

Note: The number of youths referred is determined by counting only the most serious offense for which a youth is charged during the fiscal year. This differs from the number of cases received in that the most serious offense on any given date is counted as one case. Therefore, the same youth may be referred for additional offenses on different dates throughout the year, resulting in more than one case received.

Source: State of Florida, Department of Juvenile Justice, Office of Research and Planning, *2005–06 Profile of Delinquency Cases and Youths Referred,* Internet site <http:/www.djj.state.fl.us/> (accessed 22, February 2007).

Table 22.24. JUVENILE DELINQUENCY: YOUTHS COMMITTING VIOLENT FELONY OFFENSES BY TYPE OF OFFENSE IN THE STATE, JUDICIAL CIRCUIT, AND COUNTIES OF FLORIDA, 2005–06

Judicial circuit and county	Total 1/ Number	Total 1/ Percentage change from 2004–05	Murder 2/	Sex offense	Robbery	Aggravated assault	Resisting arrest with violence	Shoot or throw a deadly missile
Florida	14,228	1.7	175	1,767	2,294	8,833	327	832
Circuit 1	475	-8.5	1	65	37	330	8	34
Escambia	328	-12.3	1	30	29	239	4	25
Okaloosa	64	-14.7	0	7	7	44	1	5
Santa Rosa	63	16.7	0	25	1	35	1	1
Walton	20	25.0	0	3	0	12	2	3
Circuit 2	330	6.1	2	46	26	235	13	8
Franklin	10	25.0	0	2	1	5	0	2
Gadsden	111	18.1	0	7	6	91	5	2
Jefferson	12	9.1	0	6	2	4	0	0
Leon	172	-2.3	2	23	14	121	8	4
Liberty	4	0.0	0	2	0	2	0	0
Wakulla	21	16.7	0	6	3	12	0	0
Circuit 3	144	-15.8	0	29	13	88	4	10
Columbia	53	-29.3	0	12	6	30	2	3
Dixie	5	-44.4	0	2	0	3	0	0
Hamilton	11	-42.1	0	1	1	7	0	2
Lafayette	0	-100.0	0	0	0	0	0	0
Madison	9	-62.5	0	0	2	7	0	0
Suwannee	49	172.2	0	11	4	31	2	1
Taylor	17	-39.3	0	3	0	10	0	4
Circuit 4	935	2.7	8	164	160	543	11	49
Clay	106	17.8	0	18	6	72	3	7
Duval	800	1.3	8	138	151	454	8	41
Nassau	29	-3.3	0	8	3	17	0	1
Circuit 5	787	12.6	8	155	67	484	12	61
Citrus	72	7.5	0	13	5	45	0	9
Hernando	102	-22.1	1	23	1	65	5	7
Lake	280	30.2	1	57	34	158	5	25
Marion	286	16.7	4	52	24	187	2	17
Sumter	47	14.6	2	10	3	29	0	3
Circuit 6	937	-5.9	6	114	127	596	27	67
Pasco	196	-9.7	0	39	26	118	3	10
Pinellas	741	-4.9	6	75	101	478	24	57
Circuit 7	798	3.9	1	97	82	554	22	42
Flagler	64	18.5	0	13	2	44	3	2
Putnam	140	7.7	0	19	15	93	2	11
St. Johns	108	25.6	0	12	8	84	2	2
Volusia	486	-2.4	1	53	57	333	15	27
Circuit 8	397	32.3	5	59	48	257	8	20
Alachua	290	47.2	2	37	43	183	8	17
Baker	29	31.8	1	6	1	21	0	0
Bradford	30	3.4	0	3	2	23	0	2
Gilchrist	11	-31.3	0	4	0	6	0	1
Levy	29	3.6	2	8	1	18	0	0
Union	8	0.0	0	1	1	6	0	0
Circuit 9	1,392	15.5	22	138	261	879	24	68
Orange	1,099	15.8	21	101	238	676	22	41
Osceola	293	14.5	1	37	23	203	2	27

See footnotes at end of table. Continued. . .

Table 22.24. JUVENILE DELINQUENCY: YOUTHS COMMITTING VIOLENT FELONY OFFENSES BY TYPE OF OFFENSE IN THE STATE, JUDICIAL CIRCUIT, AND COUNTIES OF FLORIDA, 2005–06 (Continued)

Judicial circuit and county	Total 1/ Number	Total 1/ Percentage change from 2004–05	Murder 2/	Sex offense	Robbery	Aggra- vated assault	Resisting arrest with violence	Shoot or throw a deadly missile
Circuit 10	600	-7.8	7	93	47	382	14	57
Hardee	26	-7.1	1	1	4	19	0	1
Highlands	70	-20.5	0	15	0	49	1	5
Polk	504	-5.8	6	77	43	314	13	51
Circuit 11	1,592	-7.0	35	100	391	942	29	95
Miami-Dade	1,592	-7.0	35	100	391	942	29	95
Circuit 12	440	-9.8	8	83	56	268	8	17
DeSoto	25	-30.6	0	4	4	14	1	2
Manatee	263	-3.0	5	55	39	149	6	9
Sarasota	152	-16.0	3	24	13	105	1	6
Circuit 13	1,240	6.8	14	135	182	822	19	68
Hillsborough	1,240	6.8	14	135	182	822	19	68
Circuit 14	180	8.4	1	44	19	101	5	10
Bay	96	-7.7	0	20	14	50	4	8
Calhoun	9	-25.0	0	1	0	8	0	0
Gulf	10	-9.1	0	2	0	7	0	1
Holmes	14	366.7	0	11	1	2	0	0
Jackson	36	56.5	1	5	1	27	1	1
Washington	15	15.4	0	5	3	7	0	0
Circuit 15	826	-5.1	12	86	191	480	24	33
Palm Beach	826	-5.1	12	86	191	480	24	33
Circuit 16	33	-13.2	1	2	2	23	4	1
Monroe	33	-13.2	1	2	2	23	4	1
Circuit 17	1,218	-4.1	17	106	321	648	58	68
Broward	1,218	-4.1	17	106	321	648	58	68
Circuit 18	743	18.7	9	99	95	474	15	51
Brevard	425	28.8	8	52	40	286	9	30
Seminole	318	7.4	1	47	55	188	6	21
Circuit 19	480	7.6	12	52	52	335	8	21
Indian River	51	2.0	1	7	6	34	1	2
Martin	105	-6.3	1	10	15	69	3	7
Okeechobee	38	11.8	1	9	1	25	1	1
St. Lucie	286	14.4	9	26	30	207	3	11
Circuit 20	515	9.6	5	68	101	284	13	44
Charlotte	62	14.8	0	12	7	35	2	6
Collier	123	-7.5	2	11	21	71	5	13
Glades	9	125.0	0	2	1	5	0	1
Hendry	48	26.3	0	4	3	31	0	10
Lee	273	13.3	3	39	69	142	6	14

1/ The number of youths referred is determined by counting only the most serious offense for which a youth is charged during the fiscal year. This differs from the number of cases received in that the most serious offense on any given date is counted as one case. Therefore, the same youth may be referred for additional offenses on different dates throughout the year.
2/ Includes attempted murder and manslaughter.

Source: State of Florida, Department of Juvenile Justice, Office of Research and Planning, *2005–06 Profile of Delinquency Cases and Youths Referred,* Internet site <http:/www.djj.state.fl.us/> (accessed 22, February 2007).

Table 22.30. VICTIM SERVICES: CRIMES COMPENSATION TRUST FUNDS RECEIPTS IN THE STATE, JUDICIAL CIRCUITS, AND COUNTIES OF FLORIDA FISCAL YEAR 2005–06

(rounded to dollars)

Judicial circuit and county	Total	Court costs 1/	Other 2/
Florida	25,904,766	20,306,353	5,598,413
Circuit 1	1,188,738	986,628	202,110
Escambia	451,466	345,347	106,119
Okaloosa	435,188	381,649	53,539
Santa Rosa	179,056	160,102	18,954
Walton	123,027	99,530	23,497
Circuit 2	334,860	185,508	149,352
Franklin	46,582	41,571	5,011
Gadsden	82,404	76,508	5,896
Jefferson	18,820	15,359	3,461
Leon	123,779	50	123,729
Liberty	9,249	8,582	667
Wakulla	54,025	43,438	10,587
Circuit 3	336,848	222,297	114,551
Columbia	147,448	111,562	35,886
Dixie	16,707	13,733	2,974
Hamilton	28,827	0	28,827
Lafayette	14,693	9,498	5,195
Madison	15,102	0	15,102
Suwannee	64,402	46,360	18,042
Taylor	49,669	41,144	8,525
Circuit 4	1,984,902	1,654,666	330,236
Clay	280,823	235,436	45,387
Duval	1,563,559	1,288,017	275,542
Nassau	140,520	131,212	9,308
Circuit 5	1,509,444	1,165,784	343,660
Citrus	231,183	143,147	88,036
Hernando	233,738	201,892	31,846
Lake	382,931	318,279	64,652
Marion	559,489	432,516	126,973
Sumter	102,103	69,951	32,152
Circuit 6	2,093,878	1,663,372	430,506
Pasco	569,367	490,394	78,973
Pinellas	1,524,511	1,172,978	351,533
Circuit 7	1,273,547	1,107,200	166,347
Flagler	107,711	93,584	14,127
Putnam	90,902	85,489	5,413
St. Johns	210,160	187,921	22,239
Volusia	864,773	740,205	124,568
Circuit 8	443,092	351,770	91,322
Alachua	276,762	229,924	46,838
Baker	40,572	37,820	2,752
Bradford	43,530	25,875	17,655
Gilchrist	28,524	16,442	12,082
Circuit 8 (Cont.)			
Levy	43,524	34,908	8,616
Union	10,179	6,801	3,378
Circuit 9	1,808,011	308,550	1,499,461
Orange	1,459,553	0	1,459,553
Osceola	348,458	308,550	39,908
Circuit 10	1,170,264	1,038,398	131,866
Hardee	56,668	50,189	6,479
Highlands	139,708	121,407	18,301
Polk	973,888	866,802	107,086
Circuit 11	1,930,238	1,580,145	350,093
Miami-Dade	1,930,238	1,580,145	350,093
Circuit 12	1,045,809	868,294	177,515
DeSoto	46,211	39,302	6,909
Manatee	453,300	345,003	108,297
Sarasota	546,298	483,989	62,309
Circuit 13	2,170,032	1,954,651	215,381
Hillsborough	2,170,032	1,954,651	215,381
Circuit 14	682,827	558,320	124,507
Bay	456,945	371,425	85,520
Calhoun	38,172	33,805	4,367
Gulf	30,354	25,257	5,097
Holmes	49,754	42,374	7,380
Jackson	61,878	48,891	12,987
Washington	45,723	36,568	9,155
Circuit 15	1,010,323	862,482	147,841
Palm Beach	1,010,323	862,482	147,841
Circuit 16	201,325	174,572	26,753
Monroe	201,325	174,572	26,753
Circuit 17	2,692,456	2,500,954	191,502
Broward	2,692,456	2,500,954	191,502
Circuit 18	1,512,201	1,179,459	332,742
Brevard	927,768	684,075	243,693
Seminole	584,432	495,384	89,048
Circuit 19	985,287	738,750	246,537
Indian River	198,920	162,440	36,480
Martin	274,409	197,344	77,065
Okeechobee	90,088	57,495	32,593
St. Lucie	421,871	321,471	100,400
Circuit 20	1,530,686	1,204,553	326,133
Charlotte	186,652	146,221	40,431
Collier	768,829	653,714	115,115
Glades	16,722	14,140	2,582
Hendry	84,905	68,531	16,374
Lee	473,578	321,946	151,632

1/ Mandatory court cost is $50 per conviction of which the court clerk retains $1.
2/ Includes surcharges, offense fines, interest, restitution, subrogation, refunds, and other receipts.

Source: State of Florida, Office of the Attorney General, Division of Victim Services, *Annual Report, 2005-2006,* Internet site <http://www.myfloridalegal.com/> (accessed 22, February 2007).

Table 22.50. HATE CRIMES: HATE-MOTIVATED CRIMES BY TYPE OF OFFENSE AND BY MOTIVATION IN FLORIDA, 1999 THROUGH 2005

Offense and motivation	1999	2000	2001	2002	2003	2004	2005
Offenses, total	307	269	335	306	275	334	260
Crimes against persons	212	174	207	220	186	254	185
Percentage of total	69.1	64.7	61.8	71.9	67.6	76.0	71.2
Assaults	104	131	124	156	134	177	106
Percentage of total	33.9	48.7	37.0	51.0	48.7	53.0	40.8
Motivation							
Race/color	180	155	129	161	135	190	130
Percentage of total	58.6	57.6	38.5	52.6	49.1	56.9	50.0
Religion	48	44	68	41	34	41	36
Percentage of total	15.6	16.4	20.3	13.4	12.4	12.3	13.8
Ethnicity	31	28	95	44	51	51	58
Percentage of total	10.1	10.4	28.4	14.4	18.5	15.3	22.3
Sexual orientation	48	41	42	56	55	52	34
Percentage of total	15.6	15.2	12.5	18.3	20.0	15.6	13.1

Note: A hate crime is an act committed or attempted by one person or group against another person or group, or their property, that in any way constitutes an expression of hatred toward the victim based on his or her personal characteristics. It is a crime in which the perpetrator intentionally selects the victim based on one of the following characteristics: race, color, religion, ethnicity, ancestry, national origin, or sexual orientation. Some data may be revised.

Source: State of Florida, Office of the Attorney General, *Hate Crimes in Florida, January 1, 2005 through December 31, 2005,* Internet site <http://myfloridalegal.com> (accessed 22, February 2007).

Table 22.51. LAWYERS: NUMBER AND MEMBERS IN GOOD STANDING OF THE FLORIDA BAR BY SECTION IN FLORIDA, JUNE 1, 2007

Section	Number of members	Section	Number of members
Total attorneys	98,424	Members in sections (Continued)	
		Labor and employment	2,148
Florida	60,525	International	1,023
Out-of-state	12,325	Entertainment, arts, and sports	963
Foreign	189	Health	1,352
Members in good standing, total	73,039	Public interest	498
Male attorneys	49,337	Governmental	1,093
Female attorneys	23,702	Elder	1,651
Members in sections, total	30,093	Out-of-state	1,154
Tax	2,035	Appellate practice	1,550
Real property, probate	9,669		
Trial	6,825		
Business	4,739	Delinquent members	814
General	2,160	Suspended/disbarred	240
Family	3,634	Deceased/resigned	6,651
Local government	1,688	Retired	4,323
Workers' compensation	1,553	Inactive/incapacity	8,432
Criminal	2,785	Lapsed	3,383
Environmental and land use	2,073	Young lawyers (all)	19,225
Administrative	1,218		

Source: The Florida Bar, release from the Records Department, June 1, 2007.

Table 22.52. LAWYERS: NUMBER AND MEMBERS IN GOOD STANDING OF THE FLORIDA BAR IN THE STATE AND COUNTIES OF FLORIDA, JUNE 1, 2007

County	Number of members	County	Number of members
Total	73,039	Lafayette	3
Florida	60,525	Lake	323
Out-of-state	12,325	Lee	1,159
Foreign	189	Leon	3,043
Alachua	900	Levy	38
Baker	14	Liberty	1
Bay	298	Madison	13
Bradford	27	Manatee	536
Brevard	939	Marion	481
Broward	7,869	Martin	488
Calhoun	7	Miami-Dade	12,737
Charlotte	193	Monroe	278
Citrus	130	Nassau	72
Clay	160	Okaloosa	308
Collier	868	Okeechobee	33
Columbia	105	Orange	4,793
DeSoto	26	Osceola	204
Dixie	4	Palm Beach	5,864
Duval	3,113	Pasco	419
Escambia	760	Pinellas	3,050
Flagler	72	Polk	895
Franklin	16	Putnam	87
Gadsden	46	St. Johns	383
Gilchrist	13	St. Lucie	350
Glades	4	Santa Rosa	119
Gulf	20	Sarasota	1,235
Hamilton	9	Seminole	771
Hardee	13	Sumter	48
Hendry	25	Suwannee	50
Hernando	158	Taylor	16
Highlands	87	Union	4
Hillsborough	5,338	Volusia	988
Holmes	8	Wakulla	33
Indian River	313	Walton	81
Jackson	35	Washington	15
Jefferson	30		

Note: Detail may not add to total due to nondisclosure of confidential membership data.

Source: The Florida Bar, release from the Records Department, June 1, 2007.

Table 22.55. LEGAL SERVICES: AVERAGE MONTHLY PRIVATE REPORTING UNITS, EMPLOYMENT AND PAYROLL COVERED BY UNEMPLOYMENT COMPENSATION LAW IN THE STATE AND COUNTIES OF FLORIDA, 2006

County	Number of reporting units	Number of employees	Payroll ($1,000)	County	Number of reporting units	Number of employees	Payroll ($1,000)
			Legal services (NAICS code 5411)				
Florida	18,367	92,299	552,297	Leon	375	2,847	19,009
Alachua	196	997	4,010	Levy	11	49	102
Baker	5	15	50	Madison	3	16	73
Bay	112	487	2,036	Manatee	180	771	3,237
Bradford	11	35	77	Marion	190	745	3,586
Brevard	336	1,227	5,480	Martin	145	745	4,033
Broward	2,709	11,658	68,095	Miami-Dade	3,878	19,700	140,503
Calhoun	3	11	24	Monroe	92	254	1,132
Charlotte	76	373	2,318	Nassau	30	81	361
Citrus	62	232	752	Okaloosa	140	656	2,508
Clay	61	249	854	Okeechobee	13	69	182
Collier	298	1,339	8,098	Orange	1,187	8,863	56,614
Columbia	35	122	447	Osceola	83	243	776
DeSoto	7	39	137	Palm Beach	1,910	8,736	57,124
Duval	743	4,764	28,645	Pasco	186	649	2,552
Escambia	206	1,490	7,756	Pinellas	965	4,434	20,938
Flagler	43	131	496	Polk	269	1,537	7,666
Franklin	5	15	51	Putnam	24	59	155
Gadsden	9	16	28	St. Johns	102	456	1,726
Gilchrist	6	20	41	St. Lucie	120	406	1,824
Gulf	10	33	110	Santa Rosa	36	183	814
Hardee	6	32	70	Sarasota	452	2,136	12,148
Hendry	8	25	56	Seminole	317	1,003	3,838
Hernando	65	201	639	Sumter	17	64	173
Highlands	36	214	657	Suwannee	9	35	114
Hillsborough	1,329	8,583	54,480	Taylor	10	33	109
Holmes	6	16	40	Volusia	338	1,371	6,006
Indian River	100	432	2,342	Wakulla	9	35	100
Jackson	14	55	127	Walton	51	127	357
Jefferson	7	20	44	Washington	5	10	20
Lake	133	612	3,024	Statewide 1/	22	90	774
Lee	412	2,188	11,010	Unknown 1/	133	242	1,677

NAICS North American Industry Classification System. See Glossary for definition.

1/ Reporting units without a fixed location within the state or of unknown county location.

Note: Private employment. These data include establishments which are engaged in offering legal advice or services and which are headed by a member of the Bar. Data are preliminary. Only counties for which data are disclosed are shown. Detail may not add to totals due to disclosure editing and/or rounding. See Tables 23.70, 23.72, 23.73, and 23.74 for public employment data.

Source: State of Florida, Agency for Workforce Innovation, Labor Market Statistics, "Quarterly Census of Employment and Wages" (ES-202), Annual NAICS files, Internet site <http://www.labormarketinfo.com/index.htm> (accessed 17, July 2007).

GOVERNMENT FINANCE AND EMPLOYMENT

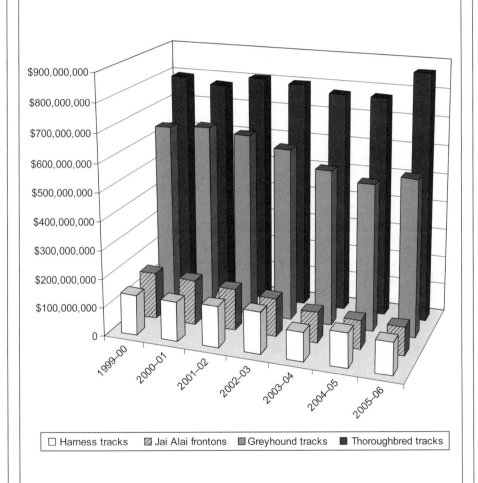

Pari-mutuel Handle by Type of Event in Florida 1999–00 Through 2005–06

Source: Table 23.54

Section 23.00
Government Finance and Employment

This section presents data about Florida's finances and public employment. Previous sections have reported private industry employment. Statistics in this section include federal, state, and local government finance, including tax collections and disbursements; defense contract awards and payroll and veteran data; state lottery sales, pari-mutuel wagering, and tobacco and alcoholic beverage licensing; state retirement system data; government employment and payroll; property valuations; and land use data.

Explanatory notes. A number of tables in the Health, Education, and Cultural Services section (20.00) contain data on property valuations, revenue, expenditure, and taxes for education by public agencies. In Section 19.00, Table 19.54 provides figures on the tourist-development/ local option tax and Table 19.70 provides information about tax collections from tourist- and recreation-related businesses.

Even though the official records of the Comptroller are used by the Census Bureau in its compilations on state and local government finances, the Census Bureau has found it necessary at times to classify and present the government financial statistics in terms of its own system of uniform concepts and categories, rather than according to the diverse terminology and structure of individual governments. This procedure explains the differences that may be found between similar data from the two sources.

Public government employment data by industry and county based on the North American Industry Classification System (NAICS) (See the introduction to Section 6.00 and the Glossary) are from the office of Labor Market Statistics in the state's Agency for Workforce Innovation.

Sources. The U.S. Census Bureau publishes a number of annual series and various other data on the Internet. Users should contact the Census Bureau for a list of current publications. Two sources for government expenditure data are *Federal Aid to States* and *Consolidated Federal Funds Report.* Other federal, state, and local revenue and expenditure data are also available on the Census Bureau Web site.

The Census Bureau conducts a *Census of Governments* every five years, coincident with the economic censuses. Results from the current 2002 census relevant to public government employment and payroll appear on Tables 23.77 and 23.78.

Information pertaining to Florida's defense contract awards and payroll appear in *Atlas/Data Abstract for the US and Selected Areas,* published on the Internet by the Statistical Information Analysis Division of the Directorate for Information Operations and Reports within the U.S. Department of Defense. Veterans' Administration expenditures appear in *Geographical Distribution of the Department of Veterans Affairs Expenditures* on the Internet.

Official records and reports of the Florida Department of Financial Services comprise the basic source of information about government finances in Florida and appear in the *Comprehensive Financial Report* and in unpublished form.

Other State of Florida agencies providing sources of data on government finances and employment include:

- Department of Revenue's, *Florida Property Valuations and Tax Data.*
- Department of Business and Professional Regulation (pari-mutuel wagering and beverage and tobacco licenses).
- Department of the Lottery Department of Highway Safety and Motor Vehicles.
- *Annual Report of the State Treasurer.*
- Division of Retirement in the Department of Management Services' *Florida Retirement System Annual Report.*
- Department of Banking and Finance, Office of the Comptroller.

Users are encouraged to search other state government agency Web sites on the Internet on the state's official Web site at www.myflorida.com.

The Florida Department of Revenue annually reviews the ad valorem tax rolls submitted by county property appraisers. Armasi, Inc., compiles data from these tax rolls, making the data available with software that displays data geographically by county. Table 23.97 presents assessed land use values by county summarized by Armasi, Inc., from the Department of Revenue files.

Section 23.00
Government Finance and Employment

Tables listed by major heading

Tables listed by major heading

Table 23.07. FEDERAL GOVERNMENT FINANCE: EXPENDITURE BY AGENCY AND BY SPECIFIED PROGRAM IN FLORIDA AND THE UNITED STATES, FISCAL YEAR 2004

(in thousands of dollars)

Item	Florida	United States
Total expenditure	120,498,450	2,110,194,884
Grants and other payments to state and local governments, total	18,174,467	408,143,442
Department of Agriculture	1,015,824	23,183,867
Agricultural Marketing Service	16,663	535,942
Cooperative State Research–Education and Extension Service	25,682	1,028,994
Extension activities	9,909	449,742
Research and education activities	15,773	579,252
Farm Service Agency	70	6,730
Food and Nutrition Service	939,644	20,220,383
Child nutrition programs	622,487	11,131,792
Commodity assistance program	5,538	169,685
Food Stamp program	82,862	4,060,040
Special supplemental food program (WIC)	228,757	4,857,959
Forest Service	5,446	602,205
Payments to states and counties	2,426	372,294
Rural community and emergency fire fighting program	157	6,953
State and private forestry	2,853	211,923
National Forest Service	10	7,410
Natural Resources Conservation Service	368	38,547
Rural development activities	27,951	663,292
Water systems and waste disposal systems grants	9,895	516,393
Department of Commerce	34,898	919,608
Economic Development Administration	15,438	373,478
National Oceanic and Atmospheric Administration	18,522	489,306
National Telecommunications and Information Administration	938	56,002
Corporation for National and Community Services	1,693	115,060
Corporation for Public Broadcasting	13,314	411,970
Department of Defense	6	327,738
Department of Education	1,814,563	31,250,823
Office of English Language Acquisition	29,851	575,427
Office of Educational Research and Improvement	18,253	432,993
Office of Special Education and Rehabilitative Services	642,028	9,483,468
Office of Vocational and Adult Education	97,322	1,500,280
Office of Elementary and Secondary Education	964,408	17,121,382
Office of Postsecondary Education	35,281	1,258,146
Office of Student Financial Assistance	27,420	879,127
Election Assistance Commmission	47,417	1,333,855
Department of Energy	12,297	807,128
Environmental Protection Agency	145,769	4,311,080
Equal Employment Opportunity Commission	1,601	29,622
Department of Health and Human Services	10,560,497	234,754,728
Administration for Children and Families	1,785,667	44,356,998
Child care and development	253,948	4,784,436
Child support enforcement	151,005	2,903,732
Children and Family Services (Headstart)	315,115	8,263,220
Safe and Stable Families	18,410	420,067
Foster care and adoption assistance	199,822	6,331,125
Low-income home energy assistance	19,532	1,755,574
Refugee and entrant assistance	83,713	382,265
Social Services Block Grant	97,185	1,751,670
Temporary Assistance to Needy Families (TANF)	642,327	17,467,859

See footnotes at end of table.

Continued . . .

Table 23.07. FEDERAL GOVERNMENT FINANCE: EXPENDITURE BY AGENCY AND BY SPECIFIED PROGRAM IN FLORIDA AND THE UNITED STATES, FISCAL YEAR 2004 (Continued)

(in thousands of dollars)

Item	Florida	United States
Grants and other payments to state and local governments (Continued)		
Department of Health and Human Services (Continued)		
Administration on Aging	87,901	1,319,999
Agency for Healthcare Research and Quality 1/	340	44,996
Centers for Disease Control and Prevention	24,238	668,303
Centers for Medicare and Medicaid Services	8,163,296	180,115,148
Health Resources and Services Administration	325,582	5,321,337
Substance Abuse and Mental Health Services Administration	173,473	2,827,792
Department of Homeland Security	270,326	5,773,246
Coast guard	3,607	53,299
Domestic preparedness and anti-terrorism programs 1/	132,509	3,121,178
Federal Emergency Management Agency	134,210	2,507,769
Disaster relief	122,832	2,032,813
Department of Housing and Urban Development	1,404,958	40,431,028
Fair housing and equal opportunity	2,712	46,098
Community planning and development	251,524	6,732,738
Housing programs	88,024	2,036,685
Public housing programs	1,015,411	29,898,609
Home ownership assistance	46,990	1,597,993
Institute for Museum and Library Services	11,944	246,216
Department of the Interior	29,473	3,917,106
Bureau of Indian Affairs	7,544	853,818
Bureau of Land Management	2,887	399,488
Fish and Wildlife Service	15,305	607,848
Minerals management service	25	1,248,693
National Park Service	3,712	116,739
Department of Justice	252,978	4,526,973
Office of asset forfeiture	24,956	236,563
Office of Justice Programs	227,295	4,283,748
Law Enforcemnt Assistance	134,324	2,766,326
Community oriented policing program (COPS)	31,768	704,421
Violence against women and children	8,908	284,652
Substance abuse programs	38,473	876,634
Department of Labor	282,798	8,748,984
Bureau of Labor Statistics	3,149	89,799
Employment and Training Administration	268,725	8,318,572
State Unemployment Insurance and Employment Service	104,665	3,404,182
Workforce Investment	132,425	3,166,369
Veterans Employment and Training Administration	8,732	183,124
National Foundation on the Arts and the Humanities	827	37,016
Neighborhood Reinvestment Corporation	2,242	76,403
Social Security Administration supplemental security income	1,600	30,878
State Justice Institute	2	1,767
Department of Transportation	1,981,531	40,079,575
Federal Aviation Administration	130,979	2,680,899
Federal Highway Administration	1,569,142	29,878,393
Highway Trust Fund	1,563,475	28,880,593
Federal Transit Administraton	262,113	6,818,074
Department of the Treasury	276,390	5,398,141
Department of Veterans Affairs	11,495	646,105

See footnotes at end of table. Continued . . .

Table 23.07. FEDERAL GOVERNMENT FINANCE: EXPENDITURE BY AGENCY AND BY SPECIFIED PROGRAM IN FLORIDA AND THE UNITED STATES, FISCAL YEAR 2004 (Continued)

(in thousands of dollars)

Item	Florida	United States
Expenditure for salaries and wages	10,394,686	225,601,344
Nondefense Civilian	6,005,001	136,618,955
Department of Defense	4,389,685	88,982,389
Other defense civilian	139,963	4,783,642
Military services	4,249,722	84,198,747
Active	2,845,392	50,932,566
Inactive	361,003	10,561,834
Civilian	1,043,327	22,704,347
Army	501,784	32,284,066
Navy	2,063,474	29,304,761
Air Force	1,684,464	22,609,920
Nondefense agencies	6,005,001	136,618,955
Agriculture	101,044	5,707,828
Commerce	54,213	2,538,313
Education	335	364,676
Energy	109	1,326,615
Environmental Protection Agency	6,875	1,494,644
Federal Deposit Insurance Corporation	5,546	502,566
General Services Administration	6,958	936,686
Health and Human Services	17,235	4,393,816
Homeland Security	583,192	8,433,962
Housing and Urban Development	20,076	812,386
Interior	79,963	4,126,443
Justice	388,134	10,133,630
Labor	31,933	1,242,288
National Aeronautics and Space Administration	155,463	1,659,774
Postal Service	2,813,123	52,030,998
Small Business Administration	5,085	255,926
Social Security Administration	135,381	3,855,721
State	25,912	1,111,956
Transportation	285,271	5,638,180
Treasury	193,421	6,835,610
Veterans Affairs	849,799	13,008,712
Other nondefense	29,233	8,097,699
Direct payments for individuals for retirement and disability	48,049,721	666,969,380
Social Security payments	36,881,522	526,594,468
Retirement insurance payments	23,987,479	315,780,113
Survivors insurance payments	5,996,244	96,551,586
Disability insurance payments	4,760,411	80,439,028
Supplemental security income payments	2,137,388	33,823,741
Federal retirement and disability benefits	8,157,046	95,989,340
Civilian	3,646,090	53,358,037
Military	4,510,956	42,631,303
Veterans benefits	2,142,769	29,312,175
Payments for service connected disability	1,623,275	22,145,959
Other benefit payments	519,494	7,166,216
Other	868,384	15,073,398

See footnotes at end of table.

Continued . . .

Table 23.07. FEDERAL GOVERNMENT FINANCE: EXPENDITURE BY AGENCY AND BY SPECIFIED PROGRAM IN FLORIDA AND THE UNITED STATES, FISCAL YEAR 2004 (Continued)

(in thousands of dollars)

Item	Florida	United States
Direct payments other than for retirement and disability	32,432,424	469,799,943
Medicare	24,949,877	300,088,651
Hospital insurance payments	12,536,415	165,968,515
Supplementary medical insurance payments	12,413,462	134,120,136
Excess earned income tax credits	2,434,876	34,454,758
Unemployment compensation	1,113,007	38,214,521
Food stamp payments	1,268,549	24,696,715
Housing assistance	128,092	4,472,029
Agricultural assistance	179,589	17,050,640
Federal employees life and health insurance	827,046	19,149,309
Other	1,531,387	31,673,319
Procurement contracts	11,447,152	339,680,775
Department of Defense	8,385,036	211,538,185
Army	2,196,022	59,332,624
Navy	2,195,055	59,586,122
Air Force	2,941,483	54,073,312
Army Corps of Engineers	273,162	3,304,576
Other defense	779,315	35,241,550
Nondefense agencies	3,062,116	128,142,590
Agriculture	60,172	4,211,683
Commerce	30,903	1,678,062
Education	23	1,528,756
Energy	32,572	22,160,730
Environmental Protection Agency	12,062	1,000,582
General Services Administration	510,079	13,718,993
Health and Human Services	19,624	7,679,801
Homeland Security	237,284	6,074,213
Housing and Urban Development	45,212	1,060,807
Interior	66,092	4,825,789
Justice	108,347	4,417,977
Labor	70,403	1,616,315
National Aeronautics and Space Administration	635,025	12,545,284
Postal Service	741,573	13,715,998
Small Business Administration	487	49,500
Social Security Administration	832	530,929
State	24,285	1,656,725
Transportation	204,154	5,166,807
Treasury	29,705	4,041,389
Veterans Affairs	199,239	12,912,531
Other nondefense	34,044	7,352,282

1/ Data are preliminary.

Note: Expenditures classified as "other" may not be specified in the table and are contained in the totals for major expenditure categories.

Source: U.S., Department of Commerce, Census Bureau, *Federal Aid to States for Fiscal Year 2004,* issued January 2006, and *Consolidated Federal Funds Report for Fiscal Year 2004, State and County Areas,* issued December 2005, Internet site <http://www.census.gov/> (accessed 19, September 2007).

Table 23.08. FEDERAL GOVERNMENT FINANCE: DIRECT EXPENDITURE BY TYPE IN THE UNITED STATES AND IN THE STATE AND COUNTIES OF FLORIDA, FISCAL YEAR 2004

(in thousands of dollars, except where indicated)

County	Total	Retirement and disability	Grants	Procure-ment	Salaries and wages	Other direct payments
United States 1/	2,162,204	666,969	460,152	339,681	225,601	469,800
Florida	121,933,502	48,049,721	19,609,519	11,447,152	10,394,686	32,432,424
Alachua	1,473,737	478,797	482,520	52,409	202,227	257,784
Baker	103,407	56,601	19,723	1,155	3,651	22,279
Bay	1,599,092	595,599	157,014	290,605	359,016	196,858
Bradford	146,356	62,851	31,738	1,794	16,611	33,363
Brevard	5,905,222	2,054,549	261,996	2,400,352	471,568	716,758
Broward	8,767,967	3,580,118	913,174	489,453	549,916	3,235,307
Calhoun	78,082	32,074	24,080	282	1,177	20,469
Charlotte	1,074,857	654,914	52,555	19,995	20,957	326,435
Citrus	886,871	568,359	41,897	3,694	13,747	259,174
Clay	722,022	533,362	47,055	10,369	23,669	107,567
Collier	1,332,323	820,625	109,623	34,369	42,958	324,747
Columbia	385,315	177,332	73,247	2,863	56,758	75,115
DeSoto	165,436	73,098	26,505	1,054	3,326	61,454
Dixie	92,298	44,892	26,617	276	1,180	19,332
Duval	6,457,599	2,064,939	855,559	745,598	1,816,719	974,783
Escambia	2,777,562	1,171,684	325,952	327,662	563,741	388,523
Flagler	386,264	289,752	13,598	5,802	8,915	68,198
Franklin	70,484	31,317	15,337	1,003	2,168	20,658
Gadsden	280,166	106,656	101,746	3,662	7,647	60,454
Gilchrist	66,816	40,467	9,166	432	1,686	15,065
Glades	31,149	17,598	4,077	68	476	8,930
Gulf	98,062	48,395	20,189	428	959	28,091
Hamilton	77,470	33,292	26,040	499	1,689	15,950
Hardee	132,177	52,172	39,266	787	3,315	36,637
Hendry	143,781	61,554	30,364	3,093	4,238	44,532
Hernando	1,094,871	670,509	57,120	7,230	20,579	339,432
Highlands	688,484	379,295	55,533	22,057	16,460	215,139
Hillsborough	7,095,092	2,552,037	1,295,937	934,642	1,003,168	1,309,308
Holmes	140,456	63,422	38,434	1,064	4,174	33,361
Indian River	900,035	501,507	63,538	36,042	25,561	273,387
Jackson	381,231	139,015	113,708	16,271	30,983	81,254
Jefferson	86,992	34,406	32,782	464	2,078	17,262
Lafayette	26,096	11,986	5,220	1,413	944	6,533
Lake	1,770,598	1,165,290	129,901	30,303	35,641	409,463

See footnotes at end of table.

Continued . . .

Table 23.08. FEDERAL GOVERNMENT FINANCE: DIRECT EXPENDITURE BY TYPE IN THE UNITED STATES AND IN THE STATE AND COUNTIES OF FLORIDA, FISCAL YEAR 2004 (Continued)

(in thousands of dollars, except where indicated)

County	Total	Retirement and disability	Grants	Procure- ment	Salaries and wages	Other direct payments
Lee	2,866,389	1,657,251	226,529	52,180	138,912	791,517
Leon	4,612,863	613,644	3,477,134	81,353	122,049	318,683
Levy	229,981	115,281	54,455	2,700	5,711	51,834
Liberty	36,371	15,030	11,016	1,456	1,680	7,188
Madison	127,970	51,082	45,131	677	2,779	28,301
Manatee	1,556,621	873,580	130,362	38,223	66,782	447,674
Marion	1,774,507	1,094,557	182,201	23,684	42,816	431,248
Martin	935,675	534,438	91,632	28,010	18,909	262,686
Miami-Dade	15,597,387	4,040,550	4,864,730	671,878	1,413,687	4,606,542
Monroe	556,691	205,243	68,964	41,525	132,468	108,490
Nassau	365,717	190,736	43,571	2,502	73,294	55,614
Okaloosa	2,766,738	886,222	112,439	945,819	652,337	169,921
Okeechobee	228,026	108,432	33,974	5,159	4,030	76,432
Orange	6,587,668	1,966,510	667,132	2,404,878	521,436	1,027,712
Osceola	714,294	417,773	64,008	20,635	21,533	190,344
Palm Beach	7,403,842	3,595,928	710,685	304,768	385,535	2,406,927
Pasco	2,302,149	1,216,723	145,018	27,364	68,405	844,639
Pinellas	7,234,202	3,205,568	633,490	815,277	438,778	2,141,089
Polk	2,769,993	1,488,012	457,217	67,469	86,898	670,396
Putnam	481,694	226,005	119,191	2,239	8,238	126,021
St. Johns	846,214	429,573	163,994	61,649	38,511	152,486
St. Lucie	1,330,991	773,930	115,696	29,056	39,049	373,260
Santa Rosa	866,023	486,157	79,165	95,536	97,753	107,411
Sarasota	2,665,830	1,596,266	139,319	38,888	62,711	828,646
Seminole	1,508,855	851,191	176,538	52,060	92,417	336,649
Sumter	365,358	173,428	33,377	24,608	62,063	71,882
Suwannee	234,266	125,422	41,673	1,232	10,230	55,709
Taylor	133,571	54,634	32,869	12,625	2,517	30,926
Union	50,467	22,611	15,789	339	1,257	10,471
Volusia	2,973,791	1,609,696	306,324	142,272	97,604	817,895
Wakulla	90,905	47,869	18,175	1,742	4,392	18,727
Walton	603,858	126,598	77,113	1,273	357,103	41,771
Washington	154,519	64,874	45,081	855	4,897	38,812
Undistributed	5,521,706	16,440	724,315	29	(NA)	4,780,924

(NA) Not available.
1/ Rounded to millions of dollars.

Source: U.S., Department of Commerce, Census Bureau, *Consolidated Federal Funds Report for Fiscal Year 2004, State and County Areas,* issued December 2005, Internet site <http://www.census.gov/> (accessed 19, September 2007).

Table 23.15. DEFENSE CONTRACTS: AWARDS AND PAYROLL IN FLORIDA, OTHER SUNBELT STATES, OTHER POPULOUS STATES, AND THE UNITED STATES, FISCAL YEARS ENDING SEPTEMBER 30, 2003 THROUGH 2005

(in thousands of dollars)

State	Contract awards 1/			Payroll 2/		
	2002–03	2003–04	2004–05	2002–03	2003–04	2004–05
			Sunbelt states			
Florida	8,108,136	8,385,549	10,317,548	8,104,532	9,333,981	8,818,528
Alabama	6,281,122	5,849,355	7,069,159	2,763,645	3,283,835	3,431,656
Arizona	7,504,719	8,430,013	9,354,653	2,314,147	2,678,171	2,650,657
Arkansas	587,546	493,589	797,149	887,735	1,127,696	1,121,645
California	28,681,160	27,875,260	31,064,740	13,271,691	15,017,113	14,937,094
Georgia	3,446,525	3,905,216	5,740,617	5,971,307	6,633,440	6,808,705
Louisiana	1,914,220	2,544,016	3,029,060	1,647,224	1,871,386	1,791,469
Mississippi	2,325,642	1,866,809	3,293,583	1,601,191	1,828,491	1,726,015
New Mexico	972,924	1,070,808	1,154,137	1,245,004	1,447,041	1,446,273
North Carolina	2,091,445	2,213,409	2,948,612	5,632,216	6,569,452	6,858,630
Oklahoma	1,514,812	1,524,233	1,993,842	2,671,191	2,975,918	3,073,845
South Carolina	1,540,474	1,598,654	2,001,329	2,807,145	3,306,218	3,288,403
Tennessee	2,189,558	2,115,771	2,803,637	1,297,197	1,614,320	1,512,629
Texas	22,867,586	21,044,024	20,696,579	9,798,528	11,082,032	10,925,284
Virginia	19,978,027	23,542,542	26,809,823	14,187,010	15,992,369	16,386,019
			Other populous states			
Illinois	2,564,632	3,003,807	3,571,661	2,497,205	3,025,482	3,132,244
Indiana	2,607,131	3,173,322	4,428,478	1,106,168	1,298,906	1,363,035
Massachusetts	6,799,599	6,961,412	8,332,707	979,872	1,102,544	1,095,667
Michigan	2,524,136	2,611,682	3,961,952	1,039,701	1,240,876	1,273,264
New Jersey	3,792,555	4,196,285	6,101,177	1,656,631	1,860,431	1,990,658
New York	4,319,529	5,243,889	5,961,812	2,016,897	2,442,780	2,548,258
Ohio	4,325,903	4,636,572	5,460,308	2,523,370	2,894,340	3,048,625
Pennsylvania	5,491,220	6,202,797	7,483,391	2,521,232	2,912,308	3,029,536
United States	191,221,965	203,388,706	236,986,557	122,270,018	139,490,361	141,018,119

1/ Data include net value of contracts for civil functions as well as military awards for supplies, equipment, RDT&E (reseach, development, test and evaluation), services, and construction.

2/ Data are estimates and cover active duty military, reserve and National Guard, retired military, and direct hire civilian personnel, including Army Corps of Engineers.

Note: Data refer to awards in year specified and to state in which prime contractor is located. Expenditure may extend over several years and work may be performed by a subcontractor in another state.

Source: U.S., Department of Defense, Directorate for Information Operations and Reports, Statistical Information Analysis Division, *Atlas/Data Abstract for the US and Selected Areas,* Internet site <http://siadapp.dior.whs.mil/> (accessed 1, October 2007).

Table 23.20. VETERANS' ADMINISTRATION: VETERAN POPULATION AND VETERANS' ADMINISTRATION (VA) EXPENDITURE BY PROGRAM IN THE STATE AND COUNTIES OF FLORIDA, FISCAL YEAR 2006

County	Veteran Population 1/	Expenditure ($1,000) Total	Compensation and pension 2/	Education 3/	Medical expenditures 4/
Florida	1,747,076	5,230,401	2,681,007	200,605	2,348,789
Alachua	18,240	97,381	35,258	5,018	57,105
Baker	2,540	8,151	3,402	144	4,605
Bay	22,161	75,214	55,472	4,916	14,827
Bradford	3,421	14,781	5,504	251	9,026
Brevard	73,928	200,560	131,858	7,380	61,322
Broward	123,496	287,664	140,525	10,599	136,540
Calhoun	1,135	4,262	2,553	43	1,666
Charlotte	27,140	57,429	33,580	648	23,202
Citrus	22,789	64,493	32,428	631	31,434
Clay	24,833	71,346	45,255	4,829	21,262
Collier	36,237	46,227	26,348	883	18,997
Columbia	7,746	59,053	19,616	654	38,783
DeSoto	3,260	6,981	3,468	63	3,450
Dixie	2,100	14,453	6,213	52	8,188
Duval	94,598	231,010	135,912	28,292	66,805
Escambia	45,584	146,873	100,006	13,686	33,181
Flagler	9,458	25,379	14,639	1,451	9,289
Franklin	1,437	3,636	1,985	43	1,609
Gadsden	3,922	13,281	6,559	305	6,418
Gilchrist	1,630	9,456	4,419	117	4,920
Glades	1,192	3,335	1,295	25	2,014
Gulf	1,899	4,382	2,964	124	1,294
Hamilton	1,303	6,525	2,619	84	3,822
Hardee	1,878	3,884	2,041	48	1,795
Hendry	2,515	6,060	2,945	92	3,023
Hernando	24,008	87,604	52,979	1,424	33,201
Highlands	13,414	38,008	20,372	429	17,207
Hillsborough	100,099	409,977	186,049	15,999	207,928
Holmes	2,324	8,446	6,339	143	1,964
Indian River	17,582	37,480	19,264	567	17,649
Jackson	5,112	16,769	10,906	352	5,511
Jefferson	1,518	5,273	2,673	424	2,176
Lafayette	673	3,838	2,153	15	1,670
Lake	35,580	89,264	49,478	1,813	37,973
Lee	64,647	132,711	72,718	2,927	57,066
Leon	19,522	49,213	25,539	6,680	16,994

See footnotes at end of table. Continued . . .

Table 23.20. VETERANS' ADMINISTRATION: VETERAN POPULATION AND VETERANS' ADMINISTRATION (VA) EXPENDITURE BY PROGRAM IN THE STATE AND COUNTIES OF FLORIDA, FISCAL YEAR 2006 (Continued)

		Expenditure ($1,000)			
County	Veteran Population 1/	Total	Compen- sation and pension 2/	Educa- tion 3/	Medical expend- itures 4/
Levy	4,924	29,377	11,004	304	18,069
Liberty	599	2,171	1,166	26	979
Madison	1,982	7,087	3,249	161	3,678
Manatee	38,431	82,924	43,510	1,755	37,659
Marion	41,756	140,528	64,758	2,175	73,596
Martin	19,765	45,510	21,738	534	23,238
Miami-Dade	71,947	296,829	106,395	12,463	177,971
Monroe	11,245	25,294	11,790	561	12,943
Nassau	8,629	15,828	9,658	596	5,573
Okaloosa	33,362	97,888	78,576	6,438	12,874
Okeechobee	3,807	14,156	5,948	92	8,115
Orange	78,532	234,513	134,374	15,131	85,008
Osceola	16,791	54,226	32,927	2,466	18,833
Palm Beach	126,456	324,241	128,734	5,103	190,404
Pasco	51,451	202,327	99,711	4,191	98,425
Pinellas	112,547	467,421	190,563	8,117	268,741
Polk	55,159	158,282	82,533	3,430	72,319
Putnam	8,697	41,037	15,609	465	24,963
St. Johns	17,554	37,285	21,969	1,421	13,895
St. Lucie	24,897	76,569	36,402	1,454	38,713
Santa Rosa	20,654	64,560	46,789	3,874	13,896
Sarasota	50,353	97,516	56,556	1,543	39,417
Seminole	39,000	92,603	56,215	5,299	31,090
Sumter	8,905	30,888	14,932	171	15,786
Suwannee	4,675	26,071	9,444	347	16,279
Taylor	2,514	7,565	3,519	108	3,939
Union	1,604	4,927	1,683	50	3,194
Volusia	60,090	169,824	98,123	7,565	64,136
Wakulla	2,845	9,031	4,238	1,514	3,279
Walton	6,401	21,780	16,030	521	5,229
Washington	2,587	11,742	7,530	1,579	2,634

GOE General Operating Expenses.
1/ Veteran population estimated as of September 30, 2006.
2/ Veterans compensation for service-connected disability; dependency and indemnity for service-connected deaths; pension for nonservice-connected disabilities; and pension to surviving spouses and children.
3/ Medical costs are shown in the county of the VA facility that has responsibility for the expenditures. Construction costs for accrued expenditure by VA facility are included.
4/ Medical expenditure includes services, administration, facility costs, educational and research support and other overhead. It does not include construction or other non-medical support activities.

Source: U.S., Department of Veterans Affairs, *Geographical Distribution of the Department of Veterans Affairs Expenditures, FY 2006,* Internet site <http://www1.va.gov/> (accessed 17, August 2007).

Table 23.29. STATE GOVERNMENT FINANCE: REVENUE, EXPENDITURE, DIRECT EXPENDITURE INDEBTEDNESS, AND CASH AND SECURITY HOLDINGS IN FLORIDA, 2005

Item	Total ($1,000)	Percentage change 2004 to 2005	Percentage of total	Per capita 1/ (dollars)
Revenue, total	77,077,664	2.3	100.0	4,332.67
General revenue	62,085,218	9.5	80.5	3,489.92
Intergovernmental	18,287,697	9.3	23.7	1,027.98
Taxes	33,894,971	11.0	44.0	1,905.30
General sales	19,056,249	11.3	24.7	1,071.19
Selective sales	6,430,205	2.4	8.3	361.45
License taxes	1,894,180	6.7	2.5	106.48
Corporate income	1,785,213	23.9	2.3	100.35
Other taxes	4,729,124	21.0	6.1	265.83
Current charges	4,032,498	9.6	5.2	226.67
Miscellaneous	5,870,052	2.5	7.6	329.97
Utility	19,593	5.7	0.0	1.10
Insurance trust	14,972,853	-19.7	19.4	841.65
Expenditure, total	70,417,744	17.4	100.0	3,958.31
Intergovernmental	17,328,518	5.2	24.6	974.07
Direct	53,089,226	22.0	75.4	2,984.24
Current operation	36,680,726	22.1	52.1	2,061.89
Capital outlay	5,160,979	8.4	7.3	290.11
Insurance benefits and repayments	8,006,384	36.9	11.4	450.05
Assistance and subsidies	1,965,308	18.0	2.8	110.47
Interest on debt	1,275,829	6.7	1.8	71.72
Exhibit: Salaries and wages	7,416,845	5.9	10.5	416.91
Expenditure, total	70,417,744	17.4	100.0	3,958.31
General expenditure	62,411,360	15.4	88.6	3,508.25
Intergovernmental	17,328,518	5.2	24.6	974.07
Direct	45,082,842	19.9	64.0	2,534.19
General expenditure by function				
Education	19,410,331	9.4	27.6	1,091.09
Public welfare	16,260,738	5.5	23.1	914.05
Hospitals	247,938	5.0	0.4	13.94
Health	2,942,651	4.0	4.2	165.41
Highways	5,636,396	17.3	8.0	316.83
Police protection	479,317	18.9	0.7	26.94
Correction	2,307,216	5.6	3.3	129.69
Natural resources	1,680,204	14.1	2.4	94.45
Parks and recreation	151,196	-1.6	0.2	8.50
Government administration	2,467,582	19.0	3.5	138.71
Interest on general debt	1,275,829	6.7	1.8	71.72
Other and unallocable	9,551,962	71.8	13.6	536.93
Utility	66,277	7.4	0.1	3.73
Insurance trust	8,006,384	36.9	11.4	450.05
Debt at end of fiscal year	25,879,751	0.5	100.0	1,454.75
Cash and security holdings	175,348,844	-1.1	100.0	9,856.67

1/ Based on U.S. Census Bureau Annual State Population Estimates.

Source: U.S., Department of Commerce, Census Bureau, Internet site <http://www.census.gov/> (accessed 22, March 2007).

Table 23.31. STATE TREASURER'S REPORT: BALANCE SHEET FOR FISCAL YEAR 2005–06

(in dollars)

Item	Assets
Currency and coins	300,000.00
Unemployment compensation investments 1/	2,306,545,431.52
Deferred compensation assets 2/	1,956,652,473.24
Bank accounts 3/	96,449,767.25
Consolidated revolving account 4/	362,994.22
Total cash, receivables, and other assets	4,360,310,666.23
Certificates of deposit	893,800,000.00
Securities 5/	20,750,337,211.78
Total investments	21,644,137,211.78
Total assets of the treasurer	26,004,447,878.01
	Liabilities
General revenue fund	6,120,818,645.23
Trust fund 6/	13,637,753,569.98
Working capital fund	0.00
Budget stabilization fund	1,078,048,784.46
Total four funds	20,836,620,999.67
Adjustments 7/	36,382,741.86
Due to special purpose investments 8/	3,174,428,669.02
Due to deferred compensation participants 2/	1,956,652,473.24
Due to consolidated revolving account agency participants 4/	362,994.22
Total liabilities	26,004,447,878.01

1/ Unemployment Trust Fund represents U.C. benefit funds invested by the federal government and due from the U.S. Treasury.

2/ All assets are held in the Deferred Compensation Trust Fund for the exclusive benefit of participants and their beneficiaries in the amount of $1,956,473.24. Of the plan assets, $69,435,127.12 are Statutory Valuation Reserves. Plan assests also include $20,782.72 in the Deferred Compensation Communications Account, and $59,324.05 in the Operating Account.

3/ Represents "Per Reconciled Cash Balance" of $113,189,999.39 as of June 30, 2006 with receipted items in transit of $159,325,020.44 and disbursed items in transit of -$142,584,788.30 which nets to $16,740,232.14. These items have cleared the bank but have not been posted to the state ledger. The total bank account figure does not include $10,711,080.99 held in clearing and/or revolving accounts outside the Treasury.

4/ The amount due to agency participants in the Consolidated Revolving Account as of June 30, 2006 is $3,467,600.91. Of this amount $362,994.22 is in a financial institution account and $3,104,606.69 is invested in Special Purpose Investment Accounts.

5/ Includes purchased interest in the amount of $1,077,461.72.

6/ Includes $7,541,872,874.72 earning interest for the benefit of trust funds, unemployment trust fund balance of $2,306,545,431.52, and the remaining balance of $3,789,335,263.74 earning interest for general revenue.

7/ Represents $36,382,741.86 in interest not yet receipted to state accounts.

8/ Represents Treasurer's Special Purpose Investment Accounts held in the Treasurer's custody and interest due to those accounts. Treasurer's Special Purpose Investment Accounts are investments on behalf of state agencies with funds outside the Treasurer's Cash Concentration System and other statutorily created entities.

Note: Total market value of all securities held by the Treasury $21,275,805,843.57.

Source: State of Florida, *Annual Report of the State Treasurer for the Fiscal Year Ending June 30, 2006.*

Table 23.40. STATE GOVERNMENT FINANCE: GOVERNMENTAL FUND REVENUE, EXPENDITURE AND CHANGES IN FUND BALANCE BY FUND TYPE IN FLORIDA, FISCAL YEAR 2005–06

(in thousands of dollars)

Item	Total governmental funds 1/	Fund type: General	Fund type: Health and family services	Fund type: Transportation 2/
Beginning fund balance, July 1, 2005	16,909,945	6,851,119	949,026	1,017,620
Revenue, total	60,622,873	32,233,584	13,697,919	4,458,296
Taxes 3/	35,317,243	31,209,623	347,416	2,270,245
Licenses and permits	1,318,920	126,645	20,518	11,104
Fees and charges	3,141,434	714,445	887,531	453,083
Grants and donations	19,567,321	15,674	12,398,317	1,685,956
Investment earnings	455,205	96,793	5,455	14,038
Fines, forfeits, settlements, and judgments	804,869	64,457	38,665	19,032
Other revenue	17,881	5,947	17	4,838
Expenditure, total	60,344,757	26,984,180	14,201,115	5,353,174
Current				
General government	7,428,922	4,524,019	177,476	261,698
Education	17,643,897	12,787,235	0	0
Human services	19,755,015	5,412,063	13,974,798	0
Criminal justice and corrections	3,673,967	3,180,109	0	0
Natural resources and environmental	4,030,076	561,366	28,708	0
Transportation	3,188,602	0	0	3,188,577
State courts	412,793	397,116	0	0
Capital outlay	2,639,161	116,012	18,356	1,900,800
Debt service				
Principle retirement	736,331	5,738	1,773	0
Interest and fiscal charges	835,993	522	4	2,099
Excess (deficiency) of revenue over expenditure	278,116	5,249,404	-503,196	-894,878
Other financing sources (uses)	2,518,015	-4,232,299	438,362	1,366,983
Net change in fund balances	2,796,131	1,017,105	-64,834	472,105
Fund balances - beginning, as restated	16,976,793	7,032,858	989,300	1,150,005
Adjustments to increase (decrease) beginning fund balances	66,848	181,739	40,274	132,385
Ending fund balance, June 30, 2006	19,772,924	8,049,963	924,466	1,622,110

1/ Includes funds not shown separately. Detail may not add to totals.
2/ Tranportation is a special revenue fund that accounts for the maintenance and development of the state highway system and other transportation-related projects.
3/ Florida levies neither a personal income tax nor an ad valorem tax on real or tangible personal property. Taxes are, however, the principal means of financing state operations.
Note: The Public Education fund was reported as a major fund in prior years. However, it no longer meets major fund criteria.

Source: State of Florida, Department of Financial Services, *Comprehensive Annual Financial Report,* Fiscal Year Ended June 30, 2006, Internet site <http://www.dbf.state.fl.us/> (accessed 22, March 2007).

Table 23.41. STATE GOVERNMENT FINANCE: TAX COLLECTIONS BY TYPE OF TAX COLLECTED IN FLORIDA AND THE UNITED STATES, 2006

Type of tax	Florida		United States 1/	
	Amount ($1,000)	Per capita 2/ (dollars)	Amount ($1,000)	Per capita 2/ (dollars)
Total	37,201,518	2,056.48	706,334,858	2,359.18
Property taxes	187,941	10.39	11,737,504	39.20
Sales and gross receipts	27,584,580	1,524.86	330,033,159	1,102.32
General sales and gross receipts	20,788,525	1,149.18	226,523,438	756.60
Selective sales taxes	6,796,055	375.68	103,509,721	345.73
Alcoholic beverages	642,926	35.54	4,925,400	16.45
Amusements	(X)	(X)	5,535,873	18.49
Insurance premiums	879,079	48.60	15,404,875	51.45
Motor fuels	2,264,350	125.17	35,754,616	119.42
Pari-mutuels	28,145	1.56	304,093	1.02
Public utilities	2,018,612	111.59	11,392,697	38.05
Tobacco products	456,794	25.25	14,479,660	48.36
Other selective sales	506,149	27.98	15,712,507	52.48
Licenses	1,899,350	105.00	45,273,416	151.21
Alcoholic beverages	35,855	1.98	406,224	1.36
Amusement	4,696	0.26	262,450	0.88
Corporation	191,716	10.60	7,577,211	25.31
Hunting and fishing	14,609	0.81	1,323,595	4.42
Motor vehicle	1,191,111	65.84	19,015,063	63.51
Motor vehicle operators	175,755	9.72	2,138,447	7.14
Public utility	31,112	1.72	465,046	1.55
Occupation and business, NEC	253,223	14.00	13,352,922	44.60
Other licenses	1,273	0.07	732,458	2.45
Income taxes	2,405,863	132.99	291,762,762	974.50
Individual income	(X)	(X)	244,370,415	816.20
Corporation net income	2,405,863	132.99	47,392,347	158.29
Other taxes	5,123,784	283.24	27,528,017	91.94
Death and gift	71,300	3.94	4,746,672	15.85
Documentary and stock transfer	4,996,694	276.21	11,897,762	39.74
Severance	55,790	3.08	10,660,498	35.61
Other	(X)	(X)	223,085	0.75

NEC Not elsewhere classified.
(X) Not applicable.
1/ Excludes the District of Columbia and territories.
2/ Per capita amounts are based on a Census Bureau July 1, 2006 estimate of 18,089,888 in Florida and 299,398,484 in the United States.

Source: U.S., Department of Commerce, Census Bureau, Internet site <http://www.census.gov/> (accessed 5, July 2007).

Table 23.43. STATE GOVERNMENT FINANCE: SALES AND USE TAX COLLECTIONS BY TRADE CLASSIFICATION IN FLORIDA, FISCAL YEARS 2005–06 AND 2006–07

Group	2005–06	2006–07	Percentage change
All classifications, total	21,723,055,182	18,202,967,026	-16.2
Food and beverage group	2,803,810,748	2,369,409,670	-15.5
Grocery stores	888,133,792	755,127,738	-15.0
Meat markets	1,249,241	945,177	-24.3
Seafood dealers	1,638,766	1,470,834	-10.2
Vegetables and fruit markets	2,656,906	2,206,446	-17.0
Bakeries	16,122,825	13,708,704	-15.0
Delicatessens	28,385,183	27,039,980	-4.7
Candy, confectionery, concession stands	31,630,750	25,255,670	-20.2
Restaurants, lunchrooms, catering services	1,670,607,295	1,408,661,823	-15.7
Taverns, night clubs, bars, liquor stores	163,385,990	134,993,298	-17.4
Apparel group	671,304,089	582,830,132	-13.2
Clothing stores	578,411,576	502,758,722	-13.1
Shoe stores	92,892,513	80,071,410	-13.8
General merchandise group	3,153,240,211	2,727,787,268	-13.5
Feed, seed, fertilizer stores	24,606,216	25,756,322	4.7
Hardware, paints, and machinery	208,292,581	170,889,609	-18.0
Farm implements and supplies	265,203,241	179,820,639	-32.2
General merchandise stores	2,594,407,647	2,295,639,947	-11.5
Second-hand stores, antique shops, flea markets	43,109,023	41,111,884	-4.6
Dry goods stores	17,621,503	14,568,867	-17.3
Automotive group	4,093,248,478	3,268,936,363	-20.1
Motor vehicle dealers, trailers, campers	3,295,166,477	2,609,502,617	-20.8
Auto accessories, tires, and parts	249,994,082	214,399,613	-14.2
Filling and service stations, car wash	79,895,340	66,879,231	-16.3
Garage and repair shops	266,970,059	223,169,243	-16.4
Aircraft dealers	21,953,048	18,717,610	-14.7
Motorboat and yacht dealers	179,269,472	136,268,049	-24.0
Furniture and appliances group	1,560,848,542	1,265,076,443	-18.9
Furniture stores, new and used	505,629,479	404,783,604	-19.9
Household appliances, dinnerware, etc.	229,588,580	186,274,765	-18.9
Store and office equipment	208,957,486	168,631,469	-19.3
Music stores, radios, and televisions	616,672,997	505,386,605	-18.0
Lumber, builders, and contractors group	1,496,516,825	1,138,171,137	-23.9
Building contractors	116,517,672	107,794,266	-7.5
Heating and air conditioning	152,159,577	124,629,309	-18.1
Electrical and plumbing	8,934,720	13,698,159	53.3
Decorating, painting, and papering	69,245,785	58,975,248	-14.8
Roofing and sheet metal	15,712,430	11,484,498	-26.9
Lumber and building materials	1,133,946,641	821,589,657	-27.5
General classification group	7,944,086,289	6,850,756,013	-13.8
Hotels, apartment houses, etc.	900,567,835	760,037,364	-15.6
Barber and beauty shops	51,353,532	38,447,459	-25.1
Book stores	67,286,717	60,155,486	-10.6
Cigar stands and tobacco shops	8,099,361	6,815,967	-15.8
Florists	23,267,618	18,549,913	-20.3
Fuel dealers, L.P. gas dealers	42,763,560	33,775,171	-21.0

See footnotes at end of table. Continued . . .

Table 23.43. STATE GOVERNMENT FINANCE: SALES AND USE TAX COLLECTIONS BY TRADE CLASSIFICATION IN FLORIDA, FISCAL YEARS 2005–06 AND 2006–07 (Continued)

Group	2005–06	2006–07	Percentage change
General classification group (Continued)			
Funeral directors, monuments	1,676,275	1,225,879	-26.9
Scrap metal and junk yards	4,113,878	3,456,881	-16.0
Itinerant vendors	33,176,600	28,164,970	-15.1
Laundry, cleaning services, alterations	18,020,119	18,563,264	3.0
Machine shops and foundries	31,652,970	31,228,909	-1.3
Horse, cattle, and pet dealers	38,603,261	20,807,765	-46.1
Photographers, photo supplies, art galleries	47,052,337	36,468,792	-22.5
Shoe repair shops	778,365	591,037	-24.1
Storage and warehousing	24,117,149	20,623,810	-14.5
Gift, card, and novelty stores, taxidermy	129,205,325	107,600,776	-16.7
Newsstands	3,317,004	3,014,467	-9.1
Social clubs and associations	31,798,143	28,190,327	-11.3
Industrial machinery equipment	173,674,954	140,314,910	-19.2
Admissions	460,700,984	391,376,053	-15.0
Holiday season vendors, Christmas trees	2,420,432	2,477,727	2.4
Rental of tangible property	461,974,126	381,625,363	-17.4
Fabrication and sales of cabinets, etc.	113,260,936	96,881,251	-14.5
Manufacturing and mining	717,207,010	584,639,355	-18.5
Bottlers (beer and softdrinks)	13,675,137	11,699,245	-14.4
Pawn shops	13,609,659	11,544,309	-15.2
Communications 1/	1,047,268,016	981,100,125	-6.3
Transportation	18,968,179	17,424,593	-8.1
Graphic arts and printing	113,061,368	96,718,518	-14.5
Insurance, banking, information services, etc.	35,367,493	31,896,003	-9.8
Sanitary and industrial supplies	73,436,184	56,812,704	-22.6
Packaging materials and paper boxes	13,920,316	12,717,701	-8.6
Repair of tangible personal property	122,950,373	101,515,431	-17.4
Advertising	20,921,655	18,059,149	-13.7
Topsoil, clay, sand, and fill dirt	50,770,783	40,090,381	-21.0
Trade stamp redemption centers	219,833	278,863	26.9
Nurseries and landscaping	50,903,892	45,527,692	-10.6
Vending machines	29,867,531	25,485,540	-14.7
Importing and exporting	56,163,119	48,320,940	-14.0
Medical, dental, surgical, hospital supplies	48,774,993	39,551,835	-18.9
Wholesale dealers	722,668,610	617,175,081	-14.6
Schools and educational institutions	8,641,440	8,166,907	-5.5
Office space and commercial rentals	1,205,189,663	1,079,333,519	-10.4
Parking lots, boat docking, and storage	31,471,535	27,809,042	-11.6
Utilities, electric or gas	458,547,220	436,509,824	-4.8
Motion picture industry	26,312,632	29,520,622	12.2
Flea market vendors	5,319,948	3,599,435	-32.3
Other professional services	25,063,739	27,524,509	9.8
Other personal services	151,399,651	135,756,516	-10.3
Other industrial services	4,806,389	4,374,818	-9.0
Commercial fisherman	113,016	204,029	80.5
Miscellaneous	199,549,579	116,265,799	-41.7
Other 2/	9,035,845	10,739,987	18.9

1/ Communications services sales and use tax collected, under Chapter 202, F.S., have been added back into communications, and the state total.

2/ Total for kind codes that have fewer than four businesses reporting.

Source: State of Florida, Department of Revenue, Internet site <http://dor.myflorida.com/> (accessed 20, July 2007).

Table 23.45. STATE GOVERNMENT FINANCE: TAX COLLECTIONS BY OR WITHIN COUNTIES BY TYPE OF TAX COLLECTED IN THE STATE AND COUNTIES OF FLORIDA FISCAL YEAR 2005–06

County	Total 1/	Sales and use taxes	Motor vehicle tags	Pari-mutuel wagering taxes
Florida	22,477,281,618	21,813,625,970	636,081,900	27,573,748
Alachua	238,541,440	232,464,560	6,076,880	0
Baker	10,394,389	9,563,943	830,446	0
Bay	209,246,632	203,797,931	5,448,701	0
Bradford	15,621,613	14,754,027	867,586	0
Brevard	519,476,301	503,183,617	16,179,531	113,153
Broward	2,110,187,473	2,055,594,362	49,419,725	5,173,386
Calhoun	5,521,995	5,135,919	386,076	0
Charlotte	173,795,666	168,100,775	5,694,891	0
Citrus	98,533,117	93,909,580	4,623,537	0
Clay	133,154,817	126,224,547	5,385,353	1,544,917
Collier	464,866,584	454,273,840	10,592,744	0
Columbia	59,433,475	57,189,501	2,243,974	0
DeSoto	19,791,848	18,570,873	1,220,975	0
Dixie	14,410,877	13,887,172	523,705	0
Duval	1,058,477,299	1,033,686,472	24,408,988	381,839
Escambia	327,423,246	318,268,280	8,650,594	504,372
Flagler	55,466,586	53,025,094	2,441,492	0
Franklin	10,306,300	9,906,193	400,107	0
Gadsden	21,044,203	19,882,122	1,162,081	0
Gilchrist	4,905,979	4,321,773	584,206	0
Glades	2,729,280	2,442,367	286,913	0
Gulf	7,472,364	6,974,973	497,391	0
Hamilton	5,023,072	4,583,592	344,678	94,802
Hardee	13,067,584	12,126,183	941,401	0
Hendry	30,273,407	28,339,440	1,933,967	0
Hernando	107,101,673	102,372,955	4,728,718	0
Highlands	89,557,044	85,843,712	3,713,332	0
Hillsborough	1,527,455,441	1,488,683,046	36,510,322	2,262,073
Holmes	7,440,279	6,874,625	565,654	0
Indian River	152,116,168	147,467,918	4,648,250	0
Jackson	31,371,728	29,840,851	1,530,877	0
Jefferson	7,897,408	6,876,711	686,293	334,404
Lafayette	4,083,816	3,825,007	258,809	0
Lake	255,723,354	246,014,751	9,708,603	0
Lee	817,505,286	795,737,816	20,342,951	1,424,519
Leon	265,444,545	258,671,098	6,773,447	0
Levy	23,714,918	22,171,274	1,543,644	0

See footnotes at end of table.

Continued . . .

Table 23.45. STATE GOVERNMENT FINANCE: TAX COLLECTIONS BY OR WITHIN COUNTIES BY TYPE OF TAX COLLECTED IN THE STATE AND COUNTIES OF FLORIDA FISCAL YEAR 2005–06 (Continued)

County	Total 1/	Sales and use taxes	Motor vehicle tags	Pari-mutuel wagering taxes
Liberty	3,871,683	3,600,838	270,845	0
Madison	9,412,656	8,845,179	567,477	0
Manatee	306,682,728	297,585,065	9,097,663	0
Marion	309,082,147	298,336,576	10,727,331	18,240
Martin	228,034,587	222,776,086	5,258,501	0
Miami-Dade	2,527,325,535	2,442,803,960	75,785,553	8,736,022
Monroe	169,447,239	166,495,359	2,951,879	0
Nassau	52,301,242	50,158,626	2,142,616	0
Okaloosa	243,179,171	236,994,137	6,185,034	0
Okeechobee	32,534,799	30,905,656	1,629,143	0
Orange	2,105,011,923	2,072,128,861	32,883,062	0
Osceola	258,037,746	250,851,397	7,186,348	0
Palm Beach	1,580,529,149	1,539,511,951	37,109,176	3,908,022
Pasco	315,720,579	301,988,687	13,731,892	0
Pinellas	986,683,012	936,939,581	47,931,888	1,811,543
Polk	527,466,577	507,010,927	20,455,650	0
Putnam	44,005,697	41,723,481	2,282,216	0
St. Johns	166,254,736	159,457,479	6,602,943	194,314
St. Lucie	207,326,743	199,535,895	7,771,328	19,520
Santa Rosa	82,879,076	78,755,302	4,123,774	0
Sarasota	488,064,275	475,629,361	12,321,607	113,307
Seminole	517,850,679	505,255,318	12,539,401	55,960
Sumter	46,295,391	43,726,096	2,569,295	0
Suwannee	22,233,531	20,829,005	1,404,526	0
Taylor	17,494,107	14,772,593	2,721,514	0
Union	4,222,561	3,774,021	448,540	0
Volusia	480,476,548	464,022,922	16,064,043	389,583
Wakulla	9,916,175	9,160,621	755,554	0
Walton	82,489,981	80,827,274	1,662,707	0
Washington	10,950,071	9,813,192	643,107	493,772
Out-of-state	1,662,410,932	1,662,410,932	0	0
Other A/	80,513,135	32,412,690	48,100,445	0

A/ Includes refunds and Department of Highway Safety and Motor Vehicle district office data.
1/ Does not include gasoline taxes.

Source: Column 2, State of Florida, Department of Revenue, Internet site <http://sun6.dms.state.fl.us/>; Column 3, State of Florida, Department of Highway Safety and Motor Vehicles, Division of Motor Vehicles, *Revenue Report, July 1, 2005–June 30, 2006,* Internet site <http://www.hsmv.state.fl.us/>; Column 4, State of Florida, Department of Business and Professional Regulation, Division of Pari-Mutuel Wagering, *75th Annual Report, Fiscal Year 2005–2006,* Internet site <http://www.state.fl.us/>. All Internet sites were accessed March 22, 2007.

Table 23.46. STATE GOVERNMENT FINANCE: GASOLINE TAX COLLECTIONS IN FLORIDA, FISCAL YEARS 1969–70 THROUGH 2005–06

Fiscal year	Gallons sold	Tax rate (cents)	Tax collected 1/ (dollars)
1969–70	3,054,891,901.3	7	213,842,433.12
1970–71	3,341,148,943.8	7	233,880,426.09
1971–72	3,685,131,310.5	7/8	291,484,318.30
1972–73	4,080,699,270.9	8	326,454,941.67
1973–74	4,157,754,572.7	8	332,617,165.82
1974–75	4,243,123,105.1	8	339,449,848.41
1975–76	4,326,195,422.0	8	346,095,633.76
1976–77	4,483,397,014.2	8	358,671,761.14
1977–78	4,721,812,693.4	8	377,745,015.47
1978–79	4,961,448,003.1	8	396,915,840.25
1979–80	4,765,935,970.1	8	381,274,877.61
1980–81	4,681,857,035.4	8	374,548,562.90
1981–82	4,746,090,470.3	8	379,687,237.63
1982–83	4,686,388,610.8	5.7/8/9.7	387,286,074.47
1983–84	4,709,246,332.0	5.7/8/9.7	455,678,899.26
1984–85	4,739,366,278.0	5.7/9.7	458,188,999.77
1985–86	5,003,004,954.0	5.7/9.7	483,953,518.77
1986–87	5,493,474,844.7	5.7/9.7	484,754,881.20
1987–88	5,869,584,946.8	5.7/9.7	569,328,353.84
1988–89	5,995,884,170.5	5.7/9.7	581,596,538.65
1989–90	6,087,306,071.0	5.7/9.7	590,082,229.69
1990–91	5,985,729,187.8	9.7/10.9/11.2	653,943,345.04
1991–92	6,065,182,815.5	9.7/10.9/11.2/11.6	689,690,791.78
1992–93	6,279,687,903.2	9.7/10.9/11.2/11.6/11.8	723,722,832.76
1993–94	6,451,928,258.1	10.9/11.2/11.6/12.1	765,014,400.64
1994–95	6,560,589,349.5	11.6/11.8/12.1/12.3	802,201,952.42
1995–96	6,780,173,415.7	12.3/12.5	830,748,648.21
1996–97	6,832,487,453.1	12.5/12.8	863,814,563.00
1997–98	7,017,565,750.3	12.8/13.0	902,439,282.00
1998–99	7,291,963,115.1	13.0/13.1	948,226,230.00
1999–00	7,495,821,226.3	13.1/13.3	984,569,718.00
2000–01	7,614,933,421.6	13.6	1,019,975,798.00
2001–02	7,835,936,471.0	13.9	1,073,613,236.00
2002–03	8,031,388,963.4	14.1	1,118,505,479.00
2003–04	8,248,890,382.3	14.3	1,166,233,647.87
2004–05	8,633,568,299.1	14.9	1,182,603,643.65
2005–06	8,648,231,126.8	15.3	1,275,154,509.02

1/ Includes collection fees.
Note: Some data may be revised.

Source: State of Florida, Department of Revenue, *Report of Fuel Tax Collections and Distributions, Fiscal Year 1994-95,* unpublished data, and Fuel Tax Statistics and State and Local Tax Receipts, FY 2005–06, Internet site <http://www.myflorida.com/> (accessed 22, March 2007).

Table 23.48. STATE FUNDS TO LOCAL GOVERNMENT: DISTRIBUTION OF SHARED TAXES BY THE FLORIDA DEPARTMENT OF REVENUE TO COUNTY AND CITY GOVERNMENTS BY MAJOR SOURCE IN THE STATE AND COUNTIES OF FLORIDA FISCAL YEAR 2006–07

(rounded to thousands of dollars)

County	Total DOR distri-bution	Half-cent sales tax distributed to– County govern-ments	City govern-ments	Emer-gency and supple-mental	Revenue sharing County	Munici-pal	County tax on motor fuel
Florida	2,519,717	1,148,992	586,496	18,504	363,000	318,541	84,184
Alachua	30,275	11,753	8,477	0	4,363	4,491	1,190
Baker	2,645	664	187	884	421	182	307
Bay	25,325	10,050	7,640	0	3,166	3,546	922
Bradford	3,125	1,011	343	825	459	279	209
Brevard	62,797	23,518	18,009	0	9,418	9,590	2,263
Broward	257,145	73,202	107,215	0	24,440	45,988	6,300
Calhoun	1,572	297	78	573	241	137	246
Charlotte	19,232	12,595	1,399	0	3,862	503	873
Citrus	12,138	7,328	623	0	3,066	464	657
Clay	16,200	9,894	1,050	0	3,905	588	763
Collier	49,769	33,873	4,378	0	8,571	1,233	1,714
Columbia	7,400	4,214	822	0	1,374	388	602
DeSoto	3,524	1,226	288	777	635	267	331
Dixie	1,739	393	60	576	286	105	319
Duval 1/	138,681	86,214	4,560	0	19,282	24,938	3,687
Escambia	36,752	21,659	4,353	0	7,219	2,180	1,342
Flagler	7,084	1,989	2,341	0	1,010	1,323	421
Franklin	1,482	576	235	0	221	125	325
Gadsden	5,588	1,285	488	1,805	818	678	515
Gilchrist	1,644	323	54	732	300	61	174
Glades	1,345	179	31	503	192	54	386
Gulf	1,769	373	176	566	237	141	277
Hamilton	1,619	350	113	534	213	138	272
Hardee	3,124	712	274	1,004	469	326	339
Hendry	4,918	1,712	568	947	756	349	587
Hernando	13,410	8,412	418	0	3,497	375	707
Highlands	9,806	5,062	1,211	0	2,050	764	719
Hillsborough	174,066	93,515	35,561	0	26,502	13,907	4,581
Holmes	2,068	419	103	806	337	152	250
Indian River	16,772	8,417	3,416	0	2,890	1,358	690
Jackson	5,953	1,819	716	1,284	845	663	627
Jefferson	1,937	632	132	529	262	90	291
Lafayette	873	135	23	330	123	44	219
Lake	29,580	13,172	6,934	0	5,090	3,093	1,291
Lee	91,290	44,466	24,676	0	12,320	7,496	2,332

See footnotes at end of table.

Continued . . .

Table 23.48. STATE FUNDS TO LOCAL GOVERNMENT: DISTRIBUTION OF SHARED TAXES BY THE FLORIDA DEPARTMENT OF REVENUE TO COUNTY AND CITY GOVERNMENTS BY MAJOR SOURCE IN THE STATE AND COUNTIES OF FLORIDA FISCAL YEAR 2006-07 (Continued)

(rounded to thousands of dollars)

County	Total DOR distri- bution	Half-cent sales tax distributed to-- County govern- ments	City govern- ments	Emer- gency and supple- mental	Revenue sharing County	Munici- pal	County tax on motor fuel
Leon	32,956	12,292	10,032	0	4,672	4,833	1,128
Levy	4,637	1,468	409	1,143	755	309	553
Liberty	949	152	24	274	130	46	323
Madison	2,280	434	112	807	343	188	395
Manatee	35,821	19,697	5,569	0	6,818	2,413	1,323
Marion	36,599	21,620	4,304	0	7,032	1,779	1,864
Martin	22,078	14,709	2,152	0	3,770	667	780
Miami-Dade	359,796	133,248	89,005	0	45,190	83,769	8,584
Monroe	18,744	8,424	5,668	0	2,042	1,557	1,053
Nassau	6,729	3,531	918	0	1,402	417	462
Okaloosa	27,744	13,510	6,396	0	4,200	2,596	1,042
Okeechobee	4,139	2,185	350	0	829	252	522
Orange	227,413	128,956	51,205	0	28,480	14,397	4,375
Osceola	31,053	15,590	6,378	0	5,062	2,488	1,535
Palm Beach	182,352	78,383	53,871	0	25,137	20,118	4,842
Pasco	38,563	23,697	2,451	0	9,343	1,443	1,629
Pinellas	119,181	41,554	38,116	0	15,846	20,543	3,122
Polk	63,780	30,093	13,039	0	11,086	6,861	2,701
Putnam	6,193	2,935	681	0	1,504	519	554
St. Johns	19,547	12,486	1,667	0	3,816	693	885
St. Lucie	24,942	8,432	7,669	0	3,784	3,978	1,079
Santa Rosa	10,581	5,640	598	0	2,995	468	881
Sarasota	52,778	28,720	10,604	0	8,601	3,458	1,395
Seminole	58,301	26,125	15,925	0	8,439	6,285	1,528
Sumter	7,114	4,018	582	106	1,453	368	587
Suwannee	4,585	1,548	315	1,158	793	350	422
Taylor	2,396	903	356	23	392	244	478
Union	1,296	266	76	515	192	117	130
Volusia	59,695	19,261	19,964	0	7,664	10,783	2,023
Wakulla	2,842	928	27	980	552	55	300
Walton	9,367	6,065	899	0	1,417	330	656
Washington	2,618	681	181	825	423	205	303

DOR Department of Revenue.
1/ Duval County is the consolidated city of Jacksonville.
Note: Detail may not add to totals due to rounding.

Source: State of Florida, Department of Revenue, Internet site <http://dor.myflorida.com/> (accessed 20, July 2007).

Table 23.50. STATE LOTTERY: SALES IN THE STATE AND COUNTIES OF FLORIDA FISCAL YEARS 2001–02 THROUGH 2006–07

(rounded to thousands of dollars)

County	2001–02	2002–03	2003–04	2004–05	2005–06	2006–07
Florida	2,422,514	2,920,648	3,137,259	3,537,951	4,030,055	4,195,388
Alachua	29,061	36,796	40,095	45,362	52,692	55,497
Baker	2,542	2,953	3,669	3,837	4,387	4,859
Bay	21,478	26,839	30,804	35,462	43,038	46,045
Bradford	4,075	4,780	5,205	5,993	6,771	8,011
Brevard	78,157	97,011	106,210	124,532	138,073	138,021
Broward	234,822	271,395	278,759	293,286	330,168	346,492
Calhoun	1,611	2,312	2,506	2,857	3,233	3,606
Charlotte	20,847	26,425	30,278	35,253	40,032	39,109
Citrus	20,410	25,350	26,711	30,480	33,803	35,670
Clay	16,231	20,448	21,638	25,784	29,741	30,611
Collier	29,616	36,955	40,011	45,529	51,926	53,794
Columbia	9,833	13,677	16,367	18,788	21,228	23,172
DeSoto	3,687	4,317	5,240	6,103	6,797	6,504
Dixie	1,348	1,654	1,894	2,272	2,732	2,731
Duval	123,351	151,796	168,968	189,307	211,216	219,060
Escambia	61,402	76,564	81,666	94,676	109,287	107,697
Flagler	9,188	10,795	12,109	14,125	16,622	18,708
Franklin	1,622	1,945	2,809	2,865	3,119	2,981
Gadsden	7,515	9,519	11,094	12,574	14,826	16,811
Gilchrist	1,333	1,697	1,909	2,412	2,995	2,988
Glades	687	1,004	1,103	1,348	1,248	1,247
Gulf	1,496	1,857	2,451	2,724	3,467	3,175
Hamilton	2,510	2,996	4,042	4,703	5,139	5,632
Hardee	2,589	3,403	3,789	5,000	6,188	6,000
Hendry	4,476	5,048	5,803	7,772	9,081	9,111
Hernando	21,850	26,271	29,335	33,493	39,313	41,289
Highlands	10,777	13,196	14,702	16,627	19,097	20,261
Hillsborough	138,698	170,722	179,085	200,277	228,951	235,741
Holmes	4,911	5,943	6,469	7,340	8,077	8,125
Indian River	20,250	24,300	26,027	30,189	32,693	32,404
Jackson	12,915	15,414	16,938	17,446	21,134	22,530
Jefferson	2,529	3,194	3,593	4,267	4,740	4,661
Lafayette	413	532	650	902	941	933
Lake	35,699	44,221	48,006	56,676	67,259	70,405

See footnote at end of table. Continued . . .

Table 23.50. STATE LOTTERY: SALES IN THE STATE AND COUNTIES OF FLORIDA
FISCAL YEARS 2001–02 THROUGH 2006–07 (Continued)

(rounded to thousands of dollars)

County	2001–02	2002–03	2003–04	2004–05	2005–06	2006–07
Lee	60,948	78,273	83,839	97,356	113,036	116,606
Leon	24,653	29,280	35,585	42,575	51,967	54,346
Levy	6,130	7,298	8,144	9,563	10,957	11,404
Liberty	834	983	1,086	1,342	1,459	1,733
Madison	2,699	3,279	3,798	4,425	4,426	5,181
Manatee	35,585	44,170	47,400	56,282	64,351	68,412
Marion	44,364	56,431	63,720	71,829	82,481	87,954
Martin	22,370	28,256	30,025	32,737	37,467	38,801
Miami-Dade	382,326	421,182	435,778	458,065	522,615	548,678
Monroe	15,118	18,165	19,033	20,748	23,496	24,050
Nassau	8,531	9,802	10,343	11,908	13,466	14,478
Okaloosa	22,324	28,549	32,174	36,692	41,782	40,913
Okeechobee	6,049	7,475	8,134	9,208	9,598	9,782
Orange	132,572	164,258	175,758	207,289	237,214	247,196
Osceola	27,648	34,186	38,118	44,562	50,372	55,477
Palm Beach	159,502	189,689	203,835	225,034	262,627	276,937
Pasco	53,615	67,525	72,044	82,441	92,085	96,408
Pinellas	143,847	174,673	183,634	204,924	230,884	237,638
Polk	75,549	94,725	102,723	125,105	138,643	142,282
Putnam	11,366	13,904	15,196	18,102	19,442	19,981
St. Johns	15,122	19,142	21,060	25,652	30,305	31,050
St. Lucie	33,397	42,128	46,182	55,156	61,912	62,906
Santa Rosa	12,547	16,389	18,891	23,329	27,237	26,531
Sarasota	41,648	50,283	55,707	66,588	74,833	78,461
Seminole	42,299	51,502	54,597	65,027	72,919	79,125
Sumter	7,531	9,584	10,369	13,378	16,535	16,466
Suwannee	4,537	6,014	7,489	9,323	10,948	12,069
Taylor	2,955	3,804	4,135	4,875	6,137	7,913
Union	1,263	1,503	1,654	1,748	1,733	2,247
Volusia	76,606	94,116	102,080	115,272	129,925	135,851
Wakulla	2,431	2,604	3,018	3,516	4,549	5,397
Walton	5,887	7,532	8,490	10,027	10,266	11,021
Washington	1,966	2,615	3,283	3,612	4,369	4,208

Note: Data are unadjusted, unaudited gross sales amounts.

Source: State of Florida, Department of the Lottery, unpublished data.

Table 23.52. TOBACCO LICENSES: NUMBER OF LICENSES ISSUED IN THE STATE AND COUNTIES OF FLORIDA, FISCAL YEARS 2005–06 AND 2006–07

County	2005–06	2006–07 Total	2006–07 Percentage change	2006–07 Issued with alcoholic beverage license	County	2005–06	2006–07 Total	2006–07 Percentage change	2006–07 Issued with alcoholic beverage license
Florida	28,173	28,128	-0.2	24,075	Lake	348	343	-1.4	311
					Lee	872	854	-2.1	769
Alachua	316	323	2.2	284	Leon	331	322	-2.7	286
Baker	40	43	7.5	41	Levy	82	77	-6.1	74
Bay	368	364	-1.1	317	Liberty	15	17	13.3	14
Bradford	45	45	0.0	40	Madison	38	34	-10.5	29
Brevard	769	761	-1.0	658	Manatee	397	405	2.0	370
Broward	2,548	2,535	-0.5	2,144	Marion	446	452	1.3	414
Calhoun	33	27	-18.2	23	Martin	216	222	2.8	205
Charlotte	182	195	7.1	168	Miami-Dade	4,886	4,847	-0.8	3,774
Citrus	190	192	1.1	168	Monroe	410	383	-6.6	337
Clay	198	196	-1.0	174	Nassau	107	112	4.7	101
Collier	444	442	-0.5	398	Okaloosa	268	267	-0.4	244
Columbia	112	107	-4.5	101	Okeechobee	80	83	3.8	75
DeSoto	44	45	2.3	43	Orange	1,618	1,612	-0.4	1,374
Dixie	33	32	-3.0	31	Osceola	365	366	0.3	302
Duval	1,361	1,355	-0.4	1,201	Palm Beach	1,729	1,726	-0.2	1,476
Escambia	492	503	2.2	447	Pasco	539	545	1.1	471
Flagler	97	97	0.0	88	Pinellas	1,561	1,559	-0.1	1,355
Franklin	42	42	0.0	37	Polk	749	744	-0.7	667
Gadsden	97	92	-5.2	85	Putnam	136	137	0.7	124
Gilchrist	20	20	0.0	18	St. Johns	233	242	3.9	220
Glades	19	19	0.0	19	St. Lucie	350	348	-0.6	307
Gulf	34	32	-5.9	29	Santa Rosa	131	144	9.9	123
Hamilton	38	39	2.6	36	Sarasota	492	488	-0.8	422
Hardee	38	40	5.3	37	Seminole	496	486	-2.0	433
Hendry	86	87	1.2	82	Sumter	82	85	3.7	77
Hernando	153	162	5.9	141	Suwannee	68	71	4.4	61
Highlands	141	144	2.1	124	Taylor	53	52	-1.9	48
Hillsborough	1,750	1,785	2.0	1,472	Union	20	20	0.0	18
Holmes	36	35	-2.8	31	Volusia	791	786	-0.6	689
Indian River	208	207	-0.5	176	Wakulla	41	40	-2.4	36
Jackson	95	91	-4.2	77	Walton	113	120	6.2	109
Jefferson	38	37	-2.6	33	Washington	32	34	6.3	28
Lafayette	11	11	0.0	9					

Source: State of Florida, Department of Business and Professional Regulation, Division of Alcoholic Beverages and Tobacco, "Number of Retail Tobacco Product Dealer Licenses Issued by County," June 30, 2007.

Table 23.53. ALCOHOLIC BEVERAGE LICENSES: NUMBER OF LICENSES ISSUED BY TYPE OF LICENSE IN THE STATE AND COUNTIES OF FLORIDA, LICENSE YEAR JULY 1, 2006 THROUGH JUNE 30, 2007

		Type of license						
County	Total	Clubs enter- tainment and tracks 1/	Package sales only 2/	Package and on- premises sales 3/	Distribu- tors 4/	Manu- factur- ers 5/	Import/ export 6/	Other clubs 7/
Florida	41,589	796	18,340	21,018	312	71	193	859
Alachua	499	7	242	242	3	0	1	4
Baker	48	0	34	13	0	0	0	1
Bay	574	9	226	320	5	1	0	13
Bradford	57	2	36	19	0	0	0	0
Brevard	1,211	19	502	634	6	4	3	43
Broward	3,823	50	1,714	1,946	41	3	28	41
Calhoun	29	0	21	8	0	0	0	0
Charlotte	323	11	136	158	1	1	0	16
Citrus	317	12	136	152	0	2	0	15
Clay	291	5	146	131	0	1	0	8
Collier	911	54	291	533	3	0	0	30
Columbia	140	2	92	41	1	0	0	4
DeSoto	64	0	30	30	0	0	0	4
Dixie	40	0	23	16	0	0	0	1
Duval	1,996	31	960	951	17	2	5	30
Escambia	716	12	346	340	7	0	0	11
Flagler	164	8	61	92	0	0	0	3
Franklin	71	1	27	42	0	0	0	1
Gadsden	105	1	72	30	2	0	0	0
Gilchrist	25	1	13	11	0	0	0	0
Glades	32	0	15	15	0	0	0	2
Gulf	48	1	22	24	0	0	0	1
Hamilton	44	0	33	11	0	0	0	0
Hardee	50	0	33	15	0	0	0	2
Hendry	114	2	60	47	0	1	0	4
Hernando	283	14	115	142	0	0	0	12
Highlands	208	6	102	85	1	1	0	13
Hillsborough	2,375	43	1,122	1,141	24	5	9	31
Holmes	39	0	31	8	0	0	0	0
Indian River	337	11	146	160	0	0	0	20
Jackson	107	0	82	25	0	0	0	0
Jefferson	46	2	28	15	0	1	0	0
Lafayette	10	0	7	3	0	0	0	0
Lake	565	12	269	265	1	2	0	16
Lee	1,514	52	572	833	5	2	4	46
Leon	508	5	238	256	2	0	3	4
Levy	120	4	65	45	1	1	0	4
Liberty	15	0	11	4	0	0	0	0
Madison	39	1	28	10	0	0	0	0
Manatee	664	13	297	332	3	1	2	16

See footnotes at end of table.

Continued . . .

Table 23.53. ALCOHOLIC BEVERAGE LICENSES: NUMBER OF LICENSES ISSUED BY TYPE OF LICENSE IN THE STATE AND COUNTIES OF FLORIDA, LICENSE YEAR JULY 1, 2006 THROUGH JUNE 30, 2007 (Continued)

County	Total	Type of license: Clubs enter- tainment and tracks 1/	Package sales only 2/	Package and on- premises sales 3/	Distribu- tors 4/	Manu- factur- ers 5/	Import/ export 6/	Other clubs 7/
Marion	629	7	329	268	8	0	0	17
Martin	421	18	167	215	1	0	0	20
Miami-Dade	5,502	53	2,540	2,707	82	2	90	28
Monroe	607	15	184	391	2	0	0	15
Nassau	182	5	79	95	0	0	0	3
Okaloosa	479	8	174	273	2	1	1	20
Okeechobee	108	1	59	42	0	0	0	6
Orange	2,503	35	1,008	1,406	24	3	5	22
Osceola	584	6	245	323	1	0	1	8
Palm Beach	2,843	56	1,136	1,531	16	5	23	76
Pasco	755	26	355	330	4	4	0	36
Pinellas	2,406	39	986	1,292	16	8	7	58
Polk	1,036	23	577	397	4	11	1	23
Putnam	175	3	90	74	0	1	0	7
St. Johns	470	18	149	288	4	1	1	9
St. Lucie	510	14	278	201	4	0	0	13
Santa Rosa	196	6	114	73	0	0	0	3
Sarasota	965	24	321	573	8	1	4	34
Seminole	822	16	349	434	4	2	3	14
Sumter	136	2	72	58	0	0	0	4
Suwannee	78	2	53	23	0	0	0	0
Taylor	68	2	38	27	0	0	0	1
Union	19	0	14	4	0	0	0	1
Volusia	1,226	22	508	650	5	1	0	40
Wakulla	62	1	31	27	0	0	1	2
Walton	246	3	74	159	4	2	1	3
Washington	39	0	26	12	0	1	0	0

1/ Beer, wine, and/or all alcoholic beverages sold in clubs (including bottle clubs), American Legion Posts, civic and performing arts centers, at race tracks and from golf carts. Licenses included in this category are: 11AL, 11C, 11CG, 11CS, 11CT, 11PA, 12RT, 14BC, and HBX.

2/ Beer, wine, and/or all alcoholic beverages sold by the package only. Licenses included in this category are: 1APS, 2APS, 3APS, 3BPS, 3CPS, 3DPS, and 3PS.

3/ Beer, wine, and/or all alcoholic beverages to consume on premises and by the package. Establishments with three or more bars (such as hotels) are included. Licenses included in this category are: 13CT, 1COP, 2COP, 4COP, 5COP, 6COP, 7COP, and 8 COP.

4/ Distributors of beer, wine, and/or liquor (including wine distributed to churches). Licenses included in this category are: JDBW, JDSW, and KLD.

5/ Manufacturers of beer, wine, and/or liquor. Licenses included in this category are: AMW, BMWC, CMB, DD, and ERB.

6/ Licenses included in this category are: BSA, IMPR, and MEXP.

7/ Clubs exempted from payment of alcoholic beverage surcharges due to exemption from federal income tax as determined by the Internal Revenue Service. License type 11CE.

Source: State of Florida, Department of Business and Professional Regulation, Division of Alcoholic Beverages and Tobacco, "Number and Series of Beverage Licenses Issued by County," June 30, 2007.

Table 23.54. PARI-MUTUEL WAGERING: PERFORMANCES, ATTENDANCE, AND REVENUE BY TYPE OF EVENT IN FLORIDA, FISCAL YEARS 1999–00 THROUGH 2005–06

Item	Number of— Days	Perform-ances	Paid attendance	Pari-mutuel handle (dollars)	Revenue to state (dollars)
All tracks and frontons					
1999–00	4,557	6,124	3,437,073	1,656,229,260	55,150,255
2000–01	4,475	6,042	3,040,755	1,602,300,077	32,812,085
2001–02	4,487	6,048	2,836,869	1,596,945,465	33,373,319
2002–03	4,243	5,744	2,742,429	1,536,568,898	30,761,630
2003–04	4,342	5,847	2,804,583	1,439,870,758	28,410,487
2004–05	4,300	5,554	2,135,044	1,383,620,482	26,045,320
2005–06	4,993	6,278	2,066,192	1,514,758,761	27,573,748
Thoroughbred tracks					
1999–00	370	370	850,684	792,644,112	11,059,490
2000–01	377	377	680,903	765,859,498	9,297,769
2001–02	359	359	739,124	799,124,075	11,261,738
2002–03	348	348	653,206	789,172,282	11,256,046
2003–04	343	343	657,427	758,928,837	10,726,132
2004–05	338	337	298,933	748,362,620	11,267,930
2005–06	356	354	282,845	853,839,589	11,623,770
Harness tracks					
1999–00	164	164	16,256	105,638,151	2,201,028
2000–01	145	145	9,908	103,940,165	1,469,118
2001–02	144	144	0	111,429,374	1,636,447
2002–03	139	139	0	112,145,058	1,657,021
2003–04	140	140	0	95,129,287	1,434,497
2004–05	148	148	0	99,851,408	1,524,838
2005–06	146	145	0	99,119,658	1,494,376
Greyhound tracks					
1999–00	3,058	4,239	2,021,771	633,230,507	39,926,544
2000–01	2,979	4,147	1,830,770	610,715,139	21,192,101
2001–02	2,986	4,125	1,622,914	575,384,174	19,635,145
2002–03	2,937	4,087	1,712,118	533,124,097	17,243,188
2003–04	3,011	4,142	1,788,241	491,924,053	15,619,680
2004–05	3,088	4,037	1,565,858	448,189,414	12,712,832
2005–06	3,513	4,490	1,488,488	477,910,496	13,816,240
Jai Alai frontons					
1999–00	965	1,351	548,362	124,716,490	1,963,193
2000–01	974	1,373	519,174	121,785,275	853,097
2001–02	998	1,420	474,831	111,007,842	839,989
2002–03	819	1,170	377,105	102,127,461	605,375
2003–04	848	1,222	358,915	93,888,581	630,178
2004–05	726	1,032	270,253	87,217,040	539,720
2005–06	978	1,289	294,859	83,889,018	639,362

Note: These data represent the distribution of revenue derived from pari-mutuel performances and do not represent the total revenue received by the Division of Pari-Mutuel Wagering. Excluded are such items as licenses, fees, escheated tickets, charity, scholarship performances, and other miscellaneous items.

Source: State of Florida, Department of Business and Professional Regulation, Division of Pari-Mutuel Wagering, *75th Annual Report, Fiscal Year 2005–2006,* and previous editions, Internet site <http://www.state.fl.us/dbpr/> (accessed 22, March 2007).

Table 23.58. STATE RETIREMENT SYSTEM: MEMBERSHIP, PAYROLL, CONTRIBUTIONS ANNUITANTS, AND BENEFITS IN FLORIDA, JUNE 30, 2006

(in millions of dollars, except where indicated)

System	Active membership 1/	Annual payroll 1/	Accumulated contributions 1/	Annuitants (number)	Annual benefits Total paid	Annual benefits Average (dollars)
Total	664,819	24,632,183	59,474	251,209	3,793,144	(X)
Average salary (dollars)	(X)	37,828	(X)	(X)	(NA)	15,100
Florida retirement system	664,731	24,626,242	53,009	243,465	3,645,888	(X)
Regular members	576,520	20,230,288	40,667	220,679	3,008,509	13,633
Senior management members	7,154	525,460	2,272	1,288	50,208	38,981
Special risk members	72,078	3,483,622	8,886	19,575	516,493	26,385
Administrative support	74	3,233	2	152	4,391	28,891
Elected official class members	2,037	162,710	1,158	1,771	66,287	37,429
Renewed membership	6,868	220,929	22	(X)	(X)	(X)
Teachers retirement system	81	5,715	6,286	5,728	135,455	23,648
Survivors' benefits	(X)	(X)	(X)	713	1,337	1,875
State and county officers and employees retirement system	7	226	179	1,229	9,147	7,443
Highway patrol pension trust fund	0	0	0	63	1,080	17,143
Judicial retirement system	0	0	0	11	236	21,439

(X) Not applicable.
(NA) Not available.
1/ Excludes Deferred Retirement Option Program (DROP) participants.
Correction: Payroll, contribution, and benefit amounts were shown as rounded to thousands of dollars in *Abstracts* prior to 2006. Those figures should have been reported as rounded to millions of dollars.

Table 23.59. STATE RETIREMENT SYSTEM: ANNUITANTS AND BENEFITS BY AGE OF RETIREMENT IN FLORIDA, JUNE 30, 2006

Retirement age	Retirees Number	Retirees Annualized benefits (dollars)	Joint annuitants Number	Joint annuitants Annualized benefits (dollars)
Total	227,941	3,527,804,787	22,555	264,002,143
Under age 40	865	8,295,595	280	3,319,165
40-44	2,222	23,924,115	593	4,316,407
45-49	9,200	146,894,666	1,697	13,861,933
50-54	34,407	671,531,138	3,363	38,112,833
55-59	55,432	960,112,830	4,866	62,716,306
60-64	85,847	1,209,460,034	6,853	84,911,913
65-69	31,036	412,953,207	3,567	43,388,580
70-74	6,549	75,519,586	890	9,814,512
75-79	1,880	15,938,443	320	2,775,670
80-84	431	2,812,069	99	659,759
85 and over	72	363,103	27	125,064

Note: Annuitants include all retired persons or survivors of retired persons who are receiving monthly benefits. Excludes DROP, General Revenue, TRS-SB, and IFAS annuitants.

Source for Tables 23.58 and 23.59: State of Florida, Department of Management Services, Division of Retirement, *Florida Retirement System: July 1, 2005–June 30, 2006 Annual Report,* Internet site <http://www.frs.state.fl.us> (accessed 23, March 2007).

Table 23.60. STATE RETIREMENT SYSTEM: ADDITIONS, DEDUCTIONS, AND BALANCES OF THE FLORIDA RETIREMENT SYSTEM, FISCAL YEARS 2004–05 AND 2005–06

(in dollars)

Item	2004–05	2005–06
Additions, total	12,498,857,205	13,859,198,910
Pension contributions, total	2,218,128,210	2,349,816,307
State	518,487,899	537,215,151
Nonstate	1,669,084,178	1,781,877,843
Employee	30,556,133	30,723,313
Transfers from other funds	19,774,370	13,591,855
Net investment income	10,608,494,383	11,647,060,269
Net appreciation/depreciation in fair value of investments	7,095,129,461	8,621,065,352
Interest income	1,540,519,246	1,313,272,444
Dividends	1,629,643,577	1,405,760,887
Net real estate operating income	291,145,707	299,270,855
Other investment income	52,056,392	7,690,729
Less investment activity expense	385,987,675	201,760,299
Net income from security lending	38,447,917	50,490,779
Deductions, total	5,225,991,089	5,604,208,198
Benefit payments	4,295,049,880	4,537,273,049
General revenue fund	10,807,423	(NA)
Refunds of contributions 1/	(NA)	3,385,597
Transfers within department	884,535	897,829
Transfer to other departments	19,047,153	12,602,108
Transfer to other funds	884,675,265	1,035,245,564
Property dispositions	6,938	85,269
Depreciation expense	223,961	154,389
Administrative expenses	15,295,934	14,564,394
Net increase/decrease	7,272,866,116	8,254,990,712
Net assets held in trust for pension benefits—Beginning of year	100,933,577,003	108,085,058,462
Net assets held in trust for pension benefits—End of year	108,206,443,118	116,340,049,175

(NA) Not available.

1/ Refund of employee contributions in the amount of $1,908,065 has been netted against pension contributions by employees in fiscal year 2004–05.

Table 23.61. STATE RETIREMENT SYSTEM: DEFERRED RETIREMENT OPTION PROGRAM (DROP) AND RETIREMENT TRUST FUND BALANCES OF THE FLORIDA RETIREMENT SYSTEM, FISCAL YEARS 2004–05 AND 2005–06

(in dollars)

Item	2004–05	2005–06
Defferred Retirement Option Program (DROP)		
Participants	31,457	31,688
Annual payroll	1,718,983,600	1,801,177,303
Employee contributions	142,924,138	155,734,264
DROP accrued liability	1,770,809,043	1,939,763,360
Trust fund balance, total	108,443,596,138	116,614,340,960
Florida Retirement System	108,206,443,118	116,340,049,175
Institute of Food and Agricultural Sciences (IFAS) Supplemental Retirement Program	15,275,088	16,228,978
Health Insurance Subsidy	159,431,704	192,817,345
State University System (SUS) Optional Retirement Program	960,847	2,081,969
Senior Management Service Optional Annuity Program	20,241	9,136
Police Officers and Firefighters' Premium Tax Trust Fund	61,465,140	63,154,357

Source for Tables 23.58 and 23.59: State of Florida, Department of Management Services, Division of Retirement, *Florida Retirement System: July 1, 2005–June 30, 2006 Annual Report,* Internet site <http://www.frs.state.fl.us> (accessed 23, March 2007).

Table 23.70. FEDERAL GOVERNMENT: AVERAGE MONTHLY EMPLOYMENT COVERED BY UNEMPLOYMENT COMPENSATION LAW BY INDUSTRY IN FLORIDA, 2005 AND 2006

NAICS		Number of employees	
code	Industry	2005 A/	2006 B/
10	All industries	128,714	127,743
44-45	Retail trade	3,695	3,465
445	Food and beverage stores	778	765
452	General merchandise stores	2,902	2,686
48-49	Transportation and warehousing	44,536	44,090
488	Support activities for transportation	1,629	1,156
491	Postal service	42,662	42,611
52	Finance and insurance	188	197
522	Credit intermediation and related activities	125	128
524	Insurance carriers and related activities	63	70
54	Professional, scientific and technical services	1,723	1,790
5413	Architectural and engineering services	1,220	1,284
5419	Other professional and technical services	502	506
56	Admininstrative and support and waste management and remediation services	35	33
5611	Office administrative services	13	14
62	Health care and social assistance	16,538	16,915
621	Ambulatory health care services	1,949	1,995
622	Hospitals	14,589	14,920
71	Arts, entertainment, and recreation	2,134	2,068
712	Museums, historical sites, zoos, and parks	663	629
713	Amusements, gambling, and recreation	1,472	1,438
72	Accommodation and food services	887	893
7211	Traveler accommodation	122	116
7213	Rooming and boarding houses	765	776
81	Other services (except public administration)	71	67
92	Public administration	58,904	58,225
921	Executive, legislative and general government	5,033	5,051
922	Justice, public order, and safety activities	12,570	12,064
923	Administration of human resource programs	3,460	3,432
924	Administration of environmental programs	1,444	1,350
925	Community and housing program administration	252	241
926	Administration of economic programs	10,319	9,972
927	Space research and technology	2,080	2,145
928	National security and international affairs	23,745	23,971

NAICS North American Industry Classification System. See Glossary for definition.
A/ Revised.
B/ Preliminary.
Note: Detail may not add to totals due to disclosure editing and/or rounding.

Source: State of Florida, Agency for Workforce Innovation, Labor Market Statistics, "Quarterly Census of Employment and Wages" (ES-202), Annual NAICS files, Internet site <http://www.labormarketinfo.com/index.htm> (accessed 17, July 2007).

Table 23.72. STATE GOVERNMENT: AVERAGE MONTHLY EMPLOYMENT COVERED BY UNEMPLOYMENT COMPENSATION LAW BY INDUSTRY IN FLORIDA, 2005 AND 2006

NAICS code	Industry	Number of employees 2005 A/	2006 B/
10	Total, all industries	196,544	192,373
101	Goods-producing	6,524	6,450
1011	Natural resources and mining	1,276	1,321
1012	Construction	5,248	5,129
102	Service-providing	190,021	185,924
1021	Trade, transportation, and utilities	31	31
1022	Information	136	130
1025	Education and health services	75,511	72,052
1026	Leisure and hospitality	1,591	1,589
1028	Public administration	112,751	112,122
11	Agriculture, forestry, fishing and hunting	1,276	1,321
23	Construction	5,248	5,129
48-49	Transportation and warehousing	31	31
51	Information	136	130
518	ISPs, search portals, and data processing	4	0
519	Other information services	132	130
61	Educational services	66,394	63,892
6111	Elementary and secondary schools	879	937
6113	Colleges and universities	65,515	62,955
62	Health care and social assistance	9,117	8,160
622	Hospitals	4,510	4,042
6222	Psychiatric and substance abuse hospitals	4,344	3,875
6223	Other hospitals	166	167
623	Nursing and residential care facilities	4,178	3,665
6231	Nursing care facilities	438	406
6232	Residential mental health facilities	2,856	2,461
6233	Community care facilities for the elderly	884	798
624	Social assistance	430	453
71	Arts, entertainment, and recreation	1,591	1,589
92	Public administration	112,751	112,122
921	Executive, legislative and general government	7,637	7,407
922	Justice, public order, and safety activities	50,224	50,653
923	Administration of human resource programs	34,992	34,564
924	Administration of environmental programs	5,380	5,478
925	Community and housing program administration	159	173
926	Administration of economic programs	14,069	13,548
928	National security and international affairs	291	298

NAICS North American Industry Classification System. See Glossary for definition.
A/ Revised.
B/ Preliminary.
Note: Detail may not add to totals due to disclosure editing and/or rounding.

Source: State of Florida, Agency for Workforce Innovation, Labor Market Statistics, "Quarterly Census of Employment and Wages" (ES-202), Annual NAICS files, Internet site <http://www.labormarketinfo.com/index.htm> (accessed 17, July 2007).

Table 23.73. LOCAL GOVERNMENT: AVERAGE MONTHLY EMPLOYMENT COVERED BY UNEMPLOYMENT COMPENSATION LAW BY INDUSTRY IN FLORIDA, 2005 AND 2006

NAICS code	Industry	Number of employees 2005 A/	2006 B/
10	All industries	727,585	744,870
22	Utilities	5,743	5,703
2211	Power generation and supply	4,350	4,277
2212	Natural gas distribution	214	217
2213	Water, sewage and other systems	1,179	1,209
23	Construction	16	14
44-45	Retail trade	43	42
447	Gasoline stations	37	38
448	Clothing and clothing accessories stores	1	1
453	Miscellaneous store retailers	4	2
4532	Office supplies, stationery, and gift stores	4	2
48-49	Transportation and warehousing	5,098	5,312
485	Transit and ground passenger transportation	2,458	2,519
4851	Urban transit systems	2,324	2,379
4853	Taxi and limousine service	36	38
4859	Other ground passenger transportation	98	102
487	Scenic and sightseeing transportation	10	10
488	Support activities for transportation	2,630	2,783
4881	Support activities for air transportation	2,537	2,668
4883	Support activities for water transportation	41	61
4884	Support activities for road transportation	53	55
51	Information	855	933
515	Broadcasting, except Internet	24	19
518	ISPs, search portals, and data processing	68	114
519	Other information services	763	801
52	Finance and insurance	18	16
522	Credit intermediation and related activities	10	10
523	Securities, commodity contracts, investments	1	1
525	Funds, trusts, and other financial vehicles	6	5
53	Real estate and rental and leasing	1,930	1,831
5311	Lessors of real estate	1,191	1,137
5312	Offices of real estate agents and brokers	146	141
5313	Activities related to real estate	594	554
54	Professional, scientific and technological services	2	5
56	Administrative and support and waste management and remediation services	1,187	1,230
561	Administrative and support services	739	769
5615	Travel arrangement and reservation services	267	287
5617	Services to buildings and dwellings	439	441
562	Waste management and remediation services	448	461

See footnotes at end of table. Continued . . .

Table 23.73. LOCAL GOVERNMENT: AVERAGE MONTHLY EMPLOYMENT COVERED BY UNEMPLOYMENT COMPENSATION LAW BY INDUSTRY IN FLORIDA, 2005 AND 2006 (Continued)

NAICS code	Industry	Number of employees 2005 A/	2006 B/
61	Educational services	382,771	390,976
6111	Elementary and secondary schools	347,046	355,048
6112	Junior colleges	35,725	35,917
62	Health care and social assistance	42,069	43,561
621	Ambulatory health care services	376	367
622	Hospitals	40,608	42,048
623	Nursing and residential care facilities	890	941
624	Social assistance	196	205
6241	Individual and family services	31	26
6242	Emergency and other relief services	84	83
6243	Vocational rehabilitation services	62	76
6244	Child day care services	20	20
71	Arts, entertainment, and recreation	4,442	4,689
711	Performing arts and spectator sports	487	512
7111	Performing arts companies	128	134
7112	Spectator sports	5	4
7113	Promoters of performing arts and sports	353	374
712	Museums, historical sites, zoos, and parks	15	15
713	Amusements, gambling, and recreation	3,940	4,162
7132	Gambling industries	2,709	2,903
7139	Other amusement and recreation industries	1,232	1,259
72	Accommodation and food services	1,905	2,147
721	Accommodation	1,894	2,134
722	Food services and drinking places	11	13
81	Other services (except public administration)	354	357
812	Personal and laundry services	133	132
813	Membership associations and organizations	221	225
8133	Social advocacy organizations	159	166
8134	Civic and social organizations	52	47
8139	Professional and similar organizations	11	12
92	Public Administration	281,153	288,054
921	Executive, legislative and general government	221,847	227,050
922	Justice, public order, and safety activities	52,426	54,013
923	Administration of human resource programs	245	252
924	Administration of environmental programs	4,121	4,147
925	Community and housing program administration	2,073	2,165
926	Administration of economic programs	440	428

NAICS North American Industry Classification System. See Glossary for definition.
A/ Revised.
B/ Preliminary.
Note: Detail may not add to totals due to disclosure editing and/or rounding.

Source: State of Florida, Agency for Workforce Innovation, Labor Market Statistics, "Quarterly Census of Employment and Wages" (ES-202), Annual NAICS files, Internet site <http://www.labormarketinfo.com/index.htm> (accessed 17, July 2007).

Table 23.74. GOVERNMENT EMPLOYMENT: AVERAGE MONTHLY EMPLOYMENT COVERED BY UNEMPLOYMENT COMPENSATION LAW BY LEVEL OF GOVERNMENT IN THE STATE AND COUNTIES OF FLORIDA, 2005 AND 2006

County	Federal	State	Local	County	Federal	State	Local
			2005 A/				
Florida	128,714	196,544	727,585	Lee	2,294	3,903	24,945
				Leon	1,699	38,223	11,935
Alachua	3,614	25,502	10,895	Levy	80	399	1,570
Baker	84	1,669	770	Liberty	49	393	361
Bay	3,215	1,219	8,594	Madison	49	479	929
Bradford	36	1,532	959	Manatee	989	791	10,080
Brevard	6,057	2,280	19,866	Marion	684	2,328	13,009
Broward	7,909	6,588	87,833	Martin	272	679	4,560
Calhoun	23	400	527	Miami-Dade	20,387	17,586	111,498
Charlotte	277	841	4,678	Monroe	1,187	706	4,068
Citrus	201	415	3,902	Nassau	577	299	2,806
Clay	333	449	5,686	Okaloosa	6,763	1,034	6,908
Collier	673	820	10,901	Okeechobee	71	433	1,440
Columbia	1,032	1,809	2,673	Orange	9,449	10,749	45,198
DeSoto	52	1,038	1,177	Osceola	364	748	9,565
Dixie	16	429	552	Palm Beach	6,165	7,746	49,608
Duval	15,901	7,941	28,539	Pasco	782	1,289	12,527
Escambia	5,970	3,928	11,847	Pinellas	6,575	4,059	35,180
Flagler	137	204	2,776	Polk	1,355	4,094	21,674
Franklin	18	377	470	Putnam	143	521	3,741
Gadsden	124	3,317	1,843	St. Johns	476	1,555	5,397
Gilchrist	30	459	647	St. Lucie	670	1,428	9,341
Glades	12	43	370	Santa Rosa	729	1,085	4,179
Gulf	16	784	595	Sarasota	967	1,943	11,293
Hamilton	32	739	558	Seminole	1,430	783	15,006
Hardee	49	511	1,150	Sumter	1,202	809	1,718
Hendry	91	509	1,828	Suwannee	118	282	1,386
Hernando	358	644	5,138	Taylor	37	581	988
Highlands	250	392	3,347	Union	18	1,879	509
Hillsborough	13,020	12,628	47,105	Volusia	1,420	3,157	18,072
Holmes	55	453	861	Wakulla	83	524	956
Indian River	382	566	4,577	Walton	142	583	1,982
Jackson	474	2,711	2,640	Washington	50	835	1,055
Jefferson	38	372	473	Statewide 1/	98	13	(NA)
Lafayette	18	434	245	Out-of-state 2/	2	222	(NA)
Lake	565	1,127	10,079	Unknown 1/	(NA)	1,235	(NA)

See footnotes at end of table.

Continued . . .

Table 23.74. GOVERNMENT EMPLOYMENT: AVERAGE MONTHLY EMPLOYMENT COVERED BY UNEMPLOYMENT COMPENSATION LAW BY LEVEL OF GOVERNMENT IN THE STATE AND COUNTIES OF FLORIDA, 2005 AND 2006 (Continued)

County	Federal	State	Local	County	Federal	State	Local
			2006 B/				
Florida	127,743	192,373	744,870	Lee	2,329	3,861	26,314
				Leon	1,679	36,517	12,105
Alachua	3,681	25,348	10,972	Levy	77	387	1,592
Baker	81	1,604	806	Liberty	48	386	376
Bay	3,175	1,253	8,825	Madison	48	496	948
Bradford	34	1,543	983	Manatee	972	776	10,446
Brevard	6,146	2,279	20,217	Marion	714	2,397	13,331
Broward	7,866	6,385	88,784	Martin	271	674	4,763
Calhoun	27	389	542	Miami-Dade	19,979	14,356	113,060
Charlotte	313	850	4,878	Monroe	1,128	667	4,153
Citrus	207	440	4,105	Nassau	582	310	2,910
Clay	336	474	6,091	Okaloosa	6,780	1,090	7,091
Collier	675	841	11,216	Okeechobee	74	447	1,473
Columbia	1,030	1,792	2,719	Orange	9,051	10,920	46,688
DeSoto	50	1,066	1,207	Osceola	401	828	10,187
Dixie	17	419	563	Palm Beach	6,180	7,858	51,012
Duval	15,428	8,045	27,725	Pasco	811	1,284	13,332
Escambia	6,008	3,947	11,944	Pinellas	6,496	3,966	35,274
Flagler	151	229	3,196	Polk	1,369	4,008	22,182
Franklin	17	499	515	Putnam	137	512	3,819
Gadsden	125	3,260	1,870	St. Johns	495	1,605	5,801
Gilchrist	32	443	677	St. Lucie	673	1,494	10,071
Glades	12	41	380	Santa Rosa	716	1,245	4,332
Gulf	16	772	636	Sarasota	972	1,996	11,669
Hamilton	32	733	564	Seminole	1,380	809	15,295
Hardee	45	494	1,171	Sumter	1,360	871	1,867
Hendry	86	493	1,916	Suwannee	120	278	1,378
Hernando	365	687	5,428	Taylor	37	640	996
Highlands	243	397	3,434	Union	19	1,928	523
Hillsborough	13,320	12,602	47,620	Volusia	1,425	3,149	18,771
Holmes	58	453	883	Wakulla	85	537	995
Indian River	380	566	4,811	Walton	144	581	2,153
Jackson	468	2,669	2,722	Washington	49	880	1,058
Jefferson	39	354	459	Statewide 1/	91	26	47
Lafayette	17	403	267	Out-of-state 2/	4	244	(NA)
Lake	571	1,140	10,738	Unknown 1/	(NA)	1,359	1

(NA) Not available.
A/ Revised. B/ Preliminary.
1/ Reporting units without a fixed location within the state or of unknown county location.
2/ Employment based in Florida, but working out of the state or country.
Note: Data are for North American Industry Classification System (NAICS) codes. See Glossary for definition. Detail may not add to totals due to rounding.
Source: State of Florida, Agency for Workforce Innovation, Labor Market Statistics, "Quarterly Census of Employment and Wages" (ES-202), Annual NAICS files, Internet site <http://www.labormarketinfo.com/index.htm> (accessed 17, July 2007).

Table 23.75. STATE AND LOCAL GOVERNMENT: GAS TAX RATE AND LOCAL OPTION GAS TAX COLLECTIONS IN THE STATE AND COUNTIES OF FLORIDA, FISCAL YEAR 2005–06

County	Certified gallons (1,000,000)	Local option collections (dollars)	Total tax imposed (cents)	County	Certified gallons (1,000,000)	Local option collections (dollars)	Total tax imposed (cents)
Florida	8,648,231,127	882,025,421	(X)	Lake	127,415,970	10,504,860	0.279
				Lee	299,544,192	38,910,654	0.329
Alachua	119,306,673	9,698,766	0.279	Leon	121,677,567	9,757,656	0.279
Baker	15,234,710	1,277,217	0.279	Levy	17,874,279	1,524,839	0.269
Bay	86,566,672	6,743,222	0.279	Liberty	3,158,901	409,637	0.279
Bradford	15,495,058	1,168,324	0.269	Madison	10,376,547	2,012,722	0.269
Brevard	251,312,392	17,913,307	0.269	Manatee	142,704,981	11,672,911	0.279
Broward	818,400,187	104,822,319	0.329	Marion	181,831,555	16,549,379	0.279
Calhoun	4,312,577	438,253	0.269	Martin	80,927,970	10,456,916	0.329
Charlotte	83,005,196	10,641,987	0.329	Miami-Dade	1,020,652,912	114,230,960	0.309
Citrus	56,595,860	5,458,921	0.329	Monroe	57,526,321	3,876,697	0.269
Clay	77,110,125	6,211,468	0.279	Nassau	29,308,896	3,276,164	0.329
Collier	144,936,267	18,487,869	0.329	Okaloosa	104,375,313	8,080,060	0.279
Columbia	45,014,243	5,616,598	0.279	Okeechobee	30,852,894	2,866,522	0.279
DeSoto	12,182,253	1,786,201	0.329	Orange	579,806,951	43,490,221	0.269
Dixie	6,030,792	666,955	0.269	Osceola	167,844,701	13,569,149	0.279
Duval	447,024,773	36,606,046	0.269	Palm Beach	552,524,506	71,587,816	0.329
Escambia	136,207,945	11,886,016	0.279	Pasco	191,359,787	15,597,281	0.279
Flagler	38,025,189	3,055,821	0.279	Pinellas	385,178,698	26,439,652	0.269
Franklin	9,055,022	619,770	0.249	Polk	239,657,780	35,565,920	0.329
Gadsden	28,640,879	4,405,824	0.269	Putnam	32,859,118	2,626,400	0.269
Gilchrist	6,430,556	527,466	0.279	St. Johns	95,219,294	7,280,880	0.269
Glades	3,525,816	457,733	0.279	St. Lucie	124,609,859	16,746,641	0.329
Gulf	5,460,784	469,873	0.269	Santa Rosa	64,755,989	4,885,328	0.269
Hamilton	10,963,958	1,206,136	0.269	Sarasota	165,928,827	21,246,493	0.329
Hardee	14,812,242	1,705,547	0.329	Seminole	202,705,682	15,965,569	0.279
Hendry	19,289,671	2,540,725	0.299	Sumter	44,743,182	5,668,661	0.279
Hernando	71,925,971	7,688,429	0.299	Suwannee	23,612,618	3,478,100	0.329
Highlands	38,489,142	5,659,264	0.329	Taylor	12,198,291	1,349,308	0.269
Hillsborough	573,752,900	49,054,977	0.279	Union	3,850,320	486,135	0.269
Holmes	8,520,241	851,395	0.279	Volusia	213,562,005	27,824,468	0.329
Indian River	67,917,232	5,465,074	0.269	Wakulla	9,692,188	902,251	0.279
Jackson	35,314,767	4,188,096	0.279	Walton	35,902,405	3,487,298	0.279
Jefferson	9,317,984	1,109,212	0.279	Washington	10,988,093	1,003,431	0.279
Lafayette	2,824,458	265,633	0.269				

(X) Not applicable.
Note: Detail may not add to totals because of rounding.
Source: State of Florida, Department of Revenue, Internet site <http://www.myflorida.com/> (accessed 23, March 2007).

Table 23.76. STATE AND LOCAL GOVERNMENT: EMPLOYMENT BY FUNCTION AND PAYROLL OF STATE AND LOCAL GOVERNMENTS IN FLORIDA AND THE UNITED STATES MARCH 2006

Item	Florida		United States	
	State and local	State only	State and local	State only
Full-time equivalent employees, all functions	867,259	215,495	16,135,699	5,127,796
General administration	73,770	29,808	1,098,904	408,154
Financial	24,515	7,282	392,632	173,646
Central	15,833	2,139	286,303	59,833
Judicial and legal	33,422	20,387	419,969	174,675
Police protection	64,887	4,477	919,277	106,377
Police with powers of arrest	41,848	2,092	685,612	65,665
Other police protection	23,039	2,385	233,665	40,712
Fire protection	27,345	(X)	327,712	(X)
Correction	43,950	28,803	717,047	471,747
Streets and highways	22,870	7,474	545,089	242,372
Air and water transportation	5,461	(X)	58,052	8,332
Airports	4,317	(X)	45,934	3,467
Water transport	1,144	(X)	12,118	4,865
Public welfare	16,431	9,759	510,841	236,680
Health	30,082	24,817	432,857	189,054
Hospitals	49,831	3,805	926,773	421,402
Social insurance administration	2,440	2,451	83,297	85,419
Solid waste management	6,797	(X)	109,392	1,930
Sewerage	9,757	(X)	127,525	1,769
Parks and recreation	22,016	1,537	267,126	39,170
Housing and community development	5,689	(X)	114,100	(X)
Natural resources	15,800	12,089	188,308	161,481
Public utilities	26,304	761	484,170	38,055
Water supply	11,864	(X)	165,915	711
Electric power	5,557	(X)	77,610	4,055
Gas supply	708	(X)	12,632	(X)
Transit	8,175	761	228,013	33,289
Education	409,192	82,378	8,625,260	2,492,612
Elementary and secondary schools	323,078	(X)	6,645,323	59,266
Higher education	82,381	78,616	1,888,819	2,335,038
Other education	3,733	3,762	91,118	98,308
Libraries 1/	6,569	(X)	128,653	722
State liquor stores	(X)	(X)	7,493	8,661
Other and unallocable	28,068	7,336	463,823	213,859
March payroll, total ($1,000)	3,022,534,925	657,005,547	60,741,155,413	16,769,427,957

(X) Not applicable, local government only.
1/ United States totals include state government amounts for some states.

Source: U.S., Department of Commerce, Census Bureau, Federal, State, and Local Governments, Public Employment and Payroll Data, March 2006, Internet site <http://www.census.gov/> (accessed 26, March 2007).

Table 23.77. LOCAL GOVERNMENT: EMPLOYMENT AND PAYROLL IN THE STATE AND COUNTIES OF FLORIDA, MARCH 2002

County	Total employ- ment	March payroll ($1,000)	Average earnings 1/ (dollars)	County	Total employ- ment	March payroll ($1,000)	Average earnings 1/ (dollars)
Florida	685,418	1,851,207	3,159	Lake	7,717	16,614	2,625
Alachua	10,579	25,078	2,806	Lee	21,569	55,456	3,060
Baker	840	1,705	2,573	Leon	11,131	27,895	3,065
Bay	8,664	18,276	2,472	Levy	1,444	2,874	2,337
Bradford	956	1,911	2,490	Liberty	288	522	2,275
Brevard	19,681	47,520	2,801	Madison	1,088	1,970	2,430
Broward	75,309	232,096	3,537	Manatee	10,948	25,851	2,756
Calhoun	547	1,068	2,447	Marion	9,385	21,260	2,552
Charlotte	4,405	10,857	2,784	Martin	4,117	10,994	2,978
Citrus	4,318	7,909	2,599	Miami-Dade	104,944	342,067	3,806
Clay	5,185	12,448	2,692	Monroe	3,988	11,320	3,146
Collier	9,216	25,770	3,248	Nassau	2,244	5,048	2,679
Columbia	2,570	5,332	2,513	Okaloosa	6,886	15,922	2,743
DeSoto	1,087	2,270	2,428	Okeechobee	1,625	3,556	2,670
Dixie	556	845	2,090	Orange	44,248	124,231	3,234
Duval	27,227	77,695	3,355	Osceola	8,034	19,881	2,856
Escambia	12,143	27,399	2,735	Palm Beach	44,623	132,315	3,432
Flagler	2,155	3,401	2,350	Pasco	11,952	26,652	2,545
Franklin	421	753	2,304	Pinellas	36,256	95,464	3,143
Gadsden	1,843	4,063	2,446	Polk	21,160	48,532	2,659
Gilchrist	652	1,213	2,396	Putnam	4,063	9,830	2,908
Glades	373	772	2,595	St. Johns	4,161	10,674	2,780
Gulf	651	1,381	2,505	St. Lucie	9,377	23,054	2,800
Hamilton	629	1,492	2,629	Santa Rosa	3,900	8,804	2,690
Hardee	1,305	2,739	2,444	Sarasota	14,713	42,454	3,276
Hendry	1,606	3,558	2,512	Seminole	13,829	33,693	2,885
Hernando	4,947	11,498	2,686	Sumter	1,591	2,999	2,420
Highlands	3,250	7,324	2,634	Suwannee	1,331	2,849	2,590
Hillsborough	43,982	113,277	3,084	Taylor	938	1,892	2,489
Holmes	815	1,532	2,323	Union	504	796	2,006
Indian River	4,134	10,656	2,975	Volusia	19,406	47,857	2,789
Jackson	3,097	5,936	2,516	Wakulla	802	1,594	2,481
Jefferson	533	935	2,170	Walton	1,781	4,231	2,710
Lafayette	292	549	2,270	Washington	1,407	2,796	2,517

1/ Average March earning of full-time equivalent employees.

Source: U.S., Department of Commerce, Census Bureau, *2002 Census of Governments, Volume 3, Public Employment: Compendium of Public Employment, 2002,* issued September 2004, Internet site <http://www.census.gov/> (accessed 11, May 2007).

Table 23.78. LOCAL GOVERNMENT: FTE EMPLOYMENT BY SPECIFIED FUNCTION IN THE STATE AND COUNTIES OF FLORIDA, MARCH 2002

County	Total FTE employment 1/	Education	Public welfare	Health and hospitals	Highways	Public safety 2/	Environment and housing 3/	Government administration	Utilities
Florida	604,011	305,856	6,341	44,746	14,361	93,513	45,325	40,444	22,615
Alachua	9,166	4,856	77	143	188	1,086	372	897	702
Baker	686	535	3	6	19	21	36	37	8
Bay	7,497	3,776	3	1,847	258	625	329	348	117
Bradford	802	513	0	0	23	89	17	72	25
Brevard	17,368	8,975	64	969	615	2,444	1,389	1,476	416
Broward	67,650	27,740	484	13,338	953	9,888	4,574	3,606	2,335
Calhoun	452	297	8	0	33	25	7	46	2
Charlotte	3,966	2,005	43	90	181	539	181	437	148
Citrus	3,166	1,973	55	32	131	315	67	242	87
Clay	4,628	3,225	3	15	170	497	141	268	44
Collier	8,291	4,583	20	227	182	1,300	523	705	201
Columbia	2,179	1,456	3	26	91	178	65	167	34
DeSoto	953	629	0	0	66	78	30	96	0
Dixie	416	298	0	24	25	12	25	15	4
Duval	23,910	12,770	215	158	527	3,509	1,505	1,378	1,994
Escambia	10,259	6,220	18	132	239	1,068	686	828	276
Flagler	1,474	1,057	4	43	77	70	67	74	11
Franklin	330	196	0	0	16	32	16	23	14
Gadsden	1,711	1,089	2	32	107	187	47	109	37
Gilchrist	516	345	1	21	23	40	14	45	2
Glades	305	132	2	20	22	33	16	28	18
Gulf	569	310	2	20	39	74	42	53	7
Hamilton	577	320	1	1	35	48	13	57	2
Hardee	1,128	583	1	17	51	180	50	86	106
Hendry	1,451	861	2	191	74	51	63	31	17
Hernando	4,340	2,224	7	16	82	538	221	265	84
Highlands	2,864	1,698	9	46	130	331	101	175	37
Hillsborough	38,301	20,368	968	342	764	4,551	2,980	2,675	1,140
Holmes	675	443	1	18	64	37	38	46	1
Indian River	3,653	1,679	7	100	212	573	319	192	248
Jackson	2,433	1,236	168	423	95	207	49	109	18
Jefferson	439	281	9	13	38	25	31	24	4
Lafayette	245	160	0	6	12	15	8	26	0
Lake	6,513	3,760	12	66	176	854	332	478	202
Lee	18,675	7,257	51	5,062	497	2,092	1,409	933	316

See footnotes at end of table. Continued . . .

Table 23.78. LOCAL GOVERNMENT: FTE EMPLOYMENT BY SPECIFIED FUNCTION IN THE STATE AND COUNTIES OF FLORIDA, MARCH 2002 (Continued)

County	Total FTE employment 1/	Education	Public welfare	Health and hospitals	Highways	Public safety 2/	Environment and housing 3/	Government administration	Utilities
Leon	9,451	4,740	12	180	453	1,041	735	768	609
Levy	1,246	830	0	38	78	138	52	38	22
Liberty	234	178	0	7	18	0	9	5	12
Madison	826	571	1	18	39	58	30	54	9
Manatee	9,658	5,135	53	222	242	1,141	619	916	169
Marion	8,550	5,394	13	33	232	1,112	427	437	220
Martin	3,777	1,903	23	0	119	611	223	389	71
Miami-Dade	93,765	42,181	2,188	10,688	1,147	12,133	7,256	6,020	4,350
Monroe	3,679	1,459	3	56	18	638	228	449	430
Nassau	1,932	1,185	1	50	106	251	99	69	1
Okaloosa	5,950	3,850	3	78	205	643	223	335	276
Okeechobee	1,318	853	12	0	47	172	12	54	50
Orange	39,274	20,249	719	1,277	888	4,948	2,688	2,569	2,354
Osceola	7,151	3,972	46	49	275	1,045	407	549	292
Palm Beach	40,311	19,851	424	824	886	5,904	3,096	3,015	1,035
Pasco	10,634	7,001	98	22	277	1,224	501	680	150
Pinellas	31,552	15,761	156	168	632	4,786	3,088	2,262	1,594
Polk	18,604	10,462	260	299	487	2,188	1,181	1,434	1,090
Putnam	3,309	1,867	2	56	76	225	105	144	53
St. Johns	3,923	2,404	10	85	109	499	211	359	17
St. Lucie	8,092	5,001	22	43	218	960	538	522	243
Santa Rosa	3,373	2,280	3	28	136	367	115	197	54
Sarasota	13,441	4,587	4	3,804	389	1,810	525	733	376
Seminole	11,960	7,393	12	67	328	1,771	608	936	254
Sumter	1,305	760	4	3	43	146	60	129	36
Suwannee	1,138	671	0	0	61	94	66	48	29
Taylor	787	512	2	1	5	90	45	62	11
Union	402	319	1	15	14	13	15	11	0
Volusia	17,353	8,671	21	2,753	467	2,447	1,112	899	273
Wakulla	670	579	1	21	2	0	13	29	4
Walton	1,606	804	4	89	141	218	35	153	14
Washington	1,152	583	0	328	8	68	16	132	10

FTE Full-time Equivalent.
1/ Includes "other" and unallocable employment.
2/ State total includes corrections.
3/ State total includes natural resources.

Source: U.S., Department of Commerce, Census Bureau, *2002 Census of Governments, Volume 3, Public Employment: Compendium of Public Employment, 2002,* issued September 2004, Internet site <http://www.census.gov/> (accessed 11, May 2007).

Table 23.81. COUNTY FINANCE: REVENUE AND EXPENDITURE AND PER CAPITA AMOUNTS IN THE STATE AND COUNTIES OF FLORIDA, FISCAL YEARS 2003–04 AND 2004–05

County	Revenue				Expenditure			
	Total ($1,000)		Per capita (dollars)		Total ($1,000)		Per capita (dollars)	
	2003–04	2004–05	2003–04	2004–05	2003–04	2004–05	2003–04	2004–05
Florida	36,239,191	40,605,038	2,069	2,266	34,763,131	37,236,028	1,985	2,078
Alachua	277,946	323,622	1,177	1,344	273,005	304,993	1,156	1,267
Baker	23,280	29,571	972	1,235	22,675	26,311	946	1,098
Bay	153,210	168,629	967	1,043	162,151	164,593	1,023	1,018
Bradford	26,876	30,244	969	1,076	27,828	27,478	1,003	977
Brevard	548,158	770,848	1,051	1,449	519,695	653,934	997	1,229
Broward	3,270,447	3,302,459	1,898	1,897	3,121,080	3,009,901	1,811	1,729
Calhoun	12,677	14,764	931	1,059	13,369	14,046	982	1,007
Charlotte	408,983	607,319	2,605	3,943	401,694	514,092	2,559	3,338
Citrus	146,087	183,658	1,131	1,385	139,457	179,309	1,080	1,352
Clay	205,731	212,312	1,259	1,252	202,911	193,375	1,241	1,140
Collier	775,203	1,117,888	2,532	3,518	711,117	840,606	2,323	2,645
Columbia	69,853	76,372	1,155	1,243	67,299	76,848	1,113	1,250
DeSoto	60,238	67,265	1,766	2,063	63,153	67,309	1,852	2,064
Dixie	20,032	22,635	1,342	1,472	20,083	21,699	1,345	1,411
Duval 1/	3,979,073	3,940,725	4,734	4,576	3,790,920	4,085,378	4,510	4,744
Escambia	338,403	592,076	1,101	1,950	337,842	565,243	1,100	1,862
Flagler	75,798	167,822	1,088	2,135	56,180	83,075	806	1,057
Franklin	22,014	27,040	2,067	2,493	21,596	25,616	2,028	2,362
Gadsden	48,649	43,790	1,038	918	41,610	44,050	888	923
Gilchrist	17,864	21,392	1,124	1,319	16,415	19,422	1,032	1,197
Glades	17,876	20,066	1,666	1,870	17,993	18,981	1,676	1,769
Gulf	19,539	26,625	1,208	1,616	20,445	23,021	1,264	1,397
Hamilton	20,305	21,736	1,420	1,518	20,789	20,047	1,453	1,400
Hardee	47,319	67,176	1,703	2,458	44,063	55,584	1,586	2,034
Hendry	13,317	61,959	356	1,615	6,903	41,838	185	1,090
Hernando	239,203	236,259	1,647	1,567	210,065	217,918	1,447	1,445
Highlands	85,358	102,819	927	1,100	85,203	87,854	926	940
Hillsborough	2,699,414	2,903,309	2,435	2,566	2,542,178	2,734,594	2,293	2,417
Holmes	12,449	13,524	655	706	12,881	12,903	678	674
Indian River	247,732	336,358	1,953	2,587	214,379	232,489	1,690	1,788
Jackson	47,020	50,796	962	1,022	46,232	43,336	946	872
Jefferson	14,622	18,617	1,040	1,308	13,610	18,450	968	1,296
Lafayette	10,053	9,401	1,334	1,179	8,702	9,656	1,155	1,211
Lake	236,300	298,860	938	1,136	208,743	262,248	829	997
Lee	1,725,400	1,661,535	3,310	3,024	1,647,558	1,577,075	3,161	2,870

See footnotes at end of table. Continued . . .

Table 23.81. COUNTY FINANCE: REVENUE AND EXPENDITURE AND PER CAPITA AMOUNTS IN THE STATE AND COUNTIES OF FLORIDA, FISCAL YEARS 2003–04 AND 2004–05 (Continued)

County	Revenue				Expenditure			
	Total ($1,000)		Per capita (dollars)		Total ($1,000)		Per capita (dollars)	
	2003–04	2004–05	2003–04	2004–05	2003–04	2004–05	2003–04	2004–05
Leon	271,140	352,472	1,027	1,300	272,476	323,968	1,033	1,195
Levy	44,981	48,591	1,200	1,279	49,893	46,724	1,331	1,230
Liberty	11,346	13,142	1,543	1,734	11,204	12,353	1,524	1,629
Madison	23,201	27,221	1,190	1,382	23,331	26,566	1,197	1,349
Manatee	686,350	641,479	2,325	2,108	525,426	584,664	1,780	1,921
Marion	385,215	414,499	1,313	1,359	318,392	383,990	1,085	1,259
Martin	290,244	359,146	2,109	2,546	266,095	319,890	1,933	2,268
Miami-Dade	7,081,264	8,370,603	2,976	3,456	7,262,214	7,680,046	3,052	3,171
Monroe	261,039	284,543	3,213	3,453	255,852	276,637	3,149	3,357
Nassau	119,978	123,188	1,845	1,873	115,199	110,189	1,772	1,676
Okaloosa	225,966	240,484	1,216	1,273	197,607	221,525	1,064	1,172
Okeechobee	71,230	74,915	1,874	1,984	73,274	68,443	1,928	1,812
Orange	1,995,109	2,091,502	1,968	2,004	1,994,543	1,959,101	1,967	1,878
Osceola	643,133	466,875	2,848	1,985	638,554	415,305	2,828	1,766
Palm Beach	2,613,706	2,964,139	2,104	2,342	2,412,150	2,624,259	1,942	2,073
Pasco	529,288	571,165	1,358	1,404	459,435	466,440	1,179	1,146
Pinellas	1,490,682	1,598,351	1,580	1,686	1,452,482	1,527,205	1,539	1,611
Polk	526,594	701,967	997	1,296	510,685	598,439	966	1,104
Putnam	88,187	99,630	1,204	1,351	82,883	102,451	1,132	1,389
St. Johns	332,930	344,710	2,229	2,192	229,647	261,694	1,538	1,664
St. Lucie	267,598	412,282	1,183	1,718	280,090	407,662	1,238	1,698
Santa Rosa	133,670	207,378	1,000	1,520	131,956	206,655	987	1,515
Sarasota	771,905	876,467	2,154	2,383	719,659	758,086	2,008	2,061
Seminole	494,140	704,964	1,225	1,712	523,948	636,468	1,299	1,546
Sumter	101,083	105,230	1,522	1,421	100,254	97,790	1,509	1,321
Suwannee	40,855	48,960	1,083	1,283	40,156	47,615	1,065	1,247
Taylor	28,541	43,566	1,363	2,044	31,577	43,806	1,508	2,056
Union	10,719	12,449	733	827	11,044	12,264	755	815
Volusia	596,871	670,291	1,233	1,355	500,761	557,299	1,034	1,127
Wakulla	37,649	40,015	1,476	1,489	37,496	38,412	1,470	1,430
Walton	97,111	117,759	1,921	2,200	85,700	121,600	1,696	2,272
Washington	51,037	27,584	2,275	1,194	39,324	25,208	1,753	1,091

1/ Duval County includes the consolidated cities of Jacksonville, Jacksonville Beach, Atlantic Beach, Baldwin, and Neptune Beach.

Note: Per capita figures computed using Bureau of Economic and Business Research April 1, 2004 and 2005 population estimates.

Source: State of Florida, Department of Banking and Finance, Office of the Comptroller, Internet site <http://localgovserver.dbf.state.fl.us/> (accessed 26, March 2007).

Table 23.83. COUNTY FINANCE: REVENUE BY SOURCE OF COUNTY GOVERNMENTS IN FLORIDA FISCAL YEAR 2004–05

(rounded to thousands of dollars)

County	Total	Taxes and impact fees	Federal grants	State and other govern- ments	Charges for services	Fines and forfeits	Other sources and transfers
Florida	40,605,038	12,755,071	1,935,588	2,842,900	10,724,437	194,925	12,152,117
Alachua	323,622	124,673	6,248	27,663	44,662	2,628	117,749
Baker	29,571	8,005	2,860	5,061	2,561	384	10,699
Bay	168,629	70,550	3,287	21,629	50,210	1,314	21,639
Bradford	30,244	8,894	1,094	5,057	3,793	285	11,120
Brevard	770,848	265,783	32,519	68,411	185,615	2,080	216,439
Broward	3,302,459	935,073	65,526	192,281	839,531	17,731	1,252,317
Calhoun	14,764	3,630	4,197	4,313	298	188	2,137
Charlotte	607,319	178,873	51,427	44,930	119,677	2,031	210,380
Citrus	183,658	81,500	11,905	18,995	36,868	1,869	32,523
Clay	212,312	94,464	4,832	21,707	18,282	1,156	71,872
Collier	1,117,888	332,208	5,633	69,469	202,451	4,407	503,720
Columbia	76,372	31,606	3,941	13,790	6,905	261	19,870
DeSoto	67,265	16,058	17,690	11,092	6,967	137	15,322
Dixie	22,635	8,369	2,220	3,526	1,790	233	6,497
Duval 1/	3,940,725	770,208	166,288	197,815	1,755,304	10,098	1,041,011
Escambia	592,076	184,486	191,641	70,039	59,119	3,183	83,609
Flagler	167,822	37,801	2,648	9,175	13,741	1,478	102,978
Franklin	27,040	11,674	1,571	3,499	1,570	67	8,659
Gadsden	43,790	13,742	1,865	10,163	2,816	34	15,169
Gilchrist	21,392	6,764	591	4,200	1,626	80	8,132
Glades	20,066	6,406	402	3,815	2,105	1,063	6,275
Gulf	26,625	12,482	1,424	4,104	1,672	180	6,762
Hamilton	21,736	6,741	748	5,905	1,302	74	6,966
Hardee	67,176	16,394	11,700	10,157	3,329	213	25,382
Hendry	61,959	22,615	592	11,819	8,129	156	18,649
Hernando	236,259	97,383	7,092	18,464	61,491	1,128	50,700
Highlands	102,819	54,351	4,116	14,142	13,886	688	15,636
Hillsborough	2,903,309	923,934	89,666	162,654	495,782	12,858	1,218,415
Holmes	13,524	4,500	2,258	3,928	826	506	1,505
Indian River	336,358	153,846	21,841	22,694	71,856	1,726	64,396
Jackson	50,796	18,157	3,372	9,684	4,771	225	14,587
Jefferson	18,617	6,991	1,489	4,673	1,313	229	3,921
Lafayette	9,401	2,765	0	2,713	1,055	64	2,804
Lake	298,860	139,411	26,804	33,638	44,515	4,565	49,927

See footnote at end of table. Continued . . .

Table 23.83. COUNTY FINANCE: REVENUE BY SOURCE OF COUNTY GOVERNMENTS IN FLORIDA FISCAL YEAR 2004–05 (Continued)

(rounded to thousands of dollars)

County	Total	Taxes and impact fees	Federal grants	State and other govern- ments	Charges for services	Fines and forfeits	Other sources and transfers
Lee	1,661,535	451,608	24,568	89,016	410,891	2,746	682,706
Leon	352,472	126,936	5,204	24,873	37,829	2,144	155,486
Levy	48,591	19,037	1,039	7,608	5,596	336	14,975
Liberty	13,142	1,822	3,151	3,319	894	114	3,842
Madison	27,221	7,896	50	5,602	2,550	196	10,926
Manatee	641,479	216,386	14,199	63,990	241,905	3,800	101,199
Marion	414,499	176,267	26,395	42,357	58,028	3,315	108,137
Martin	359,146	156,668	24,392	36,788	73,450	2,688	65,160
Miami-Dade	8,370,603	2,128,106	581,316	391,981	3,107,458	44,267	2,117,475
Monroe	284,543	104,527	31,173	22,458	56,711	2,253	67,421
Nassau	123,188	58,657	2,092	12,859	14,651	355	34,573
Okaloosa	240,484	62,601	16,676	28,354	74,404	494	57,955
Okeechobee	74,915	30,740	869	8,679	3,837	779	30,011
Orange	2,091,502	951,236	67,010	193,953	459,098	9,924	410,282
Osceola	466,875	215,431	24,143	35,454	67,181	2,297	122,369
Palm Beach	2,964,139	969,819	95,484	160,868	599,509	13,094	1,125,365
Pasco	571,165	254,943	16,153	53,943	135,052	2,884	108,191
Pinellas	1,598,351	553,982	25,723	95,035	407,755	6,740	509,117
Polk	701,967	241,560	17,603	117,602	205,443	4,353	115,407
Putnam	99,630	41,660	2,491	11,733	14,288	1,044	28,412
St. Johns	344,710	135,679	2,565	31,283	62,604	3,258	109,322
St. Lucie	412,282	145,653	56,046	24,010	57,838	3,482	125,253
Santa Rosa	207,378	52,967	60,337	23,659	49,151	279	20,985
Sarasota	876,467	357,778	16,522	60,552	230,996	3,444	207,174
Seminole	704,964	228,143	38,677	57,928	78,932	2,210	299,073
Sumter	105,230	44,111	2,912	11,406	11,542	1,696	33,564
Suwannee	48,960	18,292	1,167	12,621	4,854	602	11,424
Taylor	43,566	12,461	774	4,766	1,453	211	23,902
Union	12,449	3,116	569	3,154	784	244	4,581
Volusia	670,291	251,098	15,504	67,879	165,461	1,977	168,371
Wakulla	40,015	11,111	3,588	4,716	8,277	74	12,249
Walton	117,759	64,982	6,979	19,040	7,923	212	18,625
Washington	27,584	9,462	732	4,208	2,273	96	10,813

1/ Duval County includes the consolidated cities of Jacksonville, Jacksonville Beach, Atlantic Beach, Baldwin, and Neptune Beach.

Source: State of Florida, Department of Banking and Finance, Office of the Comptroller, Internet site <http://localgovserver.dbf.state.fl.us/> (accessed 26, March 2007).

Table 23.84. COUNTY FINANCE: EXPENDITURE BY FUNCTION OF COUNTY GOVERNMENTS IN FLORIDA, FISCAL YEAR 2004–05

(rounded to thousands of dollars)

County	Total	General govern-ment	Public safety	Physical and economic environ-ment	Trans-portation	Human services cultural and recreation	Debt service and other uses and interfund transfers 1/
Florida	37,236,028	5,025,728	7,261,012	6,144,904	4,274,122	4,584,044	9,946,219
Alachua	304,993	54,458	83,087	22,514	9,880	10,612	124,442
Baker	26,311	3,388	6,416	2,672	3,004	1,881	8,949
Bay	164,593	23,525	44,391	51,580	11,312	8,051	25,734
Bradford	27,478	3,561	6,750	2,055	2,558	1,281	11,274
Brevard	653,934	110,634	141,374	117,391	51,568	93,138	139,829
Broward	3,009,901	258,002	628,436	290,148	368,256	350,831	1,114,228
Calhoun	14,046	2,012	2,303	3,718	2,934	854	2,224
Charlotte	514,092	111,583	78,058	81,035	82,318	40,733	120,366
Citrus	179,309	36,069	46,494	18,622	31,659	24,061	22,404
Clay	193,375	35,339	51,202	13,868	13,048	9,230	70,687
Collier	840,606	122,416	190,111	122,981	110,126	79,039	215,932
Columbia	76,848	8,073	19,816	7,592	12,097	3,977	25,293
DeSoto	67,309	6,497	10,921	25,518	4,497	2,477	17,399
Dixie	21,699	2,495	6,245	2,710	1,897	1,165	7,188
Duval 2/	4,085,378	613,434	437,173	1,418,414	493,226	271,625	851,505
Escambia	565,243	71,121	328,523	32,338	31,832	14,303	87,126
Flagler	83,075	21,846	23,534	4,333	12,536	6,797	14,029
Franklin	25,616	3,267	6,269	2,548	4,287	1,264	7,980
Gadsden	44,050	6,545	15,124	1,884	10,705	4,092	5,700
Gilchrist	19,422	3,212	4,584	1,128	2,311	468	7,717
Glades	18,981	2,775	6,620	2,086	1,275	659	5,566
Gulf	23,021	4,434	4,747	3,876	1,388	1,446	7,130
Hamilton	20,047	2,659	5,943	1,868	1,967	914	6,697
Hardee	55,584	5,521	22,068	11,034	3,736	2,587	10,637
Hendry	41,838	10,254	13,096	3,850	10,436	2,426	1,776
Hernando	217,918	43,226	68,132	32,419	28,965	10,793	34,383
Highlands	87,854	17,521	30,737	11,917	12,161	6,522	8,996
Hillsborough	2,734,594	322,502	427,212	351,130	110,812	325,362	1,197,576
Holmes	12,903	2,339	3,993	1,604	2,616	645	1,707
Indian River	232,489	42,330	60,639	51,832	22,369	31,746	23,572
Jackson	43,336	5,997	10,448	3,017	9,343	2,215	12,316
Jefferson	18,450	1,829	4,621	3,797	2,847	712	4,644
Lafayette	9,656	1,396	2,161	714	1,983	429	2,974
Lake	262,248	43,631	86,456	37,498	27,842	20,924	45,897
Lee	1,577,075	211,344	182,282	198,228	275,246	95,737	614,238

See footnotes at end of table.

Continued . . .

Table 23.84. COUNTY FINANCE: EXPENDITURE BY FUNCTION OF COUNTY GOVERNMENTS IN FLORIDA, FISCAL YEAR 2004–05 (Continued)

(rounded to thousands of dollars)

County	Total	General govern- ment	Public safety	Physical and economic environ- ment	Trans- portation	Human services cultural and recreation	Debt service and other uses and interfund transfers 1/
Leon	323,968	40,299	72,338	26,291	20,370	21,188	143,482
Levy	46,724	6,175	16,019	2,886	5,420	1,877	14,347
Liberty	12,353	1,535	2,566	1,380	2,472	754	3,646
Madison	26,566	2,921	6,193	2,078	3,937	1,005	10,432
Manatee	584,664	111,491	124,541	117,740	56,234	67,509	107,148
Marion	383,990	70,925	98,223	51,000	41,671	21,725	100,446
Martin	319,890	85,499	87,056	61,535	17,762	24,027	44,010
Miami-Dade	7,680,046	757,234	1,109,753	1,177,854	1,216,018	2,113,379	1,305,808
Monroe	276,637	45,074	87,572	37,477	22,304	27,068	57,141
Nassau	110,189	20,942	26,794	8,019	9,183	8,295	36,957
Okaloosa	221,525	42,921	46,618	42,177	26,752	11,928	51,128
Okeechobee	68,443	10,174	17,702	3,387	4,274	3,908	28,999
Orange	1,959,101	166,120	462,878	379,629	159,597	182,648	608,228
Osceola	415,305	101,871	66,191	63,024	36,720	28,958	118,541
Palm Beach	2,624,259	461,127	530,608	314,805	239,509	211,656	866,555
Pasco	466,440	97,719	120,763	91,282	53,753	29,285	73,637
Pinellas	1,527,205	238,429	329,813	280,648	66,849	103,327	508,139
Polk	598,439	104,790	183,800	88,587	81,565	45,254	94,443
Putnam	102,451	19,425	24,651	12,952	16,444	4,458	24,521
St. Johns	261,694	34,839	81,981	41,855	34,656	43,378	24,986
St. Lucie	407,662	67,196	75,223	39,872	85,009	40,512	99,849
Santa Rosa	206,655	33,160	126,006	8,902	14,040	6,368	18,179
Sarasota	758,086	63,594	150,405	164,209	68,077	54,884	256,916
Seminole	636,468	67,410	121,608	88,339	75,965	16,860	266,285
Sumter	97,790	15,495	23,065	7,658	14,969	3,011	33,593
Suwannee	47,615	5,338	8,769	5,784	11,775	3,601	12,348
Taylor	43,806	3,113	6,926	2,216	3,017	2,595	25,941
Union	12,264	1,491	2,649	1,223	1,444	598	4,859
Volusia	557,299	97,218	146,682	55,576	83,227	66,512	108,086
Wakulla	38,412	3,619	11,443	3,323	3,078	2,095	14,853
Walton	121,600	28,837	27,646	23,307	21,731	4,275	15,803
Washington	25,208	4,508	4,563	1,968	3,261	2,112	8,796

1/ Includes court-related expenditures.
2/ Duval County includes the consolidated cities of Jacksonville, Jacksonville Beach, Atlantic Beach, Baldwin, and Neptune Beach.

Source: State of Florida, Department of Banking and Finance, Office of the Comptroller, Internet site <http://localgovserver.dbf.state.fl.us/> (accessed 26, March 2007).

Table 23.85. MUNICIPAL FINANCE: REVENUE AND EXPENDITURE PER CAPITA, PERSONAL SERVICES EXPENDITURE, AND BONDED INDEBTEDNESS OF CITY GOVERNMENTS SERVING A 2005 POPULATION OF 48,000 OR MORE IN FLORIDA, FISCAL YEAR 2004–05

City	Revenue Total ($1,000)	Revenue Per capita (dollars)	Expenditure Total ($1,000)	Expenditure Per capita (dollars)
Jacksonville	3,752,345,072	4,595	3,916,163,000	4,795
Miami	1,194,727,758	3,088	1,049,929,617	2,714
Tampa	1,162,181,574	3,559	910,965,468	2,790
St. Petersburg	756,382,222	2,979	685,043,691	2,698
Hialeah	339,882,847	1,475	307,300,050	1,334
Orlando	816,950,981	3,755	697,530,307	3,206
Tallahassee	1,127,736,000	6,452	1,004,396,000	5,747
Ft. Lauderdale	668,141,165	3,899	520,228,499	3,036
Pembroke Pines	341,030,437	2,258	281,133,131	1,861
Hollywood	452,173,167	3,161	372,338,668	2,603
Cape Coral	354,061,667	2,525	279,980,385	1,997
Port St. Lucie	400,756,271	3,103	287,728,676	2,228
Coral Springs	213,425,401	1,682	190,141,912	1,499
Gainesville	515,987,351	4,304	504,482,371	4,208
Clearwater	417,133,107	3,764	343,611,081	3,100
Miramar	333,864,064	3,080	261,484,896	2,413
Pompano Beach	243,136,118	2,390	198,162,750	1,948
West Palm Beach	375,168,529	3,710	320,408,217	3,169
Miami Beach	731,355,613	7,819	642,250,809	6,866
Palm Bay	130,033,270	1,415	103,706,003	1,129
Lakeland	670,706,181	7,382	610,206,635	6,717
Sunrise	236,915,854	2,640	197,149,511	2,197
Boca Raton	316,195,221	3,706	260,599,293	3,055
Plantation	164,786,447	1,935	152,257,056	1,788
Deltona	71,306,468	859	54,694,871	659
Deerfield Beach	138,725,713	1,846	124,878,328	1,661
Melbourne	144,101,261	1,920	125,117,849	1,667
Largo	128,300,106	1,714	114,434,715	1,529
Boynton Beach	157,432,550	2,400	133,320,615	2,032
Daytona Beach	167,239,485	2,568	150,406,038	2,309
Delray Beach	193,474,067	3,028	166,723,001	2,610
Ft. Myers	252,555,609	4,112	195,649,248	3,186
Weston	76,945,033	1,261	74,401,528	1,219
North Miami	125,090,777	2,074	92,543,249	1,534
Tamarac	103,742,626	1,767	87,003,098	1,482
Lauderhill	97,761,765	1,667	59,364,366	1,012
Kissimmee	103,984,000	1,786	92,582,000	1,590
Margate	85,391,629	1,553	78,310,907	1,424
Sarasota	218,640,416	3,986	176,354,530	3,215
Pensacola	288,840,312	5,268	254,857,434	4,648
Port Orange	88,957,508	1,628	68,551,027	1,255
Bradenton	104,295,940	1,921	90,001,592	1,657
Wellington	106,904,605	2,001	97,171,875	1,819
Ocala	298,351,939	6,035	272,934,402	5,521
Sanford	100,167,575	2,034	71,805,654	1,458
Pinellas Park	110,099,459	2,275	98,225,832	2,029
Coconut Creek	71,232,800	1,474	60,071,902	1,243
Jupiter	106,065,715	2,197	81,242,202	1,683

Note: Per capita figures computed using Bureau of Economic and Business Research April 1, 2005 estimates.

Source: State of Florida, Department of Banking and Finance, Office of the Comptroller, Internet site <http://localgovserver.dbf.state.fl.us/> (accessed 26, March 2007).

Table 23.86. MUNICIPAL FINANCE: REVENUE BY SOURCE OF CITY GOVERNMENTS SERVING A 2005 POPULATION OF 48,000 OR MORE IN FLORIDA FISCAL YEAR 2004-05

(rounded to thousands of dollars)

City	Total	Taxes and impact fees	Federal grants	State and other govern-ments	Charges for services	Fines and forfeits	Other sources and transfers
Jacksonville	3,752,345	745,771	164,996	189,047	1,637,493	9,299	1,005,739
Miami	1,194,728	332,116	85,084	74,543	125,060	4,980	572,944
Tampa	1,162,182	244,408	27,816	122,642	269,743	7,991	489,581
St. Petersburg	756,382	142,621	6,351	65,791	239,479	3,414	298,726
Hialeah	339,883	98,503	15,319	63,246	58,989	334	103,492
Orlando	816,951	210,585	20,346	81,830	210,151	3,031	291,008
Tallahassee	1,127,736	66,250	7,706	21,731	680,939	1,820	349,290
Ft. Lauderdale	668,141	188,453	41,760	34,851	181,629	5,764	215,683
Pembroke Pines	341,030	84,939	4,026	46,816	71,753	959	132,538
Hollywood	452,173	115,791	8,451	18,911	130,564	2,569	175,888
Cape Coral	354,062	150,178	13,422	20,365	65,072	1,521	103,504
Port St. Lucie	400,756	102,074	14,285	13,759	88,254	849	181,536
Coral Springs	213,425	65,874	2,192	15,076	51,482	2,177	76,625
Gainesville	515,987	38,649	9,844	15,210	305,077	5,263	141,944
Clearwater	417,133	84,812	2,168	24,887	176,453	2,381	126,432
Miramar	333,864	67,633	2,643	20,539	37,927	667	204,456
Pompano Beach	243,136	89,414	4,626	13,086	72,984	1,483	61,542
West Palm Beach	375,169	107,225	11,802	21,490	114,393	2,515	117,743
Miami Beach	731,356	171,398	9,251	42,811	134,593	5,977	367,325
Palm Bay	130,033	48,417	8,285	10,040	32,344	718	30,229
Lakeland	670,706	48,126	4,595	23,824	444,213	1,017	148,931
Sunrise	236,916	65,477	1,563	10,706	94,264	969	63,937
Boca Raton	316,195	102,531	7,440	30,120	69,460	1,666	104,978
Plantation	164,786	53,420	2,610	12,493	25,700	1,255	69,309
Deltona	71,306	26,829	8,985	7,437	18,648	234	9,173
Deerfield Beach	138,726	47,038	1,928	10,194	38,473	1,813	39,280
Melbourne	144,101	44,989	1,254	9,370	56,418	880	31,191
Largo	128,300	37,952	3,141	16,301	45,536	673	24,698
Boynton Beach	157,433	48,174	1,101	14,770	46,418	531	46,439
Daytona Beach	167,239	45,576	2,838	14,991	67,571	989	35,275
Delray Beach	193,474	69,100	1,231	11,416	52,039	1,067	58,620
Ft. Myers	252,556	59,650	13,263	14,274	73,759	1,366	90,243
Weston	76,945	44,923	0	5,224	19,777	355	6,665
North Miami	125,091	28,396	1,264	38,270	30,508	452	26,200
Tamarac	103,743	35,552	453	9,939	27,575	540	29,683
Lauderhill	97,762	22,314	0	10,298	22,967	363	41,821
Kissimmee	103,984	27,652	743	30,429	18,170	604	26,386
Margate	85,392	30,850	1,108	9,719	35,738	1,411	6,567
Sarasota	218,640	49,516	3,318	15,228	69,525	1,697	79,355
Pensacola	288,840	44,160	50,250	15,787	87,162	554	90,927
Port Orange	88,958	31,416	971	7,402	27,698	254	21,216
Bradenton	104,296	28,775	3,868	8,539	31,364	495	31,254
Wellington	106,905	37,980	1,058	5,544	18,819	404	43,099
Ocala	298,352	33,554	7,798	9,970	187,886	529	58,614
Sanford	100,168	25,815	6,709	6,988	32,394	288	27,974
Pinellas Park	110,099	29,971	576	8,753	35,054	491	35,255
Coconut Creek	71,233	27,435	1,189	5,907	19,374	524	16,804
Jupiter	106,066	32,454	7,814	6,521	21,271	432	37,572

Source: State of Florida, Department of Banking and Finance, Office of the Comptroller, Internet site <http://localgovserver.dbf.state.fl.us/> (accessed 26, March 2007).

Table 23.87. MUNICIPAL FINANCE: EXPENDITURE BY FUNCTION OF CITY GOVERNMENTS SERVING A 2005 POPULATION OF 48,000 OR MORE IN FLORIDA FISCAL YEAR 2004–05

(rounded to thousands of dollars)

City	Total	General govern- ment	Public safety	Physical and economic environment	Trans- portation	Human services cultural and recreation	Debt service 1/
Jacksonville	3,916,163	601,215	419,189	1,329,263	487,236	265,776	813,484
Miami	1,049,930	368,972	226,906	97,000	61,636	48,904	246,512
Tampa	910,965	110,573	194,661	219,318	97,845	77,860	210,709
St. Petersburg	685,044	142,552	119,631	155,322	21,807	67,220	178,512
Hialeah	307,300	105,910	70,366	64,086	33,301	15,763	17,875
Orlando	697,530	150,662	152,704	149,676	56,726	60,399	127,362
Tallahassee	1,004,396	322,832	69,234	354,995	78,553	30,439	148,343
Ft. Lauderdale	520,228	99,677	144,566	125,908	22,868	41,908	85,301
Pembroke Pines	281,133	59,512	69,513	58,707	10,800	64,260	18,342
Hollywood	372,339	106,435	108,409	93,464	12,647	13,757	37,626
Cape Coral	279,980	39,314	63,204	47,305	27,908	43,305	58,945
Port St. Lucie	287,729	37,861	48,919	28,414	59,483	14,337	98,715
Coral Springs	190,142	35,703	53,315	11,113	6,166	24,807	59,038
Gainesville	504,482	79,011	53,585	234,051	26,975	8,527	102,333
Clearwater	343,611	74,659	56,638	109,507	16,133	35,587	51,087
Miramar	261,485	7,711	54,250	23,953	3,710	18,575	153,287
Pompano Beach	198,163	52,553	61,496	53,290	4,024	11,189	15,611
West Palm Beach	320,408	27,141	73,484	80,246	12,727	16,844	109,966
Miami Beach	642,251	123,030	111,794	71,386	30,315	61,896	243,830
Palm Bay	103,706	21,945	31,540	15,612	13,741	4,398	16,469
Lakeland	610,207	58,666	41,878	370,653	37,181	27,421	74,407
Sunrise	197,150	26,123	41,808	73,190	4,609	12,329	39,090
Boca Raton	260,599	29,187	61,160	43,294	11,641	38,626	76,691
Plantation	152,257	24,473	40,755	26,679	5,828	13,877	40,644
Deltona	54,695	7,591	12,904	20,442	7,032	2,622	4,104
Deerfield Beach	124,878	16,888	34,357	37,331	6,215	10,536	19,551
Melbourne	125,118	17,638	27,846	33,939	24,191	9,261	12,243
Largo	114,435	19,927	30,005	34,061	2,333	21,622	6,486
Boynton Beach	133,321	24,035	42,160	32,088	1,547	13,066	20,425
Daytona Beach	150,406	26,137	36,589	42,345	14,587	10,863	19,885
Delray Beach	166,723	35,344	45,989	32,293	3,519	31,630	17,948
Ft. Myers	195,649	25,452	37,455	48,874	10,139	15,186	58,544
Weston	74,402	5,889	14,453	39,934	4,393	5,889	3,844
North Miami	92,543	29,021	14,193	32,988	3,715	8,178	4,449
Tamarac	87,003	14,523	24,776	20,605	4,915	4,462	17,722
Lauderhill	59,364	6,079	19,996	19,320	2,933	6,017	5,019
Kissimmee	92,582	20,707	23,325	5,817	13,178	7,426	22,129
Margate	78,311	8,560	28,122	20,035	2,661	6,848	12,085
Sarasota	176,355	49,023	28,647	48,128	15,571	17,082	17,904
Pensacola	254,857	42,935	72,114	57,855	19,285	15,529	47,140
Port Orange	68,551	13,620	15,946	20,045	2,916	3,225	12,798
Bradenton	90,002	11,559	18,707	27,158	3,943	10,393	18,242
Wellington	97,172	9,641	7,590	21,263	2,510	9,869	46,299
Ocala	272,934	26,619	35,847	161,140	15,977	7,905	25,446
Sanford	71,806	10,795	17,840	14,516	19,379	4,297	4,980
Pinellas Park	98,226	12,692	22,740	25,530	4,540	6,046	26,679
Coconut Creek	60,072	10,719	16,541	18,150	1,003	4,646	9,013
Jupiter	81,242	26,172	17,804	13,979	4,584	3,813	14,889

1/ Includes other uses and interfund transfers, and court related expenditures.

Source: State of Florida, Department of Banking and Finance, Office of the Comptroller, Internet site <http://localgovserver.dbf.state.fl.us/> (accessed 26, March 2007).

Table 23.89. PROPERTY VALUATIONS: NET ASSESSED VALUES OF REAL, PERSONAL, AND RAILROAD PROPERTY IN FLORIDA, JANUARY 1, 1966 THROUGH 2006

(amounts rounded to thousands of dollars)

Year	Total		Real property		Personal property		Railroad and private car lines	
	Amount	Percentage change from previous year	Amount	Percent-age of total	Amount	Percent-age of total	Amount	Percent-age of total
1966	36,253,654	21.82	31,943,021	88.11	4,036,480	11.13	274,153	0.76
1967	40,606,927	12.01	35,154,260	86.57	5,162,026	12.71	290,640	0.72
1968	42,060,610	3.58	36,637,166	87.10	5,125,541	12.19	297,903	0.71
1969	45,180,722	7.42	39,697,479	87.86	5,187,897	11.48	295,346	0.66
1970	51,247,667	13.43	45,066,274	87.94	5,915,000	11.54	266,393	0.52
1971	59,967,320	17.01	51,822,900	86.42	7,845,286	13.08	299,134	0.50
1972	67,053,619	11.82	56,610,767	84.43	10,134,332	15.11	308,520	0.46
1973	82,146,275	22.51	69,936,535	85.14	11,870,966	14.45	338,774	0.41
1974	107,894,309	31.34	92,979,953	86.18	14,570,730	13.50	343,627	0.32
1975	120,558,360	11.74	103,460,245	85.82	16,690,698	13.84	407,417	0.34
1976	128,700,512	6.75	109,217,279	84.86	19,072,710	14.82	410,523	0.32
1977	139,650,757	8.51	118,232,881	84.66	20,925,041	14.98	492,835	0.35
1978	151,271,654	8.32	129,382,344	85.53	21,393,945	14.14	495,365	0.33
1979	159,642,320	5.53	135,705,468	84.38	24,422,967	15.30	513,884	0.32
1980	187,750,045	17.61	164,755,192	87.75	22,480,384	11.97	514,470	0.27
1981	237,140,341	26.31	211,148,696	89.04	25,579,874	10.79	411,772	0.17
1982	272,997,005	15.12	244,424,808	89.53	28,194,359	10.53	377,839	0.14
1983	298,583,050	9.37	266,304,607	89.19	31,858,923	10.67	419,519	0.14
1984	323,647,775	8.39	288,392,562	89.11	34,820,448	10.76	434,765	0.13
1985	356,061,973	10.02	317,508,051	89.17	38,100,514	10.70	453,408	0.13
1986	385,126,891	8.16	343,168,089	89.11	41,389,766	10.75	569,036	0.15
1987	417,508,830	8.41	372,504,470	89.22	44,326,033	10.62	678,327	0.16
1988	446,103,804	6.85	398,216,681	89.27	47,192,039	10.58	695,085	0.16
1989	485,766,305	8.89	434,583,860	89.46	50,554,052	10.41	628,394	0.13
1990	524,248,524	7.92	469,498,829	89.56	54,114,754	10.32	634,941	0.12
1991	553,456,777	5.57	496,581,168	89.72	56,260,942	10.17	614,667	0.11
1992	560,820,605	1.33	501,638,271	89.45	58,586,918	10.45	595,416	0.11
1993	570,341,544	1.70	509,360,697	89.31	60,380,135	10.59	600,712	0.11
1994	595,216,496	4.36	530,408,830	89.11	62,835,320	10.56	1,972,345	0.33
1995	623,757,999	4.80	556,091,584	89.15	67,006,163	10.74	660,252	0.11
1996	652,462,117	4.60	580,555,689	88.98	71,217,716	10.92	688,712	0.11
1997	691,235,598	5.94	616,179,520	89.14	74,069,860	10.72	986,218	0.14
1998	736,334,987	6.52	658,425,719	89.42	77,005,107	10.46	904,162	0.12
1999	790,384,554	7.34	708,764,946	89.67	80,674,465	10.21	945,143	0.12
2000	854,130,559	8.07	769,413,004	90.08	83,779,637	9.81	950,023	0.11
2001	952,026,130	11.46	864,056,980	90.76	87,046,434	9.14	892,258	0.09
2002	1,067,805,040	12.16	978,260,540	91.61	88,676,571	8.30	867,928	0.08
2003	1,208,662,001	13.19	1,116,813,195	92.40	90,653,303	7.50	1,195,503	0.10
2004	1,384,585,482	14.38	1,290,618,036	93.21	92,594,200	6.69	1,373,246	0.10
2005	1,672,806,771	20.82	1,574,861,725	94.14	96,902,141	5.79	1,045,892	0.06
2006	2,166,874,654	29.54	2,061,519,510	95.14	104,255,939	4.81	1,099,204	0.05

Note: Net assessed value is total assessed or just value less nontaxable value of property having a classified use value. Classified use value is the value at which agricultural land and certain privately owned park and recreation land is assessed for tax purposes. The "highest and best" use principle is relaxed and assessment is based on current use only. Some data may be revised.

Source: State of Florida, Department of Revenue, *2006 Florida Property Valuations and Tax Data,* Internet site <http://dor.myflorida.com/> (accessed 26, July 2007).

Table 23.90. PROPERTY VALUATIONS: ASSESSED AND TAXABLE VALUES BY CATEGORY OF REAL PROPERTY IN FLORIDA, JANUARY 1, 2005 AND 2006

(rounded to thousands of dollars)

Category	Just value 1/			Taxable value 2/		
	2005	2006	Percent-age change	2005	2006	Percent-age change
Total 3/	1,770,557,192	2,307,039,317	30.3	1,215,977,908	1,540,158,627	26.7
Residential	928,113,313	1,235,341,017	33.1	636,859,126	810,172,870	27.2
Vacant	70,321,615	108,989,768	55.0	68,888,824	107,018,516	55.3
Single-family	857,791,698	1,126,351,249	31.3	567,970,302	703,154,354	23.8
Mobile homes	24,798,028	32,051,352	29.2	14,792,050	19,271,236	30.3
Multifamily	76,661,650	86,523,695	12.9	71,131,176	79,472,987	11.7
9 units or less	31,569,429	39,812,736	26.1	27,368,646	34,290,048	25.3
10 units or more	45,092,221	46,710,959	3.6	43,762,530	45,182,938	3.2
Condominiums	271,054,136	371,468,137	37.0	216,821,444	293,516,562	35.4
Cooperatives	3,956,297	5,159,182	30.4	3,023,853	3,892,987	28.7
Retirement homes	3,852,725	4,827,034	25.3	3,337,973	4,246,245	27.2
Commercial	191,939,029	232,440,298	21.1	186,483,449	225,717,126	21.0
Vacant	17,042,016	24,912,449	46.2	16,385,312	23,999,680	46.5
Improved	174,897,013	207,527,849	18.7	170,098,137	201,717,445	18.6
Industrial	47,657,101	57,305,439	20.2	46,534,474	56,054,355	20.5
Vacant	4,123,198	5,509,923	33.6	3,937,900	5,278,915	34.1
Improved	43,533,902	51,795,515	19.0	42,596,574	50,775,440	19.2
Agricultural	62,474,053	86,078,823	37.8	12,168,655	13,915,991	14.4
Institutional	35,754,765	41,742,179	16.7	8,433,866	9,924,228	17.7
Government	104,490,416	127,037,081	21.6	1,046,949	1,108,884	5.9
Leasehold	3,055,985	3,462,984	13.3	1,540,924	1,735,850	12.6
Miscellaneous	6,108,607	6,817,189	11.6	3,912,245	4,440,352	13.5
Nonagricultural	10,183,768	15,186,960	49.1	9,531,819	14,389,168	51.0

1/ The value of property for tax purposes as determined by the elected county property appraiser. Value is determined at the highest and best use of property, except for special classes provided for in Florida Statutes.
2/ The value against which millage rates are applied to compute the amount of tax levied. Total taxable value makes up the ad valorem tax base for units of government in Florida.
3/ Totals include centrally assessed values not shown elsewhere.

Source: State of Florida, Department of Revenue, *2006 Florida Property Valuations and Tax Data,* Internet site <http://dor.myflorida.com/> (accessed 26, July 2007).

Table 23.91. PROPERTY VALUATIONS: ASSESSED, EXEMPT, AND TAXABLE VALUES OF REAL PROPERTY IN THE STATE AND COUNTIES OF FLORIDA JANUARY 1, 2005 AND 2006

(rounded to thousands of dollars)

County	Just values 1/		Exempt and immune values		Taxable values 2/	
	2005	2006	2005	2006	2005	2006
Florida	1,768,878,963	2,306,256,430	309,964,132	363,861,161	1,212,446,922	1,537,919,858
Alachua	15,726,381	18,308,114	5,774,933	6,299,362	8,600,943	10,130,861
Baker	1,159,931	1,335,586	616,039	643,646	456,293	563,877
Bay	16,062,370	23,774,642	3,437,097	4,031,967	11,486,987	16,678,090
Bradford	1,248,360	1,810,230	665,963	1,029,866	526,210	648,021
Brevard	50,050,855	62,812,856	10,620,136	11,487,084	28,665,541	36,729,883
Broward	182,023,645	229,165,495	23,955,763	26,515,164	124,042,076	150,284,582
Calhoun	510,201	795,655	293,570	516,667	206,263	249,295
Charlotte	20,937,367	32,413,213	2,807,467	3,860,209	15,255,516	23,369,009
Citrus	10,331,779	15,252,150	2,122,250	3,055,080	6,909,743	9,701,761
Clay	10,214,009	13,151,704	2,131,907	2,341,983	6,863,146	8,563,524
Collier	76,292,993	100,200,751	7,629,181	9,297,459	59,841,656	75,240,489
Columbia	3,051,725	4,088,303	1,290,692	1,721,360	1,593,750	2,017,529
DeSoto	2,094,506	3,670,863	1,119,266	1,896,459	865,987	1,443,855
Dixie	982,536	1,858,168	449,893	1,225,049	439,125	554,279
Duval	60,415,491	70,096,837	12,555,231	13,320,422	40,671,784	47,111,708
Escambia	18,226,317	24,459,300	7,145,752	8,534,573	9,650,128	12,734,895
Flagler	10,192,039	14,335,339	1,468,137	2,051,164	7,631,455	10,566,258
Franklin	4,733,614	5,618,411	1,097,613	1,126,499	3,287,888	3,982,087
Gadsden	1,671,405	2,248,111	749,790	1,096,756	822,354	969,591
Gilchrist	930,552	1,392,802	547,925	811,958	347,936	479,834
Glades	3,035,745	4,216,777	2,517,785	3,544,133	485,171	592,445
Gulf	4,177,040	4,425,838	1,286,190	1,333,608	2,569,949	2,790,439
Hamilton	768,741	1,246,734	465,858	835,388	287,905	372,185
Hardee	1,999,273	2,689,527	1,373,175	1,857,250	594,244	736,429
Hendry	3,249,832	6,625,023	1,583,121	3,947,101	1,512,747	2,328,577
Hernando	11,004,597	14,737,836	2,725,498	3,294,725	6,904,806	9,152,765
Highlands	5,710,711	8,271,475	1,473,969	1,680,818	3,655,755	5,334,439
Hillsborough	87,321,571	110,793,363	17,824,407	19,770,332	57,220,285	70,835,689
Holmes	756,040	1,096,447	468,760	720,194	268,124	336,487
Indian River	19,253,495	25,447,211	3,167,003	4,489,272	13,581,700	17,141,193
Jackson	2,180,427	2,407,738	1,158,858	1,224,210	925,591	1,083,864
Jefferson	1,099,441	1,201,986	725,082	740,328	336,834	406,180
Lafayette	455,105	838,332	305,005	625,227	133,303	173,850
Lake	17,331,581	24,009,757	3,200,564	3,473,436	12,994,531	17,588,484
Lee	78,804,626	114,152,584	9,715,293	12,000,576	60,522,998	85,669,024
Leon	19,178,340	23,130,983	6,022,332	6,983,562	11,402,166	13,480,426

See footnotes at end of table.

Continued . . .

Table 23.91. PROPERTY VALUATIONS: ASSESSED, EXEMPT, AND TAXABLE VALUES OF REAL PROPERTY IN THE STATE AND COUNTIES OF FLORIDA JANUARY 1, 2005 AND 2006 (Continued)

(rounded to thousands of dollars)

County	Just values 1/		Exempt and immune values		Taxable values 2/	
	2005	2006	2005	2006	2005	2006
Levy	2,892,869	4,651,266	1,262,707	2,060,945	1,390,824	2,096,884
Liberty	637,783	730,584	523,258	581,125	101,421	119,691
Madison	876,007	1,022,601	457,084	460,806	386,573	496,792
Manatee	31,744,642	39,852,622	4,597,409	4,987,730	22,710,778	28,031,711
Marion	19,412,346	28,210,770	6,126,709	8,716,518	11,805,778	16,163,545
Martin	25,063,423	31,967,821	4,354,614	5,729,874	16,056,334	19,328,291
Miami-Dade	235,120,627	297,825,836	34,190,688	38,283,007	162,343,582	202,124,630
Monroe	31,452,912	38,579,528	5,921,181	6,527,238	21,168,312	25,827,512
Nassau	7,489,945	9,139,300	1,140,258	1,204,176	5,538,135	6,785,135
Okaloosa	17,978,385	24,890,535	3,265,127	4,049,747	12,783,764	17,056,877
Okeechobee	3,230,401	3,782,954	1,488,922	1,512,933	1,541,380	1,940,222
Orange	91,650,056	116,893,795	16,534,982	17,751,814	67,866,436	84,028,708
Osceola	19,435,819	27,273,326	3,639,825	4,460,476	14,717,778	20,226,914
Palm Beach	172,998,068	224,929,763	20,393,588	22,910,303	123,590,203	154,185,909
Pasco	27,816,171	37,956,299	6,189,939	7,386,835	18,035,493	23,820,408
Pinellas	87,770,598	110,368,480	13,514,199	14,744,589	58,597,865	70,995,378
Polk	27,996,940	37,942,553	6,644,340	7,403,003	18,755,146	24,979,645
Putnam	4,078,003	5,422,324	1,378,156	1,691,544	2,346,497	3,096,716
St. Johns	23,530,599	30,839,619	3,763,066	4,799,810	16,654,175	21,233,616
St. Lucie	24,275,722	35,298,381	5,435,654	7,827,310	15,751,845	22,528,072
Santa Rosa	10,264,958	13,830,161	3,207,950	3,550,585	6,102,594	8,348,770
Sarasota	61,995,123	81,694,691	7,582,822	8,361,009	44,683,354	56,964,195
Seminole	30,428,928	41,015,174	4,214,972	4,935,668	22,045,984	27,644,978
Sumter	5,142,166	6,755,285	1,589,035	1,833,336	3,045,581	4,199,218
Suwannee	1,996,333	2,843,303	1,007,155	1,326,004	825,220	1,204,464
Taylor	1,355,449	1,598,129	555,096	623,482	737,623	891,393
Union	480,821	580,580	311,475	395,547	147,585	162,025
Volusia	40,886,301	55,873,967	7,419,719	9,364,223	27,203,325	35,427,441
Wakulla	1,811,389	2,234,049	544,893	646,033	1,048,476	1,305,821
Walton	14,927,243	18,710,776	1,773,307	1,795,677	12,412,694	15,816,109
Washington	956,299	1,461,818	444,494	556,927	491,278	846,887

1/ The value of property for tax purposes as determined by the elected county property appraiser before deduction of exemptions and immunities. Value is determined at the highest and best use of property, except for special cases provided for in Florida Statutes.

2/ The value against which millage rates are applied to compute the amount of tax levied. The tax base of a unit of local government also includes the taxable value of personal property and centrally assessed property.

Note: Data for 2005 are revised.

Source: State of Florida, Department of Revenue, *2006 Florida Property Valuations and Tax Data,* Internet site <http://dor.myflorida.com/> (accessed 26, July 2007).

Table 23.92. PROPERTY VALUATIONS AND TAXES: ASSESSED, EXEMPT, AND TAXABLE VALUES, MILLAGE RATES, AND TAXES ON MUNICIPAL REAL, PERSONAL, AND RAILROAD PROPERTY IN THE STATE, COUNTIES, AND SELECTED MUNICIPALITIES OF FLORIDA, 2006

(rounded to thousands of dollars, except where indicated)

County and municipality 1/	Total assessed value	Exemption value Homestead	Exemption value Other 2/	Taxable Value	Operating millage rate	Taxes
Florida TMP	1,227,390,869	47,360,128	326,038,183	853,992,558	4.6122	3,938,772
Alachua TMP	12,493,527	596,296	5,760,687	6,136,544	4.9691	30,493
Gainesville	10,604,175	444,388	5,190,615	4,969,172	4.8509	24,105
Baker TMP	308,062	27,652	88,222	192,189	3.6500	701
Bay TMP 3/	8,382,131	268,456	1,553,892	6,559,784	0.8760	5,746
Panama City	(NA)	(NA)	(NA)	(NA)	4.1722	(NA)
Bradford TMP	376,663	37,730	122,108	216,825	3.7077	804
Brevard TMP	35,845,815	2,177,218	10,809,498	22,859,100	4.2154	96,359
Cocoa	1,749,965	94,132	522,429	1,133,404	4.5705	5,180
Melbourne	7,638,716	454,250	2,537,999	4,646,467	4.5081	20,947
Palm Bay	8,496,954	654,721	2,117,384	5,724,849	4.6000	26,334
Rockledge	2,560,715	178,729	881,905	1,500,081	4.9500	7,425
Titusville	3,596,083	290,068	1,183,220	2,122,794	4.8193	10,230
Broward TMP 3/	234,221,909	10,673,016	66,197,134	157,351,760	4.9793	783,503
Coconut Creek	5,551,586	349,390	1,816,241	3,385,956	5.3408	18,084
Cooper City	3,796,856	212,875	1,456,925	2,127,057	5.4000	11,486
Coral Springs	14,586,782	671,801	4,409,135	9,505,845	3.8715	36,802
Dania Beach	4,062,116	161,771	913,853	2,986,492	6.0679	18,122
Davie	11,985,726	529,954	3,904,678	7,551,095	4.9879	37,664
Deerfield Beach	9,372,072	491,330	2,270,848	6,609,894	5.8250	38,503
Ft. Lauderdale	39,986,620	995,286	10,622,299	28,369,036	4.8066	136,359
Hallandale	5,681,194	241,989	1,241,428	4,197,777	5.9696	25,059
Hollywood	19,143,389	844,579	5,627,622	12,671,188	6.8051	86,229
Lauderdale Lakes	1,841,628	156,274	533,399	1,151,955	6.4007	7,373
Lauderhill	4,250,982	355,995	1,219,628	2,675,359	6.0200	16,106
Margate	4,804,391	391,325	1,426,119	2,986,946	6.5611	19,598
Miramar	12,059,240	609,143	3,087,025	8,363,072	6.5500	54,778
North Lauderdale	2,381,042	180,293	657,266	1,543,483	6.4292	9,923
Oakland Park	4,791,050	238,670	1,354,623	3,197,757	5.5823	17,851
Parkland	4,478,003	133,925	1,274,341	3,069,737	3.9500	12,125
Pembroke Pines	17,145,458	1,048,873	5,457,593	10,638,992	4.5990	48,929
Plantation	12,181,653	577,795	3,676,415	7,927,443	4.5889	36,378
Pompano Beach	16,490,649	601,621	4,132,558	11,756,471	3.7250	43,793
Sunrise	9,438,669	588,881	2,750,293	6,099,495	6.1100	37,268
Tamarac	6,242,664	544,171	1,845,531	3,852,963	6.2224	23,975
Weston	10,966,261	365,200	2,760,659	7,840,403	1.5235	11,945
Calhoun TMP	104,333	15,818	27,588	60,927	1.3404	82
Charlotte TMP 3/	5,098,492	151,810	1,378,412	3,568,270	2.1772	7,769
Citrus TMP	1,552,141	71,891	499,628	980,622	5.2536	5,152
Clay TMP	1,626,630	110,209	504,788	1,011,632	3.6790	3,722
Collier TMP	36,985,052	326,204	7,970,568	28,688,280	1.2485	35,818
Naples	21,802,039	174,221	5,093,769	16,534,049	1.2450	20,585
Columbia TMP	970,650	48,973	301,945	619,732	3.4395	2,132
DeSoto TMP	427,510	29,843	175,697	221,970	7.9180	1,758
Dixie TMP	148,934	11,588	43,961	93,385	4.1005	383
Duval TMP 3/ 4/	7,168,193	291,811	2,094,806	4,781,576	3.4964	16,718
Jacksonville Beach	3,845,718	146,573	1,002,148	2,696,998	3.9071	10,537

See footnotes at end of table.

Continued . . .

Table 23.92. PROPERTY VALUATIONS AND TAXES: ASSESSED, EXEMPT, AND TAXABLE VALUES, MILLAGE RATES, AND TAXES ON MUNICIPAL REAL, PERSONAL, AND RAILROAD PROPERTY IN THE STATE, COUNTIES, AND SELECTED MUNICIPALITIES OF FLORIDA, 2006 (Continued)

(rounded to thousands of dollars, except where indicated)

County and municipality 1/	Total assessed value	Exemption value Homestead	Exemption value Other 2/	Taxable Value	Operating millage rate	Taxes
Escambia TMP	5,313,975	365,686	1,674,103	3,274,187	4.9060	16,063
Pensacola	5,252,909	358,106	1,655,056	3,239,747	4.9500	16,037
Flagler TMP	10,026,137	538,496	2,036,335	7,451,306	3.2745	24,399
Palm Coast	8,288,439	486,807	1,561,638	6,239,994	3.2500	20,280
Franklin TMP	1,279,777	43,278	337,009	899,490	3.1564	2,839
Gadsden TMP	795,741	83,685	317,199	394,857	2.5961	1,025
Gilchrist TMP	152,930	13,394	62,610	76,927	2.7180	209
Glades TMP	92,856	8,326	37,441	47,089	4.0000	188
Gulf TMP	109,742	12,003	30,450	67,290	6.0000	404
Hamilton TMP	152,624	15,481	59,447	77,697	4.1029	319
Hardee TMP	303,750	36,944	108,829	157,976	6.0698	959
Hendry TMP	932,865	49,369	376,966	506,530	4.5554	2,307
Hernando TMP	813,983	28,140	283,226	502,618	7.2910	3,665
Highlands TMP 3/	648,361	95,624	-472,183	1,024,920	6.4422	6,603
Hillsborough TMP	47,920,281	2,030,313	15,557,176	30,332,793	6.2260	188,852
Plant City	2,839,102	170,141	735,140	1,933,821	4.7000	9,089
Tampa	42,932,007	1,724,848	14,288,663	26,918,496	6.4080	172,494
Temple Terrace	2,149,172	135,324	533,372	1,480,476	4.9100	7,269
Holmes TMP	180,827	19,969	56,807	104,051	0.2524	26
Indian River TMP	10,205,984	340,580	2,372,487	7,492,917	2.0300	15,210
Sebastian	2,320,218	168,260	604,575	1,547,383	3.0519	4,722
Vero Beach	4,024,326	110,532	1,155,781	2,758,014	2.1425	5,909
Jackson TMP	634,544	70,141	207,768	356,635	2.2125	789
Jefferson TMP	132,980	13,773	34,657	84,551	7.0000	592
Lafayette TMP	42,117	4,802	16,513	20,802	2.5000	52
Lake TMP	11,393,334	788,340	2,333,381	8,271,613	4.5099	37,304
Clermont	2,638,018	154,127	466,514	2,017,377	3.7290	7,523
Eustis	1,271,558	103,484	256,527	911,548	5.5000	5,014
Leesburg	1,763,111	88,246	357,857	1,317,009	4.5000	5,927
Lee TMP	59,496,714	1,631,785	11,670,802	46,194,127	3.6519	168,698
Bonita Springs	11,856,793	276,516	1,776,753	9,803,525	0.7919	7,763
Cape Coral	29,114,085	1,019,936	6,410,779	21,683,370	4.8787	105,787
Ft. Myers	8,208,670	215,833	2,056,441	5,936,396	6.8000	40,367
Leon TMP	17,643,758	704,539	6,856,040	10,083,178	3.7000	37,308
Tallahassee	17,643,758	704,539	6,856,040	10,083,178	3.7000	37,308
Levy TMP	1,070,694	58,211	284,505	727,978	3.7256	2,712
Liberty TMP	52,231	4,712	26,318	21,201	3.0000	64
Madison TMP	159,218	19,220	42,092	97,907	7.1888	704
Manatee TMP	12,094,386	423,799	2,610,276	9,060,311	3.1677	28,700
Bradenton	4,641,589	270,662	1,110,375	3,260,553	4.7500	15,488
Marion TMP	5,723,958	278,589	1,297,460	4,147,909	5.5765	23,131
Ocala	5,166,250	237,888	1,166,214	3,762,148	5.6760	21,354
Martin TMP	6,621,229	119,461	1,828,846	4,672,922	3.5730	16,697
Stuart	3,123,841	93,786	904,834	2,125,221	5.1000	10,839
Miami-Dade TMP 3/	200,418,825	5,603,279	50,237,677	144,577,869	6.0070	868,473
Aventura	9,459,878	238,170	1,153,798	8,067,910	2.2270	17,967
Coral Gables	17,245,983	273,225	5,024,087	11,948,671	6.1500	73,484
Cutler Bay	3,565,260	215,975	1,090,332	2,258,953	2.4470	5,528
Doral	10,349,823	138,650	1,074,787	9,136,386	2.4470	22,357

See footnotes at end of table.

Continued . . .

Table 23.92. PROPERTY VALUATIONS AND TAXES: ASSESSED, EXEMPT, AND TAXABLE VALUES, MILLAGE RATES, AND TAXES ON MUNICIPAL REAL, PERSONAL, AND RAILROAD PROPERTY IN THE STATE, COUNTIES, AND SELECTED MUNICIPALITIES OF FLORIDA, 2006 (Continued)

(rounded to thousands of dollars, except where indicated)

County and municipality 1/	Total assessed value	Exemption value		Taxable Value	Operating millage rate	Taxes
		Homestead	Other 2/			
Miami-Dade TMP (Cont.)						
Hialeah	14,638,026	866,360	4,071,752	9,699,915	6.8000	65,959
Hialeah Gardens	1,664,218	101,512	410,265	1,152,441	6.1200	7,053
Homestead	3,995,091	144,463	878,565	2,972,064	6.2500	18,575
Miami	48,939,749	1,117,102	13,707,592	34,115,055	8.3745	285,697
Miami Beach	29,233,324	417,520	6,069,995	22,745,809	7.3740	167,728
Miami Lakes	4,520,926	172,175	1,276,789	3,071,962	2.7403	8,418
North Miami	4,577,059	230,174	1,559,149	2,787,736	8.3000	23,138
North Miami Beach	3,757,785	196,470	1,173,539	2,387,775	7.5000	17,908
Opa-locka	1,038,594	40,014	221,833	776,747	9.8000	7,612
Pinecrest	5,678,759	121,425	2,056,333	3,501,001	2.4000	8,402
Sunny Isles Beach	5,674,582	106,094	714,835	4,853,652	2.9500	14,318
Monroe TMP	22,004,697	207,709	7,694,716	14,102,273	2.0358	28,710
Key West	12,381,126	97,671	5,576,545	6,706,910	2.3034	15,449
Nassau TMP	2,907,288	97,595	823,328	1,986,364	3.9624	7,871
Okaloosa TMP	13,119,871	468,615	2,614,691	10,036,566	2.6722	26,820
Crestview	1,380,239	103,470	334,986	941,783	6.4989	6,121
Ft. Walton Beach	2,117,354	125,691	636,304	1,355,359	4.6458	6,297
Okeechobee TMP	436,870	28,285	104,075	304,509	7.1899	2,189
Orange TMP	57,747,875	1,802,014	14,280,251	41,665,609	4.5762	190,670
Apopka	3,296,009	218,778	755,363	2,321,869	3.7619	8,735
Maitland	2,891,341	90,645	544,358	2,256,338	3.8800	8,755
Ocoee	2,925,223	190,548	672,500	2,062,175	4.6295	9,547
Orlando	31,506,283	873,303	9,384,238	21,248,742	5.6916	120,939
Winter Garden	2,663,649	140,251	524,811	1,998,587	4.3040	8,602
Winter Park	5,641,010	181,364	1,466,515	3,993,131	4.7580	18,999
Osceola TMP	6,479,400	366,739	1,308,338	4,804,323	5.1158	24,578
Kissimmee	4,316,992	203,261	819,814	3,293,917	5.5453	18,266
St. Cloud	2,162,409	163,478	488,524	1,510,406	4.1790	6,312
Palm Beach TMP 3/	150,563,894	4,513,912	37,469,504	108,580,478	4.9508	537,557
Boca Raton	27,437,082	599,211	6,906,529	19,931,342	3.3000	65,773
Boynton Beach	8,297,640	435,619	2,267,054	5,594,967	7.1000	39,724
Delray Beach	11,986,222	422,656	3,147,520	8,416,046	6.8600	57,734
Greenacres City	3,005,256	216,515	812,592	1,976,149	5.5500	10,968
Jupiter	12,089,827	363,975	2,906,838	8,819,015	2.5417	22,415
Lake Worth	3,169,313	150,696	993,851	2,024,766	8.1500	16,502
Palm Beach Gardens	11,933,929	350,247	2,279,160	9,304,522	5.4950	51,128
Riviera Beach	5,248,854	160,584	1,305,050	3,783,220	8.7500	33,103
Royal Palm Beach	3,922,998	233,556	1,152,067	2,537,374	2.1400	5,430
Wellington	10,252,473	339,697	2,688,388	7,224,388	2.7000	19,506
West Palm Beach	17,023,994	508,502	4,506,470	12,009,022	7.8500	94,271
Pasco TMP	3,642,780	223,502	1,079,622	2,339,655	6.3419	14,838
New Port Richey	1,307,305	88,271	356,346	862,688	7.0000	6,039
Pinellas TMP	84,772,956	4,289,860	24,527,293	55,955,802	4.6792	261,830
Clearwater	15,647,110	637,308	4,351,696	10,658,106	5.2088	55,516
Dunedin	3,955,414	268,212	1,342,020	2,345,182	4.0934	9,600
Largo	6,320,457	395,552	1,547,243	4,377,661	4.2758	18,718
Pinellas Park	4,965,590	326,308	1,172,580	3,466,702	4.9788	17,260

See footnotes at end of table.

Continued . . .

Table 23.92. PROPERTY VALUATIONS AND TAXES: ASSESSED, EXEMPT, AND TAXABLE VALUES, MILLAGE RATES, AND TAXES ON MUNICIPAL REAL, PERSONAL, AND RAILROAD PROPERTY IN THE STATE, COUNTIES, AND SELECTED MUNICIPALITIES OF FLORIDA, 2006 (Continued)

(rounded to thousands of dollars, except where indicated)

County and municipality 1/	Total assessed value	Exemption value		Taxable Value	Operating millage rate	Taxes
		Homestead	Other 2/			
Pinellas TMP (Cont.)						
Safety Harbor	2,110,638	137,836	727,510	1,245,292	2.7391	3,411
St. Petersburg	26,876,288	1,602,643	8,966,320	16,307,324	6.6000	107,628
Seminole	2,025,697	142,050	569,789	1,313,859	2.7500	3,613
Tarpon Springs	2,769,950	168,959	807,645	1,793,346	4.7957	8,600
Polk TMP	16,780,912	1,020,348	4,522,324	11,238,239	5.1070	57,393
Bartow	1,129,360	87,557	408,312	633,490	4.5000	2,851
Lakeland	7,903,168	438,919	2,168,545	5,295,703	3.5450	18,773
Winter Haven	2,541,375	150,331	622,895	1,768,148	6.9000	12,200
Putnam TMP	1,165,576	74,395	453,954	637,226	8.3193	5,301
St. Johns TMP	4,178,382	116,092	1,124,630	2,937,660	4.5506	13,368
St. Lucie TMP 3/	21,992,017	1,162,122	5,884,694	14,945,201	3.8957	58,222
Ft. Pierce	4,016,507	161,885	1,120,875	2,733,747	5.9823	16,354
Port St. Lucie	17,865,941	995,429	4,730,266	12,140,246	3.4399	41,761
Santa Rosa TMP	1,802,403	97,859	654,255	1,050,289	2.0070	2,108
Sarasota TMP 3/	32,749,194	850,037	8,364,416	23,534,741	2.7267	64,172
North Port	6,494,749	334,567	1,229,045	4,931,137	3.3000	16,273
Sarasota	15,015,206	302,404	4,996,686	9,716,116	2.9022	28,198
Venice	5,577,398	159,866	1,267,218	4,150,313	3.1290	12,986
Seminole TMP	20,766,280	1,161,903	4,797,478	14,806,900	4.5586	67,499
Altamonte Springs	4,152,189	189,836	694,753	3,267,600	2.6500	8,659
Casselberry	1,978,700	139,453	424,852	1,414,394	5.0000	7,072
Oviedo	3,224,911	200,963	880,034	2,143,915	5.3350	11,438
Sanford	4,125,354	210,013	1,010,086	2,905,255	6.3250	18,376
Winter Springs	3,199,178	240,450	954,922	2,003,806	4.2919	8,600
Sumter TMP	493,418	33,627	101,309	358,482	4.9184	1,763
Suwannee TMP	280,043	29,783	77,670	172,590	6.4384	1,111
Taylor TMP	400,334	35,889	133,103	231,342	4.6675	1,080
Union TMP 3/	75,253	8,416	28,718	38,120	2.0380	78
Volusia TMP	43,729,538	2,460,419	11,963,441	29,305,677	4.4289	129,793
Daytona Beach	8,141,262	284,269	2,366,230	5,490,763	5.9939	32,911
DeBary	2,596,094	152,992	516,453	1,926,650	3.0000	5,780
DeLand	2,574,506	121,777	748,216	1,704,513	5.5977	9,541
Deltona	5,490,449	594,239	1,604,137	3,292,074	4.0145	13,216
Edgewater	1,867,683	163,825	614,438	1,089,420	5.7000	6,210
New Smyrna Beach	5,243,112	178,002	1,321,635	3,743,475	3.3671	12,605
Ormond Beach	5,564,115	294,300	1,718,706	3,551,109	3.4400	12,216
Port Orange	5,037,438	374,862	1,485,590	3,176,985	4.6600	14,805
Wakulla TMP	88,209	2,298	46,121	39,790	4.2500	169
Walton TMP	451,167	36,533	90,322	324,312	4.1534	1,347
Washington TMP	638,647	31,721	80,763	526,162	1.6594	873

(NA) Data not available.
TMP Total municipal property.
1/ Only municipalities with a 2006 population of 17,000 or more are shown. Refer to the source for data for other municipalities.
2/ Includes governmental, institutional, and miscellaneous other exempt properties.
3/ Revised value; final not yet available.
4/ Consolidated with the City of Jacksonville since 1968.

Source: State of Florida, Department of Revenue, *2006 Florida Property Valuations and Tax Data,* Internet site <http://dor.myflorida.com/> (accessed 26, July 2007).

Table 23.93. COUNTY MILLAGE: AD VALOREM MILLAGE RATES IN THE COUNTIES OF FLORIDA, JANUARY 1, 2006

County	Total county-wide millage	County government Operating millage	County government Debt service millage	District school board Operating millage	District school board Debt service millage	Other millage 1/
Alachua	19.2712	8.8887	0.2500	7.8210	0.7500	1.5615
Baker	17.3709	8.3500	0.0000	7.7610	0.0000	1.2599
Bay	11.0200	4.1620	0.0000	6.8080	0.0000	0.0500
Bradford	17.0486	9.3756	0.0000	7.6730	0.0000	0.0000
Brevard	14.9099	3.8558	0.0000	7.6670	0.0000	3.3871
Broward	15.0776	5.6433	0.4228	7.6790	0.1897	1.1428
Calhoun	15.6250	10.0000	0.0000	5.5750	0.0000	0.0500
Charlotte	11.0349	4.8409	0.0000	6.0140	0.1400	0.0400
Citrus	15.5930	6.3307	0.0000	7.4670	0.0000	1.7953
Clay	16.9946	8.7536	0.0000	7.7790	0.0000	0.4620
Collier	10.0625	3.9790	0.0000	5.5250	0.0000	0.5585
Columbia	19.3404	8.7260	0.0000	7.7350	0.0000	2.8794
DeSoto	15.3220	7.4000	0.0000	7.3050	0.0000	0.6170
Dixie	18.1124	10.0000	0.0000	7.6210	0.0000	0.4914
Duval	32.6463	24.1038	0.0000	7.7000	0.3420	0.5005
Escambia	16.7000	8.7560	0.0000	7.8940	0.0000	0.0500
Flagler	12.9831	4.6655	0.1061	7.7110	0.0000	0.5005
Franklin	7.8787	3.8437	0.0000	3.9850	0.0000	0.0500
Gadsden	17.9010	10.0000	0.0000	7.8510	0.0000	0.0500
Gilchrist	19.2834	10.0000	0.0000	7.7920	0.0000	1.4914
Glades	18.0780	10.0000	0.0000	7.4810	0.0000	0.5970
Gulf	9.0971	4.6371	0.0000	4.4100	0.0000	0.0500
Hamilton	18.2894	10.0000	0.0000	7.7980	0.0000	0.4914
Hardee	17.6333	9.0000	0.0000	7.6630	0.0000	0.9703
Hendry	18.0380	6.5000	0.0000	7.8410	0.0000	3.6970
Hernando	16.4216	7.7106	0.1000	7.7670	0.4220	0.4220
Highlands	16.8310	8.5000	0.0000	7.9090	0.0000	0.4220
Hillsborough	15.5803	6.5200	0.0953	7.8230	0.0000	1.1420
Holmes	15.5740	9.7500	0.0000	5.7740	0.0000	0.0500
Indian River	10.7750	3.1914	0.1406	7.1630	0.2800	0.0000
Jackson	13.7190	8.0000	0.0000	5.6690	0.0000	0.0500
Jefferson	17.5990	10.0000	0.0000	7.5990	0.0000	0.0000
Lafayette	18.2444	10.0000	0.0000	7.7530	0.0000	0.4914
Lake	13.8480	5.7470	0.2000	7.6480	0.0000	0.2530

See footnote at end of table.

Continued . . .

Table 23.93. COUNTY MILLAGE: AD VALOREM MILLAGE RATES IN THE COUNTIES OF FLORIDA, JANUARY 1, 2006 (Continued)

County	Total county-wide millage	County government Operating millage	County government Debt service millage	District school board Operating millage	District school board Debt service millage	Other millage 1/
Lee	12.2242	4.4752	0.0000	7.0120	0.0000	0.7370
Leon	16.4960	7.9900	0.0000	7.9200	0.5360	0.0500
Levy	15.6120	7.9000	0.0000	7.7120	0.0000	0.0000
Liberty	17.9360	10.0000	0.0000	7.8860	0.0000	0.0500
Madison	16.0114	9.2500	0.0000	6.2700	0.0000	0.4914
Manatee	15.8573	7.4021	0.1042	7.6140	0.0000	0.7370
Marion	12.4390	4.4700	0.1000	7.8690	0.0000	0.0000
Martin	12.8417	4.9280	0.1140	6.7440	0.0000	1.0557
Miami-Dade	15.2048	5.6150	0.4270	7.6910	0.4140	1.0578
Monroe	6.9261	2.5609	0.0000	3.0610	0.0000	1.3042
Nassau	14.3636	6.1821	0.0000	7.6810	0.0000	0.5005
Okaloosa	11.4860	3.6500	0.0000	7.7860	0.0000	0.0500
Okeechobee	14.1288	5.8468	0.2360	7.7660	0.0000	0.2800
Orange	12.3329	5.1639	0.0000	7.1690	0.0000	0.0000
Osceola	14.5265	6.2445	0.0000	7.7820	0.0000	0.5000
Palm Beach	14.6749	4.2800	0.1975	7.7120	0.1600	2.3254
Pasco	13.8110	5.9800	0.0000	7.1810	0.2280	0.4220
Pinellas	15.3178	5.4700	0.0000	8.2100	0.0000	1.6378
Polk	16.1030	8.3330	0.0000	7.7700	0.0000	0.0000
Putnam	17.4740	9.2000	0.0000	7.7740	0.5000	0.0000
St. Johns	14.1970	5.8475	0.0000	7.6690	0.1800	0.5005
St. Lucie	18.1691	6.7512	0.0000	7.7370	0.0000	3.6809
Santa Rosa	13.8745	6.6175	0.0000	7.2070	0.0000	0.0500
Sarasota	12.5259	3.5691	0.0749	7.2100	0.0000	1.6719
Seminole	13.3590	4.9989	0.1451	7.7530	0.0000	0.4620
Sumter	14.2790	6.4410	0.0000	7.8380	0.0000	0.0000
Suwannee	17.2854	9.0000	0.0000	7.7940	0.0000	0.4914
Taylor	15.7294	8.0760	0.0000	7.1620	0.0000	0.4914
Union	18.7864	10.0000	0.0000	7.7950	0.0000	0.9914
Volusia	13.2249	4.2563	0.0000	7.6850	0.0000	1.2836
Wakulla	16.5820	8.1800	0.0000	7.8620	0.4900	0.0500
Walton	8.0585	3.8255	0.0000	4.1830	0.0000	0.0500
Washington	15.6360	8.5000	0.0000	7.0860	0.0000	0.0500

1/ Includes county government special service districts and independent special service districts.

Source: State of Florida, Department of Revenue, *2006 Florida Property Valuations and Tax Data,* Internet site <http://dor.myflorida.com/> (accessed 26, July 2007).

Table 23.94. LOCAL GOVERNMENT FINANCE: TOTAL AND MUNICIPAL AD VALOREM TAXES IN THE STATE AND COUNTIES OF FLORIDA, JANUARY 1, 2006

(in thousands, rounded to hundreds of dollars)

County	Total taxes levied: Amount	Total taxes levied: Percentage change 2005 to 2006	Municipal taxes	County	Total taxes levied: Amount	Total taxes levied: Percentage change 2005 to 2006	Municipal taxes
Florida	30,418,773.0	18.40	4,066,248.0	Lake	344,846.6	32.14	37,571.6
Alachua	269,969.1	14.48	30,495.1	Lee	1,506,161.3	25.91	172,045.2
Baker	13,990.6	20.24	701.4	Leon	288,278.7	11.80	37,462.0
Bay	220,360.4	17.95	15,628.1	Levy	40,480.4	33.72	2,714.5
Bradford	15,015.7	15.72	785.6	Liberty	4,051.7	28.14	63.6
Brevard	671,622.2	18.14	97,226.5	Madison	10,925.5	17.33	703.8
Broward	3,499,448.0	12.48	825,140.0	Manatee	543,164.1	20.35	29,464.9
Calhoun	5,089.5	15.58	81.7	Marion	301,698.1	27.90	23,165.7
Charlotte	329,542.9	29.06	7,768.8	Martin	346,138.7	14.31	18,608.2
Citrus	194,287.4	20.74	5,151.8	Miami-Dade	4,651,070.5	17.93	882,565.3
Clay	160,522.0	21.10	3,661.1	Monroe	228,275.8	11.85	28,709.9
Collier	922,849.7	17.98	38,560.0	Nassau	122,973.2	16.24	8,355.2
Columbia	47,383.1	25.27	2,241.6	Okaloosa	249,396.9	21.84	26,819.7
DeSoto	29,562.7	37.18	1,787.1	Okeechobee	35,805.9	10.81	2,189.4
Dixie	12,772.1	18.39	366.8	Orange	1,668,743.7	18.41	194,151.0
Duval	956,500.6	12.54	16,718.2	Osceola	351,312.1	24.05	24,581.6
Escambia	270,793.6	26.50	16,540.7	Palm Beach	3,207,388.7	18.69	557,790.2
Flagler	168,114.9	30.33	24,365.2	Pasco	410,103.3	20.52	14,838.0
Franklin	35,817.8	15.63	2,839.1	Pinellas	1,603,732.8	13.79	262,013.2
Gadsden	22,997.3	12.19	1,025.1	Polk	582,959.9	22.53	57,393.5
Gilchrist	12,366.4	36.77	209.1	Putnam	78,528.5	21.56	5,301.3
Glades	14,000.5	17.47	188.4	St. Johns	360,724.9	32.08	13,367.9
Gulf	30,942.0	-7.03	1,919.5	St. Lucie	542,125.2	31.46	70,397.5
Hamilton	12,867.7	17.62	318.9	Santa Rosa	128,939.2	30.29	2,107.9
Hardee	27,374.3	12.11	958.9	Sarasota	841,794.1	19.46	70,057.7
Hendry	53,144.9	28.28	2,307.5	Seminole	516,515.7	21.83	68,316.5
Hernando	184,805.0	23.86	3,679.0	Sumter	70,769.3	23.48	1,763.2
Highlands	106,960.6	34.84	6,602.8	Suwannee	27,716.5	26.81	1,111.2
Hillsborough	1,769,454.2	17.74	188,847.2	Taylor	22,563.5	12.07	1,079.8
Holmes	6,406.7	4.30	4.3	Union	3,876.9	13.68	77.7
Indian River	270,981.7	12.99	15,210.3	Volusia	772,700.9	13.61	136,307.0
Jackson	19,002.6	9.09	791.1	Wakulla	23,805.4	20.18	169.1
Jefferson	9,574.2	12.16	591.9	Walton	146,130.2	16.20	1,347.0
Lafayette	3,950.6	23.60	52.0	Washington	16,603.5	37.11	873.1

Source: State of Florida, Department of Revenue, *2006 Florida Property Valuations and Tax Data,* Internet site <http://dor.myflorida.com/> (accessed 26, July 2007).

Table 23.95. LOCAL GOVERNMENT FINANCE: COUNTY AD VALOREM TAXES IN THE STATE AND COUNTIES OF FLORIDA, JANUARY 1, 2006

(rounded to thousands of dollars)

County	Total county taxes levied 1/	County-wide Total	County government Operating levy	County government Debt services	District school board Operating levy	District school board Debt services	Special districts 2/	Less than county-wide levied
Florida	26,352,525	23,099,543	8,927,740	219,117	12,101,257	202,390	1,649,039	3,252,982
Alachua	239,474	216,474	99,654	2,803	88,006	8,439	17,571	23,000
Baker	13,289	12,959	5,913	0	5,541	0	1,506	330
Bay	204,732	195,642	73,096	0	121,653	0	893	9,090
Bradford	14,230	13,832	7,585	0	6,247	0	0	398
Brevard	574,396	532,016	151,147	0	301,901	0	78,969	42,379
Broward	2,674,308	2,393,553	893,551	66,945	1,221,155	30,167	181,734	280,755
Calhoun	5,008	5,008	3,185	0	1,807	0	16	0
Charlotte	321,774	267,911	117,530	0	146,011	3,399	971	53,863
Citrus	189,136	180,712	73,368	0	86,537	0	20,806	8,424
Clay	156,861	156,800	80,643	0	71,887	0	4,269	61
Collier	884,290	775,816	306,714	0	426,036	0	43,065	108,474
Columbia	45,141	45,141	20,263	0	18,132	0	6,747	0
DeSoto	27,776	27,233	13,152	0	12,984	0	1,097	543
Dixie	12,405	10,752	6,012	0	4,448	0	292	1,653
Duval	939,782	939,782	489,739	0	405,658	18,018	26,368	0
Escambia	254,253	246,241	128,473	0	117,027	0	741	8,012
Flagler	143,750	142,009	50,870	1,157	84,498	0	5,485	1,741
Franklin	32,979	31,731	15,479	0	16,050	0	201	1,247
Gadsden	21,972	21,972	12,274	0	9,637	0	61	0
Gilchrist	12,157	12,157	5,924	0	5,350	0	883	0
Glades	13,812	12,214	6,750	0	5,060	0	404	1,598
Gulf	29,023	26,182	13,339	0	12,699	0	144	2,841
Hamilton	12,549	12,549	6,833	0	5,377	0	339	0
Hardee	26,415	26,415	13,112	0	11,808	0	1,495	0
Hendry	50,837	50,200	18,049	0	21,849	0	10,302	638
Hernando	181,126	163,198	76,628	994	77,189	4,194	4,194	17,928
Highlands	100,358	98,799	50,044	0	46,613	0	2,143	1,558
Hillsborough	1,580,607	1,225,348	512,396	6,638	616,340	0	89,973	355,259
Holmes	6,402	6,402	3,969	0	2,412	0	21	0
Indian River	255,771	192,593	56,957	2,509	128,118	5,008	0	63,179
Jackson	18,212	17,971	10,238	0	7,666	0	68	240
Jefferson	8,982	8,894	5,054	0	3,840	0	0	88
Lafayette	3,899	3,899	2,137	0	1,657	0	105	0
Lake	307,275	262,990	108,826	3,787	145,562	0	4,815	44,285
Lee	1,334,116	1,096,249	401,329	0	628,826	0	66,093	237,868

See footnotes at end of table.

Continued . . .

Table 23.95. LOCAL GOVERNMENT FINANCE: COUNTY AD VALOREM TAXES IN THE STATE AND COUNTIES OF FLORIDA, JANUARY 1, 2006 (Continued)

(rounded to thousands of dollars)

County	Total county taxes levied 1/	County-wide						Special districts 2/	Less than county-wide levied
		Total	County government		District school board				
			Operating levy	Debt services	Operating levy	Debt services			
Leon	250,817	243,451	117,709	0	117,079	7,924		739	7,366
Levy	37,766	36,160	18,179	0	17,981	0		0	1,606
Liberty	3,988	3,988	2,047	0	1,929	0		12	0
Madison	10,222	10,222	5,891	0	4,016	0		315	0
Manatee	513,699	485,583	226,419	3,187	233,391	0		22,585	28,117
Marion	278,532	218,419	78,490	1,756	138,173	0		0	60,114
Martin	327,531	274,592	105,323	2,436	144,252	0		22,581	52,938
Miami-Dade	3,768,505	3,180,739	1,172,321	85,809	1,613,785	86,869		221,956	587,766
Monroe	199,566	166,348	67,906	0	81,206	0		17,236	33,218
Nassau	114,618	104,412	44,904	0	55,867	0		3,640	10,206
Okaloosa	222,577	205,838	65,333	0	139,609	0		897	16,739
Okeechobee	33,617	32,062	13,238	536	17,651	0		636	1,555
Orange	1,474,593	1,138,679	476,443	0	662,236	0		0	335,914
Osceola	326,731	317,165	136,159	0	170,078	0		10,928	9,566
Palm Beach	2,649,599	2,366,173	689,012	31,811	1,244,330	25,816		375,203	283,426
Pasco	395,265	357,829	155,053	0	185,945	5,904		10,927	37,436
Pinellas	1,341,720	1,156,961	413,133	0	620,121	0		123,707	184,758
Polk	525,566	488,403	252,290	0	236,114	0		0	37,163
Putnam	73,227	68,593	35,988	0	30,635	1,970		0	4,634
St. Johns	347,357	313,921	129,165	0	169,699	3,983		11,075	33,436
St. Lucie	471,728	445,631	164,816	0	190,286	0		90,529	26,096
Santa Rosa	126,831	123,788	58,646	0	64,693	0		449	3,043
Sarasota	771,736	738,104	210,274	4,413	424,891	0		98,526	33,632
Seminole	448,199	398,287	148,608	4,333	231,548	0		13,798	49,912
Sumter	69,006	65,830	29,593	0	36,237	0		0	3,176
Suwannee	26,605	26,605	13,853	0	11,996	0		756	0
Taylor	21,484	20,145	10,343	0	9,172	0		629	1,339
Union	3,799	3,799	2,022	0	1,576	0		200	0
Volusia	636,394	505,780	162,024	0	294,750	0		49,006	130,613
Wakulla	23,636	23,636	11,643	0	11,222	699		71	0
Walton	144,783	131,021	62,172	0	68,035	0		813	13,762
Washington	15,730	15,730	8,510	0	7,170	0		51	0

1/ Includes taxes not shown separately.
2/ Special and independent districts.

Source: State of Florida, Department of Revenue, *2006 Florida Property Valuations and Tax Data,* Internet site <http://dor.myflorida.com/> (accessed 26, July 2007).

Table 23.97. LAND USE: ASSESSED VALUE AND PROPORTION OF LAND BY USE IN THE STATE AND COUNTIES OF FLORIDA, 2006

County	Residential		Commercial		Industrial	
	Value (million dollars)	Percentage of total value	Value (million dollars)	Percentage of total value	Value (million dollars)	Percentage of total value
Florida	1,330,159.00	72.8	231,939.80	12.7	57,241.26	3.1
Alachua	8,856.15	56.6	1,884.23	12.0	327.60	2.1
Baker	444.79	46.9	61.97	6.5	45.77	4.8
Bay	14,420.17	71.9	2,711.32	13.5	249.78	1.2
Bradford	583.08	61.3	86.74	9.1	14.95	1.6
Brevard	34,419.28	72.3	4,827.09	10.1	1,027.24	2.2
Broward	130,184.47	74.0	23,656.92	13.4	8,315.62	4.7
Calhoun	181.55	48.3	30.53	8.1	4.74	1.3
Charlotte	21,641.42	82.7	2,356.86	9.0	377.23	1.4
Citrus	8,905.87	72.9	1,133.03	9.3	89.72	0.7
Clay	8,144.01	77.2	1,205.02	11.4	162.88	1.5
Collier	69,009.09	83.3	5,671.10	6.8	1,093.81	1.3
Columbia	1,536.42	52.7	400.53	13.7	86.51	3.0
DeSoto	854.69	44.8	178.68	9.4	124.78	6.5
Dixie	525.86	61.8	42.27	5.0	9.93	1.2
Duval	38,389.28	65.1	10,603.03	18.0	3,279.20	5.6
Escambia	12,601.63	66.5	2,717.05	14.3	365.46	1.9
Flagler	10,231.52	84.7	791.65	6.6	92.43	0.8
Franklin	3,816.74	75.3	190.70	3.8	37.52	0.7
Gadsden	877.68	59.4	106.37	7.2	60.06	4.1
Gilchrist	408.82	57.8	23.98	3.4	30.66	4.3
Glades	375.92	25.8	71.77	4.9	6.91	0.5
Gulf	2,475.19	62.9	131.35	3.3	62.30	1.6
Hamilton	244.42	46.2	26.34	5.0	66.34	12.5
Hardee	363.32	34.4	87.03	8.2	19.02	1.8
Hendry	1,534.71	43.8	237.98	6.8	118.99	3.4
Hernando	8,595.70	73.7	1,054.42	9.0	155.00	1.3
Highlands	4,637.21	67.7	695.17	10.2	93.49	1.4
Hillsborough	56,656.75	64.1	14,086.33	15.9	4,206.21	4.8
Holmes	228.56	40.1	45.86	8.0	5.65	1.0
Indian River	15,604.90	77.8	1,782.82	8.9	298.07	1.5
Jackson	900.05	49.8	185.97	10.3	70.09	3.9
Jefferson	231.74	38.9	37.53	6.3	4.61	0.8
Lafayette	119.67	40.2	8.47	2.8	3.16	1.1

Continued . . .

Table 23.97. LAND USE: ASSESSED VALUE AND PROPORTION OF LAND BY USE IN THE STATE AND COUNTIES OF FLORIDA, 2006 (Continued)

County	Residential Value (million dollars)	Residential Percentage of total value	Commercial Value (million dollars)	Commercial Percentage of total value	Industrial Value (million dollars)	Industrial Percentage of total value
Lake	16,566.12	79.4	2,162.64	10.4	398.80	1.9
Lee	77,506.13	81.6	8,772.33	9.2	2,008.42	2.1
Leon	11,457.74	58.0	2,844.16	14.4	416.90	2.1
Levy	1,886.38	70.4	222.69	8.3	20.92	0.8
Liberty	97.14	19.3	8.55	1.7	4.14	0.8
Madison	282.58	41.4	46.07	6.8	48.89	7.2
Manatee	25,003.99	78.9	3,080.84	9.7	927.35	2.9
Marion	14,359.31	67.6	2,066.20	9.7	637.78	3.0
Martin	16,822.85	74.1	2,238.41	9.9	485.92	2.1
Miami-Dade	158,623.35	67.2	38,388.66	16.3	13,399.59	5.7
Monroe	22,848.14	70.4	3,290.29	10.1	177.18	0.5
Nassau	6,230.72	79.1	724.87	9.2	140.85	1.8
Okaloosa	15,291.41	73.9	2,340.06	11.3	314.55	1.5
Okeechobee	1,505.98	59.0	265.30	10.4	27.99	1.1
Orange	63,728.84	64.3	20,995.29	21.2	3,460.00	3.5
Osceola	16,767.20	72.1	3,741.65	16.1	330.22	1.4
Palm Beach	137,968.85	79.4	19,812.98	11.4	3,754.24	2.2
Pasco	22,045.14	76.6	3,587.69	12.5	503.11	1.7
Pinellas	61,593.19	72.2	11,560.87	13.6	3,047.01	3.6
Polk	21,461.82	69.6	4,104.25	13.3	1,529.47	5.0
Putnam	2,851.08	66.2	331.21	7.7	187.55	4.4
St. Johns	19,056.02	77.8	2,373.41	9.7	259.52	1.1
St. Lucie	19,731.65	75.2	2,333.16	8.9	710.55	2.7
Santa Rosa	8,053.72	73.1	918.37	8.3	119.64	1.1
Sarasota	52,077.32	80.8	6,462.62	10.0	1,214.92	1.9
Seminole	23,616.02	73.8	5,293.55	16.6	1,100.60	3.4
Sumter	3,844.10	74.8	558.82	10.9	64.98	1.3
Suwannee	925.24	55.5	153.08	9.2	25.45	1.5
Taylor	685.65	57.2	104.74	8.7	24.83	2.1
Union	119.42	39.0	11.56	3.8	3.43	1.1
Volusia	32,138.02	74.6	5,160.25	12.0	885.47	2.1
Wakulla	1,298.80	73.6	87.21	4.9	19.53	1.1
Walton	14,962.92	85.6	716.87	4.1	71.48	0.4
Washington	751.46	67.2	51.05	4.6	14.26	1.3

Continued . . .

Table 23.97. LAND USE: ASSESSED VALUE AND PROPORTION OF LAND BY USE IN THE STATE AND COUNTIES OF FLORIDA, 2006 (Continued)

County	Agricultural		Institutional		Government	
	Value (million dollars)	Percentage of total value	Value (million dollars)	Percentage of total value	Value (million dollars)	Percentage of total value
Florida	15,238.07	0.8	41,605.50	2.3	150,747.06	8.3
Alachua	344.41	2.2	522.92	3.3	3,705.20	23.7
Baker	135.82	14.3	28.94	3.1	230.65	24.3
Bay	55.28	0.3	325.69	1.6	2,290.58	11.4
Bradford	97.04	10.2	35.64	3.7	133.27	14.0
Brevard	129.95	0.3	1,228.28	2.6	5,995.19	12.6
Broward	236.97	0.1	3,451.22	2.0	10,088.59	5.7
Calhoun	94.60	25.2	12.51	3.3	51.92	13.8
Charlotte	138.66	0.5	385.09	1.5	1,281.15	4.9
Citrus	78.64	0.6	280.63	2.3	1,727.72	14.1
Clay	88.72	0.8	312.75	3.0	640.63	6.1
Collier	327.34	0.4	1,490.72	1.8	5,247.51	6.3
Columbia	182.96	6.3	77.20	2.6	633.48	21.7
DeSoto	302.37	15.8	49.80	2.6	399.24	20.9
Dixie	78.08	9.2	10.77	1.3	184.59	21.7
Duval	137.71	0.2	1,929.78	3.3	4,675.84	7.9
Escambia	111.46	0.6	596.07	3.1	2,552.36	13.5
Flagler	52.95	0.4	85.17	0.7	819.48	6.8
Franklin	5.43	0.1	77.50	1.5	942.90	18.6
Gadsden	163.17	11.1	50.42	3.4	218.75	14.8
Gilchrist	122.72	17.3	20.32	2.9	101.18	14.3
Glades	170.33	11.7	25.99	1.8	808.05	55.4
Gulf	36.90	0.9	41.88	1.1	1,184.65	30.1
Hamilton	75.55	14.3	14.63	2.8	101.88	19.3
Hardee	253.26	24.0	34.02	3.2	300.73	28.4
Hendry	483.21	13.8	63.39	1.8	1,066.38	30.4
Hernando	166.46	1.4	301.09	2.6	1,386.91	11.9
Highlands	355.19	5.2	307.62	4.5	757.48	11.1
Hillsborough	689.68	0.8	3,183.84	3.6	9,502.25	10.8
Holmes	152.92	26.8	37.71	6.6	99.17	17.4
Indian River	158.30	0.8	463.43	2.3	1,755.78	8.8
Jackson	210.49	11.6	101.67	5.6	339.44	18.8
Jefferson	156.99	26.4	20.09	3.4	144.55	24.3
Lafayette	74.41	25.0	11.42	3.8	80.87	27.1

Continued . . .

Table 23.97. LAND USE: ASSESSED VALUE AND PROPORTION OF LAND BY USE IN THE STATE AND COUNTIES OF FLORIDA, 2006 (Continued)

County	Agricultural		Institutional		Government	
	Value (million dollars)	Percentage of total value	Value (million dollars)	Percentage of total value	Value (million dollars)	Percentage of total value
Lake	341.23	1.6	438.48	2.1	955.14	4.6
Lee	306.47	0.3	1,784.05	1.9	4,653.72	4.9
Leon	111.99	0.6	536.03	2.7	4,396.61	22.2
Levy	277.41	10.3	53.19	2.0	220.17	8.2
Liberty	46.74	9.3	15.46	3.1	330.25	65.8
Madison	149.07	21.8	29.12	4.3	126.56	18.5
Manatee	293.54	0.9	700.50	2.2	1,698.16	5.4
Marion	868.71	4.1	501.25	2.4	2,803.58	13.2
Martin	306.71	1.4	439.22	1.9	2,423.39	10.7
Miami-Dade	1,569.40	0.7	5,616.70	2.4	18,299.08	7.8
Monroe	0.00	0.0	462.42	1.4	5,659.21	17.4
Nassau	169.60	2.2	137.40	1.7	474.87	6.0
Okaloosa	103.15	0.5	354.03	1.7	2,279.36	11.0
Okeechobee	212.16	8.3	63.21	2.5	477.62	18.7
Orange	479.60	0.5	2,296.94	2.3	8,143.41	8.2
Osceola	198.00	0.9	410.17	1.8	1,824.13	7.8
Palm Beach	1,073.98	0.6	2,776.75	1.6	8,414.69	4.8
Pasco	316.37	1.1	613.91	2.1	1,730.49	6.0
Pinellas	13.16	0.0	2,985.07	3.5	6,102.17	7.2
Polk	523.71	1.7	657.74	2.1	2,567.51	8.3
Putnam	66.33	1.5	168.72	3.9	701.78	16.3
St. Johns	181.97	0.7	538.71	2.2	2,080.89	8.5
St. Lucie	198.50	0.8	308.97	1.2	2,947.91	11.2
Santa Rosa	159.27	1.4	229.93	2.1	1,542.41	14.0
Sarasota	66.21	0.1	1,618.27	2.5	3,025.49	4.7
Seminole	43.79	0.1	761.04	2.4	1,165.05	3.6
Sumter	226.12	4.4	58.44	1.1	384.15	7.5
Suwannee	234.26	14.0	52.97	3.2	277.13	16.6
Taylor	150.63	12.6	37.70	3.1	195.26	16.3
Union	77.05	25.2	12.08	3.9	82.74	27.0
Volusia	256.36	0.6	1,184.34	2.7	3,457.43	8.0
Wakulla	70.71	4.0	17.39	1.0	270.88	15.4
Walton	137.16	0.8	135.31	0.8	1,458.51	8.3
Washington	140.72	12.6	31.79	2.8	128.97	11.5

Source: State of Florida, Department of Revenue, unpublished data. Compiled by Armasi, Inc.

ECONOMIC INDICATORS AND PRICES

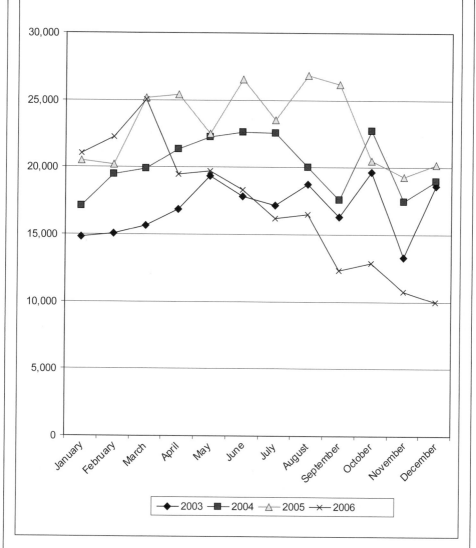

Private Residential Housing Units Authorized by Building Permits in Florida, 2003 Through 2006

Source: Table 24.20

Section 24.00
Economic Indicators and Prices

Tables in the first twenty-three sections of the *Abstract* are primarily cross-sectional or "snapshot" portrayals of a set of circumstances or a situation existing at any one time. Because many readers are interested in charting trends over time, most tables in Section 24.00 contain data over several years.

Explanatory notes. The Bureau of Labor Statistics (BLS) of the U.S. Department of Labor develops consumer price indexes and publishes them in the monthly *CPI Detailed Report* and on the BLS Web site. BLS publishes two indexes; one reflecting the buying habits of all urban households (CPI-U), and one reflecting the buying habits of urban wage earners and clerical workers (CPI-W). Both indexes are comparable with historical CPI figures; the all urban households index is used in tables in this section (except for the entry of the CPI-W index in Table 24.73). The CPI-U is based on information reflecting the buying habits of about 80 percent of the U.S. population and represents all urban residents, including professional workers, the self-employed, the poor, the unemployed, and retired persons. Excluded are persons living outside urban areas, farm families, persons in military services, and those in institutions.

BLS issues a bimonthly CPI for the Miami-Ft. Lauderdale CMSA and the Tampa-St. Petersburg-Clearwater MSA (see Table 24.74.) Both the CPI-U and the CPI-W use updated expenditure weights based on data tabulated from the consumer expenditure surveys. Also, the rental equivalence measures of home ownership costs in both the CPI-U and the CPI-W were improved to better represent both owners' and renters' shelter costs.

The series of producer prices appears in Tables 24.72 and 24.75. According to the BLS, the series measures the average changes in prices received in primary markets of the United States by producers of commodities in all stages of processing. The sample used for calculating the indexes contains nearly 2,800 commodities and about 10,000 quotations selected to represent the movement of prices of all commodities produced in the agriculture, forestry, fishing, mining, manufacturing, gas, electric, and all public utilities sectors.

Florida price indexes. The Bureau of Economic and Business Research (BEBR) prepares the *Florida Price Level Index* (FPLI) for the Florida Department of Education's Office of Education Budget and Management. BEBR also prepares the Florida County Retail Price Index (FCRPI). FCRPI data are presented in Tables 24.79 and 24.80, The FCRPI measures relative price levels across counties. Items representative of the expenditure categories used by the BLS in the CPI are surveyed in each county. Table 24.79 shows the relative weights of selected items in the survey; Table 24.80 compares the index and sub-indexes for major items across counties. Section 15.00 contains additional information on energy prices and Section 2.00 provides housing cost data for counties based on the housing component of the FCRPI.

Gross Domestic Product (GDP). The U.S. Bureau of Economic Analysis (BEA) introduced estimates of Gross State Product (GSP) by state, by component, and by industry for each state. On October 26, 2006, the GSP was renamed the Gross Domestic

Product by State (GDP) and is the state counterpart of the Nation's gross domestic product. GDP is the gross market value of goods and services attributable to labor and property located in the state. These estimates are available from the Regional Economic Information System and the BEA Web site.

Sources. Extensive series of economic indicators for the United States, Florida, and its counties are maintained in the BEBR Database. Data surveying consumer confidence are presented on Table 24.85 and published monthly by the BEBR UF Survey Research Program on the Internet at www.bebr.ufl.edu.

The U.S. Department of Commerce Census Bureau reports building permit activity in the states in *New Privately Owned Housing Units Authorized Unadjusted Units for Regions, Divisions, and States* on the Census Web site. Table 24.20 presents data from current and previous editions of this publication back to 1994.

The Florida Department of Revenue has data on sales and use tax collections and historical gross and taxable sales. The Labor Market Information office of the Florida Agency for Workforce Innovation provided unemployment rate data.

The Office of Public Affairs within the Administrative Office of the U.S. Courts publishes data on bankruptcy cases filed by type on their Web site.

Electricity price data from the Division of Research and Regulatory Review within the Florida Public Service Commission are published in *Statistics of the Florida Electric Utility Industry* on the Internet.

Section 24.00
Economic Indicators and Prices

Tables listed by major heading

Table 24.12. ECONOMIC INDICATORS: SPECIFIED INDICATORS OF THE FLORIDA ECONOMY JANUARY 2001 THROUGH DECEMBER 2006

(not adjusted for seasonal variation)

Month and year	Unemployment rate	Nonfarm wage and salary employment 1/ (1,000)	Sales and use tax collections 2/	Month and year	Unemployment rate	Nonfarm wage and salary employment 1/ (1,000)	Sales and use tax collections 2/
2001				2004			
January	4.1	7,096.7	1,502.0	January	4.9	7,332.7	1,633.1
February	3.8	7,167.7	1,302.0	February	4.7	7,404.7	1,344.7
March	3.9	7,229.5	1,319.1	March	4.7	7,470.8	1,435.1
April	4.1	7,194.7	1,446.7	April	4.5	7,507.1	1,611.5
May	3.9	7,198.5	1,314.1	May	4.5	7,511.6	1,478.1
June	4.5	7,135.1	1,287.8	June	5.1	7,444.1	1,410.2
July	4.5	7,046.0	1,315.4	July	4.9	7,405.6	1,570.0
August	4.9	7,147.1	1,256.3	August	4.8	7,493.2	1,493.2
September	4.8	7,147.8	1,281.4	September	4.7	7,471.0	1,409.0
October	5.9	7,138.8	1,206.7	October	4.6	7,555.0	1,425.4
November	5.9	7,187.0	1,279.5	November	4.5	7,657.0	1,669.2
December	5.8	7,228.0	1,334.7	December	4.2	7,736.5	1,606.4
2002				2005			
January	6.1	7,089.1	1,536.7	January	4.4	7,621.9	1,944.4
February	5.8	7,144.9	1,278.2	February	4.3	7,704.9	1,634.0
March	5.7	7,206.4	1,324.3	March	4.0	7,751.6	1,713.0
April	5.7	7,186.4	1,496.3	April	3.8	7,794.2	1,904.5
May	5.5	7,198.3	1,351.4	May	3.7	7,812.4	1,759.9
June	6.0	7,116.4	1,332.2	June	4.1	7,718.4	1,718.9
July	5.9	7,037.0	1,327.7	July	4.0	7,698.1	1,787.4
August	6.0	7,143.5	1,315.0	August	3.9	7,815.0	1,692.6
September	5.6	7,154.3	1,298.5	September	3.8	7,860.0	1,660.6
October	5.4	7,184.2	1,277.3	October	3.5	7,866.8	1,730.2
November	5.5	7,253.2	1,307.0	November	3.6	7,941.2	1,626.3
December	5.3	7,310.5	1,367.8	December	3.1	8,014.6	1,819.4
2003				2006			
January	5.6	7,176.8	1,563.9	January	3.3	7,887.6	2,103.5
February	5.3	7,232.3	1,285.7	February	3.2	7,962.3	1,784.0
March	5.2	7,287.6	1,322.8	March	3.1	8,042.8	1,831.5
April	5.1	7,262.3	1,465.6	April	3.0	8,020.4	2,067.1
May	5.2	7,266.8	1,400.7	May	3.1	8,037.0	1,862.1
June	5.9	7,184.5	1,370.8	June	3.5	7,950.8	1,848.9
July	5.6	7,116.9	1,402.9	July	3.6	7,879.0	1,866.6
August	5.6	7,217.7	1,366.4	August	3.6	7,991.0	1,741.1
September	5.4	7,238.0	1,328.5	September	3.5	8,007.7	1,718.8
October	5.0	7,283.2	1,413.8	October	3.2	8,038.3	1,727.8
November	4.9	7,331.2	1,401.6	November	3.3	8,111.0	1,736.5
December	4.5	7,403.3	1,412.2	December	3.0	8,157.0	1,815.8

1/ Data are for employment covered by unemployment compensation.
2/ Data are rounded to millions of dollars.
Note: Some data are revised.

Source: State of Florida, Agency for Workforce Innovation, Labor Market Information, Internet site <http://www.labormarketinfo.com/>, and State of Florida, Department of Revenue, Internet site <http://sun6.dms.state.fl.us/> (both accessed 26, March 2007).

Table 24.14. GROSS DOMESTIC PRODUCT BY STATE: ESTIMATES IN FLORIDA, OTHER SUNBELT STATES, OTHER POPULOUS STATES, AND THE UNITED STATES, 1997 AND 2002 THROUGH 2006

(in millions of current dollars)

State	1997	2002	2003	2004	2005	2006
			Sunbelt states			
Florida	391,451	522,719	559,021	607,201	666,639	713,505
Alabama	102,433	123,805	130,210	141,702	151,342	160,569
Arizona	127,370	171,942	182,011	194,134	212,312	232,463
Arkansas	59,182	72,203	75,685	81,752	87,004	91,837
California	1,019,150	1,340,446	1,406,511	1,515,453	1,616,351	1,727,355
Georgia	237,468	306,680	317,922	337,622	358,365	379,550
Louisiana	113,261	134,308	146,726	162,646	180,336	193,138
Mississippi	57,954	68,144	72,259	76,534	79,786	84,225
New Mexico	47,442	52,510	57,469	63,861	69,692	75,910
North Carolina	228,864	296,435	306,018	324,622	350,700	374,525
Oklahoma	78,019	97,170	103,452	111,400	121,558	134,651
South Carolina	97,397	121,582	127,885	132,348	140,088	149,214
Tennessee	153,405	191,525	200,279	214,400	224,995	238,029
Texas	599,492	783,480	828,797	904,412	989,333	1,065,891
Virginia	211,921	285,759	302,540	325,467	350,692	369,260
			Other populous states			
Illinois	403,982	487,129	510,296	534,364	555,599	589,598
Indiana	168,115	205,015	215,434	229,618	236,357	248,915
Massachusetts	221,827	284,386	293,840	309,483	320,050	337,570
Michigan	298,994	349,837	359,030	363,380	372,148	381,003
New Jersey	300,910	372,754	389,077	409,156	427,654	453,177
New York	654,750	821,577	850,243	908,308	961,385	1,021,944
Ohio	332,124	389,773	402,399	424,562	442,243	461,302
Pennsylvania	343,368	423,110	440,704	464,467	486,139	510,293
United States	8,237,994	10,398,402	10,886,172	11,633,572	12,372,850	13,149,033

Note: Data are for North American Industry Classification System (NAICS) industries. Data for 2002 through 2005 are revised. As of the October 26, 2006 BEA release, the Gross State Product (GSP) series was renamed the Gross Domestic Product (GDP) by State.

Source: U.S., Department of Commerce, Bureau of Economic Analysis, released June 7, 2007, Internet site <http://www.bea.doc.gov/> (accessed 12, June 2007).

Table 24.15. GROSS DOMESTIC PRODUCT BY STATE : ESTIMATES OF GROSS DOMESTIC PRODUCT (GDP) BY COMPONENT AND MAJOR INDUSTRIAL GROUP IN FLORIDA SPECIFIED YEARS 1992 THROUGH 2006

(in millions of current dollars)

Item	1992 A/	1997	2002	2003	2004	2005	2006
Components of GDP							
Total	283,800	391,451	522,719	559,021	607,201	666,639	713,505
Compensation of employees	163,231	(NA)	298,882	315,800	339,659	369,862	(NA)
Taxes on production and imports less subsidies	28,392	(NA)	49,222	54,035	59,874	65,437	(NA)
Gross operating surplus	92,176	(NA)	174,615	189,186	207,668	231,340	(NA)
GDP by major industry							
Agriculture forestry, and fishing	6,237	5,654	5,300	5,536	6,218	6,327	6,313
Farms	3,915	3,728	3,550	3,743	4,362	4,438	(NA)
Mining	774	610	652	689	733	879	805
Utilities	(NA)	9,318	8,588	9,685	11,054	11,688	11,685
Construction	12,517	19,076	32,166	35,859	41,195	50,095	55,839
Manufacturing	25,305	27,510	29,053	28,743	31,221	33,391	35,860
Durable goods	14,668	17,216	18,229	17,898	20,195	22,423	24,430
Nondurable goods	10,637	10,294	10,824	10,845	11,027	10,968	11,430
Wholesale trade	19,915	27,253	34,217	36,143	39,811	43,788	47,023
Retail trade	30,766	33,453	43,228	45,885	48,619	53,236	56,573
Transportation and public utilities	25,585	(NA)	(NA)	(NA)	(NA)	(NA)	(NA)
Transportation and warehousing 1/	(NA)	12,452	14,614	16,093	16,252	17,157	18,194
Information	(NA)	16,305	22,875	23,640	26,267	27,881	28,841
Finance, insurance, and real estate	57,780	(NA)	(NA)	(NA)	(NA)	(NA)	(NA)
Finance and insurance	(NA)	24,727	36,579	40,044	41,822	45,547	48,397
Real estate, rental and leasing	(NA)	59,135	82,527	89,363	100,173	112,195	122,221
Professional and technical services	(NA)	20,555	31,768	33,902	37,578	41,944	45,405
Management of companies and enterprises	(NA)	4,481	6,452	7,022	6,925	8,111	8,707
Administrative and waste services	(NA)	16,778	26,954	27,228	28,778	33,272	37,207
Educational services	(NA)	2,232	3,530	3,862	4,277	4,614	5011
Health care and social assistance	(NA)	28,810	38,756	42,153	44,888	47,961	51,299
Arts, entertainment, and recreation	(NA)	7,225	9,094	9,584	10,166	10,688	11,263
Accommodation and food services	(NA)	14,986	18,982	20,410	22,507	24,639	26,032
Other services, except government	(NA)	11,279	14,599	15,652	16,327	17,101	17,954
Government	41,199	49,613	62,786	67,527	72,390	76,123	78,875
Federal civilian	6,554	7,733	9,662	10,535	11,233	11,391	(NA)
Federal military	5,454	5,470	6,589	7,283	7,693	7,918	(NA)
State and local	29,191	36,410	46,535	49,709	53,465	56,814	(NA)

(NA) Not available.

Note: Some data may be revised. See Appendix for discussion of Gross Domestic Product (GDP) estimates. As of the October 26, 2006 BEA release, the Gross State Product (GSP) series was renamed the Gross Domestic Product (GDP) by State.

A/ Data are for Standard Industrial Classification System (SIC) industries, and may not be comparable to later years, which are for North American Industry Classification System (NAICS) industries.

1/ Excludes Postal Service.

Source: U.S., Department of Commerce, Bureau of Economic Analysis, released June 7, 2007, Internet site <http://www.bea.doc.gov/> (accessed 12, June 2007).

Table 24.20. BUILDING PERMIT ACTIVITY: PRIVATE RESIDENTIAL HOUSING UNITS AUTHORIZED BY BUILDING PERMITS IN FLORIDA AND THE UNITED STATES, 1995 THROUGH 2006

Month	1995	1996	1997	1998	1999	2000
Florida						
Annual total 1/	122,903	125,020	133,990	148,603	164,722	155,269
January	9,940	9,743	9,863	10,712	13,676	11,268
February	8,166	9,376	9,209	9,713	12,537	11,147
March	10,677	9,856	12,207	12,284	14,188	12,627
April	9,686	11,069	11,212	11,447	13,367	10,750
May	10,038	11,174	11,185	11,512	11,654	13,635
June	11,208	10,603	11,798	12,980	14,802	15,448
July	10,101	10,904	12,561	13,653	14,136	11,506
August	10,577	11,889	10,272	14,307	15,342	13,266
September	10,368	11,280	11,785	11,272	12,113	12,421
October	9,266	9,895	12,103	13,640	13,700	12,429
November	9,891	9,088	8,517	12,027	10,697	12,346
December	9,668	8,798	9,662	11,306	14,214	11,556
United States, annual total	1,332,549	1,425,616	1,441,136	1,612,260	1,663,533	1,592,267

Month	2001	2002	2003	2004	2005	2006
Florida						
Annual total 1/	167,035	185,431	213,567	255,893	287,250	203,238
January	12,487	15,347	14,836	17,131	20,519	21,067
February	11,151	15,555	15,080	19,452	20,176	22,281
March	16,146	14,756	15,644	19,876	25,177	25,024
April	12,406	13,951	16,885	21,360	25,394	19,498
May	16,902	14,407	19,376	22,240	22,529	19,734
June	13,561	16,181	17,865	22,621	26,561	18,305
July	14,643	16,840	17,206	22,554	23,529	16,206
August	16,116	16,602	18,739	20,028	26,831	16,485
September	12,385	12,896	16,349	17,595	26,167	12,359
October	11,898	17,068	19,682	22,739	20,480	12,902
November	13,383	13,028	13,293	17,477	19,308	10,776
December	13,202	13,952	18,626	18,974	20,176	9,982
United States, annual total	1,636,676	1,747,678	1,889,214	2,070,077	2,155,316	1,838,903

1/ Annual total reflects revisions not distributed to months.

Note: To arrive at state totals, data for metropolitan areas (MSAs and PMSAs) were taken from reports submitted by all places within these areas. Estimates for nonmetropolitan areas in Florida and the United States were based on a sample of the data; 19,000 for 1994 through 2003, and 20,000 for 2004 through 2006. See Glossary for metropolitan area definitions and map at the front of the book for area boundaries.

Source: U.S., Department of Commerce, Census Bureau, *New Privately Owned Housing Units Authorized Unadjusted Units for Regions, Divisions, and States, Annual 2006,* Internet site <http://www.census.gov/> (accessed 14, May 2007).

Table 24.30. GROSS AND TAXABLE SALES: SALES REPORTED AND SALES AND USE TAXES COLLECTED BY THE DEPARTMENT OF REVENUE IN FLORIDA, 1969 THROUGH 2006

(sales and taxes rounded to dollars)

Year	Gross sales	Taxable sales	Net sales taxes paid	Number of reports
1969	33,441,677,220	16,246,816,932	616,919,658	2,324,350
1970	36,834,259,466	18,339,123,013	681,920,445	2,394,366
1971	41,255,223,174	20,272,358,516	784,708,762	2,528,429
1972	49,280,284,464	23,884,881,400	947,086,120	2,508,097
1973	59,294,867,904	28,264,125,745	1,136,864,712	2,495,557
1974	65,887,520,411	29,785,250,309	1,216,071,766	2,689,313
1975	66,764,958,864	29,329,230,180	1,197,020,925	2,845,986
1976	73,791,141,256	32,215,852,176	1,323,271,879	2,962,711
1977	82,783,600,922	36,274,024,296	1,500,074,880	2,788,578
1978	98,227,927,655	43,640,280,027	1,816,192,620	2,844,083
1979	114,373,759,327	50,555,056,774	2,074,119,153	3,005,717
1980	136,318,330,861	58,177,097,809	2,383,348,768	3,177,162
1981	156,619,282,052	66,750,301,522	2,691,772,260	3,214,217
1982	161,796,458,854	66,663,022,175	3,143,878,949	3,451,004
1983	168,492,566,327	73,906,494,761	4,035,324,107	3,632,967
1984	195,758,800,411	84,639,051,288	4,498,315,417	3,735,161
1985	210,089,814,330	89,673,013,371	4,874,199,447	3,887,677
1986	223,601,586,263	98,612,192,144	5,304,286,552	4,249,174
1987	259,753,403,821	113,379,458,921	6,053,620,606	5,054,411
1988	277,485,847,435	119,103,871,758	7,299,532,184	5,115,463
1989	289,076,440,275	122,788,168,387	7,834,635,188	5,101,085
1990	303,464,877,632	127,283,343,961	8,242,720,563	5,177,182
1991	310,147,685,581	126,648,591,209	8,181,744,259	5,505,665
1992	330,770,069,551	135,959,144,438	8,778,486,852	5,747,984
1993	360,267,713,516	150,592,943,893	9,582,751,878	6,091,241
1994	385,110,859,523	159,956,354,846	10,008,966,792	5,837,879
1995	423,309,073,509	171,551,704,651	10,975,746,043	5,644,615
1996	451,908,747,292	182,117,956,958	11,461,071,670	5,569,872
1997	480,333,681,982	196,353,235,291	12,326,816,327	5,456,337
1998	495,076,575,334	208,234,872,534	13,071,502,379	6,199,782
1999	538,986,640,384	226,636,112,442	14,207,915,429	5,093,050
2000	599,682,329,270	243,137,002,604	15,210,330,319	5,229,101
2001	619,832,393,094	248,838,779,977	16,269,348,571	5,366,749
2002	609,051,742,803	244,334,874,362	15,156,303,303	5,514,848
2003	642,280,422,229	256,756,333,437	14,507,743,980	5,458,546
2004	694,212,364,366	275,409,179,618	15,135,561,092	5,309,136
2005	802,889,236,258	313,461,537,268	17,488,538,646	5,434,566
2006	895,361,247,509	334,828,571,336	18,119,337,195	5,441,897

Note: These sales were reported to the Department of Revenue for the 5 percent regular sales tax, the 5 percent use tax, and the 3 percent vehicle and farm equipment sales tax from January to December of each year. The sales occurred, for the most part, from December of the previous year through November of the posted year. In February 1988, the regular sales and use tax increased to 6 percent; this increase is reflected in the collections from March 1988. These data are not comparable with retail sales figures reported by the Census Bureau because of differences in definitions of retailers and retail sales. At various times, changes in the rate of the taxes or in the items to be taxed or excluded have been made. Data prior to 1993 are unaudited and are not comparable to later years. Some data may be revised.

Source: State of Florida, Department of Revenue, unpublished data prepared by the University of Florida, Bureau of Economic and Business Research.

Table 24.72. CONSUMER AND PRODUCER PRICE INDEXES: ANNUAL AVERAGES AND PERCENTAGE CHANGES FOR ALL URBAN CONSUMERS INDEX AND PRODUCER PRICE INDEX IN THE UNITED STATES, 1989 THROUGH 2006

	Consumer prices 1/					
	All items		Commodities		Services	
Year	Index	Percentage change	Index	Percentage change	Index	Percentage change
1989	124.0	4.8	116.7	4.7	131.9	4.9
1990	130.7	5.4	122.8	5.2	139.2	5.5
1991	136.2	4.2	126.6	3.1	146.3	5.1
1992	140.3	3.0	129.1	2.0	152.0	3.9
1993	144.5	3.0	131.5	1.9	157.9	3.9
1994	148.2	2.6	133.8	1.7	163.1	3.3
1995	152.4	2.8	136.4	1.9	168.7	3.4
1996	156.9	3.0	139.9	2.6	174.1	3.2
1997	160.5	2.3	141.8	1.4	179.4	3.0
1998	163.0	1.6	141.9	0.1	184.2	2.7
1999	166.6	2.2	144.4	1.8	188.8	2.5
2000	172.2	3.4	149.2	3.3	195.3	3.4
2001	177.1	2.8	150.7	1.0	203.4	4.1
2002	179.9	1.6	149.7	-0.7	209.8	3.1
2003	184.0	2.3	151.2	1.0	216.5	3.2
2004	188.9	2.7	154.7	2.3	222.8	2.9
2005	195.3	3.4	160.2	3.6	230.1	3.3
2006	201.6	3.2	164.0	2.4	238.9	3.8

	Producer prices 2/					
	All commodities		Farm products		Industrial commodities	
Year	Index	Percentage change	Index	Percentage change	Index	Percentage change
1989	112.2	5.0	110.9	5.7	111.6	5.0
1990	116.3	3.7	112.2	1.2	115.8	3.8
1991	116.5	0.2	105.7	-5.8	116.5	0.6
1992	117.2	0.6	103.6	-2.0	117.4	0.8
1993	118.9	1.5	107.1	3.4	119.0	1.4
1994	120.4	1.3	106.3	-0.7	120.7	1.4
1995	124.7	3.6	107.4	1.0	125.5	4.0
1996	127.7	2.4	122.4	14.0	127.3	1.4
1997	127.6	-0.1	112.9	-7.8	127.7	0.3
1998	124.4	-2.5	104.6	-7.4	124.8	-2.3
1999	125.5	0.9	98.4	-5.9	126.5	1.4
2000	132.7	5.7	99.5	1.1	134.8	6.6
2001	134.2	1.1	103.8	4.3	135.7	0.7
2002	131.1	-2.3	99.0	-4.6	132.4	-2.4
2003	138.1	5.3	111.5	12.6	139.1	5.1
2004	146.7	6.2	123.3	10.6	147.6	6.1
2005	157.4	7.3	118.5	-3.9	160.2	8.5
2006	164.7	4.6	117.0	-1.3	168.8	5.4

1/ 1982-84 = 100.
2/ 1982 = 100.
Note: Due to changes in the methodology used to compute the Consumer Price Index, caution should be used when comparing data for 1998 and following years to previous data. See the introduction to this section for discussion of consumer and producer price indexes.

Source: U.S., Department of Labor, Bureau of Labor Statistics, *CPI Detailed Report,* Annual Average Indexes, Internet site <http://stats.bls.gov/> (accessed 1, June 2007).

Table 24.73. CONSUMER PRICE INDEXES: INDEXES BY COMMODITY IN THE UNITED STATES 2005 AND 2006

(1982-84 = 100, except where indicated)

Index expenditure category and commodity	Relative importance December 2006	Annual average index 2005	Annual average index 2006	Percentage change 2005 to 2006
Wage earners and clerical workers index (CPI-W), all items	100.000	191.0	197.1	3.2
All urban consumers index (CPI-U), all items				
Expenditure category				
All items	100.000	195.3	201.6	3.2
All items (1967 = 100)	(NA)	585.0	603.9	(NA)
Food and beverages	14.992	191.2	195.7	2.4
Food	13.885	190.7	195.2	2.4
Food at home	7.896	189.8	193.1	1.7
Cereals and bakery products	1.103	209.0	212.8	1.8
Meats, poultry, fish, and eggs	2.112	184.7	186.6	1.0
Dairy and related products	0.821	182.4	181.4	-0.5
Fruits and vegetables	1.211	241.4	252.9	4.8
Nonalcoholic beverages and beverage materials	0.906	144.4	147.4	2.1
Other food at home	1.743	167.0	169.6	1.6
Sugar and sweets	0.302	165.2	171.5	3.8
Fats and oils	0.227	167.7	168.0	0.2
Other foods	1.214	182.5	185.0	1.4
Other miscellaneous foods 1/	0.327	111.3	113.9	2.3
Food away from home	5.989	193.4	199.4	3.1
Other food away from home 1/	0.281	131.3	136.6	4.0
Alcoholic beverages	1.107	195.9	200.7	2.5
Housing	42.691	195.7	203.2	3.8
Shelter	32.776	224.4	232.1	3.4
Rent of primary residence	5.930	217.3	225.1	3.6
Lodging away from home 1/	2.648	130.3	136.0	4.4
Owners' equivalent rent of primary residence 2/	23.830	230.2	238.2	3.5
Tenants' and household insurance 1/	0.369	117.6	116.5	-0.9
Fuels and utilities	5.264	179.0	194.7	8.8
Fuels	4.368	161.6	177.1	9.6
Fuel oil and other fuels	0.338	208.6	234.9	12.6
Gas (piped) and electricity	4.029	166.5	182.1	9.4
Water and sewer and trash collection services 1/	0.897	130.3	136.8	5.0
Household furnishings and operations	4.651	126.1	127.0	0.7
Household operations 1/	0.792	130.3	136.6	4.8
Apparel	3.726	119.5	119.5	0.0
Men's and boys' apparel	0.885	116.1	114.1	-1.7
Women's and girls' apparel	1.590	110.8	110.7	-0.1
Infants' and toddlers' apparel	0.177	116.7	116.5	-0.2
Footwear	0.749	122.6	123.5	0.7
Transportation	17.249	173.9	180.9	4.0
Private transportation	16.188	170.2	177.0	4.0
New and used motor vehicles 1/	7.581	95.6	95.6	0.0
New vehicles	4.982	137.9	137.6	-0.2

See footnotes at end of table. Continued . . .

Table 24.73. CONSUMER PRICE INDEXES: INDEXES BY COMMODITY IN THE UNITED STATES 2005 AND 2006 (Continued)

(1982-84 = 100, except where indicated)

Index expenditure category and commodity	Relative importance December 2006	Annual average index 2005	Annual average index 2006	Percentage change 2005 to 2006
All urban consumers index (CPI-U) (Continued)				
Expenditure category (Continued)				
Used cars and trucks	1.716	139.4	140.0	0.4
Motor fuel	4.347	195.7	221.0	12.9
Gasoline (all types)	4.303	194.7	219.9	12.9
Motor vehicle parts and equipment	0.370	111.9	117.3	4.8
Motor vehicle maintenance and repair	1.145	206.9	215.6	4.2
Public transportation	1.060	217.3	226.6	4.3
Medical care	6.281	323.2	336.2	4.0
Medical care commodities	1.446	276.0	285.9	3.6
Medical care services	4.834	336.7	350.6	4.1
Professional services	2.817	281.7	289.3	2.7
Hospital and related services	1.630	439.9	468.1	6.4
Recreation 1/	5.552	109.4	110.9	1.4
Video and audio 1/	1.719	104.2	104.6	0.4
Education and communication 1/	6.034	113.7	116.8	2.7
Education 1/	3.076	152.7	162.1	6.2
Educational books and supplies	0.204	365.6	388.9	6.4
Tuition, other school fees, and childcare	2.872	440.9	468.1	6.2
Communication 1/	2.958	84.7	84.1	-0.7
Information and Information processing 1/	2.769	82.6	81.7	-1.1
Telephone services 1/	2.225	94.9	95.8	0.9
Information technology, hardware and services 3/	0.543	13.6	12.5	-8.1
Personal computers and peripheral equipment 1/	0.203	12.8	10.8	-15.6
Other goods and services	3.476	313.4	321.7	2.6
Tobacco and smoking products	0.712	502.8	519.9	3.4
Personal care	2.764	185.6	190.2	2.5
Personal care products	0.708	154.4	155.8	0.9
Personal care services	0.677	203.9	209.7	2.8
Miscellaneous personal services	1.188	303.0	313.6	3.5
Commodity and service group				
Commodities	40.305	160.2	164.0	2.4
Food and beverages	14.992	191.2	195.7	2.4
Commodities less food and beverages	25.313	142.5	145.9	2.4
Nondurables less food and beverages	14.191	168.4	176.7	4.9
Apparel commodities	3.726	119.5	119.5	0.0
Nondurables less food, beverages, and apparel	10.465	202.6	216.3	6.8
Durables	11.122	115.3	114.5	-0.7
Services	59.695	230.1	238.9	3.8
Rent of shelter 2/	32.407	233.7	241.9	3.5
Tenants' and household insurance 1/	0.369	117.6	116.5	-0.9

See footnotes at end of table.

Continued . . .

Table 24.73. CONSUMER PRICE INDEXES: INDEXES BY COMMODITY IN THE UNITED STATES 2005 AND 2006 (Continued)

(1982-84 = 100, except where indicated)

Index expenditure category and commodity	Relative importance December 2006	Annual average index		Percentage change 2005 to 2006
		2005	2006	
Commodity and service group (Continued)				
Services (Continued)				
Gas (piped) and electricity	4.029	166.5	182.1	9.4
Water and sewer and trash collection services 1/	0.897	130.3	136.8	5.0
Household operations 1/	0.792	130.3	136.6	4.8
Transportation services	5.638	225.7	230.8	2.3
Medical care services	4.834	336.7	350.6	4.1
Other services	10.730	268.4	277.5	3.4
Special indexes				
All items less food	86.115	196.0	202.7	3.4
All items less shelter	67.224	186.1	191.9	3.1
All items less medical care	93.719	188.7	194.7	3.2
Commodities less food	26.420	144.5	148.0	2.4
Nondurables less food	15.299	170.1	178.2	4.8
Nondurables less food and apparel	11.572	201.2	213.9	6.3
Nondurables	29.183	180.2	186.7	3.6
Services less rent of shelter 2/	27.288	243.2	253.3	4.2
Services less medical care services	54.861	221.2	229.6	3.8
Energy	8.715	177.1	196.9	11.2
All items less energy	91.285	198.7	203.7	2.5
All items less food and energy	77.401	200.9	205.9	2.5
Commodities less food and energy commodities	21.735	140.3	140.6	0.2
Energy commodities	4.685	197.4	223.0	13.0
Services less energy	55.666	236.6	244.7	3.4
Purchasing power of the consumer dollar:				
1982-84 = $1.00	(NA)	0.512	0.496	(NA)
1967 = $1.00	(NA)	0.171	0.166	(NA)

(NA) Not available.
1/ Indexes on a December 1997 = 100 base.
2/ Indexes on a December 1982 = 100 base.
3/ Indexes on a December 1988 = 100 base.
Note: Some monthly categories are not seasonally adjusted. See the introduction to this section for an explanation of CPI-W and CPI-U.

Source: U.S., Department of Labor, Bureau of Labor Statistics, *CPI Detailed Report,* January 2007, Internet site <http://stats.bls.gov/> (accessed 26, March 2007).

Table 24.74. CONSUMER PRICE INDEXES: INDEXES FOR ALL URBAN CONSUMERS BY CATEGORY AND COMMODITY IN MIAMI-FT. LAUDERDALE AND TAMPA-ST. PETERSBURG-CLEARWATER FLORIDA, ANNUAL AVERAGE 2006

Expenditure category and commodity	Miami– Ft. Lauderdale		Tampa–St. Petersburg–Clearwater	
	2006	Change 1/	2006	Change 1/
All items	203.9	4.9	175.2	4.0
Food and beverages	203.6	1.7	170.4	2.7
Food	204.3	1.7	169.1	2.7
Food at home	205.6	1.7	167.3	1.7
Food away from home	206.1	2.0	172.4	4.6
Alcoholic beverages	196.9	3.1	175.2	1.7
Housing	204.5	7.4	173.2	5.2
Shelter	220.3	6.5	187.4	5.0
Renters of primary residence	210.1	7.0	182.9	5.9
Owners' equivalent rent of primary residence 2/	221.7	6.6	194.9	6.2
Fuel and other utilities	168.8	18.4	179.4	10.1
Fuels	163.2	22.5	153.7	12.7
Gas (piped) and electricity	160.6	22.6	152.0	12.7
Electricity	156.5	23.0	148.7	12.6
Utility natural gas service	246.6	1.5	290.4	1.6
Household furnishings and operations	170.1	2.5	122.2	0.0
Apparel	154.1	6.1	139.9	2.9
Transportation	185.4	3.1	167.3	5.0
Private transportation	185.6	2.8	171.0	5.0
Motor fuel	234.1	9.4	269.0	11.0
Gasoline (all types)	231.7	9.4	263.8	11.1
Medical care	325.4	4.5	256.6	5.3
Recreation 3/	114.1	2.4	112.8	2.0
Education and communication 3/	108.8	1.3	104.7	1.5
Other goods and services	254.0	2.0	223.1	2.0
Commodity and service group				
All items	203.9	4.9	175.2	4.0
Commodities	177.7	2.4	151.0	2.5
Commodities less food and beverages	160.6	2.8	139.6	2.8
Nondurables less food and beverages	182.3	7.0	191.1	4.5
Durables	137.7	-2.9	95.8	0.7
Services	225.5	6.4	197.2	5.1
Special aggregate indexes				
All items less medical care	197.9	5.0	170.3	3.9
All items less shelter	196.0	3.9	170.7	3.5
Commodities less food	162.4	2.8	142.1	2.7
Nondurables	194.5	4.1	179.8	3.3
Nondurables less food	183.8	6.7	190.5	4.2
Services less rent of shelter 2/	238.4	6.0	204.7	4.9
Services less medical care services	215.4	6.5	189.8	5.2
Energy	191.9	15.5	199.1	11.4
All items less energy	205.5	4.0	172.9	3.5
All items less food and energy	205.5	4.4	173.8	3.7

1/ Percentage change from 2005 to 2006.
2/ Indexes on a November 1982 = 100 base for Miami-Ft. Lauderdale.
3/ Indexes on a December 1997 = 100 base.
Note: Data are annual averages. The Miami-Ft. Lauderdale and Tampa-St. Petersburg-Clearwater areas are two of several metropolitan areas for which a consumer price index is issued bimonthly.
Source: U.S., Department of Labor, Bureau of Labor Statistics, *CPI Detailed Report,* Annual Average Indexes, Internet site <http://stats.bls.gov/> (accessed 26, March 2007).

Table 24.75. PRODUCER PRICE INDEXES: INDEXES BY STAGE OF PROCESSING, BY DURABILITY OF PRODUCT, AND BY COMMODITY IN THE UNITED STATES, ANNUAL AVERAGES 2004, 2005, AND 2006, AND JUNE 2007

(1982 = 100, not seasonally adjusted)

Item	Annual average 2004	Annual average 2005	Annual average 2006	June 2007 A/
All commodities	146.7	157.4	164.7	173.7
By stage of processing				
Crude materials for further processing	159.0	182.2	184.8	208.5
Intermediate materials, supplies, etc.	142.6	154.0	164.0	172.2
Finished goods 1/	148.5	155.7	160.4	167.1
Finished consumer goods	151.7	160.4	166.0	174.2
Capital equipment	141.4	144.6	146.9	149.4
By durability of product				
Durable goods	139.6	144.1	151.0	155.5
Nondurable goods	151.5	166.8	174.4	186.4
Manufactured goods, total	145.4	153.9	161.4	168.7
Durable manufactured goods	138.2	142.6	148.1	151.8
Nondurable manufactured goods	152.6	165.5	175.0	185.7
Farm products, processed foods and feeds	142.0	141.3	141.2	157.9
Farm products	123.3	118.5	117.0	141.3
Foods and feeds, processed	151.2	153.1	153.8	166.3
Industrial commodities	147.6	160.2	168.8	176.4
Chemical and allied products	174.4	192.0	205.8	215.6
Fuels and related products and power	126.9	156.4	166.7	181.7
Furniture and household durables	135.1	139.4	142.6	144.6
Hides, skins, and leather products	164.5	165.4	168.4	174.5
Lumber and wood products	195.6	196.5	194.4	193.7
Machinery and equipment	122.1	123.7	126.2	127.5
Metals and metal products	149.6	160.8	181.6	196.3
Nonmetallic mineral products	153.2	164.2	179.9	186.6
Pulp, paper, and allied products	195.7	202.6	209.8	215.3
Rubber and plastics products	133.8	143.8	153.8	154.3
Textile products and apparel	121.0	122.8	124.5	126.0
Transportation equipment 1/	148.6	151.0	152.6	154.6
Motor vehicles and equipment	131.0	131.5	131.0	131.9

A/ Preliminary.
1/ Includes data for items not shown separately.
Note: See the introduction to this section for discussion of producer price indexes.

Source: U.S., Department of Labor, Bureau of Labor Statistics, Internet site <http://stats.bls.gov/> (accessed 24, July 2007).

Table 24.76. ENERGY PRICES: NATURAL GAS, ELECTRICITY, FUEL OIL, AND GASOLINE PRICES U.S. CITY AVERAGE AND MIAMI-FT. LAUDERDALE, FLORIDA, JUNE 2006 THROUGH MAY 2007

(in dollars)

Month and year	Piped gas per 40 therms U.S. city average	Piped gas per 40 therms Miami-Ft. Lauderdale	Electricity per 500 kilowatt-hours U.S. city average	Electricity per 500 kilowatt-hours Miami-Ft. Lauderdale	#2 fuel oil per gallon– U.S. city average	All types gasoline per gallon U.S. city average	All types gasoline per gallon Miami-Ft. Lauderdale
2006							
June	54.006	77.746	59.457	63.232	2.566	2.963	2.926
July	54.146	76.159	59.621	63.232	2.597	3.046	3.007
August	54.428	73.686	59.565	63.232	2.649	3.033	3.032
September	55.291	71.036	59.568	63.232	2.531	2.637	2.701
October	51.673	69.412	58.332	63.232	2.396	2.319	2.348
November	55.279	69.638	57.532	63.232	2.375	2.287	2.323
December	56.661	73.459	57.738	63.232	2.460	2.380	2.396
2007							
January	55.986	75.689	59.043	60.505	2.368	2.321	2.303
February	55.977	76.568	59.047	60.505	2.425	2.333	2.338
March	57.001	80.854	59.297	60.505	2.505	2.639	2.641
April	56.763	80.854	59.175	60.505	2.555	2.909	2.922
May	57.327	80.152	59.779	60.670	2.567	3.176	3.128

Source: U.S., Department of Labor, Bureau of Labor Statistics, *CPI Detailed Report,* monthly releases.

Table 24.77. ELECTRICITY PRICES: COST PER KILOWATT-HOUR OF ELECTRICITY BY CLASS OF SERVICE OF THE FLORIDA ELECTRIC UTILITY INDUSTRY, 1991 THROUGH 2005

(in cents)

Year	Total	Residential	Commercial	Industrial	Other public authorities
1991	7.15	7.89	6.88	5.29	6.95
1992	6.90	7.75	6.41	5.36	6.59
1993	7.21	7.99	6.43	6.18	7.37
1994	6.95	7.78	6.33	5.56	6.43
1995	7.04	7.76	6.42	5.42	9.06
1996	7.19	8.00	6.65	5.52	6.85
1997	7.18	8.07	6.63	5.42	6.73
1998	6.99	7.89	6.21	5.61	6.46
1999	6.55	7.53	5.67	4.93	6.95
2000	6.88	7.70	5.77	6.43	7.79
2001	7.77	8.70	6.62	6.92	9.20
2002	7.39	8.24	6.21	6.85	8.94
2003	7.78	8.63	6.63	7.04	9.29
2004	8.74	9.62	7.42	8.51	10.32
2005	8.87	9.77	7.60	8.23	11.09

Note: Cost by class of service is defined as revenue by class of service/kilowatt-hour consumption by class of service. Some data may be revised.

Source: State of Florida, Public Service Commission, Division of Research and Regulatory Review, *Statistics of the Florida Electric Utility Industry, 2005,* Internet site <http://www.psc.state.fl.us/> (accessed 19, February 2007).

Table 24.78. BANKRUPTCIES: BANKRUPTCY CASES FILED BY TYPE IN FLORIDA AND THE UNITED STATES, 2006

Area	Total	Type of bankruptcy Chapter 7	Chapter 11	Chapter 12	Chapter 13
All filings, total					
United States	617,660	360,890	5,163	348	251,179
Florida	25,700	16,544	249	3	8,903
Percentage of U.S.	4.2	4.6	4.8	0.9	3.5
Business filings					
United States	19,695	11,878	4,643	348	2,749
Florida	991	711	225	3	51
Percentage of U.S.	5.0	6.0	4.8	0.9	1.9
Nonbusiness filings					
United States	597,965	349,012	520	(X)	248,430
Florida	24,709	15,833	24	(X)	8,852
Percentage of U.S.	4.1	4.5	4.6	(X)	3.6

(X) Not applicable.

Source: Administrative Office of the U.S. Courts, Office of Public Affairs, U.S. Bankruptcy Statistics, Internet site <http://www.uscourts.gov/> (accessed 18, June 2007).

Table 24.79. RETAIL PRICE INDEX: RELATIVE WEIGHTS ASSIGNED TO SELECTED ITEMS PRICED FOR THE FLORIDA RETAIL PRICE INDEX, 2005

Item	Number of items	Weight	Item	Number of items	Weight
Housing	4	44.946	Food and beverages	4	17.157
Homeowner cost index		26.343	Hamburger		1.505
Apartment rent index		5.090	French fries		1.444
Electricity, 1000 kWh		3.781	Served coffee		1.448
Air conditioning, seasonal			Served soft drink		1.453
inspection		0.495	Medical care	5	5.639
Other goods and services	8	16.641	Health insurance		0.359
Safety deposit box fee		0.120	Health care cost index		4.264
Man's haircut		0.296	Eye examination		0.116
Woman's haircut		0.296	Extraction		0.216
Dry cleaning, woman's dress		0.118	Filling		0.216
Dry cleaning, man's suit		0.118	Transportation	3	15.618
Day care service		1.228	Auto insurance		2.570
Movie rental		0.769	Lube-oil-filter		0.864
Bowling		0.769	Gasoline, unleaded, self		4.085

kWh Kilowatt hour.
Note: Items weighted one percent or more are included. See also note on Table 24.80 and discussion under this section in the Appendix.

Source: University of Florida, Bureau of Economic and Business Research, Economic Analysis Program, *2005 Florida County Retail Price and Wage Indices*, Internet site <http://www.bebr.ufl.edu/>.

Table 24.80. RETAIL PRICE INDEX: TOTAL INDEX AND INDEXES OF PRICES OF MAJOR ITEMS IN THE COUNTIES OF FLORIDA, 2005

(population-weighted state average = 100)

County	Florida County Retail Price Index		Food and beverages	Medical Care	Housing	Other goods and services 1/	Transportation
	Index	Rank among counties					
Alachua	92.47	30	100.69	89.27	85.40	99.22	97.76
Baker	91.05	47	98.72	94.55	83.35	97.33	96.84
Bay	91.73	36	102.59	90.22	84.12	98.23	95.34
Bradford	90.72	51	102.95	87.66	81.37	98.14	97.41
Brevard	93.93	18	99.92	96.40	89.00	97.63	96.68
Broward	114.12	3	99.88	107.56	129.11	100.21	103.82
Calhoun	89.55	61	103.99	85.57	79.53	96.32	96.72
Charlotte	94.46	15	100.67	98.45	88.43	99.83	97.80
Citrus	91.23	41	102.30	87.87	83.56	96.05	97.21
Clay	92.31	33	101.91	95.54	83.67	100.97	96.27
Collier	99.76	6	100.86	96.43	98.60	103.09	99.55
Columbia	91.10	44	104.66	88.95	82.29	96.44	96.63
DeSoto	92.53	29	98.21	109.10	84.21	97.91	98.49
Dixie	90.42	53	100.64	87.32	82.42	95.37	98.09
Duval	93.70	19	100.89	95.40	86.86	99.61	98.55
Escambia	91.12	42	100.18	94.61	82.97	97.88	96.16
Flagler	92.57	28	101.92	94.50	85.31	98.33	96.35
Franklin	90.93	48	100.31	107.58	81.08	96.56	96.96
Gadsden	91.78	35	105.22	94.99	81.65	98.06	98.36
Gilchrist	90.19	57	102.22	93.09	80.54	96.01	97.51
Glades	92.68	27	101.35	93.50	85.08	97.94	99.14
Gulf	91.66	37	103.44	89.90	82.85	97.26	98.72
Hamilton	88.51	67	99.64	86.03	79.66	95.37	95.35
Hardee	91.62	39	97.62	97.17	83.86	98.90	97.62
Hendry	95.00	14	103.28	91.11	89.68	98.45	98.94
Hernando	92.34	32	103.68	95.41	84.61	96.95	96.14
Highlands	90.73	50	100.23	91.53	81.52	98.71	98.03
Hillsborough	96.50	12	100.60	94.02	92.29	100.18	101.10
Holmes	88.75	65	99.33	86.35	79.60	95.84	96.81
Indian River	95.53	13	98.44	94.23	92.16	99.94	97.81
Jackson	88.98	64	100.38	87.75	79.12	97.30	96.40
Jefferson	90.14	58	98.95	92.29	81.16	98.01	97.15
Lafayette	89.36	63	101.83	92.21	78.87	95.17	98.63
Lake	92.38	31	99.19	93.45	85.62	98.27	97.71
Lee	97.47	11	99.21	96.84	96.34	99.63	96.78
Leon	93.10	22	102.63	95.33	84.95	100.46	97.41
Levy	91.12	42	106.34	87.21	82.03	95.92	96.88

See footnote at end of table.

Continued . . .

Table 24.80. RETAIL PRICE INDEX: TOTAL INDEX AND INDEXES OF PRICES OF MAJOR ITEMS IN THE COUNTIES OF FLORIDA, 2005 (Continued)

(population-weighted state average = 100)

County	Florida County Retail Price Index: Index	Florida County Retail Price Index: Rank among counties	Food and beverages	Medical Care	Housing	Other goods and services 1/	Transpor-tation
Liberty	89.57	60	102.58	88.71	79.46	96.14	97.69
Madison	89.45	62	97.47	85.28	80.08	97.46	100.60
Manatee	97.90	10	101.28	92.68	96.51	100.81	96.99
Marion	90.39	55	99.67	95.04	81.86	97.93	95.04
Martin	98.11	9	98.81	96.81	96.94	100.44	98.71
Miami-Dade	115.42	2	98.70	118.38	129.79	100.52	107.23
Monroe	130.87	1	99.87	101.23	167.97	101.98	99.66
Nassau	92.04	34	102.27	92.98	83.70	98.63	97.47
Okaloosa	91.64	38	99.78	87.02	85.48	98.40	94.91
Okeechobee	92.74	26	97.74	108.13	84.82	98.19	98.68
Orange	94.34	17	99.48	97.89	88.96	99.87	97.01
Osceola	93.49	21	100.40	93.70	87.24	99.24	97.70
Palm Beach	102.78	4	98.41	101.71	103.70	103.83	104.18
Pasco	94.43	16	99.89	95.11	89.85	98.75	96.75
Pinellas	98.73	7	100.25	96.34	97.20	101.61	99.29
Polk	92.82	25	100.66	95.56	85.53	98.79	97.80
Putnam	90.78	49	102.74	88.98	82.42	96.96	95.74
St. Johns	92.89	24	100.64	94.09	85.52	101.02	96.47
St. Lucie	100.66	5	101.01	107.28	101.47	98.75	97.57
Santa Rosa	90.55	52	97.51	94.07	83.05	96.17	97.23
Sarasota	98.20	8	101.61	96.07	96.73	101.28	96.13
Seminole	93.52	20	99.46	98.54	86.70	101.83	95.94
Sumter	91.40	40	98.05	87.97	85.00	97.25	97.52
Suwannee	90.31	56	104.56	90.20	80.30	95.59	97.87
Taylor	91.10	44	101.53	100.34	81.29	96.64	98.65
Union	89.79	59	101.43	88.02	81.19	95.11	96.73
Volusia	93.10	22	99.57	95.26	87.23	98.38	96.48
Wakulla	91.10	44	101.17	96.01	82.75	97.15	95.81
Walton	90.40	54	100.31	88.07	82.15	97.85	96.15
Washington	88.71	66	100.24	85.20	79.42	96.29	95.95

1/ Includes federal taxes and savings.

Note: The Florida County Retail Price Index is a set of numbers which reflects the price level in each county relative to population-weighted statewide average (100 for each category) for a particular point in time, August, 2005. It measures price level differences from place to place in contrast to the consumer price index prepared by the U.S. Bureau of Labor Statistics, which measures price level changes from month to month. The basis for these comparisons is one of fixed standard of living which represents the consumption pattern of a typical wage earner or clerical worker. The index measures in each county the relative cost of living by this standard. See Table 24.79 for relative weights of items priced.

Source: University of Florida, Bureau of Economic and Business Research, Economic Analysis Program, *2005 Florida County Retail Price and Wage Indices,* Internet site <http://www.bebr.ufl.edu/>.

Table 24.85. CONSUMER CONFIDENCE INDEX: TOTAL INDEX AND COMPONENTS OF THE FLORIDA CONSUMER CONFIDENCE INDEX BY MONTH, JULY 2004 THROUGH JUNE 2007

(1996 = 100)

			Index component				
Year	Month	Index 1/	Current personal 2/	Future personal 3/	U.S. one year 4/	U.S. five years 5/	Household purchases 6/
2004	7	94	83	95	91	94	107
	8	95	88	103	89	89	108
	9	93	85	100	87	90	102
	10	93	81	101	87	92	105
	11	93	85	100	88	85	109
	12	91	87	94	82	87	104
2005	1	93	85	98	87	88	110
	2	97	91	99	93	88	113
	3	92	88	93	83	84	114
	4	91	90	96	77	80	110
	5	91	87	96	79	82	111
	6	96	90	98	88	89	114
	7	95	87	100	84	88	113
	8	89	86	97	75	80	109
	9	78	80	90	56	70	91
	10	80	79	90	66	76	88
	11	84	80	92	72	78	98
	12	91	88	95	84	84	105
2006	1	95	88	99	86	90	109
	2	87	83	95	77	79	102
	3	91	89	96	81	83	106
	4	86	84	92	76	78	102
	5	86	88	92	73	75	100
	6	88	87	94	77	86	98
	7	87	80	98	76	82	100
	8	77	74	91	62	73	87
	9	83	76	89	73	77	100
	10	90	82	97	83	85	101
	11	93	84	101	88	93	101
	12	90	84	96	84	85	103
2007	1	89	80	92	83	83	106
	2	92	84	94	85	87	109
	3	86	80	90	78	81	99
	4	85	83	93	76	79	97
	5	81	77	89	74	76	90
	6	82	78	88	75	82	87

1/ Based on a monthly telephone survey of approximately 500 randomly selected Florida households. Compiled from survey responses giving views of personal financial and general business conditions.
2/ Personal financial conditions at time of survey as compared to previous year.
3/ Personal financial conditions anticipated a year from time of survey.
4/ U.S. business conditions anticipated a year from time of survey.
5/ U.S. business conditions anticipated five years from time of survey.
6/ Perception that the time of survey is a good time to buy major household items.

Source: University of Florida, Bureau of Economic and Business Research, UF Survey Research Program, *Florida Economic and Consumer Survey,* July 2007.

STATE COMPARISONS

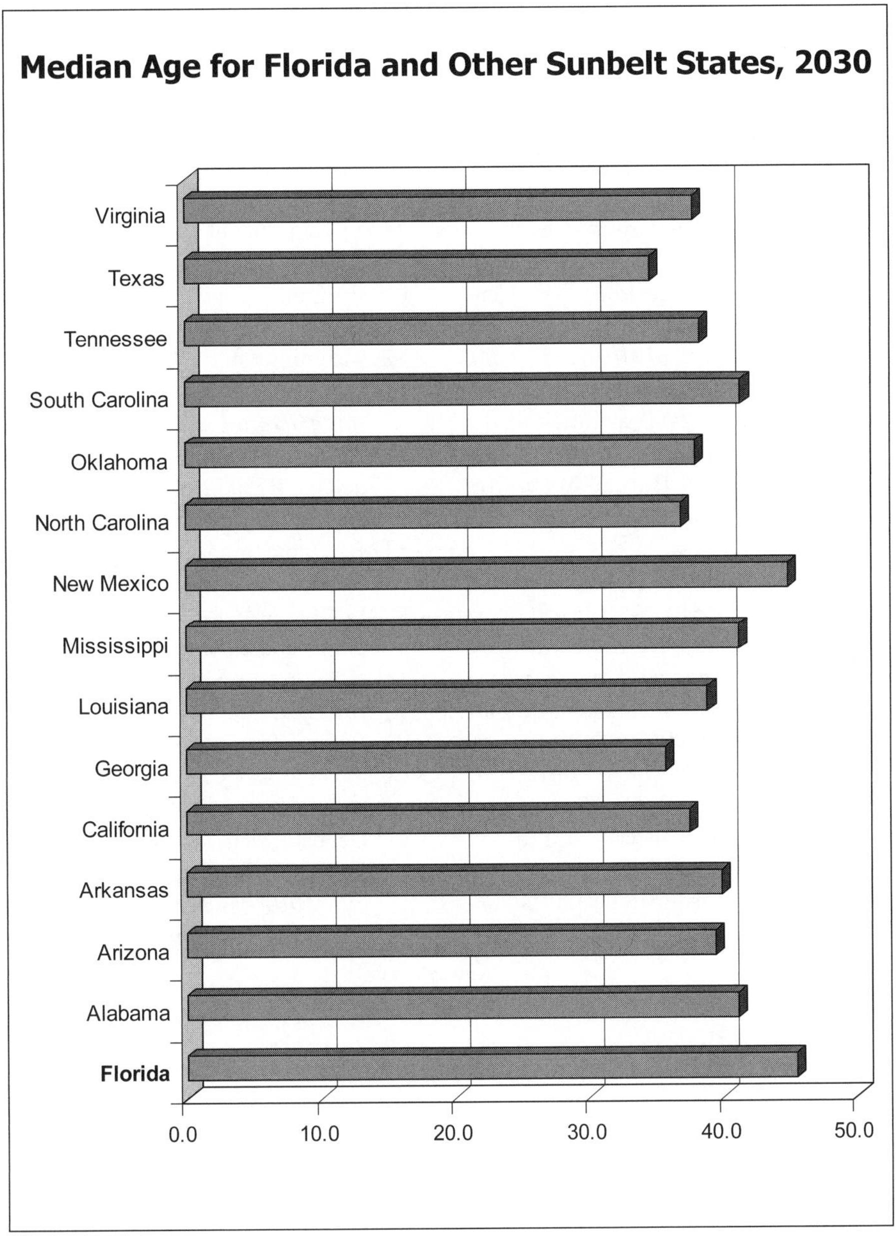

Source: Table 25.01

Section 25.00
State Comparisons

This section provides comparative data for Florida and other Sunbelt states, other populous states, and the United States among various demographic, economic, and social parameters. Both economic and non-economic factors appear in this section to permit the reader to compare aspects of life in Florida to similar living conditions in other Sunbelt and populous states.

Sources. There are numerous sources for these tables, most of which have been discussed in previous sections. The Census Bureau is a primary source for this section. The *Statistical Abstract of the United States,* the *State and Metropolitan Area Data Book,* as well as much of the other census data resources are available on the Census Bureau Web site. Sources not previously mentioned are:

- U.S. Department of Health and Human Services, *National Vital Statistics Report, Health United States with Chartbook on Trends in the Health of Americans, National MSIS Tables,* and *TANF Recipients.*
- National Education Association, Washington, DC, *Rankings and Estimates.*
- U.S. Department of Education, National Center for Education Statistics, *Digest of Education Statistics.*
- U.S. Department of Energy, Energy Information Administration, *Electric Sales and Revenue.*
- U.S. Department of the Treasury, Internal Revenue Service, *Statistics of Income: SOI Bulletin.*
- U.S. Department of Labor, Bureau of Labor Statistics, *Quarterly Census of Employment and Wages* and *Current Employment Statistics.*
- U.S. Department of Agriculture, Food and Nutrition Service, Food Stamp Program, *Annual State Level Data.*
- U.S. Department of Labor, Employment and Training Administration, *Unemployment Insurance Financial Data Handbook.*
- National Academy of Social Insurance, *Workers' Compensation: Benefits, Coverage, and Costs.*
- U.S. Department of Justice, *Bureau of Justice Statistics Bulletin: Probation and Parole in the United States* and *State Prison Expenditures.*
- U.S. General Services Administration, Office of Governmentwide Policy, *Federal Real Property Profile.*
- U.S. National Oceanic and Atmospheric Administration, National Climatic Data Center, *Comparative Climatic Data.*
- U.S. Environmental Protection Agency, *2005 TRI Public Data Release* and *National Priorities List.*

Section 25.00
State Comparisons

Tables listed by major heading

Table 25.01. SOCIAL STATISTICS AND INDICATORS: POPULATION CHARACTERISTICS OF FLORIDA, OTHER SUNBELT STATES, OTHER POPULOUS STATES AND THE UNITED STATES

State	July 1, 2006					
	Total	Rank among states	Percentage change 2000 to 2006	Persons per square mile of land area	Female (percent-age)	Aged 85 and over (percent-age)
			Sunbelt states			
Florida	18,089,888	4	12.7	335.5	50.9	2.6
Alabama	4,599,030	23	3.3	90.6	51.5	1.7
Arizona	6,166,318	16	19.3	54.3	50.0	1.7
Arkansas	2,810,872	32	4.9	54.0	51.0	2.0
California	36,457,549	1	7.2	233.8	50.0	1.5
Georgia	9,363,941	9	13.8	161.7	50.8	1.2
Louisiana	4,287,768	25	-4.1	98.4	51.4	1.6
Mississippi	2,910,540	31	2.2	62.0	51.6	1.7
New Mexico	1,954,599	36	7.3	16.1	50.6	1.6
North Carolina	8,856,505	10	9.6	181.8	51.0	1.5
Oklahoma	3,579,212	28	3.6	52.1	50.7	1.8
South Carolina	4,321,249	24	7.4	143.5	51.3	1.6
Tennessee	6,038,803	17	5.9	146.5	51.1	1.6
Texas	23,507,783	2	12.2	89.8	50.2	1.3
Virginia	7,642,884	12	7.6	193.0	50.8	1.5
			Other populous states			
Illinois	12,831,970	5	3.1	230.9	50.8	1.8
Indiana	6,313,520	15	3.6	176.0	50.7	1.8
Massachusetts	6,437,193	13	1.2	821.1	51.6	2.1
Michigan	10,095,643	8	1.4	177.7	50.8	1.7
New Jersey	8,724,560	11	3.4	1,176.2	51.1	1.9
New York	19,306,183	3	1.6	408.9	51.5	1.9
Ohio	11,478,006	7	1.0	280.3	51.2	1.9
Pennsylvania	12,440,621	6	1.3	277.6	51.4	2.4
United States	299,398,484	(X)	6.1	84.6	50.7	1.8

See footnotes at end of table.

Continued . . .

Table 25.01. SOCIAL STATISTICS AND INDICATORS: POPULATION CHARACTERISTICS OF FLORIDA, OTHER SUNBELT STATES, OTHER POPULOUS STATES AND THE UNITED STATES (Continued)

State	Age, July 1, 2006					
	Under 5	5-17	18-24	25-44	45-64	65 and over
			Sunbelt states			
Florida	1,122,849	2,898,706	1,594,516	4,868,204	4,567,909	3,037,704
Alabama	299,377	814,924	447,567	1,239,397	1,182,168	615,597
Arizona	480,491	1,147,707	588,180	1,752,098	1,407,556	790,286
Arkansas	192,891	498,295	266,780	758,800	703,685	390,421
California	2,678,019	6,854,595	3,784,128	10,767,783	8,441,510	3,931,514
Georgia	702,134	1,752,886	914,568	2,831,306	2,250,173	912,874
Louisiana	301,375	788,626	455,262	1,141,815	1,077,344	523,346
Mississippi	209,457	549,948	303,685	771,521	713,757	362,172
New Mexico	141,969	366,961	204,902	515,837	482,330	242,600
North Carolina	611,110	1,544,277	834,747	2,548,840	2,240,580	1,076,951
Oklahoma	254,718	639,316	369,119	952,911	889,603	473,545
South Carolina	283,481	756,172	423,096	1,180,743	1,124,361	553,396
Tennessee	398,252	1,044,341	548,775	1,715,517	1,562,696	769,222
Texas	1,925,197	4,568,768	2,448,736	6,894,417	5,336,206	2,334,459
Virginia	508,965	1,297,882	747,108	2,226,126	1,975,035	887,768
			Other populous states			
Illinois	887,605	2,327,639	1,281,767	3,659,718	3,140,765	1,534,476
Indiana	431,089	1,146,540	615,836	1,743,780	1,592,056	784,219
Massachusetts	387,863	1,061,021	633,278	1,822,110	1,676,959	855,962
Michigan	638,195	1,840,161	982,823	2,735,111	2,638,489	1,260,864
New Jersey	558,994	1,530,344	763,949	2,472,454	2,271,077	1,127,742
New York	1,220,468	3,293,874	1,939,099	5,423,867	4,906,189	2,522,686
Ohio	734,735	2,035,300	1,096,729	3,081,056	2,998,192	1,531,994
Pennsylvania	724,687	2,080,186	1,198,898	3,224,626	3,326,901	1,885,323
United States	20,417,636	53,317,926	29,454,784	84,082,929	74,864,857	37,260,352

See footnotes at end of table.

Continued . . .

Table 25.01. SOCIAL STATISTICS AND INDICATORS: POPULATION CHARACTERISTICS OF FLORIDA, OTHER SUNBELT STATES, OTHER POPULOUS STATES AND THE UNITED STATES (Continued)

State	July 1, 2006 Median age	Race White	Race Black	Race Other 1/	Hispanic origin 2/	Metro-area population 2000 to 2004 A/ (percentage)
			Sunbelt states			
Florida	39.6	14,503,894	2,864,423	721,571	3,646,499	8.9
Alabama	37.1	3,276,561	1,211,583	110,886	113,890	2.3
Arizona	34.6	5,380,815	231,677	553,826	1,803,378	12.2
Arkansas	36.8	2,279,839	442,155	88,878	141,053	4.0
California	34.4	28,043,733	2,445,228	5,968,588	13,074,156	6.0
Georgia	34.6	6,158,769	2,799,625	405,547	703,246	8.2
Louisiana	35.7	2,802,347	1,357,661	127,760	124,481	1.2
Mississippi	35.3	1,771,596	1,080,796	58,148	53,381	2.7
New Mexico	35.3	1,653,876	49,161	251,562	860,688	5.0
North Carolina	36.6	6,558,154	1,921,307	377,044	593,896	6.5
Oklahoma	36.0	2,803,755	278,849	496,608	247,450	2.6
South Carolina	37.1	2,958,982	1,253,131	109,136	151,289	5.0
Tennessee	37.1	4,855,937	1,019,528	163,338	194,706	3.9
Texas	33.1	19,452,577	2,804,949	1,250,257	8,385,139	8.3
Virginia	36.9	5,605,240	1,519,812	517,832	479,530	5.9
			Other populous states			
Illinois	35.7	10,169,966	1,928,153	733,851	1,886,933	2.5
Indiana	36.3	5,575,402	563,037	175,081	300,857	2.7
Massachusetts	38.2	5,568,643	446,721	421,829	511,014	1.0
Michigan	37.2	8,198,927	1,444,451	452,265	393,281	1.8
New Jersey	38.2	6,665,390	1,264,681	794,489	1,364,696	3.4
New York	37.3	14,220,047	3,352,874	1,733,262	3,139,456	1.3
Ohio	37.6	9,747,752	1,377,161	353,093	267,750	0.9
Pennsylvania	39.5	10,660,136	1,336,278	444,207	526,976	1.0
United States	36.4	239,746,254	38,342,549	21,309,681	44,321,038	4.6

See footnotes at end of table.

Continued . . .

Table 25.01. SOCIAL STATISTICS AND INDICATORS: POPULATION CHARACTERISTICS OF FLORIDA, OTHER SUNBELT STATES, OTHER POPULOUS STATES AND THE UNITED STATES (Continued)

State	Projections, July 1, 2030					
			Age			
	Total	Percentage change from 2000	18 and over	65 and over	85 and over	Median age
			Sunbelt states			
Florida	28,685,769	78.7	22,915,687	7,769,452	943,675	45.4
Alabama	4,874,243	9.5	3,761,979	1,039,160	132,070	41.0
Arizona	10,712,397	107.3	8,105,245	2,371,354	265,274	39.3
Arkansas	3,240,208	21.0	2,456,985	656,406	82,327	39.8
California	46,444,861	36.6	35,398,721	8,288,241	1,158,537	37.4
Georgia	12,017,838	46.0	8,871,214	1,907,837	224,926	35.6
Louisiana	4,802,633	7.5	3,652,694	944,212	126,215	38.8
Mississippi	3,092,410	8.6	2,380,388	634,067	73,646	41.1
New Mexico	2,099,708	15.3	1,643,900	555,184	75,629	44.8
North Carolina	12,227,739	51.4	9,147,128	2,173,173	266,881	36.8
Oklahoma	3,913,251	13.3	2,935,322	757,553	99,559	37.9
South Carolina	5,148,569	28.0	4,004,762	1,134,459	141,286	41.3
Tennessee	7,380,634	29.4	5,589,353	1,417,708	180,192	38.3
Texas	33,317,744	59.0	24,327,649	5,186,185	638,855	34.6
Virginia	9,825,019	38.3	7,504,829	1,843,988	250,366	37.8
			Other populous states			
Illinois	13,432,892	8.0	10,173,779	2,412,177	351,941	37.8
Indiana	6,810,108	11.8	5,108,684	1,231,873	169,134	37.7
Massachusetts	7,012,009	10.2	5,466,395	1,463,110	211,939	40.2
Michigan	10,694,172	7.4	8,260,843	2,080,725	287,089	40.2
New Jersey	9,802,440	16.2	7,626,688	1,959,545	290,911	40.8
New York	19,477,429	2.5	15,151,952	3,916,891	621,771	39.9
Ohio	11,550,528	1.6	8,909,857	2,357,022	322,497	40.2
Pennsylvania	12,768,184	3.9	10,021,985	2,890,068	415,436	42.1
United States	363,584,435	28.8	277,877,138	71,453,471	9,603,034	39.0

(X) Not applicable.

A/ Change in Metropolitan and Micropolitan Statistical Areas, July 1, as defined through June 30, 2004. See Glossary for definition.

1/ Includes American Indian, Alaska Native, Asian alone, Native Hawaiian, Other Pacific Islander, and persons of two or more races.

2/ Persons of Hispanic origin may be of any race.

Source: U.S., Department of Commerce, Census Bureau; Columns 1-17, "Population Estimates;" Column 18, *State and Metropolitan Area Data Book, 2006;* Columns 19-24, "Interim Projections of the Population by Selected Age Groups for the United States and States: April 1, 2000 to July 1, 2030," Internet site <http://www.census.gov/>. All data were accessed July 3, 2007.

Table 25.02. SOCIAL STATISTICS AND INDICATORS: HOUSING CHARACTERISTICS OF FLORIDA OTHER SUNBELT STATES, OTHER POPULOUS STATES, AND THE UNITED STATES

	Housing, 2005					
	Occupied households					
		Age of householder (percentage)				
State	Total	15-44	45-64	65 and over	Persons per household 1/	Vacant housing units
			Sunbelt states			
Florida	7,048,800	38.6	35.7	25.7	2.5	1,208,047
Alabama	1,788,692	41.2	37.4	21.4	2.6	293,448
Arizona	2,204,013	44.7	34.1	21.2	2.7	340,793
Arkansas	1,087,542	41.8	35.9	22.2	2.5	161,574
California	12,097,894	44.5	37.0	18.5	3.0	891,360
Georgia	3,320,278	48.4	35.9	15.7	2.7	451,188
Louisiana	1,676,599	42.7	37.4	19.9	2.7	263,800
Mississippi	1,084,034	42.0	37.1	20.8	2.7	151,462
New Mexico	727,820	41.5	38.0	20.5	2.7	110,848
North Carolina	3,409,840	45.2	35.7	19.2	2.5	530,714
Oklahoma	1,380,595	42.7	36.0	21.2	2.6	208,154
South Carolina	1,635,907	42.1	37.3	20.5	2.6	291,957
Tennessee	2,366,130	43.2	37.0	19.8	2.5	271,311
Texas	7,978,095	47.3	35.7	17.1	2.9	1,047,916
Virginia	2,889,688	43.3	38.2	18.5	2.6	285,020
			Other populous states			
Illinois	4,691,020	43.3	36.4	20.2	2.8	453,603
Indiana	2,443,010	43.3	36.4	20.2	2.6	281,419
Massachusetts	2,448,032	41.0	37.8	21.2	2.7	239,982
Michigan	3,887,994	41.6	37.8	20.5	2.7	590,513
New Jersey	3,141,956	39.4	39.1	21.5	2.9	302,025
New York	7,114,431	40.6	37.9	21.4	2.8	738,589
Ohio	4,507,821	41.2	37.6	21.2	2.6	499,270
Pennsylvania	4,860,140	37.8	38.3	23.9	2.6	562,222
United States	111,090,617	42.8	37.0	20.2	2.7	13,431,269

See footnotes at end of table.

Continued . . .

Table 25.02. SOCIAL STATISTICS AND INDICATORS: HOUSING CHARACTERISTICS OF FLORIDA OTHER SUNBELT STATES, OTHER POPULOUS STATES, AND THE UNITED STATES

	Housing, 2005 (Continued)					
	Total	Units in structure			House heating fuel 1/	
State	housing units	1-unit detached	1-unit attached	Mobile home	Utility gas	Electricity
			Sunbelt states			
Florida	8,256,847	4,410,814	485,886	866,431	366,742	6,352,266
Alabama	2,082,140	1,400,729	38,626	304,192	634,841	911,517
Arizona	2,544,806	1,529,319	133,756	306,934	795,966	1,249,793
Arkansas	1,249,116	876,082	20,281	165,557	498,494	410,227
California	12,989,254	7,503,815	920,438	536,468	8,341,302	2,768,337
Georgia	3,771,466	2,466,469	124,933	396,384	1,542,096	1,434,266
Louisiana	1,940,399	1,264,342	75,838	241,789	707,781	882,240
Mississippi	1,235,496	847,094	21,294	194,583	375,908	499,114
New Mexico	838,668	525,060	30,481	149,044	484,937	106,056
North Carolina	3,940,554	2,545,983	121,287	610,596	874,796	1,761,058
Oklahoma	1,588,749	1,152,987	34,728	154,805	810,457	399,930
South Carolina	1,927,864	1,190,272	48,556	357,491	421,490	1,016,372
Tennessee	2,637,441	1,787,193	78,163	276,184	855,545	1,274,770
Texas	9,026,011	5,828,531	244,628	714,642	3,233,765	4,270,507
Virginia	3,174,708	1,986,218	316,310	187,240	1,018,499	1,318,024
			Other populous states			
Illinois	5,144,623	3,017,210	287,822	160,944	3,805,375	590,388
Indiana	2,724,429	1,958,657	97,057	160,959	1,559,602	569,835
Massachusetts	2,688,014	1,407,960	123,309	23,591	1,142,108	312,355
Michigan	4,478,507	3,169,503	204,259	279,756	3,020,584	281,809
New Jersey	3,443,981	1,860,015	308,512	34,811	2,197,048	340,369
New York	7,853,020	3,303,050	395,040	205,967	3,677,056	602,975
Ohio	5,007,091	3,395,143	221,630	212,903	3,070,843	865,476
Pennsylvania	5,422,362	3,069,165	983,072	245,433	2,510,837	844,189
United States	124,521,886	76,112,065	7,063,608	8,737,428	56,073,178	36,134,273

See footnotes at end of table.

Continued . . .

Table 25.02. SOCIAL STATISTICS AND INDICATORS: HOUSING CHARACTERISTICS OF FLORIDA OTHER SUNBELT STATES, OTHER POPULOUS STATES, AND THE UNITED STATES

	Housing, 2005 (Continued)					
	Owner-occupied units					
			Value			
State	Total units	Median value 2/ (dollars)	Less than $100,000	$100,000 to $199,999	$200,000 to $299,999	$300,000 and over
			Sunbelt states			
Florida	4,903,949	189,500	1,033,396	1,568,575	959,870	1,342,108
Alabama	1,261,475	97,500	648,936	409,830	111,755	90,954
Arizona	1,502,457	185,400	291,977	526,470	302,612	381,398
Arkansas	736,825	87,400	428,145	217,637	52,973	38,070
California	7,070,138	477,700	424,549	469,461	734,746	5,441,382
Georgia	2,218,217	147,500	638,253	905,954	339,667	334,343
Louisiana	1,136,873	101,700	558,789	406,197	100,344	71,543
Mississippi	757,446	82,700	463,595	212,857	48,070	32,924
New Mexico	504,354	125,500	190,306	190,867	63,730	59,451
North Carolina	2,325,140	127,600	828,083	941,552	290,825	264,680
Oklahoma	937,051	89,100	538,653	297,969	61,710	38,719
South Carolina	1,146,620	113,100	503,994	400,222	122,105	120,299
Tennessee	1,638,837	114,000	699,781	627,480	170,559	141,017
Texas	5,162,604	106,000	2,426,730	1,853,115	487,644	395,115
Virginia	2,012,391	212,300	394,955	560,342	327,103	729,991
			Other populous states			
Illinois	3,277,573	183,900	761,461	1,024,828	657,414	833,870
Indiana	1,759,089	114,400	726,892	750,651	173,037	108,509
Massachusetts	1,567,885	361,500	41,233	190,965	314,414	1,021,273
Michigan	2,903,328	149,300	774,252	1,252,968	488,080	388,028
New Jersey	2,114,072	333,900	119,577	358,990	429,953	1,205,552
New York	3,936,378	258,900	899,158	777,793	423,143	1,836,284
Ohio	3,152,610	129,600	1,029,750	1,460,228	414,441	248,191
Pennsylvania	3,474,048	131,900	1,259,486	1,238,742	487,385	488,435
United States	74,318,982	167,500	20,211,661	23,046,447	11,195,025	19,865,849

See footnotes at end of table.

Continued . . .

Table 25.02. SOCIAL STATISTICS AND INDICATORS: HOUSING CHARACTERISTICS OF FLORIDA OTHER SUNBELT STATES, OTHER POPULOUS STATES, AND THE UNITED STATES

	Housing, 2005 (Continued)					
	Renter-occupied units					
		Median gross	Gross rent			
State	Total units	rent 2/ (dollars)	Less than $300	$300 to $499	$500 to $749	$750 or more
			Sunbelt states			
Florida	2,144,851	809	91,188	170,938	578,523	1,194,994
Alabama	527,217	535	61,594	139,287	168,096	93,713
Arizona	701,556	717	26,822	84,271	253,594	294,146
Arkansas	350,717	549	36,419	90,013	127,695	56,120
California	5,027,756	973	177,984	271,371	850,748	3,541,396
Georgia	1,102,061	709	73,749	151,938	347,348	453,392
Louisiana	539,726	569	57,900	118,588	195,793	106,474
Mississippi	326,588	538	42,674	80,264	101,077	58,383
New Mexico	223,466	587	19,585	53,617	73,150	57,282
North Carolina	1,084,700	635	75,957	191,833	410,388	308,572
Oklahoma	443,544	547	35,798	122,481	156,069	84,916
South Carolina	489,287	611	37,753	96,801	173,040	127,017
Tennessee	727,293	583	70,693	156,408	272,603	162,377
Texas	2,815,491	671	155,815	402,964	1,074,489	1,001,847
Virginia	877,297	812	55,705	96,538	207,342	461,101
			Other populous states			
Illinois	1,413,447	734	103,899	175,459	422,192	641,835
Indiana	683,921	615	52,178	136,432	274,320	179,508
Massachusetts	880,147	902	92,493	77,895	141,032	534,194
Michigan	984,666	655	75,347	164,710	360,455	331,214
New Jersey	1,027,884	935	65,494	50,838	160,299	711,154
New York	3,178,053	841	250,349	317,577	701,912	1,792,777
Ohio	1,355,211	613	113,972	264,398	523,724	372,257
Pennsylvania	1,386,092	647	118,353	255,318	456,511	467,295
United States	36,771,635	728	2,549,530	4,982,973	10,693,519	16,330,119

1/ Owner-occupied housing units.
2/ Constant 2005 dollars.

Source: U.S., Department of Commerce, Census Bureau, *2005 American Community Survey*, Internet site <http://www.census.gov/> (accessed 8, August 2007).

Table 25.03. SOCIAL STATISTICS AND INDICATORS: VITAL STATISTICS CHARACTERISTICS OF FLORIDA, OTHER SUNBELT STATES, OTHER POPULOUS STATES AND THE UNITED STATES

State	Live births, 2006			Rates, 2006		
	Number	Rate 1/	Fertility rate 2/	Deaths 1/	Marri- ages 1/	Divorces 1/
			Sunbelt states			
Florida	237,371	13.1	67.5	9.4	8.6	4.9
Alabama	63,296	13.8	67.1	10.2	8.6	4.8
Arizona	103,070	16.7	82.1	7.5	6.3	3.9
Arkansas	40,494	14.4	71.4	10.0	12.2	5.7
California	562,676	15.4	71.8	6.5	5.9	(NA)
Georgia	148,427	15.9	72.3	7.1	7.1	(NA)
Louisiana	60,190	14.0	67.0	9.0	(NA)	(NA)
Mississippi	46,073	15.8	75.8	9.8	5.8	4.7
New Mexico	29,867	15.3	74.6	7.7	6.9	4.3
North Carolina	128,186	14.5	69.2	8.4	6.2	4.1
Oklahoma	54,212	15.1	74.9	9.9	7.3	5.3
South Carolina	61,870	14.3	69.2	8.5	7.6	3.0
Tennessee	83,928	13.9	67.1	9.4	10.6	4.3
Texas	399,831	17.0	78.8	6.5	7.4	3.3
Virginia	108,245	14.2	66.6	7.5	7.9	4.1
			Other populous states			
Illinois	180,519	14.1	66.8	7.9	6.1	2.5
Indiana	89,461	14.2	68.9	8.8	8.1	(NA)
Massachusetts	77,610	12.1	56.8	8.3	6.0	2.3
Michigan	127,603	12.6	61.8	8.4	5.9	3.5
New Jersey	114,934	13.2	64.4	8.2	4.9	3.0
New York	254,806	13.2	62.2	7.8	6.6	2.9
Ohio	152,112	13.3	65.3	9.3	6.4	3.6
Pennsylvania	148,234	11.9	60.3	10.1	5.5	2.2
United States	4,269,000	14.3	68.6	8.1	7.2	3.6

(NA) Not available.

1/ Rate per 1,000 population calculated by the Bureau of Economic and Business Research using July 1, 2006 Census Bureau population estimates.

2/ Births per 1,000 resident female population aged 15-44 years.

Note: All data are preliminary. Birth and death rates are by place of residence and exclude nonresidents of the United States and members of the armed forces abroad. Marriage and divorce rates are by place of occurrence. Divorce rates include annulments.

Source: U.S., Department of Health and Human Services, National Center for Health Statistics, Centers for Disease Control and Prevention, *National Vital Statistics Reports*, Volume 55, Number 20, Internet site <http://www.cdc.gov/nchs/> (accessed 29, August 2007).

Table 25.04. SOCIAL STATISTICS AND INDICATORS: HEALTH CHARACTERISTICS OF FLORIDA, OTHER SUNBELT STATES, OTHER POPULOUS STATES AND THE UNITED STATES

State	Community hospital beds 2004 A/	Nursing home resident rate 2004 B/	Active physicians 2004 C/	Enrollment in managed care (percentage) Medicare 2003	Medicaid 2003	Persons without health care coverage 2002–04 D/ (percentage)
			Sunbelt states			
Florida	2.9	191.7	25.1	18.4	61	18.5
Alabama	3.4	355.2	21.1	6.4	53	13.5
Arizona	1.9	151.0	22.2	28.1	90	17.0
Arkansas	3.5	370.6	20.5	0.5	67	16.7
California	2.0	206.3	25.2	33.2	52	18.4
Georgia	2.8	377.2	22.0	3.9	84	16.6
Louisiana	3.8	473.9	25.3	11.3	59	18.8
Mississippi	4.5	407.0	18.4	0.6	45	17.2
New Mexico	1.9	235.3	23.8	15.6	65	21.4
North Carolina	2.8	314.4	24.5	4.0	70	16.6
Oklahoma	3.1	395.0	20.3	7.7	68	19.2
South Carolina	2.7	275.1	22.6	0.3	8	13.8
Tennessee	3.5	397.4	25.4	7.0	100	12.7
Texas	2.6	360.3	21.2	6.8	42	25.1
Virginia	2.3	272.8	26.5	2.0	45	13.6
			Other populous states			
Illinois	2.7	361.5	27.2	5.1	9	14.2
Indiana	3.0	386.7	21.6	2.1	71	13.7
Massachusetts	2.5	335.1	41.7	17.5	99	10.8
Michigan	2.6	236.3	27.1	1.8	66	11.4
New Jersey	2.5	274.3	31.6	7.8	67	14.4
New York	3.3	320.5	37.1	17.2	53	15.0
Ohio	2.9	385.6	27.2	13.3	29	11.8
Pennsylvania	3.2	278.4	31.7	24.0	80	11.5
United States	2.8	296.8	26.3	13.1	59	15.5

A/ Beds per 1,000 resident population. Excludes hospital units of institutions, facilities for the mentally retarded, and alcohol and drug abuse facilities.
B/ Nursing home residents (all ages) per 1,000 resident population 85 years of age and over.
C/ Nonfederal physicians per 10,000 civilian population.
D/ Persons under age 65.

Source: U.S., Department of Health and Human Services, National Center for Health Care Statistics, Centers for Disease Control and Prevention, *Health United States, 2006, with Chartbook on Trends in the Health of Americans,* Internet site <http://www.cdc.gov/> (accessed 27, March 2007).

Table 25.05. SOCIAL STATISTICS AND INDICATORS: EDUCATION CHARACTERISTICS OF FLORIDA OTHER SUNBELT STATES, OTHER POPULOUS STATES, AND THE UNITED STATES

State	School year 2005–06 A/				College enrollment, 2005 B/	
	Students enrolled per teacher	Average salary of teachers (dollars)	Receipts ($1,000)	Current expenditure per pupil in ADA (dollars)	Number	Minority (percent age)
			Sunbelt states			
Florida	16.4	43,302	24,967,922	8,105	872,662	39.9
Alabama	14.9	40,347	6,027,248	7,585	256,389	32.8
Arizona	21.8	44,672	7,979,468	5,791	545,597	31.5
Arkansas	13.5	42,093	3,915,342	7,197	143,272	22.9
California	20.0	59,345	64,054,472	8,607	2,399,833	53.8
Georgia	14.8	48,300	15,337,449	9,836	426,650	37.2
Louisiana	14.8	40,253	6,325,490	8,633	197,713	34.6
Mississippi	15.7	37,924	3,768,462	7,240	150,457	41.1
New Mexico	14.9	41,637	3,176,148	9,588	131,337	54.8
North Carolina	14.7	43,922	10,333,356	7,976	484,392	30.3
Oklahoma	15.2	38,772	4,789,409	7,236	208,053	25.1
South Carolina	14.8	43,242	6,587,609	9,073	210,444	31.1
Tennessee	15.7	42,537	6,972,142	7,625	283,070	23.6
Texas	14.9	41,744	38,512,169	7,913	1,240,707	44.1
Virginia	13.2	43,823	12,789,820	10,011	439,166	29.2
			Other populous states			
Illinois	15.4	57,819	20,735,556	10,959	832,967	31.9
Indiana	17.1	47,255	10,487,474	9,757	361,253	13.7
Massachusetts	14.3	56,587	13,455,151	13,091	443,316	21.7
Michigan	17.8	58,482	21,250,527	10,646	626,751	20.2
New Jersey	12.6	57,707	20,023,212	13,626	379,758	36.4
New York	12.3	57,354	41,346,057	13,216	1,152,081	33.4
Ohio	15.6	50,314	20,636,385	11,316	616,350	16.6
Pennsylvania	14.7	54,027	20,759,648	10,714	692,340	17.8
United States	15.6	49,109	498,066,621	9,576	17,487,475	30.9

ADA Average daily attendance.

A/ Data are estimates for public schools, grades K through 12. United States numbers include District of Columbia.

B/ Preliminary. Excludes students taking courses for credit by mail, radio, or TV, and students in branches of U.S. institutions operated in foreign countries.

Source: Columns 1-4, National Education Association, Washington, DC, *Rankings and Estimates: 2006,* Internet site <http://www.nea.org/>; and Columns 5, 6, U.S., Department of Education, National Center for Education Statistics, *Digest of Education Statistics, 2006,* Internet site <http://nces.ed.gov/>. Both Internet sites were accessed September 19, 2007.

Table 25.06. SOCIAL STATISTICS AND INDICATORS: PERSONAL FINANCES AND INCOME AND WEALTH CHARACTERISTICS OF FLORIDA, OTHER SUNBELT STATES, OTHER POPULOUS STATES, AND THE UNITED STATES

State	Personal finances: Average cost per KwH electricity 2005 A/ (cents)	Personal finances: Life insurance in force 2005 (million dollars)	Personal finances: State gasoline tax rate 2005 B/ (cents per gallon)	Income and wealth: Median family income 2005 C/ (dollars)	Income and wealth: Percent of people below the poverty level 2005 D/	Income and wealth: Average tax liability 2005 E/ (dollars)
			Sunbelt states			
Florida	9.6	1,142,814	14.5	50,465	12.8	11,305
Alabama	8.0	312,552	18.0	46,086	17.0	7,718
Arizona	8.9	351,266	18.0	51,458	14.2	9,562
Arkansas	8.0	143,915	21.7	43,134	17.2	6,701
California	12.5	2,465,865	18.0	61,476	13.3	11,828
Georgia	8.6	743,046	7.5	53,744	14.4	9,031
Louisiana	8.9	276,660	20.0	45,730	19.8	7,745
Mississippi	8.7	153,241	18.4	40,917	21.3	6,359
New Mexico	9.1	96,157	18.9	44,097	18.5	7,030
North Carolina	8.7	636,819	27.1	49,339	15.1	7,944
Oklahoma	8.0	185,160	17.0	45,990	16.5	7,699
South Carolina	8.7	270,763	16.0	48,100	15.6	7,265
Tennessee	7.0	440,441	21.4	47,950	15.5	8,107
Texas	10.9	1,579,094	20.0	49,769	17.6	10,455
Virginia	8.2	635,825	17.5	65,174	10.0	9,523
			Other populous states			
Illinois	8.3	1,194,363	19.0	61,174	12.0	10,697
Indiana	7.5	387,678	18.0	54,077	12.2	7,393
Massachusetts	13.4	631,123	21.0	71,655	10.3	12,477
Michigan	8.4	678,027	19.0	57,277	13.2	8,088
New Jersey	11.7	947,398	10.5	75,311	8.7	13,129
New York	15.7	1,750,266	23.3	59,686	13.8	12,703
Ohio	8.5	804,273	28.0	54,086	13.0	7,180
Pennsylvania	9.9	976,838	30.0	55,904	11.9	8,813
United States	9.5	22,213,142	F/ 19.3	55,832	13.3	9,870

KwH Kilowatt-hour.
A/ Residential service.
B/ Tax rates for motor fuel as of December 31.
C/ Median income for 4-person families.
D/ Sample person count, all income levels. Data are limited to household population and exclude persons in group quarters, dormitories, or institutions.
E/ Preliminary data from a sample of individual income tax forms.
F/ Weighted average based on net gallons taxed.

Source: Column 1, U.S., Department of Energy, Energy Information Administration, *Electric Sales and Revenue, 2005,* Internet site <http://www.eia.doe.gov/>; Column 2, American Council of Life Insurers, *Life Insurers Fact Book, 2006,* Internet <http://www.acli.com/>; Column 3, U.S., Department of Transportation, Federal Highway Administration, *Highway Statistics, 2005,* Internet site <http://www.fhwa.dot.gov/>; Columns 4, 5, U.S., Department of Commerce, Census Bureau, Internet site <http://www.census.gov/>; Column 6, U.S., Department of the Treasury, Internal Revenue Service, *Statistics of Income: SOI Bulletin, Spring 2007.* All Internet sites were accessed July 9, 2007.

Table 25.07. SOCIAL STATISTICS AND INDICATORS: EMPLOYMENT CHARACTERISTICS OF FLORIDA OTHER SUNBELT STATES, OTHER POPULOUS STATES, AND THE UNITED STATES

State	Labor force participation rate, 2006 A/		Annual average unemployment rate, 2006 A/		Average annual wages 2005 B/ (dollars)	Total non-agricultural employment 2006
	Male	Female	Male	Female		
			Sunbelt states			
Florida	70.1	57.5	3.2	3.3	36,800	8,007
Alabama	69.8	55.2	3.9	4.4	34,598	1,982
Arizona	73.4	56.3	3.7	4.8	38,154	2,644
Arkansas	69.3	58.0	5.4	5.1	31,266	1,200
California	73.9	56.7	4.7	5.0	46,211	15,073
Georgia	75.5	60.9	4.5	4.8	39,096	4,086
Louisiana	69.4	55.0	4.4	4.8	33,566	1,857
Mississippi	66.4	53.6	6.6	6.2	29,763	1,142
New Mexico	69.2	57.5	4.3	4.4	32,605	833
North Carolina	73.4	59.5	4.4	5.1	35,912	4,021
Oklahoma	72.1	56.6	4.5	3.3	31,721	1,552
South Carolina	71.3	57.9	6.5	6.5	32,927	1,903
Tennessee	72.5	56.9	5.1	5.3	35,879	2,783
Texas	76.4	57.7	4.5	5.2	40,150	10,053
Virginia	75.2	62.3	2.7	3.5	42,287	3,726
			Other populous states			
Illinois	75.4	59.8	4.5	4.4	43,744	5,935
Indiana	74.9	60.8	4.5	5.6	35,431	2,973
Massachusetts	73.5	61.0	5.6	4.4	50,095	3,243
Michigan	71.4	59.2	7.3	6.6	41,214	4,341
New Jersey	75.2	58.7	4.8	4.9	49,471	4,075
New York	69.6	57.3	4.8	4.0	51,937	8,612
Ohio	73.1	61.7	5.9	4.9	37,333	5,441
Pennsylvania	71.8	57.6	4.7	4.5	39,661	5,753
United States	73.5	59.4	4.6	4.6	40,677	136,174

See footnotes at end of table.

Continued . . .

Table 25.07. SOCIAL STATISTICS AND INDICATORS: EMPLOYMENT CHARACTERISTICS OF FLORIDA OTHER SUNBELT STATES, OTHER POPULOUS STATES, AND THE UNITED STATES (Continued)

	Nonagricultural employment, 2006					
		Distribution (percentage)				
State	Percentage change from 2005	Natural resources and mining	Con- struction	Manufac- turing	Trade transpor- tation, and utilities	Infor- mation
			Sunbelt states			
Florida	2.66	0.08	7.95	5.03	19.94	2.09
Alabama	1.93	0.66	5.56	15.29	19.53	1.53
Arizona	5.37	0.37	9.29	7.09	19.32	1.69
Arkansas	1.84	0.63	4.75	16.59	20.76	1.67
California	1.86	0.17	6.23	9.98	19.07	3.14
Georgia	2.08	0.30	5.36	10.98	21.23	2.83
Louisiana	-1.87	2.63	7.12	8.21	20.12	1.45
Mississippi	1.08	0.83	5.05	15.38	19.86	1.20
New Mexico	3.05	2.24	7.12	4.52	17.03	1.91
North Carolina	2.70	0.17	6.06	13.76	18.78	1.82
Oklahoma	2.61	2.71	4.54	9.61	18.32	1.92
South Carolina	1.93	0.25	6.54	13.22	19.34	1.44
Tennessee	1.46	0.15	4.70	14.38	21.85	1.80
Texas	3.21	1.84	6.00	9.21	20.34	2.21
Virginia	1.69	0.30	6.69	7.75	17.79	2.47
			Other populous states			
Illinois	1.24	0.17	4.65	11.51	20.18	1.96
Indiana	0.62	0.24	5.05	19.03	19.69	1.35
Massachusetts	0.99	0.06	4.34	9.22	17.57	2.69
Michigan	-1.12	0.18	4.15	14.94	18.31	1.54
New Jersey	0.89	0.04	4.28	7.98	21.49	2.43
New York	0.92	0.07	3.91	6.59	17.49	3.13
Ohio	0.27	0.21	4.25	14.64	19.23	1.63
Pennsylvania	0.89	0.36	4.55	11.68	19.58	1.88
United States	1.85	0.50	5.65	10.43	19.26	2.24

See footnotes at end of table. Continued . .

Table 25.07. SOCIAL STATISTICS AND INDICATORS: EMPLOYMENT CHARACTERISTICS OF FLORIDA OTHER SUNBELT STATES, OTHER POPULOUS STATES, AND THE UNITED STATES (Continued)

	Nonagricultural employment, 2006 (Continued)					
	Distribution (percentage) (Continued)					
State	Financial activities	Professional and business services	Education and health services	Lesiure and hospitality	Other services	Govern-ment
			Sunbelt states			
Florida	6.82	16.75	12.12	11.30	4.21	13.71
Alabama	4.97	10.85	10.27	8.59	4.07	18.70
Arizona	6.93	14.93	10.99	10.09	3.81	15.51
Arkansas	4.38	9.55	12.59	8.11	3.63	17.36
California	6.24	14.76	10.74	10.08	3.36	16.24
Georgia	5.65	13.46	10.71	9.36	3.90	16.22
Louisiana	5.15	10.46	12.63	9.95	3.56	18.73
Mississippi	4.05	8.21	10.75	10.40	3.24	21.03
New Mexico	4.22	12.34	12.95	10.38	3.53	23.76
North Carolina	5.12	11.77	12.12	9.24	4.37	16.79
Oklahoma	5.42	11.28	12.09	8.80	4.80	20.51
South Carolina	5.37	11.42	10.16	10.90	3.99	17.37
Tennessee	5.18	11.50	12.18	9.71	3.63	14.93
Texas	6.22	12.20	12.11	9.38	3.45	17.03
Virginia	5.25	16.84	10.86	9.07	4.87	18.09
			Other populous states			
Illinois	6.84	14.37	12.86	8.84	4.37	14.25
Indiana	4.71	9.43	12.98	9.45	3.74	14.34
Massachusetts	6.89	14.55	18.68	9.10	3.67	13.23
Michigan	4.98	13.54	13.45	9.38	4.10	15.43
New Jersey	6.89	14.78	13.96	8.31	3.94	15.92
New York	8.43	12.87	18.23	7.87	4.14	17.27
Ohio	5.65	12.07	14.29	9.21	4.10	14.72
Pennsylvania	5.83	11.77	18.34	8.52	4.52	12.97
United States	6.14	12.89	13.10	9.65	3.99	16.15

A/ Percentage of civilian noninstitutional population of each specified group in the civilian labor force. Includes persons 16 years old and over. Data are preliminary.
B/ Preliminary data for workers covered by state and federal unemployment insurance programs.

Source: U.S., Department of Labor, Bureau of Labor Statistics, Columns 1-4, *Geographic Profile of Employment and Unemployment;* Column 5, *Quarterly Census of Employment and Wages;* Columns 6-12, *Current Employment Statistics,* Internet site <http://www.bls.gov/> (accessed 18, September 2007).

Table 25.08. SOCIAL STATISTICS AND INDICATORS: MANUFACTURING AND AGRICULTURAL CHARACTERISTICS OF FLORIDA, OTHER SUNBELT STATES, OTHER POPULOUS STATES AND THE UNITED STATES

State	Manufacturing: Jobs won/lost 2000 to 2006 (1,000)	Manufacturing: Rank among states in employment 2006	Manufacturing: Percentage change in GDP 2000 to 2006	Agriculture: Farm acreage 2006 B/ (1,000)	Agriculture: Farm cash receipts 2006 A/ Amount ($1,000)	Agriculture: Farm cash receipts 2006 A/ Rank among states
			Sunbelt states			
Florida	-60.7	12	19.7	10,000	6,974,161	9
Alabama	-48.3	17	42.3	8,600	3,739,060	27
Arizona	-22.6	27	-9.2	26,100	2,879,224	29
Arkansas	-41.3	25	22.8	14,300	6,164,069	11
California	-359.5	1	-7.7	26,300	31,402,706	1
Georgia	-89.4	11	6.6	10,800	6,005,101	13
Louisiana	-24.8	30	134.6	7,800	2,186,180	34
Mississippi	-46.8	29	13.6	11,000	3,788,510	26
New Mexico	-4.0	43	6.7	44,500	2,463,526	32
North Carolina	-204.6	9	10.6	8,800	8,199,349	8
Oklahoma	-27.8	32	14.2	33,700	5,093,622	18
South Carolina	-84.6	22	11.6	4,850	1,890,661	35
Tennessee	-93.0	13	27.8	11,400	2,564,931	31
Texas	-141.7	2	50.2	129,700	16,026,756	2
Virginia	-74.8	19	1.1	8,500	2,688,669	30
			Other populous states			
Illinois	-187.5	4	12.5	27,300	8,635,700	7
Indiana	-98.6	8	21.0	15,000	5,973,217	14
Massachusetts	-104.1	18	-10.4	520	433,026	47
Michigan	-246.5	6	-10.4	10,100	4,487,765	21
New Jersey	-96.5	15	0.7	790	923,933	40
New York	-182.9	7	6.4	7,500	3,509,003	28
Ohio	-224.2	3	6.4	14,300	5,479,712	17
Pennsylvania	-192.1	5	8.4	7,650	4,691,681	20
United States	-3,066.0	(X)	12.3	932,430	239,271,907	(X)

GDP Gross Domestic Product by State, formerly the Gross State Product.
(X) Not applicable.
A/ Includes net commodity credit loans.
B/ As of June 1.

Source: Columns 1, 2, U. S., Department of Labor, Bureau of Labor Statistics, *Current Employment Statistics,* Internet site <http://stats.bls.gov/>; Column 3, U.S., Department of Commerce, Bureau of Economic Analysis, Internet site <http://www.bea.doc.gov/>; Columns 4-6, U.S., Department of Agriculture, Internet sites <http://usda.mannlib.cornell.edu/> and <http://www.ers.usda.gov/>. All Internet sites were accessed June 29, 2007.

Table 25.09. SOCIAL STATISTICS AND INDICATORS: SOCIAL INSURANCE AND WELFARE CHARACTERISTICS OF FLORIDA, OTHER SUNBELT STATES, OTHER POPULOUS STATES, AND THE UNITED STATES

State	Persons in the federal food stamp program 2006 A/	Average weekly state unemployment benefits, 2006 (dollars)	Workers' compensation payments 2005 (thousand dollars)	Average medicaid benefits per recipient 2004 (dollars)	Temporary assistance for needy families (TANF) recipients December 2006	Average monthly social security benefits 2005 B/ (dollars)
			Sunbelt states			
Florida	1,417,749	231.38	2,899,301	4,347	81,654	927.60
Alabama	546,684	183.76	608,522	4,772	46,539	860.40
Arizona	540,782	197.64	535,539	3,633	80,453	940.30
Arkansas	384,889	243.98	208,021	3,332	19,925	841.20
California	1,999,656	289.07	10,938,475	2,740	1,161,392	921.40
Georgia	946,812	255.57	1,197,521	3,600	47,051	887.30
Louisiana	829,882	191.12	667,097	3,645	25,341	834.80
Mississippi	447,710	185.84	311,796	4,564	24,907	815.10
New Mexico	244,672	237.70	230,591	4,802	38,867	842.90
North Carolina	854,407	265.08	1,398,001	4,884	52,560	898.90
Oklahoma	435,519	233.23	587,523	3,572	20,930	881.80
South Carolina	534,294	222.80	769,553	4,686	37,991	894.20
Tennessee	870,416	215.70	880,100	4,213	166,380	881.60
Texas	2,622,548	271.04	1,554,796	3,667	148,757	880.50
Virginia	506,656	255.67	853,877	4,883	70,270	907.40
			Other populous states			
Illinois	1,225,093	291.67	2,404,456	5,314	81,513	958.30
Indiana	574,696	286.32	609,596	4,589	121,963	960.20
Massachusetts	431,518	366.33	903,555	7,240	90,611	931.30
Michigan	1,133,793	293.66	1,473,598	4,278	193,989	981.80
New Jersey	405,667	344.09	1,608,345	6,900	86,001	1,026.30
New York	1,785,914	277.41	2,895,331	7,910	277,742	971.90
Ohio	1,063,920	287.03	2,447,038	5,999	170,167	926.10
Pennsylvania	1,092,298	301.27	2,677,899	5,481	210,157	950.30
United States	26,671,819	277.20	55,307,176	4,686	4,119,217	915.70

A/ Average monthly participants. Federal fiscal year ending September 30.
B/ Includes retired workers, disabled workers, survivors, and children.

Source: Column 1, U.S., Department of Agriculture, Food and Nutrition Service, Food Stamp Program, *Annual State Level Data,* Internet site <http://www.fns.usda.gov/>; Column 2, U.S., Department of Labor, Employment and Training Administration, *Unemployment Insurance Financial Data Handbook,* Internet site <http://atlas.doleta.gov/unemploy/>; Column 3, National Academy of Social Insurance, *Workers' Compensation: Benefits, Coverage, and Costs, 2005,* Internet site <http://www.nasi.org/>; Columns 4, 5, U.S., Department of Health and Human Services, Centers for Medicare and Medicaid Services, *Fiscal Year 2004 National MSIS Tables,* Internet site <http://www.cms.hhs.gov/> and Administration for Children and Families, ACF News, *TANF Recipients, December 2006,* Internet site <http://www.acf.hhs.gov/>; Column 6, U.S., Department of Health and Human Services, Social Security Administration, *Social Security Bulletin: Annual Statistical Supplement, 2006,* Internet site <http://www.ssa.gov/>. All Internet sites were accessed August 29, 2007.

Table 25.10. SOCIAL STATISTICS AND INDICATORS: ELECTION AND PUBLIC SAFETY CHARACTERISTICS OF FLORIDA, OTHER SUNBELT STATES, OTHER POPULOUS STATES, AND THE UNITED STATES

State	Elections: Percentage casting votes for presidential electors 2004	Elections: Women in state legislatures 2007 (percentage)	Elections: Hispanic elected officials 2005 A/	Public safety: Adults on probation per 100,000 resident adults 2005	Public safety: FTE police protection 2005 B/	Public safety: Average daily operating expenditure per inmate 2001 (dollars)
			Sunbelt states			
Florida	56.8	23.8	119	2,002	40,831	55.32
Alabama	54.8	12.9	0	1,121	9,838	22.27
Arizona	48.0	34.4	362	1,606	14,646	61.58
Arkansas	50.8	20.7	1	1,431	5,963	42.79
California	47.2	28.3	1,021	1,462	66,674	68.64
Georgia	50.8	19.5	7	(NA)	20,456	54.41
Louisiana	58.0	17.4	2	1,133	12,528	35.48
Mississippi	52.9	13.8	0	1,096	6,211	35.05
New Mexico	53.6	29.5	633	1,287	4,365	76.81
North Carolina	54.5	24.7	4	1,693	19,725	73.93
Oklahoma	55.0	12.8	1	1,065	7,502	44.68
South Carolina	51.0	8.8	1	1,212	10,054	45.92
Tennessee	54.0	15.9	2	1,072	13,276	49.88
Texas	45.7	20.4	2,082	2,580	45,765	37.83
Virginia	56.5	17.1	1	788	15,793	62.85
			Other populous states			
Illinois	55.7	27.7	81	1,500	37,458	59.85
Indiana	53.2	18.7	13	2,583	12,564	59.84
Massachusetts	59.1	24.5	20	3,350	19,476	103.34
Michigan	63.8	19.6	18	2,350	19,135	89.11
New Jersey	55.2	19.2	107	2,117	26,395	74.92
New York	50.8	23.6	68	810	73,003	100.92
Ohio	64.8	17.4	7	2,745	24,833	72.04
Pennsylvania	60.3	14.6	16	1,741	25,405	87.40
United States	55.5	23.5	4,853	1,858	671,717	62.05

(NA) Not available.
A/ Persons of Hispanic origin may be of any race.
B/ Full-time equivalent state and local police officers with the power of arrest.

Source: U.S., Department of Commerce, Census Bureau, Columns 1 and 3, *Statistical Abstract of the United States, 2007,* and Column 5, State and Local Government Employment and Payroll 2005, Internet site <http://www.census.gov/>; Column 2, Center for the American Woman and Politics (CAWP), Eagleton Institute of Politics, Rutgers University, *Women in State Legislatures, 2007,* Internet site <http://www.cawp.rutgers.edu/>; U.S., Department of Justice, Bureau of Justice Statistics, Column 4, *Bureau of Justice Statistics Bulletin: Probation and Parole in the United States, 2005,* and Column 6, *State Prison Expenditures, 2001,* Internet site <http://www.ojp.usdoj.gov/bjs/>. All Internet sites were accessed March 30, 2007.

Table 25.11. SOCIAL STATISTICS AND INDICATORS: GOVERNMENTAL EXPENDITURE CHARACTERISTICS OF FLORIDA, OTHER SUNBELT STATES, OTHER POPULOUS STATES, AND THE UNITED STATES

State	Federal government expenditure, by function, per capita, 2005 (dollars)					
	Total	Education	Public welfare	Health and hospitals	Highways	Police protection
			Sunbelt states			
Florida	3,963.14	1,092.42	915.16	179.57	317.22	26.98
Alabama	4,627.38	1,747.91	1,093.35	482.15	274.25	30.80
Arizona	4,024.36	1,316.27	1,037.99	223.84	292.08	34.46
Arkansas	4,911.98	1,928.24	1,183.99	321.46	344.23	35.83
California	5,802.14	1,792.09	1,454.41	401.58	247.27	34.37
Georgia	3,701.77	1,466.03	1,024.86	178.54	100.47	24.74
Louisiana	4,748.29	1,492.03	1,005.39	480.21	283.31	60.76
Mississippi	5,055.80	1,534.22	1,463.32	361.70	340.23	27.31
New Mexico	6,541.61	2,117.16	1,592.85	446.21	349.09	69.97
North Carolina	4,552.60	1,650.15	1,112.93	297.59	377.84	43.41
Oklahoma	4,433.55	1,635.33	1,064.85	197.87	303.16	37.43
South Carolina	5,347.15	1,525.38	1,234.86	439.32	339.23	39.49
Tennessee	4,027.98	1,169.97	1,562.79	229.85	274.00	25.69
Texas	3,548.80	1,280.04	860.41	168.75	318.72	21.44
Virginia	4,334.88	1,535.88	806.18	394.74	353.15	77.68
			Other populous states			
Illinois	4,360.76	1,185.89	1,138.20	274.14	277.28	30.19
Indiana	4,221.43	1,511.42	983.19	144.61	303.41	37.59
Massachusetts	5,910.60	1,345.95	1,718.88	177.14	275.59	69.90
Michigan	5,089.52	2,038.12	1,200.53	285.47	274.18	32.09
New Jersey	5,656.66	1,584.29	1,098.63	273.64	257.45	58.71
New York	7,081.61	1,657.09	2,208.93	495.40	207.76	43.18
Ohio	5,279.03	1,561.15	1,252.86	373.42	284.95	22.68
Pennsylvania	5,065.01	1,341.55	1,567.35	326.02	392.79	49.59
United States 1/	4,959.28	1,534.88	1,243.84	308.70	304.46	38.32

See footnotes at end of table. Continued . . .

Table 25.11. SOCIAL STATISTICS AND INDICATORS: GOVERNMENTAL EXPENDITURE CHARACTERISTICS OF FLORIDA, OTHER SUNBELT STATES, OTHER POPULOUS STATES, AND THE UNITED STATES (Continued)

	Federal government expenditure per capita, 2004 (dollars)					
State	Total	Grants to state and local govern-ments	Salaries and wages	Direct payments to indivi-duals 1/	Procure-ments	Other
			Sunbelt states			
Florida	7,008.82	1,127.17	597.49	2,761.93	657.99	1,864.24
Alabama	8,619.41	1,546.92	770.91	2,854.30	1,677.61	1,769.68
Arizona	7,308.59	1,456.10	628.13	2,253.24	1,705.62	1,265.49
Arkansas	7,080.08	1,701.21	548.37	2,689.63	307.90	1,832.97
California	6,474.30	1,519.32	613.74	1,785.20	1,121.47	1,434.57
Georgia	6,246.52	1,331.77	942.81	2,010.10	658.31	1,303.52
Louisiana	7,297.55	1,724.33	624.06	2,210.34	756.99	1,981.93
Mississippi	7,694.78	1,852.91	721.24	2,513.48	817.25	1,789.91
New Mexico	10,436.65	2,449.73	1,088.63	2,459.30	3,138.17	1,300.84
North Carolina	6,466.69	1,472.21	842.63	2,356.94	460.48	1,334.43
Oklahoma	7,561.66	1,495.81	982.76	2,602.22	795.77	1,685.09
South Carolina	7,158.33	1,463.79	751.77	2,575.36	998.75	1,368.66
Tennessee	7,700.53	1,671.48	589.01	2,460.03	1,375.74	1,604.26
Texas	6,307.62	1,235.77	653.19	1,857.05	1,199.14	1,362.47
Virginia	12,150.14	1,071.21	2,190.73	2,812.66	4,735.38	1,340.15
			Other populous states			
Illinois	6,042.99	1,300.27	551.12	2,013.35	517.78	1,660.48
Indiana	6,079.04	1,192.18	393.97	2,247.51	641.62	1,603.77
Massachusetts	8,278.72	2,162.57	554.39	2,210.92	1,422.44	1,928.40
Michigan	5,981.49	1,308.01	356.99	2,266.05	407.34	1,643.10
New Jersey	6,353.04	1,302.83	497.51	2,175.22	704.95	1,672.53
New York	7,484.37	2,600.94	471.74	2,143.26	462.31	1,806.11
Ohio	6,387.57	1,441.11	486.61	2,290.90	605.26	1,563.69
Pennsylvania	7,649.36	1,605.30	532.71	2,671.78	750.52	2,089.05
United States 2/	7,222.62	1,545.08	749.55	2,250.36	1,089.06	1,588.58

1/ Retirement and disability.
2/ Average.
Note: Some data may be preliminary.

Source: U.S., Department of Commerce, Census Bureau, Columns 1-6, *2005 State Government Finance Data,* issued February 2007; *Columns 7-12, Consolidated Federal Funds Report for Fiscal Year 2004, State and County Areas,* issued December 2005. All data are from Internet site <http://www.census.gov/> (accessed 4, May 2007).

Table 25.12. SOCIAL STATISTICS AND INDICATORS: GEOGRAPHY, CLIMATE, AND ENVIRONMENTAL CHARACTERISTICS OF FLORIDA, OTHER SUNBELT STATES OTHER POPULOUS STATES, AND THE UNITED STATES

State	Federally owned land 2004 A/ (percentage)	Climate 1/ Average annual days with rainfall .01 inch or more 2/	Climate 1/ Highest annual temper-ature 2/	Climate 1/ Lowest annual temper-ature 2/	Environment Chemical toxic releases 2005 (pounds)	Environment Hazardous waste sites 2005 B/
			Sunbelt states			
Florida	8.2	131	98	30	129,866,857	49
Alabama	1.6	117	106	-6	122,888,800	13
Arizona	48.1	36	122	17	65,121,394	8
Arkansas	7.2	104	112	-5	49,461,442	10
California	45.3	35	112	5	43,653,705	93
Georgia	3.8	115	105	-8	130,424,788	15
Louisiana	5.1	114	102	11	125,244,675	11
Mississippi	7.3	109	107	2	58,618,046	4
New Mexico	41.8	60	107	-17	15,105,066	12
North Carolina	11.8	111	104	-5	139,459,424	31
Oklahoma	3.6	83	110	-8	27,299,988	10
South Carolina	2.9	104	104	5	75,927,679	26
Tennessee	3.2	107	108	-13	143,793,237	13
Texas	1.9	79	113	-1	261,872,877	43
Virginia	9.9	114	105	-12	73,947,822	29
			Other populous states			
Illinois	1.8	124	104	-27	122,338,475	42
Indiana	2.0	126	104	-27	249,202,754	30
Massachusetts	1.9	127	102	-12	7,656,873	31
Michigan	10.0	135	104	-21	101,887,835	65
New Jersey	3.1	110	102	-3	23,912,385	115
New York	0.8	121	106	-15	42,447,044	86
Ohio	1.7	156	104	-20	276,920,721	30
Pennsylvania	2.5	117	104	-7	156,651,991	93
United States	28.8	(X)	(X)	(X)	4,339,463,751	1,243

(X) Not applicable.
A/ Land owned by the federal government as a percentage of total land area.
B/ Sites on the National Priority List as of December 31.
1/ Data are for a major city in each state.
2/ Period of record through 2006. Temperatures are in degrees Farenheit.

Source: Column 1, U.S., General Services Administration, Office of Governmentwide Policy, *Federal Real Property Profile as of September 30, 2004*, Internet site <http://www.gsa.gov/>; Columns 2-4, U.S., Department of Commerce, National Oceanic and Atmospheric Administration, National Climatic Data Center, *Comparative Climatic Data*, Internet site <http://www.ncdc.noaa.gov/>; Columns 5-6, U.S., Environmental Protection Agency, *2005 TRI Public Data Release,* and *National Priorities List,* Internet site <http://www.epa gov/>. All Internet sites were accessed July 25, 2007.

INTERNATIONAL COMPARISONS

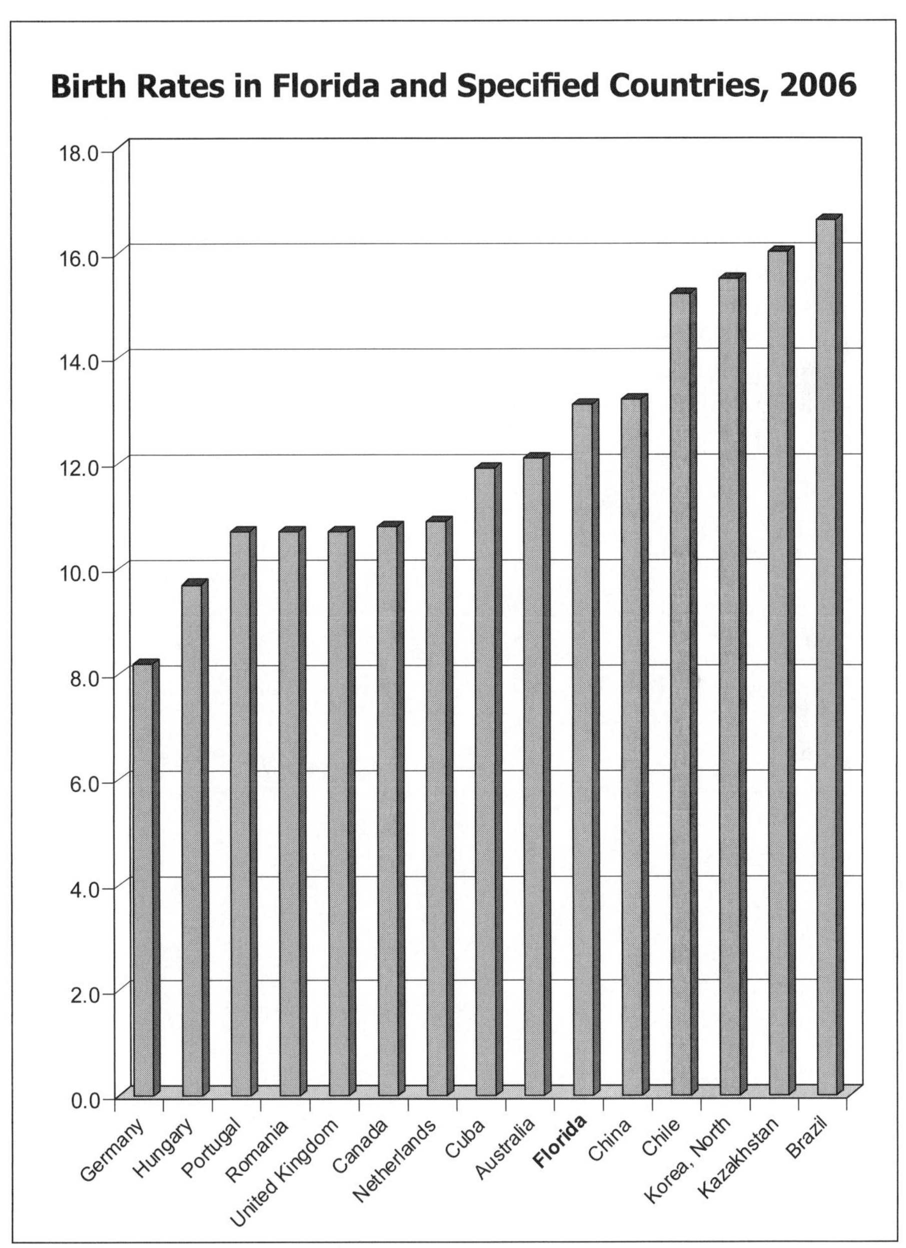

Source: Table 26.02

Section 26.00
International Comparisons

This International Comparisons section attempts to compare specified Florida characteristics to those of the United States and other countries in an effort to depict Florida globally. It is our goal to expand this section in future years as more and more relative comparative international data becomes available.

Sources. The primary source of information on statistics from other countries thus far is the U.S. Census Bureau, using data found on the Census Bureau's Web site and data from the *Statistical Abstract of the United States.* Other Census Bureau sources include "State and County QuickFacts," "International Data Base," and the Foreign Trade Statistics office's *State by Top 25 Commodities.*

The U.S. Department of Commerce's Bureau of Economic Analysis (BEA) provided data in *Survey of Current Business,* "U.S. Affiliates of Foreign Companies, Operations in 2004," and "Foreign Direct Investment in the U.S.: Financial and Operating Data for U.S. Affiliates of Foreign Multinational Companies."

The Economic Research Service office of the U.S. Department of Agriculture provided data online about agricultural exports in *State Export Data.*

Section 26.00
International Comparisons

Tables listed by major heading

Heading | Page

Table 26.01. LAND AND POPULATION: LAND AREA AND POPULATION CHARACTERISTICS IN FLORIDA, THE UNITED STATES, AND SPECIFIED OUTLYING AREAS, 2000

Item	Florida	United States	Puerto Rico	Virgin Islands	Guam	American Samoa	Northern Mariana Islands
Land area (square miles)	53,937	3,537,422	3,425	134	210	77	179
Total resident population	15,982,378	281,421,906	3,808,610	108,612	154,805	57,291	69,221
Per square mile	296.4	79.6	1,112.0	810.5	737.2	744.0	386.7
Percentage increase, 1990-2000	23.5	13.2	8.1	6.7	16.3	22.5	59.7
Male	7,797,715	138,053,563	1,833,577	51,864	79,181	29,264	31,984
Female	8,184,663	143,368,343	1,975,033	56,748	75,624	28,027	37,237
Males per 100 females	95.3	96.3	92.8	91.4	104.7	104.4	85.9
Median age (years)	38.7	35.3	32.1	33.4	27.4	21.3	28.7
Martial status, person 15 years and over	12,946,990	221,148,671	2,903,329	80,207	107,649	35,079	53,632
Never married	3,076,457	59,913,370	813,784	32,764	37,711	12,741	22,462
Married 1/	7,032,798	120,231,273	1,509,403	31,223	57,505	19,519	28,224
Separated	309,160	4,769,220	104,897	2,639	1,453	437	916
Widowed	1,026,014	14,674,500	197,123	4,078	4,253	1,570	1,121
Divorced	1,502,561	21,560,308	278,122	9,503	6,727	812	909
Households and families							
Households	6,337,929	105,480,101	1,261,325	40,648	38,769	9,349	14,055
Families	4,210,760	71,787,347	1,004,080	26,636	32,367	8,706	9,407
Husband-wife families	3,192,266	54,493,232	682,804	13,498	22,693	6,596	6,445
Nonfamily households	2,127,169	33,692,754	257,245	14,012	6,402	643	4,648
Average household size	2.5	2.6	3.0	2.6	3.9	6.1	3.7
Average family size	3.0	3.1	3.4	3.3	4.3	6.2	4.2
Births	204,125	4,058,814	59,333	1,564	3,766	1,731	1,431

1/ Includes other family types not shown separately.

Source: U.S., Department of Commerce, Census Bureau, *Statistical Abstract of the United States, 2003,* Internet site <http://www.census.gov/> and "State and County QuickFacts," Internet site <http://quickfacts.census.gov/> (accessed 8, August 2006).

Table 26.02. POPULATION AND VITAL STATISTICS: POPULATION ESTIMATES, 2006, AND PROJECTIONS, 2030, AND VITAL STATISTICS, 2006, IN FLORIDA, THE UNITED STATES AND OTHER SPECIFIED COUNTRIES

	Population, 2006					Vital statistics, 2006 A/		
	Midyear (1,000)	Persons per square kilometer	Persons aged 65 and over (percent-age)	Projec-tions 2030 (1,000)	Land area (square kilometers)	Birth rates	Death rates	Infant mortality rates
United States	298,444,215	32.6	12.5	363,811	9,161,923	14.1	8.3	6.4
Florida 1/	18,349,132	131.3	16.6	26,419	139,697	13.1	9.4	(NA)
Australia	20,264,082	2.7	13.1	23,497	7,617,931	12.1	7.5	4.6
Brazil	188,078,227	22.2	6.1	222,838	8,456,511	16.6	6.2	28.6
Cameroon	17,657,856	37.6	3.2	25,997	469,440	35.6	13.0	67.2
Canada	33,098,932	3.6	13.3	39,128	9,093,507	10.8	7.8	4.7
Chile	16,134,219	21.5	8.2	18,903	748,800	15.2	5.8	8.6
China	1,313,973,713	140.9	7.7	1,461,528	9,326,411	13.2	7.0	23.1
Cuba	11,382,820	102.7	10.6	11,579	110,860	11.9	7.2	6.2
Ecuador	13,547,510	48.9	5.0	17,946	276,840	22.3	4.2	22.9
Egypt	78,887,007	79.2	4.5	109,044	995,451	22.9	5.2	31.3
Germany	82,422,299	236.0	19.4	79,573	349,223	8.2	10.6	4.1
Ghana	22,478,658	97.3	3.5	32,641	230,940	30.5	9.7	54.9
Guatemala	12,454,747	114.9	3.6	18,643	108,430	29.6	5.4	30.8
Hungary	9,981,334	108.1	15.2	9,250	92,341	9.7	13.1	8.4
Iraq	26,783,383	62.0	3.0	43,873	432,162	32.0	5.4	48.6
Kazakhstan	15,233,244	5.7	8.2	15,979	2,669,800	16.0	9.4	28.3
Korea, North	23,113,019	192.0	8.2	26,215	120,409	15.5	7.1	23.3
Madagascar	18,872,164	32.5	3.1	38,140	581,540	38.8	8.7	58.5
Malaysia	24,385,858	74.2	4.7	35,306	328,549	22.9	5.0	17.2
Mexico	107,449,525	55.9	5.8	135,172	1,923,039	20.7	4.7	20.3
Mozambique	20,530,023	26.2	2.8	24,323	784,089	39.0	20.7	112.1
Nepal	28,287,147	197.6	3.7	42,839	143,181	31.0	9.3	65.3
Netherlands	16,491,461	486.7	14.2	17,673	33,883	10.9	8.7	5.0
Portugal	10,605,870	115.3	4.8	10,731	91,951	10.7	10.5	5.0
Romania	22,303,552	96.8	14.7	20,827	230,339	10.7	11.8	25.5
Saudi Arabia	27,019,731	13.8	2.4	38,142	1,960,582	29.3	2.6	12.8
Sri Lanka	20,717,932	320.0	7.6	22,937	64,740	17.3	6.0	19.9
Syria	18,881,361	102.6	3.3	28,349	184,051	27.8	4.8	28.6
Uganda	29,206,503	146.2	2.2	67,604	199,710	48.1	13.0	68.5
United Kingdom	60,609,153	250.9	15.8	64,304	241,590	10.7	10.1	5.1
Uzbekistan	27,307,134	64.2	4.8	39,415	425,400	26.4	7.8	70.0
Venezuela	25,730,435	29.2	5.2	33,429	882,050	21.5	5.1	21.5
Yemen	21,456,188	40.6	2.6	45,464	527,969	42.9	8.3	59.9
Zimbabwe	12,236,805	31.6	3.5	12,842	386,669	28.0	21.8	51.7

(NA) Not available.

A/ Death rates are per 1,000 population. Infant mortality rates represent deaths to children under age 1 per 1,000 live births. Fertility rates are per 1,000 females of child-bearing age.

1/ Florida's populations are for April 1.

Source: U.S., Department of Commerce, Census Bureau, "International Data Base," Internet site <http://www.census.gov/ipc/> (accessed 29, August 2007). Florida data from sources cited in previous tables throughout this publication.

Table 26.03. FOREIGN DIRECT INVESTMENT: GROSS BOOK VALUE AND EMPLOYMENT OF U.S. AFFILIATES OF FOREIGN COMPANIES IN FLORIDA, OTHER SUNBELT STATES, OTHER POPULOUS STATES, AND THE UNITED STATES
1995, 2000, AND 2004

	Gross book value 1/				Total employment				
							2004 A/		
	1995	2000	2004 A/	Percentage change 1995 to 2004	1995	2000	Number	Percentage change 1995 to 2004	Percentage of all businesses
Florida	24,865	38,755	31,731	27.6	210.0	244.2	238.4	13.5	3.6
Sunbelt states									
Alabama	10,598	16,646	17,812	68.1	60.6	65.0	70.6	16.5	4.4
Arizona	6,699	10,716	10,157	51.6	51.9	60.8	62.9	21.2	3.1
Arkansas	3,666	4,613	6,084	66.0	32.1	34.7	32.0	-0.3	3.2
California	96,576	121,040	119,815	24.1	548.6	638.9	547.0	-0.3	4.3
Georgia	22,432	29,510	29,261	30.4	180.1	199.5	175.9	-2.3	5.2
Louisiana	20,543	31,160	33,078	61.0	51.0	51.3	49.9	-2.2	3.1
Mississippi	3,055	4,121	8,016	162.4	22.6	20.0	25.5	12.8	2.8
New Mexico	4,363	5,801	3,943	-9.6	16.2	12.0	12.6	-22.2	2.1
North Carolina	21,475	29,931	27,681	28.9	225.3	239.1	198.0	-12.1	6.0
Oklahoma	5,448	7,635	8,526	56.5	34.2	34.7	31.7	-7.3	2.7
South Carolina	13,438	23,563	22,742	69.2	111.6	129.1	121.7	9.1	7.9
Tennessee	14,227	20,842	21,280	49.6	136.3	137.7	126.9	-6.9	5.4
Texas	68,142	110,032	99,878	46.6	326.4	384.9	341.2	4.5	4.2
Virginia	15,129	23,570	17,751	17.3	141.4	158.0	133.7	-5.4	4.5
Other populous states									
Illinois	34,305	48,425	47,000	37.0	237.0	277.2	235.6	-0.6	4.6
Indiana	18,782	30,179	32,966	75.5	136.9	143.8	132.5	-3.2	5.2
Massachusetts	12,707	23,875	26,126	105.6	141.5	207.7	182.9	29.3	6.3
Michigan	21,370	39,238	45,149	111.3	170.3	228.4	201.0	18.0	5.3
New Jersey	26,175	35,115	40,187	53.5	205.2	234.6	219.7	7.1	6.4
New York	52,992	68,522	75,024	41.6	343.8	415.8	377.0	9.7	5.3
Ohio	29,932	37,530	37,578	25.5	222.1	228.3	203.6	-8.3	4.3
Pennsylvania	24,432	34,106	35,817	46.6	231.6	253.9	225.6	-2.6	4.5
United States 2/	733,089	1,070,422	1,207,106	64.7	4,898.9	5,632.4	5,099.8	4.1	4.5

A/ Preliminary.
1/ Value of property, plant, and equipment.
2/ Excludes Puerto Rico, other U.S. areas, foreign, and unspecified affiliates.
Note: Gross book value and employment of U.S. affiliates of foreign companies. A U.S. affiliate is a U.S. business in which one foreign owner (individual, branch, partnership, association, trust corporation, or government) has a direct or indirect voting interest of 10 percent or more and include nonbank U.S. affiliates. Book values in millions of dollars; employment in thousands, unless otherwise indicated.

Source: U.S., Department of Commerce, Bureau of Economic Analysis, *Survey of Current Business,* "U.S. Affiliates of Foreign Companies, Operations in 2004," and "Foreign Direct Investment in the U.S.: Financial and Operating Data for U.S. Affiliates of Foreign Multinational Companies," Internet site <http://www.bea.gov/> (accessed 4, April 2007).

Table 26.04. EXPORTS: U.S. TOTAL EXPORTS AND AGRICULTURAL EXPORTS BY STATE OF ORIGIN IN FLORIDA, OTHER SUNBELT STATES, OTHER POPULOUS STATES, AND THE UNITED STATES, SPECIFIED YEARS 2000 THROUGH 2006

(amounts in millions of dollars)

	Exports 1/				Agricultural exports 2/		
	2000	2005	2006	Percentage change 2000 to 2006	2000	2006	Percentage change 2000 to 2006
Florida	26,543	33,377	38,545	45.2	1,289	1,699	31.8
				Sunbelt states			
Alabama	7,317	10,796	13,878	89.7	393	572	45.7
Arizona	14,334	14,950	18,287	27.6	394	520	32.0
Arkansas	2,599	3,862	4,265	64.1	1,235	1,912	54.8
California	119,640	116,819	127,746	6.8	6,685	10,475	56.7
Georgia	14,925	20,577	20,073	34.5	859	1,356	57.8
Louisiana	16,814	19,232	23,503	39.8	432	641	48.3
Mississippi	2,726	4,008	4,674	71.5	617	950	53.8
New Mexico	2,391	2,540	2,892	21.0	128	248	93.0
North Carolina	17,946	19,463	21,218	18.2	1,294	2,045	58.0
Oklahoma	3,072	4,314	4,375	42.4	553	754	36.3
South Carolina	8,565	13,944	13,615	59.0	266	482	81.4
Tennessee	11,592	19,070	22,020	90.0	489	924	89.0
Texas	103,866	128,761	150,888	45.3	3,063	3,805	24.3
Virginia	11,698	12,216	14,104	20.6	454	588	29.5
				Other populous states			
Illinois	31,438	35,868	42,085	33.9	2,843	3,787	33.2
Indiana	15,386	21,476	22,620	47.0	1,412	2,044	44.7
Massachusetts	20,514	22,043	24,047	17.2	117	167	42.0
Michigan	33,845	37,584	40,405	19.4	857	1,161	35.5
New Jersey	18,638	21,080	27,002	44.9	125	219	76.0
New York	42,846	50,492	57,369	33.9	481	671	39.5
Ohio	26,322	34,801	37,833	43.7	1,160	1,716	48.0
Pennsylvania	18,792	22,271	26,334	40.1	914	1,354	48.2
United States	771,994	894,631	1,023,109	32.5	50,744	68,721	35.4

1/ Based on origin of movement.
2/ Data presented on a Balance of Payment (BOP) basis.

Source: U.S., Department of Commerce, Census Bureau, Foreign Trade Statistics, *State by Top 25 Commodities, 2006,* Internet site <http://www.census.gov/>; and U.S., Department of Agriculture, Economic Research Service, *State Export Data,* Internet site <http://www.ers.usda.gov/> (both sites accessed 14, June 2007).

Appendix
Summary of Sources

State sources. Most state publications used in the *Abstract* are available free of charge either on the Internet in printable or downloadable form or from the agency issuing the report. Printed document supplies are frequently limited and sometimes requests cannot be honored unless they come from other state agencies. The agency directory and the 411 listing located in the state's Web site at www.myflorida.com is an excellent reference for contacting state agencies. Florida has a system of state depository libraries, coordinated by the Division of Library Services, Florida Department of State, R.A. Gray Building, Tallahassee. All state agency publications are required to be on file in depository libraries or available for interlibrary loan. The reference departments of most libraries are willing to answer questions about data in these publications if the requests are not too time-consuming. The Florida Division of State Library Services issues a monthly and annual summary of state agency publications called *Florida Public Documents*.

Depository libraries of the State of Florida include the public libraries of Bay, Broward, and Orange counties, Cocoa, Jacksonville, Miami Beach, Miami-Dade, Ocala, St. Petersburg, Tampa-Hillsborough, and West Palm Beach. University libraries designated as depositories are those at Central Florida, Florida Atlantic, Florida (Gainesville), Florida International, Florida State, Miami, North Florida, South Florida, West Florida, Jacksonville, and Stetson. The State Library of Florida in the R.A. Gray Building in Tallahassee also is a depository.

Federal sources. Most federal publications are available on the Internet. Many other federal reports are available without charge from the agency issuing the information. Some must be purchased from the Superintendent of Documents, U.S. Government Printing Office (GPO), Washington, D.C. 20402 or from a local Government Printing Office bookstore. The *Statistical Abstract of the United States*, available on the Internet, is similar in scope to the *Florida Statistical Abstract* and provides a comprehensive focus on state and national data. Readers interested in information about the nation, its regions, and states are referred to it.

The federal government also maintains a system of depository libraries in all fifty states, usually the same libraries as state depositories. The University of Florida is designated as a regional depository library and is required to receive and retain one copy of all depository government publications made available to depository libraries. Many of the libraries listed above as state depositories are also federal depositories and some are not listed. Refer to the annual directory printed by the University of Florida Libraries, *Federal Document Depositories and Resource Information for Florida and Puerto Rico*.

Private sources. A number of private agencies and associations issue publications or reports which have been used in this and recent editions of *Abstract*. Some are copyrighted and have been used with permission. Several have additional information that can be obtained for a fee.

American Council of Life Insurance, Washington, D.C.
American Public Power Association, Washington, D.C.
Center for the American Woman and Politics (CAWP), Eagleton Institute of Politics, Rutgers University
Enterprise Florida, Inc., Orlando, Florida
Federal Deposit Insurance Corporation, Washington, D.C.
Florida Association of Realtors
Louis de la Parte Florida Mental Health Institute, University of South Florida
Joint Center for Political and Economic Studies, Washington, D.C.
National Education Association, Washington, D.C.
National Academy of Social Insurance, Washington, D.C.
VISIT FLORIDA, Florida Commission on Tourism

BEBR Publications. The Bureau of Economic and Business Research (BEBR) at the University of Florida can supply a variety of detailed information about Florida:

Florida Estimates of Population. Intercensal estimates of the population of Florida, its counties, cities, and unincorporated areas. Also includes census counts, components of population change, and density figures. Published annually. A summary of census results is published in census years.

Florida Population Studies. Bulletins providing information on age, race, sex, and Hispanic origin components of Florida's population, household numbers and average household size, projections of population, discussions of estimation and projection methodology, and other topics related to population. Published three times a year.

Special Population Reports. The *Revised Annual Population Estimates by County in Florida, with Components of Growth, 1999-2000* is the most recent of these five releases. Previous releases include the 1995 estimates of Hispanic population with age and sex detail, revised 1980-90 population estimates by county, an evaluation of population projection errors for Florida counties, and an evaluation of 1990 population estimation. Published periodically.

Florida County Rankings. At-a-glance ranked statistics for more than 800 current data topics for all Florida counties, with a state comparison for each topic and pertinent data maps.

Florida County Perspective. Individual ranking reports, one for each of Florida's 67 counties in the same category variables used in *Florida County Rankings*, with historical state and county data summaries.

Building Permit Activity in Florida. Monthly comparisons with year-to-date data, including an annual summary, of the value and number of units permitted in the state, counties, cities, and unincorporated areas of Florida.

Annual State and County Building Permits and Housing Starts, 1976-2006. Annual number of single- and multifamily units permitted and single- and multifamily housing starts for the state and counties of Florida from 1976 forward. Data provided by the U.S. Census Bureau.

Tough Choices: Shaping Florida's Future. Jointly produced with the Leroy Collins Institute at Florida State University, this report provides a politically neutral study of Florida's tax policy to address the question of whether or not Florida's tax structure will support Floridians' future needs. Free at www.bebr.ufl.edu.

1990 Census Handbook: Florida. Over 600 pages of census information for Florida, its counties, congressional districts and most populous cities and comparisons of Florida with the other forty-nine states. No update is scheduled.

Gross and Taxable Sales Reports. Monthly and annual printouts of information from the Florida Department of Revenue reports of gross and taxable sales for the 6% sales and use taxes. Includes gross sales, taxable sales, tax collected, and reporting units. Information available in two formats: (1) a category report listing data for one category for all 67 counties and (2) a county report listing data for one county and all 99 categories. Data are provided by e-mail.

Florida Consumer Confidence Index. Monthly survey data from the UF Survey Research Center on Florida consumers' confidence in the national and local economies, buying plans, personal financial condition, and special topics. Free at www.bebr.ufl.edu.

Florida Focus. An online publication series covering a broad range of economic, demographic, and public policy topics focusing on the state of Florida. The objective of this series is to provide rigorous but readable discussions of issues and trends with particular relevance to Floridians. Free at www.bebr.ufl.edu.

BEBR Monographs. In-depth analyses of special topics relevant to an understanding of the Florida economic and business climate. Issued periodically. Current titles include *Population Projections: What Do We Really Know?*; *Local Government Economic Analysis Using Microcomputers*; *Cuban Immigration and Immigrants in Florida and the United States: Implications for Immigration Policy*; *Urban Development Issues: What is Controversial in Urban Sprawl?*; *Preparing the Economic Element of the Comprehensive Plan*; *Concurrency Management Systems in Florida: A Catalog and Analysis*; and *The Economic Impact of Local Government Comprehensive Plans*.

BEBR Data Base. A computerized data management system containing extensive economic data for the United States, Florida, and all counties. Provides PC access to current and historical data for Florida, any of its counties and Metropolitan Statistical Areas, and for the United States. Continuously updated.

For pricing and ordering information, please contact:
Bureau of Economic and Business Research
University of Florida
PO Box 117145
221 Matherly Hall
Gainesville, FL 32611-7145
(352) 392-0171 ext. 212
FAX: (352) 392-4739
www.bebr.ufl.edu

Glossary

ALIEN. Person who is not a citizen of the United States whether or not he/she is a resident, legally or illegally.

AMERICAN INDIAN, ESKIMO, OR ALEUT POPULATION. See Race.

AMERICAN INDIAN OR ALASKA NATIVE POPULATION. See Race.

ANCESTRY. A person's nationality group, lineage, or the country in which the person or the person's parents or ancestors were born before their arrival in the U.S. Different from other indicators of ethnicity, such as country of birth and language spoken in home and is a separate characteristic from race.

ASIAN OR PACIFIC ISLANDER POPULATION. See Race.

ASIAN POPULATION. See Race.

BLACK OR AFRICAN AMERICAN POPULATION. See Race.

BLACK POPULATION. See Race.

BUSINESS ESTABLISHMENT. A commercial enterprise.

CHILDREN. Sons and daughters classified as "own child of householder," including stepchildren and adopted children, who have never been married and are under age 18.

CIVILIAN LABOR FORCE. See Labor Force.

CLASS OF WORKERS. Private wage and salary workers who work for a private employer for wages, salary, commission, tips, pay-in-kind, or at price rates. Private employers include churches and other nonprofit organizations. Also includes persons who consider themselves self-employed but who work for corporations where in most cases these persons own or are a part of a group that owns controlling interest in the corporation.
Government workers who work for a governmental unit, regardless of the activity of the particular agency.
Self-employed workers who work for profit or fees in their own unincorporated business, profession, or trade, or who operate a farm. Includes owner-operators of large stores and manufacturing establishments, as well as small merchants, independent craft-persons and professionals, farmers, peddlers, and other persons who conduct enterprises of their own.
Unpaid family workers who work without pay on a farm or in a business operated by a person to whom they are related by blood or marriage.

COLLEGE STUDENTS. See Residency.

COMMUNITY HEALTH PURCHASING ALLIANCE (CHPA). Authorized by the 1993 Florida legislature to assist members of the alliance in securing the highest quality health care at the lowest possible price. Membership is voluntary and available primarily to businesses that have 50 or fewer employees. CHPAs are state-chartered, not-for-profit, private purchasing organizations and have exclusive territories.

COMMUTE. Travel back and forth regularly, usually between place of residence and place of work.

CONSOLIDATED METROPOLITAN STATISTICAL AREA (CMSA). A large metropolitan complex with a population over one million in which individual metropolitan components, Primary Metropolitan Statistical Areas (PMSAs), have been defined.

CONSUMER PRICE INDEX (CPI). A measure of the average level of prices over time in a fixed market collection of goods and services. The index is intended to represent prices of most items and services that people purchase in daily living, and is calculated to represent purchases by urban wage earners and clerical workers or by all urban consumers.

CONTRACT RENT. See Rent.

CORE BASED STATISTICAL AREA (CBSA). Established in 2003 by the U.S. Office of Management and Budget. A statistical geographic entity consisting of the county or counties associated with at least one core (urbanized area or urban cluster) of at least 10,000 population, plus adjacent counties having a high degree of social and economic integration with the core as measured through commuting ties with the counties containing the core. Metropolitan and Micropolitan Statistical Areas are the two categories of Core Based Statistical Areas. See also Metropolitan Statistical Area and Micropolitan Statistical Area.

COUNTY. An administrative subdivision of a state; a local government organization and political jurisdiction authorized and designated by a state's constitution or statutes.

DROPOUT. A student over the age of compulsory school attendance (16) who has voluntarily removed himself from the school system before graduation; or who has not met attendance requirements; or who has withdrawn from school but has not transferred to another public or private school or enrolled in any other educational program; or has withdrawn from school due to hardship without official granting of such withdrawal; or is not eligible to attend school because of reaching the maximum age for an exceptional student program.

EARNINGS. Sum of wage and salary income and net income from farm and nonfarm self-employment. Reported before deductions for personal income taxes, social security, bond purchases, union dues, and other deductions.

EDUCATIONAL ATTAINMENT. Years of school completed.

EMPLOYED PERSONS. All civilians 16 years of age and over that work at all as paid employees for an employer, or in their own business or profession, on their own farm, or who work 15 hours or more as unpaid workers in an enterprise operated by a family member and all those temporarily absent from their jobs due to such factors as illness or vacation (during a given reference week).

ENERGY. The ability to do work; can exist in many forms such as chemical, light, heat, etc.
Primary energy is energy available from conversion of original fuel rather than from a secondary form such as electricity.
Renewables are energy sources that can be used continuously or regenerated quickly such as wind, sunlight, wood, and solid waste.

FAMILY HOUSEHOLD. A householder and one or more other person(s) living in the same household who are related to the householder by birth, marriage, or adoption. All persons in a household who are related to the householder and are regarded as members of his or her family.

FAMILY HOUSEHOLD INCOME. See Income.

FARM. For the 1990 census, property of one acre or more where $1,000 or more of agricultural products were sold from the property in 1989.

FARM POPULATION. See Rural farm population.

FIRM. A business organization or entity consisting of one or more establishment(s) under common ownership or control; a commercial partnership of two or more persons.

GENERAL, SHORT-TERM ACUTE CARE HOSPITAL. Establishment that offers services more intensive than those required for room, board, personal services, and general nursing care. Offers facilities and beds for use beyond 24 hours by individuals requiring diagnosis, treatment, or care for illness, injury, deformity, infirmity, abnormality, disease, or pregnancy. Regularly makes available at least clinical laboratory services, diagnostic radiology services, and treatment facilities for surgery, medical, or obstetrical care, or other definitive medical treatment of similar extent.

GROSS STATE PRODUCT (GSP). The gross market value of the goods and services attributable to labor and property located in a state.

GROUP QUARTERS. All persons not living in households are classified by the Census Bureau as living in group quarters—institutional and noninstitutional. Institutional group quarters are all institutions offering care or custody, e.g., prisons, mental hospitals, nursing homes, juvenile institutions. Noninstitutional quarters include workers' dormitories, monasteries, convents, large rooming houses or boarding houses or communes having at least ten persons unrelated to the resident who maintains the living quarters. Noninstitutional quarters also cover certain living arrangements regardless of the number or relationship of the people in the unit such as military barracks, college dormitories, missions and emergency shelters for the homeless. Data on the homeless also include visible in street locations or predesignated street sites, (e.g., bridges, parks, bus depots) where the homeless congregate.

HISPANIC ORIGIN. Persons who classified themselves in one of the Hispanic-origin categories listed on the census questionnaire—Mexican, Puerto Rican, Cuban, or other Spanish/Hispanic origin. This latter category includes those whose origins are from Spain or the Spanish-speaking countries of Central or South America, or the Dominican Republic, or they are Hispanic-origin persons identifying themselves generally as Spanish, Spanish-American, Hispanic, Latino, etc. Origin can be viewed as the ancestry, nationality group, lineage or country in which the person or person's parents or ancestors were born before their arrival in the U.S. Persons of Hispanic origin may be of any race. Households and families are classified by the Hispanic origin of the householder.

HOMELESS POPULATION. See Group quarters.

HOMEOWNER VACANCY RATE. The proportion of the homeowner inventory which is vacant for sale. Rates are computed by dividing the vacant year-round units for sale only by the sum of the number of owner-occupied units, vacant year-round units sold but awaiting occupancy, and vacant year-round units for sale only.

HOMEOWNER VACANCY RATE. The proportion of the homeowner inventory which is vacant for sale. Rates are computed by dividing the vacant year-round units for sale only by the sum of the number of owner-occupied units, vacant year-round units sold but awaiting occupancy, and vacant year-round units for sale only.

HOUSEHOLD. The person or persons occupying a housing unit. Designation of a household as "family" or "nonfamily" is based on the householder. If the household has family members of the householder, then it is classified as a family household. If the householder is an individual unrelated to other household members, lives alone, or is living in group quarters (not institutionalized), then the household is classified as a nonfamily household.

HOUSEHOLD INCOME. See Income.

HOUSEHOLDER. Person, or one of the persons, in whose name the home is owned or rented and who is listed in column one of the census questionnaire. If there is no such person in the household, any adult household member could be designated as "householder."
Family householder is a householder living with one or more person(s) related to him or her by birth, marriage, or adoption.
Nonfamily householder is a householder living alone or with nonrelatives only.

HOUSING UNIT. A house, an apartment, a group of rooms, or a single room occupied as a separate living quarters, or if vacant, intended for occupancy as a separate living quarters.
Occupied housing unit is the usual place of residence of the person or group of persons living there at the time of the census enumeration, or the unit from which the occupants are only temporarily absent (away on vacation, etc.).
Owner-occupied housing unit is one in which the owner or co-owner lives, whether the unit is owned without lien or mortgaged.
Renter-occupied unit is any unit not classified as owner-occupied, including a unit rented for cash rent or one occupied without payment of cash rent.
Vacant housing unit has no one living in it at the time of census enumeration, unless the occupants are only temporarily absent. May be classified as "seasonal and migratory," or "year-round." Seasonal unit is intended for occupancy during only certain seasons of the year. Migratory unit is held for occupancy for migratory labor employed in farm work during crop season. Year-round vacant unit is available or intended for occupancy at any time of the year.

IMMIGRANTS. Aliens admitted for legal permanent residence in the United States, including persons who may have entered as nonimmigrants or refugees, but who subsequently changed their status to that of a permanent resident.

INCOME. The amount of money or monetary equivalent received during a specified time period in exchange for work performed, sale of goods or property, or from profits made on financial investments.
Adjusted gross income is a tax-defined concept of income. Certain kinds of income such as some portion of capital gains, social security, and in-kind transfer payments are excluded and certain types of expenses such as some trade and business expenses, alimony payments, and contributions to individual retirement plans are deducted.
Family household income and nonfamily household income are compiled by summing and treating as a single amount the money income of all family or nonfamily household members aged 15 and over.
Household income includes the money income of the householder and all other persons aged 15 and over in the household, whether related to the householder or not. Because many households consist of only one person, average household income is usually less than average family income.
Interest, dividend, or net rental income includes interest on savings or bonds, dividends from stockholdings or membership in associations, net royalties, and net income from rental of property to others and receipts from boarders or lodgers.
Labor income is an item generally used for various types of supplemental earnings in cash and in kind.
Mean income is the amount obtained by dividing the total income of a particular statistical universe by the number of units in that universe.
Median income is the amount that divides the income distribution into two equal groups, one having incomes above the median and the other having incomes below the median. For households, families, and unrelated individuals the median income is based on the distribution of the total number of units including those with no income. The median for persons is based on persons with income.
Money income is an income definition of the Census Bureau. It is the sum of amounts reported separately for wage and salary income; net nonfarm self-employment income; net farm self-employment income; interest, dividend, net royalty or rental income; social security or railroad retirement income; public assistance or welfare income; unemployment compensation; alimony; veterans' payments; and all other income. Not included are monies received from the sale of property owned by a recipient; the value of income "in-kind" from food stamps, public housing subsidies, medical care, employer contributions for

pensions, etc.; withdrawal of bank deposits; money borrowed; tax refunds; exchanges of money between relatives living in the same household; gifts and lump-sum inheritances, insurance payments, and other types of lump-sum receipts.

Personal income is an income definition of the Bureau of Economic Analysis. It is the sum of current income received by persons from all sources and is measured before deduction of personal contributions to social insurance programs and income and other personal taxes. It is reported in current dollars and includes the following categories of earnings: private and governmental wages and salaries; labor income; farm and nonfarm proprietors' income; property income; and government and business transfer payments, but excludes transfers among persons. (Also, includes some nonmonetary income such as estimated net rental values—to owner—of owner-occupied homes, and the value of services furnished without payment, and food and fuel produced and consumed on farms.)

Disposable personal income is personal income less personal tax and nontax payments. Personal taxes include income, estate, gift, personal property and license taxes. Nontax payments include fines and penalties, tuition, and donations.

Property income is net rental income, dividends, and interest.

Proprietors' income is net income of owners of unincorporated businesses (farm and nonfarm, with the latter including the income of independent professionals).

Public assistance income includes three items: supplementary security income payments made by federal or state welfare agencies to low-income persons aged 65 or over, blind, or disabled; aid to families with dependent children; and general assistance. Separate payments received for hospital or other medical care are excluded.

Social security income includes social security pensions and survivors' benefits and permanent disability insurance payments made by the Social Security Administration prior to deductions. Medicare reimbursements are not included.

INMATES OF INSTITUTIONS. See Group quarters.

INTEREST, DIVIDEND, OR NET RENTAL INCOME. See Income.

LABOR FORCE. Includes the civilian labor force, which comprises all civilians in the noninstitutional population 16 years and over classified as "employed" or "unemployed" and members of the Armed Forces stationed in the United States.

MANUFACTURED HOUSING. Any prefabricated dwelling such as a mobile home or modular housing.

MANUFACTURING ESTABLISHMENT. An enterprise usually consisting of a single physical location where raw materials are transformed into new products.

MARITAL STATUS. Classification refers to the status of persons aged 15 and over at the time of census enumeration. Couples who live together (unmarried persons, common-law marriages) were allowed to report the marital status they considered the most appropriate. Persons reported as separated are those living apart because of marital discord, with or without a legal separation. Persons in common-law marriages are classified as now married, except separated if they consider this category most appropriate; persons whose only marriage has been annulled are classified as never married; persons married at the time of enumeration (including those separated), widowed, or divorced are classified as ever married. Persons whose current marriage has not ended by widowhood or divorce are classified as now married. This category includes married persons whose spouse may have been (1) temporarily absent for such reasons as travel or hospitalization; (2) absent, including all married persons living in group quarters, employed spouses living away from home or in an institution, or absent in the Armed Forces; and (3) those who are separated.

MARKET VALUE. Amount a seller reasonably expects to obtain in a market for commodities, merchandise, services, or whatever is being sold.

MEDICAID. A jointly funded state and federal health care program for low-income persons. States establish their own eligibility criteria and may set benefits above the minimum established by federal law.

MEDICARE. Federal health insurance program for people aged 65 and over. Also covers (since 1973) eligible disabled persons of any age and persons with chronic kidney disease.

METROPOLITAN POPULATION. Population living inside Metropolitan Statistical Areas (MSAs) or Consolidated Metropolitan Statistical Areas (CMSAs).

METROPOLITAN STATISTICAL AREA (MSA). A Core Based Statistical Area associated with at least one urbanized area that has a population of at least 50,000. The Metropolitan Statistical Area comprises the central county or counties containing the core, plus adjacent outlying counties having a high degree of social and economic integration with the central county as measured through commuting.
See map at front of the book for list of counties in MSAs.

MICROPOLITAN STATISTICAL AREA. A Core Based Statistical Area associated with at least one urban cluster that has a population of at least 10,000, but less than 50,000. The Micropolitan Statistical Area comprises the central county or counties containing the core, plus adjacent outlying counties having a high degree of social and economic integration with the central county as measured through commuting.

MOBILE HOME. Movable dwelling, ten or more feet wide and thirty-five or more feet long (a movable dwelling of less than these dimensions is considered to be a travel trailer or a motor home), designed to be towed on its own chassis and without need of a permanent foundation. Does not include prefabricated or modular housing, travel trailers, and other self-propelled vehicles such as motor homes. Mobile homes or trailers to which one or more permanent rooms have been added or built are classified by the Census Bureau as single-unit, detached housing.

MILITARY PERSONNEL. See Labor force and Residency.

MILL. Unit of monetary value equal to 1/1000 of a U.S. dollar.

MILLAGE RATE. Tax rate stated in mills where one mill produces one dollar of tax for every $1,000 of taxable property.

MONEY INCOME. See Income.

MUNICIPALITY. Political subdivision within which a municipal corporation has been established to provide a general local government for a specific population concentration in a defined area. In Florida, municipalities may be called cities, towns, or villages and have been established either by special acts of the legislature or by general law.

NAICS. Abbreviation of North American Industry Classification System.

NATIVE HAWAIIAN OR OTHER PACIFIC ISLANDER POPUL.ATION. See Race.

NONFAMILY HOUSEHOLDER. See Householder.

NONMETROPOLITAN POPULATION. Population living outside of metropolitan areas (as defined by the U.S. Office of Management and Budget).

NONPUBLIC SCHOOL. See Private school.

NONRELATIVES. Any persons in the household not related to the householder by birth, marriage, or adoption. Includes roomers, boarders, partners, roommates, paid employees, wards, and foster children.

NORTH AMERICAN INDUSTRY CLASSIFICATION SYSTEM (NAICS). System for classifying industrial establishments by type of economic activity which replaces the Standard Industrial Classification System. It is a production-oriented system developed jointly by Mexico's Instituto Nacional de Estadística, Geografía e Informática, Statistics Canada, and the United States Office of Management and Budget. NAICS was designed to provide new comparability in statistics about business activity across North America and to be consistent with the United Nations' International Standard Industrial Classification for certain high-level groupings. NAICS identifies new emerging technology industries and reorganizes industries into more meaningful sectors, particularly expanding the services industries. NAICS groups the economy into 20 broad sectors, up from the 10 divisions of the SIC system. For more details, conversion tables and related products available on the subject go to www.census.gov/ and search for "NAICS" or "North American Industry Classification System."
The major industry groups and their NAICS codes are as follows:

Agriculture, forestry, fishing, and hunting (11)
Mining (21)
Utilities (22)
Construction (23)
Manufacturing (31-33)
Wholesale trade (42)
Retail trade (44-45)
Transportation and warehousing (48-49)
Information (51)
Finance and insurance (52)
Real estate and rental and leasing (53)
Professional, scientific, and technical services (54)
Management of companies and enterprises (55)
Administrative and support and waste management and remediation services (56)
Education services (61)
Health care and social assistance (62)
Arts, entertainment, and recreation (71)
Accommodation and food services (72)
Other services (except Public administration) (81)
Public administration (92)

OCCUPATIONAL LICENSING. Required operational licenses for professional persons who operate at the retail level such as dispensing opticians or pharmacists.

OCCUPIED HOUSING UNIT. See Housing unit.

OWNER-OCCUPIED HOUSING UNIT. See Housing unit.

PER CAPITA. A per capita (per person) figure is defined by taking the total for some item (e.g., government expenditures, income) and dividing it by the number of persons in the specified population.

PERSONAL INCOME. See Income.

PERSONS PER FAMILY. Number of persons living in families divided by the number of families.

PERSONS PER HOUSEHOLD. Number of persons living in households divided by the number of households.

PLACE OF BIRTH. For census enumeration, the mother's usual state or country of residence at the time of birth. Native-born persons are those born in the U.S., Puerto Rico, or an outlying area of the U.S. Includes a small number of persons born at sea or in a foreign country but with at least one American parent. Foreign-born persons are those not classified as native born.

PLACE OF WORK. Geographic location at which workers carry out their occupational activities.

POVERTY STATUS. In census publications, based on a definition developed by the Social Security Administration in 1964 and revised by a federal interagency committee in 1969 and 1980. Defined by income levels that (depending on family or household size) describe a family or household as being in extreme want of necessities. Income cutoffs or poverty thresholds used by the Bureau of the Census to determine the poverty status of families and individuals are defined by family size and by presence and number of family members aged 18 and under. Unrelated individuals and two-person families are differentiated by age of householder. If total income of a family or individual is less than the corresponding threshold, the family or individual is classified as below the poverty level. Poverty thresholds are adjusted annually to allow for changes in the cost of living as reflected in the Consumer Price Index and are computed on a national basis only. The poverty index is based on money income and does not take into account noncash benefits, such as food stamps, Medicaid, and public housing. Differences in poverty thresholds based on farm-nonfarm residence have been eliminated. Nonfarm thresholds now apply to all families. Beginning in 1987, poverty thresholds are based on revised processing procedures and are not directly comparable with prior years.

POVERTY THRESHOLD. See Poverty status.

PRIMARY METROPOLITAN STATISTICAL AREA (PMSA). A Metropolitan Statistical Area which is part of a larger urban complex with a population over one million and is designated as a Consolidated Metropolitan Statistical Area (CMSA).

PRIVATE SCHOOL. Any individual, association, co-partnership, or corporation which designates itself an education center and which includes kindergarten or a higher grade below college level. Primarily supported by private funds.

PROPERTY INCOME. See Income.

PROPRIETORS' INCOME. See Income.

PUBLIC ASSISTANCE INCOME. See Income.

PUBLIC SCHOOL. Any school controlled and supported primarily by a local, state, or federal agency.

RACE. In census enumeration, reflects self-identification by respondents and does not necessarily denote a scientific definition of biological stock.

2000 census data and subsequent intercensal figures are based on these 2000 census race categories:

American Indian or Alaska Native includes persons who are classified in one of these specific categories or who entered the name of a specific Indian tribe.

Asian includes persons having origins in any of the original peoples of the Far East, Southeast Asia, or the Indian subcontinent. Included are "Asian Indian," "Chinese," "Filipino," "Korean," "Japanese," "Vietnamese," and "Other Asian."

Black or African American includes persons having origin in any of the Black racial groups of Africa and those indicating their race as "Black, African American, or Negro" or those who provided written entries such as African American, Kenyan, Nigerian, or Haitian.

Native Hawaiian or Other Pacific Islander includes persons having origins in any of the original peoples of Hawaii, Guam, Samoa, or other Pacific Islands. Included are persons who indicate their race as "Native Hawaiian," "Guamanian or Chamorro," "Samoan," and "Other Pacific Islander."
White includes persons having origins in any of the original peoples of Europe, the Middle East, or North Africa. Included are persons who indicate their race as "White" or report entries such as Irish, German, Italian, Lebanese, Near Easterner, Arab, or Polish.
Some other race includes all other responses, including write-in entries in the "Some other race" category, such as multiracial, mixed, interracial, or a Hispanic/Latino group (for example, Mexican, Puerto Rican, or Cuban).

Two or more races refers to a combinations (57 possible) of two or more of the race groups defined above.

RENT. Contract (cash) rent is the monthly rent agreed to, or contracted for, regardless of any furnishings, utilities, fees, meals, or services that may be included. For vacant units, it is the monthly rent asked at the time of enumeration. In some tabulations, contract rent is presented for all renter-occupied housing units, as well as for "specified renter-occupied" housing units and for "specified vacant-for-rent" housing units which include renter units except one-family houses or mobile homes on 10 or more acres. Respondents were asked to exclude any rent paid for additional units or for business premises. Gross rent is the contract rent plus the estimated average monthly cost of utilities if these are paid by the renter. Renter units occupied without payment of cash rent are shown separately as no cash rent.

RENTAL VACANCY RATE. The proportion of the rental inventory which is vacant for rent. Rates are computed by dividing the vacant year-round units for rent by the sum of the number of renter-occupied units, vacant year-round units rented by awaiting occupancy, and vacant year-round units for rent.

RENTER-OCCUPIED HOUSING UNIT. See Housing unit.

RESIDENCY. The place where a person lives and sleeps most of the time is the usual residence. It may not be the person's legal or voting residence. College students are considered residents of the community in which they live while attending college. Military personnel (persons in the Armed Forces) are counted as residents of the area in which their installations are located. Persons staying only temporarily away from their usual residence (e.g., migrant workers, vacationers) are considered to have a usual home elsewhere in which they are counted for census purposes.

RETAIL TRADE. Businesses primarily engaged in selling merchandise for personal, household, or farm consumption.

RURAL FARM POPULATION. Only in rural areas and includes all persons living on places of one acre or more from which at least $1,000 worth of agricultural products were sold during 1989.

RURAL POPULATION. Population not classified as urban.

SCHOOL DISTRICT. A political organization and jurisdiction that supports and administers local public schools. There is an independent school district in each Florida county and there are 28 community college districts in the state.

SCHOOL MEMBERSHIP (ENROLLMENT). Cumulative number of students registered during a school year.

SERVICE INDUSTRIES. Establishments primarily engaged in rendering a wide variety of services to individuals and to business establishments.

SOCIAL SECURITY INCOME. See Income.

SPANISH ORIGIN. See Hispanic origin.

SPECIAL DISTRICT. A local government entity established to provide one or more specific function(s) such as fire protection, public transit, water management, libraries, or hospitals. About one-third of Florida's special districts have taxing power.

STANDARD INDUSTRIAL CLASSIFICATION SYSTEM (SIC). Former industrial classification system for classifying establishments by type of economic activity. This system was replaced. See North American Industry Classification System (NAICS).

TENURE OF HOUSING UNIT. See Housing unit.

TRANSFER PAYMENTS. General disbursements to persons for which they do not render current services. These include payments by government and business to individuals and nonprofit institutions.

UNEMPLOYED PERSONS. All civilians 16 years of age and over who do not work and who actively seek employment, and who are available to work except for temporary illness (during a given reference week).

UNRELATED INDIVIDUAL. Householder living alone or with nonrelatives or household member who is not related to the householder by blood, marriage, or adoption, or person living in group quarters who is not an inmate of an institution.

URBAN POPULATION. Comprises all persons living in urbanized areas and in places (incorporated and unincorporated) of 2,500 or more inhabitants outside urbanized areas.

URBANIZED AREA. Incorporated place and adjacent densely settled surrounding area that together have a minimum population of 50,000.

VACANT HOUSING UNIT. See Housing unit.

WHITE POPULATION. See Race.

WHOLESALE TRADE. Establishments primarily engaged in selling merchandise to retailers, to institutions, to industrial, commercial, and professional users, or to other wholesalers.

WORKERS. See Labor force and Class of workers.

WORKERS' COMPENSATION. State-administered medical care payments and income maintenance. Benefits are granted for work-caused disability, illness, injury, or death.

A

B

C

D

H

N

R

V

W

Z